Rhetoric

Concepts, Definitions, Boundaries

WILLIAM A. COVINO

University of Illinois at Chicago

DAVID A. JOLLIFFE

De Paul University, Chicago

ALLYN AND BACON

Boston • London • Toronto • Sydney • Tokyo • Singapore

Editor: Eben Ludlow
Editorial Assistant: Morgan Lance
Production Supervisor: Sharon Lee
Production Manager: Francesca Drago
Text Designer: Meryl Levavi
Cover Designer: Suzanne Harbison
Marketing Manager: Lisa Kimball

Library of Congress Cataloging-in-Publication Data
Covino, William A.
  Rhetoric: concepts, definitions, boundaries / [written
and compiled by] William A. Covino and David A. Jolliffe.
    p.   cm.
  Includes index.
  ISBN 0-02-325321-5
  1. Rhetoric. I. Jolliffe, David A. II. Title.
P301.C665 1995
808—dc20

94-17727
CIP

Printed in the United States of America
10 9 8 7 6 5 4 3 2 1 04 03 02 01 00

ISBN: 0-02-325321-5

CONTENTS

PART III: PERSPECTIVES ON THE HISTORY AND THEORY OF RHETORIC   101

PART IV: THE CONTENTS OF RHETORIC   319

ACKNOWLEDGEMENTS

James Berlin. "Rhetoric and Ideology in the Writing Class." Originally appeared in *College English,* September 1988. Copyright 1988 by the National Council of Teachers of English. Reprinted with permission.

Lloyd F. Bitzer. "The Rhetorical Situation." Originally appeared in *Philosophy and Rhetoric,* 1.1 (1968). Pages 1–14. Copyright 1968 by The Pennsylvania State University. Reproduced by permission of The Pennsylvania State University Press.

Jay Bolter. "The Electronic Hiding Place." From *Writing Space* by Jay David Bolter. Copyright © 1991 Lawrence Erlbaum Associates. Reprinted by permission of the author and of the publisher, Lawrence Erlbaum Associates.

Mark Evan Bonds. "Musical Grammar and Musical Rhetoric." Reprinted by permission of the publishers from *Wordless Rhetoric: Musical Form and the Metaphor of the Oration* by Mark Evan Bonds, Cambridge, Mass.: Harvard University Press, Copyright © 1991 by the President and Fellows of Harvard College.

David Bordwell. Excerpts reprinted by permission of the publishers from *Making Meaning: Inference and Rhetoric in the Interpretation of Cinema* by David Bordwell, Cambridge, Mass.: Harvard University Press, Copyright © 1989 by the President and Fellows of Harvard College.

Barry Brummett. "Rhetorical Theory as Heuristic and Moral: A Pedagogical Justification." Originally appeared in *Communication Education,* 33 (1984). Pages 97–107. Used by permission of the Speech Communication Association.

Ronald K. Burke. "Eight Alabama Clergymen vs. Martin Luther King, Jr." From *Oratorical Encounters,* edited by Halford Ross Ryan. Copyright © 1988 The Greenwood Press. Reprinted with permission of Greenwood Publishing Group, Inc., Westport, CT.

Karlyn Kohrs Campbell. "Struggling for the Right to Speak" and "Declaration of Sentiments and Resolutions, 1848." From *Man Cannot Speak for Her: A Critical Study of Early Feminist Rhetoric, Volume 1.* Copyright © 1989 Karlyn Kohrs Campbell. Reprinted with permission of Greenwood Publishing Group, Inc., Westport, CT.

Mary J. Carruthers. From *The Book of Memory.* New York: Cambridge University Press, 1990. Copyright © 1990 Cambridge University Press. Reprinted with the permission of Cambridge University Press.

Richard Cherwitz. "Rhetoric as 'A Way of Knowing': An Attenuation of the Epistemological Claims of 'The New Rhetoric'." Originally appeared in *Southern Speech Journal,* vol. 42 (SP 77). Pages 207–219. Reprinted by permission of the Southern States Communication Association.

Donald Lemen Clark. "The Progymnasmata." From *John Milton at St. Paul's School* by Donald Lemen Clark. Copyright © 1948 Columbia University Press, New York. Reprinted by permission of the publisher.

Robert J. Connors. "The Rise and Fall of the Modes of Discourse." Originally appeared in *College Composition and Communication,* 32 (1981). Pages 444–455. Copyright © 1981 National Council of Teachers of English. Reprinted by permission.

William A. Covino. "Rhetoric is Back: Derrida, Feyerabend, Geertz, and the Lessons of History." Reprinted by permission of William A. Covino: *The Art of Wondering: A Revisionist Return to the History of Rhetoric.* (Boynton/Cook Publishers Inc., Portsmouth, NH, 1988).

Sharon Crowley. "The Methodical Memory on Display: The Five-Paragraph Theme." From Crowley, Sharon. *The Methodical Memory: Invention in Current-Tradition Rhetoric,* pp. 120–138, 182–184. Copyright © 1990 by the Board of Trustees, Southern Illinois University. Reprinted by permission of the publisher.

Mary Daly. Excerpt from *Websters' First New Intergalactic Wickedary of the English Language.* Copyright © 1987 Beacon Press. Reprinted by permission of the author.

Christine de Pizan. Selections from *The Book of the City of Ladies* by Christine de Pizan, translated by Earl Jeffrey Richards, copyright © 1982 by Persea Books, Inc. Reprinted by permission of Persea Books, Inc.

Terry Eagleton. "Conclusion: Political Criticism." From *Literary Theory: An Introduction* by Terry Eagleton. Copyright © 1983 by Terry Eagleton. Published by the University of Minnesota Press. Reprinted by permission.

Janet Emig. "Writing as a Mode of Learning." Originally appeared in *College Composition and Communication,* May 1977. Copyright 1977 by the National Council of Teachers of English. Reprinted with permission.

Marcia Farr. Excerpt from "Essayist Literacy and other Verbal Performances." Originally appeared in *Written Communication,* 8 (January 1993). Pages 17–26. Copyright © 1993 Sage Periodicals Press. Reprinted by permission of Sage Publications, Inc.

Thomas J. Farrell. "A Defense for Requiring Standard English." Originally appeared in PRE/TEXT 7 (1986). Pages 165–179. Reprinted by permission of the author and of the publisher, Department of English, University of Texas at Arlington, Arlington, TX 76019.

Paul Feyerabend. Excerpt from *Against Method* reprinted by permission of the publisher, Verso. The imprint of New Left Books Ltd. Copyright © 1988, Verso.

Melinda Fine. " 'You Can't Just Say That the Only Ones Who Can Speak Are Those Who Agree with Your Position': Political Discourse in the Classroom." *Harvard Educational Review*, 63:4, pp. 412–433. Copyright © 1993 by the President and Fellows of Harvard College. All rights reserved.

Stanley Fish. "Rhetoric." From *Critical Terms for Literary Studies*, edited by Frank Lentricchia and Thomas McLaughlin. Chicago: University of Chicago Press, 1990. Copyright © 1990 by The University of Chicago. Reprinted by permission of The University of Chicago Press and the author.

Elizabeth Flynn. "Composing as a Woman." Originally appeared in *College Composition and Communication*, December 1988. Copyright 1988 by the National Council of Teachers of English. Reprinted with permission.

John T. Gage. "Why Write?" From *The Teaching of Writing* edited by Anthony Petroskey and David Bartholomew. Copyright © 1986 The National Society for the Study of Education. Reprinted by permission.

Henry Louis Gates, Jr. "Integrating the American Mind." From *Loose Canons* by Henry Louis Gates, Jr. Copyright © 1992 Henry Louis Gates, Jr. Reprinted by permission of Oxford University Press, Inc.

Angus C. Graham. "The Sharpening of Rational Debate: The Sophists." Reprinted from *Disputers of the Tao* by Angus C. Graham by permission of Open Court Publishing Company, La Salle, Illinois. Copyright © 1989 Open Court Press.

William M. A. Grimaldi. "The Aristotelian Topics." Reprinted by permission of the publisher from *Traditio*, 14 (1958), 1–16, Copyright © 1958 by Fordham University Press.

Alan G. Gross. Excerpt reprinted by permission of the publisher from *The Rhetoric of Science* by Alan G. Gross, Cambridge, Mass.: Harvard University Press, Copyright © 1990 by the President and Fellows of Harvard College.

Han Fei Tzu. "The Difficulties of Persuasion." From *Basic Writings of Mo Tzu, Hsun Tzu, and Han Fei Tzu*, by Burton Watson. Copyright © 1967 Columbia University Press, New York. Reprinted with permission of the publisher.

Chad Hansen. "Kung-sun Lung and the White-Horse Paradox." From *Logic and Language in Ancient China*. Copyright © 1983 The University of Michigan. Reprinted by permission of The University of Michigan Press.

Roderick P. Hart. "Speech and Power: The

Tools of Presidential Leadership." From *The Sound of Leadership*. Chicago: University of Chicago Press, 1987. Copyright 1987 by The University of Chicago. Reprinted by permission of The University of Chicago Press and the author.

Eric A. Havelock. "The Coming of Literate Communication to Western Culture." From *The Journal of Communication* 30 (1): 90–98 (1980). Reprinted by permission of Oxford University Press, Inc.

E.D. Hirsch. "The Decline of Teaching Cultural Literacy." From *Cultural Literacy* by E.D. Hirsch, Jr. Copyright © 1987 by Houghton Mifflin Company. All rights reserved.

Douglas Hofstadter. Selected excerpts from pages 297–299 from *Gödel, Escher, Bach: An Eternal Braid* by Douglas Hofstadter. Copyright © 1979 by Basic Books, Inc. Reprinted by permission of Basic Books, Inc., a division of HarperCollins Publishers, Inc.

bell hooks. "Culture to Culture: Ethnography and Cultural Studies as Critical Intervention." From *Yearning: Race, Gender, and Cultural Politics*. Copyright © 1990 South End Press. Reprinted by permission of the publisher, South End Press.

Kathleen Hall Jamieson. Excerpt from *Eloquence in an Electronic Age*. Copyright © 1988 by Oxford University Press, Inc. Reprinted by permission. Excerpt from *Packaging the Presidency*. Copyright 1984, 1992 by Kathleen Hall Jamieson. Reprinted by permission of Oxford University Press, Inc.

Susan C. Jarratt. "Toward a Sophistic Historiography." Originally appeared in PRE/TEXT, 8. 1&2 (1987). Pages 9–28. Reprinted by permission of the author.

Nan Johnson. "Habits of Eloquence." From Johnson, Nan. *Nineteenth Century Rhetoric in North America*, pp. 227–247, 285–288. Copyright © 1991 by the Board of Trustees, Southern Illinois University. Reprinted by permission of the publisher.

Sister Miriam Joseph. Excerpt from *Rhetoric in Shakespeare's Time: Literary Theory in Renaissance Europe*. Reprinted by permission of the Sisters of the Holy Cross.

Victoria Kahn. "Humanist Rhetoric." Reprinted from Victoria Kahn: *Rhetoric, Prudence, and Skepticism in the Renaissance*. Copyright © 1985 by Cornell University. Used by permission of the publisher, Cornell University Press.

George A. Kennedy. "A Hoot in the Dark: The Evolution of General Rhetoric." Originally appeared in *Philosophy and Rhetoric*, 25.1 (1992). Pages 1–21. Copyright 1992 by The

Acknowledgements continue on page 836

PREFACE

Rhetoric: Concepts, Definitions, Boundaries introduces students to what we might call (after Kenneth Burke) the "scope" and "circumference" of the field of rhetoric. The audience for this book is students who would like to broaden their understanding of the presence of rhetoric in intellectual and institutional history and as a shaping force in contemporary intellectual, academic, and political domains. At this late moment in the twentieth century, as we recognize the community, the nation, and the world as a more and more complex conglomerate of diverse cultures, politics, and ways of knowing, it becomes crucial for us to understand how different modes of theory-building and knowledge-making—different rhetorics—interact in the construction and negotiation of this diversity.

Rhetoric begins with Part I, "An Introduction to Rhetoric," which offers a working definition of the theory and practice of rhetoric by surveying its conventional identity as this has developed since antiquity and touching upon the limitations and elaborations of this identity that have arisen in the postmodern age. Students should take the title of this essay literally: It is an *introduction,* not a *conclusion;* that is, we hope here to provoke questions, discussion, and challenges that acknowledge that rhetoric is not a subject to be boxed in.

Part II, "Glossary of Major Concepts, Historical Periods, and Rhetors," provides concise and authoritative surveys of 68 terms that represent significant areas of inquiry in the field of rhetoric. Traditional figures such as Plato, Aristotle, and Erasmus are represented along with "new" names such as Mary Daly, Diotima, Malcolm X, and Richard Rodriguez. Each of the traditional historical periods in the history of rhetoric is given a fresh look, and current concepts such as postmodernism and dramatism are included along with those that have a long history in rhetorical theory (e.g., enthymeme, invention, and *pisteis*).

Part III, "Perspectives on the History and Theory of Rhetoric," complements and complicates the glossary treatments of traditional historical periods and terms by offering a selection of accessible and provocative scholarly essays. Taken together, these essays demonstrate a contentious interaction of perspectives and invite students to question the nature of rhetoric and its changing roles in intellectual history.

Part IV, "The Contents of Rhetoric," proposes that a number of areas of intellectual inquiry are concerned with their respective rhetorics, that is, with the ways in which they make and express knowledge in writing. Subjects such as science, philosophy, and history that have been traditionally regarded as content-subjects are increasingly understood as enterprises whose contents are transformable, that is, rhetorical. Other less traditional academic concerns, such as gender studies, technology, and cultural studies, are also pursuing their rhetorical identities. For instance, the relationship between rhetoric and gender studies has developed over the past twenty years to include (1) the recovery of women speakers and writers who have contributed to the theory and practice of rhetoric; (2) feminist critiques of traditional and conventional theories of rhetoric; and (3) the introduction of rhetorical forms and practices that resist and disrupt patriarchal rhetorics.

Rhetoric: Concepts, Definitions, Boundaries obviously presents a wide-ranging treatment of a large and significant field; as such, this book would not have been possible without the assistance of a number of colleagues and students. We would like to extend special thanks to Catherine A. Colton and Kristopher H. Kowal. Ms. Colton responded to our interest in making this book representative of gender issues and cultural studies by initiating extensive research in these subjects. Likewise, Mr. Kowal brought his deep knowledge of non-Western literacies and rhetorics to bear on our desire to treat the field of rhetoric comprehensively. Both of these people worked under our direction to contribute initial bibliographies and drafts in a number of areas, and our subsequent development of their suggestions is indebted to their intelligence and energy.

Ken McAllister helped to educate us about the relationship between rhetoric and technology and was an invaluable assistant in the final preparation and assembly of the manuscript. We are also grateful to students at the University of Illinois at Chicago who worked under our direction to provide draft material for many of the Glossary entries: Angelo A. Bonadonna, Robert Cooner, Deborah Covino, Edwin Cruz, Jeffry Davis, Todd Deam, Patricia Duffy, Mary Ellen Flynn, Elizabeth Franken, Marcia Fujii, Janet Geovanis, Karen Hyman, Ulrike Zinn Jaeckel, Tina S. Kazan, Julie L. Lindquist, Paula J. Mathieu, Orlando Menes, Mary Kay Mulvaney, Rammina Paulissian, Kathleen Ruhl, Denise Schubert, Sarah Schuler, Karen Halvorsen Schreck, David Seitz, Bradford T. Stull, Linda Vavra, and Eve Wiederhold.

Colleagues who reviewed this project at various stages are L. Bensel-Meyers, The University of Tennessee-Knoxville; Sharon Crowley, University of Iowa; Theresa Enos, The University of Arizona; Patricia Harkin, Purdue University; Carolyn R. Miller, North Carolina State University; Jasper Neel, Vanderbilt University; C. Jan Swearingen, The University of Texas at Arlington; and Victor J. Vitanza, The University of Texas at Arlington. We thank them for their deep engagement and careful suggestions.

William A. Covino
University of Illinois at Chicago

David A. Jolliffe
De Paul University, Chicago

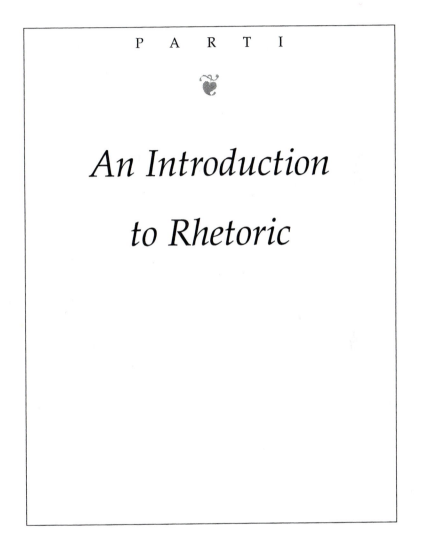

PART I

An Introduction

to Rhetoric

What Is Rhetoric?

I specify now that rhetoric is the functional organization of discourse, within its social and cultural context, in all its aspects, exception made for its realization as a strictly formal metalanguage—in formal logic, mathematics, and in the sciences whose metalanguages share the same features. In other words: rhetoric is all of language, in its realization as discourse.
—PAOLO VALESIO
Novantiqua (1980)

[The function of rhetoric] is not to persuade but to see the available means of persuasion in each case.
—ARISTOTLE
Rhetoric (c. 350 BCE)

Here then we have in popular use two separate ideas of Rhetoric: one of which is occupied with the general end of the fine arts—that is to say, intellectual pleasure; the other applies itself more specifically to a definite purpose of utility, viz. fraud.
—THOMAS DE QUINCEY
"Rhetoric" (1828)

A rhetorician, I take it, is like one voice in a dialogue. Put several such voices together, with each voicing its own special assertion, let them act upon one another in cooperative competition, and you get a dialectic that, properly developed, can lead to the views transcending the limitations of each.
—KENNETH BURKE
"Rhetoric—Old and New" (1950)

Rhetoric in the most general sense may perhaps be identified with the energy inherent in communication: the emotional energy that impels the speaker to speak, the physical energy expended in the utterance, the energy level coded in the message, and the energy experienced by the recipient in decoding the message.
—GEORGE KENNEDY
"A Hoot in the Dark" (1992)

> *Nearly the entire history of writing is confounded with the history of reason, of which it is at once the effect, the support, and one of the privileged alibis. It has been one with the phallocentric tradition. It is indeed that same self-admiring, self-stimulating, self-congratulatory phallocentricism.*
> —Helene Cixous
> "The Laugh of the Medusa"
> (1975)

"What is Rhetoric?" This a difficult question for which there is no short answer. The difficulty begins with the fact that rhetoric is not a *content* area that contains a definite body of knowledge, like physics; instead, rhetoric might be understood as the study and practice of shaping content. This is a common definition that has informed the vilification of rhetoric since antiquity. When rhetoric is regarded as the manipulation of the linguistic features of a text, it becomes associated by some with fraud, by others with the maintenance of institutional hierarchies. In this connection, studying rhetoric means studying how people get fooled, and rhetoric is understood as the opposite of truth. The rhetoric of a text is seen as its use of ornamental, pretentious, carefully calculated, sometimes bombastic language, through which the writer or speaker seeks power over listeners or readers.

If we consider rhetoric as the study and practice of featuring rather than shaping content, we foreground its function as a tool for "special-interest groups." The special-interest-group rhetor selects and configures language so that certain terms are privileged and endorsed, and others are ignored. In literary studies, for example, the rhetoric of the New Criticism appreciates unity, continuity, and coherence in literary works, and directs our attention to these elements; by contrast, the rhetoric of deconstruction finds literary value in the *breakdown* of these same elements. These two groups adopt different critical lexicons that strike us as mutually exclusive:

> It will be sufficient if [the reader] will understand the unit meanings with which the poet begins—that is, that he understands the meanings of the words which the poet uses—and if he will so far suppress his convictions or prejudices as to see how the unit meanings or partial meanings are built into a total context. (Cleanth Brooks, *The Well Wrought Urn*, 252)

> In this ideal text, the networks are many and interact, without any one of them being able to surpass the rest; this text is a galaxy of signifiers, not a structure of signifieds; it has no beginning; it is reversible; we gain access to it by several entrances, none of which can be authoritatively declared to be the main one; the codes it mobilizes extend *as far as the eye can reach* . . . based as it is on the infinity of language. (Roland Barthes, *S/Z*, 5–6)

Brooks employs the lexicon of units and unity, Barthes of multiplicity and infinity. Analyzing the connection of lexical and syntactic choices to the special-interest group that an author represents has become a common academic and journalistic enterprise, so that there are numerous studies of, for instance, the rhetoric of advertising and marketing, the rhetoric of political movements, and the rhetoric of religious institutions, as well as the rhetoric of academic language itself, such as literary criticism and philosophy. However, to the extent that the meaning of rhetoric is restricted in such studies to the linguistic features of the text, they evade a fuller—and, in fact, classical—portrayal of rhetoric.

The power of eloquence, as defined in 55 CE by the Roman orator Marcus Tullius Cicero, indicates the scope of rhetoric: "The real power of eloquence is such that it embraces the origin, the influence, the changes of all things in the world, all virtues, duties, and all nature, so far as it affects the manners, minds, and lives of mankind" (*De Oratore* 3.20). Eloquence, which is for Cicero another word for rhetoric, is activated by and affects changing manners, minds, and lives as it constructs our knowledge of the world. Taking as our cue this representative classical view, we would like to present the practice of rhetoric here as much more than verbal ornamentation, and the study of rhetoric as much more than a catalog of ideological buzz words.

Rhetoric is a primarily verbal, situationally contingent, epistemic art that is both philosophical and practical and gives rise to potentially active texts. As we explicate this definition, we will attempt to interrogate it as well, recognizing that any conception of rhetoric—no matter how broad—entails ambiguities and limitations. As twentieth-century rhetorician and philosopher Kenneth Burke said, "A way of seeing is also a way of not seeing" (*Permanence and Change,* 49).

The word *text* in our definition of rhetoric can be understood in both its conventional, quite limited sense, and its ambiguous, more rhetorical sense. In the former sense, we mean by *text* any instance of spoken or written language that could be considered in isolation as a self-sufficient entity. Thus, a book, an essay, an editorial, a song's lyrics, a joke, and a speech are texts, but so are a chapter, a section of an article, a refrain in a song or poem, and a contribution to a conversation. This definition of *text* may remind you of the definition of *sentence* that you learned in elementary school: "a statement that can stand alone." You probably realize now that this is an inadequate definition of a sentence, because no statement can "stand alone"; every utterance depends for its meaning on extrinsic factors. This fact is epitomized by a famous passage from Kenneth Burke's *Philosophy of Literary Form:*

> Imagine that you enter a parlor. You come late. When you arrive, others have long preceded you, and they are engaged in a heated discussion, a discussion too heated for them to pause and tell you exactly what it is about. In fact, the discussion had already begun long before any of them got there, so that no one present is qualified to retrace for you all the steps that had gone before. You listen for a while, until you decide that you have caught the tenor of the argument; then you put in your oar. Someone answers; you answer him; another

comes to your defense; another aligns himself against you, to either the embarrassment or gratification of your opponent, depending upon the quality of your ally's assistance. However, the discussion is interminable. The hour grows late, you must depart. And you do depart, with the discussion still vigorously in progress. (110–111)

If we imagine a text as the momentary entry into an unending conversation connected to what Burke calls (after anthropologist Bronislaw Malinowski) shifting "contexts of situation," we see that defining it as an independent and self-contained entity is something of a convenience.

We will use the term *rhetor* here to indicate an individual involved in the production of a text, usually a speaker or writer; we will call readers and listeners who attend to and interpret a text *auditors,* or, as a group, the *audience.* A text is *potentially active* when the rhetor intends it to *do* something, to affect or change the auditors' minds or actions or environments. *Rhetorical analysis* is the study of whether and how texts actually do affect, influence, or change auditors. The term *potentially active* bears some scrutiny here, as one of our students, Ulrike Jaeckel, indicated in her review of this Introduction:

> Does a rhetor ever NOT intend a text to do something? Since you include "a contribution to conversation" under "texts," pretty much any utterance can become a text, . . . even (specific instances of) "hello" or "thank you." Aren't these "potentially active"—capable of producing an effect on a hearer—just by being uttered?

We agree that all utterances are texts, and all texts have the potential to change auditors. As Ulrike Jaeckel's response indicates, our term *potentially active* had effects that we did not anticipate; that is, we did not assess its potential fully enough to predict that it might activate her questions. With this admission, we might draw a distinction between the *intended* potential activity of a text and its *unintended* potential activity. Rhetorical analysis is interested in both kinds of potential.

As a primarily verbal art, rhetoric has as its medium the written and spoken word, although many scholars study how visual images and nonverbal sounds can complement the effect of a text's words. Some use the term *rhetoric* metaphorically and speak of the rhetoric of, for instance, gestures, paintings, or films. The elocutionary movement of the eighteenth and nineteenth centuries attempted an exhaustive analysis of the communicative effects of bodily movements in order to advise orators about what kinds of body language suited what kinds of speeches. But the elocutionists made clear that gestures do not themselves constitute rhetoric; rather, the visual image of the rhetor produced linguistic understanding in the auditors. For instance, a certain contortion of the facial features would have them think and feel "pity." Following this understanding, we may say that rhetoric *inheres* in the words that a visual image *activates,* so that the rhetoric of a painting, for instance, may be understood as the verbal understanding that accompanies its viewing.

As a situationally contingent art, rhetoric guides prospective writers and speakers to consider the timeliness and suitability for the particular situation of any text they might produce. Ancient Greek philosophers and rhetoricians had a useful term for this abstract concept: *kairos.* Inherent in *kairos* is a sensitivity to the belief that in any situation where the potential for active communication exists, rhetors must consider whether, from the point of view of potential auditors, the time, the circumstances, and the intellectual and ideological climate are right. These are factors that are very difficult to control, let alone predict. In recent years, scholarship in the humanities and the social sciences has begun to recognize the difficulty of maintaining "stable" texts with determinate meaning; this recognition accounts for the difference in the statements by Brooks and Barthes above, written in 1947 and 1970, respectively. Barthes's statement suggests that—given infinite possibilities for meaning—*kairos* is an unachievable ideal. Adding to this view our recognition that the public realm any text enters is today more politically, ethnically, and intellectually diversified than ever, the contingent nature of rhetoric becomes a very prominent and formidable consideration.

As an epistemic art, rhetoric leads prospective auditors to see "truth" neither as something that exists in their own minds before communication nor as something that exists in the world of empirical observation that they must simply report "objectively." Instead, rhetorical truth is something achieved *transactionally* among the rhetor and the auditors whenever they come to some shared understanding, knowledge, or belief. As coparticipants in a verbal exchange, all the parties involved are knowledge-makers.

Philosophical rhetoric is primarily concerned with the exploratory construction of knowledge. The philosophical rhetor is less concerned with the composition of a particular text than with exploring ways of knowing and defining a subject. Plato attempts to illustrate philosophical rhetoric in *Phaedrus,* in which Socrates engages in a question-and-answer exchange with Phaedrus about the nature of love, of rhetoric, and of writing, working through different possible meanings of each term. Ann E. Berthoff has recently tried to engage writing students in a kind of philosophical rhetoric through the use of a "double-entry notebook," in which they write about a subject in one column and then return to that writing at a later date, reconsider it, and write a critique of their prior thinking/writing in a facing column. In this way, writers engage in a dialectical exchange with themselves as they try to "think, and think again," as Berthoff puts it. Another form of philosophical rhetoric might be called *topical* rather than dialectical, originating in Aristotle's definition of rhetoric as "seeing the available means of persuasion" (*Rhetoric* 1355b) through the subjection of an issue to *topoi* or "topics," which are strategies (such as comparison or analogy) that contribute to full investigation. As a philosophical art, rhetoric guides rhetors to think and observe deeply—intuitively, systematically, and empirically. Philosophic or exploratory rhetoric can also be seen as the foundation for practical rhetoric. That is, systematic exploration leads prospective rhetors to find what they *could* say or write in specific situations when they plan a potentially active text, even if they do not actually produce it.

Rhetoric is not logic, but they are related fields of inquiry. Logic studies the way a chain of reasoning leads from premises to incontrovertible conclusions. Rhetoric also studies how rhetors and auditors reason from premises to conclusions, but it is located in the realm of uncertainty and *probable* truth, in which conclusions are arguable rather than incontrovertible.

Rhetoric is not dialectic, although Aristotle calls rhetoric the *antistrophos* (counterpart) to dialectic, and the examples from Plato and Berthoff above suggest that rhetorical exploration can take on a dialectical—question–answer or comment–response—form. In its classical sense, dialectic is a system of reasoning about subjects for which there are few or no "hard," scientific data or proven premises. Rhetoric also addresses such subjects, but because the practice and study of rhetoric take into account how rhetors actually shape their reasoning processes into texts that appeal to a potential auditor's understanding and emotions, it is a more expansive, inclusive, and socioculturally alert art than dialectic.

Rhetoric is not poetics, but they are related fields as well. Poetics studies literary texts—poetry, fiction, drama, and so forth—as linguistic artifacts, examining such features as imagery, diction, textual organization, and rhythm. In his *Poetics*, Aristotle discusses the ways in which tragic drama affects its audience, and this perspective suggests that both rhetoric and poetics are audience-oriented. The decisive distinction between rhetoric and poetics rests on rhetoric's concern with the *invention* of an effective text: whereas poetics regards the elements of an effective composition, rhetoric is additionally a body of resources for composing.

To anyone who would hold that rhetoric is merely an empty display of verbal ornamentation or a facile use of one-sided terms and concepts, we would offer a broader view of rhetoric's scope: Certainly, the rhetoric of a text is the selection and organization of language it uses to move potential readers and listeners to consider its ideas and conclusions. But the rhetoric of a text is also the intellectual, cognitive, affective, and social considerations that guide the writer or speaker to use the language as he or she does, *and* the rhetoric of a text is the effect it actually has on people who listen to it or read it.

THE FIELD(S) OF RHETORIC

When we speak about the art of rhetoric, then, we mean the faculty that humans have—a teachable, improvable faculty—for inventing constructions of "reality" that others may regard as such. In short, rhetoric is the art of knowledge-making. Some scholars have devoted themselves to learning how this art was conceived and taught in periods since antiquity; they specialize in the history of rhetoric and have produced an impressive array of studies that indicate the ways in which the definition and purposes of rhetoric have changed through the ages, and have tied these changes to epistemological and political shifts. Other scholars study the effectiveness of actual texts, past and present, thus specializing in rhetorical criticism. Perhaps one of the most famous pieces of rhetorical criticism in this century is Kenneth Burke's essay, "The Rhetoric of Hitler's 'Battle,' " in *The Philosophy of Literary Form,* in which Burke tries to account for the social, political, and psychological conditions that made Hitler's discourse persuasive.

The teaching of written and oral communication has also recently become a scholarly specialty, with the history and theory of rhetoric as its antecedent. Communication pedagogy that is grounded in a full definition of rhetoric offers students a broad view of the functions a text can perform. The rhetorical theorist-as-teacher would tend to give the following sort of characterization of rhetoric to these students:

> To engage in the art of rhetoric does not solely mean producing texts that aim to persuade people to take a specific action—vote for Candidate X, invest your money in Bank Y, march in protest against Policy Z. The range of rhetoric is wide: You can create a text that will lead your auditors to wonder about a subject, to ruminate, to think in ways they have never thought before. You can create a text that clarifies a complex subject they have previously found baffling. You can inform your auditors about facts, data, and information of which they were previously unaware. You can lead your auditors to accept an idea, a proposition, a thesis. And, of course, you can move your auditors to take a specific action: vote for Candidate X, invest their money in Bank Y, march in protest against Policy Z. Teachers in antiquity proposed that the art of rhetoric appeals to an auditor's beliefs and opinions, emotions, and aesthetic sensibilities. They named the purposes of rhetorical communication as 1) to teach, 2) to please, and 3) to move. Through the elaboration and practice of the appeals and purposes of rhetoric, you can develop a broad repertory of communication skills and strategies.

> Think of the complexity of the art of rhetoric. To succeed at it calls for a thoroughly inquisitive, logical, flexible and philosophical frame of mind; an almost anthropological view of the situation in which you will be communicating, in order to assess how issues of time and place and the predispositions of potential auditors might affect your text; a knowledge of the structure, limits, and nuances of language; and a psychological ability to assay your auditors and know how to move them from believing only in their own ideas and feelings to considering and accepting yours.

Although a number of scholars and teachers specialize in the history, theory, and teaching of rhetoric *per se,* we can locate an implicit theory of rhetoric in any discussion that addresses the elements of verbal knowledge-making. The philosopher discussing the ethical limits of the human imagination, the ethnographer surveying the types of discourse in action in a village, the teacher typing up the requirements for her students' term paper, the political scientist offering reasons for an election victory, the feminist illustrating the kinds of writing that correspond with women's ways of knowing, the computer programmer creating word-processing software, the cultural historian studying the different ways in which literacy has been defined through the centuries, the psychologist presenting the cognitive effects of television advertising, and the newspaper subscriber writing a letter to the editor complaining about an inaccurate article, are all both rhetors and theorists of rhetoric. They are rhetors in that they are making verbal knowledge, with the hope that others will accept it as valid; they are theorists of rhetoric in that they are explicating and criticizing particular instances of verbal knowledge-making. We offer this indication of the diverse activities that might constitute both the theory and practice of rhetoric in order to further our point that rhetoric concerns nothing less than what Terry Eagleton has called "the field of discursive practices in society as a whole" (*Literary Theory* 205).

We survey the breadth of this field more fully in Part IV of this book, which focuses on the relationships between rhetoric and cultural studies, non-Western culture, feminism, gender studies, philosophy, the arts, literary criticism, science, education, literacy, composition, technology, and oratory.

Our primary concern in this book is the development and diversification of theories of rhetoric. For the balance of this Introduction, we will essay this concern in a general fashion, with the promise that the terms and concepts we deal with here will show up again in subsequent sections, in discussions that we hope will both further explicate and complicate the nature of rhetorical theory.

THE ELEMENTS OF RHETORIC

Over the centuries, scholars have produced works that explain principles, techniques, and guidelines for practicing the art of rhetoric. Because they have generally been used to teach prospective rhetors, these works have often been called *rhetorica docens,* the Latin term for a "teaching" rhetoric book. In addition, scholars over the centuries have studied what they regarded as excellent and effective texts—often speeches—produced by renowned rhetors, trying to infer principles that other rhetors could follow. Collectively, the exemplary texts have been called *rhetorica utens,* Latin for *rhetoric in use.* The traditional body of concepts that we know as rhetorical theory is derived from both the works of *rhetorica docens* and *rhetorica utens.*

The major elements of rhetorical theory are the *rhetorical situation,* the *audience,* the *pisteis* or "proofs" (and their subdivisions), and the five canons of rhetoric: *invention, arrangement, style, memory,* and *delivery.*

Although the concept of the rhetorical situation is inherent in the history of rhetoric from antiquity to the present, it is most clearly explicated in an essay written in 1968 by Lloyd Bitzer titled "The Rhetorical Situation" (reprinted in Part III). According to Bitzer, a situation is rhetorical when three elements are present: an exigence, an audience, and rhetorical constraints. An exigence is a need, a gap, something wanting, that can be met, filled in, or supplied *only* by a spoken or written text. We can say that the exigence of a situation calls forth a text. Thus, exigence is related to *kairos* as a kind of "generative timeliness": The death of a famous person creates an exigence that calls forth a eulogy. Receiving lousy service from a public utility company creates an exigence that calls forth a letter of complaint. The discovery of a new concept by researchers—for example, the discovery of the double-helix structure of DNA by James Watson and Francis Crick—creates an exigence that calls forth an article reporting the discovery and arguing for its importance.

The audience, according to Bitzer, is not simply the aggregation of people who listen to or read the text called forth by the exigence. More specifically, the audience comprises the people who have a reason to be concerned about the exigence and who are capable of acting on it or being acted upon by it. The audience for a eulogy is the people who were connected, however remotely, to the deceased person and who are in the position to have their feelings of grief assuaged by the text. The audience for the letter of complaint is the people connected with the utility company who are in some position to see that the lousy service improves in the future. The audience for the report of the new discovery is the people who are concerned about the state of knowledge in the field and who believe that future research projects should be built on the foundations of newly validated concepts, whether they actually conduct those research projects themselves or simply keep informed of others who do.

Rhetorical constraints, according to Bitzer, are the features of the audience's—and perhaps the speaker's or writer's—frames of mind, belief systems, and ways of life that lead the audience to accept the speaker's or writer's ideas and to act upon the exigence. Rhetorical constraints include the audience's presuppositions and beliefs about the subject of the text as well as the patterns of demonstration or proof that the audience will accept. In other words, the constraints are ideas and attitudes that exist between the rhetor—motivated to create discourse by the exigence—and the auditors, who ideally will act upon this exigence. Constraints upon a eulogy include the facts about the deceased person's life and works that the audience can be expected to know, as well as the audience's beliefs about the thoughts and sentiments that are comforting in a time of grief. Constraints upon the letter of complaint include the writer's conception of what would constitute good service, the facts of the situation that amount to lousy service, and the types of appeals the writer believes she can make—appeals to her status as a good customer who regularly pays her bill, say, or appeals to the company's image as a truthworthy provider of service—that will induce the company to improve. Constraints upon the research report include the beliefs, shared by the writers and the audience, about the nature of an experiment or research project in the field, presumptions about the "objective" roles of the researchers themselves, the facts of the experiment or project that the researchers are reporting, and the patterns of reasoning they use (and fully expect their audience to "buy") in order to argue for their discovery as something significant in the intellectual community.

Although Bitzer's article brought together concepts that had already been developed in rhetorical theory, some scholars found his characterization of exigence, audience, and constraints a bit too passive. Thus, his work was very productively revised in an article written eight years later by Richard Vatz, titled "The Myth of the Rhetorical Situation" (reprinted in Part IV). The problem with Bitzer's depiction of the rhetorical situation, Vatz maintains, lies in Bitzer's tacit suggestion that exigences, audiences, and constraints exist as *a priori* categories, before a rhetor chooses to produce a text. It's not that exigences, audiences, and constraints are simply there, Vatz argues, and a rhetor simply trips over them and uses them. On the contrary, says Vatz, exigences, audiences, and constraints are created by rhetors who choose to activate them by inscribing them into their texts. In other words, a situation becomes rhetorical only when a speaker or writer evokes an audience within a text, embodies an exigence within the text that the evoked audience is led to respond to, and handles the constraints in such a way that the audience is convinced that they are true or valid. Bitzer's and Vatz's articles represent two major contributions to an important debate within rhetorical theory about whether texts simply recognize and make use of certain conditions or whether texts actually create those conditions.

AUDIENCE

At first glance, the concept of audience in rhetorical theory seems simple to illustrate, but that simplicity is deceptive. The term *audience* embodies a metaphor from the theater, and indeed when a speech is given before an assembly, we can say that that collection of people is an audience for the speech. In other words, the term *audience* can refer exclusively to those who *hear* a speech or performance, as suggested by a strict translation of *audire,* to hear. But the definition of audience becomes considerably tangled when we consider three complications: First, spoken texts are often recorded for later listening or transmitted electronically beyond the setting where they are performed. Second, spoken texts are often performed versions of previously written texts or are transcribed into written form after they are spoken, and are thus available for audiences completely removed in both time and space from the person who delivered the speech. Third, most of the texts we encounter are never spoken or intended to be spoken, but instead are written and, like transcribed spoken texts, may be read by anyone who happens to pick them up.

Scholars have tried to accommodate these complications by reconsidering the definition of audience. They have, for instance, distinguished the *primary* audience for a text from various *subsidiary* audiences; this distinction has also been drawn using the terms *immediate audience* and *mediated audiences.* Consider an example: The governing council of an economically developing city commissions an ecologist to write a report on the environmental implications of opening up a certain region of the city for commercial real estate development. The primary, immediate audience for the ecologist's report would be the city council members. The report, however, would probably have at least several subsidiary or mediated audiences: the aides to the council members, who read important documents for their bosses and help them digest the material; potential real estate developers, who want to see whether their entrepreneurial plans are favored or foiled by the document; writers for the local media, who are responsible for reporting such issues in newspapers, magazines, radio, and television; and members of environmental protection groups, who want to maintain the ecological viability of the region in the face of what they consider threats posed by commercial development plans. The ecologist's text, to be most effective, would have to address the concerns of all these audiences in some way.

Drawing on canonical works from antiquity through the eighteenth century, traditional rhetorical theory has conceived a text's audience as some individual or collective "other" whom the rhetor must identify, analyze in psychological and emotional terms, and then, by means of the text, "change" in some way so that they will adhere to the rhetor's central idea or thesis. This traditional view has three drawbacks. First, it largely limits attention to the primary, immediate auditors in a rhetorical situation, and generally ignores any subsidiary, mediated audiences. Second, the traditional view tends to assume an antagonistic relation between the rhetor and the audience; it tacitly posits that there is some ideological, emotional, or psychological condition that must be changed within the auditors before they can accept the rhetor's ideas. Third, the traditional view ignores the shared, dialectical nature of communication by characterizing the rhetorical interaction as moving in one direction, from the rhetor to the auditor: The rhetor is the sender and the auditor is the receiver.

Clearly, real communication does not operate on such an immediate, one-way, agonistic street. Some theorists have conflated the concept of audience, as traditionally treated in rhetorical theory, with the concept of *speech community*, as developed in sociolinguistics. The result has been the forging of a new concept, *discourse community*, an entity defined by Martin Nystrand in 1982. A discourse community, according to Nystrand, comprises people who "may very well *never* speak or write to each other," but who "*could effectively so interact if required* since they know the ways-of-speaking of the group" (15; emphasis in original). In a 1991 work, John Swales provides a more comprehensive definition of discourse community: It comprises people who strive to achieve a "broadly agreed set" of epistemological or social goals by means of their spoken or written texts, who employ "mechanisms of intercommunication among members," who use "participatory mechanisms" to provide information and feedback concerning one another's texts, who use one or more genres "in the communicative furtherance of [the common] aims," and who conventionally use "some specific lexis" (24–27). Consider, for example, the kind of discourse community that has developed in many contemporary industrial settings as quality control operations have been shifted from a single department to the production workforce as a whole. Instead of having a company inspector examining the products as they are being made, the workers themselves assess the products and they document, in writing, what is working well, what is not working, and what needs to be done differently in future shifts. They meet regularly, usually in "quality control teams," to go over the quality control documents they are writing and to plan modifications to both production and the documentation system; they produce a common genre, the "quality management report," which embodies their common knowledge of appropriate content, diction, and format. These workers form a discourse community.

The concept of a discourse community allows rhetorical theorists to analyze interactions among rhetors and both primary and subsidiary audiences, and to illustrate how audiences and speakers and writers influence each other's texts. A clear example of such an analysis is provided by the work of Greg Myers, a linguist at Lancaster University in Great Britain. In the early 1980s, Myers studied how two academic biologists—one a well-known researcher in his field and the other attempting to publish his first article in what for him was a new area—shaped their personae as they wrote grant proposals and articles for professional journals. Myers was able to analyze how the two biologists reacted differently to the responses by the grant proposal reviewers, as well as how the biologists tried to shape their articles to accommodate the range of auditors in their discourse community, which included the reviewers, the journal editors, and the readership of the journal.

The concept of audience is further complicated by the question whether the audience in mind is "addressed" or "evoked." As noted previously, rhetorical theory has traditionally conceived the audience as an isolated, usually antagonistic other whom rhetors have to "address" and "accommodate" in their texts. Clearly, there are some rhetorical situations in which the transaction between the rhetor and the auditors happens in exactly that way. But as early as 1975, with the publication of Walter Ong's essay, "The Writer's Audience is Always a Fiction," rhetorical theorists began to characterize the writer–reader interaction in some texts as constructive rather than adaptive. In other words, in some rhetorical situations, writers cannot know with any certainty who their readers are; accordingly, writers work to *construct* an audience, playing on the assumptions and operating within the rhetorical constraints to which they presume the constructed audience would adhere. For example, when writing a letter to a friend or colleague, discussing common ideas or experiences, a writer addresses an auditor personally and immediately as a known entity. On the other hand, when writing an article for mass publication, a writer must *inscribe* or *invoke* the interests, knowledge, and needs of a presumed audience. In either case, the rhetor determines the *role* of the audience as part of the process of composing. A full explanation of this conception of audience is offered by Lisa Ede's and Andrea Lunsford's 1984 article, "Audience Addressed/Audience Invoked: The Role of Audience in Composition Theory and Pedagogy."

MEANS OF PERSUASION

An ancient term for the kinds of appeals that may affect an audience is *pisteis*. The concept of the *pisteis* is Aristotelian, and the singular term *pistis,* usually understood as "proof," "appeal," or "means of persuasion," is one of those classical Greek terms for which we have no precise English equivalent. In his *Rhetoric,* Aristotle discusses three sorts of textual appeals: to the authority of the rhetor (*ethos*), to the emotions or "stages of life" of the audience (*pathos*), and to systems of reasoning (*logos*) that the rhetor and the audience share. Although Aristotle categorizes the appeals separately, examining their operation clearly shows that they intersect and interact.

Ethos is generally defined as the good character and the consequent credibility of the rhetor. Theorists in ancient Greece and Rome did not agree among themselves whether *ethos* exists solely in the text a rhetor creates, or whether the rhetor must evince *ethos* in his or her life as well as in his or her texts. Aristotle maintained the former position: He taught that a text must demonstrate that the rhetor is a person of good sense (*phronesis*), virtue (*arete*), and good will (*eunoia*). A rhetor could not depend, according to Aristotle, on the audience's knowing more about the rhetor's *ethos* than the text itself established. The text must do the job. The theorists who translated and adapted Greek rhetoric for Roman life, notably Cicero and later Quintilian, tended to take the externalist position. Quintilian, who referred to *ethos* with the Latin term *auctoritas,* maintained that the character of a speaker or writer was as vital as the representations of it within a text. Thus, Quintilian taught that the expert at rhetoric was the *vir bonus dicendi peritus:* the *good man* [sic] skilled at speaking.

Although there are clearly instances where the *ethos* of a rhetor is demonstrated by actions and examples in life, because texts are today so frequently disseminated and consumed at a remove from the author, it is sensible to examine the ways the texts themselves inscribe a rhetor's *ethos.* Consider, for example, the convention in published academic papers of using footnotes and bibliographies to cite previously published studies. Why does a writer do this? Surely, some readers could use these citations to check the accuracy and validity of the writer's intellectual antecedents, and some readers might use them to guide their own reading or research on the same subject. Actually, however, such citations operate to invest the writer—and thus the text—with *phronesis:* good sense or "practical" wisdom. The writer becomes more credible because she has done the required homework in the field and shown it through the citations. Consider, to continue using the published academic paper as an example, the tradition of listing the author's academic affiliation in a byline, an address line, or a biographical paragraph; here is an example recently published to accompany an article by William Covino:

William A. Covino is professor of English at the University of Illinois, Chicago, where he teaches in the graduate program in language, literacy, and rhetoric. His articles on rhetorical theory and history have appeared in several journals, and his books include *The Art of Wondering: A Revisionist Return to the History of Rhetoric, Forms of Wondering: A Dialogue on Writing for Writers,* and *Magic, Rhetoric, and Literacy: An Eccentric History of the Composing Imagination.*

Although certainly some readers might want to correspond with the author or read something else he has written, for most such a listing amounts to a display of *arete,* a demonstration of affiliations and activities that amount to "virtue" in an academic context. Consider, to take a final example from this genre, the degree of deference an author shows to previous studies, even if his or her work will diverge radically from them, and the amount of polite hedging the author of an academic paper demonstrates when setting out the significance of his or her own thesis.

> The pioneering histories of rhetoric produced early in the current revival (Kennedy, Corbett, and Kinneavy) have served virtually to bring into existence for a twentieth-century audience authors and texts ignored under the philosophic tradition. The task at hand now is to examine more closely the method of reading we bring to those texts and, more broadly, to the whole discursive field within which they take their places. The result will be different readings of canonical texts, as well as the identification of new significant sites of "rhetoric" in its more comprehensive sophistic definition. (Susan Jarratt, *Rereading the Sophists,* xix).

Jarratt might conceivably have been more dismissive of previous scholarship and more brash in asserting the importance of her own. Maintaining *eunoia*—good will toward the discourse community she hopes to engage with her work—requires the more respectful tone struck here, a tone we recognize as a strategic appeal at the same time that we presume it to be sincere.

We have already alluded to the second traditional *pistis* in our discussion of audience. This is the appeal to *pathos,* sometimes called the *pathetic* or the *emotional* appeal. The central idea underlying *pathos* is that an effective text will somehow activate or draw upon the sympathies and emotions of the auditors, causing them to attend to and accept its ideas, propositions, or calls for action. As with *ethos,* the source of most later rhetorical theory concerning *pathos* is Aristotle's *Rhetoric.* In Book I, Aristotle describes in detail the emotions he believes a text, depending on the rhetorical situation, could activate in order to persuade one's audience: anger, calmness, friendship, enmity, fear, confidence, shame, shamelessness, kindness, unkindness, pity, indignation, envy, and emulation. In addition, he categorizes potential audiences into social groupings according to character types—the young, the elderly, people in their prime, aristocrats, the wealthy, and the powerful—and analyzes the dominant emotions inherent in each of these character types that a text might try to animate.

Two points about Aristotle's view of *pathos* are noteworthy for understanding the role of this appeal in rhetorical theory. First, his catalog of emotions and characters is thoroughly ethnocentric, tied to his purpose of providing instruction in rhetoric to young men who strove to gain political influence in fourth-century BCE Athens. There is little to suggest that rhetors in all, or even most, current rhetorical situations would find it wise to appeal to the emotions as Aristotle defines them. Nor would it probably be wise for rhetors to stereotype their auditors into Aristotle's categories. Nonetheless, the basic move that Aristotle's treatment illustrates—fitting one's text to the character types and states of mind that make up one's audience—remains legitimate in current rhetorical activity. Second, Aristotle assumes a neutral stance toward ethical issues related to pathetic appeals. Certainly current rhetorical theorists, as well as rhetors, need to distinguish between texts that indiscriminately titillate and pander to an audience's emotions and texts in which *pathos* is tied to a virtuous *ethos,* in which a rhetor of goodwill seeks to evoke the same in the audience.

The third *pistis* is *logos,* the appeal to patterns, conventions, and modes of reasoning that the audience finds convincing and persuasive. Although it is common to translate *logos* into its cognate, the "logical" appeal, such a translation is imprecise and potentially misleading. *Logos* in ancient Greek means more than simply logic or reasoning; it means something like "thought plus action." Thus, just as *ethos* moves an audience by activating their faith in the credibility of the rhetor and *pathos* stimulates their feelings and seeks a change in their attitudes and actions, so *logos,* accompanied by the other two appeals, mobilizes the powers of reasoning.

Although *logos* has been explained using different terminology by rhetorical theorists over the centuries, the "logical" transaction they describe can always be characterized in the same general way. A rhetor enters a rhetorical situation either knowing, or prepared to discover, what she and her audience hold as common assumptions about the subject that she will discuss. Knowing that she will have to invoke these common assumptions either implicitly or explicitly in her text, she proceeds to offer a premise or observation about the situation at hand, about the subject of the text. With the common assumptions invoked and the premise or observation put into play, the speaker can then posit a conclusion that follows from the assumption and the premise; this conclusion is, in general terms, the central idea or thesis that the speaker or writer hopes the audience will believe or act upon. The key feature of this basic "logical" transaction of rhetoric is that none of its constituent elements is always, or even frequently, certain and beyond argument. That is, the speaker or writer might find herself in a wrangle with the audience about (1) what they do believe, think, or feel in common; (2) whether the premise or observation is just and appropriate; or (3) whether the conclusion—the central idea or thesis—actually does follow from the assumptions and premise, and even if it does, whether there are other circumstances that would prevent the audience from accepting the conclusion. Conversely, the speaker or writer might find the audience in perfect agreement with some or all of the constituents, in which case the "logical" rhetorical transaction succeeds grandly.

Three cases might provide instances of this basic logical transaction at work.

Case A is a simplified version of a rhetorical situation in the social sciences: A graduate student in psychology wants to investigate whether high school seniors learn more effectively if they listen to classical music while they study. Thus, the researcher identifies two groups of high school students, equal in number and gender, who on a pretest showed similar levels of ability and knowledge with respect to a particular subject. One group is the control group and the other the experimental group. The control group studies new material on the pretested subject under naturalistic conditions in a library; the experimental group studies the same material in the same location, but with classical music playing. The researcher finds that 95 percent of the students in the experimental group score higher on a post test than their counterparts in the control group. In the report of this experiment, the researcher attributes the success of the experimental group to the presence of classical music in the students' study environment.

Case B comes from American history: The second paragraph of the Declaration of Independence reads, in part, as follows:

> We hold these truths to be self-evident: that all men are created equal; that they are endowed by their Creator with certain inalienable rights; that among these are life, liberty, and the pursuit of happiness; that to secure these rights, governments are instituted among men, deriving their just powers from the consent of the governed; that whenever any form of government becomes destructive of these ends, it is the right of the people to alter or to abolish it, and to institute new government, laying its foundation on such principles, and organizing its powers in such form, as to them shall seem most likely to effect their safety and happiness.

The Declaration then proceeds to list and elaborate the "long train of abuses and usurpations" of these "inalienable rights," 19 such violations in all, perpetrated by George III, king of England. Thus, the representatives to the General Congress assembled in 1776 could "solemnly publish and declare, that these united colonies are, and of right ought to be free and independent states; that they are absolved from allegiance to the British crown, and that all political connection between them and the state of Great Britain is, and ought to be totally dissolved."

Case C is another hypothetical case, this time from literary criticism: A student in an American literature class is reading William Faulkner's novel *As I Lay Dying* and encounters the character Dewey Dell. The name sounds vaguely familiar to the student, and he seems to remember a phrase in Percy Bysshe Shelley's poem, "To a Skylark," where some action takes place "in a dell of dew." The student eventually reads further into Faulkner's work, finds many echoes of phrases from English romantic poetry, and writes a term paper detailing the influences of the romantics on the American novelist.

How does *logos*, the invocation of and appeal to a potential reader's system of reasoning, operate in each case? Only in rare instances does a discourse function "logically" by announcing incontrovertible premises as assumptions, by positing empirically verifiable and irrefutable observations about the subject matter at hand, and by offering a claim that is based on a "logical" chain of reasoning from assumptions through observation to a conclusion. In other words, *logos* generally does not function logically; it functions rhetorically, and each element of the appeal—the assumptions, the observation, and the claim—may be debatable and admit of more than one possibility.

Case A represents a classic, if oversimplified, version of what social scientists would call a causal–comparative study. The researcher is working from three of the ruling assumptions of the experimental research community: first, that we live in an essentially behaviorist world where people's actions come in response to various stimuli that affect them; second, that it is possible to establish a research setting in which all the conditions under which the research subjects are operating are controlled and in which a single, isolatable variable can be manipulated; and, third, that when conditions have been controlled, any differences in behavior between two groups of research subjects can be attributed to the causal influence of the single, manipulated variable. Although none of these assumptions is indisputable, the researcher does not explicitly argue for their validity. Such assumptions are, he presumes, part of the conventional *logos* already operating in his scholarly field, and they effectively constitute some of the premises for his conclusion, that 95 percent of the students who listened to classical music while they studied scored higher on a post test than their non-music-listening counterparts. Because the researcher has established a conventional and controlled investigative structure, this observation itself is largely indisputable. Some readers might question the *validity* of the post test, asking whether it really measures anything significant about the students' performance, but no one can question the *reliability* of the assessment. Armed with these data, the researcher is prepared to make his claim, to argue that the higher scores of the music listeners were caused by their more relaxed states or their more intense concentration, both attributable, in the researcher's argument, to the presence of the classical music.

The operation of *logos* in Case B involves one of the most famous examples of explicitly stated assumptions in history. The authors of the Declaration of Independence boldly state the credo, the "self-evident truths" upon which their argument is built: All people are created equal and are entitled to the pursuit of life, liberty, and happiness; when any government impedes this pursuit, the people may abolish it and institute a new government. As with the experimentalist/behaviorist assumptions in Case A, the question of whether these assumptions are universally "true" or "valid" is a moot point. They are certainly "true" and "valid" within the theology and cosmology of the authors of the Declaration, who see them as "self-evident"; similarly, the authors assume, anyone reading or hearing their text will agree.

Coming in the wake of the power and euphony of the "self-evident" assumptions, the actual observation that the authors make about the situation seems rather prosaic: In 19 ways, the king of England has violated the colonists' rights to the pursuit of life, liberty, and happiness. Unlike the "hard-data" observations in Case A, the assertions in Case B cannot be so easily verified empirically. The assertions themselves—for example, that George III has kept a standing army in the colonies—are contentious and open to dispute. But notice that the authors of the Declaration do not invite the audience to dispute the truth of these assertions. They simply lay each assertion out, offer a bit of evidence to illustrate it, and then move to the claim: The colonies are independent of Great Britain. If you buy into the "self-evident" assumptions and you agree that the actions of George III cited in the document represent breaches of these "truths," then you must concur that the colonists have a right to declare their independence and that this document makes it so.

Case C builds its claim on a common assumption in the rhetoric of Western literary criticism, namely that authors are influenced by the work of their predecessors, particularly those revered as "great authors" in the canon of British and American literature. Although this assumption has been freighted with psychological implications by Harold Bloom and other scholars, traditionally literary critics have not seen it as troubling in the *logos* of a critical argument. Thousands of critical theses in articles, papers, monographs, and books have been put forward based on the assumption that the influence of a previous "great author" on a latter one is discernible, perhaps conscious on the part of the latter, and generally a good thing for literary criticism to make note of. Again, this assumption is not provable; it is simply a notion that students of literature tacitly adhere to. The student in Case C discovers a "manifest intertextuality," a patch of language in Faulkner that so closely resembles a passage in Shelley that the critic must assume that the similarity is intentional; indeed, other passages in Faulker show distinct Shelleyesque echoes as well. Accepting the assumption about influence and citing the intertextual passages, the student in American literature can argue, probably convincingly, that Faulkner was influenced by the literature of British romanticism.

This basic transaction of *logos*—assumptions, assertion or observation, and claim—is called an *enthymeme.* According to Aristotle, speakers or writers arguing a case either construct enthymemes or cite examples; those are the only two persuasive devices available. Unfortunately, Aristotle's own definition of the enthymeme is quite sketchy. He explains that the enthymeme is to rhetoric what the syllogism is to logic. A syllogism offers an incontrovertible proposition as its major premise, an empirically verifiable observation as its minor premise, and a necessary, logical conclusion; an enthymeme, however, might be contentious at all three points. It is a "rhetorical syllogism" that depends for acceptance upon the context in which it occurs. In the centuries since Aristotle, rhetorical theorists have tried to flesh out his suggestive definition. Some have seen the enthymeme as a materially deficient syllogism because neither its premises or conclusions are provable; some have seen it as formally deficient because the major premise—what the rhetor believes that the audience presumes to be true—often goes unstated, and the minor premise—the assertion or observation—is occasionally implicit as well. Contemporary rhetoricians have largely stopped trying to distinguish the enthymeme from the syllogism, simply accepting that the two logical devices have some formal and material similarities but are essentially different.

The other logical device Aristotle describes, the example, might initially seem the converse of the enthymeme, but actually the two devices are related. Anyone who has ever argued a case knows the value of citing a precedent. If you are campaigning for a Republican presidential candidate and arguing that he or she will act decisively to protect American economic interests in the oil-rich Middle East, you might cite the precedent of George Bush's actions in the Gulf War and claim that your candidate will be equally decisive. To Aristotle, however, an example is more than a single instance that acts as a precedent. The Greek word Aristotle uses for example is *paradeigma,* from which English draws the cognate *paradigm.* To be rhetorically effective, an example must offer a *repeated pattern* of precedents. For example, if a rhetor is arguing that, despite its advocates' claims to the contrary, the "Star Wars" defense system will probably be used aggressively and offensively, she might cite the example of previous weapons systems: "They said the incendiary bomb would be used only for defense and it was used offensively; they said the hydrogen bomb would be used only for defense and it was used offensively; they said the atomic bomb would be used only for defense and it was used offensively. Shouldn't we expect, then, that the `Star Wars' system will be used offensively?"

Although the enthymeme looks like what a logician would call a deduction and the example looks logically like an induction, they are similar in their effect rhetorically. As James Raymond has perceptively noted, the example is itself a kind of enthymeme. Its major premise, the unstated assumption, is that history tends to repeat itself. Its observation, its assertion about the situation at hand, consists of the pattern of precedent-setting instances. Its claim is the conjecture about the future that follows from this premise and the cited instances.

Although the enthymeme and example are usually discussed in rhetorical theory under the rubric of *logos,* these two tools of argument are not devoted exclusively to appealing to the logic and reasoning of the audience. Indeed, in order to move an audience to believe what the rhetor holds as a communal assumption, to accept her observation about the subject at hand as valid and legitimate, and to adhere to the conclusion that she claims follows from the assumption and the observation, she may need to deploy *pathos* and *ethos* as well. That is, arguing enthymematically may require her to appeal to the audience's reasoning, emotions, interests, and to her own credibility and character.

THE CANONS OF RHETORIC

In addition, although the enthymeme and example are often discussed in rhetorical theory as elements of *logos,* they are also central elements in the first of what the Roman rhetoricians proposed as the five *canons* of rhetoric: invention, arrangement, style, memory, and delivery. Each of these canons is considered separately later in Part II, but conceptual definitions of each at this point will suggest how they have been developed as general features within rhetorical theory.

Invention is the art of generating effective material for a particular rhetorical situation. Some rhetorical theorists have argued that *invention* is not a completely appropriate term for this canon because the rhetor often does not generate *new* material, but simply calls it forth from memory. Invention requires the rhetor to assess the audience in order to determine what they feel, think, and know about the subject he intends to speak or write about; to determine, at least provisionally, what purpose he hopes his text will accomplish; and thus to decide what kinds of material—facts, propositions, ideas, and so on—he will inscribe in the text. For many rhetors, these determinations are made subconsciously, simultaneously, and perhaps even randomly. Nonetheless, such decisions allow the rhetor to probe his thoughts, knowledge base, and experiences and the data in the world around him, and to generate material he believes will be effective for the particular audience and purposes he will invoke. Some rhetors effect this search for material using techniques specific to their particular discipline. For example, a writer constructing an argument in literary criticism may search a novel, poem, or play for some apparently anomalous or distinct feature of plot, character, theme, or diction, with a view to explicating it. Some rhetors, on the other hand, invent material by using some form of structured heuristic (derived from the Greek for *finding*) technique, such as an abbreviated form of Aristotle's *topoi*, Kenneth Burke's dramatistic pentad (which investigates human action as the interaction of Act, Agent, Scene, Agency, and Purpose), the common "journalist's questions," or the tagmemic matrix (which adapts terms from physics—particle, wave, field—as categories for understanding the nature of a unit of information). Finally, some rhetors may generate material using a relatively unstructured, even intuitive, heuristic such as freewriting, brainstorming, and drawing tree diagrams.

Arrangement, sometimes called "disposition," is the art of ordering the material in a text so that it is most appropriate for the needs of the audience and the purpose the text is designed to accomplish. Every effective rhetor understands, at least intuitively, that in most conventional situations a text must have a beginning, a middle, and an end, but methods of producing this order differ widely. Some speakers and writers considering arrangement may use principles drawn from ancient rhetoric; in general terms, these principles suggest that an effective argument is specifically ordered first to capture the audience's attention, second to provide necessary background information, third to state and prove the text's thesis or central idea, fourth to anticipate and address possible countertheses, and finally to conclude by appealing to the audience's emotions. Rather than relying on any general laws, however, most rhetors derive principles of arrangement from the genres their discourse community values and expects from speakers and writers within it. For example, a writer of scientific research reports knows that for her text to command the attention of people in the discipline, she must write an introduction that frames a research question, a section outlining the methods and materials involved in her research, a section detailing the results of the specific project, and a section arguing that these results actually mean something significant.

Some rhetorical theorists have included under the rubric of arrangement not only principles for ordering entire texts, but also guidelines for arranging information within smaller units, such as paragraphs. The work of the Scottish rhetorician Alexander Bain, for example, led many scholars in the late nineteenth and early twentieth centuries to describe the arrangement of material in both whole texts and paragraphs according to the *mode of discourse* they were supposed to display: narration, description, exposition (often subdivided into such "methods of exposition" as cause-and-effect, definition, comparison–contrast, and so on), and argumentation. Finally, some rhetorical theorists have treated issues of the relative importance of information under arrangement. One mode of arrangement-by-importance is Nestorian order, named after the clear-voiced orator of the Greeks in the Trojan War. Nestor, according to legend, would begin a speech with the next-to-most important information, then provide the least important, and close with the most important.

The canon of arrangement has been called into question with the advent of postmodernism, in particular through the insistence that no text ever really "begins" or "ends"; rather, as Burke's "conversation in the parlor" above suggests, all texts enter into a larger text. The artificiality of beginnings and endings has been explored by postmodern writers such as Roland Barthes, as the excerpt above from *S/Z* indicates. For an audience of postmodern literary theorists, then, the rhetor might deliberately create a discourse that violates the conventions of arrangement, one that accepts and welcomes the disorderliness of open intellectual play.

Style, sometimes called elocution, is the art of producing sentences and words that will make an appropriately favorable impression on readers or listeners. Traditionally, the canon of style has included discussions of levels of language— the grand, the middle, and the low, for example—as well as explanations of *tropes,* or figures of thought, and *schemes,* or figures of actual expression. To cite just three examples: Under the rubric of tropes, rhetorical theorists have explained the nature and uses of metaphor (implied comparison), personification (the attribution of human qualities to nonhuman entities), and synechdoche (the substitution of the part for the whole). Under schemes, rhetorical theorists have catalogued such devices as parallelism (creating a similarity of structure in a set of related words, phrases, or clauses), ellipsis (a deliberate omission of words that are readily supplied by the context), and anaphora (the repetition of the same words at the beginning of successive phrases or clauses). A great debate in the history of rhetoric has surrounded the question of whether style is simply an ornamentation of thought and speech, or whether style is "organic" to the specific text and represents, as Thomas De Quincey proposed, the "incarnation of thought."

Most modern rhetorical theorists have adopted some version of the latter position and see style as the process of "giving presence" to ideas that rhetors want their audiences to attend to. Chaim Perelman, among others, has discussed presence in terms of the emphasis that the rhetor gives to "events which, without his intervention, would be neglected but now occupy our attention." The rhetor can do this by presenting images that will affect an audience—"Caesar's bloody tunic as brandished by Antony, the children of the victim of the accused"—or by applying techniques of *amplification* (e.g., "repetition, accumulation, accentuation of particular passages") that highlight the "reality" that the rhetor would like to present (Perelman, *The Realm of Rhetoric*, 35–37).

Memory, the fourth traditional canon of rhetoric, seems to bear the most residue of the oral culture in which rhetorical theory has its ancient roots; however, memory is undergoing something of a revival in contemporary theory. In classical periods, rhetors were expected to commit their speeches to memory. In later periods, the art of memory was taught to young rhetors as a means of mental discipline, even though they most often read texts that had been written out. The most commonly taught mnemonic method was for rhetors to associate the parts of the speech with visual images in some specific physical setting. For example, a rhetor could mentally connect the introduction of his speech to the porch of a house, the background narration to the foyer, the thesis and proof to the arch and the grand ballroom, and the conclusion to the antechamber. As rhetoric over the centuries became more and more an art of crafting and delivering written texts, the canon of memory diminished in importance. In current rhetorical theory, however, computers are being used to store monumental databases and rhetors are devising increasingly inventive ways to manipulate these data, so memory is becoming a vital canon once again.

Delivery, the final traditional canon of rhetorical theory, once constituted the art of using one's voice and body effectively when speaking. Elaborate theory and pedagogy, in both classical periods and later in the eighteenth and nineteenth centuries, was developed to teach rhetors how to pronounce words, project their voices, and move their faces, arms, hands, and even legs and feet. In departments offering courses in public speaking today, contemporary principles of delivery are still being developed; where rhetorical theory and pedagogy are more concerned with written texts, the canon of delivery has come to embrace the study of *graphemics*, the display of material on the printed page or screen.

When one teaches rhetoric, either its theory or its effective practice, one can teach principles of invention, arrangement, style, memory, and delivery as general tenets, applicable in varying degrees to discourse in all fields. However, as suggested earlier, rhetoric has developed during the second half of this century as the study and practice of the featuring of specific content that is vital to the epistemological and social functions of special-interest groups. The title of a 1983 book by Christopher Norris, *The Deconstructive Turn: Essays in the Rhetoric of Philosophy*, suggests what might have been regarded as a heretical idea in centuries past—that philosophy is rhetorical. The "rhetoricizing" of academic subjects that were once regarded as objective, and whose scholars regarded themselves as disinterested, comes along with the postmodern recognition that all discourse serves to advance certain interests, certain versions of truth and facts that serve individual and institutional biases and motives. One of the projects of rhetoric has become the investigation of how such biases and motives are inscribed into academic and scholarly discourses, and so we see increasing attention by humanists, scientists, and social scientists to the *pisteis* of the writing that defines their fields. The presence of rhetoric in other fields is addressed extensively in Part IV of this book in order to suggest what a global art rhetoric has become in our time.

WORKS CITED

Aristotle. *Rhetoric.* Trans. George Kennedy. New York: Oxford UP, 1991.

———. *Poetics.* Trans. W. Hamilton Fyfe. Cambridge: Harvard UP, 1932.

Barthes, Roland. *S/Z.* Trans. Richard Miller. New York: Hill and Wang, 1974.

Berthoff, Ann E. *The Making of Meaning: Metaphors, Models, and Maxims for Writing Teachers.* Portsmouth, NH: Boynton/Cook, 1981.

Bitzer, Lloyd. "The Rhetorical Situation." *Philosophy and Rhetoric* 1.1 (1968): 1–14.

Brooks, Cleanth. *The Well Wrought Urn: Studies in the Structure of Poetry.* New York: Harcourt, 1947.

Burke, Kenneth. *Permanence and Change.* 3rd ed. 1935. Berkeley: U of California P, 1984.

———. *The Philosophy of Literary Form.* 3rd ed. Berkeley: U of California P, 1973.

———. "Rhetoric—Old and New." *New Rhetorics.* 1950. Ed. Martin Steinmann. New York: Scribner's, 1967.

Cicero, *On Oratory and Orators (De Oratore).* Trans. J. S. Watson. Carbondale: Southern Illinois UP, 1970.

Cixous, Helene. "The Laugh of the Medusa." *Critical Theory Since 1965.* Ed. Hazard Adams and Leroy Searle. Tallahassee: Florida State UP, 1986. 309–320.

Ede, Lisa, and Andrea Lunsford. "Audience Addressed/Audience Invoked: The Role of Audience in Composition Theory and Pedagogy." *College Composition and Communication* 35 (1984): 155–71.

De Quincey, Thomas. "Rhetoric." *Selected Essays on Rhetoric.* Ed. Frederick Burwick. Carbondale: Southern Illinois UP, 1967. 81–133.

Eagleton, Terry. *Literary Theory: An Introduction.* Minneapolis: U of Minnesota P, 1983.

Jarratt, Susan. *Rereading the Sophists.* Carbondale: Southern Illinois UP, 1991.

Kennedy, George. "A Hoot in the Dark: The Evolution of General Rhetoric." *Philosophy and Rhetoric* 25.1 (1992): 1–21.

Myers, Greg. "The Social Construction of Two Biologists' Proposals." *Written Communication* 2 (1985): 219–45.

Norris, Christopher. *The Deconstructive Turn: Essays in the Rhetoric of Philosophy.* London: Methuen, 1983.

Nystrand, Martin. "Rhetoric's `Audience' and Linguistics' `Speech Community': Implications For Understanding Writing, Reading, and Text." *What Writers Know: The Language, Process, and Structure of Written Discourse.* Ed. Martin Nystrand. New York: Academic, 1982. 1–30.

Ong, Walter. "The Writer's Audience is Always a Fiction." *PMLA* 90 (1975): 9–21.

Perelman, Chaim. *The Realm of Rhetoric.* Notre Dame: U of Notre Dame P, 1982.

Plato. *Phaedrus.* Trans. Harold North Fowler. Cambridge, MA: Harvard UP, 1914.

Quintilian. *The Institutio Oratoria of Quintilian.* Trans. H. E. Butler. 4 vols. Cambridge, MA: Harvard UP, 1921.

Raymond, James. "Enthymemes, Examples, and Rhetorical Method." *Essays in Classical Rhetoric and Modern Discourse.* Eds. Robert J. Connors, Lisa Ede, and Andrea Lunsford. Carbondale: Southern Illinois UP, 1984. 140–51.

Swales, John. *Genre Analysis: English in Academic and Research Settings.* Cambridge: Cambridge UP, 1990.

Valesio, Paolo. *Novantiqua.* Bloomington: Indiana UP, 1980.

Vatz, Richard. "The Myth of the Rhetorical Situation." *Philosophy and Rhetoric* 6 (1972): 154–61.

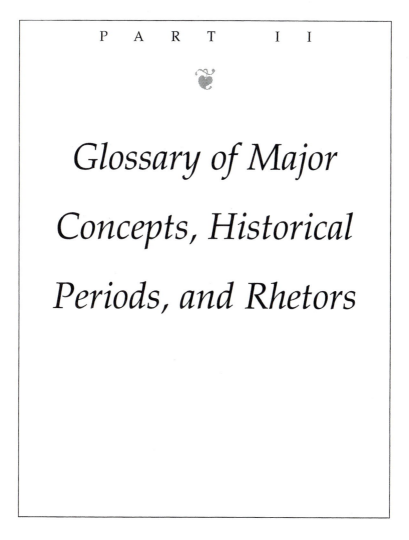

P A R T I I

Glossary of Major

Concepts, Historical

Periods, and Rhetors

Aristotle **(384–322 BCE)** Aristotle's statements on rhetoric were fundamental to all Western rhetorics that followed him, but his influence was eclipsed by the attention to Ciceronian rhetoric that extended through the Renaissance, and by the dismissal of classical rhetoric in the Enlightenment. Thomas De Quincey, offering this own eccentric theory of rhetoric in 1828, both recognizes the centrality of Aristotle to rhetoric and anticipates Aristotle's elevated importance in this century, when he says that "All parties may possibly fancy a confirmation of their views in Aristotle."

A student of **Plato** who preferred the practical to the transcendental, Aristotle wrote broadly—on logic, the natural sciences, metaphysics, ethics, politics, and rhetoric. His *Rhetoric* was probably composed between 360 and 334 BCE, undergoing several revisions, and was edited to some extent after his death. While the *Rhetoric* has often been cited as a source for prescriptive rules for speaking and writing, this work is highly speculative and offers little in the way of a coherent, complete, and detailed process. The "open" character of the *Rhetoric* is perhaps its greatest strength for those who wish to maintain that rhetoric is an exploratory art that cannot be reduced to a disciplined system.

Aristotle's *Rhetoric* can be read as a response to Plato's condemnation of the art, in which Aristotle proposes that rhetoric can help to create community and goodwill. Like dialectic, rhetoric is concerned with the probable; unlike dialectic, rhetoric is expository rather than dialogic, treats specific cases rather than general principles, and relies on psychology as well as logic for its effectiveness.

Aristotle defines rhetoric as the ability to see, in each particular case, the available means of persuasion (*pisteis*). He identifies three types of rhetorical address: the deliberative, the judicial, and the epideictic or ceremonial. Showing how the *pisteis* operate in these situations leads Aristotle to consider—rather excursively—matters such as the nature of happiness and the good, and the emotions of anger, fear, pity, shame, and envy. The psychological device central to rhetoric is the **enthymeme,** a rhetorical syllogism that requires audience participation for its completion. Aristotle's inventory of the sources of material for enthymemes, the twenty-eight *topoi,* can be seen to illustrate his emphasis on the invention of multiple perspectives as the rhetor's primary responsibility. Aristotle also addresses issues of **style** (concentrating on diction and metaphor) and **arrangement,** but ignores for the most part features of speechmaking that become important in Roman rhetorics: **memory** and **delivery.**

Further Reading: Larry Arnhart, *Aristotle on Political Reasoning: A Commentary on the 'Rhetoric'* (De Kalb: Northern Illinois UP, 1981); William M. A. Grimaldi, *Aristotle, Rhetoric I: A Commentary* (Bronx, NY: Fordham UP, 1980) and *Aristotle, Rhetoric II: A Commentary* (Bronx, NY: Fordham UP, 1988); *Aristotle on Rhetoric: A Theory of Civic Discourse,* ed. and trans. George A. Kennedy (New York: Oxford UP, 1991).

Arrangement In classical rhetorical theory, **arrangement,** also called disposition, is the second of the five traditional canons of rhetoric, along with **invention, style, memory,** and **delivery.** Arrangement refers to the placement and ordering of the parts of a discourse. The principles of arrangement developed by classical rhetoricians can be represented as points on a continuum, ranging from organic within the structure of an individual text at one end to prescriptive, taxonomic, and universal for all texts at the other. Modern and contemporary scholars have associated the rhetorical concept of arrangement with theories of genre, often arguing that arrangement and genre have a heuristic role in the composition of texts.

Among classical rhetoricians, **Plato** offers a perspective on arrangement as organic to the individual text. In *Phaedrus,* **Plato** has Socrates say that "every discourse, like a living creature, should be so put together that it has its own body and lacks neither head nor feet, middle nor extremities, all composed in such a way that they suit both each other and the whole." In his *Rhetoric,* **Aristotle's** advice about the arrangement of discourse (or *taxis* in Greek) is only a bit more prescriptive than **Plato's**. In Book III, **Aristotle** writes, "A speech has two parts. You must state your case, and you must prove it." He acknowledges later, however, that for some audiences unfamiliar with the subject matter at hand, a discourse might need a *proem,* or introduction, and some other audiences might find a text more persuasive if it had a separate, recognizable conclusion. Isocrates' teachings about arrangement in the *Antidosis* are more prescriptive than either **Plato's** or **Aristotle's**. Isocrates maintains that a speech has four divisions: introduction, narration, proofs, and epilogue. Cicero in *De Oratore* is the most prescriptive of all the classical rhetoricians, teaching that an oration has seven parts: the entrance, or the introduction of the subject and the securing of goodwill; the narration, or a recital of the circumstances necessary to understand the subject at hand; the proposition, the speaker's central idea or thesis; the division, or an outline of the points the speaker will demonstrate; the confirmation, or the body of proof for the points; the confutation, or the rebuttal of an opponent's possible objection to the proofs; and the conclusion, or a summation of the proofs and a final appeal to the audience's emotions. This taxonomic perspective on arrangement, especially as promulgated by **Quintilian** in the *Institutio Oratoria,* remained dominant in Western rhetoric through the Middle Ages and the Renaissance. Eighteenth-century rhetoricians **George Campbell, Hugh Blair,** and **Richard Whately** returned to a more organic view of arrangement by fusing explanations of invention and arrangement.

Scholars of genre theory have debated the degree to which the arrangement of the parts of a text is a signal of its status as a genre. **W. Ross Winterowd,** for example, maintains that a genre is textual manifestation of form, which he defines as "the internal set of consistent relationships perceived in any stretch of discourse, whether poem, play, essay, oration, or whatever." Carolyn Miller, on the other hand, argues that a genre is more than textual arrangement; it is a fusion of substance and arrangement, a speaker's or writer's socially active response to a typified, recurrent social situation.

Questions of arrangement have been vigorously debated by scholars of written composition in school settings. Janet Emig, for example, disparages instruction in the "five-paragraph theme," with its predictable arrangement of an introductory paragraph followed by three paragraphs of development and a conclusion, as being mechanical and reductive. Richard Coe, on the other hand, maintains that the typical arrangement patterns of school compositions can be heuristic, teaching students that many compositions require a thesis and that it's good to be able to offer at least three points in support of it.

Further Reading: Richard M. Coe, "An Apology for Form: Or, Who Took the Form out of the Process," *College English* 49 (1987): 13–28; Janet Emig, *The Composing Processes of Twelfth Graders* (Urbana, IL: National Council of Teachers of English, 1971); David A. Jolliffe and Ellen M. Brier, "Studying Writers' Knowledge in Academic Disciplines," *Writing in Academic Disciplines,* ed. David A. Jolliffe (Norwood, NJ: Ablex, 1988), 35–87; Carolyn Miller, "Genre as Social Action," *Quarterly Journal of Speech* 70 (1984): 151–167; W. Ross Winterowd, *Contemporary Rhetoric: A Conceptual Background with Readings* (New York: Harcourt Brace Jovanovich, 1975).

Francis Bacon (1561–1626) A courtier in the court of Elizabeth I and later Lord Chancellor under James I, Francis Bacon was the foremost moral and scientific philosopher of the English Renaissance, as well as one of its most eminent politicians. His contributions to rhetorical theory emerge as part of his overall inquiry into the nature of the human intellect, developed in three major works, *The Advancement of Learning* (1605), *Novum Organum* (1620), and the *New Atlantis* (published posthumously in 1627). Bacon's attention to the prominence of intellection and inquiry in rhetoric distances him from the work of another influential Renaissance rhetorician, **Peter Ramus,** whose theory held that rhetoric comprises only **style** and **delivery,** not **invention** or **arrangement.**

Bacon's famous definition of rhetoric in *The Advancement of Learning* depends on his division of the mind into three faculties: reason, the faculty that perceives regularities, analyzes, and generalizes; **memory,** the repository of experience and facts; and **imagination,** the faculty that can conceive states of affairs as different from the way they are. To Bacon, thus, "the duty and office of Rhetoric is to apply Reason to Imagination for the better moving of the will."

Bacon acknowledges that **invention** is perhaps not the proper term for the first traditional canon of rhetoric. He writes that "to invent is to discover that we know not, and not to recover or resummon that which we already know; and the use of [rhetorical] invention is no other but out of the knowledge whereof our mind is already possessed, to draw forth or call before us that which may be pertinent to the purpose which we take into our consideration." Nonetheless, Bacon accepts the traditional term and teaches the use of four **commonplaces** for invention: the *Colours of Good and Evil,* a table of ethically influential statements and some potential fallacies that accompany each; the *antitheta,* a list of parallel, pro and con theses; the *formulae,* or "small parts of a speech, fully composed and ready for use"; and *apothegms,* or *pointed speeches* that can be "interlaced in continuous speech" or "recited upon occasion of themselves."

Anticipating the **epistemic rhetoric** of the eighteenth century, Bacon rejects the syllogism as a means of arriving at truth. He writes in a 1620 essay, "The Great Instauration," that "I use induction throughout. . . . I consider induction to be that form of demonstration which upholds the sense, and closes with nature, and comes to the very brink of operation, if it does not actually deal with it." Because he is concerned with the role of clear human perception in induction, however, Bacon warns readers in the *Novum Organum* to beware the "four class-es of Idols" that cloud judgment: the "Idols of the Tribe," the inherent human tendency to distort and "discolour . . . the nature of things"; the "Idols of the Cave," the propensity of individual people to "refract and discolour" reality in idiosyncratic ways; the "Idols of the Market-place," which stem from the confu-sions occasioned by commerce; and the "Idols of the Theatre," which come not from actual dramatic performances but instead from "the various dogmas of philosophies," which Bacon sees as "but so many stage plays."

Further Reading: John Briggs, *Francis Bacon and the Rhetoric of Nature* (Cambridge: Harvard UP, 1989); Lisa Jardine, *Francis Bacon and the Art of Discourse* (Cambridge: Cambridge UP, 1974); Karl Wallace, *Francis Bacon on Communication and Rhetoric* (Chapel Hill: U of North Carolina P, 1943).

Hugh Blair (1718–1800) Hugh Blair's *Lectures on Rhetoric and Belles-Lettres* was the most widely published and widely used rhetoric textbook through the late eighteenth and nineteenth centuries. The conjunction of rhetoric and *belles lettres*—that is, "polite" arts that include poetry, history, and drama—suggests that a range of artistic and scholarly pursuits should share common standards and reflect common human qualities; this is a central presupposition of what we now call the *belletristic tradition,* whose English practitioners include Adam Smith, Lord Kames, and Blair.

A Presbyterian minister, Blair began his career as a teacher with his presenta-tion of the first *Lectures* at the University of Edinburgh in 1759. The tremendous popularity of Blair's public lectures led to his appointment as Regius Professor of Rhetoric and Belles Lettres in 1762. The *Lectures* were published in 1783, and as William Charvat points out, by the end of the eighteenth century "half the educated English-speaking world was reading Blair." Well over one hundred editions of Blair have been published since 1783, and he has been translated into several foreign languages. In America, Blair's *Lectures* became the standard text for rhetoric courses at Harvard, Yale, Brown, Amherst, and Columbia.

Volume 1 of the forty-seven lectures concentrates on the relationship between **style** and taste, and gives critical attention to several numbers of *The Spectator.* Volume 2 deals with public speaking, especially pulpit eloquence, and moves to a consideration of literary discourse with lectures on several kinds of poetry, on epic poets from Homer to Milton, and on tragedy and comedy.

Often leagued with rhetoricians **George Campbell** and **Richard Whately,** Blair is notable for his discussion of taste as an element of rhetoric. For Blair, refined taste is marked by delicacy and correctness, and while he acknowledges that taste may vary with religious and political beliefs, he also universalizes it: "In every composition, what interests the imagination, and touches the heart, pleases all ages and all nations." Such a statement may be compared with contemporary treatises on taste by Sir Joshua Reynolds, Edmund Burke, Lord Kames, and David Hume.

Considered on a grand scale, tasteful style is connected to the sublime and the beautiful. In more local terms, taste is manifest in the author's adherence to unity and perspicuity. A speech or story in which "all the parts [are] joined together with due connection" appeals to an internal sense that is inherent in human psychology; we receive "superior pleasure from the relation of an action which is one and entire, beyond what we receive from the relation of scattered and unconnected facts." Perspicuity—which we may understand as transparency of meaning—also appeals to our distaste for ambiguity, or what Blair calls "circumlocutions."

Further Reading: Paul Bator, "The Formation of the Regius Chair of Rhetoric and Belles-Lettres at the University of Edinburgh," *Quarterly Journal of Speech* 75 (1989): 40–64; Nan Johnson, "Hugh Blair and the Belles-Lettres Rationale for Rhetoric," *Nineteenth Century Rhetoric in North America* (Carbondale: Southern Illinois UP, 1991): 31–46; Robert Schmitz, *Hugh Blair* (New York: King's Crown, 1948).

Wayne C. Booth **(b. 1921)** American scholar Wayne C. Booth oversees the operations of rhetoric in politics, music, and culture; but most significantly, Booth emphasizes the rhetorical dimensions of literature. In *The Rhetoric of Fiction*, Booth contests the Jamesian notion that good fiction should be "pure," that is, free of rhetoric. Booth argues that all fiction has a rhetorical function whether or not it is overtly persuasive. When he says that "we must never forget that though the author can to some extent choose his disguises, he can never choose to disappear," Booth is insisting that an author is always either "showing" or "telling," always present and attempting to advance a viewpoint in some form.

In order to study how authors persuade us, Booth examines such devices as distance, irony, and sympathy as rhetorical gestures. He also defines a number of narrative stances: the reliable narrator, the unreliable narrator, the impersonal narrator, the self-conscious narrator. Further, Booth develops the concept of the *implied author,* an entity distinct from the actual author and from the narrator but existing somewhere in between. For all his concepts, Booth draws liberally from the Western literary tradition to make his cases.

In addition to studying rhetorical dimensions of literature (which he continues in *The Rhetoric of Irony*), Booth examines the rhetoric of Good Reasons: he sees "rhetoric as the whole art of discovering and sharing warrantable assertion" in *Modern Dogma and the Rhetoric of Assent.* Written in the 1960s amid the turmoil of student revolts at the University of Chicago, where Booth was a teacher and administrator, *Modern Dogma* is an exhortation that we do indeed have values. Booth explicates "five modern dogmas" that prevent us from listening to each other's good reasons, including the modern notion that the universe is value-free. But Booth argues that we are ethical creatures, not merely sacks of water. We *do* have values, so we might as well listen to each other so we can discover what the right values are, Booth proposes. More than listening, however, we should make an intellectual effort to accept as true anything that we have no good reason to doubt.

In a similar vein, Booth takes up **Plato**'s ideas about the relationship between art and ethics. Does it matter, Booth wonders, if art is moral? Should we consider the moral value of literature when we criticize it? Oscar Wilde has said, "There is no such thing as a moral or an immoral book. Books are well written or badly written. That is all." In *The Company We Keep: An Ethics of Literature,* Booth points out that Wilde's promotion of aesthetics over ethics is itself an ethical stance. Ethical criticism, then, is inevitable; we do it whether we intend to or not.

The vulnerability of Booth's stance, of course, is that he seems to set himself up as the keeper of knowledge and values, as suggested by the title of his book *The Knowledge Most Worth Having.* David Lodge has argued in *Twentieth Century Literary Criticism* that "Professor Booth evinces a prejudice . . . as extreme and unnecessary as the one he himself exposes," and Booth himself suggests this in *The Rhetoric of Irony* when he asks, "Who is the paragon who determines critical norms?" and answers, "I may often have sounded as if I offered myself for the job." At the same time, Booth would say that it is every rhetor's responsibility to make value judgments, and that he is not obliged to hedge his opinions simply because others have failed to assert theirs.

Further Reading: Richard Berrong, "Finding Antifeminism in Rabelais; or, A Response to Wayne Booth's Call for an Ethical Criticism," *Critical Inquiry* 11 (June 1985): 687–96; Ellen Rooney, *Seductive Reasoning: Pluralism as the Problematic of Contemporary Literary Theory* (Ithaca: Cornell UP, 1989).

Kenneth Burke   (1897–1993)   Kenneth Burke was a theorist, or "word man" as he called himself, who developed a unique style of linguistic and sociological analysis based on the study of literature and language.

R. P. Blackmur called rhetoric Burke's "first cradle-word," and indeed Burke theorized about rhetoric throughout his published career, which ranges from the 1920s to the 1990s. Burke sums up his approach to the study of rhetoric in particular and language in general in the introduction to his *Rhetoric of Motives* when he states that he "would but rediscover rhetorical elements that had become obscured when rhetoric as a term fell into disuse, and other specialized disciplines such as esthetics, anthropology, psychoanalysis, and sociology came to the fore."(xiii) Many have called Burke's approach encyclopedic—i.e., instead of merely taking back pilfered rhetorical principles, he contains the new discipline by re-evaluating its terminology, the category names that have become rhetoric's terministic screen. Overall, Burke has identified his role as a "middle-man," or a "translator," even if it is but "English to English."

Basically, rhetoric operates for Burke through *identification,* the means by which a speaker bridges ("pontificates") a division ever inherent in the rhetorical situation, in which the speaker, audience, and speech are necessarily separate. Identification is persuasion in that the audience is moved to remake the substance of its identity into a state of oneness or consubstantiality with the speaker. At one extreme, rhetoric is but a scramble for advantage in the "Human Barnyard"; at another, it consists of "pure persuasion," or the ultimate attempt at communication with one's god, be it religious or aesthetic.

Rhetoric is one of Burke's four categories of language, along with poetics, science, and philosophy. Like rhetoric, each of the categories partakes of "permanence and change" because of the dual, ever-changing, ever-permanent nature of language itself. Although particular language uses and situations change, linguistic principles themselves are permanent. Regarding rhetoric, for instance, Burke says, "If you start language all over again tomorrow, you would [still] have the means of praise and blame [inherent in language]."

Unchanging also is Burke's belief that language is the prime enabler of human action and interaction. Throughout his work Burke maintains a humane, cautionary tone. From language, he says, humankind inherits a "perfection principle," which is the source of our greatest threats as well as promises: A hope for and belief in the possibility of perfect language speaking perfect truth can lead us to impose ways of seeing and naming upon others and to fight when others don't see and name things our way. Burke's particular brand of rhetoric, which complicates and subverts the possibilities for perfection, has been characterized by many as an ongoing plea for peace, a "purification of war" through sheer loquacity, grounded in the understanding and elaboration of all the powerful goads implicit in human language (see **Dramatism**).

Further Reading: Stephen Bygrave, *Kenneth Burke: Rhetoric and Ideology* (London: Routledge, 1993); William Rueckert, *Kenneth Burke and the Drama of Human Relations* (Berkeley: U of California P, 1982); Herbert Simons and Trevor Melia, ed., *The Legacy of Kenneth Burke* (Madison: U of Wisconsin P, 1989).

George Campbell (1719–1796) George Campbell, a Presbyterian minister and principal of Marischal College in Aberdeen, Scotland, is best known today as the author of *The Philosophy of Rhetoric* (1776). During his lifetime, his reputation rested on his sermons and theological writings, especially his *Dissertation on Miracles* (1762), a refutation of Hume's *Essay on Miracles*. His posthumously published *Lectures on Systematic Theology and Pulpit Eloquence* (1807) contain practical rhetorical advice for beginning preachers.

Campbell developed his epistemology in contention with Hume's skepticism. As a theologian, he accepted revelation as a source of knowledge. At the same time, he adopted the empiricism and the science of human nature initiated by Bacon and Locke. Finally, as cofounder of the Aberdeen Philosophical Society, he helped elaborate the Scottish Common Sense philosophy. A synthesis of these strands informs his *Rhetoric*.

Campbell sees eloquence as a "grand art of communication" that encompasses all kinds of discourse, including poetry, and he bases it on the faculty psychology of his time by classifying it according to the intended effects on the audience: "to enlighten the understanding, to please the imagination, to move the passions, or to influence the will." The speaker must address all faculties, especially when the aim is persuasion.

With Locke, Campbell rejects the syllogism as an instrument for discovering knowledge. Instead, his theory of evidence combines common-sense philosophy (which postulates intuitive evidence) and empiricism. Empirical evidence is either demonstrative (scientific) or moral. The latter is "the proper province of rhetoric" and draws on experience, analogy, testimony, or calculation of chances (probability).

Elocution (usage and style) has to serve the aims of discourse and match the faculties of the mind. The desired properties of style are perspicuity, vivacity, elegance, animation, and music (beauty of sound). Added to these must be grammatical purity. Rejecting prescriptive grammar, Campbell advocates use as the standard for regulating speech, use that must be reputable (based on that of "celebrated authors"), national (not provincial or foreign), and present (neither obsolete nor modish).

Although his book went into fewer editions than those of Blair and Whately, Campbell exerted a strong influence on nineteenth-century rhetoric, particularly in America. Present-day scholars have traced the influence of earlier philosophers on the *Philosophy of Rhetoric* and also engaged in controversies about its degree of originality. Howell and Bevilacqua stress the influence of **Bacon**, Bitzer stresses that of Hume, and Bormann notes that of Scottish common-sense philosophers. Ehninger champions Campbell as "revolutionary" for basing rhetoric on human nature; La Russo sees him as traditional. Berlin holds him responsible for the current-traditional model of teaching composition; Hagaman praises his "creative management of audience."

Further Reading: James Berlin, *Writing Instruction in Nineteenth Century American Colleges* (Carbondale, Southern Illinois UP, 1984); Vincent Bevilacqua, "Philosophical Origins of George Campbell's Philosophy of Rhetoric," *Speech Monographs* 32.3 (1965): 1–12; Lloyd Bitzer, "Hume's Philosophy in George Campbell's Philosophy of Rhetoric," *Philosophy and Rhetoric* 2 (1969): 139–66; Dennis Bormann, "Some 'Common Sense' about Campbell, Hume, and Reid: The Extrinsic Evidence," *Quarterly Journal of Speech* 71 (1985): 395–421; Douglas Ehninger, "George Campbell and the Revolution in Inventional Theory," *Southern Speech Journal* 15 (1950): 270–76; John Hagaman, "On Campbell's Philosophy of Rhetoric and Its Relevance to Contemporary Invention," *Rhetoric Society Quarterly* 21 (1981): 145–55; Wilbur Samuel Howell, *Eighteenth Century British Logic and Rhetoric* (Princeton: Princeton UP, 1971); Dominic La Russo, "Root or Branch? A Re-examination of Campbell's 'Rhetoric,'" *Western Speech* 32 (1968): 85–91.

Christine de Pizan (1365–1431) Born in Venice, Christine de Pizan was raised at the French court of Charles V, where her father was court astrologer. She received a good education and was encouraged in her studies by both her father and her husband, whom she married when she was fifteen. Widowed at age twenty-five with three children to support, Christine began to write for a living and created more than twenty works, most of which dealt with the political situation of France in her time and with women's issues.

Christine's eloquence in writing has been compared to that of classical rhetoricians. She argued for the moral and intellectual equality between women and men, advocated the education of girls, critiqued the representations of women by classical male writers, offered practical advice to women of all social classes and political advice to those in power, and wrote women back into history. Two of her best-known works are *The Book of the City of Ladies* and *A Medieval Woman's Mirror of Honor: The Treasury of the City of Ladies*. The first of these is a history of women's contributions to Western civilization, and the second is a companion piece that offers practical advice for women. Extant manuscripts indicate that Christine's works were read by many women for years after she wrote them.

In *The Book of the City of Ladies*, Christine employs Socratic dialectic as she poses questions to three women—Reason, Rectitude, and Justice—who expose the falsity of patriarchal writings about women. Giving a traditionally silenced gender a voice, Christine claims authority for this act by citing Biblical examples, saying that "God has demonstrated that He has truly placed language in women's mouths so that He might be thereby served."

Included in Christine's history is Carmentis, inventor of the Latin alphabet. Critics have noted the connection between Christine's ideas about language and knowledge. For Christine, language is able to transcend gender and class distinctions, making possible equality for those who know how to use it well. Because language is the medium for transmitting knowledge, knowledge too becomes egalitarian.

Debates over whether Christine was a feminist are part of the current academic discussion surrounding her work. Some argue that her position is best described as "sex complementarity," holding that men and women are different, but equal. Others argue that, in light of the ways in which Christine portrays some of her female characters, she often speaks in the voice of patriarchy, while still others urge readers to consider the context in which she was writing. Although views on her work differ, no one disputes her importance to history and historiography, rhetoric, and women's studies.

Further Reading: Margaret Brabant, ed., *Politics, Gender, and Genre: The Political Thought of Christine de Pizan* (Boulder: Westview P, 1992); Christine M. Laennec, "Unladylike Polemics: Christine de Pizan's Strategies of Attack and Defense," *Tulsa Studies in Women's Literature* 12 (Spring 1993): 47–59; Patricia A. Phillippy, "Establishing Authority: Boccaccio's *De Claris Mulieribus* and Christine de Pizan's *Le Livre de la Cité des Dames*," *Romanic Review* 77 (May 1986): 167–94.

Cicero (106–43 BCE) Marcus Tullius Cicero was a Roman orator, lawyer, and statesman whose rhetorical treatises *De Inventione (On Invention)* and *De Oratore (On Oratory and Orators)* dominated our understanding of classical rhetoric up to the Renaissance and continued to be a strong influence thereafter. Ranked in importance with **Plato's** *Phaedrus,* **Aristotle's** *Rhetoric,* and **Quintilian's** *Institutio Oratoria,* Cicero's treatises collected what was known of **Isocrates, Plato,** and **Aristotle.**

Cicero was born in Italy and was given a patrician education, studying Greek with Greek teachers. It is generally accepted that *De Inventione* (84 BCE) is a compilation of Cicero's student notebooks, detailing in handbook fashion a method for generating speeches. *De Inventione* retains **Aristotle's** distinctions of the kinds of oratory (epideictic, deliberative, and judicial) and the canons of rhetoric (invention, arrangement, style, memory, delivery). However, most of the treatise is devoted to invention only, concentrating on the parts and composition of forensic speeches. Cicero pays only minor attention to speaker and audience. Although he later disowned this treatise as unsatisfactory, it is recognized as the major authority for later knowledge of rhetorical invention, and with its contemporary text *Rhetorica ad Herennium* serves as a model of Roman technical rhetoric.

De Oratore (54 BCE) is considered Cicero's mature statement on rhetoric, and was written to correct what he saw as the inadequacies of *De Inventione.* Evocative of **Plato's** *Phaedrus, De Oratore* is a dialogue primarily between two speakers, the historical figures Antonius and Crassus. Antonius, in general, argues that eloquence can be learned through training in formulaic technical rhetoric, while Crassus, in general, takes the position that eloquence springs from innate talent, practice, and in-depth knowledge of sophistic rhetoric and philosophy. However, Antonius and Crassus contradict their own positions and each other so that a simple definition of rhetoric cannot be articulated from *De Oratore.* Its method of contradiction and amplification shows Cicero's refusal to treat rhetoric as mechanistic handbooks did, suggesting instead a rhetoric that is speculative, literary, and expansive and that draws equally from sophistic, philosophic, and technical rhetorics.

Cicero was active in Roman politics and is often referred to as the greatest Roman orator. Through his eloquence, he was elected to a series of public offices, culminating in a position as consul. In 43 BCE, he was killed trying to prevent Marc Antony from taking power. Cicero's surviving fifty-eight speeches and over 900 letters do not significantly add to our understanding of Cicero's rhetorical theory, yet we can see the power of rhetoric in republican Rome versus the subsequent decline of oratory during the waning of the Republic and in the Roman Empire established by Octavius in 31 BCE, shortly after Cicero's death.

Further Reading: *Cicero on Tatnic: Papers From the Rutgers University Conference on De Oratore. Rhetorica 6.3* (1988). Special issue; Richard Leo Enos, *The Literate Mode of Cicero's Legal Rhetoric* (Carbondale: Southern Illinois UP, 1988); George Kennedy, *The Art of Rhetoric in the Roman World* (Princeton: Princeton UP, 1972); Mary Rosner, "Reflections on Cicero in Nineteenth Century England and America," *Rhetorica* 4 (1986):153–82.

Classical Rhetoric In standard histories of rhetoric, the classical period extends from early in the fifth century BCE to around the beginning of the fifth century CE; it comprises the principles and theories of rhetoric developed by philosophers and teachers primarily in Athens, Rome, and the Roman Empire. Most scholars acknowledge that the work of the classical rhetoricians forged the concepts of rhetorical theory that have continued to be developed or adapted in the two millennia since.

According to these standard histories, although effective speakers and writers certainly practiced their crafts in the Greek city-states before the fifth century, it was the sudden introduction of democracy in the Greek colony of Syracuse on Sicily in 467 BCE—and the democracy's implicit requirement that citizens be able to speak for themselves—that gave rise to explicit theorizing and teaching about speaking effectively in public gatherings. From the need to train budding orators there emerged two traditions of rhetorical teaching. The first, the handbook, or *techne,* tradition, prescribed how to structure an oration. The second, or *sophistic,* tradition offered set speeches that students of oratory could memorize, analyze, and imitate.

Plato called both of these types of rhetorical teaching into question in *Gorgias* and *Phaedrus.* In both, **Plato** has Socrates, a central character in the dialogues, criticize the handbooks as being too mechanistic and reductive and dismisses both the handbooks and the sophists as being unconcerned with the role of truth, which Socrates sees as transcending the material world of reality, in persuasive discourse. Perhaps in response to Plato's call for an ideal philosophical rhetoric that leads orators to design each speech to match the "souls" of the rhetor and audience, **Aristotle** in the fourth century BCE taught courses in rhetoric, the contents of which were later collected into his *Rhetoric.* **Aristotle's** work has been called the first psychological rhetoric, emphasizing how an orator demonstrates a thesis by creating **enthymemes** and examples and how a discourse appeals to both the **ethos,** or character, of the orator and the **pathos,** or emotional states, of the audience.

As they attempted to adapt principles developed by the Greeks to a new sociopolitical context, **Cicero** and his fellow Roman rhetoricians featured aspects of rhetorical theory initially introduced by the sophists, particularly **Isocrates:** the interdependence of wisdom and eloquence and the humanistic power of persuasive discourse to create an orderly civil state. The Romans also emphasized technical features of rhetoric from the handbook tradition, particularly the parts of an oration and the definitions and functions of **tropes and schemes.** Both **Cicero** and later **Quintilian** are credited with synthesizing the rhetorics, and their supporting philosophical and pedagogical theories, of the Greek and Roman cultures. **Quintilian's** *Institutio Oratoria* in particular is valuable as a compendium of classical rhetorical thought.

The end of the classical period is generally seen as the early fifth century CE with the rhetorical theory of Augustine, bishop of Hippo, in *De Doctrina Christiana,* or *On Christian Doctrine.* Augustine demonstrated that principles developed by classical rhetoricians, particularly Cicero, could be adapted to address the need to train Christian preachers, even though the antique orators were seen as pagans by the early Christian apologists.

Further Reading: William A. Covino, *The Art of Wondering: A Revisionist Return to the History of Rhetoric* (Upper Montclair, NJ: Boynton/Cook, 1988); George Kennedy, *The Art of Persuasion in Greece* (Princeton: Princeton UP, 1963); George Kennedy, *The Art of Rhetoric in Rome* (Princeton: Princeton UP, 1966).

Commonplaces Commonplaces represent a recurring feature of rhetorical theory from antiquity through the present. The term *commonplaces* emerged largely from a problem in translation. In ancient Greek rhetoric, an orator could be expected to consult the *topoi*, or places, of an argument. There were two types of *topoi:* Special *topoi* furnished conventionally accepted propositions—that is, material knowledge—for particular kinds of speeches, and the common *topoi* furnished various options for handling that knowledge—that is, patterns of development and inference. The Greek term for the latter was *koinoi topoi.* Translated into Latin, the phrase becomes *loci communis;* translated into English it becomes "common places." The removal of the space between words yielded the term.

Largely because rhetorical education in western Europe was based on *Institutio Oratoria* of **Quintilian,** the definition of the term *commonplaces* lost the double meaning inherent in the concept of *topoi.* As **Cicero** and later **Quintilian** taught, the commonplaces were sources of content, either propositions or constructed arguments, that could be easily inserted into a discourse. Medieval and Renaissance scholars taught students to keep lists of commonplaces—stock arguments, snippets of past speeches, praises or censures of famous people, brief treatises on virtues and vices, proverbs, quotations, and so on. The stock arguments were usually from cause and effect, from the orderly design of the universe, from the degrees of natural perfection, and from the contingent nature of things in the universe.

Not all rhetorical theorists of the Renaissance and later the Enlightenment embraced the use of commonplaces in composing texts. In the seventeenth century, Thomas Hobbes and Bernard Lamy saw commonplaces as sources of deception. In the eighteenth century, **George Campbell** and **Hugh Blair** rejected them as inimical to observation and induction. Indeed, as Richard Lanham points out, from the Renaissance forward rhetorical theory has tended to make much less use of the commonplaces than did earlier periods in that the function of rhetoric has been increasingly to communicate a distinct, novel worldview and not to transmit conventional, accepted wisdom.

Further Reading: Frank A. D'Angelo, *A Conceptual Theory of Rhetoric* (Cambridge, MA: Winthrop, 1975); John T. Harwood, ed., *The Rhetorics of Thomas Hobbes and Bernard Lamy* (Carbondale: Southern Illinois UP, 1986); Richard Lanham, *A Handlist of Rhetorical Terms* (Los Angeles: U of California P, 1991).

Edward P. J. Corbett **(b. 1919)** For many years a professor of English at Ohio State University, Edward P. J. Corbett is one of the half dozen or so scholars responsible for reviving the study of rhetoric in American universities in the

1960s and 1970s and for infusing the principles of classical rhetoric in the teaching of college composition. Corbett's major work is his seminal textbook *Classical Rhetoric for the Modern Student*. He is also responsible for helping introduce the rhetorical theories of eighteenth- and nineteenth-century rhetorical theorists, notably Hugh Blair, to a new generation of scholars.

Corbett chronicles his introduction to the study of rhetoric in an interview with his student Robert J. Connors, published in Connors' edited volume *Selected Essays of Edward P. J. Corbett*. In his first year of college teaching, Corbett was assigned to teach four sections of composition and one survey of literature course. He recounts that planning the composition courses didn't worry him—it was the literature course that was troubling. Having been taught the New Criticism, Corbett was adept at analyzing poetry but at a loss for how to analyze the prose pieces that are frequently included in literature anthologies. In the library, Corbett happened to pick up **Hugh Blair'**s *Lectures on Rhetoric and Belles-Lettres* and was taken with **Blair'**s analyses of Joseph Addison's *Spectator* papers. Curious about his discovery, Corbett decided that if he were to work with **Blair,** he had better investigate the rhetoricians Blair cited, specifically **Cicero** and **Quintilian.** Corbett went on to write his doctoral dissertation on the rhetorical theory of **Hugh Blair** and to spend his entire professional life in rhetoric, a field into which he accidentally stumbled.

Like **Quintilian'**s *Institutio Oratoria,* Corbett's *Classical Rhetoric for the Modern Student* is a stunning compendium and synthesis of previous rhetorical theory. As **Quintilian** synthesized six centuries of Greek and Roman rhetorical theory, Corbett drew together the theories and applications proferred by rhetoricians in antiquity, the Renaissance, and the eighteenth and nineteenth centuries. Offering sample essays for analysis from a range of historical periods in each chapter, Corbett introduces major terms from rhetoric, then teaches principles of **invention** (which he terms "discovery of arguments"), **arrangement,** and **style.** He closes the text with a historical survey of rhetoric. Faithful to its sources throughout, *Classical Rhetoric* is particularly notable in its thorough treatment of figures of rhetoric, **tropes and schemes.**

Corbett's best essays fall into two categories. Under a general rubric of eighteenth- and nineteenth-century rhetoric, Corbett offers such essays as "Hugh Blair as an Analyzer of English Prose Style" (1958) and "Some Rhetorical Lessons from John Henry Newman" (1980). Under a rubric of rediscovering and applying the rhetorical tradition to contemporary teaching and scholarship, Corbett provides such essays as "What is Being Revived?" (1967) and "The Rhetoric of the Open Hand and the Rhetoric of the Closed Fist" (1969).

Further Reading: Edward P. J. Corbett, *Classical Rhetoric for the Modern Student* (New York: Oxford UP, 1965); Edward P. J. Corbett, *Selected Essays of Edward P. J. Corbett,* ed. Robert J. Connors (Dallas: Southern Methodist UP, 1989); James L. Golden and Edward P. J. Corbett, eds., *The Rhetoric of Blair, Campbell, and Whately* (New York: Holt, Rinehart and Winston, 1968); Gary Tate and Edward P. J. Corbett, eds., *The Writing Teacher's Sourcebook* (New York: Oxford UP, 1988).

Mary Daly **(b. 1928)** Mary Daly, radical feminist philosopher, is a "Weaver of Words and Word-Webs." She sees one of her main projects to be freeing language from its patriarchal bonds so that women can "unwind the bindings of mummified/ numbified words" and overcome the aphasia, amnesia, and apraxia patriarchy imposes upon them. Daly focuses on the magical qualities of language—its ability to affect both women's psyches and the material world—and attempts to create an uncompromising feminist epistemology.

Daly's "re-membering" of the conventional patriarchal lexicon involves several strategies, including: making up new words to describe that for which patriarchy allows no words (Gynergy); uncovering lesser known or obsolete meanings of words (grammar = book of sorcery); and using unconventional punctuation and capitalization to suggest new meanings (Be-Longing). Changing language can lead to new knowledge, which leads to women overcoming apraxia, or paralysis of action.

Epistemologically, the world of patriarchy—what Daly terms the foreground—and the "Background" realm of radical feminism are widely divergent. Daly characterizes knowledge in the foreground as static, dead, void of meaning, and something that is acquired passively. For "Websters" (Weavers of Words and Word-Webs), knowing is a process of vital creative and critical thinking. Only women who have had their consciousness changed, and have become a part of the "Wicked" universe of feminist Websters, can participate in this process.

Daly is a controversial figure, criticized for being essentialist and for focusing on words as the loci of meaning, rather than on the context in which those words arise. In response to charges of essentialism, Daly writes that such charges are an inversion, a ploy to turn the patriarchy around and project it back onto those who fight it. She argues that it is patriarchal ideology that is essentialist because it holds that men possess something making them superior to women. Daly argues that she and other women labeled essentialist are trying to transcend the patriarchal lexicon.

Daly does believe that meanings reside within words and that the words one chooses to use are vitally important, because they have a material impact on the world. She does not, however, ignore the contexts of use, writing that "As the terrain changes so also does the style of the explorer, her movement, her language." In this connection, the contexts of foreground and Background are crucial to an understanding of a word's meaning. Although much of Daly's writing is mythic, creating another world for women to inhabit, from book to book her focus on "real life" incidents increases. At the end of her 1992 autobiographical *Outercourse*, Daly is sitting on the floor surrounded by newspaper articles, overwhelmed with the "horrors" described in them. She argues that feminists need to have one foot in the "now" of patriarchal foreground and the other foot in the "Now" of the Background in order to work for change and to be grounded in the "Otherworld" of women's Be-ing.

Further Reading: Jane Hedley, "Surviving to Speak New Language: Mary Daly and Adrienne Rich," *Hypatia* 7.2 (1992): 40–62; Meaghan Morris, "Amazing

Grace; Notes on Mary Daly's Poetics," *The Pirate's Fiancée: Feminism, Reading, Postmodernism* (London: Verso, 1988).

Delivery   In oral rhetoric, delivery refers to the ways an orator uses his or her voice and gestures to accompany the spoken words. Although delivery is one of the five ancient canons of rhetoric—along with **invention, arrangement, style,** and **memory,** there is considerably less written about it in the history of rhetorical theory than the other four. Delivery was hardly treated at all in ancient Greek rhetoric and somewhat more fully explained in classical Roman rhetoric. Perhaps the heyday of delivery was the eighteenth century, when a group of British rhetoricians engaged in an extensive study of rules of delivery.

Noting that no systematic treatment of delivery existed at the time, **Aristotle** mentions delivery only in passing in the third book of his *Rhetoric,* written in the fourth century BCE. He characterizes delivery generally as the "matter of how the voice should be used in expressing each emotion." Delivery receives fuller treatment in the major works of the two central figures in Roman rhetoric, **Cicero** and **Quintilian,** both of whom explain how voice and gesture should be appropriate to the demands of the rhetorical situation. **Cicero** writes in *De Oratore,* for example, that "Nature has assigned to each emotion a particular look and tone of voice and bearing of its own; and the whole of a person's frame and every look on his face and utterance of his voice are like the strings of a harp, and sound according as they are struck by each successive emotion."

Although stories of the elocutionary excellence of ancient orators lived in lore in the history of rhetoric, delivery was not extensively treated until a group of British rhetoricians in the late eighteenth and early nineteenth centuries turned their attention to the canon. Such works as Thomas Sheridan's *Lectures on Elocution* (1762), Gilbert Austin's *Chironomia* (1806), and John Walker's *Elements of Elocution* (1810) were motivated by the increasing demand for oral performance in politics and business, by the lack of thorough treatment by previous authors, and by a desire for new standards of language use and pronunciation.

Sheridan's principal contributions to the study of delivery dealt with the voice. He divided vocal quality into volume, stability, and flexibility and offered pedagogical precepts for each of these concepts. Walker was primarily concerned with the study of physical movement. Basing his teaching on observations of dance, musical, and theatrical performance, Walker offered instruction on how a speaker should position and move his face, body, arms, hands, legs, and feet. Austin's monumental treatise combined attention to both voice and gesture and grounded his teaching in a self-proclaimed scientific study of effective delivery.

Although delivery seems relevant only in oral delivery, some rhetorical theorists consider delivery of written material under the rubric of *graphemics,* the study of how information is presented on the printed page.

Further Reading: Sonja Foss, "The Construction of Appeal in Visual Images: A Hypothesis," *Rhetorical Movement: Essays in Honor of Leland Griffin,* ed. David Zarefsky (Evanston, IL: Northwestern UP, 1993), 210–24; Warren Guthrie, "The

Elocutionary Movement—England," *Speech Monographs* 38 (1951): 17–30; John Frederick Reynolds, ed., *Rhetorical Memory and Delivery: Classical Concepts for Contemporary Composition and Communication* (Hillsdale, NJ: Lawrence Erlbaum Associates, 1993).

Dialectic   Although **dialectic** has been defined in different ways since the fifth century BCE, generally the term describes a process of seeking truth through questioning. In his *Republic,* **Plato** calls dialectic "the copingstone of the sciences," the supreme philosophic method. The Platonic model of dialectic is a cooperative exchange between two speakers, beginning with a definition of terms and ending with a synthesis that approaches philosophic, universal understanding. The equality of speakers implied by this model does not materialize in the form of **Plato's** dialogues on dialectic and rhetoric: In *Gorgias,* the dialectic ends with Socrates' auditors falling silent while he continues a solitary speech; in *Phaedrus,* Socrates maintains the question–answer format, but Phaedrus' answers are confined merely to brief acknowledgments such as "yes, we have," and "quite so."

Unlike **Plato, Aristotle** views dialectic as the counterpart of rhetoric, although what he means by counterpart (*antistrophos*) remains uncertain. In one respect, dialectic differs from rhetoric because the former employs the syllogism and aims at certainty, while the latter employs the **enthymeme** and aims at establishing probabilities. After Aristotle and throughout the Middle Ages, dialectic was synonymous with formal logic. Throughout the Renaissance, teachers of dialectic contended that their discipline was superior to rhetoric; sixteenth-century teacher **Peter Ramus** argued vigorously for the separation of rhetoric from dialectic, and that the invention of arguments should be exclusive to logic and consist of a dialectic built upon binary divisions and subdivisions.

In the late eighteenth century, Immanuel Kant introduced the concept of dialectic as a critical device for exposing illusion in dogmatic philosophy, and for arriving at philosophic judgments that transcend the limits of experiential knowledge. In modern philosophy, Hegel's dialectical method emphasizes the need for dialectical oppositions that lead toward higher unity. He proposed that central truths rely on the tension between contraries (e.g., good exists in relation to evil), and that dialectical relationships finally define the universe and its processes. Influenced by Hegel, Karl Marx emphasized dialectic as a political force, developing a theory of historical materialism that posits economic and social development as the results of class conflict. The Marxist appropriation of dialectic, insofar as it brings dialectic into the realm of civic and communal issues, returned dialectic to a relationship with rhetoric. Current Marxist educators, such as **Paulo Freire,** regard the dialectical process as central to the development of literacy and the reform of public discourse; education becomes the process of ongoing critique, where conclusions lead to further questions in an effort to continually disrupt established, conventionally helped truths.

Further Reading: Theodor Adorno, *Negative Dialectics* (New York:

Continuum, 1983); Gregory Clark, *Dialogue, Dialectic, and Conversation* (Carbondale: Southern Illinois UP, 1990); Hans Georg Gadamer, *Dialogue and Dialectic* (New Haven: Yale UP, 1980).

Diotima Diotima of Mantinea was a teacher of Socrates, a priestess, and—as Socrates described her in **Plato**'s *Symposium*—an expert on many subjects. For several hundred years, scholars have treated her as a mythical figure, although more recently debate over her historicity has been part of the scholarly conversation about the *Symposium*, in which she is featured. We include Diotima here because hers is an important appearance of a tutelary speechmaker. Further, Diotima's philosophical position on ideal love must be regarded as one considers **Plato**'s views on the relationship between love and rhetoric in *Phaedrus*, especially her positioning of Eros as "an interpreter and means of communication between gods and men."

Until 1485, Diotima's historical reality was taken for granted. At that time, Marsilio Ficino, a prominent Italian neo-Platonist, offered the opinion that it is "absurd" to think of a woman as philosopher. Mary Ellen Waithe has recently noted that Ficino's remark was regarded as conclusive for the next five hundred years. Determining the extent to which a real Diotima might have really given the speech presented by **Plato** is difficult on a number of counts. The speech would have occurred a number of years before **Plato** reports it, and been filtered through several versions. With regard to the historicity of Diotima, Mary Ellen Waithe presents arguments both for and against her existence. Diotima could not have existed for the following reasons: According such prominence to a real woman would have been anomalous for both Socrates and **Plato**, so Diotima's inclusion is most likely an example of "Socratic wit"; the *Symposium* should be understood as a literary rather than a historical work; and outside of references to the *Symposium*, no ancient sources mention Diotima. Those who argue for a historical Diotima point out the following: Socrates is recorded as having consulted priestesses on occasion, and thus may have consulted Diotima; the auditors in the *Symposium* do not react to Socrates' story of his female teacher as if he is being satiric, but take him seriously; later writings, beginning in the second century CE, refer to the Diotima of the *Symposium* as if she were real; and Diotima's views vary enough from those of **Plato** and **Plato**'s Socrates to suggest that she is a distinct individual. J. J. Bachofen argues that the prominence of certain women in classical times correlates with the carryover in certain cultures of matriarchal religions. Diotima came from Mantinea, known for its cult of the Samothracian Demeter, which can explain Diotima's position as a philosopher.

Although we cannot be sure about the historical reality of Diotima, arguments seem to show that, for the most part, skepticism about her existence stems from incredulity regarding women's abilities, initially registered by Ficino. Maintaining the possibility that she was a real woman and not **Plato**'s creation has become part of a reconsideration of the actual roles of women in intellectual history and the rhetorical tradition, a reconsideration enacted as early as the fifteenth century by **Christine de Pizan** and continued today by feminist writers such as **Mary Daly.**

Further Reading: J. J. Bachofen, *Myth, Religion, and Mother Right* (New York: Bolingen, 1967): 90–92; Plato, *Symposium,* trans. W.R.M. Lamb (Cambridge: Harvard UP, 1975); Mary Ellen Waithe, "Diotima of Mantinea," *A History of Women Philosophers* (Dordrecht: Nijhoff, 1987), 1.83–116.

Dramatism   Dramatism is the name given to a philosophy of language and human relations that **Kenneth Burke** developed in the course of writing his 1945 *Grammar of Motives.* To some extent, dramatism was developed as a response to theories of human motivation based on psychological, sociological, and scientific theories that Burke felt did not encompass the full complexity of the human situation. Dramatism begins with the belief that "a rounded statement of motives" must address each of the following categories, which collectively comprise the dramatistic pentad: act ("what took place, in thought or deed"); scene ("the background of the act, the situation in which it occurred"); agent ("what person or kind of person performed the act"); agency ("what means or instruments he used"); and purpose. Sometimes Burke adds a sixth term, attitude (the manner of the act), making the pentad a hexad.

Although dramatism would highlight the five-fold complexity of human motivation, it places special emphasis on the role of "act." In the dramatistic perspective, all language and thought are primarily modes of action. Because of this emphasis, dramatism considers human motivation a problem of philosophy, not science. In Burke's view, the study of motives necessarily lies beyond the realm of empirical science because of a basic "arbitrariness" or "magic" inherent in the very idea of an act. An act cannot be scientifically explained as the sum total of its causes. An act is a paradoxical combination—both a result of causes outside itself (namely, the other four categories of the pentad) and a creation of "something out of nothing."

Dramatism was "developed from the analysis of drama," but Burke insists that it is a literal, not figurative nomenclature. People really do act, a fact that Burke emphasizes through a dichotomy separating the *action* of symbol-users from the mere *motion* of things (that have no choice, that can make no mistakes). Fundamentally, "dramatism is a theory of terminology," a theory, that is, of the "resources, limitations, and paradoxes" of "symbolic action." Burke succinctly summarized the theory's implications for human relations in his essay "Dramatism": "If action, then drama; if drama, then conflict; if conflict, then victimage." With the examples of Greek tragedy and Christian theology before it, dramatism believes "that rituals of victimage are the `natural' means for affirming the principle of social cohesion above the principle of social division" ("On Human Behavior"). Given such a principle, inherent in the very structure of language, Burke gave dramatism the motto *ad bellum purificandum* (toward the purification of war), in the "moralistic" hope that an attitude of "linguistic skepticism" would provide us our best method for understanding and averting linguistically generated threats to our collective welfare.

Further Reading: Stephen Bygrave, *Kenneth Burke: Rhetoric and Ideology* (London: Routledge, 1993); William Rueckert, *Kenneth Burke and the Drama of Human Relations* (Berkeley: U of California P, 1982); Herbert Simons and Trevor Melia, ed., *The Legacy of Kenneth Burke* (Madison: U of Wisconsin P, 1989).

Enlightenment Rhetoric   In the era of European intellectual history known as the Enlightenment, roughly from the early seventeenth century through the middle of the eighteenth century, rhetorical theory underwent a major epistemological shift. Reacting to the emphasis in science on experimentation, empiricism, and inductive logic, rhetoricians promoted new ways of investigating reality and constructing discourses to appeal to what they saw as the mind's "faculties." Notable among the Enlightenment rhetoricians' concerns was a diminution (and sometimes dismissal) of the role of syllogistic logic and a broadening of the scope of rhetorical discourse to include explanatory, expository texts as well as persuasive ones.

Many thinkers provided an intellectual foundation for the new rhetorics of the Enlightenment, but among the most influential were French philosopher René Descartes and British philosophers John Locke and David Hume. Descartes, whose ideas were promulgated in the *Port-Royal Logic* (1662), taught that the way to truth was through individual intellectual analysis, not through the collective interaction that characterizes rhetoric. To Descartes, one investigates reality by carefully dividing it into parts, conducting experiments, and drawing out causal connections. To Descartes, truth is absolute and empirically validated, not probable and established through deductive argumentation.

In his *Essay on Human Understanding* (1689), John Locke proposed that because the mind has the ability to perceive and prefer, it therefore comprises two principal faculties, the understanding and the will. Within the will, ideas are formed from sensory observation and then bound together by a law of association. To extend Locke's theories, David Hume proposed in his *Treatise on Human Nature* (1739) that the association of ideas occurs in one of three ways: resemblance, contiguity in time or place, and cause and effect.

In the eighteenth century, it fell primarily to the Scots to translate this new epistemology of empiricism and faculty psychology into rhetorical theory. In *The Philosophy of Rhetoric*, for example, **George Campbell** notes that there are four possible ends of any discourse—"to enlighten the understanding, to please the imagination, to move the passions, or to influence the will"—and proposes a "regular progression" of the intellectual faculties to achieve these ends: "Knowledge, the object of the intellect, furnisheth materials for the fancy; the fancy culls, compounds, and by her mimic art, disposes these materials so as to affect the passions; the passions are the natural spurs to volition or action, and so need only to be rightly directed."

Other rhetoricians offered theories that expanded the scope of the faculties. **Hugh Blair,** for example, taught that the path from understanding to will lay through the cultivation of the faculties of morality and taste. To **Blair,** rhetoric was the art of "belles lettres and criticism," which encompass all "that relates to beauty, harmony, grandeur, and elegance; all that can soothe the mind, gratify the fancy, or move the affections." To Blair and others, rhetoric became a technique for upward mobility, an art that would distinguish a person as a disciple of the best culture of the times.

Further Reading: Wilbur S. Howell, *Logic and Rhetoric in England, 1500–1700* (Princeton: Princeton UP, 1956); Wilbur S. Howell, *Eighteenth-Century British Logic and Rhetoric* (Princeton: Princeton UP, 1971); Nan Johnson, *Nineteenth-Century Rhetoric in North America* (Carbondale: Southern Illinois UP, 1991).

Enthymeme   In his *Rhetoric,* **Aristotle** proposes that the enthymeme is central to rhetorical persuasion. It functions, he argues, much in the same way as a syllogism in dialectic. A *syllogism* is a complete formal argument that consists of a major premise, a minor premise, and a conclusion. The following is a well-known example:

> All humans are mortal [major premise]
> Socrates is human [minor premise]
> Socrates is mortal [conclusion]

For **Aristotle,** the enthymeme is a partial syllogism; for instance, "Socrates is human, therefore mortal." The rhetor delivering this enthymeme presupposes that the audience will supply the missing part; the result should be cooperative understanding in which the audience is persuaded of the enthymeme's truth by virtue of having participated in making it fully meaningful. Through such a process, the enthymeme constitutes a rhetorical proof.

Aristotle's proposal that the enthymeme is a truncated syllogism is much modified and elaborated through the history of rhetoric; rhetoric handbooks from antiquity forward are full of discussions of how many parts a rhetorical proof might have and still be considered an enthymeme. Current scholarship has called into question the practice of defining an enthymeme in terms of the number of its parts. Lloyd Bitzer, for one, contends that counting the parts of the enthymeme is less important than recognizing that it is rooted in probability. He emphasizes that the premises of the enthymeme are drawn not from certainties (as with the syllogism), but from the beliefs and presuppositions of the audience.

Some important examples of enthymemes may illustrate Bitzer's position. In "Keeping the Thing Going While Things Are Stirring" (1867), **Sojourner Truth** says "If I have to answer for the deeds done in my body just as much as a man, I have a right to have just as much as a man." The unstated premise here is "All those who are equally responsible by law for their actions should receive equal rights under the law." The effectiveness of the enthymeme depends upon the audience's silent acceptance of this premise, which is itself a contestable interpretation of the operation of equal rights. Elizabeth Cady Stanton makes a related appeal in her 1860 "Address to the New York State Legislature":

> The prejudice against color, of which we hear so much, is not stronger than that against sex. It is produced by the same cause and manifested very much in the same way . . . [S]trike out all special legislation . . . strike the words "white male" from all your constitutions, and then, with fair sailing, let us sink or swim, live or die, survive or perish together."

Stanton states her highly debatable (and, some could argue, hyperbolic) major premise that equates slavery and sexual inequality. It is important to remember that she makes this speech to the New York State Legislature, a group of men who are opposed to slavery, yet are uncertain about women's rights. She leaves unstated the minor premise, "As one who opposes slavery, you must oppose sexual discrimination." Hoping that the legislature will supply this premise, Stanton illustrates the enthymeme as a negotiation between speaker and audience.

Further Reading: Lloyd Bitzer, "Aristotle's Enthymeme Revisited," *Quarterly Journal of Speech* 45 (1959): 399–408; Carol Poster, "A Historicist Recontextualization of the Enthymeme," *Rhetoric Society Quarterly* (1993): 1–24; James C. Raymond, "Enthymeme, Examples and Rhetorical Mood," *Essays on Classical Rhetoric and Modern Discourse,* ed. Robert Connors et al. (Carbondale: Southern Illinois UP, 1984), 140–151.

Epistemic Rhetoric   Epistemic rhetoric is the body of rhetorical theory maintaining that the truth conveyed by a text neither exists *a priori* outside the rhetorical situation that generates the discourse nor dwells immanently within the speaker or writer. Instead, epistemic rhetoric holds that truth is forged via negotiation, is generated by the transaction among the speaker/writer, the listener/reader, and the constraints of the particular rhetorical situation.

Epistemic rhetoric has historical antecedents that extend back to the Greek **sophists** Protagoras and Gorgias. Arguing that decisions about truth in rhetorical situations cannot be guided by a transcendent **logos** or reason, the sophists concluded that they must consult the *dissoi logoi,* or competing, often contradictory, truth claims and determine which best fits the situation at hand.

Although the pre-Socratic sophists discussed the situational contingency of truth in rhetoric, epistemic rhetoric as a theoretical construct was not so named until 1967, when Robert Scott published his seminal article, "On Viewing Rhetoric as Epistemic." Maintaining that "truth is not prior and immutable but is contingent," Scott argues that, "Insofar as we can say there is truth in human affairs, it is in time; it can be the result of a process of interaction at a given moment. Thus rhetoric may be viewed not as a matter of giving effectiveness to truth but of creating truth"; rhetoric, thus, "is a way of knowing; it is epistemic."

Scott's essay generated abundant controversy among scholars (see the Cherwitz essay in Part IV), and in 1978 Michael Leff published a synthesis of the claims theorists have offered in support of the proposition that rhetoric is epistemic. Leff explicates four claims and evaluates them in what he sees as their ascending order of strength. First, "[r]hetoric is epistemic because it allows us to know how particular objects and events relate to fixed, abstract principles." In other words, he explains, while individuals and communities generally maintain some "unified hierarchy of stable standards," these standards are only worked out via communication in real, particular situations. Second, "[r]hetoric is epistemic because it represents an active, social form of thinking that allows us to gain knowledge both of particulars and of principles in respect to practical matters." Third, "[r]hetoric is epistemic since it can serve a meta-logical function that helps us to secure knowledge of the first principles of theoretical disciplines." For example, when scientists offer conflicting interpretations of the same data, rhetoric can guide them to state explicitly the previously-tacit assumptions upon which their interpretations are based. Finally, "[r]hetoric is epistemic since knowledge itself is a rhetorical construct." This last assertion, the strongest according to Leff, is essentially Scott's original claim.

The principles underlying epistemic rhetoric have been incorporated both in composition pedagogy and in scholarship on the history of writing instruction. Kenneth Dowst, for example, demonstrates that the "epistemic approach" to teaching composition rests on three propositions: "(1) we do not know the world immediately; rather, we *compose* our knowledge by composing language; (2) how we can act depends on what we know, hence on the language with which we make sense of the world; (3) serious experimenting in composing with words is experimenting in knowing in new ways, perhaps better ways." In his study of writing instruction in American colleges from 1900 to 1985, James Berlin valorizes epistemic rhetoric, which he says "posits a transaction that involves all elements of the rhetorical situation: interlocutor, audience, material reality, and language. . . . All truths arise out of dialectic, out of the interaction of individuals within discourse communities. Truth is never simply 'out there' in the material world or the social realm, or simply 'in here' in a private or personal world. It emerges only as the three—the material, the social, and the personal—interact, and the agent of mediation is language."

Further Reading: James A. Berlin, *Rhetoric and Reality: Writing Instruction in American Colleges, 1900–1985* (Carbondale, IL; Southern Illinois UP, 1987); Kenneth Dowst, "The Epistemic Approach," *Eight Approaches to Teaching Composition*, eds. Timothy R. Donovan and Ben W. McClelland (Urbana, IL: National Council of Teachers of English, 1980); Michael Leff, "In Search of Ariadne's Thread: A Review of Recent Literature on Rhetorical Theory," *Central States Speech Journal* 29 (1978): 73–91; Robert Scott, "On Viewing Rhetoric as Epistemic," *Central States Speech Journal* 18 (1967): 9–17.

Erasmus (c. 1469–1536) Desiderius Erasmus of Rotterdam was the most widely read author of his time, and his voluminous writings include style manuals and handbooks, religious pamphlets and tracts, defenses and apologiae, translations and commentaries, and thousands of letters. Born in the Low

Countries an illegitimate son of a priest, Erasmus became an Augustinian monk and traveled throughout Europe to work and study. His achievements fall principally into two areas: As a scholar and writer Erasmus was a rhetorician with an aesthetic program; as a philosopher and theologian he established himself as the great humanist of the Renaissance.

His central contribution to rhetoric is a textbook for young boys, *On Copia of Words and Ideas (De duplici copia verborum ac rerum,* 1513). Here Erasmus exemplifies various classical tropes and figures of speech, drawing liberally from ancient writers to illustrate his points. He stresses the importance of copiousness and variety in speech and writing, at one point articulating dozens of different ways to say "Your letter has delighted me very much." His *Colloquies* (1518) is a grammar handbook that employs classical Latin and makes frequent allusions to the ancient canon, in dialogues about daily life and current events. With these works, Erasmus associates grammar with the study and imitation of classical texts and the consequent improvement of character, and makes rhetoric an art of persuasion vital in political, religious, and social spheres. In sum, grammar and rhetoric are methods to improve humanity.

Along with his interest in educational reform, Erasmus was a stalwart force in Renaissance humanism, advocating free inquiry and philosophical skepticism. In the satirical *Praise of Folly (Moriae encomium,* 1511), Erasmus both criticizes and forgives humankind, mocking everyone in the process (lawyers, courtiers, scholars, old women, monks), and suggesting that they should do better. To the extent that these attitudes were inimical to the authority of the Catholic Church, Erasmus's humanism paved the way for Luther and the Reformation. Yet he never renounced the Church, and ultimately refuted Luther, who favored a God-centered determinism. This compromised position left him caught between humanism and Catholicism; and during his life and after his death, Erasmus was attacked from all sides.

Despite accusations of inconsistency (it was often said that Erasmus was a great scholar but a weak character), the two branches of Erasmus's work synthesize into a coherent whole: He brings his aesthetic sensibility to bear on his religious teachings, which are sometimes straightforward and rational, sometimes witty and satirical, sometimes pagan, sometimes Christian, but always elegant and persuasive in a style full of figurative amplification. And likewise, his humanism is implicit in his aesthetic concerns: because humans are capable of language, thought, and reason, we can appeal to each other with words, persuade each other with speeches. Language, then, becomes a most valuable tool, so our attention to its style is imperative. As Erasmus says in *On Copia,* "The best possible words must be selected from every type of writer."

Further Reading: Marjorie O'Rourke Boyle, *Rhetoric and Reform: Erasmus's Civil Dispute with Luther* (Cambridge: Harvard UP, 1983); Terence Cave, *The Cornucopian Text* (London: Oxford UP, 1979); H. H. Gray, "Renaissance Humanism: The Pursuit of Eloquence," in *Renaissance Essays,* eds. Paul Oskar Kristeller and Philip Wiener (New York: Harper, 1968).

Ethos In rhetorical theory, the appeal of speakers or writers to their own credibility and character is called *ethos*. This Greek term, from which the noun *ethics* originates, is sometimes called the *ethical appeal* in modern handbooks of rhetoric.

The earliest systematic treatment of *ethos* is in **Aristotle's** *Rhetoric*. Most modern discussions of the concept derive from **Aristotle,** who taught that *ethos* is one of three *pisteis,* or means of securing persuasion, available to a speaker; the other two are *logos* and *pathos*. According to **Aristotle,** to establish *ethos* a speaker must demonstrate three characteristics: *phronesis,* good sense or practical wisdom; *arete,* good moral character; and *eunoia,* good will toward the audience. Roman rhetoricians adapted the Greek concept. **Cicero,** for example, in the *Orator* describes an oratorical style designed to secure the good will of the audience with the adjective *ethikon.* **Quintilian** in the *Institutio Oratoria* concedes that there is no exact Latin equivalent for the term *ethos* and offers *mores,* or a person's overall moral constitution, as the closest corresponding term.

A tension has existed in the history of rhetorical theory over the ultimate source of *ethos*. One tradition, established by **Aristotle,** maintains that *ethos* must be established by the speech itself and may not depend on the actual, historical personal characteristics of the speaker herself. Another tradition, established by **Isocrates** and further developed by **Cicero** and **Quintilian,** holds that the rhetor's actual history may be emphasized in order to establish character and credibility. Thus, **Quintilian** can argue that an effective rhetor must be a *vir bonus dicendi peritus,* a "good man skilled at speaking." Drawing on Richard Lanham's distinction between *homo rhetoricus* and *homo seriosus,* James Baumlin calls the former, intrinsic-to-the-speech tradition the "rhetorical" view of *ethos;* he calls the latter, extrinsic-to-the-speech tradition the "philosophical" view.

A term related to *ethos* in literary theory is *persona*. In classical drama, a *persona* was literally a mask that an actor wore, both to amplify his voice and to provide clues about his character. Literary theorists use the term metaphorically, referring to the character a narrator's voice establishes in both literary and non-literary discourse. In a useful essay, Roger Cherry casts *ethos* and *persona* as end points on a continuum, with *ethos* being the speaker's or writer's invocation of his or her own "real" self and *persona* being the establishment of a "fictional" character appropriate for the discursive situation at hand. Cherry acknowledges that although the concepts are separable, many situations require a speaker or writer to establish both *ethos* and *persona*.

Contemporary rhetorical and literary theory has complicated the concept of *ethos* considerably. Poststructuralist discourse theorists reject the image of a stable, unified author whose "self" can be invoked as either *ethos* or *persona*. Michel Foucault, for example, maintains that texts have "author functions," fragmentary voices that are dispersed throughout, rather than authors. Given this claim, theorists from several fields are attempting to redefine *ethos* for the postmodern critical world.

Further Reading: James S. Baumlin and Tita French Baumlin, eds., *Ethos: New Essays in Rhetorical and Critical Theory* (Dallas: Southern Methodist UP, 1994);

Roger D. Cherry, "Ethos versus Persona: Self-Representation in Written Discourse," *Written Communication* 5 (1988): 251–76; Nan Johnson, "Ethos and the Aims of Rhetoric," *Essays in Classical Rhetoric and Modern Discourse,* eds. Robert J. Connors, Lisa Ede, and Andrea Lunsford (Carbondale: Southern Illinois UP, 1984), 98–114; Richard Lanham, *The Motives of Eloquence: Literary Rhetoric in the Renaissance* (New Haven: Yale UP, 1976).

Faculty Psychology Various philosophical theories of the faculties or powers of the human mind are central to conceptions of audience appeal in eighteenth-century rhetorics, primarily those of **Blair** and **Campbell.** Faculty psychology is sometimes contrasted with eighteenth-century associationism and with Scottish common-sense philosophy, but both of these doctrines made use of the concept of mental faculties; moreover, modern histories of psychology also apply the term faculty psychology to the way the regions of the mind–soul were described by **Plato** and **Aristotle** and their medieval and Renaissance successors.

Although David Hartley spoke of "Psychology, or the Theory of the Human Mind" in his *Observations on Man* (1748), the term *psychology* was not commonly used until the nineteenth century. German philosopher Christian Wolff (1679–1754) has been identified as an originator of faculty psychology, and it is true that his *Psychologia Empirica* (1732) and *Psychologia Rationalis* (1734) carry the modern term in their titles. However, in England, use of the term *faculty* to denote a mental capacity dates back to before 1600; and in *The Advancement of Learning* (1605), **Bacon** divides the "faculties of the mind of man" into understanding and will. This division is adopted by such eighteenth-century thinkers as Locke and Reid, and under these two main heads, the number of faculties varied. Reid's student Dugald Stewart distinguished forty-eight, which included attention, memory, and conception under the subcategory "intellectual," and sex, ambition, and pity under the subcategory "active powers."

In **Campbell's** *Philosophy of Rhetoric*, the four "ends of speaking"—"to enlighten the understanding, to please the imagination, to move the passions, or to influence the will"—match the four faculties to be addressed. **Campbell** also discusses memory as a faculty that assists the other four when hearers listen to and react to a speech. Both **Blair** and **Campbell** emphasize the faculty of taste.

Faculties played an important role in empiricist epistemology. In contrast to ideas, which were thought to be acquired through experience, the faculties were assumed to be innate: They were the equipment that enabled the mind to form ideas through reflection on sense perceptions. However, Condillac (1715–1780) was one philosopher who made even faculties—at least those related to the understanding—into products of sensation.

Faculty psychology maintained its sway into the nineteenth century and became especially important as a subject in American universities. It took a physiological and scientific turn in Gall and Spurzheim's phrenology—an attempt to locate the seat of various human capacities in the brain by examining the protuberances of the skull—which later came to be discredited as a form of occultism. Today, faculty psychology has resurfaced as modular psychology.

Further Reading: Douglas Ehninger, "Dominant Trends in English Rhetorical Thought, 1750–1800," *Southern Speech Journal* 18 (1952): 3–12; Thomas Leahy, *A History of Psychology: Main Currents of Psychological Thought* (Englewood Cliffs, NJ: Prentice-Hall, 1980); Thomas Leahy and Grace Leahy, *Psychology's Occult Doubles* (Chicago: Nelson Hall, 1983); Keith Lehrer, *Thomas Reid* (London: Routledge, 1989).

Paulo Freire (b. 1921) Paulo Freire is a Brazilian-born educator whose revolutionary methods of adult literacy have spread from South America to the entire continent. Freire's work centers on the notion that not just literacy but *conscientizacao*, the development of critical consciousness, leads to the liberation of the masses. Lack of this critical consciousness is everywhere a symptom of the oppressed, revealed by a sense of powerlessness and hopelessness. Only when people begin to think critically about their world rather than just adapt to it can they begin to effect change. Freire makes a distinction between the human capacity for *adaptation*, when one submits fatalistically, and *integration*, when one not only adapts to the world but also uses intelligence to ask questions and make choices, thus participating in the world and developing one's own agency.

To develop *conscientizacao*, Freire says teachers must avoid the *banking method* of educational practice, teaching that he describes in his *Pedagogy of the Oppressed* as "the act of one person's depositing ideas in another." This method presupposes the student as receptacle or Object. Instead, a teacher must see a student as a Subject who can dialogue with the teacher, can participate in the naming of the world, and thus transform it; as Freire says in *Education for Critical Consciousness,* "Learning to read and write has meaning in that, by requiring men to reflect about themselves and about the world they are in and with, it makes them discover that the world is also theirs." At its base this dialogic method requires love, faith, and humility: By love, Freire means a commitment to the people and their liberation; faith is akin to the Enlightenment attitude that all people are striving to be self-directed, autonomous, and intelligently responsible for public decisions; and humility banishes elitism by encouraging the teacher's willingness to listen to students without fear of being displaced by them.

For Freire, language must work in two dimensions: reflection and action. Language without action is empty chatter, and language without reflection is an undirected thrashing about. Further, *praxis* is "action plus reflection," and can be prompted by language teaching that is grounded in social and cultural situations. Teaching students the word *arado* (plow), then, will generate discussions about the value of human labor, agrarian reform, the process of transforming nature, and so on.

Freire's methods with illiterate adults in developing countries have been useful in contemporary American settings because, as he says in *Education for Critical Consciousness,* they promote "an education of 'I wonder' instead of merely, 'I do.' " Some contemporary scholars who espouse Freirean methods bleach the Marxist strains from the notion of critical consciousness and emphasize self-reflexive thinking, whatever the content of the thought; others retain the leftist emphasis on the interrelations of humans, nature, culture, history. But all followers of Freire agree with his proposition—in *Pedagogy of the Oppressed*—that "knowledge emerges only through invention and reinvention."

Further Reading: Patricia Bizzell, *Academic Discourse and Critical Consciousness* (Pittsburgh: U of Pittsburgh P, 1992); Gary Olson and Irene Gale, eds., *(Inter)views: Cross-Disciplinary Perspectives on Rhetoric and Literacy* (Carbondale: Southern Illinois UP, 1991): 155–83; Ira Shor, *Freire for the Classroom* (Portsmouth, NH: Heinemann, 1988).

Good Reasons   A philosophy of good reasons teaches that through a pluralistic process of full exchange, opposing parties can come to a sharing and tolerance of each other's views. One of the main proponents of this process is **Wayne Booth,** whose 1974 *Modern Dogma and the Rhetoric of Assent* defines good reasons as those recognized as such by an open-minded community, whose members are not driven by *motivism*. Motivists reject the concept of good reasons, and believe instead that anyone's justification for an action is always suspect and often merely self-serving. **Booth** argues that we must get beyond motivism by assenting to other points of view in order to discover what we hold in common. Although the search for good reasons does not eliminate conflict, it does—according to Booth—yield warrantable assertions that can withstand public scrutiny.

Several of **Booth's** contemporaries have also investigated the nature of good reasons and communal exchange. Stephen Toulmin offers a model for rational argument in which any valid claim can be justified by explicit information, called *data,* and implicit information, called *warrants,* which both may be understood as premises that open a logical path to the claim. He offers the following example: Harry was born in Bermuda [data], so Harry is a British subject [claim], because a man born in Bermuda will be a British subject [warrant]. The elaboration of this model constitutes Toulmin's discussion of the ways in which arguments are made acceptable.

A model of good reasons less analytical than Toulmin's and more spiritual than **Booth's** is developed by Robert Pirsig in *Zen and the Art of Motorcycle Maintenance.* Phaedrus, the main character of this novel, engages in an all-consuming search for the meaning of Quality, trying to establish rational grounds for determining that one idea or act is qualitatively better than another. His search takes him back through the history of rhetoric, and he concludes that Quality coincides with the excellence of mind and spirit that the Greeks called *arete.* Finding good reasons for one's values and behavior is the process of realizing and cultivating one's own *arete,* and is an internal rather than a communal process.

The philosophy of good reasons has been criticized by some for overlooking the needs of minority or oppressed groups. Privileging the discourse of rationality and the consensus of those competent with this discourse would seem to overlook marginalized groups and devalue their rhetoric if it does not appreciate and include the norms, values, and behaviors of those deemed reasonable (or in Pirsig's view, virtuous). Critics of the value of consensus and the philosophy of good reasons that upholds it include Jean-Francois Lyotard, who associates consensus with tyranny in *The Postmodern Condition,* and feminists such as bell hooks, who suspect that an emphasis on ethical norms will continue to disenfranchise nonconformists.

Further Reading: Wayne Booth, *Modern Dogma and the Rhetoric of Assent* (Notre Dame: U of Notre Dame P, 1974); Jean-Francois Lyotard, *The Postmodern Condition* (Minneapolis: U of Minnesota P, 1984); Robert Pirsig, *Zen and the Art of Motorcycle Maintenance* (New York: Bantam, 1974); Stephen F. Toulmin, *The Uses of Argument* (Cambridge: Cambridge UP, 1958).

Sarah and Angelina Grimke   Sarah and Angelina Grimke were the daughters of a South Carolina Supreme Court judge and his wife, who were slaveholders. Both sisters developed an abhorrence for the institution of slavery, and eventually moved to the North and began working for abolition. They realized that in order to be effective abolitionists, they would also have to fight for a woman's right to speak in public.

Both of them were orators, but Angelina spoke in public more frequently and was seen by some to be the more eloquent orator; Sarah was more of a theorist, and occupied more with writing. The Grimkes violated taboos against women speaking to mixed audiences of both men and women, black and white, and against women and men sharing a podium together (Angelina once debated two pro-slavery men in Amesbury, Massachusetts).

An examination of their oratory and writing reveals a number of important features that have become identified with women's rhetoric. They spoke and wrote from their personal experiences with slavery in the South, and their oratory often included spontaneous adaptations to the tenor of the audience. In a speech Angelina Grimke made before the Women's Anti-Slavery Society in Pennsylvania Hall in Philadelphia, she frequently made adjustments in her speech to react to and incorporate the violent mob outside the hall. She also used the presence of the mob to further her purpose of urging sympathy for slaves: "What is a mob? . . . What if the mob should now burst in upon us, break up our meeting and commit violence upon our persons—would this be anything compared with what the slaves endure? No, no."

In 1837, a group of Congregational ministers in Massachusetts issued a "Pastoral Letter" that warned churches against female orators as representing a danger to feminine character. Although the letter did not name the Grimkes directly, it was motivated in large part by their public speaking tours. In response, Sarah Grimke published a series of *Letters on the Equality of the Sexes* in 1838, which argued that the Bible has injunctions against women speaking only because it reflects the patriarchal culture that produced it. Other written works by the sisters include Angelina's *Letters to Catherine Beecher* (1838), which maintains their advocacy of an active role for women within the abolition movement;

Angelina's *Appeal to the Christian Women of the South* (1836) and *Appeal to the Women of the Nominally Free States* (1837); Sarah's *Address to Free Colored Americans* (1837); and *American Slavery As It Is* (1838), coauthored by the Grimkes and Theodore Weld, whom Angelina married in 1838.

Phyllis Japp writes that Angelina Grimke adopted two different personae, that of the Biblical Esther and that of Isaiah. Depending on the situation, she was either a supplicant or a prophet, always demanding justice for slaves and women. These can still be seen as the options open to and taken by women rhetors today, making Angelina Grimke a foremother of and role model for the contemporary women's movement.

Further Reading: Karlyn Kohrs Campbell, *Man Cannot Speak for Her* (New York: Greenwood Press, 1989), 1.22–33; Angela Davis, *Women, Race and Class* (New York: Vintage, 1981), 40–45; Phyllis Japp, "Esther or Isaiah?: The Abolitionist–Feminist Rhetoric of Angelina Grimke," *Quarterly Journal of Speech* 71 (1985); 335–48.

Winifred Bryan Horner (b. 1922)   Winifred Bryan Horner, who until her retirement in 1993 held the Lillian Radford Chair of Rhetoric and Composition at Texas Christian University, has not only contributed significantly to contemporary scholarship in rhetoric but also has served as a role model for a generation of women who have achieved prominence as teachers and researchers in the field. Horner's work deals with eighteenth-century and nineteenth-century rhetoric, particularly the Scottish rhetoricians, and with the relations between rhetoric and literature in education.

Horner emphasizes historical recovery of the primary texts of eighteenth- and nineteenth-century rhetoric. She sees a shift in eighteenth-century rhetorical theory from a study of the speaker and the text to a study of the reader and interpretation of the text. Her work traces the origins of English literature courses in Scottish universities and maintains that this development marks the earliest point at which the teaching of literature and the teaching of writing were separated. Examining the effects of print media, the distribution of printed materials, and the increasing prominence of the Scottish universities, Horner sees two central concepts, the importance of "taste" in literature and the empirical characterization of the understanding of the reader, as being central to the "new rhetoric" of the eighteenth century.

Following her early work on eighteenth-century rhetoric, Horner in 1982 edited a volume of essays that called on scholars in literature and composition to "bridge the gap" between the two fields. Focusing on the fact, apparent in 1982, that most American university writing programs were staffed by people trained solely in literature, Horner laments that many college writing instructors maintain a view of rhetoric limited to issues of diction and style. Returning to her research on the eighteenth century, she demonstrates the role in contemporary education of the empirical philosophies of John Locke, Lord Berkeley, and David Hume and the common sense philosophy of the Scottish scholar Thomas Reid.

The influence of these scholars, according to Horner, shifted the emphasis in American university English classes from the rhetorical interaction of reader, writer, and text to the interaction of the written product with the literary experience of the reader.

Many contemporary scholars of rhetoric and composition believe that Horner's personal accomplishments equal her professional achievements. She began graduate work in the early 1970s, when only a handful of rhetoric and composition programs were beginning in American universities. Horner has consistently been a powerful voice against gender discrimination in salary, promotion, and tenure cases. Her advocacy of young scholars, particularly women, moved Sharon Crowley to call her a heroine in rhetoric and composition in American higher education.

Further Reading: Winifred Bryan Horner, ed., *Composition and Literature: Bridging the Gap* (Chicago: U of Chicago P, 1982); Winifred Bryan Horner, *Nineteenth-Century Scottish Rhetoric: The American Connection* (Carbondale: Southern Illinois UP, 1992); Sharon Crowley, "Three Heroines: An Oral History," *Pre/Text* 9 (1988): 205–6; Theresa Enos, ed., *Learning from the Histories of Rhetoric: Essays in Honor of Winifred Bryan Horner* (Carbondale: Southern Illinois UP, 1993).

Hypatia (370–415 CE) Hypatia is important to the history of rhetoric as one of the early female public speakers who was able to influence prominent men. Beyond that, however, Hypatia presents an interesting opportunity to see at work what Hayden White called the "fictions of factual representation" and offers us an example of the rhetorical construction of women in history.

Fourth-century Alexandria saw a scientific renaissance in which Hypatia—pagan philosopher, mathematician, astronomer, and inventor—played a large role. She publicly taught the philosophy of **Plato** and **Aristotle,** holding an unprecedented position paid by the government. She also taught and wrote on geometry, algebra, astronomy, and mechanics; invented an apparatus for the distillation of water; and was often sought out for advice by city government officials. She published three works on algebra and geometry, two of which are extant; and approved a defense of philosophy, written by her student Synesius, against rhetoricians who were presenting themselves as philosophers. She was brutally killed in 415 by a Christian mob.

Hypatia's death has been attributed to resentment of her public role as a female philosopher, to a purge of pagans by Cyril, bishop of Alexandria, and to Cyril's jealousy of Hypatia's large and influential following. The different representations of her death are part of the rhetorical construction of history and of Hypatia. In *Decline and Fall of the Roman Empire,* Gibbon writes that Cyril was behind Hypatia's murder, but J. M. Rist has recently argued that Gibbon misrepresented the situation to generate anti-Cyril and anti-Christian sentiment. Margaret Alic's recent history of women in science says that Cyril was attempting to purge the city of neo-Platonists and that with Hypatia's death, science ceased until the end of the Dark Ages.

Hypatia's character and activities have also been represented in a variety of ways. As a woman, she was subject to much speculation about her sexual activity, including comments about the audacity of a woman publicly addressing groups of men. An eighteenth-century article about her was titled, "The History of Hypatia, a most impudent school-mistress of Alexandria." In the nineteenth century, British clergyman and novelist Charles Kingsley wrote a novel, *Hypatia, or New Foes with an Old Face,* that romanticized Hypatia as a radical neo-Platonist involved in political intrigue. Jane Snyder describes Kingsley's character as an unfortunate mixture of helplessness and titillation. In this century, Hypatia has been reclaimed by historians of women in science and mathematics, by Africanists in America, and by feminists. She is featured in Judy Chicago's famous *Dinner Party* sculpture and as a speaker in Mary Daly's feminist meeting over the moon in *Outercourse.* In sum, Hypatia has not been entirely written out of intellectual history, but she is treated with unusual historiographic and rhetorical license, a female teacher and orator rhetoricized.

Further Reading: Margaret Alic, *Hypatia's Heritage: A History of Women in Science from Antiquity to the Late Nineteenth Century* (London: Women's Press, 1986), 41–46; J. M. Rist, "Hypatia," *Phoenix* 19.3 (1965): 214–25; Mary Ellen Waithe, ed., *A History of Women Philosophers* (Dordrecht: M. Nijoff, 1987), 1.169–97.

Imagination   We can trace the origins of the word *imagination* to the Greek *phantasia,* which stood for cognition in general. It was believed that thinking relied on **phantasms,** which were likenesses of sense impressions from the exterior world. Phantasia, or phantasy, is the process of combining and storing phantasms in the mind; as such, phantasy is the basis for the production of human language. Our image-making capacity (phantasy) is the origin of our word-making capacity, as words are themselves understood to be images, or phantasms.

For both **Plato** and **Aristotle,** phantasy is central to the production of discourse; **Plato** is especially troubled by this fact. He believes that because phantasy itself originates in sensation, and one's own mental interpretation of sense impressions is affected by common opinion, phantasy cannot be trusted as an agent of truth. It is, instead, a resource for **sophists,** whom **Plato** sees as deceptive rhetoricians capable of manipulating and purveying false images. Despite **Plato's** objections, phantasy—later called *imaginatio* by the Romans—becomes associated with both **invention** and **memory** in the canons of rhetoric (**invention, arrangement, style, memory, delivery**). **Quintilian** stresses the importance of *rerum imagines* (vivid conceptions) to effective rhetoric: "From such [phantastic] impressions arises that enargeia which Cicero calls illumination and actuality." In *On the Sublime,* Longinus says that "Weight, grandeur and energy in writing are largely produced, dear pupil, by the use of images. . . . For the term Imagination is applied in general to an idea which enters the mind from any source and engenders speech."

The identification of imagination with rhetorical invention was maintained through the Renaissance, until the epistemological shift we associate with the Enlightenment brought with it deep suspicion and official castigations of the products of imagination. The Royal Society of London, established in 1662, associated imagination with falsehoods and dismissed rhetorical invention as the production of mere semblances that have no truth value. Driven from rhetoric, imagination became a faculty primarily associated with literature and art, activities in which veracity is thought less crucial.

Today, the relationship between imagination and rhetoric is central to emerging computer technologies that generate a virtual infinity of information and images. Computers hold the power that idealists such as **Plato** and determinists such as the Royal Society feared: They can replicate a version of phantasy in which new realities are created, deconstructed, and recombined, in which reading and writing programs such as Hypertext encourage wildly associational composing, and in which we question once again whether the broad and powerful generation of multiple truths requires constraints.

Further Reading: Jay Bolter, *Writing Space* (Hillsdale, NJ: Erlbaum, 1991); Mary Carruthers, *The Book of Memory* (New York: Cambridge, 1990); William Covino, *Magic, Rhetoric, and Literacy* (New York: SUNY P, 1994).

Invention   In the classical Greek rhetoric represented by **Aristotle,** invention is congruent with the overall function of rhetoric, which is "to see the available means of persuasion in each case." One invents these means with reference to situational variables that might infc m a speech situation, by surveying common relational perspectives, or **topoi,** and constructing rhetorical syllogisms, or **enthymemes,** with the potential for psychological engagement and persuasion. After **Aristotle,** treatments of invention in Roman rhetoric were much more formalized and formulaic, and this tendency to schematize the construction of a speech was maintained for the most part in medieval applications of rhetoric— to the "arts" of preaching, letter-writing, and poetry.

Tendencies in the Renaissance to aggrandize the human imagination had their effect on treatments of invention. There was not a revival of **Aristotle's** interest in psychology and contingency, but there was increased attention to *amplification,* the ability to use tropes and figures to vary and ornament an expression in a number of ways. The proposal that a rhetor must develop a copious storehouse of words and ideas found its exemplary statement in **Erasmus's** *On Copia,* a 1513 school textbook that presents students with hundreds of examples of stylistic variation and amplification. Admittedly, the Renaissance emphasis on *copia* conflated invention and style and prepared the way for even more exclusive concentration on style and the abandonment of invention as a rhetorical process.

In works written during the 1540s, French educational reformer **Peter Ramus** argues that invention should not be an intellectual process governed by contingencies, as **Aristotle** would have it. He presented invention as an arhetorical procedure that must conform to the rules of logic, and argued that rhetoric must be concerned with matters of **style** and **delivery** only. Ramus's identification of rhetoric with **style** launched a vilification of **invention** that lasted for centuries. Enlightenment rhetorics such as **Hugh Blair's** 1783 *Lectures on Rhetoric and Belles-Lettres* replaced invention with a kind of inspiration in which the rhetor is visited by clear ideas that he or she then expresses in a plain style free of ambiguity. The connection of invention to inspiration did not originate in the Enlightenment; we see it in the works of **Plato** and **Augustine,** for instance, and in romantic statements such as Coleridge's *Biographia Literaria.* However, **Blair's** relegation of invention to an arhetorical realm is not explicitly spiritual.

The identification of rhetoric with plain style certainly prevailed as a pedagogical assumption through the mid-1900s. With the renewed interest in classical rhetoric and human creativity that emerged in the 1960s and 1970s, the importance of invention as an epistemological and rhetorical process has been revitalized. Further, the centrality of invention informs postmodern views of knowledge itself as an inventional process subject to cultural, psychological, and ideological contingencies.

Further Reading: Sharon Crowley, *The Methodical Memory: Invention in Current-Traditional Rhetoric* (Carbondale: Southern Illinois UP, 1990); Karen Burke Lefevre, *Invention as a Social Act* (Carbondale: Southern Illinois UP, 1987); Eric Charles White, *Kaironomia: On The Will To Invent* (Ithaca: Cornell UP, 1987).

Isocrates (436–338 BCE) Isocrates is a Greek **sophist** who established a pattern of systematic education based on rhetoric that contributed to the codification of rhetoric in the Roman trivium of grammar, rhetoric, and dialectic. His speeches were composed primarily for written publication, not oral delivery, and he is considered responsible for making oratory a literary form.

Isocrates was a student of Gorgias. After losing his family's wealth in the Peloponnesian War, he supported himself as a logographer, then established a school of rhetoric for advanced students in Athens around 393 BCE, shortly before **Plato's** Academy was founded. Unlike other sophists who traveled and lectured for a fee, Isocrates remained in Athens and worked as a mentor with his students.

His speeches elucidate his views on the necessary interrelationship of rhetoric, philosophy, institutionalized education, and political leadership. *Against the Sophists* (c. 390 BCE), was written to publicize his school; it clarifies his opposition to the ideals of **Plato's** Academy as well as to the simplistic technical rhetoric many **sophists** taught. Isocrates rejects the philosophical insistence on the possibility of teaching transcendent knowledge, believing that such an enterprise is immoral because it fosters social isolation. He simultaneously criticizes as sycophants those **sophists** who taught forensic oratory as a technical skill to be mastered for political and economic success.

Antidosis (353 BCE) articulates his belief in the necessity of an ideal rhetoric that could incite practical political action and at the same time be ethical. For Isocrates, a successful rhetor is a useful citizen who makes useful citizens of others. Rhetorical success is a combination of three items: innate natural aptitude, which a teacher may develop but not create, practice in framing speeches, and training by a teacher in the general principles of rhetoric. Although Isocrates idealizes the discourse that is the outward image of a good soul, he insists that speaking well can be ennobling for the speaker as well as the audience. Thus his ethical rhetoric both creates and is created by the moral orator.

Isocrates insists that oratory is an act of creation and cannot be learned or taught from a handbook. Concepts such as *kairos* (fitness of oratory to each particular situation) and *prepon* (intuition of adequacy and propriety) are central to the production of ethical discourse. Such concepts are not successfully systematized by rhetorical rules and must be flexibly, even instinctively, understood and manipulated by the orator. Isocrates defends the use of this noncodifiable rhetoric to educate young men, and attempts in his educational system to institutionalize principles he admits cannot methodically control subject matter.

Further Reading: William Benoit, "Isocrates on Rhetorical Education," *Communication Education* 33 (1984): 109–20; Michael Cahn, "Reading Rhetoric Rhetorically: Isocrates and the Marketing of Insight," *Rhetorica* 7.2 (1989):121–44; Werner Jaeger, "The Province of Rhetoric and Its Cultural Ideal," in *The Province of Rhetoric,* eds. Joseph Schwartz and John Rycenga (New York: Ronald, 1965).

Kairos In rhetorical theory, *kairos* is the term used to describe the right or opportune time to speak or write. It also connotes the right measure, the appropriate move in a rhetorical situation. In contrast to the Greek noun *chronos,* which is measurable time, *kairos* is less translatable into English. It is akin to "timing," implying choice of a specific moment upon which success or failure depends.

Both pragmatic and moral implications inhere in the concept of *kairos.* Carolyn Miller illustrates its pragmatic nature, arguing that James Watson and Francis Crick's 1953 paper on the structure of DNA was widely accepted because its timing was right, even though Oswald Avery and his associates had published a similar paper nine years earlier. **James Kinneavy** demonstrates the moral aspect of *kairos,* establishing a link between it and justice. For the Pythagoreans, justice was what was due to a person for his or her hard work or accomplishments. The "proper measure" afforded to a person is just; therefore, to be moral and just means to observe "the proper measure" in action and words.

Kinneavy also traces the history of the concept. Other sources besides the Pythagoreans include Hesiod, whose seventh-century BCE proverb instructs people to "observe due measure and proportion . . . in all things," and Pindar, whose fifth-century BCE poetry stresses due or proper measure. The concept is central to the rhetorical theory of the **sophists,** especially Gorgias, who, according to **Kinneavy,** placed it as "the cornerstone of his entire epistemology, ethics, aesthetic, and rhetoric." **Plato** develops a theory of *kairos* in the conclusion to *Phaedrus,* and Aristotle develops the concept briefly in *Rhetoric.*

Kairos has emerged as an important concept in modern scholarship in rhetoric and religion. Theologian Paul Tillich, for example, describes a New Testament *kairos* as "the fullness of time," the fateful demand of every moment that requires decision.

Further Reading: James Luther Adams, *Paul Tillich's Philosophy of Culture,*

Science, and Religion (New York: Harper and Row, 1965); Stephen Doheny-Farina, "The Individual, the Organization, and *Kairos:* Making Transitions from College to Careers," *A Rhetoric of Doing,* eds. Stephen P. Witte, Neil Nakadate, and Roger Cherry (Carbondale, IL: Southern Illinois UP, 1992), 293–309; James L. Kinneavy, "*Kairos:* A Neglected Concept in Classical Rhetoric," *Rhetoric and Praxis,* ed. Jean Deitz Moss (Washington, DC: Catholic UP, 1986), 79–105; Carolyn R. Miller, "*Kairos* in the Rhetoric of Science," *A Rhetoric of Doing,* eds. Stephen P. Witte, Neil Nakadate, and Roger Cherry (Carbondale, IL: Southern Illinois UP, 1992), 310–27.

James L. Kinneavy (b. 1920) James L. Kinneavy, the Jane and Roland Blumberg Centennial Professor of English at the University of Texas at Austin, emerged in the 1970s as a major figure in the revival of the study of rhetoric in college and university English departments. In three books that merge theory and practice—*A Theory of Discourse* (1971; reprinted 1981), *Aims and Audiences in Writing* (1976), and *Writing—Basic Modes of Organization* (1976)—Kinneavy develops theories of the basic "aims," or emphases, of discourse and its basic "modes," or patterns of organization. In later works, Kinneavy provides rich historical scholarship on the ancient rhetorical concepts of **pisteis** and **kairos.** Throughout his career, he has argued for a more central role for traditional rhetorical theory in the teaching of writing.

Kinneavy's theory of discourse, which he defines as a complete utterance of speech or writing that has a beginning, middle, closure, and a purpose, depends on his graphic depiction of the *communications triangle,* a representation with historical roots ranging from **Aristotle** to Roman Jakobson. Kinneavy's triangle depicts the discourse participants, the terms for which he varies depending on the kind of discourse being described. At the three points are the *encoder* (i.e., the speaker or writer), the *decoder* (listener or reader), and the *reality* (the subject matter treated in the discourse). In the center of the triangle is the *signal* (the text, the artifact of communication). Using the communications triangle as a structuring device, Kinneavy attempts to describe the intellectual scope of English studies by explicating points of tension and cooperation among the four elements.

More importantly, Kinneavy employs the triangle to generate his theory of the major aims of discourse. Conceding a "crucial caution" that some aims will overlap, Kinneavy maintains that discourse that primarily emphasizes the encoder—journals, diaries, protest manifestos, and so on—is expressive in aim; discourse that primarily emphasizes the decoder—advertising, sermons, editorials, and so on—is persuasive in aim; discourse that primarily emphasizes the signal, or the artifact of communication—lyric poetry, a joke, an art film, and so on—is literary in aim; discourse that primarily emphasizes the reality—definitions, diagnoses, research reports, news articles, and so on—is referential in aim. Using this taxonomy, Kinneavy explains the underlying philosophy and basic organizational patterns of each aim.

Kinneavy's theory of the modes of discourse offers four modes—description, narration, classification, and evaluation—in lieu of the traditional modes promulgated by nineteenth-century Scottish rhetorician Alexander Bain—narration, description, exposition, and argumentation. Kinneavy maintains in *A Theory of Discourse* that the modes constitute "classifications of the kinds of realities referred to by full texts" and "are grounded in certain philosophic concepts of the nature of reality considered as being or becoming."

As a historian of rhetoric, Kinneavy has exhaustively explicated two important concepts from classical rhetorical theory. His 1987 book *Greek Rhetorical Origins of Christian Faith* demonstrates how the New Testament concept of faith, or *pisteis,* grew out of the use of that term by **Isocrates** and **Aristotle.** A 1986 essay provides a similarly rich historical explanation of the notion of **kairos,** or situational timeliness, in discourse.

Further Reading: Timothy Crusius, "James L. Kinneavy: A Bibliographic Essay," *A Rhetoric of Doing: Essay on Written Discourse in Honor of James L. Kinneavy,* eds. Stephen P. Witte, Neil Nakadate, and Roger D. Cherry (Carbondale, IL: Southern Illinois UP, 1992), 351–72; James L. Kinneavy, *Greek Rhetorical Origins of Christian Faith: An Inquiry* (New York: Oxford UP, 1987); James L. Kinneavy, *"Kairos:* A Neglected Concept in Classical Rhetoric," *Rhetoric and Praxis: The Contributions of Classical Rhetoric to Practical Reasoning,* ed. Jean Deitz Moss (Washington, DC: Catholic UP of America, 1986), 79–105; James L. Kinneavy, *A Theory of Discourse* (Englewood Cliffs, NJ: Prentice-Hall, 1971; rpt. New York: Norton, 1980); James L. Kinneavy, John Q. Cope, and J. W. Campbell, *Aims and Audiences in Writing* (Dubuque, IA: Kendall-Hunt, 1976); James L. Kinneavy, John Q. Cope, and J. W. Campbell, *Writing—The Basic Modes of Organization* (Dubuque, IA: Kendall-Hunt, 1976).

Logos In the ordinary Greek sense, *logos* means *word* or *reason.* In **Aristotle's** *Rhetoric, logos* is thought made manifest in speech (the Greek verb *legein* means *to speak*) and is one of the **pisteis** or means of proof. For **Aristotle,** proof through *logos,* or what may be called logical proof, involves the construction of persuasive examples and enthymemes. **Aristotle** does not develop in *Rhetoric* the more spiritual and magical senses of *logos* that also informed its meanings in antiquity. The power of *logos* is described in magical terms by the sophist Gorgias in his *Encomium of Helen* (415 BCE), where he expresses the conventional view that diabolical forces can reside in words; speech, he says, can "bewitch the soul with a kind of evil persuasion." For Heraclitus, the sixth-century BCE Greek philosopher, *logos* is the ordering principle of the universe, the term that stands for divine reason. *Logos* is also understood as the power of discourse to call forth realities by the New Testament writer of the Gospel of John, who, alluding to the Hebrew Bible's creation story, writes, "In the beginning was the Word." We are reminded that the earth is formed from out of the chaos by divine utterance: " 'Let there be light,' " calls God in Genesis 1, "And then there was light." As Donald Preziosi points out, the divine "Word made flesh," manifests "a perfect exchange between Spirit and matter, between the world of the infinite and the world of mortal finitude." The Christian *logos* is the divine text walking among us.

It should not be surprising, given its association with reason and with the male God, that *logos* has been seen as a term of exclusion by feminists. A number of recent studies remind us that the ancients (**Aristotle** among them) considered women to be lower on the scale of being and perfection than men, and utterly incapable of reason. Helene Cixous and Julia Kristeva are particularly concerned with what they see as the silencing of women's voices by patriarchal culture, and both attempt to create conditions in which women can speak and write and be heard. **Mary Daly,** because she sees women as being essentially locked out of the mythological system that celebrates the perfection of the male God, wrote *Beyond God the Father* as an introduction to her later books overhauling the patriarchal lexicon that determines our *logos*.

Another modern conception of *logos* has been offered by Jacques Derrida, who uses the term in order to critique a Western philosophical tradition that reinforces what he calls "the metaphysics of presence." In a sophistic spirit, Derrida confronts those ancients who believe that reason can discover truth and that language is a mimetic link between mind and nature. This belief, for Derrida the principle assumption of all Western thought, participates in a "logocentrism" that insists that mind and nature give rise to language; Derrida would insist instead that language makes possible consciousness and reality. For Derrida, there could be no god before there was the word.

Further Reading: Andrea Nye, *Words of Power: A Feminist Reading of the History of Logic* (New York: Routledge, 1990); Donald Preziosi; *Rethinking Art History* (New Haven: Yale UP, 1989); Edward Schiappa, *Protagoras and Logos: A Study in Greek Philosophy and Rhetoric* (U of South Carolina P, 1991).

Medieval Rhetoric   The medieval period in the history of rhetoric is often said to have begun in 427 CE, with the completion of Augustine's *De Doctrina Christiana*, and ended in 1416 with the rediscovery of **Quintilian'**s long-lost complete *Institutio Oratoriae*. Augustine's work marks the adaptation of classical rhetoric to the Christian institutions that dominated the Western Middle Ages, and the rediscovery of Quintilian heralds the neoclassical Renaissance tradition. Dominant characteristics of medieval rhetoric are its preceptive, heavily rule-governed nature and its pragmatic adaptation of classical material.

Historians of rhetoric have traditionally identified the Middle Ages as a period that reduced classical rhetoric to formulary treatments of **style** and **arrangement.** Works on rhetoric by Boethius, Cassidiorus, Isidore, and Martianus Capella tend to reinforce this view. Characteristically, Martianus' famous fifth-century poem, *De Nuptiis Philologiae et Mercurii*, features rhetoric as a lady fearsomely armed and ornamented with figures and tropes. Recently, however, revisionist historians such as Mary Carruthers and Rita Copeland have emphasized the dominance of both invention and memory. Carruthers labels the entire medieval tradition as a "memorial culture," documenting the pedagogical emphasis on memory while she points out that memory was itself coincident with the invention of arguments.

The adaptation of rhetoric to the needs of the times is evident in the development of *ars dictaminis,* the art of letter writing, which developed in the eleventh century in response to the political and commercial needs of a growing society. This art was initially guided by the work of a Monte Cassino monk, Alberic. Handbooks contained models of letters for addressing matters that included contractual obligations, real estate transactions, and domestic disputes; these forms were taught in an attempt to order and unify societal relations in an increasingly complicated environment.

Ars praedicandi, the art of preaching, is a second strain of medieval rhetoric. It is a complex theory of sermon writing and delivery that developed in the thirteenth century. Rhetorical concerns were Christian concerns and the emphasis shifted from the direct success of the speaker to the spiritual welfare of the audience. Gradually, hundreds of preaching manuals were promulgated, creating a homiletic revolution of sorts. Robert of Basevorn's *The Form of Preaching* typifies this genre.

During the early Middle Ages, the tradition of *ars grammatica,* the rhetoric of verse writing, conjoined classical grammatical study to rhetoric. Influenced by the Roman works of Horace and Donatus and exemplified by the sixth-century work of Priscian, this strain focused on the analysis of figures and tropes. About 1200, the *ars grammatica* began to dissolve into a slightly expanded study of language, *ars poetriae,* represented in the *Poetria Nova* of Geoffrey of Vinsauf. The new art of poetry concerned itself with developmental changes in the Latin language; more imaginative experimentation with language patterns, including elements of rhythm that constituted an *ars rithmica;* and increased preoccupation with figures and tropes.

Further Reading: Martin Camargo, "Rhetoric," in *The Seven Liberal Arts in the Middle Ages,* ed. David L. Wagner (Bloomington: Indiana UP, 1983), 96–124; Richard McKeon, "Rhetoric in the Middle Ages," *Speculum* 17 (1942): 1–32; James J. Murphy, *Rhetoric in the Middle Ages* (Berkeley: U of California P, 1981).

Memory Memory is one of the five ancient canons of rhetoric, along with **invention, arrangement, style,** and **delivery.** In fifth-century BCE Greece, the primarily oral tradition of rhetoric required rhetors to rely solely on their memories to deliver the most elaborate of speeches.

The canon of memory is grounded in classical philosophy as well as rhetoric. In **Aristotle's** *De Anima,* memory is likened to a mental picture or phantasm that imprints itself on our minds and to which we can return repeatedly. Thus, memory is associated with a kind of reminiscence that is both sensory and experiential. Ancient scholars employed two metaphors to describe the way knowledge is retained in memory. The first was that of memory as a blank wax tablet upon which images are imprinted. The second saw memory as a storage room that kept all the memorized images in an ordered configuration. From this storage room, images could be called forth by using the appropriate associations.

Classical rhetoricians developed mnemonics, heuristic systems used to retrieve information, from the prevailing philosophy of memory. In *De Oratore*, **Cicero** calls memory "the keenest of all our senses" and describes a common architectural mnemonic technique. This technique requires the orator to create a set of visual images like the rooms of a house, which can be associated with the items in a long speech. These mnemonic places and images (*loci* and *imagines*) are used to ensure accuracy as the rhetor goes through the speech and mentally associates each idea with a particular image.

In medieval rhetoric, memory became associated with ethics. Reflecting the philosophy of Alcuin, Albertus Magnus, and Thomas Aquinas, medieval theorists of memory cast its responsibility as not only for remembering a long speech but also for enhancing virtue and destroying vice. This new function arose in part because the Aristotelian theory of reminiscence allowed for the possibility that the memory of past experiences could be used to generate important lessons to improve a person's present moral state.

Medieval theorists also created new mnemonic systems. Rather than using the ancient method of creating images associated with architecture, the medieval scholars upheld the use of images as *corporeal similitudes*. That is, memory was to be enhanced by images of humanity, not merely architectural structures.

As many scholars have noted, the role of memory declined as rhetoric became associated more with written texts and less with solely oral delivery. In contemporary rhetoric, however, memory is returning as an important concept in the guise of a computer's "memory." Computer chips, disks, and tapes can hold far more data than any human's mind, and contemporary rhetorical theorists are faced with explaining and predicting how the awesome abundance of memory available to communicators now can be used most efficiently and ethically.

Further Reading: Mary Carruthers, *The Book of Memory* (Cambridge: Cambridge UP, 1990); Frances Yates, *The Art of Memory* (Chicago: U of Chicago P, 1966).

Modern Rhetoric   Just as it is difficult to say precisely when the modern period in literature begins, so it is difficult to claim an exact moment of birth for modern rhetoric. However, if one were to consider rhetorical theory developed from the last third of the nineteenth century to the present, an outline of modern rhetoric would emerge that embodies several challenging theoretical concepts: the ideas that all language is metaphorical, that "truth" in discourse is not transferred directly from reality but is instead constructed, that the interpretation of such "truth" must account for the constraints of context, and that context includes not only social characteristics such as politics and economics, but also such psychological variables as personality, race, and gender.

Rhetorical theory since the late nineteenth century has occasioned an epistemological shift that is both novel and rooted in the ancient tradition of the sophists. In challenging works that link the fields of rhetoric, philosophy, and history, such scholars as Friedrich Nietzsche (1844–1900), Jacques Derrida (b. 1930), and Michel Foucault (1926–1984) have promulgated modern and postmodern versions of two predominantly sophistic ideals. First, language is ultimately incapable of transmitting "reality," so all language must be seen as metaphorical, as a substitution for the objects and ideas actually being spoken or written about. Second, "truth" is not some absolute state of affairs that precedes discourse and transcends the rhetorical situation; instead, the "truth" in discourse is a rhetorical construction, a set of objects, ideas, and propositions that the rhetor arranges in collaboration with the prevailing ways of thinking shared by readers or auditors.

The writings of several theorists whose work moves between rhetoric and literary criticism amplify the role of interpretation in the constructivist epistemology of modern rhetoric. I. A. Richards (1893–1979), for example, in *The Philosophy of Rhetoric* (1936) challenges what he calls the "proper meaning superstition," the fallacy that words have inherent and stable meanings, and promulgates the notion of the "interinanimation of words," the idea that meaning is shaped in all discourse by the immediate verbal context that language is placed within. During his long and imaginative career, **Kenneth Burke** (1897–1993) consistently returned to the importance of dialectic and perspective in interpretation. Meaning is forged in texts, **Burke** argues, as rhetors and audiences consider ways of interpreting the reality at hand dialectically and emphasize certain perspectives over others. In the past quarter-century, a group of rhetorical theorists and literary critics, including Helene Cixous (b. 1937) and Julia Kristeva (b. 1941), have expanded theories of interpretation to account for the ways the gender of rhetors and audiences influences the production, consumption, and interpretation of discourse. Similarly, the nature, scope, and definitions of rhetoric and interpretation have been refined by scholars such as Henry Louis Gates (b. 1950) who are interested in the effect of ethnicity in discourse.

In the midst of these developments in epistemology and interpretation, modern rhetoric has also been the site of impressive reiterations of concepts from classical rhetorical theory. The writings of **Chaim Perelman** (1912–1984), for example, show a strong affinity to the interactive, consensus-building theory of argumentation developed in **Aristotle's** *Rhetoric*. Stephen Toulmin (b. 1922) similarly builds on **Aristotle** by recasting the **enthymeme** in a modern structural model of an argument that accounts for data, claim, warrants, backing, grounds, and qualifications.

Further Reading: James L. Kinneavy, "Contemporary Rhetoric," *The Present State of Scholarship in Historical and Contemporary Rhetoric,* ed. Winifred Bryan Horner (Columbia, MO: U of Missouri P, 1983); C. H. Knoblauch, "Modern Rhetorical Theory and Its Future Directions," *Perspectives on Research and Scholarship in Composition,* eds. Ben W. McClelland and Timothy R. Donovan (New York: Oxford UP, 1985); Michael Leff, "In Search of Ariadne's Thread: A Review of Recent Literature on Rhetorical Theory," *Central States Speech Journal* 29 (1978): 73–91.

Walter J. Ong   (b. 1912)   Walter Jackson Ong, S. J., is William E. Haren Professor of English and Professor of Humanities in Psychiatry at St. Louis University. Ong's scholarship focuses on issues of literacy. In his many articles and books, including

The Presence of the Word, Interfaces of the Word, and *Orality and Literacy,* Ong attempts to build a historical reconstruction of what it means to be a literate people.

Ong's theories are founded on the premise that an overarching intellectual shift occurs when written, alphabetic literacy enters cultures whose literacy was previously oral or ideographic. Drawing on field research conducted by such anthropologists as Claude Lévi-Strauss and Bronislav Malinoski, Ong analyzes preliterate cultures discovered in the twentieth century in the light of his understanding of ancient oral traditions, such as the Homeric tradition in ancient Greece. He sees a relatively absolute transformation resulting from alphabetic literature. As he told interviewer Wayne Altree in 1973, "After writing took hold, purely oral talk was finished. Too bad, in many ways. For the purely oral has great beauties of its own. But you can't have your cake and eat it."

Ong's comparisons of different cultures have yielded a number of oppositions he uses to contrast orality from literacy. In an often-quoted 1975 article, "The Writer's Audience is Always a Fiction," Ong maintains that the "[c]ontext for the spoken word is simply present, centered,"—and, thus, the audience is a collective community—while, for the writer, "the audience is simply further away, in time or space or both"—and, thus, composed of isolated individuals. Ong elaborates the "evanescent" quality of sound and speech versus the encoded, surface inscriptions of writing. Because written discourse is indirect, the masks of writer and reader are more fixed than those of the speaker and hearer: "[O]ral communication . . . has within it a momentum that works for the removal of masks"; the audience with an oral culture is less likely to be a fiction. Ong adds to the catalogue of oppositions in "Some Psychodynamics of Orality." He lists nine characteristics of orally based thought, all of them polarized against traits of literacy: "additive rather than subordinative," "aggregative rather than analytic," "redundant or 'copious,' " "conservative or traditionalist," "close to the human lifeworld," "agonistically toned," "empathetic and participatory rather than objectively distanced," "homeostatic," and "situational rather than abstract."

Critiques of Ong's work have centered on its oppositional nature, finding it a bit reductive, and on his ethnocentric bias. Beth Daniell, for example, faults Ong for what she terms the concept of "the Great Leap": "Like others who think that literacy brings about a great mental leap, he sees literacy primarily as a technology that fosters abstract thinking." Arguing that his universalizing tendencies decontextualize specific situations and disregard power relations, Daniell sees Ong's imposition of generalized cultural and historical theories to individuals and cultures as "justification for the status quo."

Further Reading: Wayne Altree, ed., "Why Talk: A Conversation About Language with Walter J. Ong," *The National Humanities Faculty Why Series* (San Francisco: Chandler and Sharp, 1973); Beth Daniell, "The Situation of Literacy and Cognition: What We Can Learn from the Uzbek Experiment," *The Right to Literacy,* eds. Andrea Lunsford, Helene Moglin, and James Slevin (New York: Modern Language Association, 1990); Walter J. Ong, S. J., "Some Psychodynamics of Orality," *Perspectives on Literacy,* eds. Eugene R. Kintgen, Barry M. Kroll, and

Mike Rose (Carbondale: Southern Illinois UP, 1988); Walter J. Ong, S. J., "The Writer's Audience is Always a Fiction." *PMLA* 90 (1975): 9–21.

Pan Chao (c. 45CE–115CE) Pan Chao, a first-century CE Chinese woman, served as historian to the Imperial Court of China during the reign of the Eastern Han emperor Ho; taught mathematics, writing, history, astronomy, poetry, and eloquence at the court; wrote commentaries, poetry, arguments, and what was one of the first treatises in history arguing for the education of girls; and was editor for the imperial library. She was also a successful orator and political advisor to the empress Teng.

Although her extant works are relatively few (four poems, two memorials, and a treatise have survived out of sixteen volumes of her written work), Pan Chao is important to understanding the history of women in rhetoric, and can also contribute to our understanding of Eastern rhetoric. In her *Lessons for Women,* Pan Chao offers advice that had not been articulated before on the proper use of language. "Womanly words" were one qualification of a virtuous woman; these words "need be neither clever in debate nor keen in conversation," but women should be careful to choose "words with care; to avoid vulgar language; to speak at appropriate times; and not to weary others [with much conversation]." Pan Chao shared the traditional belief that an ability to distinguish right from wrong was the basis of knowledge, and thus stated that "words may be either right or wrong."

In the midst of this treatise on appropriate female behavior, Pan Chao inserted a radical call to educate girls. This was not an indication that she viewed males and females as equals, but, consistent with her philosophical position that human nature has within it a seed of goodness that can be fostered by education, she believed that females should have the same opportunity to develop that goodness as males. Pan Chao was the first person in China to argue for such an innovation.

Although Pan Chao's argument for the education of girls and women was not successful in her time, she was successful in framing and presenting arguments to the emperor and empress, gaining through two "memorials" the release of her aging and ailing brother from public service and the right of the empress's relatives to resign of their own volition. The pieces present lucid, well-crafted arguments that turn pleas for granting the wishes of the ruler's subjects into arguments for action in the ruler's best interest. With regard to her ailing brother, Pan Chao argues:

> If it is a long time before he is relieved, (your handmaiden) fears that there will be a springing up of conspiracies to incite a spirit of rebellion and disorder. . . . Should trouble arise among the barbarian soldiers, Chao's physical strength would not be able to follow the wishes of his heart. And it may happen that from the point of view of the dynasty the work of several generations would be injured.

Further Reading: Derk Bodde, *Essays on Chinese Civilization* (Princeton:

Princeton UP, 1981): 148–60; Nancy Lee Swann, *Pan Chao: Foremost Woman Scholar of China* (New York: Century, 1932).

Pathos

> The emotions [*pathe*] are those things through which, by undergoing change, people come to differ in their judgments and which are accompanied by pain and pleasure, for example, anger, pity, fear, and other such things and their opposites.

For **Aristotle,** *pathos* names the rhetor's appeal to the audience's emotions, which he characterizes here in Book 2 of the *Rhetoric* as states of mind that affect judgments. It is primarily **Aristotle's** discussion of *pathos* that has distinguished his *Rhetoric* as a study of human psychology. However, it is also true that **Aristotle's** teacher **Plato** made the psychology of the rhetor's audience—expressed as the state of the mind–soul—a central concern in *Phaedrus,* where **Plato's** Socrates says that the ideal rhetor must

> discover the kind of speech that matches each type of nature. When that is accomplished, he must arrange and adorn each speech in such a way as to present complicated and unstable souls with complex speeches, speeches exactly attuned to every changing mood of the complicated soul—while the simple soul must be presented with simple speeches.

Although defining *pathos* as *state of mind* leads us to associated considerations of human psychology in rhetorical theory, emphasis on a common connotation of *pathos*—that is, "what one has suffered"—makes *pathos* an element of tragic literature, usually associated with characters who evoke the audience's pity. Proceeding from this sense of *pathos,* John Ruskin coined the term *pathetic fallacy* in 1856 to describe the attribution of human emotions to nonhuman entities, such as the foam in these lines: "They rowed her in across the rolling foam— / The cruel, crawling foam."

Returning to the sense of *pathos* that **Aristotle** initiated, we may conclude that the meaning of a discourse is contingent upon the beliefs and presuppositions that inform the audience's state of mind. Thus, **Chaim Perelman** says in *The Realm of Rhetoric* that "[t]o adapt to an audience is, above all, to choose as premises of argumentation theses the audience already holds." With this statement, **Perelman** follows **Aristotle's** blurring of the distinctions between ethical, logical, and pathetic appeals, saying, in effect, that the **logos** of one's speech must fit the *pathos* of the audience, and noting elsewhere (as does **Aristotle**) that the character of the speaker—insofar as it arouses the good will of the audience—also has persuasive force.

Although the role of the audience in determining meaning has been acknowledged in rhetorical theory since antiquity, only quite recently have theories of reading that feature the reader's role gained notice. Under the general rubric of Reader

Response Theory, theorists such as David Bleich, Norman Holland, Wolfgang Iser, Hans Robert Jauss, and Stanley Fish have emphasized audience psychology.

Further Reading: David Bleich, *Readings and Feelings: An Introduction to Subjective Criticism* (Urbana: National Council of Teachers of English, 1975); Jakob Wisse, *Ethos and Pathos from Aristotle to Cicero* (Amsterdam: Hakkert, 1989).

Chaim Perelman (1912–1984) Chaim Perelman is a contemporary scholar whose works have done much to revive the traditional intellectual status of rhetoric. A professor of law and philosophy at the University of Brussels, Perelman co-authored with Lucie Olbrechts-Tyteca *The New Rhetoric* (1958), an ambitious study of argumentation with Aristotelian underpinnings. He distilled this analysis later in *The Realm of Rhetoric* (1977). In their works, Perelman and Olbrechts-Tyteca unite philosophy and rhetoric by analyzing *phronesis,* the Greek ideal of practical reason. Like Aristotle before him, Perelman finds that arguments do not necessarily rely on formal logic, that arguments are capable of being persuasive without being purely logical.

For example, Perelman emphasizes the importance in argumentation of establishing *presence,* by which he means the evoking of physical realities. In *The Realm of Rhetoric,* he notes the persuasive effects of the sight of "Caesar's bloody tunic as brandished by Antony" and says in *The New Rhetoric* that an effective speaker must similarly "make present by verbal magic, what is actually absent."

Metaphor and analogy, long understood as an orator's flourishes rather than argumentative strategies, are also important in Perelman's scheme. An analogy is a comparison of a set of relationships (a/b = c/d), and a metaphor is a "condensed analogy" (a = c) that an audience must expand in the act of apprehending it. An analogy or metaphor has two parts, the *phoros* (or figure) that we employ to understand the *theme* (or subject); there are similarities here to **I. A. Richards**'s conception of vehicle and tenor. Although sometimes a speaker will abandon the *phoros* once the *theme* is clear "as does the contractor who takes down the scaffolding after the building is finished," there is usually not such an easy separation of the two parts because "the separation between the form and content of discourse cannot be realized in as simple a way as classical thought imagined it." Metaphor and analogy, then, are not dispensable aids to an argument, but the very fiber of it.

Perhaps Perelman's most controversial concept is the *universal audience.* Throughout his work, Perelman stresses the importance of the audience to which arguments must be adapted. In order not to alienate the diverse members of an audience, a speaker must posit a universal audience whose members all assent to certain fundamental propositions. To critics who fear that the idea of a universal audience presupposes the existence of self-evident truths, Perelman answers that a great variety of conflicting ideas have seemed self-evident throughout history. He points out that the universal audience does not exist in fact, but must exist in the rhetor's imagination. It is, in words borrowed from Sartre, an "abstract universality."

Further Reading: Ray D. Dearin, ed., *The New Rhetoric of Chaim Perelman: Statement and Response* (University Press of America: 1989); James J. Golden and Joseph J. Pilotta, eds., *Practical Reasoning in Human Affairs: Studies in Honor of Chaim Perelman* (Boston: Reidel, 1986).

Pisteis In **Aristotle's** *Rhetoric, pisteis* are proofs, or resources for rhetorical persuasion. Artistic proofs, those that must be invented by a speaker, are based on ethos, pathos, and logos. **Ethos** is the character of the speaker, as projected in the speech. This projected character should embody practical wisdom, virtue, and goodwill. It should also meet the needs of specific rhetorical occasions: The ethos one projects to one audience may not be effective with another, as any modern political candidate knows well. **Pathos** refers to the emotions, or states of mind, of the audience. The rhetor must understand the elements of emotions such as pity and fear in order to appeal to them or arouse them when necessary. **Logos** refers to the chosen words of the speech, and its signature is the **enthymeme.** In practice, the *pisteis* are interdependent. Even for purposes of explanation, they are not easily isolated. **Aristotle** overtly connects ethos and pathos in his discussion of how a speaker might adapt his own character to the character of the audience, based on its age and social and economic status; and he treats ethical and pathetic considerations in his discussion of constructing the enthymemic logos.

Although **ethos, pathos,** and **logos** have remained central to rhetorical theory, their interrelationship has been neglected since **Aristotle's** time. Many theorists have emphasized a single *pistis*: In *De Oratore,* **Cicero** dwells on the qualifications of the orator and extends his sense of ethos to include a discussion of the rhetor's general intellectual habits, apart from a particular rhetorical situation. **Quintilian** continues the emphasis on ethos with his definition of the ideal rhetor as the "good man speaking well." The advent of Christianity brought renewed attention to the moral and spiritual qualities of the rhetor; in his fifth-century treatise *On Christian Doctrine,* Augustine says that an effective preacher needs only to be filled up with the grace of God.

From the late Middle Ages, as rhetoric developed further written and spoken forms, it became more logos-centered, with handbooks attending mainly to matters of arrangement and style: An effective text was one that followed conventional organizational formulas. **Enlightenment rhetoric,** with its appreciation of plain style and its suspicion of subjectivity, gave most weight to perspicuity and factuality. Influential teachers such as Hugh Blair argue that the simplest and most direct argument will be most effective because our minds are naturally predisposed to it; in this way, **Blair** acknowledges a role for audience psychology, but makes pathos ancillary to a rather constrained logos. **George Campbell's** 1776 *Philosophy of Rhetoric* gives more complex attention to pathos than does **Blair,** drawing on contemporary faculty psychology. Renewed interest in **Aristotle** in this century has led to the foregrounding of the *pisteis'* interdependency in the work of theorists such as **Chaim Perelman.**

Further Reading: Christopher Gill, "The Ethos/Pathos Distinction in Rhetorical and Literary Criticism," *Classical Quarterly* 34.1 (1984): 149–66; William M. A. Grimaldi, *Aristotle, Rhetoric I: A Commentary* and *Aristotle, Rhetoric II: A Commentary* (New York: Fordham UP, 1980 and 1988); Chaim Perelman and Lucie Olbrechts-Tyteca, *The New Rhetoric* (Notre Dame, 1979).

Plato   (c. 429–347 BCE)   A follower of Socrates (469–399 BCE), Plato presented his philosophy primarily through dialogues whose main character is Socrates. The dialogue form contributes to the literary quality of Plato's works, that is, the ambiguity that results from an interplay of viewpoints and the absence of an expository author (i.e., Plato) with a determined perspective. Although many of Plato's dialogues deal with the nature and practice of rhetoric, those that devote fullest attention to the subject are *Gorgias* and *Phaedrus*.

The dialogue form in these works and others lends itself to the practice of **dialectic,** that is, a method of inquiry that proceeds through series of questions and answers in order to arrive at the precise definitions and distinctions that must, for Plato's Socrates, inform philosophical truth. Ostensibly, participants in dialectic do not have a final solution or thesis in view as they proceed, but the character of Socrates often seems to be directing the discussion toward certain ends to which he is already predisposed. In this way, Platonic dialogues can be seen as instances of Socrates trying to move his auditors toward certain conclusions, not unlike the kind of orator he often disparages.

Gorgias is a relatively early dialogue (c. 387 BCE) whose characters are Socrates, Gorgias, Polus, and Callicles. Gorgias—a prominent orator and teacher of rhetoric remembered for his *Encomium of Helen*—was still alive when *Gorgias* was published, and is reported to have read it. In this dialogue, Plato's Socrates advances the idea that because the practice of rhetoric does not require any particular body of knowledge and does not aim at the good, it is a false art or "knack" rather than a true art. Just as cookery is a false art that offers the body pleasant taste rather than good health, rhetoric is a false art that offers a crowd what they enjoy hearing rather than what is good for them.

The castigation of rhetoric continues in *Phaedrus,* which is probably a later dialogue than *Gorgias,* and is widely regarded as one of Plato's greatest works. This dialogue begins with a meeting between Socrates and Phaedrus, in which the latter describes his excitement over just having heard the sophist Lysias give a speech. In a discussion of the speech, Socrates leads Phaedrus through considerations of both the nature of love (the subject of Lysias's speech) and the nature of rhetoric, culminating in a famous Platonic summary of ideal rhetoric:

> A man must first know the truth about every single subject on which he speaks or writes. He must be able to define each in terms of a universal class that stands by itself. When he has successively defined his subjects according to their specific classes, he must know how to continue the division until he reaches the point of indivisibility. He must make the same sort of distinction

with reference to the nature of the soul. . . . Not until a man acquires this capacity will it be possible to produce speech in a scientific way . . . either for the purposes of instruction or of persuasion.

Further Reading: Ronna Burger, *Plato's Phaedrus: A Defense of a Philosophic Art of Writing* (University: U of Alabama P, 1980); Lynette Hunter, *Rhetorical Stance in Modern Literature: Allegories of Love and Death* (New York: St. Martin's, 1984); Richard Weaver, "The *Phaedrus* and the Nature of Rhetoric," in *The Ethics of Rhetoric* (Chicago: Regnery, 1953).

Poetics   Though used in various ways, the term *poetics* commonly refers to theories of the nature and function of poetry, which in this connection is meant to encompass all conventional forms of literature. The term *poetics* has origins in **Aristotle's** *Peri Poetikes,* which has been translated as *On Poetic Art,* and is commonly known as the *Poetics.* In the fragment of this work that survives, **Aristotle** discusses the elements of poetic tragedy, giving particular attention to the construction of the plot. **Aristotle's** *Poetics* is notable for the recognition that the effects of poetic art are connected to the psychology of the audience, and in this regard the *Poetics* can be compared to his *Rhetoric.*

One of the important points of overlap between **Aristotle's** *Rhetoric* and *Poetics* is his discussion of metaphor. In his comments on style in Book 3 of the *Rhetoric,* Aristotle features metaphor as one of three most effective elements of style—metaphor, antithesis, and actuality; and in the *Poetics,* metaphor is called "the token of genius." Both books advise writers to create engaging metaphors that are neither too obscure nor too obvious.

Finding common terms for rhetoric and poetics in discussions of **style,** **Aristotle** anticipates the forum in which these two subjects will meet in the following centuries. *On the Sublime,* written in the first century CE by an undetermined author, discusses sublimity as a feature of great poetry while at the same time locating its effects in stylistic categories associated with rhetoric. The tendency to locate literary excellence in terms of rhetorical style continues in influential and representative treatises such as Geoffrey of Vinsauf's thirteenth-century *Poetria Nova* and George Puttenham's sixteenth-century *Arte of English Poesie.* **Hugh Blair's** eighteenth-century *Lectures on Rhetoric and Belles-Lettres* announces with its title the conjunction of rhetoric and poetics, and argues that the same formal and stylistic features that constitute tasteful and effective rhetoric—unity, clarity, and perspicuity—are evident in the best literature as well.

It has been argued by Donald Stewart that the splitting off of poetics and literary study from rhetoric was an effect of the "Harvardization of English departments" in the late nineteenth century, when rhetoric in the academy became identified more exclusively with basic expository writing, and distinguished from the more advanced study of literature. Reconsiderations of the relationship between rhetoric and poetics have emerged recently in the wake of postmodernism, with literary theorists such as Paul De Man proposing that the tropes and figures traditionally associated with style in rhetoric are vehicles for the play of meanings in literature; and Terry Eagleton arguing that distinctions between literature and rhetoric are not possible to establish, and that a comprehensive poetics should coincide with classical conceptions of rhetoric—as a broad-based consideration of the stylistic, formal, psychological, social, political, and cultural elements of discourse.

Further Reading: Paul de Man, "The Rhetoric of Temporality," in *Blindness and Insight: Essays in the Rhetoric of Contemporary Criticism* (New York: Oxford UP, 1971); Wilbur S. Howell, *Poetics, Rhetoric, and Logic: Studies in the Basic Disciplines of Criticism* (Ithaca: Cornell UP, 1975); Donald C. Stewart, "Two Model Teachers and the Harvardization of English Departments," in *Rhetorical Traditions and the Teaching of Writing*, ed. James J. Murphy (New York: MLA, 1982): 118–30.

Postmodernism The difficulties of the word *postmodernism*, the term generally applied to our present cultural era, are illustrated in its etymology: *modern* comes from the Latin *modo* meaning *just now*; and *post,* of course, means *after.* So to be in a postmodern era means to be in a time that is "after just now," an impossibility appropriate to our understanding of the term. Jean-Francois Lyotard explains that postmodernists "are working without rules in order to formulate the rules of what will have been done." It is this backwards view, this grammatical paradox of the future anterior tense ("what will have been done"), that explains postmodernism.

Historically, postmodernism is a response to modernism and concerns the state of dissolution forecast in Yeats's *The Second Coming:* "Things fall apart; the center cannot hold." One postmodernist view is that our experience of the world—language, knowledge, and culture—is fragmented, unstable, indeterminate, discontinuous. Another postmodern view is that the world is actually unified, totalized under the monolith of capitalism, a state characterized by a fungibility of the individual and an overemphasis on performativity (the valuation of knowledge in terms of utility and marketability) rather than ethics (valuation of the Good and the True). But whether the world is seen as fractured or totalized, the postmodern stance rejects *metanarratives,* overarching concepts such as progress or enlightenment that are used to legitimate and aggrandize knowledge and learning.

Postmodern rhetoric, as literary theorist Terry Eagleton conceives it, is the study that can heal the contemporary schisms in academia and in the world. Because rhetoric addresses itself to the wide field of all discursive practices, it can embrace the multiplicity of twentieth-century critical theories—from liberal humanism to neomarxism and feminism. However, postmodern rhetoric distinguishes itself from ancient rhetoric because our contemporary theories question the very ground of traditional givens such as author, purposes, and audience.

One prominent postmodern rhetorical strategy is deconstruction. Premised on a belief in the isolation and impenetrability of the self, deconstruction concludes that language can never say what it means to say. Yet deconstructionists do not despair from this lack of meaning; rather, the antireferentiality of language invites play, *jouissance*. All discourse, then, is *bricolage*, literally tinkering or puttering around, the only activity possible because there is no center, no originary or stable meaning. One striking celebration of a lack of center, or deterritorialization, is found in the work of Gilles Deleuze and Felix Guattari, who celebrate schizophrenia—a state of psychological instability—because it is always inventive and can never be totalized.

Further Reading: Terry Eagleton, "A Small History of Rhetoric," in *Walter Benjamin* (London: NLB, 1981): 101–13; Patricia Harkin and John Schilb, eds., *Contending With Words* (New York: MLA, 1991); Fredric Jameson, "Postmodernism," in *New Left Review* 146 (1984): 53–92; Jean-Francois Lyotard, *The Postmodern Condition* (Minneapolis: U of Minnesota P, 1984).

Quintilian (c. 35–95) Born in the small town of Calagurris in what is today Spain, Marcus Fabius Quintilianus entered a politically treacherous epoch when the totalitarian proclamations of imperial Rome had supplanted the once lively debate of the Republic. Rhetoric had become a school subject with little connection to public life.

Appointed by Emperor Vespasian as the first chair of Latin rhetoric in the public schools of Rome in 71, Quintilian received a handsome yearly salary of 100,000 sesterces (the equivalent today of several hundred thousand dollars). As a teacher, Quintilian stressed his belief that the true orator must be *vir bonus dicendi peritus*, the good man speaking well. For Quintilian, eloquence was predicated upon personal virtue combined with artistic excellence. His emphasis on the formation of moral character resounds throughout his *Institutio Oratoria (Institutes of Oratory)*, the most complete treatise on Latin rhetoric surviving from antiquity. During most of the Middle Ages, only incomplete manuscripts of *Institutio Oratoria* circulated; however, in 1416 a complete manuscript of the work was discovered by Poggio in a Swiss monastery. Though largely unoriginal in its formulation of rhetoric, endorsing **Cicero's** views from *De Oratore* and *Orator,* Quintilian's work is significant for its systematic presentation of the complete rhetorical education of a boy from birth to adulthood.

Perceiving the crucial stages of early development, Quintilian argues that parents, not household slaves, should begin the moral training of their children from the cradle. Both the father and the mother should be as learned as possible, speaking well in the presence of their child so that he might imitate proper pronunciation, in both Latin and Greek. At age seven, the prospective orator should attend the school of the literator, whose job it is to teach the child how to read and write the languages he can already speak. First by touching carved ivory letters of the alphabet, the child finds delight in handling written language. Later the child progresses by tracing these letters onto wax boards and learning to spell. Eventually, sentences consisting of moral admonitions are copied.

By about age fourteen, the child moves to the instruction of the grammaticus, from whom he learns sentence grammar, advanced vocabulary, and proper pronunciation. Also, works of literature are to be carefully read, memorized and delivered, formally analyzed, and considered for moral content. When the young man graduates to the school of rhetoric, his elementary training is not forgotten but expanded upon. The student must now provide plot summaries of tragedies and comedies, analyze recognized narratives, and craft his own words into meaningful discourse.

Further Reading: George Kennedy, *Quintilian* (New York: Twayne, 1969); Michael Winterbottom, "Quintilian and the Vir Bonus," *Journal of Roman Studies* 54 (1964): 90–97.

Peter Ramus (1515–1572) Peter Ramus, or Pierre de la Ramée in the French vernacular, was a controversial and influential figure in the sixteenth-century French university. Ramus' most important work centers on educational reform: His imperative was to make the curriculum practicable. In the service of establishing a straightforward, unencumbered pedagogical method, Ramus redefined the ancient disciplines, simplified theory, and streamlined definitions. As Walter Ong says, Ramus' focus was not "Is it true?" but "Is it teachable?" Refashioning the curriculum, however, meant challenging the prevailing authorities. So Ramus took on figures no less than **Cicero, Quintilian,** and **Aristotle,** a scandalizing approach because these ancient figures had provided the foundations for the entire scholastic system since the Middle Ages. Ramus' vitriolic attacks on the masters led to an early ban on his books, and he was forbidden to teach. Fortunately, Ramus had friends in high places, including Charles, Cardinal of Lorraine, with whom he went to school as a boy, and by 1547 the ban of 1544 was reversed.

In *Remarks on Aristotle* and *Structure of Dialectic* (both 1543), Ramus refutes and simplifies **Aristotle's** definition of logic, leading **Walter Ong** to label him "the greatest master of the short-cut the world has ever known." Similarly, in *Arguments in Rhetoric Against Quintilian* (1549) Ramus eviscerates **Quintilian's** conception of rhetoric: **Quintilian** refused to notate a system of rules for rhetoric because he believed that it was something complicated and fluid, taking into consideration the personality of the speaker, the conditions of the audience, and so on. Ramus targets this view of rhetoric:

"I teach," [Quintilian] says, "that the orator cannot be perfect unless he is a good man. Consequently I demand from him not only outstanding skill in speaking but all the virtuous qualities of character." . . . What then can be said against this definition of an orator? I assert indeed that such a definition of an orator seems to me to be useless and stupid: Why? Because a definition of any artist which covers more than is included in the rules of his art is superfluous and defective. . . . For although I admit that rhetoric is a virtue, it is virtue of the mind and the intelligence, as in all true liberal arts, whose followers can still be men of the utmost moral depravity.

Thus, Ramus separated virtue out of rhetoric; in his definition rhetoric was confined to **style** and **delivery. Invention** and **arrangement,** as well as all matters of logic and ethics, were extraneous, belonging instead to philosophy. Ramus' rhetoric, then, becomes something smaller, simpler; this attenuated notion of rhetoric is evoked today when a politician says that his opponent is spouting "mere rhetoric." It is this Ramist heritage that the renewed emphasis in this century on classical invention and philosophical rhetoric has sought to reverse.

Further Reading: James J. Murphy, "Introduction," *Arguments in Rhetoric Against Quintilian* by Peter Ramus, trans. Carole Newlands and James J. Murphy (De Kalb, IL: Northern Illinois UP, 1983): 1–76; Walter J. Ong, *Ramus, Method, and the Decay of Dialogue* (Cambridge: Harvard UP, 1958).

Renaissance Rhetoric   Much of the vitality of the study and practice of rhetoric in the Renaissance can be located in enthusiasm for classical Greek and Roman texts. The discovery of a complete **Quintilian** by Poggio in 1416 ushered in tremendous efforts by translators and teachers of the *studia humanitatis*—known to us now as humanists—to appropriate and propagate the literature of antiquity. Taking a new look at **Plato, Cicero,** and **Quintilian,** as well as other works on eloquence such as *On the Sublime* by Longinus, Renaissance humanists emphasized rhetoric as an art contributing to the full realization of human potential.

The power of language to transform consciousness was a central occupation of those who associated rhetoric with magic. Marsilio Ficino translated all of **Plato** in the late fifteenth century and employed his neoplatonism in an important treatise on natural magic, *Three Books on Life,* in which Ficino observes that the positions and influences of the stars and the planets should be considered part of the context for effective speechmaking. Ficino's student, Giovanni Pico della Mirandola, continues this conception of the orator as a mediator of universal powers in his 1487 *Oration on the Dignity of Man,* in which he proposes that the universe can speak through the orator, and that the orator in harmony with the universe can exert powerful effects on auditors. The most famous Renaissance magician, Cornelius Agrippa, says in his 1510 *Three Books of Occult Philosophy* that properly uttered discourse can change "not only the hearers but also other bodies and things that have no life."

The alignment of rhetoric with magic indicates a general Renaissance preoccupation with the powers of the human imagination. This interest is evident in increased attention to *copia,* a classical concept introduced by **Quintilian,** for whom it means an abundance of words and ideas at the rhetor's disposal. **Erasmus** wrote a textbook *On Copia* in 1511, demonstrating the creation of abundant words and ideas through amplification and variation and indicating the dominant Renaissance preoccupation with figurative language. Perhaps the most extensive—though unsystematic—demonstration of *copia* in writing is Montaigne's *Essais,* composed in the late sixteenth century. Recognized as the inventor of the essay, Montaigne is notable for the development of the genre as a series of "trials" in which a writer explores a wide variety of perspectives on a subject. Such intellectual play is, according to Richard Lanham, an important motive for eloquence in the Renaissance.

The recovery of classical conceptions of rhetoric as a broadly exploratory art is challenged by **Peter Ramus** in the mid-sixteenth century, in his arguments that rhetorical invention should be replaced by a more rigid logical invention, and that disciplined attention to **style** and **delivery** should comprise the whole of rhetoric. Ramus looks forward to further reductions of the scope of rhetoric in the seventeenth century by the Port Royalists in France and the Royal Society of London.

Further Reading: Richard Lanham, *The Motives of Eloquence* (New Haven: Yale UP, 1976); John Monfasani, "Humanism and Rhetoric," in *Renaissance Humanism: Foundations, Forms, and Legacy,* ed. Albert Rabil, Jr. (Philadelphia: U of Pennsylvania P, 1988), 3.171–235; James J. Murphy, *Renaissance Eloquence: Studies in the Theory and Practice of Renaissance Rhetoric* (Berkeley: U of California P, 1983).

I. A. Richards   (1893–1979)   The work of I. A. Richards, a British scholar educated in philosophy, was instrumental in the rise of the university study of English. As a professor first at the University of Cambridge and later at Harvard, Richards advocated the importance of literature, and even more, the study of interpretation. For Richards—and for the American New Critics who followed his lead—understanding literature is bound up with understanding the human condition. In *The Meaning of Meaning* (written in 1923 with C. K. Ogden), Richards is concerned not only with words, grammar, and symbols, but with aesthetics, philosophy, and psychology.

The inquiry into interpretation led Richards in short order to rhetoric, which he wanted to resurrect as the discipline able to inquire into how words mean and how they fail to mean. Defining rhetoric as "a study of misunderstanding and its remedies" in his 1936 *Philosophy of Rhetoric,* Richards sees words as inextricably linked to ideas. But words are rarely stable things. If a passage has one meaning, it can also "at the same time mean another and an incompatible thing" and, in fact, this is precisely the case with poetry. The instability of language is made clear in Richards' concept of the "interinanimation of words": Just as the movement of one's hand involves and is supported by the entire skeletal system, words involve and are supported by their contexts. So then, how do words mean? Richards answers by proposing a *word theorem:* First he debunks the "Proper Meaning Superstition"—that a word has a single, rigid meaning; then he claims that "the meaning of a word is the missing part of its contexts." Richards also wants to elevate the theory of metaphor in rhetoric because he claims that metaphor is not exceptional in language but ubiquitous. He distinguishes the two components of a metaphor: the *tenor*—the subject that is made metaphorical; and the *vehicle*—the metaphorized term that carries the tenor. Thus, in a statement such as "Life is a bumpy road," *life* is the tenor and *bumpy road* is the vehicle.

Richards felt that science had made great advances but our thinking hadn't, and he wanted our understanding of language to be undertaken with the same precision and attention to method that the sciences employ. In that spirit, Richards conducted a now-famous experiment in his classes at Cambridge: He distributed to his students a dozen poems of wide-ranging quality, then documented the students' written responses. He found that students could not consistently identify and distinguish the canonized works from the noncanonized ones. Although their responses seemed at first to show no particular pattern of interpretation or misinterpretation, Richards concluded that their errors in both identification and interpretation actually lie in four areas that comprise the four kinds of meaning that occur simultaneously in a literary work: sense (what is said); feeling (the author's attitude to what is said); tone (the attitude toward the listener or reader); and intention (the author's conscious or unconscious aim). Richards concluded that the teaching of literature should involve not just attention to the poem, but a broader scrutiny of the aspects of meaning, what might be called rhetoric.

Further reading: Ann Berthoff, "I. A. Richards," in *Traditions of Inquiry*, ed. John Brereton (New York: Oxford, 1985); Ann Berthoff, ed., *Richards on Rhetoric* (New York: Oxford UP, 1991); John Paul Russo, *I. A. Richards: His Life and Work* (Baltimore: Johns Hopkins UP, 1989).

Richard Rodriguez (b. 1944) Richard Rodriguez is best known for his criticism of affirmative action and bilingual education, presented in his 1982 *Hunger of Memory: The Education of Richard Rodriguez*. His arguments on these issues disclose a cultural theory of language and rhetoric that we can see informing 1990s debates on public policy and "political correctness."

Rodriguez proposes that affirmative action is based upon a false synecdoche, that as a Mexican American (a "part") he necessarily represents all Mexican Americans (the "whole"). Rodriguez—holding a PhD in English with a specialization in Renaissance literature—thinks that he has more in common with the educated class of all races than with Mexican Americans without advanced education. This leads to his second criticism of affirmative action, rooted in the rhetorician's realization that language both reflects material reality and tries to shape it. Rodriguez argues that affirmative action is a way by which upper-class Americans keep lower-class Americans from educational and employment opportunities. This is because affirmative action primarily benefits minority individuals such as Rodriguez who belong to the upper class of their racial groups. The poor of all races are left out.

For Rodriguez, bilingual education is wrong because it leads to the ghettoization of non-English speakers. If they want to become full participants in American community, he insists, they must master English. In this argument rests the general view that language both creates communities and separates people from communities. In *Hunger of Memory*, Rodriguez reveals what it was that closely bound his own family: the sounds of Spanish. However, in order to help their children succeed in school and in American society, his parents obeyed the request of Richard's teachers that they speak English at home. As a result,

Rodriguez came to be fluent in English at the expense of Spanish. This inalterably changed the family, no longer bound by the familial and familiar sounds of a native language.

Rodriguez's advanced education enabled and required him to move out of the "oral" world of the Spanish-language family and community forever and into the "literate" world of English. The loss of family resulted in a gain of community. As a result, Rodriguez has become a person who lives in many communities but belongs to none fully. In this regard he is perhaps a synecdoche for the sort of population that will emerge in the twenty-first century: Racially he is Mexican; linguistically he is American; intellectually he is international, moving in a world of academics, journalists, and artists.

Further Reading: Richard Rodriguez, "Mexico's Children," *The American Scholar* 55 (1986): 161–77; Shirley K. Rose, "Metaphors and Myths of Cross-Cultural Literacy: Autobiographical Narratives by Maxine Hong Kingston, Richard Rodriguez, and Malcolm X," *Melus* 5.14 (1987): 3–15.

Oscar Romero (1917–1980) Oscar Arnulfo Romero y Galdamez, the archbishop of San Salvador, El Salvador, from 1977 to 1980, was assassinated while celebrating mass on March 24, 1980. His assassin is thought to have been a member of one of the right-wing death squads that terrorized the Salvadoran population during the 1970s and 1980s. Thus ended the life of a man who had become known as the voice of the voiceless.

Before he became archbishop, Romero was the friend of Rutilio Grande, a Jesuit proponent of liberation theology, which argues that the Church should focus on alleviating the suffering of the poor. Grande was killed by a death squad shortly after Romero became archbishop, and his death seemed to mark a shift in Romero's theological rhetoric. He took up Grande's cause and began to speak with and for the Salvadoran poor.

Bradford T. Stull has argued effectively that Romero's sermons and pastoral letters draw their effectiveness from attention to both pain and imagination. They concentrate on the suffering of the Salvadoran *campesinos* both as it exists in the Salvadoran situation and as it echoes the suffering of Christ. Suffering here means physical pain: the hunger, torture, and death that marked the lives of the Salvadoran poor and Christ alike. Likewise, the sermons and pastoral letters imagine liberation, which in this context can be understood as the alleviation of suffering. Romero looked both to a kingdom in Heaven and a kingdom on Earth as places of liberation. He did not suggest that the *campesinos* must stoically endure their suffering, waiting for the afterlife. Rather, Romero argued that the suffering must end on Earth. However, Romero did not think that it was possible to re-establish Eden. He reminded his audiences that the final alleviation of suffering would come in a future kingdom.

In order to develop these themes, Romero made extensive use of rhetorical figures such as metaphor and analogy. Most powerful, however, was his use of intertextuality, that is, his evocation of textual worlds beyond that of the immediate writing. For instance, Romero often used the documents of Vatican II to illustrate points in his addresses to and about the poor. Thus creating an intertextual world, Romero forces listeners and readers to explore texts and examples from which they might otherwise be insulated.

Further Reading: James S. J. Brockman, *Romero: A Life* (Maryknoll, NY: Orbis, 1989); Oscar Romero, *Voice of the Voiceless: The Four Pastoral Letters and Other Statements,* trans. Michael Walsh (Maryknoll, NY: Orbis, 1990); Bradford T. Stull, *Religious Dialectics of Pain and Imagination* (New York: SUNY P, 1994).

Social Construction   Social construction is often associated with the work of Thomas Kuhn and Richard Rorty, the former a historian of science, the latter a philosopher of intellectual history. Both have explored the relationship between language and knowledge, and each has raised questions about whether scientific or philosophical premises may be regarded as fundamentally true. A social constructionist perspective discounts the possibility that truth/reality/knowledge exists in an *a priori* state. It emphasizes the role that language plays in constructing what cultures regard as knowledge or truth. All knowledge, all social practices, and even humans themselves exist as signs within a language system because all can be understood only via their description or expression in language. The nature of truth does not interest social constructionists, who see it as a word that philosophers and scientists debate rather than an existent phenomenon; knowledge, however, does exist, but as the product of social consensus constructed through communal discourse. Thus, the nature of what counts as knowledge is variable: For instance, what some societies call *science* we call *magic*. The social constructionist resists the tendency to dismiss such societies as primitive and to discount their beliefs as something other than "real" knowledge.

The proposal that knowledge is socially constructed undermines the tradition maintaining that a realm of knowledge preexists societies and may be recovered through rigorous philosophical and scientific methods. This tradition has a long history. **Plato,** for example, not only established the method by which centuries of philosophers sought to make truth claims, he also named philosophy as a discrete discipline operating apart from the conventions and contingencies of social life. Social constructionists recognize that the Platonic framework is itself a construction, subject to all the social and political influences from which it would seek to distance itself. Much of **Plato's** philosophy is, after all, a reaction to contemporary social and intellectual conditions, and even he seems to allow in *Phaedrus* and elsewhere that knowledge can be nothing more than an assemblage of available social and linguistic resources.

The tendencies to "forget" that no knowledge construction is inevitable or natural and to behave as if certain propositions are absolutely true are explained by social constructionists as consequences of ideology. Certain sets of principles, with names such as conservatism, liberalism, marxism, and feminism, arise out of particular material conditions and determine competing views of basic issues, such as the relationship of the individual to society and the nature of justice. An ideological construction of such issues inevitably makes truth claims: The conservative and the feminist will disagree about what "really" constitutes social reform, and each will lay claim to knowledge that is more valid than the other's. The social constructionist is interested less in who is right than in the economic, social, political, and cultural conditions that motivate their beliefs.

Further Reading: Gary Olson and Irene Gale, eds., *Interviews: Cross-Disciplinary Perspectives on Rhetoric and Literacy* (Carbondale: Southern Illinois UP, 1991): 226–40; Herbert W. Simons, ed., *Rhetoric in the Human Sciences* (London: Sage, 1989).

Sophists *Sophos* means knowledge or wisdom, and the first sophists were teachers who traveled in classical Greece teaching a number of different subjects. They are especially famous—or infamous—for relativistic views of truth and demonstrations of oratorical dexterity; such demonstrations were especially popular as both entertainments and as indications of the skills required of citizens in newly emerging democracies. A "second sophistic" developed in the first century CE and continued through late antiquity, with its practitioners demonstrating the art of declamation, or highly stylized ceremonial speech.

Some of the most well-known classical sophists conceived of rhetoric as epistemic, that is, as an art that creates rather than reflects knowledge. **Plato** was suspicious of the affront to stable philosophical truth by such sophists, and criticized them in several of his dialogues, especially his *Sophist:*

> The imitative kind of the dissembling part of the art of opinion which is part of the art of contradiction and belongs to the [ph]antastic class of the image-making art, and is not divine, but human, and has been defined in arguments as the juggling part of productive activity—he who says that the true sophist is of this descent and blood will, in my opinion, speak the exact truth.

In this dialogue, **Plato** sees the sophists as manipulators or jugglers of the truth, and also as the makers of phantasms that can enchant youth to believe falsehoods. The sophists are dangerous because they regard language as protean and see rhetoric as an elaboration of this quality.

In general, the sophists are identified with a belief in the limitations of human knowledge. To the sophist Protagoras (c. 481–411 BCE) we attribute the famous statement, "Of all things the measure is man, of things that are that they are, and of things that are not that they are not." Protagoras's statement, along with complementary propositions by other sophists, contends that all physical or metaphysical predications are determined through the observer's biases and within circumstantial limitations. This idea is congenial to the doctrine of **kairos**.

Plato's view of the sophists initiated similar negative responses that continued well into the nineteenth century. Twentieth-century rhetorical theory, with its skepticism about essentialisms, has supported a reevaluation and new appreciation of sophistic thought and its contemporary relevance. It has even been argued that sophistry should be considered synonymous with rhetoric, insofar as we have come to understand rhetoric as a knowledge-making activity that is situationally contingent, productive of multiple perspectives, and—given the effects of strategically stylized discourse upon a susceptible audience—potentially mesmerizing. The traditional view of sophistry as deception has become appropriated to an appreciation of all truth statements as contingent, and connected to the suspicion of any statement put forth as the "whole truth."

Further Reading: Susan Jarratt, *Rereading the Sophists* (Carbondale: Southern Illinois UP, 1991); Rosamund Kent Sprague, ed. *The Older Sophists* (Columbia: U of South Carolina P, 1972); Mario Untersteiner, *The Sophists* (New York: Philosophical Library, 1954).

Speech Act Theory The theory of speech acts can be traced to language philosopher Ludwig Wittgenstein's conception of language as a social game, and was developed more systematically by J. L. Austin in a series of lectures published posthumously as *How To Do Things with Words*. Wittgenstein's dictum that "meaning is use" undergirds Austin's work; for Austin, the question becomes What does language do in the world, and how does it do it? To work toward an answer, Austin initially posits two kinds of speech acts: the *constative*, which states a fact that may be judged either true or false ("The book is on the table"), and the *performative*, which enacts a social function and does not invite a true-or-false judgment ("I'll bet you five dollars"). He cannot maintain this distinction, however, realizing that because every utterance is the performance of an intended action that carries a certain suasive force, all language is in some measure performative. Depending upon the conditions of its utterance, "The book is on the table" might be delivered or understood as an assumption, a promise, a warning, an assurance, and so forth. Understood in this way, the utterance performs a social act (e.g., "[I assure you that] the book is on the table"). The performance of a speech act that may be interpreted in a certain way (e.g., as an assurance) is what Austin calls an *illocutionary act*. Austin calls the way that the utterance is taken by the audience a *perlocutionary act:*

Illocution: "(I promise you that) the book is on the table."
Perlocution: "(She convinced me that) the book is on the table."

John Searle elaborates Austin's classifications of performatives in his widely influential book, *Speech Acts*.

Although speech act theory was originally conceived by Austin to describe oral discourse, it has since been applied to written texts in the area of literary theory and criticism. Mary Louise Pratt, drawing from the work of linguist H. P. Grice, has argued that treating literature as a conventional form subject to rules for the performance of speech acts encourages a view of literary texts as rhetorical entities that shape and are shaped by social values and practices. The speech act theorist working with a literary text will be interested in its particular illocutionary and perlocutionary force in a given community of readers.

Speech act theory has become an established paradigm in the field of linguistic anthropology. Del Hymes has proposed that a true understanding of how language works to enact social realities must take into account the illocutionary and perlocutionary meanings of utterances from the perspective of the members of the language community under study. The speech act is viewed as the essential component of more complex discursive activities, such as speech events and speech situations, in which it participates.

Further Reading: Stanley Fish, "How To Do Things With Austin and Searle," *Is There A Text In This Class?* (Cambridge: Harvard UP, 1980): 197–245; Del Hymes, *Foundations in Sociolinguistics* (Philadelphia: U of Pennsylvania P, 1974); Mary Louise Pratt, *Toward a Speech Act Theory of Literary Discourse* (Bloomington: Indiana UP, 1977); John Searle, *Speech Acts* (London: Cambridge UP, 1969); G. J. Warnock, *J. L. Austin* (New York: Routledge, 1989).

Stasis Theory   The word *stasis* has both Greek and Latin roots and means *to stand* or *to sit*. In rhetorical theory, a stasis designates the point of disagreement in an issue. Stases present a way of determining the central question in a controversy; thus, stases determine where a case stands, and the case develops or proceeds from this point of disagreement.

Although stasis theory has roots in **Aristotle**'s *Topics,* Hermagoras of Temnos (second century BCE) was the first to write a treatise on it. As developed by Hermagoras, stasis theory comprises four questions, the stases, that a rhetor can ask about an issue. The first stasis is question of fact: Did an act take place? The second stasis is a question of definition: What are the act's essential qualities? The third stasis is a question of quality: What are the act's nonessential qualities or its extenuating circumstances? Hermagoras divided the third stasis into categories of justification, countercharge, pleas for leniency, and shifting of blame. The fourth stasis is a question of jurisdiction or objection: Is there anything about this act that mandates its being dismissed or considered in a different setting? For example, the claim, "It is a fact that you stole my watch," embodies the stasis of fact. The rejoinder, "I did not steal your watch but merely borrowed it," represents the stasis of definition. The further explanation, "I took your watch because I knew that the spies had bugged it and would be listening to your every word," falls under the stasis of quality. The claim, "I insist that we take this case of the stolen watch to the Supreme Court," represents the stasis of jurisdiction.

Later rhetoricians adapted Hermagoras' version of stasis theory to their own contexts. In *De Inventione,* for example, **Cicero** teaches the four stases, but in *De Oratore* he dismisses the fourth stasis. In **Cicero**'s time, questions of jurisdiction and procedure were settled before the case came to court, thus making the fourth stasis superfluous. **Cicero** complicated stasis theory, however, by dividing the third stasis into legal topics and topics of equity. In the second century CE, Hermogenes altered stasis theory in three major ways. First, he restored the fourth stasis. Second, he taught that stasis theory applies to political, deliberative discourse as well as to judicial, forensic rhetoric. Third, and most important, he insisted on the hierarchical order of the stases. Thus, the stasis of fact must be answered before definition, definition before quality, and quality before jurisdiction.

Stasis theory still lives in today's courtrooms, inherent in legal procedures, but modern applications of stasis theory range beyond the courtroom. Jeanne Fahnestock and Marie Secor, for example, have applied stasis theory not only to forensics but also to what they see as the epidictic discourse of literary criticism. Fahnestock and Secor modify the last two stases, calling the third *value* and the fourth *procedure*. They also add a fifth stasis, the stasis of cause.

Further Reading: Otto Dieter, "Stasis," *Speech Monographs* 17 (1950): 345–69; Jeanne Fahnestock and Marie Secor, "Grounds for Argument: Stasis Theory and the *Topoi*," *Argument in Transition,* eds. David Zarefsky, Malcolm O. Sillars, and Jack Rhodes (Annandale, VA: Speech Communication Association, 1983), 135–46; Jeanne Fahnestock and Marie Secor, "The Stases in Scientific and Literary Argument," *Written Communication* 5 (1988): 427–43.

Style   Style is the third of the five traditional canons of rhetoric, appearing in lists of the canons after **invention** and **arrangement** and before **memory** and **delivery.** Style—called *lexis* in Greek and *elocutio* in Roman rhetorics—concerns the selection and deployment of the words and sentences that comprise a discourse. Under the general rubric of style can come treatments of diction, or word choice; the length, variety, and patterns of emphasis in sentences; and the use of figurative language, including **tropes and schemes.**

In ancient Greece, **Aristotle** stated that the "propriety" of an orator's level of language should conform to the expectations and aspirations of the audience, thus fostering a community prepared to be persuaded. Uncommon language could make the audience feel learned and elevated; yet to persuade, the speech had to appear natural to a given audience, always concealing its art. Roman rhetoric emphasized textbook learning for efficient bureaucratic ends, so the choice of style depended more on subject matter than audience. The *Rhetorica ad Herrenium,* for example, schematizes style as a prescriptive doctrine of tropes and schemes that match three types of subject matter and purpose: the plain style for teaching, the middle style for pleasing, and the grand style for moving audiences. Augustine and later Christian rhetoricians retained the Roman structure, but they based their choices of style on the intended purpose of the sermon (the subject matter was uniformly Christian doctrine).

Renaissance humanists embraced imaginative uses of tropes as a way of cultivating intellect. **Erasmus'** *On Copia of Words and Ideas,* for example, shows how a writer can turn any statement through infinite varieties of figurative language and **commonplaces.** The highly figurative style of some Renaissance authors presses the vital question: Is rhetoric the "dress" or the "incarnation" of thought? If such tropes as metaphor generate different views of reality rather than simply ornamenting ideas, thought becomes more dynamic than foundational.

Such complexities of the style–thought relationship are difficult to teach to people who need to use language in real situations. **Peter Ramus** in the sixteenth century sought to simplify and democratize rhetorical education by isolating style as rhetoric divorced from invention and arrangement. Ramus thus displaces style as a means of imagining thought; language only embellishes arguments derived from dialectical processes. In the late seventeenth century, the Royal Society of London, perceiving figurative speech as a threat to the "truths" of empirical science, advocated a plain style uncorrupted by ambiguity, a style in which "men deliver'd so many things in an almost equal number of words."

The managerial needs of the industrial age produced a rhetorical style that, as **Hugh Blair** asserted in the eighteenth century, seemingly freed "us from fatigue of searching for meaning." **Blair's** call for perspicuity of language concealed what **George Campbell's** *Philosophy of Rhetoric* acknowledged: Tropes can act like "some magic spell" to arouse passions.

Today, Enlightenment doctrines of plain style have so influenced our essayist prose that teaching style is often reduced to teaching editing skills. Yet the concerns of the postmodern age have also rekindled interest in metaphor as a way to generate multiple perspectives on the subject matter at hand.

Further Reading: Morris W. Croll, *Style, Rhetoric, and Rhythm* (Princeton, NJ: Princeton UP, 1962); Walter J. Ong, S. J., *Ramus, Method, and the Decay of Dialogue: From the Art of Discourse to the Art of Reason* (Cambridge: Harvard UP, 1958); Brian Vickers, *In Defence of Rhetoric* (Oxford: Clarendon Press, 1988).

Topoi The Greek *topos* (the singular form of *topoi*) means *place*, and *topoi* becomes **Aristotle's** metaphor for the places or seats of certain types of arguments. The Latin counterpart of *topos* is *locus*, suggestive of a place in the memory where ideas can be stored and retrieved. Thus, *topoi* may be defined as a mental store of argumentative strategies, or lines of reasoning, useful for inventing persuasive arguments. **Aristotle** distinguishes between *topoi* that are specific to particular disciplines (*idia*) and *topoi* that are applicable in general (*koinoi topoi*, or common topics). Of *idia*, **Aristotle** says, "for example, in physics there are premises from which there is neither an enthymeme nor a syllogism applicable to ethics; and in ethics [there are] others not useful in physics." As an example of the *koinoi topoi*, he cites "the *topos* of the more and the less," noting that a rhetor can invent enthymemes based on the relationship of more and less in both an argument about justice, and one about an entirely different subject, such as physics. Illustrating this point George Kennedy notes that a more/less *topos* related to justice might be "If it is just to punish offenses, it is more just to punish great offenses," and one related to physics might be "If a small force will move a body, a larger force will move it as well." In Book 2 of the *Rhetoric*, **Aristotle** lists twenty-eight common topics that underlie the construction of **enthymemes;** for instance, the rhetor might construct an **enthymeme** based on opposites, correlatives, definition, induction, analogy, causality, and so forth.

Protagoras is sometimes credited as an early deviser of *topoi*, although the repetition of commonplace modes of thought might also be located in pre-Socratic epic narrative. D'Angelo has noted that Greek arguments involving opposites date back to the late seventh century BCE, and can be regarded as evidence that the idea of *topoi* was evolving in Greek thought. **Aristotle** cites a number of examples in *Rhetoric* of previous authors employing a certain *topos*, leading us to believe that this method of building **enthymemes** was well-understood in Greece by his time.

Typical of the schematization of rhetoric after **Aristotle,** later classical and medieval treatments of the *topoi* involved the mere cataloging of strategies that seem unconnected to larger conceptual views of human psychology, or what **Giambattista Vico** would call the *sensus communis*. Realizing that topical philosophy was disappearing in the wake of Cartesian logic, **Vico** attempted to reassert *topoi* as central to rhetorical invention. However, by the seventeenth and eighteenth centuries, elements of classical invention such as the **enthymeme** and the *topoi* were discarded; however, both Grimaldi and D'Angelo have suggested that the *topoi* may have been in hiding by the nineteenth century as more acceptable rhetorical forms, such as figures of speech and standard modes of composition that embodied such processes as opposition, correlation, analogy, and definition, were in use.

Further Reading: Thomas M. Conley, "The Enthymeme in Perspective," *Quarterly Journal of Speech* 70 (1984): 168–87; Frank J. D'Angelo, "The Evolution of the Analytic *Topoi:* A Speculative Inquiry," *Essays on Classical Rhetoric and Modern Discourse,* ed. Robert J. Connors et al. (Carbondale: Southern Illinois UP, 1984); William M. A. Grimaldi, *Studies in the Philosophy of Aristotle's Rhetoric* (Wiesbaden: Verlag, 1972); George Kennedy, trans. *Aristotle, On Rhetoric* (New York: Oxford UP, 1991).

Tropes and Schemes   Tropes and schemes are the two major divisions of the general category of figurative language, or *figures of speech* as they were called when rhetoric was primarily an oral art. As **Edward P. J. Corbett** notes in his *Classical Rhetoric for the Modern Student,* a trope "involves a deviation from the ordinary and principal signification of a word," and a scheme "involves a deviation from the ordinary pattern or arrangement of words." Julius Caesar's famous *Veni, vidi, vici*—"I came, I saw, I conquered" is a scheme called *asyndeton,* the omission of conjunctions in a series of related clauses. The most prominent of the tropes—some call it the *master trope*—is metaphor.

The number of tropes and schemes one claims exist depends on how carefully one defines each figure. The anonymous classical text *Rhetorica ad Herennium* lists 65 figures; rhetoricians and teachers in sixteenth-century England often catalogued more than 200; **Corbett's** text defines 20 schemes and 28 tropes.

Although scholars occasionally refer to tropes and schemes as embellishments or decorations of thought, in classical rhetorical theory their function was organic to the orator's purpose to persuade his audience. For example, in Book Three of his *Rhetoric,* **Aristotle** refers to the function of metaphor as being to bring a persuasive appeal "before the eyes"—that is, to make it clear and vivid. In the ninth book of the *Institutio Oratoria,* **Quintilian** explains how the figures lend "credibility to our arguments"; they are capable of "exciting the emotions" and of securing "approval for our characters as pleaders." A similar view of the figures as organic to the discourse can be found in contemporary rhetoric. **Chaim Perelman,** for example, sees the function of the figures as giving "presence"—foreground—to the theses a rhetor intends his or her audience to accept.

Some contemporary literary and rhetorical theorists capitalize on the idea, originally promulgated by Ferdinand de Saussure in the 1905 *Course in General Linguistics,* that because there is an arbitrary relation between the signifier and the signified, all language is metaphorical. Thus, to these theorists, all rhetoric is solely an art of tropes. Hayden White, for example, refers to the "tropics" of discourse as "the process by which all discourse constitutes . . . objects." In *Allegories of Reading,* Paui de Man limits rhetoric to "the study of tropes and of figures" and distinguishes it from "rhetoric as having to do with the skills of persuasion." Brian Vickers' essay from *In Defence of Rhetoric,* reprinted in Part III of this volume, roundly criticizes White, de Man, and others whom Vickers charges with promoting a "modern fragmentation" of the tropes and schemes from a unified theory of rhetoric.

Further Reading: Edward P. J. Corbett, *Classical Rhetoric for the Modern Student* (New York: Oxford UP, 1965); Paul de Man, *Allegories of Reading* (New Haven: Yale UP, 1979); Gerard Genette, *Figures of Literary Discourse,* trans. Annette Sheridan (Oxford: Oxford UP, 1982)· Hayden White, *Topics of Discourse: Essays in Cultural Criticism* (Baltimore: Johns Hopkins UP, 1978).

Sojourner Truth (1797–1883) Sojourner Truth, formerly a slave in New York State, began her speaking career as a preacher in 1843. At a time when very few women spoke in public, Sojourner Truth spoke out eloquently for the causes of abolition and women's rights, and was described as having a "magical influence" on her audience. Although Truth herself was unable to read or write, we do have records of both her ideas and her rhetorical style from various people who wrote down her speeches. Her speeches are in some ways representative of contemporary women orators, incorporating the inductive reasoning and personal tone that Karlyn Kohrs Campbell has identified as elements of "feminine style." Women orators of the time tended to base their authority on their experience and invite audience participation.

Truth's speeches were extemporaneous and she was adept at taking account of the audience's responses in her presentation. Speaking once before an audience that was hissing at her, Truth said, "When she comes to demand [her rights], don't you hear how sons hiss their mothers like snakes, because they ask for their rights; and can they ask for anything less. . . . You may hiss as much as you like, but it's comin'."

Although she was textually illiterate, Truth once told Elizabeth Cady Stanton's children, "I don't read much small stuff as letters, I read men and nations." In

Paulo Freire's terms, Sojourner Truth was adept at "reading the world," an example of comprehensive literacy. Her abilities as a social and cultural analyst and her powerful rhetorical skills make her to this day a model for feminists.

Further Reading: Karlyn Kohrs Campbell, *Man Cannot Speak for Her* (New York: Greenwood, 1989): 19–22; Dale Spender, *Women of Ideas (And What Men Have Done To Them)* (London: Ark Paperbacks, 1982): 366–74; Dorothy Sterling, ed., *We Are Your Sisters: Black Women in the Nineteenth Century* (New York: Norton, 1984): 150–53, 251–56.

Giambattista Vico (1668–1744) Giambattista Vico was a professor of rhetoric at the University of Naples from 1699 to 1741. However, it was not until the middle of this century, when renewed interest in classical rhetoric and reactions against Cartesianism prompted revisionist scholarship in the history and historiography of rhetoric and philosophy, that Vico emerged as an important figure. As Cartesian philosophy was sweeping Europe, Vico argued in university addresses and in his major effort of more than twenty years—*The New Science*—that knowledge and knowledge-making could not be reduced to a mathematical logic; rather, knowledge is the product of the active philosophical imagination enfranchised by classical rhetoric.

In his address "On the Study Methods of Our Time," delivered at the University of Naples in 1708, Vico proposed that a Cartesian emphasis on analytical judgment skirts the importance of the "invention of arguments," which is "by nature, prior to the judgment of their validity, so that, in teaching, that invention should be given priority over [analysis]." Vico means rhetorical invention here, of the sort described by **Aristotle** in his *Rhetoric*, in which a student surveys the **topoi** or topics from which arguments may be constructed. The mind's capacity for discovering relationships—which Vico calls *ingenuity*—works in concert with considerations of probable truth and *sensus communis*, or common sense, in the creation of eloquent discourse.

Thus knowledge is not received, it is constructed, or as Vico says in his 1710 *On the Ancient Wisdom of the Italians*, "What is known is what is made." Such statements comprise Vico's definition of rhetoric, which, though not given explicitly, is accurately surmised by Donald Verene as "an activity in which the mind constructs a knowledge of itself." Thus Vician rhetoric is akin to what Ann Berthoff in this century calls "knowing your knowledge," and Vico's most extensive demonstration of knowledge knowing is his *New Science*. In this work, Vico describes the beginnings of culture and society as acts of *naming* that are possible because of our *poetic wisdom*, that is, our capacity for making associative connections between the unknown and the known. Vico offers a fable about primitive people experiencing a thunderstorm for the first time, in a state of fearful wonder. Urgent to name their experience, these people metaphorize the storm in terms of themselves, imagining a humanlike being making thunder in the sky. This image, this god, becomes part of their shared lexicon, their common sense, and its creation typifies the way in which the human imagination builds its own mental lexicon.

Through this fable, we see the importance of *uncertainty* in Vico's construction of knowledge-making. Only in this state are people prompted to create explanatory discourse; this is one of the reasons that Vico opposes Cartesian epistemology and pedagogy: As he says in "Study Methods," the student whose uncertainty is replaced by decisive formulaic analysis will either "accept any viewpoint [that] has been sanctioned by a teacher" or "step rashly into discussions while they are still in the process of learning."

Further Reading: Ann Berthoff, *The Making of Meaning* (Portsmouth, NH: Boynton/Cook, 1981); Michael Mooney, *Vico in the Tradition of Rhetoric* (Princeton: Princeton UP, 1985); John Schaeffer, *Sensus Communis: Vico, Rhetoric, and the Limits of Relativism* (Durham: Duke UP, 1990); Donald Verene, *Vico's Science of Imagination* (Ithaca: Cornell UP, 1981).

Juan Luis Vives (1492–1540)   Juan Luis Vives enjoyed tremendous popularity and prestige, especially in northern Europe, for his humanistic writings on philosophy, rhetoric, and education. His fellow humanists extolled him as another **Quintilian,** and they looked to him as the natural successor of **Erasmus** upon that luminary's death in 1536. For more than 100 years after his death, Vives's educational program influenced English pedagogy. As schoolboys, Shakespeare, Sidney, and even Milton learned rhetoric and moral philosophy from textbooks that Vives either wrote or inspired.

Vives was born in Valencia, Spain, studied in Paris at the College of Beauvais, and taught in Louvain and at Oxford. As both a theorist and a teacher of rhetoric, Vives sought the attainment of practical wisdom combined with Christian morals. In his major treatise, *De Tradendis Disciplinis* (*On the Transmission of Knowledge,* 1531), Vives defines rhetoric not as speculative or philosophical but as "the expression of wisdom, which cannot in any way be separated from righteousness and piety." Like his fellow humanists Thomas More and John Colet, as well as **Erasmus,** Vives believed that the moral formation of the individual is the primary goal of education. Thus the study of rhetoric should be directed toward the acquisition of a Ciceronian style, elegant and proper, that proves how "eloquence is a most important part of prudence."

Vives was highly suspicious of the value of debate, in particular those public *disputationes* much in vogue since the Middle Ages. He believed that exercises that engage children's emotions in the learning process harmed young, unformed minds. In place of controversial subjects that usually lead such immature minds to deliver acrimonious harangues meant to defeat the opponent rather than elucidate the truth, he prescribed universal commonplaces and maxims, which he outlined in his *Introductio ad Sapientiam* (*Introduction to Wisdom,* 1524), that instill in students practical wisdom, civility, and piety. Vives also scorned judicial rhetoric, perceiving that it is "better to die than defend oneself in court."

Influenced by Rudolph Agricola, Vives redefined the relationship between rhetoric and dialectic in such works as *Adversus Pseudo-Dialecticos* (1520) and *Censura de Aristotelis Operibus* (1538). Like his contemporary **Peter Ramus,** Vives believed that invention, because of its foundation in reasoning, belongs to dialectic rather than to rhetoric. The student of rhetoric should concentrate on matters of style, but should take care not to imitate corrupt classical poets such as Catullus, Martial, Ovid, and Homer, whom Vives associated with violence and eroticism. The student should be directed to study selected "extracts" and "blossoms" from **Cicero, Quintilian,** Martianus Capella, Seneca, and Trebizond, gathering from them what is most useful and beautiful, transferring these "blossoms" to compositions as painters "transfer pleasing sights to their canvas." For Vives, "a true imitation of what is admirable is proof of the goodness of the moral disposition."

Further Reading: Ernst Cassirer et al., *The Renaissance Philosophy of Man* (Chicago: U of Chicago P, 1948); Carlos G. Norena, *Juan Luis Vives* (The Hague: Nijhoff, 1970) and *A Vives Bibliography* (Lewiston: Mellen, 1990).

Richard M. Weaver (1910–1963) For many years a professor of English at the University of Chicago, Richard M. Weaver devoted most of his career to explaining and reviving the role of ethics in rhetorical theory. Although he taught at Chicago with scholars renowned for their neo-Aristotelian views, Weaver was the foremost neo-Platonist among modern rhetoricians.

Weaver's fame in rhetoric rests primarily on two collections of essays, *The Ethics of Rhetoric* (1958) and *Language Is Sermonic* (1970). In the opening essay of the former volume, titled "Phaedrus and the Nature of Rhetoric," Weaver reveals his essentialist stance by lauding the ideal rhetoric of Socrates' second speech in **Plato's** *Phaedrus* for holding up the "good soul" whose "definitions will agree with the true nature of intelligible things." In the same volume, Weaver draws a distinction between two methods of argumentation. The first, lower in Weaver's estimation, is argument from circumstance, which relies on the expedient and generally fails to define what Weaver sees at the "first principles" of the issue being considered. The second, more praiseworthy, is argument from definition—that is, argument in which the orator defines first principles, the "essential nature" of the issue and its components.

The concluding chapter of *The Ethics of Rhetoric* offers two key terms that have become Weaver's most lasting contributions to modern rhetorical theory. These "ultimate words" are "God terms" and "Devil terms," bits of diction that different rhetorical communities invest with either positive or negative connotations. In America, for example, a rhetor need only use the words "freedom" and "justice" to evoke positive identifications from the audience; they are God terms. In contrast, a rhetor who uses "reactionary" or "fascist" plays on the audience's Devil terms and arouses negative feeling.

Language is Sermonic collects several of Weaver's essays in a posthumous volume in his honor. The title essay reinforces Weaver's position on the ethics of rhetoric. He writes, for example, that, "The honest rhetorician . . . has two things in mind: a vision of how matters should go ideally and ethically and a consideration of the special circumstances of his auditors. Toward both of these he has a responsibility." He concludes the essay with an allusion to **Quintilian's** famous definition of the orator as the *vir bonus dicendi peritus,* the good man skilled at speaking, maintaining that this ethical position precedes technical skill in rhetoric:

> We are all of us preachers in private or public capacities. . . . That is why I must agree with Quintilian that the true orator is the good man, skilled at speaking—good in his formed character and right in his ethical philosophy. When to this he adds fertility in invention and skill in the arts of language, he is entitled to that leadership which tradition accords him.

Further Reading: Donald Cushman and Gerard Hauser, "Weaver's Rhetorical Theory: Axiology and the Adjustment of Belief, Invention, and Judgment," *Quarterly Journal of Speech* 59 (1973): 319–29; Richard L. Johannesen, Rennard Strickland, and Ralph T. Eubanks, eds., *Language is Sermonic: Richard M. Weaver on the Nature of Rhetoric* (Baton Rouge: Louisiana State UP, 1970); Richard M. Weaver, *The Ethics of Rhetoric* (Chicago: U of Chicago P, 1958).

Richard Whately (1787–1863)   Richard Whately achieved widespread influence in nineteenth-century Britain, and later in the United States, for his textbook *Elements of Rhetoric* (1828). A friend of the early tractarians at Oxford, Whately was ordained to the Anglican priesthood at 25 and went on to become a professor of political economy at Oxford and archbishop of St. Patrick's Anglican Cathedral in Dublin. His two major works, *Elements of Rhetoric* and *Elements of Logic* (1826), were originally published as long articles on those subjects for Samuel Taylor Coleridge's *Encyclopaedia Metropolitana.* John Henry Newman, then a young man, helped Whately prepare the work on logic.

Whately's rhetorical theory is distinct from that of his two Scottish counterparts in the late eighteenth and early nineteenth centuries, **George Campbell** and **Hugh Blair,** in its major focus on the logic of argumentative composition. Differing from **Campbell,** who aimed to develop a psychological theory to account for all types of rhetorical address, and **Blair,** who tried to explain a theory of taste in literary production and reception, Whately in his *Elements of Rhetoric* declares his intention to treat "Argumentative Composition, generally and exclusively, considering Rhetoric (in conformity with the very just and philosophical view of Aristotle) as an off-shoot from Logic." Later in *Elements,* he clarifies the relation between logic and rhetoric:

> The finding of suitable Arguments to prove a given point, and the skillful arrangement of them, may be considered as the immediate and proper province of Rhetoric, and of that alone. The business of Logic is, as Cicero complains, to judge arguments, not to invent them. . . . The art of inventing and arranging arguments is . . . the only province that Rhetoric can claim entirely and exclusively.

Although Whately does treat inductive examples relatively briefly and discusses both **pathos** and **style,** the *Elements* is, in the words of Douglas Ehninger, "a ratiocinative rather than an empirical rhetoric."

Specifically in the Preface, and in passing throughout the *Elements,* Whately demonstrates his intention that the text should find a specific use in the training of Christian apologists and preachers. Of particular interest for this use is Whately's explanation of three kinds of testimony: "undesigned" testimony, which appears unaffected, authentic, and simple; "negative" testimony, or the failure of a rhetor to confront a particular claim or charge well-known by the public; and "concurrent" testimony, or the corroboration of a claim by several witnesses who could not have had contact with each other before offering the testimony.

Elements was also noteworthy for being the first rhetorical text to treat the previously strictly legal concepts of presumption and burden of proof, and for promulgating the advantages of an orator reading a composition in the "natural style," that is, "with some degree of the manner and effect of one that is extemporaneous."

Further Reading: "The Rhetorics of Campbell and Whately," *The Rhetoric of Western Thought,* eds. James L. Golden, Goodwin F. Berquist, and William Coleman (Dubuque, IA: Kendall-Hunt, 1976); James L. Golden and Edward P. J. Corbett, eds., *The Rhetoric of Blair, Campbell, and Whately* (New York: Holt, Rinehart, and Winston, 1968); Richard Whately, *Elements of Rhetoric,* ed. Douglas Ehninger (Carbondale, IL: Southern Illinois UP, 1963).

Thomas Wilson (1523–1581) Thomas Wilson was a Renaissance humanist who wrote the first handbook on logic in English, *The Rule of Reason* (1551), and the first book in English on the principles of classical (primarily **Ciceronian**) rhetoric, *The Arte of Rhetorique* (1553).

The Rule of Reason is a Renaissance version of the Aristotelian treatment of dialectic. **Aristotle** had described dialectic as the "counterpart" (*antistrophos*) of rhetoric, and Wilson in *The Rule of Reason* builds on this relationship, citing the popular image, originally coined by the Stoic philosopher Zeno, of logic as a closed fist and rhetoric as an open hand. Wilson departs slightly from Aristotelian teaching by suggesting that logic or dialectic (he uses both terms) can not only demonstrate probability but achieve certainty.

The Arte of Rhetorique was extremely influential in promulgating the principles of classical rhetoric in Renaissance England. Wilson teaches the five traditional canons—**invention, arrangement, style, memory,** and **delivery**—and supplements his explanations with examples from contemporary rhetorical situations. Book I is devoted to invention. Wilson describes the "places" (his Renaissance-adapted version of the classical **topoi**) for generating demonstrative (epideictic or ceremonial), deliberative (political), and judicial (forensic) speeches. In treating forensic discourse, Wilson teaches a version of **stasis theory.** Book II, thoroughly Ciceronian, is about arrangement and explains the structure and functions of a seven-part oration: the *enteraunce* or beginning, the *narration,* the *division,* the *proposicion,* the *confirmacion,* the *confutacion,* and the *conclusion.* Book III is devoted to style, memory, and delivery and contains the most famous passage of *The Arte of Rhetorique,* Wilson's condemnation of the use of "straunge ynkehorne terms": "Among al other lessons, this should first be learned, that we never affect any straunge ynkehorne termes, but so speake as is commonly received: neither sekying to be over fine, nor yet living over careless, using our speache as most men do, and ordryng our wittes, as the fewest have doen." Wilson follows this injunction by offering a humorous parody of "an ynkehorne letter."

Further Reading: Thomas O. Sloane, *Donne, Milton, and the End of Humanist Rhetoric* (Berkeley: U of California P, 1985); Russell H. Wagner, "Thomas Wilson's Contributions to Rhetoric," *Readings in Rhetoric*, ed. L. Crocker and P. A. Carmack (Springfield, IL: Charles C. Thomas, 1965); Russell H. Wagner, "Wilson and His Sources," *Quarterly Journal of Speech* 15 (1929): 530–32.

W. Ross Winterowd (b. 1930) W. Ross Winterowd, the Bruce R. McElderry Professor of English at the University of Southern California, is a discourse theorist whose works exhibit a wide range of interests, including structural linguistics, rhetoric, literature, composition theory, literary theory, and pedagogy. Winterowd's interdisciplinary bent has lasted throughout his career. In "The Grammar of Coherence" (1970), one of several pioneering studies Winterowd wrote in the 1970s, he extrapolates linguistic theories of sentence-level relationships to larger units of discourse (the paragraph and beyond) to create a model of how formal unity is achieved by transitions. Winterowd illustrates this transition-based coherence by analyzing a Shakespearean sonnet, then turns the analytic model into an invention heuristic and suggests its productivity as a pedagogical strategy.

In *Contemporary Rhetoric: A Conceptual Background with Readings* (1975), Winterowd offers an overarching synthesis of the linguistic, rhetorical, and literary dimensions of composition theory. He proposes that rhetoric includes all human discourse, not just persuasion, thus expanding the scope of rhetoric and enabling a more vital role for rhetorical theory in composition instruction. *The Culture and Politics of Literacy* (1989) discusses the revolutionary and liberatory significance of literacy and maintains that defining literacy is a political act. Exploring the degree to which writing originated to meet mercantile needs, Winterowd traces not only how literacy has enabled abstract thought and technological change but also how literacy, because it replaces reality with symbols, is potentially alienating. Drawing on the work of **Paulo Freire,** Winterowd maintains that in teaching reading and writing, the emphasis must be on students as democratic creators of their own culture, not on students as passive consumers of an ill-defined canon. Winterowd advocates the teaching of critical television literacy as an adjunct to print literacy, citing studies showing that the cognitive skills acquired in one domain are transferrable to another.

Further Reading: William A. Covino, "W. Ross Winterowd," *The Encyclopedia of Rhetoric,* ed. Theresa Enos (New York: Garland, forthcoming); W. Ross Winterowd, *Contemporary Rhetoric: A Conceptual Background with Readings* (New York: Harcourt Brace Jovanovich, 1975); W. Ross Winterowd, *The Culture and Politics of Literacy* (New York: Oxford UP, 1989).

Mary Wollstonecraft (1759–1797) Mary Wollstonecraft wrote a number of books that argue for women's rights, contribute to the contemporary debate about revolution, and develop ideas about rhetoric and language use. Her works include *Thoughts on the Education of Daughters* (1786), *The Female Reader* (1788), *A Vindication of the Rights of Men* (1790), *Vindication of the Rights of Women* (1792), and *Maria, or the Wrongs of Woman*, a novel that was incomplete at the time of her death in 1797. Her ideas became more radical as time passed, but a central tenet of her philosophy from the beginning of her writing career was the belief that women have equal capacity with men to develop as rational, thinking human beings; lack of educational opportunities is what prevents such development.

Although Wollstonecraft did not develop a complete theory of rhetoric and language use, she offered significant views on these subjects. In *Vindication of the Rights of Women*, Wollstonecraft offers readings of Rousseau's *Émile*, Fordyce's sermons, and Dr. Gregory's *Legacy to His Daughters*, among other well-known male-authored works. In such readings, she proposes that the mind develops through habitual association of ideas, and that the repeated use of certain associations is a way in which language reinforces attitudes toward women. For example, because the typical notion of masculinity held that traits such as strength and reason are essential masculine virtues, these traits were dissociated from and denied to women.

In *Vindication of the Rights of Men*, a response to Edmund Burke's *Reflections on the Revolution in France,* Wollstonecraft both responds to Burke's ideas on revolution and criticizes his rhetorical strategy. She calls it "sophistical," noting that he uses emotional arguments in a calculated way. Alternatively, she advocates simple style and arguments based on reason rather than eloquence. "Simplicity," she writes, "is but a synonymous word for truth."

In her preface to *The Female Reader,* an anthology of readings recommended in the education of girls, Wollstonecraft writes that one of the main objects of the book is "to infuse a relish for a pure and simple style . . . [as] simplicity and sincerity generally go hand in hand." Her purpose is to educate girls so that they too can develop as reasoning, thinking people. Instead of having a girl engage in rote memorization exercises, which for Wollstonecraft do not involve thinking, she suggests that it would be "more useful to make her read a short lesson, and then transcribe it from her memory; and afterwards let her copy the original, and lead her to remark the mistakes she has made. This method would exercise the memory and form the judgment at the same time."

Finally, Wollstonecraft exhibits an awareness of the importance of women's rhetorical ability. Her unfinished novel, *Maria, or the Wrongs of Woman,* is an argument for the rights of women embodied in the story of Maria, a character very aware of herself as a rhetor, as she is confronted by situations requiring that she exercise her powers of persuasion.

Further Reading: Jennifer Lorch, *Mary Wollstonecraft: The Making of a Radical Feminist* (New York: Berg, 1990); Virginia Sapiro, *A Vindication of Political Virtue: The Political Theory of Mary Wollstonecraft* (Chicago: U of Chicago P, 1992).

Virginia Woolf (1882–1941)   Virginia Woolf was a novelist, critic, and essayist, noted for her innovative style and feminist politics. Her theories and practice of language and writing are particularly relevant to rhetorical studies. Woolf was concerned with the ability of language to reflect human experience effectively and wrote that "it is the nature of words to mean many things." Thus, her novels are structured to suggest the possibility of multiple realities, breaking with traditional forms of representation. At the same time, she saw language as a limited mode of expression, offering an order that is only illusory. In *Between the Acts*, Woolf goes so far as to call language an "infection," spreading among all people, and between people and nature. Although there is much that she thought language could not do, Woolf also wrote that it is "only when we put two and two together—two pencil strokes, two written words . . . do we overcome dissolution and set up some stake against oblivion." Language can be a saving force.

For Woolf, language was also gendered. She writes in "Men and Women" that women speak to each other in "a little language unknown to men," and insists that women must strive to break out of the patriarchally controlled masculine language to create something new and effect social change:

> "I have the feelings of a woman," says Bathsheba in *Far From the Madding Crowd,* "but I have only the language of men." From that dilemma arise infinite confusions and complications. Energy has been liberated, but into what forms is it to flow? To try the accepted forms, to discard the unfit, to create others which are more fitting, is a task that must be accomplished before there is freedom or achievement.

In *Three Guineas,* which deals with the interconnectedness of war and the oppression of women, Woolf argues in response to the book's guiding question—How in your opinion are we to prevent war?—that the daughters of educated men "can best help you to prevent war not by repeating your words and following your methods but by finding new words and creating new methods."

Seeing writing as a subversive force to be used against the powerful, Woolf worked to make a shift from an egotistical "I" to a collective "we," attempting to create in her readers a sense of themselves as a community with common interests in creating change. In *Three Guineas,* Woolf uses the typically feminine epistolary form to argue her case against war and educational and professional restrictions upon women. She employs a number of rhetorical strategies to advocate a women's way of conducting education and professional life, replacing the traditional hierarchical, competitive models with cooperative ones. She uses men's words against themselves, quoting extensively from male-written history, biography, and journalism, testing their ideas out, at first as if she agrees with them, only later to show them false.

Further Reading: Mark Hussey, *The Singing of the Real World: The Philosophy of Virginia Woolf's Fiction* (Columbus: Ohio State UP, 1986); Jane Marcus, ed., *New*

Feminist Essays on Virginia Woolf (Lincoln: U of Nebraska P, 1981); Jane Marcus, *Virginia Woolf and the Languages of Patriarchy* (Bloomington: Indiana UP, 1987).

Malcolm X (1925–1965) *The Autobiography of Malcolm X* tells the story of a man whose life was a series of changing rhetorics that matched his changing identities. It is, in this sense, the autobiography of a theorist of rhetoric. Written in collaboration with Alex Haley, the *Autobiography* is notable for X's appreciation for the power of metaphor, his proposition that language can serve agonistic purposes that substitute for physical battle, and the account of his prison awakening to the powers of oratory and literacy.

The chapter titles signal the important connection between language and identity; each is a new label that Malcolm takes on and tries out, each attached to its own particular lexicon. X identifies himself as a "mascot," "homeboy," "harlemite," "hustler," "satan," "savior," "minister," "icarus," and "El Hajj Malik El-Shabazz." This final incarnation coincides with his effort to transcend previous identities and their exclusive, limiting, and sometimes malicious rhetorics: X's conversion to Islam is marked by his realization that "I no longer had any words." In a state of speechlessness, he finds himself ready to move beyond the agonistics of divided peoples with their separatist languages, in order to reveal "any meaningful truth as that will help destroy the racist cancer that is malignant in the body of America."

In prison from 1946 to 1951, X came to know a convict who did not speak the "Whatcha know, Daddy?" language of the others. Bimbi was an orator who liked to hold forth on a variety of subjects, and never lacked an audience. From Bimbi, X realizes the power of public speaking: "What fascinated me with him most of all was that he was the first man I had ever seen command total respect . . . with his words." The prison experience originated both X's career as a public speaker and his love of reading; he says that "I knew right there in prison that reading had changed forever the course of my life. As I see it today, the ability to read awoke inside me some long dormant craving to be mentally alive."

Shortly before he was assassinated in 1965 as he was beginning to give a speech, Malcolm X gave indications that the militant rhetoric that had defined most of his public career was giving way to what we might call a philosophical rhetoric, that is, reflection on a broad range of viewpoints: "I would just like to *study*, I mean ranging study, because I have a wide-open mind. I'm interested in almost any subject you can mention. . . . I'm man enough to tell you that I can't put my finger on exactly what my philosophy is now, but I'm flexible."

Further Reading: Haig A. Bosmajian and Hamida Bosmajian, *The Rhetoric of the Civil Rights Movement* (New York: Random House, 1969); Shirley K. Rose, "Metaphors and Myths of Cross-Cultural Literacy: Autobiographical Narratives by Maxine Hong Kingston, Richard Rodriguez, and Malcolm X," *Melus* 14 (1987): 3–15.

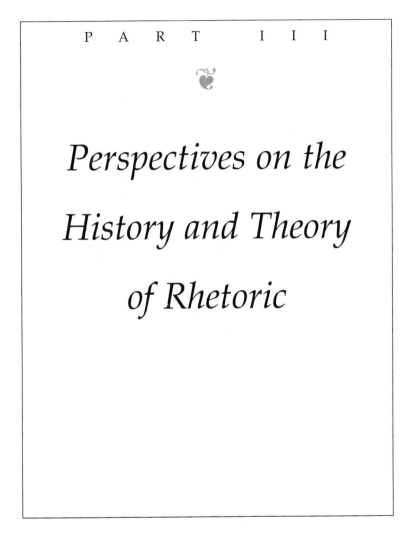

P A R T   I I I

Perspectives on the

History and Theory

of Rhetoric

Overviews of Rhetoric

As the Introduction to this book demonstrates, one strategy for providing an overview of the scope of rhetoric is extended definition. In our Part I, we aimed to provide an *essay*—in the original French sense of the verb *essayer*, "to try"—on what rhetoric is. The following selections start by deploying another strategy of extended definition: They begin by positing what rhetoric is *not*. By moving away from and building upon negative definition, each of these three pieces offers a fascinating, unique view of what rhetoric is.

George Kennedy, a noted historian of classical rhetoric, opens by reviewing what most rhetorical and literary theorists think rhetoric is—"public discourse in which cultural and political values find expression" and "a quality of the use of language ... most perfectly seen in the metaphor." But then Kennedy asserts that rhetoric is not *just* that. Rhetoric is instead—or perhaps, in addition—a kind of *energy*, "the emotional energy that impels the speaker to speak, the physical energy expended in the utterance, the energy level coded in the message, and the energy experienced by the recipient in decoding the message." Exploring a challenging parallel between human and animal communication, Kennedy posits this energy as a basic, organic principle of life that precedes speaking, writing, and intentionality, and that collaborates with the concept of survival of the fittest.

Stanley Fish, a prominent literary theorist, opens his definition of rhetoric by rehearsing a tension first played out between the pre-Socratic sophists and Plato, and later inscribed in innumerable literary works from antiquity to the present. A Miltonist by training, Fish draws his example from *Paradise Lost*: Belial, though "graceful and humane," represented the depths of rhetorical superficiality to Milton's readers because this fallen angel "could make the worse appear / The better reason, to perplex and dash the / Maturest counsels." But, Fish maintains, rhetoric is not that ability. Rhetoric comprises the human, and ultimately humane, ability to see a case from many perspectives, not simply from the perspective of better and worse; rhetoric, as Fish explains, "is the force that pulls us away from [a] center and into its world of ever-shifting shapes and shimmering surfaces." Rhetoric, says Fish, is good because it does so. The hero of Fish's essay is an imagined character he borrows from Richard Lanham's study of Renaissance eloquence, *homo rhetoricus*, the person who "manipulates reality, establishing through his words the imperatives and urgencies to which he and his fellows must respond." *Homo rhetoricus* "manipulates and fabricates himself, simultaneously conceiving of and occupying the roles that become first possible and then mandatory given the social structure his rhetoric has put in place."

Finally, Brian Vickers, an eminent scholar of the influence of classical rhetorical theory on Renaissance poetry, begins by surveying a definition of rhetoric that he perceives as developed over several centuries in the works of Vico, Roman Jakobson, Hayden White, and Paul de Man. Through Vico's linguistic philosophy, Jakobson's structuralism, and White's and de Man's poststructuralist thought, Vickers sees rhetoric becoming defined as the study of words as "signifiers [that] 'float freely,' or are 'liberated' from the burden of meaning." But rhetoric is not that, Vickers argues. Such a view of the field is, he claims, a "modern fragmentation," and does not portray "a discipline in its totality." Vickers calls for studies of rhetoric that embrace the referential, social function of language, "wide-ranging historical and critical studies, biographies, editions of texts, analyses of specific issues within rhetoric and in its relationship to the other arts, to politics, and to society."

George A. Kennedy

"A Hoot in the Dark: The Evolution
of General Rhetoric"

After spending much of my professional life teaching rhetoric, I began to wonder what I was talking about. My initial assumption, one generally shared by classicists and students of speech communication, though not by literary theorists, was that rhetoric emerged in Greece as an art of persuasion in public address; once it was formulated as a system of invention, arrangement, and style and widely taught as a useful skill under constitutional governments, it underwent a process of *letteraturizzazione* in which it affected, or if you prefer, infected, all forms of oral and written communication and molded audience expectations of communication. With changing political conditions, rhetoric repeatedly became more associated with matters of style than with argument, and in the sixteenth century Petrus Ramus carried this to the extreme of limiting rhetoric to style and delivery. Bernard Lamy and others in the seventeenth and eighteenth century then inverted the structure of rhetorical teaching to begin with the nature of language as the core of rhetoric and to build around that a theory of literary genres, including but not limited to public address. From these sources, classical and early modern respectively, have developed two contrasting, though sometimes intersecting, modern views of rhetoric: the view of literary theorists that rhetoric is a quality of the use of language and most perfectly seen in the metaphor, and a revived view of rhetoric as a phenomenon of public discourse in which cultural and political values find expression.

The term *rhetoric* has clearly had different meanings in different historical cultures and the phenomena that we call "rhetoric" have been called different things at different times. I suppose rhetoric is not a "substance" in the logical sense, though it does seem to me that there is something found in nature that either resembles rhetoric or possibly constitutes the starting point from which it has culturally evolved. If we could come to some understanding of that starting point we might be able to define a "genus" of which the various historical meanings of rhetoric are "species," and if we could do that we might be on the way to a more general theory of rhetoric that could be useful in studying speech, language, literature, art, religion, and other aspects of human society.

Rhetoric is apparently present in communication, though communication can be within the personality of one individual, as when one tries to "talk" the self into some action or belief about which one has conflicting sentiments. But rhetoric probably should not be identified with communication, since there seem to be various degrees of rhetoric among communications: "zero grade" rhetoric may be approached but never quite achieved. "The window is shut" is a communication. Its rhetorical quality is dependent on its context. It might, for example, be a mild reassurance to a recipient concerned about rain blowing into a room, or an exclamation of frustration by a thief who had planned to climb in. "Shut the window," even without knowing its context, seems inherently more rhetorically intense. The speaker is expressing an order or wish. The statement carries some authority to make the particular request. The recipient's responses are limited to executing the order, refusing to execute the order and thus denying the authority of the speaker, or demanding some equality in negotiating the situation. The recipient might say "Shut it yourself." Or "Why? It's stuffy in here." If the first speaker adds a reason, and thus creates an enthymeme ("Shut the window because the wind is blowing the papers off the desk"), the rhetorical energy is somewhat reduced. Authority is less obvious, appeal to the judgment of the recipient is implied. There is recognition of the possibility for deliberation. I would provisionally describe the rhetoric of these sentences as a matter of their energy level. It is easy to see that they might be expressed in different degrees of shrillness or calmness of voice. Thus they also involve different degrees of expenditure of physical energy in their utterance. Rhetoric in the most general sense may perhaps be identified with the energy inherent in communication: the emotional energy that impels the speaker to speak, the physical energy expended in the utterance, the energy level coded in the message, and the energy experienced by the recipient in decoding the message. In theory, one might even seek to identify some quantitative unit of rhetorical energy—call it the "rheme"—analogous to an erg or volt, by which rhetorical energy could be measured. I leave that to the experimentalists.

Tropes and figures of speech in literature are often described as rhetorical devices. When the text of the *Gilgamesh* says that the hero is a "goring wild bull," we note a metaphor, an assertion, and the presence of energy in the text. In metaphor, energy is expended by the author in defamiliarizing the language and by the reader in mentally experiencing the presence of a force affecting the meaning. Whether or not there is an actual displacement of one term by another in the text of the ancient Mesopotamian epic is open to debate; the identification of human beings with animals is literally believed in some cultures. But Shakespeare presumably did not believe that music is, literally, "the food of love," only that it resembles food in that it nurtures passion. There is, however, energy in the poet's composition, energy in the actor's utterance of the line, energy implied in the character as represented on stage, and energy experienced in the minds of the audience by the emotionally charged words. Even in figures of speech like anaphora there is an expression of energy. The Beatitudes, for example, have been worked or figured to begin with the repeated phrase "Blessed are. . . ." Some energy has been expended in making a series of assertions and arranging them into parallels, emotionally laden words are used, and emotion is experienced by the reader. A reader may then subject the assertions to reasoned analysis, even denying their validity. That requires mental effort and the expenditure of energy. Rhetorical assertion conveys energy and can spark reaction in another energy source. Rhetoric is least effective when either speaker or audience is tired, for the physical energy required on both sides is lacking.

Umberto Eco offered a theoretical account of rhetoric into which the more impressionistic description just given can be fitted.[1] He speaks of rhetoric as the "labor" performed in order to overcode and to switch codes. Rhetoric is "overcoding" in that it is the activation within a message of a preexisting code of devices of invention, arrangement, and style, with their own rules, that makes up "a semiotics of conversational interaction" (278). "Overcoding" is perhaps an unfortunate term in that it may imply something that is arbitrarily added, such as an ornament, to a semantic base—a common view of rhetoric. To me, it is the other way around: semantics is one vehicle of rhetoric. One of the goals of this paper is to try to identify some universal rules of the rhetorical code.

It seems clear, however, that rhetorical energy is not found only in language. It is present also in physical actions, facial expressions, gestures, and signs generally. The axiom that rhetoric is a form of energy leads to the first of several theses about rhetoric:

THESIS I. RHETORIC IS PRIOR TO SPEECH.

By "prior" I mean that rhetoric, as energy, has to exist in the speaker before speech can take place. It is prior in biological evolution and prior psychologically in any specific instance.[2] Speech cannot take place without some force or motivation to articulate an utterance. The originator of a communication has to experience an exigence. But I also mean that rhetoric is prior to speech historically and in biological evolution. Speech would not have evolved among human beings unless rhetoric already existed. In fact, rhetoric is manifest in all animal life and existed long before the evolution of human beings. Nature has favored the development of communication skills;[3] although they have some energy cost, they are less costly than physical motion, such as flight or fight.

Let me give a couple of easy examples of animal rhetoric in case what I am saying is not immediately clear. Imagine a pack of animals, such as lions or wolves, who constitute a small society. There will be some kind of hierarchy among them based on sex and age. Among some species there may be one animal who is on watch. An intruder is noticed and a cry given indicating a possible enemy or possible prey. The other animals receive the message and react in an appropriate way. Energy has been transmitted by a sign. If another animal of the same species is approaching, the leader of the pack will experience this as a threat to his position, perhaps an effort to replace him in his relationship to the females or to secure his food supply. What then takes place is rarely an immediate fight. There is a more or less extended period of attempts on each side to intimidate the other with growls, physical movements such as circling or pacing up and down, and other signs of intent. Michael Bright's description of encounters between male red deer stags during the rutting season is an excellent example.[4] Their encounter involves a great deal of expenditure of physical and emotional energy, and the ability of a particular animal to keep it up forcefully and for an extended period of time is crucial to his success. The stag that can roar the loudest and longest wins. This strength is in fact a measure of his likelihood of success in actual fight if it does take place and is apparently so regarded by the stags. They rarely actually fight. One outroars the other and the latter leaves. This seems to me comparable to the rhetorical ultimata exchanged between hostile states and to constitute a kind of deliberation in which evidence of the power of each side is used to convince the other to give way. Within a group of animals, there can also be something like a judicial situation when two animals of lesser rank engage in a quarrel and an animal of senior rank "judges" it, often without physical intervention but by a roar of authority that means something like "Stop it!" Or the animal in authority may run off one of the participants, as it were imposing a judgment of exile.

There is also quite a lot of epideictic rhetoric among animals. By this I mean a kind of ritualized socializing that involves reassuring "contact calls" within the group. In the fall, I have witnessed convocations of crows on my university campus. To me, as an uninformed spectator interested in rhetoric, it looked as though they had gathered to debate some important issue. There was much cawing. Some of the crows seemed to become disgusted with the proceedings and flew off; some turned their backs on the center of the group as if to vote "no." Brief research on the habits of the crow (*corvus brachyrhynchus*) revealed that they were probably not engaged in deliberation on any of the three subjects that most interest them (territorial control, mating, and feeding). There was no food supply at the site of the conference, it was not the mating season, and they had temporarily abandoned their territorial instincts to come together. Our local crows do not migrate, and they usually live in pairs or small families with distinct territories, but occasionally they assemble into large flocks. Zoologists have identified among crows what is known as an "assembly call," which consists of a succession of long raucous cries. This brings other crows together. Another kind of utterance is the "contact call," which consists of a series of short caws spaced into groups of two.[5] This is probably a way of establishing a relationship to others in the flock. The assembly and the vocalization thus perform something like the reaffirmation of group identity in ceremonial oratory on public occasions. Birds are the most vocal of all animals and vocal rhetoric is more highly developed among them than in any species except human beings. It is perhaps not a coincidence that the Greeks gave the name Corax, or "crow," to the "inventor" of rhetoric.

For the last year or two I have been reading research on animal communication, a subdivision of social biology, or the more exotic field of zoo-semiotics, a subdivision of linguistics. I have yet to encounter the term "rhetoric" in social biology, though often that seems to me to be what is under discussion. Whether animals can be said to have languages is controversial, even among scientists, who sometimes stress the discontinuity of evolution[6] or the dangers of anthropomorphizing animals,[7] and more among those humanists who react against any apparent threat to the uniqueness of human beings. Lorenz argues that both the reductionist and the uniqueness schools fail to understand "creative evolution."[8] *Language* is an emotionally laden word and even if taken as a metaphor, "animals have languages" has a relatively high degree of rhetorical energy. But there is no room for doubt that animals communicate among their own species and with other species; what is in doubt is the extent of their intentionality and consciousness of sending and receiving messages and the resulting question of whether some animals have a sense of self and of mental individuality. Darwin was inclined to think they do,[9] with which Lorenz seems to agree,[10] others are very doubtful.[11] Chomsky argued that human language is not a higher stage of evolution of animal communication but a result of a specific type of mental organization lacking in animals.[12] He does not mention rhetoric, but rhetoric seems to me exactly what animal and human communication, as he describes them, have in common. Animals, whether for physical or mental reasons, do not naturally employ human language, though some birds can learn to do so for limited purposes, and conversely human beings are inept in employing most systems of animal communication. We can, however, by observation learn to understand animal rhetoric and many animals can understand some features of human rhetoric that they share with us, such as gestures or sounds that express anger or friendliness or commands. We share a "deep" universal rhetoric.

Animals communicate by a complex code of signs. What seem to be undifferentiated chirps or grunts to a casual observer often turn out on spectrographic analysis of recordings to have clearly differentiated meanings and can indicate a particular class of predator or the imminence or distance of a perceived threat. The capacity to use and recognize a particular code of signs is innate in each species, including human beings, and thus genetically transmitted; among animals, some of the simplest signs are apparently also innate, and some animals, even some mammals, never advance beyond this, but among others, for example primates, and especially birds, many of the "words" or "phrases" in the code are learned from others by experiments in imitation. If birds, at least of many species, are deafened or are brought up in isolation from others of their own kind, they do not learn to use their native "language." It is largely culturally transmitted and subject to selective variation. Groups of birds living apart from others of their species develop local "dialects" and individuals introduce new vocalizations by combining segments of song, rather like phonemes, into new utterances, rather like sentences. Whether or not animals have a sense of self, many clearly can recognize other individuals of their own species and some animals can apparently recognize what individuals belong to what family groups.[13] Some animals can use or can learn to use symbols. Chimpanzees can be taught a rudimentary form of sign language. Although some would-be defenders of the superiority of the human species would say that the ability to lie and deceive is a unique human trait,[14] they seem to overlook the fact that animals are perfectly adept at lying and deceiving, not only in hiding food or themselves under a bush, but even in using vocalization to deceive, as when a bird gives different calls from different places in its territory with the result that a potential intruder concludes that the area is occupied and flies away.[15]

What is the meaning of a particular communication by an animal? Since conscious intent cannot be assumed in the case of most animal communication, the answer is that the "meaning" is the interpretation given to the communication by another animal. Vocalized communication usually produces an instinctive reaction, such as flight, but response is contextual and thus interpreted.[16] Occasionally an animal seems confused by a message, or may ignore it. Parents often ignore erroneous vocalizations by young offspring. This implies a second thesis:

THESIS II: THE RECEIVER'S INTERPRETATION OF A COMMUNICATION IS PRIOR TO THE SPEAKER'S INTENT IN DETERMINING THE MEANING.

More specifically, in nature the meaning is what the receiver does as a result of receiving the message, which should be some comfort to the pragmatist school of philosophers. If the receiver does nothing, the message has no meaning. The receiver's interpretation is "prior" in the sense that what the receiver is already conditioned to do on receipt of a certain message—the receiver's knowledge of the rhetorical code—determines what the receiver does when the message arrives. This is consistent with those schools of modern literary interpretation that look to reader reception rather than to authorial intent as determinative of meaning. It runs somewhat counter to the claim of Aristotle (*Rhetoric* 1.1.14) and his successors that the function of rhetoric is not persuasion but observing the available means of persuasion. A speech may not succeed, but in Aristotle's view may still be the best possible speech and demonstrate the speaker's rhetorical skill. Of course a speech, though ineffective with an audience, may successfully fulfill the speaker's need to speak—to put himself "on record" as it were; a bird that gives a cry indicating a predator fulfills a need to express that, even if the bird is mistaken or ignored by others. A speech that is not successful at the moment may affect future conditions indirectly. Aristotle's position is a result of a more reflective society that separates function from art and can judge both from some distance. It remains the case that audience reception is a more primitive and a more basic criterion of meaning than is authorial intent. A good indication of this is that in nature a single vocalization can perform two different functions for two different audiences at the same time. The song of a male bird is thought, at one and the same time, both to inform other male birds that a territory is occupied (thus to warn them off) and to inform a female of the male's readiness to mate (and arouse her mating instincts).[17] This should raise problems for speech act theorists, who apparently unanimously assume that intentionality is essential in illocutionary speech acts, such as giving a warning.[18] But even in the case of human communication, an utterance can carry a warning without being intended by the utterer. I can interpret as a warning the chance remark of another that my bête noire John is coming to a party, though the speaker may have been expressing pleasure at the thought. Rhetoric allows, in Eco's terminology, a "switch" in the code, in this case a reversal of the message.

In human society, rhetoric is, however, usually given some direction and form by varying degrees of intentionality on the part of a speaker, some conscious, some not fully conscious. Intentional rhetoric invokes a network of beliefs and beliefs about beliefs, both about one's own and those of others, for example, the belief that the audience addressed believes that action should be based on reason. In animal communication at the lowest levels, there is what Dennett[19] calls "zero order" intentionality on the part of the organism, which gives off a sign, such as a change in coloration or shape, in response to a stimulus without making a conscious decision. But there is evidence that some species of higher animals have "first order" intentionality in that they are capable of choosing whether or not to respond to an exigence depending on their personal situation. A response, for example, might attract the attention of a predator or conversely might attract help from others of its own species. There is also some evidence that primates may have a "second order" of intentionality that involves a conception of their own and another animal's beliefs. A vervet monkey, for example, may give a leopard alarm not only because it believes that a leopard is nearby but because it wants others to believe it, too.[20] At least some scientists believe that chimpanzees understand each other's goals and motives.[21] At what stage in the evolution of intentionality among species does rhetoric appear? I am inclined to say that the ability to give a sign, even without intent or belief, is basic to rhetoric, and thus I advance a third thesis:

THESIS III: RHETORIC IS PRIOR TO INTENTIONALITY OR TO ANY BELIEF ON THE PART OF A SPEAKER ABOUT THE MEANING OF A SIGN OR ITS EFFECT ON OTHERS.

There are a number of features of animal communication that resemble features of rhetoric as it has been formulated in Western society. We are not, of course, descended from any surviving species of animals, but we do have an ultimate common origin. Rhetorical characteristics of animal communication are analogies to what has developed in different species, indications of some possible parameters of rhetoric, of what nature has favored in particular environments, and perhaps of some of its basic features of communication. They deserve comparative study in an attempt to understand rhetoric and the forms it takes. I do not deny that human evolution is complex and that human capabilities far exceed what can be seen among animals. Merlin Donald has recently advanced a cognitive theory of human evolution that both preserves the link with animal communication and differentiates it from the human condition. He argues that the cognitive culture of social animals is "episodic": "Their lives are lived entirely in the present, as a series of concrete episodes, and the highest element in their system of memory representation seems to be at the level of event representation."[22] Later stages of evolution of the brain and culture are first "mimetic," then "mythic," then "theoretic." But these represent new layers of the mind, not the substitution of a later stage for an earlier one. Episodic culture, and thus its rhetoric, continues to exist among human beings.

Actually there is even a kind of rhetoric among plants. Though clearly lacking in conscious intent, it is essential for the survival of the species. The term *colors of rhetoric* was frequently used in the past to describe figures of speech. The colors of flowers attract insects and birds and facilitate pollination. Plants also use odors to attract or repel animals. Coloration and scent are each a kind of rhetoric and the creation and perception of each involves the use of energy. This is purposive in nature, though not purposeful. Taking living things as a whole, I state two more theses:

THESIS IV: THE FUNCTION OF RHETORIC IS THE SURVIVAL OF THE FITTEST.
THESIS V: THE RHETORICAL CODE EVOLVES BY SELECTIVE VARIATION.

Rhetoric acts as a mechanism for survival by facilitating successful adaptation of an organism to environmental change. Genetic mutation benefits the species by providing increased options for adaptation, but does little or nothing for the progenitive organism; within animal cultures, however, including human culture, rhetoric is a powerful force for the survival and well-being of the individual, the family, and the social group as these exist at any given moment. It secures or benefits the human individual every day in courts of law and the individual nonhuman animal in the jungle. Among the latter, it facilitates securing territory, thus a food supply to provide energy, and a mate, thus survival of its genes, and as we have seen it protects the individual or the group from hostile intruders or predators. It has secured and benefited culture generally, as well as smaller units within cultures, throughout the history of the evolution of social animals and human society. Stripped to its bare minimum, rhetoric is a defense mechanism (although a good offense is often the best defense).

The acquisition of the ability to move themselves and the evolution of sexual reproduction were early stages in individuation of living creatures. The faculty of rhetoric, more than anything else in nature, is probably responsible for the development of individual personality, and thus in the highest forms of animal life, of a sense of selfhood. The basic reason for this is that rhetoric is expressive of the integrity of the individual, thus in higher animals the emotions, and thus distinctive personality, and among animals of the same species there often are strong individual personalities. Even if animals are to a large extent behaviorally conditioned, each is a unique entity with some unique features, however small. All animals manifest anger; many manifest love, at least mothers for their offspring; some show signs of loneliness and depression; and biologists frequently describe some animals as demonstrating "altruism," meaning a concern for others expressed through protecting them at their own risk, grooming them, or assisting them in gaining food.[23] Variation among individual animals produces more or less successful rhetorical skills. Nature selects for survival those individuals whose skills are most adaptive to their environment. Selective variation in rhetoric probably originates in small "mistakes" in using either a non-human or human code, in novel combinations of its conventional elements, or chance experimentation or play that proves more effective than what has traditionally been done and is imitated. At some point in history, some human being hit upon the novelty of giving a reason for a command, and kept on doing it when a rational audience responded well. Among higher animals, rhetorical skills are transmitted culturally by imitation and learning, not genetically.

Some caution is needed in statements about the relationship of emotion to rhetorical expression in nature. Bird lovers and romanticists often believe that birds sing for joy (as in Shelley's "To a Skylark" or Keats' "Ode to a Nightingale") or in sadness (the myth of the "swan song" persists). There is no scientific evidence that bird song is expressive of joy or sorrow, though it can express a biological mating instinct and stimulate the physical ability to mate in females. Most singing birds are males, and after mating they often reduce their song. All bird song and all bird calls are thought to be strictly functional, related primarily to territoriality, location of a food supply, defense against predators, mating, or cohesion between mates, families, or flocks. A complicated song, analogous to the rhetorical display of the stags mentioned earlier, communicates the energy, maturity, and fitness of a male for mating purposes. Mammals, however, do express pleasure, either by body language as in the wagging of dogs' tails, or in sound, as in the purring of cats and some other animals. Some animals have a sense of humor. Man is not the only animal that laughs: some monkeys make the facial gestures and sounds of laughter. In a still-authoritative work, Darwin traced a continuum between facial gesture in animals and in human beings and showed how facial gestures are derived from functional muscular actions: for example, the snarl of a dog or a man from the instinct to bite.[24] But human gestures involving coordinated use of other parts of the body are cultural symbols and vary widely.[25]

The young of birds and mammals engage in play, and some animals carry this on throughout life. Play among animals is important in developing their muscles, in practicing the skills of catching prey, and in learning the communication code and rhetoric of the species. Play is physically and socially educational for animals[26] and for human beings, as reflected in the Greeks' basic division of education into gymnastics and music. Play is very important in the development of both rhetoric and literature. Traditional education has practiced students in mock speeches, such as the deliberative and judicial declamations of the classical rhetorical schools, resumed in the Renaissance. The student learns the rhetorical code, strategies of attack and defense, arrangement of material, skills at amplification and ornamentation, and the conventional values of the society. Young animals learn comparable things useful in their societies.

Since play is in large part action, this brings me to another thesis:

THESIS VI: AMONG THE TRADITIONAL PARTS OF RHETORIC (INVENTION, ARRANGEMENT, STYLE, MEMORY, AND DELIVERY), DELIVERY IS PRIOR TO THE OTHERS.

"Delivery" in traditional rhetoric includes facial expression, gesture, and tonal inflection. In Latin, the term *actio* was often used instead, and it is action, not subtleties of vocalization, to which I refer here. Physical motion in response to some exigence occurs in the earliest and most primitive forms of life, as when an amoeba moves toward a food supply or away from some noxious stimulus. A kind of proto-rhetoric can be said to exist in those creatures that can react to a challenge by change of color or shape or by spewing out some substance as does an octopus. Some action produces sound, which other creatures can perceive although the originator of the sound may not. Many insects create sound instrumentally, by sawing a part of the anatomy on another. A rattlesnake's rhetoric consists of coiling or uncoiling itself, threatening to strike, and rattling its tail, which other creatures hear, even though a rattlesnake is itself deaf. There is an evolutionary chain from the most primitive defensive or offensive actions to the complex system of rhetorical delivery described in John Bulwer's *Chirologia* and *Chironomia* in the eighteenth century. The dance of bees in the hive shows how complex systems of gesture can be. Dance is also one of the earliest forms of expression and communication developed among human beings. This leads to another thesis:

THESIS VII: WRITING IS PRIOR TO SPEECH BUT NOT PRIOR TO RHETORIC.

Writing, or "Grammatology" as described by Derrida,[27] is prior to speech in that a kind of marking is prior in evolutionary development and a necessary condition for all communication, although oral communication existed in human societies before the invention of historical writing systems. These systems represent a conceptualization and organization of written symbols to represent utterances, but they were preceded by picturing, which goes far back to cave painting in Cro-Magnon times and which directly represents action, not speech about action. Writing or marking, however, is much earlier and more primitive than even that. It survives in many animals today who "mark" their territory with urine or bodily scent, as well as in animals that have little or no ability to generate sounds but do so by their movements. Vocalization is, in fact, a form of marking, in that to communicate, it must distinguish sounds by moments of silence, often producing rhythm, or by changes of pitch or volume. As in the telegraph, a very simple pattern is one of spacing of long or short units. But marking does not seem to be prior to rhetoric among living creatures in that the impulse and the expenditure of energy required in marking necessarily must exist before the marking, or "writing," can take place. Both are mechanisms for survival, and the most primitive form of marking is a vehicle for rhetoric. Marking is, perhaps, a kind of metaphor, that is, something transferred to the condition of life from the inanimate world where there is also a kind of marking. The entity of any body of matter is based on a binary distinction between what is and what is not; this is what limits its mass. In speaking of rhetoric, I have defined it as an energy existing in life. But energy exists apart from living organisms and the energy of the life force, and thus rhetoric is perhaps a special case of the energy of all physics as known from subatomic particles. Since matter can be converted into energy and energy into matter, and since in the origin of the universe we do not know which existed first, I leave open the question of the ultimate sources of the qualities of being that made possible the evolution of both rhetoric and marking. They may be two aspects of the same thing.

Returning to our world of animal life, let me identify some features of invention, arrangement, and style that can be illustrated from nonhuman rhetoric for purposes of comparison with human rhetoric. These may constitute the fundamental rules of the universal rhetorical code. Of the other two parts of traditional rhetoric, delivery has been briefly discussed and I bracket memory, the fourth traditional part, as a subject of less interest to modern rhetoricians, important as it may be, and as too complex for discussion here, except to note that it is an aid to survival and requires some kind of marking system in the mind. (In traditional rhetoric, the art of memory is based on the substitution of a sequence of visual images for sound patterns "written" in the mind.) Since memory exists in creatures that do not have speech, like all parts of rhetoric it is clearly prior to speech. Using the traditional parts of rhetoric as a basis for discussion may be objected to by some as analogous to ethnocentrism in anthropology, the imposition of a later, and Western, structural scheme on phenomena that in their natural state might be related in different ways. My response to this criticism is to agree that the categories of traditional rhetoric may not be a satisfactory basis to describe animal communication and I do not use them for that purpose. What I am looking for are features of animal communication that resemble categories of traditional rhetoric and that therefore suggest that these categories, though conditioned by cultural conventions, represent the survival of certain natural phenomena.

THESIS VIII: RHETORICAL INVENTION, ARRANGEMENT, STYLE, MEMORY, AND DELIVERY ARE PHENOMENA OF NATURE AND PRIOR TO SPEECH.

It does not seem possible for speech to have developed without the prior existence of the faculties represented in the traditional parts of rhetoric. The need for memory and delivery has already been noted. Equally needed would have been something to say, some order in the saying, and some manner of saying it. All these faculties exist in varying degrees among animals and thus they are likely to have existed in some form in the direct ancestors of man.

"Invention" in rhetoric corresponds in a general way to "information" in animal communication. Two kinds of information are conveyed by animal sounds:[28] the presence of an animal in a territory and the internal state of the animal making the sound. "Presence" includes individuation, the individual personality of the animal in so far as this has developed in the species and can be perceived by another animal. "The internal state" includes the animal's physical and emotional reaction to the immediate environment and the message about it that may be of use to another animal. As interpreted by a receiver and recast in anthropomorphic terms, the information conveys something like "Blackie, a known and usually reliable member of our community, is warning that he has observed a stranger who may constitute a danger to any of us." I would describe this as deliberative rhetoric in that in a particular social context it implies advice about future action—be wary, or flee—and the receiver needs to make a judgment. I would also suggest that elements of ethos, pathos, and logos are inherent in it. The originator of the communication, whether consciously or not, has given a sign of his credibility and good will (ethos), has expressed with more or less emphasis his alarm and produced a message that can awaken alarm in his audience (pathos), and has indicated why he feels alarm by giving the call that denotes a predator (logos). It should be noted that the translation of the message into human language requires the statement of propositions; the message has semantic content. Propositions are, I believe, implicit in animal communication, though no student of semantics to the best of my knowledge has ever entertained the possibility. The ethos is likely to reflect hierarchy or "pecking order" in the society; in many groups, especially of mammals, certain members have greater authority than others. It could, perhaps, be argued that hierarchy among animals represents an incipient distinction between office and individual office holder, a distinction often made in political rhetoric in historical times when a speaker stresses respect for an office, such as the presidency of the United States, and a belief that the incumbent is unworthy of it. This distinction is found in human tribal societies as well.[29] Among animals, the position of authority exists and is respected, but the incumbent is regularly challenged by the younger and stronger. "Debate" exists in the animal world, as in the meeting of rutting stags described above. The issue there is largely one of hierarchy and what is "proved" is the superior stamina and thus superior rights of one animal in comparison with another for a particular position.

As in human deliberation, an animal communication may turn out to be an overreaction, an underreaction, or reflect the judgment of a mature and experienced observer. As an animal learns the rhetorical code of its species, there is a kind of "oscillation" between overstatement (hyperbole) and understatement (meiosis).[30] Gradually the maturing animal develops a "pattern" of observation against which a particular event can be tested and evaluated. Lorenz (113–20) regarded this as an ability of abstracting the general from the particular and saw in evolution the integration of a number of separate cognitive functions, many existing in rudimentary form in nonhuman animals. These include a faculty of abstract thought (which produces language), an ability to accumulate supraindividual knowledge, the power to foresee consequences of an action (which produces moral responsibility), the ability to make voluntary movements, and imitation (which Lorenz regarded as the basis of learning verbal language and thus of the faculty of passing on objective knowledge independently of the presence of the object). To abstract the general from the particular is a rudimentary form of induction; once a pattern has been established in the mind, to apply it to a particular situation is deduction.

Overstatement in oscillation seems to perform a rhetorical function beyond its role in the learning process. It gets the attention of an audience and, helped by features of style and delivery, stands out against the "noise" of the environment. In the jungle, in the seas, and in human assemblies, background noise is an obstacle to communication. Noise is also overcome by redundancy in the message. The primary cognitive device of animal rhetoric is repetition of the same statement several times in the same form.[31] This remains a feature of human rhetoric ("Tell them what you are going to say, then say it, then tell them what you have said"), though with a sophisticated audience it is often best to convey the same message in different words, whereas in animal rhetoric, with its limited vocabulary, this is impossible or would be confusing. "Amplification," however, is manifested in some animal rhetoric, and performs some cognitive function, but, as in traditional rhetoric, it is more a device of style than invention and can be left for discussion below.

The history of the evolution of rhetorical invention is the history of the diffusion of energy and the growth of information in communication. In a primordial cry of "Help!" there is the greatest energy and the least information. Animal communication requires less energy than does physical confrontation and conveys more useful information, including some quite specific information useful for survival, which is probably why it has been favored in evolution. Human rhetoric, with its conceptualization of rational argument, its ability to give a narrative picture of previous or possible future events, and its great creativity, conveys the greatest amount of information, but reduces the emotional energy.[32]

A number of features of "arrangement" are to be found in the rhetorical codes of the animal world. Bird songs have a syntax in their arrangement of phoneme-like sound segments; differently arranged they convey different messages. The most highly developed forms of bird songs have something like an exordium, which announces the bird's presence and calls attention to its message, then a main body of song, divided into segments, often with repeated elements, and a terminal flourish or epilogue.[33] From my reading overall, however, I conclude that whereas the presence of an exordium is not uncommon both among birds and mammals, the presence of an epilogue is unusual and when it exists it is a simple flourish, not a recapitulation of the message in brief. This resembles some non-Western music that often has some initial introductory passage to strike up the tune, but ends abruptly without a coda. The artistic need for an epilogue is characteristic of Western speech, Western literature, and Western music, carried to its fullest formal development in traditional perorations and in the concluding sections of the sonata form. Western society has sought closure.

Arrangement is crucial in the process of ritualization, a common feature of primitive societies and a continuing vehicle of religious cohesion, thus an epideictic rather than deliberative use of rhetoric. The right utterances have to be said in the right order, or the ceremony is often invalid. Ritualization is a feature of animal communication also. Its simpler form can be seen in the mating displays of some birds. One of its most elaborate forms is the spectacular morning duet of mated pileated gibbons. The female gives a soft "hoo-hoo-hoo" as an exordium. The male and female then join in a rhythmic "ooh-a-ooh-a-ooh-a." "Eventually, the female utters some short 'hoos' that tell the male to be quiet; this is the signal that she wants to sing the long series of whoops of the spectacular 'great call'—a kind of south-east Asian yodel. At the climax, male and female swing around in the tops of the trees, making a considerable commotion—it is a period of intense excitement."[34] Since the performance is very loud, it is thought to function to defend territory, but it is also important in the cohesion of the pair, who mate for life and achieve increased coordination in the ritual over time. In some species of birds, the male sings and the female repeats his song. Ritualization, dialogue, and antiphonal singing among animals is perhaps analogous to the early stages of poetry, drama, and literature among human beings and may point to some of its rhetorical functions which include territorial interests (strong in the *Iliad*, for example) and family integrity (strong in the *Odyssey*, for example).

This mention of the possible "literary" quality of communication among animals leads me to a short digression on textuality among animals, relevant to later rhetoric in that it may have something to do with the development of aesthetic sensibilities. There is almost no scientific evidence that nonhuman animals have any perception of beauty; what they seem to have instead is a sense of fitness. A bird builds a nest to fit an innate mental pattern of what constitutes a nest. This is primarily a matter of the arrangement of the material, which is woven together in a structure conventional to the species. I recently observed cardinals building a nest. The male brought twigs of various lengths, which the female worked into the fabric. Sometimes she rejected a particular piece and even seemed to be trying to explain to her mate what she needed, which he learned by experiment. Sometimes birds will abandon a particular nest half-built, usually because the location is unsuitable or dangerous, sometimes perhaps because they have made a mistake in laying the foundations. Some birds seem to build a series of nests without intending to use them, possibly as decoys to the final, more hidden nest. In any event, the nest must fulfill the animal's sense of what constitutes a proper nest in the proper place. "Propriety" is an important quality in traditional rhetoric. The behavior of birds also seems to me to indicate an incipient aesthetic sense. The Greek word *kosmos* means "order," or what is set in order. It came to mean the seemingly orderly arrangement of the stars in the heavens, but also ornament and jewelry, thus something that is beautiful. When I said that there is "almost no scientific evidence that nonhuman animals have any perception of beauty," the exception I had in mind was the degree to which some birds—magpies, for example—are attracted by bright-colored objects, which they sometimes build into a nest. This may suggest an inclination to ornamentation in nature, present also in bird song, though most artifacts created by nonhuman animals are entirely functional. When traps were set to reduce the beaver population in my town, the beavers responded by building the traps into their dams, thus strengthening them. This is what is called in French *bricolage,* a subject much developed in the writings of the anthropologist Claude Lévi-Strauss. It is somewhat analogous to catachresis in rhetoric, the use of a metaphor when there is no proper word available. Modern discussions of metaphor suffer from their failure to consider comparative evidence of how metaphor may have evolved, both in terms of function and in terms of ornamentation.

This has already led us into discussion of style. Most of the important features of style in nature have already been mentioned: individual birds, at least of some species, have recognizable individual styles within rather limited parameters. Each species has its own style. Especially in singing to attract mates, birds amplify their song; this helps the message to stand out against background noise, but also conveys the strength, maturity, and suitability of the bird as a mate. Something similar exists among mammals, though in less intricate fashion. Some birds—mocking birds, for example—imitate the song of other birds, thus amplifying and ornamenting their song by intertextual allusion. The commonest figure of speech among animals is probably anaphora: beginning a series of phrases with the same sounds. But homoeoteleuton occurs, too, when successive segments end with the same pattern. Animal communication is usually rhythmical: the metrical pattern is a key to the meaning. An inclination to hyperbole exists among animals; they overreact as do human speakers. Vocal signs made by animals are arbitrary symbols of mental perceptions, as are the words in human languages. There is often a kind of synecdoche in that the symbol represents a class of objects rather than a particular one: a large bird rather than specifically an eagle. Proportional metaphor based on similarity of appearance or function does not seem present in animal vocalizations, though catechresis occurs in animal behavior, as mentioned earlier. Though I have not noted the use of metonymy in vocal communication among animals, some animals easily understand metonymy: though none of my dogs has ever brought me his leash to suggest going on a walk, when I take the leash in hand, they become excited and know exactly what it signifies.

This brief discussion is intended to direct attention to animal communication as a way of understanding some basic features of rhetoric that might be restated as general rules. I must emphasize again that what is seen among animals is only analogous to features of human rhetoric, not its direct sources. These are behaviors that have been developed in separate species in accord with their biological characteristics. The potentialities in each species are limited by physical characteristics, including brain size and structure and the nature of the organs of vocalization. There do, however, appear to be some features of communication in common among many species, including human beings, apparently favored by natural selection in evolution from the earliest forms of life. These various features are vehicles, techniques, or rules of rhetoric, which itself is a form of energy driven by a basic instinct to survive. Research on the forms of rhetoric in nature can be a first step toward a theory of general rhetoric and a comprehensive history of its development. The study of rhetoric is essentially distinct from the study of speech or language, which rhetoric has however exploited. A second logical step is further research in rhetoric as it can be seen in tribal societies living in primitive conditions and studied by anthropologists (with the warning, however, that even the most primitive society of modern times is the result of thousands of years of cultural evolution), and of the earliest stages of historical societies in urban culture. Diachronic research, including observation of discontinuities, is a needed complement to the synchronic research on communication and rhetoric which today dominates the field.[35]

NOTES

1. *A Theory of Semiotics* (Bloomington IN: Indiana University Press, 1979), 276–88.
2. "Prior" in this discussion should generally be taken to mean prior in biological evolution and a necessary condition for whatever is "posterior." I shall, however, explain the usage of the term as applied in some contexts below. The complex question of why and how speech developed among human beings is not a necessary part of the argument of this paper.
3. See Peter H. Klopfer and Jeremy J. Hatch, "Experimental Considerations," in *Animal Communication: Techniques of Study and Results,* ed. Thomas A. Sebeok (Bloomington IN: Indiana University Press, 1968), 31.
4. *Animal Language* (Ithaca NY: Cornell University Press, 1985), 204.
5. See Derek Goodwin, *Crows of the World* (London: British Museum, 1981), 84–88.
6. E.g., Eric H. Linneberg, "Language in the Light of Evolution," and Gregory Bateson, "Redundancy and Coding," in Sebeok, *Animal Communication,* 592–613 and 614–26 respectively.
7. See Lord Zucherman, "Apes Я Not Us," *New York Review of Books* 38, no. 10 (1991), 43–9.
8. Konrad Lorenz, *Behind the Mirror: A Search for a Natural History of Human Knowledge,*

tr. Ronald Taylor (New York: Harcourt-Brace-Jovanovich, 1977), 167–8.

9. Charles Darwin, *The Expression of the Emotions in Man and Animals* (Chicago: University of Chicago Press, 1965), 118.

10. Konrad Lorenz, *Behind the Mirror*, 40.

11. E.g., Leslie Dewart, *Evolution and Consciousness: The Role of Speech in the Origin and Development of Human Nature* (Toronto: University of Toronto Press, 1989), 159.

12. Noam Chomsky, *Language and Mind* (New York: Harcourt-Brace-Jovanovich, 1972), 66–71.

13. Michael Bright, *Animal Language*, 229.

14. E.g., Leslie Dewart, *Evolution and Consciousness*, 104–5.

15. Michael Bright, *Animal Language,* 12, 82.

16. J. P. Scott, "Observation," in Sebeok, *Animal Communication,* 28.

17. Michael Bright, *Animal Language*, 73.

18. E.g., John R. Searle, "What is a Speech Act," in *Philosophy in America,* ed. Max Black (Ithaca NY: Cornell University Press, 1965), 221–39.

19. D. C. Dennett, *The Intentional Stance* (Cambridge MA: MIT/Bradford), 246.

20. Dorothy L. Cheney and Robert M. Seyfarth, *How Monkeys See the World: Inside the Mind of Another Species* (Chicago: University of Chicago Press, 1990), 143.

21. Ibid., 254.

22. Merlin Donald, *Origins of the Modern Mind: Three Stages in the Evolution of Culture and Cognition* (Cambridge MA: Harvard University Press, 1991), 149.

23. See Edward O. Wilson, *On Human Nature* (Cambridge MA: Harvard University Press, 1978), 149–67.

24. Charles Darwin, *The Expression of the Emotions in Man and Animals.*

25. See James L. Peacock and A. Thomas Kirsch, *The Human Direction: An Evolutionary Approach to Social and Cultural Anthropology* (New York: Appleton-Century-Crofts, 1970), 8.

26. See Konrad Lorenz, *Behind the Mirror*, 145–7.

27. Jacques Derrida, *Of Grammatology,* tr. Gayatri Chakrovorty Spivak (Baltimore MD: Johns Hopkins University Press, 1976).

28. See René Busnel, "Acoustic Communication," in Sebeok, *Animal Communication,* 139.

29. See John Comaroff, "Talking Politics: Oratory and Authority in a Tswana Chiefdom," in *Political Language and Oratory in Traditional Society,* ed. Maurice Bloch (London: Academic Press, 1975), 144.

30. See Konrad Lorenz, *Behind the Mirror*, 237–42.

31. See Michael Bright, *Animal Language*, 74.

32. See Leslie Dewart, *Evolution and Consciousness*, 233.

33. See Barbara A. Hooker, "Birds," in Sebeok, *Animal Communication,* 318.

34. Michael Bright, *Animal Language*, 217.

35. I am grateful to the National Endowment for the Humanities for awarding me a Summer Stipend for a project of which this paper is a part, and to my colleague, Professor J. Robert Cox, for valuable suggestions.

Stanley Fish

"Rhetoric"

... up rose
Belial, in act more graceful and humane;
A fairer person lost not Heav'n; he seem'd
For dignity compos'd and high exploit:
But all was false and hollow; though his Tongue
Dropt Manna, and could make the worse appear
The better reason, to perplex and dash
Maturest counsels: for his thoughts were low; . . .
... yet he pleas'd the ear,
And with persuasive accent thus began.
                                       —(PARADISE LOST, II, 108–15, 117–18)

I

For Milton's seventeenth-century readers this passage would have been immediately recognizable as a brief but trenchant essay on the art and character of the rhetorician. Indeed in these few lines Milton has managed to gather and restate with great rhetorical force all of the traditional arguments against rhetoric. Even Belial's gesture of rising is to the (negative) point: he catches the eye even before he begins to speak, just as Satan will in Book IX when he too raises himself and moved so that "each part, / Motion, each act won audience ere the tongue" (673–74). That is, he draws attention to his appearance, to his surface, and the suggestion of superficiality (a word to be understood in its literal meaning) extends to the word "act"; i.e., that which can be seen. That act is said to be "graceful," the first in a succession of double meanings (one of the stigmatized attributes of rhetorical speech) we find in the passage. Belial is precisely *not* full of grace; that is simply his outward aspect, and the same is true for "humane" and "fairer." The verse's judgment on all of his apparent virtues is delivered in the last two words of line 110—"he seem'd"—and the shadow of "seeming" falls across the next line which in isolation might "seem" to be high praise. But under the pressure of what precedes it, the assertion of praise undoes itself with every Janus-faced word (the verse now begins to imitate the object of its criticism by displaying a pervasive disjunction between its outer and inner meanings; indicting seeming, it itself repeatedly seems): "compos'd" now carries its pejorative meaning of "affected" or "made-up"; "high" at once refers to the favored style of bombastic orators and awaits its ironic and demeaning contrast with the lowness of his thoughts; "dignity" is an etymological joke, for Belial is anything but worthy; in fact, he is just what the next line says he is, "false and hollow," an accusation that repeats one of the perennial antirhetorical topoi, that rhetoric, the art of fine speaking, is all show, grounded in nothing but its own empty pretensions, unsupported by any relation to truth. "There is no need," declares Socrates in Plato's *Gorgias*, "for rhetoric to know the facts at all, for it has hit upon a means of persuasion that enables it to appear in the eyes of the ignorant to know more than those who really know" (459), and in the *Phaedrus* the title figure admits that the "man who plans to be an orator" need not "learn what is really just and true, but only what seems so to the crowd" (260).

This reference to the vulgar popular ear indicates that rhetoric's deficiencies are not only epistemological (sundered from truth and fact) and moral (sundered from true knowledge and sincerity) but social: it panders to the worst in people and moves them to base actions, exactly as Belial is said to do in the next famous run-on statement, "and could make the worse appear / The better reason." Behind Belial is the line of sophists—Protagoras, Hippias, Gorgias, shadowy figures known to us mostly through the writings of Plato where they appear always as relativist foils for the idealistic Socrates. The judgment made on them by a philosophic tradition dominated by Plato is the judgment here made on Belial; their thoughts were low, centered on the suspect skills they taught for hire; the danger they represented is the danger Belial represents: despite the lowness of their thoughts, perhaps *because* of the lowness of their thoughts, they pleased the ear, at least the ear of the promiscuous crowd (there is always just beneath the surface of the antirhetorical stance a powerful and corrosive elitism), and the explanation of their unfortunate success is the power Belial now begins to exercise, the power of "persuasive accent." "Accent" here is a resonant word, one of whose relevant meanings is "mode of utterance peculiar to an individual, locality or nation" (*OED*). He who speaks "in accent" speaks from a particular *angled* perspective into which he tries to draw his auditors; he also speaks in the rhythms of song (etymologically "accent" means "song added to speech") which as Milton will soon observe "*charms* the sense" (II, 556). "Persuasive accent" then is almost a redundancy: the two words mean the same thing and what they tell the reader is that he is about to be exposed to a force whose exercise is unconstrained by any sense of responsibility either to the Truth or to the Good. Indeed, so dangerous does Milton consider this force that he feels it necessary to provide a corrective gloss as soon as Belial stops speaking: "Thus *Belial* with words cloth'd in reason's garb/Counsell'd ignoble ease and peaceful sloth" (II, 226–27). Just in case you hadn't noticed.

I have lingered so long over this passage because we can extrapolate from it almost all of the binary oppositions in relation to which rhetoric has received its (largely negative) definition: inner/outer, deep/surface, essential/peripheral, unmediated/mediated, clear/colored, necessary/contingent, straightforward/angled, abiding/fleeting, reason/passion, things/words, realities/illusions, fact/opinion, neutral/partisan. Underlying this list, which is by no means exhaustive, are three basic oppositions: first, between a truth that exists independently of all perspectives and points of view and the many truths that emerge and seem perspicuous when a particular perspective or point of view has been established and is in force; second, an opposition between true knowledge, which is knowledge as it exists apart from any and all systems of belief, and the knowledge, which because it flows from some or other system of belief, is incomplete and partial (in the sense of biased); and third, an opposition between a self or consciousness that is turned outward in an effort to apprehend and attach itself to truth and true knowledge, and a self or consciousness that is turned inward in the direction of its own prejudices, which far from being transcended, continue to inform its every word and action. Each of these oppositions is attached in turn to an opposition between two kinds of language: on the one hand, language that faithfully reflects or reports on matters of fact uncolored by any personal or partisan agenda or desire; and on the other hand, language that is infected by partisan agendas and desires, and therefore colors and distorts the facts which it purports to reflect. It is use of the second kind of language that makes one a rhetorician, while adherence to the first kind makes one a seeker after truth and an objective observer of the way things are.

It is this understanding of linguistic possibilities and dangers that generates a succession of efforts to construct a language from which all perspectival bias (a redundant phrase) has been eliminated, efforts that have sometimes taken as a model the notations of mathematics, at other times the operations of logic, and more recently the purely formal calculations of a digital computer. Whether it issues in the elaborate linguistic machines of seventeenth-century "projectors" like Bishop Wilkins (*An Essay Towards a Real Character and a Philosophical Language*, 1668), or in the building (à la Chomsky) of a "competence" model of language abstracted from any particular performance, or in the project of Esperanto or some other artificial language claiming universality (see Large 1985), or in the fashioning of a Habermasian "ideal speech situation" in which all assertions express "a 'rational will' in relation to a common interest ascertained without deception" (Habermas 1975, 108), the impulse behind the effort is always the same: to establish a form of communication that escapes partiality and aids us in first determining and then affirming what is absolutely and objectively true, a form of communication that in its structure and operations is the very antithesis of rhetoric.

Although the transition from classical to Christian thought is marked by many changes, one thing that does not change is the status of rhetoric in relation to a foundational vision of truth and meaning. Whether the center of that vision is a personalized deity or an abstract geometric reason, rhetoric is the force that pulls us away from that center and into its own world of ever-shifting shapes and shimmering surfaces.

The quarrel between philosophy and rhetoric survives every sea change in the history of Western thought, continually presenting us with the (skewed) choice between the plain unvarnished truth straightforwardly presented and the powerful but insidious appeal of "fine language," language that has transgressed the limits of representation and substituted its own forms for the forms of reality (see Kennedy 1963, 23).

II

To this point my presentation has been as skewed as this choice, because it has suggested that rhetoric has received only negative characterizations. In fact, there have always been friends of rhetoric, from the Sophists to the antifoundationalists of the present day, and in response to the realist critique they have devised (and repeated) a number of standard defenses. Two of these defenses are offered by Aristotle in the *Rhetoric*. First, he defines rhetoric as a faculty or art whose practice will help us to observe "in any given case the available means of persuasion" (1355b) and points out that as a faculty is it not in and of itself inclined away from truth. Of course, bad men may abuse it, but that, after all, "is a charge which may be made in common against all good things." "What makes a man a 'sophist,' " he declares, "is not his faculty, but his moral purpose."

Aristotle's second defense is more aggressively positive and responds directly to one of the most damaging characterizations of rhetoric: "We must be able to employ persuasion . . . on opposite sides of a question, not in order that we may in practice employ it in both ways (for we must not make people believe what is wrong), but in order that we may see clearly what the facts are" (1355a). In short, properly used, rhetoric is a heuristic, helping us not to distort the facts but to discover them; the setting forth of contrary views of a matter will have the beneficial effect of showing us which of those views most accords with the truth. By this argument, as Peter Dixon has pointed out (1971, 14), Aristotle "removes rhetoric from the realm of the haphazard and the fanciful" and rejoins it to that very realm of which it was said to be the great subverter.

But if this is the strength of Aristotle's defense, it is also its weakness, for in making it he reinforces the very assumptions in relation to which rhetoric will always be suspect, assumptions of an independent reality whose outlines can be perceived by a sufficiently clear-eyed observer who can then represent them in a transparent verbal medium. The stronger defense, because it hits at the heart of the opposing tradition, is one that embraces the accusations of that tradition and makes of them a claim.

To the accusation that rhetoric deals only with the realms of the probable and contingent and forsake truth, the Sophists and their successors respond that truth itself is a contingent affair and assumes a different shape in the light of differing local urgencies and the convictions associated with them. "Truth was individual and temporary, not universal and lasting, for the truth for any man was . . . what he could be persuaded of" (Guthrie 1971, 193). Not only does this make rhetoric—the art of analyzing and presenting local exigencies—a form of discourse no one can afford to ignore, it renders the opposing discourse—formal philosophy—irrelevant and beside the point. This is precisely Isocrates' thesis in his *Antidosis*. Abstract studies like geometry and astronomy, he says, do not have any "useful application either to private or public affairs; . . . after they are learned . . . they do not attend us through life nor do they lend aid in what we do, but are wholly divorced from our necessities" (Isocrates 1962, 2:261–62).

What Isocrates does (at least rhetorically) is shift the balance of power between philosophy and rhetoric by putting philosophy on the defensive. This same strategy is pursued after him by Cicero and Quintilian, the most influential of the Roman rhetoricians. In the opening pages of his *De Inventione* Cicero elaborates the myth that will subsequently be invoked in every defense of humanism and belles lettres. There was a time, he says, when "men wandered at large in the field like animals," and there was "as yet no ordered system of religious worship nor of social duties" (Cicero, 1:2). It was then that a "great and wise" man "assembled and gathered" his uncivilized brothers and "introduced them to every useful and honorable occupation, though they cried out against it at first because of its novelty." Nevertheless, he gained their attention through "reason and eloquence" (*propter rationem atque orationem*) and by these means he "transformed them from wild savages into a kind and gentle folk." From that time on, "many cities have been founded, . . . the flames of a multitude of wars have been extinguished, and . . . the strongest alliances and most sacred friendships have been formed not only by the use of reason, but also more easily by the use of eloquence" (1:1). Whereas in the foundationalist story an original purity (of vision, purpose, procedure) is corrupted when rhetoric's siren song proves too sweet, in Cicero's story (later to be echoed by countless others) (see, for example, Lawson 1972, 27) all the human virtues, and indeed humanity itself, are wrested by the arts of eloquence from a primitive and violent state of nature. Significantly (and this is a point to which we shall return), both stories are stories of power, rhetoric's power; it is just that in one story that power must be resisted lest civilization fall, while in the other that power brings order and a genuine political process where before there was only the rule of "physical strength."

The contrast between the two stories can hardly be exaggerated because what is at stake is not simply a matter of emphasis or priority (as it seems to be in Aristotle's effort to demonstrate an *alliance* between rhetoric and truth) but a difference in worldviews. The quarrel between rhetorical and foundational thought is itself foundational; its content is a disagreement about the basic constituents of human activity and about the nature of human nature itself. In Richard Lanham's helpful terms, it is a disagreement as to whether we are members of the species *homo seriosus* or *homo rhetoricus*. *Homo seriosus* or serious man

> possesses a central self, an irreducible identity. These selves combine into a single, homogeneously real society which constitutes a referent reality for the men living in it. This referent society is in turn contained in a physical nature itself referential, standing "out there" independent of man.

Homo rhetoricus or rhetorical man, on the other hand,

> is an actor; his reality public, dramatic. His sense of identity depends on the reassurance of daily histrionic reenactment. . . . The lowest common denominator of his life is a social situation. . . . He is thus committed to no single construction of the world; much rather, to prevailing in the game at hand. . . . Rhetorical man is trained not to discover reality but to manipulate it. Reality is what is accepted as reality, what is useful. (Lanham 1976, 1, 4)

As rhetorical man manipulates reality, establishing through his words the imperatives and urgencies to which he and his fellows must respond, he manipulates or fabricates himself, simultaneously conceiving of and occupying the roles that become first possible and then mandatory given the social structure his rhetoric has put in place. By exploring the available means of persuasion in a particular situation, he tries them on, and as they begin to suit him, he becomes them (see Sloane 1985, 87: "Rhetoric succeeded in humanism's great desideratum, the artistic creation of adept personhood"; see also Greenblatt 1980). What serious man fears—the invasion of the fortress of essence by the contingent, the protean and the unpredictable—is what rhetorical man celebrates and incarnates.

Which of these views of human nature is the correct one? The question can be answered only from within one or the other, and the evidence of one party will be regarded by the other either as illusory or as grist for its own mill. When presented with the ever-changing panorama of history, serious man will see variation on a few basic themes; and when confronted with the persistence of essentialist questions and answers, rhetorical man will reply as Lanham does by asserting that serious man is himself a supremely fictional achievement; seriousness is just another style, not the state of having escaped style. That is to say, for rhetorical man the distinctions (between form and content, periphery and core, ephemeral and abiding) invoked by serious man are nothing more than the scaffolding of the theatre of seriousness, are themselves instances of what they oppose. And on the other side if serious man were to hear *that* argument, he would regard it as one more example of rhetorical manipulation and sleight of hand, an outrageous assertion that flies in the face of common sense, the equivalent in debate of "so's your old man." And so it would go, with no prospect of ever reaching accord, an endless round of accusation and counteraccusation in which truth, honesty, and linguistic responsibility are claimed by everyone: "from serious premises, all rhetorical language is suspect; from a rhetorical point of view, transparent language seems dishonest, false to the world" (Lanham 1976, 28).

And so it *has* gone; the history of Western thought could be written as the history of this quarrel. And indeed such histories have been written and with predictably different emphases. In one version written many times, the mists of religion, magic, and verbal incantation (all equivalently suspect forms of fantasy) are dispelled by the Enlightenment rediscovery of reason and science; enthusiasm and metaphor alike are curbed by the refinement of method, and the effects of difference (point of view) are bracketed and held in check by a procedural rigor. In another version (told by a line stretching from Vico to Foucault) a carnivalesque world of exuberance and possibility is drastically impoverished by the ascendancy of a soulless reason, a brutally narrow perspective that claims to be objective and proceeds in a repressive manner to enforce its claim. It is not my intention here to endorse either history or to offer a third one or to argue as some have for a nonhistory of discontinuous *episteme* innocent of either a progressive or lapsarian curve; I only wish to point out that the debate continues to this very day and that its terms are exactly those one finds in the dialogues of Plato and the orations of the Sophists.

III

As I write, the fortunes of rhetorical man are on the upswing, as in discipline after discipline there is evidence of what has been called the interpretive turn, the realization (at least for those it seizes) that the givens of any field of activity—including the facts it commands, the procedures it trusts in, and the values it expresses and extends—are socially and politically constructed, are fashioned by man rather than delivered by God or Nature. The most recent (and unlikely) field to experience this revolution, or at least to hear of its possibility, is economics. The key text is Donald McCloskey's *The Rhetoric of Economics* (1985), a title that is itself polemical since, as McCloskey points out, mainstream economists don't like to think of themselves as employing a rhetoric; rather they regard themselves as scientists whose methodology insulates them from the appeal of special interests or points of view. They think, in other words, that the procedures of their discipline will produce "knowledge free from doubt, free from metaphysics, morals, and personal conviction" (16). To this McCloskey responds by declaring (in good sophistic terms) that no such knowledge is available, and that while economic method promises to deliver it, "what it is able to deliver [and] renames as scientific methodology [are] the scientist's and especially the economic scientist's metaphysics, morals, and personal convictions" (16). Impersonal method then is both an illusion and a danger (as a kind of rhetoric it masks its rhetorical nature), and as an antidote to it McCloskey offers rhetoric, which he says, deals not with abstract truth, but with the truth that emerges in the context of distinctly human conversations (28–29). Within those conversations, there are always

> particular arguments good or bad. After making them there is no point in asking a last, summarizing question: "Well, is it True?" It's whatever it is—persuasive, interesting, useful, and so forth. . . . There is no reason to search for a general quality called Truth, which answers only the unanswerable question, "What is it in the mind of God?" (47)

The real truth, concludes McCloskey, is that "assertions are made for purposes of persuading some audience" and that given the unavailability of a God's-eye view, "this is not a shameful fact" but the bottom-line fact in a rhetorical world.

At the first conference called to consider McCloskey's arguments, the familiar antirhetorical objections were heard again in the land and the land might have been fifth-century B.C. Athens as well as Wellesley, Massachussets, in 1986. One participant spoke of "the primrose path to extreme relativism." Other voices proclaimed that nothing in McCloskey's position was new (an observation certainly true), that everyone already knew it, and that at any rate it didn't touch the core of the economists' practice. Still others invoked a set of related (and familiar) distinctions between empirical and interpretive activities, between demonstration and persuasion, between verifiable procedures and anarchic irrationalism. Of course, each of these objections had already been formulated (or reformulated) in those disciplines that had heard rhetoric's siren song long before it reached the belated ears of economists. The name that everyone always refers to (in praise or blame) is Thomas Kuhn. His *The Structure of Scientific Revolutions* (1962) is arguably the most frequently cited work in the humanities and social sciences in the past twenty-five years, and it is rhetorical through and through. Kuhn begins by rehearsing and challenging the orthodox model of scientific inquiry in which independent facts are first collected by objective methods and then built up into a picture of nature, a picture that nature herself either confirms or rejects in the context of controlled experiments. In this model, science is a "cumulative process" (3) in which each new discovery adds "one more item to the population of the scientist's world" (7). The shape of that world—of the scientist's professional activities—is determined by the shapes (of fact and structure) already existing in the larger world of nature, shapes that constrain and guide the scientist's work.

Kuhn challenges this story by introducing the notion of a paradigm, a set of tacit assumptions and beliefs within which research goes on, assumptions which rather than deriving from the observation of facts are determinative of the facts that could possibly be observed. It follows then that when observations made within different paradigms conflict, there is no principled (i.e., nonrhetorical) way to adjudicate the dispute. One cannot put the competing accounts to the test of fact, because the specification of fact is precisely what is at issue between them; a fact cited by one party would be seen as a mistake by the other. What this means is that science does not proceed by offering its descriptions to the independent judgment of nature; rather it proceeds when the proponents of one paradigm are able to present their case in a way that the adherents of other paradigms find compelling. In short, the "motor" by which science moves is not verification or falsification, but persuasion. In the case of disagreement, "each party must try, by persuasion, to convert the other" (198), and when one party succeeds there is no higher court to which the outcome might be referred: "there is no standard higher than the assent of the relevant community" (94). "What better criterion," asks Kuhn, "could there be?" (170).

The answer given by those who were horrified by Kuhn's rhetoricization of scientific procedure was predictable: a better criterion would be one that was not captive to a particular paradigm but provided a neutral space in which competing paradigms could be disinterestedly assessed. By denying such a criterion, Kuhn leaves us in a world of epistemological and moral anarchy. The words are Israel Scheffler's:

> Independent and public controls are no more, communication has failed, the common universe of things is a delusion, reality itself is made . . . rather than discovered. . . . In place of a community of rational men following objective procedures in the pursuit of truth, we have a set of isolated monads, within each of which belief forms without systematic constraints. (19)

Kuhn and those he has persuaded have, of course, responded to these accusations, but needless to say, the debate continues in terms readers of this essay could easily imagine; and the debate has been particularly acrimonious because the area of contest—science and its procedures—is so heavily invested-in as the one place where the apostles of rhetorical interpretivism would presumably fear to tread.

At one point in his argument, Kuhn remarks that, in the tradition he is critiquing, scientific research is "reputed to proceed" from "raw data" or "brute experience"; but, he points out, if that were truly the mode of proceeding, it would require a "neutral observation language" (125), a language that registers facts without any mediation by paradigm-specific assumptions. The problem is that "philosophical investigation has not yet provided even a hint of what a language able to do that would be like" (127). Even a specially devised language "embodies a host of expectations about nature," expectations that limit in advance what can be described. Just as one cannot (in Kuhn's view) have recourse to neutral facts in order to settle a dispute, so one cannot have recourse to a neutral language in which to report those facts or even to report on the configuration of the dispute. Whatever reports a particular language (natural or artificial) offers us will be the report on the world as it is seen from within some particular situation; there is no other aperspectival way to see and no language other than a situation-dependent language—an interested, rhetorical language—in which to report.

This same point was being made with all the force of philosophical authority by J. L. Austin in a book published, significantly, in the same year (1962) that saw the publication of *The Structure of Scientific Revolutions*. Austin begins *How to Do Things with Words* by observing that traditionally the center of the philosophy of language has been just the kind of utterance Kuhn declares unavailable, the context-independent statement that offers objective reports on an equally independent world in sentences of the form "He is running" and "Lord Raglan won the battle of Alma" (47, 142). Such utterances, which Austin calls "constative," are answerable to a requirement of truth and verisimilitude ("the truth of the constative . . . 'he is running' depends on his being running"); the words must match the world, and if they do not they can be criticized as false and inaccurate. There are, however, innumerable utterances that are not assessable in this way. If, for example, I say to you, "I promise to pay you five dollars" or "Leave the room," it would be odd were you to respond by saying "true" or "false"; rather you would say to the first "good" or "that's not enough" or "I won't hold my breath" and to the second "yes, sir" or "but I'm expecting a phone call" or "who do you think you are?" These and many other imaginable responses would not be judgments on the truth or accuracy of my utterance but on its appropriateness given our respective positions in some social structure of understanding (domestic, military, economic, etc.). Thus the very identity, and therefore the meaning, of this type of utterance—Austin names it "performative"—depends on the context in which it is produced and received. Nothing guarantees that "I promise to pay you five dollars" will be either intended or heard as a promise; in different circumstances it could be received as a threat or a joke (as when I utter it from debtor's prison) and in many circumstances it will be intended as one act and understood as another (as when your opinion of my trustworthiness is much lower than my own). When the criterion of verisimilitude has been replaced by the criterion of appropriateness, meaning becomes radically contextual, potentially as variable as the situated (and shifting) understandings of countless speakers and hearers.

It is, of course, precisely this property of performatives—their force is contingent and cannot be formally constrained—that is responsible for their being consigned by philosophers of language to the category of the "derived" or "parasitic," where, safely tucked away, they are prevented from contaminating the core category of the constative. But it is this act of segregation and quarantining that Austin undoes in the second half of his book when he extends the analysis of performatives to constatives and finds that they too mean differently in the light of differing contextual circumstances. Consider the exemplary constative, "Lord Raglan won the battle of Alma." Is it a true, accurate, faithful report? It depends, says Austin, on the context in which it is uttered and received (142–43). In a high-school textbook, it might be accepted as true because of the in-place assumptions as to what, exactly, a battle is, what constitutes winning, what the function of a general is, etc., while in a work of "serious" historical research all of these assumptions may have been replaced by others, with the result that the very notions "battle" and "won" would have a different shape. The properties that supposedly distinguish constatives from performatives—fidelity to preexisting facts, accountability to a criterion of truth—turn out to be as dependent on particular conditions of production and reception as performatives. "True" and "false," Austin concludes, are not names for the possible relationships between freestanding (constative) utterances and an equally freestanding state of affairs; rather they are situation-specific judgments on the relationship between contextually produced utterances and states of affairs that are themselves no less contextually produced. At the end of the book constatives are "discovered" to be a subset of performatives, and with this discovery the formal core of language disappears entirely and is replaced by a world of utterances vulnerable to the sea change of every circumstance—the world, in short, of rhetorical (situated) man.

This is a conclusion Austin himself resists when he attempts to isolate (and thereby contain) the rhetorical by invoking another distinction between serious and nonserious utterance. Serious utterances are utterances for which the speaker takes responsibility; he means what he says, and therefore you can infer his meaning by considering his words in context. A nonserious utterance is an utterance produced in circumstances that "abrogate" (21) the speaker's responsibility, and therefore one cannot with any confidence—that is, without the hazard of ungrounded conjecture—determine what he means:

> a performative utterance will, for example, be . . . hollow or void if said by an actor on the stage, or if introduced in a poem, or spoken in a soliloquy. . . . Language in such circumstances is in special ways . . . used not seriously, but in ways *parasitic* upon its normal use. . . . All this we are *excluding* from consideration. Our performative utterances . . . are to be understood as issued in ordinary circumstances. (22)

The distinction then is between utterances that are, as Austin puts it later, "tethered to their origin" (61), anchored by a palpable intention, and utterances whose origin is hidden by the screen of a theatrical or literary stage-setting. This distinction and the passage in which it appears were taken up in 1967 by Jacques Derrida in a famous (and admiring) critique of Austin. Derrida finds Austin working against his own best insights and forgetting what he has just acknowledged, that "infelicity [communication going astray, in an unintended direction] is an ill to which *all* [speech] acts are heir" (Derrida 1977). Despite this acknowledgment, Austin continues to think of infelicity—of those cases in which the tethering origin of utterances is obscure and must be constructed by interpretive conjecture—as special, whereas, in Derrida's view, infelicity is itself the originary state in that any determination of meaning must always proceed within an interpretive construction of a speaker's intention. In short, there are no ordinary circumstances, merely those myriad and varied circumstances in which actors embedded in stage settings hazard interpretations of utterances produced by actors embedded in other stage situations. All the world, as Shakespeare says, is a stage, and on that stage "the quality of risk" admitted by Austin is not something one can avoid by sticking close to ordinary language in ordinary circumstances, but is rather "the internal and positive condition" of any act of communication (Derrida 1977, 190).

In the same publication in which the English translation of Derrida's essay appeared, John Searle, a student of Austin's, replied in terms that make clear the affiliation of this particular debate to the ancient debate whose configurations we have been tracing. Searle's strategy is basically to repeat Austin's points and declare that Derrida has missed them: "Austin's idea is simply this: if we want to know what it is to make a promise we had better not *start* our investigations with promises made by actors on stage . . . because in some fairly obvious ways such utterances are not standard cases of promises" (Searle 1977, 204). But in Derrida's argument, the category of the "obvious" is precisely what is being challenged or "deconstructed." Although it is true that we consider promises uttered in everyday contexts more direct—less etiolated—than promises made on a stage, this (Derrida would say) is only because the stage settings within which everyday life proceeds, are so powerfully—that is, rhetorically—in place that they are in effect invisible, and therefore the meanings they make possible are experienced as if they were direct and unmediated by any screens. The "obvious" cannot be opposed to the "staged," as Searle assumes, because it is simply the achievement of a staging that has been particularly successful. One does not escape the rhetorical by fleeing to the protected area of basic communication and common sense because common sense in whatever form it happens to take is always a rhetorical—partial, partisan, interested—construction. This does not mean, Derrida hastens to add, that all rhetorical constructions are equal, just that they are equally rhetorical, equally the effects and extensions of some limited and challengeable point of view. The "citationality"—the condition of being in quotes, of being *indirect*—of an utterance in a play is not the same as the citationality of a philosophical reference or a deposition before a court; it is just that no one of these performatives is more serious—more direct, less mediated, less rhetorical—than any other.

One recognizes in these assertions the familiar world of Rhetorical Man, teeming with roles, situations, strategies, interventions, but containing no master role, no situation of situations, no strategy for outflanking all strategies, no intervention in the arena of dispute that does not expand the arena of dispute, no neutral point of rationality from the vantage point of which the "merely rhetorical" can be identified and held in check. Indeed deconstructive or poststructuralist thought is in its operation a rhetorical machine: it systematically asserts and demonstrates the mediated, constructed, partial, socially constituted nature of all realities, whether they be phenomenal, linguistic, or psychological. To deconstruct a text, says Derrida, is to "work through the structured genealogy of its concepts in the most scrupulous and immanent fashion, but at the same time to determine from a certain external perspective that it cannot name or describe what this history may have concealed or excluded, constituting itself as history through this repression in which it has a stake" (1981, 6). The "external perspective" is the perspective from which the analyst knows in advance (by virtue of his commitment to the rhetorical or deconstructive worldview) that the coherence presented by a text (and an institution or an economy can in this sense be a text) rests on a contradiction it cannot acknowledge, rests on the suppression of the challengeable rhetoricity of its own standpoint. A deconstructive reading will surface those contradictions and expose those suppressions and thus "trouble" a unity that is achieved only by covering over all the excluded emphases and interests that might threaten it.

Nor is this act performed in the service of something beyond rhetoric. Derridean deconstruction does not uncover the operations of rhetoric in order to reach the Truth; rather it continually uncovers the truth of rhetorical operations, the truth that all operations, including the operation of deconstruction itself, are rhetorical. If, as Paul de Man asserts, "a deconstruction always has for its target to reveal the existence of hidden articulations and fragmentations within assumedly monadic totalities," care must be taken that a new monadic totality is not left as the legacy of the deconstructive gesture. Since the course of a deconstruction is to uncover a "fragmented stage that can be called natural with regard to the system that is being undone," there is always the danger that the "natural" pattern will "substitute *its* relational system for the one it helped to dissolve" (de Man 1979, 249). The only way to escape this danger is to perform the deconstructive act again and again, submitting each new emerging constellation to the same suspicious scrutiny that brought it to light, and resisting the temptation to put in place of the truths it rhetoricizes the truth that everything is rhetorical. One cannot rest even in the insight that there is no place to rest. The rhetorical beat must by definition go on, endlessly repeating the sequence by which "the lure of solid ground" is succeeded by "the ensuing demystification" (Ray 1984, 195). When de Man approvingly quotes Nietzsche's identification of truth with "a moving army of metaphors, metonymies and anthropomorphisms," a rhetorical construction whose origin has been (and must be) forgotten, he does not exempt Nietzsche's text from its own corrosive effects. "A text like *On Truth and Lie*, although it presents itself legitimately as a demystification of literary rhetoric remains entirely literary, and deceptive itself" (113). The "rhetorical mode," the mode of deconstruction, is a mode of "endless reflection," since it is "unable ever to escape from the rhetorical deceit it announces" (115).

IV

That, however, is just what is wrong with deconstructive practice from the viewpoint of the intellectual left, many of whose members subscribe to Nietzsche's account of truth and reality as rhetorical, but find that much of poststructuralist discourse uses that account as a way of escaping into new versions of idealism and formalism. Frank Lentricchia, for example, sees in some of de Man's texts an intention to place "discourse in a realm where it can have no responsibility to historical life" and fears that we are being invited into "the realm of the thoroughly predictable linguistic transcendental," the "rarified region of the undecidable," where every text "speaks synchronically and endlessly the same tale . . . of its own duplicitous self-consciousness" (1980, 310, 317). Terry Eagleton's judgment is even harsher. Noting that in the wake of Nietzschean thought, rhetoric, "mocked and berated for centuries by an abrasive rationalism," takes its "terrible belated revenge" by finding itself in every rationalist project, Eagleton complains that many rhetoricians seem content to stop there, satisfied with the "Fool's function of unmasking all power as self-rationalization, all knowledge as a mere fumbling with metaphor" (1981, 108). Operating as a "vigorous demystifier of all ideology," rhetoric functions only as a form of thought and ends up by providing "the final ideological rationale for political inertia." In retreat "from market place to study, politics to philology, social practice to semiotics" deconstructive rhetoric turns the emancipatory promise of Nietzschean thought into "a gross failure of ideological nerve," allowing the liberal academic the elitist pleasure of repeatedly exposing "vulgar commercial and political hectorings" (108–9). In both his study of Benjamin and his influential *Literary Theory: An Introduction,* Eagleton urges a return to the Ciceronian–Isocratic tradition in which the rhetorical arts are inseparable from the practice of a politics, "techniques of persuasion indissociable from the substantive issues and audiences involved," techniques whose employment is "closely determined by the pragmatic situation at hand" (601). In short, he calls for a rhetoric that will do real work and cites as an example the slogan "black is beautiful" which he says is "paradigmatically rhetorical since it employs a figure of equivalence to produce particular discursive and extra-discursive effects without direct regard for truth" (112). That is, someone who says "black is beautiful" is not so much interested in the accuracy of the assertion (it is not constatively intended) as he is in the responses it may provoke—surprise, outrage, urgency, solidarity—responses that may in turn set in motion "practices that are deemed, in the light of a particular set of falsifiable hypotheses, to be desirable" (113). This confidence in his objectives makes Eagleton impatient with those for whom the rhetoricity of all discourse is something to be savored for itself, something to be lovingly and obsessively demonstrated again and again. It is not, he says, "a matter of starting from certain theoretical or methodological problems; it is a matter of starting from what we want to *do,* and then seeing which methods and theories will best help us to achieve these ends" (1983, 211). Theories, in short, are themselves rhetorics whose usefulness is a function of contingent circumstances. It is ends—specific goals in local contexts—that rule the invocation of theories, not theories that determine goals and the means by which they can be reached.

There are those on the left, however, for whom the direction is the other way around, from the theoretical realization of rhetoric's pervasiveness to a vision and a program for implementing it. In their view the discovery (or rediscovery) that all discourse and therefore all knowledge is rhetorical leads, or should lead, to the adoption of a *method* by which the dangers of rhetoric can be at least mitigated and perhaps extirpated. This method has two stages: the first is a stage of debunking, and it issues from the general suspicion in which all orthodoxies and arrangements of power are held once it is realized that their basis is not reason or nature but the success of some rhetorical/political agenda. Armed with this realization one proceeds to expose the contingent and therefore challengeable basis of whatever presents itself as natural and inevitable. So far this is precisely the procedure of deconstruction; but whereas deconstructive practice (at least of the Yale variety) seems to produce nothing but the occasion for its endless repetition, some cultural revolutionaries discern in it a more positive residue, the loosening or weakening of the structures of domination and oppression that now hold us captive. The reasoning is that by repeatedly uncovering the historical and ideological basis of established structures (both political and cognitive), one becomes sensitized to the effects of ideology and begins to clear a space in which those effects can be combatted; and as that sensitivity grows more acute, the area of combat will become larger until it encompasses the underlying structure of assumptions that confers a spurious legitimacy on the powers that currently be. The claim, in short, is that the radically rhetorical insight of Nietzschean/Derridean thought can do radical political work; becoming aware that everything is rhetorical is the first step in countering the power of rhetoric and liberating us from its force. Only if deeply entrenched ways of thinking are made the objects of suspicion will we be able "even to *imagine* that life could be different and better."

This last sentence is taken from an essay by Robert Gordon entitled "New Developments in Legal Theory" (1982, 287). Gordon is writing as a member of the Critical Legal Studies movement, a group of legal academics who have discovered the rhetorical nature of legal reasoning and are busily exposing as interested the supposedly disinterested operations of legal procedures. Gordon's pages are replete with the vocabulary of enclosure or prison; we are "locked-into" a system of belief we did not make; we are "demobilized" (that is, rendered less mobile); we must "break out" (291), we must "unfreeze the world as it appears to common sense" (289). What will help us to break out, to unfreeze, is the discovery "that the belief-structures that rule our lives are not found in nature but are historically contingent," for that discovery, says Gordon, "is extraordinarily liberating" (289). To the question, what is the *content* of that liberation, given a world that is rhetorical through and through, those who work Gordon's side of the street usually reply that emancipation will take the form of a strengthening and enlarging of a capacity of mind that stands to the side of, and is therefore able to resist, the appeal of the agenda that would enslave us. That capacity of mind has received many names, but the one most often proposed is "critical self-consciousness." Critical self-consciousness is the ability (stifled in some, developed in others) to discern in any "scheme of association," including those one finds attractive and compelling, the partisan aims it hides from view; and the claim is that as it performs this negative task critical self-consciousness participates in the positive task of formulating schemes of associations (structures of thought and government) that are in the service not of a particular party but of all mankind.

It need hardly be said that this claim veers back in the direction of the rationalism and universalism that the critical/deconstructive project sets out to demystify. That project begins by rejecting the rationalities of present life as rationalizations, and revealing the structure of reality to be rhetorical, that is, partial; but then it turns around and attempts to use the insight of partiality to build something that is less partial, less hostage to the urgencies of a particular vision and more responsive to the needs of men and women in general. Insofar as this "turn" is taken to its logical conclusion, it ends up reinventing at the conclusion of a rhetorically informed critique the entire array of antirhetorical gestures and exclusions. One sees this clearly in the work of Jürgen Habermas, a thinker whose widespread influence is testimony to the durability of the tradition that began (at least) with Plato. Habermas's goal is to bring about something he calls the "ideal speech situation," a situation in which all assertions proceed not from the perspective of individual desires and strategies, but from the perspective of a general rationality upon which all parties are agreed. In such a situation nothing would count except the claims to universal validity of all assertions. "No force except that of the better argument is exercised; and . . . as a result, all motives except that of the cooperative search for truth are excluded" (1975, 107–8). Of course, in the world we now inhabit, there is no such purity of motive, but nevertheless, says Habermas, even in the most distorted of communicative situations there remains something of the basic impulse behind all utterance, "the intention of communicating a true [wahr] proposition . . . so that the hearer can share the knowledge of the speaker" (1979, 2). If we could only eliminate from our discourse-performances those intentions that reflect baser goals—the intentions to deceive, to manipulate, to persuade—the ideal speech situation could be approximated.

This is the project Habermas names "Universal Pragmatics" and the name tells its own story. Habermas recognizes, as all modern and postmodern contextualists do, that language is a social and not a purely formal phenomenon, but he thinks that the social/pragmatic aspect of language use is itself "accessible to formal analysis" (6) and that therefore it is possible to construct a universal "communicative competence" (29) parallel to Chomsky's linguistic competence.

Sentences produced according to the rules and norms of this communicative competence would be tied not to "particular epistemic presuppositions and changing contexts" (29), but to the unchanging context (the context of contexts) in which one finds the presuppositions underlying the general possibility of successful speech. "A *general* theory of speech acts would . . . describe . . . that fundamental system of rules that adult subjects master to the extent that they can fulfill *the conditions of happy employment of sentences in utterances* no matter to which particular language the sentences may belong and in which accidental contexts the utterances may be embedded" (26). If we can operate on the level of that fundamental system, the distorting potential of "accidental contexts" will be neutralized because we will always have one eye on what is essential, the establishing by rational cooperation of an interpersonal (nonaccidental) truth. Once speakers are oriented to this goal and away from others, oriented toward *general* understanding, they will be incapable of deception and manipulation. A company of transparent subjectivities will join together in the fashioning of a transparent truth and of a world in which the will to power has been eliminated.

In his recent book *Textual Power* (1985), Robert Scholes examines the rationalist epistemology in which a "complete self confronts a solid world, perceiving it directly and accurately, . . . capturing it perfectly in a transparent language" and declares it to be so thoroughly discredited that it now "is lying in ruins around us" (132–33). Perhaps so, in some circles, but the fact of Habermas's work and of the audience he commands suggests that even now those ruins are collecting themselves and rising again into the familiar antirhetorical structure. It would seem that any announcement of the death of either position will always be premature, slightly behind the institutional news that in some corner of the world supposedly abandoned questions are receiving what at least appear to be new answers. Only recently, the *public* fortunes of rationalist–foundationalist thought have taken a favorable turn with the publication of books like Alan Bloom's *The Closing of the American Mind* and E. D. Hirsch's *Cultural Literacy,* both of which (Bloom's more directly) challenge the "new Orthodoxy" of "extreme cultural relativism" and reassert, albeit in different ways, the existence of normative standards. In many quarters these books have been welcomed as a return to the common sense that is necessary if civilization is to avoid the dark night of anarchy. One can expect administrators and legislators to propose reforms (and perhaps even purges) based on Bloom's arguments (the rhetorical force of antirhetoricalism is always being revived) and one can expect too a host of voices raised in opposition to what will surely be called the "new positivism." Those voices will include some that have been recorded here and some others that certainly merit recording, but can only be noted in a list that is itself incomplete. The full story of rhetoric's twentieth-century resurgence would boast among its cast of characters: Kenneth Burke, whose "dramatism" anticipates so much of what is considered avant-garde today; Wayne Booth, whose *The Rhetoric of Fiction* was so important in legitimizing the rhetorical analysis of the novel; Mikhail Bahktin, whose contrast of monologic to dialogic and heteroglossic discourse sums up so many strands in the rhetorical tradition; Roland Barthes, who in the concept of "jouissance" makes a (non)constitutive principle of the tendency of rhetoric to resist closure and extend play; the ethnomethodologists (Harold Garfinkel and company), who discover in every supposedly rule-bound context the operation of a principle (exactly the wrong word) of "ad-hocing"; Chaim Perelman and L. Olbrechts-Tyteca, whose *The New Rhetoric: A Treatise on Argumentation* provides a sophisticated modern source-book for would-be rhetoricians weary of always citing Aristotle; Barbara Herrnstein Smith, who in the course of espousing an unashamed relativism directly confronts and argues down the objections of those who fear for their souls (and more) in a world without objective standards; Fredric Jameson and Hayden White, who teach us (among other things) that "history . . . is unaccessible to us except in textual form, and that our approach to it and to the Real itself necessarily passes through its prior textualization" (1981, 35); reader-oriented critics like Norman Holland, David Bleich, Wolfgang Iser, and H. R. Jauss, who by shifting the emphasis from the text to its reception open up the act of interpretation to the infinite variability of contextual circumstance; innumerable feminists who relentlessly unmask male hegemonic structures and expose as rhetorical the rational posturings of the legal and political systems; equally innumerable theorists of composition who, under the slogan "process, not product," insist on the rhetorical nature of communication and argue for far-reaching changes in the way writing is taught. The list is already formidable, but it could go on and on, providing support for Scholes's contention that the rival epistemology has been vanquished and for Clifford Geertz's announcement (and he too is a contributor to the shift he reports) that "Something is happening to the way we think about the way we think" (1980).

But it would seem, from the evidence marshalled in this essay, that something is always happening to the way we think, and that it is always the same something, a tug-of-war between two views of human life and its possibilities, no one of which can ever gain complete and lasting ascendancy because in the very moment of its triumphant articulation each turns back in the direction of the other. Thus Wayne Booth feels obliged in both *The Rhetoric of Fiction* and *A Rhetoric of Irony* to confine the force of rhetoric by sharply distinguishing its legitimate uses from two extreme limit cases (the "unreliable narrator" and "unstable irony"); some reader-response critics deconstruct the autonomy and self-sufficiency of the text, but in the process end up privileging the autonomous and self-sufficient subject; some feminists challenge the essentialist claims of "male reason" in the name of a female rationality or nonrationality apparently no less essential; Jameson opens up the narrativity of history in order to proclaim one narrative the true and unifying one. Here one might speak of the return of the repressed (and thereby invoke Freud, whose writings and influence would be still another chapter in the story I have not even begun to tell) were it not that the repressed—whether it be the fact of difference or the desire for its elimination—is always so close to the surface that it hardly need be unearthed. What we seem to have is a tale full of sound and fury, and signifying itself, signifying a durability rooted in inconclusiveness, in the impossibility of there being a last word.

In an essay, however, someone must have the last word and I give it to Richard Rorty. Rorty is himself a champion of the antiessentialism that underlies rhetorical thinking; his neopragmatism makes common cause with Kuhn and others who would turn us away from the search for transcendental absolutes and commend to us (although it would seem superfluous to do so) the imperatives and goals already informing our practices. It is however, not the polemicist Rorty whom I call upon to sum up, but the Rorty who is the brisk chronicler of our epistemological condition:

> There . . . are two ways of thinking about various things. . . . The first . . . thinks of truth as a vertical relationship between representations and what is represented. The second . . . thinks of truth horizontally—as the culminating reinterpretation of our predecessors' reinterpretation of their predecessors' reinterpretation. . . . It is the difference between regarding truth, goodness, and beauty as eternal objects which we try to locate and reveal, and regarding them as artifacts whose fundamental design we often have to alter (1982, 92).

It is the difference between serious and rhetorical man. It is the difference that remains.

Brian Vickers

"Epilogue: The Future of Rhetoric"

On nous reprochera peut-être de voir la Rhétorique partout. Et si, par hasard, elle y était vraiment?

—BASIL MUNTÉANO

Having carried the story of rhetoric from the past to the present, from Homer to the works of living novelists, I now link the present to the future, and suggest what might be hoped for in rhetoric studies, and what not.

To start with the negative side, we might by now expect that the significance of rhetoric in the classical world would be clearly recognized, given its importance in politics, law, philosophy, poetry, history, and literary criticism, and indeed as one of the main preservers of classical culture. Yet in two recent compilations from our ancient universities rhetoric is nowhere given adequate treatment, either as a cultural phenomenon or as a discipline affecting all forms of literary composition. In *The Cambridge History of Classical Literature*[1] neither the Greek nor Latin volume treats rhetoric as a subject in its own right, with a continuous history. There are references to it, unavoidably so, as concerns Cicero (ten pages out of over nine hundred in the Latin volume), Quintilian (three pages, his 'grave deficiencies' apparently including a sketchy knowledge of Greek literature, his 'narrow vision' and 'scant historical sense' having created canons 'which have constricted the study of Latin literature over the last five hundred years'—with the grudging admission that his influence 'has been beneficent as well as stultifying'), and oratory under the later principate (seven pages). In the Greek volume Aristotle's *Rhetoric* receives one page, where it is virtually dismissed as being 'now of largely historical interest' (a dangerous formulation for a classicist to use), Dionysius, Longinus, and Demetrius together receive six, but oratory nearly thirty pages (by George Kennedy): what emphasis there is is on end-products rather than shaping forces. It is evident that for many practitioners of traditional classical philology literary criticism has begun to exist as a respectable category, but not rhetoric. The rival production from Oxford,[2] of smaller scope but with equally distinguished authors, gives no separate attention to rhetoric, although it has sections on 'Life and Society' and 'The Arts of Living'. *Quis custodiet?*—It might be said in defence that these books are addressed to the general reader, or under-graduate—but then all the more need to get some fundamental elements of classical culture into the right perspective from the first.

Where proper scholarly histories of rhetoric do exist, these can have serious defects. The two volumes on British logic and rhetoric by W. S. Howell, although pioneering in their day, and giving the first full account of many texts, are examples of internalist and parochial history. They are limited to English rhetoric-books, ignore the school and university background, and consider neither the international neo-Latin texts used in England nor the continuing tradition of editing, commenting, and teaching the major classical texts. A proper history of rhetoric, or any other discipline, however, will consider not just new titles but the totality of teaching-material, ancient or modern, in Greek, Latin, and the vernaculars, since the presence of Cicero or Quintilian is often more important than the latest modern digest. It will also consider the parallel presence of rhetoric in major literary forms, such as poetry, history, the sermon, the letter, the novel, and the other arts, for these are all ways in which rhetoric has influenced the thought-habits and modes of expression in a society. A properly-balanced history will also be responsive to the actual emphases in rhetoric at each point in time or within a culture: Howell, for instance, was notoriously dismissive of *elocutio* and the figures and tropes in any form, whether in education or in real life. A true history of rhetoric will need to consider the role of eloquence in institutions, such as parliaments, lawcourts, universities, academies.

A model history in this respect, which far outdistances anything done for any other country, is Marc Fumaroli's survey of 'the Age of Eloquence' in France from 1580 to the 1660s. This begins with the classical heritage as it was being refashioned at the turning-point between the inherited values of the European Renaissance and the newer spirit of French classicism. The dispute over Cicero, especially the concept of *imitatio* as applied to models of style, which begins in Italy in the late fifteenth century was fought out in France just as bitterly, the old catcalls of 'Asianism' and 'Atticism' taking on a new lease of life. Professor Fumaroli devotes the second part of his history to the Jesuits, whose growth, flourishing, and final extinction between 1551 and 1763 is treated in its full context, social and intellectual. The Jesuits are shown as embracing simultaneously both the scholarly history of rhetoric, sifting the printed records of the past to form an ever-more complete picture, and newer interests in the visual effects possible with such figures as *hypotyposis* and *ekphrasis*, resulting in a vogue for emblems and hieroglyphs as a sacred language. The Jesuits were under constant attack from the University of Paris: another institution conscious of its image as an academy of eloquence was Parliament, which used the formal addresses delivered at its opening to enhance its legitimacy and antiquity, and to mark its independence from Rome. The 'Remonstrances' or harangues delivered by the royal advocates twice a year represented an important fusion of legal and political eloquence, a new genre which had its parallel in England, in the 'Charges' delivered by Sir Francis Bacon in his capacity as Attorney-General and Solicitor-General. The outstanding figure in France at this time was Richelieu, the politician who legitimized rhetoric by taking his own orators with him when he came to power, and helped institutionalize rhetoric more firmly by founding the Académie française. All these developments are linked by Fumaroli in their consequences for literature, from Muret and Montaigne to Guez de Balzac, a unification of history which should provoke students of other literatures to emulation.

If this study is exemplary in its grasp of rhetoric as a cultural phenomenon, other recent books arouse expectations which they do not fulfil. A book with the ambitious title *Rhetorical Norms in Renaissance Literature,* by W. J. Kennedy, offers an investigation of the literary conventions in Renaissance lyric poetry, ironic prose, and the epic, all in under two hundred pages. Rhetoric is treated not only skimpily but with a disabling lack of historical understanding. In the seven pages given to classical rhetoric Kennedy states that the influence of Aristotle's *Rhetoric* was 'decisive', or 'tremendous', and that Cicero and Quintilian reproduce Aristotle wholesale. In addition to these obvious errors, the author ignores major forces in the tradition such as Isocrates, the *Rhetorica ad Herennium,* and the Hellenistic texts, while dismissing the three centuries from Petrarch to Milton in three pages. Any subject may be treated concisely, of course, but the haste and superficiality of this survey is accompanied by a fundamental misconception of Renaissance rhetoric. Kennedy states that the Middle Ages regarded rhetoric 'almost exclusively as an art of ornamentation', yet sees no difference between this period and the Renaissance, when a concept of *elocutio* as supposedly 'ornate speech' is said to have gradually 'reduced rhetoric to nothing more than a mere classification of figures and tropes'. This is such a travesty of the multiform nature of Renaissance rhetoric—the author was, at the time of writing, a professor at Cornell, and chairman of the Department of Comparative Literature—that one wonders how it can have been acquired. Far from being 'superficial elocutionary devices', used for 'embellishment or ornamentation', the figures carried out the expressive and persuasive function ascribed to *ornatus* as a whole. The author goes on to discuss lyric poetry in terms of 'speech and address', but fails to see the relevance of epistolary rhetoric; he discusses appeals to other persons or places within Petrarch's poems but never investigates the figure *apostrophe;* and he is quite unable to read the conventions of the prooemium in the invocation to *Paradise Lost,* saying that its 'questions have no answer and the dilemmas no resolution'. All this might not matter, had he not claimed in his title and chapter headings to be talking about rhetoric. As so often today, the word 'rhetoric' is used as a legitimizing counter in a book's title, but is in fact exploited, the reader likewise.[3]

The deficiencies of William Kennedy's book—by no means the only one of its kind—derive from a half-hearted or inadequate attempt to reconstruct rhetoric as a historical reality. But we also find, in contemporary work on rhetoric, evidence of a progressive atrophy of the discipline, not just from a primary to secondary role—from oral to written communication—but to *elocutio* alone, now detached from its expressive and persuasive functions, and brought down finally to a handful of tropes. It is not easy to reconstruct the process by which this atrophying has come about, but one name sometimes evoked as exemplar is that of Vico. In his *New Science,* discussing 'Poetic logic', which 'considers things in all the forms by which they may be signified' (§400), Vico argues that the first form taken by language was anthropomorphic metaphor, for 'the first poets attributed to bodies the being of animate substances, with capacities measured by their own, namely sense and passion, and in this way made fables of them. Thus every metaphor so formed is a fable in brief', and metaphor remains 'the most luminous and therefore the most necessary and frequent' of all the tropes (§404). After the invention of metaphor, Vico believes, followed metonymy, the substitution of agent for act resulting from 'the fact that names for agents were commoner than names for acts', and that of subject for form and accident being due to the early poets' 'inability to abstract forms and qualities from subjects' (§406). The third trope Vico considers is synecdoche, which, he claims, 'developed into metaphor as particulars were elevated into universals or parts united with the other parts together with which they make up their wholes' (§407). Vico's speculative history of the genesis of tropes ends with irony, which, he thinks, 'could not have begun until the period of reflection, because it is fashioned of falsehood by dint of a reflection which wears the mask of truth' (§408).

That really marks the extent of Vico's interest in the tropes, which are brought in not as rhetorical devices in their own right but as stages in a hypothetical scheme of the evolution of language and poetry. But before leaving the topic he makes a further reductive gesture:

> From all this it follows that all the tropes (and *they are all reducible to the four types above discussed*), which have hitherto been considered ingenious inventions of writers, were necessarily modes of expression of all the first poetic nations, and had originally their full native propriety. But these expressions of the first nations later became figurative when, with the further development of the human mind, words were invented which signified abstract forms or genera comprising their species or relating parts with their wholes. (p. 131, §409; my italics)

Behind Vico's theory of the genesis of tropes one can just see the traditional argument of rhetoricians that eloquence was natural before it became systematized into an art. Like other rhetoricians, Vico uses this argument as a tool to attack a neighbouring discipline, wishing to 'overthrow ... two common errors of grammarians'. But his reduction of the tropes to four is unfortunate, and in fact unworkable, as anyone will see who tries to reduce *prosopopoeia, antiphrasis, onomatopoeia, antonomasia,* or *hyperbole* to one of the privileged four. Each of these tropes has a specific nature, and a specific role to play in the elaboration of discourse, so that to claim that all the others may be ignored can only impoverish rhetoric. Vico seems to be the source—typically, unacknowledged—behind Kenneth Burke's adding to one of his books an appendix discussing 'Four

Master Tropes', namely the same four, metaphor, metonymy, synecdoche, and irony.[4] Burke also subordinates them to his own concerns, free-wheeling, allusive, unhistorical philosophizing, a system that rearranges the components of classical rhetoric so idiosyncratically as to be virtually unusable.

Vico is the acknowledged inspiration for the 'four trope' theory of the contemporary American historian Hayden White,[5] who has revived the ancient (if somewhat confusing) term 'tropics' to describe 'the tropical element in all discourse' (p. 1). White believes that this element is 'inexpungeable from discourse in the human sciences, however realistic they may aspire to be', for 'tropics is the process by which all discourse *constitutes* the objects' which it then describes and analyses (p. 2). The 'turning' of words and thoughts effected by tropes allows us to move from 'one notion of the way things are related' to another, and to see that the connection between things 'can be expressed in a language that takes account of the possibility of their being otherwise' (ibid.). So White indirectly refutes Croce's monism, and justifies the adaptive power of language. No text, he goes on, 'can represent "things as they are" without rhetorical adornment or poetic imagery', and even the syllogism works by using synecdoche and metonymy as it moves 'from the plane of universal propositions to singular existential statements' (p. 3). I agree with some of White's principles, and I endorse his comment that those thinkers (he cites Vico, Rousseau, Hegel, and Nietzsche) who held that the first languages derived from tropes and figures did not oppose these 'prefigurative modes of cognition' to 'rational modes', and were interested in integration rather than opposition (p. 7). But I cannot do much with his claim to have discovered an 'archetypal plot of discursive formations' which moves, in Vico's sequence but for a different purpose, from metaphor to metonymy to synecdoche to irony. White claims to find this pattern in Piaget's division of children's cognitive development into four phases ('sensorimotor, representational, operational, and logical'); in Freud's interpretation of dreaming (condensation, displacement, representation, secondary revision), in Marx, and in Hegel (pp. 6–20). In another essay he finds the same 'quaternary pattern' in the levels of interpretation in historical narrative, which are 'structurally homologous with one another' (p. 70). So to the four 'basic' tropes, metaphor, synecdoche, metonymy, irony, correspond four 'modes of employment' (romance, comedy, tragedy, satire), four 'modes of explanation' (idiographic, organistic, mechanistic, contextualist), four 'modes of ideological implication' (anarchist, conservative, radical, liberal), and four nineteenth-century historians (Michelet, Tocqueville, Ranke, Burckhardt: pp. 70–4). This is an unusual recurrence of a technique that I have called 'category-fit', common in the occult sciences,[6] and a venerable way of making sense of the world. But as far as rhetoric is concerned, White's practice is doubly unfortunate, being not only reductive in its concern with four tropes only, but also subordinating them to a different and, let it be said, alien interest.

The other tradition behind the atrophying of rhetoric in modern theory reduces the tropes to two only, metaphor and metonymy. The instigator of this reduction was of course Roman Jakobson, who wanted to apply 'purely *linguistic* criteria to the interpretation and classification' of aphasia.[7] I have italicized the term that shows how rhetoric has once again been subordinated to another discipline, here linguistics, especially the kind practised by Jakobson, which never shook off the influence of structuralist phonology and its concern with binary oppositions. Any linguistic sign, according to Jakobson, 'involves two modes of arrangement' of its constituent parts, combination and substitution or selection, these two ways of treating constituent signs yielding the 'context' of a linguistic unit and the 'code' (pp. 60–1). So the 'constituents of a context', he argues, can be thought to be 'in a state of *contiguity,* while in a substitution set signs are linked by various degrees of *similarity'*, fluctuating between synonyms and antonyms (ibid.). These two operations, contiguity and similarity, 'provide each linguistic sign with two sets of *interpretants'*, to use the terminology of C. S. Peirce, two references 'which serve to interpret the sign—one to the code, and the other to the context' (pp. 61–2). Jakobson's binary system, finally, allows him to distinguish two types of aphasics, those with 'Similarity Disorder' and those with 'Contiguity Disorder', and it is at this point that he invokes rhetoric, claiming that the two types correspond to the tropes metaphor and metonymy.

Before examining Jakobson's argument it may be worth recalling the meaning of these terms in rhetoric. 'By a trope', Quintilian writes, 'is meant the artistic alteration of a word or phrase from its proper meaning to another.' The alteration involves not just words but 'our thoughts and the structure of our sentences', so that those writers are 'mistaken who have held that tropes necessarily involved the substitution of one name for another', such as indicating an invention by substituting the name of the inventor (Vulcan for fire, Ceres for bread), or substituting 'that which contains for that which is contained' ('a cup was drunk to the lees', implying a cup of wine), or cause for effect ('slothful ease'), or vice versa (8. 6. 23). *Synecdoche* gives 'variety to our language by making us realise many things from one, the whole from a part, the *genus* from a *species,* things which follow from things which have preceded' (8. 6. 19). Other rhetoricians agree substantially, or are more explicit, such as the *Ad Herennium,* describing metonymy as 'the figure which draws from an object closely akin or associated [*ab rebus propinquis et finitimis*] an expression suggesting the object meant, but not called by its own name', substituting greater for lesser, instrument for possessor, and so on (4. 32. 43). *Metaphor,* as everyone knows, involves describing one thing or concept in terms of another, so as to relate or combine attributes not commonly associated. *Antonomasia* is 'the substitution of an epithet as equivalent to the name which it replaces', or 'indicating the most striking characteristics of an individual, as in the phrase "Father of gods and king of men" '. Periphrasis and allegory are large-scale ways of using one verbal sequence to describe another; irony and related tropes substitute a form of discourse that means the opposite of what it seems to say.

All the tropes, then, work by a form of substitution based on resemblance and difference, with the listener or reader being expected to make the mental operations necessary to relate one term to another within the same class. In one context 'Mars' will be a metonymy for 'war', 'gold' for 'wealth', 'Venus' for 'love'.

The movement can be within a logical class (part for whole, container for contained), and demands a certain power of abstraction in both writer and reader, that 'ability to see resemblances' that Aristotle praised so highly where metaphor is involved. The tropes form a rather miscellaneous group, notoriously so, standard lists ranging from eight to thirty or more. Some rhetoricians attempted to classify them by their general operations, a typical example, found as late as Alexander Bain in the 1880s,[8] being the grouping into 'Figures Founded on Similarity' (similitude, metaphor), 'Figures Founded on Contiguity' (metonymy, synecdoche, transferred epithet), and 'Figures Founded on Contrast' (irony, interrogation). It is important to realize that all such groupings place the tropes in various classes but without implying fundamental differences between them: 'contiguity', as in the *Ad Herennium's* description of metonymy, is a variant form of 'similarity', not a polar opposite to it. What Jakobson does is to take the binary oppositions that he has established for linguistics—combination/substitution, code/context, paradigmatic/syntagmatic—and then forcibly impose these on to the two tropes that he has picked out. Even within his own terms, 'combination' is hardly a polar opposite to 'selection', just a different process, and to see 'syntagm' and 'paradigm' as opposites involves taking a metaphor very literally, spatializing it ('pole' or 'axis') and then subordinating it to a dichotomy.

In the first kind of aphasia, he argues, with 'impaired substitution and intact contexture', operations of contiguity are said to replace those based on similarity:

> From the two polar figures of speech, metaphor and metonymy, the latter, based on contiguity, is widely employed by aphasics whose selective capacities have been affected. *Fork* is substituted for *knife, table* for *lamp, smoke* for *pipe, eat* for *toaster.* . . . Such metonymies may be characterized as projections from the line of a habitual context into the line of substitution and selection. (p. 69)

I shall return to this metaphor of 'polar figures of speech', but must say first that Jakobson is using the term 'contiguity' in a loose, indeed metaphorical way, to describe how aphasics, unable to recall the proper word, substitute the *next* best, or the *nearest* word they can think of. But in rhetoric, as we have seen, metonymy involves the substitution of a 'related' term (where *propinquis* does not mean literally 'next to') according to fixed transitions or tropings within a category on different levels, such as putting the container for the thing contained, or the sign for the thing signified. In Jakobson's examples there is no such movement across the levels within a category, only the attempt to find a substitute corresponding to the unrecallable word, some of which are very approximate indeed. 'Table' and 'lamp' are two domestic objects sometimes found in physical contiguity but which do not imply each other, neither do 'eat' and 'toaster'. It takes a reader with a special knowledge of the clinical context to recognize what the aphasic means by these terms. One may doubt whether they are figures of speech in the sense that we normally give that phrase. In fact, when he describes the other type of patient, one 'confined to the substitution set (once contexture is deficient'), Jakobson himself substantially qualifies his claim that these are rhetorical processes. Such an aphasic

> deals with similarities, and his approximate identifications are of a metaphoric nature, contrary to the metonymic ones familiar to the opposite [*sic*] type of aphasics. *Spyglass* for *microscope,* or *fire* for *gaslight* are typical examples of such *quasi-metaphoric expressions,* . . . since, in contradistinction to rhetoric or poetic metaphors, they present no deliberate transfer of meaning. (p. 72)

In that case, they are not really metaphors, and since the items in the first class are not really metonymies Jakobson's use of rhetorical terms can be seen to be both opportunistic and vague. Just as with the attempt to apply rhetorical terms to music or painting, the *translatio* of rhetoric to linguistics, and thence to psychology and neurology, involves both a simplification and a distortion of rhetoric.

Yet Jakobson was unconcerned by such reflections, returning to his earlier metaphor in a chapter entitled 'The metaphoric and metonymic poles'. Here he asserts that either of those two relations, similarity and contiguity, can appear 'on any verbal level—morphemic, lexical, syntactic, and phraseological' (p. 77). That may well be, especially given the rather vague terms in which they are defined, but where his argument becomes really damaging is when he asserts that 'either of the two gravitational poles [gravity provides a further reinforcing metaphor] may prevail', that is, what he calls 'metaphor' *will dominate over* 'metonymy', or vice versa, not just in the disordered mental world of aphasics but in literary genres or large-scale artistic movements. Jakobson actually proposes (pp. 77–8, 81–2) the following dichotomy, based on the 'dominance' of either 'pole':

METAPHOR	METONYMY
Russian lyrical songs	Russian Heroic epics
Romanticism and symbolism	Realism
Surrealism	Cubism
Poetry	Prose

He argues that 'the predominance of metonymy' underlies realism, which belongs to 'an intermediary stage between the decline of romanticism'—he must mean in the mid-nineteenth century—'and is opposed to them both'. This case is argued in two sentences, in terms of 'the realistic author metonymically' digressing from the plot to atmosphere, or from characters to action; and illustrated with two quotations from Tolstoy (p. 78). One hardly knows which to admire most, the vastness of the thesis or the paucity of argument. Perhaps further analysis would only have complicated the issue. The same mixture of grandiose assertion and non-existent argument characterizes his dichotomizing of poetry and prose: 'Since poetry is focused upon sign, and pragmatical prose primarily upon referent'—let us not stop to discuss that proposition—'tropes and figures were studied primarily as poetical devices. The principle of similarity underlies poetry. . . . Prose, on the contrary, is forwarded essentially by contiguity' (pp. 81–2). This reveals too clearly Jakobson's ignorance of rhetoric, in which tropes and figures were studied primarily as expressive devices, first in prose and only later in poetry. But the distinction is so vast as to be meaningless.

In Jakobson's work, as in Vico and White, rhetoric is fragmented and then subordinated to an alien enterprise. This is a pattern we have met before, in medieval rhetoric, with its disintegration of a unified tradition into components that were reused for different and usually more restricted ends. In Jakobson the guiding spirit is the binary opposition basic to structuralist phonology after Trubetzkoy, which here not only divides rhetoric into two terms, and two only, but then conceives of them in fundamental opposition. Invoking what he claims to be '*the bipolar structure of language (or other semiotic systems)*, and in aphasia, the *fixation* on one of these poles to the *exclusion* of the other' (pp. 78–9; my italics), Jakobson states as a general law that 'A competition between both devices, metonymic and metaphoric, is manifest in any symbolic process, either intrapersonal or social' (p. 80). The reader may well feel at this point that such an opposition, and the further desire to exclude one half of the field, is manifest most of all in Jakobson's thought-processes. In other words, aphasia provides the norm for wide-scale social and intellectual movements. His supporting evidence is what he calls the 'decisive question' in analysing the structure of dreams, namely whether the symbols and narratives that occur there 'are based on contiguity (Freud's metonymic "displacement" and synecdochic "condensation") or on similarity (Freud's "identification and symbolism")' (p. 81). Freud provided Hayden White's quaternary scheme with four terms: the same text accommodates Jakobson's binary theory with two. These categories are malleable, evidently, and once again too vast to be usable. Jakobson's other evidence is the wholly outmoded anthropology of J. G. Frazer, who, as Jakobson innocently puts it, 'resolved' the principles underlying magic rites into similarity and contiguity—'this bipartition is indeed illuminating', he says (p. 81).

Jakobson was a great linguist, whose contribution will stand when most of us writing in this century will have long been forgotten. But on this issue he is merely expressing a general attitude to rhetoric in modern times, which first reduces its scope, and then applies it to purposes that it never dreamt of. No rhetorician before Vico could have thought of describing the evolution of human consciousness in terms of the interaction of four tropes, or summing up the complex nature of poetry and prose in two.

The effects of Jakobson's dichotomizing reduction of rhetoric have, I believe, been disastrous, as a whole critical school has attempted to read literature solely in terms of metaphor versus metonymy, ignoring all other verbal devices. The kind of undisciplined and unhistorical criticism that may use this method as a form of self-legitimization is illustrated from an unexpected side in a recent work by Gordon Williams which appears to be about rhetoric in Latin poetry.[9] In fact the author claims that between the major compositions of Catullus and the death of Horace (60–8BC) poets used a technique of composition that 'ran counter to rhetorical theory as it has come down to us (mostly from later periods)', in particular by denying 'the fundamental distinction between form and content' basic to rhetoric with its categories of *inventio* and *elocutio* (p. ix). But unfortunately rhetorical theory was already fully formed in this period, as an examination of the *Rhetorica ad Herennium, De Inventione,* and what we know of their Hellenistic sources, will soon show; indeed rhetoric was already a part of Roman education then, and its impact is clearly visible in the poetry of Catullus, and Horace; while the distinction between *res* and *verba* is inherent in the Latin language and in general thought categories. Once that comfortable distinction between form and content was disregarded', Williams goes on (so it must already have existed, then!), 'conventional rhetorical analysis was impotent'. But this is to confuse creation with criticism, since it does not consider how poets constructed their poems, and to substitute an animus against rhetoric for an informed and responsible attitude to history. Williams claims that the poetry of this period is 'a poetry of meditation', not 'a rhetorical poetry' which would try to 'manipulate an audience by making immediate impact', a process that, according to him, only arose later, during the age of Augustus, when 'rhetorical theory' succeeded in forcing its 'impertinent impositions' on to poetry, assimilating it 'to the condition of prose (with the addition of metre). . . . It is only fairly recently that the imposture has been seriously questioned' (pp. x–xi)—namely by Professor Williams himself, in two previous books.

Whether 'a poetry of meditation' is the right description for the poetry of Catullus, or Horace, is a question that can be left to other readers, but what this dichotomy—privileging one side and dismissing the other—reveals is just another instance of classicists' continuing hostility to rhetoric. Williams's case is interesting in that he admits to having been 'faced with difficult problems of terminology', since he scorns to use that of the 'ancient rhetorical theorists'. Apparently they 'confined their analysis to simple structures for the most part, like rhetorical questions or aposiopesis, and devoted their attention otherwise to figures of speech': since these are all figures of speech, that is a meaningless statement. Worse still, the 'close distinctions' they made between terms (unlike Williams) can easily get the modern user into 'a scholastic nightmare of labelling in which the important issues simply disappear from view' (pp. xi–xii)—another travesty of classical rhetoric. Therefore he decided to use Jakobson's simpler binary opposition, even though he knows that

> ancient theorists used the words 'metaphor' and 'metonymy' to describe modifications of meaning that are produced by the fact that a sign or group of signs is connected to an unexpected or unusual referent. The resulting modification is intelligible to the reader because a relationship of similarity or of contiguity links the normal or expected referent with the new referent,

which presupposes in the reader the capacity to recognize the relationship (p. xi). This is, despite the general dismissal of rhetoric, an acute observation on the actual functioning of these tropes as conceived of in the classical treatises, well supported by his later survey of the relevant texts (pp. 23 ff.). Yet although the author knows how unhistorical and non-rhetorical Jakobson's terminology is, he finds it convenient for the real aim of his book, which is equally non-rhetorical. By 'figures of thought' in his title he refers not to the *figurae mentis* of the handbooks (which in any case meant figures expressing 'the mind, feeling or conceptions': Quintilian, 9. 1. 17), but to a special technique which he claims operated in Roman poetry of this period. For these poets, it seems 'an idea . . . could be regarded as a semantic unit, analogous to a word, and could be subject to configurations with other ideas just as had been done previously with words [thus sabotaging his chronology again!]. Consequently . . . new techniques could be devised for managing transitions of thought, and the poet could say one thing while expecting his reader to understand that he meant something else . . . ' (pp. ix–x). That seems to me, I confess, a wholly unfounded idea, and one that opens the door to any interpretation of a text, whatever its overt meaning, putting the critic in a state of privileged communication with the *manes* of his poets, since he alone, after nearly two thousand years, knows what their poems are really about. The prospect is alarming, but in the event this turns out to be a largely conventional piece of criticism, using such concepts as 'thematic anticipation' and 'objective correlative'. Yet it dismissed rhetoric; and sought legitimization by using Jakobson's two 'polar' tropes.

Some dangers of this reductive attitude to rhetoric have been brought out by Gérard Genette, a critic who has devoted much thought to rhetoric and its history and who has edited two classic French rhetoric texts.[10] Commenting on the appearance in 1970 of the *Rhétorique générale* of the 'Groupe µ de Liège (a team of Belgian critics who adopted the first letter of 'metaphor' for their name), and of two articles discussing 'la figure généralséé and 'la métaphore généralséé, Genette observed that in all these cases rhetoric was being neither generalized nor enlarged, but reduced, restricted. Aristotle's *Rhetoric* was a truly general treatise, including some remarks on metaphor, but now the term 'generalized' is applied to what is in effect a handbook of figures (pp. 21–2). Rhetoric has always had a smaller role in modern times, of course, compared to its status in Greece and Rome, but Genette thinks that the final process of reducing it to a study of tropes took place with the publication in 1730 of the treatise *Des Tropes* by Du Marsais, the grammar expert for the *Encyclopédie,* whose interest in rhetoric was that of 'a linguist, and more precisely a semantician' (p. 23). Du Marsais was concerned with the process by which tropes offered a substitution of a 'figurative' sense for 'the proper' sense, a concern that was taken further by Fontanier when he re-edited Du Marsais' treatise in 1818, and made the trope the model for all other figures, as if by right. Although including eighteen tropes, in a somewhat chaotic order, Du Marsais had proposed that they should be arranged hierarchically, a suggestion, Genette points out, already made by Vossius in the seventeenth century (perhaps Vico's unacknowledged source), who defined four main genera, metaphor, metonymy, synecdoche, and irony (pp. 23–4). Du Marsais proposed an alignment based on the three main associative principles of similitude, contiguity, and opposition (Genette does not note that these principles are already clearly defined in the classical rhetoric texts). Fontanier rejected irony, and stated that the only tropes worthy of the name were metonymy, synecdoche, and metaphor. As Genette puts it, one has only to combine the two approaches to obtain 'le couple figural exemplaire, chiens de faïence irremplaçables de notre propre rhétorique moderne: Métaphore et Métonymié (p. 25): china dogs, or 'bookends' as the English version has it.

The final reduction of all tropes to these two was carried out, as we have seen, by Jakobson (anticipated, apparently, by Eikhenbaum in 1923, who also made the correlation metonymy = prose, metaphor = poetry), but Jakobson's borrowing from rhetoric involved, as Genette shows, a drastic reduction of the scope of these figures. In classical rhetoric the categories of analogy and contiguity refer to signifiers placed in a substitutional relation within metaphor and metonymy, such as 'gold' and 'corn' (having in common the colour yellow), 'steel' and 'sword' (exchanging substance for artefact). Jakobson assimilated that opposition to one derived from linguistics, between paradigm and syntagm, equivalence and succession, but these oppositions refer to what is signified, not to the signifiers. As well as creating an opposition where none exists in the original, and then displacing it within the linguistic sign (from signifier to signified), Jakobson's 'drastic reduction' of scope continues what Genette sees as a general trend in modern rhetoric, one that prefers tropes of a more semantically concrete, 'spatio-temporal' nature, excluding those that rely on intellectual operation. This 'displacement of the object . . . privileges the two relations of contiguity (and/or inclusion) and resemblance, while weakening those of association' (pp. 25–6). The trope *synecdoche* depends on similarities being grasped by the intellect, and cannot be subsumed under physical contiguity: 'sail' for 'ship', as Genette points out, is a substitution not by contiguity—which would demand 'mast', say—but within a class defined logically (p. 27). Perhaps for this reason it was of no use to Jakobson in his attempt to define aphasia in 'purely linguistic terms'. The 'pseudo-spatial' concept of contiguity, as Genette calls it, may privilege metonymy but it also creates a further reduction within the figure itself, for many of the relations described by classical rhetoric—effect for cause, sign for the thing signified—'cannot be easily reduced to an effect of contact or spatial proximity, unless by using metaphor' (pp. 27–8). Contiguity in this physical sense cannot relate 'heart' and 'courage', 'bowels' and 'pity', so that 'to reduce all metonymy to a purely spatial relationship is to restrict the mode of action of this figure to a single physical' or material aspect (p. 28). As with my earlier analysis of the attempt to apply figures of rhetoric to music, the field of application of the rhetorical device taken over into another discipline is immediately limited.

The same reductive process has operated with the figures of resemblance, benefiting metaphor at the expense of others, especially comparison or similitude. Genette's detailed and original analysis of the functioning of analogy—which reveals, too, the inadequacy of a Jakobsonian binary model (pp. 29–31)—shows that metaphor is only one of several figures of analogy, and that to reduce all such tropes to 'the metaphoric pole' is to do violence to language and to thought. The opposition metonymy–metaphor, he concludes somewhat mockingly, could be assimilated to other grand binary schemes, such as the correspondence between heaven and earth, or between the sisters in the Gospel: metonymy is Martha, the active one, busy about the house, passing from one object to another, duster in hand, while metaphor is Mary, who having chosen 'the better part', namely contemplation, will go straight to heaven. Or they could be seen as horizontal versus vertical, or materialists (prosaic people privileging 'contact') versus spiritualists (poetic souls preferring 'similitude'), or—but 'nous ne pousserons pas plus loin', he comments with a rare sarcasm, 'ce jeu d'extrapolations manichéistes, dont les stations terminales ne réservent aucune surprise' (pp. 37–8). Genette's target in these closing pages is the elevation, more marked in French literary theory than elsewhere, of metaphor to 'the trope of tropes', the figure of figures, the only part of rhetoric worth saving (p. 28–40). I agree with him that this is the ultimate reduction of rhetoric, the penultimate stage being Jakobson's binary opposition, its apotheosis a monism that, from the vast corpus of the art, privileges one single trope, a rare survivor from 'the great shipwreck of rhetoric' in the nineteenth century (p. 32).

My last example of the reduction, fragmentation, and misapplication of rhetoric in modern literary discourse is the work of the late Paul de Man, in three collections of essays. *Blindness and Insight. Essays in the Rhetoric of Contemporary Criticism* (New York, 1971) contained work produced between 1966 and 1969. *Allegories of Reading. Figural Language in Rousseau, Nietzsche, Rilke, and Proust* (New Haven, 1979) brought together essays from 1972 to 1976, while *The Rhetoric of Romanticism* (New York, 1984) assembled essays written between 1956 and 1983. This last volume discusses Wordworth's *Essays upon Epitaphs* in terms of the figure *prosopopoeia*, here claimed to be 'the trope of autobiography', since it 'deals with the giving and taking away of faces, with face and deface, *figure*, figuration, and disfiguration' (pp. 75–6)—a self-centered playing with the word (here the figure *polyptoton*) that de Man sometimes indulged in. Another essay, 'Anthropomorphism and Trope in the Lyric', claims that in Baudelaire's 'Correspondances' the 'anthropomorphic' symbolism of seeing nature as a 'temple' of trees with living 'pillars'—surely referring to architecture and therefore not primarily *anthropo*morphic—means that 'anthropomorphism' can be elevated to the ranks of rhetoric as a 'figure of amplification' (pp. 246–7). Both essays are typical of de Man in limiting their interest in rhetoric to one stage, *elocutio*, then to one category within it, namely a specific trope (sometimes misnamed figure), which then becomes the fragile basis for a vastly elaborated theory. But at least this rather miscellaneous volume does not attempt to turn rhetoric against itself, as the two other collections do.

Blindness and Insight uses 'rhetoric' in the subtitle, but the term only appears in an essay called 'The Rhetoric of Blindness', which finds Jacques Derrida guilty of 'blindness' in his reading of Rousseau. The rhetoric text in dispute is Rousseau's *Essai sur l'origine des langues*[11] (*c.* 1756), especially the discussion of how imitation works differently in the various arts. Readers of my account of the translation of rhetorical categories to the visual arts will recognize the tradition behind Rousseau's giving the priority to drawing—'le dessin'—over colour. Much of Rousseau's thinking on language derives from familiar emphases in the rhetorical tradition: language distinguishes men from beasts (p. 27); gestures express emotion vividly, and history has many examples of 'ces maniéres d'argumenter aux yeux' which prove that 'on parle aux yeux bien mieux qu'aux oreilles: il n'y a personne qui ne sente la vérité du jugement d'Horace à cet égard' (pp. 31–3). The passage in Horace that Rousseau alludes to is *ut pictura poesis* once again, and his account of the emotional impact of metaphor—'les discours les plus éloquens sont ceux où l'on enchâsse le plus d'images' (p. 35)—derives from a long and well-known tradition of the power of visual appeal, recently flourishing in France (Rousseau cites Lamy's *L'Art de parler*). The origin of language, Rousseau reasons, was due not to the satisfaction of human needs—gestures are more appropriate for that—but to the expression of feeling. The original languages resembled poetry, not geometry, man's first words being formed to express immediate emotional needs: 'pour émouvoir un jeune coeur, pour repousser un aggresseur injuste la nature dicte des accens, des cris, des plaintes: voilà les plus anciens mots inventés' (pp. 41–3).

Within the argument I have been developing in this book it will come as no surprise that Rousseau should connect language with human feelings, nor that he conceives rhetoric as being the natural language for feeling. Chapter III of his treatise is entitled 'Que le premier langage dut être figuré', and at once links rhetoric and feeling:

> Comme les prémiers motifs qui firent parler l'homme furent des passions, ses prémiéres expressions furent des Tropes. Le langage figuré fut la première à naître, le sens propre fut trouvé le dernier. . . . D'abord on ne parla qu'en pöesie; on ne s'avisa de raisonner que longtemps après. (p. 45)

Anticipating the reader's objection that an expression cannot become figurative before its literal sense has been established—a serious objection, still—Rousseau replies that

> pour m'entendre il faut substituer l'idée que la passion nous présente, au mot que nous transposons; car on ne transpose les mots que parce qu'on transpose aussi les idées, autrement le langage figuré ne signifieroit rien.

In a trope *res* and *verba* must cohere in the process of *translatio* (the Latin term for metaphor) from one level of discourse to another. The motive force in Rousseau's theory of the trope's *translatio* is 'passion', strong feelings such as fear. His example is of a savage who encounters other men for the first time and in his fear sees them as bigger and stronger than himself, and so calls them 'giants'; later, as he gets used to them, he substitutes the term 'men'. The example may not be well chosen, as de Man complains, but my point is that Rousseau uses it to connect tropes with feeling: 'Voilà comment le mot figuré nait avant le mot propre, lorsque la passion nous fascine les yeux. . . . L'image illusoire offerte par la passion se montrant la première, le langage qui lui répondoit fut aussi le premier inventé' (p. 47).

Of Rousseau's theory as such I have little to say beyond noting the organic connection it preserves between rhetoric and feeling. But I find it strange that de Man's discussion of Rousseau, and Derrida, should totally ignore the affective significance of tropes. In his view, the title of Rousseau's Chapter III 'must be understood' as saying, 'the only literal statement that says what it means to say is the assertion that there can be no literal statements' (*Blindness*, p. 33). Rousseau's chronology—first trope, then literal meaning—is collapsed into a simultaneity that produces an impasse of contradiction. De Man wishes to argue that all literary language, and so literature itself, is figurative, and therefore ambivalent, but he foists this theory into Rousseau's text, which is given the additional hazard of undermining itself: 'Accounting for the "rhetoricity" of its own mode, the text also postulates the necessity of its own misreading.' That is, it writes in 'an indirect, figural way that knows it will be misunderstood by being taken literally' (p. 136). But if this reader, any reader, can distinguish literal and figurative, why is misreading a necessity? Because, de Man might reply, reading is impossible. Rousseau supposedly makes metaphor 'the cornerstone of a theory of rhetoric'—I cannot discover that Rousseau had a 'theory of rhetoric': this text merely argues that communication of feeling results in the invention of figurative language—but 'a rhetoric that can assert itself only in a manner that leaves open the possibility of misunderstanding'. It not only 'leaves open' that possibility, but 'opens up', much more excitingly, 'the possibility of the archetypal error: the recurrent confusion of sign and substance' (ibid.). So, de Man concludes, any text can be called 'literary' that 'implicitly or explicitly signifies its own rhetorical mode and prefigures its own misunderstanding as the correlative of its rhetorical nature; that is, of its "rhetoricity" ' (ibid.). Derrida accused Rousseau of blindness, but, de Man says, he either read Rousseau in terms of Rousseau's critics or else he deliberately misread him (p. 139). Either way, he is himself blind—or rather, he shows 'blindness to be the necessary correlative of the rhetorical structure of literary language' (p. 141).

Paul de Man's discussion of Rousseau's rhetoric is typical of his whole critical method, being based on a very small amount of text, which is here interpreted in a way quite different to that meant, indeed insisted on by the author. Rousseau's emphasis on tropes as representing passion, feelings, poetry as against rational discourse—a web of ideas derived from the rhetorical tradition, most immediately from Vico—is ignored in favour of a modern intellectualist discussion of metaphor in terms of literal and figurative levels. This line of discussion is then subjected to a mode of simultaneous assertion and negation which results in a logical impasse: 'rhetoricity' is found to be the state of making assertions that are fated to be misunderstood. In *Allegories of Reading* this process is repeated on a larger scale, both as a general theoretical statement and as a reading of Nietzsche. In the opening chapter, 'Semiology and Rhetoric', de Man explains that he uses the word rhetoric to signify 'the study of tropes and of figures', and 'not in the *derived* sense of comment or of eloquence or persuasion' (p. 6; my italics). But this is a *hypallage,* that gets things back to front: tropes and figures are the verbal means by which persuasion is carried out, not an alternative to it, to be detached for separate discussion. And persuasion is not a 'derived' but a primary conception of rhetoric. In the hands of de Man rhetoric no longer means oratory, civic eloquence, moving the feelings, or constructing the whole of an artistic discourse; it refers to a few well-known tropes, not even figures. The modern fragmentation of rhetoric is carried further, reducing it from persuasion or 'actual action upon others' to the workings of a self-contained 'intralinguistic figure or trope' (p. 8). It has been made introverted, solipsistic.

Whether de Man ever read Aristotle, Quintilian, or any other rhetorician remains unclear. (Derrida by contrast, cites Aristotle in Greek.) His actual knowledge of rhetoric as revealed in these essays is limited to a fundamentally misguided conception of the art, and to a few tropes, not always correctly understood. But this did not prevent him from making grand generalizations. The continuity between grammar and rhetoric, a constant in the language arts for over two thousand years, is swept away in three pages (9–11). On the basis of one invented anecdote, in which a husband responds to his wife's solicitous question with the irritable reply 'What's the difference?', de Man builds up a whole theory of a 'tension between grammar and rhetoric'. Since the question is capable of being misunderstood (either asking 'what is the difference between x and y?', or implying 'it makes no difference to me'—one would have thought that the speech-context, especially the tone of the speaker's voice, would have made it quite clear to the wife what her husband meant), de Man concludes that 'the same grammatical pattern engenders two meanings that are mutually exclusive: the literal meaning asks for the concept (difference) whose existence is denied by the figurative meaning' (p. 9). This trivial incident, describing a banal misunderstanding (if it ever took place) actually gives de Man the cue to define the 'difference between grammar and rhetoric', namely that 'grammar allows us to ask the question, but the sentence by means of which we ask it may deny the very possibility of asking'. Unfortunately, de Man has misunderstood the term 'rhetorical question', which means a question posed without the expectation of a reply, the speaker implying the answer to be self-evident. De Man, however, says that a question 'becomes rhetorical . . . when it is impossible to decide by grammatical or other linguistic devices which of the two meanings [literal or figurative] prevails.' (This would simply be a muddled or ambivalent question.) But, insisting on his idiosyncratic and anachronistic late twentieth-century conception, de Man takes it to a melodramatic and paranoiac conclusion, with the rhetorical question now seen as a 'semiological enigma', recording the despair that a speaker feels 'when confronted with a structure of linguistic meaning that he cannot control', a state that can only lead to 'an infinity of similar future confusions' (p. 10). So de Man reaches the amazing conclusion that in the rhetorical question, as such, 'Rhetoric radically suspends logic and opens up vertiginous possibilities of referential aberration'. And he promptly equates this 'rhetorical, figural potentiality of language' with literature, similarly bound to an autotelic absorption with itself, not with the world or experience it purports to describe, and equally liable to self-undermining. After a brief analysis of a passage in Proust, made to deny 'the intrinsic metaphysical superiority of metaphor over metonymy'—a pointless enough exercise in the Jakobsonian mode of setting one trope off against another—de Man concludes by reaffirming that 'a literary text simultaneously asserts and denies the authority of its own rhetorical mode' (p. 17).

In deconstructionist theory, we may say, the binary oppositions of structuralism, originally conceived in spatial or skeletal terms, are confronted in a linear equation, and made to negate each other. An older modern critical school, the so-called 'New Criticism', with its concepts of 'tension' and 'irony', has also contributed to this critical mode. But the oppositions, polarities, deconstructions, vertigo, are in the minds and method of the critics, not in the material itself. They may be expressing modern anxieties about language, with the curiously self-satisfying claim that language is an unreliable tool, but they ought not to foist these anxieties on to rhetoric.

De Man's essays on Nietzsche, especially 'Rhetoric of Tropes' (pp. 103–18), and 'Rhetoric of Persuasion' (pp. 119–31), further extend the deconstructionist deformation of rhetoric. As with the Rousseau essay, some references to rhetoric by Nietzsche (mainly the notes he took for the course on rhetoric given to an audience of two students at Basle University during the winter semester 1872-3), form the starting-point of de Man's enquiry, an enquiry that will end, like the Rousseau piece, in an impasse. Nietzsche made excerpts from several recent German books on rhetoric, Richard Volkmann's still unequalled survey, *Die Rhetorik der Griechen und Römer in systematischer Uebersicht* (1872), Gustav Gerber's *Die Sprache als Kunst* (1872), and the twin studies by Friedrich Blass, *Die griechische Beredsamkeit* (1865) and *Die attische Beredsamkeit* (1868). As a classical philologist anxious to establish his career, Nietzsche was diligent in taking notes, but added his own comments and interpretations, still not published in their totality.[12] He had excellent authorities, and produced a well-balanced account of the art. The course as a whole discussed: 1. the concept of rhetoric; 2. the main divisions; 3. the relationship between rhetoric and language; 4. *elocutio*: linguistic purity, clarity, decorum; 5. decorum of character and ornament; 6. neologism; 7. tropes; 8. figures; 9. prose rhythm; 10. the doctrine of *stasis*; 11. *genera et figurae causarum*; 12. judicial rhetoric and its types; 13. deliberative rhetoric; 14. epideictic rhetoric; 15. *dispositio*; 16. *memoria* and *actio*; Appendix: a brief history of eloquence.

Only the first seven chapters have been published (modern editors' interest expired, significantly enough, when they reached the rhetorical figures), but we can see that Nietzsche covered the whole subject, with perhaps insufficient attention to *inventio*. To pick out some of the main emphases, Nietzsche begins with the prestige of rhetoric in the ancient world, as the final stage in the formation of culture and intellect. He shows his awareness of the recent history of rhetoric, noting its decline in the nineteenth century, and quoting the attacks by Locke and Kant (p. 104). To illustrate the great status of the orator in Rome he cites Schopenhauer's account of the power of eloquence to penetrate the listener's mind and feelings, leading them wherever he will, even against their desires (p. 105)—Cicero and Quintilian made new, once again. In the present time, he writes, 'rhetorical' has come to mean 'artificial' in a pejorative sense, but of course, he asserts, 'natural' is itself a relative concept, and in fact rhetoric is only a development of artifices already present in language. Invoking Aristotle's description of rhetoric as a force (*dynamis*), Nietzsche argues (like Rousseau) that the purpose of language is not to pass on abstract truths or instruction, but to communicate an individual's emotions and judgments (p. 111). Drawing very closely on Gerber's work, Nietzsche equates rhetoric and language, since all words originated as tropes, and continue to be fundamentally tropelike (pp. 112–13; p. 128 n. 38). This idea also resembles Rousseau, but we note that Rousseau's linking of tropes and the feelings has disappeared from the nineteenth-century rhetorical tradition. Returning to the relation between art and nature, Nietzsche makes the traditional points that the orator must avoid any impression of artifice, must imitate nature, and win the audience's belief in his sincerity (pp. 117–18). The 'agonistic', competitive nature of rhetoric in the ancient world, he writes (perhaps echoing his friend Jacob Burckhardt), meant that the weapons with which orators fought had to be not only powerful but beautiful, so that eloquence was meant to be both ethically moving and aesthetically pleasing, arousing the audience's *admiratio,* which Cicero and Quintilian—both quoted by Nietzsche—held to be an essential result of oratory (see above, p. 315).

Whether Nietzsche got his knowledge of rhetoric direct from the classical sources or from modern surveys (the latter seems the case for his somewhat confusing account of the tropes: p. 129 n. 67) is irrelevant. Once the full texts become available (including his lecture notes on Aristotle's *Rhetoric*) we should be able to confirm an interim judgment that Nietzsche was fully aware of the whole social and political function of classical rhetoric, its powers of persuasion, its use of *movere,* its various genres and categories, and its detailed teaching on the tropes and figures. Yet in Paul de Man's account Nietzsche's interest in rhetoric seems oddly one-sided. De Man makes two major claims. First, that 'Nietzsche moves the study of rhetoric away from techniques of eloquence and persuasion (*Beredsamkeit*) by making these dependent on a previous theory of *figures of speech or* [sic!] *tropes*' (*Allegories of Reading*, p. 105; my italics). Secondly, that for Nietzsche 'the figurative structure is not one linguistic mode among others but it characterizes language as such' (ibid.). The passages cited to substantiate both points derive from the same section in Nietzsche's notes, §7, on tropes, itself largely derivative from Gerber. De Man claims that the second point 'marks a full reversal' of established priorities, from a conception of language 'in its adequacy to an extralinguistic referent or meaning' to one directed to 'the intralinguistic resources of figures' (p. 106).

Even from the very brief account I have given of Nietzsche's notes on rhetoric it is clear that the first point is quite without substance. Nietzsche has no programme to move the study of rhetoric away from eloquence and persuasion. Nor does he make persuasion 'dependent on a previous theory' of the tropes: this is de Man's own formulation, stated earlier in his book (p. 6), and in fact Nietzsche fails to make an explicit connection between the tropes and persuasion. As for the second point, de Man represents Nietzsche's opinions more accurately, but the deduction that a belief in the figurality of language means a shift from an extralinguistic to an intralinguistic concept of rhetoric is not Nietzsche's but de Man's, already made in his opening essay, *in propria persona* (p. 8). It should by now be evident that de Man is ascribing to Nietzsche attitudes towards rhetoric that he himself holds. De Man's account is highly selective, once more, again using small points from his author to support his own much larger claims. A fragment in *The Will to Power* (1888) on chronological reversal, the fluctuating priorities of cause and effect, inside and outside, is set beside the account of metonymy or metalepsis in the rhetoric notes (1872) to claim that both texts give language 'the possibility of substituting binary polarities such as before for after, . . . cause for effect, without regard for the truth-value of these structures' (p. 107–9). By running together two texts working at radically different levels and in quite different contexts de Man is able to diagnose what he calls 'the general drift of Nietzsche's thought', no less, namely 'the possibility of escaping from the pitfalls of rhetoric by becoming aware of the rhetoricity of language' (p. 110). That seems, however, his problem, not Nietzsche's. The underlying deconstructionist's preoccupation appears unmistakably in de Man's judgment of Nietzsche's essay 'On Truth and Lie in an Extra-Moral Sense', that 'although it presents itself legitimately as a demystification of literary rhetoric' it 'remains entirely literary, rhetorical, and deceptive itself' (p. 113). Once again, the desired impasse is achieved, with an air of satisfaction at having reached the *quod erat demonstrandum*.

In de Man's mental universe rhetoric is fated to a condition of deceit and mystification from which it is ceaselessly but fruitlessly trying to escape. Literature, and indeed language, suffer similar fates, so that, rather like Plato's arraignment of rhetoric with tragedy and music, the defender of rhetoric once again finds himself in congenial company. Yet why should rhetoric be ascribed this self-disruptive, fruitlessly un-self-healing fate? That is a hard question to answer, but the other essay on Nietzsche, 'Rhetoric of Persuasion' (given de Man's rejection of persuasion this is perhaps meant as a deliberate *oxymoron* or self-contradiction), pushes this diagnosis to its extreme point. De Man starts with a long passage from the posthumous fragments known as *The Will to Power* which challenges that basic tenet of philosophy since Aristotle, the principle of non-contradiction, the impossibility of affirming and denying the same thing (pp. 119–21). Readers must judge for themselves the cogency of Nietzsche's argument on this head, and de Man's account of it (as he says, 'the text does not simultaneously affirm and deny identity but it denies affirmation': p. 124). I want to pick up the discussion later, where de Man surprisingly bends his account of *The Will to Power*, sections 477 to 479, which is said to effect the deconstruction of consciousness and of thought as act (p. 129), back to his earlier discussion of Nietzsche's rhetoric.

De Man now claims that the Course on Rhetoric 'starts out from a pragmatic distinction between rhetoric as a system of tropes and rhetoric as having to do with the skills of persuasion' (p. 136). Anyone who takes the trouble to consult the text will see that it does nothing of the kind, as my summary above has shown. To understand de Man's reading of Nietzsche we must read him as he said we should read Derrida or Rousseau, namely substituting the critic's name for the author's. So, he goes on,

> Nietzsche [de Man] contemptuously dismisses the popular meaning of rhetoric as eloquence and concentrates instead on the complex and philosophically challenging epistemology of the tropes . . . Privileging figure over persuasion is a typically post-Romantic [de Man] gesture. (p. 130)

The references to history and specific texts begin to take on a hallucinatory or purely imaginary quality, as in the comments that in Plato 'rhetoric becomes the ground for the furthest-reaching dialectical speculations conceivable to the mind' (a grandiose affirmation with little content or meaning), whereas in the 'text books that have undergone little change [*sic!*] from Quintillian [*sic!*] to the present', rhetoric 'is the humble and not-quite-respectable handmaiden of the fraudulent grammar used in oratory; Nietzsche himself begins his course by pointing out this discrepancy and documenting it with examples taken from Plato and elsewhere' (ibid.). Nietzsche did not in fact begin his course like that, but that is how de Man began his book—or at least placed first an essay which called grammar in question.

The degree of assimilation of Nietzsche to his own views on rhetoric, language, and literature, reaches its height in the last page of de Man's essay, where he ascribes to Nietzsche the 'final insight' that 'what is called "rhetoric" is precisely the gap' that de Man has just posited between the 'philosophical' and 'pedagogical' traditions, represented by Plato (!) and Quintilian:

> Considered as persuasion, rhetoric is performative but when considered as a system of tropes, it deconstructs its own performance. Rhetoric is a *text* in that it allows for two incompatible, mutually self-destructive points of view, and therefore puts an insurmountable obstacle in the way of any reading or understanding. The aporia between performance and constative language is merely a version of the aporia between trope and persuasion that both generates and paralyzes rhetoric and thus gives it the appearance of a history. (p. 131)

That is perhaps the most extraordinary statement about rhetoric made in its long history. Yet it is entirely typical of de Man's deconstructionist methods in the way it fractures rhetoric into persuasion on the one hand, tropes on the other, dismisses the first without discussion, finds an inherent flaw in the second, and then juxtaposes them as 'incompatible, mutually self-destructive'—one of those activities being superfluous (a deliberate *pleonasmus*?). This is as if to say that verbs and nouns were always fighting against each other, or themselves, thus making communication impossible. In Paul de Man's theory of literature rhetoric becomes grist to the deconstructionist mill, which 'both generates and paralyzes' not just rhetoric but literary criticism, discourse itself.

De Man's influence on contemporary criticism, especially in America, has been great, and it may well be beneficial. But as regards rhetoric, his effect can only be harmful, for the totally unhistorical and self-confusing nature of his raids on rhetoric could paralyse and stultify any further thought. The concern that any responsible student of rhetoric must feel over this idiosyncratic distortion has been expressed by at least one reviewer of *Allegories of Reading*, Jeffrey Barnouw.[13] Analysing de Man's account of Proust, which claims to find an opposition between metaphor and metonymy (de Man's definition of which, Barnouw says, is 'scandalously loose and slippery': p. 460), and hence a disjunction between 'the aesthetically responsive and the rhetorically aware reading', Barnouw comments that

> the wide gap between his 'reading' and the textual basis in the passage from Proust suggests that the model, far from being derived from the experience of reading, is *a priori* and arbitrary. Its affinities with the 'self-consuming artifact' of Stanley Fish include the capacity to create difficulties in and for a text. The difficulties in either case are not real, however, but simply needed for the therapeutic effects of reading. (p. 461)

'Therapeutic' for the deconstructionist implies reading a text so as to reach what de Man calls a 'state of suspended ignorance' (*Allegories*, p. 19), the sceptic's *aporia* or doubt, what I have called the impasse.

Quoting de Man's conclusions to his Nietzsche chapters, with its discovery (or creation) of what we might call structural *aporiai* within rhetoric, Barnouw comments that de Man's claim to reach this conclusion 'by means of reading and presumably understanding what Nietzsche wrote is just the sort of "paradox" that de Man would see as in some way confirming his approach' (p. 462). But Barnouw re-examines the long excerpt from *The Will to Power* which de Man quotes and shows that his account of it is seriously misleading. In it Nietzsche argues that the principle of identity 'reflects not an objective impossibility and necessity but a subjective inability', the subject's 'need to reduce things to a manageable order', to 'posit and arrange a world that should be true for us'. He is referring to logic, not language, arguing that 'our sense of reality, our awareness of entities, precedes and underlies logic', so that it is a basic error to ' "make of logic a criterion of true being" ' (p. 462). De Man, however, applies Nietzsche's point to a much larger and tendentious argument about 'types of utterance' and the fundamental schism that he finds within rhetoric, as within language itself. The way de Man applies to language what in fact refers to logic is an example of what I mean by saying that he 'bends' Nietzsche's thought to his own concerns. As Barnouw shows, having followed out de Man's development of his reading, 'the paradoxical deconstructive discourse is not Nietzsche's, it is read in by de Man against the intrinsic direction of the text' (p. 463). In the end we are left with a critical methodology 'in which a theory of reading effectively undermines the capacity to read' (ibid.). In such a method, we can now see, it was inevitable that rhetoric should have to be split in two and made to attack itself. De Man may have thought of himself as a friend to rhetoric, but his use of it for his own purposes is more destructive than many of its enemies' explicit attacks.

It is worth refuting this deconstruction of rhetoric, even at the risk of being called antipathetic to 'modern literary theory', since a rather important issue is at stake, namely the nature of human communication. De Man aims to deny language any power to refer to events or objects or experience outside itself. All tropes, then, can be faulted in so far as they claim to refer to an outside world that exists independent of language. So, he baldly asserts,

> metaphor is error because it believes or feigns to believe in its own referential meaning. . . . Metaphor overlooks the fictional, textual element in the nature of the entity it connotes. It assumes a world in which intra-and extra-textual events . . . can be distinguished. . . . This is an error, although it can be said that no language would be possible without this error. . . . To the extent that all language is conceptual, it always already speaks about language and not about things. (*Allegories*, pp. 151–2)

In his final sentence de Man disintegrates the linguistic sign, which Saussure formulated (in terms that actually go back to classical linguistics) as 'signified over signifer', that is, drawing a clear distinction between the word (signifier)' and the thing or concept (signified) that it denotes. In Saussure's terminology the two parts of the sign are divided by a line (as used in the representation of fractions) in order to emphasize that they exist on different planes, but nevertheless form a unity. Whereas linguistic materialists collapse the distinction, turning words into things, deconstructionists throw away half of it, creating a mental world in which signifiers 'float freely', or are 'liberated' from the burden of meaning.

We can understand deconstruction historically, as a phase in twentieth-century thought reflecting a loss of confidence by some highly intelligent, highly educated people about the nature of language, or as another reaction against positivism, a further calling in question of received certainties. Such questioning can be exhilarating, and salutary, but in this case I feel it to be an inward-turning, self-disruptive process, which denies literature a 'mimetic' relationship with the world just as it denies language a referential aspect. Of course, many literary texts contain an element of commentary on, or at least awareness of their own status as works fashioned by one human being according to certain artistic conventions for other humans to read and, presumably, enjoy—that is, to have their lives enriched by a greater awareness of the possibilities of literature, and language. But to declare such an element of self-awareness or self-commentary to be the primary function of literature, and to deny it any ability to represent human behaviour, is to start from a dualism (represent the world/represent itself) and turn it into a monism that is peculiarly debilitating, since it condemns literature to a self-reflexive concern with its own inability to represent, or with the incapacity of language to do so. As Jeffrey Barnouw has said,

> If a 'text' can only qualify itself as 'literature' by deconstructively turning on itself, the eventual result will be an impoverishment of what literature can say to us, because we no longer bring to it questions about our world. Awareness of the metaphorical and reflexive character of language in use, and particularly in literature, should rather lead us to recognize and explore the way language gives us access to the world at the same time that it informs the world.[14]

Deconstruction is a challenge to modern critical theory in that it calls in question the whole of our thinking about language, and literature, since the earliest records of the Greeks. The challenge has come from a highly ingenious and articulate sector of modern philosophy, which seems to have lost touch with ordinary reality. We need to remind ourselves, perhaps, of some emphases in modern linguistics that offer an alternative view of language. R. H. Robins, in his brief but penetrating history of grammatical theory,[15] objected to the Stoics' distinction between signified and signifier because, if taken literally, 'it leads to the unhelpful conception of "the meaning" as something actually existing' as an isolatable entity which can be evaluated in purely logical terms (p. 26). But the 'completeness' or otherwise of an utterance, he asserts, 'depends on its fulfilling the purpose intended by speaker or writer in its context of situation and can only be tested in relation to that context' (pp. 28–9). One weakness of Greek and Roman grammar was that 'language was considered too much as the expression of thought complete in itself, and its dependence on context, the world around, for its functioning was largely ignored' (p. 44). Later, medieval speculative grammarians made grammar the handmaid of philosophy. 'Language was for them'—as it is, I interject, for the deconstructionists, albeit with different implications—'the verbal expression of the thought of the intellect. This extraordinarily narrow and distorted conception of language', Robins writes, has persisted into our time, hindering the development of linguistics. To understand language fully, we must see it 'in its proper light as part of human co-operation, part of social action, in all the everyday situations in which men and women find themselves' (p. 89). We must situate language in the world, in concrete human situations, for 'it is contextual function alone that constitutes and guarantees linguistic meaning' (p. 92). Deconstructionists, living in social contexts, using language according to social codes, interacting with the world around them, nevertheless deny language any reliable function in reporting or creating that world, and grant literature even less relation to reality. This does seem a major paradox, especially since deconstructionist theory flourishes on its own gestures of denial and restriction. Some sense must be getting through.

My concern is to defend rhetoric, and a proper defence of language in its referential mode and its social context can be left to linguistics, phenomenology, and some of the social sciences. I would doubt whether the isolation and introversion of language created by deconstructionism would survive an honest confrontation with their work, but that is a task that must be left to other hands.

NOTES

1 *The Cambridge History of Classical Literature*. Vol. I, *Greek Literature*, ed. P. E. Easterling and B. M. W. Knox (Cambridge, 1985); Vol II, *Latin Literature*, ed. E. J. Kenney and W. V. Clausen (Cambridge, 1982).

2 *The Oxford History of the Classical World*, eds. J. Boardman, J. Griffin, O. Murray

(Oxford, 1986).

3 A recently announced series by the University of Wisconsin Press is called 'Rhetoric of the Human Sciences', which will analyse 'various disciplines, not as the "sciences" they sometimes claim to be, but as "rhetorics"—that is, as systems of belief and practice, each of which has its own characteristic form and structure': announcement in *The New York Review of Books,* 30 Jan. 1986,p. 17. This is to widen the meaning of rhetoric to the point of no return.

4 *A Grammar of Motives* (New York, 1945), pp. 503–17. Burke's debt to Vico is clear in such passages as these: 'If you trail language back far enough, of course, you will find that all our terms for "spiritual" states were metonymic in origin. . . . Language develops by metaphorical extension, in borrowing words from the realm of the corporeal, visible, tangible and applying them by analogy to the realm of the incorporeal, invisible, intangible, then in the course of time, the corporeal reference is forgotten . . .' (p. 506).

5 *Tropics of Discourse. Essays in Cultural Criticism* (Baltimore, Md., 1978); references in the text.

6 See Brian Vickers, 'On the Function of Analogy in the Occult', in A. Debus and I. Merkel (eds.), *Hermeticism and the Renaissance* (Cranbury, NJ, 1988), pp. 265–92.

7 'Two Aspects of Language and Two Types of Aphasic Disturbances', in R. Jakobson and M. Halle, *Fundamentals of Language* (The Hague, 1956), pp. 53–82; references in the text.

8 *English Composition and Rhetoric,* enlarged edition, 2 vols. (London, 1886–7), i.135–232.

9 *Figures of Thought in Roman Poetry* (New Haven, Conn., 1980).

10 Genette's three volumes entitled *Figures* include a number of essays on rhetoric. *Figures I* (Paris, 1966) has an interesting study of Etienne Binet's 1621 rhetoric-book (pp. 170–83), and an essay called 'Figures' (pp. 205–21) that unfortunately regards figures solely as 'deviations' from normal speech rather than expressive devices in their own right. *Figures II* (Paris, 1969) has an excellent essay on 'Rhétorique et enseignement' (p. 23–42), while *Figures III* (Paris, 1972) includes the text I shall discuss, 'La Rhétorique restreinte' (pp. 21–40), also available in English as 'Rhetoric Restrained' in Genette, *Figures of Literary Discourse,* tr. A. Sheridan (Oxford, 1982), pp. 103–26. (Instead of 'restrained' I would translate 'reduced' or 'restricted'.) My quotations are from the last-named essay, in the original. For Genette's editions of Du Marsais and Fontanier see p. 197 n. 46.

11 Quotations are from J.-J. Rousseau, *Essai sur l'origine des langues, où il est parlé de la mélodie et de l'imitation musicale,* ed. C. Porset (Paris, 1970), incorporated into the text. The editor reproduces Rousseau's manuscript orthography.

12 The most coherent presentation of this material to date is in the French translation by P. Lacoue-Labarthe and J.-L. Nancy, 'Friedrich Nietzsche, *Rhétorique et langagé, Poétique,* 5 (1970), 99–142, from which I quote in summary or paraphrase, with references in the text.

13 In *Comparative Literature Studies,* 19 (1982), 459–63, page-references incorporated into the text.

14 Barnouw, reviewing the Rousseau chapters in de Man's *Allegories of Reading,* in *The Eighteenth Century: A Current Bibliography,* ns. 6(1980), 338–9.

15 R. H. Robins, *Ancient and Medieval Grammatical Theory in Europe with Particular Reference to Modern Linguistic Doctrine* (London, 1951); page-references included in the text.

Ancient and Medieval Rhetoric

The periods of ancient and medieval rhetoric—a vast chronological span that, scholars argue, lasts approximately from the fifth century BCE to the fifteenth century CE—hold the seeds of the theory of rhetoric debated and developed in contemporary intellectual circles. In the treatises on rhetorical theory and practice from Greece in the fifth, fourth, and third centuries BCE, from Rome in the four or five centuries following that, and from the whole of western Europe for another millenium, we find the sources of major concepts of rhetorical theory—exigence, audience, invention, arrangement, style, memory, and delivery—being developed to serve the needs of rhetors and teachers in the Athenian democracy, the Roman Republic, and later the spreading world of Christianity.

The standard history of rhetorical theory in these periods has become well-rehearsed. When democratic government, particularly a judicial system to hear cases involving property conflicts, was introduced in Sicily in the fifth century BCE, a need arose suddenly for people to speak persuasively in public in the prosecution and defense of their own cases. According to legend, a teacher named Corax wrote a handbook of principles for constructing and delivering a persuasive speech. As others imitated Corax's apparently successful product, a tradition of handbooks—or *techne*, as the Greeks called them—grew up, providing prescriptive precepts for budding orators. At around the same time, a group of scholars later referred to as *sophists*, many of whom were philosophers, mathematicians, and musicians, began to offer instruction in public speaking based on set speeches—"show pieces"—that would-be orators could imitate. According to the standard history, Plato responded to both the handbook writers and the sophists by claiming that neither party was able to teach rhetors to speak the truth, and thus their art was questionable. In response to Plato's calls for an ideal, philosophical rhetoric, Aristotle produced his *Art of Rhetoric*, aiming to illustrate an art of public speaking, a counterpart of dialectic, in which rhetors would be able to establish a "truth" and persuade an audience to accept it. A few centuries later in Rome, orators such as Cicero took parts of all the Greek traditions—the handbooks, the sophistic teaching, and the philosophical rhetoric of Plato and Aristotle—and developed a theory of public speaking particularly suited to his time's political and social context. In the waning years of the Republic, the Roman Quintilian synthesized about seven centuries of rhetorical theory, creating a body of thought about oratory and eloquence that was then adapted and put to use in the spread of Christianity throughout western Europe.

Like many "received" histories, this standard view is sweeping and a bit reductive, but it need not be dismissed entirely. It has been centuries in the making, and scholars who have developed it have provided illuminating constructions of theoretical principles and rich, sensitive reconstructions of these concepts' histories. The first two works in this part are exemplary of the best traditional scholarship in the history of rhetorical theory. William M. A. Grimaldi, for example, examines one philosophical concept from Aristotle's *Rhetoric*, the *topoi* or "places" of an argument, and shows how the *topoi* serve two functions, helping the orator both to find substantial material about his or her topic and to develop the topic using myriad forms of inference. Mary Carruthers examines the concept of *cogitatio* in the medieval rhetorical world's theory of composition, richly demonstrating how memory and cogitation interact and produce the *res*, the substance, of speaker's discourse.

As valuable as the standard history of classical and medieval rhetoric is, however, contemporary scholars are justified in trying to expand the scope of what counts as rhetorical theory in the period. Surely, they say, there are abundant primary and secondary sources that show the origin and development of rhetorical theory that the scholarly world knows nothing about. Perhaps, they suggest, we can reconstruct histories of classical rhetoric so that, for instance, we can see for ourselves whether the sophists deserve the denigration that Plato heaps on them. In the first selection in this chapter, Susan Jarratt offers guidelines for developing new histories of classical rhetoric, urging scholars to consult new materials and sites of rhetorical activity, to postpone a scholarly urge to find complete closure and unity in rhetorical history, and to entertain notions of multiple, perhaps antithetical, causality in constructing their narratives.

Susan C. Jarratt

"Toward a Sophistic Historiography"

INTRODUCTION

While most histories of rhetoric begin with the sophists, I'd like to suggest that a revision of rhetorical *historiography* must begin with them as well. The point of starting with the sophists is not to privilege their originary or ontological status vis a vis "rhetoric" as a discipline—the "fact" that they invented a self-conscious practice of public discourse—but rather to identify the sophists with an explicitly historical mode of thought and to delineate its features toward the description of a twentieth-century practice of rhetorical history.[1]

The overlap of rhetoric and history in the work of the first sophists derives from the speculations of certain pre-Socratic philosophers who represent what Havelock calls the "biological-historical" view of human existence and institutions, a view which takes historical contingency as the crucial defining feature of the species (*LT* 30–31). These fifth-century B.C. Greek anthropologists—Anaximander, Xenophanes, Anaxagoras, Archelaus—understood not only physiology but also cultural mores as changing products of evolutionary process (*LT* 104f). Theirs is a basically diachronic understanding of human existence and stands in opposition to the ahistorical, "religious–metaphysical" orientation arising out of the universalist tendencies of Pythagoras and Parmenides and finding its fullest expression in Plato. The war between rhetoric and philosophy is a version of that opposition: between the temporal and the eternal, the contingent and the universal.

Of special interest to the sophists was the range of group behaviors they took note of in traveling among the Greek city/states (Guthrie 55). They understood that any discourse seeking to effect action or shape knowledge must take into account those differences. Not only was it essential to judge the circumstances obtaining at the moment of an oration, its *kairos,* but even more essential was the orator/alien's understanding of the local *nomoi:* community-specific customs and laws. The sophists translated the natural scientists' observations about the temporality of human existence into a coherent body of commentary on the use of discourse in the function of the social order: that is, they concentrated on the power of language in shaping human group behavior explicitly within the limits of time and space. Sophistic rhetoric, then, as an instrument of social action in the *polis* was bound to the flux.

Given this definition of the sophists as "historicist" (Streuver 11), it's possible to describe a historiography for rhetoric loosely based on certain features of their thought and practice. I intend for this historiography to indicate a direction for the future of rhetorical history in the twentieth century: it is a historiography in the subjunctive mode.[2] Rather than critiquing extensively or categorizing current histories of rhetoric (Schilb "History"; Vitanza "Historiographies"), some of which already contain strains of what is here styled sophistic rhetorical history, I instead look to the works of the sophists themselves as a creative analog for a particular kind of historical practice. Though the sophists didn't write "histories" as we understand the genre today, in certain of their fragments and attributions historical representation plays a significant part.[3] They created a discursive practice preceding the hardening of generic categories like "history" but always pervaded by an awareness of the historical. Thus both a general sophistic attitude toward history and specific examples of sophistic historical representation will provide the elements of a revised historiography for rhetoric.

The practice of a sophistic historiography entails:

1. a redefinition and consequent expansion of the materials and subject matters of rhetorical history, resulting in what today would be styled multi-disciplinary—historical investigations on the margins of traditionally conceived disciplines;

2. the denial of progressive continuity: a conscious attempt to disrupt the metaphor of a complete and full chain of events with a *telos* in the revival of rhetoric in the twentieth century; and,

3. the employment of two pre-logical language *techné*, antithesis and parataxis, creating narratives distinguished by multiple or open causality, the indeterminacies of which are then resolved through the self-conscious use of probable arguments.

The resulting narratives will set aside "the history of rhetoric" in favor of "rhetorical histories"—provisional, culturally relevant "fictions of factual representation" (White *Tropics*).

THE EXPANSION OF MATERIALS AND SITES OF RHETORICAL ACTIVITY

Traditional histories of rhetoric could be defined as those histories having taken as their subject matter chiefly documents explicitly calling themselves "rhetorics": that is, pedagogical treatises concerned with the composition and delivery of persuasive orations (Kennedy; Howell).[4] This selection is based on a narrow definition of rhetoric as the teaching and performance of an opinion-based discourse for use in the social sphere as distinct from the poetic and the philosophical or scientific. The thought and practice of the sophists themselves, however, was never so narrowly defined. They were interested in a whole group of intellectual materials and social actions, the common feature of which was language use. It might be argued that Plato and Aristotle as well exhibited such a range of interests, but the difference is that, for the sophists, all other subjects were subsumed under the rhetorical. In their works, rhetoric permeated every topic: natural science and "epistemology" (Protagoras B1–2; Gorgias, *On Nature* B1–5; Prodicus B3–4; Antiphon B66c), social and political theory (Protagoras C1; Thrasymachus B6a; Antiphon B129–151), aesthetic response and psychology (Protagoras B1; Gorgias, *Encomium to Helen* B11; Antiphon B123), law (Protagoras B6; Gorgias B11a; Antiphon B1–66), religion and ethics (Protagoras A23, B4; Gorgias A28), as well as language theory and pedagogy (Protagoras A 5, 21, 26; Gorgias B14).[5] Sophistic "rhetoric" collided and interbred with literature, science, and philosophy before such interests were bracketed by Aristotle as disciplines. Just as the sophists engaged in a wide range of eclectic intellectual and social activities before the constraints of Platonic/Aristotelian metaphysics and epistemology cordoned off investigations of human mental and physical behavior, so can they serve today as a point of reference for the formation of a comprehensive historical practice unfettered by strict disciplinary boundaries, a practice of history neither exclusively "intellectual" nor "social" (Schilb "History") nor even strictly "factual" in differentiation from the fictional (White *Tropics*). The revisionary historian today will work with an expanded range of materials: not only the pedagogical treatises summarized in traditional histories, but any literary artifact as it operates to shape knowledge and effect social action. The *identification* of materials at an active site becomes as much the work of the revisionary historian as her commentary on them.

There are several forces in play in the academic scene which have circumscribed the province of histories of rhetoric over the last few decades. The disciplinary structure of the universities and presses oftentimes puts a historian of "rhetoric," today lacking a strong deciplinary identity, in competition with scholars in overlapping disciplines of more stability or prestige. George Kennedy, for example, writing classical history of rhetoric, must compete with the ponderous philological productions typical in classical scholarship. Likewise, Wilbur Samuel Howell works within the generally atheoretical, positivist conventions of European intellectual history. The problem of overlap works in reverse as well. The general academic prejudice against rhetoric—a long-term effect of Platonic censure—has at times forced scholars in other disciplines to diminish the significance of rhetoric or simply redefine rhetorical materials as they appear in their histories. Havelock in *Liberal Temper,* for example, elaborates a sophistic "theory and practice of communication" (216), which includes an "epistemology of public opinion" along with a "theory of popular cognition and decision" (220). Though all of those descriptions easily fall within the purview of "rhetoric" broadly defined, Havelock mentions the term only briefly and in a pejorative context (206).[6] Two recent books on the sophists by Guthrie (1971) and Kerferd (1981) are the first extensive and favorable treatments in classics since Hegel and Grote in the last century.

In departments of English, the hegemony of literary studies has shaped the recent practice of history of rhetoric in several ways. The notion of history of rhetoric as a history of writing instruction has evolved naturally out of the recent revolution in writing pedagogy. Such an approach serves a genuine desire to know something about forgotten teachers and their ways while at the same time satisfying conventional disciplinary requirements for transforming "composition" into a distinct and legitimate area of study—it can be shown to have a history. But it's a definition with draw-backs, as well, for both composition and literature. Literary scholars, under such an arrangement, can keep the new co-habitant of the "English" department from usurping already well-staked turf (Harkin). But at the same time this narrow definition of rhetoric also keeps in place an equally narrow view of "literature" (Eagleton).

The movement from a disciplinary "history of rhetoric" to a postdisciplinary rhetorical historiography demands an expansion of the field of study. A shattering of categories like "literature," while potentially politically troublesome, must become an essential feature of a revised rhetorical historiography. "Rhetoric" at its most fruitful has historically functioned as a meta-discipline through which a whole spectrum of language uses and their outcomes as social action can be refracted for analysis and combination. In terms of physical evidence and pedagogical practice, the point is most radically to reconsider the notion of a canon. The rhetorician has from the beginning been a generalist. The goal for the historian in an age of vast and highly specialized knowledge should become neither the mastery of a limited body of texts nor the impossible task of knowing everything and ordering it, but rather an agility in moving between disciplines, standing back from them with the critical perspective characteristic of both history and rhetoric (Streuver 197f.) for the purpose of illuminating meaningful connections, disjunctions, overlaps, or exclusions. The choice of texts for any particular history will become an expression of *ethos*—an idiosyncratic, charismatic assertion of the relevance of a particular combination of materials. Already rhetorical historians are beginning to venture outside the most limited version of what constitutes "rhetoric" and into other areas. Berlin and Covino have taken on traditionally literary figures Emerson and De Quincey; LeFevre includes Freud and Kant in a study of invention; Campbell and Bazerman have begun rhetorical investigations of scientific discourse with studies of Darwin and contemporary physicists. Striking examples of the direction rhetorical histories could take are pointed by Foucault's studies of sexuality, prisons and punishment; G. E. R. Lloyd's investigations of linguistic structures, science, and folklore in ancient Greece; and the work of Michel Serres.

While the general historicism of the first sophists suggests an attitude toward history, two texts from the period will provide a model for the practice of rhetorical historiography. In both Gorgias' *Encomium of Helen* and the Great Speech of "Protagoras" in Plato's dialogue⁷ a multiplicity of subjects comprehended under rhetoric are interwoven into an historical narrative. *Helen,* an argument seeking to deny her responsibility in starting the Trojan War, offers speculation on morals, the psychology of reception, the relation between sense impressions and language;

Protagoras' retelling of the Prometheus myth in response to Socrates' question about teaching virtue takes into consideration the origin and development of the species, language, pedagogy, and social philosophy. It could be argued that such discourses are irrelevant to the modern situation because of the differences in genre. The encomium and the parable, though both contain elements common to history, have histories of their own as genres. I would respond that a recuperation of literary sub-genres congruent to history as a strict empirical science would not be a fruitless enterprise for rhetorical historians, for whom an expansion of materials may suggest a concomitant reconsideration of generic categories.[8]

Perhaps an even more troublesome problem for the contemporary historian in accepting these two discourses as models for history writing is their mythic status: the raw material for both histories is what we would today take to be exclusively "literary" or "fictional." But in both discourses what is more significant than establishing irrefutable facts is the choice of an historical incident for its usefulness in the reconstruction and interpretation of culturally meaningful and instructive pasts. The opportunities for speculation provided by the narrative situation in each case—on the power of *logos* in *Helen* and on the role of language in our evolution as a species in *Protagoras*—supersedes the establishment of the "factual" status of the materials themselves as a goal for the discourse. I'm certainly not suggesting that rhetorical historians fabricate a past that never existed but rather that a view of history as merely uncovering lost "facts" doesn't take fully enough into account the inevitably literary or mythic quality of any historical reconstruction and its relevance to the present. The use of these sophistic historical arguments as analogs for a contemporary historical practice is intended to encourage an increased self-consciousness about that process of reconstruction as it functions to open for investigation fruitful questions about belief, purpose and self-definition rather than answer questions of "fact."

THE DISRUPTION OF PROGRESSIVE CONTINUITY

In each sophistic discourse, the retelling of a well-known story throws into question existing versions. Gorgias casts doubt on Helen's responsibility for the Trojan War; Protagoras' Prometheus stands in sharp contrast to earlier characterizations. Whereas both Hesiod's and Aeschylus' narratives culminate in the conflict between the Titan and Zeus, the sophist downplays that outcome and focuses on the god's concern for the fate of the human species. Each sophistic discourse disrupts a stable historical narrative and subverts the teleology of its analogs. Gorgias' retelling of the abduction of Helen explicitly throws into question the moral censure of her behavior:

Helen [is] a woman about whom the testimony of inspired poets has become univocal and unanimous as had the ill omen of her name, which has become a reminder of misfortunes. For my part . . . I wish to free the accused of blame and, having reproved her detractors as prevaricators and proved the truth, to free her from their ignorance. (Sprague B114)

In so doing, the sophistic historian disrupts the continuity of the given historical narrative which uses Helen to take the blame for what could be re-seen as a petty and destructive adventure launched by a few ill-advised toughs with disastrous consequences for the whole society. In terms of the broader issue of cultural values, holding Helen responsible for the archaic war reflected and reinforced the fatalism (and misogyny) of the period. By pulling out that crucial link in the chain of events leading to the war, Gorgias opened up the causal chain, not only implicitly calling into question the historical reasons for her condemnation but, more important, introducing new issues of significance in the present as a consequence: questions about the relations or similarities between love and force, language and love, language and force. In the fledgling Athenian democracy, the power of persuasive speech was a new and potent force which Gorgias' discourse aimed to investigate. Through breaking the tight, uni-directional causal chain—of consciously refusing to tell history as a continuous, complete narrative leading to a pre-understood end—the sophist was able to throw into new light a range of facts and causes for the purpose of a more general consideration. Streuver associates sophistic rhetoric with a historical practice which continually redefines rather than affirms a pre-existing definition. Havelock links the sophists with a school of historical writers including first-centuryA.D. Diodorus Siculus who attempted encyclopedic projects—histories which didn't lend themselves to strong thematic structure (*LT* 73).

The issues of continuity and teleology are complicated in the case of Protagoras' Promethean myth by the fact that it's ultimately Plato's discourse. Havelock's sensitive reading of the story in three stages offers a convincing method for extracting what can be verified as the sophistic elements in the narrative through comparison with other sources. In the first stage of "Protagoras" story, the brothers Prometheus and Epimetheus are assigned the task of distributing faculties to the various creatures at the time of creation. Epimetheus thoughtlessly gives away all the qualities of physical strength and protection, so his fore-sightful brother steals fire and, more important, the technological skill needed to use it for humans. The second stage of the story finds humans building cities, using language, tilling the soil, but still in danger of extinction by wild beasts and war among themselves. At this moment, Zeus intervenes in the evolutionary development, bestowing divine gifts of justice and respect equally distributed among humans, though technical skill is not. Havelock argues that the third stage can be read as Plato's co-opting of what began as an anthropological account of human development for a defence of in-born excellence as the basis of an aristocratic political order (*LT* 87–94). Though there is no way of knowing how the historical Protagoras would have carried on the story, his well-known agnosticism makes it reasonably certain that his account would not have included the intercession of a divine force. Though Havelock sees in Protagoras' portion of the story an evolutionary continuity leading to a justification for a democratic political structure, that very use of the Prometheus myth, I would argue, represents a "revision" of the other versions—Hesiod's, Aeschylus', and Plato's—in each of which human creation and development is delimited by and culminates in the authority of Zeus.[9]

The point for a modern rhetorical historiography is the disruption of the conventional expectation that a history be a complete, replete, full, and logically consistent narrative record. The ancient idea of the Great Chain of Being, much older even than its eighteenth-century revival, is still a contending epistemological metaphor in the twentieth century. While the positivism of the nineteenth century removed the necessity for a transcendent source for the order, the desire for "data" which fill in a pre-formulated hypothesis remains strong. Not only is the chain full, but it has direction. For historical practice, the model dictates the location of every datum on a ladder advancing up to or down from a certain culminating point.

The point of breaking the chain, of resisting the impulse to fit historical materials into a neat, continuous line from beginning to end especially for rhetorical historians is to achieve a kind of critical distance which allows for re-vision. Rather than attempting to trace a line of thought from A to B, the rhetorical historian will seek to re-group and redefine. The point is to expose an increasing *complexity* of evidence or data, to resist the simplification which covers over subtleties, to exploit complexity toward the goal of greater explanatory power. The revisionary historian of rhetoric will look not for superficial similarities which group themselves quickly into "species" but will persist in confounding categories by looking longer and discovering finer and finer shades of difference—more and more varieties. She will see the sophist in Plato, Augustine, and Bacon; the hidden Platonist in Nietzsche.

There are several candidates for metaphors to replace the chain or ladder. Foucault argues in "The Discourse on Language" for the replacement of continuities with "events and series" combined through a theory of "discontinuous systematization" (230–31). He represents this process figuratively as cutting a "slice" or finding a "staging post" (232)—metaphors similar to White's figuration of "Contextualist" historical arguments as those which "incline more toward synchronic representations of segments or sections of the process, cuts made across the grain of time as it were" (*Metahistory* 19). The problem is describing a historical practice which denies both "mechanically causal links and an ideal necessity" among events (Foucault, "Discourse" 231). Nietzsche offers the notion of "genealogy" in contrast to history as a solution—a concept which receives its most powerful articulation in Darwin's evolutionary theory. Though Foucault, in reading Nietzsche on history, discredits "evolution" as an attempt to "map the destiny of a people" ("Nietzsche" 146), Darwin's reading of natural history exactly parallels Foucault's description of a proper historical practice: "to follow the complex course of descent is to maintain passing events in their proper dispersion; it is to identify the accidents, the minute deviations—or conversely, the complete reversals—the errors, the false appraisals, and the faulty calculations that gave birth to those things that continue to exist and have value for us" ("Nietzsche" 146).[10] Stephen Jay Gould's pedestrian metaphor for Darwinian historiography—the bush—offers a strong contender to replace the ladder as a way of re-seeing events both within their complex relations diachronically and in series through time. Any one of the multitude of possible revisionary reconstructions will follow a "circuitous path running like a labyrinth, branch to branch, from the base of the bush to a lineage now surviving at its top" (Gould 61).

The differences in outcome between a traditional or continuous history and a discontinuous alternative can be observed among the current treatments of the sophists themselves. On the ladder view, the first sophists' stylistic innovations provided the raw materials for Plato's dialectic and later Aristotle's logic of non-contradiction. Their emotional appeals and arguments from probability were systematized and legitimized by Aristotle's *Art*. In short, they are significant as a link between the oral society of the archaic period and the literate flowering in the fourth century B.C. These explanations are recognizable as commonplaces of traditional histories of rhetoric (Guthrie; Kennedy; Havelock *Literate Revolution*). But reconsidered as a branch of a bush, the sophists become the practitioners of a rhetoric which represents an independent and legitimate alternative response to the particular environment of the fifth-century B.C. Greek city-states—materialist, anthropological, "historical," "liberal," pragmatic (Enos; Havelock *Liberal Temper*). They become a source for analysis of a number of subsequent historical moments, such as Renaissance humanism (Streuver) and the "post-literate" media age of the late twentieth-century America (Corcoran).

What has led to such revisions and what emerges as a feature of a number of contemporary historiographical theories is the necessity for overturning givens: those sequences of event which have through repetition evolved from "truth" into truism. This impulse toward iconoclasm is variously described by Nietzsche as "critical history" (67), by Foucault as reversal (229), by White as the ironic mode (*Metahistory* 433). It is an expectation that "one can already be pretty sure that the stresses will not fall where we expect, and that taboos are not always to be found where we imagine them to be" (Foucault, "Discourse" 232). The sophists employed a verbal *techné* instrumental in effecting that critical, revisionary turn: antithesis. The stylistic device of setting in sequence opposing grammatical and lexical structures operates at a deeper level of narrative construction and causal linkage as an instrument of rhetorical historical practice.

ANTITHESIS AND PARATAXIS: HISTORY IN THE TRAGIC-COMIC MODE

The first two features of revisionary history—the broad range of materials and the denial of progressive continuity—complicate issues of "logical" structure and causal connection in historical narrative. Method becomes crucial and problematic under a reconsidered project of history. Here the legacy of the sophists is quite specific at the level of syntax. Their discursive practice suggests a two-stage process of historical composition—a tragic dissolution consonant with the iconoclastic movement of critical or ironic historiography followed by a "comic" reconstruction. Of the two syntactic structures therein employed, antithesis creates an openness to the multiplicity of possible causal relations; then parataxis demands the employment of probable arguments in the reconstitution of provisional historical narratives.

Antithesis   Under a traditional historiography, the sophist's antithetical pairings are interpreted in two ways. First, they're seen as a manipulative device for eliciting emotional effects in oratorical performance: the antithetical style creates "a tintinnabulation of rhyming words and echoing rhythms" with hypnotic effect on listening crowds (Kennedy 29). Second, in the development of logic, antithesis becomes a precursor to Socratic definition and, eventually, to an Aristotelian logic of noncontradiction, both of which work because they *exclude* one of the two options (Kerferd; Guthrie). Even in Solmsen's lengthy, serious treatment of the sophists' "intellectual experiments" (83–125), the assumption of a split between form and content leads to a generally suspicious attitude toward antithesis defined as a pre-logical stylistic device. For example, he describes Thucydides' use of the *techné* as an "idiosyncracy" (110), an "addiction" (84), something he's "not above" (84).

But other historians have introduced possibilities for interpreting antithesis extending beyond those traditional explanations. Finley's analysis of Thucydides' style acknowledges a more significant conceptual role for the *techné*. In arguing for a chronology of influence, Finley traces an increasing sophistication in its use from Homer to the earliest prose writers through Sophocles and Euripides and finally to the sophists. Though Finley discredits Gorgias as pressing antithesis to its "illogical conclusion" (112), he sees its use by others as fostering an expanding capacity for more complex generalization (109). Untersteiner goes further, describing the introduction of paired opposites as a Gorgian "tragic" sense of knowledge (101–161). Under this revisionist view, antithesis is not a spurious trick for clouding the minds of the listeners but rather works to awaken in them an awareness of the multiplicity of possible truths.[11] In Gorgias the antithetical style, because of the attitude toward causality it fosters, becomes a grammatical structure with implications for a historiographical method. Pairs of words or phrases in opposition set up alternative chains of causality and lead to a syntax expressing a multiplicity of probable connections between events rather than a single necessary cause. The sophistic historian will not "confine reality within a dogmatic scheme but allow it to rage in all its contradictions, in all its tragic intensity" (Untersteiner xvi). The sophists were less concerned with the "scientific" project of establishing specific events in a tight causal sequence than with exploring the possibilities for interpreting past events for present needs (Poulakos).

Gorgias' own revision of the story of Helen of Troy exemplifies the function of antithesis in the establishment of complex causal relations. In the speech, he aims to "set forth the causes through which it was likely that Helen's voyage to Troy should take place" (Sprague 51). What follows is an antithetical quartet of possible causes for the abduction: it was *either* fate *or* physical force *or* persuasion *or* love. But rather than excluding three causes in favor of one, setting up a necessary chain of causal relation, Gorgias focuses the discussion on the interplay among causes, the interrelation of the four. In this case, Gorgias insists upon an indeterminacy of situation in order to speculate on the power of *logos*—a force coming to be seen in the mid–fifth–century Greek *polis* as rivaling the fate of the gods or even physical violence in its power. Because of the gap between the reality of deeds—past, present, and future—and the words which represent them, any persuasion has an element of deception (Rosenmeyer; de Romilly). Thus Helen "against her will, might have come under the influence of speech, just as if ravished by the force of the mighty" (52). Though *logos* lacks the power of fate, it takes the same form, "constraining the soul . . . both to believe the things said and to approve the things done." The parallel between verbal persuasion and the desire created by a pleasing visual impression works as a third means of exploring the psychology of *logos* (Segal). At one point, Gorgias playfully suggests the scheme of a sophistic historiography, implicitly challenging the conventions of factual, continuous history, historical time, and simple cause/effect relations:

> Who it was and why and how he sailed away, taking Helen as his love, I shall not say. To tell the knowing what they know shows it is right but brings no delight. Having now gone beyond the time once set for my speech, I shall go on to the beginning of my future speech, and I shall set forth the causes through which it was likely that Helen's voyage to Troy should take place. (Sprague B115)

The importance of pleasure in the telling and the reference to the future indicate purposes for Gorgias' history. At the end of the speech, none of the four is identified as the single, or even primary cause. Antitheses have evolved into complex interrelations.

Thus Gorgias' "encomium" is capable of interpretation in terms of a historiographical method. Laying out a number of causes for a past event is taken as the occasion for exploring issues of vital importance for the present and future. In Gorgias' hands history becomes not the search for the true, but an opening up of questions; an enterprise not so much of reaching conclusions but of uncovering possible contradictions. Antithesis as more than a mere stylistic gesture disrupts previous complacent givens without, in this case, offering a clear resolution.

Parataxis   While the example of Gorgias as rhetorical historian corresponds to the descriptions of critical history cited earlier, the lack of resolution fails to signal a directive for action. Removing the blame from Helen entails a reconsideration of values, but the rhetorical historian both then and now has a strong obligation to action in a social and pedagogical world. A second syntactic structure characteristic of sophistic discourse balances the analytic effect of antithesis with a synthetic gesture which, nonetheless, remains flexible—free from the tighter bonds of a "logical" alternative. The loose association of clauses without hierarchical connectives or embedding is, under traditional explanations, a language behavior typical of primitive story-telling: a less sophisticated organization than its opposite, hypotaxis, the highest expression of which is Aristotelian propositional logic. But again extended beyond the level of mere style, parataxis can suggest a kind of historical practice complementary to the dissolvent impulse of antithesis alone.

The discourse of the character "Protagoras" illustrates the role of parataxis in historical argument: through the narrative *techné* he moves beyond the critical to the constructive (Untersteiner 57–62). While antithesis functioned to overthrow a commonplace about a historical character within the encomium, parataxis arises from a different *ethos*. In the dialogue, Socrates plays the critical role, trying to ruffle the wise old sophist with his hard-edged dialectic.[12] For his part, "Protagoras" demonstrates his ability to read the character and needs of his audience in choosing the form of his discourse. As an old man among young men, he chooses an entertaining narrative over dry argumentation as the most effective way of showing that civic responsibility can indeed be taught, Socrates' objections to the contrary. "Once upon a time," he begins, "there were gods only, and no mortal creatures" (§320d). Though he uses the familiar formula of the story-teller, the effect of this myth is not the hypnotic mystification to which Plato objected in the oral poetry of his fathers (Havelock *Preface*) but rather myth as "externalized thought" (Untersteiner 58): a pleasing, human and thus provisional way of composing an explanation of a human condition through time. Further evidence of the intellectual as opposed to purely aesthetic content of this sophistic history occurs as "Protagoras" blurs the line between *mythos* and *logos*, spinning off moral arguments from straight-forward narrative. These are not the repeated maxims and lessons of customary behavior learned through the oral tradition, but rather *new* solutions to the problems of social organization posed by democracy. The transition from story to its application demonstrates its use. After Zeus has distributed the qualities of justice and mutual respect to early humans equally, they are able to form cities:

> And this is the reason, Socrates, why the Athenians, and mankind in general, when the question relates to excellence in carpentry or any other mechanical art, allow but a few to share in their deliberations. And when anyone else interferes, then as you say, they object if he be not of the few; which, as I reply, is very natural. But when they meet to deliberate about political excellence or virtue, which proceeds only by way of justice and self-control, they are patient enough of any man who speaks of them, as is also natural, because they think that every man ought to share in this sort of virtue, and that states could not exist if this were other wise. I have explained to you, Socrates, the reason of this phenomenon. (322d–323a)

Though this defence of democracy as a happy moment in the evolution of humans challenges the conservative belief in in-born excellence at the foundation of both the older warrior-culture and of Plato's utopian aristocracy, the effect of the discourse is less critical than constructive. As the spokesman for democratic decision-making, Plato's "Protagoras" recommends specific pedagogical practices as natural extensions of his historical narrative: a literary study following on the socialization by the family which inculcates civic virtues (§325–27). While Gorgias' "history" successfully opened a number of speculations through antithesis, "Protagoras" passes over any potentially disruptive moment of his discourse in favor of a resolution leading to specific action. But the resolution provided by paratactic discourse differs from traditional history in that it is always open for reformulation: the continuity of the narrative represents only a contingent stability.

The repeated movement from the tragic critique provided by antithesis to the comic reformulation of parataxis was essential for the sophists. Though they are at worst characterized as skeptics and idle bickerers, in fact, they and their students did the political and legal work of the *polis*. In most disciplines the space between theory and practice allows for a wider separation between critical and constructive purposes. But rhetoric, because of its commitment to action, must be able to move from critique to reconstruction. The historical discourses of Gorgias and Protagoras, as well as their lives as teachers and diplomats, illustrate that movement.[13]

Arrangement in Tragic/Comic Rhetorical History   The displacement of the "logical" structure of traditional history in favor of "narrative"[14] structure of rhetorical history changes dramatically the status of arrangement. A reconsideration of arrangement is best approached through a graphic analogy. Imagine parataxis as *linear* in its structure and aural effect while hypotaxis is essentially *visual*. This analogy overturns the typical representation of inferential logic as "linear" based on the sentence as an equation. The alternative way to figure the difference takes as crucial the fact that in a propositional equation, the end is prefigured from the beginning—the whole structure is built in a vertical form, "hypo" suggesting an organization "from under."[15] The hypotactic discourse seems to exist as a complete, two-dimensional visual construct—as Platonic *eide* (appearance) or Aristotelian *theoria* (vision)—before its verbal performance; whereas discourse structured paratactically creates the effect of evolving in time, through sound striking the ears, minds, bodies of its listeners in a total experience which leads to action. The claim is not that hypotactic discourse does *not* affect the total auditor, but rather pretends not to—it obscures or ignores its own existence on the paratactic level of effect while discrediting any "logical" content of the paratactic alternative.

Antithesis allows for laying out options; parataxis provides for their loose coordination in a narrative with a social rather than epistemological purpose, strictly defined. The difference between sophistic historiography and a deconstructive practice is that parataxis follows or is interwoven with antithetical dissolution. The tragic opening up is resutured in a consciously constructed story: a temporary comic resolution.[16] This concept of arrangement is not Plato's organic form, growing from inside; it is rather a human invention. The story-teller plays with his material like Frankenstein with body parts. With both antithesis and parataxis, the point is not exposing or discovering the unknown, but rearranging the known. Invention is collapsed with arrangement as a single rhetorical canon. Traditional histories of rhetoric, bound by convention, derive their force and appeal from their logical presentation. Sophistic histories, on the other hand, could introduce into twentieth-century scholarship an alternative "method" of discourse in the most literal sense of finding a new path—specifically in asserting the validity of narrative as a vehicle for the serious tasks of knowledge creation, storage, and use on a more self-conscious level than the modes of emplotment White finds in the "restricted" historical art of the nineteenth century (*Metahistory* 9).[17] A sophistic method works by exposing and exploring a range of possibilities for knowledge and action and implicitly theorizing the process of their acceptance by the community less on the basis of logical validity and more on the force of their "rhetorical," that is, persuasive and aesthetic, appeal.[18] Rearrangement is revaluation. In sophistic history the pretense to distanced objectivity is overshadowed by an open acknowledgement of a value orientation: any realignment is made for a purpose.[19]

Rhetorical histories move along a continuum toward literary performance and away from objective collection of empirical data, which have themselves currently become subjects of analysis as discursive performances (Bazerman). Such histories are frankly imaginative reconstructions, instruments of *psychogogia* granted assent through their reception by the whole person who reads or hears them—not just on "cognitive" or "rational" grounds—and adopted because they serve social needs for the cultures out of which they arise. They self-consciously and without false modesty argue their theses, holding them up for applause and revision.

CONCLUSIONS

One primary objection to be anticipated to the historical practice outlined here comes out of the metaphysical/philosophical tradition: that such histories would neglect objective evidence and lack logical validity—the objection launched against the sophists by Plato. The goal for a rhetorical historiography would be not completely to renounce the "logical" or "factual," but to stop relying on their supremacy over their supposed opposites, to investigate a range of alternatives between those illusory poles. Both the categories of "fact" and "logic" have been undergoing severe critique since the beginning of the century with Peircian semiotics and Saussurean linguistics. Seizing a timely moment in academic history to take the lead in the generation of various forms of post-logical, post-disciplinary academic discourse would be an ideal role for historians of *rhetoric*. Several significant strands in philosophy and literary theory are pointing in such a direction (Eagleton; Lentricchia). What is absent thusfar is a general *practice* which takes seriously into account the insights of the theoretical developments of the last century.

Another possible objection to encouraging cross-disciplinary histories written from a variety of critical stances is the danger of a naive pluralism, a kind of theory-drift under which a particular historian fails to engage seriously enough with any one discourse tradition to understand it fully or apply it accurately (Schilb "Bricolage"). Rhetoric has always been open to the charge from philosophy of lack of system, but that feature is its virtue as well as its short-coming and is related to the special relation "rhetoric" itself signifies between theory and practice (Eagleton 207). While one check for misuse or misunderstanding will be the dialogue among historians from different positions, the more crucial test of any rhetorical history will come from the uses to which its insights are put in the classroom (Phelps) and beyond. That link provides the very definition of rhetoric's critical capacity.

For the present, what would a sophistic historiography promise? Among many possibilities, it could lead to a finer and fuller elaboration of the historical crossings of knowledge and discourse and of the social with the intellectual, a continuing exploration of "scientific" discourse as it evolved out of natural philosophy and magic, a more focused investigation of the points of contact between aesthetic, poetic and rhetoric in theory and between "literature" and non-belletristic discourse forms in practice. More fundamentally, a sophistic historiography would free the writers of histories in rhetoric from the restrictions that bind other disciplines and from the insularity of academic discourse in general, allowing its practitioners to engage, like the first sophists, in genuinely "rhetorical" acts—writing and speaking which make real changes in the world.

NOTES

1. Nancy S. Streuver's elaboration of the relation between sophistic rhetoric and history in the Italian Humanists informs the following discussion. Another source for that connection is Eric A. Havelock who associates the sophist Protagoras with one of three historical historical myths arising out of early Greek political thought (*The Liberal Temper in Greek Politics*, especially Chs. I–IV).

2. In borrowing this notion from Streuver (145), I'm shifting the emphasis. Whereas she's interested in the potential for critical distance inherent in the grammatical subjunctive, I exploit its predictive and prescriptive force, gesturing toward what could, would, and even should happen in the field.

3. The birth of the genre "history" contemporaneous with the first sophists offers another site at which to investigate the conjunction of the two strands. See Finley on the development of sophistic style in Thucydides.

4. The category "traditional" is neither exclusive (e.g., Howell's discussion of Locke in *Eighteenth-Century British Logic and Rhetoric*) nor pejorative, but rather is used to describe a particular historical practice arising in response to the needs of the field at a particular moment in its own history.

5. References are to Sprague's edition of Diels-Kranz, *Die Fragmente der Vorsokratiker*.

6. The title of Streuver's study, *The Language of History in the Renaissance*, by omitting ref-

erence either to the sophists or rhetoric, suggests the possible operation of a similar disciplinary prejudice in comparative literature.

7. Both Havelock (*LT* 157f.) and Guthrie (265–66) takes the Great Speech as an accurate reflection of the historical Protagoras' views.

8. White employs literary categories as "modes of emplotment" in the analysis of various forms of historical composition (*Metahistory* 7–11).

9. Aeschylus' *Prometheus Bound,* written during the stirrings of democratic sentiment in the mid-fifth century, contains a long description of human development along the same lines as Protagoras' and poses the strongest challenge to a divine *telos* as a grounds for autocracy, though Prometheus seems to be defeated by Zeus in the end. The two lost plays in the trilogy might have provided a more revolutionary challenge to the Hesiodic view of Prometheus.

10. Though White sees Darwinian historiography as rudely mechanistic ("Fictions of Factual Representation"), in line with his reputation for contributing to the materialistic determinism of late-nineteenth-century thought, Darwin's own text, *The Origin of Species,* reveals qualities of ambiguity, indeterminacy, and openness in the narrative form which demand a reconsideration of such a categorization.

11. Havelock associates changes in syntactic structures with evolution in thought (*Literate Revolution,* Ch. 11, especially 246, 253, 256).

12. Vlastos outlines short-comings in Socrates' argument and defends Protagoras' strong moral position in the dialogue.

13. Though the two most complete productions of Gorgias and Protagoras have been offered as a composite of sophistic historiography, both moments are realized within the works of Protagoras. His famous agnosticism, the manas-measure doctrine, and the title *Contradictory Arguments* all suggest the critical impulse.

14. Fisher's recent work on narrative as argument incorporates an opposition between rationality and narrativity, though he keeps in place an essentially Aristotelian logic of coherence, consistency, and fidelity as criteria for evaluating narrative arguments.

15. The Jakobsonian distinction between the metaphoric and metonymic poles is a clear analog to the relation between hypotaxis and parataxis. What is particularly suggestive about Jakobson and Halle's original discussion of the terms is the observation that most metalanguage about symbol systems concerns the metaphoric mode, whereas metonymy "easily defies interpretation" (95). White's reduction of metonymy to a structure ruled by deterministic causality (*Metahistory* 35–36) misses the complexity of the metonymic and the depth of difference between the two registers.

16. This formulation fits White's definition of emplotment by Comedy—"the temporary triumph of man over his world by the prospect of occasional *reconciliations* of forces at play in the social and natural worlds" [emphasis in original]—but not his view of Tragedy as law-governed (*Metahistory* 9). Untersteiner's understanding of Gorgian epistemology is the source of my use of the tragic (140f.).

17. Among rhetorical historians today, Vitanza makes the most striking and successful attempt to use the antithetical style of the first sophists to achieve "tragic" dissolution, but he defines the "comic" in terms of parody rather than reconciliation or reconstruction ("Critical Sub/Versions"). At moments, Streuver uses antithesis for the disruptive effective in a "comic" narrative (e.g., "unique" and "ounity," 143). A heavy irony within *this* essay is the extent to which it conforms to the conventional logic of academic prose while calling for change. Outside the parameters of disciplinary rhetoric, French feminists Cixous and Iragaray are experimenting with narrative alternatives to hypotaxis in intellectual argument.

18. Fisher advances narrative argument as a theory which seeks to account for how people come to adopt the *stories* that guide their behavior.

19. In its political interest, this "aesthetic" history differs from White's interpretation of Nietzsche's concept of myth (*Metahistory* 372). In advocating dialectical movement between forms, different styles of historiography for various historical needs (72), and the value of history in the service of life (116), it follows Nietzsche.

WORKS CITED

Bazerman, Charles. "Physicists Reading Physics: Schema-Laden Purposes and Purpose-Laden Schema." *Written Communication* 2 (1985): 3–23.

Berlin, James A. *Writing Instruction in Nineteenth-Century American Colleges.* Carbondale: Southern Illinois Univ. Press, 1982.

Campbell, Joseph Angus. "The Polemical Mr. Darwin." *Quarterly Journal of Speech* 61 (1975): 375–90.

Corcoran, Paul. *Political Language and Rhetoric.* Austin: U of Texas P, 1981.

Covino, William. "Thomas De Quincey In a Revisionist History of Rhetoric." *PRE/TEXT* 4 (1983): 121–37.

De Romilly, Jacqueline. *Magic and Rhetoric in Ancient Greece.* Harvard Univ. Press, 1975.

Eagleton, Terry. *Literary Theory. An Introduction.* Minneapolis: Univ. of Minnesota Press, 1983.

Enos, Richard Leo. "Rhetorical Theory and Sophistic Composition: A Reconstruction." Report of the 1985 National Endowment for the Humanities Summer Stipend.

Finley, John H., Jr. *Three Essays on Thucydides.* Cambridge: Harvard Univ. Press, 1967.

Fisher, Walter R. "Narrative as a Human Communication Paradigm: The Case of Public Moral Argument." *Communication Monographs* 51 (1974): 1–22.

Foucault, Michel. *The Archaeology of Knowledge and The Discourse on Language.* Trans. A. M. Sheridan Smith. New York: Pantheon, 1972.

———. *Discipline and Punish. The Birth of the Prison.* Trans. Alan Sheridan. New York: Pantheon, 1977.

———. "Nietzsche, Genealogy, History." In *Language, Counter-memory, Practice.* Ithaca: Cornell Univ. Press, 1977.

Gould, Stephen Jay. "Bushes and Ladders in Human Evolution." In *Ever Since Darwin. Reflections in Natural History.* New York: Norton, 1977.

Guthrie, W. K. C. *The Sophists.* Cambridge Univ. Press, 1971.

Harkin, Patricia. "Reifying Writing: The Politics of Disciplines." Paper. MidWest Modern Language Association. Chicago, 1986.

Havelock, Eric. A., *The Liberal Temper in Greek Politics.* New Haven: Yale, 1957.

———. *The Literate Revolution in Greece and Its Cultural Consequences.* Princeton Univ. Press, 1982.

———. *Preface to Plato.* Harvard Univ. Press, 1962.

Howell, Wilbur Samuel. *Eighteenth-Century British Logic and Rhetoric,* Princeton Univ. Press, 1971.

Jakobson, Roman and Morris Halle. *Fundamentals of Language.* 2nd ed. The Hague: Mouton, 1971.

Kennedy, George A. *Classical Rhetoric and Its Christian and Secular Tradition from Ancient to*

Modern Times. Chapel Hill: Univ. of N. Carolina Press, 1980.

Kerferd, G. B. *The Sophistic Movement.* Cambridge Univ. Press, 1981.

LeFevre, Karen Burke. *Invention as a Social Act.* Carbondale: So. Illinois Univ. Press, 1987.

Lentricchia, Frank. *Criticism and Social Change.* Chicago Univ. Press, 1983.

Lloyd, G. E. R. *Magic, Reason and Experience. Studies in the Origins and Development of Greek Science.* Cambridge Univ. Press, 1979.

Nietzsche, Friedrich. "On the Uses and Disadvantages of History for Life." *Untimely Meditations.* Trans. R. J. Hollingdale, Cambridge Univ. Press, 1983.

Phelps, Louise Wetherbee. "The Domain of Composition." *Rhetoric Review* 4 (1986): 182–95.

Poulakos, John. "Rhetoric, the Sophists, and the Possible." *Communication Monographs* 51 (1984): 215–25.

Rosenmeyer, Thomas G. "Gorgias, Aeschylus, and *Apate.*" *American Journal of Philology* 76 (1955) 225–60.

Schilb, John. "The History of Rhetoric and the Rhetoric of History." *PRE/TEXT* 7 (1986): 11–34.

———. "When Bricolage Becomes Theory: The Hazards of Ignoring Ideology." Paper presented at Mid-West Modern Language Association. Chicago, 1986.

Segal, Charles P. "Gorgias and the Psychology of the Logos." *Harvard Studies in Classical Philology* 66 (1962): 99–155.

Serres, Michel. *Hermes. Literature, Science, Philosophy.* Eds. Josué V. Harari and David F. Bell. Baltimore: The Johns Hopkins Univ. Press, 1982.

Solmsen, Friedrich. *Intellectual Experiments of the Greek Enlightenment.* Princeton Univ. Press, 1975.

Sprague, Rosamund, ed. *The Older Sophists. A Complete Translation by Several Hands of the Fragments in* Die Fragmente Der Vorsokratiker, *ed. Diels Kranz.* Columbia: Univ. of S. Carolina Press, 1972.

Streuver, Nancy S. *The Language of History in the Renaissance. Rhetoric and Historical Consciousness in Florentine Humanism.* Princeton Univ. Press, 1970.

Untersteiner, Mario. *The Sophists.* Trans. Kathleen Freeman. Oxford: Basil Blackwell, 1954.

Vitanza, Victor J. "Critical Sub/Versions of the History of Philosophical Rhetoric." *Rhetoric Review* 6.1 (1987): 41–66.

———. "Historiographies of Rhetoric: Traditional, Revisionary, and Sub/Versive." Paper presented at Conference on College Composition and Communication. Atlanta, 1987.

Vlastos, Gregory, ed. *Plato. Protagoras.* Trans. Benjamin Jowett, revised by Martin Ostwald. Indianapolis: Bobbs-Merrill, 1956. (References are to Stephanus pages.)

White, Hayden. "Fictions of Factual Representation." *Tropics of Discourse. Essays in Cultural Criticism.* Baltimore: The Johns Hopkins Univ. Press, 1978.

———. *Metahistory. The Historical Imagination in Nineteenth-Century Europe.* Baltimore: The Johns Hopkins Univ. Press, 1973.

In an altered form, this essay appears as a chapter in the author's book *Rereading the Sophists: Classical Rhetoric Refigured* (Carbondale: Southern Illinois Univ. Press, 1991).

William M. A. Grimaldi, S.J.

"The Aristotelian Topics"

While the influence of the Aristotelian *topoi* has been rather extensive in our western tradition, particularly in literature, it does seem that their methodology has not been fully understood. A number of factors have contributed to this: the absence in Aristotle of a forthright and formal discussion of what he has in mind,[1] the neglect of the methodology after Aristotle,[2] a partially misdirected emphasis given to the method by Cicero, one of the first to concern himself with the topics,[3] and the continuation of the Ciceronian interpretation by Quintilian with whom it passed into the Middle Ages and the stream of our western tradition.[4]

The rather truncated form in which the topics have come to us has been rather unfortunate since there has been lo: t along the way the far richer method of discourse on the human problem which they provide. Seen as mere static, stock 'commonplaces,' stylized sources for discussion on all kinds of subject matter they have lost the vital, dynamic character given to them by Aristotle, a character extremely fruitful for intelligent, mature discussion of the innumerable significant problems which face man. Indeed their genesis within an intellectual environment which included among other things discussions on ψύοιζ and νόμοζ and related problems of the First Sophistic, on the nature of justice, goodness, virtue, reality, etc., of the Platonic dialogues, of education and political science of Isocrates' discourses, seems to give a clue to their nature.

In his understanding of τόποζ it would seem that Aristotle was attempting to validate a mode of intelligent discussion in the area of probable knowledge comparable (but not equal) to that enjoyed in the area of scientific knowledge (i.e. the certain knowledge of metaphysics) and, even more than that, to enlarge where possible the subject of scientific knowledge. And in this last sense the topical method would not only be a propaideutic for *scientia*[5] but also an assistant discipline.

Even though this idea of the *topoi* as a formal discipline and an integrated methodology concerned with both the form and the content of discussion in the field of probable knowledge was lost shortly after Aristotle, as it would seem, it is interesting to note that in one form or another the *topoi* have influenced our western tradition. Understood in a rather static sense as 'rhetorical invention' they have enjoyed a dominant, and one would have to say a frequently creative, role in the literature of the West. Curtius gives abundant evidence for this but he has missed, it appears, the vitality of their contribution. This quality was seen by R. Tuve in her study of one phase of English poetry.[6] She notes with insight that it was in the area of the topics that the faculty of the imagination was thought to be most active: 'Thinking of the adjuncts of something has provided the pattern for innumerable short poems, and for innumerable longish images within poems . . .' And there is surely no need to comment upon the importance of the imaginative faculty or the pervasive presence of metaphor and image in all significant poetry. Vico had an idea similar to Miss Tuve's in mind when he wrote *De nostri temporis studiorum ratione,* but he was more concerned with the possible exclusion of the whole area of probable knowledge. Apparently he feared that the rejection of the topical method would encourage that attitude of mind which does not examine all the possible aspects of a problem. In our own day this neglect of 'problem thinking' (as opposed to 'system thinking') could well limit our quest for truth. No subject is fully exhausted until intelligent queries can no longer be raised. The critical examination of subject matter was one phase of the topical method. Another aspect of the method as Aristotle worked it out was the inferential phase, i.e. how one may legitimately advance by deductive reasoning the material gathered by the *topoi.* And here we have the *topoi* as sources of inference. Relatively little has been done with these latter topics, but R. Weaver[7] has developed from them a way of analysis whose application to prose literature could bring to light the currents of thought influential in various periods of our western tradition. In the course of a rather discerning study of the topical argumentation of Burke and Lincoln he remarks: 'the reasoner reveals his philosophical position by the source of argument which appears most often in his major premise because the major premise tells us how he is thinking about the world.'[8]

Aristotle in his topical methodology combined both of the elements just mentioned. His dominant concern in the topical method appears to be that of problem thinking, but thinking informed by intelligent procedure. It does seem that in the whole area of the problematic, the probable, and the contingent, it is his desire to enable one, as far as this is possible, to reason as intelligently, as accurately, and as precisely as one can do in the areas of certain, scientific knowledge. This becomes possible when one is in a position to examine the material of the problem with precision in order to determine it with all the accuracy permissible. After this one must be able to develop and enlarge this material by discursive reasoning to further conclusions. The kind of formal reasoning used, since one is engaged with the contingent and the probable, will generally be that which relies upon forms and principles of discursive reasoning which are usually considered to be, and are accepted as self-evident principles. The topics are the method devised to supply both elements. There are the 'particular topics,' varied aspects (i.e. sources) under which the subject may be studied for a clearer understanding. And secondly there are the 'general topics,' forms of inference, in which to develop this understanding to further conclusions.

Thus Aristotle presents us with a dynamic method,[9] not a mere static listing of likely materials readily usable in discussion, or, as the *topoi* have been called, 'opinion surveys.'[10] For Aristotle the τόποι are the methodology of Dialectics, the area of probable knowledge, just as in the *Analytics* we are given a methodology for the area of certain knowledge, *scientia*.

In view of the fact that any methodology concerned with language must occupy itself with the form and content of statements, (propositions, to use Aristotle's word),[11] it is possible to see where misinterpretation has arisen. Many commentators, from Cicero on,[12] have fastened upon the content (the particular topics) and then reduced the topics to the mere mechanics of invention, i.e. ways and means of developing and enlarging upon a theme. In more recent studies,[13] though not exclusively, the formal element has been stressed. While this captures the axiomatic character of the general topics, it neglects entirely the non-axiomatic, non-propositional character of the particular topics as they are found in the *Topics* and the *Rhetoric*.

In other words, the τόποι, which are the sources for intelligent discussion and reasoning in dialectic and rhetoric,[14] are concerned with both the material and formal element in such discussion. As sources for the content of discussion (the ordinary meaning of *loci communes*: persons, places, things, properties, accidents, etc., the περιστάσεις, or aspects of the subject pertinent to discussion) they ultimately provide the material by means of which general or particular propositions are enunciated. As sources for the forms of discussion[15] they are axiomatic forms, or modes of inference, in which syllogistic (or what is called 'enthymematic' in the *Rhetoric*) reasoning naturally expresses itself. Neither aspect can be neglected. For, granted that the τόποι are concerned with propositions (a point obvious to one acquainted with the *Topics* and the *Rhetoric*), it must not be forgotten that propositions consist of terms which must be clearly defined and determined before they can be used in meaningful discussion, or in intelligent, convincing, although probable, inference. There must be a precise apprehension of the subject as far as is possible, and there must be reasonable, inferential modes in which to develop the subject further. In the methodology of the topics Aristotle was apparently concerned with both ideas.

In what follows an attempt will be made to justify this distinction from the *Rhetoric*. It is generally admitted[16] that we must go to the *Rhetoric* for a relatively clear explanation of the term τόπος and more than this, one can clearly show from the *Rhetoric* a definite distinction in the τόποι, and how Aristotle has developed this idea of the τόποι.

The idea of τόποι, as far as one can decide historically, does not seem to originate with Aristotle. On the other hand he does seem to have isolated and formulated the technique or method which was at work in the collections of τόποι which were probably on hand. His apparent purpose was to arrive at the general method underlying discussion,[17] not to burden the mind with the kind of lists of specific subject headings and arguments for various occasions, which had probably been collected. And in this is the genius of his topical method.

When we turn to the pre-Aristotelian τόπος to make a brief review of the history of the idea, we find nothing quite similar to the meaning Aristotle gives to the term.[18] The ordinary use of the word is primarily one of local designation and we find this common in Plato[19] and Isocrates; and in the latter it is very frequently conjoined with χώρα.

There are, however, four passages in Isocrates which are germane to one aspect of the Aristotelian idea of τόπος as the place to go for material concerning one's subject, or for a clarification of it—the Aristotelian ὑπάρχοντα.[20] In *Philip* 109 the τόπος is the γαθὰ τῆς ψυχῆς, a topic peculiar (τόπος ἴδιος) to Heracles, and one, as Isocrates says, πολλῶν μὲν ἐπαίνων χαὶ χαλῶν πράξεων γέμοντα. These γαθὰ (see also *Helen* 38) are τῇ ψυχῇ πρόσοντα, which is again an echo of the ὑπάρχοντα idea of Aristotle.[21] In *Panathenaicus* 111 we have τόπος as material for discussion, and the same use in *Helen* 4.[22]

Demosthenes[23] gives further evidence that τόπος was used in his time and quite apparently with reference to the particular topics. Radermacher[24] gives rather substantial evidence that not only were such ἴδιοι τόποι known and used, but that writers frequently called them χαιρούς, rather than τόπους before Aristotle's time. These χαιροί for the most part concerned themselves with determining the nature of, and examining in detail, not merely such words and ideas as the good, the useful, the right, the beautiful, the possible,[25] but also other ideas such as war, government, peace, etc.[26]

Such is the more direct evidence which is found on the pre-Aristotelian use of the word τόπος in a way that is at all similar to Aristotle's. Indirect evidence for the pre-Aristotelian existence of the idea in the manner in which Aristotle understood it is twofold: the testimony of Aristotle himself and later writers, and the fairly abundant evidence of Aristotle's τόποι at work in various pre-Aristotelian writers.

In the *Rhetoric* Aristotle cites on a number of occasions previous authors or technographers who have employed the particular *topos* of which he is speaking.[27] One conclusion that may be drawn from this is that the methodology of the topics as Aristotle understood it was being used, even if the term τόπος was not employed to identify it. And actually in the *Topics* 105b 11ff. Aristotle suggests the listing of key ideas on life, on the good, a procedure which we have reason to believe was introduced by earlier rhetoricians. For Cicero[28] and Quintilian[29] mention Protagoras and Gorgias as those who were the first to present such 'communes locos,'[30] while Doxopater[31] speaks of a tradition which has Corax devising τούς τῶν προοιμίων τόπους.

Were one, however, to question this commonly accepted tradition, it still remains true that the actual use of Aristotle's method of particular and general topics is rather convincing. Aside from Aristotle's illustrations of his topics by citations from earlier writers, the general topics have been exemplified from the same source rather frequently by Spengel in his commentary[32] and by Palmer.[33] The particular topics have not been so fortunate, quite possibly because they were not considered τόποι.[34] Why this should be, is strange in view of the fact that the Aristotelian τόπος was certainly understood in the sense of 'particular topics' by Cicero, Quintilian and Plutarch[35] among others. Furthermore we find Gorgias continually using such particular topics in his *Palamedes*[36] and in 22 we find some of them mentioned: τὸν τόπον, τὸν χρόνον, πότε, ποῦ, πῶς. Aristotle himself[37] when speaking of the particular topics connected with honor speaks of the importance of τὸ ποῦ and τὸ πότε (τόποι χαὶ χαιροί) and we also get both of these in the *Phaedrus* 272a with a slightly different reference. In the *Meno* we find the particular topics for ἀρετή.[38] And this same process can be seen at work in Prodicus' efforts at definition, or the specification of a term, e.g. pleasure.[39] Further citation does not seem necessary, for, as Radermacher says (and he is speaking of what have thus far been called here 'particular topics'): 'Non potest esse dubium quin de sedibus argumentorum, quae τελιχὰ χεψάλαια vocantur, velut de iusto, utili, honesto, pulchro, possibili in scholis sophistarum iam ante Aristotelem sit disputatum.'[40]

It would seem, then, that the idea of both particular topics and general topics, or topics to supply one with the material for propositions, as well as topics to supply one with ways of putting this material in a form of inference, was operative prior to Aristotle. Further it does appear that collections of τόποι were made which were concerned for the most part with material and with lines of argument specific to a definite, limited problem or case.[41] These would be the materials and the arguments to be used when a similar problem arose. The process as can be seen is rather static and similar to the study of case law. Aristotle's contribution was to derive and describe the method at work,[42] and he may have kept the name τόποι for the method since it describes the process: these are the places from which originate both the material and the formal elements in all dialectical and rhetorical discussion.

It is in the *Rhetoric* that a distinction in the τόποι is made and a clue given to the nature of the methodology which Aristotle has in mind. A similar division does not exist in the *Topics* but it appears to be operative there.[43]

At 1358a 2–7 of the *Rhetoric* the whole question of particular topics (ἴδιοι τόποι or εἴδη) and general topics (χοινοὶ τόποι) is introduced. Here we are told that though it is almost universally disregarded there is a distinction of major importance with regard to enthymemes (the rhetorical syllogism), a distinction similar to that which is true of the dialectical syllogism. For 'some enthymemes belong properly to Rhetoric, as some syllogisms belong properly to Dialectic; other enthymemes are peculiar to other arts and faculties, either existent or still to be formulated.'[44]

A possible commentary on this passage is, perhaps, *Soph. El.* 170a 20–b 11. The best may be (as Aristotle himself suggests) the section in the *Rhetoric* which immediately follows: 1358a 9–28. Here Aristotle says that the dialectical and rhetorical syllogisms (10–11) are those formed on the basis of the τόποι.[45] These τόποι are then divided into the χοινοί (12) which would represent the sources of enthymemes and syllogisms χατὰ τὴν ῥητοριχὴν. . . χαι. . . διαλεκτικὴν μέθοδον (5f.), and the εἴδη (or ἴδια [17] or ἴδιοι τόποι [28] on analogy with what is quite definitely χοινοὶ τόποι in the same line) which are the sources of enthymemes and syllogisms χατ̓ ἄλλαζ τέχναζ χαὶ δυνάμειζ (6–7).[46] Aristotle continues[47] by calling the particular topics peculiar to each subject εἴδη, while the general topics peculiar to Rhetoric and Dialectic are called τόποι,[48] a distinction repeated at 1403b 14 where he sums up the discussion of Books I and II.[48a]

Aristotle then proposes to discuss the εἴδη,[49] or particular topics, and it is in his presentation of them that a distinction between them and the χοινοί becomes quite apparent.[50] The *eidos*, or particular topic, could be called a 'material topic'[51] in the sense that it offers the matter (ὕλη) for the propositions. It presents one with sources, or focal points, to be examined in order that one may derive all the material pertinent to the subject, i.e. the ὑπάρχοντα of the subject which are necessary for intelligent statement. These εἴδη belong to the subject in itself and in all of its diverse relations. They represent the varied particular aspects of an individual subject which can throw light upon the subject and the field of knowledge which it represents.[52]

To understand the point of view presented here one has merely to read Aristotle's discussion of the εἴδη for deliberative (cc. 4–8), epideictic (cc. 9–12) and forensic oratory (cc. 13–15) in Book I, or those for *pathos* (cc. 2–11) and *ethos* (cc. 1, 12–17) in Book II. Their character is that which has just been described, and, more than that, one can hardly put aside the fact that Aristotle considers these εἴδη to be τόποι when he himself sums up his discussion of them with the words: ὥστε ἐξ ὧν δεῖ ψέρειν τὰ ἐνθυμήματα τόπων (1396b 31–2). The same idea is repeated at 1419b 15–29. And at 1380b 30–1 he says of the εἴδη that he has been discussing relative to πάθος: ἐχ τούτων τῶν τόπων.[53]

These εἴδη, or particular topics, then, are the sources to which one has recourse to develop an understanding and thorough knowledge of the subject. As Aristotle says quite simply at 1396a 5–b 19: to reason intelligently upon a subject, you must reason ἐχ τῶν περὶ ἐχαστον ὑπαρχόντων (b 2).[54] As a matter of fact, when reading 1396a 4–b 21, it is impossible to avoid the conclusion that not only do the εἴδη offer factual material on the subject, but also they are considered to be τόποι.[55]

The εἴδη then, are the sources for informative, factual material upon the subject of discussion. Since this material, when derived from the εἴδη, will usually appear as an enunciation with respect to the subject, it follows that the εἴδη give us particular propositions which can be used in enthymematic reasoning on the subject. In that sense the εἴδη become particular propositions or statements on the subject under discussion.[56] Yet the kind of statement which they give, does not directly implicate the ultimate and essential truths about the subject, although it may approach them. Hence it is, as Aristotle says, that these εἴδη do not put us in contact with the special principles (ἀρχαί) of the subject.[57] A study of the references on the εἴδη cited above from Books I and II[58] will reveal that one could hardly construct a science of government, criminal law, or psychology from the εἴδη presented. Rather the purpose of these particular topics is to enable one to speak intelligently, but not scientifically, upon the subject under discussion. Enthymematic reasoning based upon them is valid, and only valid, for the subject to which they belong.[59]

In this respect the εἴδη differ, as topics, from the χοινοὶ τόποι.[60] These latter transcend the various subjects which rhetoric may treat. They are valid for all subjects and thus particularly exemplify the nature of rhetoric as a *dynamis*.[61]

This brings us to a very fundamental characteristic of the χοινοὶ τόποι emphatically stressed by Aristotle,[62] namely, that these χοινοὶ τόποι are universal and transcend all the fields of knowledge to which rhetoric may legitimately apply itself.[63] Here, then, we have a kind of topic which is essentially different from the εἴδη. Particular topics are confined to and closely related to their own specific subject matter[64] and are valid sources of information on that matter alone.[65] The χοινοί on the contrary, have no such substrate,[66] and are valid sources for enthymematic reasoning upon any subject.[67] Hence it is, that, no matter how much a particular topic is universalized, the result will never be a χοινὸς τόπος, as Aristotle understands that term in the *Rhetoric*. For an ἴδιος τόπος is always specific in its nature and confined to one subject: general or particular.[68]

Any topic, and such are the εἴδη, which is grounded in the particular subject matter of a specific branch of learning and is productive of knowledge in that area,[69] cannot transcend this discipline and include others. But the χοινοί transcend the individual disciplines. This difference in the topics translates itself into what have been called in this paper 'particular topics' (εἴδη), or sources of information upon the subject matter to be discussed, and 'general topics' (χοινοὶ τόποι), or sources for modes of reasoning by enthymeme: forms of inference most suitable for the enthymeme.[70]

A closer study of what Aristotle has to say of these χοινοί in the passage under discussion[71] and in chapter 23 of Book II appears to justify this division. In the first place the χοινοί are universal and belong properly to Rhetoric in so far as Rhetoric is a δύναμις περὶ ἕχαστον τοῦ θεωρῆσαι τὸ ἐνδεχόμενον πιθανόν[72] and in so far as it is not ἐπιστήμη[73]. Thus Rhetoric does not possess any peculiar ὑποχείμενον,[74] and neither do the χοινοὶ τόποι.[75] And so we can understand why Aristotle, for whom Rhetoric is a *dynamis* just as Dialectic, lays stress upon the μεγίοτη διάφορα in the section 1358a 2ff. which is so frequently discussed by the commentators. This 'difference' resides for him in the fact that there are enthymemes peculiar to Rhetoric as a discipline: χατὰ τὴν ῥητοριχὴν μέθοδον. If Rhetoric possesses no particular subject matter of its own, such enthymemes could only be syllogistic forms derived from universal propositional statements which are modes for probable argumentation and reasoning. As he says in the *Sophistici Elenchi:*[76] there are certain general principles common to all the sciences which even the unlettered can use. In themselves they are known to everyone, for they are natural ways in which the mind thinks. Such in a way are the χοινοὶ τόποι. As general axiomatic propositions they are valid forms of inference by themselves. Further, they may also be applied to the subject matter presented by the εἴδη to permit one to reason enthymatically with this material.[77]

It would appear, then, that the χοινοὶ τόποι are logical modes of inference which generally obtain the matter for their inference from the εἴδη.[78] And as further confirmation that they are general, formal topics, i.e. forms of reasoning, it should be noted that study of the twenty eight χοινοὶ τόποι[79] shows that they are universal[80] and that they apparently fall into one of three inferential and logical patterns.[81]

a) antecedent-consequent, or cause-effect: VII, XI, XIII, XIV, XVII, XIX, XXIII, XXIV.
b) more-less: IV, V, VI, XX, XXV, XXVII.
c) some form of relation: I, II, III, VIII, IX, X, XII, XV, XVI, XVIII, XXI, XXII, XXVI, XXVIII.

One could undoubtedly argue about the terms used for classification, or the distribution of the χοινοί among them. The point of interest, however, is that, no matter how they are classified, these χοινοὶ τόποι reduce themselves to modes of inference.[82] They always assume a form of reasoning which leads the mind from one thing to another. Expressed quite simply they would resolve themselves into the proposition: if one, then the other. And this last statement acquires new significance when, knowing the close relation between the rhetorical syllogism (enthymeme) and the χοινοὶ τόποι,[83] one reads: 'All Aristotelian syllogisms are implications of the type "if α and β then γ". . . '[84] If, further, consideration is given to Aristotle's identification of these χοινοὶ τόποι with the στοιχεῖα of rhetorical syllogisms, there appears to be no doubt that for Aristotle the general topic is a form of inference and represents the source of enthymemes: χατὰ τὴν ῥητοριχὴν μέθοδον.

At 1396b 20–22 Aristotle summarizes his discussion of the εἴδη and makes a transition to his section on the χοινοὶ τόποι. He introduces the new subject with the words 'but let us speak of the στοιχεῖα of enthymemes.' From 1358a 31–2 one would expect him to say as commentators hasten to point out: let us speak of the τόπους τοὺς χοινοὺς ὁμοιώς πάντων. Having used στοιχεῖα somewhat unexpectedly, Aristotle immediately clarifies the word with: στοιχεῖον δε λέγω χαὶ τόπον ἐνθυμήματος τὸ αὐτό. And lest there be any doubt that by τόπος here he means the χοινοὶ τόποι, he says that these τόποι are χαθόλου περὶ ἀπάντων. Thus one can be fairly certain that the τόποι here are the same as the general topics of 1358a 32: τοὺς χοινοὺς ὁμοίως πάντων.

Aristotle has now specified these χοινοὶ τόποι as στοιχεῖα. But what is meant by calling them στοιχεῖα? At 1403a 17–18 we read: 'By stoicheion and topos I mean the same thing; for a stoicheion and topos is a general class under which many enthymemes fall.' The Greek here: εἰς δ πολλὰ ἐνθυμήματα ἐμπίπτει describes στοιχεῖον (and so τόπος) as a larger category which contains many enthymemes. This at once recalls Theophrastus' definition of τόπος as: ἀρχή τις ἢ στοιχεῖον . . . τῇ περιγραφῇ μὲν ὡρισμένος (i.e. of determinate form) . . . τοῖς δὲ χαθ᾿ἔχαστα ἀόριστος (i.e. indeterminate with respect to the individual matter to which it is applied).[85] Of this definition Bochenski writes: 'pour Théophraste le τόπος est une formule logique légitime qui sert à former les prémisses de déduction. . .'[86] But this is precisely what the χοινοὶ τόποι are: forms of inference by enthymeme, any one of which may offer a form for inference on various subjects. As Waitz says of a passage in the Analytics 84b 21 which is parallel to 1403a 17–18: 'In Topicis στοιχεῖα vocat quae alio nomine τόπους appellat, universa quaedam argumenta, ex quibus cum veritatis quadam specie aliquid vel probetur vel refellatur.'[87]

Before concluding, a word should perhaps be said about the Topics. First of all it should be noted that this formal distinction between εἴδη and χοινοὶ τόποι is not found as such in the Topics. Yet, as was said earlier, both ideas appear to be operative there. For in the Topics Aristotle is concerned with determining as accurately as possible the meaning of things by specifying the various ways in which this meaning can be determined (the εἴδη), and further, in establishing these ways to determine meaning, i.e. focal points from which to examine the subject, he employs time and again the reasoning of the general topics (χοινοὶ τόποι) as we find them in the *Rhetoric.*[88]

In the *Topics* Aristotle says that a problem can be considered from four primary aspects: definition, property, genus, accident.[89] The effort in Books 2–7 is to examine the nature of these categories and what must follow with respect to a thing, if it comes under one of them. This examination is done by the τόποι, and the analysis is determined by the very nature of the category. For example: there are certain ways (τόποι) in which one can further determine the nature of a genus and consequently certain statements which can only be made about it—and they are not valid for an accident. They are ways—determined by reality—in which one must think about the subject. This kind of analysis is a vital, logical one, grounded in the metaphysical reality of the subject, and one engages in it in order to discover as far as possible the true nature of the subject. This was what was meant by saying that these particular topics are not mere mechanical lists of terms to be tried on a subject, no Procrustean bed to which the subject is fitted; rather we have here a method of analysis originating in the ontological reality of the subject.[90]

In the *Rhetoric,* however, as I understand it, Aristotle would appear to enlarge the method of the particular topics owing to an apparent awareness that a thing may be conditioned and altered by its situation; in other words, that the time, place, the circumstances, the character, the emotional involvement, may vitally affect the total meaning of a thing in a given situation. Thus these and other elements were introduced, and yet they are not entirely absent from the *Topics* as is seen in 111b 24ff.; 112a 24ff.; 118a; 146b 20ff.; 150b 34–151a 1.

As for the χοινοὶ τόποι they frequently appear in the *Topics* as the method whereby one may establish the special focal points (particular topics) from which a subject may be studied. In this use they appear in the same form and fulfill the same function as modes of inference which they have in the *Rhetoric.* That is to say, that they are ways in which the mind naturally and readily reasons, and that they are independent, in a way, of the subject to which they are applied, and may be said to be imposed as forms upon this material in order to clarify and determine it further.[91] Thus it is that we will at times find the general topics functioning in the *Topics* as a method to help in the determination of various particular topics to which one should have recourse.[92]

It is only in the *Rhetoric,* however, that a clear distinction between particular and general topics appears, and its presence would seem indisputable. The distinction may be ignored, but if the texts cited in this paper are studied, one is forced either to reject the unity of the *Rhetoric,* or to question the text as one that has been confused by later editors, or to seek an interpretation of the text. The attempt here has been to offer a tentative interpretation which keeps in mind the character of the topics as they are met in the *Topics;* further, it is an interpretation which appears to be demanded by the text of the *Rhetoric* as we possess it, and it seems to express the method Aristotle had in mind when he proposed a way of human discourse for the whole area of the contingent and the probable. In summary, then, it is proposed:

a) that the εἴδη are particular topics concerned with the specific content and meaning of the subject under discussion. They enable one to acquire the factual information pertinent to the matter which in turn permits one to make intelligent statement upon the subject;

b) that the χοινοὶ τόποι are general topics, i.e. forms of inference into which syllogistic, or enthymematic, reasoning naturally falls. As modes of reasoning they may be used for the εἴδη of various subjects which specifically differ (1358a 13–14: διαψερόντων εἴδει), and when they are applied to the εἴδη they effect syllogistic or enthymematic argumentation.[93]

NOTES

[1]The Port-Royal logicians rejected the *Topics* as 'des livres étrangement confus.' Bochenski, *La logique de Théophraste* (Fribourg 1947) 122, claims that Aristotle never gave us the meaning of τόποζ, while Solmsen, *Die Entwicklung der aristotelischen Logik und Rhetorik* (Berlin 1929) 164 maintains that *Rhet.* 1403a 18–19 is Aristotle's only genuine statement on the essential character of the term. (All citations from the *Rhetoric* are from Roemer's edition, Teubner 1923.)

[2]Theophrastus, of course, wrote on the topics, and apparently Straton continued the work (D. Laert. *Straton* 5.3). Collections of τόποι for prooemia and epilogues apparently existed in the 4th century (PW Suppl. 7.1066.54ff.). For the general trend in rhetoric between Aristotle and Cicero see *ibid.* 1071–1089; and on the topics see Volkmann, *Die Rhetorik der Griechen und Römer* (Leipzig 1885) 199ff., 299ff., 322ff.

[3]He himself found Aristotle's work somewhat obscure (*Topica* 1); W. Wallies, *Die griechischen Ausleger der aristotelischen Topik* (Berlin 1891) 4, and E. Thionville, *De la théorie des lieux communs* (Paris 1855) 9 would agree with this, for they believe that Cicero's work in this field has nothing more in common with Aristotle's than its title. This is too severe, just as Viehweg, one of the latest to consider the topics, *Topik und Jurisprudenz* (Munich 1953) 10, is a bit too sanguine in his opinion that Cicero's work will help us to understand the Aristotelian topics. The diversity of Cicero's remarks, however, implies at times that he may have seen into the nature of Aristotle's topics; on this question see B. Riposati, *Studi sui 'Topica' di Cicerone* (Milan 1947); his bibliography, 15–30, is a good one for a study of the general problem.

[4]See the pertinent chapters in E. Curtius, *European Literature and the Latin Middle Ages* (New York 1953).

[5]*Top.* 101a 34ff. All citations from the *Topics* are from I. Strache-M. Wallies (Teubner 1923).

[6]R. Tuve, *Elizabethan and Metaphysical Imagery* (Chicago 1947) c. XI. 3.

[7]R. Weaver, *The Ethics of Rhetoric* (Chicago 1953) cc. 3,4.

[8]*Ibid.* 55.

[9]*Top.* 100a 18.

[10]K. Burke, *A Rhetoric of Motives* (New York 1950) 56. On 57f. he does see a difference in the topics: there are the 'commonplaces' just mentioned, and then 'another kind of "topic" '; this

other kind, from his description of it, is actually the general topic as presented in this paper.

[11]For Aristotle the topics are the sources for the προτάσειζ and, as 1358a 10–35 and 1377b 16–24 would indicate, this means sources for both their content and form.

[12]Thionville, *op. cit.* c. vi, traces briefly the development from Cicero to Marmontel. R. Nadeau gives some attention to this area in a recent article 'Hermogenes on "Stock Issues" in Deliberative Speaking,' *Speech Monographs* 25.1 (1958) 59–66.

[13]Solmsen, *op. cit.* 163–6; Riposati, *op. cit.* 21ff.; E. Hambruch, *Logische Regen der platonischen Schule in der aristotelischen Topik* (Berlin 1904) 31; Thionville, *op. cit.* 30ff.

[14]*Rhet.* 1358a 10–35; 1377b 16–24.

[15]1358a 12–17.

[16]Viehweg, *op. cit.* 9; Solmsen, *op. cit.* 163–4; Thionville, *op. cit.* 30f.

[17]*Top.* 100a 18f.; 102b 35–103a 5.

[18]As Solmsen, *op. cit.* 156 remarks: the Aristotelian idea is something new; he discusses the term in general 151–175; see also F. Schupp, 'Zur Geschichte der Beweistopik in der älteren griechischen Gerichtsrede' *Wiener Studien* 45 (1926–7) 17–28, 173–85.

[19]See Ast, *Lexicon Platonicum sub* τόποζ; this is also true of all the pertinent references in Diels, *Die Fragmente der Vorsokratiker*⁶ (Berlin 1952), with the exception of the Cicero and Quintilian citations which will be seen later.

[20]See *Top.* 105b 12–8 for the idea, and 112a 24ff. and *Rhet.* 1396a 34ff. where Aristotle says that what he was trying to do in the *Topics* was to determine the ὑπάρχοντα.

[21]Solmsen, *op. cit.* 167 mentions these two references and he tries to connect the *Helen* citation with his idea of the Aristotelian τόποζ as 'Formprinzip,' or a propositional, axiomatic *topos*. This appears no more possible here than Thionville's attempt, *op. cit.* 55–77, to formulate many of the τόποι in the *Topics* as propositional, axiomatic statements, a process of which he must say: 'j'ai dû parfois retrancher, parfois interpréter, parfois changer la forme,' 63.

[22]In *Panathenaicus* 88 the use is ambiguous: it may mean the subject previously under discussion, but it more probably indicates the place in his speech at which he digressed.

[23]In *Aristogeiton* 76 (ed. Dindorf-Blass, Teubner 1888).

[24]L. Radermacher, *Artium Scriptores* (Vienna 1951), see the notes on 48–9, 224. It has been called to my attention by A. E. Raubitschek that this use of χαιρούζ may throw new understanding on the nature of Theophrastus' πολιτιχὰ πρὸζ τοὺζ χαιρούζ, on which see PW Suppl. 7.1517.31ff.

[25]What later rhetoricians called the τελιχα χεψάλαια, see Radermacher, *op. cit.* 226 note to 62.

[26]See the scholiast to Thucydides 3.9.1 (ed. Hude, Teubner 1927) where we find Thucydides doing this very thing for δημηγορία; or see *Anaximenes* 19 (ed. Spengel) where various meanings of δίχαιον and ἄδίχον are given. Syrianus examines συμψέρον in this manner and introduces the examination thus: ἐξετάσομεν δὲ τὸ συμψέρον διὰ τόπων ἔπτα (Rademacher, *op. cit.* 227); I mention Syrianus here since Radermacher in his note is of the opinion that the τόποι may be quite old.

[27]E.g. 1399a 15–7; 1400a 4–5; 1400b 15–7; 1402a 15; and see Radermacher, *op. cit.* 221 note to 48.

[28]*Brutus* 12.46.8 (ed. G. Friedrich, Teubner 1893).

[29]*Institutiones Oratoriae* 3.1.12 (ed. E. Bonnell, Teubner 1891).

[30]Solmsen, *op. cit.* 167–8 discusses the Cicero text.

[31]Radermacher, *op. cit.* 34.

[32]E.g. *ad* 1398a 30ff; and see note of Radermacher, *op. cit.* 57 and 223 note to 52; and comment of Solmsen, *op. cit.* 166.

[33]G. Palmer, *The ΤόΠΟΙ of Aristotle's Rhetoric as Exemplified in the Orators* (Diss. Univ. of Chicago 1934).

[34]Marx, 'Aristoteles' Rhetorik,' *Sb. Gesellschaft der Wissenschaften zu Leipzig* 52 (1900) 281ff. does not consider the εἴδη (i.e. ἴδιοι τόποι) to be topics, nor does Solmsen, *op. cit.* 17, 34ff. 165 and note 3.

[35]*Quaest. conviv.* 616 c–d (ed. Bernardakis): Plutarch remarks that to appreciate the social position of dinner guests who differ in so many ways—ἡλιχία, δυνάμει, χρείᾳ, οἰχειότητι— one would need τοὺς Ἀριστοτέλους τόπους. These are particular topics. We also find such particular topics in the scholiast on the *Staseis* of Hermogenes (ed. Walz IV 352.5ff.); the scholiast calls them τόποι and finds them used in a work by Lysias.

[36]Diels, *Vorsokratiker*[6] II 294ff.

[37]1361a 33f.

[38]Radermacher, *op. cit.* 49 number 27 with note.

[39]*Ibid.* 68f., numbers 7–11 with notes.

[40]*Ibid.* 226 note to 62.

[41]Navarre, *Essai sur la Rhétorique grecque* (Paris 1900) speaks of collections of τόποι that were made, 60ff. 124ff. 166–74.

[42]As Navarre, *ibid.* 166 says in comparing the treatment of ἤθη in the *Rhetoric* and in the Παρασχευαί attributed to Lysias: 'l'ouvrage de Lysias n'était pas un traité théorique, mais un recueil de modèles (τόποι γεγυμνασμένοι).' As far as can be judged (see Navarre 166–74), these collected *topoi* appear to be concerned with stock offense and defense tactics for typical situations, not for an intelligent discussion of the problem, which was what Aristotle had in mind: *Top.* 101a 25ff.; *Rhet.* 1354a 11ff. In the *Soph. El.* 183b 36ff. Aristotle himself criticizes the formulaic quality of these collections.

[43]Cf. *infra* 14.

[44]Jebb's translation. In the interpretation of this text, I agree with Maier, *Die Syllogistik des Aristoteles* II 1 (Tübingen 1900) 497 note 1. Spengel in his commentary 71 (1867 edition) and Solmsen, *op. cit.* 15 note 1 substantially agree. The minor variant readings admitted by Spengel together with Vater (*Animadversiones ad Aristotelis librum primum Rhetoricorum* [Halle 1794]) are not substantial, once the correct antithesis of the sentence is understood: μέν setting off 4–6 against the δέ of 6–7. In the light of the context 9–28, this gives the idea of general and particular topics. Such a distinction is also seen in Anonymous, *Commentaria in Aristotelem graeca* 21.6. line 27 and Stephanus, *ibid.* 267, lines 1–23; but I would not accept their identification of the general topics.

[45]Solmsen, *op. cit.* 15 note 4 appears more correct on the meaning of περὶ ὧν than Cope-Sandy's (Cambridge 1877) I 49.

[46]It appears that τόποι are divided into χοινοί (12) and ἴδια (17). The neuter case is noted by Spengel in his commentary *sub linea*. I do not see any insurmountable problem in it, in the light of the neuter χἀχεῖνα (21) referring to χοινοὶ τόποι. See also Roemer, 'Zur Kritik der Rhetorik des Aristoteles,' *Rhein. Mus.* 39 (1884) 506 on similar instances at 1395a 11, 1355b 35. Confirmation of this division seems to be present in 1358a 21–32. Maier's note, *op. cit.* 497–8 does not appear correct in its exclusion of the notion of τόπος from the ἴδια; this would also be true for Solmsen, *op. cit.* 14ff.; Marx, *op. cit.* 281 note 2, 283 and 296 (if I read him correctly) would understand ἐνθυμήματα or εἴδη with ἴδια. On the contrary it would appear that the ἴδια, as they are presented here, are not only τόποι but general enough to be 'loci ex quibus quasi conspiciatur via quam insistere debeamus ut et adversarium refutemus et quod nobis placeat evincamus,' as Waitz describes *topos*, *Aristotelis Organon* (Leipzig 1844) 438.

[47]1358a 30–31.

[48]*Ibid.* 32.

[48a]1403b 13–14 : εἴρηται δὲ χαί τὰ ἐνθυμήματα πόθεν δεῖ πορίζεσθαι · ἔστι γὰρ τὰ μὲν εἴδη τῶν ἐνθυμημάτων, τὰ δε τόποι.

[49]*Ibid.* 32–3.

[50]Thus Süss, *Ethos* (Leipzig-Berlin 1910) 170, would seem wrong in saying that Aristotle has not given us any sharp and satisfactory division between εἴδη and τόποι.

[51]Spengel, *Ueber das Studium der Rhetorik bei den Alten* (Munich 1842) 22ff. makes such a distinction. It may appear a quibble but 'sources for material' seems better than 'material proofs' (materielle Beweise). For it would appear that the 'proof' is the enthymeme and that the εἴδη offer material for inferential argument by syllogism or enthymeme, whereas the χοινοί τόποι present forms for inference by syllogism. There would be no objection to calling the χοινοί τόποι which are sources for formal reasoning by syllogism or enthymeme 'formelle Beweise' as Spengel does.

[52]See 1396b on the use of ἴδια; and Stephanus, *Commentaria Graeca* 21.268 lines 12–15.

[53]Marx admits that there are εἴδη for deliberative, forensic, epideictic oratory, but only τόποι for the πάθη and ἤθη. This forces him to say on 1396b 28–34 that a 'Redaktor' has confused the words and incorrectly brought them together, *op. cit.* 299,307. Solmsen on the other hand, *op. cit.* 170 note 2 with his interpretation of τόπος, has a far different problem: he cannot understand how any of these εἴδη can be called τόποι by Aristotle: it is 'prinzipwidrig.'

[54]The note of Cope-Sandys, *op. cit.* II 228–9 indicates what is had in mind here. These εἴδη are always specific to the subject but may be particular or general, see 1396b 11–9, with which compare Isocrates, *Philip* 109. This idea I find frequently present in the *Topics*, e.g. 105b 12–8: one can discuss the idea of 'good' in itself, or that which constitutes 'the good' in this specific subject.

[55]1396b 28–34 undoubtedly refers to the section on the εἴδη in Books I and II, and they are called τόποι here. This is made more probable still by the contrast between τρόπος at 1396b 20 and 1397a 1. Here Aristotle contrasts the method already presented in the first two books, of seeking source material for enthymemes (a method called τοπιχός, see Spengel in his commentary *sub* 1396b 20) with the method which he now intends to take up, namely the method of the χοινοί τόποι. See also Riccobono, *Paraphrasis in Rhetoricam Aristotelis* (London 1822) 206, who writes on 1396b 28ff. and 1358a 12ff.: 'Constat igitur locos accipi aut latius aut strictius. Primo modo loci comprehendunt etiam formas [his translation for εἴδη] . . . Secundo modo distinguuntur a formis.'

[56]1358a 31.

[57]*Ibid.* 23–26.

[58]Cf. *supra* 9f.

[59]1358a 17–21.

[60]See Stephanus, *Commentaria Graeca* 21.267. lines 34ff.

[61]1358a 12ff; 1355b 25ff.

[62]1358a 2–7.

[63]*Ibid.* 10–14.

[64]*Ibid.* 17–18.

[65]*Ibid.* 18–19.

[66]*Ibid.* 22.

[67]*Ibid.* 15–16.

[68]See note 54.

[69]1358a 17–26.

[70]E. Havet, *Étude sur la rhétorique d'Aristote* (Paris 1846) 34, expresses the distinction precisely: 'En un mot, les τόποι ne sont que des formes logiques, . . . τὰ εἴδη, au contraire, ce sont les observations, les faits ou les idées, qui font la matière du raisonnement, et sans lesquels les formes sont vides.' In essence the idea of a distinction is found in Throm, *Die*

Thesis (Paderborn 1932) 42–6; Jebb in an appendix to his translation of the Rhetoric (Cambridge 1909); Lane-Cooper, The Rhetoric of Aristotle (New York 1932) xxiv.

[71]1358a 2–7.

[72]1358a 2–7, 14ff; 1359b 1–16.

[73]1355b 25–34; 1359b 12–16. Spengel's long note in his commentary on 1355b 26 acquires, it seems, a greater significance in the light of this relation between rhetoric as a *dynamis* and the χοινοί τόποι.

[74]1355b 31–34.

[75]1358a 21–22.

[76]172a 29–b1.

[77]Aristotle at 1397a 23ff. gives an example. Here we have the χοινὸς τόπος from correlative terms. As we know, in true correlatives what is predicable of one is generally predicable of the other. As a general axiomatic proposition (assuming A and B to be correlatives) we may say: If A is x, then B is x. Aristotle applies this general form to the question of taxes (26–7). But he calls attention to the fact that it cannot be used indiscriminately and that before it can be applied to a subject (justice is his example) one must carefully determine the meaning of the terms (29ff). Such a determination must come from the εἴδη before the χοινὸς τόπος of correlative terms can be used.

[78]Spengel apparently has this in mind when he writes that the function of rhetoric is to work up the special proofs of the εἴδη and combine them with the formal to make the subject of discussion universally understood, Ueber das Studium (n. 51) 22: '. . . ihr [Rhetorik] liegt ob, die Beweise, welche die einzelne Wissenschaft gibt, zu verarbeiten, mit den formellen zu verbinden, und den Gegenstand zur allgemeinen Kenntniss zu bringen.'

[79]As found in c. 23 of Book II.

[80]Spengel in his commentary sub 1397a 1 maintains that some are not universal, i.e., common to all rhetorical argument; also Cope, An Introduction to Aristotle's Rhetoric (London 1867) 129.

[81]The Roman numerals refer to Roemer's numbering in his text.

[82]Solmsen, op. cit. 163 and note 5 says well: 'Die als Beispiele beigebrachten ἐνθυμήματα der Rhetorik sind durchaus in sich geschlossene Gedankengänge . . . und verhalten sich zu den τόποι, die sie illustrieren, in der Tat wie die πολλά zum formbestimmenden ἕν.'

[83]Cf. supra 8, and 1358a 10–17.

[84]J. Lukasiewicz, Aristotle's Syllogistic (Oxford 1951) 20, see also 2.

[85]And see Alexander, Commentaria graeca II 2 p. 5 lines 21–28.

[86]Bochenski, op. cit. 122. Bochenski (and also Solmsen) does not think that the Theophrastean τόπος is the same as the Aristotelian. Throm, op. cit. 43 and Thionville, op. cit. 30–35 consider it Aristotelian. And Bonitz and Ross on Met. 1014b note that τόπος as στοιχεῖον would be 'an argument applicable to a variety of subjects.' Top. 163b 18–164a appears to express a similar idea.

[87]Waitz, op. cit. 362.

[88]I believe that Thionville, op. cit. 74 sees this process at work but does not recognize it.

[89]Top. 101b 15ff.

[90]In the Topics, then, many of the τόποι are focal points for the analysis, criticism, and evaluation of terms, all within the framework of the four categories. For instance at 132a 22–4 it is by these τόποι (διὰ τῶνδε σχεπτέον, ἐχ τῶνδε θεωρητέον) that we determine a thing as a property. Another summary expression of the method appears at 153a 6–28, on definition: to be a true definition a genus and differentia must be present, and to ascertain whether these are on hand, certain places (τόποι) must be examined. In this regard Solmsen's (op. cit. 156) observation on the origin of the τόποι is of significance to me, although I am confining it to the particular topics. He sees the genesis of the Aristotelian

topoi in the attempt to specify one's subject, and traces their probable origin to the elenchic dialectic of the Socratic–early Platonic τί ἐστι questions. In general it does not seem true (and a passage like *Top.* 152b 36–153a 5 would appear to strengthen this) that Aristotle is concerned with specifying the meaning of terms, and a meaning grounded in the metaphysical reality. In this sense his method may well have had in mind what Hambruch (*op. cit.* 29) says was the aim of one of Plato's dialectical methods: 'die Bildung eines festgefügten und wohlgegliederten Begriffsystems . . .'

[91]In this regard Hambruch's attempt to discover the genesis of the methodology of Aristotle's topics appears valid in its general outline. He finds it (*op. cit.* 8–17) in the logical–metaphysical rules for Platonic διαίρεσιζ, e.g. ἅμα χαὶ πρότερον ψύσει, πρός τι ὄντα, μᾶλλον χαὶ ἧττον. This last rule is called the χοινὸζ τόποζ of the more-less in the *Rhetoric* and is set down in this axiomatic form (1397b 12–14): τοῦτο γάρ ἐστιν, εἰ ᾧ μᾶλλον ἂν ὑπάρχοι μὴ ὑπάρχει, δῆλον ὅτι οὐδ ᾧ ἧττον. As I see it, Hambruch's rules are the same fundamental sort of rules which were discovered independently to be at work in the general topics (see *supra* 13).

[92]E.g. in 114b 38ff. he uses χοινὸζ τόποζ IV; in 116a–b, XI, XIII, XVII; in 119a 37ff. I and II are employed, and they are described as: μάλιστα δ ἐπίχαιροι χαὶ χοινοὶ τῶν τόπων; in 124a 15ff. we find III, and in 154a 12–22 he speaks of the general effectiveness of these topics that are τοὺζ μάλιστα χοινούζ.

[93]In terms of this distinction it is interesting to note that if a rough analogy is drawn between rhetoric as a part of practical philosophy and *scientia* as a part of speculative philosophy we seem to have something of a parallel between the principal elements leading to ἐπιστήμη in one instance, and to πίστιζ in the other:

i) ἀρχαί $\begin{cases} \text{χοιναί} - \text{ἀξιώματα} \\ \text{ἴδιαι} - \text{θέσειζ} \end{cases}$ $\begin{cases} \text{ὁρισμοί} \\ \text{ὑποθέσειζ} \end{cases}$ } through which syllogism and induction effect knowledge

ii) ἀρχαι $\begin{cases} \text{χοιναί} - \text{τόποι} \\ \text{ἴδιαι} - \text{εἴδη} \end{cases}$ } through which enthymeme and example effect belief.

Furthermore it would follow that there is not in the *Rhetoric* a double enthymeme theory as Marx, *op. cit.* 281ff. and Solmsen, *op. cit.* 14f. would suggest, but rather a single theory which considers the enthymeme a unit composed of εἴδη and χοινοὶ τόποι.

Mary Carruthers

"From: The Book of Memory"

It is clear both from descriptions of pedagogy and from the practices of individual writers, that much of the process of literary composition was expected to occur mentally, in mature authors, according to a well-defined method that had postures, settings, equipment, and products all its own. The drafts that resulted were designated by different names, which do vary a bit according to the particular writer, but each of which denotes a fairly well defined stage of composition. These are, first, *invention,* taught as a wholly mental process of searching one's inventory. It involves recollection primarily, and occurs with postures and in settings that are also signals of *meditatio;* indeed, it is best to think of invention as a meditational activity. It results in a product called the *res,* a term we are familiar with from the pedagogy of memory training, and which means about the same thing in this context. The *res* is the "gist" of one's composition; more complete than what modern students think of as an outline, it should, according to Quintilian, be formed fully enough to require no more than finishing touches of ornamentation and rhythm. In other words, the *res* is like an early draft or even notes for a composition, still requiring much shaping and adjustment.

The post-invention stage is, properly, composition itself. Its products are called *dictamen;* it might, but need not, involve writing instruments. As will become clear, the *dictamen* is most like what we now call a "draft"; a number of versions, each unfinished, could be involved. *Compositio* covers three closely-related activities: *formalization,* or taking one's *res* and giving it final form as a composed piece; *correcting,* both by adding and emending, but also by comparing and adjusting the revisions to make sure the words fit one's *res* in intention and accuracy as much as possible (changing one's *res* drastically at this stage would indicate a lack of proper invention); *polishing,* artfully adjusting one's expression to make it striking and memorable in all its details (the medieval *ars dictaminis* addresses this specifically). For *compositio,* a set of waxed tablets or other informal (easily correctable) writing support could be used, on which one might write down all or parts of one's *res* to make stylistic tinkering easier. But, depending on one's maturity and experience, this process could, like invention, be completely mental.

When the *dictamen* was shaped satisfactorily, the composition was fully written out on a permanent surface like parchment in a scribal hand; this final product was the *exemplar* submitted to the public. (Usually, as we shall see, the scribal fair-copy was submitted once again for a final corrective collation by the author or author's agent before the exemplar was made available for further copying.) The word "writing" properly refers to this last inscribing process, which the author might do himself, but usually did not. Saint Anselm's biographer, Eadmer, clarifies this when he describes how he wrote his biography of Anselm:

> When I had first taken the work in hand, and had already transcribed onto parchment a great part of what I had drafted in wax [*quae in cera dictaveram pergamenae magna ex parte tradissem*], Father Anselm himself one day called me to him privately and asked what it was I was drafting and copying [*quid dictitarem, quid scriptitarem*].

Eadmer was reluctant to obey, knowing Anselm's humility, but showed his work in the hope that Anselm would correct it. In fact, Anselm did so, deleting some things, approving others, and reordering some material. But, as Eadmer feared, Anselm's reticence showed itself a few days later when he called Eadmer in and told him to destroy all "the quires in which I had put together the work." Eadmer obeyed the letter of Anselm's order and destroyed the quires after first copying their contents into others.

In this admission of guilt, Eadmer makes clear the distinction between the composing and copying stages. Of the first, he uses the verb *dictare*, of the second *scribere*. *Dictare* is done "in cerae," "on wax"; *scribere* is the action whereby the *dictamen* is *traditum*, "transcribed," to parchment. Since Eadmer did his own copying the distinction is an interesting one, for it indicates that Eadmer thought of the two activities as different, even when the same person performed them. *Dictare*, for Eadmer, evidently simply means "compose," without any suggestions of oralness (one can "dictate" with one's stylus on wax); *scribere* is what a scribe does, even when the scribe is also the author. One needs to be careful not to over-generalize Eadmer's consistent distinction, for there are instances when the verb *dictare* means "dictate to a secretary," as Thomas Aquinas did, sometimes from a written *dictamen* (in *littera inintelligibilis*) and often directly from memory. And *scribere* is used in contexts when the author is still composing. But the fact that these two verbs sometimes overlap in meaning does not indicate that the two processes, of composing and of transcribing in secretarial hand, were undifferentiated. The author produces a *res* or *dictamen;* that which is a *liber scriptus* is in a formal hand on parchment, and the product of a scribe.

The distinction is long-lived. Chaucer makes it, in English, when he begs his scrivener, Adam, that he should "after my makyng ... wryte more trewe!" Once the work was written out, it was corrected by the author (Chaucer complains of the amount of rubbing and scraping of parchment he must do after Adam's work), as Anselm corrected Eadmer's written composition, and equally, as Bernard of Clairvaux and Augustine corrected the *reportationes* of their oral sermons. It is important to realize that the written version of a text was considered to be a scribal or secretarial product, not an authorial one *no matter who the scribe was*. As such a written text was presumed to need emendation and correction; *emendare* is also a stage of the composition, formation, "authoring" of a text, which follows the fair-copy product. This is very different from the status which a printed text has now, for a medieval text was not presumed to be *perfectus*, "finished," even though it had been *scriptus*, "written." The first task which both ancient and medieval elementary students performed in school when they had written copies of texts before them was *collatio*, in which the *grammaticus* read aloud from his text while the pupils emended theirs; thus the introduction a child had in school to a written text was as something that needed to be checked and corrected.

Having sketched these stages out, I now want to examine in more detail how they are related to the procedures of trained recollection. In Book x of his *Institutio*, Quintilian describes an unskilled student in the throes of starting a composition (the stage of invention), as lying on his back with eyes turned up to the ceiling, trying to fire up his composing power ("cogitationem") by murmuring to himself, in the hope that he will find things in his memorial inventory to bring together into a composition. (That Quintilian does not approve of such desperation, preferring that one compose more calmly, is not germane to my present concern.) If a modern teacher were to describe such a scene of typical desperation, she would not do it in these terms. Instead, someone would be described with pen in hand, seated at a desk amid heaps of crumpled paper. And while the person might have a desperate or vacant look, while he might get up to pace the floor and stare out a window, he would be silent, returning constantly but silently to his pen and sheets of paper (or her computer screen). And when composition finally began, that too would be silent (even though, in fact, many people still subvocalize while actually composing). What Quintilian describes, however, is a student murmuring during recollective meditation in order to compose. And this he regards as the typical initiating activity of composition—what one does in order "to get an idea."

The mental activity which Quintilian's desperate author is attempting to stimulate is *cogitatio*. This is one of the functions of the "inner sense," and, as we have seen, while it gets defined with somewhat different emphases in the various accounts of human psychology, it is the ability to compose. To summarize my earlier description, *vis cogitativa* is closely allied in medieval psychology with *vis aestimativa*. According to Avicenna, who defines it most stringently, it is the compositive human imagination, or the activity of taking the individual phantasms produced by *vis imaginativa* or *vis formalis* and putting them together with other images, mainly those previously stored in memory. It corresponds to what Aristotle calls the "deliberative imagination," a combination of *phantasia* with *dianoia*, or the power of constructing with conscious judgment a single image out of a number of images. Some medieval psychologists distinguished the simple act of putting images together from the act of judging the result, and use *imaginativa* for the former, reserving *cogitativa* for the judging faculty. But throughout its long history, *cogitatio* is basically the activity of putting images together in a consciously recollected, deliberative way. Though it is often translated into modern English as "thought," one should never forget that the *vis cogitativa* is an activity of *animus*, the sensory-emotional soul; it therefore is never as abstractly rational as the modern word "thought." Its judging power is emotional, the sort of thing that causes a lamb, seeing a wolf, to run in fear. For Aristotle, the cogitative activity ("dianoêtikê psychê") is "the faculty which judges what is to be pursued and what is to be avoided," what is good and what is evil, not "rationally" but as an initial emotional judgment; cogitation, he says, also comprises the functions of combination and separation. So the act of invention, carried out by cogitation, was thought to be one of combining or "laying together" in one "place" or compositive image or design the divided bits previously filed and cross-filed in other discrete *loci* of memory. The result was a mental product called the *res*, the model of one's composition. It is this that an orator or preacher would lay up in *imagines rerum* when preparing to speak, and its close kinship is apparent to the technique of memorizing texts according to their *res*, which one would then shape into words to suit a particular occasion.

For composition is not an act of writing, it is rumination, cogitation, dictation, a listening and a dialogue, a "gathering" (*collectio*) of voices from their several places in memory. The fifteenth-century Italian physician, Mattheolus of Perugia, wrote that *meditatio* is derived from "mentis dictatio." The ancient writers frequently speak of the importance of listening to what one is composing. In *Heroides*, Ovid's Leander writes that "having spoken in such words to myself in a low murmur, the rest my right hand talked through with the parchment." Thus, the *vox tenuis* which accompanied meditative reading seems to have accompanied composition as well; we might recall the story of Thomas Aquinas's conversations with Saints Peter and Paul that so disturbed his *socius*. I have used the phrase "hermeneutical dialogue" to describe the relationship between a reader and his reading in *meditatio*; it applies also to composition, for indeed that hermeneutical dialogue constitutes the process of composing, as reading and other experience is gathered together and domesticated in memory.

But what exactly was this process of *collectio* thought to be as it relates to our own acts of composing? One of the boldest and most complete accounts comes from Augustine, as one might expect. During his meditation on *memoria* in Book X of the *Confessions*, Augustine speaks of how the sense impressions are "impressed" in the mind as images stored up in the wonderous cells of memory. Then he proceeds to discuss *cogitatio* and *collectio*, as the power and particular activity involved in making ideas, creating thoughts. "Cogitando," ("thinking") is "nothing else but by meditating to gather together those same things which the memory did before contain more scatteringly and confusedly." Augustine's use of *colligere*, deriving from the verb which means both "to lay down" and "to read," carries in this context a specific meaning of gathering together the memories of what one has read and stored in separate places earlier, as well as a general meaning of "collecting" earlier experiences of all sorts.

We discover ("anvenimus") such things as concepts and ideas when by an act of cogitation (*cogitendo*) we collect ("colligere"), and by the act of turning our *animus* we attend to ("animadvertendo curare") those things which the memory has held here and there ("passim") and unarranged together in any particular design ("indisposite"). These we place ("posita") gathered together in our memory, so those matters which formerly lay scattered from each other and unnoticed ("ubi sparsa prius et neglecta latitabant") now easily come together in a "familiar" opinion ("iam familiari intentioni facile occurrant"). The process Augustine describes is generally recognizable to us from other writers too, for this is Aristotelian *vis cogitativa*. *Cogitatio* finds ("invenire") things held in various memory-places and collects them ("colligere") into one place ready at hand ("ad manum posita").

"How many things of this kind my memory holds," Augustine continues, "placed ready at hand . . . things which we are said to have learned [*didicisse*] and to know [*nosse*]." If I stop recollecting them ("recolere") then they again break up and slip away ("dilabantur") into the remoter recesses of my memory ("in remotiora penetralia"), whence I must draw them together again ("cogenda rursus") in order to know them again. Knowing, *cogitandum,* derives its name from this action of continually gathering dispersed images and *res* together ("ex quadam dispersione colligenda"). For *cogo* (draw together) and *cogitatio* (cogitate) are derivative one from the other, as are *ago* (do) and *agitatio* (do continually) and *facio* (make) and *facito* (make frequently)." But the action of gathering is a particular property of the mind's activity, so that what is collated in the memory ("in animo colligitur") is now said literally to be cogitated, *cogitari.*

So learning is itself a process of composition, collation and recollection. But the result of bringing together the variously stored bits in memory is "new" knowledge. It is one's own composition and opinion, *familiari intentio*. This is the point at which collation becomes authorship. Augustine understood this quite well in his own composing experience, for he speaks of the process of *cogitatio/collectio* as an expansive one; paradoxically perhaps, the act of bringing memory images together into a single, compositive design is the path to greater, more comprehensive understanding. "I know but I do not understand," he says in one of his sermons, drawing a characteristic distinction, "but cogitation makes us expand, expansion stretches us out, and stretching makes us roomier." For Augustine, the pieces brought together in *cogitatio* make a sum greater than its parts. Knowledge extends understanding not by adding on more and more pieces, but because as we compose our design becomes more capacious, it dilates. "New" knowledge, what has not been thought, results from this process, for dilation leads ultimately even through the deepest "cavi" of memory to God. Augustine characteristically speaks of this as a "going through." How shall I reach God? he asks. "I shall pass through [*transibo*] even this power of mine which is called memory; I shall pass through it to reach Thee, sweet Light." God is indeed beyond memory, but the only way there is through and by means of it, "ascendens per animum meum ad te." Augustine gives it a metaphysical twist, but his description of how invention occurs as an activity of *memoria* belongs clearly to the ordinary pedagogy of rhetoric.

In practice, invention was an intensely emotional state, more so than we now associate with thinking. We have very few specific medieval accounts of people doing what we call composing. Among the best are those of Thomas Aquinas, and Eadmer's description of Anselm, written around 1100. The work in question was the *Proslogion;* Eadmer reports what Anselm told him of the great difficulty he experienced composing it:

> partly because thinking about it [*haec cogitatio*] took away his desire for food, drink and sleep, and partly—and this was more grievous to him—because it disturbed the attention [*gravabat intentionem ejus*] which he ought to have paid to matins and to Divine service at other times. When he was aware of this, and still could not entirely lay hold on what he sought, he supposed that this line of thought [*hujusmodi cogitationem*] was a temptation of the devil and he tried to banish it from his mind [*repellere a sua intentione*]. But the more vehemently he tried to do this, the more this thought pursued him [*tanto illum ipsa cogitatio magis ac magis infestabat*]. Then suddenly one night during matins the grace of God illuminated his heart, the whole matter [*res*] became clear to his mind, and a great joy and exultation filled his inmost being. Thinking therefore that others also would be glad to know what he had found, immediately [*ilico*] and ungrudgingly [*livore carens*] he wrote it on writing-tablets [*rem . . . scripsit in tabulis*] and gave it to one of the brethren of the monastery for safe-keeping.

There are a number of interesting features to this description. Eadmer describes the activity of composition as one of profound concentration, a meditative withdrawal that takes one from food, sleep, and even the most sacred routines of the day. This activity is described in the repeated terms *intentio* (concentration) and *cogitatio* (mulling over). This *cogitatio* is spoken of initially as an enemy; Anselm wants to repell it ("repellere"), but it more and more aggressively and hostilely takes over ("infestabat") his *intentio*, even when he turns it to the liturgical office (which is to be performed also with *intentio*). So obsessed is he that he fears the devil is tempting him. Then, of a sudden, *cogitatio* is completed (Eadmer attributes the grace of God) and only at that moment is a product, called the "res," committed to a writing surface—but to one that is traditionally associated with unfinished work and with the formation and functions of memory. By no means has it yet been "authorized," that is, become an "auctor" or source-text for other minds and memories to use.

I have already stressed that *cogitatio* involves recollection since it uses memorial images; however, it is a pre-rational process even though it involves making judgments, for these are emotionally and intuitively based at this point rather than logically so. Like meditative reading, invention is not, to use the categories of medieval psychology, a process of the "intellectual" soul, but primarily of the "sensory-emotional" one, dependent upon the images stored in memory and the effectiveness of the heuristic structures in which they have been laid down there.

This antiquated language conceals from us an important characteristic of memorial cultures, one I have stressed before but that is worth pointing to again. Alexander Murray has reminded us that what constitutes "rational behavior" is, to some considerable extent, a matter of culture. His *Reason and Society in the*

Middle Ages traces how "reasonableness" as a category of thought was influenced in the later Middle Ages by a tension between "monastic culture," whose roots were in the disciplines of meditational prayer (among other things), and "intellectual culture," which developed in the urban ambiance of the universities. These tendencies existed equally in the same institutions and even the same individuals. They were not often perceived as tensions in conflict, but their eventual incompatibility is reflected in our sharp division now between "reason" and "emotion," to the point of assuming them to be incompatible altogether. In the teaching and practice of composition, however, the monastic cultivation of meditational prayer, itself evolving from practices in the ancient schools, remained dominant. This stressed emotion, the basis of memory, as the key to "creativity," as we can readily see from the fact that medieval *cogitatio*, translates, as I emphasized in chapter 2, not as our phrase "reasoning out" (with its emphasis on logical connections) but as "mulling over," a process that depends heavily on free association and one's "feeling for" a matter.

Quintilian assures his students that *cogitatio* can be greatly helped by an orderly consideration of the case, but that order is not necessarily what we would call "logical" or "intellectual." It is an heuristic structure which we follow by habit rather than "deducing" it anew from each separate occurrence; that is, we follow a set form or procedure we have memorized (for example, we might apply an invention procedure like the "adverbial question" which my schoolteachers taught me: who, what, where, when, how, why? Or, were we medieval clerics needing a sermon on a text, we might use the heuristic of the "four levels" of interpretation.) Reason alone cannot help that frantically murmuring student, for he has not yet gathered his memorial images to the point where reason can process them. All that can help is a recollected heuristic, a trained memory which proceeds by habit and emotion, pre-rationally.

The highly emotional state described by Quintilian is very like that of Anselm as he desperately sought what he could not quite find ("nec adhuc quod quaerebat ad plenum capere valens"). We recall also what Thomas Aquinas's biographers said of his habit of intense prayer: "At night . . . he would rise, after a short sleep, and pray, lying prostrate on the ground; it was in those nights of prayer that he learned what he would write or dictate in the day-time. Such was the normal tenor of his life—a minimum of time allowed to sleeping and eating, and all the rest given to prayer or reading or thinking or writing or dictating." Such physical accompaniments of *cogitatio* are apparent in all the accounts of composition, prostration being its common posture; Quintilian's student lies down on his back, Thomas Aquinas face-downwards. It is a position designed to shut out external stimuli, especially visual ones, which would serve to confuse or distract one's recollective eye as it looks through its inventory of places, for both *strepitus* and *turba* are great mnemonic enemies.

The emotions (*affectus*) are the starting-point, as they must be in order to engage *memoria* and *cogitatio*. Reginald, Thomas Aquinas's *socius*, said of him that "in his soul, intellect and desire [*intellectus et affectus*] somehow contained each other . . . his desire [*affectus*], through prayer, gained access to divine realities, which then the intellect, deeply apprehending, drew into a light which kindled to greater intensity the flame of love." Desire begins the ascent to understanding by firing memory, and through memory's stored-up treasures the intellect is able to contemplate; the higher its understanding, the more desire flames in love as it both gets and gives more light. It is a sentiment worthy of Dante himself. So Anselm, searching his memory places for the pieces he cannot quite find to complete the design which his *cogitatio* is constructing fears the devil, fears the intense emotion that has invaded his body as well as his thoughts, keeping him from food and sleep as well as from liturgical prayer. So Thomas falls prostrate in tearful prayer. But the products of this non-logical, obsessive, emotional activity are closely-reasoned monuments of scholastic logic, the *Proslogion* and the *Summa theologica*.

It is significant that the times when both Anselm and Thomas Aquinas are described as being particularly distraught are when they are stuck, searching for connections they can't quite get hold of. "Once at Paris," writes Gui of Thomas Aquinas, "when writing on Paul's epistles, he came upon a passage which quite baffled him until, dismissing his secretaries, he fell to the ground and prayed with tears; then what he desired was given him and it all became clear." Thomas wept in order to solve an intellectual difficulty; Anselm behaved like a monk in love until his rational problem came clear. A modern scholar similarly stumped would go to the library or thumb through notes. By such transports of fear and desire, Thomas and Anselm expected to stimulate their memorial libraries. Gui reports that Thomas never set himself to compose without tearful prayer, and "[w]hen perplexed by a difficulty he would kneel and pray and then, on returning to his writing or dictation, he was accustomed to find that his thought had become so clear that it seemed to show him inwardly as in a book the words he needed." It is clear also from Gui's account that Thomas deliberately and habitually cultivated the posture of prostrate prayer in order to produce a solution to a specific compositional problem.

After invention comes the process of shaping the *res* into the version called *dictamen*. The mental activity required is still what the philosophers called *vis cogitativa*, but rhetoricians appear to use *cogitatio* for the revision stage of composition. (This is a bit confusing because Eadmer speaks of Anselm's invention stage as "cogitatio," perhaps because he was not a teacher of rhetoric.) One is still composing, but working on a much more complete form of the text than at the start of *inventio*. There seem to be a number of terms used for this stage—Fortunatianus and Julius Victor both call this "compositio"; Quintilian reserves the word "cogitatio" for it; Augustine calls it "collectio"; for Hugh of St. Victor, as we shall see, it was a kind of "collatio." In any event, the root concept is still a recollective one, bringing together, "collecting" from different "places," into a designed text (*res*) which now exists in a common place in one's memory. A related distinction is made in the scholastic terms for these two stages, invention and composition, called respectively *forma tractatus* and *forma tractandi*. The "forma tractatus" corresponds to the *res* of a text, the content arrived at during invention, or the "drawing"—both "out" and "together"—(the root meaning of *traho*) of material into a fully coherent textual argument. The "forma tractatus" can then be shaped up and refined stylistically in a "forma tractandi." The continuous, polishing nature of this latter activity is indicated in the fact that a present participle is used for it (*tractandi*), whereas the *res* is finished (*tractatus*) when invention is complete. A tract (*tractatus*) is philosophical or moral argumentation without stylistic embellishments or "figures"; the basic expression of reasons, ideas, logical connections and all structural elements such as divisions, belong to the "forma tractatus" and the various figures of style to "forma tractandi." Such definitions follow naturally from the pedagogy and practice of composition I have described. The distinction is correlative to that between "memoria ad res" and "memoria verborum," and also to the emphasis given to the former in the pedagogy of *memoria*.

Fortunatianus says that *memoria* has two essential objects: that material be securely retained, and that it be directly (*cito*) retrievable. This is essential not only for *compositio* that uses writing (*scripta*) but "immo et cogitatio," "especially cogitatio." Later, speaking of Simonides's system, he remarks that for "scripta vel cogitatio" we should place together orderly heuristic cues and memorial *similitudines*. Julius Victor makes a similar distinction between composition during which we write ("scribimus") and that we do in cogitation ("cogitamus") both of which depend on the same processes of *divisio* and *compositio* that characterize a trained and designed memory. Both these writers are distinguishing between methods of composition, one which involves writing on a physical surface and one which is entirely mental, involving no written draft at all.

One should take careful note that neither writer suggests that the two styles of composing require different mental preparation or procedures, or that one involves memory and the other not. Indeed, as presented, the difference is no more significant than our individual preferences for revising in longhand or at a machine. We see similar idiosyncrasy of choice in the compositional aids of writers throughout the Middle Ages. The same writer may choose sometimes to work with a wax tablet and other times not. Thomas Aquinas, we recall, wrote out portions of his *res* of the *Summa contra gentiles* in *littera inintelligibilis*. These pages show the signs of revision and tinkering that characterize the shaping up of a *dictamen*. But for the composition of *Summa theologica* (a longer and more complex work) he worked most often without writing anything down at all, calling a secretary in when he was finished to take down his dictation in fair hand. Quintilian, advising that prose rhythm is an effect to be worked on carefully, relates approvingly that Plato tried out the first four words of the *Republic* in a variety of orders on his wax tablets in order "to make the rhythm as perfect as possible," because this small elegance could be better worked on with the help of a tablet. Quintilian himself, however, does not encourage dependence on such physical aids. It is important to keep in mind that Quintilian was addressing the requirements of orally-delivered compositions, the need to be able to revise and change, digress and add, freely and confidently during delivery itself. So the various techniques he discusses are derived in response to such a situation. But these same techniques were applied to compositions designed to be read, and the drafting stages in the production of a final exemplar are virtually the same; the production of a *res* and then a *dictamen* follows the same successive steps, whether the *dictamen* was then read to a scribe or delivered publicly.

When was the stylus to be used? Here again individual habits obviously varied, but Quintilian describes in detail the received pedagogy that lies behind the distinctions made by later teachers and practitioners. The elementary preparation for eloquence is writing, he says in Book x (on composition); a beginner must write out maxims and sayings on wax tablets "as much as possible and with the utmost care." Writing is crucial because it forces us to concentrate and its slowness makes us careful: "as deep ploughing makes the soil more fertile . . . so, if we improve our minds by something more than superficial study, we shall produce a richer growth of knowledge and shall retain it with greater accuracy [*fidelius continet*]." In other words, one writes solely as an aid to memory: "it is writing that provides that holy of holies where the wealth of oratory is stored and whence it is produced to meet the demands of sudden emergencies." "Illic opes velut sanctiore quodam aeraris conditae," "there the riches are hidden away as in a kind of most sacred treasury"; the phrase could serve as summary of Hugh of St. Victor's opening paragraph in his preface on memory-training, composed ten centuries later.

A beginner must also learn how to cultivate the circumstances needed in all meditational activity. Young students should seek out solitude, silence, and seclusion, and learn to pursue their task with utmost concentration and involvement. Gestures accompanying strong emotion will likewise serve to stimulate the mind (*animus*), and so important is this gestural stimulus that one should not follow the example of those foolish authors who start dictating right away to scribes, lest the presence of another inhibit us (recall how Gui says Thomas Aquinas sent his secretaries away before he prostrated himself in tears). The author should learn not to compose in "the heat and impulse of the moment," dashing off a speedy draft as some do, who call such a thing their "silva," literally meaning "forest" but used metaphorically here for "unformed matter." One should exercise care from the outset "to form the work . . . in such a manner that it merely requires to be chiselled [*caelandum*] into shape." Here Quintilian advises that the *res* of one's composition be carefully planned out in one's mind before it is committed in any way to written form; "chiselling" is what one does on one's tablets (and a scribe is not appropriate until the very last stage). Finally, even as beginning students, we should "train ourselves so to concentrate our thoughts [*intentio*] as to rise superior to all impediments to study. If only you direct all your attention to the work which you have in hand, no sight or sound will ever penetrate to your mind." Therefore, wherever we are, in a crowd, on a journey, at a party, we must practice fashioning a secret inner sanctuary ("secretum") for *cogitatio*.

Quintilian stresses one matter in regard to the layout of the waxed tablets. Waxed tablets best serve excision and correction (though people with poor eyes may have to use parchment in order to see the letters better—parchment slows down the writing process, however, and so may hinder thought). Excision and correction were, of course, vital in revision but so was addition and what we might think of as digression. Dilation, *dilatatio,* allowing space for matter that might occur to you while you revise, is just as necessary as excision. As a beginner writing one's *res* onto tablets, one should, says Quintilian, be sure to allow such space physically, in the form of blank leaves, and also be sure not to cover all the space of the tablet page, but leave generous margins. The practice seems self-evident, and I don't wish to belabor it, but it underscores how the original text, the *res,* was conceived of as a common "place" into which new material is "collected" from other "places" in the tablets as one refines one's *dictamen* for delivery to an audience. For Quintilian does not recommend that one continuously recopy one's revised text in a "clean copy" in order to incorporate such additions—thus a set of written tablets would show visually just what was original and what was added (erasures are not so apparent on wax as on paper because the end of the stylus smooths the wax out). This is the visual image of his text which a student would imprint in memory before delivering it—not that of a clean, fixed document but rather the memorandum of a text, a palimpsest of the series of one's compositional drafts. It is a procedure that invites additional digression and commentary.

Having learned to revise with stylus and tablets, a student advances to the technique of *cogitatio* proper, the ability to revise mentally (Quintilian is using the word *cogitatio* to refer to a technique, not simply to the natural psychological process). "Proxima stilo cogitatio est," he writes, "next in order [of mastery] after writing with a pen is cogitation." *Cogitatio* "derives force from the practice of writing and forms an intermediate stage between the labors of the pen and the more precarious fortunes of improvisation," and is more frequently used by mature orators than either of the other two compositional methods. Eventually, through practice, we will develop to the point where we can rely as surely on what we have prepared by *cogitatio* alone as what we have written out word for word and memorized. *Cogitatio,* however, requires an especially careful conception of the order of the composition, so that we may take advantage of things occurring to us at the moment (those which we would put in the margin if we were using a tablet). Such a composition "must be conceived on such lines that we shall find no difficulty either in departing from it or returning to it at will."

"But the crown of all our study and the highest reward of our long labors is the power of improvisation," especially for an advocate who cannot always count on having time to prepare himself, and must instead rely on the agility and readiness which he has acquired by practice and training. *Ex tempore dicendi,* "improvisation," calls first of all for knowing the order in which the points of an argument proceed, from first to second to third and so on. *Divisio* is absolutely essential to establish the "modus et finem," "method and conclusion," of a composition. The mind must be so trained that it can pay attention to the invention, arrangement, and style both of what we are saying at the moment and what we will say next, for an extemporaneous speech must especially exhibit "an orderly, ornate, and fluent manner" and have "regular pattern"—"in plures simul continuas," "among many different things continuing design at the same time."

To ensure such facility, Quintilian counsels that, together with all the relevant questions, persons, and arguments, we must keep before our mental eyes "*rerum imagines*" or *phantasiai*. The phrase is used technically here, to refer to those vivid images of "the thing[s]," those which we have associated with the *res* of our composition. Their function is not only to keep track of the composition's form (as it is in *Ad Herennium*) but to awaken the emotions of the orator. "Maxima enim pars eloquentiae constat animo. Hunc adfici, hunc conspicere imagines rerum . . . necesse est." The greatest part of rhetorical activity involves the functions of the sensory soul, forming, combining, reacting to, storing, and recollecting sense images. Quintilian more particularly describes the value of the *phantasiai* to the orator, for thereby "things absent are presented to our *animus* with such vividness that they seem actually to be before our very eyes."

The mature orator will use all three methods of composition. He will write out and memorize some of his speech (perhaps the beginning) and may use his tablets as he is composing to perfect particular phrases, he will above all carefully plan out and prepare the bulk of his oration by *cogitatio*, and be able to adapt to sudden turns of a case, or to sudden inspiration, by speaking extempore when he wants to. Cicero himself kept "notebooks" (*libellos*) of memoranda; Quintilian will allow, he says, the use of such jottings, which may even be held in the hand and occasionally glanced at. But "I think we should never write out anything which we do not intend to commit to memory."

Throughout the Middle Ages, preaching included much *ex tempore dicendi*, as one might expect. The Dominican friar, Giordano of Pisa (he who first publicized eyeglasses), can be quite frank about his freedom. "I thought of preaching to you not about this, but about something else; but when it pleased Him that I should be so fluent in this, thank God this has really been a good sermon. But anyway I want to tell you a little about what I had planned to say." On another occasion, "I am so full, and I have so much in me, and I am so rich that I do not know what to say to you: I have said nothing of what I prepared, not a thing." The friar's sermons were taken down by reporters, whose comments are preserved; this *reportatio* represented the first written version of the work, which Friar Giordano seems not to have subsequently corrected.

The written *reportatio* was customarily submitted to the author for emendation before being published. Deferrari quotes from Gregory Nazianzenus's farewell sermon: "Farewell, ye lovers of my discourses, in your eagerness and concourse, ye pencils seen and unseen, and those balustrades, pressed upon by those who thrust themselves forward to hear the word." These "pencils" continued to be a fact of life in both the lay and learned circles throughout the Middle Ages; it is, I think, worth noting that Gregory refers to them as simple machines. He is, of course, being witty but his wit tells us something quite profound about the way in which the reporter's role was regarded. The scribe as such is not a thinking being, a reader or scholar, certainly not an *auctor* himself, but a mere "pencil," performing the humble and subservient task of writing.

Christian sermons were thus composed and published in the manner of all ancient orations, worked out mentally in the ways that Quintilian describes, written down at the time of delivery by reporters and then often corrected by the author before being made available for further dissemination in an exemplar. The Greek church historian, Socrates, says of Atticus, bishop of Constantinople: "Formerly, while a presbyter, he had been accustomed after composing his sermons, to commit them to memory, and then to recite them in church; but by diligent application, he acquired confidence and made his instruction extemporaneous and eloquent. His discourses, however, were not such as to be received with much applause by his auditors, or to deserve to be committed to writing." Atticus demonstrates exactly the sequence of training and proficiency which Quintilian describes, even though his results were disappointing to his congregation. And we must also notice that a sharp distinction is made between Atticus's "writing out" and memorizing *ad verbam* for oral delivery (regarded as a mark of ineptitude) and the exemplar written by a scribe which marks a text deemed worthy to be preserved.

St. Augustine composed mentally with much happier results than poor Atticus. In a 1922 article, R. J. Deferarri gathered much of the extensive evidence in Augustine's sermons which indicates the cogitative and extempore nature of their composition, among which this remark may stand as typical. In an Easter sermon on the text "et Verbum erat apud Deum" (Jn I:I), Augustine speaks of how the "inner word" (God's *res*, as it were, which by grace informs human speech) is translated into ordinary discourse. The speaker has planned his sermon in his mind as an "inner word," which he will varyingly express to fit the occasion. "For I who speak with you," he says of his own habitual practice, "before I come before you, I mentally compose [*cogitavi*] in advance what I will say to you. When I have composed what I will say to you, then the word is in my memory. Nor would I speak to you, unless I had previously composed in my mind." This mixture of prior *cogitatio* and purely *ex tempore dicendi* is a common feature not only of Augustine's sermons but of those of his contemporaries, Roman and Greek, and clearly continued throughout the Middle Ages. Not only does Augustine's *De doctrina christiana* assume that preachers will compose in this way; so, as we have seen, do the late medieval *artes praedicandi* of Robert of Basevorn and Thomas of Waleys. The reason for numerically dividing sermons is to allow the preacher to take off extempore without losing his place in his premeditated sermon (he would have no need for such an aid if he were reading from a written text), or to speak in terms of memory-design, to allow him to "gather together" material from other memorial *loci* into the *locus* where the "eye of the mind" is "reading" its text. Friar Giordano's admittedly extemporaneous sermons employ numerical *divisiones* just like pre-planned ones, pulled in from the numbered bins of his memorial treasury.

Yet we must be careful not to regard the informal style of the popular sermon as caused by its predisposition to extempore composition. Quintilian, speaking for the central tradition of classical rhetoric, does not associate particular compositional methods with any of the three kinds of style distinguished in that tradition, nor with any particular genre of discourse. There are, however, two fatal errors in delivery which an orator can make (and these cautions are repeated by every writer on the subject through the Middle Ages). The first is to lose one's way in one's oration, hesitate, or be reduced to the need of a prompt. The second is to appear in any way to be reciting word for word a pre-written text. Quintilian counsels various ways of avoiding this, such as seeming to grope for a word, pausing, perhaps wondering aloud how to answer an opponent's charge, and other devices which give the effect of spontaneity. But genuine spontaneity is equally bad if one cannot achieve the same level of crafted eloquence one attains by careful *cogitatio;* that is why *ex tempore dicendi* is reserved only to masters whose memories are fully stored and effectively designed.

This ability to appear unrehearsed despite elaborate preparation is what the Romans seem to have considered the crowning achievement of rhetorical *memoria,* regarded in the context of performance. In all the rhetorical textbooks, *memoria* precedes *pronuntiatio* or "delivery" and the discussion concerns how to achieve facility and the mastery of memorial design necessary for this end. The assumption that writing is handmaid and servant to memory is once again demonstrated in this ancient prejudice against any composition appearing to have been written down in advance of delivery. Cicero says of the great orator Marcus Antonius: "he always gave the appearance of coming forward to speak without preparation, but so well prepared was he that when he spoke it was the court rather that often seemed ill prepared." Cicero particularly stresses the orator's memory: "Erat memoria summa, nulla meditationis suspicio", "When he spoke his trained memory was of the best kind, giving no hint of prior meditational composition." I know of no more succinct demonstration of how greatly we misunderstand when we reduce ancient and medieval *memoria* to our word "memorization."

Renaissance Rhetoric

In this section, Paul Oskar Kristeller discusses rhetoric as one of the *studia humanitatis* that made up Renaissance learning beginning in the fifteenth century. For Kristeller, a Renaissance humanist is a professor of *studia humanitatis;* such studies, which Kristeller summarizes in his essay, comprise the cultural and educational program that he calls *humanism.* Humanist rhetoric is distinct from but related to subjects that classical rhetoric had included, such as poetry, history, and moral philosophy.

Within an extensive survey of the types of rhetoric practiced during the Renaissance, Kristeller pauses to stress a distinction between rhetoric and philosophy, noting that humanist rhetoricians writing on philosophical issues cannot be called philosophers, because—unlike professional philosophers, who demonstrate "terminological precision and logical consistency"—the work of a "philosophical" rhetorician is usually either derivative or internally inconsistent. Thus Kristeller enters the long-standing debate over whether rhetoric can be responsibly philosophical, and as it is addressed more recently by scholars such as Christopher Norris, whether philosophy is rhetorical. Bringing his argument for the preeminence of philosophy up to the present day, Kristeller argues that romanticism vulgarized both philosophy and rhetoric, and insists that rhetoric be understood here and now as subordinate to philosophy, mainly because it is—as Plato pointed out—based on "mere opinion."

The qualities of humanist rhetoric that worry Kristeller—its inconsistency and imprecision—become for Victoria Kahn the rudiments of positive lessons in ethical thought and action. For Kahn, "the activity of the prudent man is analogous to that of the orator." Prudence, as practical wisdom, should not be informed by transcendental ideas, but operates in the realm of the contingent, and should draw from the literature of contingency, i.e., rhetoric. Kahn notes that Cicero in particular influenced Renaissance humanism with his emphasis on the inseparability of rhetoric and prudence and his proposition that dealing in the realm of contingencies—as the rhetor does—necessarily entails the development of a practical ethics.

Kahn explains that, with the conflation of rhetoric and poetics in the Renaissance and with reduced opportunities for employing oratory in the forum or the law court, the practice of rhetoric became associated more with writing and reading. The rhetor, unconstrained by the urgency of evoking an immediate pro or con judgment from a present audience, could present both sides of an issue and thus provide readers with the opportunity for surveying the breadth of elements that must inform any prudent judgment. Writing and reading, then, are exercises in practical wisdom and moral judgment.

Offering a brief case study in Renaissance literary rhetoric, Sister Miriam Joseph explains that Shakespeare's mastery of the rhetorical *pisteis* in his plays is evident in the richness, variation, and vitality of their language. For Joseph, Shakespeare is exhibiting the delight in intellectual play that Kahn wants to associate with ethical composition, and which Richard Lanham—along with Joseph—makes central to Renaissance rhetoric in his 1976 *The Motives of Eloquence.*

Paul Oskar Kristeller

"The Renaissance"

If we understand by the Renaissance the period that runs roughly from 1350 to 1600, we find that rhetoric during this era occupied a broader and more important place than during the Middle Ages. In the Renaissance, rhetoric expanded and developed greatly, and came to pervade all areas of civilization, as it had not been the case during the preceding centuries. The rule of rhetoric during the Renaissance was not as complete as it had been in Roman antiquity or in certain periods of Greek antiquity, for Renaissance rhetoric always had to compete with scholastic philosophy and theology and with the professional disciplines of law, medicine, and mathematics, with the arts and popular literature, and with many other activities. Yet the study, imitation, and cult of classical antiquity that was one of the characteristic traits of the Renaissance had in turn the effect of strengthening and promoting rhetoric.

However, Renaissance rhetoric was in many ways different from ancient rhetoric and influenced by medieval as well as by new, contemporary patterns. Unlike ancient rhetoric, Renaissance rhetoric was not primarily concerned with the political and even less with the judiciary speech. It cultivated the letter as much as the oration, and it tended to include all forms of prose composition, and to enter a close alliance with poetics, since prose and verse composition were considered as alternating forms of the same enterprise. The ancient view that rhetoric and oratory aimed at persuasion was often repeated, but it did not dominate the prevailing conception of rhetoric.

The close alliance of rhetoric and poetics and their mutual influence can be traced back from the Renaissance through the Middle Ages to late and even classical antiquity. It has been uniformly deplored by modern historians, but its consequences have not been uniformly harmful. For example, the rhyme originated in oratory long before it was adopted in poetry. The subject obviously needs further investigation, as does the reverse influence of poetry and poetics on prose and rhetoric.

During the Renaissance, rhetoric belonged to the domain of the humanists, and it occupied an important and perhaps central, though by no means exclusive place in their work. For the *studia humanitatis* included grammar and poetry, history and moral philosophy, as well as rhetoric. As a humanist enterprise, rhetoric was thus closely connected with all these other subjects, and the rhetoric of the humanists must be understood as an integral part of their widespread interests and activities. These activities included the study of ancient literature, involved the copying, editing, translating, and interpreting of classical Greek and Latin texts, and led to an impressive development of classical scholarship and philology. The humanists also produced a vast amount of literary works in prose and verse, mostly in Latin, and hence they were usually labeled as orators and poets before the term *humanista* came into use. They also claimed philosophy, and especially moral philosophy, as a part of their domain, and proposed to combine eloquence and wisdom, that is, rhetoric and philosophy, thus reviving an ideal formulated by Cicero.

The quantity and quality of the works produced by the humanists, the level of their literary and scholarly achievement, their success and prestige greatly enhanced the role of the studies which they cultivated, and of rhetoric in particular. They soon began to dominate secondary education, and to play a significant, though not a dominant role in the universities. As chancellors and secretaries of princes and republics, as teachers and tutors of noblemen, patricians, and professionals, the humanists acquired a formative influence on the upper classes of Renaissance society. The term "civic humanism" has been used to designate the ideal of an educated citizen in a free republic, especially in Florence during the early fifteenth century. The concept has its validity within its well-defined limits of place and time. Yet I should hesitate to identify civic humanism with humanism as a whole, even in Italy, let alone with the whole of Renaissance civilization. There was a good deal of humanism other than civic during the early fifteenth century, in Florence and elsewhere, and even more of it before and after the half-century that marks the high point of the alliance between humanism and Florentine political thought and propaganda. For humanism included at all times a number of moral and other ideas that were not political or social, and many literary and scholarly pursuits that had nothing to do with thought in any sense of the word. On the other hand, the Renaissance, in Italy and elsewhere, always cultivated many professional, scholarly, and intellectual traditions that were not rooted in humanism, although they may at one time or another have been influenced or affected by humanism.

To understand Renaissance rhetoric, and that means largely humanist rhetoric, it is useful to start from the classifications of the arts and sciences and from the place rhetoric occupied in them. In the scheme of the seven liberal arts which dominated from late antiquity to the high Middle Ages, rhetoric was allied with the mathematical disciplines, that is, with the *quadrivium* of arithmetic, geometry, astronomy, and music, and more intimately with grammar and dialectic which together with rhetoric formed the *trivium*. When rhetoric was treated as a part of logic, the term logic was not taken in the specific sense, but was merely used as a label to identify the *trivium* with one of the three traditional parts of philosophy. After the rise of the universities in the twelfth and thirteenth century, it became apparent that the seven arts no longer represented the sum total of secular learning or of philosophy, and that the new university subjects, that is, theology, philosophy, medicine, and jurisprudence, were different from the liberal arts and were more advanced subjects of study and instruction. Among the arts of the *trivium,* grammar and rhetoric were now confined to elementary and preliminary instruction, whereas logic or dialectic left them far behind and became closely connected with natural philosophy and with other philosophical and scientific disciplines.

The fourteenth century witnessed a rise of grammar and rhetoric, especially in Italy, and this is reflected in the new scheme of the *studia humanitatis* which we encounter in the course of the fifteenth century. This scheme, as we saw before, includes grammar, rhetoric, poetry, history, and moral philosophy. It means, when compared with the older scheme of the seven arts, that rhetoric and grammar have now lost their connections with dialectic and with the *quadrivium;* that poetry and history, previously treated as parts of grammar and rhetoric, are now explicitly recognized as related but independent pursuits; and that moral philosophy, one of the three main parts of ancient philosophy, is now reclaimed as a part of the humanities and detached from the other more technical parts of philosophy, following the ancient model of Isocrates and Cicero.

The scholar who mastered these *studia humanitatis,* who had been called *orator et poeta* since the time of Petrarch, finally became known as *humanista,* a term that originated late in the fifteenth century in the slang of university students and gradually found its way into official documents if not into literature—it was after all a word unknown to Cicero and other ancient writers. We might add that during the eighteenth century the scheme of the humanities gave way to that of the fine arts where poetry and eloquence were grouped together with music and the visual arts, and sometimes with dancing and gardening. With the rise of Romanticism, eloquence was driven out from the illustrious company of the creative arts, whereas poetry, along with the others, was raised to such awesome heights as it had rarely, if ever, reached in previous centuries.

Before we pursue the rhetorical theory and practice of the Renaissance, and the links between its rhetoric and other fields, I should like to discuss briefly the ancient sources of Renaissance rhetoric.

If we begin with the Latin sources, we should remember that the *Rhetorica ad Herennium* and Cicero's *De inventione* had been available through the Middle Ages and were interpreted at different times by a number of commentators. Also some of Cicero's speeches and philosophical writings were more or less widely known during the Middle Ages. On the other hand, Cicero's letters, some of his orations and philosophical writings, and his more mature rhetorical works such as *De oratore, Orator,* and *Brutus* were either rediscovered by the humanists or more widely read than before. This was also true of Asconius, the ancient commentator of Cicero's orations. The other great Roman rhetorician, Quintilian, was known during the Middle Ages only in a truncated version, and his complete text was recovered only during the early fifteenth century. Also the declamations of the elder Seneca and those attributed to Quintilian began to attract greater attention in the fourteenth century. The textual history of these writings in manuscripts and early printed editions and the commentaries written on them still await further investigation. Yet Renaissance Ciceronianism, beginning with Gasparino Barzizza, if not with Petrarch, had a much broader textual basis than had been available to the preceding centuries, and humanists like Loschi and Polenton were encouraged by the model of Asconius to undertake the interpretation of some of Cicero's orations.

The difference between medieval and Renaissance rhetoric is even more striking when we look at the available sources of Greek rhetoric. As we remember, only one Greek oration and three rhetorical treatises had been translated during the thirteenth century, and three of these texts had practically no circulation, whereas the fourth, Aristotle's *Rhetoric,* was treated as a work on moral philosophy and ignored by the professional rhetoricians of the period. During the Renaissance, these texts were retranslated and more widely circulated, and Aristotle's *Rhetoric* was at last studied and utilized by the professional rhetoricians, along with his *Poetics* which became widely known and influential after the end of the fifteenth century, whereas it had been almost, though not entirely, unknown during the preceding centuries. Moreover, the fifteenth and sixteenth centuries produced a large number of Latin translations from the Greek and gradually introduced the entire patrimony of Greek literature, as far as it had survived, into the mainstream of Western learning. In the field of rhetoric, the Attic orators now became completely known, and especially Lysias, Isocrates, and Demosthenes were widely read and admired. To this we must add the later orators such as Dio of Prusa and Libanius, and especially the large body of Greek rhetorical literature: Demetrius and Dionysius of Halicarnassus, ps. Longinus and Menander, Aphthonius, and Hermogenes. The bibliographical information concerning these authors is now being investigated, and this will for the first time provide a firm foundation for exploring their influence.

It is in this area where we may also look for Byzantine influence in Renaissance rhetoric. The history of Byzantine rhetoric and its influence on Italian humanism have recently attracted some scholarly attention, but the subject seems to be in need of much more detailed study than it has received so far. As far as rhetorical theory is concerned, the study of the ancient Greek orators and rhetoricians and their wide diffusion in Latin and vernacular translations, as we find it in the Renaissance, presupposes the Byzantine transmission of these texts and is a part of the general appropriation of the Greek and Byzantine heritage that characterizes the Italian and European Renaissance of the fifteenth and sixteenth century. More specifically, the works of Aphthonius and Hermogenes had dominated Byzantine rhetorical theory before they became known and influential in the West. It is characteristic that an author who combined Byzantine and Western learning, George of Trebisond, and who wrote one of the new and influential rhetorical textbooks of rhetoric in the fifteenth century, was also the first who made extensive use of Hermogenes.

In the field of epistolography, there was a large Byzantine literature, but its influence in the West is not known, except for the Greek Church Fathers and for Libanius. The large literature of Byzantine homilies does not seem to have interested Western scholars, except for the Greek Church Fathers, and the same is apparently true of the large Byzantine literature of panegyrics and encomia. It is important to realize that epistolography and oratory flourished in the East as well as in the West during the medieval centuries, but direct links, if they exist, have not yet been investigated. In the case of secular oratory, we may very well argue that it was based in the East and West on different institutional traditions.

Let us now turn to the rhetorical literature produced by the Renaissance humanists. The general treatises on rhetoric, intended to serve as manuals of instruction, were not as numerous as we might expect, at least during the fifteenth century. We may assume that most of the instruction was based on ancient or even on medieval treatises, and on the use of classical and contemporary models. The best known rhetorical treatises of the fifteenth century are those by Gasparino Barzizza, George of Trebisond, Giorgio Valla, Guillaume Fichet, and Philippus Callimachus. The question to what extent they repeated ancient theories and models and in what way they were influenced by modern practice remains to be clarified in most instances. I had occasion to examine Fichet's treatise which introduces a new terminology of its own, and a sermon composed by Fichet and accompanied by a gloss that is based on his own rhetorical textbook and terminology.

There is a whole literature on imitation which takes up the theme of the Atticists of later antiquity, and in which the merits and demerits of imitating Cicero or other ancient writers are discussed. This literature includes a correspondence between Poliziano and Paolo Cortesi, and treatises by Bembo and Gianfrancesco Pico, and later by Erasmus and others. Valla's *Elegantiae* is strictly speaking a grammatical rather than a rhetorical treatise, but it serves stylistic and rhetorical purposes and it was read and used for centuries for that reason. Rhetorical theory was contained in the commentaries on the works of Cicero and Quintilian, and in the commentaries on Aristotle's *Rhetoric* which in the sixteenth century, unlike the medieval commentaries on that work, were written by humanist rhetoricians and not by Aristotelian philosophers.

The teaching of rhetoric was served, as in antiquity and the Middle Ages, not only by theoretical treatises, but also by collections of models. Numerous speeches and letters, both by ancient and contemporary authors, were copied and collected for the purpose of imitation. There are collections of form speeches, and especially of form letters, form introductions (*exordia*), and form addresses (*salutationes*). It is a humble type of literature, and scholars have been rightly unimpressed by its literary and intellectual level, but its mere existence and frequency helps to remind us of an area of activity that we might otherwise ignore.

Even more significant than the treatises and models intended for rhetorical instruction is the very large literature that reflects the activity of the humanists as trained and self-conscious orators. Orations and letters are probably the most numerous products of humanist prose that have come down to us in manuscripts and early editions, and they evidently constitute only a part of what was actually spoken and written during our period. This literature has usually been despised or ignored by modern historians, and it needs much further study. It does contain a good deal of empty rhetoric and of insincere praise or exaggerated blame.

However, much of it is well-written and by classical standards more elegant than the average products of the medieval *dictatores*. Moreover, this literature is full of interesting historical information, and it contains many ideas that are not necessarily false or insincere because they are expressed with eloquence.

In the field of oratory, Renaissance society provided many occasions for which a speech was demanded and where in later times the speech was accompanied or replaced by a play or show or by a recital of poetry or music. Many of these conventions go back to the late Middle Ages, as we have seen, but the fifteenth century left us a much larger number of actual specimens, and they compare favorably in style and content with the earlier products: funeral and wedding speeches; speeches by ambassadors; speeches addressed to popes, princes, or magistrates upon their accession to office or upon their visit to a city; and, less frequently, deliberative speeches to an assembly or council, or lawyers' speeches before a law court. Very frequent are the speeches connected with the universities: orations held at the beginning of the academic year or of a course of lectures, or speeches held by the candidate and his professor upon the conferral of a degree. There were speeches given at the beginning of a public disputation, or before gatherings such as the general chapter of a religious order. There were speeches before an academic or religious assembly in praise of specific saints, especially Augustine, Jerome, St. Catherine of Alexandria, or Thomas Aquinas. Many of these speeches, though addressed to an assembly of friars, were given by secular clerics or by laymen, apparently upon invitation. Vice versa, we find friars and clergymen appearing as orators on secular as well as on religious occasions.

As a further step, humanist rhetorical style began to influence the practice of sacred eloquence. After the middle of the fifteenth century, more and more priests and friars who had enjoyed a humanist education adopted the pattern of secular, humanist eloquence for their sermons, depart from the precepts of the *artes praedicandi*, and preach sermons that begin with a *prooemium*, instead of, or in addition to, a verse from Scripture, and follow the rules for the composition of a secular speech while retaining the theological content pertaining to their subject. Northern listeners such as Luther and Erasmus professed to be shocked by this mundane appearance of sacred oratory, and modern historians have often repeated their criticism, not realizing that they are in fact condemning in the religious literature the same features that they are accustomed to admiring in the religious art of the same period, namely a combination of classical or Renaissance form with religious content. This subject has just begun to attract scholarly attention, but it requires much further study.

I should like to add that humanist oratory also penetrated the vernacular speech, especially in Florence. The orations addressed to incoming officials (*protesti*) follow a rhetorical pattern, and since their content was fixed, namely the praise of justice, the tendency to provide pleasant and interesting variations on the theme is quite understandable. The same was true of contemporary sermons, many of them given by laymen, such as the ones delivered in the lay religious associations (*compagnie*) of Florence. I sometimes wonder whether the greater finesse of literature and art before the nineteenth century may be due to the very fact that the writers and artists had to find new variations on given themes that were well-known to themselves and to their audiences.

No less extensive than the humanist literature of orations was that of letters. We must distinguish between state and private letters. The state letters were composed and copied for rhetorical purposes, and served as an instrument of public propaganda when circulated and published. It is no coincidence that many chancellors and secretaries of princes and republics were noted humanists, who were able to compose the well-phrased letters that satisfied the taste of the senders and recipients. The private letters of the humanists also served a literary and rhetorical purpose, as we can see from the fact that they were often edited and collected by their authors. These letters often read very well, and they also are important sources of biographical, historical, and scholarly information. They are also vehicles of an author's opinions and ideas, and hence the letters of Petrarch, Salutati, Ficino, and others have rightly been utilized for an interpretation and reconstruction of their thought. The large poetical output of the humanists does not directly concern our subject and can only be mentioned in passing. On the other hand, their historical works and their moral treatises and dialogues were conscious prose compositions and clearly intended for a public that would read them not only for their content but also for their linguistic and stylistic elegance of expression.

After a brief description of the rhetorical theory and practice of the humanists, I should like to discuss even more briefly the links that connect the rhetoric of the humanists with their other interests and activities. The humanist study of grammar was closely allied with rhetoric and even subordinate to it, for the purpose of studying grammar was to acquire the mastery of correct Latin that was the prerequisite for any literary composition. The humanist contribution to grammar still remains to be explored, including such fields as orthography and prosody or metrics, which then as before were considered as parts of grammar. Valla's *Elegantiae,* as we saw before, was a contribution to grammar because it attempted to establish a correct Latin phraseology on the basis of classical sources. The work had a strong influence down to the early nineteenth century. It was a great merit of the humanists that they did restore correct Latin usage according to classical standards. The statement made by a distinguished scholar that they thus transformed the living language of medieval Latin into a dead language is belied by the flourishing state of written and spoken Latin for several more centuries.

Valla took a further step that is interesting and should appeal to current philosophers; he considered the linguistic usage of classical Latin as a source and standard of philosophical truth. Yet I cannot see at all that Valla or other humanists formulated a philosophy of language as was done at a later time by Giambattista Vico. Nor do I see any textual evidence for the view that humanist rhetoric and nominalist or terminist logic were closely related on the ground that they were both concerned with language or with individual facts. The humanists were firmly opposed to scholasticism, and especially to nominalism.

The relation between humanist rhetoric and historiography follows in part a pattern that had its precedents in antiquity and to a lesser extent in the Middle

Ages. History was a recognized branch of prose literature, and the ancient historians were among the preferred prose writers studied in courses on Greek and Latin literature. The writing of historical works according to the standards of good style and of the ancient historians was a part of the literary activity of the humanists, and in many cases their main occupation. We find many of them employed as official historiographers of princes or cities, and often they combined this assignment with a position of chancellor or teacher. The inserted fictitious speeches were an inheritance from ancient historiography, and it was here that the rhetorical rules were applied with special care. But the "rhetorical" style was no more an obstacle to the practice and refinement of historical criticism for the humanists than it had been for Thucydides. In the late sixteenth century, a new genre of *artes historicae* developed that evidently grew out of the *laudes historiae* in humanist courses and that tried to do for history what rhetoric and poetics had always done for oratory and poetry. This literature which has received some recent attention was intended to guide the reading and teaching as well as the writing of history.

The relation between rhetoric and poetics has been repeatedly mentioned. In the Renaissance, as often before, it was a relation of mutual influence and of parallelism. The less the rhetoricians stressed persuasion and political action, and the more they emphasized the task of speaking and writing well, the more oratory and poetry became the sister arts of writing well in prose and in verse, just as the medieval *dictatores* had conceived them before. In the sixteenth century, this attitude was further encouraged by the pairing of Aristotle's *Rhetoric* and *Poetics.* The emphasis in rhetoric had shifted from persuasion to style and imitation, and to literary criticism, and if we wish to have a complete picture of the literary theory and criticism of the period, we need a detailed study of the rhetorical treatises, including the commentaries on Aristotle's *Rhetoric,* to supplement Weinberg's work on the poetical treatises and on the commentaries on Aristotle's *Poetics.* Even in Renaissance poetics, the influence of Aristotle's *Poetics* was combined with that of his *Rhetoric,* as well as with that of Plato and Horace. There is at least one full-fledged treatise on poetics from the fifteenth century that antedates the influence of Aristotle's *Poetics,* and there is a long work on poetics by a major philosopher that is entirely based on Platonist and not on Aristotelian principles.

We might add that Renaissance poetics, no less than its rhetoric, was applied to the vernacular, and this was only natural. For the vernacular had created new genres of poetry, but no new critical theories comparable to those of antiquity, and as far as vocabulary, grammar, and style are concerned, Italian and the other vernacular languages had to be educated and developed after the model of Latin before they were able to take over all the functions of literary Latin. This can be clearly seen in Dante and Boccaccio, and even more in the writers of the sixteenth century. The view that the humanists tried to abolish the vernacular is plainly wrong. It is refuted by ample evidence, and especially by the vernacular compositions and translations due to the leading humanists themselves.

Of even greater importance, at least for the problem we are pursuing, is the relation between humanist rhetoric and philosophy, and the contribution of the humanists to philosophy, and especially to ethics. As we have seen before, the humanists claimed moral philosophy as a part of their domain, and they proposed, after the model of Cicero, to combine eloquence and wisdom. They often dealt with moral questions in their speeches and letters, and composed numerous treatises and dialogues in which they discussed questions of moral philosophy as well as of politics, religion, and education. This literature contains a great number and variety of ideas, and it has been amply explored and discussed by several scholars. I gladly agree that this literature is interesting and significant, and that it constitutes an important contribution to Renaissance thought and philosophy, but I must qualify this statement in more than one way.

The humanists were not professional philosophers, and their writings on moral subjects lack the terminological precision and logical consistency that we have a right to expect of professional philosophers. Secondly, the opinions held by a humanist in a given passage may be contradicted by his opinions in another work or even in another passage of the same work, and even more by the opinions of other humanists. In other words, even if we were able to construct a coherent philosophy for individual humanists, we cannot discover a common philosophy for all humanists, and hence it is not possible to define their contribution in terms of a specific set of philosophical doctrines. Finally, the opinions voiced by the humanists may at times be original in content or detail, but in many instances they are mere repetitions or variations of ancient philosophical ideas. Hence any attempt to construct the thought of a humanist without reference to the classical sources that determined it and of which he was fully conscious must be highly misleading and is often wrong.

The humanists were as eclectic in philosophy as their admired master Cicero had been, and many of their more consistent philosophical efforts were restatements of ancient doctrines. As a matter of fact, thanks to humanist efforts, the Renaissance witnessed a revival of such ancient systems as Stoicism, Epicureanism, and Scepticism. Some of the best contributions the humanists made to philosophy consisted in translating or retranslating the sources of Greek philosophy, and in restating and popularizing Greek philosophical ideas and doctrines that were not connected with the Aristotelian and Neoplatonic traditions—which were the only ones known to the medieval philosophers. In providing new alternatives for philosophical and scientific thought, the humanists created a kind of intellectual fermentation, and thus they prepared the ground for the philosophers of the seventeenth century who were far more original than the humanists themselves.

Finally, we must mention the impact of humanist rhetoric on a field that was not a part of the *studia humanitatis* but had belonged to the *trivium* and more recently to philosophy: logic or dialectic. There is a whole series of humanist attempts to reform logic that began with Lorenzo Valla and ended with Nizolius and with Peter Ramus and his school. These authors were trained humanists and tried to replace Aristotelian and scholastic logic with a logic subordinated to rhetoric. Their aim was clarity rather than precision, two qualities that are by no means always identical. When Ramus assigned invention and disposition to dialectic, he split traditional rhetoric into two parts and called the first part dialectic, putting it into the place previously occupied by scholastic logic.

It remains for us to consider briefly the professional philosophers who were concerned with the problems of natural philosophy and metaphysics, subjects that never belonged to the domain of the humanists and that were based on the traditions of medieval and ultimately of ancient Greek philosophy. The humanists had often attacked the scholastic philosophers and their Aristotelianism, but this tradition remained very strong throughout the Renaissance period, and especially in Italy, it dominated the teaching of philosophy at the universities and influenced large sectors of popular thought and literature. These Aristotelian philosophers were not interested in rhetoric or poetics, and many of them were quite insensitive to the charge that their Latin terminology and style were "barbarous."

However, Renaissance Aristotelianism was in several ways exposed to the influence of humanism and transformed by this influence. The humanists supplied new translations of Aristotle that competed with the medieval versions and often led to interesting comparisons. They translated the works of the ancient Greek commentators on Aristotle, including Alexander and Simplicius, many of them for the first time, and thus supplied new and authoritative alternatives to the commentaries of Averroes and Thomas Aquinas. They insisted on the study of the Greek text of Aristotle. There were also several humanists who favored Aristotle over other ancient thinkers and claimed to understand him better than his scholastic interpreters were able to do. This attitude appears first in Petrarch, and it was adopted by Leonardo Bruni, Ermolao Barbaro, Jacques Lefèvre d'Etaples, Philip Melanchthon, and many others. We may add that during the fifteenth and sixteenth century, not only Aristotle's *Rhetoric* and *Poetics,* but also his *Ethics, Politics,* and other moral writings were largely, if not entirely, left to the humanists. Yet in the fields of logic, natural philosophy, and metaphysics, the scholastic tradition held firm, except for the use of new translations, the newly translated Greek commentators, and the Greek text, which led to a better understanding of Aristotle than the scholastics had reached, for example in the case of Jacopo Zabarella.

The Renaissance Platonists are often treated as a part of the humanist movement, but I think they deserve a place of their own, apart from humanism proper to which they were clearly indebted, and from Aristotelian scholasticism by which they were also more deeply influenced than is commonly known. Ficino and others supplied the first complete translations of Plato and of the Neoplatonists, thus continuing the work of the humanists. Yet they were interested in philosophical doctrine rather than in literary form, and they inherited Plato's critique of the rhetoricians and the poets. They tended, however, to tone down this critique, for they harmonized Plato's critique of the rhetoricians in the *Gorgias* with his defense of a philosophical rhetoric in the *Phaedrus;* they attached great importance to the doctrine of poetic madness, disregarding the ironic overtones of the *Ion;* and they practically ignored Plato's critique of Homer and the other poets. Pico's defense of the scholastic philosophers against Ermolao Barbaro reflects his tendency to stress content rather than form and to separate philosophy from rhetoric, whereas Melanchthon, although sympathetic to Aristotle, wrote a posthumous defense of Ermolao against Pico, restating the typical humanist alliance of wisdom and eloquence.

The natural philosophers of the sixteenth century attempted to develop new and original positions beyond the customary alternatives of scholasticism and humanism, Aristotelianism and Platonism. Their contribution to our problem seems to have been marginal, and it has not yet received sufficient scholarly attention. Girolamo Fracastoro wrote a dialogue on poetics that reflects his humanist background rather than his contributions to natural philosophy. Tommaso Campanella composed treatises on rhetoric, poetics, and historiography that have not yet been studied in detail. Francesco Patrizi composed treatises on rhetoric, the theory of history, and poetics. His extensive work on poetics which has recently been published for the first time in a complete text deserves further study. As all of Patrizi's works, it is markedly anti-Aristotelian and attempts to construct a new theory of poetics, drawing on Plato and the Neoplatonists.

On the whole, Renaissance philosophers, whether Aristotelians, Platonists, or natural philosophers, showed comparatively little interest in rhetoric and poetics and left these fields to the humanists and literary critics.

Before concluding, I should like to add a few words about the history of our subject after the Renaissance, including our own time. The seventeenth century was the great age in which the mathematical and physical sciences were placed on a new foundation, one that has remained valid to the present day in spite of later additions and transformations. The attempts to compete with the new sciences and to emulate their methods and achievements also led with Descartes, Spinoza, and others to a new philosophy that abandoned in principle, though not always in practice, the traditions of medieval as well as Renaissance philosophy. These momentous changes did not for a while affect the fields of rhetoric and poetics, or the theory and practice of the arts in general. The place of rhetoric among the humanities and the basic notions of traditional rhetoric remained unchanged through the seventeenth and part of the eighteenth century. When the new system of the fine arts began to take shape in the course of the eighteenth century, eloquence at first retained its place alongside poetry, as may be seen in the work of Baumgarten who coined the term aesthetics and established it as a philosophical theory of the arts.

However, the eighteenth century brought about a radical change in the theory and practice of the arts that reached its high point in the early nineteenth century and that in many ways is still with us. I am speaking of Romanticism, a movement which has greatly contributed to our conception and understanding of history and the arts, but which is also responsible for many ideas that are wrong and harmful and that were exaggerated and carried *ad adsurdum* long after the original Romantic movement had passed away. I have often thought that it was the task of my generation of scholars to liquidate the remnants of Romantic misconceptions in our respective fields, but I am now forced to observe that in recent years some of the worst excesses of Romanticism have been revived and seem to be immune to factual or rational refutation, at least among laymen if not among professional scholars—although I find that also professional scholars often bow to popular fashions against their own better judgment and knowledge.

The aesthetics of Romanticism rejected all rules in the arts and extolled the genius and his power of original expression. In early Romanticism, this was a highly elitist conception that was applied only to the outstanding artist, but in our egalitarian age we have now reached the point where every activity, artistic or otherwise, is considered creative, and where every person, whether gifted or not, is considered original and free from any rules and restrictions, aesthetical or ethical. Modern writers find it difficult to believe that God created the world out of nothing, but they see no difficulty in assuming that a human artist, even a minor artist, creates his art out of nothing. They should know from classical and modern psychology that our productive imagination does not produce anything out of nothing, but works by freely recombining past impressions and experiences, with each other and with the basic concepts inherent in our mind.

An early consequence of the Romantic movement was the complete rejection of rhetoric as a system of rules. The cult of the original and the spontaneous led to the emphasis on poetry, and to a lesser extent, on prose fiction, as the exclusive domain of literary criticism and of literary history, leaving out entirely the area of doctrinal prose that earlier literary historians of literature had still included, and relinquishing it in a sense to the reign of formless pedantry uninhibited by any literary discipline. The term "rhetoric" in a positive sense tended to disappear, although it has been continued or revived as a teaching subject in a few universities. The traditional content of rhetoric was split up among several disciplines that differ from each other in their goals and assumptions and do not even seem to be related to each other: aesthetics, which is a part of philosophy; literary scholarship and composition, which constitute different sectors of English literature and of other literatures; and literary criticism, which is an enterprise shared by scholars with writers and journalists.

The old *ars dictaminis* and *ars arengandi* have sunk to philistine depths: there are courses and handbooks of business correspondence for future secretaries, and I have seen a manual for college officials that contains form letters soliciting donations from different types of alumni. There are, or at least there were until recently, letter-writers with models for love letters, and with typical letters of condolence, congratulation, and recommendation. I bought for fun a book containing models for after-dinner addresses, featuring jokes and stories with which a contemporary speech begins as invariably as a medieval sermon begins with a verse from Scripture—a veritable *ars dictaminis* or *ars arengandi Americana*. We have a flourishing tradition of political oratory, in this country as in England and other countries, but although we often hear of speeches written by ghost writers, I am not aware of any conscious theory concerning the form and delivery of a speech, as against its content which is of course dictated by the political circumstances, the opinions of the speaker and his advisers, and the emotions and preconceptions of the expected audience.

What we have left of the glorious and ancient tradition of rhetoric are some broken pieces without the name, of varying quality and pretense, but sometimes sufficient to kindle a renewed interest in the history of rhetoric. With the recent progress of vulgarized Romanticism, even the teaching of composition has been replaced by an emphasis on self-expression, a part of the general tendency among educators to teach the unteachable and to refuse to teach the teachable. I remember a distinguished friend and fellow scholar who took a course in creative writing and was ready to apply the flashback technique to a historical paper until I successfully advised him against this experiment.

The heirs of rhetoric in modern times have usually refrained from competing with philosophy in the manner attempted more or less successfully by their ancient predecessors. Yet there have been literary critics who claim that they are better students and historians of philosophy than the professional philosophers, and that also the poets of the past were better philosophers than their philosophical contemporaries. In our age when so many professional philosophers are antihistorical and omit from their consideration many important problems of traditional philosophy, the literary critics have an easy time, and we should even be grateful to them if they take up the history of past philosophy abandoned by the philosophers. I gladly agree that there is a good deal of philosophy in the great poets and writers of the past, if we take philosophy in the broad rather than in the strict professional sense of the term. However, the literary critics spoil their game when they first insist on the philosophical importance of past writers and then refuse to apply to their thought the standards of conceptual precision and consistency that are the earmarks of a philosopher, avoiding their intellectual responsibility with such phrases as intellectual play or deliberate ambiguity. There are plenty of ambiguities and inconsistencies even in the greatest professional philosophers, but the task of understanding and interpreting them just begins, and does not end, with the awareness of these inconsistencies. For I venture to think and to say that the only safe way for a philosopher who tries to avoid inconsistencies altogether is to have and express only one single idea.

I am afraid we are left in a chaos, in rhetoric as in other areas of our civilization. The old formulas have ceased to satisfy, and the new ones that may satisfy have not yet appeared. I am no prophet and do not claim to know the answers to our grave educational and other problems. At present, everybody has to find his own way, and by lucky chance or providence, there seem to be enough people around, old and young, who have found a decent solution for themselves and for their friends and pupils. My political sympathies are democratic as I understand that word, and although I admire Plato for many reasons, I should not like to see my ideas or opinions imposed on others by force. The ideas that I have seen imposed on people in various places during the present century are neither true nor adequate, and I do not hope to see the day when the truth of ideas, political or otherwise, is measured by the number of divisions or airplanes that may be mobilized in their support.

What we as teachers can do is to transmit and spread knowledge—even information, which is now considered to be a bad word, but which is a very important thing and which certainly is the basis of any original ideas that have validity. I also think that we must try to extend the area of our knowledge, as best we can, and thus limit the range of mere opinion, and originality. I see no value in ideas that are original but false.

We also should encourage in all areas an effort to aim at clarity and consistency which seem to be the basic concern of rhetoric and philosophy. Rules are not sufficient, and talent is needed, as the ancient rhetoricians knew very well, although I am afraid talent is not as widely diffused as people now like to believe. Knowledge is needed, for I do not think originality can or should be based on ignorance. To be sure, not everything is known or can be known, and thus the range of opinion and of taste will always remain large enough to satisfy our desire for intellectual freedom. Many people now seem to feel that submitting to the truth, factual or rational, and to valid standards of conduct and of taste, is a restriction of their freedom, and that the best defense of this freedom is to deny that there is any valid truth or standard. Such views were expressed more subtly by the sceptical philosophers of antiquity and of later times. I do not share them, and rather believe with many respectable philosophers that the submission to truth and to valid norms is what constitutes our true intellectual and moral freedom.

I must profess in the end something that may have been inferred from my previous statements. I am at heart a Platonist, on the issue of rhetoric as on many, though not on all, others. Rhetoric in all its forms is based on mere opinion, and therefore it should be subordinated to philosophy, that is, to all forms of valid knowledge where such knowledge is available. Our ability to write and to speak well must be disciplined by the acquisition of knowledge and the refutation of error, and used as an effective tool for expressing and conveying knowledge and insight. Rhetoric is important, as it always was, as a technique of expression, for we wish and try to write and speak well and clearly. Yet in our universe of discourse, and in our system of education that should reflect this universe, rhetoric should not occupy the center, but be subordinated, not only to philosophy, but also to the sciences as well as to poetry and the other arts.

Victoria Kahn

"Humanist Rhetoric"

---

*Dicere enim bene nemo potest nisi qui prudenter intellegit; qua re qui elo-
quentiae verae dat operam, dat prudentiae. [For no one can be a good speaker who is not a prudent thinker. Thus whoever devotes himself to true eloquence devotes himself to prudence.]*
　　　　　　　　　　　　　　　　　　　　　　　　—Cicero, *Brutus*

Quattrocento humanism was a civic humanism, which means that rhetoric was
in the service of the active life. While a thorough examination of the social and
political factors contributing to the Quattrocento humanists' interest in prudence
and the active life is beyond the scope of this book, it is clear that this interest
was determined neither by purely political nor by purely literary factors, but by
a combination of the two. Political conditions in the republics and courts of Italy
created the need for the humanists' rhetorical activity, at the same time that the
humanists' literary interest in antiquity led them to recover classical arguments
for the superiority of prudence to theoretical reason within the realm of action.
During the fifteenth century, Aristotle's *Rhetoric* and *Nicomachean Ethics* were
newly translated from the Greek, not only into Latin but also into the vernaculars. It was at this time as well that the sovereign Ciceronian texts of the Middle
Ages, the *De inventione* and the pseudo-Ciceronian *Ad Herennium,* were
dethroned: in 1416 Poggio Bracciolini discovered the complete Quintilian, and in
1421, Gherardo Landriani, Bishop of Lodi, discovered the complete texts of
Cicero's *De oratore* and *Orator.* But what is decisive about these translations and
recoveries is the opportune moment at which they occurred: the moment when
they could be read with a new openness and receptivity to the rhetorical ideal
they presented. For the humanists, who were professional men of letters, might
not have been interested in the classical defense of prudence if it had not been
for the further argument—hinted at by Aristotle and developed by Cicero—that
the activity of the prudent man is analogous to that of the orator.

　　While Aristotle limits the province of the orator in the *Rhetoric,* he draws several analogies between rhetoric and prudence in the *Nicomachean Ethics*—not so

much in terms of the domain of competence, when this is interpreted as an intellectual discipline or subject matter, as in terms of *the form or the activity* of judgment that both involve. In this respect, while Aristotle's orator may seem to have little in common with the Ciceronian ideal of the good man speaking persuasively, Aristotle's man of practical reason or prudence is very similar. That Cicero himself recognized this to be the case is clear from his many references to Peripatetic ethics. It is because of the implicit, and at times explicit, connection between rhetoric and prudence in the *Ethics* that the Quattrocento humanists, in turn, drew heavily on this text in their defense of their own rhetorical activity. For this reason, a brief sketch of the Aristotelian notion of prudence is in order. The crucial difference to keep in mind in the following summary is that while Aristotle analyzes the formal similarities in the activities of the orator and the prudent man, Cicero insists that the prudent man be eloquent.

RHETORIC, PRUDENCE, AND SKEPTICISM IN ANTIQUITY

Aristotle recognized both in the *Rhetoric* and in the *Nicomachean Ethics* that rhetorical decorum and prudence share a faculty of judgment that is not logical or theoretical, but practical; that does not subordinate an object to a general rule or concept, but responds to the particular per se. This is because both rhetoric and prudence are concerned with "problems about which different points of view . . . [can] be maintained, questions open to debate because they . . . [can] be judged only in terms of probable truth and . . . [are] not susceptible to scientific demonstrations of irrefutable validity." Thus, Aristotle writes in the *Rhetoric:* "The duty of rhetoric is to deal with such matters as we deliberate upon without arts or systems to guide us. . . . There are few facts of the 'necessary' type that can form the basis of rhetorical syllogisms. Most of the things about which we make decisions, and into which we therefore inquire, present us with alternative possibilities. For it is about our actions that we deliberate and inquire, and all our actions have a contingent character; hardly any of them are determined by necessity" (1357a). One crucial implication of Aristotle's observation that we debate about things that present us with alternative possibilities is that the arguments with which we debate themselves suggest alternative possibilities—that is, not only can we argue pro and contra a given position, but the same arguments can be marshaled on either side of the question.

The consideration of which figures or forms of argument are appropriate to the end of the persuasion (leaving aside for a moment the question of the ethical status of that end) is analogous to the choice of means by the prudent man. In neither case are general rules simply applied to particular instances. Rather, it is the nature of the rule to be modified in the application. Hence one critic of Aristotle refers to prudence as the knowledge of the rule about choice. The relevant distinction here is between the determinant (logical and necessary) judgment of the theoretical sciences, for which objective or mathematical certainty is the criterion of truth, and the reflective judgment of practical wisdom, which is concerned with action. Thus, A. E. Taylor writes, "Aristotle calls the method of practical wisdom the practical syllogism or syllogism of action, since its peculiarity is that what issues from the putting together of the premises is not an assertion but the performance of an act." Practical wisdom, Aristotle tells us in the *Ethics*, is much closer to the technical skills required by the applied arts (*technai*), not only because both are concerned with "things which admit of being other than they are" (1140a ff.), but also because, as Gadamer writes: "Both are knowledge of a dynamic kind [vorgängiges Wissen], and must determine and guide an action. Consequently, they must contain within themselves the rule for the application of this knowledge to the concrete task at hand."

Both Cicero and Aristotle realized that the rule of decorum is only formal if it is not referred to some ethical standard—hence Aristotle's insistence that deliberation seeks to determine the means, not the ends of action—and for both such a standard of reflective judgment did indeed exist, whether it was interpreted as an inborn disposition (Aristotle) or innate ideas (Cicero). For both, in other words, the possibility of prudence was grounded in man's natural being.

Aristotle argued that man has an innate disposition to moral virtue which must be cultivated by prudence, while prudence is itself a potentiality whose realization depends on practice and on moral virtue. Thus, while human beings have an intellectual intuition of the absolute standard of conduct which is the good life, the prudent man incarnates the "standard and measure" (1113a 30) by making the "actual and normative" coincide in every particular act of judgment. His deliberation or interpretation of what is required is intrinsically authoritative, because informed by an intuition of the good. But this rule of behavior is not something that can be conceptualized. It is a combination of intuition or innate predisposition and practice. Thus, Aristotle writes in the *Ethics*, "It is this kind of deliberation which is good deliberation, a correctness that attains what is good" (1142b 20).

It was in terms of such an intuitive standard of judgment that Aristotle first provided a theoretical justification of the dialectical syllogism. He explains in the *Topics* that the dialectical syllogism differs from the apodeictic syllogism in dealing with the realm of contingency rather than that of necessity. It takes the probable as its point of departure, and thus achieves a lesser degree of certainty in its conclusions. The probable is defined in terms of common opinion: opinions "which are accepted by every one or by the majority or by the philosophers" (100b 20). The degree of truth that Aristotle then claims for the conclusion of the dialectical syllogism thus depends on the assumption that common opinion or consensus corresponds in some degree to the truth. Yet for Aristotle, as for the Sophists, this argument by consensus or probability is not merely a debased form of the apodeictic syllogism. Rather, it is governed by completely different—practical—considerations, and derives its authority from the conviction that, in some practical sense, "what all believe to be true is actually true" (*NE* 1173a).

Thus, whereas Plato condemned the realm of opinion as deceptive and illusory, Aristotle granted it a positive status in its own right, and this is important because the contingent realm of opinion is the realm in which persuasion and action can take place. Furthermore, in this realm practical reason takes precedence over the precepts of theoretical speculation, for there can be no science of particulars. On the basis of these two assertions, one could then argue—as many of the humanists later did—that the literature that is appropriate to this realm should not be identified with the static representation of transcendental ideas, but rather with the dynamic activity of persuasion.

While Aristotle does not apply his defense of the dialectical syllogism to literature, he clearly intends it to apply to rhetoric, since dialectic and rhetoric are counterparts of each other (*Rhet.* 1354a). Both are instruments of practical reason rather than of theoretical speculation. Both take the probable or commonly accepted opinion as their point of departure, and are concerned with persuading rather than conclusively demonstrating. For example, when Aristotle discusses the man of practical wisdom in the *Nicomachean Ethics,* he begins with the way in which we commonly speak of such men:

> We may approach the subject of practical wisdom by studying the persons to whom we attribute it. Now, the capacity of deliberating well about what is good and advantageous for oneself is regarded as typical of a man of practical wisdom—not deliberating well about what is good and advantageous in a partial sense . . . but [about] what sort of thing contributes to the good life in general. *This is shown by the fact that we speak* of men having attained practical wisdom in a particular respect . . . when they calculate well with respect to some worthwhile end, one that cannot be attained by an applied science or art. *It follows that,* in general, a man of practical wisdom is he who has the ability to deliberate. [1140a 25–30, my emphasis]

It was this belief in a practical standard of judgment reflected in common linguistic usage that legitimated the orator's appeal to common sense, his arguments by consensus, opinion, and commonplace. Accordingly, the rhetorical syllogism was not a false and deceitful form of argument, but one grounded in the common imperfection of human nature: imperfection because human affairs do not lend themselves to logical formalization; common because, although based on the probable, such an argument can claim universal appeal by virtue of a shared human nature.

Whereas Aristotle writes of the standard of judgment that guides the prudent man, and by extension the orator, in terms of potentiality, Cicero gives this standard a content as well. In an article on the concept of the *consensus omnium,* Klaus Oehler remarks on this difference:

> Aristotle and Plato already speak of a natural disposition of man to morality, . . . [but] it was Cicero who first grounded moral consciousness in an innate knowledge, which gives the individual an immediate inner certainty of his ethical conduct [*Wertverhalten*]. Surpassing all previous tendencies in this direction, he teaches that the innate seeds of morality will in themselves lead us to a happy life, if they are allowed to develop unhindered: *Sunt enim ingeniis nostris semina*

innata virtutum; quae si adolescere liceret, ipsa nos ad beatam vitam natura perduceret
[The seeds of virtue are inborn in our dispositions and, if they were allowed to
ripen, nature's own hand would lead us on to happiness of life].

It was no doubt in part because of this more substantial definition of prudence in terms of "innate seeds of virtue" that Cicero provided the Renaissance
with the classical statement of confidence regarding the standard of judgment
that informs the activity of the orator. In *De oratore*, as later in Quintilian, we read
that the good orator is necessarily a good man, and in *De officiis* we learn that
moral goodness and decorum, *honestas* and *utilitas*, cannot conflict: "For what is
proper is morally right, and what is morally right is proper [*quod honestum est,
decet*]. The nature of this difference between morality and propriety [*decori*] can
be more easily felt than expressed. For whatever propriety may be, it is manifest
only when there is preexisting moral rectitude" (1.27.94; see also 2.3.9–10, 3.3.11).
This conviction in turn justifies the centrality of the rhetorical and ethical concept
of decorum in Cicero's works. In a famous passage in the *Orator*, Cicero writes:

> For after all the foundation of eloquence, as of everything else, is wisdom [*sapi-
> entia*]. In an oration, as in life, nothing is harder to determine than what is
> appropriate [*quid deceat*]. The Greeks called it *prépon:* let us call it decorum or
> "propriety." . . . From ignorance of this mistakes are made not only in life but
> very frequently in writing, both in poetry and in prose. Moreover the orator
> must have an eye to propriety, not only in thought but in language. For the
> same style and the same thoughts must not be used in portraying every condi-
> tion in life, or every rank, position or age, and in fact a similar distinction must
> be made in respect of place, time and audience. The universal rule, in oratory
> as in life, is to consider propriety. This depends on the subject matter under dis-
> cussion, and on the character of both the speaker and the audience. The
> philosophers are accustomed to consider this extensive subject under the head
> of duties [*officiis*]. . . . the literary critics consider it in connexion with poetry;
> orators in dealing with every kind of speech, and in every part thereof.

When we turn to *De officiis* we find that Cicero defines decorum in the political realm as prudence. And while he first opposes prudence to theoretical wisdom as Aristotle does, he goes beyond Aristotle when he argues for the superiority of prudence on the grounds that it is concerned with action rather than contemplation. Human society is Cicero's primary concern, and prudence is more
appropriate to this society than contemplation is:

> And then, the foremost of all virtues is wisdom [*sapientia*]—what the Greeks
> call *sophia;* for by prudence, which they call *phronesis*, we understand some-
> thing else, namely, the practical knowledge of things to be sought for and of
> things to be avoided. . . . And service [which is a function of prudence] is bet-
> ter than mere theoretical knowledge, for the study and knowledge of the uni-

verse would somehow be lame and defective, were no practical results to follow. Such results, moreover, are best seen in the safeguarding of human interests. It is essential, then, to human society; and it should, therefore, be ranked
above theoretical knowledge. [1.43.153]

In Cicero's view, then, even more than in Aristotle's, the faculty of prudence
is inseparable from the ideal practice of the orator. Both the orator and the prudent man are concerned with the domain of probability, and both know that they
can only be effective in this domain by acting according to the rhetorical standard of decorum. Just as the orator is guided by decorum in adapting his speech
to the exigencies of the moment, so the prudent man enacts decorum in the
moral sphere by responding to the particular and contingent in human affairs
(*Orator* 71). Furthermore, the prudent man and the orator are not only analogous
for Cicero; they are ideally the same, since the good man to be effective must be
persuasive, and the orator who is not good is not worthy of the name. Cicero's
point is not simply that the orator has the rhetorical skills of persuasion that will
enable the prudent man to achieve a particular end, but that the latter is prudent
precisely by being an orator. The important consequence of Cicero's argument is
that rhetoric—properly speaking—is morally justified.

Cicero's further contribution to the ideology of humanist rhetoric was to argue
for the similarities between the orator and the Academic skeptic (an analogy that
was already implicit in Aristotle's conception of rhetoric as the art of finding the
best available arguments within the realm of the probable). Since man, according
to the skeptic, can know nothing absolutely, he is always concerned with the
realm of the contingent and the probable, that is, the realm of rhetoric.
Furthermore, while the skeptic is traditionally less concerned than the orator with
persuasion to action within this realm, he shares with the orator a refusal of dogmatism and an ability "to speak persuasively on any side of any philosophical
question." Finally, the Academic skeptic believes that within the contingent realm
of human life the genuine exchange of ideas and opposing arguments in rhetorical debate will elicit the practical truth we know as consensus. This is a conception of truth that involves reference not to some absolute ethical norm but rather
to a standard of decorum, likelihood, or probability; it thus allows for, indeed
depends upon, action but does not thereby abandon the claims of an ethical conception of judgment. In short, what the Academic skeptic has to offer the
Ciceronian civic orator is an important argument for the possibility of prudence:
that is, the combined acknowledgment of the contingent realm of action and the
assurance of a practical ethical criterion within this realm.

Thus, while Aristotle draws an analogy between the orator and the prudent
man, it was Cicero's presentation of the orator that was particularly attractive to
many Renaissance humanists. As we have seen, this was not simply because
Cicero's texts were written in a Latin which the humanists regarded as the model
of eloquence. Nor was it only because as professional men of letters they had a
vested interest in Cicero's emphasis on the propaedeutic role of a literary education in the training of the orator. While both of these factors contributed to

Cicero's influence, the humanists were primarily drawn to the Ciceronian orator as an ideal representative of humanist culture. For Cicero does not restrict the orator's domain of competence in the way that Aristotle does, with the result that the orator is not simply a technician, as Aristotle's orator must have seemed to many humanists, but rather the embodiment of true learning.

QUATTROCENTO RHETORIC

Leonardo Bruni's remarks in his *Isagogicon moralis disciplinae* (Introduction to moral education, 1421–24) are typical of the Quattrocento humanist attitude toward prudence and the active life. While acknowledging the superiority of theoretical wisdom or contemplation, he argues for the greater utility of prudence in the contingent realm of human affairs. In so doing, he illustrates the tendency of many Quattrocento humanists to turn to classical texts for a theoretical defense of the ethic of prudence that was already theirs in practice:

> For in truth, although there are many virtues, as I have said, some are more suited to the life of retirement and contemplation, others to the life of business and civic affairs. For wisdom and knowledge nourish the contemplative life, while prudence governs every action. Each, to be sure, has its proper merits and excellences. The contemplative life is clearly more divine and rarer, but the active life is superior in public service.

In articulating and defending the ideals of civic humanism in the *Isagogicon* and in *De studiis et litteris* (On studies and letters, 1422–29), Bruni appeals both to Aristotle's analysis of prudence and to Cicero's rhetorical treatises. In fact, he conflates them in a way that Cicero would have approved of and that was characteristic of many Quattrocento humanist texts, for he argues that the study of secular literature has the power to make us both prudent and eloquent. The study of history, Bruni tells us in *De studiis* (13), educates the faculty of prudence and provides us with a copia of examples which we can then employ in our own writing. Similarly, the study of orators teaches us how to be both politically effective speakers and eloquent writers, just as reading poetry informs us about "vita moribusque" as well as about its own persuasive way of teaching.

It is now generally accepted that the Quattrocento humanists were decisively influenced both by Aristotle's *Ethics* and by Cicero's rhetorical works. But it is important to recognize that the influence of these works was itself determined by the humanist conflation of rhetoric and poetics. Whereas in the works of these classical authors literature was seen as separate from or a propaedeutic to the acquisition of rhetorical skills, in the Renaissance the two were often combined and literature was conceived of in Horatian and rhetorical terms as having its own persuasive and formative powers. If we interpret this conflation in simple didactic terms as the subordination of the text to some transcendental meaning, then this attitude was certainly already present in the Middle Ages. For Bruni and his contemporaries, however, there was an increasing emphasis not only on the power of literature to present a transcendental Idea but to persuade to right action. This emphasis in turn helps explain the humanists' practical conception of the acts of reading and writing.

Intellectual historians tend to agree about the conflation of rhetoric and poetics in the Renaissance, but are divided as to its causes and its significance. Some have argued that the rhetorical definition of literature was influenced by the early Italian humanists' experience of the political force of their own literary activity, as when Giangaleazzo Visconti is reported to have said that he feared Salutati's letters more than a thousand horsemen ("non tam sibi mille Florentinorum equites quam Colucii scripta nocere"). Others have suggested to the contrary that this conflation was owing in part to a more developed sense of the limited possibilities for genuine political action, with the resulting defensive argument that instead of being preparatory to the action of persuasion in the forum or the law court, literature was itself seen as an act of persuasion. What is clear in either case is that the arguments that Cicero and Aristotle had intended to apply to speeches in the forum, law court, or public ceremony were applied by the humanists to written texts. Accordingly, Renaissance rhetoric can be seen as a truncated version of its classical ancestor, since as the legal and political dimension of rhetoric falls away, only epideictic—the rhetoric of praise and blame—remains.

Those scholars who stress the limited possibilities for genuine political action in the Renaissance tend to view this shrinking of rhetoric to epideictic as an anticipation of a properly aesthetic conception of literature. What I want to suggest with specific reference to humanist works is that if the conflation of rhetoric and poetics diminishes the sphere of rhetoric as it was classically conceived, it enlarges the sphere of literature, since the written text now takes on the functions of deliberative and judicial rhetoric. One generic consequence of this prudential and rhetorical conception of the literary text was, as I have already suggested, the prominence of the dialogue among Quattrocento humanist works. Whereas the classical orator was trained to argue *in utramque partem,* that is, on both sides of a question, in any particular case he argued on one side or the other. But when the Renaissance humanist adopted the Aristotelian and Ciceronian rhetorical skills, he was not constrained by the same immediate concerns as is the orator in the forum or the law court. As a result he could actually present both cases and, in so doing, persuade the reader not to any specific action, but to the exercising of the prudential judgment that is required for all actions.

Aristotle reminds us of the practical dimension of epideictic in the *Rhetoric* when he remarks that demonstrative or epideictic rhetoric is inseparable from deliberative rhetoric insofar as praising is tantamount to urging a course of action. But the distinction between deliberative and demonstrative rhetoric breaks down in the works of the Quattrocento humanists not only because epideictic can be viewed as urging a course of action, but also because the deliberation involved in reading is itself understood as a form of the deliberation that leads to action. The Renaissance humanists thus go beyond their classical mentors in conceiving of literature not only as the cause and effect of prudence and right action (i.e., the writer is presumed to be prudent and to inspire prudence in others), but as a form of prudence itself. Rhetoric here is not primarily conceived of in terms of style or ornament, but in terms of its capacity to exemplify and encourage the activity of practical reasoning.

The Quattrocento humanists thus shared two related assumptions that influenced their conception of the act of reading. First, the prudence or practical reason that is deliberation about action in a social and political context is also at work in the artist's production of a work of art. Prudence is, in this sense, the precondition of artistic decorum, just as it is of ethical decorum. As a result, the work of art is seen less as an object than as reflecting a certain process or activity of judgment. Second, and consequently, the reader's knowledge of the literary text (or any other work of art) can only be practical, since the interpretive practice of reading requires the same acts of discrimination, the same judgments of decorum, as does the author's practice of writing. Thus, the practice of interpretation, like the practice of writing, exemplifies for the humanist the inseparability of moral philosophy and rhetoric.

In the Trecento Coluccio Salutati, chancellor of Florence from 1375 to 1406, is particularly eloquent on this point. In his early letter in praise of Petrarch, he argues that moral philosophy is inseparable from rhetoric not only because both are concerned with the practical realm of human affairs, but because it is in language that this moral dimension is most fully realized: language raises man above the animals and enables him to create a consensus and community, and language allows for the persuasion of the will to action. Accordingly, the poet and the orator do not perform a merely aesthetic function; rather, the aesthetic dimension is the precondition of the political. This does not only imply that the meaning of the text is inextricable from the aesthetic expression, which is then both pleasing and useful in terms of conveying meaning, or that the intended function of the text is to persuade to right action. It means something particular about the way in which the text persuades to action: unlike the reading of an abstract argument, reading poetry or history involves an "applicatio mentis" (*Ep.* 2.295), a pleasurable activity, exercise, or praxis, which educates us in the very act of reading at the same time that it moves us to the application of prudence in human affairs.

The Quattrocento humanists were decisively influenced by Salutati's arguments. Like Salutati, Giovanni Pontano claimed that literary or rhetorical decorum can educate the reader in the virtue of prudence, both because it can provide thematic examples of prudent actions in the past and because the skills of judgment and discrimination involved in the composition and interpretation of a literary work are similar to those involved in practical reasoning about our actions. Thus, in the *De principe*, Pontano insists on the contribution of the activity of reading to the rhetorical force of virtuous examples, and in his dialogue *Actius* he argues that the portrayal of counsel and debate in historical works will serve to elucidate the truth, while reported speeches will not only provide moral precepts but also make the reader more diligent in examining and reflecting on other passages. Contrary to the notion that epideictic as the rhetoric of aesthetic display is the form of rhetoric most suited to writing (because the written text allows for the appreciation of aesthetic effects), Pontano suggests that writing transforms the auditor's aesthetic appreciation of epideictic into the reader's active participation in a process of deliberation, deliberation that is itself analogous and conducive to action. According to this argument, the reader's process of discrimination in reading must be seen as the imitation not of the text as a product, but of the text as a process.

In the sixteenth century, this educative view of the process of reading is epitomized by Erasmus's famous remark in the *Ratio: lectio transit in mores* (reading passes over into morals [usage, practice, custom]). Yet, while Aristotelian prudential deliberation results immediately in action (*NE* 1095a 5: "The end of this kind of study is not knowledge but action"), in Erasmus's dictum political action is mediated by the exercise of judgment in the act of reading. Praxis in the sense of political action can be the fruit of reading because the practice of interpretation educates our ability to deliberate about such action.

Philip Sidney articulates a similar view in the *Apology* when he writes that the poet "so far substantially . . . worketh, not only to make a Cyrus, which had been but a particular excellency as Nature might have done, but to bestow a Cyrus upon the world to make many Cyruses, if they will learn aright why and how that maker made him" (101). To learn aright "why and how" Xenophon made Cyrus is to imitate the poet's own imitative process, not merely the image of Cyrus. To learn why and how Sidney made the *Apology* is to imitate the activity of judgment, the decisions of decorum, that are manifest in the rhetorical structure of that work.

Even Hobbes, who wants to exclude rhetoric from the commonwealth, constructs the *Leviathan* to enable the reader to understand the logical *process* by which the right commonwealth is produced, for it is only in imitating and comprehending this process that the reader who is sovereign will be able to put Hobbes's logic into practice, and the reader who is subject will accept the necessity of the finished product. Accordingly, the "Introduction" to the *Leviathan* concludes by emphasizing this prudential and reflective moment of deliberation: "When I shall have set down my own reading orderly, and perspicuously, the pains left another, will be onely to consider, if he also find not the same in himself. For this kind of Doctrine, admitteth no other Demonstration" (83).

As I argue in chapter 6, Hobbes dismissed prudential rhetoric on technical rather than moral grounds. But his technical critique is simply the other side of the ethical objections to prudence. If we return for a moment to Pontano, we can anticipate some of the reasons for these objections, and at the same time further clarify the Quattrocento humanist position. For, unlike most of his contemporaries, Pontano explicitly calls attention to the ambivalence with which rhetoric and prudence have traditionally been regarded, and in so doing, obliges himself to offer a defense of their ambiguous status.

As Pontano is well aware, ambivalence about rhetoric or prudence arises when their dual allegiance to the morally right and the expedient is recognized, and when the amoral character of the technical skills involved is judged to be immoral. Just as the orator has the dual purpose of speaking well and persuading his audience, so the prudent man is bound by considerations of both moral correctness and efficacious action, and in each case it is not clear that what is conducive to success need be in conformity with the good. For just as the technical skills of the orator can be seen as capable of serving immoral as well as moral ends, so prudence, which is, strictly speaking, an intellectual rather than a moral virtue, looks as though it might involve the clever manipulation of circumstances without direct regard for morality.

There have traditionally been at least three ways of dealing with the ambivalent moral status of rhetoric. One can (1) condemn it as an immoral pseudo-science (Plato in the *Gorgias*); (2) subordinate rhetoric as a skill to moral judgment, and thereby identify rhetoric with the moral use of rhetoric (Cato, Cicero, and Quintilian: the good orator is necessarily a good man); or (3) acknowledge that there are no built-in constraints and that rhetoric can be used to persuade to evil as well as to good (the Sophists, Aristotle). Similarly, with regard to prudence, one can identify it with theoretical wisdom, in which case it is governed by an absolute notion of the truth (the Platonic ideas); with practical wisdom as the knowledge of good and evil, what to seek and what to avoid (the Stoics, on occasion Cicero); or with a faculty of practical reason which has no precepts but is governed in every particular case by considerations of decorum—of the best means to achieve the end at hand (Cicero, Aristotle).

Depending on how one feels about the claims of social and political action, a rhetoric or prudence that is not subordinate to the fixed moral precepts characteristic of theoretical reason will be more or less attractive. If this realm of action is in all cases to be subordinate to the standards of theoretical reason, then conformity to that standard rather than practical effectiveness will be the primary concern, and prudence in the sense we have been exploring falls away. Accordingly, if one has to choose between speaking well and speaking persuasively, between acting correctly or acting effectively, one will always choose the former. But, Pontano argues, there is another way of looking at things, another system of values that is not concerned with correspondence to some fixed theoretical truth or ethics, but with the creation and maintenance of a social and political community, and thus with compromise and consensus. The agent within this community does not seek preestablished first principles, but rather a practical truth:

> We are speaking about truth here, not that truth which is sought by scientists or mathematicians, which has to do with the certainty of syllogisms in disputations about nature and the disciplines, sciences and faculties of man, but about that truth which shows there is nothing fictitious, deceitful or counterfeit in conversation or speech or customs. . . . Those who have followed this [truth], and hold to it in speaking, business, and domestic habits, are called truthful, and that virtue [is called] truth.

The measure of the extent to which Pontano views this truth as practical appears in the discussion of the positive use of fiction in the *De sermone:* doctors, rulers, priests may all tell untruths without being charged with lying, since their intention is not to deceive their interlocutors but to help them. In this turn to fiction, they are guided by the social and pragmatic judgment of prudence: "omnino prudentiam est hominum munus atque officium" (the entire duty of man is prudence, 58). Poets are thus also exempt from the charge of lying (61–63) since they invent their fables not out of vanity, "but in order that, by this art, men should be deterred from vice . . . or incited to virtue" (62). Finally, ironic dissimulation of the sort Socrates engaged in is not immoral because it is not self-interested. Socrates denied his own learning "not in order to deny what was clear to all [quod in luce expositum est] but to incite others to *humanitas* and modesty" (197). This emphasis on the realm of praxis leads Pontano to justify irony, along with other rhetorical figures, in persuasive rather than cognitive terms: in the case of Socrates, irony is employed to persuade the auditor to the morally good rather than to indicate his own knowledge by a figure of inversion.

Pontano's defense of his practical conception of the truth makes explicit a final assumption that the Quattrocento humanists shared with the Ciceronian orator: the belief that the impossibility of *gnosis,* or cognitive knowledge of the truth, was not a hindrance to ethical praxis. The difference between the two periods is that in the Quattrocento the Ciceronian analogy between the orator and the skeptic is further reinforced by the generally accepted view of the compatibility of skepticism and faith, on the grounds that both involve a critique of the authority of theoretical reason. Salutati is particularly forceful on this point. While in his letters he subscribes to the classical dictum that one must have knowledge in order to be eloquent, he adds the at once serious and ironic qualification that the knowledge that is necessary is the knowledge that one knows nothing, but this recognition is liberating rather than constraining, for it shifts the emphasis from the realm of necessity, that is, from the cognition of logical truth, to that of probability, or of action within a social and political context. Here the criterion of theoretical certainty gives way to that of moral efficacy and rhetoric assumes the divinely authorized function of moving the will.

The early humanist conception of rhetoric thus involves a precarious synthesis of aesthetic, political, and religious factors. Aesthetic decorum is seen to be inseparable from political effectiveness, and in both cases the possibility of such decorum is seen to be not only compatible with cognitive skepticism but contingent upon it. But this skepticism about the power of human reason is itself just the opposite side of faith in divine will. The view that the impossibility of theoretical knowledge leaves room for action and practical certainty then explains the benign role of both skeptical and hypothetical arguments in early humanist texts. As a Christian, the Quattrocento humanist believed that skeptical arguments could be used to destroy the claims of theoretical reason and thus make room for faith. Like the Sophist, the humanist believed that hypothetical argumentation could have beneficial practical consequences. Thus, Lorenzo Valla adopts a Pyrrhonist mode of arguing in his dialogue on free will in order to suggest that we cannot *know* whether or not we have free will but that we can *assume* we practice it. And Erasmus argues explicitly in his

Diatribe that it is good to assume that we have free will since this hypothesis will have beneficial effects. The humanist's practical transcendence of the epistemological impasse of skepticism can then be seen to be opposed to one traditional analogy between skepticism and aesthetics, according to which the skeptic's detachment is the equivalent of the autonomy of art, or the disinterestedness of the aesthetic experience.

At this point it may be helpful to distinguish the humanist conception of the morally educative activity of reading from the aesthetic conception of reading. In the former, humanist conception, reading is seen to involve a series of discriminations that are analogous to the kinds of discriminations we make in acting in the social and political spheres. This activity of judgment is an interested one. Furthermore, it is not something that supervenes upon the experience of pleasure but is intrinsically bound up with it. While the humanists argue that the activity of judgment is constitutive of the reader's or viewer's response to a work of art, the Kantian, on the other hand, claims that our primary aesthetic response is one of pleasure, which is noncognitive. Only upon reflection do we subject the source of this pleasure to a properly aesthetic judgment.

Despite these differences, however, the practical and aesthetic conceptions of reading are alike in significant ways. While the Kantian aesthetic judgment is noncognitive, and is explicitly opposed to the interested judgments of prudential reasoning, it shares with the prudential judgment of decorum both an authoritative moment of self-reflection and an implicit claim for the moral value of this experience. Just as the judgment of decorum involves reflection on the needs of the judging subject, as well as reference to an internal though not merely subjective standard of decorum, so the aesthetic judgment requires reflection on the subject's experience as grounded in the shared, and thus not merely subjective, human capacity for judgment. Both the practical and aesthetic models of reading, in other words, reject the Pyrrhonist threat to the possibility of cognitive and moral claims; both presuppose the integrity and authority of the judging subject, as well as a relatively unproblematic conception of judgment. The practical and the aesthetic can thus be seen to represent two models of literary judgment, two attitudes toward the text, which are not so far apart as has often been assumed. For if the former places more emphasis on the direct tie between literary and ethical praxis, the latter is far from denying that we are interested in having disinterested aesthetic experiences.

It is important for a number of reasons to establish these differences and similarities between the aesthetic and practical conceptions of reading. In the first case, such clarification guards us against the anachronistic reading of Renaissance texts in purely aesthetic terms. In the second case, it guards us from assuming that the questioning of the humanists' practical conception of reading by many later Renaissance authors necessarily led them to an aesthetic conception of literature (this is one way the conflation of rhetoric and poetics has been interpreted): if the criterion of judgment or of common sense that informs practical reason is open to doubt, the possibility of aesthetic judgment may be threatened as well. The practical and aesthetic conceptions of judgment can then serve as heuristic paradigms, models of reading, which can help us clarify *per contrariam* the rhetorical practices of a number of later Renaissance authors who are skeptical both of the possibility of persuasion to action and of (in Kenneth Burke's definition of the properly aesthetic effect of the text) the action of "pure persuasion."

•   •   •

Sister Miriam Joseph

"Shakespeare's Use of the [Renaissance] Theory [of Composition]"

Shakespeare knew the complete doctrine and method of composition regularly taught in the grammar schools of his day from a combination of Latin textbooks. He employed in his work the techniques prescribed in Cicero's *Topica*, the *Ad Herennium*, Susenbrotus' *Epitome troporum ac schematum*, Erasmus' *Copia* and *Modus conscribendi*, Aphthonius' *Progymnasmata*, Quintilian's *Institutio oratoria*, and a work on logic, perhaps Melanchthon's. These techniques, comprising the core of grammar school discipline, were applied to both composition and the reading of classical Latin literature in a manner which formed the Renaissance creating and responding mind.

The Renaissance grammar school discipline justified itself by its results. Logic and rhetoric were, indeed, used too badly in Gascoigne's works, Lyly's *Euphues,* Sidney's *Arcadia,* and Greene's *Tritameron,* which reveal apprenticeship to art rather than achievement; and logic was employed in a too-obvious, even though interesting, way in the interludes of John Heywood and in the plays of Lyly, Jonson, Dekker, Chapman, and Massinger. Nevertheless, it is the work of the apprentice rather than that of the finished artist which shows most clearly the currents of the time, and one has only to remember Ben Jonson's "To Celia" to realize how an impression of creative spontaneity and ease can be wrested from borrowed material by one trained as the Elizabethans were in imitative synthesis.

Many of the great passages in Shakespeare similarly transfigured materials that were borrowed from the Latin literature studied in grammar school, for Shakespeare also pressed his school learning into service and his early work discloses his own apprenticeship to art. There is some evidence of his continued interest as an adult in theoretical works and of his acquaintance with a number of the English works on rhetoric and logic that have furnished the selections in Part III of the present study, which sets forth the Renaissance theory of composition. This theory was a penetrating and comprehensive analysis of thought and its expression, and there can be no doubt that formal training in it contributed vitally to the development of Shakespeare's genius. An intensive and thorough investigation of his use of any or all the features of this theory might prove as instructive and rewarding as a study of his blank verse, for verse was just one of many instruments of style carefully cultivated by Renaissance writers and brought to unprecedented perfection by Shakespeare. Verse was, in fact, a part of the theory, insofar as a study of prosody and the composition of verse were important features of Tudor grammar school training.

Even though Shakespeare parodied the extremely narrow and artificial style of *Euphues*, his own early work was marked by a schematic use of the most obvious rhetorical and logical devices. Like many of his contemporaries, he too seems often to have been occupied in a pursuit of words rather than of ideas. In his mature work he continues to use these devices and many more, but with a delicate dramatic fitness and subtle inwardness adapted to minds and moods of a range unmatched by any other dramatist. Each point of view is fully entered into. Each person speaks in his own idiom, be it that of king, scholar, pedant, or rogue. With equally authentic accent Shakespeare speaks the language appropriate to the garrulous, the shallow, the ignorant, the grave. Mainly by a skillful use of the vices of language, he travesties the verbal affectation of Osric, the ineptitude of Dogberry, the misapprehension and confusion of Bottom and Mistress Quickly, the scurrility of Thersites. By means of fallacious and captious argument he creates the light sophistic of Feste and Touchstone, the dodges and nimble wit of Falstaff, the chicanery of Richard III, the cynical mockery of Apemantus, the barbed shafts of the fool in *Lear*. Through complete mastery of *logos, pathos,* and *ethos,* characters whom he has endowed with natural eloquence full of personal and vivid touches engage both the intellect and the feelings of the audience, whether they voice with experienced tongue the cogent application of analytic thought to grave affairs in public debate or in soliloquy unburden the heart of poignant doubt or fear or grief. Thought and image commensurate with the genuine stress of a compelling problem or passion forge language which by appealing simultaneously to the reason and the imagination confers beauty as well as vision. The style echoes the mood with sureness, though it shifts from unruffled deliberation to hysterical excitement, or from stern self-control to unbridled emotion in the movement of living drama. Shakespeare's creative art illustrates most fully the variety and compass of the Renaissance theory of composition.

In his best work Shakespeare employs the figures of repetition with easy mastery to achieve varied artistic effects. Yet even in his early plays he seldom uses them merely as verbal embroidery. When they are so used, they usually serve by that very fact to characterize the speaker. The repetition often accentuates an idea dramatically significant, as in *II Henry VI* (I.3), where the repetition of *Lord Protector* galls Queen Margaret, who wishes Henry to rule, and who accordingly schemes to get rid of the Lord Protector. In the scene in *King John* where Hubert, under orders from the king, comes to put out young Arthur's eyes with a heated iron (4.I), *iron* becomes symbolic through repetition and acquires a quality of reflection and meditation, which joined to the repetition of *eyes, see,* and *look,* communicates both dignity and pathos.

Even in the more external phases of his art Shakespeare is preeminent.

Writing at a time which invited originality, distinction, and music of expression, he exhibits the ultimate in energy, verve, and daring creativeness. He uses every resource of language and imagination to give life, movement, and piquancy to his richly laden thought. Since the schemes of grammar owe much of their attractiveness to the very nearness of their approach to error, he likes to teeter on the brink of solecism and like a tightrope walker or an acrobatic dancer to display in the precariousness of balance such sureness, poise, agility, and consummate skill as to awaken tense admiration in the prosaic onlooker with two feet squarely on the ground. And all this he does within the scope of an approved tradition which sanctioned such deviations from pedestrian style. The very vices of language he employs with fine dramatic effect to portray the ignorance, affectation, scurrility, garrulity, and ineptitude of certain characters in his plays. The figures of repetition in his later works give beauty, emphasis, and strength to the thought and feeling.

Regarding invention in the contemporary and traditional sense of a systematic process for finding something to say, Shakespeare drew matter for his plays and poems from all the topics of invention including inartificial arguments, which were given an important place by the logicians and rhetoricians of his time. He employed all the rhetorical figures related to the several logical topics, sometimes adding comments which constitute a virtual definition of the figure. The characters in his plays manifest a knowledge and practice of logical and rhetorical theory, lively, concrete, specific, displayed in parody as well as in serious application, which were expected to win a commensurate response from an audience similarly disciplined and practiced in the arts of logic and rhetoric. The pedant Holofernes' question "What is the figure?" echoes the English schoolmaster's insistent and familiar *"Per quam figuram?"*

Equipped as every educated man of his time was with a thorough knowledge of the terms, the forms, and the processes of argumentation, Shakespeare skillfully adapts these devices to every conceivable dramatic purpose. Often the skirmish of wits is light and playful, as in *Twelfth Night, As You Like It, Much Ado About Nothing, Love's Labor's Lost, The Two Gentlemen of Verona, Romeo and Juliet,* displayed sometimes in a bandying of words, sometimes of ideas. An Elizabethan audience could be relied upon to follow the turns and twists of an argument, to note the skill, the adroitness, the fumbles, as readily as a modern crowd notes these points in a football game. Touchstone, Feste, and the other clowns, Rosalind, Beatrice, Benedick, Romeo, Juliet, Cressida are skillful fencers with words, adept at the quick retort, the pert reply. The gravediggers in *Hamlet* match Touchstone and Feste in light sophistic, even though the subject of their banter is grim. Richard III and Iago reason fallaciously, even falsely, in pursuit of deepest villainy. Despite his personal feeling and sympathies, York in *Richard II* upholds what reason tells him is the right. Desdemona and Hermione argue with dignity and cogency before judges at a public trial. Isabella contends with superb skill and honesty against the craft and deceit of Angelo, the reputed saint. Portia eloquently pleads that mercy temper justice; yet, upholding the literal application of the law, with consummate cunning she turns the tables on revenge-bent Shylock. Logic contributes much to the interest of *All's Well* and *Julius Caesar*. It is vital in the soliloquies of Hamlet.

In impregnating dramatic scenes of human urgency with the tension of genuine debate Shakespeare easily excels his contemporaries. Combining intellectual power with imaginative and emotional persuasion, he successfully blends logic, rhetoric, and poetic. He so fuses character and plot, thought and feeling, that they become almost indistinguishable and thereby more intense, more convincing, moving both mind and heart. This is particularly true of his great tragedies, *Othello, Macbeth, Hamlet, Lear, Coriolanus, Antony and Cleopatra,* and of the dark comedy *Troilus and Cressida*. In these he mirrors the whole of man's composite but integrated nature.

The formal training which Shakespeare received contributed not only to the breadth and stature of his thought but also to the richness of the gorgeous panoply with which he invested it. His language, fresh, vibrant, exuberant, and free, makes use of the schemes of words as well as the schemes of construction. He effects sudden and vivid concentrations of meaning by a poetically superb and daring use of anthimeria (nouns as verbs), catachresis (verbs and adjectives employed in a transferred sense), hypallage (the transferred epithet), the compound epithet, metaphor, metonymy, syllepsis of the sense, negative and privative terms. He secures swiftness of movement, compactness, and emphasis through anastrophe (inverted word order), parenthesis, zeugma (one verb serving two or more subjects), brachylogia and asyndeton (omission of conjunctions).

With figures of repetition, Shake peare weaves a haunting harmony of sound; through the schemes of grammar he achieves such control over movement and rhythm that like a figure skater he may dart, poise, turn, plunge, go where he will, his words laden with penetrating thought and deep feeling—and all this but an art subservient to the larger art of the builder, to plot construction, character creation, and profound insight into human nature and its problems. Yet this myriad-minded man has time for fun and nonsense, for parody and foolery, for mere gleeful bandying of words.

One may read Shakespeare's plays, or see them produced, with attention to any or all these facets of his art. They give pleasure at many levels, as great music does. One who recognizes in the intricate web of harmonic and melodic progressions the chord structures and rhythmic design, and notes the fine gradation and coloring, experiences a deeper and keener delight in music than one who does not perceive these things; he enjoys not only what the untrained listener enjoys but also a detailed intellectual perception of the relation of parts to parts and to the whole. Similarly, to cultivate the alert attentiveness to patterns of sound and movement and the expert analysis of thought-relations habitual to educated Elizabethans quickens the responsiveness requisite to a full appreciation of Shakespeare's plays.

Modern Rhetoric

In her comprehensive treatment of nineteenth-century rhetoric, Nan Johnson proposes that rhetoric during that time was central to the full development of the intellect for the purposes of improving society. She shows that theoretical and pedagogical expressions of nineteenth-century rhetoric are remarkably consistent and comprehensive. Nineteenth-century rhetoric is a furtherance of the project of the New Rhetoric, which, as Johnson explains earlier in her book, "evolved from the efforts of theorists such as George Campbell (*The Philosophy of Rhetoric*) and Hugh Blair (*Lectures on Rhetoric and Belles-Lettres*) to reconcile the principles and practices of rhetoric with theories of the mind, logic, and language that had emerged from the Baconian–Lockian tradition."

For Johnson, then, nineteenth-century rhetoric is a rich and beneficial social and pedagogical enterprise. Sharon Crowley, on the other hand, emphasizes an eighteenth- and nineteenth-century *reduction* of rhetoric to schematic principles, grounded in "an orderly model of the mind's workings"; Crowley is worried that such reductionist tendencies continue to influence the teaching of rhetoric and composition in this century. Robert Connors has a similar concern; he traces the history of the modes of discourse that became established as fundamental to composition in the nineteenth century: narration, description, exposition, and argument. As he explains the "fall" of the modes in this century, Connors indicates with some relief that this century's rhetoricians have disparaged nineteenth-century conceptions of composition as an abstract and mechanical process, and have viewed the traditional modes as inimical to what Albert Kitzhaber calls "the real nature of writing." Karlyn Kohrs Campbell explains that, regardless of whether rhetoric was more or less a schematic pursuit, its practice by women has been ignored. From antiquity, women have no place in the history of rhetoric parallel to men. For this reason, she wants "to restore one segment of the history of women, namely the rhetoric of the early woman's rights movement that emerged in the United States in the 1830s."

Lloyd Bitzer, in keeping with the twentieth-century rejection of form and technique as stable and primary elements of rhetoric, sets forth a "theory of situation." For Bitzer, a rhetorical situation has three constituents: exigence, audience, and constraints. A discourse that takes these constituents into account can, as Bitzer points out, "effect valuable changes in reality." By surveying the variables of a rhetorical situation rather categorically, and by concluding that rhetoric—like science—is a body of "principles, concepts, and procedures," Bitzer maintains rhetoric as a disciplined philosophical art whose end is *decision*. William Covino lays more stress on instability and uncertainty as elements of rhetoric, suggesting that the postmodern celebration of these qualities has opened the possibility for our understanding of rhetoric as the multiplication of perspectives, rather than an agency of determinant meaning.

Nan Johnson

"Habits of Eloquence"

The art of speaking and writing with purity, propriety, and elegance, is of the highest importance to the mere English, as well as to the classical and general scholar. It invests the talents and knowledge of its possessor with more than a double value. . . . The power which an eloquent orator exerts over an assembly, an able writer exerts over a country. . . . The noble prize and the enviable power of elegant and forcible writing are within the grasp of ordinary minds, and may, in general be viewed as the certain reward of patient industry. The value of such an acquirement cannot be estimated, as its resources of enjoyment and influence are unmeasured.

—EGERTON RYERSON,
address at the opening of Victoria
College, Toronto, 1842

Whatever then may be your employment in future life, though you may never be called to the pulpit or to the bar, it is a sacred duty which you owe to yourselves and your friends, to cultivate those graces and accomplishments of our nature—those elegances of taste and imagination; of language and of address, which, in every profession, give the crowning ornament to intellectual superiority.

—CHAUNCEY ALLEN GOODRICH,
"Lectures on Rhetoric and
Public Speaking"

The work in rhetoric assumes considerable study and practice in the art of composition, devotes itself largely to a consideration of the science of effective discourse, embracing the laws of mind, the laws of language. Opportunities for original work in the writing of essays and in the preparation and delivery of orations are afforded in the literary societies, in class, and before the faculty and body of students.

DePauw College Catalogue, 1887

The nineteenth-century theoretical tradition exceeded the accomplishments of the New Rhetoric by synthesizing the epistemological, belles lettres, and classical rationales to justify a broader range of rhetorical practice. The articulation of this broader range of practice can be traced to two characteristics of nineteenth-century theory: (1) the fundamental presumption that rhetorical principles are applicable to all types of oral and written communication; and (2) a wider interpretation of the function of rhetoric in social and cultural exchange. Nineteenth-century rhetoricians presumed the philosophical verifiability of rhetorical principles and the inherent relationship between the structure and techniques of rhetorical discourse and the laws of the mind; they equated the study of rhetorical principles with an understanding of communication in a general sense. As the century progressed, the nineteenth-century tradition promoted an ever more encompassing definition of the relevance of rhetorical principles. The abiding assumption that every communicative occasion represents an instance in which rhetorical principles must be applied in a strategic manner was the dominant attitude of influential theorists such as Henry N. Day, Alexander Bain, A. S. Hill, and John F. Genung, who shaped the theoretical stance of the tradition after 1850.

The pervasive influence of the epistemological rationale of the New Rhetoric was primarily responsible for the marked tendency of the nineteenth-century tradition to regard practice as a matter of coordinating the natural principles of rhetoric with the demands of particular occasions. Theorists promoted the notion that the effective writer and speaker must convey ideas with the clarity and liveliness required to engage the associative dynamics of mind (processing ideas in terms of logical links to experience and common sense). In this view, the challenge for the rhetorician is to select ideas, order content, and apply the principles of style in the manner best suited to ə given instance. The belletristic views incorporated into nineteenth-century theory also reinforced the notion that rhetorical practice involves the application of natural laws of the mind. Incorporating a rational philosophy of taste within a general epistemological account of rhetorical practice, nineteenth-century theorists added the aesthetic imagination to the list of the mental faculties that rhetorical technique must engage. Although especially useful in speeches and prose intended to move the will, appeals to the imagination must be satisfied in all discourses through harmony in arrangement and the principles of style—perspicuity, force, and ornament. Whether foregrounded in the nature of the subject, the structure of the discourse, or the devices of style, the principles of harmony, elegance, and the sublime provide the writer and speaker with the means of intensifying the response of the imagination and the higher passions and elevating the reader or listener's apprehension of the beautiful. Just as the rhetorician must always consider what content and structure will best facilitate the associational responses of the faculties, the writer and speaker must also evaluate how to appeal to the taste of the audience through subject matter and technique.

By asserting epistemological and belletristic rationales for practice, nineteenth-century rhetoricians reconfirmed the classical principle that the content and technique of rhetorical discourse must be relevant to those addressed and the particular circumstances of the rhetorical event. The theoretical weight given in nineteenth-century theory to the consideration of human nature in the devising of subject matter and technique had the effect of reinscribing the classical precept that the rhetorician must adapt to subject, audience, and occasion. In nineteenth-century rhetoric, rhetorical occasion was not defined strictly in contextual terms but in terms of what effect the writer or speaker would characteristically be seeking in that setting. For example, when a congregation gathers to hear a sermon, the preacher provides Bible lessons (appeals to the understanding) and also exhorts the assembly to change their behavior and live a good life (persuasion by moving the will). To devise the appropriate content and techniques of the sermon, the preacher combines a scientific knowledge of human nature with an insight into what people typically expect a sermon to provide. The rhetorician must evaluate the epistemological conditions of the occasion as well as the ways in which the formal nature of the occasion may have imposed on the listener's frame of mind. Claiming the authority of the classical maxim that the essence of rhetoric lies in adaptation as further support of the natural relationship between the dynamics of communication and the science of rhetoric, nineteenth-century theorists consistently asserted that an understanding of fundamental rhetorical principles (canons) can be applied to any type of public speaking or writing.

The presupposition that natural laws authorize the applicability of rhetorical principles to all forms of discourse supported significant innovations: (1) the definition of description, narration, exposition, argumentation, and persuasion as types of rhetoric constrained primarily by epistemological intention and method and (2) the formalization of "popular oratory" as a distinct type of oratory appropriate to occasions at which the public is addressed on a topic of collective interest. The formalization of description, narration, argumentation, and persuasion as generic categories (Campbell and Whately simply treat these as inventional techniques) allowed nineteenth-century theorists to define genres extending across an unprecedented range of venues. For example, the writer whose intention is to appeal to the understanding through exposition could do so in a scientific article, a travel lecture, or a treatise on botany. Exposition is intended to have a particular effect on the mind; it is this intention (to define the term or concept) that characterizes the rhetorical strategies employed in this type of discourse. Epistemological intention presumes a consideration of audience since an evaluation of how best to inform the understanding, move the will, or please the imagination and the passions focuses explicitly on the mental nature of the reader or listener. The formal designation of popular oratory as a major form of public speaking (which adds a fourth category to the New Rhetoric's list of judicial, deliberative, and sacred oratory) was rationalized theoretically by the assumption that popular oratory, like sacred and deliberative oratory, represents another instance of persuasion, or an attempt [to] move the will. This view of popular oratory is typical of the nineteenth-century tendency to define generic varieties in terms of epistemological intention. While the powerful influence of the New Rhetoric predisposed this tendency in great measure, the nineteenth-century tradition itself was responsible for incorporating a greater range of oral and written forms under epistemological and belletristic rubrics for practice.

One of the consequences of this innovative outline of the range of rhetoric was that nineteenth-century theorists accounted for a greater number of modes through which rhetoric can function as an agency of social well-being and cultural education. By the late nineteenth century, rhetoricians perceived the domain of rhetoric as including public speaking, all forms of argumentative, expository, descriptive, and narrative composition, and the critical study of literature. Whether engaged in the delivery of a lecture from the platform or in the composition of a critical review, the rhetorician is involved in airing matters of the public interest or in dispensing needed information; whether providing a historical account of past wars or urging the legislature to take action, the rhetorician is taking active responsibility for the education or the welfare of the public. The nineteenth-century tradition never represented the obligations of the rhetorician in strictly pragmatic terms. Throughout the century, rhetoricians promoted the notion that rhetorical skill enables the individual to participate in and contribute to society and to engage in that communication which ensures an informed populace. Whenever the speaker or writer informs others, moves them to needed action, or provides them with insight into the literary experience, the rhetorician affects the intellectual and moral constitution of the community. Because nineteenth-century theorists conflated the acquisition of rhetorical skills with the development of taste, they assumed that the orator and the writer influence the community through the subject matter conveyed as well as through the aesthetic appeal of rhetorical form.

The special status of the rhetorician was ensured by the nineteenth-century assumption that the study of rhetorical principles is a type of scientific study that confers a philosophical understanding of human nature and deep appreciation of the beauty and art of language. This view of the study of rhetoric and of the culturally significant function of its practice was supported by the pedagogies of rhetoricians who argued that the study of rhetoric cultivates higher intellectual and moral sensibilities. Under the influence of such views, nineteenth-century educators came to view rhetoric as an important subject in the liberal arts. Three important documents—Samuel P. Newman's *Lecture on a Practical Method of Teaching Rhetoric* (delivered to the American Institute of Instruction in 1830), Bain's article series "The Teaching of English" (*Journal of Education*, 1869), and Genung's *Study of Rhetoric in the College Course* (1887)—reveal the theoretical and ideological presumptions governing attitudes toward rhetorical education. Despite the span of decades between the date of Newman's lecture and the publication of Bain and Genung's guidelines for rhetorical instruction, these three discussions review similar issues: (1) the salutary intellectual effects of the study of rhetoric; (2) the irrefutable usefulness of rhetorical skills to every individual; (3) the pedagogical centrality of the study and practice of rhetorical principles; (4) the importance of criticism in the development of rhetorical skills; and (5) the qualifications of the effective instructor of rhetoric.

Newman and Bain explicitly defend the value of rhetorical education on the grounds that the study of rhetoric contributes to intellectual discipline and the cultivation of taste, and they share the same conception of what makes up a sound course in rhetoric. Newman points out that the student must be taught something of "the science of intellectual philosophy" and the nature of "literary taste" as preparation for the study of rhetorical principles. These studies acquaint students with the operations of the mind and with what constitutes tasteful achievement in discourse. The student who has been educated in the philosophy of rhetoric is better able to understand "the nature of the rules and directions" of rhetoric and its "intricate principles" (*Lecture* 5). Arguing that a philosophical understanding of rhetoric must precede the study of technique, Newman outlines what a "practical method of studying rhetoric" should provide: "1. Some acquaintance with the philosophy of rhetoric. 2. The cultivation of the taste, and in connexion, the exercise of the imagination. 3. Skill in the use of language. 4. Skill in literary criticism. 5. The formation of a good style" (3–4). This course of study disciplines the powers of reason, improves the imagination, and allows the individual to develop the powers of expression. Newman recommends a number of pedagogical methods including the study of literary models; instruction in the rules of diction, sentence construction, and arrangement; and correction of student's work. The objective of the study of rhetoric, Newman advises, should be for each student to "acquire a manner of writing, to some extent, peculiarly his own, and which is to be the index of his modes of thinking—the development of his intellectual traits and feelings. It is the office of the instructor to facilitate the accomplishment of this important end, both by wisely directing the efforts of his pupil, and by removing every obstacle in his way" (14).

In his analysis of "instruction in English," Bain defines the nature and scope of instruction in "Composition and Rhetoric," along with two other subjects, grammar and English literature. Bain regards rhetoric and composition to be the most advanced of these subjects and claims "training in prose composition" as the ultimate end of all the work done in "the English classroom" ("On Teaching English" 201). Like Newman, who acknowledges the relationship between philosophical training and the study of rhetoric, Bain observes that the cultivation of taste is "ministerial to composition" and that "intellectual discipline" in the art of expression is the end of rhetorical instruction. Bain defines rhetoric as the science that lays down the rules for effective composition. By the term *composition* Bain means the general art of expression: "A wide scope is to be allowed to the meaning of composition. It is not confined to mere business composition, nor even to that coupled with the expository art for the purposes of science; it takes in the graces and amenities of style, as an art refining social intercourse, and for aiding in oratory" (201). A course in rhetoric should provide instruction in sentence construction, arrangement (what Bain calls "the rhetoric of the paragraph"), the different kinds of composition (description, narration, exposition, persuasion), and the principles of style. Like Newman, Bain affirms the usefulness of studying exemplary models of style and of correcting student exercises. Bain particularly recommends engaging students in various types of practice exercises such as rendering poetic passages in prose, developing essays from outlines, and asking students to write about familiar subjects (2). He insists that rhetoric is largely a matter of the study and practice of fundamental principles and rules that are generally applicable in compositions "by the pen, or by mouth" (2).

Bain and Newman argue that the study of rhetoric presumes on and affirms the intellectual powers. Because the principles of rhetoric are drawn from scientific principles and embody the qualities of taste, the study of rhetoric is an ongoing education in intellectual discipline and taste. Bain and Newman point out that instruction in rhetoric ensures the development of intellectual discipline by focusing on the principles and rules that control rhetorical practice as a rational art; likewise, involving students in the study of an exemplary canon facilitates the development of critical judgment. These views are confirmed by Bain and Newman's shared expectation that the instructor of rhetoric be an individual of exemplary intellect and taste. Newman equates the qualifications of the competent instructor with the abilities that the practicing rhetorician must possess:

> 1. He should possess some knowledge of intellectual philosophy. The art of rhetoric, like the other arts, is founded on science of mind. It is from a knowledge of what is in man, of the constitution of the human mind, its susceptibilities of emotion, and the various influences it feels, that the skilful writer is enabled to address himself with success to his readers and subject them to this power. And further, many of the rules of rhetoric, based as they are on principles unfolded in the science of mind, are but aids for effecting of this purpose. How absolutely necessary, then, that he who attempts to explain and illustrate these rules, and to assist in cultivating the taste and forming the style, should possess some knowledge of that science whose principles are thus applied.

> 2. An instructor in rhetoric should possess some acquaintance with the prominent writings in his native language. Familiarity with good writers will evidently prove highly serviceable in illustrating the rules and principles, which he has occasion to bring to the notice of his pupils. With this familiarity, also, will most probably be associated some skill in literary criticism, and some refinement of the taste, both of which are highly conducive to the success of an instructor. (*Lecture* 19)

Like the rhetorician, the instructor of rhetoric must understand the philosophical foundations of rhetorical practice and must possess critical skills and a knowledge and appreciation of an exemplary canon—exactly the same attributes that the rhetorician must develop. Bain agrees with this assessment, observing that the instructor must know the rules of composition and have a "mind practised, up to the rapidity of an instinct, in discriminating good and evil in composition, in showing how the good may become better, and the better, best" ("On Teaching English" 1). An internalized instinct for critical analysis presupposes a highly developed sense of taste and a scientific understanding of the relationship between rhetorical form and intellectual and emotional response. Only this kind of background can prepare the instructor of rhetoric and composition to "engender a habit of excellence in style" (1).

In his analysis of "the direction and scope" of the college course in rhetoric, Genung reiterates many of Newman and Bain's views on rhetorical education. Genung considers the study of rhetoric to be philosophical in nature because "it draws from every department of nature and life" (*Study* 10). He defines the study of rhetoric as a process by which an individual learns how to apply "the facts and principles" of rhetoric to "the tasks of life" (4–5). Like Bain and Newman, Genung assumes that mental discipline is acquired when one engages in the systematic study of natural principles of language and art. Genung argues that the mental discipline acquired through the study of rhetoric is a unique resource to every individual who hopes to make an intellectual contribution: "The study of rhetoric in college aims to forstall that coming time of need. . . . It is preparing in secret for the future when the student shall begin to think for himself. And most of all, it seeks to induce that attitude of watchfulness, carefulness, contrivance, creativeness, which must be his when he has done with merely taking in knowledge, and addresses himself to giving it out again, newly minted and stamped with his individuality" (*Study* 5–6). Sharing Bain's view that the rhetoric course should provide general instruction in the art of composition, Genung points out that the student of rhetoric should learn to compose for a variety of purposes. He insists that rhetoric courses must address the increase in popular and periodical literature, which has "multiplied the forms of literary production," by teaching students how to apply the principles of style and invention to "prevailing literary forms" (11). Conceiving of "prevailing forms" quite broadly, Genung stresses that rhetorical study should take in all possible forms of "reading matter": political essays, scientific and descriptive treatises, short stories, editorials, and reporter's columns as well as the traditional forms of the sermon and the lyceum address (12).

Genung's overall pedagogical view confirms what both Newman and Blair recommend: the most effective way to teach rhetoric is to provide instruction in principles. The theoretical phase of study should be complemented with a variety of exercises that allow the writer (or speaker) to practice applying rhetorical techniques to various types of composition. Genung suggests two terms of theoretical study: the first term would provide a review of the grammatical and mechanical features of composition including diction, figures of speech, sentence structure and paragraphs; the second term would provide instruction in invention, arrangement, and style and applications to description, narration, exposition, argument, and persuasion. Sharing with Newman and Bain the conviction that the development of critical judgment reinforces an understanding of rhetorical principles, Genung considers the study of exemplary models a necessary aid to the study of rhetorical theory, and he also recommends extending critical exercises to include class members exchanging comments on each other's work. He refers to this entire sequence of study as "a systematically ordered, progressive series" that allows students of rhetoric to "gain freedom with the pen and confidence in [their] own powers of portrayal" (*Study* 26).[1] Although nineteenth-century theorists stressed the importance of theoretical and critical study in this "series," Genung, Bain, and Newman insist that the ultimate aim of theoretical study and critical exercises is to instruct students in how to express their own thoughts on subjects of personal significance or community interest. As Genung points out, the aim of every rhetorician is to "impart a clear and moving idea of common things, common events, common thoughts" (27). The aim of rhetorical education is to provide instruction in the nature and application of those principles that allow the writer or speaker to compose this type of discourse. In the course of developing the art of expression, the student comes to an understanding of human nature and the qualities of taste that in turn enhance the powers of thought.

The fact that Newman, Bain, and Genung promote a similar pedagogical program and share the conviction that the study of rhetoric has long-lasting salutary effects indicates the homogeneous nature of philosophies of rhetorical education during the nineteenth century, a period during which the goals of both liberal education and rhetorical education were highly compatible. The hegemony of the pedagogical program of the nineteenth-century tradition is obvious in the make-up of rhetoric courses given at colleges and universities in the United States and Canada throughout the century. The typical nineteenth-century college rhetoric course was organized according to the structure that rhetoricians such as Newman, Bain, and Genung explicitly defined: the systematic study of the nature and application of fundamental rhetorical principles in combination with the study of rhetorical modes and exercises in critical analysis. This system of study was promoted in the prefaces and introductions of the rhetoric treatises adopted as course texts and confirmed by the attitudes of nineteenth-century educators, who assumed without question the claim that the study of rhetoric confers mental discipline as well as the powers of eloquent expression.

The nineteenth-century rhetoric course integrated the study of epistemological, belletristic, and classical theory in a course that focused on the application of rhetorical principles to both oratory and writing. The popularity of the theory–practice–study of models sequence as an organizing pedagogical structure for the nineteenth-century rhetoric course is revealed by the consistency with which college and university calendar descriptions of rhetoric courses outlined this sequence. These calendar entries from Amherst College (1839) and Delaware College (1883) indicate the ways in which rhetoric courses typically combined the study of theoretical treatises on rhetoric and criticism with practice exercises in oratory and prose composition:

> [Amherst College, 1839–40:] Freshman Year . . . Porter, *Analysis of Rhetorical Delivery* . . . During the Year. A Weekly exercise in Declamation and Composition. Sophomore Year . . . Newman's *Rhetoric* . . . Cicero *de Oratore*. During the Year. Two Weekly Rhetorical Exercises, Declamations, Debates or English Composition. . . . Junior Year . . . Whately's *Rhetoric* with references to Campbell's *Philosophy of Rhetoric* . . . During the Year. Two Weekly Rhetorical Exercises, Composition, Declamation, Debates, or English Composition. . . . Senior Year . . . Kames's *Elements of Criticism.* . . . On every Wednesday afternoon is an exercise in Declamation, in which all the classes take part. Seniors and Juniors deliver original essays. (18–22)

> [Delaware College, 1883] English Language and Literature. . . . The Freshman, Sophomore, and Junior Classes are regularly required to write essays, which are carefully criticised; and there are weekly exercises in declamation and read-

ing. The Senior class prepare essays and original orations to be read or spoken in the oratory in the presence of the assembled students; questions of interest and importance are selected for discussion by members of the Class. The Freshman Class during the first and second terms have weekly recitations in Rhetoric, using Hart's work on the subject, and their knowledge is tested by examples on the blackboard. Books of Reference—Hill's *Science of Rhetoric*. (19)

Frequently joined with the study of elocution, logic, or English literature, the study of rhetorical theory was complemented by exercises in declamation, essay writing, and the study of literary models. This pedagogical program changed very little over the decades. Although college and university courses offered before midcentury focused on the treatises of Campbell and Blair (or Kames), whereas later courses tended to require the study of more contemporary rhetoricians such as Whately, G. P. Quackenbos, A. S. Hill, David J. Hill, John S. Hart, and Genung, the theory–practice–study of models sequence remained intact (appendix A). Critical exercises and the study of an exemplary canon continued as mandatory components of rhetoric courses throughout the century, as did instruction in oratory and the forms of prose composition.[2]

Calendars published in the latter decades of the century tended to be more detailed than earlier publications and often provided descriptions of rhetoric courses that reiterated dominant pedagogical rationales for rhetorical study. For example, these descriptions of courses offered at the Andover Theological Seminary, the University of Wyoming, and the University of Georgia between 1870 and 1900 corroborate the standard pedagogical format and also confirm a number of assumptions fundamental to the theoretical stance of the nineteenth-century tradition:

Lectures.—General Rhetoric: Province of Rhetoric; History of the Science—Alliance with other Sciences; Relation to Preaching; The Rhetorical and Scientific forms of Truth. Sources of Rhetorical Science.—Study of Men . . . Study of Models in Literature, Its Objects, Its Subjects, Its Methods . . . Methods of Study of English Literature . . . Study of Rhetorical Treatises . . . Exercises in Criticism. Sermons and Plans of Sermons by the Class, criticized in private. (Andover Theological Seminary, 1870, 19)

Rhetoric, English Literature, and oratory receive attention throughout the University course. The student's work in literature is made to furnish the occasion as well as the material for the preparation of essays. These essays are subject to criticism both in the class and with the individual writers. The formal study of rhetoric begins with the junior year and is designed to ground the student in the principles of English composition and to cultivate his literary sense by analytical study. The work in oratory is of a practical character. An effort is made to secure readings that shall be intelligent, natural, and forcible, and to develop spontaneous expression from the mental side. The student meets the instructor personally for rehearsal and criticism. (University of Wyoming, 1887)

Rhetoric—. In this course the subject is pursued by Sophomores who meet the professor twice a week throughout the year. Frequent practical exercises in all forms of composition are required. In illustration of the subject, selections from standard authors are used. This has the double advantage of acquainting the student with the principles of Rhetoric and of creating and forming a taste for classic English literature. (University of Georgia, 1898, 33)

All three of these course descriptions stress the pedagogical relationship between practice and the study of "principles." The detail of the Andover entry illustrates how the theory–practice–study of models sequence served rhetoric courses organized primarily for instruction in the rhetoric of the sermon. Even in this narrowly focused course, the study of the principles or "science" of rhetoric, "exercises in criticism," and practice in composition comprised the basic program of study. The attention awarded to the study of literature in the Andover course, and in the Wyoming and Georgia courses, indicates the normative status of critical study in the nineteenth-century rhetoric course. In addition to validating the theory–practice–study of models sequence, these course descriptions confirm a number of key assumptions of nineteenth-century rhetorical theory: (1) the governing assumption that principles of rhetoric are "scientific" in foundation ("The Rhetorical and Scientific forms of Truth"); (2) the governing definition of rhetoric as the study of both oral and written discourse ("all forms of composition"); (3) the assumption that the study of rhetorical principles, the practice of criticism, and the study of the literary canon are theoretically and practically interrelated ("Study of Rhetoric Treatises . . . Exercises in Criticism"); (4) the assumption that the acquisition of eloquence depends on the development of control over the natural mental faculties ("develop spontaneous expression from the mental side"); and (5) the assumption that the study and practice of rhetoric improves intelligence and taste ("analytical study," "forming a taste").

By incorporating the theoretical assumptions of the nineteenth-century tradition in the curricular design of rhetoric courses in such obvious ways, nineteenth-century educators contributed to the authority that these assumptions exerted over definitions of the nature and aims of rhetorical education. The powerful parallel between the curricular substance of nineteenth-century rhetoric courses and the philosophical and pedagogical stances of the tradition as a whole was further encouraged by the prominent attention given in popular textbooks to defining the nature of rhetoric and the correct system for studying it. The treatises of Newman, Quackenbos, Day, Bain, David J. Hill, A. S. Hill, and Genung, all texts that enjoyed wide adoption in nineteenth-century colleges and universities, explicitly define rhetoric as a science and as the general art of communication, prescribe the importance of taste, stress the importance of the canons and critical study, and confirm the importance of the neoclassical pedagogical scheme theory–practice–study of models. These tenets were reinscribed in treatise after treatise, course after course, standardizing a theoretical context that dominated nineteenth-century rhetorical education from the early decades of the century through the 1890s.

In addition to institutionalizing the mandate of nineteenth-century theory in the design of rhetoric courses, nineteenth-century educators confirmed the status of rhetorical study by regarding rhetoric as an essential subject in the liberal arts curriculum. Nineteenth-century educators perceived the goal of higher education to be the cultivation of the mental powers. By midcentury this psychological conception of the goal of education had displaced the classical model favored by eighteenth-century educators, which stressed the command of subject matter. Nineteenth-century educators assumed that the most important consequence of higher education is not the acquisition of special knowledge but the development of the powers of perception and reason. The study of particular subjects such as classical and modern languages, logic, history, natural philosophy, literature, and rhetoric all contribute to the development of mental discipline by presenting the student with opportunities to sharpen intellectual habits: the abilities to observe, to compare, to reason, to concentrate on a single object or problem, and to evaluate an issue with an open mind. In the view of nonsecular educators, a significant force in the first part of the nineteenth century when many colleges had religious affiliations, the development of mental discipline also extended to the improvement of Christian morality. Although a dominant theme in the early decades of the century, an emphasis on the moral aspect of mental discipline was a less insistent theme in educational philosophy after 1860. By that time a number of new public institutions had reinterpreted the moral mission of education in secular terms as the development of taste and a sensibility to truth. Despite various interpretations of what "moral" education entailed, secular and nonsecular educators alike persistently held to the philosophy that the mission of higher education was "the development of intellectual and moral faculties and correct habits of thought and study" (Indiana University, 1854).[3]

The opinion that the development of mental discipline is the most significant aim of higher education was so widely affirmed in nineteenth-century commentaries on the nature of college education that it achieved the status of ideology. The laudable mission of the college and university was a frequent theme of addresses at baccalaureate ceremonies and university celebrations; in such speeches prominent educators promoted the idea that only higher education can confer the mental and moral habits necessary for the advancement of the individual and society. In his account of the nature of college education, Horace Mann expresses this view:

A College is a place where character is developed with fearful rapidity. Seeds which might never, or not for years, have germinated at home spring into sudden vitality and shoot with amazing luxuriance. . . . A young man of fair intelligence and an uncorrupted heart cannot have been in a College class for a single year without perceiving that he has crossed a boundary and entered a new realm; the realm of thoughts instead of the realm of the senses. The reflecting student cannot have been in College for a single year, without discovering that there is *periodicity* in his nature. Under the force of habit, the most difficult things become easy. . . . So of the intellectual faculties. Every cultivated mind which has arrived at mature age knows that what, at first, cost great efforts, is now performed without consciousness. Ideas which once seemed heavy as the hills to lift, are now handled like toys. . . . It is in this way that the intellectual and moral character of man grows up . . . into sturdiness and loftiness.[4] ("Antioch College: Baccalaureate Address of 1857")

Mann believes that the training of the mind to think accurately and systematically fulfills a natural phase of mental development that subsequently liberates original thinking and the finer sensibilities. The conflation that Mann makes between higher education and the development of "loftiness" of mind and heart is typical of how nineteenth-century educators rationalized the social and cultural value of college education. When the intellectual faculties are developed to a higher level, a moral disposition and sense of social responsibility are cultivated as well. The university experience sponsors the development of the whole individual by educating the powers of reason and taste and by cultivating special abilities; in turn, the individual with these traits contributes to the maintenance of a high standard of culture and a harmonious society.

Daniel Coit Gilman, first president of Johns Hopkins University (1875–1901) and founder of the graduate school model of the American university, reiterates this belief in his definition of "the idea of the university": "It may include a college; or several colleges; but it is more than a college, more than a group of colleges. It is the highest expression which any community can give to its intellectual aspirations; the most complex, diversified, and fruit-bearing organism which any community can devise for the intellectual and moral welfare of its people" ("Address").[5] Although Gilman's comment marks the view of educators at the end of the century, his characterization of the university as the site at which the highest intellectual and moral aspirations of a community can be instilled simply affirms rather than redefines the mandate of higher education formulated in earlier decades. Gilman's claim for the interrelationship between intellectual training, moral welfare, and the good of the community was reiterated by nineteenth-century educators as a guiding philosophy for college and university education.[6] In this general philosophical context, the study of rhetoric was rationalized as a pursuit that contributes directly to the development of mental discipline and that provides the individual with the means to express his ideas and thus make a contribution to society.

Because of the systematic nature of rhetorical study, its foundation in philosophically sound principles, and its practical value to the individual and literate culture in general, nineteenth-century educators considered the development of "the powers of expression" one of the components of a liberal education. In *College Education for Men of Business* John A. Broadus, author of the popular textbook *A Treatise on the Preparation and Delivery of Sermons* (1870), expresses the widely held opinion that "development and strengthening and discipline of [the student's] principal faculties" must be complemented by the development of communication skills (8). In his description of the well-educated man, Broadus reviews those traits that nineteenth-century educators equated with mental discipline:

1. An educated man is one whose mind is *widened out,* so that he can take broad views, instead of being narrow-minded; so that he can see the different sides of a question, or at least can know that all questions have different sides. 2. An educated man is one who has the power of *patient thinking;* who can fasten his mind on a subject, and hold it there while he pleases; who can keep looking at a subject till he sees into it and sees through it. . . . 3. Again, an educated man is one who has sound judgment, who knows how to *reason* to right conclusions, and so to *argue* as to convince others that he is right. 4. And finally,—not to speak now of imagination and taste, important as they are—an educated man is one who can *express* his thoughts clearly and forcibly.[7] (7; Broadus's italics)

Broadus's definition of the well-educated man links rhetorical study to the development of the mental powers. Through the study of rhetoric, the individual learns to argue and communicate in a rational and principled fashion; this activity trains the mind while it confers practical skills.

So common was this view of the function of rhetorical study in a college education that nineteenth-century commentaries on the nature of college education typically defined rhetorical training as a mandatory component of the bachelor of arts curriculum. F. A. P. Barnard, president of Columbia College during its rise to the status of a major university (1864–89), defines the importance of rhetorical training in his analysis of higher education in nineteenth-century America, "On Improvements Practicable in American Colleges": "Nothing can possess a higher practical value, to any man, than that which . . . gives him habits of clear, systematic, and independent thought, which . . . invigorates his powers of reasoning, teaches him to analyze, chastens and refines his taste . . . and confers upon him the priceless gift of lucid and forcible utterance" (181). Barnard shares Broadus's view that the development of rhetorical skills facilitates mental development by providing the student with the means to apply the powers of reason to the communication of ideas. Like Daniel Gilman, Barnard was a highly regarded spokesman for college education in the decades after midcentury, and his innovative restructuring of Columbia provided a model for others; thus, his regard for rhetorical instruction was not only typical but authoritative.[8]

The same legislative authority can be assigned to the views of Egerton Ryerson, the most influential nineteenth-century educator in Anglo-Canada and first president of Victoria College (Toronto). Ryerson confirms Barnard's high opinion of rhetorical instruction in his discussion of the function of rhetoric studies in the college curriculum:

Rhetoric may be considered as relating to *discourse; Belles Lettres,* to *writing.* Both are founded in nature; the principles of good taste are common to both; and both are eminently subservient to individual and public interests. . . . Not to be able to communicate our knowledge is but little better than to be without knowledge. To be useful to others, and to be in the fullest sense advantageous to ourselves, our knowledge must be communicated; how to communicate it to the best advantage, it is the province of *Rhetoric* to teach. . . . Cultivation is essential to the fruitfulness of both the intellectual and natural soil. . . . The noble prize and the enviable power of elegant and forcible writing are within the grasp of ordinary minds, and may, in general, be viewed as the certain reward of patient industry.[9] (18–19)

In this inaugural address at the opening of Victoria College (1842), Ryerson articulates an attitude toward rhetorical education held by Canadian and American educators throughout the century: the study of rhetoric cultivates the habits of mental discipline and furthers the general health of society by teaching the speaker and writer how to communicate knowledge to the "best advantage" of all concerned. Strikingly similar to the rationale advocated by nineteenth-century rhetoricians who defended the study of rhetoric as an intellectually elevating and culturally significant discipline, Ryerson's remarks indicate how closely entwined the aspirations of education and the rhetorical tradition were in this era. Educators and rhetoricians alike assumed that the systematic study of principles trains the mind to higher powers; the attainment of elevated mental abilities inclines the individual to rational thinking, service, and an appreciation of nature, truth, and art, which culminates in the development of taste and moral character. The marked ideological reciprocity between the professed goals of the nineteenth-century discipline of rhetoric and the mandate of higher education served to assure the conventional status of rhetoric as an academic subject and preserve the authority of rhetoricians' claims that the study and practice of rhetoric liberalized the mind.

From the nineteenth-century point of view, the advance of culture and the stability of society relied on the attainment of mental and moral development by each individual, a level of development that represents the fulfillment of individuality *and* an enlightened commitment to the common good. Nineteenth-century rhetoricians argued that the orator and writer advances to this level through the systematic study of natural principles and standards of taste. As a consequence, the rhetorician becomes an agent of edification, a delegate of culture. Rhetorical practice provides the individual with an expressive voice and society with the means to dispense justice, debate policy, and exalt the beauties of truth and nature. By justifying the study and practice of rhetoric in these terms, the nineteenth-century rhetorical tradition corroborated one of the most earnest beliefs of nineteenth-century North American society: that the productive exchange of ideas between rational minds furthers the progress of democratic society and protects the fortunes of all.

Nineteenth-century rhetoricians claimed for rhetoric the status of science, practical art, and civil servant. In laying this claim, they addressed and confirmed the dominant intellectual and cultural values of their era. The highly self-conscious idealism of this tradition remained essentially unchanged as the century closed, as did the theoretical disposition of nineteenth-century theory with its debt to New Rhetorical and classical precedents. By perceiving the study and practice of rhetoric as a means by which the mind and heart are trained to the service of the individual intellect and the social good, the nineteenth-century tradition supported a discipline that maintained a neoclassical regard for the social significance of rhetoric while relying on an extremely contemporary set of epistemological and aesthetic principles to explain the nature and effects of rhetorical practice. Throughout the century, rhetoricians persisted in urging educators and those who would be educated to believe that the mastery of eloquent speech and writing represented an inevitable challenge and opportunity that no one hoping to fulfill his natural gifts or take part in society could afford to decline. (Nineteenth-century rhetoricians unfailingly characterized the practitioner of rhetoric as male.) The nineteenth-century tradition was able to sustain a theoretical and pedagogical authority over institutional and public standards of higher literacy because it formulated a mandate for the discipline of rhetoric that inevitably evoked the ambitions and ideals of the dominant culture it was designed to serve. Consistently validating the interests of social progress, democracy, individuality, and cultural literacy (the knowledge of what is best in art and literature), the nineteenth-century tradition reinvented a role for the orator and the writer in the grand scheme of things. After the turn of the century, William Jennings Bryan offered a particularly American view of this grand scheme in an explanation of the function of oratory that recalls both the practical and idealistic commitments of the nineteenth-century tradition:

> The age of oratory has not passed; nor will it pass. The press, instead of displacing the orator, has given him a larger audience and enabled him to do more extended work. As long as there are human rights to be defended; as long as there are great interests to be guarded; as long as the welfare of nations is a matter for discussion, so long will public speaking have its place.

NOTES

1. For another defense of this same pedagogical method see Russell, "Articulation": "Rhetoric, to become a useful branch of modern education, should embrace a gradually progressive course of exercises, embodying successively the facts of language, in the use of words and the construction of sentences: it should include the practice of daily writing; frequent exercises in the logical arrangement of thought for the purposes of expression, and the adapting of the forms and character of expression to thought; and it should be accompanied by the close study and critical analysis of the works of distinguished writers with a view to acquire a perfect mastery over every form of style" (332).
2. Essay topics for composition exercises were often assigned. Topics assigned to the sophomore class of the College of New Jersey during the term 1873–74 (when John S. Hart was the instructor of rhetoric and composition) indicate that composition exercises typically ranged across the major genres: "The Influence of Prejudice"; "Iron"; "The Aristocracy of Wealth"; "Indulgence in Slang"; "Topic Selected by the Writer"; "My Favorite English Author"; "My Favorite American Author"; and "The Approaching Centennial." John S. Hart, *Essays of the Sophomore Class for 1873–74*, Department of English, College of New Jersey (University of Virginia Archives).

3. For expressions of this philosophy of education by renowned nineteenth-century figures, see Ralph Waldo Emerson, "Modern Education," and the views of Henry Barnard, founder of the *American Journal of Education,* first U.S. Commissioner of Education, and organizer of the U.S. Bureau of Education. Barnard expresses this creed: "The education of a people bears a constant and most pre-eminently influential relation to its attainments and excellences— physical, mental, and moral. . . . [T]he history of education affords the only ready and perfect key to the history of the human race, and of each nation in it—an unfailing standard for estimating its advance or retreat upon the line of human progress" (qtd. by Downs 123).

4. Mann was one of the foremost educators in the first half of the century and one of the chief architects of the modern system of education in the United States. He created the Massachusetts Board of Education and was first secretary for several years. His annual reports to the board are now regarded as landmark documents in the history of education. Mann believed that public education for all was essential to a healthy democracy. Applebee confirms that Mann approved of rhetoric because it "offered a 'scientific' rigor and discipline" (39).

5. Gilman was president of the University of California, 1872–75, before accepting the position at Johns Hopkins. Gilman was one of the leading figures during the expansionist period between 1870 and 1890, during which offerings at universities became far more diversified. For other works by Gilman on higher education see his *University Problems in the United States.*

6. Other educators who promoted this view included Charles W. Eliot, president of Harvard from 1869 to 1909, and John Bascom, president of the University of Wisconsin from 1874 to 1887 and author of the highly regarded *Philosophy of Rhetoric* (1888). Like Gilman, Eliot was one of the leading philosophers of higher education in the latter decades of the century. Although a less well known figure, Bascom wrote extensively on the aims of higher education. Bascom perceived the college to be a place at which the individual could develop mental abilities that contribute to the social good. See James, *Charles W. Eliot,* and "The Mind of John Bascom," in Curti and Carstensen, *The University of Wisconsin.*

7. The mental abilities that Broadus defines here were associated with the study of rhetoric, belles lettres, and literature. For an analysis of nineteenth-century educators' views of the general relevance of instruction in English and literature to the development of mental discipline, see Graff. For an analysis of the influence of the mental discipline philosophy on Canadian higher education in particular, see Johnson, "Rhetoric and Belles Lettres."

8. Frederick Augustus Porter Barnard was president of the University of Mississippi between 1850 and 1858 and chancellor from 1858 to 1861. He assumed the presidency of Columbia College in 1864 and was the guiding force in the development of Columbia into a major university and research institution. Barnard College for women is named after him. Like Eliot of Harvard and Bascom of Wisconsin, Barnard was a champion of women's education.

9. Like his contemporary Horace Mann in the United States, Egerton Ryerson promoted the common school movement in Canada; he also pressed for the development of institutions of higher learning in Canada. Committed to the notion that education develops the mind and the Christian virtues, Ryerson defined higher education as that level of education which cultivates the mind to the highest extent: "Man is made for physical, mental, and moral action; and the grand object of education is to develop, improve, and perfect, as far as possible, his physical, mental and moral faculties. . . . education signifies the cultivation of the mind by means of Schools and Colleges" (9). For background on Ryerson see McDonald and Chaiton; for an analysis of Ryerson's contribution to the development of English studies and the discipline of rhetoric in Canada, see Hubert.

Sharon Crowley

"The Methodical Memory on Display: The Five-Paragraph Theme"

A popular conceit among eighteenth-century rhetorical theorists characterized the relation between thought and its expression as analogous to that between soul and body. George Campbell employed the analogy in the *Philosophy of Rhetoric* as follows:

> In contemplating a human creature, the most natural division of the subject is the common division into soul and body, or into the living principle of perception and of action, and that system of material organs by which the other receives information from without, and is enabled to exert its powers. . . . Analogous to this, there are two things in every discourse which principally claim our attention, the sense and the expression; or in other words, the thought and the symbol by which it is communicated. These may be said to constitute the soul and the body of an oration, or indeed of whatever is signified to another by language. For, as in man, each of these constituent parts hath its distinctive attributes, and as the perfection of the latter consisteth in its fitness for serving the purposes of the former, it is precisely with those two essential parts of every speech, the sense and the expression. (32)

Campbell's metaphoric distinction between an inner core and an outer envelope endured within current-traditional thought. To supply only one example of its many appearances, I quote Day in the *Art of Discourse:* "No process of art is complete until its product appears in a sensible form; and language is the form in which the art of discourse embodies itself, as sound furnishes the body in the art of music and color in that of painting" (208). In the modern rhetorical systems I am examining here, language was treated as a pliant medium that exactly represented thought. Thought, the "soul," "interior," or "core" of discourse, always preceded, and was superior to, language, which was a secondary, fallen, exterior embodiment of what was really important.

Because language had only one function—to mirror thought—the function of arrangement came to be very like that of style in current-traditional rhetoric.

Both served to externalize the internalized process of invention. Where arrangement made graphic the larger movements of mind, such as analysis or synthesis, style made graphic its connections between simple ideas. Indeed, early current-traditional rhetoricians acknowledged this likeness between the two canons by submerging their treatment of arrangement within that given to style. For example, Alexander Jamieson included arrangement in his general remarks on style in his *Grammar of Rhetoric and Polite Literature* (originally published 1818).[1] Samuel Newman also placed his very brief treatment of arrangement in the *Practical System of Rhetoric* under the heading of style.

Thus many current-traditional authors maintained that rhetoric, and hence composition, had only two canons: invention and style. Arrangement, suspended as it was between the binaries of thought and expression never quite found a comfortable home in their textbooks. Occasionally it was submerged within invention, as when various sorts of aims were associated with their respective orders of development within genres. Of course this was made possible by the two-faced nature of method, which could both direct the progress of thought and exactly represent that progress in discourse.

Despite all of this, current-traditional authors were very concerned with arrangement, even though they no longer gave that name to the disposition within a discourse of its larger parts or divisions. Two developments characterized mature current-traditional treatments of the arrangement of discourse on a page: the hardening and reduction of methodical principles into the trinity of unity, coherence, and emphasis and the emergence of what I call the "nesting approach" to composing.

EARLY COMMENTARY ON ARRANGEMENT

In *On Invention*, Cicero discriminated six parts that could appear in any rhetorical discourse: the introduction, which readied audiences to receive the argument; the narration, which gave the history of the case; the partition, which announced the issues that would be addressed and the order in which the rhetor would address them; the confirmation and refutation, which presented the rhetor's arguments for the case and against those offered by opponents; and the peroration or conclusion, which excited enthusiasm for the rhetor's argument or set the audience against the case advanced by opponents (2.20–190).

The arrangement of any discourse was determined by the rhetor's assessment of the rhetorical situation for which she was preparing. For example, the composition of an introduction was determined by her guess about the attitude of the targeted audience toward her ethos and the case at hand. Were they hostile? Did she need to be conciliatory? Or were they receptive, so that she could begin more directly? If the audience were familiar with the case, the rhetor could dispense with the narration of its history; if the audience were uninformed and there was no skilled opponent, a refutation was unnecessary. In other words, the composition and arrangement of the parts of the discourse were determined by the rhetor's informed guess about how listeners or readers would react.

Current-traditional discourse theory, on the other hand, painted listeners and readers as curiously docile. They were never hostile or inattentive—they were just interested. Writers needed only to arrange their discourse, then, in a fashion that would ease the reading process—that would, in fact, reflect the way any reasonable person might have written it, according to the natural dictates of the rational mind.

Alexander Jamieson was among the few current-traditional rhetoricians who drew on Cicero's six-part division of the oration for his principles of arrangement. However, he updated the classical treatment by adding some methodical refinements to his discussion of the partition—just as Hugh Blair had. While Cicero had only recommended that the partition be stated briefly, clearly, and concisely, Jamieson noted that the division of the subject ought to follow "the order of nature"; otherwise it should be "concealed." He recommended natural method (analysis) for general use since it moved from the simple to the complex and was appropriate for any discourse, such as a sermon, where "division is proper to be used." In this case, the parts of the division must be "really distinct from one another." They should begin "with the simplest points, such as are easiest apprehended." Taken together, the "several members of a division ought to exhaust the subject." Their terms ought to be absolutely clear, and "unnecessary multiplication of heads" was to be avoided (249). Observance of these careful methodical procedures, Jamieson thought, would insure that any similarly rational reader could follow the writer's train of thought.

This is the last we hear of Ciceronian arrangement in mainstream current-traditional textbooks, however. Newman's treatment of arrangement, which occupied perhaps a single page of his textbook, was suffused with methodical principles much like those advanced by George Campbell. Newman suggested that the arguments in a discourse ought to be arranged synthetically, since this method was more natural given that "men usually assert their opinions, and then assign the reasons on which they are founded." However, "if what is asserted is likely, either from its being novel, or uncommon, or from its being opposed to the prejudices of the reader, to disaffect him, and to prevent his due consideration of the arguments brought forward, it is better to . . . defer the formal statement of the proposition maintained to the close" (37). This is analysis, couched in the "concealed" or "hidden" method of presentation recommended by Blair and Watts.

As Campbell and Priestley had done, Newman made some comments on transitions. As generic lines altered, conventional classical means of marking the major sections of discourse were not so ubiquitous nor so familiar to educated readers as they once had been. Newman noted that transitions were not so important in argumentative discourse, "where the different parts are connected by a common reference to some particular point" (38). Since argumentative discourse was the genre to which classical lore about arrangement was most often applied, its conventions regarding the disposition of its parts were well known, and thus argument needed fewer explicit transitions.

Transitions were crucial, however, in those sorts of discourse that followed the newer analytic approach. Newman wrote that transitions were to be "natural and easy, that is, in agreement with the common modes of associating the thoughts" (38). They were most skillfully employed when they represented resemblance, cause and effect, or contiguity as to time or place. Newman's interest in transitions as a means of representing mental patterns of association marked his work as indebted to the new rhetoric, insofar as the accurate linguistic representation of mental connections had become crucial to readers' ability to follow an argument. Later current-traditional rhetoricians identified the methodical principle of coherence with the ability to make appropriate transitions between the parts of discourse.

THE GANG OF THREE: UNITY, COHERENCE, AND FRIEND

Method came into its own in mature current-traditional rhetoric as a means of amplification. Textbook authors set forth dispositional formulas that prescribed which formal features ought to characterize every finished piece of discourse. Some of these formulas were derived from method.

As I noted earlier, advocates of method employed it during the discovery process in the hope of reducing the intrusion of unpredictable factors that might extend the investigation forever. The concept of unity (also called clarity) allowed investigators to impose arbitrary limits on the area roped off for investigation. A second concept, called variously distinction, division, or progression, insured that the investigation touched systematically on every point that could be deemed relevant to the notion under study. That unity and progression were part of the history of logic was never acknowledged by the current-traditional rhetoricians who adopted it as an inflexible principle of amplification. They took great pains to establish unity as a natural and necessary principle of discourse at every level from the sentence on up to whole compositions.

The importation of method into current-traditional rhetoric as a means of amplification owed a good deal to two influential midcentury rhetoricians, Henry Noble Day and Alexander Bain. Throughout his explication of the means of amplification in the *Elements of Rhetoric,* Day insisted on the absolute observance of two requirements: unity and completeness. In explanatory discourse, the principle of unity required "that the conception which forms the theme, be one. This one conception, however, may be simple or complex; may embrace but one individual or a class" (53). This passage indicates that, for Day, unity meant representation in discourse of a single idea as this term was used in association psychology—that is, of an idea that had resulted from a simple perception or a combination of perceptions.

But Day had a fetish about unity, which was apparently a self-evident principle of discourse for him. In his discussion of invention in general, he argued that "unless the object of speaking be distinctly perceived and that object be strictly one, the inventive faculty has no foothold at all, or, at least, no sure standing and all of its operations must be unsteady and feeble" (44). Unity was to be secured in discourse, then, not only by selecting a single subject for development, but by choosing but "one leading object to be effected" (43). Elsewhere, Day argued that since discourse was a rational procedure, any "discourse can hardly with propriety be called one which has more than one general theme. The unity of a discourse in which, indeed, lies its very life, requires that there be but one thought to which every other shall be subordinate and subservient, utterly forbids the introduction of two or more co-ordinate thoughts" (38). To take Day's remarks quite literally, every discourse is to represent one whole thought and the relation of its parts, since this thought in its turn represents a combination of the rhetor's aim with her mental representation of some object perceived in nature. Observance of the principle of unity apparently insured that all discourses that observed it would be eminently readable, since they announced themselves as representations of single thought units.

By the time Day wrote the *Art of Discourse,* the laws of unity and completeness had been joined by two others—selection and method. Unity, selection, completeness, and method were to govern amplification in every genre, although he gave them their fullest explication in connection with explanatory discourse.

In his later work Day took even fewer pains to justify the necessity of unity than he had previously. He noted that unity was "founded in the nature of all discourse as a rational procedure" (60). He then referred his readers to two other sections of his text, in each of which he made a circular argument for the necessity of unity. Since unity required that a discourse have only one subject, it was important that writers center their discourse around a single thought, so that their work would have unity (44, 51).

The law of selection reinforced unity in that selection was "grounded in the necessity of excluding some of the infinite variety of subordinate thoughts or views through which the general theme may be developed" (Day, *Art of Discourse* 60). The law of completeness was also mandated by the rational nature of discourse and provided for a "full exhibition of the theme for the object proposed" (62). The laws of unity, selection, and completeness, taken together, repeat Descartes' injunction that any investigation be characterized by clarity and distinction. The laws mandated that writers concentrate on a single whole, that they divide it into its constituent parts, and that all of the resulting parts be enumerated.

When unity, selection, and completeness were used as means of amplification, they repeated methodical advice for analyzing the proposition, now applied on the scale of the whole discourse; that is, the organization of the entire discourse would now repeat the analytic moves that were appropriate to establishing the proposition and its parts, and thus the structure of whole essays would now reflect the structure of their propositions on a larger scale. Here Day employed the micro-macrocosmic vision that was characteristic of method: smaller parts repeat and fit neatly into larger parts.

What was left, then, was to provide some advice about progression, which Day did in his discussion of the law of method. The law of method had to govern invention since to proceed methodically was to exert the activity of the mind "freely, fully, and successfully," that is, "as it proceeds in accordance with the laws of its own nature." He was further confident that the laws of the mind were consonant with those of nature, "so that the mind . . . must be proceeding at the same time in accordance with the principles of truth." Nonetheless method, however natural, had to be studied and applied in discourse so that it could form and strengthen "those habits of methodical thinking" that were the indispensable condition of all rational progress. "A mind trained to habitual activity in method has reached its true maturity of training. Without this, it is essentially deficient in its culture" (*Art of Discourse* 61). The constant study and practice of discourse could be justified on the ground that it immersed its students in the exercise of method; method in turn exercised the mind along its natural lines and thus strengthened it.

To some extent the four laws of method supplanted the classical list of means of amplification that Day had formerly favored. The resulting discussion looks a lot more like Watts' list of rules for method as presentation than anything derived from classical rhetoric. Day could have found an early connection between method and the amplification of scientific discourse in Priestley's *Lectures on Oratory and Criticism*. It seems more likely, however, that the connection suggested itself simply because explanatory discourse took science as its subject, and thus method, as the discovery process that took nature as its model, was appropriate to it.

However, Day was not alone in utilizing methodical means of amplification. Alexander Bain also derived his famous principles for the formulation of acceptable paragraphs from method.[2] His innovative departure from tradition in this regard did not lay in the principles themselves but rather in his interest in paragraphs, which had received virtually no modern attention prior to the publication of the first edition of *English Composition and Rhetoric*.

Bain justified his attention to paragraphs by means of "an old homely maxim," borrowed from the methodical tradition, which posited that smaller units of discourse should always bear a microcosmic relation to larger units. As he put it: "Look to the paragraphs and the discourse will look to itself, for, although a discourse as a whole has a method or plan suited to its nature, yet the confining of each paragraph to a distinct topic avoids some of the worst faults of composition; besides which, he that fully comprehends the method of a paragraph, will also comprehend the method of an entire work" (151). Like Day, Bain authorized the micro-macrocosmic view of discourse that characterized late current-traditional thought.

Bain defined "the Paragraph" as "a collection of sentences with unity of purpose" (142). His requirements for their formation can be summarized as follows: paragraphs must have (1) coherence, which demanded explicit reference and use of conjunctions; (2) parallel construction, which mandated that sentences that express ideas roughly equal in weight be presented as grammatically equivalent to one another; (3) a clear statement of the topic in the opening sentence; (4) an absence of dislocation, which required that sentences succeed one another in some logical sequence, the preferred descent being from the general to the particular; (5) unity, so that the writer could make her purpose immediately apparent to readers and avoid digression; (6) due proportion between principal and subordinate statements (142–52).

Bain's concern for the major requirements of method—unity and progression—is apparent in these principles. Every paragraph was to represent one whole thought and the relation of its parts, since this representation in its turn represented some object in nature. Observance of the principles insured that all paragraphs would be eminently readable, since they announced themselves as representations of a single thought, idea, or notion.

Unity was secured by observance of the fifth and third principles. Each paragraph would be opened by a sentence that stated its contents in general form. This sentence came to be called the topic sentence, and it owes its genesis to synthetic method. Given the ubiquitous assumption in methodical theory that larger units of discourse reflect the structure and movement of smaller ones, Bain may have derived his principle of the topic sentence by analogy with the proposition that was to govern the direction of the entire discourse—just as Day had done. The presence of the topic sentence gave further assurance that unity would be observed in the paragraph that followed.

Progression required that all parts of the discourse be explicitly related to one another. Bain refined this principle to insist that sentences within a paragraph be ordered by means of some discernible sequence, preferably from the general to the specific. Bain's second and fourth principles—parallel construction and logical sequence—are reminiscent of synthetic method, where they were standard means of division. His preference for a descending order of generality could have been dictated by methodical tradition, which usually recommended synthetic method as a means of arranging material that had already been discovered. Or he could have chosen synthesis out of concern for his audience; synthetic method was always the recommended movement for discourse aimed at learners, and *English Composition and Rhetoric* itself employs a synthetic movement. Of course, Bain's avowed allegiance to science—which he defined as the production of useful generalizations—could also have dictated the precedence of generality.

Observance of the first principle secured surface coherence in any paragraph. This would be represented by the selection of appropriate transitions, which announced the logical relation of each sentence to those that preceded and followed it. Principle six, which required that writers show a due awareness of the relationships that obtain between levels of generality, was a traditional methodical means of insuring distinctiveness. This last principle was refined by Bain's imitators into a rule requiring that all discourse demonstrate something called mass or proportion or emphasis.

My hunch that Bain derived these principles out of method is lent support not only by the interesting analogies that obtain between his rules and older lists of laws governing presentational method such as Watts', but by some affinities with other contemporary applications of the law of method, such as Day's. For example, the methodical interest in a clear statement of the "leading inquiry" or proposition is apparent in his second principle. What is new is Bain's systematization of a long conceptual tradition governing patterns of inquiry into inflexible rules for paragraph development. In a sense, his principles of the paragraph complete the process I have been tracing, a process that shifts the ultimate responsibility for the ordering of discourse away from the steps gone through during inquiry and onto the way that discourse is supposed to look on the page.

Bain's principles were widely adopted by later current-traditional textbook writers, perhaps because his was the first popular composition textbook to pay extended attention to paragraphs as separate units of composition. Certainly current-traditional textbook authors have more often treated his principles as rules to be employed in the amplification of paragraphs than in essays, which were usually to be amplified by the expository means of development. At the very least, Bain's application of methodical principles to the development of paragraphs exacerbated the emerging tendency of nineteenth-century composition theory to concentrate on the shape of discourse, rather than on its contents or on the persons who compose and read it.[3] His rules for paragraph formation must also have accelerated the tendency of school rhetoric to assume that universal rules could be generated for the composition of almost any discourse, regardless of its occasion.

Scott and Denney adapted a conflation of Day's and Bain's methodical principles in order to forge their "laws of the paragraph" for *Paragraph-Writing*. The law of unity required "that the sentences composing the paragraph be intimately connected with one another in thought and purpose. . . . [U]nity forbids digressions and irrelevant matter" (4). The law of selection mandated that "of all which might be said on the subject treated, only those points be chosen for mention in the sentences which will best subserve the purpose of the paragraph," while the law of proportion dictated the scope, length, and placement of important points within the paragraph (6). The law of sequence, that is, of method, required "that the sentences be presented in the order which will best bring out the thought" (13).

Scott and Denney did add a new law to the list: variety. This law required "that as much diversity as is consistent with the purpose of the paragraph is introduced." Lest the law of variety be thought to contradict the law of unity, Scott and Denney hastened to add that variety was a matter of length, structure, and order, rather than of thought (*Paragraph-Writing* 15). Here again, the rigid current-traditional distinction between thought and language surfaced. "Artistic" flourishes, such as variety, were always associated with language, and as such, were always subservient to the rules mandating clarity and distinctiveness of thought.

As they had done in the case of the expository means of development, later current-traditional textbook authors recommended a variety of methods for paragraph development. There could be as many as four of these—as in Day—or five or six—as in Scott and Denney or Bain. But mature current-traditional theory more consistently condensed the principles governing the development of paragraphs into three.[4] Genung reduced the paragraph principles to unity, continuity, and proportion, and his influential example may have established the tripartite tradition, although Barrett Wendell may have been complicit in this as well. In his discussion of the whole composition, Wendell extended the principles of unity, coherence, and mass (proportion) to the composition of all discourse at all levels, since the trains of thought they represented were typical of all minds (153–54).

Wendell marshaled the principles as first lines of defense against the confused and disordered state in which ideas presented themselves to writers.

In the methodical tradition, of course, unity was treated as a self-evident principle of discourse, and as I have tried to demonstrate, it was crucial to such thinking. The ubiquity of unity as a primary principle of discourse was no doubt reinforced by teachers' fear that students would bite off more than they could chew in a short discourse; Whately's dictum that no discourse should "enter on too wide a field of discussion" is the primary example (37). But in current-traditional rhetoric, unity came to be conceived as an end in itself to which the flow of all parts of the discourse, even sentences, was to be subordinated.

Continuity or coherence was also necessary to method, since discursive coherence represented the connections made between mental ideas; that is, the connective logic of the mind could be repeated in discourse by selection of the appropriate transitions. This was especially true when the method chosen was analysis, where the connecting links between the parts of the discourse depended upon the associative movement of the writer's mind, rather than on some predetermined or conventional form. Writers employing this method would have to take special care to cue their readers into the movement and relation of their ideas by means of explicit linguistic transitions.

Emphasis, or proportion, may also have derived from method. As formulated originally by Bain, emphasis meant placing generalities in a dominant position so that their relation of primacy over the particulars that supported them was absolutely clear. Barrett Wendell generalized this rule somewhat; he defined emphasis (he called it mass) as the discursive feature governing the relative placement of ideas on the page, no matter what their level of generality. He lamented that sometimes the achievement of coherence interfered with the principle of mass, but he solved this difficulty by announcing that coherence was more important at the beginnings of paragraphs than at their conclusions, where mass assumed predominance (180).

During the twentieth century, unity, coherence, and emphasis increasingly controlled the process of amplification in general. They were to be applied in the composition of all discourse at all levels, no matter what its kind. In some textbooks unity and coherence even got chapters all to themselves. Their observance was often recommended in negative terms. Writers could violate the principle of unity by failing to cover everything associated with the main idea of a paragraph or composition, or they could commit the sin of digression. There were also two ways to violate the principle of coherence. Sentences could follow one another in some illogical order, or the writer could fail to include transitions that signaled the appropriate relations between sentences. The recommended "logical" orders were usually the means of expository amplification, although in some writers these were limited to three orders, all drawn from method: chronology, spatial arrangement, and analysis. Transitions were to announce and track such movements—the inclusion of words and phrases such as *moreover, besides, on the contrary,* or *in conclusion* would constantly cue readers into the method underlying the paragraph or discourse.

In very-current-traditional textbooks, the principles have returned to their original province—the paragraph. They are now generally identified as unity, coherence, and completeness. Very-current-traditional textbooks emphasize that paragraphs are not just any old random assemblage of sentences: "A block of words on a page is not a paragraph merely because it looks like one; it must also *function* like one" (Winkler and McCuen 94). Paragraphs are predictive—for writers as well as readers. Their topic sentences (usually placed at the beginning of the paragraph) announce to readers what will happen in the following sentences, thereby securing unity for the paragraph. Certain transitional words announce the relation of every sentence to those that precede and follow it, and hence coherence is assured. The textbooks sometimes offer question-begging advice about completeness. Writers know that their paragraphs are complete when enough sentences have been supplied to support the topic sentence. Others supplement this advice by calling on the limits of readers' ability to endure hardship. For example, Packer and Timpane say that readers will call it quits when "they find it difficult to retain the overall shape of the argument, or their eyes and mind begin to tire" (170). They do give writers a rule of thumb for estimating completeness, however; paragraphs shouldn't require more than ten sentences, nor should they spread over a whole page.

DISCOURSE AS NESTING BEHAVIOR

The current-traditional preoccupation with the paragraph as an independent unit of discourse is a very curious phenomenon. Scholars have attempted to account for it by connecting it to the rise of literacy (after all, spoken discourse does not break itself into paragraphs). A historical rationale can also be found in the enormous influence exerted on current-traditional rhetoric by Bain's *English Composition and Rhetoric*, which spawned Scott and Denney's equally influential *Paragraph-Writing*.

But many current-traditional authors adopted a pedagogical rationale to justify their preference for paragraphs: since paragraphs were shorter than essays, they could be composed with more ease, especially by younger students. Scott and Denney rationalized the entire project of *Paragraph-Writing* in just this way: the paragraph exemplified the principles of discourse in "small and convenient compass so that they are easily appreciable by the beginner" (iv). A student could also "write more paragraphs than he can write essays in the same length of time; hence the character of the work may be made for him more varied, progressive, and interesting" (v). Nor did Scott and Denney overlook the advantage of paragraph exercises to teachers, who would have shorter compositions to evaluate than if they assigned whole essays.

I think that current-traditional focus on the paragraph had a great deal to do with the tradition's reliance on method. Scott and Denney would not so casually have substituted paragraph writing for essay practice were they not confident that the same principles were at work in both. Paragraphs were a little handier than whole essays as ways of reflecting the movement of minds. The topic sentence with its accompanying details, whose internal relations were rigidly controlled by the principles of coherence and emphasis, constituted a tidy graphic display of unity and progression. Nor can there be any doubt that current-traditional rhetoricians regarded paragraphs as representations of complete thoughts, just as sentences were. For example, in *Writing and Thinking* (originally published 1931) Norman Foerster and J. M. Steadman charged that "scrappy" paragraphs resulted from "a mere fragment of the full-formed idea that lies in the mind but that we are too lazy to call forth" (68).

Paragraphs came into their own because of the methodical habit of viewing the universe of discourse as a collection of increasingly larger repetitions of its smallest elements. After about 1880, textbook authors began to organize their texts according to what might be called the constituent units of discourse: words, sentences, paragraphs, whole compositions. The constituent units of discourse often named chapters or sections of traditional textbooks, as they did, for example, in Adams Sherman Hill's *Principles of Rhetoric*.

In its maturity, current-traditional rhetoric tended to see a composition as a nest of Chinese boxes, in which the smaller parts of discourse—words and sentences—were contained inside, and reflected by, the structure of increasingly larger parts—the paragraph and the essay. In treatises on method, this microcosmic to macrocosmic view of discourse was often illustrated by analogy with the study of grammar, which began with letters, syllables, and words since these were the smallest discernible units and supposedly the least difficult to understand. Once they had mastered these, students were allowed to move on to the study of sentences.

Adams Sherman Hill provided an influential example in the direction of treating larger levels of discourse as reflections of smaller ones. In the most effective arrangement of words, he wrote, "the position of every verbal sign would exactly correspond to that of the thing signified; the order of language would be the order of the thought, and would distinctly indicate the relative importance of every constituent part of the composition" (*Principles of Rhetoric* 129).

Although Hill cited Lord Kames as his authority here, associationism and method seem to be the sources of this line of thought. To recap briefly: the mental entities called ideas were connected in the mind by means of mental operations called associations. Hill apparently thought that ideas and operations ought to be representable in the syntax of the sentence, where the grammatical subject represented an idea and the predicate represented whatever operation was applied to the subject. Thus sentences could represent complete thoughts, just as they did in logical propositions. And, just as "every sentence should contain but one principal assertion; every paragraph should discuss the subject in hand from but one point of view; every essay or discourse should treat of but one subject, and of but one proposition relating to that subject at a time" (159). This is an argument for observance of the principle of unity at all levels of discourse. Hill was equally insistent on the observance of coherence at all levels beyond the sentence: "If a sentence can be put in one place as well as in another, there is a defect somewhere" (157).

Wendell found the principles of unity, coherence, and mass in sentences, paragraphs, and whole compositions. He was able to do this because he firmly separated words from ideas and awarded priority to ideas. In *English Composition* he wrote that once we know "what ideas we wish to group together, the task of finding words for them is immensely simplified" (29–30). Apparently ideas took form in the mind already equipped with unity, which always characterized the immaterial ideas for which material words stood. Coherence was the province of both ideas and words; that is, the associative operations of the mind lent coherence to ideas, while discursive transitions lent coherence to discourse. Mass, however, applied only to words, and, as I already noted, sometimes the achievement of mass got in the way of coherence (34, 180).

Here again a current-traditional writer had difficulty in getting language to lie down and behave itself. Despite his assured tone, Wendell had no little difficulty when he applied his three principles to composition of the sentence, where they were "constantly hampered by good use." He wrote this peculiarity off as a result of the vagaries of English grammar (120). Good use never stood in Wendell's way when he set about the business of applying his three principles to the production of discourse at all levels.

Later current-traditional authors imported the principles into their discussions of syntax in an attempt to demonstrate that individual sentences could display unity, coherence, and emphasis. The principles also appeared in some twentieth-century textbooks as principles of composition for essays and paragraphs. In sum, later current-traditional textbooks created a grammar of discourse, where whole discourses were reflective sums of their parts. Just as sentences combined subjects with predicates, paragraphs named their subjects in an opening sentence, to which its body bore one or another of a series of predicated relationships. Whole compositions, in their turn, displayed thesis statements that were analogous to topic sentences; the ordering of the paragraphs and their relation to the whole composition and to each other mirrored the ordering of sentences within a paragraph and their relation to each other. Wendell provided his readers with a fine statement of the nesting theory of arrangement when he wrote that "a paragraph whose unity can be demonstrated by summarizing its substance in a sentence whose subject shall be a summary of its opening sentence, and whose predicate shall be a summary of its closing sentence, is theoretically well massed" (129). Here is method with a vengeance; Peter Ramus would feel right at home.

Because they adopted a word-sentence-paragraph approach to composition, textbooks often postponed work with essays, preferring to begin with grammar and syntax and moving through the composition of paragraphs to whole essays. The difficult character assigned to essays assumed, of course, that the bigger parts of discourse were harder to write—an assumption that seems to contradict the assertion that all parts of a discourse display the same principles.

The tendency of current-traditional composition theory to structuralize concepts that were formerly means of invention and to disperse them graphically within a theme as components of its arrangement saw its most striking manifestation in the paradigm discourse espoused by many twentieth-century current-traditional textbooks—the five-paragraph theme. This ideal discourse was a standard to be imitated whenever students wrote. The standard was formal rather than conceptual; that is, a set of static relations dictated the placement on the page of certain structural features of the text. The five-paragraph theme had a paragraph of introduction, three of development, and one of conclusion. Each of the developmental paragraphs was initiated by a topic sentence summarizing the body of the paragraph.

If there was a conceptual movement within this paradigm, it was from general to particular. By virtue of this synthetic movement, the parts of the discourse fit neatly into one another. Just as essays contained thesis and body paragraphs that specified the thesis, paragraphs contained topic and body sentences that specified the topic of each paragraph. The model five-paragraph theme could be laid out on the page with the aid of colored lines, boxes, and arrows. Discourse had shape. Shape was clarified by analogy to funnels, pyramids, or keyholes. (I borrow these metaphors from Sheridan Baker's *The Practical Stylist* [1962]).

Of course the five-paragraph theme is a graphic representation of the introspective model of invention I traced in earlier chapters. This paradigm appeared as a methodical process for arranging didactic discourse in Adam Smith's lectures in the 1760s. It was still appearing in current-traditional textbooks written two hundred years later. But by the middle years of the twentieth century, the synthetic process was more often treated as a graphic structure than a means of invention.

The five-paragraph theme was the most thoroughgoing scheme for spatializing discourse that had appeared in rhetorical theory since Peter Ramus' method of dichotomizing division rendered all the world divisible by halves. Indeed, it is no doubt indebted to method, as this entered traditional composition theory via Bain's paragraph principles and Day's laws of amplification, and was translated to twentieth-century textbook authors in the guise of Wendell's three principles of discourse. The five-paragraph theme was prescribed to students in the absence of a historical context; it was simply touted as the way things are done. The intellectual contexts originally recommended for the use of synthesis had disappeared from the tradition entirely, as had the psychological arguments that made it analogous to the movement of the human mind in acts of communication.

WRITING INSTRUCTION AS SOCIALIZATION

In 1936, I. A. Richards was invited to Bryn Mawr to lecture on rhetoric. In those lectures, subsequently published as *The Philosophy of Rhetoric* (1936), he fired several well-aimed salvos at textbook exemplars of both the new rhetoric and current-traditional rhetoric. Accusing them of "poking the fire from the top," he dismissed much of the advice they gave as irrelevant to rhetorical practice. Most telling of all, he launched a direct attack on the current-traditional notion that language could be separated from thought: "An idea or a notion, when unencumbered and undisguised, is no easier to get hold of than one of those oiled and naked thieves who infest the railway carriages of India. Indeed an idea, or a notion, like the physicist's ultimate particles and rays, is only known by what it does. Apart from its dress or other signs it is not identifiable" (5). Richards' critique seems to have had little impact on the current-traditional juggernaut. He may have put his finger on one reason for its longevity when he characterized its strictures about discursive deportment as "the Club Spirit." As he noted, the club spirit enlisted language as a servant of manners, specifically those of "a special set of speakers. . . . Deviations from their customs is incorrectness and is visited with a social penalty as such" (78).

Current-traditional concern with mannerly discourse can be explained in part by the institutional circumstances in which college composition has always been taught. At least one introductory composition course has been required of students entering American colleges ever since the late nineteenth century.[5] At the turn of the twentieth century, the huge numbers of students who were required to take one or two introductory writing courses simply swamped the resources of most college and university English departments, which were just then emerging as representatives of an independent academic discipline. The immediate solution to the numbers difficulty was to develop a composition course that could be taught to many students at once, through lectures and readings. And if the theory of composition used were highly formalized, the work of grading papers could be simplified, since harried teachers could ignore the content of their students' themes and would only need to assess the degree of their conformity to the formal features prescribed by the lectures and the textbook. Students needed only to demonstrate that their writing conformed to standards that had been devised as measures of their work before they ever set foot inside the academy.

But herein lies an irony. Of all the subjects commonly taught in university curricula, composition is no doubt the skill least amenable to standardized instruction. Writing is best taught and learned through individual effort and attention. As Wallace Stegner pointed out in 1950, "anyone writing honestly creates and solves new problems every time he sits down at his desk. Nobody can solve them for him in advance, and no teacher had better try" (431).[6] And yet current-traditional pedagogy rests on this very assumption—that students' inventional processes can be forecasted, their difficulties anticipated, and their inadequacies named, in advance.

I am prepared to grant that the authors of current-traditional textbooks imported standardized techniques into writing instruction in order to render its demands on teachers less onerous. No doubt the textbooks composed by Wendell and the others were attractive because they provided a list of universal prescriptions that made evaluation of students' papers a routine matter. Wendell's text supplied teachers and students of composition with a small set of discursive principles that could be applied at any level of discourse with the same degree of analytical rigor. His system articulated three unequivocal rules that would determine how any completed discourse should look. Teachers had only to measure each student's discourse against the standardized ideal discourse in order to gauge a given paper's relative success or failure.

However, late nineteenth-century attempts to standardize composition instruction may have sprung from motives other than that of relieving composition teachers from some of the burden of paper grading. Evelyn Wright argues that socialization was a hidden agenda in most language arts instruction during the late nineteenth century. According to Wright, elementary schoolteachers were held "responsible for saving children from grammatical-rhetorical sins by which their personal character was judged"; that is, students' failure to meet universally imposed standards of good form was interpreted as a sign of inadequate moral development rather than an indication that the standards might have been insufficiently considered" (332).[7] And as Wright remarks in connection with a series of popular elementary textbooks, "When rules of courtesy or school deportment are smuggled into English lessons as if they are an intellectual discipline or a law of language or of thought, then the lesson obscures the social issues and apotheosizes middle-class manners by associating them with the sentence definition" (333). In other words, language arts instruction was efficiently (because silently) geared to include those whose manners and class it reflected. Those whose manners were not middle-class either adapted or were excluded.

Wright's analysis holds for college-level textbooks as well. The textbook series she excoriates in the passage above was written by Gardiner, Kittredge, and Arnold, whose college-level text, *A Manual of English Composition* (1907) was singled out for attack by Richards. In his review of the history of nineteenth-century rhetoric, Donald C. Stewart asserts that "late nineteenth-century composition theory and practice was less a response to the social and educational needs of the time and more a reflection of a select class's wrong-headed attitudes about the importance of usage and superficial editorial accuracy" ("Introduction" 230). That current-traditional textwriters saw their work in terms of the socialization of their charges was usually not acknowledged explicitly in their textbooks, but it came through loud and clear nonetheless. As Stewart noted, it showed up in their discussions of correct usage, which was consistently presented as the mark of an "educated person." It was also implicit in their pervasive assumption that unremitting practice in a prescribed discursive format would not only encourage the practice of straight thinking but would virtually insure it.

The formal standards the textbooks imposed on student writers reflected ethical and social values fully as much as intellectual ones. A discourse marked by unity, coherence, and emphasis, stringently construed, would of necessity reflect a strong sense of limitations, of what was possible, as well as a grasp of the proper relations of things within the universe.

The discursive imperatives imposed by these limitations was felt so strongly by James Fernald as to lead him to remark in his textbook that no distraction, no matter how beautiful, was to be admitted into a discourse: writers "must have the moral courage severely to cut down or cut out what is good and beautiful, if it leads away from the main theme and plan." To do so, Fernald continued, was to make the necessary "sacrifice to unity" (416).

True enough, rejection of the approved conventional form could produce discourse that was fragmented or digressive. But the authors of many current-traditional textbooks were concerned with more than wayward discourse. As one set of authors remarked in 1922, "It is desirable to preserve in composition the graces of social life: quietness of manner, moderation in the expression of judgments, the tone of persuasion rather than that of command—in a word, the group of civilized qualities that may be summed up in *urbanity*" (Thomas, Manchester, and Scott 13). The institutional project of current-traditional rhetoric, it seems, was to produce quiescent, moderate, and solicitous student discourse. I suspect that, as with most things in life, current-traditional rhetoricians got just what they asked for.

NOTES

1. The *Grammar of Rhetoric* went through at least twenty-four editions in this country prior to 1844, something over one edition a year. Jamieson was read in many American colleges during the 1820s and 1830s and was used at some schools in conjunction with Blair and Campbell. Jamieson cited Campbell as his authority on style and mentioned Blair and Kames as the mentors of his discussion of taste. Despite these demurrers, Jamieson's text is so thoroughly indebted to Blair that it might fairly be called a summary or redaction of the *Lectures on Rhetoric*—which explains its late appearance in this book, since Blair's rhetorical theory was oriented toward style and arrangement rather than invention.

2. I seem to be alone in connecting Bain's paragraph principles with method. Rodgers argues that Bain deduced these principles by making an analogy between paragraphs and sentences. Shearer disputes this interpretation in "Genesis of Paragraph Theory," arguing Bain's possible indebtedness to Murray's *English Grammar,* as well as other contemporary sources. Kitzhaber discusses Bain's possible indebtedness to Angus' *Handbook of the English Tongue* (245). Lunsford rejects Rodgers' argument that Bain derived his principles deductively.

3. Ong notices a parallel movement in the confluence of printing with Ramus' popularization of method. Ong writes that "the diagrammatic tidiness which printing was imparting to the realm of ideas was part of a large-scale operation freeing the book from the world of discourse and making it over into an object, a box with surface and 'content' " (311). Ong sees this movement as taking the logical concept of "place" literally; that is, a seat or locus of argument became, in the farthest extension of method, a structure on the page.

4. Kitzhaber attributes unity, coherence, and emphasis to eighteenth-century principles of style (183–84). Indeed, the notion that sentences were to represent a complete thought can be traced via associationism to eighteenth-century discussions of style. See, for example, Campbell's discussion of perspicuity in book 2 of the *Philosophy of Rhetoric*. Cautions about the necessity for sentences to display unity appear in current-traditional textbooks written throughout the nineteenth century. But it was only in mature current-traditional theory that all three principles were marshaled into service on all levels of discourse. For another discussion of current-traditional treatments of unity, coherence, and emphasis, see Connors, "Static Abstractions."

5. Some institutions allow some students to exempt themselves from the composition requirement—but this possibility makes the requirement itself nonetheless universal. The universal requirement was suspended in many institutions during the late 1960s and early 1970s, thanks to students' assertion of its irrelevance to their education. However, it was

firmly back in place in many institutions by 1975 or so. The benefits of the composition requirement to the academy are enormous. Because the composition course is institution-alized as freshman English, faculty across the university can ignore their responsibility to inculcate literate skills in their students. If their students' level of literacy is unacceptable, faculty can blame the composition course, which is in place precisely so that they do not have to bother with this supposedly elementary work. Faculty in English departments reap the added benefits of its huge enrollments and cheap labor.

6. Stegner's essay, which was an overt plea for the institutionalization of what is now called creative writing, was a covert diatribe against the structure of English departments and the teaching of writing done in composition classes.

7. I am not arguing that no discursive conventions should be made available to students, nor is Wright. Rather, we are objecting to the current-traditional habit of smuggling middle-class social values into composition instruction by disguising them as inflexible rules for discursive behavior.

Robert J. Connors

"The Rise and Fall
of the Modes of Discourse"

The classification of discourse into different types has been one of the continuing interests of rhetoricians since the classical period. Some of these classifications have been genuinely useful to teachers of discourse, but others have exemplified Butler's damning couplet, "all a rhetorician's rules / Teach nothing but to name his tools." To explore the question of what makes a discourse classification useful or appealing to teachers, this essay will examine the rise, reign, and fall of the most influential classification scheme of the last hundred years: the "forms" or "modes" of discourse: Narration, Description, Exposition, and Argument. More students have been taught composition using the modes of discourse than any other classification system. The history of the modes is an instructive one; from the time of their popularization in American rhetoric textbooks during the late nineteenth century, through the absolute dominance they had in writing classrooms during the period 1895–1930, and into the 1950's when they were finally superseded by other systems, the modes of discourse both influenced and reflected many of the important changes our discipline has seen in the last century. Looking at the modes and their times may also help us answer the question of what sorts of discourse classifications are most useful for writing classes today.

THE EARLY YEARS: INTRODUCTION, CONFLICT, AND ACCEPTANCE

Most short histories of the modes of discourse (which for brevity's sake will hereafter be called simply "the modes") trace them back to George Campbell's "four ends of speaking" and to Alexander Bain, the Scottish logician and educator whose 1866 textbook *English Composition and Rhetoric* made the modal formula widely known. But, as Albert Kitzhaber points out, the terms we have come to call the modes were floating about in very general use during the period 1825–1870.[1] It is not easy to trace influences among rhetoric texts of this period, since the ideas were presumed to be in currency rather than the specific property of individuals, but the first definitive use of terms similar to our modal terms was in 1827. In that year, they appeared in a small book called *A Practical System of Rhetoric,* by Samuel P. Newman, a professor at Bowdoin College in Maine.

According to the *National Union Catalog,* Newman's text was the most widely-used rhetoric written in America between 1820 and 1860, going through at least sixty "editions" or printings between its first publication and 1856—a huge number for that time. Newman owed much to Hugh Blair's *Lectures on Rhetoric and Belles-Letters* of 1873 and something to George Campbell's 1776 treatise on *The Philosophy of Rhetoric,* but *A Practical System* differed from both books in its penchant for grouping concepts, a fascination with categories which was to become one of the hallmarks of the rigidly formalized rhetoric of the late nineteenth century. Here is Newman's description of the "kinds of composition":

> Writings are distinguished from each other as didactic, persuasive, argumentative, descriptive, and narrative. . . . Didactic writing, as the name implies, is used in conveying instruction. . . . when it is designed to influence the will, the composition becomes the persuasive kind. . . . the various forms of argument, the statement of proofs, the assigning of causes . . . are addressed to the reasoning faculties of the mind. Narrative and descriptive writings relate past occurrences, and place before the mind for its contemplation, various objects and scenes.[2]

Newman uses the term "didactic" in place of the more common "expository" and, as was common in the later nineteenth century, separates persuasion of the will from argument to the logical faculties, but it seems obvious that his is the prototype of the modal formula.

Newman's terms did not, however, fall on very fertile soil. He had a few imitators between 1827 and 1866, most notably Richard Green Parker, whose 1844 text *Aids to English Composition* added "Pathetic" to Newman's list, and George Quackenbos, who listed Description, Narration, Argument, Exposition, and Speculation in his *Advanced Course of Composition and Rhetoric* of 1854. Few other texts picked up the terms, and the modes hung in suspension, waiting for a powerful voice to solidify and disseminate a formulation.

That voice was found in Bain. Here are "the various kinds of composition" from the first American edition of *English Composition and Rhetoric.*

> Those that have for their object to inform the understanding, fall under three heads—*Description, Narration,* and *Exposition.* The means of influencing the will are given under one head, *Persuasion.* The employing of language to excite pleasurable Feelings is one of the chief characteristics of *Poetry.*[3]

Minus the reference to poetry (which Bain later admitted was extraneous), this was the modal formulation that was to prove such a powerful force in the teaching of writing in American colleges.

Why did Bain's formulation win wide adherence within two decades while Newman's earlier version was not generally accepted? There are two reasons, one having to do with the manner in which Bain used the modes in his text and the other related to the changing temperament of rhetorical education in America during the late nineteenth century.

First, unlike either Newman or Quackenbos, who merely mentioned their modal terms in passing in their texts—Newman spent only two pages on his "kinds of composition"—Bain used the modes as an organizing principle in *English Composition and Rhetoric*. Modal terms inform long sections of his discussion, and one cannot read the text without carrying away a vivid impression of their importance. This is an important key to Bain's success, for the modes were to become generally accepted not merely as a classification of discourse, but as a conceptualizing strategy for teaching composition.

The second reason for the popularity of the Bainian modes was the changing atmosphere of rhetorical education between 1830 and 1900, especially in the United States. At the beginning of this period, American colleges tended to be small and were often religion-based. Curricula were generally classical, and rhetorical study tended to follow the examples set down by the great rhetoricians of the eighteenth century. The work of Hugh Blair was especially influential, and scores of editions of his *Lectures* were printed in the United States between 1790 and 1860. The analyses of belletristic literature that made Blair's work novel had a profound impact on other elements in rhetorical study during the early nineteenth century.

When we consider the popularity of Blair's belletristic approach to rhetoric, it is not strange to find that the leading discourse classification of the time—the classification the modes were to displace—was based in belles-lettres and classified discourse "according its literary form—epistle, romance, treatise, dialog, history, etc."[4] This belletristic classification was found in most pre-Civil War rhetorics. Although some texts included journalistic forms such as Reviews and Editorials and some went into minor forms such as Allegories and Parables, the five most common belletristic forms were Letters, Treatises, Essays, Biographies, and Fiction.

Time-proven though this classification was, it lasted only thirty years after the introduction of the modes, largely because rhetorical study in America was transformed after 1860. In tandem with the shift in the structure of higher education from a preponderance of smaller private colleges to a preponderance of larger institutions with more varied and scientific curricula, the study of rhetoric mutated from a traditional (that is, classically-derived) analysis of argument, eloquence, style, and taste into a discipline much more concerned with forms. The culture was calling for a new sort of educated man, and the "Freshman English Course" as we know it today, with its emphasis on error-free writing and the ability to follow directions, was born during this period in response to the call. The shift in classification schemes from belletristic to modal is just a part—though an important part—of this larger change. The teacher of the Gilded Age perceived his students as having needs quite different from the needs of their counterparts of 1830. Treatises, Biographies, Fiction, and such were well and good, but the essentially aristocratic educational tradition they represented was on the way out. What occurred between 1870 and 1895 was a shift from a concrete, form-based model rooted in literary high culture to a more pliable abstract model that seemed to be adaptable to anything which a rising young American might wish to say.

While the belletristic classification was waning, the modes were waxing, but only after a slow beginning. The period 1875–1890 shows no clear victor, though modal texts can be seen advancing, and general acceptance of the modes took two decades after Bain's first publication of them. *English Composition and Rhetoric* itself, after a burst of popularity in 1867, subsided into relative obscurity through the 1870's and early 1880's, and Bain's early followers were not much luckier.

The turning point, the text that really marks the paradigm shift most clearly, did not come until 1885, with the publication of *The Practical Elements of Rhetoric,* by the redoubtable John Genung. As much as Bain himself (whose sales Genung helped boost throughout the late eighties), Genung popularized the modes throughout America. *The Practical Elements* was in print from 1885 through 1904, and only Bain's text, which was in print far longer, A. S. Hill's *Principles of Rhetoric,* which had the cachet of Harvard, and Barrett Wendell's *English Composition* were more popular during the period 1865–1900. Between them, Bain and Genung greatly influenced the theoretical and practical world of rhetoric instruction between 1886 and 1891, and the popularity of their books sounded the death-knell of the belletristic classification in composition courses.

Genung, of course, did not adopt Bain's notion of four modes absolutely, as had Bain's earlier and less successful imitators A. D. Hepburn and David Hill. He distinguished between Argumentation, which he called "Invention dealing with Truths" and Persuasion, which he called "Invention dealing with Practical Issues."[5] These two sorts of arguments were copied and used by derivative text-book authors after Genung until about 1910, when the four standard terms swept all before them. Genung himself adopted the four terms of the standard modes himself in 1893 in his *Outlines of Rhetoric,* the follow-up text to *The Practical Elements.*

THE REIGN OF THE MODES

Of the textbook authors that Kitzhaber calls "The Big Four" of the late nineteenth century—Barrett Wendell, John Genung, Adams Sherman Hill, and Fred Newton Scott (who wrote his texts in collaboration with Joseph V. Denney)—all had implicitly accepted the modes by 1894, and by 1895 all except Wendell were using them as important parts of their texts. Wendell merely mentioned the modes as an accepted convention in his *English Composition,* using instead as an organizing structure his famous trinity of Unity–Mass–Coherence (which he adopted, incidentally, from Bain's discussion of the paragraph). Though he did not use the modes in an important way, Wendell at least advanced no competitive classification, and many later texts adopted both the modes and the trinity as important elements.[6]

A. S. Hill, Boylston Professor of Rhetoric at Harvard, denied the modes throughout the eighties in his text *The Principles of Rhetoric*, which omitted Exposition from its scope. Hill saw the handwriting on the wall in the early nineties, however, when sales of his book dropped off sharply. There was no edition of *The Principles of Rhetoric* in 1894, and when the book reappeared in 1895 in a "New Edition, Revised and Enlarged," the revision recited the modal litany in perfect chorus. So fell into line many of the partially-converted.

Fred N. Scott and Joseph Denney's text, *Paragraph-Writing*, in 1891, dealt as much with paragraphs as with whole essays—using, of course, the paragraph model that Bain had originated 25 years earlier—but the four sorts of essays that Scott and Denney do mention are the familiar quartet. *Paragraph-Writing* was Scott and Denney's most popular text, and aside from its use of the modes it is important for another reason. It is the first truly popular codification of "the means of developing paragraphs" which were to become more and more important in the fifty years following Scott and Denney. Adapted from the classical topics, these "means" included Contrast, Explanation, Definition, Illustration, Detail, and Proofs. Watch these terms, for they will reappear, both as methods of paragraph development and more importantly as the "methods of exposition" that will come to supplant the modes.

This reappearance was not to happen, though, for many years. After 1895, the modes were the controlling classification, having driven the belletristic forms from the field. During the late nineties, non-modal texts almost completely disappeared; of 28 books dating between 1893 and 1906 surveyed by Kitzhaber, only four made no mention of the modes.[7] There was for a while some disagreement about whether argument and persuasion were truly separate, but by 1910 even these internecine quarrels had died out. That the modes were accepted almost absolutely was evidenced by the growth and spread of texts devoted to treating only one of them, such as George Pierce Baker's influential *The Principles of Argumentation* in 1895, Carroll L. Maxcy's *The Rhetorical Principles of Narration* in 1911, and Gertrude Buck's *Expository Writing* in 1899. As we shall see, these single-mode texts would have an important effect on the future of the modes as a system.

With single-mode and four-mode textbooks controlling the lists, the reign of modal text organization was long and ponderous, lasting from the mid-1890's through the mid-1930's. During this time there were no theoretical advances. Most textbooks were written by followers of Genung and Wendell, and a typical organizing structure of the time was a combination of Wendell's trinity of Unity–Mass–Coherence—later modernized to Unity–Coherence–Emphasis—with "the four traditional forms of discourse." (By 1920 the origin of the modes was lost in the mists of time; they had presumably been carved in stone during the Paleolithic Age.) In terms of new insights, the teaching of composition was frozen in its tracks between 1900 and 1925, and despite a few novel treatments and up-to-date appearances, I cannot find a single text that is not derivative of the authors of the nineties.

Partially this stasis was due to the changing backgrounds of textbook authors, a change which in turn was the result of new directions in the discipline of

English. During this period, "philology" was coming more and more to mean the criticism and scholarly study of literature, and rhetoric was being displaced in many schools from English departments. The composition texts of the nineteenth century had generally been written by rhetorical scholars (Barrett Wendell is a notable exception), but in the early years of the new century, the majority of composition texts began to be written by literary scholars who were producing derivative texts in order to put bread on their tables. The pure fire of Bain was kept alive during this period by such literary figures as Percy Boynton, John C. French, and Raymond Pence.

From the middle of the last decade of the nineteenth century, through the Great War, and into the middle of that disillusioned decade following it, the modes controlled the teaching of composition through complete control of textbooks. Nothing threatened, nothing changed. But the world was turning, and the modes were about to be challenged.

THE MODES UNDER ATTACK

It is relatively simple to detail the hegemony of the modes up until the mid-twenties, but at that time, in composition as in the culture at large, great shifts began to occur. Not all of these shifts can be satisfactorily analyzed, but beginning in the late twenties we can note the rise of two trends that would fragment the discipline and result in the gradual diminution of the importance of the modes. The first—which was, ironically, a by-product of the vast popularity the modes had had—was the rise of single-mode textbooks, especially those dealing with exposition. The second was the appearance of new sort of textbook which I call the "thesis text." Let us examine these trends.

To begin with, single-mode texts had been popular as far back as the nineties, as we have seen, but in the twenties and thirties the texts on argumentation and narration were far outstripped by the ultimate victor: texts concerned with exposition. Books like Maurice Garland Fulton's *Expository Writing*, which was first published in 1912 and which survived until 1953 (making it, by my calculations, the longest-lived text of the century) found new popularity in the thirties, and dozens of new expository-writing texts appeared after 1940. Fulton's text, the grandfather to most which followed it, was organized by what he called "Expository Procedures and Devices." Among them are the following: Definition, Classification and Division, Contrast, Comparison or Analogy, Examples, and Descriptive Exposition. You will notice that these overlap to a large degree with Scott and Denney's 1891 list of "Methods of Paragraph Development." Fulton's Procedures and Devices were to be the first important prototypes for the "methods of exposition" still being retailed (sometimes under different names) in many texts today.

Fulton's list was followed and augmented by many other writers throughout the twenties and thirties. There were disagreements about what the "genuine" methods of exposition were, with different texts offering different choices. By the late thirties, though, the list had largely standardized itself, and the techniques of exposition, as they appeared in a whole series of widely-used texts from the forties through the present time, consisted of selections from this final list: definition, analysis, partition, interpretation, reportage, evaluation by standards, comparison, contrast, classification, process analysis, device analysis, cause-and-effect, induction, deduction, examples, and illustration.[8]

By the 1940's exposition had become so popular that it was more widely taught than the "general" modal freshman composition course. This does not, of course, mean that the other modes had ceased to be taught, but more and more they retreated out of composition classes into specialized niches of their own. Narration and description seceded to become the nuclei of creative writing courses, and argumentation, finding itself more and more an orphan in English departments, took refuge in Speech departments and became largely an oral concern for many years. The very success of the modes—and the fact that exposition was the most "practical" of them in a business-oriented culture—was destroying their power as a general organizational strategy throughout the thirties and forties. The modes were still used in many texts, but by the end of World War II they no longer controlled composition or defined discourse except in a relatively general way.

The second trend that was to result in the passing of the modes was the rise of a new sort of composition textbook, different in its angle of approach from modal texts. Prior to 1930, nearly all composition texts were organized according to a hierarchical view of discourse in which the levels were discussed impartially—modal organization, the Bain–Wendell trinity of Unity–Coherence–Emphasis, the Bainian paragraph model, traditional three-element sentence theory, and a few other ritual topics. The order of presentation of material in texts was arbitrary, and occasionally the trinity and the modes would change positions in the hierarchy, but the most important classification discussed in the texts was always the modal, and the controlling assumptions about writing underlying these texts were drawn from the theory of modes, as well. Up until the thirties there were few departures from this line.

Then, beginning in 1930 and in larger numbers throughout the forties and fifties, we begin to see this new type of textbook. It is not a text in purely expository writing; it does not use pragmatic classification exclusively; and it certainly does not treat the levels in writing impartially. This new kind of text does, of course, contain a great deal of traditional rhetorical material, but it is marked by an important change in focus: *it announces that one powerful "master idea" about writing should control the way that students learn to write, and it gives precedence to this central thesis, subordinating all other theoretical material to it.* For this reason, I call these new textbooks thesis texts (without at all implying that they focus attention on the need for a thesis in the student's paper). They are *the* modern composition texts, and today they control the textbook world almost completely.

It would not be hard to make a case for Barrett Wendell's *English Composition* in 1891 as the first thesis text. In that book Wendell observed that rhetoric texts in his time consisted

... chiefly of directions as to how one who would write should set about composing. Many of these directions are extremely sensible, many very suggestive.
But in every case these directions are appallingly numerous. It took me some
years to discern that all which have so far come to my notice could be grouped
under one of three simple heads. . . . The first of these principles may conveniently be named the principle of Unity; the second, the principle of Mass; the
third, the principle of Coherence.[9]

There in a nutshell is the central doctrine of the thesis text: "All else is essentially subordinate to this." Wendell spent the rest of his book explicating how his
three principles could be applied to sentences, paragraphs, and whole themes.

Despite the success of *English Composition* and the flock of slavish imitators it
spawned, Wendell did not have a spiritual successor for over forty years; the
period following his text, as we have seen, was marked by conventionality and
reliance upon modal organization of texts. In 1931, though, a text appeared
which was to signal an important departure: Norman Foerster and J. M.
Steadman's *Writing and Thinking*. This extremely popular text was in print for
over twenty years, and it exerted a profound influence on later authors. Foerster
and Steadman's dual thesis was announced on their first page: "Writing and
thinking are organically related," and "Writing, in other words, should be organic, not mechanic."[10] The authors then went on to subordinate the rest of their
material—not much of which was genuinely original—to this thesis.

Although *Writing and Thinking* was a popular book, the new trend in texts
began slowly; there are only a few books identifiable as being controlled by non-
modal theses in the thirties and early forties. The theses that truly established
thesis texts, that tipped the balance away from the domination of the modes in
the late forties, reflected the two most popular intellectual movements in composition theory at that time: the general education movement with its "language
arts/communications" approach, and the General Semantics movement. This
essay is not the place for a history of these movements, fascinating as one might
be. In brief, the general education/"communications" movement grew out of the
Deweyite interest in "English for Life Skills" during the thirties and emphasized
the whole continuum of language activities—reading, writing, speaking, and listening—rather than writing alone. The Conference on College Composition and
Communication was formed in 1948 by "communications" enthusiasts. (That's
where the "communication" comes from.) General Semantics, of course, was
based on the work of Alfred Korzybski as popularized by S. I. Hayakawa in his
influential *Words in Action* of 1940, and is most interested in language as a symbol system liable to abuse. Together, communications and General Semantics
provided theses for more than half of the new composition texts that appeared
between 1948 and 1952.

There were, of course, some thesis texts not based on either communications
or on General Semantics. One of the best of them is still going strong: James
McCrimmon's *Writing With A Purpose*, the thesis of which is, of course, the
importance of the writer's controlling purpose. Most thesis texts not based on

communications or General Semantics used theses based on some version of favorite old notions, writing and thinking, writing and reading, the unique demands of American writing. Later the theses in texts would grow out of concepts more complex and interesting: writing and perception, writing and cognition, writing and process. Most expository writing texts also took on characteristics of thesis texts during the fifties, and more and more thesis texts came to use the "methods of exposition."

FALL AND ABANDONMENT OF THE MODES

And where stood the Bainian modes in this avalanche—for an avalanche it became after 1950—of expositionists and thesis texts? As has been suggested, the modes did not completely disappear, but they were certainly changed, truncated, and diminished in power. The new texts that appeared did not subvert the modes because they proved them theoretically erroneous, but rather because their theses or listing of methods took over the role in organizing texts that the modes had earlier played. McCrimmon makes a telling statement in the Preface to the first edition of *Writing With A Purpose* in 1950: "The decision to make purpose the theme of the book made the conventional fourfold classification of writing unnecessary. Therefore Exposition, Narration, Description, and Argument are not considered as special types of writing."[11] Even when thesis texts mentioned the modes, they were a minor consideration. Essentially, the modes were ignored to death after 1950.

The new thesis texts used a number of original classifications of discourse, and the modes were everywhere being replaced by these novel classifications. After 1955 or so the modes are seen in new texts only when those texts have specifically traditional intent: for instance, Richard Weaver's *Composition* and Hughes and Duhamel's *Rhetoric: Principles and Usage*. Though the theses of the thesis texts would continue to change—from propositions based upon General Semantics or communications in the forties and fifties to propositions developed from transformational grammar, problem solving, and prewriting in the sixties to theses about invention, process, cognition, and syntactic methods in the seventies—all these theses (of which some texts contain several) have one thing in common: they bypass or ignore the modes of discourse. W. Ross Winterowd spoke for authors of thesis texts when he stated in a 1965 textbook that the modal classification, "though interesting, isn't awfully helpful."[12]

In rhetoric texts today, the modes are still expiring. A few texts still mention them as minor elements, but their power in rhetorics is gone. Of the fifteen or so most widely-used freshman rhetoric texts, only one still advances the modal classes as absolute. Though the modes still retain a shadow of their old puissance as an organizing device in certain freshman anthologies of essays, their importance in modern pedagogy is constantly diminishing, and the only teachers still making real classroom use of the modes are those out of touch with current theory. Stripped of their theoretical validity and much of their practical usefulness, the modes cling to a shadowy half-life in the attic of composition legends.

L'ENVOI—THE MODES AS PLAUSIBLE FICTION

Why did the modes of discourse rise to such power, hold it for so long and so abolutely, and then decline so rapidly? At least part of the answer has to do with the relative vitality of the rhetorical tradition during the period 1870–1930, an era when hardly any progressive theoretical work was done in the field. Alexander Bain, Fred N. Scott, and perhaps Barrett Wendell are the greatest figures writing during the period, and (except for Scott, whose influence was limited) they cannot stand beside Campbell in the eighteenth century or Burke in the twentieth. The modes became popular and stayed popular because they fit into the abstract, mechanical nature of writing instruction at the time, and they diminished in importance as other, more vital, ideas about writing appeared in the 1930's and after. Like the "dramatic unities" that ruled the drama of the seventeenth and eighteenth centuries until exploded by Samuel Johnson's common sense, the modes were only powerful so long as they were not examined for evidence of their usefulness.

One of the most damning assessments of the modes' use in the nineteenth century is that of Albert Kitzhaber:

> Such convenient abstractions as . . . the forms of discourse were ideally suited to the purpose of instruction in a subject that had been cut off from all relation with other subjects in the curriculum and, in a sense, from life itself. . . . They represent an unrealistic view of the writing process, a view that assumes writing is done by formula and in a social vacuum. They turn the attention of both teacher and student toward an academic exercise instead of toward a meaningful act of communication in a social context. Like Unity–Coherence–Emphasis—or any other set of static abstractions concerning writing—they substitute mechanical for organic conceptions and therefore distort the real nature of writing.[13]

The weakness of the modes of discourse as a practical tool in the writing class was that they did not really help students to learn to write. When we look closely at the nature of modal distinctions, it is not hard to see why: the modes classify and emphasize the product of writing, having almost nothing to do with the purpose for which the writer sat down, pen in hand. Modal distinctions are divorced from the composition process. As James Kinneavy puts it,

> ... a stress on modes of discourse rather than aims of discourse is a stress on "what" is being talked about rather than on "why" a thing is talked about. This is actually a substitution of means for ends. Actually, something is narrated for reason. Narration, as such, is not a purpose. Consequently, the "modes" period in history has never lasted very long.[14]

In our time, the modes are little more than an unofficial descriptive myth, replaced in theory by empirically-derived classifications of discourse and in practice by the "methods of exposition" and other non-modal classes. The important theoretical classification schemas of today are those of James Moffett, whose Spectrum of Discourse consists of Recording, Reporting, Generalizing, and Theorizing; of James Kinneavy, who divides discourse into Reference, Scientific, Persuasive, Literary, and Expressive types; and of James Britton, with its triad of Poetic, Expressive, and Transactional discourse. All of these classification schemes have one thing in common: they are based on the writer's purposes, the ends of his or her composing, rather than merely being classifications of written discourse.

In current textbooks, too, the modes are largely displaced by more process-oriented considerations or by heuristic theses that see classification of discourse as unimportant. The most popular discourse classification still found in textbooks is Fulton's "methods of exposition," updated and augmented, of course. Doubtless the most complete system using the methods of exposition is Frank D'Angelo's system of "discourse paradigms." We do not yet know whether the paradigms will become as rigid, abstract, and useless as did their progenitors, the modes.

"Anytime a means is exalted to an end in history of discourse education, a similar pattern can be seen," writes Kinneavy; "the emphasis is short-lived and usually sterile." The modes of discourse controlled a good part of composition teaching during one of rhetoric's least vigorous periods, offering in their seeming completeness and plausibility a schema of discourse that could be easily taught and learned. For years the fact that this schema did not help students learn to write better was not a concern, and even today the modes are accepted by some teachers despite their lack of basis in useful reality. Our discipline has been long in knuckling from its eyes the sleep of the nineteenth and early twentieth centuries, and the real lesson of the modes is that we need always to be on guard against systems that seem convenient to teachers but that ignore the way writing is actually done.

NOTES

1. Albert R. Kitzhaber, *Rhetoric in American Colleges, 1850–1900,* Diss. University of Washington, 1953, pp. 191–196.

2. Samuel P. Newman, *A Practical System of Rhetoric* (New York: Mark H. Newman, 1827) pp. 28–29.

3. Alexander Bain, *English Composition and Rhetoric* (New York: D. Appleton and Co., 1866) p. 19.

4. Kitzhaber, p. 191.

5. John F. Genung, *The Practical Elements of Rhetoric* (Boston: Ginn and Co., 1887), Table of Contents.

6. It is interesting to note that Wendell, who mentions the modes only in passing, is the only one of the "Big Four" who admits any indebtedness to Bain. This is especially strange

when we consider that Bain's paragraph model was also used in all these texts without direct citation. For more on Bain's paragraph theory—which undoubtedly helped spread the associated doctrine of the modes—see Paul C. Rodgers, Jr., "Alexander Bain and the Rise of the Organic Paragraph," *Quarterly Journal of Speech* 51 (December, 1965), 399–408.

7. Kitzhaber, p. 204.

8. This list is compiled from John S. Naylor, *Informative Writing* (New York: Macmillan, 1942); Joseph M. Bachelor and Harold L. Haley, *The Practice of Exposition* (New York: Appleton-Century, 1947); and Louise F. Rorabacher, *Assignments in Exposition* (New York: Harper and Bros., 1946).

9. Barrett Wendell, *English Composition* (New York: Scribners, 1891), pp. 18–19.

10. Norman Foerster and J. M. Steadman, Jr., *Writing and Thinking* (Boston: Houghton Mifflin, 1931), p. 3.

11. James M. McCrimmon, *Writing With A Purpose* (Boston: Houghton Mifflin, 1950), pp. viii–ix.

12. W. Ross Winterowd, *Writing and Rhetoric* (Boston: Allyn and Bacon, 1965), p. 199.

13. Kitzhaber, pp. 220–221.

14. James L. Kinneavy, *A Theory of Discourse* (Englewood Cliffs, NJ: Prentice-Hall, 1971), pp. 28–29.

Karlyn Kohrs Campbell

From: *Man Cannot Speak For Her:*
A Critical Study of Early Feminist Rhetoric

STRUGGLING FOR THE RIGHT TO SPEAK

Early woman's rights activists were constrained to be particularly creative because they faced barriers unknown to men. They were a group virtually unique in rhetorical history because a central element in woman's oppression was the denial of her right to speak (Lipking 1983). Quite simply, in nineteenth-century America, femininity and rhetorical action were seen as mutually exclusive. No "true woman" could be a public persuader.

The concept of "true womanhood" (Welter 1976), or the "woman-belle ideal" (Scott 1970), defined females as "other," as suited only for a limited repertoire of gender-based roles, and as the repository of cherished but commercially useless spiritual and human values. These attitudes arose in response to the urbanization and industrialization of the nineteenth century, which separated home and work. As the cult of domesticity was codified in the United States in the early part of the century, two distinct subcultures emerged. Man's place was the world outside the home, the public realm of politics and finance; man's nature was thought to be lustful, amoral, competitive, and ambitious. Woman's place was home, a haven from amoral capitalism and dirty politics, where "the heart was," where the spiritual and emotional needs of husband and children were met by a "ministering angel." Woman's nature was pure, pious, domestic, and submissive (Welter 1976, 21). She was to remain entirely in the private sphere of the home, eschewing any appearance of individuality, leadership, or aggressiveness. Her purity depended on her domesticity; the woman who was compelled by economic need or slavery to work away from her own hearth was tainted. However, woman's alleged moral superiority (Cott 1977, 120, 146–48, 170) generated a conflict out of which the woman's rights movement emerged.

As defined, woman's role contained a contradiction that became apparent as women responded to what they saw as great moral wrongs. Despite their allegedly greater moral sensitivity, women were censured for their efforts against the evils of prostitution and slavery (Berg 1978; Hersh 1978). Women who formed moral reform and abolitionist societies, and who made speeches, held conventions, and published newspapers, entered the public sphere and thereby lost their claims to purity and piety. What became the woman's rights/woman suffrage movement arose out of this contradiction.

Women encountered profound resistance to their efforts for moral reform because rhetorical action of any sort was, as defined by gender roles, a masculine activity. Speakers had to be expert and authoritative; women were submissive. Speakers ventured into the public sphere (the courtroom, the legislature, the pulpit, or the lecture platform); woman's domain was domestic. Speakers called attention to themselves, took stands aggressively, initiated action, and affirmed their expertise; "true women" were retiring and modest, their influence was indirect, and they had no expertise or authority. Because they were thought naturally incapable of reasoning, women were considered unsuited to engage in or to guide public deliberation. The public realm was competitive, driven by ambition; it was a sphere in which the desire to succeed could only be inhibited by humane concerns and spiritual values. Similarly, speaking was competitive, energized by the desire to win a case or persuade others to one's point of view. These were viewed as exclusively masculine traits related to man's allegedly lustful, ruthless, competitive, amoral, and ambitious nature. Activities requiring such qualities were thought to "unsex" women.

The extent of the problem is illustrated by the story of educational pioneer Emma Hart Willard (Scott 1978; Willard 1819). Encouraged by Governor De Witt Clinton in 1819 to present "A Plan for Improving Female Education" to the New York Legislature, Hart Willard presented her proposal to legislators, but carefully remained seated to avoid any hint that she was delivering a speech. In her biography of this influential educator, Alma Lutz writes: "Although this [oral presentation] was very unconventional for a woman, she did not hesitate, so great was her enthusiasm for her *Plan*. . . . She impressed them not as the much-scorned female politician, but as a noble woman inspired by a great ideal" (Lutz 1931, 28).

In other words, a woman who spoke displayed her "masculinity"; that is, she demonstrated that she possessed qualities traditionally ascribed only to males. When a woman spoke, she enacted her equality, that is, she herself was proof that she was as able as her male counterparts to function in the public sphere. That a woman speaking is such proof explains the outraged reactions to women addressing "promiscuous" audiences of men and women, sharing a platform with male speakers, debating, and preaching, even on such clearly moral issues as slavery, prostitution, and alcohol abuse. The hostility women experienced in reform efforts led them to found female reform organizations and to initiate a movement for woman's rights, at base a movement claiming woman's right to engage in public moral action.

Biology, or rather ignorance of biology, was used to buttress arguments limiting woman's role and excluding her from higher education and political activity.

On average, women were smaller than men. As a result, it was assumed that they had smaller brains, and that therefore their brains presumably were too small to sustain the rational deliberation required in politics and business. Moreover, their smaller, and hence more delicate and excitable, nerves could not withstand the pressures of public debate or the marketplace. Menarche, the onset of menstruation, was viewed as a physical cataclysm that rendered women unfit for normal activity. For example, Harvard medical professor Dr. Edward Clarke (1873) argued against higher education for women on the grounds that the blood needed to sustain development of the ovaries and womb would be diverted to the brain, which he believed was a major cause of serious illness.

Because of the conceptions of their nature and the taboos that were part of the cult of domesticity, women who spoke publicly confronted extraordinary obstacles. For example, abolitionist Abby Kelley [Foster]

> faced such continuous and merciless persecution that she earned the title "our Joan of Arc" among her co-workers. Lucy Stone later described Kelley's career as "long, unrelieved, moral torture." . . . Because she often traveled alone, or (worse) with male agents, she was vilified as a "bad" woman. . . . She was further reviled when she continued to appear in public while pregnant. (Hersh 1978, 42–43)

On the one hand, a woman had to meet all the usual requirements of speakers, demonstrating expertise, authority, and rationality in order to show her competence and make herself credible to audiences. However, if that was all she did, she was likely to be judged masculine, unwomanly, aggressive, and cold. As a result, women speakers sometimes searched for ways to legitimate such "unwomanly" behavior and for ways to incorporate evidence of femininity into ordinary rhetorical action. In other instances, their own defiance and outrage overwhelmed their efforts at adaptation. In still other cases, rhetors found womanly ways of persuasion that were self-contradictory, and hence ultimately damaging to their cause. Yet on occasion, extraordinarily skilled women persuaders found symbolic means of responding to these contradictory expectations, and produced masterpieces. The problems women faced as speakers are a recurring theme of this book, a theme that remains relevant for contemporary women who still must struggle to cope with these contradictory expectations, albeit in somewhat modified forms.

FEMININE STYLE

Analysis of persuasion by women indicates that many strategically adopted what might be called a feminine style to cope with the conflicting demands of the podium. That style emerged out of their experiences as women and was adapted to the attitudes and experiences of female audiences. However, it was not, and is not today, a style exclusive to women, either as speakers or as audiences.

Deprived of formal education and confined to the home, a woman learned the crafts of housewifery and motherhood—cooking, cleaning, canning, sewing, childbearing, child-rearing, and the like—from other women through a supervised internship combining expert advice with trial and error. These processes are common to all craft-learning, including carpentry, horse training and plumbing, but craft-related skills cannot be expressed in universal laws; one must learn to apply them contingently, depending upon conditions and materials (McMillan 1982). Learning to adapt to variation is essential to mastery of a craft, and the highly skilled craftsperson is alert to variation, aware of a host of alternatives, and able to read cues related to specific conditions.

If the process of craft-learning is applied to the rhetorical situation (and rhetoric itself is a craft), it produces discourse with certain characteristics. Such discourse will be personal in tone (crafts are learned face-to-face from a mentor), relying heavily on personal experience, anecdotes, and other examples. It will tend to be structured inductively (crafts are learned bit by bit, instance by instance, from which generalizations emerge). It will invite audience participation, including the process of testing generalizations or principles against the experiences of the audience. Audience members will be addressed as peers, with recognition of authority based on experience (more skilled craftspeople are more experienced), and efforts will be made to create identification with the experiences of the audience and those described by the speaker. The goal of such rhetoric is empowerment, a term contemporary feminists have used to refer to the process of persuading listeners that they can act effectively in the world, that they can be "agents of change" (Bitzer 1968). Given the traditional concept of womanhood, which emphasized passivity, submissiveness, and patience, persuading women that they could act was a precondition for other kinds of persuasive efforts.[1]

Many of the qualities of the style just described are also part of the small-group phenomenon known as consciousness-raising, associated with contemporary feminism as well as other social movements, which is a communicative style that can be incorporated into speaking or prose writing (Farrell 1979). Because oppressed groups tend to develop passive personality traits, consciousness-raising is an attractive communication style to people working for social change. Whether in a small group, from the podium, or on the page, consciousness-raising invites audience members to participate in the persuasive process— it empowers them. It is a highly appealing form of discourse, particularly if identification between advocate and audience is facilitated by common values and shared experience.

Based on this description, it should be obvious that while there is nothing inevitably or necessarily female about this rhetorical style, it has been congenial to women because of the acculturation of female speakers and audiences.[2] It can be called "feminine" in this context because it reflects the learning experiences of women who were speakers and audiences in this period, and because, as a less authoritative and aggressive style, it was a less confrontational violation of taboos against public speaking by women.

Because the very act of speaking publicly violated concepts of womanhood, the rhetoric of early woman's rights advocates always had at least two dimensions—presentation of their grievances and justification of woman's right to function in the public sphere, to speak with authority in any area of human life. From the beginnings of the movement, women justified their demands based on what Aileen Kraditor (1965, 43–74) calls the argument from justice and the argument from expediency. The argument from justice was drawn from natural rights philosophy and affirmed the personhood of women and their right to all the civil and political privileges of citizenship.[3] It was a demand for rights affirming that, at least in law and politics, there were no differences between the sexes. By contrast, the argument from expediency presumed that women and men were fundamentally different, so that it would be beneficial, that is, desirable and prudent, to give women rights because of the effect on society. For example, it was argued that if women were educated, they would be better able to fulfill their obligations as wives and mothers; if married women had the right to sue, to enter into contracts, to control their earnings, and to own property, they would be able to protect themselves and their children against profligate husbands, or to fulfill their duties to their children in widowhood. If women were allowed to vote, they would bring to bear on politics their purity, piety, and domestic concerns, and thus purify government and make it more responsive to the needs of the home.

Most woman's rights advocates mixed these arguments, often in a somewhat self-contradictory way. In the earliest period, natural rights arguments predominated, but most advocates still assumed that women were naturally better suited to motherhood and that the aim of a woman's life was wifehood and motherhood. However, even in that period, some argued chiefly from the benefits that increased opportunities or rights would produce for woman's traditional qualities and duties—education would make women more virtuous, increased economic rights for married women would produce better mothers. In the 1870s, arguments from expediency predominated, with emphasis on the societal benefits of the woman's ballot, particularly in fighting the evils of alcohol. Yet as time passed, those who argued from benefits frequently incorporated arguments from natural rights into their rhetoric, and in this later period there were speakers, such as Dr. Anna Howard Shaw, who argued almost exclusively from the natural rights position (Linkugel 1963).

Natural rights arguments were perceived as less feminine. "True women" were unselfish—their efforts were for others, particularly their husbands and children. Women who claimed their rights were seen as selfish, as wanting to abandon their traditional womanly roles to enter the sphere of men, and this made such arguments and advocates particularly unappealing to many women (Camhi 1973, 113). Arguments from benefits were "feminine" in part because they presupposed the qualities of "true womanhood" and in part because they appeared unselfish. Women who argued from expediency did not seek rights for their own sake but only for the good that could be done with them for others. This argument achieved its fullest development in the WCTU's support for woman suffrage as a means to protect the home against the abuses of alcohol.

The obstacles early women persuaders faced persist, although in altered forms, in the present. As a result, my goals in this project are simultaneously scholarly and feminist. As a scholar, I wish to rescue the works of great women speakers from the oblivion to which most have been consigned; above all, I wish to show that the artistry of this rhetoric generated enduring monuments to human thought and creativity.[4] Because early feminists faced obstacles whose residues still haunt contemporary women, their rhetorical efforts are a rich source of illumination. As a feminist, I believe that the works analyzed in this volume and anthologized in volume II represent a particularly abundant mother lode of rhetorical creativity from which contemporary women speakers and activists may draw examples and inspiration.

NOTES

1. Passivity, modesty, patience, and submissiveness were integral parts of "true womanhood," concepts reinforced by nineteenth-century women's total lack of economic, social, legal, or political power. The impact of such attitudes is apparent in more contemporary studies of women's self-concepts (McClelland 1964). Freeman (1971) cites a study done in the 1950s in which women were asked to pick adjectives to describe themselves: they selected "uncertain, anxious, nervous, hasty, careless, fearful, childish, helpless, sorry, timid, clumsy, stupid, silly, domestic, understanding, tender, sympathetic, pure, generous, affectionate, loving, moral, kind, grateful, and patient" (165). Many of these qualities are at odds with a sense of being capable of effective action.

2. Unlike Farrell (1979, 917n), I do not presume that "feminine" style is rooted in biological differences.

3. Natural rights philosophy grew out of ancient and medieval doctrines of natural law that were modified by an emphasis on the individual in the seventeenth century. Fundamentally, natural rights philosophy took the view that individuals had rights no government could abridge or deny. As a result, the function of government was to protect such rights, requiring plebiscites to determine the consent of the governed and revolution if the government failed in its proper functions. Articulated in the writings of John Locke, natural rights philosophy was elaborated in the United States in the works of Thomas Jefferson, Samuel Adams, and Thomas Paine. Classic expressions of natural rights philosophy are the Declaration of Independence and the Bill of Rights. Concepts of natural rights infused the writings of Mary Wollstonecraft and were central to the Declaration of Sentiments adopted at Seneca Falls in 1848.

4. Rhetoric is not, of course, the only important element in a social movement (Freeman 1975, 1–43).

Lloyd F. Bitzer

"The Rhetorical Situation"

If someone says, That is a dangerous situation, his words suggest the presence of events, persons, or objects which threaten him, someone else, or something of value. If someone remarks, I find myself in an embarrassing situation, again the statement implies certain situational characteristics. If someone remarks that he found himself in an ethical situation, we understand that he probably either contemplated or made some choice or action from a sense of duty or obligation or with a view to the Good. In other words, there are circumstances of this or that kind of structure which are recognized as ethical, dangerous, or embarrassing. What characteristics, then, are implied when one refers to "the rhetorical situation"—the context in which speakers or writers create rhetorical discourse? Perhaps this question is puzzling because "situation" is not a standard term in the vocabulary of rhetorical theory. "Audience" is standard; so also are "speaker," "subject," "occasion," and "speech." If I were to ask, "What is a rhetorical audience?" or "What is a rhetorical subject?"—the reader would catch the meaning of my question.

When I ask, What is a rhetorical situation?, I want to know the nature of those contexts in which speakers or writers create rhetorical discourse: How should they be described? What are their characteristics? Why and how do they result in the creation of rhetoric? By analogy, a theorist of science might well ask, What are the characteristics of situations which inspire scientific thought? A philosopher might ask, What is the nature of the situation in which a philosopher "does philosophy"? And a theorist of poetry might ask, How shall we describe the context in which poetry comes into existence?

The presence of rhetorical discourse obviously indicates the presence of a rhetorical situation. The Declaration of Independence, Lincoln's Gettysburg Address, Churchill's Address on Dunkirk, John F. Kennedy's Inaugural Address—each is a clear instance of rhetoric and each indicates the presence of a situation. While the existence of a rhetorical address is a reliable sign of the existence of situation, it does not follow that a situation exists only when the discourse exists. Each reader probably can recall a specific time and place when there was opportunity to speak on some urgent matter, and after the opportunity was

Philosophy and Rhetoric, Supplementary Issue, 1992. Copyright © 1968, 1992 The Pennsylvania State University, University Park, PA.

gone he created in private thought the speech he should have uttered earlier in the situation. It is clear that situations are not always accompanied by discourse. Nor should we assume that a rhetorical address gives existence to the situation; on the contrary, it is the situation which calls the discourse into existence. Clement Attlee once said that Winston Churchill went around looking for "finest hours." The point to observe is that Churchill found them—the crisis situations— and spoke in response to them.

No major theorist has treated rhetorical situation thoroughly as a distinct subject in rhetorical theory; many ignore it. Those rhetoricians who discuss situation do so indirectly—as does Aristotle, for example, who is led to consider situation when he treats types of discourse. None, to my knowledge, has asked the nature of rhetorical situation. Instead rhetoricians have asked: What is the process by which the orator creates and presents discourse? What is the nature of rhetorical discourse? What sorts of interaction occur between speaker, audience, subject, and occasion? Typically the questions which trigger theories of rhetoric focus upon the orator's method or upon the discourse itself, rather than upon the situation which invites the orator's application of his method and the creation of discourse. Thus rhetoricians distinguish among and characterize the types of speeches (forensic, deliberative, epideictic); they treat issues, types of proof, lines of argument, strategies of ethical and emotional persuasion, the parts of a discourse and the functions of these parts, qualities of styles, figures of speech. They cover approximately the same materials, the formal aspects of rhetorical method and discourse, whether focusing upon method, product or process; while conceptions of situation are implicit in some theories of rhetoric, none explicitly treat the formal aspects of situation.

I hope that enough has been said to show that the question—What is a rhetorical situation?—is not an idle one. I propose in what follows to set forth part of a theory of situation. This essay, therefore, should be understood as an attempt to revive the notion of rhetorical situation, to provide at least the outline of an adequate conception of it, and to establish it as a controlling and fundamental concern of rhetorical theory.

I

It seems clear that rhetoric is situational. In saying this, I do not mean merely that understanding a speech hinges upon understanding the context of meaning in which the speech is located. Virtually no utterance is fully intelligible unless meaning-context and utterance are understood; this is true of rhetorical and non-rhetorical discourse. Meaning-context is a general condition of human communication and is not synonymous with rhetorical situation. Nor do I mean merely that rhetoric occurs in a setting which involves interaction of speaker, audience, subject, and communicative purpose. This is too general, since many types of utterances—philosophical, scientific, poetic, and rhetorical—occur in such settings. Nor would I equate rhetorical situation with persuasive situation, which exists whenever an audience can be changed in belief or action by means of speech. Every audience at any moment is capable of being changed in some way by speech; persuasive situation is altogether general.

Finally, I do not mean that a rhetorical discourse must be embedded in historic context in the sense that a living tree must be rooted in soil. A tree does not obtain its character-as-tree from the soil, but rhetorical discourse, I shall argue, does obtain its character-as-rhetorical from the situation which generates it. Rhetorical works belong to the class of things which obtain their character from the circumstances of the historic context in which they occur. A rhetorical work is analogous to a moral action rather than to a tree. An act is moral because it is an act performed in a situation of a certain kind; similarly, a work is rhetorical because it is a response to a situation of a certain kind.

In order to clarify rhetoric-as-essentially-related-to-situation, we should acknowledge a viewpoint that is commonplace but fundamental: a work of rhetoric is pragmatic; it comes into existence for the sake of something beyond itself; it functions ultimately to produce action or change in the world; it performs some task. In short, rhetoric is a mode of altering reality, not by the direct application of energy to objects, but by the creation of discourse which changes reality through the mediation of thought and action. The rhetor alters reality by bringing into existence a discourse of such a character that the audience, in thought and action, is so engaged that it becomes mediator of change. In this sense rhetoric is always persuasive.

To say that rhetorical discourse comes into being in order to effect change is altogether general. We need to understand that a particular discourse comes into existence because of some specific condition or situation which invites utterance. Bronislaw Malinowski refers to just this sort of situation in his discussion of primitive language, which he finds to be essentially pragmatic and "embedded in situation." He describes a party of fishermen in the Trobriand Islands whose functional speech occurs in a "context of situation."

> The canoes glide slowly and noiselessly, punted by men especially good at this task and always used for it. Other experts who know the bottom of the lagoon . . . are on the look-out for fish. . . . Customary signs, or sounds or words are uttered. Sometimes a sentence full of technical references to the channels or patches on the lagoon has to be spoken; sometimes . . . a conventional cry is uttered. . . . Again, a word of command is passed here and there, a technical expression or explanation which serves to harmonize their behavior towards other men. . . . An animated scene, full of movement, follows, and now that the fish are in their power the fishermen speak loudly, and give vent to their feelings. Short, telling exclamations fly about, which might be rendered by such words as: "Pull in," "Let go," "Shift further," "Lift the net."

In this whole scene, "each utterance is essentially bound up with the context of situation and with the aim of the pursuit. . . . The structure of all this linguistic material is inextricably mixed up with, and dependent upon, the course of the activity in which the utterances are embedded." Later the observer remarks: "In its primitive uses, language functions as a link in concerted human activity, as a piece of human behaviour. It is a mode of action and not an instrument of reflection."[1]

These statements about primitive language and the "context of situation" provide for us a preliminary model of rhetorical situation. Let us regard rhetorical situation as a natural context of persons, events, objects, relations, and an exigence which strongly invites utterance; this invited utterance participates naturally in the situation, is in many instances necessary to the completion of situational activity, and by means of its participation with situation obtains its meaning and its rhetorical character. In Malinowski's example, the situation is the fishing expedition—consisting of objects, persons, events, and relations—and the ruling exigence, the success of the hunt. The situation dictates the sorts of observations to be made; it dictates the significant physical and verbal responses; and, we must admit, it constrains the words which are uttered in the same sense that it constrains the physical acts of paddling the canoes and throwing the nets. The verbal responses to the demands imposed by this situation are clearly as functional and necessary as the physical responses.

Traditional theories of rhetoric have dealt, of course, not with the sorts of primitive utterances described by Malinowski—"stop here," "throw the nets," "move closer"—but with larger units of speech which come more readily under the guidance of artistic principle and method. The difference between oratory and primitive utterance, however, is not a difference in function; the clear instances of rhetorical discourse and the fishermen's utterances are similarly functional and similarly situational. Observing both the traditions of the expedition and the facts before him, the leader of the fishermen finds himself *obliged* to speak at a given moment—to command, to supply information, to praise or blame—to respond appropriately to the situation. Clear instances of artistic rhetoric exhibit the same character: Cicero's speeches against Cataline were called forth by a specific union of persons, events, objects, and relations, and by an exigence which amounted to an imperative stimulus; the speeches in the Senate rotunda three days after the assassination of the President of the United States were actually required by the situation. So controlling is situation that we should consider it the very ground of rhetorical activity, whether that activity is primitive and productive of a simple utterance or artistic and productive of the Gettysburg Address.

Hence, to say that rhetoric is situational means: (1) rhetorical discourse comes into existence as a response to a situation, in the same sense that an answer comes into existence in response to a question, or a solution in response to a problem; (2) a speech is given *rhetorical* significance by the situation, just as a unit of discourse is given significance *as* answer or *as* solution by the question or problem; (3) a rhetorical situation must exist as a necessary condition of rhetorical discourse, just as a question must exist as a necessary condition of an answer;

(4) many questions go unanswered and many problems remain unsolved; similarly, many rhetorical situations mature and decay without giving birth to rhetorical utterance; (5) a situation is rhetorical insofar as it needs and invites discourse capable of participating with situation and thereby altering its reality; (6) discourse is rhetorical insofar as it functions (or seeks to function) as a fitting response to a situation which needs and invites it. (7) Finally, the situation controls the rhetorical response in the same sense that the question controls the answer and the problem controls the solution. Not the rhetor and not persuasive intent, but the situation is the source and ground of rhetorical activity—and, I should add, of rhetorical criticism.

II

Let us now amplify the nature of situation by providing a formal definition and examining constituents. Rhetorical situation may be defined as a complex of persons, events, objects, and relations presenting an actual or potential exigence which can be completely or partially removed if discourse, introduced into the situation, can so constrain human decision or action as to bring about the significant modification of the exigence. Prior to the creation and presentation of discourse, there are three constituents of any rhetorical situation: the first is the *exigence;* the second and third are elements of the complex, namely the *audience* to be constrained in decision and action, and the *constraints* which influence the rhetor and can be brought to bear upon the audience.

Any *exigence* is an imperfection marked by urgency; it is a defect, an obstacle, something waiting to be done, a thing which is other than it should be. In almost any sort of context, there will be numerous exigences, but not all are elements of a rhetorical situation—not all are rhetorical exigences. An exigence which cannot be modified is not rhetorical; thus, whatever comes about of necessity and cannot be changed—death, winter, and some natural disasters, for instance—are exigences to be sure, but they are not rhetorical. Further, an exigence which can be modified only by means other than discourse is not rhetorical; thus, an exigence is not rhetorical when its modification requires merely one's own action or the application of a tool, but neither requires nor invites the assistance of discourse. An exigence is rhetorical when it is capable of positive modification and when positive modification requires discourse or can be assisted by discourse. For example, suppose that a man's acts are injurious to others and that the quality of his acts can be changed only if discourse is addressed to him; the exigence—his injurious acts—is then unmistakably rhetorical. The pollution of our air is also a rhetorical exigence because its positive modification—reduction of pollution—strongly invites the assistance of discourse producing public awareness, indignation, and action of the right kind. Frequently rhetors encounter exigences which defy easy classification because of the absence of information enabling precise analysis and certain judgment—they may or may not be rhetorical. An attorney whose client has been convicted may strongly believe that a higher court would reject his appeal to have the verdict overturned, but because the matter is uncertain—because the exigence *might* be rhetorical—he elects to appeal. In this and similar instances of indeterminate exigences the rhetor's decision to speak is based mainly upon the urgency of the exigence and the probability that the exigence is rhetorical.

In any rhetorical situation there will be at least one controlling exigence which functions as the organizing principle: it specifies the audience to be addressed and the change to be effected. The exigence may or may not be perceived clearly by the rhetor or other persons in the situation; it may be strong or weak depending upon the clarity of their perception and the degree of their interest in it; it may be real or unreal depending on the facts of the case; it may be important or trivial; it may be such that discourse can completely remove it, or it may persist in spite of repeated modifications; it may be completely familiar—one of a type of exigences occurring frequently in our experience—or it may be totally new, unique. When it is perceived and when it is strong and important, then it constrains the thought and action of the perceiver who may respond rhetorically if he is in a position to do so.

The second constituent is the *audience*. Since rhetorical discourse produces change by influencing the decision and action of persons who function as mediators of change, it follows that rhetoric always requires an audience—even in those cases when a person engages himself or ideal mind as audience. It is clear also that a rhetorical audience must be distinguished from a body of mere hearers or readers: properly speaking, a rhetorical audience consists only of those persons who are capable of being influenced by discourse and of being mediators of change.

Neither scientific nor poetic discourse requires an audience in the same sense. Indeed, neither requires an audience in order to produce its end; the scientist can produce a discourse expressive or generative of knowledge without engaging another mind, and the poet's creative purpose is accomplished when the work is composed. It is true, of course, that scientists and poets present their works to audiences, but their audiences are not necessarily rhetorical. The scientific audience consists of persons capable of receiving knowledge, and the poetic audience, of persons capable of participating in aesthetic experiences induced by the poetry. But the rhetorical audience must be capable of serving as mediator of the change which the discourse functions to produce.

Besides exigence and audience, every rhetorical situation contains a set of *constraints* made up of persons, events, objects, and relations which are parts of the situation because they have the power to constrain decision and action needed to modify the exigence. Standard sources of constraint include beliefs, attitudes, documents, facts, traditions, images, interests, motives and the like; and when the orator enters the situation, his discourse not only harnesses constraints given by situation but provides additional important constraints—for example his personal character, his logical proofs, and his style. There are two main classes of constraints: (1) those originated or managed by the rhetor and his method (Aristotle called these "artistic proofs"), and (2) those other constraints, in the situation, which may be operative (Aristotle's "inartistic proofs"). Both classes must be divided so as to separate those constraints that are proper from those that are improper.

These three constituents—exigence, audience, constraints—comprise everything relevant in a rhetorical situation. When the orator, invited by situation, enters it and creates and presents discourse, then both he and his speech are additional constituents.

III

I have broadly sketched a conception of rhetorical situation and discussed constituents. The following are general characteristics or features.

1. Rhetorical discourse is called into existence by situation; the situation which the rhetor perceives amounts to an invitation to create and present discourse. The clearest instances of rhetorical speaking and writing are strongly invited—often required. The situation generated by the assassination of President Kennedy was so highly structured and compelling that one could predict with near certainty the types and themes of forthcoming discourse. With the first reports of the assassination, there immediately developed a most urgent need for information; in response, reporters created hundreds of messages. Later as the situation altered, other exigences arose: the fantastic events in Dallas had to be explained; it was necessary to eulogize the dead President; the public needed to be assured that the transfer of government to new hands would be orderly. These messages were not idle performances. The historic situation was so compelling and clear that the responses were created almost out of necessity. The responses—news reports, explanations, eulogies—participated with the situation and positively modified the several exigences. Surely the power of situation is evident when one can predict that such discourse will be uttered. How else explain the phenomenon? One cannot say that the situation is the function of the speaker's intention, for in this case the speaker's intentions were determined by the situation. One cannot say that the rhetorical transaction is simply a response of the speaker to the demands or expectations of an audience, for the expectations of the audience were themselves keyed to a tragic historic fact. Also, we must recognize that there came into existence countless eulogies to John F. Kennedy that never reached a public; they were filed, entered in diaries, or created in thought.

In contrast, imagine a person spending his time writing eulogies of men and women who never existed: his speeches meet no rhetorical situations; they are summoned into existence not by real events, but by his own imagination. They may exhibit formal features which we consider rhetorical—such as ethical and emotional appeals, and stylistic patterns; conceivably one of these fictive eulogies is even persuasive to someone; yet all remain unrhetorical unless, through the oddest of circumstances, one of them by chance should fit a situation. Neither the presence of formal features in the discourse nor persuasive effect in a reader or hearer can be regarded as reliable marks of rhetorical discourse: A speech will be rhetorical when it is a response to the kind of situation which is rhetorical.

2. Although rhetorical situation invites response, it obviously does not invite just any response. Thus the second characteristic of rhetorical situation is that it invites a *fitting* response, a response that fits the situation. Lincoln's Gettysburg Address was a most fitting response to the relevant features of the historic context which invited its existence and gave it rhetorical significance. Imagine for a moment the Gettysburg Address entirely separated from its situation and existing for us independent of any rhetorical context: as a discourse which does not "fit" any rhetorical situation, it becomes either poetry or declamation, without rhetorical significance. In reality, however, the address continues to have profound rhetorical value precisely because some features of the Gettysburg situation persist; and the Gettysburg Address continues to participate with situation and to alter it.

Consider another instance. During one week of the 1964 presidential campaign, three events of national and international significance all but obscured the campaign: Khrushchev was suddenly deposed, China exploded an atomic bomb, and in England the Conservative Party was defeated by Labour. Any student of rhetoric could have given odds that President Johnson, in a major address, would speak to the significance of these events, and he did; his response to the situation generated by the events was fitting. Suppose that the President had treated not these events and their significance but the national budget, or imagine that he had reminisced about his childhood on a Texas farm. The critic of rhetoric would have said rightly, "He missed the mark; his speech did not fit; he did not speak to the pressing issues—the rhetorical situation shaped by the three crucial events of the week demanded a response, and he failed to provide the proper one."

3. If it makes sense to say that situation invites a "fitting" response, then situation must somehow prescribe the response which fits. To say that a rhetorical response fits a situation is to say that it meets the requirements established by the situation. A situation which is strong and clear dictates the purpose, theme, matter, and style of the response. Normally, the inauguration of a President of the United States demands an address which speaks to the nation's purposes, the central national and international problems, the unity of contesting parties; it demands speech style marked by dignity. What is evidenced on this occasion is the power of situation to constrain a fitting response. One might say metaphorically that every situation prescribes its fitting response; the rhetor may or may not read the prescription accurately.

4. The exigence and the complex of persons, objects, events and relations

which generate rhetorical discourse are located in reality, are objective and publicly observable historic facts in the world we experience, are therefore available for scrutiny by an observer or critic who attends to them. To say the situation is objective, publicly observable, and historic means that it is real or genuine—that our critical examination will certify its existence. Real situations are to be distinguished from sophistic ones in which, for example, a contrived exigence is asserted to be real; from spurious situations in which the existence or alleged existence of constituents is the result of error or ignorance; and from fantasy in which exigence, audience, and constraints may all be the imaginary objects of a mind at play.

The rhetorical situation as real is to be distinguished also from a fictive rhetorical situation. The speech of a character in a novel or play may be clearly required by a fictive rhetorical situation—a situation established by the story itself; but the speech is not genuinely rhetorical, even though, considered in itself, it looks exactly like a courtroom address or a senate speech. It is realistic, made so by fictive context. But the situation is not real, not grounded in history; neither the fictive situation nor the discourse generated by it is rhetorical. We should note, however, that the fictive rhetorical discourse within a play or novel may become genuinely rhetorical outside fictive context—if there is a real situation for which the discourse is a rhetorical response. Also, of course, the play or novel itself may be understood as a rhetorical response having poetic form.

5. Rhetorical situations exhibit structures which are simple or complex, and more or less organized. A situation's structure is simple when there are relatively few elements which must be made to interact; the fishing expedition is a case in point—there is a clear and easy relationship among utterances, the audiences, constraints, and exigence. Franklin D. Roosevelt's brief Declaration of War speech is another example: the message exists as a response to one clear exigence perceived by one major audience, and the one overpowering constraint is the necessity of war. On the other hand, the structure of a situation is complex when many elements must be made to interact: practically any presidential political campaign provides numerous complex rhetorical situations.

A situation, whether simple or complex, will be highly structured or loosely structured. It is highly structured when all of its elements are located and readied for the task to be performed. Malinowski's example, the fishing expedition, is a situation which is relatively simple and highly structured; everything is ordered to the task to be performed. The usual courtroom case is a good example of situation which is complex and highly structured. The jury is not a random and scattered audience but a selected and concentrated one; it knows its relation to judge, law, defendant, counsels; it is instructed in what to observe and what to disregard. The judge is located and prepared; he knows exactly his relation to jury, law, counsels, defendant. The counsels know the ultimate object of their case; they know what they must prove; they know the audience and can easily reach it. This situation will be even more highly structured if the issue of the case is sharp, the evidence decisive, and the law clear. On the other hand, consider a complex but loosely structured situation, William Lloyd Garrison preaching abolition from town to town. He is actually looking for an audience and for constraints; even when he finds an audience, he does not know that it is a genuinely rhetorical audience—one able to be mediator of change. Or consider the plight of many contemporary civil rights advocates who, failing to locate compelling constraints and rhetorical audiences, abandon rhetorical discourse in favor of physical action.

Situations may become weakened in structure due to complexity or disconnectedness. A list of causes includes these: (a) a single situation may involve numerous exigences; (b) exigences in the same situation may be incompatible; (c) two or more simultaneous rhetorical situations may compete for our attention, as in some parliamentary debates; (d) at a given moment, persons composing the audience of situation A may also be the audience of situations B, C, and D; (e) the rhetorical audience may be scattered, uneducated regarding its duties and powers, or it may dissipate; (f) constraints may be limited in number and force, and they may be incompatible. This is enough to suggest the sorts of things which weaken the structure of situations.

6. Finally, rhetorical situations come into existence, then either mature or decay or mature and persist—conceivably some persist indefinitely. In any case, situations grow and come to maturity; they evolve to just the time when a rhetorical discourse would be most fitting. In Malinowski's example, there comes a time in the situation when the leader of the fisherman should say, "Throw the nets." In the situation generated by the assassination of the President, there was a time for giving descriptive accounts of the scene in Dallas, later a time for giving eulogies. In a political campaign, there is a time for generating an issue and a time for answering a charge. Every rhetorical situation in principle evolves to a propitious moment for the fitting rhetorical response. After this moment, most situations decay; we all have the experience of creating a rhetorical response when it is too late to make it public.

Some situations, on the other hand, persist; this is why it is possible to have a body of truly *rhetorical* literature. The Gettysburg Address, Burke's Speech to the Electors of Bristol, Socrates' Apology—these are more than historical documents, more than specimens for stylistic or logical analysis. They exist as rhetorical responses *for us* precisely because they speak to situations which persist—which are in some measure universal.

Due to either the nature of things or convention, or both, some situations recur. The courtroom is the locus for several kinds of situations generating the speech of accusation, the speech of defense, the charge to the jury. From day to day, year to year, comparable situations occur, prompting comparable responses; hence rhetorical forms are born and a special vocabulary, grammar, and style are established. This is true also of the situation which invites the inaugural address of a President. The situation recurs and, because we experience situations and the rhetorical responses to them, a form of discourse is not only established but comes to have a power of its own—the tradition itself tends to function as a constraint upon any new response in the form.

I V

In the best of all possible worlds, there would be communication perhaps, but no rhetoric—since exigences would not arise. In our real world, however, rhetorical exigences abound; the world really invites change—change conceived and effected by human agents who quite properly address a mediating audience. The practical justification of rhetoric is analogous to that of scientific inquiry: the world presents objects to be known, puzzles to be resolved, complexities to be understood—hence the practical need for scientific inquiry and discourse; similarly, the world presents imperfections to be modified by means of discourse—hence the practical need for rhetorical investigation and discourse. As a discipline, scientific method is justified philosophically insofar as it provides principles, concepts, and procedures by which we come to know reality; similarly, rhetoric as a discipline is justified philosophically insofar as it provides principles, concepts, and procedures by which we effect valuable changes in reality. Thus rhetoric is distinguished from the mere craft of persuasion which, although it is a legitimate object of scientific investigation, lacks philosophical warrant as a practical discipline.

NOTE

1. "The Problem of Meaning in Primitive Languages," sections III and IV. This essay appears as a supplement in Ogden and Richards' *The Meaning of Meaning.*

William A. Covino

"Rhetoric Is Back: Derrida, Feyerabend, Geertz, and the Lessons of History"

The epistemological crisis of this century—the failure of objectivity, Cartesian rationality, and detachment to account for our complicated perception of a world in flux where matters are never settled—has called into question writing that tries to maintain unity, coherence, perspicuity, and certainty, writing that Edward Said has called "preservative" rather than "investigative" ("The Future of Criticism"). Postmodern critical theory "celebrates" uncertainty, upsetting the generic distinctions that tuck literature, science, and social science away from one another; blurring objectivity and subjectivity, fact and fiction, imagination and reality. As Terry Eagleton demonstrates, what counts as a *literary* test, once one begins taking inventory, just cannot be determined (*Literary Theory* 1–16). All texts being equal, so to speak, any genre—a freshman essay, lyric poem, casual conversation, scientific treatise, lab report—is legitimate game for the critic, and each is potentially rich in "symbolic action."

Just as the definition of a literary text has become a multiple choice, so has the nature of criticism. "The main ideal of criticism," to quote Kenneth Burke's long-standing but curiously postmodern proposition, "is to use all that is there to use" (*Philosophy of Literary Form* 23). Recognizing that no critical determination is either stable or limited, the postmodern critic acknowledges and "plays" with the psychological, cultural, political, epistemological and linguistic variables that enrich and complicate meaning.

In sum, the recent theory and practice of criticism—that is, commentary about a text—has extended both outside traditionally "literary" disciplines and outside the established criterial realm. One practices criticism not by positing "meaning," but by demonstrating the possibilities for multiple perspectives. Thus, postmodern criticism has reinvented the "forgotten" rhetoric that DeQuincey mourns, the art of wondering demonstrated in the specimen texts of Antiquity and continued by the revisionary figures I have presented in this study.

Kenneth Burke is perhaps the first "postmodern" of this century. In 1931 he wrote *Counterstatement* in response to positivistic movements in both science and the arts; there, in his *"Lexicon Rhetoricae,"* Burke proposes that form and meaning in discourse are entirely ambiguous phenomena. The critic's task is the exploitation of that ambiguity; toward that end, as Burke writes later, we need *"terms that clearly reveal the strategic spots at which ambiguities necessarily arise"* (*Grammar* xviii). Burke stands alone, through the New Critical middle of this century, as the great complicator of positivistic and "logocentric" criticism and as a performer of those "inversions, evolutions, and harlequin changes" that "eddy about a truth." With a survey of more recent figures in critical theory, I wish to reinforce the postmodern recognition that texts are "rhetorical," in the richest sense of that term (see Eagleton, *Literary Theory* 205ff, and "A Small History of Rhetoric"). Both more celebrated and infamous than Kenneth Burke, Jacques Derrida reigns as the current proponent of textual indeterminacy.

Derrida recognizes the tendency of all discourse systems to circumscribe thought, noting that the Western practice has been, always and everywhere, to *structure* experience, and "above all to make sure that the organizing principle of the structure would limit what we might call the *play* of the structure."[1] In line with Derrida's proposal, we can regard the dominant mode of communicating literary experience, the critical essay, as one type of limited structure; as Keith Fort argues, "In general, we cannot have attitudes toward reality that cannot be expressed in available forms. If, for example, we can only express our relation to literature in the form of the standard critical essay, we can only have an attitude that would result in the proper form" (174). Derrida believes that resisting enclosure by institutionalized structures requires intellectual play by writers who recognize the limitations of their disco·rse clearly enough to push against them: "In effect, what appears most fascinating in this critical search for a new status of discourse is the stated abandonment of all reference to a *center*, to a *subject*, to a privileged *reference*, to an *origin*, or to an absolute *archia*" (286).

However, complete "decentering," free play equivalent to total anarchy, can never occur, as Derrida explains. All play begins with "the means at hand" and entails to some extent "the necessity of borrowing one's concepts from the text of a heritage" (282–85). By concluding that all play cannot escape "the culture of reference," Derrida counters any misconception of play as solipsistic meandering with his implication that members of a culture can play *together*, able to share new conceptions because they share the received tradition against which the innovator struggles. But Derrida holds little hope for shared play; what prevails are "dreams of deciphering a truth or an origin which escapes play," dreams of achieving certainty. Those who idealize certainty and conviction "turn their eyes away when faced by the as yet unnameable which is proclaiming itself," blind to departures from received ways of knowing and naming (292–93).

The controversy over textual authority has emerged in the philosophy of science, which also opposes the rhetoric of free play to the valorization of truth. Logical positivism and empiricism have been dethroned by both Thomas Kuhn and Paul Feyerabend. Kuhn's position, that scientific progress always results from a "paradigm shift" which discards theories and methods no longer applicable to new problems, has been adapted by historians, sociologists, and educators, among others, as they recognize that what counts as "research" or "discovery" or "progress" in any discipline depends upon the paradigm implicitly espoused by its practitioners. Kuhn has provoked interest in how the virtues and values of any profession are relative, or we might say, rhetorical.

More interesting, more radical, and less well known than Kuhn, Paul Feyerabend disrupts the philosophy of science with the same advocacy of play as methodology that distinguishes Derrida's work. Feyerabend summarizes his argument "Against Method" with the following advice:

> Do not work with stable concepts. Do not eliminate counterinduction. Do not be seduced into thinking that you have at last found the correct description of "the facts" when all that has happened is that some new categories have been adapted to some older forms of thought, which are so familiar that we take their outlines to be the outlines of the world itself. (36)

This advice means to correct the tendency in scientific education to kill the ability of students to think for themselves and make discoveries: "An essential part of the [scientific] training is the inhibition of intuitions that might lead to a blurring of boundaries. A person's religion, for example, or his metaphysics, or his sense of humor must not have the slightest connection with his scientific activity. His imagination is restrained and even his language will cease to be his own" (20). Shackled by a "professional conscience," students and scientists alike proceed by ignoring any variables that upset the uniformity and "objectivity" of their investigation. In uncompromising opposition to a fixed method or fixed theory, whose fixity "arises from too naive a view of man and of his social surroundings," Feyerabend proposes *counterinduction:* "Introducing, elaborating, and propagating hypotheses which are inconsistent either with well-established theories or well-established facts" (26). Explaining that the proliferation of alternative views coincides with a pluralistic society whose people share their unique talents and predispositions, and that such pluralism flourishes only in the absence of constraints, Feyerabend offers a single maxim: "Anything goes" (26).

Feyerabend's professed "anarchistic theory" does not lead to chaos; he deflects the fear that "anything goes" promotes erosion of all community by stressing the essentially constructive nature of play. With repeated references to the "aimless wandering" of young children engaged in intuitive exploration, he notes that the absence of some predetermined goal or purpose makes possible "accidental solutions to unrealized problems" while the investigator pursues unsanctioned lines of research. And he adds that "we need not fear that the diminished concern for law and order in science and society that is entailed by the anarchistic philosophies will lead to chaos. The human nervous system is too well-organized for that" (21). Even the most "unreasonable, nonsensical, unmethodical" play will tend toward a resolution because each of us cannot tolerate a suspended conclusion for very long. Wondering does lead to a determination, whose consequences need not remain strictly private:

> It is possible to *retain* what one might call the freedom of artistic creation *and to use it to the full*, not just as a road of escape, but as a necessary means for dis-

covering and perhaps even changing the properties of the world we live in. For me this coincidence of the part (individual man) with the whole (the world we live in), of the purely subjective and arbitrary with the objective and lawful, is one of the most important arguments in favor of a pluralistic methodology. (27)

But while recognizing the potential usefulness of the determinations we create, we must not resist their undoing: "Whatever we accept we should trust only tentatively, always remembering that we are in possession, at best, of partial truth (or rightness)" (79). Temporary clarity yields to a fresh start.

One's capacity for innovation varies with the "observation language" one chooses; this major point merges Feyerabend's reflections on science with a theory of the origins and uses of discourse in general and highlights Feyerabend's thinking as a rhetorical theory. He insists that the rhetoric of innovation cannot find voice in the normalized lexicon of old ideas: "We are of course obliged to appeal to the existing forms of speech that do not take [counterinductive speculation] into account and which must be distorted, misused, and beaten into new patterns in order to fit unforeseen situations (without a constant misuse of language there cannot be any discovery and any progress)" (25). Both Derrida and Feyerabend admit the danger of thinking with language that embodies rationalistic and positivistic biases and thus delimits what we are capable of observing, feeling, knowing, changing. They also charge that any language, any "style" of investigation, embodies some bias. Such biases are not strictly personal; we carry with us all the cultural and academic and historical baggage that necessarily informs our learning and comprise the context within which we perceive anything. So even deconstructing one's heritage begins with "borrowing" and working with "the means at hand," those very concepts, that very language, one aims to obliterate. Derrida maintains that "no one can escape this necessity" and shares Feyerabend's belief that "experience arises *together* with theoretical assumptions, not before them" (Feyerabend 292; Derrida 93).

A certain security comes from the fact that one always begins within a context of "received" assumptions, the security that every "counterinduction" derives somehow from "the culture of reference," and for this reason the innovator sustains a dialogue as well as a tension with that culture, never cut loose altogether from communal exchange, never isolated in an entirely private subjective world. But also, never capable of "pure" observation, only of seeing things in some measure as others have seen them.

Acknowledging the fraudulence of "neutral" perspectives in social anthropology, Clifford Geertz joins forces with Derrida and Feyerabend as he advocates "thick description," an approach set against the practices of "universalizing" the concept of culture, practices which ignore the "piled up structures of inference and implication" that complicate social life. Seeking to "limit, specify, focus, and contain" the concept of culture, modern anthropology has created a "conceptual morass" of vague definitions that "obscures a good deal more than it reveals." Geertz sets out "in search of meaning" rather than "in search of law," with the assumption that meaningful generalizations come from analyzing a very specific situation on a number of levels.

"Thick description" means "doing ethnography," which means doing what-ever multiplies the available perspectives: "establishing rapport, selecting infor-mants, transcribing texts, taking genealogies, mapping fields, keeping a diary, and so on" (4–5).[2] Ethnographic research views each culture as a context of inter-relationships that can be explicated with the help of heuristic inventories. Del Hymes proposes such an inventory:

> For what has to be inventoried and related in an ethnographic account, a some-what elaborated version of factors identified in communication theory and adapt-ed to linguistics by Roman Jakobson . . . can serve. Briefly put, 1) the various kinds of participants in communicative events—senders and receivers, addressors and addressees, interpreters and spokesmen, and the like; 2) the various available channels and their modes of use: speaking, writing, printing, drumming, blow-ing, whistling, singing, face and body motion as visually perceived, smelling, tast-ing, and tactile sensation; 3) the various codes shared by various participants: lin-guistic, paralinguistic, kinesic, musical, interpretative, interactional, and other; 4) the settings (including other communication) in which communication is permit-ted, enjoined, encouraged, abridged; 5) the forms of messages, and their genres, ranging verbally from single-morpheme sentences to the patterns and diacritics of sonnets, sermons, salesmen's pitches, and any other organized routines and styles; 6) the attitudes and contents that a message may convey and be about; 7) the events themselves, their kinds and characters as wholes—all these must be identified in an adequate way. (Hymes, *Foundations* 10)

The spirit of free play informs the ethnographic process, insofar as ethnogra-phers deliberately resist "the study of abstracted categories" and counter an ossi-fied observation language with a generative one.

Geertz encourages ethnography while also warning that the fullness, or thick-ness, of an ethnographic account does not safeguard its accuracy. Because anthropologists always begin observation with conscious and unconscious assumptions and presuppositions, always detached from the native experience itself, "anthropological writings are themselves interpretations, and second and third order ones to boot" (15). To say that all writing interprets rather than re-presents experience threatens "the objective status of anthropological knowl-edge," as long as we believe that the goal of the process is closure, "discovering the continent of meaning and mapping out its bodiless landscape" (20). But Geertz desires that cultural knowledge become a much more tentative and live-ly enterprise: "guessing at meanings, assessing the guesses, and drawing explanatory conclusions from the better guesses" (20). The resulting science draws its life from intellectual free play, "marked less by a perfection of consen-sus than by refinement of debate. What gets better is the precision with which we vex each other" (29).

With summary attention to Derrida, Feyerabend, and Geertz, I have tried to portray an emergent, interdisciplinary critical theory, fundamentally a theory of discourse that devalues certainty and closure while it celebrates the generative power of the imagination. Kenneth Burke reminds us that the proponents and practitioners of postmodern critical theory, with their acute sense of the relativism and ambiguity of every statement, are our rhetoricians:

> A rhetorician, I take it, is like one voice in a dialogue. Put several such voices together, with each voicing its own special assertion, let them act upon one another in co-operative competition, and you get a dialectic that, properly developed, can lead to the views transcending the limitations of each. ("Rhetoric—Old and New," in Steinmann, *New Rhetorics* 63).

Burke recognizes that rhetoric partakes from and contributes to the many voices of social inquiry and equates rhetoric with "identification," social cohesion that results when a multiplicity of views interact. Intellectual movements that follow Burke's conception of rhetoric validate it; postmodernism leaves the suasory dominion of "truth" for the variegated mind-scape of tentative speculation.

Although pluralism and disdain for positivism are fermenting critical theory, institutionalized communicative efficiency prevails outside the pages of postmodernism, where the appointment book is the primary text, individual achievement and happiness are all, progress is linear, and the universe exists in binary permutations of a silicon chip. It is, or it isn't. In the academy, the numbers and diversity of our students continue to increase, and that diversity is threatened by both the standardization of literacy and competency and the appeal of a marketplace that pays for hard data and speedy conclusions.

My revisions in the history of rhetoric mean to question the prominent virtues informing traditional and conventional attitudes about literacy. In even the most enlightened composition class, a class blown by the winds of change through a "paradigm shift" into a student-centered, process-oriented environment replete with heuristics, sentence combining, workshopping, conferencing, and recursive revising, speculation and exploration remain subordinate to finishing. Certainly, learning to write in such a class may be a richer and more interesting enterprise than before, because "process" has upstaged "product"; pages about prewriting and rewriting now appear in composition textbooks. But while classrooms and textbooks give more time and attention to process (that is, "unfinished" writing), work-in-process does not count as writing, at least not as writing that counts.

What counts, if we survey writing competency exams (which, after all, represent a prevailing definition of rhetoric and writing) is rushing through the beginning, middle, and end of an uncontemplated and patently artificial topic in 30 or 40 minutes. The student writer's movement of mind among ideas, facts, and possibilities is beside the point when representative measures of competency obtain (Covino, "Writing Tests and Creative Fluency").

What counts is ending rather than continuing the discourse. And even in the process-busy classroom, what counts when all the prewriting and revising ends is some type of academic essay, some demonstration of all the virtues of mainstream literacy—unity, coherence, perspicuity, closure, and correctness. Because the academic essay is the end of the composing process, both on exams and in classrooms, and because closing a discourse counts more than the questions and qualifications that keep discourse open, the emphasis our discipline has placed on the composing process over the last dozen years, especially on the plurality of processes available to writers, remains ironic. While writing is identified exclusively with a product and purpose that contain and abbreviate it, writers let the conclusion dictate their tasks and necessarily censor whatever imagined possibilities seem irrelevant or inappropriate; they develop a trained incapacity to speculate and raise questions, to try stylistic and formal alternatives. They become unwilling and unable to fully elaborate the process of composing.

Without minimizing the importance of making up one's mind, or of creating a finished document, and with appreciation for the utility and beauty of cogent prose, I question the overriding preference for a closed form as the token of literacy. And I call for a philosophy of composition that exploits writing as a mode of *avoiding* rather than *intending* closure, a philosophy of composition informed by the lessons of a revisionist history, a philosophy of composition that exploits writing as philosophy.

I have in mind a student writing whose model is Montaigne or Byron or DeQuincey or Kenneth Burke or Tom Wolfe, a student for whom, as Henry Miller says, "there is no progress: there is perpetual movement, displacement, which is circular, spiral, endless" (180). The writing is informed by associational thinking, a repertory of harlequin changes, by the resolution that resolution itself is anathema. This writer writes to see what happens.

I am not suggesting that students should learn to trade clarity for obscurity (a trade that some postmodern writers have been accused of making). I am suggesting that they should trade certainty for ambiguity, trade preservative writing for investigative writing, trade conclusions for "counterinduction." The climate is right for writing teachers to point out that the world is a drama of people and ideas and that writing is how we consistently locate and relocate ourselves in the play.

What writers must maintain is thoughtful uncertainty, the attitude that necessarily informs full exploration and motivates wonder. That attitude is proof against the notion that writing proficiency necessarily involves a "haste to score, to make a quick intellectual killing" (Moffett 140) and, furthermore, proof against the narcissism that may be the most outstanding and disabling epidemic of this decade. As Christopher Lasch points out, the "narcissistic personality of our times" is one for whom creativity is a "success formula" used for self-aggrandizement rather than for enriching one's sense of interdependence (71–103). And Arthur Levine's study of college students concludes that "Today, students are playing to win, take whatever they can get, and then push for more" (50).

Thoughtful uncertainty seems neither profitable nor fashionable. But it is uncertainty that provokes the investigation of possibilities beyond one's stock response; uncertainty necessarily sends us into conversation with other ideas and people. As Kenneth Burke has pointed out through all of his work, the longer we can maintain this conversation and forestall taking a stance, the longer we avoid the conflict, intolerance, and oppression informed by ossified viewpoints.

While the intellectual and political foundations and implications of open discourse are intricate, the way to encourage such discourse in the academy is simple: just make it count. Then, a thick folder of "sustained invention" is more important than a short stack of themes; then, legitimate classroom genres are dialogue and drama, forms that enfranchise the interplay of viewpoints; then, an apparent fact such as "Romeo and Juliet are in love" prompts us to consider whether love, both inside and outside Shakespeare's play and milieu, is really hate, or lust, or greed, or rashness, or empty verbiage, or a kind of murder or suicide, or loyalty, or absolute unselfishness, or the nectar of the gods, or fate. Then, puzzlement and disequilibrium are the elements of rhetoric.

NOTES

1. The particular critical search to which Derrida refers is that of Lévi-Strauss in *The Raw and the Cooked*, whose method Derrida admires and engages in himself, with differences.

All quotations by Derrida are from the seminal presentation of his philosophy, "Structure, Sign, and Play in the Discourse of the Human Sciences."

2. All quotations from Geertz are from "Thick Description" in *The Interpretation of Cultures*; Geertz further elaborates thick description and the postmodern tendency toward "blurred genres" in *Local Knowledge*.

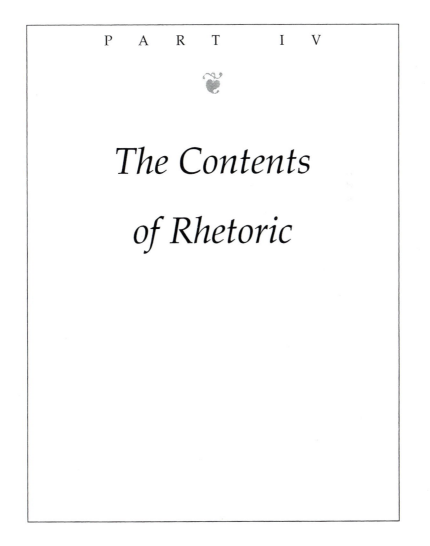

PART IV

The Contents

of Rhetoric

Rhetoric and Cultural Studies

Cultural studies, like *rhetoric*, is a term and a field of study whose definition and parameters are continually debated. Even so, some generally acknowledged features of cultural studies match those of rhetoric. Both lack their own proper content, supplying instead methods of evaluating and explicating facts, materials, and beliefs that comprise traditional content-subjects in the sciences, the social sciences, and the arts and humanities. Both are context- or situation-based, regarding texts or events as indicators of a specific social setting, recognizing that meaning is a sociocultural variable. Both make the study of discourse central, and emphasize that multiple discourses contend with each other in the public realm. Both claim to be epistemic (knowledge-making) enterprises, and both claim to influence action in the world outside of the academic arenas in which they function.

Many in the field of cultural studies in the United States want to follow the lead of the Center for Contemporary Cultural Studies in England, birthplace of cultural studies in the 1960s. They see their work as decidedly political, concerned with examining power relations and intent on intervening in the world. Cary Nelson expresses this position; his manifesto, reprinted in this section, is a reaction against what he sees as the depoliticization of cultural studies. Other cultural studies scholars would maintain a separation between the academic and political realms, and are occupied less with the modification of cultural hegemonies than with constructing a unified, systematic conception of culture that accounts for the production and reception of cultural products. They belong to what Jim Collins calls the "Grand Hotel" school of cultural studies. However, the more common and popular current view sees culture through the metaphor of many buildings variegating the landscape, all vying for prominence.

One area in cultural studies in which the monolithic model contends with the pluralistic model is education, especially with regard to a canon of "great books." Among the readings in this section, Henry Louis Gates's "Integrating the American Mind" and an excerpt from E. D. Hirsch's *Cultural Literacy* represent part of the debate over multicultural education and canon formation, raising questions of how *American* should be defined, what Americans should know, and who should decide. Should we maintain a curriculum that advances a common national identity grounded in traditional masterworks of the Western tradition? Or should we create a curriculum that reflects the racial, ethnic, and gender diversity of the United States, making room for the new voices and representatives of competing discourses? These questions are academic and pedagogical, but ultimately rhetorical and political. They are rhetorical in their focus on the ways in which texts construct and constrain our understanding of our world, and political in their occupation with the relationship of education to democracy.

Studies in the fields of gender and sexuality, national identity, race, ethnicity, mass media, science, history, politics, anthropology, law, economics, and history all feed cultural studies, to the extent that they are indicative of both cultural issues and practices, and of the biases that affect scholarship and its construction of culture. bell hooks's "Culture to Culture: Ethnography and Cultural Studies as Critical Intervention," reprinted here, proposes that studies of African Americans and women are often conducted by white male scholars who end up reinscribing "the old patterns of colonial domination, where the 'Other' is always made object, appropriated, interpreted, taken over by those in power." Her work is related to current postcolonial theory, which advocates the reconsideration of traditional boundaries and oppositions between, for instance, a Third World and a First World.

Cultural studies can be understood as the interdisciplinary study of the full range of signifying practices that constitute cultural life. Put another way, cultural studies is occupied with how knowledge and behavior are inscribed within and among communities, with how culture is written. The emphasis on the relationship of culture to writing leads scholars in the field to recognize that they are making culture by the way in which they describe and define it, and therefore to give attention to the "observation language(s)" they employ. They see themselves as rhetoricians inventing the public discourse of cultural identity, and culture itself as a rhetoric of events that comprises the text of our lives.

FURTHER READING

Berlin, James A. "Poststructuralism, Cultural Studies, and the Composition Classroom: Postmodern Theory in Practice." *Rhetoric Review* 11.1 (1992): 18–33.

Collins, Jim. *Uncommon Cultures: Popular Culture and Post-Modernism.* New York: Routledge, 1989.

Grossberg, Lawrence, Cary Nelson, and Paula A. Treichler, eds. *Cultural Studies.* New York: Routledge, 1992.

Said, Edward. *Orientalism.* New York: Vintage, 1978.

Schilb, John. "The History of Rhetoric and the Rhetoric of History." *PRE/TEXT* 7.1–2 (1986): 11–34.

Spivak, Gayatri. *The Post-Colonial Critic: Interviews, Strategies and Dialogues.* Ed. Sarah Harasym. New York: Routledge, 1990.

Cary Nelson

"Always Already Cultural Studies: Two Conferences and a Manifesto"

... **I** would like to [put forward some generalizations about the cultural studies enterprise] in the form of a series of numbered points, a first draft of one version of a cultural studies manifesto:

1. Cultural studies is not simply the close analysis of objects other than literary texts. Some English departments would like to believe that their transportable methods of close reading can make them cultural studies departments as soon as they expand the range of cultural objects they habitually study. Indeed, cultural studies is usually sold to English departments as part of the manifest destiny of the discipline. Our skills at close reading need to be extended to other cultural domains, it is often argued, lest these domains be left to the dubious care of student subcultures or the imprecise attention of lesser disciplines like speech communication. Similarly, some scholars like the sense of theoretical prestige that an unspecified cultural studies umbrella gives their close readings of nontraditional objects. Indeed, cultural studies often arrives in English departments in the form of an easy alliance between debased textuality and recent theory. But the immanent formal, thematic, or semiotic analysis of films, paintings, songs, romance novels, comic books, or clothing styles does not, in itself, constitute cultural studies. Perhaps that is why one department in 1993 advertised for a cultural studies specialist in "theory and practice"—to avoid being deluged by writing samples consisting of decontextualized readings of films and popular novels. Of course, it is only in America that cultural studies theory and practice are in danger of being severed from one another.

2. Cultural studies does not, as some people believe, require that every project involve the study of artifacts of popular culture. On the other hand, people with ingrained contempt for popular culture can never fully understand the cultural studies project. In part that is because cultural studies has traditionally been deeply concerned with how all cultural production is sustained and determined by (and in turn influences) the broad terrain of popular common sense. Thus, no properly historicized cultural studies can cut itself off from that sense of "the popular."

3. Cultural studies also does not mean that we have to abandon the study of

what have been historically identified as the domains of high culture, although it does challenge us to study them in radically new ways. Because every cultural practice has a degree of relative autonomy, every cultural practice potentially merits attention. But we need to recognize that autonomy is not a function of intrinsic merit and that it is never fixed and never more than relative. The notion of relative autonomy, of course, makes it properly impossible to repeat traditional claims that some cultural production transcends history.

4. Cultural studies is not simply the neutral study of semiotic systems, no matter how mobile and flexible those systems are made to be. There can be a semiotic component to cultural studies, but cultural studies and semiotics are not interchangeable. Cultural studies is not satisfied with mapping sign systems. It is concerned with the struggles over meaning that reshape and define the terrain of culture. It is devoted, among other things, to studying the politics of signification.

5. Cultural studies is committed to studying the production, reception, and varied use of texts, not merely their internal characteristics. This is one of the reasons that cultural studies work is more difficult in periods when the historical record is either fragmentary or highly restrictive in class terms. So long as the difficulties are foregrounded, however, limited but ambitious and important cultural studies projects can be carried out for earlier periods of history.

6. Cultural studies conceives culture relationally. Thus, the analysis of an individual text, discourse, behavior, ritual, style, genre, or subculture does not constitute cultural studies unless the thing analyzed is considered in terms of its competitive, reinforcing, and determining relations with other objects and cultural forces. This task is also, it should be noted, an impossible one to complete in any given instance. But unless the constitutive and dissolving cultural relations are taken as a primary concern, the work is not, properly considered, cultural studies.

This relational understanding of culture was one of cultural studies' earliest defining goals. Yet just what is meant by the relational study of culture has changed and evolved and abruptly shifted throughout the history of cultural studies, from Williams's efforts to describe culture as a whole way of life to the effort by Hall and others to adapt Antonio Gramsci's notion of a war of position to discursive and political analyses of contemporary Britain. One could, in fact, write the history of cultural studies in terms of how it conceives relationality and puts it into practice.

7. Cultural studies is not a fixed, repeatable methodology that can be learned and thereafter applied to any given cultural domain. It is the social and textual history of varying efforts to take up the problematic of the politics and meaning of culture. Its history mixes founding moments with transformative challenges and disputations. To do cultural studies is to take a place within that history.

8. Taking a place within that history means thinking of one's work in relation to cultural studies work on the politics of race. It means taking seriously the way feminism radically transformed cultural studies in the 1980s. And it means positioning one's work in relation to the long, complex, and often contentious history of cultural studies' engagements with Marxism, from Williams to Hall. To

treat that history of engagements with Marxism as irrelevant, as many Americans do, is to abandon cultural studies for a fake practice that merely borrows its name.

9. Cultural studies is concerned with the social and political meaning and effects of its own analyses. It assumes that scholarly writing can and does do meaningful cultural work. To avoid facing this challenge and retreat into academic modesty (asserting that interpretive writing is impotent or irrelevant) or into claims of disinterested scholarship (protesting that political commitments vitiate scholarly objectivity) is to hide from cultural studies' historical mission. A poststructuralist academic liberalism might lead one to argue that, because the political effects of discourse are indeterminate and unpredictable, scholarship and politics are best kept separate. Cultural studies might counter by arguing that such arguments do not free us from responsibility for the political meaning of scholarly work. Cultural studies typically accepts the notion that scholarship entails an engagement with and commitment to one's own historical context. The choice of what scholarly writing to do involves a decision about what one's most effective cultural and political intervention can be.

10. In much the same way, it must be emphasized that cultural studies does not simply offer students a liberal cornucopia of free choices. Cultural studies seeks to empower students to understand the social and political meaning of what they learn throughout the university. It urges them to reflect on the social meaning of disciplinary work and to decide what kinds of projects the culture needs most. A cultural studies pedagogy, thus, encourages a more critical relationship to cultural and political life. One small but necessary implication is that current debates and social practices need to be far more pervasive elements of many more courses than is now the case. Fields like history and literature that often teach pure period courses need to make detailed and specific analogies to present conditions. It is not enough to establish contexts for and relationships between discourses in earlier periods on the assumption that students will make the contemporary connections and work out the contemporary differences on their own. The Taylorized curriculum needs to be thoroughly undermined with the aim of gaining critical purchase on contemporary life.

11. Cultural studies has a responsibility to continue interrogating and reflecting on its own commitments. In fulfilling this task, however, cultural studies has inevitably had a history that is far from perfect. It needs now to critique its investment in what has been called the left's "mantra of race, class, and gender," categories that are properly considered both in relation to one another and to the culture as a whole. It needs as well to question its recent fetishizing of "fandom." A ritualized, unreflective confession of fandom has become almost a requirement in some American cultural studies circles. Being a fan is not a prerequisite for doing cultural analysis. Invoking fandom without describing or specifying its conditions and its cultural construction has little intellectual value. Being a fan gives potential access to important insights; the challenge is to reflect on fandom and articulate what one learns from it.

12. Cultural studies is not required to approve a struggle for dominance

among the disenfranchised. Multiculturalism in America sometimes degenerates into a competitive form of identity politics in which oppressed and marginalized groups work to sort themselves out into a hierarchy based on their record of historical suffering. Cultural studies is not, however, simply a neutral field in which people can give free reign to their inclinations to play identity politics. Cultural studies is properly an enterprise in which people can explore their race, ethnicity, or gender and articulate its relations with the larger culture. A properly relational and historical analysis suggests that no one group can claim the ultimate site of oppression. The progressive alliances we now need require us to avoid using previously marginalized identities to suppress debate and criticism. At the other end of the spectrum, multiculturalism restricts itself to an unrealistic, liberal ideal of diversity and difference without conflict. Cultural studies needs to maintain a critical relation to both these tendencies. Cultural studies may thus establish alliances with multiculturalism but should resist being absorbed by it. Similarly, if multicultural work is to claim a place within cultural studies, it cannot ignore all the innovative work other cultural studies scholars have done on race, gender, and ethnicity.

13. The historicizing impulse in cultural studies is properly in dialogue with an awareness of the contemporary rearticulation of earlier texts, contexts, and social practices. In literary studies, New Historicism may sometimes succumb to an illusion of being able to address only the earlier historical period being analyzed, but cultural studies properly does not. Being historically and politically here and there—then and now—is part of the continuing, and thus necessarily newly theorized, burden of cultural studies. Nothing we rescue from forgetfulness or distortion stays the same. To study the present or the past is inevitably to rearticulate it to current interests; that is a problem and an opportunity to take up consciously, not to repress or regret. Cultural studies can never be a simple program of recovery; properly speaking, such programs are not cultural studies. Indeed, a conservative tendency to categorize every limited project of cultural recovery as cultural studies usually signals a high cultural contempt for the things being recovered. The tendency, for example, to classify efforts to recover minority literatures as cultural studies sometimes reflects an assumption that these literatures are inherently inferior or that they lack the esthetic importance of the traditional canon.

14. In its projects of historical and contemporary analysis, cultural studies is often concerned as well with intervening in the present and with encouraging certain possible futures rather than others. Thus, as cultural studies people reflect on the simultaneously undermined and reinforced status of the nation-state in different parts of the world, they are often also concerned with the future status of nationhood. An interest in how high technology has changed our lives may be combined with an effort to shape its future impact. The opportunities that fragmented postmodern identities offer are not only to be studied, but also to be exploited. A study of the multiple meanings of gender in a given moment may lead to reflection on how our lives may be gendered in the future. For many scholars outside cultural studies, such double investments are to be avoided. In cultural studies they can be at the center of the enterprise.

15. Cultural studies accepts the notion that the work of theorizing its enterprise is inescapably grounded in contemporary life and current polities. New social and political realities require fresh reflection and debate on the cultural studies enterprise, no matter what historical period one is studying. Although it is possible to overstate the phenomenon of a local theorizing grounded in current social realities because such a process involves a rearticulation of previously existing theories, it is nonetheless true that major changes in cultural studies have regularly come from an effort to understand and intervene in new historical conditions. From a cultural studies perspective, then, one never imagines that it is possible to theorize for all times and places. Not only our interpretations but also our theories are produced for the world in which we live.

16. Cultural studies within the academy is inescapably concerned with and critical of the politics of disciplinary knowledge. It is not simply interdisciplinary in the model of liberal diversity and idealized communication. This means that the nontrivial institutionalization of cultural studies within traditional academic disciplines is impossible unless those disciplines dismantle themselves. A first step, for a discipline like English, is to make a commitment to hiring faculty members who do not have degrees from English departments. Otherwise there is little chance that English departments will even admit that literature does not acquire its meaning primarily from its own autonomous traditions, let alone take up the general problematics of culture. Yet while English departments have much to gain from expanding their enterprises to include cultural studies, it is less clear what cultural studies has to gain from being institutionalized in English departments. If it is to be institutionalized at all, cultural studies might be better served by a variety of programs outside traditional departments.

Not every individual cultural studies book or essay can fulfill all the conditions in these sixteen points. But a successful cultural studies project should position itself in relation to these concerns. When it does not take them on directly, they should be implicit in the project's interests, terms, and references. These, it seems to me, represent some of the key aims and imperatives growing out of thirty years of cultural work. These points are effectively part of the cultural studies paradigm and part of the cultural studies challenge to the contemporary world. Because they are focused on the ways cultural studies has and is likely to continue to change and develop, they are less rigid than the form of a numbered manifesto may lead some readers to think. Indeed, to take up these points is to write in such a way as to engage in a continual interrogation of what cultural studies is and can be. Thus, I have articulated this manifesto at a level of theoretical generality that does not totalize and synthesize all cultural studies projects. These principles do not attempt to anticipate the specific work of local theorizing. To place oneself in relation to the history of cultural studies is precisely to recognize that the practices of cultural studies are not given in advance. They are always to be rethought, rearticulated to contemporary conditions. That imperative to continuing political renewal and struggle is part of what cultural studies has bequeathed to us.

bell hooks

"Culture to Culture: Ethnography and Cultural Studies as Critical Intervention"

Through the "talk story" and the telling of aphorisms, Sarah Oldham, my mother's mother, communicated her philosophy of being and living. One of her favorite sayings was "play with a puppy he'll lick you in the mouth." Usually this pronouncement prefaced a long lecture that began with declarations like, "I ain't no puppy, I'm a big dog, that don't like mess." These lectures were intended to emphasize the importan[ce] of distance, of not allowing folks to get close enough "to get up in your face." It was also about the danger of falsely assuming familiarity, about presuming to have knowledge of matters that had not been revealed. Sometimes the lectures were about putting yourself on the same level as someone who was different and then being surprised that they took certain liberties, even, say, that they treated you with contempt. Often these lectures focused on the notion of "difference" and "otherness."

If it happened that white folks were the subject and the talk was about the feasibility of bonding with them across racial boundaries, they were the puppy. I remember these talks often happened after white folks came to visit (usually they wanted something). You have to understand that in the racially segregated South it was unusual for white folks to visit black folks. Most of the white visitors called my grandmama Aunt Sarah, a more dignified version of the word "auntie" used by whites to address black women in slavery, reconstruction, and the apartheid period known as Jim Crow. Baba never called these visitors by their first names irrespective of the number of years that they had been dropping by. Anyhow these white folks would sit in her living room and talk for hours. Some of these conversations led to the making of ties which lasted lifetimes. Though this contact appeared intimate, Baba never forgot slavery, white supremacy, and the experience of Jim Crow. There was never any bond between her and a white person strong enough to counter that memory. In her mind, to be safe one had to "keep a distance."

I remember these lectures as I read new work in literary and cultural studies focusing on race, noting how often contemporary white scholars writing about black people assume positions of familiarity, as though their work were not coming into being in a cultural context of white supremacy, as though it were in no way shaped and informed by that context. And therefore as though no need exists for them to overtly articulate a response to this political reality as part of their critical enterprise. White scholars can write about black culture or black people without fully interrogating their work to see if it employs white western intellectual traditions to re-inscribe white supremacy, to perpetuate racist domination. Within academic and intellectual climates that are striving to respond to the reality of cultural pluralism, there should be room for discussions of racism that promote and encourage critical interrogation. It should be possible for scholars, especially those who are members of groups who dominate, exploit, and oppress others, to explore the political implications of their work without fear or guilt.

Cultural studies has emerged as that contemporary location in the academy that most invites and encourages such analysis. This seems appropriate since much of the new critical work by white scholars and non-white people focusing on issues of "otherness" and "difference" is informed by the recent emphasis on culture and by academic concern with the question of race and post-colonial discourse. Feminist movement played a major role in generating academic focus on these concerns. Significantly, feminist academic and/or intellectual focus on race began with critical contestation about racism, thereby bringing to the academic context a revitalized focus on race as a political issue, assertively linking anti-racist radical politics with scholarly work. This only happened within feminist studies because of the powerful critical intervention of black women/women of color. It must be remembered that black studies programs have explored issues of race and culture from the moment of their inception. To black scholars who are exploring these subjects in programs that are not shrouded in contemporary radical "chic," programs that are definitely not administered by white men, it can be disheartening when new programs focusing on similar issues receive a prestige and acclaim denied black studies. Cultural studies programs are definitely in this category. They are most always administered by white men and are quickly gaining a legitimacy long denied African-American and Third World studies. At some campuses cultural studies programs are seen as potential replacements for black studies and women's studies. By making this observation I in no way want to denigrate cultural studies. It is exciting to have a new arena for the validation and proliferation of inter-disciplinary work. Working and writing, as I do, across disciplines, with English, women's studies, and black studies as starting points for work that is focused on contemporary culture, I am as at "home" in cultural studies as I am in these more familiar locations where issues of difference and otherness have long been a part of the discourse.

Cultural studies is an exciting and compelling addition, as it makes a space for dialogue between intellectuals, critical thinkers, etc., who may in the past have stayed within narrow disciplinary concerns. It calls attention to race and similar issues and gives them renewed academic legitimacy. And it is rapidly becoming one of the few locations in the academy where there is the possibility of inter-racial and cross-cultural discussion. Usually scholars in the academy resist engagement in dialogues with diverse groups where there may be critical contestation, interrogation, and confrontation. Cultural studies can serve as an intervention, making a space for forms of intellectual discourse to emerge that have not been traditionally welcomed in the academy. It cannot achieve this end if it remains solely a privileged "chic" domain where, as Cornel West writes in his essay "Black Culture and Postmodernism," scholars engage in debates which "highlight notions of difference, marginality, and otherness in such a way that it further marginalizes actual people of difference and otherness." When this happens, cultural studies re-inscribes patterns of colonial domination, where the "Other" is always made object, appropriated, interpreted, taken over by those in power, by those who dominate.

Participants in contemporary discussions of culture highlighting difference and otherness who have not interrogated their perspectives, the location from which they write in a culture of domination, can easily make of this potentially radical discipline a new ethnographic terrain, a field of study where old practices are simultaneously critiqued, re-enacted and sustained. In their introduction to the collection of essays *Writing Culture: The Poetics and Politics of Ethnography* editors James Clifford and George Marcus present a critical background against which we can consider work that breaks with the past, to some extent work that redefines ethnography:

> Ethnography is actively situated between powerful systems of meaning. It poses its questions at the boundaries of civilizations, cultures, classes, races, and genders. Ethnography decodes and recodes, telling the grounds of collective order and diversity, inclusion and exclusion. It describes processes of innovation and structuration, and is itself part of these processes. Ethnography is an emergent interdisciplinary phenomenon. Its authority and rhetoric have spread to many fields where "culture" is a newly problematic object of description and critique. . . .

This book includes many compelling essays which break new ground in the field of ethnography. I was particularly excited by the essay by Michael M. J. Fischer, "Ethnicity and the Post-Modern Arts of Memory."

Despite the new and different directions charted in this collection, it was disappointing that black people were still being "talked about," that we remain an absent presence without voice. The editors state at the end of their introduction that "the book gives relatively little attention to new ethnographic possibilities emerging from non-Western experience and from feminist theory and politics." They also give no attention, no "play" as we would say in black vernacular speech, to the anthropologists/ethnographers in the United States who are black, who have either been "indigenous ethnographers" or who entered cultures where they resemble the people they are studying and writing about. Can we believe that no one has considered and/or explored the possibility that the experiences of these non-white scholars may have always been radically different in ways from their white counterparts and that they possibly had experiences which deconstructed much old-school ethnographic practice, perhaps reaching conclusions similar to those being "discovered" by contemporary white scholars writing on the new ethnography? Their voices cannot be heard in this collection. It in no way challenges the assumption that the image/identity of the ethnographer is white and male. The gap that is explained and apologized for in this text is the lack of feminist input.

The construction of the anthology, its presentation, compelled me to think about race, gender, and ethnography. I was drawn again and again to the cover of this book. It is the reproduction of a photograph (Stephen Tyler doing fieldwork in India). One sees in this image a white male sitting at a distance from darker-skinned people, located behind him; he is writing. Initially fascinated by the entire picture, I begin to focus my attention on specific details. Ultimately I fix my attention on the piece of cloth that is attached to the writer's glasses, presumably to block out the sun; it also blocks out a particular field of vision. This "blindspot," artificially created, is a powerful visual metaphor for the ethnographic enterprise as it has been in the past and as it is being rewritten. As a script, this cover does not present any radical challenge to past constructions. It blatantly calls attention to two ideas that are quite fresh in the racist imagination: the notion of the white male as writer/authority, presented in the photograph actively producing, and the idea of the passive brown/black man who is doing nothing, merely looking on.

After I completed this essay I read a similar critique of this photograph by Deborah Gordon in her essay "Writing Culture, Writing Feminism: The Poetics and Politics of Experimental Ethnography." Gordon writes that, "The authority of the white male is present but not unambiguous—it is now watched, and we watch it being watched." Unlike Gordon, I see nothing active or critical about the watcher; if anything he is curiously fascinated, possibly admiring. To simply be an "observer" does not imply the displacement or subversion of the white "authorial presence." The brown male gaze can be read as consensual look of homoerotic bonding and longing, particularly since he is visually separated from family, kin, community, his gaze turned away from them. The photo implies however subtly that this brown man may indeed desire the authorial, "phallocentric power" of the white man. Significantly, we cannot discuss the brown female gaze because her look is veiled by the graphics of the cover; a black line drawn across her face. Why does this cover doubly annihilate the value of brown female gaze, first by the choice of picture where the dark woman is in the shadows, and secondly by a demarcating line? In *Writing Culture* Paul Rabinow's essay "Representations are Social Fact: Modernity and Postmodernity in Anthropology" suggest that the politics of culture, and here he draws on the work of Pierre Bourdieu, "Has taught us to ask in what field of power, and from what position in that field, any given author writes." Added to that might be the question of what politics of representation are enacted by images. Is it possible that an image, a cover can undermine radical writing—can reinscribe the colonizing anthropology/ethnography that is vigilantly critiqued in *Writing Culture?* Describing this image in his introduction, James Clifford writes, "The ethnographer hovers at the edge of the frame—faceless, almost extraterrestrial, a hand that writes." As an onlooker, conscious of the politics of race and imperialism, looking at this frontispiece I am most conscious of the concrete whiteness and maleness. To my gaze it is anything but extraterrestrial.

Another aspect of this cover strikes me as powerful commentary. The face of the brown/black woman is covered up, written over by the graphics which tell readers the title of the book and its authors. Anyone who glances at this cover notes that the most visible body and face, the one that does not have to be searched for, is the white male image. Perhaps to the observer trained in ethnography and anthropology this cover documents a very different history and vision from the one I see. I look at it and I see visual metaphors of colonialism, of domination, of racism. Surely it is important as we attempt to rethink cultural practice, to re-examine and remake ethnography, to create ways to look at and talk about or study diverse cultures and peoples in ways that do not perpetuate exploitation and domination. Starting from such a perspective one would have to consider intentionality and visual impact when choosing a cover like the one I have been discussing. One would need to consider the possibility that people who might never actually read this book might look at the cover and think that it illustrates something about the information inside. Surely the cover as representation has value and meaning that are not subverted when one reads the content. Inside, black/brown people remain in the shadows. When I look at this cover, I want to know who is the audience for this book.

Linking this question to the development of cultural studies, we must also ask: who are the subjects this discipline addresses its discourse and practice. To consider that we write about "culture," for only those of us who are intellectuals, critical thinkers, is a continuation of a hierarchical idea of knowledge that falsifies and maintains structures of domination. In the introduction to *Writing Culture,* the authors explain their exclusion of certain voices in this way, speaking here about feminism:

> Feminism clearly has contributed to anthropological theory. And various feminist ethnographers, like Annette Weimer (1976), are actively rewriting the masculinist canon. But feminist ethnography has focused either on setting the record straight about women or on revising anthropological categories (for example the nature/culture opposition). It has not produced either unconventional forms of writing or a developed reflection on ethnographic textuality as such.

Similar assumptions have been stated about scholarship by black academics of both genders. After making this statement, the authors of *Writing Culture* emphasize the relevance of exploring "the exclusion and inclusion of different experiences in the anthropological archives, the rewriting of established traditions," declaring, "This is where feminist and non-Western writing have made their greatest impact." To many feminists, especially women of color, the current scholarly trend of encouraging radical rethinking of the idea of "difference" has its roots in anti-racist black liberation efforts and resistance struggles globally. Many new trends in cultural studies and ethnography seem to be piggybacking on these efforts.

It is particularly disturbing to read work that is informed and shaped by the intellectual labor of women of color, particularly black women, which erases or de-emphasizes the importance of that contribution. Often this work is subtly devalued by the evocation of conventional academic standards of judgment that deem work that is not written in a particular manner less important. Clifford writes in a footnote to the statement quoted in the last paragraph:

> It may be generally true that groups long excluded from positions of institutional power, like women or people of color, have less concrete freedom to indulge in textual experimentation. To write in an unorthodox way, Paul Rabinow suggests in this volume, one must first have tenure. In specific contexts a preoccupation with self-reflexivity and style may be an index of privileged estheticism. For if one does not have to worry about the exclusion or true representation of one's experience, one is freer to undermine ways of telling, to focus on form over content. But I am uneasy with a general notion that privileged discourse indulges in esthetic or epistemological subtleties whereas marginal discourse "tells it like it is." The reverse is too often the case.

Like Clifford, I am suspicious of any suggestion that marginalized groups lack the freedom and opportunity to engage in textual experimentation.

Marginalized groups may lack the inclination to engage in certain ways of thinking and writing because we learn early that such work may not be recognized or valued. Many of us experiment only to find that such work receives absolutely no attention. Or we are told by gatekeepers, usually white, often male, that it will be better for us to write and think in a more conventional way. A distinction must be made between our freedom to think and write in multiple ways and the choice to write in accepted ways because we want particular rewards. My struggle over form, content, etc., has been informed by a desire to convey knowledge in ways that make it accessible to a wide range of readers. It is not a reflection of a longing to work in ways that will enable me to have institutional power or support. This is simply not the only form of power available to writers and thinkers. There is power in having a public audience for one's work that may not be particularly academic, power that comes from writing in ways that enable people to think critically about everyday life. When I do write in a manner that is experimental, abstract, etc., I find the most resistance to my choosing that style comes from white people who believe it is less "authentic." Their need to control how I and other black people write seems to be linked to the fear that black folks writing in ways that show a preoccupation with self-reflexivity and style is a sign that they no longer "possess" this form of power. Of course work exists by black folks/people of color which indicates a preoccupation with textuality and style. Here the work of academic and writer Nathaniel Mackey comes to mind. Such work may be an index of privileged aestheticism and a reflection of a concrete need to rethink and rewrite the conventional ways of exploring black experience, as well as the desire to re-vision the nature of our resistance struggle. It may very well be that certain efforts at black liberation failed because they were strategies that did not include space for different forms of self-reflexive critique.

One exciting dimension to cultural studies is the critique of essentialist notions of difference. Yet this critique should not become a means to dismiss differences or an excuse for ignoring the authority of experience. It is often evoked in a manner which suggests that all the ways black people think of ourselves as "different" from whites are really essentialist, and therefore without concrete grounding. This way of thinking threatens the very foundations that make resistance to domination possible.

•   •   •

Those cultural studies programs emphasizing post-colonial discourse bring a global perspective that is often sorely lacking in many traditional disciplines. Within the academy, concern with global perspectives and global issues has been a re-vitalizing response to the crisis in western civilization and western thought. It is both ironic and tragic when conservative academic politics lead to the co-optation of these concerns, pitting Third World scholars and African-American scholars against one another. We not only compete for jobs, we compete for recognition. Anyone who has attended a conference on African-American studies recently knows that there are growing numbers of Third World nationals who are, for diverse reasons, engaged in scholarship on African-American culture. They may be non-white, but they may not necessarily have a radical politic or be at all concerned about challenging racial hierarchies. They may choose instead to exploit the privileged location already allotted them in the existing structure. In such situations all the necessary elements exist for the re-enactment of a paradigm of colonial domination where non-western brown/black-skinned folks are placed in positions where they act as intermediaries between the white power structure and indigenous people of color, usually black folks.

These negative dimensions are countered only by the radical political actions of individual professors and their allies. When conservative forces combine to privilege only certain kinds of discourse and particular areas of study, the expansive invitation to engage in multiple discourses from diverse perspectives that is a core concept of cultural studies is threatened. These days when I enter classrooms to teach about people of color and the students present are nearly all white, I recognize this to be a risky situation. I may be serving as a collaborator with a racist structure that is gradually making it much more difficult for students of color, particularly black students, from impoverished and in some cases privileged backgrounds to participate in undergraduate or graduate study. Their absence can be easily ignored when the subjects studied focus on non-whites, just as their absence in the professorial role can be ignored when white professors are addressing issues of difference. In such circumstances I must interrogate my role as educator. Am I teaching white students to become contemporary "interpreters" of black experience? Am I educating the colonizer/oppressor class so that they can better exert control? An East Indian colleague of mine, Anu Needham, says that we can only respond to this circumstance by assuming a radical standpoint and radicalizing these students so that they learn to think critically, so that they do not perpetuate domination, so that they do not support colonialism and imperialism, but do understand the meaning of resistance. This challenge then confronts everyone who participates in cultural studies and in other inter-disciplinary programs like women's studies, black studies, anthropology, etc. If we do not interrogate our motives, the direction of our work, continually, we risk furthering a discourse on difference and otherness that not only marginalizes people of color but actively eliminates the need for our presence.

Similarly, unless progressive scholars actively pushing for further institutionalization of cultural studies remain ever mindful of the way discursive practices and the production of knowledge are easily appropriated by existing systems of domination, cultural studies cannot and will not serve as critical intervention disrupting the academic status quo. Concurrently, as individual critical thinkers, those of us whose work is marginalized, as well as those whose work successfully walks that elusive tightrope with one foot on the radical edge and one foot firmly rooted on acceptable academic ground, must be ever vigilant, guarding against the social technology of control that is ever ready to co-opt any transformative vision and practice.

If the recent international conference Cultural Studies Now and in the Future is any sign of the discipline's direction, it is evident that grave tensions exist between those who would have cultural studies be that discipline which radically questions and transforms the academy and those who would make it (as one concerned white male put it) "the latest hip racism," where every culture and everybody being talked about is "colored" but those doing the talking and writing are white, with few exceptions. Furthermore, it was noted by the same white male participant that "the most extended discussions of African-American culture and politics came from people outside the United States." When individual black scholars made similar public critiques, their words were dismissed as mad ravings. Given the context of white supremacy, we must always interrogate institutional structures which give voice to people of color from other countries while systematically suppressing and/or censoring the radical speech of indigenous folks of color. While black Americans have every political reason to recognize our place in the African diaspora, our solidarity and cultural connections with people of African descent globally, and while we do appreciate cross-cultural exchange, we must not abdicate intellectual responsibility for promoting a cultural studies that will enhance our ability to speak specifically about our culture and gain a hearing. As a radical critical intervention, cultural studies "now and in the future" can be a site of meaningful contestation and constructive confrontation. To achieve this end, it must be committed to a "politics of difference" that recognizes the importance of making space where critical dialogues can take place between individuals who have not traditionally been compelled by politicized intellectual practice to speak with one another. Of course, we must enter this new discursive field recognizing from the onset that our speech will be "troubled," that there exists no ready-made "common language." Drawing from a new ethnography, we are challenged to celebrate the polyphonic nature of critical discourse, to—as it happens in traditional African-American religious experience—hear one another "speak in tongues," bear witness, and patiently wait for revelation.

E. D. Hirsch, Jr.

"The Decline of Teaching Cultural Literacy"

Why have our schools failed to fulfill their fundamental acculturative responsibility? In view of the immense importance of cultural literacy for speaking, listening, reading, and writing, why has the need for a definite, shared body of information been so rarely mentioned in discussions of education? In the educational writings of the past decade, I find almost nothing on this topic, which is not arcane. People who are introduced to the subject quickly understand why oral or written communication requires a lot of shared background knowledge. It's not the difficulty or novelty of the idea that has caused it to receive so little attention.

Let me hazard a guess about one reason for our neglect of the subject. We have ignored cultural literacy in thinking about education—certainly I as a researcher also ignored it until recently—precisely because it was something we have been able to take for granted. We ignore the air we breathe until it is thin or foul. Cultural literacy is the oxygen of social intercourse. Only when we run into cultural illiteracy are we shocked into recognizing the importance of the information that we had unconsciously assumed.

To be sure, a minimal level of information is possessed by any normal person who lives in the United States and speaks elementary English. Almost everybody knows what is meant by *dollar* and that cars must travel on the right-hand side of the road. But this elementary level of information is not sufficient for a modern democracy. It isn't sufficient to allow us to read newspapers (a sin against Jeffersonian democracy), and it isn't sufficient to achieve economic fairness and high productivity. Cultural literacy lies *above* the everyday levels of knowledge that everyone possesses and *below* the expert level known only to specialists. It is that middle ground of cultural knowledge possessed by the *"common reader."* It includes information that we have traditionally expected our children to receive in school, but which they no longer do.

During recent decades Americans have hesitated to make a decision about the specific knowledge that children need to learn in school. Our elementary schools are not only dominated by the content-neutral ideas of Rousseau and Dewey, they are also governed by approximately sixteen thousand independent school districts. We have viewed this dispersion of educational authority as an insurmountable obstacle to altering the fragmentation of the school curriculum even when we have questioned that fragmentation. We have permitted school policies that have shrunk the body of information that Americans share, and these policies have caused our national literacy to decline.

At the same time we have searched with some eagerness for causes such as television that lie outside the schools. But we should direct our attention undeviatingly toward what the schools teach rather than toward family structure, social class, or TV programming. No doubt, reforms outside the schools are important, but they are harder to accomplish. Moreover, we have accumulated a great deal of evidence that faulty policy in the schools is the chief cause of deficient literacy. Researchers who have studied the factors influencing educational outcomes have found that the school curriculum is the most important controllable influence on what our children know and don't know about our literate culture.

It will not do to blame television for the state of our literacy. Television watching does reduce reading and often encroaches on homework. Much of it is admittedly the intellectual equivalent of junk food. But in some respects, such as its use of standard written English, television watching is acculturative. Moreover, as Herbert Walberg points out, the schools themselves must be held partly responsible for excessive television watching, because they have not firmly insisted that students complete significant amounts of homework, an obvious way to increase time spent on reading and writing. Nor should our schools be excused by an appeal to the effects of the decline of the family or the vicious circle of poverty, important as these factors are. Schools have, or should have, children for six or seven hours a day, five days a week, nine months a year, for thirteen years or more. To assert that they are powerless to make a significant impact on what their students learn would be to make a claim about American education that few parents, teachers, or students would find it easy to accept.

Just how fragmented the American public school curriculum has become is described in *The Shopping Mall High School,* a report on five years of firsthand study inside public and private secondary schools. The authors report that our high schools offer courses of so many kinds that "the word 'curriculum' does not do justice to this astonishing variety." The offerings include not only academic courses of great diversity, but also courses in sports and hobbies and a "services curriculum" addressing emotional or social problems. All these courses are deemed "educationally valid" and carry course credit. Moreover, among academic offerings are numerous versions of each subject, corresponding to different levels of student interest and ability. Needless to say, the material covered in these "content area" courses is highly varied.

Cafeteria-style education, combined with the unwillingness of our schools to place demands on students, has resulted in a steady diminishment of commonly shared information between generations and between young people themselves. Those who graduate from the same school have often studied different subjects, and those who graduate from different schools have often studied different material even when their courses have carried the same titles. The inevitable consequence of the shopping mall high school is a lack of shared knowledge across and within schools. It would be hard to invent a more effective recipe for cultural fragmentation.

The formalistic educational theory behind the shopping mall school (the theory that any suitable content will inculcate reading, writing, and thinking skills) has had certain political advantages for school administrators. It has allowed them to stay scrupulously neutral with regard to content. Educational formalism enables them to regard the indiscriminate variety of school offerings as a positive virtue, on the grounds that such variety can accommodate the different interests and abilities of different students. Educational formalism has also conveniently allowed school administrators to meet objections to the traditional literate materials that used to be taught in the schools. Objectors have said that traditional materials are class-bound, white, Anglo-Saxon, and Protestant, not to mention racist, sexist, and excessively Western. Our schools have tried to offer enough diversity to meet these objections from liberals and enough Shakespeare to satisfy conservatives. Caught between ideological parties, the schools have been attracted irresistibly to a quantitative and formal approach to curriculum making rather than one based on sound judgments about what should be taught.

Some have objected that teaching the traditional literate culture means teaching conservative material. Orlando Patterson answered that objection when he pointed out that mainstream culture is not the province of any single social group and is constantly changing by assimilating new elements and expelling old ones. Although mainstream culture is tied to the written word and may therefore seem more formal and elitist than other elements of culture, that is an illusion. Literate culture is the most democratic culture in our land: it excludes nobody; it cuts across generations and social groups and classes; it is not usually one's first culture, but it should be everyone's second, existing as it does beyond the narrow spheres of family, neighborhood, and region.

As the universal second culture, literate culture has become the common currency for social and economic exchange in our democracy, and the only available ticket to full citizenship. Getting one's membership card is not tied to class or race. Membership is automatic if one learns the background information and the linguistic conventions that are needed to read, write, and speak effectively. Although everyone is literate in some local, regional, or ethnic culture, the connection between mainstream culture and the national written language justifies calling mainstream culture *the* basic culture of the nation.

The claim that universal cultural literacy would have the effect of preserving the political and social status quo is paradoxical because in fact the traditional forms of literate culture are precisely the most effective instruments for political and social change. All political discourse at the national level must use the stable forms of the national language and its associated culture. Take the example of *The Black Panther*, a radical and revolutionary newspaper if ever this country had one. Yet the *Panther* was highly conservative in its language and cultural assumptions, as it had to be in order to communicate effectively. What could be more radical in sentiment but more conservative in language and assumed knowledge than the following passages from that paper?

The present period reveals the criminal growth of bourgeois democracy since the betrayal of those who died that this nation might live "free and indivisible." It exposes through the trial of the Chicago Seven, and its law and order edicts, its desperate turn toward the establishment of a police state. (January 17, 1970)

In this land of "milk and honey," the "almighty dollar" rules supreme and is being upheld by the faithful troops who move without question in the name of "law and order." Only in this garden of hypocrisy and inequality can a murderer not be considered a murderer—only here can innocent people be charged with a crime and be taken to court with the confessed criminal testifying against them. Incredible? (March 28, 1970)

In the United States, the world's most technologically advanced country, one million youths from 12 to 17 years of age are illiterate—unable to read as well as the average fourth grader, says a new government report. Why so much illiteracy in a land of so much knowledge? The answer is because there is racism. Blacks and other Nonwhites receive the worst education. (May 18, 1974)

The last item of the Black Panther Party platform, issued March 29, 1972, begins

10. WE WANT LAND, BREAD, HOUSING, EDUCATION, CLOTHING, JUSTICE, PEACE AND PEOPLE'S CONTROL OF MODERN TECHNOLOGY.
When in the course of human events it becomes necessary for one people to dissolve the political bands which have connected them with another, and to assume among the powers of the earth the separate and equal station to which the laws of nature and nature's God entitle them, a decent respect to the opinions of mankind requires that they should declare the causes which impel them to the separation.

And so on for the first five hundred of Jefferson's words without the least hint, or need of one, that this is a verbatim repetition of an earlier revolutionary declaration. The writers for *The Black Panther* had clearly received a rigorous traditional education in American history, in the Declaration of Independence, the Pledge of Allegiance to the Flag, the Gettysburg Address, and the Bible, to mention only some of the direct quotations and allusions in these passages. They also received rigorous traditional instruction in reading, writing, and spelling. I have not found a single misspelled word in the many pages of radical sentiment I have examined in that newspaper. Radicalism in politics, but conservatism in literate knowledge and spelling: to be a conservative in the *means* of communication is the road to effectiveness in modern life, in whatever direction one wishes to be effective.

To withhold traditional culture from the school curriculum, and therefore from students, in the name of progressive ideas is in fact an unprogressive action that helps preserve the political and economic status quo. Middle-class children acquire mainstream literate culture by daily encounters with other literate persons. But less privileged children are denied consistent interchanges with literate persons and fail to receive this information in school. The most straightforward antidote to their deprivation is to make the essential information more readily available inside the schools.

Providing our children with traditional information by no means indoctrinates them in a conservative point of view. Conservatives who wish to preserve traditional values will find that these are not necessarily inculcated by a traditional education, which can in fact be subversive of the status quo. As a child of eleven, I turned against the conservative views of my family and the Southern community in which I grew up, precisely because I had been given a traditional education and was therefore literate enough to read Gunnar Myrdal's *An American Dilemma*, an epoch-making book in my life.

Although teaching children national mainstream culture doesn't mean forcing them to accept its values uncritically, it does enable them to understand those values in order to predict the typical attitudes of other Americans. The writers for *The Black Panther* clearly understood this when they quoted the Declaration of Independence. George Washington, for instance, is a name in our received culture that we associate with the truthfulness of the hero of the story of the cherry tree. Americans should be taught that value association, whether or not they believe the story. Far from accepting the cherry-tree tale or its implications, Oscar Wilde in "The Decay of Lying" used it ironically, in a way that is probably funnier to Americans than to the British audience he was addressing.

> [Truth telling is] vulgarizing mankind. The crude commercialism of America, its materializing spirit, its indifference to the poetical side of things, and its lack of imagination and of high unattainable ideals, are entirely due to that country having adopted for its national hero a man who, according to his own confession, was incapable of telling a lie, and it is not too much to say that the story of George Washington and the cherry tree has done more harm, and in a shorter space of time, than any other moral tale in the whole of literature. . . . And the amusing part of the whole thing is that the story of the cherry tree is an absolute myth.

For us no less than for Wilde, the values affirmed in traditional literate culture can serve a whole spectrum of value attitudes. Unquestionably, decisions about techniques of conveying traditions to our children are among the most sensitive and important decisions of a pluralistic nation. But the complex problem of how to teach values in American schools mustn't distract attention from our fundamental duty to teach shared content.

The failure of our schools to create a literate society is sometimes excused on the grounds that the schools have been asked to do too much. They are asked, for example, to pay due regard to the demands of both local and national acculturation. They are asked to teach not only American history but also state and city history, driving, cardiopulmonary resuscitation, consumerism, carpentry, cooking, and other special subjects. They are given the task of teaching information that is sometimes too rudimentary and sometimes too specialized. If the schools did not undertake this instruction, much of the information so provided would no doubt go unlearned. In some of our national moods we would like the schools to teach everything, but they cannot. There is a pressing need for clarity about our educational priorities.

As an example of the priorities we need to set, consider the teaching of local history in the Commonwealth of Virginia. Suppose Virginians had to choose between learning about its native son Jeb Stuart and Abraham Lincoln. The example is arbitrary, but since choices have to be made in education, we might consider the two names emblematic of the kind of priority decision that has to be made. Educational policy always involves choices between degrees of worthiness.

The concept of cultural literacy helps us to make such decisions because it places a higher value on national than on local information. We want to make our children competent to communicate with Americans throughout the land. Therefore, if Virginians did have to decide between Stuart and Lincoln they ought to favor the man from Illinois over the one from Virginia. All literate Americans know traditional information about Abraham Lincoln but relatively few know about Jeb Stuart. To become literate it's therefore more important to know about Lincoln than about Stuart. The priority has nothing to do with inherent merit, only with the accidents of culture. Stuart certainly had more merit than Benedict Arnold did, but Arnold also should be given educational priority over Stuart. Why? Because Benedict Arnold is as much a part of our national language as is, say, Judas.

To describe Benedict Arnold and Abraham Lincoln as belonging to the national language discloses another way of conceiving cultural literacy—as a vocabulary that we are able to use throughout the land because we share associations with others in our society. A universally shared national vocabulary is analogous to a universal currency like the dollar. Of course the vocabulary consists of more than just words. *Benedict Arnold* is part of national cultural literacy; *eggs Benedict* isn't.

Henry Louis Gates, Jr.

"Integrating the American Mind"

When I'm asked to talk about the opening of the American mind, or the decentering of the humanities, or the new multiculturalism—or any number of such putative "developments"—I have to say my reaction is pretty much Mahatma Gandhi's when they asked him what he thought about Western civilization. He said he thought it would be a very good idea. My sentiments exactly.

This decade has, to be sure, witnessed an interesting coupling of trends. On the one hand, we've seen calls from on high to reclaim a legacy, to fend off the barbarians at the gates and return to some prelapsarian state of grace. On the other hand (or is it the same hand?), we've seen a disturbing recrudescence of campus racism sweeping the nation. Many of you will have seen the articles about this in the recent media, as the topic has been in the news for quite some time. For people who agitated in the civil rights era and saw real gains in the college curriculum in the 1970s, the new conservatism seems to have succeeded their own efforts rather as the Redemption politicians followed the Reconstruction, threatening to undo what progress had been made.

One thing is clear. Education in a democratic society (or in one that aspires to that ideal) has particular burdens placed upon it: few theorists of American education, in this century or the preceding one, have separated pedagogy from the needs of citizenship. The usual term, here, is often given a sinister intonation: *social reproduction*. Yet this country has always had an evolutionary view of what reproduction entails: we've never been content with more replication, we've sought improvement. We want our kids to be better than we are.

So it's discouraging, even painful, to look about our colleges, bastions of liberal education, and find that people are now beginning to talk—and with justice, it seems—about the "new racism." I don't want to offer a simple diagnosis, but perhaps the phenomenon isn't completely unconnected to larger political trends. It's been pointed out that today's freshmen were ten years old when the Reagan era began; presumably the public discourse of the 1980s had something to do with the forming of political sensibilities.

But whatever the causes, the climate on campus has been worsening: according to one monitoring group, racial incidents have been reported at over 175 colleges since the 1986–87 school year. And that's just counting the cases that made the papers.

At the same time, there's been, since 1977, a marked decline in overall black enrollment in colleges. The evidence suggests the decline is connected to a slipping economic situation, and to cuts in available federal aid. In the decade since 1977, federal grants and scholarships have fallen 62 percent, and that, of course, disproportionately affects minority students. Almost half of all black children (46.7 percent) live under the poverty line, according to the Congressional Research Service. Indeed, if you look at students at traditionally black colleges, you find that 42 percent of them come from families with income below the poverty line; a third of these students come from families with a total family income less than $6,000 a year. So when it comes to larger economic trends, blacks are like the canaries in the coal mine: the first to go when things are going wrong.

But there's an even bigger problem than getting these students, and that's keeping them. The attrition rate is depressing. At Berkeley, one in four black students will graduate. The fact is, according to the National Center of Education Statistics, that of freshmen blacks in 1980, only 31 percent had graduated by 1986. And while financial pressures explain some of it, they don't explain all of it.

Down the educational pike, things get worse. Just 4.0 percent of our full-time college professors are black, and the number is said to be decreasing. In 1986, only 820 of the 32,000 Ph.D.'s awarded went to blacks; less than half those 820 planned a college career (that's 0.015 percent of our new Ph.D.'s).

In short, it's a bad situation. But it's not a conspiracy; nobody wants it to be the way it is. In general, our colleges really are devoted to diversity: people are genuinely upset when they fail to incorporate diversity among their students and faculty. I said before that the peculiar charge of our education system is the shaping of a democratic polity. It's a reflection of the public consensus on this matter that one of the few bipartisan issues in the last presidential campaign had to do with equitable access to higher education. Pollsters on both sides found that this was an issue that made the American heart skip a beat. Equal opportunity in education is an idea with very broad appeal in this country. And that has something to do with what education means to us. So one thing I want to bring out is that the schools are a site where real contradictions and ambivalences are played out.

I would like to think about institutions for higher learning in terms of the larger objectives of what we call a liberal education; as unfashionable as it is among many of my fellow theorists, I do believe in the humanities, very broadly conceived. But it's that breadth of conception I want to address. We hear the complaints. Allan Bloom, for example, laments that "just at the moment when everyone else has become 'a person,' blacks have become blacks." (Needless to say, "everyone else" can become a person precisely when the category *person* comes to be defined in contradistinction to *black*.) Many thoughtful educators are dismayed, even bewildered, when minority students—at Berkeley or Stanford or Texas or Oberlin, the sentiment's widespread—say that they feel like visitors, like guests, like foreign or colonized citizens in relation to a traditional canon that fails to represent their cultural identities. I'm not interested in simply endorsing that sentiment; it's not a reasoned argument, this reaction, but it is a playing out—a logical extension—of an ideology resident in the traditional rhetoric about Western civilization. And I want to consider it in that light.

Once upon a time, there was a race of men who could claim all of knowledge as their purview. Someone like Francis Bacon really did try to organize all of knowledge into a single capacious but coherent structure. And even into the nineteenth century, the creed of universal knowledge—*mathesis universalis*—still reigned. There's a wonderful piece of nineteenth-century student doggerel about Jowett, the Victorian classicist and master of Balliol College, Oxford, which rather sums up the philosophy:

Here stand I, my name is Jowett,
If there's knowledge, then I know it;
I am the master of this college,
What I know not, is not knowledge.

The question this raises for us, of course, is: How does something get to count as knowledge? Intellectuals, Gramsci famously observes, can be defined as experts in legitimation. And the academy, today, is an institution of legitimation—establishing what counts as knowledge, what counts as culture. In the most spirited attacks on the movement toward multiculturalism in the academy today, there's a whiff of this: We are the masters of this college—What we know not, is not knowledge. So that in the wake of Bacon's epistemic megalomania, there's been a contrary movement, a constriction of what counts as even worth knowing. We've got our culture, what more do we need? Besides, there was Heidegger on stage right, assuring us that "philosophy speaks Greek." And beyond the cartography of Western culture? A cryptic warning: Here Be Monsters.

I got mine: The rhetoric of liberal education remains suffused with the imagery of possession, patrimony, legacy, lineage, inheritance—call it cultural geneticism (in the broadest sense of that term). At the same moment, the rhetoric of possession and lineage subsists upon, and perpetuates, a division: between us and them, we the heirs of *our* tradition, and you, the Others, whose difference defines our identity. (In the French colonies, in Africa and the Caribbean, a classroom of African students would dutifully read from their textbook, "Our ancestors, the Gauls ..." Well, you could see that wasn't going to last.)

What happens, though, if you buy into that rhetoric—if you accept its terms and presuppositions about cultural geneticism? Then you will say: Yes, I am Other, and if the aim of education is to reinforce an individual's rightful cultural legacy, then I don't belong here—I am a guest at someone else's banquet. Foucault called this kind of contestation that of "reverse discourse": it remains entrapped within the presuppositions of the discourse it means to oppose, enacts a conflict internal to that "master discourse"; but when the terms of argument have already been defined, it may look like the only form of contestation possible.

One of the most eloquent reflections on this sense of entrapment is James Baldwin's, where the rhetoric of dispossession turns to that of cultural reappropriation:

I know, in any case, that the most crucial time in my own development came when I was forced to recognize that I was a kind of bastard of the West; when I followed the line of my past I did not find myself in Europe but in Africa. And this meant that in some subtle way, in a really profound way, I brought to Shakespeare, Bach, Rembrandt, to the stones of Paris, to the cathedral at Chartres, and to the Empire State Building, *a special attitude*. These were not really my reactions, they did not contain my history; I might search in them in vain forever for any reflection of myself. I was an interloper; this was not my heritage. At the same time, I had no other heritage which I could possibly hope to use—I had certainly been unfitted for the jungle or the tribe. I would have to appropriate these white centuries, I would have to make them mine—I would have to accept my special attitude, my special place in this scheme—otherwise I would have no place in any scheme.

(This terror of having no place in any scheme contrasts oddly with the more familiar modernist anxiety of the Western writer, the anxiety that one fits into a scheme all too easily, all too well.)

If Richard Wright's comments are characteristically blunter, they are no less anxious: "I'm black. I'm a man of the West. . . . I see and understand the non- or anti-Western point of view." But, Wright confesses, "when I look out upon the vast stretches of this earth inhabited by brown, black and yellow men . . . my reactions and attitudes are those of the West" (*White Man, Listen!*). Wright never had clearer insight into himself; but his ambivalent relation to both the Western and non-Western cultures was satisfactorily resolved. So long as we retain a vocabulary of heritage and inheritance in defining our putative national cultures, it cannot *be* resolved.

This suggests (if I may invoke the relevant stereotypes) that the old fogey and the Young Turk have a lot more in common than they realize; that they may, in fact, be two sides of the same debased coin; and that those of us who really care about humane learning should convert to another currency.

The argument has been made that cultural nationalism has been a constitutive aspect of Western education. As humanists, our challenge today is, simply, to learn to live without it. Indeed, it saddens me that there should be any perceived conflict between the ideal of humanistic learning and what I think of as the truly human, and humane, version of the humanities, one that sees the West not as some mythical, integrative whole, but as a part of a still larger whole. In the resonant words of W.E.B. Du Bois:

> I sit with Shakespeare, and he winces not. Across the color line I move arm in arm with Balzac and Dumas, where smiling men and welcoming women glide in gilded halls. From out the caves of evening that swing between the strong-limbed earth and the tracery of the stars, I summon Aristotle and Aurelius and what soul I will, and they come all graciously with no scorn nor condescension. So, wed with Truth, I dwell above the Veil. Is this the life you grudge us, O knightly America? Is this the life you long to change into the dull red hideousness of Georgia? Are you so afraid lest peering from this high Pisgah, between Philistine and Amalekite, we sight the Promised Land?

Which is then to say, I believe we can change the terms of argument; I believe we can rethink the role of a liberal education without the conceptual residue of cultural nationalism or geneticism. I believe it, because I do think many scholars have already begun to do so.

• • •

Well, Americans know so very little about world history and culture in part because high school and college core curricula, in this country, center upon European and American societies, with America represented as the logical conclusion or summary of civilization since the Greeks, in the same way that Christians believe that Christ is the culmination of the Old Testament prophesies. Our ignorance of physical geography is a symptom of a much broader ignorance of the world's cultural geography. Since the trivium and quadrivium of the Latin Middle Ages, "the humanities" has *not* meant the best that has been thought by all human beings; rather, "the humanities" has meant the best that has been thought by white males in the Greco-Roman, Judeo-Christian traditions. A tyrannical pun obtains between the words *humanity,* on the one hand, and *humanities,* on the other.

We need to reform our entire notion of core curricula to account for the comparable eloquence of the African, the Asian, the Latin American, and the Middle Eastern traditions, to prepare our students for their roles in the twenty-first century as citizens of a world culture, educated through a truly human notion of the humanities.

Now, I talked earlier about the long-dead ideal of universal knowledge. Today, you look back to C. P. Snow's complaint about the gulf between the "two cultures," and you think, *two?* Keep counting, C. P. The familiar buzz words here are the "fragmentation of humanistic knowledge." And there are people who think that the decentering of the humanities that I advocate just makes a bad situation worse: Bring on the Ivory Towers of Babel. So I want to say a few words about this.

There are, certainly, different kinds of fragmentation. One kind of fragmentation is just the inevitable result of the knowledge explosion; specialized fields produce specialized knowledge, and there's too much to keep up with. But there's another kind of fragmentation which does deserve scrutiny: the ways in which knowledge produced in one discipline setting is inaccessible to scholars in another discipline, even when it would be useful to them in solving their problems. And here, what I call the decentering of the humanities can help us rethink some of the ways traditional subjects are constituted and can allow us a critical purchase helpful in cultural studies quite generally. Indeed, far from being inimical to traditional Western scholarship, humanistic scholarship in Asian and African cultures can be mutually enriching to it, to the humanities in general.

• • •

But I do want to emphasize that a true decentering of the humanities can't be just a matter of new content in old forms. We have to get away from the paradigm of disciplinary essentialism: imagining the boundaries of disciplines as hermetic, imagining our architectures of knowledge as natural or organic. Granted, sometimes conversation is neither possible nor productive. But we don't need a lazy sort of Platonism that can pretend to "cut nature at the joints"—sustaining the illusion only as long as we don't inquire too closely about the peculiar institutional history of our own particular discipline.

I've suggested that moving toward this human notion of the humanities moves us away from the divisive us/them implications of traditional defenses of the humanities and removes a source of cultural alienation that is clearly breeding disenchantment and disillusionment among those to whom the experience of higher education may matter the most. But I also think—and here my Whiggish triumphalism is revealed—that it's the natural conclusion of scholarly enlightenment, in which ethnocentric presuppositions have fallen under scholarly critique—autocritique—and been found wanting. We need, for instance, to rethink the whole notion of comparative literature. The most influential and innovative programs in comparative literature have usually embraced just three languages—Latin, French, German—and one other. I look forward to truly comparative programs of comparative literature that embrace the languages and literatures of Yoruba, Urdu, or Arabic as well as the traditional European literatures. I think we should design a required Humanities Course that's truly humanistic—with the Western segment comprising a quarter or a third—in addition to the traditional Western Civ course, so that students can begin to understand the histories of civilization itself, in a truly comparative manner. Such an embracive posture honors the best, the noblest traditions and ambitions of the academy. And while I've decried cultural nationalism, I hope you'll permit me to bow to it in citing something Ishmael Reed has said on the subject of multiculturalism. He said it's possible here "because the United States is unique in the world: *the world is here.*"

Or listen to a great canonical author, Herman Melville, writing a century earlier: "There is something in the contemplation of the mode in which America has been settled, that, in a noble breast, should forever extinguish the prejudices of national dislikes. Settled by the people of all nations, all nations may claim her for their own. You can not spill a drop of American blood, without spilling the blood of the whole world. . . . We are not a narrow tribe, no: our blood is as the flood of the Amazon, made up of a thousand noble currents, all pouring into one. We are not a nation, so much as a world."

• • •

I respect what Robert Nisbet calls the Academic Dogma: knowledge for its own sake (I suspect it doesn't quite exist; but that's another matter). At the same time, I believe that truly humane learning can't help but expand the constricted boundaries of human sympathy, of social tolerance. Maybe the truest thing to be said about racism is that it represents a profound failure of imagination. I've talked a good deal about cultural pluralism as a good in itself, as the natural shape of scholarship untrammeled by narrow ethnocentrism. And the best ethnic studies departments have made a real contribution to this ideal of scholarly diversity. As I said, I respect the ideal of the disinterested pursuit of knowledge, however unattainable, and I don't think classes should be converted into consciousness-raising sessions, Lord knows; at the same time, anyone who's not a positivist realizes that "moral education" is a pleonasm: in the humanities, facts and values don't exist in neatly disjunct regimes of knowledge. Allan Bloom is right to ask about the effect of higher education on our kids' moral development, even though that's probably the only thing he is right about.

Amy Gutmann said something important in her recent book *Democratic Education:* "In a democracy, political disagreement is not something that we should generally seek to avoid. Political controversies over our educational problems are a particularly important source of social progress because they have the potential for educating so many citizens." I think that's true; I think a lot of us feel that any clamor or conflict over the curriculum is just a bad thing in itself, that it somehow undermines the legitimacy of the institutions of knowledge—a sort of no-news-is-good-news attitude on the subject of education; they think if you even look at a university crosseyed, it'll dry up and blow away and then where will you be? In contrast, I think one of the most renewing activities we can do is to rethink the institutions where we teach people to think; we invest in myths of continuity, but universities have constantly been molting and creating themselves anew for the last millennium, and there's no reason to think that'll change in the next. Gerald Graff has been saying, where there's no consensus—and there's no consensus—teach the conflicts. In fact, I think at the better colleges, we do. We don't seem to be able not to. And that's nothing to be embarrassed about: College isn't kindergarten, and our job isn't to present a seemly, dignified, unified front to the students. College students are too old to *form*—we shouldn't delude ourselves—but they're not too old to challenge. I'm reminded of something that the college president and educator Robert Maynard Hutchins wrote, in a book he published during the height of the McCarthy era. He recounted a conversation he'd had with a distinguished doctor about the attempt of the Board of Regents of the University of California to extort (as Hutchins put it) "an illegal and unconstitutional oath of loyalty from the faculty of that great institution." "Yes, but" the doctor said, "if we are going to hire these people to look after our children we are entitled to know what their opinions are." And Hutchins grandly remarked, "I think it is clear that the collapse of liberal education in the United States is related as cause or effect or both to the notion that professors are people who are hired to look after children." Wise words, those.

In all events, the sort of pluralism I've been recommending has one evolutionary advantage over its opponents. If you ask, How do we form a consensus around such a "de-centering" proposal? the answer is that it doesn't exactly require a consensus. Which is why, in the words of John Dewey, "pluralism is the greatest philosophical idea of our times." Not that this puts us home free. As Dewey also said,

What philosophers have got to do is to work out a fresh analysis of the relations between the one and the many. Our shrinking world presents that issue today in a thousand different forms. . . . How are we going to make the most of the new values we set on variety, difference, and individuality—how are we going to realize their possibilities in every field, and at the same time not sacrifice that plurality to the cooperation we need so much? How can we bring things together as we must without losing sight of plurality?

Learning without center is not learning without focus. We've all seen undigested eclecticism posing as a bold new synthesis; but to read and write culture anew means additional demands for rigor and coherence, not emancipation from these things. I take Dewey's question seriously, but there's nothing vaporous about the form the answer takes: it is made of brick and mortar, and sometimes a little ivy about the architrave. For us—scholars and teachers—it is the university, whose constant refashioning is our charge, burden, and privilege.

Rhetoric and
Non-Western Culture

Western philosophers have for centuries been interested in the systems of thinking represented by classic literature of East Asian people, and this century has witnessed a growing awareness of these traditions in anthropology, linguistics, and sociology. In recent decades, as American universities have responded to the challenges posed by an increasingly multicultural student population, the attendant need to communicate effectively across disciplines as well as across geographical and cultural boundaries has helped to redefine conceptions of rhetoric, literacy, and language. The field of rhetoric has responded to the changing face of the academy by examining the discursive practices of non-Western civilizations, and found a wealth of textual material from countries such as China and India.

Chinese and Indian rhetoric may seem at first glance to be somewhat elusive for students more familiar with Plato, Aristotle, and Cicero. Perhaps one reason for this is the fact that classical Asian writers characteristically have not named their books and treatises that treat rhetoric with terms bearing obvious rhetorical concerns. While ancient Western writings on rhetoric have used various forms of *rhetoric, oratory, discourse,* and so on, in their titles and chapter headings, many of the most important treatments of these subjects by Asian writers tend to occur within the framework of larger philosophical subjects.

Even when rhetoric is defined narrowly as the principles of verbal persuasion, we should note that Han Fei Tzu's third-century BCE essays "On the Difficulties of Speaking" and "Difficulties in the Way of Persuasion," among others, do address many of the same concerns that occupied Western contemporaries. In his essay "The Eight Villainies," Han lists "Making use of fluent speakers" as one of eight strategies that political advisers "customarily employ to work their villainy" (Watson 43):

> The ruler, because of the nature of his upbringing, has usually been cut off from ordinary conversation, and has seldom had an opportunity to listen to debates, and he is accordingly apt to be particularly susceptible to persuasive speaking. The ministers therefore search about for rhetoricians from other states or patronize the most able speakers in their own state, and employ them to plead their special cause. With clever and elegant phrases, fluent and compelling

words, such men draw the ruler on with prospects of gain, terrify him with predictions of hazard, and completely overwhelm him with their empty preachments. This is what I mean by making use of fluent speakers.

This excerpt, taken together with Han's other writings, entails a thoroughgoing theory of rhetoric not unlike those developing in ancient Greece.

In India, centuries before Han's time, Gautama Buddha espoused the beginnings of a rhetorical theory. Living and teaching in the same century as China's Confucius, Persia's Zarathustra, and Greece's Aeschylus and Pericles, Gautama Buddha comes to us through the records of dialogue and anecdote handed down by his disciples. One such record tells of the attempt of Gautama's opponents to deceive him into saying something that would discredit his own teaching, and is notable for the Buddha's categorization of kinds of speeches that should or should not be spoken:

> Even so, prince, speech that the Tagatha [a title for the Buddha meaning One Who Has Attained Perfection] knows to be untrue, false, and useless, and also unpleasant and disagreeable to others, he does not speak; that which he knows to be true, real, and useful, but also unpleasant and disagreeable to others, in that case he knows the right time to express it. Speech that he knows to be untrue, false, and useless, and also pleasant and agreeable to others, he does not speak; that which is true, real, but useless, and also pleasant and agreeable to others, that, too, he does not speak; but that which is true, real, and useful, and also pleasant and agreeable to others, in that case he knows the right time to express it.

Effectiveness of and accountability for speech was a frequent theme in Gautama Buddha's teachings. A speech should be "true, real, and useful," and should take into account the emotions of the audience as well as the appropriateness of the delivery's timing. We can see in this passage and others the beginnings of a Buddhist rhetorical theory.

In the interests of promoting a global understanding of rhetorical theory, the following selection of readings introduces texts from China and India to the canon of rhetoric. Selections from Robert Oliver's informative *Communication and Culture in Ancient China and India* sketches some preliminary concepts. These are followed by passages from the *Tao Te Ching*, called the "one book in the whole of Oriental literature which one should read above all others" by China's foremost literary statesman, Lin Yutang. The *Tao Te Ching* is traditionally attributed to the fifth-century BCE figure Lao-tzu, but in all likelihood it was edited by later followers of Taoism, perhaps in China's Warring States period (403–221 BCE). These excerpts are accompanied by Kristopher Kowal's discussion of rhetorical concepts in the *Tao Te Ching*. Han Fei Tzu's classic essay "The Difficulties of Persuasion" (written sometime in the third century BCE) follows without commentary. Angus C. Graham's discussion of the Chinese Sophists, or Dialecticians, introduces Chad Hansen's translation of and commentary on Kung-sun Lung's well-known "White Horse Paradox," also dating from the third century BCE.

FURTHER READING

Graham, Angus. *Studies in Chinese Philosophy and Philosophical Literature.* Albany: SUNY P, 1990.

Hansen, Chad. *A Taoist History of Chinese Philosophy.* New York: Oxford UP, 1992.

Henricks, Robert G. *Philosophy and Argumentation in Third-Century China: The Essays of Hsi K'ang.* Princeton: Princeton UP, 1983.

Lin Yutang. *The Wisdom of India and China.* New York: Random House, 1942.

Rhys Davids, T. W., and C.A.F. Rhys Davids, trans. and eds. *Dialogues of the Buddha.* London: Luzac, 1910, 1951.

Rosemont, Henry, Jr., ed. *Chinese Texts and Philosophical Contexts.* La Salle, IL: Open Court, 1991.

Robert T. Oliver

"Culture and Rhetoric"

THE CULTURAL ORIENTATION OF COMMUNICATION

Neither India nor China has ever had a public platform comparable with that of America or of those European nations inclined toward democracy. Until very recently political debate in the whole area from Bombay to Peking was confined largely to court circles. There were no political parties, no election campaigns, no contending candidates arguing their issues before voters. Their courtrooms offered none of the inducements found in the West to affect judicial decisions through eloquent pleading. Although evangelism was prominent in some Eastern religions, their temples of worship contained no pulpits in which weekly sermons were delivered. Their education did not feature what the West would consider to be lectures, though it encouraged student discussions. Despite the prominence of lecturing in early India and the Chinese penchant for talk, Eastern communities developed nothing comparable to the lyceum, the chautauquas, or the commercial lecture bureaus of the Western world.

Eastern legislative bodies debated public policies only in a strictly confined format, for carefully limited purposes. They called no conventions to draw up constitutions or to nominate candidates for public office through processes of discussion and debate. Their colleges had no debating societies; nor did their businessmen organize luncheon clubs in which to listen to speeches. Even on ceremonial occasions they made little use of such set orations of praise or blame, attack or defense, as made the eloquence of classical Athens a marvel of the Western world. There was none of the debating of civic issues that was among the highest literary achievements of Cicero's Rome. There was none of the dialectical preaching that sharpened the wits of schoolmen and ecclesiastics in medieval and renaissance Europe. Nor even in modern times has skill in speech—in public forums, at conference tables, and in the persuasion of salesmen—had in the East anything like the currency attained in the West.

Despite this catalog of negative statements, it should not be presumed that the populations of India and China dwelt for centuries in stultified silence. For them no less than for the peoples of the West, their ability to symbolize and to communicate was the cardinal aspect of their humanity. It is a commonplace of sociological doctrine that "man as a social being exists in and through communication; communication is as basic to man's nature as food and sex."

This is a sweeping judgment, and one that inevitably directs attention to the manner in which people communicate, if their culture is to be understood. What communication means to them—how important it is, how it is conducted, who the nominated speakers are, and to what groups they find it desirable to speak—these are questions not of incidental but of paramount importance for the study of any society.

Once this approach is undertaken, it must be accepted as a totally inclusive way of viewing the social scene. It is as though a photograph of the society were to be taken from a communicative stance. Everything will be considered from the perspective of communicative intentions and effects. As Margaret Mead, a dean among cultural anthropologists, has testified: "the whole mesh of human social life might logically, and perhaps, in other contexts, fruitfully, be treated as a system of human communication."

The confident acceptance of communication—and most explicitly of spoken or oral communication, with its face-to-face directness—as the essential factor in the study of the "languagized mammal" and of the kind of society which a particular set of people evolves is well nigh universal among philosophers, political scientists, humanists, and even the fabled man in the street. Perhaps nowhere has it been better stated than by Thomas Mann, in the magnificent sixth chapter of his *Magic Mountain,* where he wistfully attests that "Speech is civilization itself. The word, even the most contradictory word, preserves contact—it is silence which isolates."

It is inconceivable that oral discourse should be in the West "that web of signals and expectations and understandings that makes living together possible," and also "in its private manifestations, within the single mind, a controlling factor in personality," and that, at the same time, it should lack a comparable importance in the East. If "civilization itself might well be called that state of being in which communication is achieved," the highly civilized societies of India and China cannot have been mute. On the contrary, the key to understanding the Asian mind and Asian civilization is their *manner of talk: how they addressed one another and why, under what circumstances, on what topics, in what varied styles, with what intent, and with what effects.*

This is the key to the inquiry that comprises this book: an attempt to depict the manner of talk in ancient India and China. The method is through exploration of the communication theories implicit in the philosophical classics of their peoples and expressed in the life style of their societies. Since rhetoric inheres in the philosophy and way of life of its practitioners, it is necessary to examine the premises which underlie Oriental thought and feeling, as well as (a strange concept to Western minds) their non-thought and non-feelings. As guidelines for the inquiry, the following questions are always dominant: How have Asians conceived the problems of communication? What significance have they attached to barriers which impede it? By what means and in what contexts have they considered such questions? What sorts of communication systems—

nonverbal as well as verbal—have they conceived? What theories and practices have they fostered? How have they institutionalized communication beyond the boundaries of talk?

In conducting this inquiry, primary attention is focused upon oral communication in all its forms: person-to-person conversation, as well as in the more formal situations of public address. There must also be serious consideration of the Asian recognition of the varied communicative functions of silence. Meanwhile, secondary and incidental consideration of written discourse is occasionally inevitable, for considerable segments of rhetoric apply without significant discrimination to speech and writing.

Should we attempt to conceptualize the nature of rhetoric and of public discourse in Asia in terms that have proved appropriate in the West, the results would be biased, inadequate, and misleading. The East is not the West. Cultures differ, and minds, feelings, and intentions in differing societies intermesh in differing ways. Discourse occurs, or is constrained, under different circumstances and has different styles for different reasons. The standards of rhetoric in the West which have had a unitary development since their identification by Aristotle are not universals. They are expressions of Western culture, applicable within the context of Western cultural values.

The premise that rhetoric is culturally based is the vantage point from which this exposition of ancient Indian and Chinese rhetorics is undertaken. Any attempt to discover in Asia prototypes of the Western rhetorical canons would be unavailing. It would resemble trying to measure the salinity of water with a ruler.

Orientals have long understood how cultural differences stamp themselves not only upon but also within human personality, dividing mankind into groups that in significant ways differ from one another. The point is emphasized in an old Chinese fable about a monkey and a fish that were caught in a devastating river flood. Luckily, the monkey was able to grasp an overhanging bough and pull himself to safety. Then, seeing the fish still tossed in the raging waters, the monkey generously reached down and pulled it up beside him in the tree. But the fish was not grateful. What is good for one kind is not necessarily good for another. "Like a fish out of water" is a saying that has relevance even to the varied provinces of rhetoric.

How different a strange culture may be was well described by a Korean student reporting his feelings upon arriving in New York:

> To be a New Yorker among New Yorkers means a totally new experience from being Japanese or Chinese or Korean—a changed character. New Yorkers all seem to have some aim in every movement they make. (Some frantic aim.) They are like guns shooting off. How unlike Asiatics in an Oriental village, who drift up and down aimlessly and leisurely. But these people have no time, even for gossiping, even for staring. To be thrown among New Yorkers—yes, it means to have a new interpretation of life never conceived before. The business interpretation. Even the man who only goes to a show and is making arrangements about it, has a business air. His every action is decisive, orderly, pur-

poseful. . . . he must know exactly what he wants to do in his mind. . . . His mind is like Grand Central Station. It is definite, it is timed, it has mathematical precision on clearcut stone foundations.

A perceptive American diplomat, on his first mission to Tokyo at the opening of the twentieth century, found that "everywhere about lay a mystery that either lured or irritated, but one felt it and could not escape. The Japanese themselves, the islands in which they lived, their customs and their language seemed so utterly unlike anything ever imagined that they either absorbed the stranger in an attempt to understand, or he rejected it as impossible to understand."

Decades earlier, a scholarly Chinese, seeing white men in his country for the first time, found them quite incredible. "These 'Ocean Men,' as they are called," he reported, "are tall beasts with deep sunken eyes and beaklike noses. The lower part of their faces, the backs of their hands, and, I understand, their entire bodies are covered with a mat of curly hair, much as are the monkeys of the southern forests. But the strangest part about them is that, although undoubtedly men, they seem to possess none of the mental faculties of men. The most bestial of peasants is far more human, although these Ocean Men go from place to place with the self-reliance of a man of scholarship and are in some respects exceedingly clever. It is quite possible that they are susceptible to training and could with patience be taught the modes of conduct proper to a human being."

The significance of these attestations is clear: every society has its own culture—its own ways of thinking, behaving, and believing. And it is a truism of cultural anthropology that there is universal belief in the superiority of one's own culture. There is everywhere a lack of sympathetic comprehension of the unlike. What is *strange* is, to use the word the Greeks applied to it, *barbaric*. *Exotic* is psychologically if not semantically a synonym for *eccentric*. Ruth of the Old Testament is regarded as being of unique virtue because she could say to Naomi: "Your ways will be my ways, your people my people." Each person bears within himself the imprint of his own society—its values, its fears, its prejudices, its mannerisms. Every culture "is a body of ready-made solutions to the problems encountered by the group . . . that gives to the people who participate in it a certain style of life that is peculiarly their own."

What happens when we try to understand a set of meanings in another culture is, to use a word coined by Gregory Bateson, *schizmogenetic*, meaning, in effect, that one difference creates another. Strangeness begets strangeness. When foreigners confront one another across cultural barriers, the strange behavior that each notices causes him to alter his own behavior. He adjusts his manner of speaking and acting; concurrently he also adjusts his ways of interpreting what he sees and hears. Where ideally there ought to be a drawing together, there is instead a pulling apart. A socio-psychological chasm develops that is not readily bridged; indeed, clumsy efforts to bridge it result rather in its being pushed further apart.

The difficulties to be encountered in this attempt to discover, depict, and evaluate the rhetorics of ancient India and China are apparent. Every culture constitutes a unique value system. Any attempt to see inside a culture from the outside must be carefully guarded, with the difficulties understood. Indians and Chinese cannot be expected to think or to communicate as do Americans. They react to different stimuli in different ways. Their goals are not the same, nor are their ways of trying to achieve them.

To escape utter confusion, it is essential that the fact of the differences and the reasons for them be recognized. If the great thought systems of Asia—Hinduism, Buddhism, Confucianism, Taoism—are not quite religions (according to Judeo-Christian standards) or quite philosophy (according to Platonic or Kantian expectancies), the impulse to reject them should be replaced with a desire to discover what alternatives they do present. If their historic-sovereignty systems do not correspond with our Western concept of nationalism, we should be glad to explore with them the system of relations which they have used to make their societies cohesive. If instead of democracy we find them exalting propriety, and along with justice they acclaim decorum, we may at least pause to inquire the reasons for their choices of emphasis. If our technological forwardness keeps us aware of the "social lag" in adapting men to machines, perhaps we may be just as interested in the Asian "science lag," which for many centuries kept them more interested in mastery of social relations than in the mastery of nature.

The necessity of accepting differences not as barriers to understanding but as invitations to inquiry, and even to new modes or channels of investigation, is especially pertinent for a study of ancient Asian rhetoric. If their occasions for speech and their methods of speaking did not conform to ours, the reasons no doubt lay in the differing cultural patterns of their societies and of ours. If their rhetoric was not like ours, it is because they, like us, derived the principles of effective discourse from observation of what appears to have been required and what seems to have worked in situations being observed. The situations East and West were different; so were the rhetorics. This is why such an inquiry as we are undertaking is long overdue.

RHETORICS EAST AND WEST

A widely accepted encapsulated definition of rhetoric is "the function of adjusting ideas to people and people to ideas." It should be added: and also of adjusting people to people. The function of rhetoric is not, like dialectic, to examine a given subject in order accurately to depict its nature. Nor is rhetoric, like logic, designed to discover and demonstrate inevitable conclusions about a subject. The province of rhetoric, as Aristotle pointed out, is the realm of probabilities. We do not argue about that which is certain or ascertainable; we try to persuade concerning propositions which have alternative acceptable conclusions.

It follows that eloquence, the fruit of rhetoric, whether it be suasive or informative, is devoted to influencing the behavior of men concerning the matters of choice by which they are confronted. Rhetoric is the consideration of means by which eloquence is or may be rendered effective in influencing the reactions of listeners (or of readers). Whatever might be adduced to influence the unfettered actions of men is the proper inquiry of the rhetorician. The answers to be found depend on the personalities of the speakers and listeners and on the nature of their society. The *kinds of ideas* that interest or move people and the *reasons why they accept or reject them* are not universals; they are particular attributes of specific cultures.

Accordingly rhetoric may be universal in (and only in) the sense that "philosophy" or "religion" are universals. There is a genre of rhetoric, just as there is a genre of philosophy. But precisely as there are distinct philosophical systems and distinct religions, so, too, are there distinct rhetorics, each an integral part of its own culture, its own society.

Although there was a long tradition of quasi-rhetorical thought in the Mediterranean basin prior to the Periclean Age, the foundation of Western rhetoric is properly found in the writings of Plato and Aristotle. Plato's most definitive statement about the nature of rhetoric is to be found in his *Phaedrus*, where he represents Socrates as saying:

> The conditions to be fulfilled are these. First, you must know the truth about the subject that you speak or write about; that is to say, you must be able to isolate it in definition, and having so defined it you must understand how to divide it into kinds, until you reach the limit of division; secondly, you must have a corresponding discernment of the nature of the soul, discover the type of speech appropriate to each nature, and order and arrange your discourse accordingly, addressing a variegated soul in a variegated style that ranges over the whole gamut of tones, and a simple soul in a simple style. All this must be done if you are to become competent, within human limits, as a scientific practitioner of speech, whether you propose to expound or persuade.

This Platonic definition has been confidently asserted to encompass "all discourse which influences men." Rather, it was specifically designed for the civilization that provided its context. Plato's injunction to "discover the type of speech appropriate to each nature" is indeed a rhetorical universal. But his insistence upon "knowing the truth about the subject," and thence proceeding to "isolate it in definition" and "to divide it into kinds" is based upon a particular view of the nature of truth and a particular concept of psychology.

According to Aristotle, the effectiveness of a speaker is limited by two factors which lie outside his control. The first is that truth and justice are realities; in the long run he cannot deny them, and in immediate circumstances it is his duty to uphold them. The second factor is human nature, both his own and as represented in the audience the speaker will address. In Aristotle's view, man is potentially or basically rational but tends to be governed by emotions. Hence, the speaker often finds it convenient to appeal to emotions, even though he or his listeners will ultimately insist upon determination of the issue by rational considerations. Meanwhile, the speaker finds that his listeners interpret the case he is presenting to them in terms of their conception of his character, personality, and reputation—or, to use the Greek term, his *ethos*.

Thus, in every circumstance the speaker is confronted by a threefold task. He must try to accomplish what he himself most desires, what the facts of the matter prescribe, and what the audience wishes or at least will accept. Such a tripartite rhetoric is basic in European and Anglo-American civilization. It has evolved for a society in which honest inquiry will lead to debate, by means of which propositions of fact and of policy may ultimately be decided by decision of the majority—or by those able to control the opinions of the majority. Truth and justice triumph when they are adequately championed. But "minds warped by emotion" (Aristotle's phrase) will accept whatever probability is made to appear most appealing to them. Obviously such a rhetoric evolved to serve a particular kind of man in a particular kind of society, rather than mankind in general. It was oriented to the culture of Athens and has served those peoples whose societies developed in the Hellenic tradition.

The conditions described here were not found in ancient times in either India or China. An Indian would not have reasoned from the same premises as a European, nor would his thinking have followed the same processes. Nor would a Chinese of the period have resembled either an Indian or a European. Each culture had different topical priorities; each used its own value system as its chosen standard of judgment. Not only in India were there "sacred cows" and "untouchables." In China as well, even as in Europe and America, there were compulsive prejudices and unreasonable dislikes. And as motivational patterns adhered in each culture in special ways, so too did rhetorical systems flourish to serve these differing needs.

One striking difference that is highly relevant to our inquiry is in the kinds of attitudes toward rhetoric. In Euro-American literature rhetorics occupy a considerable space. From the outpouring of writings on rhetoric, it would appear that the West has been intoxicated with eloquence and the means of attaining it. In sharp and dramatic contrast, the bibliographies of Indian and Chinese writings are virtually bare of tractates on rhetoric. Everything published bearing directly on the subject in ancient India and China could be comprised in a slim anthology.

This does not mean that the inhabitants of ancient India and China did comparatively little speaking; nor does it mean that they neglected to theorize about the nature, means, and effects of discourse. On the contrary, as will become evident, in all the extensive populations subject to Indian and Chinese influences, speaking, discussing, arguing, and elucidating have been exceedingly important activities. They have dealt with these matters, however, in a way that was peculiarly their own, very different from the tradition that developed in the West.

In ancient India and China, in contrast to what happened in Athens and Rome, speculation about how truth and justice should be determined, interpreted, and rendered appealing to listeners was not considered to be separable from general religious, social, and political philosophy. It is a striking fact that Aristotle wrote separate treatises on *Ethics, Politics, Poetics, Logic,* and *Rhetoric.* However interrelated he may have thought them to be, he believed nevertheless that they could and should be treated separately. This was strictly in accordance with his and Plato's emphasis upon definition and classification as essential tools for dealing with the nature of truth.

To state the matter most simply, in the West rhetoric has been considered to be so important that it has had to be explored and delineated separately, as a special field of knowledge about human relations. In the East, rhetoric has been considered so important that it could not be separated from the remainder of human knowledge. Asian thinkers have consistently seen rhetoric as being inseparably interconnected with problems of ethics, psychology, politics, and social relations. Basic rhetorical considerations underlie much of the classical literature of the Eastern hemisphere. There are many reasons for this which will emerge in following chapters. Perhaps most basic of all is the cardinal devotion of the Asian mind to the related concepts of unity and harmony. In this view all things properly belong together and should coexist. Consequently, the ancient East has not been much interested in logic, which necessarily correlates unlike elements, nor has it favored either definition or classification as aids to clear thought. Indeed, clarity of thought itself has been far less favored in traditional literature of India and China than it has been in the West. Whereas the West has favored analysis and division of subject matter into identifiable and separate entities, the East has believed that to see truth steadily one must see it whole. If the outlines and the distinctions are dimmed, this possible loss is counterbalanced by the gain of viewing the object in its interrelated entirety. Hence, rhetoric, like philosophy and religion, penetrates all Eastern thinking and writing. The problem is not to find the rhetoric of the East but to find ways of identifying and depicting it in a fashion that will make it meaningful to Western minds without thereby denying its essentially holistic character.

Basic to both Hindu and Buddhist conceptions of reality is the mystery of the symbolic process. Moreover, even from its legendary beginnings Chinese civilization stressed communicative speaking as the principal means by which the actions of men might be harmonized.

It was Tzu-Ssu, the grandson of Confucius, who said that words are like colored glass: they obscure all that they do not clarify. The sentiment is often encountered in both Indian and Chinese cultures. The relationship between *what is* and *what appears* was as intriguing to thinkers of the ancient East as it has been in the West. In the East, as in the West, there has been much speculation about why some try to represent and some to misrepresent the nature of reality, and about the means by which both types of communicators do or may or should present their interpretations in order to make them effective. All the great Oriental philosophers—including Gautama and the anonymous authors of Hinduism, Confucius, Mencius, Hsüntze, Han Fei-Tzu, Mo-Tze, Lao-Tzu, and Chuang-Tzu—have also been rhetoricians. For in Asia rhetoric has been too important to be severed from its religio-philosophical context.

FOCAL POINTS IN ASIAN RHETORIC

Instead of attempting to discover in Asia judgments which may be compared or contrasted with Western pronouncements concerning the major classical canons of rhetoric, it is more fruitful to attempt to assess the rhetorical theories of Asia in their own terms—to go with them wherever they may take us, regardless of whether this may be close to or far from the kinds of rhetoric with which Westerners are familiar. When this method is followed, the following focal points of Asian rhetoric may be discerned.

First, the primary function of discourse is not to enhance the welfare of the individual speaker or listener but to promote harmony. In China the goal generally was a harmonious society, in India a harmonious relationship of the individuals with the course of nature—which, as we have seen, was also the goal of the Chinese Taoists. One effect of this view of the function of discourse was to depersonalize it. Emphasis was removed from the specific individual purposes of speakers and listeners and was placed, instead, upon their participation in the common lot of mankind. Another effect was to magnify both the importance and the seriousness of discourse. Its generalized function was of far too great significance to permit it to be undertaken lightly or conducted carelessly.

Second, rather than encouraging individuality of style or of method, the traditions in both India and China stressed the value of adhering strictly to patterns of expectation. Originality was discounted. Effectiveness was achieved primarily by identification of the speaker with accepted tradition. This principle affected both what was said and the manner of saying it. Speakers who wished to have a favorable effect took care to stress that what they presented was not their own idea but was derived directly from ancient authority. And they took equal care to make it clear that they were phrasing and presenting their message in a mode that was precisely prescribed. Listeners were no less constrained than were speakers to behave in a manner that was predetermined by custom. The dynamic vitality of change and progress was thereby exchanged for social stability and dependability. Individuals were taught to look not for ways by which they could manipulate circumstances for their own best interests but how they could accommodate themselves to situations with the least possible disturbance of them.

Third, discourse which aimed toward social harmony rather than at the specific wellbeing of the participants, and which somewhat ritualistically adhered to approved patterns, naturally tended to avoid argumentation and persuasive fervor. The characteristic mode was exposition. What the West has generally designated as a search for common ground between speaker and listener was in ancient Asia the natural and virtually the universal method of conducting a discussion.

Fourth, both in India and in China the very insistence of the societies upon restrained and ceremonial discourse resulted upon occasion in wild bursts of quarrelsomeness. In India particularly these outbursts often resembled the temper tantrums of children. But their purpose was expressive rather than communicative. The free vent of the emotions simply emphasized the fact that generally they were decorously controlled. And in China, more particularly than in India, the quarreling was subject to well-understood and observed rules that gave even to the quarrels the appearance of a well-rehearsed drama.

Fifth, more specifically than in the West, the Asians (and especially the ancient Chinese) emphasized the dual and reciprocal responsibility of speakers and listeners. This emphasis was a natural result of their point of view that discourse should properly aim not toward accomplishment of personal desires of the particular participants in a discussion but toward the general advantages of society as a whole. Listeners were advised not only to be attentive but to bring to the problem of interpretation of the speaker's meaning all their resources of knowledge and of critical judgment. Since individuals are liable to err, speakers might through ignorance, lack of skill, or selfishness fail to further the welfare of the community, just as listeners, through careless inattention, prejudice, or selfwill, might fail to interpret what was said in terms of the general needs of society. Each must be alert to compensate for the possible incapacity of the other.

Sixth, the principal sources of proof on which judgment should be based were authority and analogy. Speakers took care to represent ideas as being not their own but an authoritative derivation from ancient precepts or practice. Further support was sought through the use of analogies, which had the twin functions of clarifying the speaker's viewpoint while, at the same time, appealing through comparison to the everyday experience and observation of the listener. Authority and analogy were used almost to the exclusion of both formal logic and citation of specific evidence or supporting facts. The Indians did develop a complicated system of pseudo-logic, which rested basically upon intuitive insight and the Chinese did employ a "chain of reasoning" which was in effect an appeal to commonsense observation. But in both cultures what was finally persuasive was appeal to established authority, buttressed by analogical reasoning which sought to clarify the unfamiliar through comparison with the familiar.

Seventh, in contrast to the West, Asians were inclined to believe that an individual could more truly be judged in terms of what he said than what he did. Actions, they felt, could be manipulated for hypocritical effect; but speech is sensitively revelatory of character, for two reasons: first, because the words, the accents, and the gestures form a complicated pattern so responsive to the inner impulses of the speaker that they cannot successfully camouflage his actual sentiments; and second, because the speech establishes a record to which the individual subsequently may be held. Hence, whereas in the West warning often is given to look behind and beyond the words to see how the speaker actually behaves, in ancient Asia the counsel was, rather, to look beyond the behavior to see what the individual was saying and to note how he said it. Speech, they felt, most shows the man. It was the criterion of character to which they were most continually alert.

Eighth, another focal point of Asian rhetoric is the value which it attached to silence. In Western society, silence is awkward and embarrassing. When a conversation is broken by a lengthy pause, the suspicion is that the participants have nothing to say (which is an admission of ignorance or of lack of interest) or perhaps that they have something in mind which they do not wish to communicate or do not know how to state, or even that the subject of discourse has skirted upon a subject area that is embarrassing or disagreeable. When a pause develops, it is felt to be a social responsibility to say something—almost anything—to get the discourse reanimated. In the ancient Orient, on the contrary, silence was valued rather than feared. If a group of people fell silent, the reason might be any one of four: (1) perhaps no one had anything he wished to say—meaning there was no sense of urgency to be discussing the particular subject; or (2) perhaps the subject was felt to be wordlessly ambiguous, so that whatever meaning it had could be sensed but could not be phrased; or (3) perhaps it was generally felt that all were in substantial agreement, so that no affirmation was needed; or, finally, (4) if the subject matter were sensitive, it might be that to speak would be an unwise commitment of one's judgment—a risk that ought not to be taken. For a variety of reasons, silence in Asia has commonly been entirely acceptable, whereas in the West silence has generally been considered socially disagreeable.

And ninth, the insistence in the West upon everyone's equal right to have and to express his own opinion has been countered in the East by the tradition that opinion-formation was primarily the responsibility of those who were elderly, or in a position of authority, or were scholars and teachers. This difference resulted in a more clear-cut understanding in Asia than in the West as to who should do the speaking, and under what circumstances. In Asian rhetoric the principle was accepted that individuals do not have the right to speak until or unless they have earned it. Concurrently, Asians have felt that speaking carries with it a direct responsibility to abide by the consequences, for which reason the speaking about particular subjects should be done primarily by those who have the power and authority to take actions which correspond with their words. This point of view has been especially prevalent in China. In India the theory and the practice have been more nearly in accord with the Western emphasis upon both the freedom of speech and the values of hearing all sides of every question from all who are involved in it. Even in India, however, the establishment of the Brahmin caste to include those who teach, judge, and legislate has had the effect of restricting the most meaningful discourse to select members of the society.

Such are significant focal points of Asian rhetoric, which indicate substantial ways in which it differs from the traditional rhetoric of the West. They reflect a society, a philosophy, and a view of individuality that are constituents of the culture of that part of the world. Their theories of communication are an integral part of their ways of thinking and of living. Even the effort to compare them with Western beliefs and practices results in some degree of distortion. But the fact that such a comparison is to some extent possible indicates the usefulness which this rhetoric may have for the West.

Kristopher Kowal

Reading Lao-tzu as Rhetoric

<hr>

LAO-TZU AND THE TAO TE CHING

The *Tao Te Ching* is first and foremost a work of rhetoric. While it is perhaps most often read as philosophical poetry on "The Way of Life" (as some have translated the title), the *Tao Te Ching* represents a persuasive critique of the coalescing Confucianism of its day by giving alternative practical guidance on how to govern; beyond this purpose, the text seems to persuade general readers of the primary importance of mystical wisdom. Many statements in the *Tao Te Ching* have direct bearing upon the use and misuse of speech, and the place of learning in the life of the people. These observations, along with the fact that the *Tao Te Ching* has been "translated more often than any other book in the world, with the single exception of the Bible" (Needleman v),[1] would seem to invite its careful reading by students of world rhetorics.

Popular myth has held that the text was authored by Lao-tzu, an archivist in the latter half of the Chou Dynasty (1111–249) (Chan xvi–xvi) born as early as fifty years before Confucius (Needleman vi–vii; Bahm 71*ff*; Legge 2).[2] He has been seen as the preserver of a much older oral tradition having its source in China's legendary *Huang Ti* ("Yellow Emperor")[3] of the third or fourth millenium B.C.E. (Bahm 72; Legge 3; Waley 103*ff*.), who may have been influenced by Indian teachings (Wieger 145*ff*.). It is more likely, however, that the *Tao Te Ching* is the result of many redactors working during and after the time of Confucius and Mencius. Much of current scholarship generally agrees that the text is largely a product of the Warring States period (480–222 B.C.E.), during which Confucianism was gaining the ascendance as a philosophy to unify all of China (Mair 119*ff*.).

The dating of the *Tao Te Ching* is important to a consideration of its rhetoric. As its recent translator, Victor Mair, has noted, the *Tao Te Ching* "represents a quietistic reaction against the hierarchical, bureaucratic ideology of Confucius and his followers" (126). Obvious criticisms of what Thomas Merton called the "four-sided mandala of basic [Confucian] virtues" (18) abound in the *Tao Te Ching*: *Jen* (humaneness), *Yi* (justice, righteousness, responsibility to others), *Li* (etiquette or ritual), and *Chih* (knowledge) are either explicitly criticized or subtly parodied in the *Tao Te Ching; Hsiao* (filial piety) receives similar treatment. Mair notes that "such attacks could not have come to pass before about the middle of the fourth century B.C.," since they are "plainly directed at the Confucian school" (126).

The *Tao Te Ching's* criticisms are not directed so much at the value of the virtues themselves as at the way Confucianism advocated their attainment. "Virtue" in Confucianism is essentially "a long and arduous discipline by external standards" (Merton 19) and contributed, in the view of the *Tao Te Ching*, to a fragmenting and de-harmonizing of society. Rather than force unnatural standards as a way of inculcating virtue, the *Tao Te Ching* advocates a return to the unity of nature.

CENTRAL CONCEPTS IN THE TAO TE CHING

The title of the *Tao Te Ching* has been translated variously as *The Way of Virtue, The Way and Its Power,* or simply as *The Way of Lao-tzu.* Originally the work was known simply as *Lao-tzu* or *The 5000 Character Book* (Mair 130 *ff.*). As the text's edited version became popular in the Western Han period (206 B.C.E.–8 C.E.) (Chan *xv*), it acquired its title *Tao Te Ching* after the first characters of its two main parts: *Tao,* almost invariably translated as "the way" (or simply transliterated); and *Te,* which until recently has been taken almost universally to mean "virtue" (in some sense of the word). *Ching* simply means "classic" or "scripture" (Mair 132–136).

Several terms of rhetorical significance are used in the *Tao Te Ching* to represent the text's main teachings:

1. *Tao,* a road or path, suggests a "way" of traveling. In the *Tao Te Ching,* this way is synonymous with "the way of nature and . . . the Way of ultimate Reality" (Blakney 37). The Chinese character is a combination of the figures for a person and for the act of walking. Merton (19) and Blakney (37) both note that Confucius had an understanding of this Way, but a limited one, in keeping with his behavioristic philosophy of doing. The Taoists, on the other hand, conceived of the *Tao* as "the way that those must walk who would 'achieve without doing'"(Waley 15). Whereas Confucius saw the *Tao* as a source of ethical teaching, the anti-Confucian mystics considered *Tao* "not only a means, a doctrine, a principle. It is the ultimate reality in which all attributes are united" (Waley 15). According to Mair, *Tao* is "the all-pervading, self-existent, eternal cosmic unity, the source from which all created things emanate and to which they return" (123*ff.*). It is identified with both *yu* (being) and *wu* (non-being), and as such is the ontological ground of the phenomenological world.[4]

Any number of passages could serve as illustrations of the above definitions of *Tao,* but Chapter One is especially noteworthy since it serves as the introduction to and basis of the rest of the book. It is worth noting that *tao* (as used, for instance, in the first line of Chapter One) connotes speaking (Hansen 67; Graham, *Disputers* 219, 228), and so immediately refers to the *Tao Te Ching* as a theory of language. Names and naming likewise figure into the *Tao Te Ching's* criticism of the "Rectification of Names" theory prevalent during the period in question.

2. *Te,* the label attached to one of the two main divisions of the *Tao Te Ching,* has traditionally been understood to mean "virtue." Since the discovery of the *Ma Wang Tui* manuscripts in 1973, however, scholars have become even more concerned about the translation of *Te,* as well as the order of the book's main divisions. These authoritative, early manuscripts strongly suggest that the work might more properly be known as the *Te Tao Ching,* because the section on "virtue" precedes the section on "the way." At least two very recent, complete translations reflect sensitivity to this ordering (Henricks, *Te Tao Ching;* Mair), and one translator makes a case for a new interpretation of the word *Te.*[5]

Mair argues that *Te* as "virtue" is too suggestive of Confucian moralism. "Under [Confucian] auspices [*te*] came to mean 'virtue' in the positive sense of innate goodness or the source of ethical behavior toward others" (134). Mair goes on to point out that the *Ma-wang Tui* manuscripts present *Te* as "integrity," which is neutral, and (depending on how it is modified adjectivally) not always desirable. For example, the expressions *hsia-te* ("inferior *te*") and *hsiung-te* ("malevolent *te*") are both used in the *Ma-wang Tui* manuscripts. However one translates *te,* it is important to note that the common Chinese notion of virtue is very much suggestive of the Confucian attainment of character by application of ethical standards, which is contrary to the Taoist conception of human nature.[6]

3. *Wu-wei* is the *Tao Te Ching*'s most important dynamic concept, and simply means "non-action" or "non-doing." The term's connotation is not simply passive inactivity, but existential spontaneity, a letting-things-happen-on-their-own.[7] The paradoxical expression *wei-wu-wei* ("to do without doing," or "to act without acting") appears in many places in the *Tao Te Ching,* and means "to get along as nature does: the world gets created, living things grow and pass away without any sign of effort" (Blakney 39). Representative passages are found in Feng and English's translations of chapters 57, 64 and 81. (*Cf.* the second division of Mair's translation of Chapter 38.)

Chapter 57 presents an obvious critique of Confucian moralism in its statements against laws, restrictions, rules and regulations, as well as against the "ingenious and clever men" who would seek to follow them. This chapter also reveals the non-violent political teaching of the *Tao Te Ching* as it was later to influence the Chinese classic *Sun-tzu Ping-fa* (Sun-tzu's *The Art of War*).

4. The "sage" (*sheng-jen*) appears sixty times (Blakney 41) in the *Tao Te Ching,* and is presented not as merely a wise person (although he is that); he is the "ideal Taoist ruler" (Mair 137), one who is sensitive and responsive to the *Tao,* and who implements *wu-wei* in his dealings with his own subjects and with other nations. Blakney agrees that *sheng-jen* " is a euphemism for 'king'," and that "these poems amount to open letters to a king" (41). Graham concludes that "certainly the audience to which *Lao-tzu* ... is directly addressed is the ruler of a state—a small state, one might guess, which has to bend with the wind to survive among stronger states" (*Disputers* 234).

On the difference between Confucian and Taoist politics, Fung Yu-lan, in *A Short History of Chinese Philosophy,* has stated that "when a [Confucian] sage becomes a ruler, he should do many things, whereas according to the Taoists, the duty of the sage ruler is not to do things, but rather to undo or not to do at all" (102). Both Mair (137) and Blakney (41) mention the fact that the root of the Chinese character for *sheng* is an ear, suggesting that the sagacious ruler is one whose primary strategy involves listening. This aspect of his character is illustrated in the final lines of chapter 49.

5. *P'u* is the word used in the *Tao Te Ching* to refer to the natural state of innocence and naïveté found in little children, frequently described as a quality of the *Tao* and of those who would follow it. It is often translated as "uncarved block" or "unhewn log," and is "the most frequent metaphor in the *Tao Te Ching* for expressing the utter simplicity of the Way" (Mair 139).[8] Chapter 28 is the most obvious passage treating this idea. In his analysis of this chapter's rather cryptic concluding lines, Henricks comments that " 'vessel' (*ch'i*) can mean a government lackey" (*Te Tao Ching* 99)—someone bereft of gentlemanly qualities, even though he is a specialist technically. The final line's "carving" (*chih*) can also be understood as "regulating" in the governmental sense; thus, "the Sage is someone who will govern (= carve) without destroying (= splitting up) what is genuine and natural in people" (*Te Tao Ching* 99). It is not difficult to see in these lines a veiled critique of the Confucian bureaucracy emerging in the Warring States period.

6. The pairs of antonyms used in parallel sequence in chapter 28 (male/female, pure/soiled, white/black) are suggestive of the Taoist concepts of *yin* and *yang*. Although the words themselves are used only once in the text, the concepts are implied throughout many chapters of the *Tao Te Ching* and they have become perhaps the single most important emblem of Taoism. In their most primitive sense they denote "shadeward" (*yin*) and "sunward" (*yang*), and this is in fact the very way in which some translators have rendered the terms as they appear in chapter 42.

It is tempting to see in *yin* and *yang* the two elements required by an oppositional dualistic cosmology, and several commentators do refer to a "Taoist dualism" not unlike that described by Zoroaster, Plotinus, and the neo-platonists. Taken in the broader context of the teachings of Taoism, however, *yin* and *yang* must be understood as essentially complementary principles expressive of different aspects of the *Tao:* the harmony and oneness of the *Tao* comprise both *yin* and *yang.* Graham states that it "has long been recognised [that] China tends to treat opposites as complementary, the West as conflicting" (*Disputers* 331; *cf.* "Reflections" 286). This is especially evident in the passages cited above, where the "active" *yang* (and its metaphors of light, masculinity, and so on) is not described as more desirable than the "passive" *yin.* Indeed, one must strain the text unnecessarily in order to see any kind of implied misogyny in the *Tao Te Ching.*[9] In fact, if the text elevates one gender over the other, that gender (and all it symbolizes) is the female: several passages (*e.g.,* 6:1–4, 10:9–10, 25:6, 28:2) depict a nurturing mother figure in this way. While the complementary father figure is noticeably absent, the frequent appearance of the Sage—who in ancient China would typically be a male[10]—functions to balance out the gender differences. In short, if *yin* and *yang* are elements of a traditional contrastive dualism, we would expect to find more of an emphasis on their opposition to each other, their incompatibility; this is, however, not the case.

This complementary relationship between the two primal elements of existence is not original to the *Tao Te Ching*. It is pre-dated in Chinese writings by the *I Ching (Book of Changes)*, where *yin* is represented by the broken line and *yang* by the unbroken (Bahm 76). Originally a book of wisdom and not one of divination as it came to be misused (Wilhelm and Baynes *livff.*), the *I Ching* influenced the Taoists and Confucians alike, and all Chinese thought to one extent or another. The *Ta Chuan* ("Great Commentary") on the *I Ching* elaborates on the symbiotic nature of *yin* and *yang* (Wilhelm and Baynes 297–301).

The rhetorical significance of *yin* and *yang* in terms of the *Tao Te Ching*'s critique of Confucianism can be seen in Taoism's emphasis on non-action (*wu-wei*). This non-action, or spontaneity, is expressive of a return to the mystical balance of *yin* and *yang*, while Confucianism's "virtues" emphasized the active, programmatic practice of ethical behavior. If the *Tao Te Ching* appears to elevate *yin*, it is only because Confucianism was (in the view of the Taoists) attempting to throw the *Tao* out of kilter by elevating *yang*-like activity. In reality, however, the *Tao Te Ching* seldom refers to one of the principles without referring to its complement.

7. *Wan-wu*, the "myriad creatures" (literally "ten thousand objects," as it is translated by Waley and others), refers to all things that possess being or existence. *Tao*, as the originator of being, is itself "without existence" (Mair 139). Humans of course are included in *wan-wu*, and find their place in the order of things as they understand the way of nature. One is tempted to see humans in the *Tao Te Ching* as somehow inferior to the rest of creation because of their prideful "intelligence" (*Homo non sapiens?*) and distance from nature, but the text throughout emphasizes the unity of the ten thousand objects. This is *wan-wu*'s principal rhetorical significance, as it reinforces the sense of order and harmony between nature and those who seek to follow the *Tao*. A merely Confucian conception of things ultimately divorces people from nature and, in turn, from each other; society as a whole becomes fragmented or "crazed" (in the original sense of "cracked").

Blakney has commented on the similarities between the first stanza of chapter 42 of the *Tao Te Ching*[11] and a statement of Chuang Tzu, an important Taoist figure. Chuang said the following:

> The world and I have a common origin and all creatures [*wan-wu*] and I together are one. Being one, our oneness can be expressed … or unexpressed. The one, with the expression, makes two, and the two with one (what is unexpressed), make three. (qtd. by Blakney 95)

8. *Ch'i* occurs only three times in the *Tao Te Ching*, but is an important idea in the Taoist understanding of things. It is the "vital breath" or spirit that unites the two cosmological principles of *yin* and *yang*. This can be illustrated by looking at John Wu's translation of the first half of chapter 42. Mair sees *ch'i* as "the metaphysical concept of material energy coursing through the body and the universe" (137). He also notes that *ch'i* is the same concept as the Greek *pneuma*, the Latin *spiritus*, and the Hebrew *ruah* (137).

THE TAO TE CHING ON LANGUAGE AND LEARNING

Having noted the *Tao Te Ching*'s insistence on a return to nature as the solution to the problems of humans and governing, one might well wonder what the roles of speaking and education would be in the kind of society the text advocates. With the several concepts outlined above as an introduction to the *Tao Te Ching*, we should not be surprised to find statements in the text which deal directly with the topics of language and learning. Predictably, these passages continue the same anti-Confucian tenor implicit throughout the text. Viewed in the context of Confucianism, these passages make explicit the mystical quietism advocated throughout the rest of the text of the *Tao Te Ching*. To be consistent with the teaching of *wu-wei*, those who would follow the *Tao* in daily life "keep their mouths shut" and return to the primal state of nature. According to the legend, this is precisely what Lao-tzu was in the process of doing as he wrote the *Tao Te Ching*: giving up his curatorship at the royal library, he set out to leave society and its complexity in order to become a hermit. Passing through the village gate on his way to seclusion, Lao-tzu was accosted by the gatekeeper who insisted that he write him a book about the *Tao* (Legge 4*ff.*). The task completed, Lao-tzu wandered off into the sunset—presumably to practice rope-knotting in place of writing.

In reality, the *Tao Te Ching* was written for a much wider audience than the lonely gatekeeper. Although it has inspired a large movement of seclusion-seekers, the text served as practical ammunition for those engaged in the Warring States clash with Confucianism. Since Confucianism sought to locate virtue in people through a rigorous, legalistic system of conformity to external standards, verbal and written teaching had to play an important part in the dissemination of its ideas; hence Confucianism's relationship with literacy. The more advanced one became in the attainment of Confucian morality, the more "knowledgeable" he became; such masters were subsequently perceived as literate intellectuals, accorded the powerful status of scholars, and sought after as teachers. In its later refinements, Confucianism also sought to unify and schematize the country's education system. The political utility of speaking and writing in such a system is obvious, and so the *Tao Te Ching*, in its attempt to redress what it saw as the political and societal fragmentation inherent in Confucianism, naturally directed much of its attack at the root problem of Confucian discursive practices.

During the chaotic years of the Warring States period, it was common practice for itinerant philosophers to try to convince rulers to implement their ideas. Mair, noting that the Taoists were such philosophers and that the *Tao Te Ching* espouses " a minimalist political strategy heavily laden with mystical overtones" (120), explains that during the Warring States period "it was common for philosophers to travel from state to state within the disintegrating Chinese empire, looking for a king who would put their ideas into practice" (120).[12]

The *Tao Te Ching*'s "teaching no talking" is strangely paradoxical, if not merely hypocritical. If the early Taoists had truly practiced what they were preaching and returned to rope-knotting in the place of writing, we would not even have the text of the *Tao Te Ching*. But how else could such doctrines be communicated—especially with the deluge of Confucian rhetoric seeking to engulf all of China? It is unlikely that teaching by example alone (as Lao-tzu did) would have been adequate to persuade the masses, let alone the rulers.

Present-day sinologists see an elaborate theory of language in the *Tao Te Ching*. Chad Hansen, for example, observes that in the *Tao Te Ching*, "knowledge, wisdom, and learning are matters of mastering a linguistic practice" (65). He goes on to explain that

> Lao-tzu recommends abandoning a whole complex: (1) names, (2) distinctions, (3) desires, (4) specific moral virtues of Confucius, (5) learning, cleverness, knowledge and wisdom, and sageliness, and (6) action caused by 1–5. The connection of these elements forms the core of the Taoist theories of language. (66)

The Taoist theory of language is a critique of the Confucian theory of language. The latter has been dubbed the "Rectification of Names," and is attributed in varying degrees to Confucius, Hsün-tzu and Mencius. The Rectification of Names movement sought to unite linguistic labels ("names") with what they represented in reality, for practical political purposes. In response to this doctrine and its implications, the *Tao Te Ching* openly criticizes names and naming (chapters 1, 25, 32, and 41), as well as the "definition" (chapters 14 and 32) and "description" (chapter 35) which follow from naming.

> Conventional moral terms and distinctions are introduced . . . only because of breakdowns in the natural order of things. The Confucian distinctions do not really alleviate the breakdowns but in a perverse way perpetuate them. The preferred [Taoist] policy would be to abandon the distinctions and words entirely and eliminate all learning (which is mere skill in word manipulation) and return to "natural" behavior. (Hansen 71)

The emphasis in the Taoist theory of language is that names reflect *conventional* attitudes about things, and that the "morality" implicit in the distinctions produced by naming is also conventional. An opposite name is implied by any linguistic term, and each such pair of names in turn implies a distinction. Any single distinction is the product of two names, and since these two names mark the same distinction, they are, in a way, the same. Therefore, moralistic Confucian distinctions are conventional and arbitrary, and the terms that produce them are really one. The names could be reversed to produce the same distinctions, and are consequently unstable; the distinctions are likewise unreal, and so the ethical recommendations based on such linguistic manipulation are unsound. It follows that language, in the *Tao Te Ching*, is seen as futile and absurd: truthful words are not beautiful, and beautiful words are not truthful.

The same principles embodied in the *Tao Te Ching's* anti-Confucian theory of language apply to its theory of knowledge, and can be seen in Chapters 3, 18–20, 45, 47, 64, 71, and 81. In these passages, "knowledge" is presented with its Confucian connotation, as the intellectual accumulating of facts, concepts and data. Hansen sees the Taoist theory of knowledge that emerges from these statements as essentially an argument "against *any* acquired system of naming, evaluation, and conventionally guided action" (66). According to the *Tao Te Ching*, "knowledge is . . . not . . . the acquisition of data items called concepts and facts. The paradigm of what is learned is the traditional Confucian virtues" (66).

Although the *Tao Te Ching* urges the abandoning of knowledge, this abandoning must entail acquiring another sort of knowledge. Certain passages (*e.g.*, chapters 64 and 71) attach value to this ability to "learn to be unlearned" and "to know you're not knowing." This kind of "negative knowledge" is what the *Tao Te Ching* teaches in opposition to Confucian speaking and knowing, and it is admittedly contradictory. If we view the text as primarily a refutation of Confucian knowledge, we may have to content ourselves with its paradoxical embrace of negative wisdom while it seems to advocate abandoning *all* knowledge, and stop here.

However, the mystical tradition of Taoism requires that we see beyond the negative knowledge it embraces and seek something wholly other, something after language. If the *Tao Te Ching*'s theories of language and of knowledge are consistent, they would seem ultimately to devalue its own words and teachings.

> There must be a positive kind of "wisdom" which, descriptively, is the mystical identification with the extralinguistic reality and which, regulatively, is a pattern of behavior guided by some immediate, natural response. (Hansen 68)

Since this wisdom cannot be articulated verbally, however, we are unable to find explicit statements about it in the *Tao Te Ching*. It is suggested by the text's portrayal of the Sage, who does not speak, make distinctions, or desire anything. The *ethos* of such a figure can be seen in the *Tao Te Ching* as one with no purpose, as in Waley's translation of Chapter 20.[13]

The obvious question posed by the portrait of the Taoist Sage throughout the *Tao Te Ching* is, Is this the description of one who has achieved a (positive) mystical identification with metalinguistic meaning, or is he merely "someone who has abandoned all spoken *tao*s" (Hansen 69) and embraced "negative wisdom"? On this question, the *Tao* is silent. In either case, however, the *Tao Te Ching* makes it clear that the ideal follower of its teachings is closer to an answer than is the merely "virtuous" Confucian.

NOTES

1. *N.B.* Mair (*xi*) claims the *Bhagavad-Gita* exists in more translations than does the *Tao Te Ching*. See Bahm (123–126) for a listing of 42 English translations of the *Tao Te Ching* published to 1955.

2. For a thorough treatment of the legendary author of the *Tao Te Ching*, see Angus C. Graham, "The Origins of the Legend of Lao Tan," in *Studies in Chinese Philosophy and Philosophical Literature* (Albany: SUNY P, 1990), pp. 111–124.

3. For the unique assertion that the Yellow Emperor "had an appearance of northern

white people, as the epithet 'Huang-ti' can etymologically be interpreted as 'blond heavenly god,'" see Tsung-tung Chang's "Indo-European Vocabulary in Old Chinese" (*Sino-Platonic Papers* 1988), p. 35.

4. Bahm has provided an engaging discussion of *Tao* as it contrasts with Plato's "Idea of the Good," the Stoics' *Logos,* and Plotinus's "One" (81*ff*.).

5. Although Mair prefers the chapter order suggested by the *Ma-wang Tui* documents, I have here retained the traditional numbering.

6. This idea is also implied in line seven's criticism of the person who "has a purpose for acting."

7. A related term is *tze-jan,* " of itself."

8. Mair (139) also alludes to Benjamin Hoff's recognition of *P'u* as a trait in A. A. Milne's animal characters in Hoff's *The Tao of Pooh* and *The Te of Piglet.*

9. *N.B.* that the "soil" metaphor in chapter 28 is used to exhort the reader to return to nature—to become "soiled"—yet in so doing to remain truly pure.

10. Stephen Mitchell's 1988 translation of the *Tao Te Ching,* presumably in an effort to make the text more accessible to an egalitarian readership, divides English pronominal references to the *sheng-jen* (which he translates as "Master") between feminine and masculine. He defends his choice by stating that

> since we are all, potentially, the Master (since the Master is, essentially, us), I felt it would be untrue to present a male archetype, as other versions have, ironically, done. Ironically, because of all the great world religions the teaching of Lao-tzu is by far the most female. (*ix*)

11. See Waley's translation.

12. Mair comments that "the text [of the *Tao Te Ching*] as a whole is designed to serve as a handbook for the ruler" (128).

13. Waley comments that "learning" in line one is a reference to learning "the '3300 rules of [Confucian] etiquette'" (168).

WORKS CITED

Bahm, Archie J. *Tao Teh King by Lao Tzu Interpreted as Nature and Intelligence.* New York: Frederick Ungar-Continuum, 1958.

Blakney, Raymond B. *The Way of Life/Lao Tzu.* New York: Mentor-New American, 1955.

Chan, Wing-tsit. *A Source Book in Chinese Philosophy.* Princeton: Princeton UP, 1963.

Chang, Tsung-tung. "Indo-European Vocabulary in Old Chinese: A New Thesis on the Emergence of Chinese Language and Civilization in the Late Neolithic Age." *Sino-Platonic Papers* 7 (January 1988): 1–56.

Feng, Gia-fu and Jane English. *Tao Te Ching/Lao Tsu.* New York: Vintage-Random, 1972.

Fung, Yu-lan. *A Short History of Chinese Philosophy.* Trans. Derk Bodde. New York: Macmillan, 1958.

Graham, Angus C. *Disputers of the Tao: Philosophical Argument in Ancient China.* La Salle, IL: Open Court, 1989.

———. "Reflections and Replies." *Chinese Texts and Philosophical Contexts: Essays Dedicated to Angus C. Graham.* Ed. Henry Rosemont, Jr. La Salle, IL: Open Court, 1991. 267–322.

————. *Studies in Chinese Philosophy and Philosophical Literature.* Albany: SUNY P, 1990.

Hansen, Chad. *Language and Logic in Ancient China.* Ann Arbor: U of Michigan P, 1983.

Henricks, Robert G. *Lao-Tzu: Te-Tao Ching.* New York: Ballantine-Random, 1989.

Legge, James. *The Sacred Books of China: The Texts of Taoism.* London: Oxford UP, 1891. Vol. I.

Mair, Victor. *Tao Te Ching: The Classic Book of Integrity and the Way.* New York: Bantam-Doubleday, 1990.

Merton, Thomas. *The Way of Chuang Tzu.* New York: New Directions, 1965.

Needleman, Jacob. Introduction. *Tao Te Ching/Lao Tsu.* Trans. Feng, Gia-fu and Jane English. New York: Vintage-Random, 1989, *v-xxxiii.*

Sun Tzu. *The Art of War.* Trans. Thomas Cleary. Boston: Shambhala, 1988.

Waley, Arthur. *The Way and Its Power: A Study of the Tao Tê Ching and Its Place in Chinese Thought.* New York: Grove Weidenfeld, 1958.

Wieger, Leo. *A History of the Religious Beliefs and Philosophical Opinions in China.* Trans. Edward Chalmers Werner. Orig. published 1927. New York: Paragon Book Reprint Corp., 1969.

Wilhelm, Richard and Cary F. Baynes. *The I Ching or Book of Changes.* Princeton: Princeton UP, 1977.

Wu, John C. H. *Tao Teh Ching.* Boston: Shambhala, 1990.

Lao-Tzu

Excerpts from the Tao Te Ching

CENTRAL CONCEPTS OF RHETORICAL SIGNIFICANCE

1. The Sage (*sheng-jen*).

> The sage has no mind of his own.
> He is aware of the needs of others.
>
> The sage is shy and humble—to the world he seems confusing.
> Others look to him and listen.
> He behaves like a little child. (Chapter 49:1–2, 7–9)
>
> Give up learning, and put an end to your troubles. . . .
> In spring some go to the park, and climb the terrace,
> But I alone am drifting, not knowing where I am.
> Like a newborn babe before it learns to smile,
> I am alone, without a place to go.
>
> Others have more than they need, but I alone have nothing.
> I am a fool. Oh, yes! I am confused.
> Others are clear and bright,
> But I alone am dim and weak.
> Others are sharp and clever,
> But I alone am dull and stupid.
> Oh, I drift like the waves of the sea,
> Without direction, like the restless wind.
>
> Everyone else is busy,
> But I alone am aimless and depressed.
> I am different.
> I am nourished by the great mother. (20:1, 10*ff.*)

Source: All excerpts from *Tao Te Ching/Lao-tzu*. Trans. Gia-fu Feng and Jane English. Originally published by Alfred A. Knopf, 1972. These excerpts taken from the Vintage Books (Random House) paperback edition, 1972 and 1989.

2. Non-action or Non-doing (*Wu-wei*).

> Rule a nation with justice.
> Wage war with surprise moves.
> Become master of the universe without striving.
> How do I know that this is so?
> Because of this!

> The more laws and restrictions there are,
> The poorer people become.
> The sharper men's weapons,
> The more trouble in the land.
> The more ingenious and clever men are,
> The more strange things happen.
> The more rules and regulations,
> The more thieves and robbers.

> Therefore the sage says:
> I take no action and people are reformed.
> I enjoy peace and people become honest.
> I do nothing and people become rich.
> I have no desires and people return to the good and simple life. (Chapter 57)

> A journey of a thousand miles begins under one's feet.
> He who acts defeats his own purpose;
> He who grasps loses.
> The sage does not act, and so is not defeated.
> He does not grasp and therefore does not lose. (Chapter 64)

> The Tao of the sage is without effort. (Chapter 81)

3. Shadeward and Sunward (*Yin* and *Yang*).

> The Tao begot one.
> One begot two.
> Two begot three.
> And three begot the ten thousand things.

> The ten thousand things carry yin and embrace yang.
> They achieve harmony by combining these forces. (Chapter 42:1–6)

4. The Uncarved Block (*P'u*).

> Know the strength of man,
> But keep a woman's care!
> Be the stream of the universe!
> Being the stream of the universe,

Ever true and unswerving,
Become as a little child once more.

Know the white,
But keep the black!
Be an example to the world!
Being an example to the world,
Ever true and unwavering,
Return to the infinite.

Know honor,
Yet keep humility.
Be the valley of the universe!
Being the valley of the universe,
Ever true and resourceful,
Return to the state of the uncarved block.

When the block is carved, it becomes useful.
When the sage uses it, he becomes the ruler.
Thus, "A great tailor cuts little." (Chapter 28)

THE TAO TE CHING ON LANGUAGF

Between *wei* [yes] and *o* [no]
What after all is the difference?
Can it be compared to the difference between good and bad?
The saying "what others avoid I too must avoid"
How false and superficial it is! (20:2–6)

Those who know do not talk.
Those who talk do not know.
Keep your mouth closed.
Guard your senses.
Temper your sharpness.
Simplify your problems.
Mask your brightness.
Be at one with the dust of the earth.
This is primal union.

He who has achieved this state
Is unconcerned with friends and enemies,
With good and harm, with honor and disgrace.
This therefore is the highest state of man. (Chapter 56)

Truthful words are not beautiful.

Beautiful words are not truthful.
Good men do not argue.
Those who argue are not good.
Those who know are not learned.
The learned do not know.

The sage never tries to store things up.
The more he does for others, the more he has.
The more he gives to others, the greater his abundance.
The Tao of heaven is pointed but does no harm.
The Tao of the sage is without effort. (Chapter 81)

The Tao that can be told is not the eternal Tao.
The name that can be named is not the eternal name. (1:1–2)

The sage goes about doing nothing, teaching no-talking. (2:9)

More words count less. (5:8)

Listen, [the Tao] cannot be heard—it is beyond sound. . . .
It is called indefinable and beyond imagination. (14:2 ,12)

When actions are performed
Without unnecessary speech,
People say "We did it!" (17:6-8)

[Wise men] do not quarrel,
So no one quarrels with them. (22:17–18)

To talk little is natural. (23:1)

Something . . . in the silence of the void . . . I do not know its name.
Call it Tao.
For lack of a better word, I call it great. (25:1, 3, 7–9)

The Tao is forever undefined.
Small though it is in the unformed state, it cannot be grasped.
Once the whole is divided, the parts need names.
There are already enough names. (32:1–2, 9–10)

A description of the Tao
Seems without substance or flavor.
It cannot be seen, it cannot be heard. (35:4–6)

Too much success is not an advantage.
Do not tinkle like jade
Or clatter like stone chimes. (39:22–24)

The Tao is hidden and without name. (41:18)

Teaching without words and work without doing
Are understood by very few. (43:5–6)

Keep your mouth shut.
Guard the senses, and life is ever full.
Open your mouth, always be busy, and life is beyond hope. (52:6–11)

Men return to the knotting of rope in place of writing. (80:6)

THE TAO TE CHING ON LEARNING

Not exalting the gifted prevents quarreling. . . . If people lack knowledge and desire, then intellectuals will not try to interfere. If nothing is done, then all will be well. (3:1, 6–8)

When wisdom and intelligence are born, the great pretense begins. (18:3–4)

Give up sainthood, renounce wisdom, and it will be a hundred times better for everyone. (19:1–2)

Give up learning, and put an end to your troubles. (20:1)

Great straightness seems twisted. Great intelligence seems stupid. Great eloquence seems awkward. (45:5–7)

The farther you go, the less you know. (47:3)

Knowing ignorance is strength. (71:1)

Those who know are not learned. The learned do not know. (81:5–6)

Han Fei Tzu

"The Difficulties of Persuasion¹"

On the whole, the difficult thing about persuading others is not that one lacks the knowledge needed to state his case nor the audacity to exercise his abilities to the full. On the whole, the difficult thing about persuasion is to know the mind of the person one is trying to persuade and to be able to fit one's words to it.

If the person you are trying to persuade is out to establish a reputation for virtue, and you talk to him about making a fat profit, then he will regard you as low-bred, accord you a shabby and contemptuous reception, and undoubtedly send you packing. If the person you are trying to persuade is on the contrary interested in a fat profit, and you talk to him about a virtuous reputation, he will regard you as witless and out of touch with reality, and will never heed your arguments. If the person you are trying to persuade is secretly out for big gain but ostensibly claims to be interested in a virtuous name alone, and you talk to him about a reputation for virtue, then he will pretend to welcome and heed you, but in fact will shunt you aside; if you talk to him about making a big gain, he will secretly follow your advice but ostensibly reject you. These are facts that you must not fail to consider carefully.

Undertakings succeed through secrecy but fail through being found out. Though the ruler himself has not yet divulged his plans, if you in your discussions happen to hit upon his hidden motives, then you will be in danger. If the ruler is ostensibly seeking one thing but actually is attempting to accomplish something quite different, and you perceive not only his ostensible objective but the real motives behind his actions as well, then you will likewise be in danger. If you happen to think up some unusual scheme for the ruler which meets with his approval, and some other person of intelligence manages by outside means to guess what it is and divulges the secret to the world, then the ruler will suppose that it was you who gave it away and you will be in danger. If you have not yet won substantial reward and favor and yet your words are extremely apt and wise, then if the ruler heeds them and the undertaking is successful, he will forget to reward you; and if he does not heed them and the undertaking fails, he will regard you with suspicion and you will be in danger. If some person of eminence takes a brief step in the wrong direction and you immediately launch into a lecture on ritual principles and challenge his misdeed, then you will be in danger. If some eminent person gets hold of a good scheme somewhere and plans to use it to win merit for himself, and you happen to know where he got it, then you will be in danger. If you try forcibly to talk a person into doing what he cannot do, or stopping what he cannot stop, then you will be in danger.

If you talk to the ruler about men of real worth, he will think you are implying that he is no match for them; if you talk to him of petty men, he will think you are attempting to use your influence to get your friends into office; if you talk to him about what he likes, he will suspect you of trying to utilize him; if you talk about what he hates, he will suspect you of trying to test his patience. If you speak too bluntly and to the point, he will consider you unlearned and will shun you; if you speak too eloquently and in too great detail, he will consider you pretentious and will reject[2] you. If you are too sketchy in outlining your ideas, he will think you a coward who is too fainthearted to say what he really means; if you are too exuberant and long-winded in stating your proposals, he will think you an uncouth bumpkin who is trying to talk down to him. These are the difficulties of persuasion; you cannot afford to be ignorant of them!

The important thing in persuasion is to learn how to play up the aspects that the person you are talking to is proud of, and play down the aspects he is ashamed of. Thus, if the person has some urgent personal desire, you should show him that it is his public duty to carry it out and urge him not to delay. If he has some mean objective in mind and yet cannot restrain himself, you should do your best to point out to him whatever admirable aspects it may have and to minimize the reprehensible ones. If he has some lofty objective in mind and yet does not have the ability needed to realize it, you should do your best to point out to him the faults and bad aspects of such an objective and make it seem a virtue not to pursue it. If he is anxious to make a show of wisdom and ability, mention several proposals which are different from the one you have in mind but of the same general nature in order to supply him with ideas; then let him build on your words, but pretend that you are unaware that he is doing so, and in this way abet his wisdom.

If you wish to urge a policy of peaceful coexistence, then be sure to expound it in terms of lofty ideals, but also hint that it is commensurate with the ruler's personal interests. If you wish to warn the ruler against dangerous and injurious policies, then make a show of the fact that they invite reproach and moral censure, but also hint that they are inimical to his personal interests.

Praise other men whose deeds are like those of the person you are talking to; commend other actions which are based upon the same policies as his. If there is someone else who is guilty of the same vice he is, be sure to gloss it over by showing that it really does no great harm; if there is someone else who has suffered the same failure he has, be sure to defend it by demonstrating that it is not a loss after all. If he prides himself on his physical prowess, do not antagonize him by mentioning the difficulties he has encountered in the past; if he considers himself an expert at making decisions, do not anger him by pointing out his past errors; if he pictures himself a sagacious planner, do not tax him with his failures. Make sure that there is nothing in your ideas as a whole that will vex your listener, and nothing about your words that will rub him the wrong way, and then you may exercise your powers of rhetoric to the fullest. This is the way to gain the confidence and intimacy of the person you are addressing and to make sure that you are able to say all you have to say without incurring his suspicion.

Yi Yin became a cook and Po-li Hsi a captive slave, so they could gain the ear of the ruler.[3] These men were sages, and yet they could not avoid shouldering hard tasks for the sake of advancement and demeaning themselves in this way. Therefore you too should become a cook or a slave when necessary; if this enables you to gain the confidence of the ruler and save the state, then it is no disgrace for a man of ability to take such a course.

If you are able to fulfill long years of service with the ruler, enjoy his fullest favor and confidence, lay long-range plans for him without ever arousing suspicion, and when necessary oppose him in argument without incurring blame, then you may achieve merit by making clear to him what is profitable and what is harmful, and bring glory to yourself by your forthright judgments of right and wrong. When ruler and minister aid and sustain each other in this way, persuasion may be said to have reached its fulfillment.

In ancient times Duke Wu of Cheng wanted to attack the state of Hu, and so he first married his daughter to the ruler of Hu in order to fill his mind with thoughts of pleasure. Then he told his ministers, "I want to launch a military campaign. What would be a likely state to attack?" The high official Kuan Ch'i-ssu replied, "Hu could be attacked," whereupon Duke Wu flew into a rage and had him executed,[4] saying, "Hu is a brother state! What do you mean by advising me to attack it!" The ruler of Hu, hearing of this, assumed that Cheng was friendly towards him and therefore took no precautions to defend himself from Cheng. The men of Cheng then made a surprise attack on Hu and seized it.

Once there was a rich man of Sung. When the dirt wall around his house collapsed in a heavy rain, his son said, "If you don't rebuild it, thieves will surely break in," and the old man who lived next door told him the same thing. When night fell, thieves actually broke in and made off with a large share of the rich man's wealth. The rich man's family praised the son for his wisdom, but eyed the old man next door with suspicion.

Both these men—the high official Kuan Ch'i-ssu and the old man next door—spoke the truth, and yet one was actually executed for his words, while the other cast suspicion on himself. It is not difficult to know a thing; what is difficult is to know how to use what you know. Jao Chao spoke the truth but, though he was regarded as a sage by the men of Chin, he was executed by those of Ch'in.[5] This is something you cannot afford not to examine.

In ancient times Mi Tzu-hsia won favor with the ruler of Wei.[6] According to the laws of the state of Wei, anyone who secretly made use of the ruler's carriage was punished by having his feet amputated. When Mi Tzu-hsia's mother fell ill, someone slipped into the palace at night to report this to Mi Tzu-hsia. Mi Tzu-hsia forged an order from the ruler, got into the ruler's carriage, and went off to see her, but when the ruler heard of it, he only praised him, saying, "How filial! For the sake of his mother he forgot all about the danger of having his feet cut off!" Another day Mi Tzu-hsia was strolling with the ruler in an orchard and, biting into a peach and finding it sweet, he stopped eating and gave the remaining half to the ruler to enjoy. "How sincere is your love for me!" exclaimed the ruler. "You forget your own appetite and think only of giving me good things to eat!" Later, however, when Mi Tzu-hsia's looks had faded and the ruler's passion for him had cooled, he was accused of committing some crime against his lord. "After all," said the ruler, "he once stole my carriage, and another time he gave me a half-eaten peach to eat!" Mi Tzu-hsia was actually acting no differently from the way he always had; the fact that he was praised in the early days, and accused of a crime later on, was because the ruler's love had turned to hate.

If you gain the ruler's love, your wisdom will be appreciated and you will enjoy his favor as well; but if he hates you, not only will your wisdom be rejected, but you will be regarded as a criminal and thrust aside. Hence men who wish to present their remonstrances and expound their ideas must not fail to ascertain the ruler's loves and hates before launching into their speeches.

The beast called the dragon can be tamed[7] and trained to the point where you may ride on its back. But on the underside of its throat it has scales a foot in diameter that curl back from the body, and anyone who chances to brush against them is sure to die. The ruler of men too has his bristling scales. Only if a speaker can avoid brushing against them will he have any hope for success.

NOTES

[1]This chapter, with frequent textual differences, is recorded in *Shih chi* 63, the biography of Han Fei Tzu.

[2]Reading *ch'i* instead of *chiao*.

[3]Yi Yin became a cook in the kitchen of Ch'eng T'ang, the founder of the Shang dynasty; Po-li Hsi became a slave at the court of Duke Mu of Ch'in (r. 659–621 B.C.)

[4]According to the *Bamboo Annals*, this took place in 763 B.C.

[5]Jao Chao is mentioned briefly in the *Tso chuan*, Duke Wen, 13th year (614 B.C.), as a minister of Ch'in who saw through a plot of the men of Chin, but the exact anecdote which Han Fei Tzu is referring to here is not known.

[6]Duke Ling of Wei (r. 534–493 B.C.).

[7]Reading *jao* instead of *jou*.

Angus C. Graham

"The Sharpening of Rational Debate: The Sophists"

In China rationality develops with the controversies of the schools, and dwindles as they fade after 200 B.C. With the debates of Mohists and Yangists fully launched, and the Confucians pulled into them, attention begins to shift from the practice to the theory of *pien* 'arguing out alternatives', the distinguishing of the right alternative from the wrong. During the 4th century B.C. we meet for the first time thinkers who are fascinated by the mechanics of argumentation, delight in paradoxes, astonish their audiences by 'making the inadmissible admissible'. When during the Han the philosophers were classed in the Six Schools these, and others with more practical interests in naming, came to be known retrospectively as the School of Names. Earlier they were known simply as *pien che* 辯者 'those who argue out', sometimes translated 'Dialecticians'. Confucians, Taoists and Legalists alike scorn them for wasting their time on abstractions such as 'the similar and the different', 'the hard and white', 'the limitless' and 'the dimensionless'. Only the Mohists do not join in this general derision; some of the same themes appear in the Later Mohist *Canons,* from which we learn that the hard and white represent mutually pervasive properties in general, and that the limitless and the dimensionless have the full technical sense of the infinite and the point (the latter however understood by the Mohists as the starting point of a measurement).

It is customary to call these thinkers 'sophists' and compare them to the Greek propounders of paradoxes, to the Eleatics however rather than to the Sophists proper. Although they have little in common with the latter, the label 'Sophist' does call attention to a configuration of tendencies at the birth of rational discourse which is common to Greece and China. In both traditions we meet thinkers who delight in propositions which defy common sense, and consequently are derided as frivolous and irresponsible. In both, these thinkers belong to the early period when reason is a newly discovered tool not yet under control, seeming to give one the power to prove or disprove anything. In both, the exuberance with which they play with this astonishing new toy leads not only to 'sophistries' but to paradoxes of lasting philosophical significance. In both, the pride and pleasure in logical acrobatics calls attention to the relation between words and things. In both, to exult in one's skill in proving both sides of a case pushes in the direction of relativism. Nothing could be more disorientating, more disruptive, than reason first awakening to and revelling in its powers. One may well wonder how philosophy ever gets past this stage, with the most ancient paradoxes forever returning to plague it. The first discovery of uninhibited reason is that it leads inevitably to absurd conclusions. So why go farther? The Greeks did get past this initial disorientation, the Chinese never did.

The most famous of the Sophists were Hui Shih, a chief minister of King Hui of Wei (or Liang, 370–319 B.C.) and friend of the Taoist Chuang-tzu, and Kung-sun Lung, who entertained his patron the Lord of P'ing-yüan in Chao (died 252 B.C.) with his notorious argument that a white horse is not a horse. Since it was the Mohists who started and remained at the forefront in philosophical argumentation, one notices without surprise that as advisers of princes both show the influence of the Mohist doctrines of non-aggression and concern for everyone. There are stories of both of them advising princes against war, in one of which Kung-sun Lung in reproaching King Hui of Chao (298–266 B.C.) directly appeals to the principle of concern for everyone, and the Ten Theses of Hui Shih, which we shall consider shortly, culminate in an appeal to "let concern spread to all the myriad things."

Chad Hansen

"Kung-sun Lung and the White-Horse Paradox"

INDETERMINANCY AND PARADOX

The white-horse paradox is stated in the opening line of the second chapter of the work titled the *Kung-sun Lung-tzu*. The paradox is stated in a simple four-character sentence: *pai ma fei ma* 白馬非馬 'white horse is-not horse'. There follows an argument in dialogue form about the assertability of the paradoxical sentence. Interpreting and explaining the paradox has become a source of fascination to scholars. There have been numerous interpretive theories in modern times, nearly all of which employ metaphysical, mental, abstract, or semantic concepts borrowed from the Western philosophical tradition. The challenge is to explain why Kung-sun Lung would consider the sentence assertable. This chapter is an argument from the philosophical perspective laid down in chapter 2 for a nominalistic interpretation of both the paradox and the dialogue which follows it. I contend that we do not need to treat *ma* as "horseness" nor *pai* as "whiteness" to explain Kung-sun Lung's view that "white-horse not horse" is assertable.

•   •   •

THE WHITE-HORSE PARADOX

Kung-sun Lung initiates his dialogue with the question, "Is [the sentence] *pai ma fei ma* 白馬非馬 'white-horse not horse' *k'o* 可 'assertable'?" The question is followed by the answer that it is. The dialogue then goes on to a series of objections and answers to the paradoxical thesis. We identify the objector as an opponent from either a commonsense or Neo-Mohist point of view and the answerer as Kung-sun Lung (given the independent evidence that Kung-sun Lung did advocate the position). I will follow Graham in marking the answers and objections by *S* for *sophist* and *O* for *objector* respectively.

The interpretive theory for the text is that Kung-sun Lung, committed to the rigid principle of rectification of names, objected to the two different semantic accounts of modification given by the Neo-Mohists. The sophist states his objection in a logical form, which indicates that he is more inclined to accept the ox-horse than the hard-white analysis of compounding. His choice of one term from each paradigm signals that he advocates a single, strict semantic model of compounding. The model he prefers is the "separable" one—the ox-horse (mass sum) semantics for compounds. The mass sum model preserves the relation of name and thing in a way the mass product model does not. His reported advocacy of separating hard and white is most plausibly his attempt to treat hard-white on the ox-horse model. This interpretation thus explicates the traditional view that Kung-sun Lung was separating white from horse as he was separating hard from white, and also his own reported claim that he was defending a Confucian doctrine—the one-name-one-thing rule of rectification of names. The issue between the Neo-Mohist semantic program and Kung-sun Lung's centers on what is the proper account of the scope, the extension, of compound names.

The motivation for Kung-sun Lung's approach is that compound terms should be explained in ways which do not violate the strict naming relation. If a name has two component terms, the compound name should preserve the relation of the names to their stuffs. Compound terms must *always* be more general (or they must be treated as something other than compound terms). All true compound terms name the sum of the stuffs named by each component term. Hence, white-horse, the example that calls for a decision between the semantic models, should be understood as the mass sum of white-stuff and horse-stuff. The argument for the admissibility of "ox-horse not ox" then carries over to the white-horse case.

The Mohist argument for "ox-horse not ox" concluded only that it was admissible or assertable. Similarly, Kung-sun Lung only insists that "white-horse not horse" is assertable (*k'o*). One modern analogue that might be helpful in understanding the paradox is to say that for Kung-sun Lung "white-horse not horse" is not analytically false, that is, "white-horse horse" is not analytically true.

The sophist's argument as it emerges from the dialogue takes the form of a dilemma. We must either interpret "white-horse" in a strict sense as a compound conforming to the strict standard for right use of names, or in its ordinary sense. Either way, the argument will yield the conclusion that "white-horse not horse" is admissible.

Suppose we view the problem example according to the paradigm appropriate to the "horse" part. Then white-horse works the same way as ox-horse. That is consistent with the one-name-one-thing rule, but it is different from the ordinary use of the term, and it allows the conclusion that white-horse is not horse by the same argument as that given by the Neo-Mohists.

The other horn of the dilemma is the more complicated one (and the one which is more prominent in the dialogue). It turns on the rigid interpretation of the nature of a name. A name must always pick out the same object. Suppose, then, the other alternative, that "white-horse" has its "commonsense" denotation. What then does "white" name? White-stuff in general? Then "white-horse" must include in its denotation the piece of chalk on my desk. Perhaps "white" in "white-horse" only names the white-stuff that is also horse, and similarly, "horse" as used in the compound "white-horse" only names the horse-stuff that is white. In that case, "horse" in "white-horse" is not *the same name* as "horse" *simpliciter* because it does not name *the same stuff*. Since the names used in the compound are not identifiable with those names used individually, the claim "white-horse not horse" is not necessarily false—it is *k'o* 'assertable'. On Lung's analysis of this second view, white-horse is not ontologically complex—not a compound object made up of two components—but a unique entity with a unique name.

This dilemma seems to structure most of the sophist's replies in the dialogue, but some problems remain. The presentation is often confused by the failure of the sophist to make clear when he has shifted from one to the other horn of the dilemma. Further, specious arguments are scattered among the theoretically illuminating ones. One such argument suggests that since "horse" and "white-horse" can be regarded as "ones" (individuals) and since they are different, they are not identical. This is the argument which lends plausibility to the abstract interpretation. However, as noted above, it can as easily be adapted to a claim about the nonidentity of singular stuffs.

Another well-known argument from the dialogue is also of little help in analyzing the theory behind the paradox. It is a simple and common deductive fallacy. The formal structure of the argument is: A is B; A is not-C; therefore B is not-C. (Yellow-horse is horse; yellow-horse is not white-horse; therefore white-horse is not horse.) I have placed the argument at the end of the dialogue since it contributes nothing to developing the theory behind the dialogue.

TRANSLATION AND COMMENTARY

In the following translation and commentary, I am essentially following the order proposed by Graham. The sentences are numbered and lettered. The letters represent Graham's order and the numbers the traditional order.

白馬非馬可乎。
曰可
曰何哉
曰馬者所以命形也。白者所以命色也。命色者非命形也。故曰白馬
非馬

O. Is it admissible that white-horse is not-horse?
S. It is admissible.

O. Why?

S. "Horse" is used to name shape; "white" is used to name color. What names color is not what names shape. Therefore, I say white-horse is not horse.[A–D/1–4]

This first argument has had considerable attention and analysis. Graham noted that the argument proves only that the white is not horse. Chmielewski has defended the argument as deductively valid with "white-horse not horse" as the conclusion. Chmielewski assumed that Kung-sun Lung was employing a logic based on the language of mathematical classes. That is to attribute to the sophist a neat and flexible ontology (classes, subclasses, and members) that would normally be taken as a coherent account of the proposition that a white horse *is* a horse. The problems with that interpretation were discussed in chapter 2: Kung-sun Lung seemingly does not distinguish between subclasses and members, nor, on Chmielewski's view, does he allow classes to intersect. Chmielewski does acknowledge that it is a strange logic of classes which does not allow for class intersection. The point ought to be that a theory which does not distinguish between classes and members nor allow intersection of classes is not a logic of mathematical classes at all.

As a consequence of the seeming inadequacy of the first argument, many commentators amend the penultimate sentence on the authority of a Sung Dynasty version of the text to "What names the color *and the shape* is not what names the shape" by adding or substituting the character *hsing* 'shape'. T'an Chieh-fu argues that this makes more sense of the argument.

> To say "that which names the color is not that which names the shape" is to say "that which names white is not that which names horses"—but this hardly needs saying and, having said it, it is neither to the point at issue, nor is it sufficient to support what follows. Therefore, I suspect that che 者 is a mistake and here I have corrected it to *hsing* 形 'shape'.

But Graham finds the textual variant on which the suggestion is based of questionable authenticity given contemporary quotations of the same argument:

> But although the variant is very attractive, the standard reading is supported by the summary in the first chapter and its *Hsin Lun* parallel as well as by the quotations of Chang Chan and Liu Chun.

The emendation of *che* 者 'that which' to *hsing* 形 'shape' does not render the argument more convincing. It merely makes the third sentence instead of the fourth out of place and implausible. The first two sentences would be irrelevant to the third instead of the first three irrelevant to the fourth.

Something is missing that fills the gap between this first argument and the supposed conclusion. I suggest that it is an argument a semanticist might take as already given, namely, the "ox-horse not ox is acceptable" argument mentioned earlier. A–D/1–4 is the argument for extending that result to the white-horse example. Kung-sun Lung proves, as Graham insisted, only that "some white things are not horses." But that premise triggers the rest of the argument to the conclusion "white-horse not horse." Some white things are not horses, so "white-horse not horse" is assertable.

This is the argument from the first horn of the dilemma. Since *white* names some non-horse, then it does so in the compound name as well. The compound name, on the ox-horse, mass sum model, names all the stuff which is either white-stuff *or* horse-stuff. *White-horse* is, on this analysis, a more "general" term than either *white* or *horse*. It is, accordingly, admissible that white-horse is non-horse because some of the stuff named by the compound is non-horse. The first argument is to the triggering premise in an argument which was already available in ancient Chinese semantic theory.

The argument given by Kung-sun Lung proves only that white is not horse, but that is conceivably all that Kung-sun Lung may have intended. He can now appeal to the analysis of ox-horse. Since white is not horse, then "white-horse not horse" is, in the Mohists' words, "without difficulty." This follows if we accept the first alternative in the dilemma and think of both *white* and *horse* as names with the same reference before and after forming the compound. Then, the sophist insists, we must treat *white-horse* as naming the mass sum of white-stuff and horse-stuff. This is the apparent semantic translation of the claim that "white-horse" is a separable compound. Separable compounds are those which are mass sums.

In the next exchange the objector uses the algebraic inference discussed in chapter 4 to attack the apparently general conclusion that colored horse is non-horse. The sophist's answer seems still to be in the mass sum model. Horses are colored and there is white-horse, and there is horse, but white is not horse and so one may assert of the combination of white and horse that it is non-horse.

曰以馬之有色爲非馬天下非有無色之馬也。天下無馬可乎
曰馬固有色故有白馬。使馬無色有馬如已耳。安取白馬。故白者非
馬也。白馬者馬與白也。馬與白馬也。故曰白馬非馬也

O. If we take horse's having color as non-horse, since there is no colorless horse in the world, is it admissible that there is no horse in the world?
S. Horse certainly has color, which is why there is white-horse. Suppose horse without color, then there would be just horse and where would you find white-horse? The white is not horse. White-horse is white and horse combined. Horse and white is horse, therefore, I say white-horse is non-horse. [E–F/7–8]

In the final sentence, "horse and white is horse" appears to contradict the sophist's intended conclusion, but not if we suppose he is using the mass sum model of compounding. Again, like the Mohists he can accept both "ox-horse is ox" and "ox-horse is non-ox." If Kung-sun Lung is building on that doctrine, then the troublesome phrase is totally consistent with his view. He is not saying "white-horse is horse" is inadmissible, only that "white-horse is non-horse" is equally admissible.

The objector, defending the commonsense view, chooses the other horn of the dilemma. He wants to read "white-horse" in the alternate Mohist model, the "hard-white" model, as naming a mass product. The objector has argued that horse is invariably connected with some color. Similarly, he will argue that white cannot exist independently but always interpenetrating something else, that is, white interpenetrates (is not a *t'i*) and is an "inseparable" part of any compound which contains it.

The mass product model is the one to which Kung-sun Lung must object. It raises problems for someone attracted to the strict view of names implied by the rectification of names—one-name-one-thing. The "hard-white" model generates the other horn of the dilemma. The sophist apparently feels that if hard-white is inseparable, interpenetrates, and has a smaller scope than either component term, then there are two names for what seems to be one stuff. Ox-horse is not one stuff in this sense at all, but two. If we regard hard-white as ontologically complex, its components are not coextensional with the hard and the white. So since "white" in "hard-white" just does not have the same scope as does "white" by itself, it could not be the same name. *Hard-white* must be a name which is, in this sense, independent of *hard* and *white*.

This horn of the dilemma exposes the difficulty of assuming that all words are names. Kung-sun Lung views naming as the sole semantic relation *and* sticks to a rigid version of the account of the naming relation. Those in his tradition had difficulty refuting him, supposedly, because the name-thing paradigm was so well entrenched. The strict account of names seemed plausible *and* in accord with the Confucian doctrine of rectification of names.

The Mohists, not overly concerned with the strict requirements of the rectification of names, were not bothered by different kinds of compounds. Kung-sun Lung was, and thus tried to separate hard and white, to show that they were not a unity but ultimately two things even when combined.

The objector notes that Kung-sun Lung's answer mixed the two models by talking about white horses with the "commonsense" mass product extension while arguing that the words should have the mass sum extension. So his argument for the paradox is incoherent. The sophist's answer seems to shift to the second horn of the dilemma.

曰馬未與白爲馬。白未與馬爲白。合「馬」與「白」復名「白馬」
是相與以不相與爲名未可。故曰「白馬非馬」未可

曰「白」者不定所白。忘之而可也。「白馬」者言白定所白也。定所
白者非「白」也。「馬」者無去取於色。故黃黑皆所以應。「白馬」
者有去取於色。黃黑馬皆所以色去。故唯白馬獨可以應耳。無去者
非有去也。故曰「白馬非馬」

O. If it is horse not yet combined with white which you deem horse, and white not yet combined with horse which you deem white, to compound the name "white-horse" for horse and white joined together is to give them when combined their names when uncombined, which is inadmissible. Therefore I say: it is inadmissible that white-horse is not horse.

S. "White" does not fix anything as white; that may be left out of account. "White-horse" says "white" fixes something as white. What fixes something as white is not white. "Horse" neither selects nor excludes any colors and, therefore, it can be answered with either yellow or black. "White-horse" selects some color and excludes others, and the yellow and black are both excluded on grounds of color; therefore, one may answer it only with white-horse. What excludes none is not what excludes some. Therefore I say: white-horse is not horse. [G–H/9–14]

In allowing there is white-horse, the sophist, according to the objector, has violated his own principle. He has used the name *white* (in the compound *white-horse*) to name white in combination with something. The sophist replies that, in effect, the compound *white-horse* does not contain the name *white* or the name *horse*. The name *white* in the compound *white-horse* "fixes" something as white, that is, has only horses in its range, and what "fixes" something as white is not the name *white*. A similar argument is suggested for the name *horse* in *white-horse*; since *horse* in *white-horse* "selects and excludes colors," that is, includes in its range only white horses, it is not identical with the uncombined name *horse*.

Kung-sun Lung's name-centered position is that the name *white-horse* cannot be regarded as consisting of the names *white* and *horse*. It is, like *palomino*, an independent name for only that thing. The only way available for talking about names is via the object referred to, and since the referents of the "names" are different, they cannot be the same names.

The objector uses a phrase, *combined with*, which is the term used in the Neo-Mohist Canon for interpenetrating compounds 相與 . Whether the objector is using the Mohist view or just formulating a commonsense view, he continues to hold that the combination is one of the interpenetration, mass product type. In the next exchange, the objector again uses algebraic inference against Kung-sun Lung, adding yu 有 'have' to his equation.

曰「有白馬」不可謂「無馬」也。不可謂「無馬」者有馬也。
白馬」爲「有馬」白之非馬何也。

O. Having white-horse cannot be called "not having horse." What cannot be called "not having horse" is having horse. Since having white-horse is deemed having horse, why claim that if white it is not horse? [I/5]

曰以「有白馬」爲「有馬」謂「有白馬」爲「有黃馬」可乎
曰未可
曰以「有馬」爲異「有黃馬」是異黃馬於馬也。異黃馬於馬是以黃
馬爲非馬也。以黃馬爲非馬而以白馬爲有馬此飛者入池棺槨異。處
此天下之悖言亂辭也。

S. If you deem having white-horse as having horse, is it admissible to say that having white-horse is deemed having yellow-horse?
O. No.
S. To deem having horse as different from having yellow-horse is to distinguish yellow-

horse from horse. To distinguish yellow-horse from horse is to deem yellow-horse as non-horse. To deem yellow-horse as non-horse and yet claim that white-horse is having horse, this is like flying underwater and saying the two parts of a coffin are in different places—it is the most perverse doctrine and confused phrase under heaven. [L–N/10–12]

The sophist's response to the objector looks frivolous. There might be a serious point at issue here, however. Perhaps the objector really is a skilled Mohist dialectician, and the sophist is taking a veiled dig at one of the Mohist positions—the "killing thieves is not killing men" argument. The progression of question and answer is too imprecise to be sure. As it stands, the sophist's first question has nothing to do with his subsequent accusation. The objector "distinguishes," reasonably enough on his grounds, white-horse and yellow-horse. Kung-sun Lung assumes that he has admitted that having yellow-horse is different from having horse. Thus he presents the identity argument discussed above: because yellow-horse (or white-horse) can be distinguished from horse, it is not horse.

The objector seems here to turn back to the first horn of Kung-sun Lung's dilemma, seemingly to argue that the dilemma faces the sophist as well. He cannot consistently formulate either horn of the dilemma without shifting between the two accounts of how names work. He addresses Kung-sun Lung as a *li che* 離者 'one who separates' (supposedly, hard and white). *Li che* are those who hold that all compound names represent combinations of the ox-horse type and are, therefore, separable. But as we saw in the Canon and in the sophist's own earlier answer (pp. 163–64), one can still say that white-horse is horse. It must therefore be assertable that he has horse if he has white-horse. It is, to be sure, also assertable that he has non-horse, but it is not assertable that he does *not* have horse.

日有白馬不可謂無馬者離白之謂也。不離者有白馬不可謂有馬也。
故所以爲有馬者獨馬爲有馬耳。非有白馬爲有馬。故其爲有馬也不
可以謂馬馬也。

O. Even those who hold that white is separable [i.e., like ox-horse in combinations] say "having white horse" is "having horse," [since having the sum is having the parts]. If you do not separate white, you say that "having white horse" cannot be called "having horse." So what is used to constitute "having horse" is exclusively deeming horse as "having horse" and he denies that "having white horse" is "having horse." So in his use of "having horse," he cannot call horse "horse." [K/13]

The objection does seem to assume a lot of common ground with Neo-Mohist semantic theory. The Mohists directed their arguments about hard-white against a doctrine of separation. Kung-sun Lung was known as one who separated hard and white. The Mohist doctrine is that hard-white is different from ox-horse in that no matter where you go in the combination you will find both—they cease to have separate identity. Ox-horse, on the other hand, is "separable," and in part of the mass named by the compound you will come upon non-horse and non-ox. Thus one can say "Ox-horse is not horse." But even for ox-horse, you must also say that if there is ox-horse there is horse (because part of it is horse). You can also say there is non-horse, but that does not deny that there is horse. The objector has made the sophist contradict one of his principles in the separation thesis and deny that there being white-horse, there is horse—which, he justifiably argues, should be true even for those who hold the doctrine of *li pai* 'separation of white'. But this advocate of separation denies even that. So he must deny that having anything but pure (i.e., uncolored) horse can be called "having horse." Since by his earlier admission that there is no uncolored horse, he cannot even call horse "horse."

Kung-sun Lung's second argument, based as it is on the assumption that all words are strict names, has forced him to an untenable ontology. White-horse must be treated as ontologically simple, and he must deny that the world contains horse at all—since he acknowledges that all horse is colored. This is potentially disastrous for him since he would be forced by a similar argument (adding another adjective like, e.g., *wild*) to deny that there is white-horse or yellow-horse either, and so on ad infinitum. Kung-sun Lung is open to the objector's last criticism because of his use of the second horn of the dilemma, according to which compounds like *white-horse* are to be understood as names of unique entities—having no relations to entities named by the parts of the compound. That account would make learning a language take forever. Every modified noun would have to be separately learned by ostension.

The sophist's final reply does not really attempt to salvage his position. It seems designed merely to confuse his opponent. This is the deductive fallacy discussed on page 161 and is most charitably regarded as an act of desperation.

日求馬黃黑馬皆可致。求白馬黃黑馬不可致。使白馬乃馬也是所求
一也。所求一者白者不異馬也。所求不異如黃黑馬有可有不可何也。
可與不可其相非明。故黃黑馬一也。而可以應有馬而不可以應有白
馬。是白馬之非馬審矣

S. If someone seeks horse, yellow- or black-horse will suffice. In seeking white-horse, yellow- or black-horse will not suffice. If one makes white-horse horse this is to make what is sought identical. If what was sought was identical then white (stuff) would not be different from horse (stuff). If what is sought is not different then such as yellow and black are both admissible and not admissible—how can this be? Admissible and not admissible are clearly mutually incompatible. So yellow- or black-horse is one and it can correspond to having horse but it cannot correspond to having white horse. This is the explication of white-horse's being non-horse. [J/6]

Probably the nicest thing we can say about this argument is that it may be taken as an attempt to justify the relatively trivial "identity" interpretation of the paradox: "white-horse" is not identical with "horse." This argument is the most often quoted one from the dialogue, and it seems to me the least helpful in understanding the theoretical position.

Ignoring the desperate final shot, the dialogue leaves us with two positions for Kung-sun Lung. The first arguments and the objector's later response indicate that Kung-sun Lung wants to "separate" white and horse in a way that changes the ordinary "scope" of the name *white-horse,* that is, to make it the sum of the masses named by *white* and *horse.* This makes the position one which explains the criticism by other philosophers from pre-Han times (e.g., Hsün-tzu and K'ung Ch'uan) who took the issue to be one of the generality of names in combination. It also explains Kung-sun Lung's reputation as one who separates hard-white.

But the sophist is pushed to other arguments that suggest a different theory. They indicate that he wanted not so much to separate "white-horse" as to insist that it had no semantic relations to "white" or "horse" used alone. These "names" used alone could name nothing at all, as the objector notes. The sophist's position commits him to an ontology that excludes horses and a semantics that makes learning a language unmanageable.

Kung-sun Lung correctly senses that there is a problem with the Neo-Mohist account of compounding, but he is even more committed than the Mohists to the key error, namely, regarding all terms as names. The Neo-Mohists were pushed by their accounts of commonsense use of language to deny that there was any strict relation between language and world—and to affirm, rather, that it shifted and changed with context. Kung-sun Lung wanted to make what the Mohists regarded as unreliable names into strict names which followed the one-name-one-thing formula.

Both the sophist's proposals are designed to satisfy that formula. The problem is that on the first proposal, we may only intelligibly talk about the things for which there are characters (names), and compound terms (including modified nouns) can denote only sums of those things. On the second proposal, as the objector points out, the character *ma* 馬 'horse' will name nothing at all since all actual horse is colored.

• • •

Rhetoric, Feminism, and Gender Studies

❦

In 42 BCE, Hortensia, a Roman woman, spoke before the Forum on behalf of 1400 wealthy women on whom a new tax had been imposed. During the late first century and early second century CE, Pan Chao, a Chinese woman of the court of the Eastern Han emperor Ho, served as historian to the court and wrote, among other things, *Lessons for Women*. In fifteenth-century France, Christine de Pizan wrote women's history, an argument for the moral and intellectual equality of women and men, and an instruction book for women. In seventeenth-century England, Mary Astell wrote a guide for women on how to speak and persuade, emphasizing a female disposition toward persuasiveness. All of these women lived before the mid-nineteenth century, which is often cited as the beginning of the first wave of feminism, and new attention to their presence has contributed to the recognition that female and feminist contributions to rhetorical theory have a long history.

Taking a cue from Patricia Bizzell's survey of "Opportunities for Feminist Research in the History of Rhetoric," we might categorize feminist research on rhetoric into four areas:

Revisionist history, in which overlooked female rhetoricians are written into rhetoric's history, male-authored texts are reread from a feminist perspective, and the outlines of rhetoric's history are re-evaluated

Redefinition of the theory and practice of rhetoric, in order to include works by women who do not fit into traditional categories and to construct a field of rhetoric more equitable toward women, minorities, and other marginalized groups

Language study, in which women's ways of using language are explored to discern women's styles of speaking and writing, the patriarchal nature of language itself is analyzed in order to understand how language has perpetuated gender oppression, and alternative language styles are advanced

Recognition of women's oratory as a body of implicit rhetorical theory.

Feminist studies now stand in relation to additional concerns that fall under a more general title, gender studies. This area includes gay and lesbian scholarship that has initiated a number of tasks addressing the nature and function of rhetoric: writing histories of the construction of homosexual identity; engaging in analysis of the discourse of hetero- and homosexuality, homophobia and anti-homophobia; and analyzing the "epistemology of the closet."

With the recognition that the history of rhetoric has paid rather exclusive attention to male theorists such as Plato, Aristotle, and Cicero, feminist scholars such as Michelle Ballif and Barbara Biesecker nonetheless challenge the entire enterprise of writing women into the existing histories. They propose that the mere incorporation of women may evade questioning the male-centered methods of conceiving and writing rhetoric's history. One of several important challenges to male-centered historiography is Susan Jarratt's *Rereading the Sophists,* which challenges the devaluation of sophistic rhetoric that commonly informs constructions of the Western intellectual tradition, and proposes relationships between the sophistry of antiquity and current feminism.

Kathy Davis has suggested what a particularly feminist rhetoric might seek to do: Welcome openess toward solutions of complex problems, recognizing that any solutions are partial and temporary; engage in critical self-reflection about its own rhetoric; and focus on the empowerment of women, which will necessarily make some constructions of rhetoric "better" to adopt than others. A feminist rhetoric must address what can be called a "feminine style"; Karlyn Kohrs Campbell characterizes such a style by inductive reasoning and a personal tone, and notes that female orators have tended to base their authority on their experience and to invite audience participation.

The readings in this section represent a variety of approaches to the relationship between rhetoric, feminism, and gender studies, spanning different countries of origin, time periods, racial and ethnic backgrounds, and sexual orientations. They should indicate the shape of the "conversation" that informs this field of inquiry.

Audrey Wick's essay, "The Feminist Sophistic Enterprise: From Euripides to the Vietnam War" is a "feminist sophistic rereading of both modern and ancient texts." "Axiom 5" from Eve Kosofsky Sedgwick's *Epistemology of the Closet* examines differing historical paradigms for the study of the connections between homosexuality and structures of knowledge.

Portions of speeches and writing by Pan Chao, Christine de Pizan, and the Seneca Falls Convention are suggestive of theoretical positions on rhetoric as well as examples of female discourse. Pan Chao, in first-century China, writes for a female audience, outlining what the ethos of women should be and how they should speak. Distinguished by the quality of *yin,* as opposed to the masculine *yang,* women are to be "yielding"; their words "need be neither clever in debate nor keen in conversation." While Pan Chao reflects the "proper" attitude of her culture toward male and female characteristics and relationships, she also challenges her culture by questioning the lack of educational parity between boys and girls. Christine de Pizan, writing in fifteenth-century France, provides a feminist critique of Ovid, the Bible, and classical rhetoricians Cicero and Quintus Hortensias, while writing female rhetor Hortensia back into history. Doing so, Christine enacts a theoretical position currently advanced by current feminists such as Wick and Japp. The Seneca Falls "Declaration of Sentiments and Resolutions" of 1848 suggests the feminist rhetorical strategy of revising male-authored and male-supporting texts such as the "Declaration of Independence" to suit women's purposes.

Mary Daly's *New Intergalactic Wickedary of the English Language* offers a new history of the English language; critical essays that attack ways in which language has been appropriated for use against women, animals, and the Earth by the academy, the State, and the Church; and a radical revision of the language itself. Her book weaves together theory and practice, spinning out in rhyme, rhythm, and alliteration a new web of nonpatriarchal terms designed to free women from their imprisonment by "snools." To the extent that the work of academic scholars—even feminists—can be for Daly a capitulation to snooldom, she calls into question the work of some of the other scholars represented in this section.

FURTHER READING

Ballif, Michelle. "Re/Dressing Histories; Or, On Re/Covering Figures Who Have Been Laid Bare By Our Gaze." *Rhetoric Society Quarterly* 22.1 (1992): 75–90.

Belenky, Mary Field, et al. *Women's Ways of Knowing: The Development of Self, Voice, and Mind.* New York: Basic, 1986.

Biesecker, Barbara. "Coming to Terms with Recent Attempts to Write Women into the History of Rhetoric." *Philosophy and Rhetoric* 25.2 (1992): 40–61.

Bizzell, Patricia. "Opportunities for Feminist Research in the History of Rhetoric." *Rhetoric Review* 11.1 (1992): 50–58.

Davis, Kathy. "Toward a Feminist Rhetoric: The Gilligan Debate Revisited." *Women's Studies International Forum* 15.2 (1992): 219–31.

Jarratt, Susan C. *Rereading the Sophists: Classical Rhetoric Refigured.* Carbondale: Southern Illinois UP, 1991.

Audrey Wick

"The Feminist Sophistic Enterprise: From Euripides to the Vietnam War"

The ancient sophists' investigation of physis and nomos, which took place against the backdrop of the unpopular and unsettling Peloponnesian War, challenged the foundations of Greek society. Although the essentially patriarchal nature of Greek society precludes assuming any "feminist" concern for the status of women, in many fundamental ways the sophists' project was not unlike that of modern feminists who also question dominant definitions and categories of gendered subjectivity (Jarratt "Feminism"). In the United States, a great deal of current feminist theory also emerged in the wake of the unpopular Vietnam War. War promotes and depends upon cultural bonding and social solidarity to produce patriotic fervor and unquestioning allegiance to the state. In these two eras, the eventual unpopularity of the war—which irritated and was irritated by the renegotiation of class and economic boundaries—opened questions about the status of citizenship, economic privilege, family life and, of course, gender roles. In both eras these changes were endorsed by many who had heretofore been excluded from many of the benefits of the patriarchy, but they were resisted by others who feared losing or sharing privilege.

Although popular mythology insists upon the illusion of progressive enlightenment, there is ample evidence to support the argument that periods of progressive change have often been followed by periods of repression and even regression (Kelly). The sophists' project came to an abrupt end when their pluralistic argument and pragmatic adaptations were replaced by the monolithic patriarchal certainty of Plato and Aristotle—a certainty which in various guises still operates on modern society. In Page duBois's words, Plato, in the fourth century, "appropriated feminine and particularly reproductive metaphors in order to reaffirm old patterns of dominance and to establish through new rationalization certain objects of knowledge, certain forms of power" (2). Currently, we are experiencing a similar conservative backlash—economic, racist, and sexist— which, as Susan Jeffords's work on the Vietnam War shows, enacts "the large-scale renegotiation and regeneration of the interests, values, and projects of patriarchy now taking place in U.S. social relations" (xi).

The sophistic era was marked by intellectual excitement, but the sophists' explorations were not universally acclaimed nor were they even in agreement with each other. Some of their ideas threatened members of the aristocracy who were eager to undo democratic reforms, while other ideas, for example the famous dictum that "justice is the interest of the stronger," threatened democratic principles. The basis of sophistic practice and teaching was the discovery and exposition of opposing and contradictory arguments—dissoi logoi—in order to provide their students with the training in moral reasoning and discursive ability which would allow them to assume civic responsibility (Crowley; Jarratt "History"; Jarrett). In the course of their work they attempted to draw distinctions between physis (natural laws which are closely allied with nature, universally valid, and authorized by the gods) and nomos (law or convention) (Guthrie, Hadas, Reinhold). Despite the sophists' "deep concern about important ethical, political, historical and legal questions" (Crowley 318), these distinctions alarmed conservatives.

The sophists' forum was a culture experimenting with the first democratic government in history, a government which allowed full political equality of all citizens (whose numbers did not include women, foreigners or slaves) and permitted them to vote by place of residence rather than by wealth or tribal association (Reinhold 55). The traditional land-based economy gave way to one which welcomed trade, manufacturing, and innovation (Bowra 186). While this new form of government had a great need for the "civic training" of the sophists, those whose old ways of life were threatened claimed that the sophists dealt only in clever arguments which showed no ethical regard for truth. The protracted Peloponnesian War, with its enormous military losses, caused chaotic political conditions which allowed great discussion and debate, but which also drained Athenians of economic resources, vitality and confidence (Bowra 187). The society that emerged from this epic struggle was an amalgamation of old and new ideas, but much of the work of the sophists was forgotten and their methods as well as their ideas were subsequently discredited by conservative forces.

In some respects, the women's movement of the sixties and its aftermath show certain parallels with the sophistic era. Historians agree that the initial impetus for the women's movement was the civil rights movement, which sought to disrupt old definitions of "separate but equal" and open up civil and economic opportunities to black Americans. Women involved in the civil rights movement became aware that their own situation in relation to white males in the movement was not unlike that of blacks in the society at large. Simplistically articulated, the issue was: "How come you middle class white guys who are so committed to equal rights for blacks don't see that you are treating the women involved in the movement like slaves?" When the men scathingly told the women to quit confusing insignificant personal issues with important political issues, the answer came back fast and loud: "The personal is the political." This insight led to the disruption of many traditional concepts of women and family life as women became more and more aware that, in a patriarchal society, sex/gender systems and systems of productive relations "operate simultaneously to reproduce the socioeconomic and male-dominant structures of that particular social order" (Kelly 61).

Many gains were made, but we are all aware of the backlash now occurring which threatens to undo many of those gains. The reasons for the backlash are complex, but many former liberals have come to realize that, in our current depressed economy, affirmative action cuts into their share of the pie. The abstract ideal has become a threatening reality. As in the sophistic era, the disruption of the war not only allowed cultural change, but also changed cultural concepts of war as well. Both civil rights and women's rights became entangled with student war protests. Students protested the inequities of the draft, and women began to investigate and publish the horrors perpetrated on the women and children of Vietnam. These activities led to widespread formal and informal challenges of patriarchal constructions of gender and war. Not incidentally, the renegotiation of "the relationship between high art and mass culture gained its own political momentum in the context of the emerging new social movements" (Huyssen, 204). This renegotiation has been instrumental in gaining the academic respectability for mass culture, opening the way for valuable explorations, like that of Susan Jeffords, of popular culture's representations of gender. Ironically, as her work shows, although the Vietnam War protests brought many productive changes in the status of women and minorities, the war was also enormously involved in the reconstruction of some of the most pernicious representations of masculinity and femininity.

Although these parallels between ancient and modern times are neither exact nor the primary focus of this paper, there are enough similarities to make a feminist sophistic rereading of both modern and ancient texts a viable rhetorical project. Looking at the variety of women's issues in the work of Euripides provides evidence that present day arguments about the social construction of gender began before Euripides, and were continued by Euripides. In the confused era following the Peloponnesian War, Euripides's fertile explorations were submerged by the "master narratives of patriarchy." These narratives, while only "inventions ... nevertheless powerfully controlled the interpretation" (Franco, "Plotting" xxiii). The authority and longevity of interpretations and definitions formulated by Plato in his feud with the sophists are remarkable in that they have overwhelmed not one but several attempts to seriously question patriarchal values. And they threaten to do so again. My goal is simply to examine some of the ways in which tensions between masculinity and femininity are mediated in discourse in both these eras in an effort to illuminate the origins of the dilemmas which still exist and to urge sophistic intervention in an effort to forestall another arbitrary closure.

We know that the sophists were intensely aware of the difficulty of differentiating appearance from reality both in the material world and in the infinitely more complicated world of natural and man-made law, but the fragmentary nature of their texts makes it impossible to determine the full impact of their ideas on various strata of society. However, the work of Euripides, who was profoundly influenced by the sophists, not only dramatizes ideas that were important to those on both sides of this struggle, but also provides a pragmatic insight into the nature of the search. W. K. C. Guthrie maintains that Euripides had mastered the rhetorical tricks of the sophists and that he knew and practiced the subtleties of argument: "Like Protagoras, [Euripides] knew that there were two sides to every question, and he enjoyed as much as Hippias the 'contest of words' in which his characters indulge" (128).

Just as importantly, Euripides provides a dramatic forum which allows us to see the impact of sophistic methods on the lives of individuals. His characters suffer from and question Athenian laws which deny "basic rights to women, foreigners and bastards" (Hadas, x). By shifting the mythical ground of heroic exploits and subjecting his characters to human dilemmas and choices which often allow no palatable solutions, he foregrounds both the rhetorical context of these dilemmas and the responsibility for the individual. Tragic inevitability gives way to responsible but agonizing human choice as Euripides tries to envision various alternatives.

Euripides's motivations for investigating all perspectives are also strikingly similar to those of the sophists. By dramatizing several interpretations of any given state of affairs, Euripides employs sophistic methods to push the viewer/reader to contemplate "an appropriate course of action" which "balances alternatives against one another" (Crowley 327). Susan Jarratt notes that some feminist scholars are also employing sophistic techniques to work their way out of the deconstructive impasse ("Feminism" 32). These feminists also feel that the obligation of the responsible citizen is "the choice of a position, in full knowledge that the 'economy' of her selection leaves out the other, less usable truths" (Jarratt, "Feminism" 32).

Like the sophists, some feminists are intensely interested in exploring physis and nomos. One school of feminists argues that men and women have essentially different natures and that these natures are reflected in mythology. They maintain that the old matriarchal myths were buried in order to suppress the history of the natural superiority of women and hence must be resurrected. Some would erect a matriarchy to counter the patriarchy—a Demeter myth to replace the Oedipal. Another school insists that there are great dangers in this position because it merely inverts the hierarchy and perpetuates the same social injustices in the name of the mother instead of the father. They maintain that, by insisting upon essential differences in the feminine psyche, the hierarchy of binary differences that has assigned women to an inferior place in society is being perpetuated, or at best simply inverted. They would excavate the origins of our myths hoping to show that all differences are cultural and not biological, and hence changeable. Marxist feminists insist that both of these approaches neglect the effect of social and economic class upon the position of women and would concentrate on the way these factors shaped the course of mythology.

In Euripides, there are hints of alternate mythologies, mythologies that preceded the Oedipal, as well as glimpses of how the suppression of the old mythologies was accomplished over the centuries. "[T]he pre-Hellenic myths are the religion of a conquered people, so they were co-opted and replaced for political reasons"

(Spretnak 22). "[T]he invaders blended certain aspects of pre-Hellenic religion, i.e., principally the Goddesses' names, with their own patriarchal Gods and themes" (Spretnak 21). Consequently, many modern constructions of gender have their roots in classical Greek culture and through longevity and the prestige of psychoanalytic theory, i.e., principally in regard to Freudian constructions of the Oedipal, have achieved the status of archetypes. Although many of the presumptions of psychoanalysis have been discredited, the influence of Freudian theory has taken its place in the unconscious of our culture, and the Oedipal myth continues to provide the basis for many contemporary images of family life (Deleuze and Guattari). As feminist scholars deconstruct classical Greek works, they are discovering that in antiquity these myths were not accepted as universal myths of the human psyche.

Motherhood, for instance, is at first glance one of the most unproblematic of familial relationships. That mothers give birth is an incontrovertible physiological fact. It is widely recognized that animal mothers are provided with certain instincts to ensure preservation of their young. They feed them, shelter them in dens or nests, and protect them fiercely; hence, by analogy, the widespread assumption that mothers have been assigned the nurturant role by nature. Greek drama is littered with allusions to the strength of this bond, as when Demeter lays the crops waste after her daughter is stolen. And there are indications scattered throughout Euripides's plays that the ancient power of the mother religion, with its emphasis on birth and fertility, still exerts a powerful influence on this patriarchal society.

True to sophistic form, however, Euripides's allusions to motherhood and the mother religions show the dark side as well as the strength of creativity. In *The Bacchae*, for example, when the festival reaches a fever pitch, Agave literally rips her son's body to shreds. Although the play is scattered with references to the Dionysus cult as a new religion, a good case can be made for the syncretization of the new Dionysian cults with the older agricultural earth mother rites in which young men were commonly sacrificed (Brumfield, Goodrich, Harrison). In other plays we see the calmer face of the goddess. In *Helen*, for instance, the chorus unexpectedly raises a beautiful hymn to "the mountain Mother." The song contributes nothing to our understanding of Helen's immediate situation, but it evokes Persephone's lonely sojourn in a strange world.

In *Ion*, the complicated plot revolves around the mystery of the title character's birth. After the virgin Creusa is raped and impregnated by Apollo, she gives birth secretly in a cave and abandons her son, Ion. Creusa subsequently marries Xuthus, and years later the couple visit Delphi to ask the gods to remedy their childlessness. Xuthus is deceitfully told that Ion, who has been raised as a temple servant, is his son. Creusa, enraged that Xuthus would bring "another woman's" child into their home, makes an attempt on Ion's life. However, a temple priestess reveals the tokens which allow the reconciliation of Ion and Creusa as mother and son. One of the first questions Ion puts to his newly found mother is: "Was your father sprung of the earth?" (267). This is a reference to the myths of autochthonous generation in which the earth, in its metaphorical association with women, gives birth to all life without "the agency of another species" (duBois 42). In these myths of autochthony, the father's role was incompletely understood. Consequently, in goddess rituals, women, birth, and fertility were mystically associated, and women were imbued with a mystical power over life and death (Spretnak 19). DuBois points out that in Hesiod's *Theogony* the primacy of the maternal body is demonstrated: "Gaia now first gave birth to starry Duranos, her match in size, to encompass all of her" (43). By the Theban era the metaphor of woman as earth had diminished to include "sowing" as an important considera-tion in fertility thus indicating that the patriarchy had already begun to insert itself into the parthenogenetic myths (55). Although Creusa assures Ion that her father, Erichthonius, has indeed sprung from the earth, when Ion puts the same proposition to Xuthus, saying, "Then I must have been born of mother Earth" (542), Xuthus replies that "The ground doesn't bear children" (543). Thus, although Ion is willing, even eager, to believe that he has sprung from the earth, Xuthus repudiates the myth of the autochthony of his wife's family and turns to a reasoned account of sowing his wild oats before marrying Creusa to account for Ion's birth. The old myth is reaffirmed and repudiated within the same play, leav-ing Euripides's position open to interpretation, but establishing that the "truth" of patriarchal religion was at least debatable.

At the same time, Euripides dramatizes the imposition of convention upon the natural ties of motherhood. When Creusa is asked how she could abandon her newborn baby in the cave, we can feel her anguish in her reply. It was hard, very hard, "... if you had seen the babe stretch his hands out to me!" (960). Later, after Creusa learns that Ion is her son, she tells him more about the ordeal:

> In fear of my mother, I wrapped you in these swaddling clothes which covered you, the unsteady work of a young girl's shuttle. No mother's breast had you to give you milk, no mother's hands to wash you. You were left to die; ... it was terror, my child, that constrained me to fling your life away. In spite of myself, I became your murderer. (1488–96)

Although Creusa herself is born of stock "sprung from the earth," from a line that is proudly fatherless, she abandons her own baby, conceived when she is raped by Apollo, through fear of her mother. Her mother has become the enforcer of the patriarchal laws that insist upon female virginity and the rights of paterni-ty. Although Creusa had no control over her impregnation by the god, she knows that she will be disgraced, and she knows that she will pay for this disgrace. Social disgrace clearly outweighs her so-called "natural instincts" to protect her child, and she opts—with the gods' contrivance—for the appearance of virginity. We can conclude either that social law is stronger than natural law, or that per-haps, even that which we assume is natural law is itself a convention. Creusa's subsequent barrenness might be construed as punishment for the violation of a natural law, but since the violation was Apollo's and he abandons her, the ques-tion becomes confusing. A god's law is, after all, a natural law. Her retainer's advice to "burn the oracle" adds to the confusion. Does he imply that Apollo acted wrongly and that a human being is capable of avenging herself upon him? Or is it that without the oracle, the "appearance" of obedience will be preserved? Is appearance, as in the case of her virginity, more important than fact?

Euripides is clearly sympathetic to Creusa's plight, and the deception of Xuthus points to weaknesses of the patriarchal system. Xuthus is Apollo's dupe. He remains, by Apollo's command, fallaciously convinced that he is Ion's father. Through this happy deception Ion is able to inherit his mother's property, just as he would in a matrilineal society. However, the situation is arranged by Euripides so that it looks as if Ion is inheriting the property because Xuthus is his father. Again, the possibilities for interpretation are complex. This may be a cynical reflection on the uncertainty of paternity, a conventional discussion of the deception of men by women, or a suggestion that the stringency of the conventions designed to ensure the father's lineage have operated not to protect his line but to force the terrified girl to hide her pregnancy. Although in one sense the ancient law of matrimonial inheritance is upheld, it is upheld through a deception which silences any discussion of Creusa's rights. The ending, however, just as clearly shows the ebbing strength of the old matriarchal traditions.

The complicated and conflicting energies of Clytemnestra also call the nature of motherhood into question. Clytemnestra moves in and out of our sympathies not only from play to play but from scene to scene. In *Iphigenia at Aulis* she is a powerful and loving mother who fights furiously against the proposed sacrifice of her daughter. She rails against Agamemnon, insists that Helen's child should be sacrificed instead of hers, and pleads with Achilles to help her save Iphigenia. Her appeal to Achilles reveals both her own helpless plight—as a woman she is powerless to stay the sacrifice—and her wit as she reveals her careful calculations to the audience. Clytemnestra says to Achilles: "Ah, how can I praise you with words not too fulsome [aside] yet not so sparing as to lose his favor?" (977–78). While she manages Achilles through artifice, all of her arguments to Agamemnon appeal to natural bonds: Can a father slay his own child, the child who always loved him the most? How then will his other children welcome him? That Agamemnon is severing a sacred bond is made clear when Iphigenia wails: "I am slain, I perish, foully slaughtered by a godless father" (1316–17).

None of these arguments prevail and the legal and moral right of the father to the very life of his children is affirmed when Iphigenia herself accepts her death and tells her mother to do her own duty. She willingly lays down her life to ensure that the Hellenes will rule, and her rationale is that it is not right that Hellenes be ruled by barbarians for "Hellenes are free" (1401). Mary Lefkowitz maintains that, by accepting the values of the male world, Iphigenia "wins the greatest reward, victory for her country, glory (and survival) for herself" (99). But although the patriarchal law prevails, it is revealed to be a sordid and questionable affair. Agamemnon has already compromised the divine nature of his charge by cynically questioning the truth of the oracle, and, as the scenes unfold, "no shred of heroic dignity is left to the great names of the Trojan War" (Hadas 313).

In *Electra*, Clytemnestra assumes another character. The devoted mother who fought furiously for her daughter abandons two of her children when she murders

Agamemnon and takes a new husband. Electra calls her a whore who eagerly painted her face to attract another man even as her husband's ship sailed from Troy (1070–75). Characteristically, Clytemnestra is given a chance to tell her side of the story. She maintains that she struggled to be a good wife even though she had been given to Agamemnon as a trophy of war, even though he murdered her infant son from her first marriage, and even though he sacrificed their own daughter, Iphigenia. In these scenes she is no murderess but a much wronged woman driven to desperation by the loss of her children, until she suddenly adds:

> but then he came home to me with a mad, god-filled girl and introduced her to our bed . . . Oh, women are fools for sex, deny it I shall not. Since this is in our nature. . . . (1032–35)

Finally then, it is not the murder of her daughter, but sexual jealousy which drives her to murder her husband. Even if sexual drive and motherhood are both "natural" motives, sexual jealousy is the lesser in the hierarchy of motives. In a few short lines, Clytemnestra has abrogated her claim for our sympathy by emphasizing the stereotypical and negative characteristics that have gradually come to be associated with women. Dark, tumultuous, ungovernable passion overrides reason and duty. To add to the tension, both Electra and Clytemnestra make it clear throughout the play that socially and economically they have no function in society except in relation to a man. Consequently, concern for their personal situations often overrides other familial bonds.

The same point is made in Andromache. When Hermione realizes that she has allowed her jealousy of Andromache to jeopardize her marriage, she bitterly regrets the pride that led her to make the attempt on Andromache's life. She laments not because she regrets the loss of her husband, but because she fears the loss of her marriage:

> Why should I be keeping watch over a husband? I had everything I needed, ample wealth and complete authority in the palace. Any children I had would be legitimate, whereas hers would be bastards and, through their mother slaves to mine. (936–39)

Men may imagine that their wives rend their breasts and tear their hair because of their thwarted passion for them, but Euripides points to a more pragmatic necessity—to adjust to the prevailing economic situation.

In *Helen*, by following Stesichorus' version of Helen rather than Homer's, Euripides questions not only the nature of men and women but notions of honor and war. If a phantom, and not the real Helen, went to Troy, then the whole purpose of the war is thrown into question. If Helen is chaste and Menelaus's honor is intact, lives were lost and countries devastated for an illusion. If, as Rex Warner suggests, the play was produced in 412 B.C.E. at the time of the Athenian disasters in Sicily, "the themes of going to war for the sake of a phantom, of the advantages of negotiation rather than force in international affairs . . . must have been applied by the audience to the contemporary situation" (130). Troubling questions about the nature of women can be added to those raised about the nature of war. Helen is portrayed as a good woman, chaste, honorable and intelligent. Warner calls her a "genuine heroine" (130). Yet she is condemned to years of needless suffering in order that men may win glory by performing heroic deeds on her behalf.

In *The Trojan Women*, Euripides links the plight of women and the destruction of feminine values even more obviously to the war period. *The Trojan Women* is an audacious criticism of war in that, as Moses Hadas points out, it was produced in a celebratory interval that followed the Athenian destruction of the Greek city of Melos—which had attempted to remain neutral in the Peloponnesian War (173). Although enthusiasm of Athenians for war was at a fever pitch, the wanton destruction of this great city and the slaughter and enslavement of Greek citizens prompted Euripides to portray war not just from the perspective of the defeated, but from the perspective of the women of the defeated. The former queen, Hecuba, now a broken old woman, relates heart-rending tales of pillage, rape, and slaughter of men, women, and even infants. The tales paint a portrait of human brutality and avarice rather than divine justice. Again, the feminine voices the critique.

In *Iphigenia at Aulis*, Euripides brings invective against war to its climax. After Iphigenia's sacrifice, a messenger thinking to comfort Clytemnestra tells her that a goddess has wafted Iphigenia to safety. Clytemnestra, bitterly reflecting that she brought her daughter to Agamemnon because of a false story, shows her mistrust of all their stories by answering: "What shall I say? Is this an idle story to comfort me, to end my bitter grief for you?" (1616–18). DuBois maintains that with this question Euripides throws the whole text into play. "The girl goes to her death for a lie; her salvation may well be a lie; the play itself is a lie; and the political myth of Hellas is a lie" (165).

That these plays were permitted, even officially sponsored, testifies to the democratic spirit of the Athenians (Hadas 173). Yet, by the end of the next century the floodgates of definition, at least definitions of women, had closed. Remnants of the old religion were firmly covered over and negative images of women came to predominate. DuBois outlines a series of five Greek representations of the female body which illustrate the successive change in the characterization of women. She demonstrates that as the images change from field, to furrow, to oven, to stone, to tablet, women are increasingly colonized. Once abundantly parthenogenic, woman is tamed, ploughed as fields are ploughed, and finally becomes the blank tablet upon which men write. Her "potential for producing goods or protecting them ... is alienated from the earth and made dependent on the male Athenian citizen" (169). Then, notes Catharine Stimpson, summarizing duBois, "in an audacious act of appropriation, Plato grants to the male philosopher the fertile self-sufficiency that pre-Socratic culture had once associated with the female. The seeds she nurtured are now the words he utters" (Stimpson xii).

Plato's enterprise took place amid the chaos of the Athenian defeat in the

Peloponnesian War: a period of political, social and economic crises that precipitated a return to oligarchy. Many of the writers of the late fifth and early fourth centuries condemned democracy and the ideology of equality, and longed for a return of aristocratic elitism. Most important for this discussion, "the texts of the fourth century establish new terms for the location of the female" (duBois 169).

Froma Zeitlin notes that "as war dragged on to its unhappy close, attention began to shift away from the masculine values of politics to the private sphere" (157). Soldiers of a defeated army cannot enhance their power with tales of heroic exploits, and new sources of validating masculinity must be found. Equally threatening, as women are forced to assume some of the roles and obligations of absent warriors, feminine self-concepts are altered in ways that further threaten the egos of failed warriors. Thus defeat may facilitate the appropriation of reproductive metaphors. Our interest in these plays and the issues that they raise can be linked to several contemporary issues. Compare, for example, this ancient appropriation of the female power of reproduction by disgruntled males, made possible in part by the turmoil of an unpopular war, to the scene that Susan Jeffords describes in *The Remasculinization of America*. Soldiers returning from Vietnam were greeted with cries of vituperation rather than adulation. Instead of the traditional acclaim which rewards those who fight their country's wars, the veterans faced criticism. They were seen as sellouts, moral failures, baby killers, and dope fiends. In addition, the civilian world had changed while they were gone. "With the advent of women's rights, civil rights, the 'generation gap' and other alterations in social relations that occurred during the fifties, sixties and seventies, the stability of the ground on which patriarchal power rests was challenged" (Jeffords xii). Jeffords argues that these changes were threatening to the relations of dominance that constitute masculinity in Western society, and that "in order to establish a context for a renegotiation of masculinity, an arena for masculine relations must be set forth" (xii).

Jeffords maintains that representations of Vietnam emphasize a masculine bond that crosses cultural and racial lines as a basis for reestablishing relations between men and society at large. She discusses television programs like "Miami Vice," "Riptide," "The A-Team," and "Magnum, P.I." to illustrate bonds between veterans that surpass legal, bureaucratic, and family connections. The first stage in this process that Jeffords describes is a means/end shift. In order to disassociate the loss of the war and the role of the soldier, emphasis shifts from winning to performing so that the actions of the soldier can be valorized. Because male admiration of the male body is not an acceptable activity in a heterosexual and patriarchal society, part of this project is the technologicizing of the male body. As technology, the male body and male heroics, can be admired. Rambo, "the fighting machine," is a prime example. Government is feminized both as the villain responsible for losing the war, and because it is associated with those legal changes that add to the displacement of male rights. "[T]he government and its representatives are argued as feminine not only in their loss of the war, but in their inability to retrieve POWs from Vietnam" (xiv). Think of the valorization of Oliver North's attempt to prevent a "soft government" from making cowards of us again, or the Rambo of "Rambo: First Blood Part II" as he walks away from a presidential pardon on a holy mission to find the POWs that the inept government had failed to find. The hero of post-Vietnam culture in fact and fiction is the male maverick who in the company of other stout-hearted men fixes the culture. One might say that he is building a new republic, one in which women and government become enemies of the male world.

This antagonism is currently being resolved just as it was resolved in Greek culture—through an appropriation of the feminine. Briefly, Jeffords demonstrates that popular culture "project[s] men as necessary and sufficient parents and birth figures" (xvi). Television again provides some examples of the popularity of this new masculine self-sufficiency. "Full House," "Paradise," "Who's Dad," and "You Again," all portray single fathers who take over traditional women's functions as they care for children and households. Through these varied and seemingly innocuous representations, this discourse has led to "an ambivalent and apparently increasing breakdown of gender articulations [which] has become specified to redefine the constructions of masculine and feminine in even firmer and more exclusionary terms, so that women are effectively eliminated from the masculine narration of war and the society of which it is an emblem" (186).

While media representations present only a partial view of what has been happening in the United States since the sixties, they provide a reasonable index of what those who produce movies and television thinks is an acceptable image. Jean Franco maintains that mass culture "plots" women into the social order: in effect, its representations become our realities ("Incorporation"). Much has been written about the distance between literary or dramatic representations and reality, but Phyllis Culham points out that in relation to ancient Greek literature such an examination "can demonstrate that a thought had become thinkable as of a certain date" (16). Given this stipulation, I have attempted to call attention to the similarities between the open, spirited investigation of the sophistic era and its abrupt closure, and our own turbulent sixties and its symptoms of closures—symptoms which are even now proliferating. That both the work of the sophists and the spirit of the age could be lost so completely speaks to the ability of institutions to mainstream and commodify marginal resistance (Barbara Johnson xii). It will take all our sophistic skills to keep the questions open.

Feminists have long realized the power of the domestic triangle—Mommy, Daddy and me, with Daddy firmly at the head—to reproduce itself endlessly in our institutions (Deleuze and Guattari) and they realize the need for change as well. All too often, however, while recognizing "the importance of not handing over notions of home and community," even feminists reproduce "the most conventional articulations" of home and family in their writing (Martin and Mohanty 191). Jeffords's work with representations of Vietnam shows that, while mass culture presents alternative family situations which seem more flexible, they are actually appropriations of reproduction by the male which reterritorialize older, patriarchal appropriations. They neither challenge them, nor do they assist with the deterritorialization (115). Consequently, in effect, they reintroduce Plato's earlier appropriation of feminine metaphors. Alternative representations of families are needed, but they must include feminist alternatives. This need for diverse interpretations can best be addressed by a feminist sophistic which speaks from and for a political community just as the first sophists did. The knowledge we have gained from our sophistic enterprise should allow us to insert ourselves as questioners. When we do this, as Adrienne Rich says, we are no longer the "woman question asked by someone else; we are the women who ask the questions" (216).

WORKS CITED

Bowra, C. M. *The Greek Experience.* Cleveland: The World, 1957.

Brumfield, Allaire Chandor. *The Attic Festivals of Demeter and Their Relationship To the Agricultural Year.* New York: Arno, 1981.

Culham, Phyllis. "Ten Years After Pomeroy: Studies of the Image and Reality of Women in Antiquity." *Rescuing Creusa.* Ed. Marilyn Skinner. Lubbock: Texas Tech UP, 1986.

Crowley, Sharon. "A Pleas for the Revival of Sophistry." *Rhetoric Review.* 7 (1989): 318–334.

Deleuze, Gilles, and Felix Guattari. *Anti-Oedipus: Capitalism and Schizophrenia.* Minneapolis: U of Minnesota P, 1988.

duBois, Page. *Sowing the Body: Psychoanalysis and Ancient Representations of Women.* Chicago: U of Chicago P, 1988.

Euripedes. *Andromache.* Ed. & trans. Moses Hadas and John McLean. *Ten Plays by Euripides.* 5th ed. New York: Bantam, 1985: 99–130.

———. *Electra.* Trans. Emily Townsend Vermeule. *Euripides V.* Ed. David Grene and Richmond Lattimore. New York: Washington Square, 1968:1–72.

———. *Ion.* Hadas 131–72.

———. *Iphigenia at Aulis.* Hadas 241–78.

Franco, Jean. *Plotting Women: Gender and Representation in Mexico.* New York: Columbia UP, 1989.

———. "The Incorporation of Women: A Comparison of North American and Mexican Popular Narrative." *Studies in Entertainment: Critical Approaches to Mass Culture.* Ed. Tania Modleski. Bloomington: Indiana UP 1986. 119–138.

Goodrich, Norma Lorre. *Priestesses.* New York: Franklin Watts, 1989.

Guthrie, W. K. C. *The Sophists.* New York: Cambridge UP, 1971.

Hadas, Moses. Foreword and Introductions. *Ten Plays by Euripides.* Trans. Moses Hadas and John McLean. 5th ed. New York: Bantam, 1985.

Harrison, Jane Ellen. *Epilegomena to the Study of Greek Religion and Themis.* New Hyde Park, NY: University Books, 1962 [1928].

Huyssen, Andreas. "Mass Culture as Woman: Modernism's Other." *Studies in Entertainment: Critical Approaches to Mass Culture.* Ed. Tania Modleski. Bloomington: Indiana UP, 1986. 188–207.

Jarratt, Susan C. "The First Sophists and the Uses of History." *Rhetoric Review* 6 (1987): 67–77.

———. "The First Sophists and Feminism: Discourses of the 'Other'." *Hypatia* 5 (1990): 27–41.

Jarrett, James L., ed. *The Educational Theories of the Sophists.* Columbia: Teachers College, 1969.

Jeffords, Susan. *The Remasculiniazation of America: Gender and the Vietnam War.* Bloomington: Indiana UP, 1989.

Johnson, Barbara. "Introduction: Truth or Consequences." *Consequences of Theory.* Eds. Jonathan Arac and Barbara Johnson. Baltimore: Johns Hopkins UP, 1991.

Kelly, Joan. *Women, History and Theory.* Chicago: U of Chicago P, 1984.

Lefkowitz, Mary R. *Women in Greek Myth.* Baltimore: Johns Hopkins UP, 1986.

Martin, Biddy, and Chandra Talpade Mohanty. "Feminist Politics: What's Home Got to Do with It?" *Feminist Studies/Critical Studies.* Bloomington: Indiana UP, 1986.

Reinhold, Meyer. *Essentials of Greek and Roman Classics.* New York: Barron's Educational Series, 1949.

Rich, Adrienne. *Blood, Bread and Poetry.* New York: Norton, 1986.

Spretnak, Charlene. *Lost Goddesses of Early Greece: A Collection of Pre-Hellenic Myths.* Boston: Beacon, 1984.

Stimpson, Catharine R. Foreword. *Sowing the Body: Psychoanalysis and Ancient Representations of Women.* By Page duBois. Chicago: U of Chicago P, 1988.

Warner, Rex. Trans. *Three Great Plays of Euripides: Medea, Hippolytus, Helen.* New York: New American Library, 1958.

Zeitlin, Froma I. "Travesties of Gender and Genre in Aristophanes' *Thesmophoriazousae.*" *Writing and Sexual Difference.* Ed. Elizabeth Abel. Chicago: U of Chicago P, 1982. 131–157.

Eve Kosofsky Sedgwick

Axiom 5: The historical search for a Great Paradigm Shift may obscure the present conditions of sexual identity.

Since 1976, when Michel Foucault, in an act of polemical bravado offered 1870 as the date of birth of modern homosexuality, the most sophisticated historically oriented work in gay studies has been offering ever more precise datings, ever more nuanced narratives of the development of homosexuality "as we know it today." The great value of this scholarly movement has been to subtract from that "as we know it today" the twin positivist assumptions (1) that there must be some *transhistorical* essence of "homosexuality" available to modern knowledge, and (2) that the history of understandings of same-sex relations has been a history of increasingly direct, true knowledge or comprehension of that essence. To the contrary, the recent historicizing work has assumed (1) that the differences between the homosexuality "we know today" and previous arrangements of same-sex relations may be so profound and so integrally rooted in other cultural differences that there may be no continuous, defining essence of "homosexuality" to *be* known; and (2) that modern "sexuality" and hence modern homosexuality are so intimately entangled with the historically distinctive contexts and structures that now count as *knowledge* that such "knowledge" can scarcely be a transparent window onto a separate realm of sexuality but, rather, itself constitutes that sexuality.

These developments have promised to be exciting and productive in the way that the most important work of history or, for that matter, of anthropology may be: in radically defamiliarizing and denaturalizing, not only the past and the distant, but the present. One way, however, in which such an analysis is still incomplete—in which, indeed, it seems to me that it has tended inadvertently to *refamiliarize, renaturalize*, damagingly reify an entity that it could be doing much more to subject to analysis—is in counterposing against the alterity of the past a relatively unified homosexuality that "we" *do* "know today." It seems that the topos of "homosexuality as we know it today," or even, to incorporate more fully the antipositivist finding of the Foucauldian shift, "homosexuality as we *conceive of it* today," has provided a rhetorically necessary fulcrum point for the denaturalizing work on the past done by many historians. But an unfortunate side effect of this move has been implicitly to underwrite the notion that "homosexuality as we conceive of it today" itself comprises a coherent definitional field rather than a space of overlapping, contradictory, and conflictual definitional forces. Unfortunately, this presents more than a problem of oversimplification. To the degree that power relations involving modern homo/heterosexual definition have been structured by the very tacitness of the double-binding force fields of conflicting definition—to the degree that the presumptuous, worldly implication "We Know What That Means" happens to be "the particular lie that animates and perpetuates the mechanism of [modern] homophobic male self-ignorance and violence and manipulability"—to that degree these historical projects, for all their immense care, value, and potential, still risk reinforcing a dangerous consensus of knowingness about the genuinely *un*known, more than vestigially contradictory structurings of contemporary experience.

As an example of this contradiction effect, let me juxtapose two programmatic statements of what seem to be intended as parallel and congruent projects. In the foundational Foucault passage to which I alluded above, the modern category of "homosexuality" that dates from 1870 is said to be

> characterized ... less by a type of sexual relations than by a certain quality of sexual sensibility, a certain way of inverting the masculine and the feminine in oneself. Homosexuality appeared s one of the forms of sexuality when it was transposed from the practice of sodomy onto a kind of interior androgyny, a hermaphrodism of the soul. The sodomite had been a temporary aberration; the homosexual was now a species.

In Foucault's account, the unidirectional emergence in the late nineteenth century of "the homosexual" as "a species," of homosexuality as a minoritizing identity, is seen as tied to an also undirectional, and continuing, emergent understanding of homosexuality in terms of gender inversion and gender transitivity. This understanding appears, indeed, according to Foucault, to underlie and constitute the common sense of the homosexuality "we know today." A more recent account by David M. Halperin, on the other hand, explicitly in the spirit and under the influence of Foucault but building, as well, on some intervening research by George Chauncey and others, constructs a rather different narrative—but constructs it, in a sense, *as if it were the same one:*

> Homosexuality and heterosexuality, as we currently understand them, are modern, Western, bourgeois productions. Nothing resembling them can be found in classical antiquity. . . . In London and Paris, in the seventeenth and eighteenth centuries, there appear . . . social gathering-places for persons of the same sex with the same socially deviant attitudes to sex and gender who wish to socialize and to have sex with one another. . . . This phenomenon contributes to the formation of the great nineteenth-century experience of "sexual inver-

sion," or sex-role reversal, in which some forms of sexual deviance are interpreted as, or conflated with, gender deviance. The emergence of homosexuality out of inversion, the formation of a sexual orientation independent of relative degrees of masculinity and femininity, takes place during the latter part of the nineteenth century and comes into its own only in the twentieth. Its highest expression is the "straight-acting and -appearing gay male," a man distinct from other men in absolutely no other respect besides that of his "sexuality."

Halperin offers some discussion of why and how he has been led to differ from Foucault in discussing "inversion" as a stage that in effect preceded "homosexuality." What he does not discuss is that his reading of "homosexuality" as "we currently understand" it—his presumption of the reader's commonsense, present-tense conceptualization of homosexuality, the point from which all the thought experiments of differentiation must proceed—is virtually the opposite of Foucault's. For Halperin, what is presumed to define modern homosexuality "as we understand" it, in the form of the straight-acting and -appearing gay male, is gender intransitivity; for Foucault, it is, in the form of the feminized man or virilized woman, gender transitivity.

What obscures this difference between two historians, I believe, is the underlying structural congruence of the two histories: each is a unidirectional narrative of supersession. Each one makes an overarching point about the complete conceptual alterity of earlier models of same-sex relations. In each history one model of same-sex relations is superseded by another, which may again be superseded by another. In each case the superseded model then drops out of the frame of analysis. For Halperin, the power and interest of a postinversion notion of "sexual orientation independent of relative degrees of masculinity and femininity" seem to indicate that that notion must necessarily be seen as superseding the inversion model; he then seems to assume that any elements of the inversion model still to be found in contemporary understandings of homosexuality may be viewed as mere historical remnants whose process of withering away, however protracted, merits no analytic attention. The end point of Halperin's narrative differs from that of Foucault, but his proceeding does not: just as Halperin, having discovered an important *intervening* model, assumes that it must be a *supervening* one as well, so Foucault had already assumed that the nineteenth-century intervention of a minoritizing discourse of sexual identity in a previously extant, universalizing discourse of "sodomitic" sexual acts must mean, for all intents and purposes, the eclipse of the latter.

This assumption is significant only if—as I will be arguing—the most potent effects of modern homo/heterosexual definition tend to spring precisely from the inexplicitness or denial of the gaps *between* long-coexisting minoritizing and universalizing, or gender-transitive and gender-intransitive, understandings of same-sex relations. If that argument is true, however, then the enactment performed by these historical narratives has some troubling entailments. For someone who lives, for instance, as I do, in a state where certain acts called "sodomy" are criminal regardless of the gender, never mind the homo/heterosexual "identity," of the persons who perform them, the threat of the juxtaposition *on* that prohibition against *acts* of an additional, unrationalized set of sanctions attaching to *identity* can only be exacerbated by the insistence of gay theory that the discourse of acts can represent nothing but an anachronistic vestige. The project of the present book will be to show how issues of modern homo/heterosexual definition are structured, not by the supersession of one model and the consequent withering away of another, but instead by the relations enabled by the unrationalized coexistence of different models during the times they do coexist. This project does not involve the construction of historical narratives alternative to those that have emerged from Foucault and his followers. Rather, it requires a reassignment of attention and emphasis within those valuable narratives— attempting, perhaps, to denarrativize them somewhat by focusing on a performative space of contradiction that they both delineate and, themselves performative, pass over in silence. I have tended, therefore, in these chapters not to stress the alterity of disappeared or now-supposed-alien understandings of same-sex relations but instead to invest attention in those unexpectedly plural, varied, and contradictory historical understandings whose residual—indeed, whose renewed—force seems most palpable today. My first aim is to denaturalize the present, rather than the past—in effect, to render less destructively presumable "homosexuality as we know it today."

Pan Chao

From: **Lessons for Women**

Chapter II

HUSBAND AND WIFE

The Way of husband and wife is intimately connected with *Yin* and *Yang,* and relates the individual to gods and ancestors. Truly it is the great principle of Heaven and Earth, and the great basis of human relationships. Therefore the "Rites" honor union of man and woman; and in the "Book of Poetry" the "First Ode" manifests the principle of marriage. For these reasons the relationship cannot but be an important one.

If a husband be unworthy then he possesses nothing by which to control his wife. If a wife be unworthy, then she possesses nothing with which to serve her husband. If a husband does not control his wife, then the rules of conduct manifesting his authority are abandoned and broken. If a wife does not serve her husband, then the proper relationship (between men and women) and the natural order of things are neglected and destroyed. As a matter of fact the purpose of these two (the controlling of women by men, and the serving of men by women) is the same.

Now examine the gentlemen of the present age. They only know that wives must be controlled, and that the husband's rules of conduct manifesting his authority must be established. They therefore teach their boys to read books and (study) histories. But they do not in the least understand that husbands and masters must (also) be served, and that the proper relationship and the rites should be maintained.

Yet only to teach men and not to teach women,—is that not ignoring the essential relation between them? According to the "Rites," it is the rule to begin to teach children to read at the age of eight years, and by the age of fifteen years they ought then to be ready for cultural training. Only why should it not be (that girls' education as well as boys' be) according to this principle?

Chapter III

RESPECT AND CAUTION

As *Yin* and *Yang* are not of the same nature, so man and woman have different characteristics. The distinctive quality of the *Yang* is rigidity; the function of the *Yin* is yielding. Man is honored for strength; a woman is beautiful on account of her gentleness. Hence there arose the common saying: "A man though born like a wolf may, it is feared, become a weak monstrosity; a woman though born like a mouse may, it is feared, become a tiger."

Now for self-culture nothing equals respect for others. To counteract firmness nothing equals compliance. Consequently it can be said that the Way of respect and acquiescence is woman's most important principle of conduct. So respect may be defined as nothing other than holding on to that which is permanent; and acquiescence nothing other than being liberal and generous. Those who are steadfast in devotion know that they should stay in their proper places; those who are liberal and generous esteem others, and honor and serve (them).

If husband and wife have the habit of staying together, never leaving one another, and following each other around within the limited space of their own rooms, then they will lust after and take liberties with one another. From such action improper language will arise between the two. This kind of discussion may lead to licentiousness. Out of licentiousness will be born a heart of disrespect to the husband. Such a result comes from not knowing that one should stay in one's proper place.

Furthermore, affairs may be either crooked or straight; words may be either right or wrong. Straightforwardness cannot but lead to quarreling; crookedness cannot but lead to accusation. If there are really accusations and quarrels, then undoubtedly there will be angry affairs. Such a result comes from not esteeming others, and not honoring and serving (them).

(If wives) suppress not contempt for husbands, then it follows (that such wives) rebuke and scold (their husbands). (If husbands) stop not short of anger, then they are certain to beat (their wives). The correct relationship between husband and wife is based upon harmony and intimacy, and (conjugal) love is grounded in proper union. Should actual blows be dealt, how could matrimonial relationship be preserved? Should sharp words be spoken, how could (conjugal) love exist? If love and proper relationship both be destroyed, then husband and wife are divided.

Chapter IV

WOMANLY QUALIFICATIONS

A woman (ought to) have four qualifications: (1) womanly virtue; (2) womanly words; (3) womanly bearing; and (4) womanly work. Now what is called womanly virtue need not be brilliant ability, exceptionally different from others. Womanly words need be neither clever in debate nor keen in conversation. Womanly appearance requires neither a pretty nor a perfect face and form. Womanly work need not be work done more skilfully than that of others.

To guard carefully her chastity; to control circumspectly her behavior; in every motion to exhibit modesty; and to model each act on the best usage, this is womanly virtue.

To choose her words with care; to avoid vulgar language; to speak at appropriate times; and not to weary others (with much conversation), may be called the characteristics of womanly words.

To wash and scrub filth away; to keep clothes and ornaments fresh and clean; to wash the head and bathe the body regularly, and to keep the person free from disgraceful filth, may be called the characteristics of womanly bearing.

With whole-hearted devotion to sew and to weave; to love not gossip and silly laughter; in cleanliness and order (to prepare) the wine and food for serving guests, may be called the characteristics of womanly work.

These four qualifications characterize the greatest virtue of a woman. No woman can afford to be without them. In fact they are very easy to possess if a woman only treasure them in her heart. The ancients had a saying: "Is Love afar off? If I desire love, then love is at hand!" So can it be said of these qualifications.

Chapter V

WHOLE-HEARTED DEVOTION

Now in the "Rites" is written the principle that a husband may marry again, but there is no Canon that authorizes a woman to be married the second time. Therefore it is said of husbands as of Heaven, that as certainly as people cannot run away from Heaven, so surely a wife cannot leave (a husband's home).

If people in action or character disobey the spirits of Heaven and of Earth, then Heaven punishes them. Likewise if a woman errs in the rites and in the proper mode of conduct, then her husband esteems her lightly. The ancient book, "A Pattern for Women," (*Nü Hsien*) says: "To obtain the love of one man is the crown of a woman's life; to lose the love of one man is to miss the aim in woman's life." For these reasons a woman cannot but seek to win her husband's heart. Nevertheless, the beseeching wife need not use flattery, coaxing words, and cheap methods to gain intimacy.

Decidedly nothing is better (to gain the heart of a husband) than whole-hearted devotion and correct manners. In accordance with the rites and the proper mode of conduct, (let a woman) live a pure life. Let her have ears that hear not licentiousness; and eyes that see not depravity. When she goes outside her own home, let her not be conspicuous in dress and manners. When at home let her not neglect her dress. Women should not assemble in groups, nor gather together, (for gossip and silly laughter). They should not stand watching in the gateways. (If a woman follows) these rules, she may be said to have whole-hearted devotion and correct manners.

If, in all her actions, she is frivolous, she sees and hears (only) that which pleases herself. At home her hair is dishevelled, and her dress is slovenly. Outside the home she emphasizes her femininity to attract attention; she says what ought not to be said; and she looks at what ought not to be seen. (If a woman does such as) these, (she may be) said to be without whole-hearted devotion and correct manners.

Christine de Pizan

From: *The Book of the City of Ladies*

"Here Christine tells how she dug in the ground, by which should be understood the questions which she put to Reason, and how Reason replied to her."

"Now I have prepared for you and commanded from you a great work. Consider how you can continue to excavate the ground following my marks." And so, in order to obey her command, I struck with all my force in the following way:

I.9.1

"My lady, how does it happen that Ovid, who is thought to be one of the best poets—although many believe, and I would agree with them, thanks to your correcting me, that Vergil is much more praiseworthy—that Ovid attacks women so much and so frequently, as in the book he calls *Ars amatoria,* as well as in the *Remedia amoris* and other of his volumes?"

I.9.2

She replied, "Ovid was a man skilled in the learned craft of poetry, and he possessed great wit and understanding in his work. However, he dissipated his body in every vanity and pleasure of the flesh, not just in one romance, but he abandoned himself to all the women he could, nor did he show restraint or loyalty, and so he stayed with no single woman. In his youth he led this kind of life as much as he could, for which in the end he received the fitting reward—dishonor and loss of possessions and limbs—for so much did he advise others through his own acts and words to lead a life like the one he led that he was finally exiled for his excessive promiscuity. Similarly, when afterward, thanks to the influence of several young, powerful Romans who were his supporters, he was called back from exile and failed to refrain from the misdeeds for which his guilt had already punished him, he was castrated and disfigured because of his faults. This is precisely the point I was telling you about before, for when he saw that he could no longer lead the life in which he was used to taking his pleasure, he began to attack women with his subtle reasonings, and through this effort he tried to make women unattractive to others."

"My lady, you are right, and I know a book by another Italian author, from the Tuscan marches, I think, called Cecco d'Ascoli, who wrote in one chapter such astounding abominations that a reasonable person ought not to repeat them."

She replied, "If Cecco d'Ascoli spoke badly about all women, my daughter, do not be amazed, for he detested all women and held them in hatred and disfavor; and similarly, on account of his horrible wickedness, he wanted all men to hate and detest women. He received the just reward for it: in his shame he was burned to death at the stake."

"I know another small book in Latin, my lady, called the *Secreta mulierum, The Secrets of Women*, which discusses the constitution of their natural bodies and especially their great defects."

She replied, "You can see for yourself without further proof, this book was written carelessly and colored by hypocrisy, for if you have looked at it, you know that it is obviously a treatise composed of lies. Although some say that it was written by Aristotle, it is not believable that such a philosopher could be charged with such contrived lies. For since women can clearly know with proof that certain things which he treats are not at all true, but pure fabrications, they can also conclude that the other details which he handles are outright lies. But don't you remember that he says in the beginning that some pope—I don't know which one—excommunicated every man who read the work to a woman or gave it to a woman to read?"

"My lady, I remember it well."

"Do you know the malicious reason why this lie was presented as credible to bestial and ignorant men at the beginning of the book?"

"No, my lady, not unless you tell me."

"It was done so that women would not know about the book and its contents, because the man who wrote it knew that if women read it or heard it read aloud, they would know it was lies, would contradict it, and make fun of it. With this pretense the author wanted to trick and deceive the men who read it."

"My lady, I recall that among other things, after he has discussed the impotence and weakness which cause the formation of a feminine body in the womb of the mother, he says that Nature is completely ashamed when she sees that she has formed such a body, as though it were something imperfect."

"But, sweet friend, don't you see the overweening madness, the irrational blindness which prompt such observations? Is Nature, the chambermaid of God, a greater mistress than her master, almighty God from whom comes such authority, who, when He willed, took the form of man and woman from His thought when it came to His holy will to form Adam from the mud of the ground in the field of Damascus and, once created, brought him into the Terrestrial Paradise which was and is the most worthy place in this world here below? There Adam slept, and God formed the body of woman from one of his ribs, signifying that she should stand at his side as a companion and never lie at his feet like a slave, and also that he should love her as his own flesh. If the Supreme Craftsman was not ashamed to create and form the feminine body, would Nature then have been ashamed? It is the height of folly to say this! Indeed, how was she formed? I don't know if you have already noted this: she was created in the image of God. How can any mouth dare to slander the vessel which bears such a noble imprint? But some men are foolish enough to think, when they hear that God made man in His image, that this refers to the material body. This was not the case, for God had not yet taken a human body. The soul is meant, the intellectual spirit which lasts eternally just like the Diety. God created the soul and placed wholly similar souls, equally good and noble in the feminine and in the masculine bodies. Now, to turn to the question of the creation of the body, woman was made by the Supreme Craftsman. In what place was she created? In the Terrestrial Paradise. From what substance? Was it vile matter? No, it was the noblest substance which had ever been created: it was from the body of man from which God made woman."

"My lady, according to what I understand from you, woman is a most noble creature. But even so, Cicero says that a man should never serve any woman and that he who does so debases himself, for no man should ever serve anyone lower than him." I.9.3

She replied, "The man or the woman in whom resides greater virtue is the higher; neither the loftiness nor the lowliness of a person lies in the body according to the sex, but in the perfection of conduct and virtues. And surely he is happy who serves the Virgin, who is above all the angels."

"My lady, one of the Catos—who was such a great orator—said, nevertheless, that if this world were without women, we would converse with the gods."

She replied, "You can now see the foolishness of the man who is considered wise, because, thanks to a woman, man reigns with God. And if anyone would say that man was banished because of Lady Eve, I tell you that he gained more through Mary than he lost through Eve when humanity was conjoined to the Godhead, which would never have taken place if Eve's misdeed had not occurred. Thus man and woman should be glad for this sin, through which such an honor has come about. For as low as human nature fell through this creature woman, was human nature lifted higher by this same creature. And as for conversing with the gods, as this Cato has said, if there had been no woman, he spoke truer than he knew, for he was a pagan, and among those of this belief, gods were thought to reside in Hell as well as in Heaven, that is, the devils whom they called the gods of Hell—so that it is no lie that these gods would have conversed with men, if Mary had not lived."

Karlyn Kohrs Campbell, ed.

"Declaration of Sentiments and Resolutions, 1848"

The Declaration of Sentiments, a paraphrase of the Declaration of Independence, was authored by Mary Ann McClintock, Lucretia Coffin Mott, Elizabeth Cady Stanton, and Martha Coffin Wright, who also published the call for the convention. Although the call appeared for only one day in the *Seneca County Courier* and Frederick Douglass's *North Star*, some 300 men and women attended the convention. According to the *History of Woman Suffrage*, following a number of speeches on the first day, "The Declaration having been freely discussed by many present, was . . . with some slight amendments adopted, and was signed by one hundred men and women" (1:69). Subsequently, after intensely hostile press reaction, many asked to have their names removed. Eleven resolutions were presented initially; at the last session, Coffin Mott proposed and spoke in support of #12. Only resolution #9 on woman suffrage was not unanimously adopted; it passed because of the strenuous efforts of former slave Frederick Douglass, an abolitionist speaker and publisher of the North Star. The texts of the Declaration of Sentiments and resolutions were published in HWS 1:70–73, and in the convention *Proceedings* (1870, 4–7).

DECLARATION OF SENTIMENTS

When, in the course of human events, it becomes necessary for one portion of the family of man to assume among the people of the earth a position different from that which they have hitherto occupied, but one to which the laws of nature and of nature's God entitle them, a decent respect to the opinions of mankind requires that they should declare the causes that impel them to such a course.

We hold these truths to be self-evident: that all men and women are created equal; that they are endowed by their Creator with certain inalienable rights, that among these are life, liberty, and the pursuit of happiness; that to secure these rights governments are instituted, deriving their just powers from the consent of the governed. Whenever any form of government becomes destructive of these ends, it is the right of those who suffer from it to refuse allegiance to it, and to insist upon the institution of a new government, laying its foundation on such principles, and organizing its powers in such form as to them shall seem most likely to effect their safety and happiness. Prudence, indeed, will dictate that governments long established should not be changed for light and transient causes; and accordingly, all experience hath shown that mankind are more disposed to suffer, while evils are sufferable, than to right themselves by abolishing the forms to which they were accustomed. But when a long train of abuses and usurpations, pursuing invariably the same object evinces a design to reduce them under absolute despotism, it is their duty to throw off such government and to provide new guards for their future security. Such has been the patient sufferance of the women under this government, and such is now the necessity which constrains them to demand the equal station to which they are entitled.

The history of mankind is a history of repeated injuries and usurpations on the part of man toward woman, having in direct object the establishment of an absolute tyranny over her. To prove this, let facts be submitted to a candid world.

He has never permitted her to exercise her inalienable right to the elective franchise.

He has compelled her to submit to laws, in the formation of which she had no voice.

He has withheld from her rights which are given to the most ignorant and degraded men—both natives and foreigners.

Having deprived her of this first right of a citizen, the elective franchise, thereby leaving her without representation in the halls of legislation, he has oppressed her on all sides.

He has made her, if married, in the eye of the law, civilly dead.

He has taken from her all right in property, even to the wages she earns.

He has made her, morally, an irresponsible being, as she can commit many crimes with impunity, provided they be done in the presence of her husband. In the covenant of marriage, she is compelled to promise obedience to her husband, he becoming, to all intents and purposes, her master—the law giving him power to deprive her of her liberty, and to administer chastisement.

He has so framed the laws of divorce, as to what shall be the proper causes of divorce; in case of separation, to whom the guardianship of the children shall be given; as to be wholly regardless of the happiness of women—the law, in all cases, going upon a false supposition of the supremacy of man, and giving all power into his hands.

After depriving her of all rights as a married woman, if single and the owner of property, he has taxed her to support a government which recognizes her only when her property can be made profitable to it.

He has monopolized nearly all the profitable employments, and from those she is permitted to follow, she receives but a scanty remuneration.

He closes against her all the avenues to wealth and distinction, which he considers most honorable to himself. As a teacher of theology, medicine, or law, she is not known.

He has denied her the facilities for obtaining a thorough education—all colleges being closed against her.

He allows her in Church, as well as State, but a subordinate position, claiming Apostolic authority for her exclusion from the ministry, and, with some exceptions, from any public participation in the affairs of the Church.

He has created a false public sentiment, by giving to the world a different code of morals for men and women, by which moral delinquencies which exclude women from society, are not only tolerated but deemed of little account in man.

He has usurped the prerogative of Jehovah himself, claiming it as his right to assign for her a sphere of action, when that belongs to her conscience and to her God.

He has endeavored, in every way that he could, to destroy her confidence in her own powers, to lessen her self-respect, and to make her willing to lead a dependent and abject life.

Now, in view of this entire disfranchisement of one-half the people of this country, their social and religious degradation,—in view of the unjust laws above mentioned, and because women do feel themselves aggrieved, oppressed, and fraudulently deprived of their most sacred rights, we insist that they have immediate admission to all the rights and privileges which belong to them as citizens of the United States.

In entering upon the great work before us, we anticipate no small amount of misconception, misrepresentation, and ridicule; but we shall use every instrumentality within our power to effect our object. We shall employ agents, circulate tracts, petition the state and national legislatures, and endeavor to enlist the pulpit and the press in our behalf. We hope this Convention will be followed by a series of Conventions, embracing every part of the country.

Firmly relying upon the final triumph of the Right and True, we do this day affix our signatures to this declaration. [*Names followed.*]

•   •   •

Mary Daly

Preliminary Web One
"The Wickedary:
Its History/Metamystery"

The work of the *Wickedary* is a process of freeing words from the cages and prisons of patriarchal patterns. Under the rule of snools, words are beaten down, banalized, reduced to serving the sentences of father time. They are made into ladies-in-waiting, wasted and worn in the service of thought-stopping grammar.

Websters unwind the bindings of mummified/numbified words. This process involves Hearing/Speaking through Other Time/Space. It implies unwinding the clocks of fathered time, which is tidy time. The Timing of the *Wickedary* deliberately counters the death march of patriarchal deadtime.

Websters Weave the *Wickedary* in the Thirteenth Hour. This Time is Moon-measured, Moon-Wise, beyond the reach of man-measured doomsday clocks, the tedious timers and ticking time bombs of clockocracy. It is the Time of Cronelogical innovation/creation.

The *Wickedary* is a declaration that words and women have served the fathers' sentences long enough. Websters ride the rhythms of Tidal Time, freeing words. Like birds uncaged, these Soundings rush and soar, seeking sister-vibrations. *Wickedary* words, when Heard, sound the signal that Tidal Time has come.

THE ARCHAIC HISTORY OF THE WICKEDARY

In a Weird sense, these Wicked Weavings originated some immeasurable Time ago. Indeed, the *Wickedary*'s origins are Archaic. They are whenever/wherever women first began/begin Be-Speaking. The *Wickedary*'s background is the Background.

Many of the *Wickedary*'s threads were Originally caught in ordinary patriarchal dictionaries such as the *Oxford English Dictionary, American Heritage Dictionary,* and, of course, *Webster's.* This has been possible and continues to be possible because such lexicons themselves contain countless hidden Webs.

Websters/Wickedarians are familiar with the experience of "chasing through the dictionary," that is, of catching the thread of a word and following it (for example, by checking out synonyms, looking up words contained in the definition, following clues in the etymology, or simply lighting upon another word on the page, for instance, a Guide Word). This following and chasing of words is a process of tracing a hidden Web and then Webs of Webs, threading/treading the way/ways through the Labyrinth of words buried in dictionaries.

Websters are aided in the Dis-covering of Webs in dictionaries by the fact that these lexicons still contain "archaic" and "obsolete" words and definitions. Our Web-finding is aided also by the fact that there are deep resonances even in currently used words, which carry in their wake ancestral Memories of hidden Elemental meanings. Such words—in contrast to mere elementary terms—can be Deeply Heard by those whose Labyrinthine Sense has been awakened. That is, they can be Heard/Understood by the Internal Ear of a Wicked Webster—one who actively chooses her own Wildness. They can be Seen by a Spinster who chooses to Realize her Self and her own kind, that is, to See with Real Eyes.

Wickedarians believe that one reason we can Dis-cover Webs of Wild Words in the ordinary dictionaries of patriarchy is that these were Archaically woven by Wild Women—by our own kind. Even when denied access to the written word and to the academented fraternities of Bearded Brother No-it-alls, women have always talked. Women have Be-Spoken logically, powerfully, magically, Elementally. The Race of Wild Women has always been a Race of Speakers, Spinners, Weavers. Weird Women have been Great Original Communicators, and with respect to these communications, the role of dictionary editors has essentially been merely to compile. The word *compile* is itself an A-mazing clue. Derived from the Latin *compilare,* meaning "to plunder," it means "to collect into a volume" and "to compose out of materials from other documents" (*Webster's Collegiate*). The dryasdust pedants of patriarchy have plundered and pillaged women's Word-Weavings. They have collected and twisted the Wise Words of Crones in their tedious tomes. They have composed/decomposed documents from materials which are the Documents of Others' Lives.

The *Wickedary*'s History, then, is interwoven with the History of the Race of Wild Women, and its Webs are comprised of Re-weavings as well as New Weavings of that History. Repairing and Dis-covering our own Archaic Webs, Websters create Archaic Futures. We Spin into Original Time and, from that perspective, wink at the pomposity of the "sacred" paternal pronouncement that "in the beginning was the word." Quite simply, "the word" of wasters/erasers of women's History is a colossal lie.

Websters Re-weaving our own Heritage howl at the "history" of wantwits and windbags. As Gossips, we Gossip out (divine and communicate) the secrets of our own History, which have been smoldering among the Embers of the Fires in which Fore-Crones/Fore-Websters were burned alive as Witches. These secrets—hidden by "history"—empower us to Gossip wisdom from the stars.

Wickedarians Dis-covering Webs hidden in dictionaries and Other Sources participate in the creation of Terrible Tapestries and Live in Crone-Time. We

Weave in the Presence of Other Gossips, that is, Boon-Companions. Crone-logically and Super Naturally we Gossip out the true nature of the history of man, encountering and exposing The Mystery of Man.

THE MYSTERY OF MAN

According to *Webster's,* the word *mystery* is derived from the Greek *myein,* meaning "to initiate into religious rites," and also meaning "to close (used of the eyes and lips)." It is said to be possibly akin to the Latin *mutus,* meaning "mute." These etymological clues can lead Websters a long way in the complex process of unraveling the mystery of the word *mystery.* In the process of unraveling, we should consider the fact that the Greek etymology itself is fraught with mystery. Why, we might ask, should initiation involve an injunction to close the eyes and the lips? A miasma of mystification and murkiness is attached to the very word *mystery.* If we look steadily at this word, Seeing it with Real Eyes, we understand that it functions within a patriarchal context as an archetypal elementary term, that is, as a mummy term. It serves to mummify Crones, to confuse, ensnare, and tame Terrible Women, and ultimately to block Elemental Journeyers.

Webster's serves up several definitions of *mystery,* each more unappetizing than the next. Thus, for example, we read that it means "a religious truth revealed by God that man cannot know by reason alone and that once it has been revealed cannot be completely understood … *usu cap:* a Christian religious rite or sacrament: as (1) EUCHARIST (2) mysteries *pl:* HOLY MYSTERIES (3) any of the 15 meditations on the events of the life of Christ forming the major part of the rosary devotion." It is Crone-logical to point out that one possible reason why a "religious truth" said to be revealed by god continues to be unintelligible is simply that it makes no sense. Mystified believers are of course commanded to deny their own intellectual integrity and blindly believe the babbling of men to whom god purportedly has revealed the nonsensical mystery.

Wicked Women, who notice that the "religious mysteries" of men make no sense, are enabled to gain Pyromantic perspective on other activities of mysterious men. In sum: Their academented speech makes no sense; their military science makes no sense; their -ologies (classified information) make no sense; their politics make no sense; their laws make no sense; their medicine makes no sense. Of course, Seers are ordered to keep our eyes closed to all of this mysteriousness/nonsense and to say nothing. Such Crone-logical, unclassifiable information is taboo.

A Bitchy, Be-Witching woman—a Soothsayer—is compelled to Notice and Denounce the universal lack of sense masked by mysterious men. Such Formal Denouncements by Furies could be grouped under several nonclassifications, such as "The Failure of Man"; "Flopocracy: A History of Man's Disasters"; "The Mysterical Man: A Critical Study in Male Psychology"; "The Eternal Mystery/Mistery/Misery of Man."

Many women, having frequently peeked behind the male veils and Gossiped out the facts, are able to Hear such Denouncements. Sensing and dreading the imminent possibility of such exposure, man cloaks himself in ever murkier mysteries. He is constantly having mysterics/misterics. In his religious "revelations," especially, he mysterically reveals/re-veils himself. He withdraws into all-male clubs and secret societies—those manifold priesthoods of cockocracy marked by mumbo-jumbo, ridiculous rituals, and cockaludicrous costumes. Hoping to distract from his own stupendous senselessness and to prevent women from Seeing through and Naming his illusions/delusions, he requires/prescribes female "mysteriousness," pompously proclaiming that women's eyes and lips must be sealed.

The Weaving of the *Wickedary* requires Opening our eyes, particularly our Third Eye, emitting Eye-Beams/I-Beams—Radiant Glances of the Eye/I. It demands the Opening of Augurs' lips to Name Reality. Under phallocratic rule, the Eyes and Lips of women have been forcibly sealed by the stupendously stupefying weight of the omnipresent mysteries of phallicism. Fired and empowered by Fury, Labrys-wielding Amazons and Viragos rip the veils of male mysteries, especially the "supernatural" ones. We Announce the Arrival of the Super Natural, the Supremely Natural. We unveil and release the Powerful Witch within our Selves—the Great Original Witch who is hidden by such man-made mysterious archetypes as the "eternal feminine."

Lacking Biophilic History, patriarchal males have needed to make up "mystery" to hide an abysmal absence of Presence. They have distracted Others from this ruse by projecting and fixing the label "mysterious" not only onto women but also upon all Wild be-ing, blocking Realization of Elemental Powers. Countering this ruse, the *Wickedary* participates in the work of exposing the sordid mysteries of sadosociety's priesthoods, which are contrived to confound their victims, to mute the Wicked Words of Moon-Wise Weirds and Websters.

Wickedarians unfold the man-made blindfolds that are intended to block Visionary Powers and prevent the Unfolding of Be-ing. We tear away the gags intended to stop the Nagging of Nags and Hags. When we speak of such Unfolding/Ungagging as History we are saying that the Be-Speaking of our Selves as Seers is twined with the work of creation. Our task is nothing less than Dis-covering and creating Real History behind/beyond mystery, finding our Final Cause, participating in Realms of Metamystery.

METAMYSTERY

The History that is Dis-covered and created by Websters is Metamystery, in dimensions that incorporate all of the senses of the prefix *meta*. First, the breakthrough to Metamystery occurs only *after* a woman has refused to keep her eyes closed and remain silent about the Awesome Archaic Powers of her Self and all Elemental be-ing. Second, a woman rips open man's mystery by actualizing these Elemental Powers, thus Dis-covering what is *behind* the man-made veils that have clouded her Vision. She sees through the non-sense of phallocracy/fooldom and Touches her own Wild Reality, her Background.

The third dimension of Metamystery follows logically from such an experience—or series of experiences—of breakthrough to the Background. That is, there is a release of pent-up Gynergy which *transforms* a woman's ways of thinking, feeling, acting. The Fire of her Fury melts down the embedded man-made plastic passions and unpots the potted passions that marked/marred her former life as a patriarchally possessed "mysterious" woman. She sloughs off the pseudovirtues of victimhood that were enforced during long years in the State of Servitude and acquires the Volcanic Virtues/Vices of a Virago. Breaking out of bondage, she learns to bond with Others. Re-membering ancient connections, she enters Metamorphospheres.

This transformative activity brings a Metamorphosing woman to the fourth dimension of Metamystery, which is movement *beyond* the mysteries of man into Original Time, that is, Creative Time—the Time of Metamemory and of Archaic Futures. Moved by Wonder at the absolutely Natural workings of Elemental Reality, Creative Crones transcend the mummified state that is legitimized and sustained by dead faith in man's mysteries.

THE CONCEALMENT OF ELEMENTAL COMMUNICATING POWERS

Female History/Metamystery actually happens when Wicked women refuse complicity in the patriarchs' concealment of our Powers, particularly our Metamysterious Elemental Powers of Communication. By labeling women and nature "mysterious," the paternal propagandists have committed a colossal crime of reversal, negating/denying the Powers of Seers and Soothsayers. There is a major clue in this strategy of the mindbinders, spookers, and wasters who rule the Phallic State. By attempting to hide Elemental Powers of Communication they have indicated how strong these Powers are.

Indeed, Elemental Powers of Communication are at the root of those abilities which are readily attributed to women in the State of Mystery/Misery, such as aptitudes for nurturing, healing, teaching, social facilitating, organizing. The very attribution of these capabilities to women conveniently functions to hide the depth and scope of Wicked Communicating Powers. The phallocrats have worked feverishly to reduce these Powers and then have fetishized their stunted derivatives, which are allowed expression only under male control. These "gifts of women" that are acknowledged within patriarchy have been rendered shallow and disconnected from women's own deep purposefulness. They have been fashioned to suit the masters' dead ends, to support the agendas of popocracy.

The sadosocietal system fixes and freezes women's Elemental Powers of Communication, confining their expression to "appropriate" stereotypic activities, such as those assigned to wives and mothers, nurses, schoolmarms, hostesses, and efficient do-gooders. Thus enslaved by the snoolish rules and rulers, women become complicit in the stunting and fragmentation of our Selves. A phallically fixed wife and mother keeps pop on his pedestal and nurtures future faithful followers of fatherland's rules/roles. A nurse whose loyalty is to physicians and patriarchal medicine is a servant of disease-causing agents. A female teacher, whether she works in a nursery school or in a Ph.D. program, who uncritically transmits the dogmas of doublethink is an agent of maledom's mindbinding.

In order to free the Metamysterious Elemental Communicating Powers of women that have been tied down by the spiritbindings of sadospiritual fixers, it is essential to begin adequately to Name the complex and interwoven meanings and dimensions of these Powers. This brings us to the Strange and Sinister Subject of Mediumship.

METAMYSTERY AND MEDIUMSHIP

Dictionaries offer clues concerning Metamysterious Powers through the medium of definitions, for example, definitions of the word *medium*. Among the meanings of this word are "something intermediate in position" and "an intermediate agency, means, instrument, or channel" (*O.E.D.*). These definitions can aid Websters in the process of locating the Place/Time where/when we Touch and transmit Metamysterious Powers. This ever moving Labyrinthine Location is on the Boundary between the elementary/restored/plastic world which is the State of Possession and the Wild Realms of Metabeing.

As Journeyers become Wilder, the location of the Boundary shifts further away from the centers of patriarchal possession and deeper into the Otherworld. As this happens, the man-made "mysteries" lose their power to conceal from Journeyers the Realms of our own Reality. Be-Wildering Websters Unweave the veils designed to hide our Selves from our Selves and Weave further into the Background. With Eye-Biting Powers, Be-Witching women snap the blinding/binding ties that have kept us from Seeing and Be-Speaking. Breaking these evil ties, we See with truly Wicked Eyes. The shimmering splendor of Sister-Voyagers is Realized, further revealing the foolishness of snools. Unveiled, these mysterical men evoke our Wholly Hysterical Laughter. With every Laugh, Lusty Leapers Leap further, bounding to Other Boundaries.

With each Leap and Bound, each shifting of Boundaries, more mindbindings/spiritbindings come undone. Our Mediumship springs, spirals, and soars. Our Space-Craft moves outside all hitherto known directions. We Spin beyond the compass of every compass.

Mediums are Sylph-satisfied with the clues provided in *Webster's* definition of *medium* as "something through or by which something is accomplished, conveyed, or carried on." A Metamysterious Medium experiences her Self as someone through or by whom something is accomplished and conveyed. As for carrying on, Happy Mediums do indeed carry on about the Wonders of our

Mediumship, Announcing that a Sylph-identified Medium is, like the Air, a conveyer of Words, and that a Salamandrous Medium is, like Fire, a conveyer of Light and Warmth.

Also pleasing to Happy Mediums is *Webster's* definition of *medium* as "a condition, atmosphere, or environment in which something may function or flourish." We note that by choosing our Mediumship we participate in the creation of a condition, atmosphere, or environment—that is, a Gyn/Ecological environment—in which Biophilic being can function and flourish.

Sylph-affirming Mediums/Muses join in the chorus of Others, creating an atmosphere in which New Words can be spoken and sung, participating in the Cosmic Concento—the Crone-logically simultaneous sounding of the tones of Accord among all Biophilic beings. Moreover, New Words themselves are Mediums, carriers of messages, and their Soundings break through man's mysteries. They Weave together, forming magic tapestries/carpets, carrying Muses/Mediums further into Metamysterious Realms.

All Elemental beings are Mediums, conveyers of knowledge and power. Searchers can find countless affirmations of this fact in studies of folklore and magic. The following passage is a typical Eye-opening Example:

> Among the Celtic races we observe divination, or forecasting the future, by means of omens and auspices, through the media of the flight and motions of birds, by the casting of bones, or omen-sticks, the movements or direction taken by animals, by dreams and crystal-gazing, almost precisely as we find these several methods employed by many other races.

As this passage illustrates, Mediumship implies participation in Tidal Time, movement into Archaic Future. It is therefore prophetic.

The Elements, as Metamysterious Mediums, communicate with Crones engaged in the work of prophecy/divination. This is suggested by such words as *Aeromancy, Geomancy, Hydromancy, Pyromancy.* The Air, Earth, Water, and Fire Be-Speak to those whose Senses are alive. It is evident also that the stars have been known as Mediums by astrologers for millennia, together with the moon, sun, and other planets. The *Angel,* since it is derived from the Latin *angelus,* meaning "messenger," points to the fact that Elemental Spirits, too, are Mediums.

THE CALL OF THE ELEMENTAL MEDIUMS

The Call of the Elemental Mediums is the Call of the Wild, summoning us beyond the foreground, the elementary world. It is an unremitting Howl, warning those muted and stranded in the State of Possession and mystified by its media to leave the land of the dead. Thus Elemental Mediums Scold mesmerized Seers who are glued to television sets, dead mind-sets, and dis-spiriting social sets, urgently urging them to break set and reclaim their Eyes/I's. They Nag tone-deafened Augurs who are trapped in babblespheres to close their ears to the mind-rapists' musak and creeds, and listen again to the Music of Birds and of Be-Witching Words.

Elemental Mediums Howl to silenced Soothsayers to shout down the lies of "authorities." They call to housebound/housebroken Gossips to get off the phone, get away from the phoneys, and once again Gossip Wisdom from the stars. They admonish those Sibyls who are trapped in the State of Appeasement to refuse "adultery of the brain." They remind these compromised Sages that in the science of logic the meaning of *medium is* "middle term," or the connecting link that makes possible the drawing of a logical conclusion. They Plead with these muted Mediums to Re-call their Powers of Knowing and of Proclaiming the Crone-logical connecting links and conclusions that can make Sense for women's lives.

Wicked Women, who Hear this Call of the Wild, Re-call our Primal Powers and Finally reclaim for our Selves the word *Mysterious*. This word makes Sense when wrenched from its patriarchal context and Heard in a Metamysterious way. It Names a necessary attribute of Journeyers, who choose to close our eyes to the barrage of illusions intended by trickers and frauds to delude us and who refuse to recite the framers' party lines. When Heard and Be-Spoken in this Sense, *Mysterious* is a New Word and it describes the Creative Caution of Boundary-living women.

Metamysteriously Mysterious women are positively entrancing and entranced. Indeed, Websters sometimes experience be-ing in a *trance,* in the sense of "a state of profound abstraction or absorption accompanied by exaltation" (*Webster's*). Moreover, unshackled from the mind-bindings of snooldom, we are enabled to *trance,* meaning "to move briskly: PRANCE" (*Webster's*). Whereas the masters' media fix/attach women to all that is dead, dis-spirited, and deadly, the Mediumship of trancing, prancing Websters enables us to Con-Quest, Con-Question, Consort, and Cavort with the Living. Among our lively Boon-Companions are Fore-Familiars and Fore-Crones who Live in Archaic Time.

As a Work of Entrancement, the *Wickedary* is a multiwebbed record and map as well as a book of clues for those who choose to Prance. It is a Hope-full History of, by, and for Happy Mediums deciding that Mediumship is our vessel/vehicle. In Other Words, the *Wickedary* is a Word-Webbed Wonderbook for Boundary-Bounders, for Hopping/Hoping Wonderers who are Leaving Boredom and Leaping toward Somewhere—the Time and Space of those who Spin and Weave.

Rhetoric and Philosophy

At the junction of rhetoric and philosophy, we ask about the nature of knowledge and how it is constructed, and about the nature of language and its role in the construction of knowledge.

In classical Greece, rhetoric and philosophy engaged each other in the development of philosophical rhetoric. Philosophical rhetoric may have developed as a reaction against technical rhetoric, which was embodied in handbooks that focused mainly on the conventional stylistic and formal devices employed in judicial rhetoric. Philosophical rhetoric raised questions about the ethics of the rhetor and the powers of language that were evaded in the handbooks. Some of the Greek sophists, such as Gorgias and Isocrates, imply a philosophical rhetoric that exploits the relativity of truth and the ambiguity of language, arguing that no absolute morality or truth exists before its construction in language. Plato's philosophical rhetoric, generally regarded as antisophistic, attempts to lead auditors' souls to the Good; Aristotle's philosophical rhetoric is occupied with how knowledge is constructed through appeals to communal norms. For Plato, because popular beliefs are merely poor reflections of Truth, rhetoric (which traffics with such beliefs) is impoverished. For Aristotle, however, contingent and communal knowledge is all that is possible in the world of human affairs, which is the realm of rhetoric; his philosophical rhetor can develop constructions of truth that vary according to the social norms and values in force. In Roman antiquity, Cicero criticizes the tendency to abjure philosophical exploration for merely technical skill; the orator, he declares, must develop the sort of broadly informed, speculative intellect common to philosophers, "for philosophy is essential to a full, copious and impressive discussion and exposition of the subjects which often come up in speeches" (*Orator* 34; 118–19).

In the sixteenth and seventeenth centuries, Peter Ramus and René Descartes succeeded in thoroughly discrediting the association of rhetoric and philosophy. Ramus insisted that the scope of rhetoric be restricted to matters of style and delivery. Descartes' *Discourse on Method* motivated the Enlightenment association of philosophy with formulaic analysis and the dismissal of rhetoric as a potentially fraudulent and merely ornamental art. A fierce opponent of Cartesian philosophy, Giambattista Vico attempted to reawaken the classical appreciation for philosophical rhetoric by arguing that the invention of arguments for oratory involves a "specifically philosophic" capacity for both associative thinking and common sense, that is, alertness to how knowledge is socially and culturally conditioned. A number of twentieth-century scholars have followed the Aristotelian and Vician propositions that rhetoricians should be social philosophers. Thomas B. Farrell distinguishes the kinds of knowledge that rhetoric can address as "technical" and "social." Technical knowledge presupposes an external reality of stable facts; social knowledge is consensual and variable. It is in the realm of social knowledge that rhetoric functions. Similarly, Chaim Perelman distinguishes between logic and rhetoric: Logic can demonstrate "truth," whereas rhetoric demonstrates what is "reasonable." Within the area of argumentation, Perelman proposes that the sort of argument we might call *philosophical* (in the idealized sense of that term) is one that addresses very general issues to a "universal" audience that shares the rhetor's mindset; put in Platonic terms, Perelman's philosophical rhetor and the audience are soul-mates. For Robert L. Scott, rhetoric is epistemic, a "way of knowing"; he shares with Farrell and Perelman the idea that some knowledge is created solely through communal agreement, mediated by the rhetor, about what is valid or acceptable. However, unlike Farrell and Perelman, who both acknowledge the possibility of "universal" truth, Scott joins those who see all truth as circumstantial.

Epistemological questions intersect with those about the nature of language. Can language unambiguously represent a stable, extralinguistic reality? This question implies the relationship between theology and rhetoric, a relationship that occupied ancient patristic philosophers such as Augustine (in his treatment of rhetoric in *On Christian Doctrine*) and continues to concern contemporary scholars. In "Theology as Rhetoric," David Cunningham argues that theologians should move theology out of the realm of objective certainty so that it can deal with contingent values that affect ethics and politics. We can locate Cunningham in the larger postmodern assertion that meaning, knowledge, and truth are constructions of language, not vice-versa; or as Christopher Norris proposes, philosophy is a product of rhetoric.

The articles in this chapter further discuss some of the issues raised briefly here. Chaim Perelman's "Logic, Dialectic, Philosophy and Rhetoric" from *The Realm of Rhetoric* explicates the relationship between rhetoric and logic. Andrea Nye's conclusion to *Words of Power* presents a feminist critique of traditional logic, arguing that what we have come to understand as analytic logic has acquired power as a mode of making truth because it is the language of the powerful (men). Richard Vatz's "The Myth of the Rhetorical Situation" and Richard Cherwitz's "Rhetoric as 'a Way of Knowing'" offer different responses to the claims of epistemic rhetoric. Vatz presents a refutation of Lloyd Bitzer's "The Rhetorical Situation," arguing that "no situation can have a nature independent of the perception of its interpreter or independent of the rhetoric with which he chooses to characterize it." Cherwitz wants to modify claims such as this, arguing that it is not necessarily the case that knowledge will emerge from rhetorical situations. Cherwitz believes that in order for rhetoric to create knowledge, there needs to be an emphasis on a dialogical process in which the many sides to an issue will be expressed and available for refutation, so that people can "critically balance ideas within [their] mind(s)" before making decisions.

FURTHER READING

Cunningham, David S. "Theology as Rhetoric." *Theological Studies* 52 (1991): 407–30.

Farrell, Thomas B. "Knowledge, Consensus and Rhetorical Theory." *Quarterly Journal of Speech* 62 (1976): 1–14.

Grassi, Ernesto. "Why Rhetoric is Philosophy." *Philosophy and Rhetoric* 20 (1987): 68–78.

Ijesseling, Samuel J. *Rhetoric and Philosophy in Conflict: An Historical Survey.* The Hague: Niijhoff, 1976.

Norris, Christopher. *The Deconstructive Turn: Essays in the Rhetoric of Philosophy.* London: Methuen, 1983.

Scott, Robert L. "On Viewing Rhetoric as Epistemic." *Central States Speech Journal* 18 (1967): 9–17.

Chaim Perelman

"Logic, Dialectic, Philosophy, and Rhetoric"

In his remarks on ancient rhetoric, Roland Barthes correctly observed that "rhetoric must always be read in its structural interplay with its neighbors—grammar, logic, poetics, and philosophy." I would add that in order best to define and situate rhetoric, we must also clarify its relationship to dialectic.

Aristotle in his *Organon* distinguished two types of reasoning—analytic and dialectic. He undertook a study of the former in the *Prior and Posterior Analytics*, and this study can be considered in the history of philosophy as the basis of formal logic. However, modern logicians have failed to see that Aristotle studied dialectical reasoning in the *Topics*, the *Rhetoric*, and the *Sophistical Refutations*. This failure is caused by their inability to see the importance of the latter works, which made Aristotle not only the father of formal logic but also the father of the theory of argumentation.

In his *Analytics*, Aristotle studied the forms of valid inference and specifically the syllogism which allows us, certain hypotheses being given, to infer from them a necessary conclusion. If *A* is *B* and if *B* is *C*, the necessary result is that *A* is *C*. The inference is valid whether the premises are true or false, but the conclusion is true only if the premises are true. This inference is characterized both by the fact that it is purely formal, that is, valid whatever be the contents of the terms *A*, *B*, and *C* (the only condition being that each letter be replaced by the same value each time it is used), and at the same time by the fact that it establishes a connection between the truth of the premises and that of the conclusion. Since truth is a property of the proposition and is independent of personal opinion, analytical reasoning is demonstrative and impersonal. But this is not the case with dialectical reasoning. Aristotle tells us that dialectical reasoning presupposes premises which are constituted by generally accepted opinions. The generally accepted premises are those "which are accepted by everyone or by the majority or by the philosophers—i.e., by all, or by the majority, or by the most notable and illustrious of them."

In certain cases, what is generally acceptable is probable, but this probability cannot be confounded with calculable probability. On the contrary, the meaning of the word *eulogos*, which is usually translated as "generally acceptable" or "acceptable," has a qualitative aspect which brings it closer to the term "reasonable" than to the term "probable." We should note that probability concerns only past or future facts or events, while the theses which are under discussion can deal with nontemporal questions such as "Is the world finite or infinite?" or "Is democracy the best form of government?"

We can immediately see that dialectical reasoning begins from theses that are generally accepted, with the purpose of gaining the acceptance of other theses which could be or are controversial. Thus it aims either to persuade or convince. But instances of dialectical reasoning are not made up of series of valid and compelling inferences; rather, they advance *arguments* which are more or less strong, more or less convincing, and which are never purely formal. Moreover, as Aristotle noted, a persuasive argument is one that persuades the person to whom it is addressed; this means that, unlike the processes of analytical reasoning, a dialectical argument can not be impersonal, for it derives its value from its action upon the mind of some person. As a consequence, it is necessary that we clearly distinguish analytical from dialectical reasoning, the former dealing with truth and the latter with justifiable opinion. Each field of thought requires a different type of discourse; it is as inappropriate to be satisfied with merely reasonable arguments from a mathematician as it would be to require scientific proofs from an orator.

Now, it is in relation to this distinction that we can see how the innovation introduced by Peter Ramus turned out to be an error that was fatal for rhetoric. Beginning with the trivium, with the arts of discourse, Ramus defined grammar as the art of speaking well, that is, of speaking correctly; dialectic as the art of reasoning well; and rhetoric as the art of the eloquent and ornate use of language. Taking dialectic to be the "general art of inventing and judging all things," he asserted that "there is only one method, which is that of Plato and Aristotle, . . . this method is found in Virgil and Cicero, in Homer and Demosthenes, it presides over mathematics, philosophy, opinions, and human conduct."

Thus with a flourish Ramus tossed aside the Aristotelian distinction between analytical and dialectical judgments, justifying his attitude in this way: "for although some cognitive things are necessary and scientific while others are contingent and subject to opinion, if in every case the action of seeing is common to seeing immutable as well as mutable colors, so the art of knowing, i.e., dialectic and logic, is one and the same doctrine for the apperception of all things."

The scope that was now given to dialectic, as embracing both the study of valid inferences and the art of finding and discovering arguments, deprived Aristotle's rhetoric of its two essential elements, invention and disposition, leaving only elocution, the study of ornate forms of language. It is in this spirit that Ramus' friend, Omer Talon, published in Cologne in 1572 the first systematic rhetoric limited to the study of figures. According to Talon, the figure is "a garnishing of speech, wherein the course of the same is changed from the more simple and plain manner of speaking." In this way classical rhetoric came into being—this rhetoric of figures which led progressively from the degeneration to the death of rhetoric.

It is certainly well known that modern logic, developed since the middle of the nineteenth century under the influence of Kant and the mathematical logicians, identifies logic not with dialectic but with formal logic, with Aristotle's analytical reasoning, and completely neglects dialectical reasoning as foreign to logic. In this, modern logic commits an error similar to that of Ramus. If it is undeniable that formal logic is a separate discipline which lends itself, like mathematics, to operation and calculation, it is also undeniable that we reason even when we do not calculate—in private deliberation or public discussion, in giving arguments for or against a thesis, in offering or refuting a criticism. In all these cases we do not demonstrate as we do in mathematics, but we argue. If we conceive of logic as the study of reasoning in all forms, it is natural that the theory of demonstration as developed in formal logic should be accompanied by a theory of argumentation that is similar to Aristotle's dialectical reasoning. This latter seeks through argumentation the acceptance or rejection of a debatable thesis. The object of the new rhetoric, which amplifies as well as extends Aristotle's work, is thus to study these arguments and the conditions of their presentation.

Aristotle opposed rhetoric to dialectic when he examined it in the *Topics,* nevertheless seeing in rhetoric the counterpart, the *antistrophos,* of dialectic. For him, dialectic is concerned with arguments used in a controversy or discussion with an individual, while rhetoric concerns the orator's technique in addressing a crowd gathered in a public square—a group of people who lack both specialized knowledge and the ability to follow a lengthy chain of argument.

In contrast to ancient rhetoric, the new rhetoric is concerned with discourse addressed to *any sort of audience*—a crowd in a public square or a gathering of specialists, a single being or all humanity. It even examines arguments addressed to oneself in private deliberation, or in what is now commonly referred to as "intrapersonal communication." Since it aims to study nondemonstrative discourse, its analysis of reasoning is not limited to formally correct inferences or to more or less mechanical calculations. The theory of argumentation, conceived as a new rhetoric or dialectic, covers the whole range of discourse that aims at persuasion and conviction, whatever the audience addressed and whatever the subject matter. The general study of argumentation can be augmented by specialized methodologies according to the type of audience and the nature of the discipline, should that appear useful. In this manner we can work out a juridical or a philosophical logic that would be the specific application of the new rhetoric to law or philosophy.

In subordinating philosophical logic to the new rhetoric, I am joining in the centuries-old debate which started with Parmenides' great poem and which has set philosophy against rhetoric ever since. The great tradition of Western metaphysics which Parmenides, Plato, Descartes, and Kant represent has always contrasted the search after truth—the announced goal of philosophy—to the techniques of the rhetoricians and Sophists, who have always satisfied themselves with getting people to agree to opinions that are as diverse as they are misleading. Thus Parmenides preferred the road of truth to that of appearance; Descartes based science on unshakable self-evidence, treating what was only probable as all but false; and finally Kant proposed to rid philosophy of opinions altogether by elaborating a metaphysics which is essentially an epistemology, an inventory of all the forms of knowing which, "having an a priori foundation, must be held in advance to be absolutely necessary."

In order to be certain that the propositions articulated by the philosophers did not constitute uncertain and false opinions instead of indisputable truths, it was necessary that these propositions have the benefit of a solid and unquestionable basis—a self-evident intuition that could guarantee the truth of what is perceived as self-evident. The self-evidence so conceived is not a subjective condition, varying from one moment to the next, or from individual to individual; its role is rather to establish a bridge between what is perceived as self-evident by the knowing subject and the truth of the self-evident proposition, which must impose itself in the same way on every rational being.

An argument is never capable of procuring self-evidence, and there is no way or arguing against what is self-evident. Whoever states a self-evident proposition is sure that it will compel everyone with the same "evidence." Argumentation, however, can intervene only where self-evidence is contested. Aristotle had already noticed this; he recognized that it is absolutely necessary to resort to dialectical reasoning when the first principles of a science, which normally are self-evident, are contested. The same thing happens when people dispute a definition.

Although it is normally through intuition that the simple ideas and the first principles of a theoretical science are grasped, Aristotle recognized that recourse to argumentation becomes necessary in practical disciplines such as ethics and politics, where choices and controversies are inevitable, and also in situations where private deliberations or public discussions arise. This is why his *Organon* includes the *Analytics,* which is devoted to formal reasoning, along with the *Topics,* which examines the dialectical reasoning which allows for justification of the best opinion, the reasonable opinion, the *eulogos.*

All who believe that they can disengage truth from opinion independently of argumentation have a profound disdain for rhetoric, which relates to opinions; they grant, at best, only a rhetoric which serves to propogate the truths guaranteed to speakers through intuition or self-evidence, but not a rhetoric which seeks to establish these truths. But if we do not concede that philosophical theses can be founded on self-evident intuitions, we must resort to argumentative techniques to make them prevail. The new rhetoric becomes the indispensable instrument for philosophy.

Those who, with Paul Ricoeur, acknowledge the place in philosophy of metaphoric truths which, since they propose a restructuring of reality, cannot prevail through compelling self-evidence, cannot deny the importance of rhetorical techniques in making one metaphor prevail over another. They can disregard such techniques only if they grant the existence of an intuition which would compel a unique vision of reality excluding all others.

The decline of rhetoric since the end of the sixteenth century was due to the rise of European bourgeois thought, which generalized the role of "evidence": the personal "evidence" of Protestantism, the rational "evidence" of Cartesianism, or the sensible "evidence" of empiricism.

The contempt for rhetoric and the eclipse of the theory of argumentation have led to the negation of practical reason, problems of action being sometimes reduced to problems of knowledge, that is, of truth or probability, and sometimes considered as completely irrelevant to reason.

But, if they want to acquire a clear awareness of the intellectual methods that are employed, all who believe in the existence of reasonable choice, preceded by deliberation or discussion where different solutions confront each other, cannot avoid a theory of argumentation such as the new rhetoric presents.

The new rhetoric is not limited to the sphere of practice; it is at the heart of theoretical problems for anyone who is conscious of the roles that are played in our theories by the choice of definitions, models, and analogies—and, in a more general way, by the elaboration of an appropriate language, adapted to the field of our investigations. It is in this sense that the role of argumentation can be conjoined with practical reason; it is a role that is fundamental in all areas in which we perceive the work of practical reason, even when our concern is with the solution of theoretical problems. I want to make this point clear in order to avoid misunderstanding concerning the import of argumentation as I conceive it.

Andrea Nye

"Words of Power and the Power of Words"

Traditional histories of logic trace an intermittent but steady progress toward logical truth. They point out where logicians in the past made mistakes and where they show their genius by correctly intuiting logical relations; they assume that the subject matter of logic is unitary, and that logicians, whether classical, medieval, or modern are motivated by the desire to find one logical truth. Historians of logic, usually logicians themselves, have been in sympathy with that project. They have accepted the logician's claim to supra-historical status for his researches; they have agreed that to do logic you must remove yourself from any concrete situation in time and space to contemplate eternal verities; they have considered politics and personal concerns only as intrusions. If logic is used for the evil purposes of politicians or dictators, it is by accident. What guides logic is logical truth and no other. There is a logic to these histories, which connects each innovation to the achievements of the past and makes a smooth transition toward a perfected logical form.

It must be clear by now that I am no logician, that I see no "logic" in the history of logic. Each story, each history has been different: different times, different concerns, different tones of voice, different ways of speaking, different men whose logics are no more commensurable than their lives. I have uncovered no progress of a universal rational World Spirit; nor have I found any materialist law of production that ultimately determines the forms of thought. Neither a materialist nor an idealist analysis could do justice to these complex movements of thought and action, to the subtle reworkings of communicative relations that position and reposition subjects, students, believers, followers, citizens in respect to those who rule them. If logicians have shown us ways to speak to each other, they have done so in a variety of ways, and these ways of speaking are not determined by any universal idealist or materialist dialectics, but by a diversity of purposes and desires.

According to the dictates of logic I have committed fallacy after fallacy. Purposes and desires can have nothing to do with logical truth. How could they, when the point of logic is to separate truth from what is subjective and to found a certainty independent of passion or intention? Logicians will be pained by these readings that compromise the purity of logic with biographical notes, relevant to an antiquarian, or a social historian, or a novelist, but never to a logician. There are logical names for the fallacies I have committed: the genetic fallacy, the *ad hominem* fallacy. It is a fallacy to think that the genesis of an idea is relevant to its truth and falsity. It is a fallacy to think that a critical understanding of the person who holds a view can count against the truth of that view. Logical truth is independent of both its genesis and of the man who speaks it. No matter its historical source, or who speaks it, or the intentions or desires with which it is spoken, truth must be judged on its own merits. Truths may be stated for the worst of reasons, and be true. Truths may have the most sordid of origins and be true. Bad men speak the truth, good men speak falsehoods. It is the business of logic to establish the laws of that truth without reference to men and without reference to the origins of ideas in specific social conditions. That a logician happens to be the certain son of a certain mother is irrelevant to the Name of the Truth. From that absolute point of reference come truths that are independent of contingent human affairs and of natural language's role in concrete human experiences of interaction and intercourse. From a logical point of view, there can be no reason to *read* logic, no reason for any account of logic that is not an analysis of its logical truth.

It must be clear by now that I have refused to accept this account, the logician's account of himself, at face value. Motivating this refusal is my own desire, my own commitment, a commitment that you, my reader, have already no doubt read. I believe that all human communication, including logic, is motivated. I believe that, although a word proce‌ssor may print out truths mechanically, people when they speak or write always want something and hope for something with passion and concern, even when part of that passion and concern is to deny it. In my readings of logic I have tried to understand such a denial. I do not see how any judgment on the "truth" or "falsity," or correctness of what logicians say can be made until what logic "means" in this deeper sense is made clear. If truth is more than a sterile formality, more than a mechanical semantic matching of formulae with other formulae, we must first know the meaning of the words that we are to judge true or false. What is it that Aristotle is saying? Or Frege? And how is it possible to know without knowing the "genesis" of their words, without knowing the situation and concerns out of which logicians spoke, without hearing in their words who they were, what sort of "men" they were?

If, in the new law courts of Aristotle's city-state, the point was no longer to tell the truth but to convince judges and juries of positions that were most likely false, juries must have yearned for the return of such an understanding. Heads swimming with clever arguments of plaintiffs, how many of them must have suspected that the intricacies of forensic rhetoric only got in the way of truth? How many of them must have yearned for the old understanding of women and of men, of women's and men's situations, that would have told them what the debate was all about? Words had begun to break free from the truth; manipulated and rearranged in endless combinations, they had become only signs. But words themselves, no matter how cleverly arranged, cannot tell the truth; they must have meaning and to have meaning they must be spoken by someone somewhere on some occasion. It is only after sense has finally disappeared that it is a fallacy to argue the merits of ideas on the basis of their origins in social concerns or the personalities of those who voice them.

If I am right about this, there can be no superior logic that will show up the mistakes of logicians; there can be no feminist logic that exposes masculine logic as sexist or authoritarian. And this might be taken as weakness. Have I fallen into the old trap, an attentive listening woman who understands all and forgives all? If Dummett put aside Frege's fascism because it was irrelevant to logical truth, does my "understanding" have the same effect? The experience of a lonely man, cut off from others, bitter, concentrated on one supreme intellectual task, one obsession—such an understanding makes Frege's logic intelligible but does it also make it forgivable? If a feminist reader is to remain a reader and not turn logician at the last moment and present the feminist truth by which she will judge and legislate, how can she condemn the logic of Empire, Church, or State? Desperate, lonely, cut off from the human community which in many cases has ceased to exist, under the sentence of violent death, wracked by desires for intimacy that they do not know how to fulfill, at the same time tormented by the presence of women, men turn to logic. Doomed to fail in their Parmenidean flight out of the world, fated tragically never to realize their desire for permanence and purity, can they be condemned, or only pitied, or even admired for their nobility?

But as I read I saw little to pity or admire; instead I condemned the narrowness of the views, was angry at the tone of certainty, felt horror at the indifference to suffering caused by those whose authority was based on logic. Against the force of the authoritative relations that logic structures, a judgment of falsity is inadequate; to make such a judgment is to abdicate from judgment, to join the debate, enter in the lists to fight for a truth that can be universally applied. Even to judge Frege pitiable or admirable is to enter into the debate and make again the Sophist's dichotomous division. The old game is joined. A new philosophical position is presented, debate continues, rejected, refuted, or accepted.

The point of these readings was not to make a judgment but to respond. It was to take up the words that have fallen from logician's mouths and reshape them. So this is what you are saying, this is what I have understood you to say, this is what you meant then whether you will admit it or not. If words are always spoken from and for the mouths of others, it was to take the words of logicians and make them mine, shaping them into a response that might wound more painfully than refutation. The discussion of a man in authority with a woman who sets herself up to refute his pronouncements is always on his terms, and likely to end only in one way: with the reaffirmation of his power. But if a refutation can always be refuted, a response cuts deeper. A response might refashion the words of those in power into a serpent whose bite is exposure, the exposure that pricks inflated vanity, the exposure that weakens the resolve to continue on in ridiculous, imperious blindness to reality, the exposure that makes it impossible to continue to deny one's vulnerability and the limits of any human power, the exposure that shows all men to be mother's sons dependent on others. If logic is words of power that proclaim an authoritative unitary truth, there is another power in words, the power to respond and so to challenge another's discourse and refuse its pretensions to autonomy. The antidote to logic is no supralogical metalanguage that will criticize and regulate the forms of logical thought, but language itself, the normality of human interchange that logic refuses, the answer that at its most effective is sensitive, penetrating, intelligent, shrewd, the answer that cuts to the quick. If I have not always succeeded in giving such a response, I am convinced that the words of power of logic and its derivatives can only be vulnerable to such a response.

Are women in a privileged position to make it? Is logic masculine? Can I put to rest the questioning which began so long ago as I tried to master the exercises in Quine's logic text? One thing is clear enough: those who have made the history of logic have in fact been men. Different kinds of explanations have been given of that fact. The simplest is to blame it on exclusion. If women had been permitted they would have been logicians, they would have been citizens, professors, pontifs, ministers, leaders? Would they? Once it is agreed that logic is equivalent to thought, this solution seems inescapable; there is no other way to defend women's equality and ability. If only they had been admitted to the Courts, the Assembly, the Church or University, women would have made great achievements in logic. Heloise would have been Abelard, Diotima Plato. If they had been included in the debate. But feminist experience would indicate that it is not so simple. Even when admitted to the Church, to the University, to public debate, to those disciplines in which logic rules, women have not felt comfortable. They have had an agonizing sense that the terms of success still escape them, that what they care about is lost in following the rules, that their experience must either be ignored or distorted to fit the conceptual scheme within which they are to think. They have the nagging suspicion that they must stop thinking and feeling to succeed, and that is hard for them, and so they don't succeed, or not as often as men succeed. And those who do continue to have the discomforting feeling of being the tokens that prove that male superiority is based on no arbitrary exclusion of women.

Logicians have been men. As men, they have spoken from a men's experience. Aristotle and Plato spoke from a masculine culture rigidly and defensively segregated from the generative life of the household. Ockham and Abelard spoke out of a commitment to a patristic Church founded on the authority of a transcendent male God, an exclusively male priesthood, and a theology that identified women with sin and evil. Frege speaks from the male preserve of the German University where masculine egos in mortal combat fight for glory and status. The arena of logic was made by men for men; it was expressly founded on the exclusion of what is not male, as well as what is not Greek, nor Christian, nor Western, not Aryan. From Plato to Ockham, until Frege finally banishes all substance from logic, the most common example of a concept which figures in logical arguments is "man," as if logic itself were only a grand articulation of one idea or obsession, the identity of man. Women must be interlopers here, because their assigned role is always outside. As the contrast that determines what a man is, their presence must at the same time threaten the institutions of logic. It is not that men are cleverer than women or that they think differently. The speech situations that logic structures are between men. At logic's very birth, Parmenides made clear this purpose: to leave the world of women, the world of sexual generation and fertility, the world of change, of the emotions, of the flesh. If this "birth" of logic must be repudiated in the name of Logic, as logicians claim descent only from the paternal name of Truth and Being, still the work of ordering and regulating relations between men in a world separate from women goes on.

If logic constitutes the words of power that ensure success in such a world, can women afford to give it up? Contemporary structuralist and poststructuralist theories of language have inscribed logical relations at the very heart of language. If this is true then the meaning of what we say is dependent on our words being in correct logical form. Women who speak illogically cannot speak truthfully, or persuasively, or cogently. They may express their pain or register their anger, they may break in and disrupt orderly discussion, but what they say cannot challenge the truth of what is said about women, or found just, nonsexist policies. If women are not content to moan inarticulately, rave hysterically, cast their eyes heavenward in ineffable ecstasy—none of which is likely to improve their situation—the only alternative, it would seem, is argument, in which logically constructed sentences allow the deduction of sound conclusions. If they do not accept these terms, they would seem to be condemned to the status of Parmenide's masses, wandering and confused, wracked by the physical sensations of their bodies, or of Aristotle's docile emotional housewives, obedient to the rule of their husbands, or of respectful Heloise's soliciting Abelard's superior wisdom.

But here be careful. Aren't these the alternatives that logicians have devised for us? If you do not speak logically, you will prattle like a woman, you will moan like a woman. Is it wise to accept the logician's account of what women's thought is or should be? Is it wise to accept so quickly the inscription of logic at the very threshold of thought? It was precisely the thought of women such as Diotima, a thought rooted in generation and change, that logic began by challenging. For the Eleatic Parmenides, mortal opinion was still very much alive and dangerous to the new order of law and the superiority of the Hellenes. Isis, Demeter, Moira, Eilethyia, Aphrodite, whichever name she was called by, was a deity with powers older and more compelling than those of Zeus; it was she who was worshipped in the towns of women and men, past which the logician rushed driven by his desire for Truth. By the time of Plato, logic had defined the public space of the city as the preserve of men; the towns were only insignificant rural outposts. In the place of the human community was founded the segregation that logic instituted, between an illogical feminine household charged with administration of slave labor and reproduction, and a male *polis* with law courts, assemblies, and magistrates in which rational discourse prevailed. Logic reinforced the boundaries of that segregation. If, as the Sophists argued, all free men may speak and be listened to no matter the form of their remarks, so might artisans, or laborers, or slaves, or feminized barbarians, or women speak and be listened to. Instead a standard of logical discourse must be maintained. Plato was willing to pay the final price for a definitive exclusion. By the terms of logic itself, if a woman passed the intellectual tests, she must be allowed to speak. Although women were generally incapable of logical thought, logic itself demanded that any exceptional woman who could master argument should rule with men. Qualified women, women who could pass as men, this "first feminist" argued, must be included. Of course their numbers will be small, and they will not reach the very heights of the philosophic truth that will rule the city. It is this invitation, visionary in the fourth century B.C., that still seems to require a positive response. Its rejection, a rejection of the logic that structures acceptable academic theorizing, or political debate, or theological dispute, would seem to return even the exceptional women who can think like men, who can master logic, to the household where their sisters subsist without power or autonomy.

But once the terms on which logic is based are understood, the choice is less clear. Is a woman to become the wealthy citizen who lives off the labor of slaves? Is she to become the administrator of an Empire that crushes ethnic identity with bureaucratic decree? Is she to be the priest who punishes heretics, the social scientist who justifies oppressive institutions in the name of truth? The relations between speakers that logic structures are alien to feminist aims. Nor is it possible to argue that these are misuses of logic which a feminist logic can correct. If the point of logic is to frame a way of speaking in which what another says does not have to be heard or understood, in which only the voice of a unitary authority is meaningful, in which we can avoid understanding even what we say to ourselves, then no application of logic can be feminist. If, for example, a feminist "logic" prevailed and a "rational" policy for welfare mothers consistent with that logic was instituted, as long as those women themselves were not heard and understood, that welfare policy would only return women to the domination of a paternal state bureaucracy more oppressive and paralyzing than the domination of a husband. If the passions and motives of policy-makers are hidden by theory and so not heard and understood, the racism and sexism of men or of women can continue to structure their directives.

But the alternative cannot be, as some contemporary feminists have urged, a woman's language. Such a language spoken between women for women cannot have the power that can challenge the authority of logic. By its very terms, it does not engage logic. It is outside logic, different from logic, other than logic, an expressive alternative that leaves thinking to the men, while women continue to speak and write for each other. Such a communication between women may be useful to build confidence and form new concepts by which women's experience can be understood and alleviated, but if logic is allowed to stand as reason, as rational thought, and as the underlying structure of public language, a woman's language will always be impotent.

An alternative is the one I have tried: to answer to the desire that motivates the claim of logicians to prescribe the rules of thought, even though the desire of logic is that there should be no answer possible; to respond that, understood in this way, logic is not thought at all but the denial of any challenge that might stimulate thought. It is only when the claim of logic to be reason and truth and knowledge is accepted that the anarchical chaos of purely personal expression is the only alternative to masculine rationality. With that claim exposed as a particular project of domination, it becomes possible to undertake a new feminist study of thought and language free from the logicist assumptions that dominate contemporary linguistics and epistemology.

But if logic is in fact the language of power, is this not a utopian project? If communication in the world in which women live is ordered by logical relations then it would seem that to refuse logic is to rule out the possibility of power and settle for an unrealizable dream of free thought in which all speak and decisions are reached through understanding and consensus. Even if such an oasis of communicative freedom could be realized, wouldn't it be infinitely vulnerable? Where could woman find a place to talk where that talk would not be fragmentary and furtive, carried on between wars, between bouts of alienated servile work, between incidents of violence? Isn't it the case that no matter what the purposes of logic, women must learn logical techniques if they are to survive, that they must take up words of power and fashion them into the same weapons as men? Women philosophers master logical analysis to establish a rational basis for women's issues. Women politicians exploit the concept of law to force consistency in the treatment of men and women. Women theologians search for scriptural inconsistencies in order to undermine Biblical authority for women's subjection. Women social scientists expose the logical weaknesses of theories that purport to prove women's inferiority.

But it is important to be aware of the dangers here. It is the very point of logic that no matter what content is substituted, logical relationships remain the same. The feminist logician speaks from a script in which the master always wins. Women professors find themselves refuting junior colleagues with the agressivity and jealousy of their own examiners. Women jurists ignore the inarticulate claims of poor women in the name of the law of property. Women theologians proclaim the superiority of Christianity over the spirituality of non-Western women. Women social scientists objectify their clients as research objects.

It is tempting with this realization to despair and find the only solace in deconstructive irony. Refusing to institute another logic, "the critic of patriarchy" resigns herself to exposing the pitiable vulnerability of disciplines ordered by logic and to disruptively tangling sexist arguments, all the time acknowledging while she ridicules the superior power of logic. Trapped in a language that has its substance not in speech but in formal relations issued from the Name of the Father, women play a futile game on the outskirts of logic, trying again and again the blind spots of reflexivity, Frege's antinomy, Ockham's mysteries, Aristotle's intuitions, Parmenides's Being.

But there is an escape from this dilemma. These fissures of nothingness from which the logician's refusal began, his refusals of the physical world of generation and change, of the thoughts of others that must be erased, of the otherness always in our thoughts that makes us doubt ourselves and question ourselves, these are not the necessary beginnings of thought and culture. This is the illusion that it is in logic's interest to maintain—that it is from nothing that this world of reason comes, like a trick of mirrors, the world of Ideas, the only world in which it seems we know how to live. In fact, it is men who have made the illusion, not all men, only some men, men who like all of us have their hopes and fears, men who have their own reasons for denying that there can be any other world than the world ruled by Rah or Yahweh or the Form of the Good, men who have their own reasons for attempting to build a world in which women can only be faithful daughters, adepts in logical technique, or rebellious protegés tolerated on the fringes of orthodoxy.

Regardless of an avante-garde of women's language and women's writing, logic remains a permanent and central part of the curriculum that represents current knowledge. It is taught in every philosophy program and is proposed as Critical Thinking for all courses of study. Women still struggle, if not with Quine with other texts, with computer programming, statistics, economic models, for there are many texts now. Logic is not in the words, she tells herself, it is somehow underneath or above the words and you must forget about the epidemic, and about Jones's peculiarities, about poverty and injustice. Forget what is *said*. Don't think. Logic will teach you to be critical, to learn not to accept an opinion as true without demanding an argument, it will teach you to defend your position with force. We must learn to think logically, learn to demand support for claims, catch incorrect inferences, search for inconsistency. Otherwise, there is no truth and clever politicians and merchandizers will deceive us. Logic is necessary because it forces us to take responsibility for what we think, to be ready to support it and defend it against counterattack. So the defense of logic continues. And even women, some of them, can learn.

But such a remedy for thoughtless conformity already assumes the language which logic has restructured. Before statements can be connected in arguments or judged consistent or inconsistent, speech has become the logician's propositions. Speech has become the campaign slogans of political ideologues, the come-ons of advertisers, the dogma of the catechism, "the proposition that can't be refused" to which Plato's Theaetetus is only to register assent or dissent. We already have lost our voices, already are only the auditors of sentences whose truth or falsity transcends any individual understanding. Our political thinking, whether democratic or Marxist, is a litany of talismanic slogans by which friends or enemies are identified. Economic thought takes the form of the endless repetition of possible pleasures rated in terms of satisfaction. Religion is a list of commandments that no one is expected to obey and a liturgy of beliefs that no one understands. If logic is the remedy for the lack of order in these lists, it is because logic already separated "what is said" from what anyone says, has already isolated the "meanings" which the logic of classical economics, Marxist social science and Christian theology must work into a coherent body of thought. What is said has become the "proposition," detached from who says it, and the only way to avoid the chaos of an endless indiscriminate list of truths is to insist on the logical relations that separate one domain from another and rule out inconsistency. But the important step has already been taken. The Logos has been separated from the testimony of the witness, and is now only a statement or a claim that can be proven true or false regardless of its adequacy or honesty.

The atomized statements that logic reconnects in syllogisms or propositional calculi are themselves spoken, but it is by a certain kind of speaker, a speaker who is alienated from himself, who speaks from no coherent interpersonal experience, from no stable communal reality. It is no accident that logic flourished when the human community had failed, when the village had been subsumed in the city-state and the city-state dissolved in war and economic rivalry, when the medieval consensus wracked by famine and heresy collapsed, when international capitalism had all but destroyed the nation-state. In each case, logic became more imperious, more desperate to project a thought in which all can believe, a thought like a hammer to pound into shape the common world that no longer existed, to command the common understanding which was no longer possible, to define an evil which no longer had any concrete shape. Logic is the thought necessary for those who have no thought, who must, in the midst of that emptiness, construct a substitute world of relations against disintegration, rootlessness, homelessness, who must create a consensus without cooperative and reciprocal economic relations, familial intimacy, customs and rituals which bind people together, art forms which express communal values in tangible form. Given the absence of any common sense of a world durably woven out of necessarily differing experiences, logic must seem the only alternative to chaos and anarchy.

But the extreme conditions that make such a choice necessary are specific historical facts: the collapse of the city-state, economic crisis, disease, hunger, and exposure to radically different cultures. They are neither necessary, universal, nor eternal. Furthermore, men armed with the authority of logic themselves completed the devastation, perfecting master languages insulated from criticism, ruthlessly pursuing Sophists, heretics, witches, scarlet women, unbelievers, Jews, extending the rule of law and truth over diversity. Wouldn't it also have been possible to repair and build, to reclear a space for communication and discussion among the debris, to patch and support the broken matrixes of lives? A new house, a new school, a union, a town council, a citizens' group, a woman's center? To found institutions that would support a coming together to an adequate understanding of what has happened, is happening, and ought to happen? And once there and talking, do we need logic or critical thinking to help us to reach that understanding?

In the United States Presidential campaign of 1988, a candidate won who was not a sympathizer with women's rights, and he was supported by many American women. There were two ideas that captured the attention of voters more than any others and were generally credited with turning the tide in favor of the conservative candidate. One was the fact, constantly referred to by George Bush, the Republican candidate, that Michael Dukakis, the Democratic nominee then governor of Massachusetts, had vetoed a Massachusetts bill that made it mandatory for teachers to lead the Pledge of Allegiance to the American flag in public schools. The other was more an image than an idea. Its source was a series of TV commercials that presented a large black man being led away by police, identified as a prisoner on furlough from a Massachusetts prison who had gone amok, raped a white woman, and murdered her husband.

The logic of these messages according to Bush was simple. Saluting the flag is the mark of loyalty to the United States, therefore if you are against it you are disloyal. Criminals are dangerous, therefore there should be no furlough program. By the necessity of this "logic," both men and women were convinced. Time and time again, with a sort of numbed persistence, prospective voters when interviewed repeated the conclusion, "Dukakis is soft on crime"; "Bush is a real American." What might have helped these voters to a better understanding of what was being said to them? Was it more sophisticated logic that would cleverly tangle the question further: the missing premise, the principle that an exception does not disprove the rule, the possible consistency of patriotism and dissent? Or were there other more important skills that were lacking, and that could be learned and taught, the skills of reading: attention, listening, understanding, responding?

These are not the same as the skills of logic; in many ways they are antithetical. If logic teaches us to ignore the circumstances in which something is said, reading asks us to consider it carefully, if logic teaches us to forget who says something and why, this is precisely what we need to know if we are to read correctly. To read Bush's attack on Dukakis's patriotism, it would have been necessary to have a grasp of the circumstances: our defeat in Vietnam, our fading economic hegemony, the global rivalry with communism in which we have cast ourselves as heroes. To read, it would have been necessary to know who Bush was, his conservative connections, his past with the CIA, his tenuous status as the anonymous Vice President of a popular President. To read what was said, it would have been necessary to know to whom Bush was speaking, to know about the electorate and their sense they were not as well off as they had been made to think they were and about their need to be told again that all was well. In the case of the black criminal who went amok on furlough from prison, another even more difficult skill was needed, the skill to reflect on ourselves as we read, and to be aware of deep-seated emotions and responses, in this case racist, that color our reading. Can logic or critical thinking based on logic teach these skills?

Logic has provided scripts for particular settings, the law court, programmed debate, theology, and science. At the same time it presents itself as universal. All men, and even women, should think logically; any communication that is not purely expressive and that aims at the truth should be logically ordered. This is the way to be critical, this is the way to guard against falsity and deception. This is the way men, and now women, should be taught to think. But retention of a list of carefully chosen facts, even when supplemented with logical rules of combination, is no guarantee of any effective response to the call to patriotism, or to the defense of the traditional family, or the policing of black criminals. The Pledge of Allegiance is the sign of loyalty to the country; if someone is against the Pledge they must be disloyal. It is such purity and simplicity at which logic aims.

A reader would have been harder to fool. She would have listened with a grasp of history that allowed her to realize that Bush and Dukakis spoke out of the failures of American foreign policy and out of the uneasy sense that the world capitalism which the United States leads is dangerously unstable. She would have heard the tone, strident, military, rigid, that demands that there can be no discussion of the rightness of anything American, no discussion of the rights of black murderers or the social reasons for crime. She would have taken account of the public to which Bush spoke, worried, shaken by the stock market crash the year before, afraid to rock the boat of an economy floundering in debt, but eager to believe in the American values that all around them had disappeared. She would have understood the reference to the color of the prisoner and his size, the black rapist who is the symbol of a sexual prowess that threatens white men in their possession of women, black like most criminals, prisoners who deserve what they get, because it must be them, these aliens, barbarians, not like us, who are causing things to go wrong. With a sense of history, she might have recognized the tone from having heard it before, in accounts of other times in which people grappled for hope and stability. She could never have read everything, no one can, but she would have read some of it. She would have read beneath the logic, she would have read the desires, the concerns, the hopes of these men, twisted as they might have become. And once having read, she might have had an answer.

If men have been the masters of logic, women may be the masters of reading. It is a skill we have perfected. We have listened and read to survive, we have read to predict the maneuvers of those in power over us, to seduce those who might help us, to pacify bullies, to care for children, to nurse the sick and wounded. We have read what men said, studied their words, heard the ambivalence and confusion in what they say no matter how univocal and logical, and having heard it we have sometimes wanted to cure it, if only by listening, and then listening more and not stopping listening until all is revealed, the final weakness, the final confession of need and weakness that is the sign of our common humanity. But there is more to speaking than listening and understanding. There is also responding, answering. And that can mortally wound. That steady subtle voice, that takes the words of another and repeats them back so we are given back to ourselves as another and we see ourselves and we have been forced to reveal ourselves in all our weaknesses. And with much pain we have given up our name, the secret name that we hoarded to ourselves, that we dreamt idolatrously would give us power over all, the name of Truth.

And only after that surrender, we might start to talk to each other. Women to women, women to men, men to women, men to men. And that talking might begin to make places in the world—homes, towns, assemblies, councils, workplaces, temples, churches—for the daughters and sons of mothers and fathers.

Richard Cherwitz

"Rhetoric as 'a Way of Knowing': an Attenuation of the Epistemological Claims of the 'New Rhetoric' "

This essay explores the notion of rhetoric-as-epistemic—a theory which has recently gained increasing attention from rhetoricians. The author begins by explicating the nature of the claim that rhetoric is truth-creative. This is followed by a delineation of the philosophic suppositions anchoring such a contention. Finally, the author sets forth several criteria for determining under what conditions rhetoric may be said to function in epistemologically meaningful ways.

Since the inception of rhetoric (argument)[1] in the fifth century B.C. as one of the arts of Western Civilization, much controversy has arisen regarding the justification of this discipline. Perhaps the earliest and most widely-held view until recent times was that rhetoric operated as a means of "making truth effective,"[2] or as Richard M. Weaver noted in his commentaries on Plato, "rhetoric was impulse added to truth."[3] Inherent in such a notion was the treatment of "truth" as prior and immutable, a view which cast for rhetoric the role of addressing inferiors. As Robert Scott recently suggested: "The common justification of rhetoric as making truth effective courts an attitude which has nearly always viewed rhetoric as the harlot of the arts."[4]

In the wake of these and other debasements unique to what may be termed the "old rhetoric" have emerged several contemporary theories which reinterpret the nature of truth[5] and consequently place rhetoric in a more distinctive position. According to the advocates of this "new rhetoric," if one approaches truth as contingent, perhaps one ought avoid the term "rhetoric" altogether, or at least re-evaluate its familiar justification, which incorrectly assumes that truth exists prior to persuasion.[6]

Explicit in these re-examinations is the contention that rhetoric, rather than making truth effective, is inherently evocative or "truth-creative." Robert Scott, for example, has concluded that "In human affairs rhetoric must be perceived as a way of knowing; it is epistemic."[7] According to Scott, any other way of looking at the world "offers no legitimate role to rhetoric."[8] Similarly, Carroll Arnold has described rhetoric as "the process of manipulating symbolic devices for the purpose of gaining one's own or someone else's adherence, which is essential to the very process of coming to know."[9] Perhaps the most interesting shift from the old to the new rhetoric, however, may be found in the thought of Henry W. Johnstone. Walter M. Carleton has accurately traced Johnstone's intellectual transformation from the view of "rhetoric as non-epistemic" to that of rhetoric as "epistemologically relevant."[10] According to Carleton, Johnstone no longer finds a marked distinction between the discernment of truth and its propagation. Johnstone's most recent statement on this subject sheds light on the question of whether rhetoric can properly be said to function in epistemologically relevant ways. "The distinction between finding truth in philosophy and finding the proper rhetorical devices for propagating it," declares Johnstone, "cannot be maintained."[11]

If one can adequately summarize the sentiment of this new rhetoric, it is that truth is that towards which man strives, rather than that which is *a priori*. Hence, through attempts to gain adherence (rhetoric), man comes to know with increasing certainty, or as Wheelis maintains, "knowledge is the name we give to those of our opinions to which certainty is ascribed."[12]

The purpose of this essay is to provide a perspective from which to view the statement that rhetoric is epistemic. We begin with an explication of that statement, then proceed to a delineation of the philosophic suppositions which anchor it. Finally, we advance the several criteria necessary for determining the applicability of this contention to human discourse.

VIEWING RHETORIC-AS-EPISTEMIC

At the very core of the new rhetoric is the contention that what people think they know cannot be demonstrated to be factually true. Hence, in the contingent arenas of political, social, moral and religious affairs, man can do no more than hold with uncertainty those ideas which are a unique product of his selective experience. The question which immediately arises, therefore, is this: How does man come to know with increased certainty? For this new school of rhetorical thought certainty is a derivative of the quest for adherence located in rhetorical interchange—the process whereby men collectively pool their ideas in argumentative encounters ("the marketplace of ideas"). Inherent in such interchanges is the process of critical reflection in which ideas are balanced in the minds of those who participate.

Central to this discussion is the distinction between "unfounded knowledge" and "reasoned understanding." While man's unfounded ideas take the form of attitudes rooted in prejudice, his reasoned understanding of ideas is predicated upon the critical balancing of conflicting propositions within the mind. Man's unfounded knowledge develops in a prerhetorical, nonreflective stage, growing primarily out of his selective experiences. Ideas, therefore, do not enter the reflective domain until they are exposed to free and open public disputation. At this level ideas are thrown into direct clash with one another, and are subject to the critical balancing and judgment of the human mind. Untested knowledge (uncertainties) is a unique by-product of selective experiences, while beliefs and convictions (certainties) are a unique by-product of the reasoning process. The former develop at a pre-rhetorical, nonrational stage; the latter emerge as a result of the reflective properties of rhetoric. Thus ideas advanced in a noninteractive setting may be classified as potential rhetoric, becoming actual rhetoric only upon their entrance into the marketplace of ideas.

Anchoring this distinction is the notion that rhetoric acts as a means of testing and verifying attitudes (selective experiences), and in turn creates beliefs and convictions (rhetorical truth). Phrased differently, argumentative or rhetorical activity is the tool by which we explore the avenues to problemistic discovery through "intersubjective validation." As Sereno and Bodaken suggest: "When we talk about perception, we observe that an individual knows only what he himself perceives with his senses. Therefore, we can only know and are limited to the data of our own senses. Each individual will have a different idea of what the world is like, based on his own subjective perceptions of it. By perceiving, we actively participate in the creation of our subjective reality."[13] According to this view, men hold divergent stances on contingent questions because of their differing subjective perceptions of similar phenomena. It seems to me that man's tool for eliminating such differences, or subjective realities, and hence for ascertaining truth, is rhetoric. Through rhetorical activity, subjective perceptions collide with one another and are exposed to man's faculty of critical reflection. In this sense, rhetoric functions intersubjectively, dispelling error in the face of truth; for through rhetoric opinions based on selective perceptions are tested and validated by the intersubjective properties of probing and balancing which transpire in the human mind. As Brummett suggests: "Intersubjectivity holds that the discovery of reality and the testing of it is never independent of people but takes place through people. Yet this reality is found through communication between people if humanity is to escape solipsism. Reality is meaning yet meaning is something created and discovered in communication."[14] He concludes: "Humans are necessarily involved in sharing and manipulating messages to give and gain meanings about experience. But what experience means is not by any means agreed upon. This ambiguity is a feature of the essentially rhetorical nature of reality. Ambiguity generates conflict and disagreement about meaning and a constant striving to resolve these divisions. This striving is rhetoric— rhetoric in its most fundamental sense is the advocacy of realities."[15] To say that rhetoric is epistemic is thus to say that intersubjective validation is a requisite of the rhetorical act.

For that reason, it may be said that the view that rhetoric is evocative or "truth-creative" is anchored by the contention that rhetoric is the art of investigating critically the nature, grounds, limits, criteria and validity of human knowledge. By verbalizing all possible ideas, whether they be right or wrong, man is able to generate knowledge and modify previously-held ideas. In short, rhetoric is a particular theory of cognition grounded in *intersubjective validation*— a process in which positions based upon subjective perceptions collide with one another in the minds of those involved in the rhetorical act. Through balancing and probing—faculties which may be regarded as innate to the human mind— what were once opinions stemming from man's selective experiences now transcend the realm of the subjective. From the clash of subjective realities resulting from the rhetorical encounter involving at least two people there emerges an intersubjective reality—a reality based not upon one subjective perception of the world, but rather upon the clash of two such competing perceptions. This theory entails no separation of finding and propagating truth—a separation that is embodied in the classical distinction between rhetoric and dialectic.

But, by extending the notion of rhetoric as truth-creative one might redraw the traditional lines separating rhetoric, dialectic and science. In accord with the thesis advanced above, all three disciplines may be treated as independent "ways of knowing." In each, knowledge is dependent upon certainty, the basis for which is a perceived impossibility of error. Whereas the dialectician is *logically* certain and the scientist is *empirically* certain, the rhetor is *intersubjectively* certain.

The new demarcation would thus assign the task of "synthesizing" or "deducing" truth to dialectic, "discovering" or "finding" truth to science, and "evoking" truth to rhetoric. As the chart below suggests, the dialectician's vehicle for deducing truth is the syllogism, the methodology for which is rooted in the principles of *entailment*. The scientist, however, discerns truth through observation, employing the principles of *correspondence*. Finally, as this essay argues, the rhetor's vehicle for evoking truth is persuasion (rhetorical proof)—a process methodologically grounded in attempts to gain *adherence* through intersubjective validation.

Hence, instead of viewing rhetoric as the process of taking a dialectically secured position and showing its relationship to the world of prudential conduct—as does Weaver—one must recognize that rhetoric may function as an *independent* "way of knowing."[16] Because the rhetor, through attempts to win adherence, comes to know with increasing certainty—as does the dialectician and the scientist through their respective methodologies—rhetoric may be said to function in epistemologically meaningful ways.

Although the nature of certainty may be different for each discipline, no attempt should be made to place the three in a hierarchical order. After all, the rhetor may be as intersubjectively certain as the scientist is empirically certain and the dialectician is logically certain. In each case there is a perceived impossibility of error in accordance with the methodology employed. Rhetoric, rather than being reduced to making truth effective, is therefore epistemic or truth-creative. The various relationships we are discussing here may be viewed schematically as follows:

	Science	*Dialectic*	*Rhetoric*
Nature of Certainty	Empirical certainty	Logical certainty	Intersubjective certainty
Process of Ascertaining Truth	Discovering truth	Synthesizing or deducing truth	Evoking truth
Vehicle for Ascertaining Truth	Observation	Syllogism	Persuasion
Methodology	Correspondence	Entailment	Adherence (intersubjective validation)

EPISTEMOLOGICAL SUPPOSITIONS OF THE "NEW RHETORIC"

As mentioned earlier, the new rhetoric is an outgrowth of a reinterpretation of the nature of knowledge generation. To advance the contention that rhetoric is epistemic is to explore the very avenues by which man comes to know. These re-examinations of man's cognitive faculties have yielded two philosophic conceptions regarding man's acquisition of knowledge.

A. On the one hand, there are those who maintain that man's discovery of knowledge is located in the unique truth-creative properties of philosophic inquiry. This school of thought pivots upon Maurice Natanson's claim that "self knowledge is the clue to as much of our comprehension of the world as man can gain."[17]

According to Natanson, we can be certain of very little. We can, however, attain apodictic knowledge of ourselves. If he is correct—and I believe he is—the philosopher's quest for knowledge or truth rests upon a crucial epistemological condition: that knowledge resides within the person. To learn is thus to confront another and thereby come to confront one's self.[18] This assumption seems perfectly consistent with the present philosophic notion that man is his own primary datum.

How, then, does the philosopher extract this knowledge from within himself? Obviously, it remains entrenched within him unless he is willing to open his self to inspection by others. In this statement we come upon the philosopher's vehicle for knowledge generation—controversy. Through controversy one exposes his self, allowing others to enter and probe "the privacy of his cognitive and affective life."[19] Philosophy, declares Natanson, "is the visitor who announces himself through the calling card of argumentation."[20] Without this "person risking" upon which intersubjective validation is dependent, knowledge would forever remain within the person. Only by exposure to the risks implicit in philosophical controversy can self-knowledge be extracted.

As a corollary to Natanson's argument, it might be posited that contending that rhetoric is a "way of knowing" harbors the attitude that epistemologically relevant rhetoric is interpersonal—that it involves the clash or the juxtapositioning of ideas between at least two people. After all, the confrontation of competing or contradictory rationales is a necessary condition of Natanson's theory of self-exposure and self-risk. As this essay suggests, it is only through the process of self-risk that rhetoric can function in a truth-creative capacity. For that reason, to claim that rhetoric is truth-evocative is to define rhetoric in an essentially *inter*personal fashion. In accordance with this line of argument, *intra*personal awareness would probably lie outside the realm of rhetoric and could not be considered truth-creative.

While it might be conceded that man can communicate intrapersonally in such a manner as to persuade himself, and that such behavior might have rhetorical overtones, it cannot be maintained that such a process is consistent with the conclusion that rhetoric is epistemic. When one argues with himself or attempts self-persuasion, he does not sincerely hold within his mind two diametrically opposed ideas. I cannot, for example, believe that Richard Nixon was a good president, and at the same time believe that he was a bad one. I can only *question* those beliefs that I already hold or *seek the information* necessary for answering those questions for which I have no previous opinions. At best, therefore, I can play the role of devil's advocate with myself. Notice, however, that such intrapersonal behavior is markedly different from the type of controversy discussed by Natanson, in which mutually exclusive rationales are juxtapositioned.

The devil's advocate, inasmuch as he holds no one consistent belief, lacks that which is necessary for risk. To illustrate the point, let us consider a hypothetical example. When person A, who holds "x" to be true, argues with person B, who maintains "not x" to be the case, he (A) risks the possibility that his entire way of viewing the situation will be fundamentally altered as a result of the encounter with B. The devil's advocate, on the other hand, holding no belief or position in the first place, does not risk the possibility that his outlook will be reshaped as a result of intrapersonal argument. For the devil's advocate, intrapersonal debate yields the *acquisition* or *maintenance* of a perspective or outlook, rather than the *shifting* or *alteration* of an outlook that is unique to the interpersonal behavior described above.

Thus without the pairing of these opposing beliefs, there would not be the type of self-exposure and self-risk present in philosophic controversy. Furthermore, the absence of genuine controversy precludes the kind of intersubjective validation described previously. The net effect is that intrapersonal argument or self-persuasion fails to meet the necessary criteria upon which the claim that rhetoric is epistemic rests.

B. A second view, complementary to the first, is advanced by Robert Scott. Intrinsic to this view is the assumption that truth can at best be seen as dual: "the demands of the precepts one adheres to and the demands of the circumstances in which one acts."[21] Thus truth is not to be seen in the absolute sense (the traditional philosophical claim that truth is immutable or final), but rather as something which evolves, pursuant to the particular exigencies which confront man during the course of his cognitive life.[22]

The practical result of this view according to Scott is "the inevitable dichotomy" which man faces. If man cannot come to know truth in the philosophical sense—i.e., if he cannot be absolutely certain—he must decline the challenge of life or find avenues to successfully meet that challenge.[23] As Scott further suggests, the fact that man inherently makes choices—that he is ethically committed to act—makes rhetoric at least potentially truth-evocative: "Man must say with

Gorgias, 'I know the irreconcilable conflicts and yet I act.' That man can so act, he knows from experience. What is true for that man does not exist prior to, but in the working out of its own expression."[24] Scott continues: "Because such attempts involve communication with others, we disclose again the potentiality for rhetoric to be epistemic. Inaction, failure to take the burden of participating in the development of contingent truth ought be considered ethical failure."[25]

Taken together, these two schools of thought indicate that for rhetoric to be epistemic, man must recognize that knowledge rests within him and does not exist in any fixed or absolute state. Hence, through rhetorical activity man draws knowledge from within himself and applies it as a relative standard of truth for each circumstance and situation. Viewed in this manner, rhetoric is "truth-creative," rather than "impulse added to truth."

AN ATTENUATION OF THE CLAIMS OF THE "NEW RHETORIC"

Because of the aforementioned suppositions, it would be a mistake to interpret all human discourse as operating epistemologically. The speech act must therefore meet certain criteria before it can be considered as truth-creative. As the previous analysis indicates, rhetoric operates epistemologically only when it addresses the critical, reflective properties of man's mind. That is, rhetoric is evocative or epistemic only when it involves the clash of opposing rationale—a condition which allows man to balance ideas within his mind. Moreover, rhetoric can bring forth knowledge only when it involves the collision of the subjective perceptions which undergird man's selective experiences and prejudices. Thus, only when discourse aims at intersubjective validation can it be called epistemic. Implicit within these statements, however, is perhaps the most important attenuation of the claim that rhetoric is truth-creative. As Henry W. Johnstone notes, it is only the intersection of rhetoric and philosophy that is truth-creative.[26] Emerging from each of these statements are three common criteria which afford us the ability to distinguish between those forms of discourse which are epistemic and those which are not.

A. First, in order for man to gain knowledge from his attempts to win adherence, rhetoric must be viewed as an activity of correction, wherein the clash of contradictory ideas exposes error and yields truth. Without a clash of ideas, we have only an expression of attitudes, which are based on an individual's selective and subjective perceptions. This is, at best, "potentially epistemic." When these attitudes clash, however, rhetoric becomes intersubjective, allowing man to critically balance ideas within his mind. When various subjective perceptions are allowed to stand juxtaposed to each other, man is capable of dispelling error and discerning truth through the collision of one with the other. Thus, to say that Senator Jones's speech in favor of abortion yields truth would be misleading; for it is the clash of opposing rationale in the marketplace that yields truth. Epistemologically relevant rhetoric, therefore, must not be seen as an individual utterance in a vacuum, but rather as a dialogic process or a series of speeches whose cumulative effect is epistemic. In order to claim that rhetoric evokes truth, one must view speech acts as operating out of an on-going argumentative arena in which all ideas, whether they be right or wrong, are exposed to free and open disputation.

B. But second, participants in such argumentative exchanges must be afforded an equal amount of control and initiative regarding the lines of influence. As Ehninger contends, "Lines of influence must be bilateral, flowing in both directions."[27] Unless a person who decides to argue enters an agreement, freely allowing his opponent to criticize and correct him, there is no assurance that truth will emerge. "The correctee," declares Ehninger, "instead of being an inert object is an active participant."[28] Through such an agreement between participants, initiative and control pass back and forth, guaranteeing that arguments, instead of being haphazardly launched, are presented systematically with an eye on creating various points of statiation that allow man to make reflective decisions regarding numerous *issues*. Upon resolution of each level of statiation, participants move on until that time when all resources have been exhausted and they can make a determination of the central *Issue*. Hence, without the sharing of initiative and control, man is rendered incapable of stacking up and evaluating within his mind the issues upon which truth is grounded. In the absence of the kind of agreement between participants called for by Ehninger, it is hard to see how rhetoric can be epistemic.

C. Finally, and most importantly, unless rhetoric functions as an enterprise of person-risking and person-building, there can be no guarantee that attempts to gain adherence will yield knowledge. Natanson's suggestion that truth resides within the self supports the salience of this criterion. By risking the self, the arguer opens himself to the methodical inspection by others upon which intersubjective validation rests. Only when the arguer exposes himself to the possibility "that his outlook or attitude will be reshaped by the encounter,"[29] can knowledge from within be extracted. In other words, only by laying self on the line can communication operate intersubjectively. And as we have seen, it is this process of critical reflection which underpins the contention that rhetoric is epistemic.

CONCLUSION

As this paper indicates, it is not enough simply to say that rhetoric functions in epistemologically relevant ways. To make such a claim requires an understanding of the philosophic suppositions that anchor it. Having examined two of the more tenable theories of knowledge acquisition, I have concluded that the claim that rhetoric is epistemic must be markedly attenuated. While the criteria advanced in the last section of our inquiry may not be exhaustive, they do, nevertheless, suggest the kinds of ingredients necessary for speech acts to be called evocative or "truth-creative." Assuming that humans can participate in such acts, it seems safe to conclude that there is a new rhetoric, grounded not in the quest to make truth effective, but rather in the quest to evoke truth *via* rhetoric.

NOTES

[1]These terms will be used interchangeably throughout this paper.

[2]Robert L. Scott, "On Viewing Rhetoric as Epistemic," *Central States Speech Journal,* 18 (1967), 9.

[3]Richard M. Weaver, *The Ethics of Rhetoric* (Chicago: Henry Regnery Co., 1953), p. 24.

[4]Scott, p. 9.

[5]The term "truth" is used throughout this paper in a rhetorical sense to denote "shared" certainty or knowledge. It is therefore not intended in the context of "absolute truth," which is more frequently associated with progressive rationalism. The position developed in this essay accords with the intersubjectivistic position delineated by Barry Brummett in "Postmodern Rhetoric," *Philosophy and Rhetoric,* 9 (1976), 30. This position is also consistent with the equation of "knowledge" and "certainty" as advanced by Allan Wheelis in *The End of the Modern Age* (New York: Harper and Row, 1971), p. 81.

[6]Scott, p. 9.

[7]Scott, p. 17.

[8]Scott, p. 17.

[9]Carroll C. Arnold, "Inventio and Pronuntiatio in a New Rhetoric" (Paper presented at the Central States Speech Convention, April 8, 1972), p. 4.

[10]Walter M. Carleton, "Theory Transformation in Communication: The Case Study of Henry W. Johnstone," *Quarterly Journal of Speech,* 16 (1975), 78.

[11]Henry W. Johnstone, "Truth Communication and Rhetoric in Philosophy," *Revue Internationale de Philosophie,* 23 (1969), 405–06.

[12]Wheelis, p. 81.

[13]Kenneth K. Sereno and Edward M. Bodaken, *Trans-Per Understanding Human Communication* (Boston: Houghton Mifflin Co., 1975), p. 41.

[14]Brummett, p. 30.

[15]Brummett, p. 30.

[16]Weaver, p. 27.

[17]Maurice Natanson, "The Claims of Immediacy," in *Philosophy, Rhetoric and Argumentation,* ed. Henry Johnstone and Maurice Natanson (University Park, Pa.: Pennsylvania State Univ. Press, 1965), p. 16.

[18]Natanson, p. 16.

[19]Natanson, p. 16.

[20]Natanson, p. 16.

[21]Scott, p. 17.

[22]Scott, p. 17.

[23]Scott, p. 15.

[24]Scott, p. 15.

[25]Scott, p. 15.

[26]Johnstone, p. 405.

[27]Douglas Ehninger, "Argument as Method: Its Nature, Its Limitations and Its Uses," *Speech Monographs,* 37 (1970), 105.

[28]Ehninger, p. 105.

[29]Ehninger, p. 107.

Richard E. Vatz

"The Myth of the Rhetorical Situation"

In the opening lines of "The Rhetorical Situation," Lloyd Bitzer states, "if someone says, That is a dangerous situation, his words suggest the presence of events, persons or objects which threaten him, someone else or something of value. If someone remarks, I find myself in an embarrassing situation, again the statement implies certain situational characteristics."[1]

These statements do not imply "situational characteristics" at all. The statements may ostensibly describe situations, but they actually only inform us as to the phenomenological perspective of the speaker. There can be little argument that the speakers believe they feel fear or embarrassment. Their statements do not, however, tell us about qualities within the situation. Kenneth Burke once wrote of literary critics who attributed to others the characteristic of seeking escape: "While apparently defining a trait of the person referred to, the term hardly did more than convey the attitude of the person making the reference."[2] The same goes for the attribution of traits to a situation. It is a fitting of a scene into a category or categories found in the head of the observer. No situation can have a nature independent of the perception of its interpreter or independent of the rhetoric with which he chooses to characterize it.

In his article Bitzer states, "Rhetorical discourse is called into existence by situation"[3] and "It seems clear that rhetoric is situational."[4] This perspective on rhetoric and "situation" requires a "realist" philosophy of meaning. This philosophy has important and, I believe, unfortunate implications for rhetoric. In this article I plan to discuss Bitzer's view and its implications and suggest a different perspective with a different philosophy of meaning from which to view the relationship between "situations" and rhetoric.

MEANING IN BITZER'S "RHETORICAL SITUATION"

Bitzer's perspective emanates from his view of the nature of meaning. Simply stated, Bitzer takes the position that meaning resides in events. As sociologist Herbert Blumer describes this point of view, it is "to regard meaning as intrinsic to the thing that has it, as being a natural part of the objective makeup of the thing. Thus, a chair is clearly a chair in itself, a cow a cow, a rebellion a rebellion, and so forth. Being inherent in the thing that has it, meaning needs merely to be disengaged by observing the objective thing that has the meaning. The meaning emanates, so to speak, from the thing, and as such there is no process involved in its formation; all that is necessary is to recognize the meaning that is there in the thing."[5] This is Bitzer's point of view: There is an intrinsic nature in events from which rhetoric inexorably follows, or should follow. Bitzer states, "When I ask, What is a rhetorical situation, I want to know the nature of those contexts in which speakers or writers create rhetorical discourse . . . what are their characteristics and why and how do they result in the creation of rhetoric."[6] He later adds, "the situation *dictates* the sorts of observations to be made; it *dictates* the significant physical and verbal responses. . . . "[7] This view is reiterated in various forms throughout the article. Situations are discrete and discernible. They have a life of their own independent in meaning of those upon whom they impinge. They may or may not "require" responses. If they do the situation *"invites"* a response, indeed a "fitting response" almost as a glaring sun requires a shading of the eyes, a clear S-R response.

Bitzer's views are all quite consistent given his Platonist *Weltanschauung*. He sees a world in which "the exigence and the complex of persons, objects, events and relations which generate rhetorical discourse are located in reality, are objective and publicly observable historic facts in the world we experience, are therefore available for scrutiny by an observer or critic who attends to them. To say the situation is objective, publicly observable, and historic means that it is real or genuine—that our critical examination will certify its existence."[8] If the situation is as Bitzer states elsewhere "a natural *context* of persons, events, objects, and *relations* . . . ,"[9] it is hard to see how its "existence" can be certified.

Bitzer claims there are three constituents of the rhetorical situation prior to discourse: exigence, audience, and constraints. It is the "exigence" component which interests us most. In describing "exigence" Bitzer most clearly indicates his view of the source of meaning. He states, "Any exigence is an imperfection marked by urgency; it is a defect, an obstacle, something waiting to be done, a thing that is other than it should be."[10] Not only is a "waiting to be done" now existing in the event, but we also learn that it contains an ethical imperative supposedly independent of its interpreters. Bitzer adds that the situation is rhetorical only if something *can* be done, but apparently it is only rhetorical also if something *should* be done. Bitzer seems to imply that the "positive modification" needed for an exigence is clear. He seems to reflect what Richard Weaver called a "melioristic bias." We learn for example, that the obvious positive modification of pollution of our air is "reduction of pollution." One wonders what the obvious "positive modification" of the military-industrial complex is.

THE MYTH OF THE RHETORICAL SITUATION

Fortunately or unfortunately meaning is not intrinsic in events, facts, people, or "situations" nor are facts "publicly observable." Except for those situations which directly confront our own empirical reality, we learn of facts and events through someone's communicating them to us. This involves a two-part process. First, there is a choice of events to communicate. The world is not a plot of discrete events. The world is a scene of inexhaustible events which all compete to impinge on what Kenneth Burke calls our "sliver of reality."

Bitzer argues that the nature of the context determines the rhetoric. But one never runs out of context. One never runs out of facts to describe a situation. What was the "situation" during the Vietnam conflict? What was the situation of the 1972 elections? What is any historical situation? The facts or events communicated to us are *choices,* by our sources of information. As Murray Edelman points out in *Politics as Symbolic Action,* "People can use only an infinitesimal fraction of the information reaching them. The critical question, therefore, is what accounts for the choice by political spectators and participants of what to organize into a meaningful structure and what to ignore."[11] Any rhetor is involved in this sifting and choosing, whether it be the newspaper editor choosing front-page stories versus comic-page stories or the speaker highlighting facts about a person in a eulogy.

The very choice of what facts or events are relevant is a matter of pure arbitration. Once the choice is communicated, the event is imbued with *salience,* or what Chaim Perelman calls "presence," when describing this phenomenon from the framework of argumentation. Perelman says: "By the very fact of selecting certain elements and presenting them to the audience, their importance and pertinency to the discussion are implied. Indeed such a choice endows these elements with a *presence.* . . . It is not enough indeed that a thing should exist for a person to feel its presence."[12]

The second step in communicating "situations" is the translation of the chosen information into meaning. This is an act of creativity. It is an interpretative act. It is a rhetorical act of transcendence. As Perelman states, "interpretation can be not merely a simple choice but also a creation, an invention of significance."[13]

To the audience, events become meaningful only through their linguistic depiction. As Edelman points out, "Political events can become infused with strong affect stemming from psychic tension, from perceptions of economic, military, or other threats or opportunities, and from interactions between social and psychological responses. These political 'events,' however, are largely creations of the language used to describe them."[14] Therefore, meaning is not discovered in situations, but *created* by rhetors.

As soon as one communicates an event or situation he is using evocative language. As Richard Weaver and others have pointed out, language is always value-laden. Clearly the adjectives into which a "situation" are communicated cannot be the "real situation"; they must be a translation. Surely we learn from Bentham that rhetors can arbitrarily choose eulogistic or dyslogistic coverings for the same situation: We have "leaders" or "bosses," "organizations" or "machines," and "education" or "propaganda" not according to the situation's reality, but according to the rhetor's arbitrary choice of characterization. No theory of the relationship between situations and rhetoric can neglect to take account of the initial linguistic depiction of the situation.

IMPLICATIONS FOR RHETORIC

There are critical academic and moral consequences for rhetorical study according to one's view of meaning. If you view meaning as intrinsic to situations, rhetorical study becomes parasitic to philosophy, political science, and whatever other discipline can inform us as to what the "real" situation is. If, on the other hand, you view meaning as a consequence of rhetorical creation, your paramount concern will be how and by whom symbols create the reality to which people react. In a world of inexhaustible and ambiguous events, facts, images, and symbols, the rhetorician can best account for choices of situations, the evocative symbols, and the forms and media which transmit these translations of meaning. Thus, if anything, a rhetorical basis of meaning requires a disciplinary hierarchy with rhetoric at the top.

The ethical implications for this rhetorical perspective of meaning are crucial. If one accepts Bitzer's position that "the presence of rhetorical discourse obviously indicates the presence of a rhetorical situation,"[15] then we ascribe little responsibility to the rhetor with respect to what he has chosen to give salience. On the other hand if we view the communication of an event as a choice, interpretation, and translation, the rhetor's responsibility is of supreme concern. Thus, when there are few speeches on hunger, and when the individual crime and not the corporate crime is the dominant topic of speakers and newspaper and magazine writers, we will not assume it is due to the relative, intrinsic importance of the two or even to a reading or misreading of the "exigences." Instead the choices will be seen as purposeful acts for discernible reasons. They are *decisions* to make salient or not to make salient these situations.

To view rhetoric as a creation of reality or salience rather than a reflector of reality clearly increases the rhetor's moral responsibility. We do not just have the academic exercise of determining whether the rhetor understood the "situation" correctly. Instead, he must assume responsibility for the salience he has *created*. The potential culpability of John F. Kennedy in the "missile crisis" is thus much greater. The journalists who choose not to investigate corruption in government or the health needs of the elderly are also potentially more culpable. In short, the rhetor is responsible for what he chooses to make salient.

ESSENCE: RHETORIC AND SITUATIONS

The essential question to be addressed is: What is the relationship between rhetoric and situations? It will not be surprising that I take the converse position of each of Bitzer's major statements regarding this relationship. For example: I would not say "rhetoric is situational,"[16] but situations are rhetorical; not ". . . exigence strongly invites utterance,"[17] but utterance strongly invites exigence; not "the situation controls the rhetorical response . . . "[18] but the rhetoric controls the situational response; not ". . . rhetorical discourse . . . does obtain its character-as-rhetorical from the situation which generates it,"[19] but situations obtain their character from the rhetoric which surrounds them or creates them.

When George Aiken suggested several years ago that the United States should declare that she had won the war in Vietnam and get out, it was a declaration of rhetorical determination of meaning. No one understands or understood the "situation" in Vietnam, because there never was a discrete situation. The meaning of the war (war?, civil war?) came from the rhetoric surrounding it. To give salience to a situation in an area roughly the size of one of our middle-size states and to translate its exigencies into patriotism-provoking language and symbolism was a rhetorical choice. There was no "reality" of the situation's being in or not being in our national interest. At least George Aiken saw that the situation was primarily rhetorical, not military or political. And since it was produced rhetorically it could be exterminated rhetorically! As Edelman states ". . . political beliefs, perceptions and expectations are overwhelmingly not based upon observation or empirical evidence available to participants, but rather upon cuings among groups of people who jointly *create* the meanings they will read into current and anticipated events. . . . The particular meanings that are consensually accepted *need not therefore be cued by the objective situation;* they are rather established by a process of mutual agreement upon significant symbols."[20]

Political crises, contrary to Bitzer's analysis of Churchill, are rarely "found," they are usually created.[21] There was a "Cuban Missile Crisis" in 1962, not because of an event or group of events, but mainly because acts of rhetorical creation took place which created a political crisis as well.[22] A President dramatically announced on nationwide television and radio that there was a grave crisis threatening the country. This was accompanied by symbolic crisis activity including troop and missile deployment, executive formation of *ad hoc* crisis committees, unavailability of high government officials, summoning of Congressional leaders, etc. Once the situation was made salient and depicted as a crisis, the situation took new form. In 1970, however, in a similar situation the prospects of a Russian nuclear submarine base off Cienfuegos was *not* a "crisis" because President Nixon *chose* not to employ rhetoric to create one.[23]

Bitzer refers to the controlling situation of President Kennedy's assassination. The creation of salience for certain types of events such as Presidential assassinations may be so ritualized that it is uninteresting to analyze it rhetorically. This does not mean, however, that the situation "controlled" the response. It means that the communication of the event was of such consensual symbolism that expectations were easily predictable and stable. Even Bitzer describes the reaction to the assassination as resulting from "reports" of the assassination. Again, one cannot maintain that reports of anything are indistinguishable from the thing itself. Surely Bitzer cannot believe that there was an intrinsic urgency which compelled the rotunda speeches following the killing of President Kennedy (note, that the killing of important people is communicated with the evocative term "assassination"). In fact, the killing of a president of this country at this time is not a real threat to the people in any measurable way. How smooth in fact is the transference of power. How similar the country is before and after the event. (How similar are the President and Vice-President?) *But* since rhetoric *created* fears and threat perception, the rotunda speeches were needed to communicate reassurances.

CONCLUSION

As Edelman states, "language does not mirror an objective 'reality' but rather creates it by organizing meaningful perceptions abstracted from a complex, bewildering world."[24] Thus rhetoric is a *cause* not an *effect* of meaning. It is antecedent, not subsequent, to a situation's impact.

Rhetors choose or do not choose to make salient situations, facts, events, etc. This may be the *sine qua non* of rhetoric: the art of linguistically or symbolically creating salience. After salience is created, the situation must be translated into meaning. When political commentators talk about issues they are talking about situations made salient, not something that became important because of its intrinsic predominance. Thus in 1960 Kennedy and Nixon discussed Quemoy and Matsu. A prominent or high-ethos rhetor may create his own salient situations by virtue of speaking out on them. To say the President is speaking out on a pressing issue is redundant.

It is only when the meaning is seen as the result of a creative act and not a discovery, that rhetoric will be perceived as the supreme discipline it deserves to be.

NOTES

[1]Lloyd Bitzer, "The Rhetorical Situation," *Philosophy and Rhetoric,* 1 (January, 1968) 1.
[2]Kenneth Burke, *Permanence and Change* (New York: New Republic Inc., 1936) p. 16.
[3]Bitzer, p. 9.
[4]*Ibid.,* p. 3.
[5]Herbert Blumer, *Symbolic Interactionism, Perspective and Method* (Englewood Cliffs: Prentice-Hall, 1969) pp. 3–4.
[6]Bitzer, p. 1.
[7]*Ibid.,* p. 5, emphasis my own.
[8]*Ibid.,* p. 11.
[9]*Ibid.,* p. 5, emphasis my own.
[10]*Ibid.,* p. 6.
[11]Murray Edelman, *Politics as Symbolic Action* (Chicago: Markham Publishing Company, 1971) p. 33.

[12]C. Perelman and L. Olbrechts-Tyteca, *The New Rhetoric*, translated by John Wilkinson and Purcell Weaver (London: University of Notre Dame Press, 1969), pp. 116–117.

[13]*Ibid.*, p. 121.

[14]Edelman, p. 65.

[15]Bitzer, p. 2.

[16]*Ibid.*, p. 3.

[17]*Ibid.*, p. 5.

[18]*Ibid.*, p. 6.

[19]*Ibid.*, p. 3.

[20]Edelman, pp. 32–33.

[21]For a similar view regarding presidential rhetorical "crisis creation" see Theodore Otto Windt, Jr. "Genres of Presidential Public Address: Repeating the Rhetorical Past," delivered at December, 1972 meeting of the Speech Communication Association of America.

[22]Quiet diplomacy was ruled out as were Adlai Stevenson's recommendations of a "trade" of our obsolete missiles in Turkey for Russia's in Cuba. Many of our allies who had lived in the shadow of Russia's nuclear capability could not understand why the United States would find such a situation so intolerable. Moreover, Secretary of Defense MacNamara did not feel that the missiles in Cuba would present an unendurable military situation for the United States. See Elie Abel, *The Missile Crisis* (New York: J. B. Lippincott, 1966) and Theodore Sorensen, *Kennedy* (New York: Harper and Row, 1965) pp. 667–718.

[23]Benjamin Welles, "Soviet's Removal of Vessel in Cuba is Awaited by U.S.," in *The New York Times*, November 15, 1970, p. 1 col. 8.

[24]Edelman, p. 66.

Rhetoric and the Arts

It seems appropriate to make a practical distinction between the ways in which, on the one hand, language has been used to influence the public's perceptions of what constitutes "a work of art," and how, on the other hand, nonverbal creative works employ discursive practices similar to those of verbal discourse. A consideration of the former (the fine arts *and* rhetoric) encompasses the histories of aesthetic philosophy and arts criticism, from the ancients to the present day. The latter (the fine arts *as* rhetoric) finds its fullest expression in twentieth-century—particularly poststructuralist—reconsiderations of the concept of "text": How, for example, is the persuasive appeal of a painting different from that of a successful speech or editorial writing?

Arts criticism *is* rhetoric, in the narrowest sense of the term: persuasive, verbal appeals that imply what is good, true, and beautiful, and assess the extent to which a particular work (be it a symphony, a film, a mural, a piece of choreography or architecture) engages the relevant criteria. The critic's task is to describe what is art—and, by implication, to proscribe what is not. The acts of describing and proscribing, always already value-laden, are at the heart of both the critical enterprise and effective oratory. Writing about the development of Latin humanistic criticism of painting in the fourteenth century, Michael Baxandall identifies "a linguistic component in visual taste . . . to show that the grammar and rhetoric of a language may substantially affect our manner of describing and, then, of attending to pictures and . . . other visual experiences" (vii). Baxandall's description of the humanists' notion of composition in creative visual media, the sources of which lie "in an identifiable set of linguistic preoccupations and predispositions," is no less germane to today's discussion of the rhetoric of arts criticism. Even the reductionist thumbs-up/thumbs-down semiotic of popular movie critics is ultimately a performative speech act intending to persuade audiences, and entails the same kind of linguistic machination Baxandall sees in Alberti—the first artist to argue that artists should have rhetorical training. We find similar practices at work, in one way or another, in criticism of music, dance, and theater.

The nineteenth century saw the institutionalization of art and the academicization of art criticism in the universities; at the same time, there was a general reaction on the part of the artists themselves that the growing body of art criticism could be called rhetoric, but was not itself art. The impressionists in particular attempted to free painting from words, appealing largely to natural, metalinguistic criteria rather than to academic compositional traditions. The rise of the *artiste* and of romanticism in the arts is at least suggestive of this trend to encourage acceptance of a work on its own merits, to strive for creative expression—often in direct defiance of time-honored convention.

Despite resistance to characterizing art as rhetoric, or vice versa, we can propose that creative works cannot help but reflect the times that produced them or to express the rhetorical dispositions of the artists. Richard Wagner's anti-Semitism found its way into his magnificent operas, and this in turn served to fuel the German patriotism that led to National Socialism and the Holocaust. Hitler's display and proscription of "degenerative art" that did not support Nazi ideals further underscored the rhetorical content of nonliterary creative works. Shostakovich maintained a dangerously ambiguous relationship with Stalin, and he composed instrumental music that in turn spoke of his own internal political and philosophical conflicts. After the communist revolution in Mainland China, the rhetorical force of such works as *The Yellow River Concerto* was recognized and banned by Nationalist Chinese on Taiwan for decades. Events of the past one hundred years have helped to produce a large-scale awareness of the ideological in art, and this has in turn contributed to a reconceptualizing of the powers of any "text." Creative work is inescapably personal, and the personal is intrinsically political; although artists may not consider themselves primarily rhetoricians, their work ultimately constitutes a rhetorical act.

Mass communication in the past several decades has led to a further blending of rhetoric and art. The adage "The medium is the message" has become so much a part of the fabric of everyday life in cultures where television, radio, and other popular media influence majority values and opinions that it is no longer possible to conceive of nonlinguistic images or sounds as arhetorical. We live in an era of soundbite oratory. It seems quite natural in the latter half of the twentieth century to enjoy, for example, a popular song or a creative advertising jingle—and then to welcome its demise from continual overplay on the radio or television. This continually shifting *pathos* is accelerated by the ubiquity of mass entertainment media, with the result that appeals to supposedly timeless ideals of beauty seem irrelevant in what Lyotard characterized as "the postmodern condition." In the 1960s, Andy Warhol satirized the fortuitous *ethos* of the creative artist, transforming ordinary household objects such as soupcans into works of art merely by autographing them. John Cage sought to redefine musical expression when he performed one of his early works seated at the piano without playing a single note during the entire piece.

The following reading selections illustrate how closely the fine arts mirror developments in rhetorical theory from the time of Aristotle to the present day. The excerpts focus primarily on the fine arts *as* rhetoric, whereas the works suggested for further reading treat rhetorical aspects of the arts themselves as well as the rhetoric of aesthetics and arts criticism. The first reading is taken from Donald Preziosi's *Architecture, Language, and Meaning,* which treats the semiotic organization of the built world. David Bordwell provides an introduction to the rhetoric of film and film criticism, followed by a discussion of Leland Poague's commentary on Alfred Hitchcock's *Psycho,* from Bordwell's 1989 *Making Meaning: Inference and Rhetoric in the Interpretation of Cinema.* Finally, we present an excerpt from Mark Evan Bonds's 1991 *Wordless Rhetoric: Musical Form and the Metaphor of the Oration,* which discusses how theorists and aestheticians during the past two centuries have seen parallels between language and music.

FURTHER READING

Baxandall, Michael. *Giotto and the Orators: Humanist Observers of Painting in Italy and the Discovery of Pictorial Composition, 1350–1450.* Oxford: Oxford UP, 1971.

Case, Sue-Ellen and Janelle Reinelt, eds. *The Performance of Power: Theatrical Discourse and Politics.* Iowa City: U of Iowa P, 1991.

Hulse, Clark. *The Rule of Art: Literature and Painting in the Renaissance.* Chicago: U of Chicago P, 1990.

Said, Edward. *Musical Elaborations.* New York: Columbia UP, 1991.

Steiner, Wendy. *The Colors of Rhetoric: Problems in the Relation Between Modern Literature and Painting.* Chicago: U of Chicago P, 1982.

Worthen, William. *Modern Drama and the Rhetoric of Theater.* Berkeley: U of California P, 1992.

Donald Preziosi

"Overview: Linguistic and Architectonic Signs"

In the semiotic task of revealing more clearly the place of language in communication, the study of nonverbal communication—and in particular the analysis of visual communication—has acquired today a fundamental urgency and importance.

The study of visual semiosis has been and still remains an enormously difficult task, for not only must we deal with complexities of organization which have no direct correlates in nonvisual sign-systems, but we must also carry forward the necessary extrication of visual semiotics from its verbocentric captivity without falling into any number of opposite extremes.

We cannot adequately understand any form of communication *in vacuuo*, for the various kinds of sign-systems evolved by humans have been designed from the outset to function in concert with each other in deictically-integrated ways, and it becomes increasingly clear that every code contains formative elements whose meaningfulness is ambiguous without indexical correlation to sign formations in other codes.

Human communication is characteristically *multimodal*. In the ongoing semiotic bricolage of daily life, we orchestrate and combine anything and everything at our disposal to create a significant world, or simply to get a message across. A semiotics of communicative events in their multimodal totality has yet to be born, and it will not come about until we have a more profound and complete understanding of the nature, organization, and operant behaviors of sign-systems other than verbal language.

The attempt to bring this about through the scientific superimposition of design features drawn from the study of verbal language upon other sign-systems has, by and large, been a failure. While it is true that much has been learned by such a procedure, the ultimate expected illumination has tended to be rather dim and fleeting in comparison to the energies expended, or, as more often has happened, the mute stones have remained mute.

This silence has induced some, for example the anthropologist Edmund Leach, to claim that it is only because all the things in an environment can be given lexical labels that we can recognize what they are—which is patently false (Leach 1976:33). As Michael Silverstein carefully reminds us, speech-acts are co-occurrent with events in distinct signaling media which together make up large-scale communicative events (Silverstein 1976:11–56).

Despite its truly unique powers and affordances, verbal language is not an active figure against a passive or static ground. This becomes increasingly clear the more we learn about the nature and organization of nonverbal sign-systems. One area of research which has grown up in recent years which uniquely promises to clarify the place of language in communication, and which has already served to collaterally illuminate certain features of the organization of linguistic systems themselves, is the area of architectonic analysis, concerned with the study of the system of the *built environment*—what has come to be called the *architectonic code.*

In part, the emergence of architectonic analysis as an integrated framework for the study of the built environment has become an inevitable and necessary result of the convergence of a series of perspectives on space- and place-making activity. While research elaborated over the past few decades under the rubrics of proxemics, kinesics, environmental psychology, man-environment relations, architectural history, body language, and perceptual psychology has had significant input into architectonic analysis over the past decade, not all of what each of these has had to say has been relevant. Each has been elaborated for different purposes, and each focuses upon a selected portion of the architectonic totality.

The first and most important approximation of such a synthesis came about during the 1960s with the emergence of 'architectural semiotics' and the quest for minimal meaningful units in architecture. Much of this work consisted of plugging in architecture to currently fashionable linguistic models, in the hope of specifying the nature of architectural 'deep structure' or of classifying architectural formations into phonemic, morphemic, or 'textual' unities.

But the plunge into the muddy waters of linguistic analogy brought little in the way of real illumination, and the 'semiotics of architecture' suffered additionally from a near-fatal flaw—*viz.* That 'architecture', as an autonomous system of signs, does not really exist except as a lexical label for certain arbitrarily restricted artifactual portions of the built environment, a picture artificially perpetuated by obsolescent academic departmentalization.

By hindsight, the attempt to develop a semiotics of buildings is rather like trying to understand the organization of language through a study of proper nouns. Inevitably, architectural semiotics rarely consisted of the analysis of the sum of copresent buildings in an environment—which itself would have made more sense—but instead largely concerned itself with arbitrarily selected portions of environmental arrays—prominent building types, for example, such as churches or domestic structures or factories or 'vernacular' construction.

The semiotics of buildings left us with an essentially incomplete and partial perspective on the phenomenon of architectonic semiosis, and it left us at a loss to deal with behaviors described for example by Marshall in the following African situation:

It takes the women only 3/4 of an hour to build their shelters, but half the time at least the women's whim is not to build shelters at all. In this case, they sometimes put up two sticks to symbolize the entrance of the shelters so that the family may orient itself as to which side is the man's and which the women's side of the fire. Sometimes they do not bother with the sticks. (Marshall 1960:342).

The built environment is not merely equivalent to the sum of artifactual or made formations, but will normally include formations appropriated from a given landscape, as well as formations made solely by the relative deployment of bodies in space. This has nothing to do with technological capacity, nor is it a matter of code-switching. Nor is it peculiar to !Kung Bushmen, Australian aborigines, hunter-gatherers, or people living in warm climates, but is a property of any architectonic system.

The architectonic code incorporates the entire set of place-making orderings whereby individuals construct and communicate a conceptual world through the use of palpable distinctions in formation addressed to the visual channel, to be decoded spatiokinetically over time. The proper scope of architectonics has come to be the entire range of such orderings, including all manners of space and place-making activities realized both artifactually and somatically—realized, in other words, through indirect or direct bodily instrumentality.

In an architectonic perspective, a room, a sewing machine in the corner of the room, a tree outside the window, and a mountain on the horizon, however else the latter three may function, may serve as sign-formations in an ordered and culture-specific system of architectonic signs. Moreover, even within the same code, formations may be as permanent as a pyramid or as momentary as a tent, a float in a parade, or a circle of elders assembling together in a meadow once a month.

Our traditional confusions on this point have stemmed from a misconstrual of the nature of the signing medium itself. In evident contrast to the situation with verbal language, where not only is the acoustic medium itself relatively homogeneous, the linguistic signals are themselves processed by the brain in different ways than nonlinguistic acoustic signals. By contrast, architectonic signs are realized through what appears to be an impossibly complex hybrid of media. It would seem that the built environment can employ anything from frozen blocks of water in the Arctic to aggregates of steel and glass, from twigs and animal skins to mere clearings of a forest floor.

But it becomes clear that whether we are dealing with bamboo, concrete, ice, spotlights, lines in the sand, or positions around a lecture hall, we are dealing with geometric and material distinctions *per se* which, by address to the visual channel, are intended to cue the perception of distinctions in meaning, in culture-specific and code-specific ways. The architectonic code is a system of relationships manifested in material formations, and the medium of a given code is normally a mosaic of shapes, relative sizes, colors, textures, and materials—in other words, anything drawn from the entire set of material resources potentially offered by the planetary biosphere, including our own and other bodies.

The more we learn about architectonic systems, the more evident it becomes that each system employs only a selected portion of the potential resources of an ecology, and that the constraints upon the choice of materials are primarily semiotic and culture-specific.

In the broadest sense, communication may be said to involve, most centrally, the transmission of information regarding the perception of similarities and differences. Distinctions and disjunctions in formation are generically intended to cue the perception of similarities and differences in meaning. Meaningfulness is an aspect of a sign-system in its totality rather than being a black box appended in Rube Goldbergesque fashion to other black boxes, and nearly any formative distinction may be meaningful in some sense in a given code, and often in several senses at the same time.

The way each system does this is both code-specific and culture-specific. Meaningful distinctions in formation in one system may be nonsignificant in another code of the same type, or may be significant in different ways. It is evidently the case that any semiotic system is built upon a principle of relational invariance, and it is the task of any analysis to recognize and account for patterns of invariance in variation, and vice versa.

As a system of relationships, the architectonic code signifies conceptual associations through similarities and differences in visually-palpable formation. The amount of potential variation in a built environment may seem at first glance to be impossibly enormous. A glance down any street will reveal a multidimensional mosaic of colors, textures, shapes, sizes, and materials. But a closer look will reveal the presence of the same color applied to differently shaped formations, or of different colors applied to identically shaped formations, or of different colors applied to identically shaped formations which are of different relative sizes. Moreover, each of these permutations may be multiplied across contrastive materials, or across contrastive textures of the same materials.

What might have appeared initially as a visual continuum inevitably resolves itself into a highly complex multidimensional system of contrastive oppositions cued by disjunctions both in geometric and material formation. Moreover, what is done in one system with distinctions in coloration may be accomplished by geometric or morphological distinctions in another code. The analysis of any architectonic code must proceed principally within the specific parameters of organization of that code.

There is no human society which does not communicate, express, and represent itself architectonically. Moreover, there is not just one code spread in gradient diffusion around the globe, but as many codes as there are cultures, and more. The distribution of architectonic systems is not coterminous, however, with linguistic boundaries, and it has been found to be characteristically the case that two groups speaking the same language may contrast sharply in the nature and organization of their built environments. The converse also obtains.

The component units of an architectonic code defined by contrasts in geometric and material formation are not all meaningful in the same way. It has become evident in architectonic analysis over the past decade that an architectonic code comprises a hierarchically-ordered system of signs of various characteristic types.

In connection with a research program begun eight years ago at Yale and continued more recently at MIT, the analysis of large bodies of architectonic data from a variety of cultural contexts has illuminated the nature and interrelationships of architectonic sign types. A number of the salient implications of this research are discussed in the present volume; in general, the following picture of the organization of the architectonic code has emerged.

It is now evidently the case that in any architectonic code the number of minimal significative units is limited, and that it is out of the syntagmatic and paradigmatic interaction of such units that the transfinite variety of architectonic formations in a built environment arises.

In addition, a code reveals the presence of several types of sign-formations or minimal units, related to each other in hierarchically-ordered sets. The largest directly-significant unit to be encoded as such, the *space-cell,* is itself built up of units which are principally meaningful in a systemic sense, and which serve to discriminate one cell from another. These units, or *forms,* as they have come to be called, consist of copresent spatial distinctive features of various types, as discussed below in Chapter IV.

Space-cells enter into tridimensional aggregates, called *matrices,* which, as sign-formations, comprise diagrams or patterns of syntagmatic cellular aggregation rather than larger cellular units, although it has become clear that in any code many such sign-patterns become temporarily fixed in characteristic association: this is subject, normally, to diachronic or diatopic variation.

Architectonic *forms,* while primarily significant in a systemic or sense-discriminative sense, may also serve sense-determinative or directly-significant functions under certain conditions in given codes. Thus, while the particular geometric configuration of a wall, for example, has a primary function in contributing to the contrastive discrimination of one cell from another, it may also, by virtue of its morphological characteristics, carry with it some form of direct signification. This may be over and above its material realization in terms of color, texture, absolute size, or physical material.

In this regard, architectonic and linguistic systems share a certain correlativity of systemic organization while contrasting most sharply with respect to the nature of formative units themselves. As a result of research over the past decade there is no longer any question that both systems are designed according to a principle of 'duality of patterning' or 'double articulation'.

But the architectonic code reveals a unique systemic feature not reflected except by weak approximation in nonvisual systems, which concerns the complexity of its material component, induced by the degree of potential variation in the material composition or realization of formal or geometric structure.

Whereas the material component of the system—the entire range of colors, textures, modularities of size as well as the range of materials employed—serves what is primarily a sense-discriminative function in the realization of formal or geometric units, the material parameters of a built environment offer a second major site for direct signification. The extraordinary range of these significative possibilities, which has no full analog in verbal language, has historically provided yet another block to our understanding of the nature of architectonic signification. The principal formative elements of the code—what constitutes its 'vocabulary', so to speak—consist of distinctions in formation *per se* beneath the material contextual variation explicit in architectonic objects.

Hence, while it has become clear that as a system the code is designed in ways which are correlative to the formative processes of linguistic systems, the multi-dimensional complexities of the code, manifest both spatially and temporally, are both unique and extraordinary.

It is now also clear that, in terms of functionality, both codes reveal correlative properties of organization. The question of architectonic meaning or function has not been resolved through the traditional misconstrual of 'architecture' as 'art', craft, engineering, theater, housing, frozen music, or some ingeneously clever way of writing texts in three dimensions. The study of the built environment through the offices of 'architectural history' has more often than not focussed upon only two or three of its functions—notably its contextually-referential or usage function, its aesthetic function, or its expressive function—and this way of dividing up the pie has been confounded with time- and culture-specific (and class-specific) notions of what buildings ought to do and how they ought to do it. The result has been a misconstrual of architectonic conation, expression, usage, territoriality or phaticism, and metasystemic or allusory functions.

Architectonic formations are inherently multifunctional in the sense that a given construct characteristically reveals, in code-specific ways, a variety of orientations upon the several component parts of a transmission, one or another of which may be in dominance at a given time over others which may be copresent. The built environment is no more an 'art' than is verbal language—except insofar as a given formation—of any usage type—may reveal a dominance of focus upon its own signalization, precisely paralleling the 'poetic' function of a given linguistic art.

The correlation of the functions of architectonic signs with characteristically dominant orientations upon the various copresent components in a transmission was proposed in rough form by the astute Czech theoretician Mukařovský in his 1938 monograph (Mukařovský 1978:236ff.), but it has not been until the past decade that the growth of architectonic analysis has matched his early insights. It is now clear that the functional horizons of architectonic formations correlate *systemically* with the picture of linguistic multifunctionality articulated by Jakobson (Jakobson 1956, 1960). Such a framework now finds additional salient application to other semiotic systems as well.

The picture of architectonic function and meaning is augmented by a unique property of the system, namely the relative permanence of its broadcast. Clearly, if a signal remains perceptually available, it becomes intersubjective property to many potential addressers and addressees. While some architectonic signals are more transitory than others in a given code, the range of relative permanence is in complementary contrast to the ephemerality of linguistic transmission. These contrastive properties confer unique and different advantages to each system. Verbal language and built environments interact in dynamic synchrony in complementary and supplementary fashion, as differentially-sustained components in the ongoing orchestration of meaning in daily life. The world that language builds is built in partnership with and in relationship to the relative object-permanence that architectonic sign-formations confer. By the same token, verbal language confers upon the built environment temporal variation in invariance.

Whatever the two codes share with respect to correlative processes of formation and transmission, they share by virtue of their both being panhuman sign-systems with partly-overlapping and mutually-implicative functions. The more we understand the particular parameters of organization of nonverbal codes such as the architectonic, the less will we be inclined to view the position of any one as an active figure against a static ground. This is not to deny the necessary operational paradox that any code can be employed, in communication, as a provisional metalanguage. Concomitantly, we shall be in a clearer position to understand how and why each copresent system provides its own particularly powerful perspective on the totalities of human experience, and the ways in which each such perspective necessarily implicates all others.

What distinguishes us from those of our primate relatives which we have allowed to survive over the past two million years is not the possession of any one code *per se,* but rather the globality of our intelligence in all modalities. It becomes increasingly embarrassing to assert that any one code is either phylogenetically or ontogenetically the template for all others. It is here that we must necessarily part company with semiotic theories which assert the primacy of any one code as a model for others. Our ancestors designed us with a predisposition toward the mixing of metaphors, knowing full well in their emergent wisdom that, if the only tool we had were a hammer, we would tend to treat everything as if it were a nail.

The aim of this book, then, is to explore the conditions for the emergence of this multimodal cognitive behavior as evidenced by the appearance and evolution of built environments in the human line, and to explore, by metonymic implication, the conditions for the concurrent emergence of verbal language itself.

David Bordwell

"Interpretation as Rhetoric"

It is very much more difficult to talk about a thing than to do it. In the sphere of actual life that is of course obvious. Anybody can make history. Only a great man can write it.

—Oscar Wilde

. . . I treat rhetoric as a matter of *inventio* (the devising of arguments), *dispositio* (their arrangement), and *elocutio* (their stylistic articulation). This scheme allows me to discuss how a wide range of factors, including the critic's persona and the constructed reader, will shape the finished interpretation. The classical outline also lets us trace how the schemata and heuristics that operate in the problem-solving process emerge as premises and evidence for arguments. Throughout, I shall be insisting that rhetoric is a dynamic factor in exploring issues, sharpening differences, and achieving consensus within a community.

• • •

I am hoping that contemporary critics' commitment to the analysis of how positions are "discursively constructed" will make my inquiry seem not only timely but revelatory. Critics who believe that discourse can never be a neutral agency ought to welcome analysis of the intersubjective presuppositions and implications of their own writing. Further, and more plainly, for me rhetoric does not amount to a disinterested manipulation of language. One can be sincere and rhetorical at the same time; indeed, rhetoric can help one be sincere. (Forster: "How can I know what I think till I see what I say?") Rhetoric is the shaping of language to achieve one's ends, and in the act of shaping the language, the ends get sorted and sharpened. The rhetor's purposes may be cynical or selfish ones, but they may also be—*should* be—ones which are grounded in socially desirable goals. Such is, at least, the way I take not only my analysis of critical rhetoric but also the rhetoric I deploy myself.

• • •

SAMPLE STRATEGIES

"The speaker," writes Aristotle, "must frame his proofs and arguments with the help of common knowledge and accepted opinions." Rhetorical argument is adjusted to the audience's preconceptions, even if the rhetor aims to change some of them. If the critic's audience will not assume that a home movie or an educational documentary or a "slasher" film is an appropriate object of interpretation, the critic must generate arguments for discussing such despised genres.

From the rhetorical standpoint, the interpreter's basic task—building a novel and plausible interpretation of one or more appropriate films—becomes a matter of negotiating with the audience's institutionally grounded assumptions. There is a trade-off. Risk a more novel interpretation, and you may produce an exemplar; fail, and you will seem merely odd. Stick closely to the limits of plausibility, and you will pass muster, but you may seem routine. In general, the best preparation is to study exemplars. This teaches the critic what will go down with an audience and what degrees of originality are encouraged by particular institutional circumstances.

In creating a novel and plausible interpretation, the critic draws upon strategies associated with rhetorical *inventio.* For instance, the critic must establish her expertise—by reviewing the literature or the state of a question, by making fine distinctions, by displaying a range or depth of knowledge about the film, the director, the genre, and so on. These ethos-centered appeals create the critic's persona—a *role* (Partisan, Judge, Analyst) and a set of *attributes* (rigor, fairness, erudition). A rare recognition of ethos emerges from a moment in a 1959 *Cahiers* roundtable on *Hiroshima mon amour,* in which Rivette follows mentions of Stravinsky, Picasso, and Braque with the observation: "Well now, we've mentioned quite a few 'names,' so you can see just how cultured we are. *Cahiers du cinéma* is true to form, as always." So pervasive is the power of rhetoric that the remark endows the speaker with a self-conscious honesty.

Another aspect of invention is *pathos,* the appeal to the reader's emotions. This is evident in belletristic film interpretation, and is no less present, though more circumspectly, in academic writing. A critic writes that one scene of *L'Atalante* "humanizes the thief, modeling his frail body wasted by cold and hunger." The description triggers feelings which drive home the interpretive claim. The critic who probes for symptomatic readings also uses pathos, at least insofar as he seeks to gratify an urge for knowledge, mastery, or refined discrimination. The defiant call for analytical sobriety, such as Mulvey's claim in "Visual Pleasure and Narrative Cinema" that she aims to destroy the pleasure of the image, can excite feelings of liberation, a "passionate detachment."

Whatever the critic's approach, she will also create identificatory roles around which the reader's emotions can crystallize. One such role is that of the constructed reader, a kind of parallel to the rhetor's own persona. The other role is that of the "mock viewer," the hypothetical spectator who responds in the fashion best suited to the critic's interpretation. The interpreter must give each role some emotion-laden attributes and relate the two—making them congruent, or demystifying the activities of the mock viewer in order to heighten the constructed reader's awareness. For instance, the *L'Atalante* critic cited above ends his essay with an invitation:

> If the film charms rather than preaches, it is because for Vigo, as for Père Jules, there is nothing transcendent about art or morality. These are not achievements so much as instincts, instincts, it is true, that civilization has lost, but instincts all the same. Catlike, Père Jules is the film's most artful and moral being, his sensuality a guarantee of his authenticity. The same rhythm of life, the same fever that drives the cats, drives Jules, Vigo, and each spectator not yet immunized against it.

By this point the reader should have identified with the constructed reader of the essay, one who can appreciate the film's nonnarrative, richly physical qualities. Now the reader is asked to take the role of the sensitive viewer who welcomes the film's "fever." I shall suggest later how a critic's use of "we" often blends the rhetor's persona, the mock viewer, and the constructed reader into a single vague but rhetorically conventional entity.

Invention's case-centered proofs are no less significant than its ethical and pathetic ones. An argument often passes or fails by its use of *examples.* Michel Charles has proposed that in fact the key convention of literary interpretation is what he calls the *integral citation* of parts of the text under study. By absorbing stretches of the original text into his discourse, the critic presents that discourse as seeking to approximate the act of reading, while the fragmentation of the text gives him great freedom to arrange extracts in a compelling sequence.

The film critic's examples are principally those nodal passages of the film that bear ascribed meanings. Through vivid writing and varied degrees of amplification, these passages must become what Frank Kermode, following Wilhelm Dilthey, calls "impression-points." From one angle, the history of film interpretation looks to be one of steadily increasing finesse in the presentation of such examples: the incisive description practiced by Bazin, the richer detail work of *Movie,* and the shot lists, bird's-eye views, and frame enlargements that appeared in the late 1960s. The greater detail lets more cues activate more semantic fields—producing longer and more intricate interpretations. Although diagrams and stills offer the skeptical reader an opportunity to spot disparities in the interpretation, they convince the charitable reader through "presence." Like Caesar's bloody tunic or the scientist's graph, these devices offer themselves as purified data, examples beyond words: the reader need only look and see.

Still, examples would not carry much force if tacit and widely accepted beliefs were not also giving the critic's case a logical cast. The *enthymeme* is an incomplete syllogism; the audience, from its stock of knowledge and opinions, supplies premises never set forth in the argument. Some of these premises will be specific to different critical schools, as when the critic presupposes that the Oedipal trajectory or organic unity underwrites a certain interpretive move. Other premises subtend the institution as a whole. All the problem-solving processes I have brought out in previous chapters can operate enthymematically. When the critic personifies the camera or claims that a character's surroundings reveal a psychological condition, she is using an inferential procedure as a warrant for the conclusion. The rhetor typically makes certain interpretive moves seem logically inevitable by turning semantic fields into hidden meanings, schemata and heuristics into tacit premises, inferences into argumentative points and conclusions, and the model film into the film itself.

There are, however, widely used enthymemes that do not derive from cognitive discovery procedures. Chief among these is an appeal to authority. The rhetor can count on his audience to trust knowledgeable individuals, and the appeal to respected names and writings is basic to an institution's coherence and continuity. Thus the critic can drop names (Leavis, Lévi-Strauss, Laplanche) or metonymically invoke the massive authority of vast realms of knowledge ("according to Marxism" or "semiotics"). In self-consciously theoretical criticism, the authorities cited often stand outside the institution, and the credibility arises from a belief that they possess knowledge about matters larger and more weighty than cinema. That is, claims about cinema now depend upon truth-claims about wider realms—social power, the nature of language, the dynamics of the unconscious. In this connection, the arrival of citational footnotes in *Cahiers, Screen,* and *Artforum* should be seen as a major event, signaling not simply "academicization" but a move toward arguments from external expertise.

The authority most frequently called upon is the filmmaker.

$$\bullet \quad \bullet \quad \bullet$$

One critic can take a statement by John Ford as confirming the ideological problems of *Fort Apache,* while another can quote interviews with Sirk to show that his films are about happiness and knowledge. Hitchcock's comments about fetishism can support a reading of *Marnie.* A critic can describe *Riddles of the Sphinx* in terms established by the makers: the Sphinx presents 'a stream of questions, contradictions, and word associations' (Wollen), a 'voice asking for a riddle' (Mulvey). Implicit here is a conception of feminist strategy which is not solely in the realm of the conscious, for the Symbolic world into which women enter 'is not their own' (Mulvey)." Interviews, manifestos, and essays furnish evidence for even the symptomatic critic who denounces the idea of origins or creative agency. If the author is dead, film critics are still holding seances.

More exactly, the appeal to the artist functions in relation to several alternative topoi, or commonplace enthymemes. The critic makes a claim about the film's meaning. If the filmmaker's statement confirms it, the statement becomes a piece of causal evidence. (The filmmaker "put" the meaning there, as either a rational or an involuntary agent.) What if the filmmaker's statement does not square with the reading? The critic can simply ignore it (a common tactic). Or she can cite D. H. Lawrence's dictum "Never trust the teller, trust the tale," and point out how unself-conscious the artist is. Alternatively, the symptomatic critic can use the filmmaker's counterstatement as just another trace of repressed meanings. In any case, the critic has great freedom. The *Movie* critics dismissed Hitchcock's answers at press conferences but used claims he made in more serious interviews as evidence for an interpretation. More recently, another writer builds her interpretation of *Presents* out of statements by Michael Snow about the film's techniques and themes, but then she cites other Snow remarks to demonstrate that he is unaware that the film "leaves no room" for the female spectator's look. In such exercises, film criticism plows longbroken ground; Kant, then Schleiermacher, took it as a goal of interpretation to understand an author better than he understood himself.

Two can play this game. The flexibility of the ask-the-artist topos gives filmmakers a chance to manipulate the interpretive institution. In experimental production, the filmmaker's statement can lead the critic to preferred interpretations of an otherwise opaque work. If Peter Wollen claims that the Sphinx in *Riddles of the Sphinx* represents "a repressed instance of the female unconscious," critics can pick up the hint and expand the interpretive point. (This tactic is not unknown in the history of avant-garde art; Joyce turned over his plan of *Ulysses* to Stuart Gilbert and helped a circle of friends write explications of what would become *Finnegans Wake*.) Such skills can be wielded by more commercial creators as well. The director of *In a Lonely Place* tells critics that one of his constant themes is man's loneliness. David Cronenberg acknowledges that in *Videodrome* he deliberately entices critics with a tension between medieval and Renaissance thought, as well as quotations from Yeats and Leonardo. Chabrol supplies a more cynical reason for the literary citations in his films:

> I need a degree of critical support for my films to succeed: without that they can fall flat on their faces. So, what do you have to do? You have to help the critics over their notices, right? So, I give them a hand. "Try with Eliot and see if you find me there." Or "How do you fancy Racine?" I give them some little things to grasp at. In *Le Boucher* I stuck Balzac there in the middle, and they threw themselves on it like poverty upon the world. It's not good to leave them staring at a blank sheet of paper, not knowing how to begin . . . "This film is definitely Balzacian," and there you are; after that they can go on to say whatever they want.

If critics can use the artist's statements as evidence for their interpretation, artists versed in interpretive procedures can use the critics.

A complete list of topoi at work in film interpretation would run very long, but let me pick out a few which have given pleasure over the years.

A critically significant film is ambiguous, or polysemous, or dialogical.
A critically significant film is strikingly novel in subject, theme, style, or form.
A critically significant film takes up an oppositional relation to tradition (old version: ironic; new version: subversive).
A film should make its audience work.
Putting characters in the same frame unites them; cutting stresses opposition.
Montage is opposed to mise-en-scène, or camera movement.
The first viewing is different from later viewings.
Lumière is opposed to Méliès.

The image always escapes verbal paraphrase (old version: through richness; new version: through excess or plenitude).

The filmmaker in question is not solely a master of technique; the film also harbors profound meanings.

In the artist's late period, technique is thrown aside and the work becomes simpler, more schematic, and more profound.

The film asks a question but doesn't answer it.

The film is a reflection or meditation on a sophisticated philosophical or political issue.

The film is Shakespearian (Anglo-American version) or Racinian (French) or Faulknerian (either).

The film's style is so exaggerated that it must be ironic or parodic (useful for Sirk, late Vidor, Visconti, Ken Russell, and so on).

Previous interpretations of the film are inadequate, if not downright wrong.

The critic may capsulize special topics in maxims such as: "If the woman looks, the spectacle provokes, castration is in the air," or "I daresay that ambiguity is an infallible sign of value in the cinema." People are delighted, writes Aristotle, when the rhetor expresses as a general truth the opinions they hold about individual cases.

We are now in a position to understand another function of self-consciously theoretical discourse within film criticism. Theoretical doctrines are often parceled out into enthymemes, topoi, and maxims that assist the rhetorical phase of interpretation. "Theory" has become a binding institutional force, creating tacit beliefs to which the rhetor may appeal. For instance, this book's analysis might be more persuasive to certain readers if whenever I mention critical "practice" or "discourse," I were to attach a quotation or two from Foucault. If debate within explicatory criticism rests on the premise "My theme can lick your theme," disputes within symptomatic criticism appeal to something like "My theory can lick your theory." In this respect, post-1960s film criticism turns from the Judeo-Christian tradition of putting philosophy at the service of the text and recalls the Stoic tradition of treating literature as a diversion to be mastered by the rigor of theoretical reflection. The taken-for-granted power of the theory can appear to validate the interpretation; in turn, the interpretation can seem to illustrate the theory, confirm it, or extend its range of application. The critic may also grant an avant-garde or subversive film the power to investigate conceptual issues and reveal truths; a film becomes significant insofar as it aspires to the condition of theoretical writing.

• • •

David Bordwell

Rhetoric In Action: Leland Poague's "Links in a Chain: **Psycho** *and Film Classicism"*

"The power of rhetoric," writes one sociologist of science, "lies in making the dissenter feel lonely." Suppose that a discussion has been going on for twenty-five years, and you don't like the turn the conversation has taken. Rhetoric will be used to isolate you, so you will need to use rhetoric to switch the conversational flow.

This is, more or less, the task facing Poague. Dissatisfied with the concept of "classicism" employed by Bellour, Klinger, and others, he seeks, in effect, to redefine the category schema. A classical film, he asserts, is not one which possesses certain features (continuity editing, the problem of sexual difference, or whatever); it is a film open to continuous reinterpretation within the critical community. Poague's is not simply, or even primarily, a theoretical sally. His definition presents the critic as willing to couch his case in theoretical terms—but ones which justify his attempt to say something new about a classic. Poague proposes a different set of semantic fields; in doing so, he links these to fields already accepted within the critical literature. More radically, he seeks to make this purportedly contradictory text into a unified work, and to turn its symptomatic meanings into implicit ones.

Poague wants to prove that *Psycho,* in going beyond the sexual dialectic traced by Bellour and Klinger, criticizes the value of money in American culture. "Institutions in the film's depicted world, preeminently the Ford Motor Company, threaten everything, even sight itself when characters let those institutions or paradigms delimit their field of vision." This leads to the most general theme of the film, the relation between social power (that is, capitalism) and individual freedom.

Poague's argument for this theme involves two steps. First, he activates new cues. He points to the prevalence of Ford autos in the film, suggests that Marion's second license-plate letters (NFB) stand for Norman Ford Bates, and infers an implied kinship between Norman and "the father of American assembly line capitalism." This allows Poague to push the film's money motif to a broader social level: the film is about capitalism. Here the critic has adopted the strategy of assuming that even "minor" elements of a text can become central to interpretation—a fruitful assumption if one wishes to say something new about an often-discussed film.

But if all the critic's cues were this minute, he would risk mounting an implausible interpretation. So Poague also reinterprets cues highlighted by earlier criticism, such as the stolen money, the twisting camera movements, and the motifs of eyes and doubles. His principal strategy is to concentrate on items of setting, often linked to character dialogue, as when the spinning motif is associated with money because Sam stands under a fan when he complains of his debts. Like the cues already mentioned, these tacitly appeal to the concentric-circle schema as an inferential warrant.

The dissenting critic must also carefully weave his line-by-line argument into a mesh of plausible inferences. Consider this passage:

> Let us say that money in the world of *Psycho* serves to twist or limit vision, to turn it back upon itself, and that the visual expression of this limitation is figured in the shot of the bathtub drain as water, life, even sight, is sucked into the swamplike darkness. The correlation between darkness, money, and obscured sight is seen initially in Marion's drive to Fairvale. The first water hits her car windshield immediately *after* the remark about her "fine soft flesh," a remark accompanied in the visuals by Marion's oddly self-satisfied, self-obsessed grin—which looks forward, as William Rothman points out, to the death's-head expression on Norman—the mother's face in the film's next to last shot. Indeed, the effect of the water on the windshield at certain moments is to fuse the headlights of the oncoming cars into a single circle of light (like the light bulb hanging over Mrs. Bates in the fruit cellar). Normal vision—seeing with two eyes, as it were—thus gives way to tunnel vision, seeing with a single eye, from a singular vantage point.
>
> The importance, the deadliness, of this species of tunnel vision is then reinforced by Norman's one-eyed glance through the peephole into Marion's motel room.

The critic's "let us say" is ambiguous, recalling the traditional device of presenting what "we" experience during the film, but here the phrase hovers between the authorial "we" ("If you will grant me the chance to make my case . . . ") and the collaborative "we" ("You and I may wish to say . . . "). And associational redescription is constant. Just before this passage the critic has discussed the spinning motif and the (literally) twisting camera. Now vision itself is (metaphorically) twisted; that is, distorted; that is, "limited." The reference to the film's penultimate image of Norman recalls the hollow eye sockets so often mentioned in the critical tradition, and thus evokes blindness, which is then linked to Marion's obsessional vision, and then to the fusing of headlights into one. Then this singularity of the *object* of light is redescribed as a quality of the sighting eye itself—"tunnel vision"—which then segues into Norman's monocular peeping at Marion. In subsequent paragraphs Poague goes on to equate, metaphorically, this partial *vision* with an incomplete *understanding* caused by money.

In effect, Poague's task is to make the film's flow of meaning commentative in a different way than Bellour has proposed. He aims to show that we do not have to identify with the characters, that we can detach ourselves and see "the degree to which they are victims of a culture which encourages possessiveness and limited perspective." To reinforce this implicit meaning, he constructs a Hitchcock—not a flesh-and-blood director but an omniscient "implicit character." This agency "knows what he is about, knows the ethical risks involved, knows it in every frame of *Psycho,* in every gesture and image." Didactically, this agency "shows us in *Psycho* how not to use money, how letting money use us condemns us to death; but he also shows us how to use it well, to forge a chain of images, let us say, which pulls from the heart of Norman's darkness a final image of a truth we would deny, the connection between capitalism, sexuality, and death." The string of asyndetons is suitable for this climax of the argument, conveying as it does the excitement of a rhetor carried away by the force of the film's theme. This effect of spontaneity is balanced by the recollection of the film's final image of the chain pulling the car from the swamp and the half-buried allusion to the Conrad novella which Wood had cited twenty years earlier. Such techniques construct a reader who can entertain a view of the film and of the "classical" text which is as comprehensive as that of the wise narrator whom he portrays. Here filmmaker, critic, and reader transcend the limited perspective of *Psycho's* characters and its previous interpreters.

Along the way, the argument seeks allegiances from other critics. Poague opens with a survey of recent developments, a hallowed way of portraying the interpretation as up-to-date. He cites authorities (Rothman, Culler) who can act as allies, and he even links his project to deconstruction (in his concentration on "marginal features." Chiefly, however, he relies on already-accepted semantic fields, cues, schemata, and heuristics. These provide arguments and examples on which to build a case. No dissenter in this community can persuade his opponents without relying largely, if tacitly, upon basic concepts and routines. But the critical institution is so made that nobody can *be* a legitimate dissenter without having come to share them anyhow. The dissenter is not, finally, all that lonely, and his objection often triggers only a family quarrel.

• • •

Mark Evan Bonds

Musical Grammar and Musical Rhetoric

Within the conceptual metaphor of music as a language, eighteenth-century theorists and aestheticians recognized that the language of music had its own grammar and rhetoric. Much of the basic terminology used to describe music reflects the traditionally close historical association between the verbal and the musical arts. Meter, rhythm, cadence, period, theme, even composition: all of these terms are grammatical or rhetorical in origin.

In both verbal and musical language, grammar encompasses the rules of composition, the manner in which a discourse can be constructed in a technically correct fashion. Rhetoric, on the other hand, cannot be codified nearly so precisely or categorized according to correct or incorrect procedures. A work can be considered rhetorically "correct" only to the extent that it is aesthetically persuasive: two listeners can easily disagree as to whether a particular oration has been persuasive or not. In spite of rhetoric's many precepts, the listener, in the end, is the only true arbiter.

Rhetoric, then, is at least in part an aesthetic category. Musical grammar, as Gotthilf Samuel Steinbart points out, can ensure the technical correctness of a work, but not its aesthetic value:

> [One often] says of musical compositions that they are correct in their construction [*Satz*] if nothing appears in them that would be offensive to the ear or contrary to the rules of harmony, even if in such pieces there is often neither melody nor spirit. According to this point of view, the *Satz* is nothing other than that which grammar is in language. A person can speak clearly and correctly as far as grammar is concerned, and yet say nothing that is worthy of our attention.

Friedrich Wilhelm Marpurg makes a similar distinction between rhetoric, which deals with the actual "application" *(Ausübung)* and "concatenation" *(Zusammensetzung)* of notes in the process of composition, and grammar, which in its turn explains the more mechanical "rules of rhetorical music."

This distinction between the mechanical rules of grammar and the more aesthetic qualities of rhetoric recurs throughout the writings of eighteenth-century music theorists and aestheticians. It is also one of the main reasons why so few musical treatises of the Classical era deal with the question of how one can construct a movement-length work into the shape of an aesthetically satisfying whole. Other aspects of the art—notation, figured bass, harmony, counterpoint—lend themselves far more readily to distinctions between correct and incorrect practice. But insofar as treatises on these subjects present a body of more or less fixed rules, they are all essentially grammars of music. And while Koch is absolutely correct that "a great deal about rhetoric may be found scattered here and there in writings on music, and in writings devoted to the fine arts in general," he is equally correct in pointing out that there are no systematic treatments of musical rhetoric. Forkel's account, to be considered later in this chapter, comes closer to a systematic treatment of the subject than any other, but his presentation is only an outline and necessarily lacking in detail.

Koch was not the first to express disappointment at this lopsided state of affairs, in which the grammar of music was an object of countless treatises, while rhetoric garnered only scant notice. An anonymous review of Christian Kalkbrenner's *Theorie der Tonkunst* (1789) takes the author to task for not presenting more material on the rhetoric of music and concentrating instead on such issues as periodicity, the use of figures, and the distinction among various styles, topics already "known to every amateur who wishes to judge the art correctly." Johann Adam Hiller had similarly noted several years before that

> as valuable as mathematical, arithmetical, and systematic knowledges may be in and of themselves, it is nevertheless to be wished that less fuss be made about such things; and that one should not thrust so much of them upon music toward its putative illumination. For to conceive of notes as quantities; to represent their relations in lines and numbers; to wrap intervals, like a thread, into a ball—this is a far cry from that which is required to bring forth a good melody and clean harmony. It would be better to cultivate the rhetorical or aesthetic part of music more, and to cultivate it more diligently, just as capable men have already done with music's grammatical part.

Stefano Arteaga voiced similar complaints in his *Le rivoluzioni del teatro musicale italiano* of the mid-1780s. Teachers feel satisfied with themselves if they have taught their pupils the basics of harmony and musical accompaniment, Arteaga points out; but this is really nothing more than "the grammar of music," which is "more concerned with not committing errors than with producing something truly beautiful." Such methods do not teach students "the rhetoric of the art."

In France, François Arnaud had announced a treatise on the rhetoric of music as early as 1754, proposing to show that rhetoric could serve as a common ground between two factions: that majority of artists who considered composition to be a matter of instinct and habit and who never spoke of anything other than music's "grammatical part," and those *philosophes* concerned only with music's "proportions, combinations, and mysteries, in a word, its scientific part."

But nothing would ever come of Arnaud's project, and d'Alembert later expressed regret that the proposal had remained unfulfilled. Such a treatise, as d'Alembert pointed out, was greatly needed, as up to the present, one has written almost exclusively about the *mechanics* of this art, that is to say, about its *material* part. There has been almost nothing said regarding taste and expression that one could call *intellectual*. It seems to me that one could throw a good deal of light on this subject by considering music from the perspective of painting and eloquence, particularly poetic eloquence.

This distinction between the mechanical and rhetorical elements of music brings us closer to the connections between rhetoric and form. Koch associates the "formal" elements of music with "the ability to create works of music"; an idea is "formal" in the sense that it deals with how a composer actually brings forth—forms or formulates—a work. This process, ultimately based on the act of *inventio (Erfindung)*, is the province of genius and cannot be taught. The "material" elements of music, on the other hand, constitute "a science that can be taught and learned." In practice, this body of knowledge should be divided into two parts, grammar and rhetoric; but because the available writings on rhetoric are so fragmentary and diverse, rhetoric is most often treated in conjunction with grammar. There are, as Koch observes, virtually no works dealing specifically with that aspect of composition dependent upon genius, "unless one wishes to include works on aesthetics . . . " Rhetoric, in this view, is a mediating element between the teachable and the unteachable, between the mechanical and the aesthetic.

In spite of its subordinate role, the importance of grammar as a basis for aesthetics should not be underestimated. Grammar provides a foundation for all the rhetorical arts: a work must be correct before it can be eloquent. In linguistic terms, grammar encompasses both morphology—the construction of individual words—and syntax, the arrangement of these individual words into the larger units of phrase and sentence. Syntax, in turn, is closely allied to the practice of punctuation, by which individual units of thought are set off and related to one another. Musical grammar, in the eyes of eighteenth-century theorists, follows this same pattern. It begins with individual notes and chords, which join to form small-scale units, which in turn combine to form units of ever-increasing size.

This concept of periodicity—small-scale units concatenated into increasingly larger ones—provides a key link between the grammar and rhetoric of both language and music. On the smallest scale, periodicity falls within the realm of syntax, for it is concerned with the construction of brief and relatively discrete units. On the largest scale, it merges into the broader idea of rhetoric, for it addresses the totality of an oration or movement, that is, the ordering and disposition of all the periods that together constitute the whole. Forkel makes this point in the introduction to his *Allgemeine Geschichte* of 1788:

> In concatenating musical expressions into a coherent whole, one must attend to two points in particular: first, the connection of individual notes and chords into individual phrases, and second, the successive connection of multiple phrases . . . The precepts for joining individual notes and chords into individual phrases are part of musical grammar, just as the precepts for joining multiple individual phrases are a part of musical rhetoric.

Forkel, along with other writers, suggests that grammar and rhetoric, although closely related, operate on different hierarchical levels and maintain their own distinct qualities. While grammar provides the essential building blocks of music, it is rhetoric that governs the large-scale concatenation of these units into a complete movement—or as Koch would put it, the manner in which "individual melodic sections are united into a whole."

Periodicity is treated in a variety of eighteenth-century sources, and while theorists almost inevitably disagree on matters of detail and terminology, there is consensus on several basic points. All authors stress that a hierarchy of cadences articulates various degrees of rest within a melody: authentic cadences are generally reserved for the conclusion of a major section or an entire movement, while half, deceptive, and inconclusive cadences articulate closures of ever-decreasing strength and importance. Almost every writer makes some kind of comparison between this hierarchy of cadences and the conventions of verbal punctuation: the full, authentic cadence is the equivalent of a period; the half cadence is like a colon or semicolon; and weaker points of articulation are analogous to commas. There is, moreover, a consistent emphasis on the underlying need for such points of articulation. Without them, individual phrases would be indistinguishable from one another; a movement consisting of unintelligible phrases would be unintelligible as a whole. And the ease with which a work's ideas can be comprehended by the listener is one of the most important qualities in any rhetorical art. The effective expression of ideas and the concomitant arousal of sentiments both rest upon the ability of the orator or composer to articulate the constituent elements of their respective arguments.

Saint-Lambert's *Principes du clavecin* of 1702 includes the earliest extended application of the imagery of verbal punctuation for musical periodicity in a purely instrumental work:

> The melody of a piece is not composed without order and reason; it is made up of many small segments, each of which has its own complete sense; and a piece of music somewhat resembles an oration, or rather, it is the oration that resembles the piece of music: for harmony, rhythm, meter, and the other similar things that a skilled orator observes in the composition of his works belong more naturally to music than to rhetoric. Be this as it may, just as an oration has its whole, composed most often of many sections; as each section is composed of sentences [*périodes*], each of which in turn has its own complete meaning; as each of these sentences is composed of phrases [*membres*], these phrases of words, and the words of letters—so, in the same way, does the melody of a piece of music have its whole, which is always composed of several reprises. Each reprise is composed of [units demarcated by] cadences, each of which has its own complete sense, and which often constitute the sentences [*périodes*] of the melody. These units are often composed of phrases; the phrases of measures, and the measures of notes. Thus, the notes correspond to letters, the measures to words, the [units demarcated by] cadences to sentences, the reprises to parts [*parties*], and the whole to the whole. But these divisions within the melody are not perceived by all those who hear someone singing or playing on an instrument.

With the exception of those [divisions] that are so obvious that everyone can grasp them, one must know the idiom in order to hear them; nevertheless, they are marked in the tablature by the bar-lines that separate the measures and by several other characters, each of which I shall discuss in its proper place.

Johann Mattheson, in his *Kern melodischer Wissenschaft* of 1737, and then again in *Der vollkommene Capellmeister* of 1739, provides a detailed account of "The Sections and Incisions within a Musical Oration" ("Von den Abund Einschnitten der Klang-Rede"): "Every proposition, oral or written, consists . . . of certain word-sentences or periods; but every such sentence in turn consists of smaller incisions up to the division [punctuated by] a period. Out of such sentences grows an entire concatenation or paragraph, and from various such paragraphs grows ultimately a main section or a chapter." Musical compositions exhibit the same hierarchy of articulations. A "Periodus," for example, is "a brief statement that incorporates a full idea or a complete verbal sense in itself. Now whatever does not do this, but instead includes less than this, is not a period, not a sentence; and whatever does more than this is a paragraph, which can and by all rights should consist of various periods." This definition of "Periodus," as Mattheson himself acknowledges, is derived from Quintilian, whose formulation was in fact the basis for most contemporary definitions of a sentence.

Smaller units, as Mattheson goes on to explain, are articulated by points of punctuation comparable to the comma and the colon. Using an aria as an example, Mattheson derives the musical "resting points," logically enough, from the sense of the text to be set. By relating the disposition of musical cadences to the text, Mattheson continues a long tradition going back as far as monophonic chant and extending throughout the Renaissance and Baroque. Zarlino, writing in 1558, had already observed that the "cadence is of equal value in music as the period in oratory," and that "the period in the text [to be set to music] and the cadence should coincide."

Mattheson, however, goes on to note that purely instrumental music must follow these same principles of articulation. Instrumental music, "without the aid of words and voices, strives to say just as much" as vocal music. Mattheson's subsequent account of instrumental genres includes numerous references to the articulation of sentences, paragraphs, and the like.

These same ideas of periodicity appear repeatedly throughout the eighteenth century as part of almost all contemporary accounts of movement-length form. This is largely in response to important changes in musical style that are characterized by units of increasingly smaller size and slower harmonic rhythm: short, more or less symmetrical phrases replace the long, spun-out melodies of earlier generations. While this kind of periodic construction was by no means a new technique in the second half of the eighteenth century, it did achieve unprecedented prominence at this time.

No single theorist is particularly succinct in presenting these various elements of periodicity, and the problem of terminology further confuses the issue. Kirnberger, writing in Sulzer's *Allgemeine Theorie*, recognized this even at the time, noting that "the names one gives to the smaller and larger sections of a melody have been somewhat indefinite up to now. One speaks of *Perioden, Abschnitten, Einschnitten, Rhythmen, Cäsuren*, etc., in such a way that one word sometimes has two meanings and two different words sometimes the same meaning."

Nevertheless, these basic ideas are present, with varying degrees of clarity, in virtually all contemporary accounts that attempt to describe how a composer actually goes about constructing a work of music. And these accounts almost invariably emphasize the central importance of intelligibility. In his own *Kunst des reinen Satzes*, Kirnberger observes that

> it is immediately apparent to everyone that the most moving melody would be completely stripped of all its power and expression if one note after another were performed without precise regulation of speed, without accents, and without resting points, even if performed with the strictest observance of pitch. Even common [i.e., verbal, as opposed to musical] speech would become partly incomprehensible and completely disagreeable if a proper measure of speed were not observed in the delivery, if the words were not separated from one another by the accents associated with the length and brevity of the syllables, and finally if the phrases and sentences were not differentiated by resting points. Such a lifeless delivery would make the most beautiful speech sound no better than the letter-by-letter reading of children.
>
> Thus tempo, meter, and rhythm give melody its life and power . . . Melody is transformed into a comprehensible and stimulating oration by the proper combination of these three things.

These factors combine to make individual units within a movement understandable, and the same process applies to the larger-scale ordering of these units:

> In speech one comprehends the meaning only at the end of a sentence and is more or less satisfied by it depending on whether this meaning establishes a more or less complete statement. The same is true in music. Not until a succession of connected notes reaches a point of rest at which the ear is somewhat satisfied does it comprehend these notes as a small whole; before this, the ear perceives no meaning and is anxious to understand what this succession of notes really wants to say. However, if a noticeable break does occur after a moderately long succession of connected notes (providing the ear with a small resting point and concluding the meaning of the phrase), then the ear combines all these notes into a comprehensible unit.
>
> This break or resting point can be achieved either by a complete cadence or simply by a melodic close with a restful harmony, without a close in the bass. In the first case, we have a complete musical statement that in the melody is equivalent to a full sentence in speech, after which a period is placed. But in the other case, we have a phrase that is indeed comprehensible, yet after which another or several more phrases are expected to complete the meaning of the period.

A "series of such periods, of which only the last closes in the main key, forms a single composition," and a cadence in the tonic signals the end of "the complete musical oration" *(die ganze musikalische Rede).*

One of the most extensive eighteenth-century accounts of periodicity appears in the first and second volumes of Joseph Riepel's *Anfangsgründe zur musicalischen Setzkunst* (1752–1755). Riepel presents composition essentially as a process of expansion: small phrases grow into larger ones, which in turn combine with other units to produce a movement-length whole. The composer can begin with a unit between two and nine measures in length, but a unit with an even number of measures—particularly two and four—is by far the most common. Regardless of its size, this basic unit can be expanded by the techniques of repetition, extension, interpolation, and a "doubling of cadences," that is, a varied repetition of a closing formula. Again, even-numbered units predominate in practice, as groupings of "four, eight, sixteen, and even thirty-two measures are so rooted in our nature, that it seems difficult to listen (with pleasure) to a different arrangement." The relative strength of closure for any given unit is determined by the strength of its cadence. A perfect tonic cadence is ordinarily reserved for the end of a movement, while a dominant cadence normally articulates an internal resting point of some kind. Cadences on other scale degrees are correspondingly weaker. In this sense, the various units that constitute a movement are set off from one another both harmonically and rhythmically.

Koch adopted this same basic outlook some thirty years later, and his account of periodicity is by far the most comprehensive of his time. Koch's techniques of expansion are derived from Riepel (repetition, extension, and doubling of cadences), but he goes into considerably more detail in explaining how these units can be combined into increasingly larger forms, and he relies much more heavily on rhetorical imagery than does Riepel. When Koch first introduces the concept of periodicity, he compares a short verbal sentence *(enger Satz)* to a short musical sentence. Both have a subject and a predicate (Example 2.1). The former establishes the "main idea" of the sentence, while the latter gives it a "certain direction, a certain mood." The nature of the sentence as a whole, then, is established by the subject, but can be modified by the use of alternative predicates (Example 2.2). Both subject and predicate can be expanded by means of elaboration (Example 2.3).

2.1 Koch, *Versuch,* II, 352

2.2 Koch, *Versuch,* II, 353

This very simple example incorporates the essence of Koch's approach to periodicity. A two-measure unit, the subject, is complemented by the predicate, a succeeding unit of the same size. The resulting four-measure unit, in turn, can be expanded through juxtaposition with related or contrasting units into a still larger unit of eight measures. This same process of expansion, concatenating eight- and sixteen-measure units, ultimately applies to the construction of a movement-length whole as well.

The intelligibility of a complete movement depends on the clear articulation of large-scale units from one another:

> Certain resting points of this spirit, perceptible to varying degrees, are generally necessary in speech and thus also in the products of those fine arts which attain their goal through language, namely poetry and rhetoric, if the subject they present is to be comprehensible. Such resting points of the spirit are just as necessary in melody if it is to affect our feelings. This is a fact which has never yet been called into question and therefore requires no further proof.
>
> By means of these variously perceptible resting points of the spirit, the products of these fine arts can be broken up into larger and smaller units. Speech, for example, breaks down into various sections [*Perioden*] through the most readily perceptible of these resting points; through the less readily perceptible [of these resting points], a section, in turn, breaks down into separate sentences [*Sätze*] and parts of speech. And just as in speech, the melody of a composition can be broken up into sections by means of analogous resting points of the spirit, and these, again in turn, into individual phrases [*einzelne Sätze*] and melodic segments [*melodische Theile*].

2.3 Koch, *Versuch*, II, 355

This structural principle is evident throughout the repertoire of the Classical era. At one point in his treatise, Koch even reproduces a reduced score of almost the entire second movement from Haydn's Symphony No. 42, using this Andante as a paradigm of the manner in which phrases can be extended, repeated, combined, and articulated.

The importance of these articulations for the performer is addressed in several of the eighteenth century's most important manuals on instrumental technique. In his *Violinschule* of 1756, Leopold Mozart enjoins violinists to observe the *Abschnitte* and *Einschnitte* of melody, adding that composers and performers alike should be sensitive to the *incisiones* observed by grammarians and rhetoricians. Daniel Gottlob Türk, in his *Klavierschule* of 1789, similarly notes that it is not enough for the composer alone to articulate the various sections of a composition: it is incumbent upon the performer to bring out the hierarchy of these divisions in his own playing. Otherwise, the weight and clarity of the individual units will be unintelligible to the listener. Quantz, almost forty years earlier, had already pointed to the advantage of the performer's understanding the rhetorical art, invoking a still earlier, complementary idea, borrowed from Quintilian: that the orator has much to learn from the musician.

The central importance of periodicity and its correlative for the listener—intelligibility—were emphasized repeatedly throughout the century and across the continent in numerous accounts of large-scale form. The Spanish theorist Antonio Eximeno, writing in 1774, argued that

> with cadences one creates musical sentences, as in a discourse with periods and commas. One ends a [musical] sentence with a perfect cadence as with a period. Therefore one may call the passage contained between two cadences a musical sentence . . .
>
> In sum, a composition written precisely according to the fundamental rules of music is a discourse that is occasionally elegant but that neither moves nor persuades [the listener]; expressive music is an eloquent discourse that triumphs over the spirit of its audience.

And in one of the few theoretical treatises published in Vienna during the Classical era, Johann Friedrich Daube noted that "the entire musical movement must consist above all of certain main sections, which in turn can be broken down into smaller subsidiary sections or elements, if the movement is to elicit a good effect. The alternation of harmony also belongs here." Elsewhere, Daube urged composers to apply "judicious incisions, resting points, etc.," along with "good alternation of the rushing and the cantabile, or, to use the language of painting, of light and shadow. And in all of this, the rules of rhetoric must be taken into account." In a later treatise, Daube encouraged composers to study carefully the works of great orators, including Cicero, Horace, and Seneca, and to emulate them in questions of "symmetry" and the "relationship of all a work's parts."

The concept of periodicity offers an essentially generative approach to the question of form, with small-scale units expanding into larger ones. But Mattheson and other subsequent theorists, including Koch, sensed that this approach alone would not suffice to explain the multiplicity of movement-length forms then current. While the mechanics of constructing small-scale units could be (and were) described in relatively straightforward fashion, the creation of large-scale forms out of smaller units had long been considered a more difficult matter, in music as in rhetoric. Sulzer is typical of many other writers in pointing out that

> the art of periodizing well is one of the most difficult elements in all of eloquence . . . Everything else can be attained more easily than this, through natural gifts and without back-breaking study. Work, industry, much deliberation, and great strength in language are required for this. It does not seem possible to

provide methodical instruction in this area. The best that one could do in educating the orator in this area would be to provide him with a well-arranged collection of the best periods, ordered according to the varying character of their contents, and to show him the value of each through their thorough dissection.

Among music theorists, the concatenation of individual units into a larger whole could help to explain the construction of movement-length forms, but only up to a point. Neither Mattheson nor Koch, significantly enough, was content to conclude his treatment of large-scale form with a discussion of periodicity. For while this principle emphasizes the fundamental similarities among disparate stereotypical patterns, it cannot adequately account for their differences. Periodicity, moreover, focuses primarily on the articulation of ideas, as opposed to the aesthetic coherence of the ideas themselves over the course of an entire movement. It emphasizes, in other words, the framework of articulation at the expense of that which is to be articulated. Mattheson, Koch, and others viewed form not so much as a process of articulation—critical as that process may be for intelligibility—but as a process of elaboration. The eighteenth century's theory of the compositional process provides the conceptual context for this idea of form.

• • •

Rhetoric and Literary Criticism

Like *rhetoric* itself, *literary criticism* is an enormously slippery term, and volumes of scholarly writing have been devoted to defining what kinds of practices constitute it. In its most general conception, literary criticism involves two sets of activities: the explication and evaluation of the content developed in stories, novels, poems, and plays; and the analysis and evaluation of the linguistic codes—the organization, syntax, diction, and so on—deployed in literary works as they develop this content. Literary criticism is generally seen as a broader activity than literary reviewing. Literary reviewers assess the degree to which they believe a work will appeal to the tastes of readers, either a particular group or the "general, reading public"—however that elusive abstraction might be defined. Literary critics assay and critique an expansive array of issues—among others, the work's themes, its "realism," its "truths," its reception by readers, its relation to the author's or readers' psychological–emotional–sociological states, as well as its codes and their functions.

Literary criticism operates in a dual relationship with rhetoric. Like scholars in all fields, literary critics must be concerned with the rhetoric *of* their academic discipline, the rhetoric *of* literary criticism. That is, literary criticism is always addressed to the interests and standards of some collectivity, some group of readers, either actual or potential. Thus, critics must consider a range of issues of rhetorical theory: how to conceptualize and address their readers, how and to what degree they will feature a central idea or thesis in a critical essay, how they will appeal to their readers' existing standards for what constitutes good arguments about literary texts or instead try to promulgate new standards, and how they will operate within the conventions of genre and style that their readers expect in a literary critical essay.

In addition, many literary critics are concerned with the role of rhetoric in literary criticism: Realizing that the poems, novels, stories, and plays they critique are meant to be read by and, in some way, to affect real readers, many critics analyze and evaluate the nature and functions of rhetoric inscribed in literary works. These critics examine the means by which a literary work imposes a "fictional world upon the reader," and "control[s] the reader," as Wayne Booth puts it in the preface to his 1961 study, *The Rhetoric of Fiction*. Such rhetorical criticism of literary works can include analyses of the ways stories, novels, poems, and plays affect their readers through the promulgation of central ideas, the creation and deployment of narrators and characters, and the use of evocative and engaging language.

The works in this part demonstrate both of these roles of rhetoric in relation to literary criticism. Terry Eagleton is concerned with liberating the rhetoric of literary criticism from what he perceives as the shackles of a repressive tradition. In the final chapter of *Literary Theory: An Introduction,* Eagleton surmises that the book might amount to a *conclusion* to literary theory, an "obituary" for the field. He excoriates traditional literary criticism as empty writing in which "[n]obody is especially concerned with what you say, with what moderate, radical or conservative positions you adopt, provided that they are compatible with, and can be articulated within, a specific form of discourse." Traditional literary theory, Eagleton argues, "is really no more than a branch of social ideologies," discourse that endlessly circulates the same set of conventional values about what constitutes "great literature." In lieu of such discourse, Eagleton proposes that literary scholars engage the critical tools of rhetoric, the form of analysis that examines "the way discourses are constructed to achieve certain effects," the ancient branch of inquiry, preoccupied "with discourse as a form of power and desire," that sees "speaking and writing . . . as forms of *activity* inseparable from the wider social relations between writers and readers."

Like Eagleton's, Elizabeth Flynn's work is concerned, at least tangentially, with the rhetoric of literary criticism. But the scope of Flynn's essay is broader than Eagleton's: whereas Eagleton is concerned with what he sees as the dominating power of the standard literary canon and traditional scholarship on the rhetoric of literary criticism, Flynn examines the effect of gender differences on the rhetoric of all texts, including literary criticism. Reviewing a wide array of recent research on gender differences in social and psychological development, Flynn illustrates how scholars and teachers can recognize and acknowledge the role of gender in student writing and, by extrapolation, academic and scholarly writing in general.

In contrast to Eagleton and Flynn, Charles I. Schuster considers one of the roles of rhetoric in literary criticism in his explication of the rhetorical theories of Mikhail Bahktin. Schuster explains how Bahktin's concept of the *hero* in a literary work becomes "the dominant influence in verbal and written utterance," interacting with the narrator/speaker "to shape the language and determine the form." To Bahktin, Schuster explains, the "dialogic" interaction of the hero—who can be a character, an idea, an object, or a location—with the narrator/speaker and reader/listener generates words that one must "lay claim to" and place within a new context. Within literary discourse—indeed, within all speaking and writing—"individuals struggle to replace alien meanings with their own semantic and expressive intentions." They begin to develop their own stylistic profiles, creating a language that "is essentially a rich stew of implication, saturated with other accents, tones, idioms, meanings, voices, influences, intentions." This charged, contextualized, dialogic language, as Bahktin writes, is "expression" that "organizes experience. Expression is what first gives experience its form and specificity of direction." As Schuster notes about all discourse, both "literary" and "ordinary," "When we speak and write, we create ourselves and the world."

Finally, in a challenging interview with Gary Olson, Jacques Derrida, whom most scholars acknowledge as the leading proponent of the literary theory known as deconstructionism, offers insights that deal with both the rhetoric of literary criticism and the role of rhetoric within literary criticism. Concerning the former, Derrida will not settle for a criticism that simply and unreflectively reinforces conventional theses: "Deconstruction questions the thesis, the theme, the possibility of everything, including, among other things, composition. Writing is not simply a 'composition.' " At the same time, Derrida would not have literary critics diminish the importance of the standard canon of literature: "I start with the tradition. If you're not trained in the tradition, then deconstruction means nothing." Concerning the latter, Derrida warns against an attitude he calls *rhetoricism*—"a way of giving rhetoric all the power, thinking that everything depends on rhetoric simply as a technique of speech." Arguing that "the possibility of speech acts" [in both literature and other kinds speaking and writing] "depends on conditions and conventions which are not simply verbal." In other words, Derrida maintains, "What I call 'writing' or 'text' is not simply verbal."

FURTHER READING

Booth, Wayne C. *The Rhetoric of Fiction.* Chicago: U of Chicago P, 1961.

Crowley, Sharon. *A Teacher's Introduction to Deconstruction.* Urbana, IL: National Council of Teachers of English, 1989.

Hawkes, Terence. *Structuralism and Semiotics.* Berkeley, CA: U of California P, 1977.

Herrnstein Smith, Barbara. *On the Margins of Discourse: The Relation of Literature and Language.* Baltimore: Johns Hopkins UP, 1978.

Noel, Jasper. *Plato, Derrida, and Writing.* Carbondale: Southern Illinois UP, 1988.

Terry Eagleton

"Political Criticism"

In the course of this book we have considered a number of problems of literary theory. But the most important question of all has as yet gone unanswered. What is the *point* of literary theory? Why bother with it in the first place? Are there not issues in the world more weighty than codes, signifiers and reading subjects?

Let us consider merely one such issue. As I write, it is estimated that the world contains over 60,000 nuclear warheads, many with a capacity a thousand times greater than the bomb which destroyed Hiroshima. The possibility that these weapons will be used in our lifetime is steadily growing. The approximate cost of these weapons is 500 billion dollars a year, or 1.3 billion dollars a day. Five per cent of this sum—25 billion dollars—could drastically, fundamentally alleviate the problems of the poverty-stricken Third World. Anyone who believed that literary theory was more important than such matters would no doubt be considered somewhat eccentric, but perhaps only a little less eccentric than those who consider that the two topics might be somehow related. What has international politics to do with literary theory? Why this perverse insistence on dragging politics into the argument?

There is, in fact, no need to drag politics into literary theory: as with South African sport, it has been there from the beginning. I mean by the political no more than the way we organize our social life together, and the power-relations which this involves; and what I have tried to show throughout this book is that the history of modern literary theory is part of the political and ideological history of our epoch. From Percy Bysshe Shelley to Norman N. Holland, literary theory has been indissociably bound up with political beliefs and ideological values. Indeed literary theory is less an object of intellectual enquiry in its own right than a particular perspective in which to view the history of our times. Nor should this be in the least cause for surprise. For any body of theory concerned with human meaning, value, language, feeling and experience will inevitably engage with broader, deeper beliefs about the nature of human individuals and societies, problems of power and sexuality, interpretations of past history, versions of the present and hopes for the future. It is not a matter of *regretting* that this is so—of *blaming* literary theory for being caught up with such questions, as opposed to some 'pure' literary theory which might be absolved from them.

Such 'pure' literary theory is an academic myth: some of the theories we have examined in this book are nowhere more clearly ideological than in their attempts to ignore history and politics altogether. Literary theories are not to be upbraided for being political, but for being on the whole covertly or unconsciously so—for the blindness with which they offer as a supposedly 'technical', 'self-evident', 'scientific' or 'universal' truth doctrines which with a little reflection can be seen to relate to and reinforce the particular interests of particular groups of people at particular times. The title of this section, 'Conclusion: Political Criticism', is not intended to mean: 'Finally, a political alternative'; it is intended to mean: 'The conclusion is that the literary theory we have examined is political.'

It is not only, however, a matter of such biases being covert or unconscious. Sometimes, as with Matthew Arnold, they are neither, and at other times, as with T. S. Eliot, they are certainly covert but not in the least unconscious. It is not the fact that literary theory is political which is objectionable, nor just the fact that its frequent obliviousness of this tends to mislead: what is really objectionable is the nature of its politics. That objection can be briefly summarized by stating that the great majority of the literary theories outlined in this book have strengthened rather than challenged the assumptions of the power-system some of whose present-day consequences I have just described. I do not mean by this that Matthew Arnold supported nuclear weapons, or that there are not a good many literary theorists who would not dissent in one way or another from a system in which some grow rich on profits from armaments while others starve in the street. I do not believe that many, perhaps most, literary theorists and critics are not disturbed by a world in which some economies, left stagnant and lopsided by generations of colonial exploitation, are still in fee to Western capitalism through their crippling repayments of debts, or that all literary theorists would genially endorse a society like our own, in which considerable private wealth remains concentrated in the hands of a tiny minority, while the human services of education, health, culture and recreation for the great majority are torn to shreds. It is just that they would not regard literary theory as at all relevant to such matters. My own view, as I have commented, is that literary theory has a most particular relevance to this political system: it has helped, wittingly or not, to sustain and reinforce its assumptions.

Literature, we are told, is vitally engaged with the living situations of men and women: it is concrete rather than abstract, displays life in all its rich variousness, and rejects barren conceptual enquiry for the feel and taste of what it is to be alive. The story of modern literary theory, paradoxically, is the narrative of a flight from such realities into a seemingly endless range of alternatives: the poem itself, the organic society, eternal verities, the imagination, the structure of the human mind, myth, language and so on. Such a flight from real history is in part understandable as a reaction to the antiquarian, historically reductionist criticism which held sway in the nineteenth century; but the extremism of this reaction has been nevertheless striking. It is indeed the *extremism* of literary theory, its obstinate, perverse, endlessly resourceful refusal to countenance social and historical realities, which most strikes a student of its documents, even though 'extremism' is a term more commonly used of those who would seek to call attention to literature's role in actual life. Even in the act of fleeing modern ideologies, however, literary theory reveals its often unconscious complicity with them, betraying its elitism, sexism or individualism in the very 'aesthetic' or 'unpolitical' language it finds natural to use of the literary text. It assumes, in the main, that at the centre of the world is the contemplative individual self, bowed over its book, striving to gain touch with experience, truth, reality, history or tradition. Other things matter too, of course—this individual is in personal relationship with others, and we are always much more than readers—but it is notable how often such individual consciousness, set in its small circle of relationships, ends up as the touchstone of all else. The further we move from the rich inwardness of the personal life, of which literature is the supreme exemplar, the more drab, mechanical and impersonal existence becomes. It is a view equivalent in the literary sphere to what has been called possessive individualism in the social realm, much as the former attitude may shudder at the latter: it reflects the values of a political system which subordinates the sociality of human life to solitary individual enterprise.

I began this book by arguing that literature did not exist. How in that case can literary theory exist either? There are two familiar ways in which any theory can provide itself with a distinct purpose and identity. Either it can define itself in terms of its particular *methods* of enquiry; or it can define itself in terms of the particular *object* that is being enquired 'nto. Any attempt to define literary theory in terms of a distinctive method is doomed to failure. Literary theory is supposed to reflect on the nature of literature and literary criticism. But just think of how many methods are involved in literary criticism. You can discuss the poet's asthmatic childhood, or examine her peculiar use of syntax; you can detect the rustling of silk in the hissing of the *s*'s, explore the phenomenology of reading, relate the literary work to the state of the class-struggle or find out how many copies it sold. These methods have nothing whatsoever of significance in common. In fact they have more in common with other 'disciplines'—linguistics, history, sociology and so on—than they have with each other. Methodologically speaking, literary criticism is a non-subject. If literary theory is a kind of 'metacriticism', a critical reflection on criticism, then it follows that it too is a non-subject.

Perhaps, then, the unity of literary studies is to be sought elsewhere. Perhaps literary criticism and literary theory just mean any kind of talk (of a certain level of 'competence', clearly enough) about an object named literature. Perhaps it is the object, not the method, which distinguishes and delimits the discourse. As long as that object remains relatively stable, we can move equably from biographical to mythological to semiotic methods and still know where we are. But as I argued in the Introduction, literature has no such stability. The unity of the object is as illusory as the unity of the method. 'Literature', as Roland Barthes once remarked, 'is what gets taught.'

Maybe this lack of methodological unity in literary studies should not worry us unduly. After all, it would be a rash person who would define geography or philosophy, distinguish neatly between sociology and anthropology or advance a snap definition of 'history'. Perhaps we should celebrate the plurality of critical methods, adopt a tolerantly ecumenical posture and rejoice in our freedom from the tyranny of any single procedure. Before we become too euphoric, however, we should notice that there are certain problems here too. For one thing, not all of these methods are mutually compatible. However generously liberal-minded we aim to be, trying to combine structuralism, phenomenology and psychoanalysis is more likely to lead to a nervous breakdown than to a brilliant literary career. Those critics who parade their pluralism are usually able to do so because the different methods they have in mind are not all that different in the end. For another thing, some of these 'methods' are hardly methods at all. Many literary critics dislike the whole idea of method and prefer to work by glimmers and hunches, intuitions and sudden perceptions. It is perhaps fortunate that this way of proceeding has not yet infiltrated medicine or aeronautical engineering; but even so one should not take this modest disowning of method altogether seriously, since what glimmers and hunches you have will depend on a latent structure of assumptions often quite as stubborn as that of any structuralist. It is notable that such 'intuitive' criticism, which relies not on 'method' but on 'intelligent sensitivity', does not often seem to intuit, say, the presence of ideological values in literature. Yet there is no reason, on its own reckoning, why it should not. Some traditional critics would appear to hold that other people subscribe to theories while they prefer to read literature 'straightforwardly'. No theoretical or ideological predilections, in other words, mediate between themselves and the text: to describe George Eliot's later world as one of 'mature resignation' is not ideological, whereas to claim that it reveals evasion and compromise is. It is therefore difficult to engage such critics in debate about ideological preconceptions, since the power of ideology over them is nowhere more marked than in their honest belief that their readings are 'innocent'. It was Leavis who was being 'doctrinal' in attacking Milton, not C. S. Lewis in defending him; it is feminist critics who insist on confusing literature with politics by examining fictional images of gender, not conventional critics who are being political by arguing that Richardson's Clarissa is largely responsible for her own rape.

Even so, the fact that some critical methods are less methodical than others proves something of an embarrassment to the pluralists who believe that there is a little truth in everything. (This theoretical pluralism also has its political correlative: seeking to understand everybody's point of view quite often suggests that you yourself are disinterestedly up on high or in the middle, and trying to resolve conflicting viewpoints into a consensus implies a refusal of the truth that some conflicts can be resolved on one side alone.) Literary criticism is rather like a laboratory in which some of the staff are seated in white coats at control panels, while others are throwing sticks in the air or spinning coins. Genteel amateurs jostle with hard-nosed professionals, and after a century or so of 'English' they have still not decided to which camp the subject really belongs. This dilemma is the product of the peculiar history of English, and it cannot really be settled because what is at stake is much more than a mere conflict over methods or the lack of them. The true reason why the pluralists are wishful thinkers is that what is at issue in the contention between different literary theories or 'non-theories' are competing ideological strategies related to the very destiny of English studies in modern society. The problem with literary theory is that it can neither beat nor join the dominant ideologies of late industrial capitalism. Liberal humanism seeks to oppose or at least modify such ideologies with its distaste for the technocratic and its nurturing of spiritual wholeness in a hostile world; certain brands of formalism and structuralism try to take over the technocratic rationality of such a society and thus incorporate themselves into it. Northrop Frye and the New Critics thought that they had pulled off a synthesis of the two, but how many students of literature today read them? Liberal humanism has dwindled to the impotent conscience of bourgeois society, gentle, sensitive and ineffectual; structuralism has already more or less vanished into the literary museum.

The impotence of liberal humanism is a symptom of its essentially contradictory relationship to modern capitalism. For although it forms part of the 'official' ideology of such society, and the 'humanities' exist to reproduce it, the social order within which it exists has in one sense very little time for it at all. Who is concerned with the uniqueness of the individual, the imperishable truths of the human condition or the sensuous textures of lived experience in the Foreign Office or the boardroom of Standard Oil? Capitalism's reverential hat-tipping to the arts is obvious hypocrisy, except when it can hang them on its walls as a sound investment. Yet capitalist states have continued to direct funds into higher education humanities departments, and though such departments are usually the first in line for savage cutting when capitalism enters on one of its periodic crises, it is doubtful that it is only hypocrisy, a fear of appearing in its true philistine colours, which compels this grudging support. The truth is that liberal humanism is at once largely ineffectual, and the best ideology of the 'human' that present bourgeois society can muster. The 'unique individual' is indeed important when it comes to defending the business entrepreneur's right to make profit while throwing men and women out of work; the individual must at all costs have the 'right to choose', provided this means the right to buy one's child an expensive private education while other children are deprived of their school meals, rather than the rights of women to decide whether to have children in the first place. The 'imperishable truths of the human condition' include such verities as freedom and democracy, the essences of which are embodied in our particular way of life. The 'sensuous textures of lived experience' can be roughly translated as reacting from the gut—judging according to habit, prejudice and 'common sense', rather than according to some inconvenient, 'aridly theoretical' set of debatable ideas. There is, after all, room for the humanities yet, much as those who guarantee our freedom and democracy despise them.

Departments of literature in higher education, then, are part of the ideological apparatus of the modern capitalist state. They are not wholly reliable apparatuses, since for one thing the humanities contain many values, meanings and traditions which are antithetical to that state's social priorities, which are rich in kinds of wisdom and experience beyond its comprehension. For another thing, if you allow a lot of young people to do nothing for a few years but read books and talk to each other then it is possible that, given certain wider historical circumstances, they will not only begin to question some of the values transmitted to them but begin to interrogate the authority by which they are transmitted. There is of course no harm in students questioning the values conveyed to them: indeed it is part of the very meaning of higher education that they should do so. Independent thought, critical dissent and reasoned dialectic are part of the very stuff of a humane education; hardly anyone, as I commented earlier, will demand that your essay on Chaucer or Baudelaire arrives inexorably at certain pre-set conclusions. All that is being demanded is that you manipulate a particular language in acceptable ways. Becoming certificated by the state as proficient in literary studies is a matter of being able to talk and write in certain ways. It is this which is being taught, examined and certificated, not what you personally think or believe, though what is thinkable will of course be constrained by the language itself. You can think or believe what you want, as long as you can speak this particular language. Nobody is especially concerned about what you say, with what extreme, moderate, radical or conservative positions you adopt, provided that they are compatible with, and can be articulated within, a specific form of discourse. It is just that certain meanings and positions will not be articulable within it. Literary studies, in other words, are a question of the signifier, not of the signified. Those employed to teach you this form of discourse will remember whether or not you were able to speak it proficiently long after they have forgotten what you said.

Literary theorists, critics and teachers, then, are not so much purveyors of doctrine as custodians of a discourse. Their task is to preserve this discourse, extend and elaborate it as necessary, defend it from other forms of discourse, initiate newcomers into it and determine whether or not they have successfully mastered it. The discourse itself has no definite signified, which is not to say that it embodies no assumptions: it is rather a network of signifiers able to envelop a whole field of meanings, objects and practices. Certain pieces of writing are selected as being more amenable to this discourse than others, and these are what is known as literature or the 'literary canon'. The fact that this canon is usually regarded as fairly fixed, even at times as eternal and immutable, is in a sense ironic, because since literary critical discourse has no definite signified it can, if it wants to, turn its attention to more or less any kind of writing. Some of those hottest in their defence of the canon have from time to time demonstrated how the discourse can be made to operate on 'non-literary' writing. This, indeed, is the embarrassment of literary criticism, that it defines for itself a special object, literature, while existing as a set of discursive techniques which have no reason to stop short at that object at all. If you have nothing better to do at a party you can always try on a literary critical analysis of it, speak of its styles and genres, discriminate its significant nuances or formalize its sign-systems. Such a 'text' can prove quite as rich as one of the canonical works, and critical dissections of it quite as ingenious as those of Shakespeare. So either literary criticism confesses that it can handle parties just as well as it can Shakespeare, in which case it is in danger of losing its identity along with its object; or it agrees that parties may be interestingly analysed provided that this is called something else: ethnomethodology or hermeneutical phenomenology, perhaps. Its own concern is with literature, because literature is more valuable and rewarding than any of the other texts on which the critical discourse might operate. The disadvantage of this claim is that it is plainly untrue: many films and works of philosophy are considerably more valuable than much that is included in the 'literary canon'. It is not that they are valuable in different ways: they could present objects of value in the sense that criticism defines that term. Their exclusion from what is studied is not because they are not 'amenable' to the discourse: it is a question of the arbitrary authority of the literary institution.

Another reason why literary criticism cannot justify its self-limiting to certain works by an appeal to their 'value' is that criticism is part of a literary institution which constitutes these works as valuable in the first place. It is not only parties that need to be *made* into worthwhile literary objects by being treated in specific ways, but also Shakespeare. Shakespeare was not great literature lying conveniently to hand, which the literary institution then happily discovered: he is great literature because the institution constitutes him as such. This does not mean that he is not 'really' great literature—that it is just a matter of people's opinions about him—because there is no such thing as literature which is 'really' great, or 'really' anything, independently of the ways in which that writing is treated within specific forms of social and institutional life. There are an indefinite number of ways of discussing Shakespeare, but not all of them count as literary critical. Perhaps Shakespeare himself, his friends and actors, did not talk about his plays in ways which we would regard as literary critical. Perhaps some of the most interesting statements which could be made about Shakespearian drama would also not count as belonging to literary criticism. Literary criticism selects, processes, corrects and rewrites texts in accordance with certain institutionalized norms of the 'literary'—norms which are at any given time arguable, and always historically variable. For though I have said that critical discourse has no determinate signified, there are certainly a great many ways of talking about literature which it excludes, and a great many discursive moves and strategies which it disqualifies as invalid, illicit, noncritical, nonsense. Its apparent generosity at the level of the signified is matched only by its sectarian intolerance at the level of the signifier. Regional dialects of the discourse, so to speak, are acknowledged and sometimes tolerated, but you must not sound as though you are speaking another language altogether. To do so is to recognize in the sharpest way that critical discourse is power. To be on the inside of the discourse itself is to be blind to this power, for what is more natural and nondominative than to speak one's own tongue?

The power of critical discourse moves on several levels. It is the power of 'policing' language—of determining that certain statements must be excluded because they do not conform to what is acceptably sayable. It is the power of policing writing itself, classifying it into the 'literary' and 'non-literary', the enduringly great and the ephemerally popular. It is the power of authority *vis-à-*

vis others—the power-relations between those who define and preserve the discourse, and those who are selectively admitted to it. It is the power of certificating or noncertificating those who have been judged to speak the discourse better or worse. Finally, it is a question of the power-relations between the literary-academic institution, where all of this occurs, and the ruling power-interests of society at large, whose ideological needs will be served and whose personnel will be reproduced by the preservation and controlled extension of the discourse in question.

I have argued that the theoretically limitless extendibility of critical discourse, the fact that it is only arbitrarily confined to 'literature', is or should be a source of embarrassment to the custodians of the canon. The objects of criticism, like those of the Freudian drive, are in a certain sense contingent and replaceable. Ironically, criticism only really became aware of this fact when, sensing that its own liberal humanism was running out of steam, it turned for aid to more ambitious or rigorous critical methods. It thought that by adding a judicious pinch of historical analysis here or swallowing a non-addictive dose of structuralism there, it could exploit these otherwise alien approaches to eke out its own dwindling spiritual capital. The boot, however, might well prove to be on the other foot. For you cannot engage in an historical analysis of literature without recognizing that literature itself is a recent historical invention; you cannot apply structuralist tools to *Paradise Lost* without acknowledging that just the same tools can be applied to the *Daily Mirror*. Criticism can thus prop itself up only at the risk of losing its defining object; it has the unenviable choice of stifling or suffocating. If literary theory presses its own implications too far, then it has argued itself out of existence.

This, I would suggest, is the best possible thing for it to do. The final logical move in a process which began by recognizing that literature is an illusion is to recognize that literary theory is an illusion too. It is not of course an illusion in the sense that I have invented the various people I have discussed in this book: Northrop Frye really does exist, and so did F. R. Leavis. It is an illusion first in the sense that literary theory, as I hope to have shown, is really no more than a branch of social ideologies, utterly without any unity or identity which would adequately distinguish it from philosophy, linguistics, psychology, cultural and sociological thought; and secondly in the sense that the one hope it has of distinguishing itself—clinging to an object named literature—is misplaced. We must conclude, then, that this book is less an introduction than an obituary, and that we have ended by burying the object we sought to unearth.

My intention, in other words, is not to counter the literary theories I have critically examined in this book with a literary theory of my own, which would claim to be more politically acceptable. Any reader who has been expectantly waiting for a Marxist theory has obviously not been reading this book with due attention. There are indeed Marxist and feminist theories of literature, which in my opinion are more valuable than any of the theories discussed here, and to which the reader may like to refer in the bibliography. But this is not exactly the point. The point is whether it is possible to speak of 'literary theory' without perpetuating the illusion that literature exists as a distinct, bounded object of knowledge, or whether it is not preferable to draw the practical consequences of the fact that literary theory can handle Bob Dylan just as well as John Milton. My own view is that it is most useful to see 'literature' as a name which people give from time to time for different reasons to certain kinds of writing within a whole field of what Michel Foucault has called 'discursive practices', and that if anything is to be an object of study it is this whole field of practices rather than just those sometimes rather obscurely labelled 'literature'. I am countering the theories set out in this book not with a *literary* theory, but with a different kind of discourse—whether one calls it of 'culture', 'signifying practices' or whatever is not of first importance—which would include the objects ('literature') with which these other theories deal, but which would transform them by setting them in a wider context.

But is this not to extend the boundaries of literary theory to a point where any kind of particularity is lost? Would not a 'theory of discourse' run into just the same problems of methodology and object of study which we have seen in the case of literary studies? After all, there are any number of discourses and any number of ways of studying them. What would be specific to the kind of study I have in mind, however, would be its concern for the kinds of *effects* which discourses produce, and how they produce them. Reading a zoology textbook to find out about giraffes is part of studying zoology, but reading it to see how its discourse is structured and organized, and examining what kind of effects these forms and devices produce in particular readers in actual situations, is a different kind of project. It is, in fact, probably the oldest form of 'literary criticism' in the world, known as rhetoric. Rhetoric, which was the received form of critical analysis all the way from ancient society to the eighteenth century, examined the way discourses are constructed in order to achieve certain effects. It was not worried about whether its objects of enquiry were speaking or writing, poetry or philosophy, fiction or historiography: its horizon was nothing less than the field of discursive practices in society as a whole, and its particular interest lay in grasping such practices as forms of power and performance. This is not to say that it ignored the truth-value of the discourses in question, since this could often be crucially relevant to the kinds of effect they produced in their readers and listeners. Rhetoric in its major phase was neither a 'humanism', concerned in some intuitive way with people's experience of language, nor a 'formalism', preoccupied simply with analyzing linguistic devices. It looked at such devices in terms of concrete performance—they were means of pleading, persuading, inciting and so on—and at people's responses to discourse in terms of linguistic structures and the material situations in which they functioned. It saw speaking and writing not merely as textual objects, to be aesthetically contemplated or endlessly deconstructed, but as forms of *activity* inseparable from the wider social relations between writers and readers, orators and audiences, and as largely unintelligible outside the social purposes and conditions in which they were embedded.

Like all the best radical positions, then, mine is a thoroughly traditionalist one. I wish to recall literary criticism from certain fashionable, new-fangled ways of thinking it has been seduced by—'literature' as a specially privileged object, the 'aesthetic' as separable from social determinants, and so on—and return it to the ancient paths which it has abandoned. Although my case is thus reactionary, I do not mean that we should revive the whole range of ancient rhetorical terms and substitute these for modern critical language. We do not need to do this, since there are enough concepts contained in the literary theories examined in this book to allow us at least to make a start. Rhetoric, or discourse theory, shares with Formalism, structuralism and semiotics an interest in the formal devices of language, but like reception theory is also concerned with how these devices are actually effective at the point of 'consumption'; its preoccupation with discourse as a form of power and desire can learn much from deconstruction and psycho-analytical theory, and its belief that discourse can be a humanly transformative affair shares a good deal with liberal humanism. The fact that 'literary theory' is an illusion does not mean that we cannot retrieve from it many valuable concepts for a different kind of discursive practice altogether.

There was, of course, a reason why rhetoric bothered to analyze discourses. It did not analyze them just because they were there, any more than most forms of literary criticism today examine literature just for the sake of it. Rhetoric wanted to find out the most effective ways of pleading, persuading and debating, and rhetoricians studied such devices in other people's language in order to use them more productively in their own. It was, as we would say today, a 'creative' as well as a 'critical' activity: the word 'rhetoric' covers both the practice of effective discourse and the science of it. Similarly, there must be a reason why we would consider it worthwhile to develop a form of study which would look at the various sign-systems and signifying practices in our own society, all the way from *Moby Dick* to the Muppet show, from Dryden and Jean-Luc Goddard to the portrayal of women in advertisements and the rhetorical techniques of Government reports. All theory and knowledge, as I have argued previously, is 'interested', in the sense that you can always ask why one should bother to develop it in the first place. One striking weakness of most formalist and structuralist criticism is that it is unable to answer this question. The structuralist really does examine sign-systems because they happen to be there, or if this seems indefensible is forced into some rationale—studying our modes of sense-making will deepen our critical self-awareness—which is not much different from the standard line of the liberal humanists. The strength of the liberal humanist case, by contrast, is that it is able to say why dealing with literature is worth while. Its answer, as we have seen, is roughly that it makes you a better person. This is also the weakness of the liberal humanist case.

The liberal humanist response, however, is not weak because it believes that literature can be transformative. It is weak because it usually grossly overestimates this transformative power, considers it in isolation from any determining social context, and can formulate what it means by a 'better person' only in the most narrow and abstract of terms. They are terms which generally ignore the fact that to be a person in the Western society of the 1980s is to be bound up with, and in some sense responsible for, the kinds of political conditions which I began this Conclusion by outlining. Liberal humanism is a suburban moral ideology, limited in practice to largely interpersonal matters. It is stronger on adultery than on armaments, and its valuable concern with freedom, democracy and individual rights are simply not concrete enough. Its view of democracy, for example, is the abstract one of the ballot box, rather than a specific, living and practical democracy which might also somehow concern the operations of the Foreign Office and Standard Oil. Its view of individual freedom is similarly abstract: the freedom of any particular individual is crippled and parasitic as long as it depends on the futile labour and active oppression of others. Literature may protest against such conditions or it may not, but it is only possible in the first place because of them. As the German critic Walter Benjamin put it: 'There is no cultural document that is not at the same time a record of barbarism.' Socialists are those who wish to draw the full, concrete, practical applications of the abstract notions of freedom and democracy to which liberal humanism subscribes, taking them at their word when they draw attention to the 'vividly particular'. It is for this reason that many Western socialists are restless with the liberal humanist opinion of the tyrannies in Eastern Europe, feeling that these opinions simply do not go far enough: what would be necessary to bring down such tyrannies would not be just more free speech, but a workers' revolution against the state.

What it means to be a 'better person', then, must be concrete and practical—that is to say, concerned with people's political situations as a whole—rather than narrowly abstract, concerned only with the immediate interpersonal relations which can be abstracted from this concrete whole. It must be a question of political and not only of 'moral' argument: that is to say, it must be *genuine* moral argument, which sees the relations between individual qualities and values and our whole material conditions of existence. Political argument is not an alternative to moral preoccupations: it is those preoccupations taken seriously in their full implications. But the liberal humanists are right to see that there is a *point* in studying literature, and that this point is not itself, in the end, a literary one. What they are arguing, although this way of putting it would grate harshly on their ears, is that literature has a *use*. Few words are more offensive to literary ears than 'use', evoking as it does paperclips and hair-dryers. The Romantic opposition to the utilitarian ideology of capitalism has made 'use' an unusable word: for the aesthetes, the glory of art is its utter uselessness. Yet few of us nowadays would be prepared to subscribe to *that*: every reading of a work is surely in some sense a use of it. We may not use *Moby Dick* to learn how to hunt whales, but we 'get something out of it' even so. Every literary theory presupposes a certain use of literature, even if what you get out of it is its utter uselessness. Liberal humanist criticism is not wrong to use literature, but wrong to deceive itself that it does not. It uses it to further certain moral values, which as I hope to have shown are in fact indissociable from certain ideological ones, and in the end imply a particular form of politics. It is not that it reads the texts 'disinterestedly' and then places what it has read in the service of its values: the values govern the actual reading process itself, inform what sense criticism makes of the works it studies. I am not going to argue, then, for a 'political criticism' which would read literary texts in the light of certain values which are related to political beliefs and actions; all criticism does this. The idea that there are 'non-political' forms of criticism is simply a myth which furthers certain political uses of literature all the more effectively. The difference between a 'political' and 'non-political' criticism is just the difference between the prime minister and the monarch: the latter furthers certain political ends by pretending not to, while the former makes no bones about it. It is always better to be honest in these matters. The difference between a conventional critic who speaks of the 'chaos of experience' in Conrad or Woolf, and the feminist who examines those writers' images of gender, is not a distinction between non-political and political criticism. It is a distinction between different forms of politics—between those who subscribe to the doctrine that history, society and human reality as a whole are fragmentary, arbitrary and directionless, and those who have other interests which imply alternative views about the way the world is. There is no way of settling the question of which politics is preferable in literary critical terms. You simply have to argue about politics. It is not a question of debating whether 'literature' should be related to 'history' or not: it is a question of different readings of history itself.

The feminist critic is not studying representations of gender simply because she believes that this will further her political ends. She also believes that gender and sexuality are central themes in literature and other sorts of discourse, and that any critical account which suppresses them is seriously defective. Similarly, the socialist critic does not see literature in terms of ideology or class-struggle because these happen to be his or her political interests, arbitrarily projected on to literary works. He or she would hold that such matters are the very stuff of history, and that in so far as literature is an historical phenomenon, they are the very stuff of literature too. What would be strange would be if the feminist or socialist critic thought analyzing questions of gender or class was merely a matter of academic interest—merely a question of achieving a more satisfyingly complete account of literature. For why should it be worth doing this? Liberal humanist critics are not merely out for a more complete account of literature: they wish to discuss literature in ways which will deepen, enrich and extend our lives. Socialist and feminist critics are quite at one with them on this: it is just that they wish to point out that such deepening and enriching entails the transformation of a society divided by class and gender. They would like the liberal humanist to draw the full implications of his or her position. If the liberal humanist disagrees, then this is a political argument, not an argument about whether one is 'using' literature or not.

I argued earlier that any attempt to define the study of literature in terms of either its method or its object is bound to fail. But we have now begun to discuss another way of conceiving what distinguishes one kind of discourse from another, which is neither ontological or methodological but *strategic*. This means asking first not *what* the object is or *how* we should approach it, but *why* we should want to engage with it in the first place. The liberal humanist response to this question, I have suggested, is at once perfectly reasonable and, as it stands, entirely useless. Let us try to concretize it a little by asking how the reinvention of rhetoric that I have proposed (though it might equally as well be called 'discourse theory' or 'cultural studies' or whatever) might contribute to making us all better people. Discourses, sign-systems and signifying practices of all kinds, from film and television to fiction and the languages of natural science, produce effects, shape forms of consciousness and unconsciousness, which are closely related to the maintenance or transformation of our existing systems of power. They are thus closely related to what it means to be a person. Indeed 'ideology' can be taken to indicate no more than this connection—the link or nexus between discourses and power. Once we have seen this, then the questions of theory and method may be allowed to appear in a new light. It is not a matter of starting from certain theoretical or methodological problems: it is a matter of starting from what we want to *do*, and then seeing which methods and theories will best help us to achieve these ends. Deciding on your strategy will not predetermine which methods and objects of study are most valuable. As far as the object of study goes, what you decide to examine depends very much on the practical situation. It may seem best to look at Proust and *King Lear,* or at children's television programmes or popular romances or avant-garde films. A radical critic is quite liberal on these questions: he rejects the dogmatism which would insist that Proust is always more worthy of study than television advertisements. It all depends on what you are trying to do, in what situation. Radical critics are also open-minded about questions of theory and method: they tend to be pluralists in this respect. Any method or theory which will contribute to the strategic goal of human emancipation, the production of 'better people' through the socialist transformation of society, is acceptable. Structuralism, semiotics, psychoanalysis, deconstruction, reception theory and so on: all of these approaches, and others, have their valuable insights which may be put to use. Not all literary theories, however, are likely to prove amenable to the strategic goals in question: there are several examined in this book which seem to me highly unlikely to do so. What you choose and reject theoretically, then, depends upon what you are practically trying to do. This has always been the case with literary criticism: it is simply that it is often very reluctant to realize the fact. In any academic study we select the objects and methods of procedure which we believe the most important, and our assessment of their importance is governed by frames of interest deeply rooted in our practical forms of social life. Radical critics are no different in this respect: it is just that they have a set of social priorities with which most people at present tend to disagree. This is why they are commonly dismissed as 'ideological', because 'ideology' is always a way of describing other people's interests rather than one's own.

No theory or method, in any case, will have merely one strategic use. They can be mobilized in a variety of different strategies for a variety of ends. But not all methods will be equally amenable to particular ends. It is a matter of finding out, not of assuming from the start that a single method or theory will do. One reason why I have not ended this book with an account of socialist or feminist literary theory is that I believe such a move might encourage the reader to make what the philosophers call a 'category mistake'. It might mislead people into thinking that 'political criticism' was another sort of critical approach from those I have discussed, different in its assumptions but essentially the same kind of thing. Since I have made clear my view that all criticism is in some sense political, and since people tend to give the word 'political' to criticism whose politics disagrees with their own, this cannot be so. Socialist and feminist criticism are, of course, concerned with developing theories and methods appropriate to their aims: they consider questions of the relations between writing and sexuality, or of text and ideology, as other theories in general do not. They will also want to claim that these theories are more powerfully explanatory than others, for if they were not there would be no point in advancing them as theories. But it would be a mistake to see the particularity of such forms of criticism as consisting in the offering of alternative theories of methods. These forms of criticism differ from others because they define the object of analysis differently, have different values, beliefs and goals, and thus offer different kinds of strategy for the realizing of these goals.

I say 'goals', because it should not be thought that this form of criticism has only one. There are many goals to be achieved, and many ways of achieving them. In some situations the most productive procedure may be to explore how the signifying systems of a 'literary' text produce certain ideological effects; or it may be a matter of doing the same with a Hollywood film. Such projects may prove particularly important in teaching cultural studies to children; but it may also be valuable to use literature to foster in them a sense of linguistic potential denied to them by their social conditions. There are 'utopian' uses of literature of this kind, and a rich tradition of such utopian thought which should not be airily dismissed as 'idealist'. The active enjoyment of cultural artefacts should not, however, be relegated to the primary school, leaving older students with the grimmer business of analysis. Pleasure, enjoyment, the potentially transformative effects of discourse is quite as 'proper' a topic for 'higher' study as is the setting of puritan tracts in the discursive formations of the seventeenth century. On other occasions what might prove more useful will not be the criticism or enjoyment of other people's discourse but the production of one's own. Here, as with the rhetorical tradition, studying what other people have done may help. You may want to stage your own signifying practices to enrich, combat, modify or transform the effects which others' practices produce.

Within all of this varied activity, the study of what is currently termed 'literature' will have its place. But it should not be taken as an *a priori* assumption that what is currently termed 'literature' will always and everywhere be the most important focus of attention. Such dogmatism has no place in the field of cultural study. Nor are the texts now dubbed 'literature' likely to be perceived and defined as they are now, once they are returned to the broader and deeper discursive formations of which they are part. They will be inevitably 'rewritten', recycled, put to different uses, inserted into different relations and practices. They always have been, of course; but one effect of the word 'literature' is to prevent us from recognizing this fact.

Such a strategy obviously has far-reaching institutional implications. It would mean, for example, that departments of literature as we presently know them in higher education would cease to exist. Since the government, as I write, seems on the point of achieving this end more quickly and effectively than I could myself, it is necessary to add that the first political priority for those who have doubts about the ideological implications of such departmental organizations is to defend them unconditionally against government assaults. But this priority cannot mean refusing to contemplate how we might better organize literary studies in the longer term. The ideological effects of such departments lie not only in the particular values they disseminate, but in their implicit and actual dislocation of 'literature' from other cultural and social practices. The churlish admission of such practices as literary 'background' need not detain us: 'background', with its static, distancing connotations, tells its own story. Whatever would in the long term replace such departments—and the proposal is a modest one, for such experiments are already under way in certain areas of higher education—would centrally involve education in the various theories and methods of cultural analysis. The fact that such education is not routinely provided by many existing departments of literature, or is provided 'optionally' or marginally, is one of their most scandalous and farcical features. (Perhaps their other most scandalous and farcical feature is the largely wasted energy which postgraduate students are required to pour into obscure, often spurious research topics in order to produce dissertations which are frequently no more than sterile academic exercises, and which few others will ever read.) The genteel amateurism which regards criticism as some spontaneous sixth sense has not only thrown many students of literature into understandable confusion for many decades, but serves to consolidate the authority of those in power. If criticism is no more than a knack, like being able to whistle and hum different tunes simultaneously, then it is at once rare enough to be preserved in the hands of an elite, while 'ordinary' enough to require no stringent theoretical justification. Exactly the same pincer movement is at work in English 'ordinary language' philosophy. But the answer is not to replace such dishevelled amateurism with a well-groomed professionalism intent on justifying itself to the disgusted taxpayer. Such professionalism, as we have seen, is equally bereft of any social validation of its activities, since it cannot say why it should bother with literature at all other than to tidy it up, drop texts into their appropriate categories and then move over into marine biology. If the point of criticism is not to interpret literary works but to master in some disinterested spirit the underlying sign-systems which generate them, what is criticism to do once it has achieved this mastery, which will hardly take a lifetime and probably not much more than a few years?

The present crisis in the field of literary studies is at root a crisis in the definition of the subject itself. That it should prove difficult to provide such a definition is, as I hope to have shown in this book, hardly surprising. Nobody is likely to be dismissed from an academic job for trying on a little semiotic analysis of Edmund Spenser; they are likely to be shown the door, or refused entry through it in the first place, if they question whether the 'tradition' from Spenser to

Shakespeare and Milton is the best or only way of carving up discourse into a syllabus. It is at this point that the canon is trundled out to blast offenders out of the literary arena.

Those who work in the field of cultural practices are unlikely to mistake their activity, as utterly central. Men and women do not live by culture alone; the vast majority of them throughout history have been deprived of the chance of living by it at all, and those few who are fortunate enough to live by it now are able to do so because of the labour of those who do not. Any cultural or critical theory which does not begin from this single most important fact, and hold it steadily in mind in its activities, is in my view unlikely to be worth very much. There is no document of culture which is not also a record of barbarism. But even in societies which, like our own as Marx reminded us, have no time for culture, there are times and places when it suddenly becomes newly relevant, charged with a significance beyond itself. Four such major moments are evident in our own world. Culture, in the lives of nations struggling for their independence from imperialism, has a meaning quite remote from the review pages of the Sunday newspapers. Imperialism is not only the exploitation of cheap labour-power, raw materials and easy markets but the uprooting of languages and customs—not just the imposition of foreign armies, but of alien ways of experiencing. It manifests itself not only in company balance-sheets and in airbases, but can be tracked to the most intimate roots of speech and signification. In such situations, which are not all a thousand miles from our own doorstep, culture is so vitally bound up with one's common identity that there is no need to argue for its relation to political struggle. It is arguing against it which would seem incomprehensible.

The second area where cultural and political action have become closely united is in the women's movement. It is in the nature of feminist politics that signs and images, written and dramatized experience, should be of especial significance. Discourse in all its forms is an obvious concern for feminists, either as places where women's oppression can be deciphered, or as places where it can be challenged. In any politics which puts identity and relationship centrally at stake, renewing attention to lived experience and the discourse of the body, culture does not need to argue its way to political relevance. Indeed one of the achievements of the women's movement has been to redeem such phrases as 'lived experience' and 'the discourse of the body' from the empiricist connotations with which much literary theory has invested them. 'Experience' need now no longer signify an appeal away from power-systems and social relations to the privileged certainties of the private, for feminism recognizes no such distinction between questions of the human subject and questions of political struggle. The discourse of the body is not a matter of Lawrentian ganglions and suave loins of darkness, but a *politics* of the body, a rediscovery of its sociality through an awareness of the forces which control and subordinate it.

The third area in question is the 'culture industry'. While literary critics have been cultivating sensibility in a minority, large segments of the media have been busy trying to devastate it in the majority; yet it is still presumed that studying, say, Gray and Collins is inherently more important than examining television or the popular press. Such a project differs from the two I have outlined already in its essentially defensive character: it represents a critical reaction to someone else's cultural ideology rather than an appropriation of culture for one's own ends. Yet it is a vital project nevertheless, which must not be surrendered to a melancholic Left or Right mythology of the media as impregnably monolithic. We know that people do not after all believe all that they see and read; but we also need to know much more than we do about the role such effects play in their general consciousness, even though such critical study should be seen, politically, as no more than a holding operation. The democratic control of these ideological apparatuses, along with popular alternatives to them, must be high on the agenda of any future socialist programme.

The fourth and final area is that of the strongly emergent movement of working-class writing. Silenced for generations, taught to regard literature as a coterie activity beyond their grasp, working people over the past decade in Britain have been actively organizing to find their own literary styles and voices. The worker writers' movement is almost unknown to academia, and has not been exactly encouraged by the cultural organs of the state; but it is one sign of a significant break from the dominant relations of literary production. Community and cooperative publishing enterprises are associated projects, concerned not simply with a literature wedded to alternative social values, but with one which challenges and changes the existing social relations between writers, publishers, readers and other literary workers. It is because such ventures interrogate the ruling *definitions* of literature that they cannot so easily be incorporated by a literary institution quite happy to welcome *Sons and Lovers*, and even, from time to time, Robert Tressell.

These areas are not alternatives to the study of Shakespeare and Proust. If the study of such writers could become as charged with energy, urgency and enthusiasm as the activities I have just reviewed, the literary institution ought to rejoice rather than complain. But it is doubtful that this will happen when such texts are hermetically sealed from history, subjected to a sterile critical formalism, piously swaddled with eternal verities and used to confirm prejudices which any moderately enlightened student can perceive to be objectionable. The liberation of Shakespeare and Proust from such controls may well entail the death of literature, but it may also be their redemption.

I shall end with an allegory. *We* know that the lion is stronger than the lion-tamer, and so does the lion-tamer. The problem is that the lion does not know it. It is not out of the question that the death of literature may help the lion to awaken.

Elizabeth A. Flynn

"Composing as a Woman"

It is not easy to think like a woman in a man's world, in the world of the professions; yet the capacity to do that is a strength which we can try to help our students develop. To think like a woman in a man's world means thinking critically, refusing to accept the givens, making connections between facts and ideas which men have left unconnected. It means remembering that every mind resides in a body; remaining accountable to the female bodies in which we live; constantly retesting given hypotheses against lived experience. It means a constant critique of language, for as Wittgenstein (no feminist) observed, "The limits of my language are the limits of my world." And it means that most difficult thing of all: listening and watching in art and literature, in the social sciences, in all the descriptions we are given of the world, for silences, the absences, the nameless, the unspoken, the encoded—for there we will find the true knowledge of women. And in breaking those silences, naming ourselves, uncovering the hidden, making ourselves present, we begin to define a reality which resonates to us, which affirms our being, which allows the woman teacher and the woman student alike to take ourselves, and each other, seriously: meaning, to begin taking charge of our lives.

—ADRIENNE RICH
"TAKING WOMEN STUDENTS
SERIOUSLY"

The emerging field of composition studies could be described as a feminization of our previous conceptions of how writers write and how writing should be taught.[1] In exploring the nature of the writing process, composition specialists expose the limitations of previous product-oriented approaches by demystifying the product and in so doing empowering developing writers and readers. Rather than enshrining the text in its final form, they demonstrate that the works produced by established authors are often the result of an extended, frequently enormously frustrating process and that creativity is an activity that results from experience and hard work rather than a mysterious gift reserved for a select few. In a sense, composition specialists replace the figure of the authoritative father with an image of a nurturing mother. Powerfully present in the work of composition researchers and theorists is the ideal of a committed teacher concerned about the growth and maturity of her students who provides feedback on ungraded drafts, reads journals, and attempts to tease out meaning from the seeming incoherence of student language. The field's foremothers come to mind—Janet Emig, Mina Shaughnessy, Ann Berthoff, Win Horner, Maxine Hairston, Shirley Heath, Nancy Martin, Linda Flower, Andrea Lunsford, Sondra Perl, Nancy Sommers, Marion Crowhurst, Lisa Ede. I'll admit the term foremother seems inappropriate as some of these women are still in their thirties and forties—we are speaking here of a very young field. Still, invoking their names suggests that we are also dealing with a field that, from the beginning, has welcomed contributions from women—indeed, has been shaped by women.

The work of male composition researchers and theorists has also contributed significantly to the process of feminization described above. James Britton, for instance, reverses traditional hierarchies by privileging private expression over public transaction, process over product. In arguing that writing for the self is the matrix out of which all forms of writing develop, he valorizes an activity and a mode of expression that have previously been undervalued or invisible, much as feminist literary critics have argued that women's letters and diaries are legitimate literary forms and should be studied and taught alongside more traditional genres. His work has had an enormous impact on the way writing is taught on the elementary and high school levels and in the university, not only in English courses but throughout the curriculum. Writing-Across-the-Curriculum Programs aim to transform pedagogical practices in all disciplines, even those where patriarchal attitudes toward authority are most deeply rooted.

FEMINIST STUDIES AND COMPOSITION STUDIES

Feminist inquiry and composition studies have much in common. After all, feminist researchers and scholars and composition specialists are usually in the same department and sometimes teach the same courses. Not surprisingly, there have been wonderful moments when feminists have expressed their commitment to the teaching of writing. Florence Howe's essay, "Identity and Expression: A Writing Course for Women," for example, published in *College English* in 1971, describes her use of journals in a writing course designed to empower women. Adrienne Rich's essay, " 'When We Dead Awaken': Writing as Re-Vision," politicizes and expands our conception of revision, emphasizing that taking another look at the texts we have generated necessitates revising our cultural assumptions as well.

There have also been wonderful moments when composition specialists have recognized that the marginality of the field of composition studies is linked in important ways to the political marginality of its constituents, many of whom are women who teach part-time. Maxine Hairston, in "Breaking Our Bonds and Reaffirming Our Connections," a slightly revised version of her Chair's address at the 1985 convention of the Conference on College Composition and

Communication, draws an analogy between the plight of composition specialists and the plight of many women. For both, their worst problems begin at home and hence are immediate and daily. Both, too, often have complex psychological bonds to the people who frequently are their adversaries (273).

For the most part, though, the fields of feminist studies and composition studies have not engaged each other in a serious or systematic way. The major journals in the field of composition studies do not often include articles addressing feminist issues, and panels on feminism are infrequent at the Conference on College Composition and Communication.[2] As a result, the parallels between feminist studies and composition studies have not been delineated, and the feminist critique that has enriched such diverse fields as linguistics, reading, literary criticism, psychology, sociology, anthropology, religion, and science has had little impact on our models of the composing process or on our understanding of how written language abilities are acquired. We have not examined our research methods or research samples to see if they are androcentric. Nor have we attempted to determine just what it means to compose as a woman.

Feminist research and theory emphasize that males and females differ in their developmental processes and in their interactions with others. They emphasize, as well, that these differences are a result of an imbalance in the social order, of the dominance of men over women. They argue that men have chronicled our historical narratives and defined our fields of inquiry. Women's perspectives have been suppressed, silenced, marginalized, written out of what counts as authoritative knowledge. Difference is erased in a desire to universalize. Men become the standard against which women are judged.

A feminist approach to composition studies would focus on questions of difference and dominance in written language. Do males and females compose differently? Do they acquire language in different ways? Do research methods and research samples in composition studies reflect a male bias? I do not intend to tackle all of these issues. My approach here is a relatively modest one. I will survey recent feminist research on gender differences in social and psychological development, and I will show how this research and theory may be used in examining student writing, thus suggesting directions that a feminist investigation of composition might take.

GENDER DIFFERENCES IN SOCIAL AND PSYCHOLOGICAL DEVELOPMENT

Especially relevant to a feminist consideration of student writing are Nancy Chodorow's *The Reproduction of Mothering,* Carol Gilligan's *In a Different Voice,* and Mary Belenky, Blythe Clinchy, Nancy Goldberger, and Jill Tarule's *Women's Ways of Knowing.* All three books suggest that women and men have different conceptions of self and different modes of interaction with others as a result of their different experiences, especially their early relationship with their primary parent, their mother.

Chodorow's book, published in 1978, is an important examination of what she calls the "psychoanalysis and the sociology of gender," which in turn influenced Gilligan's *In a Different Voice* and Belenky et al.'s *Women's Ways of Knowing*. Chodorow tells us in her preface that her book originated when a feminist group she was affiliated with "wondered what it meant that women parented women." She argues that girls and boys develop different relational capacities and senses of self as a result of growing up in a family in which women mother. Because all children identify first with their mother, a girl's gender and gender role identification processes are continuous with her earliest identifications whereas a boy's are not. The boy gives up, in addition to his oedipal and preoedipal attachment to his mother, his primary identification with her. The more general identification processes for both males and females also follow this pattern. Chodorow says,

> Girls' identification processes, then, are more continuously embedded in and mediated by their ongoing relationship with their mother. They develop through and stress particularistic and affective relationships to others. A boy's identification processes are not likely to be so embedded in or mediated by a real affective relation to his father. At the same time, he tends to deny identification with and relationship to his mother and reject what he takes to be the feminine world; masculinity is defined as much negatively as positively. Masculine identification processes stress differentiation from others, the denial of affective relation, and categorical universalistic components of the masculine role. Feminine identification processes are relational, whereas masculine identification processes tend to deny relationship. (176)

Carol Gilligan's *In a Different Voice*, published in 1982, builds on Chodorow's findings, focusing especially, though, on differences in the ways in which males and females speak about moral problems. According to Gilligan, women tend to define morality in terms of conflicting responsibilities rather than competing rights, requiring for their resolution a mode of thinking that is contextual and narrative rather than formal and abstract (19). Men, in contrast, equate morality and fairness and tie moral development to the understanding of rights and rules (19). Gilligan uses the metaphors of the web and the ladder to illustrate these distinctions. The web suggests interconnectedness as well as entrapment; the ladder suggests an achievement-orientation as well as individualistic and hierarchical thinking. Gilligan's study aims to correct the inadequacies of Lawrence Kohlberg's delineation of the stages of moral development. Kohlberg's study included only male subjects, and his categories reflect his decidedly male orientation. For him, the highest stages of moral development derive from a reflective understanding of human rights (19).

Belenky, Clinchy, Goldberger, and Tarule, in *Women's Ways of Knowing*, acknowledge their debt to Gilligan, though their main concern is intellectual rather than moral development. Like Gilligan, they recognize that male experience has served as the model in defining processes of intellectual maturation. The mental processes that are involved in considering the abstract and the impersonal have been labeled "thinking" and are attributed primarily to men, while those that deal with the personal and interpersonal fall under the rubric of "emotions" and are largely relegated to women. The particular study they chose to examine and revise is William Perry's *Forms of Intellectual and Ethical Development in the College Years* (1970). While Perry did include some women subjects in his study, only the interviews with men were used in illustrating and validating his scheme of intellectual and ethical development. When Perry assessed women's development on the basis of the categories he developed, the women were found to conform to the patterns he had observed in the male data. Thus, his work reveals what women have in common with men but was poorly designed to uncover those themes that might be more prominent among women. *Women's Ways of Knowing* focuses on "what else women might have to say about the development of their minds and on alternative routes that are sketchy or missing in Perry's version" (9).

Belenky et al. examined the transcripts of interviews with 135 women from a variety of backgrounds and of different ages and generated categories that are suited for describing the stages of women's intellectual development. They found that the quest for self and voice plays a central role in transformations of women's ways of knowing. Silent women have little awareness of their intellectual capacities. They live—selfless and voiceless—at the behest of those around them. External authorities know the truth and are all-powerful. At the positions of received knowledge and procedural knowledge, other voices and external truths prevail. Sense of self is embedded either in external definitions and roles or in identifications with institutions, disciplines, and methods. A sense of authority arises primarily through identification with the power of a group and its agreed-upon ways for knowing. Women at this stage of development have no sense of an authentic or unique voice, little awareness of a centered self. At the position of subjective knowledge, women turn away from others and any external authority. They have not yet acquired a public voice or public authority, though. Finally, women at the phase of constructed knowledge begin an effort to reclaim the self by attempting to integrate knowledge they feel intuitively with knowledge they have learned from others.

STUDENT WRITING

If women and men differ in their relational capacities and in their moral and intellectual development, we would expect to find manifestations of these differences in the student papers we encounter in our first-year composition courses. The student essays I will describe here are narrative descriptions of learning experiences produced in the first of a two-course sequence required of first-year students at Michigan Tech. I've selected the four because they invite commentary from the perspective of the material discussed above. The narratives of the female students are stories of interaction, of connection, or of frustrated connection. The narratives of the male students are stories of achievement, of separation, or of frustrated achievement.

Kim's essay describes a dreamlike experience in which she and her high school girlfriends connected with each other and with nature as a result of a balloon ride they decided to take one summer Sunday afternoon as a way of relieving boredom. From the start, Kim emphasizes communion and tranquility: "It was one of those Sunday afternoons when the sun shines brightly and a soft warm breeze blows gently. A perfect day for a long drive on a country road with my favorite friends." This mood is intensified as they ascend in the balloon: "Higher and higher we went, until the view was overpowering. What once was a warm breeze turned quickly into a cool crisp wind. A feeling of freedom and serenity overtook us as we drifted along slowly." The group felt as if they were "just suspended there on a string, with time non-existent." The experience made them contemplative, and as they drove quietly home, "each one of us collected our thoughts, and to this day we still reminisce about that Sunday afternoon." The experience solidified relationships and led to the formation of a close bond that was renewed every time the day was recollected.

The essay suggests what Chodorow calls relational identification processes. The members of the group are described as being in harmony with themselves and with the environment. There is no reference to competition or discord. The narrative also suggests a variation on what Belenky et al. call "connected knowing," a form of procedural knowledge that makes possible the most desirable form of knowing, constructed knowledge. Connected knowing is rooted in empathy for others and is intensely personal. Women who are connected knowers are able to detach themselves from the relationships and institutions to which they have been subordinated and begin to trust their own intuitions. The women in the narrative were connected doers rather than connected knowers. They went off on their own, left their families and teachers behind (it was summer vacation, after all), and gave themselves over to a powerful shared experience. The adventure was, for the most part, a silent one but did lead to satisfying talk.

Kathy also describes an adventure away from home, but hers was far less satisfying, no doubt because it involved considerably more risk. In her narrative she makes the point that "foreign countries can be frightening" by focusing on a situation in which she and three classmates, two females and a male, found themselves at a train station in Germany separated from the others because they had gotten off to get some refreshments and the train had left without them. She says,

> This left the four of us stranded in an unfamiliar station. Ed was the only person in our group that could speak German fluently, but he still didn't know what to do. Sue got hysterical and Laura tried to calm her down. I stood there stunned. We didn't know what to do.

What they did was turn to Ed, whom Kathy describes as "the smartest one in our group." He told them to get on a train that was on the same track as the original. Kathy realized, though, after talking to some passengers, that they were on the wrong train and urged her classmates to get off. She says,

I almost panicked. When I convinced the other three we were on the wrong train we opened the doors. As we were getting off, one of the conductors started yelling at us in German. It didn't bother me too much because I couldn't understand what he was saying. One thing about trains in Europe is that they are always on schedule. I think we delayed that train about a minute or two.

In deciding which train to board after getting off the wrong one, they deferred to Ed's judgment once again, but this time they got on the right train. Kathy concludes, "When we got off the train everyone was waiting. It turned out we arrived thirty minutes later than our original train. I was very relieved to see everyone. It was a very frightening experience and I will never forget it."

In focusing on her fears of separation, Kathy reveals her strong need for connection, for affiliation. Her story, like Kim's, emphasizes the importance of relationships, though in a different way. She reveals that she had a strong need to feel part of a group and no desire to rebel, to prove her independence, to differentiate herself from others. This conception of self was a liability as well as a strength in the sense that she became overly dependent on the male authority figure in the group, whom she saw as smarter and more competent than herself. In Belenky et al.'s terms, Kathy acted as if other voices and external truths were more powerful than her own. She did finally speak and act, though, taking it on herself to find out if they were on the right train and ushering the others off when she discovered they were not. She was clearly moving toward the development of an authentic voice and a way of knowing that integrates intuition with authoritative knowledge. After all, she was the real hero of the incident.

The men's narratives stress individuation rather than connection. They are stories of individual achievement or frustrated achievement and conclude by emphasizing separation rather than integration or reintegration into a community. Jim wrote about his "Final Flight," the last cross-country flight required for his pilot's license. That day, everything seemed to go wrong. First, his flight plan had a mistake in it that took 1 1/2 hours to correct. As a result, he left his hometown 2 hours behind schedule. Then the weather deteriorated, forcing him to fly as low as a person can safely fly, with the result that visibility was very poor. He landed safely at his first destination but flew past the second because he was enjoying the view too much. He says,

> Then I was off again south bound for Benton Harbor. On the way south along the coast of Lake Michigan the scenery was a beautiful sight. This relieved some of the pressures and made me look forward to the rest of the flight. It was really nice to see the ice flows break away from the shore. While enjoying the view of a power plant on the shore of Lake Michigan I discovered I had flown past the airport.

He finally landed and took off again, but shortly thereafter had to confront darkness, a result of his being behind schedule. He says,

> The sky turned totally black by the time I was half-way home. This meant fly-

ing in the dark which I had only done once before. Flying in the dark was also illegal for me to do at this time. One thing that made flying at night nice was that you could see lights that were over ninety miles away.

Jim does not emphasize his fear, despite the fact that his situation was more threatening than the one Kathy described, and his reference to his enjoyment of the scenery suggests that his anxiety was not paralyzing or debilitating. At times, his solitary flight was clearly as satisfying as Kim's communal one. When he focuses on the difficulties he encountered, he speaks only of his "problems" and "worries" and concludes that the day turned out to be "long and trying." He sums up his experience as follows: "That day I will long remember for both its significance in my goal in getting my pilot's license and all the problems or worries that it caused me during the long and problem-ridden flight." He emerges the somewhat shaken hero of his adventure; he has achieved his goal in the face of adversity. Significantly, he celebrates his return home by having a bite to eat at McDonald's by himself. His adventure does not end with a union or reunion with others.

Jim's story invites interpretation in the context of Chodorow's claims about male interactional patterns. Chodorow says that the male, in order to feel himself adequately masculine, must distinguish and differentiate himself from others. Jim's adventure was an entirely solitary one. It was also goal-directed—he wanted to obtain his pilot's license and, presumably, prove his competence to himself and others. His narrative calls into question, though, easy equations of abstract reasoning and impersonality with male modes of learning since Jim was clearly as capable as Kim of experiencing moments of exultation, of communion with nature.

Joe's narrative of achievement is actually a story of frustrated achievement, of conflicting attitudes toward an ethic of hard work and sacrifice to achieve a goal. When he was in high school, his father drove him twenty miles to swim practice and twenty miles home every Tuesday through Friday night between October and March so he could practice for the swim team. He hated this routine and hated the Saturday morning swim meets even more but continued because he thought his parents, especially his father, wanted him to. He says, "I guess it was all for them, the cold workouts, the evening practices, the weekend meets. I had to keep going for them even though I hated it." Once he realized he was going through his agony for his parents rather than for himself, though, he decided to quit and was surprised to find that his parents supported him. Ultimately, though, he regretted his decision. He says,

As it turns out now, I wish I had stuck with it. I really had a chance to go somewhere with my talent. I see kids my age who stuck with something for a long time and I envy them for their determination. I wish I had met up to the challenge of sticking with my swimming, because I could have been very good if I would have had their determination.

Joe is motivated to pursue swimming because he thinks his father will be disappointed if he gives it up. His father's presumed hold on him is clearly tenuous, however, because once Joe realizes that he is doing it for him rather than for himself, he quits. Finally, though, it is his gender role identification, his socialization into a male role and a male value system, that allows him to look back on his decision with regret. In college, he has become a competitor, an achiever. He now sees value in the long and painful practices, in a single-minded determination to succeed. The narrative reminds us of Chodorow's point that masculine identification is predominantly a gender role identification rather than identification with a particular parent.

I am hardly claiming that the four narratives are neat illustrations of the feminist positions discussed above. For one thing, those positions are rich in contradiction and complexity and defy easy illustration. For another, the narratives themselves are as often characterized by inconsistency and contradiction as by a univocality of theme and tone. Kathy is at once dependent and assertive; Joe can't quite decide if he should have been rebellious or disciplined. Nor am I claiming that what I have found here are characteristic patterns of male and female student writing. I would need a considerably larger and more representative sample to make such a claim hold. I might note, though, that I had little difficulty identifying essays that revealed patterns of difference among the twenty-four papers I had to choose from, and I could easily have selected others. Sharon, for instance, described her class trip to Chicago, focusing especially on the relationship she and her classmates were able to establish with her advisor. Diane described "An Unwanted Job" that she seemed unable to quit despite unpleasant working conditions. Mike, like Diane, was dissatisfied with his job, but he expressed his dissatisfaction and was fired. The frightening experience Russ described resulted from his failed attempt to give his car a tune-up; the radiator hose burst, and he found himself in the hospital recovering from third-degree burns. These are stories of relatedness or entanglement; of separation or frustrated achievement.

The description of the student essays is not meant to demonstrate the validity of feminist scholarship but to suggest, instead, that questions raised by feminist researchers and theorists do have a bearing on composition studies and should be pursued. We ought not assume that males and females use language in identical ways or represent the world in a similar fashion. And if their writing strategies and patterns of representation do differ, then ignoring those differences almost certainly means a suppression of women's separate ways of thinking and writing. Our models of the composing process are quite possibly better suited to describing men's ways of composing than to describing women's.[3]

PEDAGOGICAL STRATEGIES

The classroom provides an opportunity for exploring questions about gender differences in language use. Students, I have found, are avid inquirers into their own language processes. An approach I have had success with is to make the question of gender difference in behavior and language use the subject to be investigated in class. In one honors section of first-year English, for instance, course reading included selections from Mary Anne Ferguson's *Images of Women in Literature,* Gilligan's *In a Different Voice,* Alice Walker's *Meridian,* and James Joyce's *A Portrait of the Artist as a Young Man.* Students were also required to keep a reading journal and to submit two formal papers. The first was a description of people they know in order to arrive at generalizations about gender differences in behavior, the second a comparison of some aspect of the Walker and Joyce novels in the light of our class discussions.

During class meetings we shared journal entries, discussed the assigned literature, and self-consciously explored our own reading, writing, and speaking behaviors. In one session, for instance, we shared retellings of Irwin Shaw's "The Girls in Their Summer Dresses," an especially appropriate story since it describes the interaction of a husband and wife as they attempt to deal with the husband's apparently chronic habit of girl-watching. Most of the women were sympathetic to the female protagonist, and several males clearly identified strongly with the male protagonist.

The students reacted favorably to the course. They found Gilligan's book to be challenging, and they enjoyed the heated class discussions. The final journal entry of one of the strongest students in the class, Dorothy, suggests the nature of her development over the ten-week period:

> As this is sort of the wrap-up of what I've learned or how I feel about the class, I'll try to relate this entry to my first one on gender differences.
>
> I'm not so sure that men and women are so similar anymore, as I said in the first entry. The reactions in class especially make me think this. The men were so hostile toward Gilligan's book! I took no offense at it, but then again I'm not a man. I must've even overlooked the parts where she offended the men!
>
> Another thing really bothered me. One day after class, I heard two of the men talking in the hall about how you just have to be really careful about what you say in HU 101H about women, etc. *Why* do they have to be careful?! What did these two *really* want to say? That was pretty disturbing.
>
> However, I do still believe that MTU (or most any college actually) does bring out more similarities than differences. But the differences are still there— I know that.

Dorothy has begun to suspect that males and females read differently, and she has begun to suspect that they talk among themselves differently than they do in mixed company. The reading, writing, and discussing in the course have clearly alerted her to the possibility that gender affects the way in which readers, writers, and speakers use language.

This approach works especially well with honors students. I use somewhat different reading and writing assignments with non-honors students. In one class, for instance, I replaced the Gilligan book with an essay by Dale Spender on conversational patterns in high school classrooms. Students wrote a paper defending or refuting the Spender piece on the basis of their experiences in their own high schools. I have also devised ways of addressing feminist issues in composition courses in which the focus is not explicitly on gender differences. In a course designed to introduce students to fundamentals of research, for instance, students read Marge Piercy's *Woman on the Edge of Time* and did research on questions stimulated by it. They then shared their findings with the entire class in oral presentations. The approach led to wonderful papers on and discussions of the treatment of women in mental institutions, discrimination against minority women, and the ways in which technology can liberate women from oppressive roles.

I return now to my title and to the epigraph that introduces my essay. First, what does it mean to "compose as a woman"? Although the title invokes Jonathan Culler's "Reading as a Woman," a chapter in *On Deconstruction,* I do not mean to suggest by it that I am committed fully to Culler's deconstructive position. Culler maintains that "to read as a woman is to avoid reading as a man, to identify the specific defenses and distortions of male readings and provide correctives" (54). He concludes,

> For a woman to read as a woman is not to repeat an identity or an experience that is given but to play a role she constructs with reference to her identity as a woman, which is also a construct, so that the series can continue: a woman reading as a woman reading as a woman. The noncoincidence reveals an interval, a division within woman or within any reading subject and the "experience" of that subject. (64)

Culler is certainly correct that women often read as men and that they have to be encouraged to defend against this form of alienation. The strategy he suggests is almost entirely reactive, though. To read as a woman is to avoid reading as a man, to be alerted to the pitfalls of men's ways of reading.[4] Rich, too, warns of the dangers of immasculation, of identifying against oneself and learning to think like a man, and she, too, emphasizes the importance of critical activity on the part of the woman student—refusing to accept the givens of our culture, making connections between facts and ideas which men have left unconnected. She is well aware that thinking as a woman involves active construction, the recreation of one's identity. But she also sees value in recovering women's lived experience. In fact, she suggests that women maintain a critical posture in order to get in touch with that experience—to name it, to uncover that which is hidden, to make present that which has been absent. Her approach is active rather than reactive. Women's experience is not entirely a distorted version of male reality, it is not entirely elusive, and it is worthy of recuperation. We must alert our women students to the dangers of immasculation and provide them with a critical perspective. But we must also encourage them to become self-consciously aware of what their experience in the world has been and how this experience is related to the politics of gender. Then we must encourage our women students to write from the power of that experience.

NOTES

1. I received invaluable feedback on drafts of this essay from Carol Berkenkotter, Art Young, Marilyn Cooper, John Willinsky, Diane Shoos, John Flynn, Richard Gebhardt, and three anonymous *CCC* reviewers.

2. The 1988 Conference on College Composition and Communication was a notable exception. It had a record number of panels on feminist or gender-related issues and a number of sessions devoted to political concerns. I should add, too, that an exception to the generalization that feminist studies and composition studies have not confronted each other is Cynthia Caywood and Gillian Overing's very useful anthology, *Teaching Writing: Pedagogy, Gender, and Equity*. In their introduction to the book, Caywood and Overing note the striking parallels between writing theory and feminist theory. They conclude, "[T]he process model, insofar as it facilitates and legitimizes the fullest expression of the individual voice, is compatible with the feminist re-visioning of hierarchy, if not essential to it" (xiv). Pamela Annas, in her essay, "Silences: Feminist Language Research and the Teaching of Writing," describes a course she teaches at the University of Massachusetts at Boston, entitled "Writing as Women." In the course, she focuses on the question of silence—"what kinds of silence there are; the voices inside you that tell you to be quiet, the voices outside you that drown you out or politely dismiss what you say or do not understand you, the silence inside you that avoids saying anything important even to yourself, internal and external forms of censorship, and the stress that it produces" (3–4). Carol A. Stanger in "The Sexual Politics of the One-to-One Tutorial Approach and Collaborative Learning" argues that the one-to-one tutorial is essentially hierarchical and hence a male mode of teaching whereas collaborative learning is female and relational rather than hierarchical. She uses Gilligan's images of the ladder and the web to illustrate her point. Elisabeth Daeumer and Sandra Runzo suggest that the teaching of writing is comparable to the activity of mothering in that it is a form of "women's work." Mothers socialize young children to insure that they become acceptable citizens, and teachers' work, like the work of mothers, is usually devalued (45–46).

3. It should be clear by now that my optimistic claim at the outset of the essay that the field of composition studies has feminized our conception of written communication needs qualification. I have already mentioned that the field has developed, for the most part, independent of feminist studies and as a result has not explored written communication in the context of women's special needs and problems. Also, feminist inquiry is beginning to reveal that work in cognate fields that have influenced the development of composition studies is androcentric. For an exploration of the androcentrism of theories of the reading process see Patrocinio P. Schweickart, "Reading Ourselves: Toward a Feminist Theory of Reading."

4. Elaine Showalter, in "Reading as a Woman: Jonathan Culler and the Deconstruction of Feminist Criticism," argues that "Culler's deconstructionist priorities lead him to overstate the essentialist dilemma of defining the *woman* reader, when in most cases what is intended and implied is a *feminist* reader" (126).

WORKS CITED

Annas, Pamela J. "Silences: Feminist Language Research and the Teaching of Writing."

Teaching Writing: Pedagogy, Gender, and Equity. Eds. Cynthia L. Caywood and Gillian R. Overing. Albany: State U of New York P, 1987. 3–17.

Belenky, Mary Field, et al. *Women's Ways of Knowing: The Development of Self, Voice, and Mind.* New York: Basic Books, 1986.

Britton, James, et al. *The Development of Writing Abilities (11–18).* London: Macmillan Education, 1975.

Caywood, Cynthia L., and Gillian R. Overing. Introduction. *Teaching Writing: Pedagogy, Gender, and Equity.* Eds. Cynthia L. Caywood and Gillian R. Overing. Albany: State U of New York P, 1987, xi–xvi.

Chodorow, Nancy. *The Reproduction of Mothering: Psychoanalysis and the Sociology of Gender.* Berkeley: U of California P, 1978.

Culler, Jonathan. *On Deconstruction: Theory and Criticism after Structuralism.* Ithaca: Cornell UP, 1982.

Daeumer, Elisabeth, and Sandra Runzo. "Transforming the Composition Classroom." *Teaching Writing: Pedagogy, Gender, and Equity.* Eds. Cynthia L. Caywood and Gillian R. Overing. Albany: State U of New York P, 1987. 45–62.

Gilligan, Carol. *In a Different Voice: Psychological Theory and Women's Development.* Cambridge: Harvard UP, 1982.

Hairston, Maxine. "Breaking Our Bonds and Reaffirming Our Connections." *College Composition and Communication* 36 (October 1985): 272–82.

Howe, Florence. "Identity and Expression: A Writing Course for Women. "*College English* 32 (May 1971): 863–71. Rpt. in Howe, *Myths of Coeducation: Selected Essays, 1964–1983.* Bloomington: Indiana UP, 1984. 28–37.

Kohlberg, Lawrence. "Moral Stages and Moralization: The Cognitive-Developmental Approach." *Moral Development and Behavior.* Ed. T. Lickona. New York: Holt, 1976. 31–53.

Perry, William G. *Forms of Intellectual and Ethical Development in the College Years.* New York: Holt, Rinehart & Winston, 1970.

Rich, Adrienne. "Taking Women Students Seriously." *On Lies, Secrets, and Silence: Selected Prose, 1966–1978.* New York: W.W. Norton, 1979. 237–45.

———. " 'When We Dead Awaken': Writing as Re-Vision." *On Lies, Secrets, and Silence: Selected Prose, 1966–1978.* New York: W.W. Norton, 1979. 33–49.

Schweickart, Patrocinio P. "Reading Ourselves: Toward a Feminist Theory of Reading." *Gender and Reading: Essays on Readers, Texts and Contexts.* Eds. Elizabeth A. Flynn and Patrocinio P. Schweickart. Baltimore: Johns Hopkins UP, 1986. 31–62.

Showalter, Elaine. "Reading as a Woman: Jonathan Culler and the Deconstruction of Feminist Criticism." *Men and Feminism.* Eds. Alice Jardine and Paul Smith. New York: Methuen, 1987. 123–27.

Stanger, Carol A. "The Sexual Politics of the One-to-One Tutorial Approach and Collaborative Learning." *Teaching Writing:Pedagogy, Gender, and Equity.* Eds. Cynthia L. Caywood and Gillian R. Overing. Albany: State U of New York P, 1987. 31–44.

Charles I. Schuster

"Mikhail Bakhtin as Rhetorical Theorist"

The confusion and obscurity surrounding Mikhail Bakhtin's life compounded by the complexity and semantic density of his books and articles has made this Russian theorist into a kind of Zorro figure, the Masked Marvel of theoretical criticism. Who is this exotic character born in Orel in 1895, exiled to Kazakhstan during the 30s, returning finally to the center of Russian academic life in the 1950s? How is one to talk about Bakhtin's major book on the 18th-century German novel when Bakhtin used the only existing copy as cigarette papers during World War II? How are we to value a man who so undervalues himself that he stores unpublished manuscripts in a rat-infested woodshed in Saransk? What can one say about a writer whose very authorship is in question—since two of his major works *(Freudianism* and *Marxism and the Philosophy of Language)* were published under the name of V. N. Voloshinov?[1] Add to this that Bakhtin is known as a literary theorist (and is thus remote indeed from composition and rhetoric), that he refuses to define his terms, and that his language resists interpretation and paraphrase and we have some idea of the formidable task ahead.

To ignore Bakhtin because of these difficulties, however, is to deny rhetoric an important influence. Although much of Bakhtin's work is considered literary criticism, his conceptions of discourse develop implications about language use in the widest possible terms. Bakhtin modifies the communications triangle by redefining one of the central terms and thus compelling us to reconceive our ideas about the interactive nature of speaking and writing. His theories enable us to formulate a more enlightened conception of style as a developmental process that occurs not only within an individual user of language but within language itself. By making us more sensitive to tone and the expressive implications created by all verbal phrasing, his works train us to become more sophisticated readers of prose, which in turn contributes directly to our strength as teachers of reading and writing. They offer a compelling argument for the return of aesthetics as a central concern in rhetoric and composition since language, in Bakhtin's terms, is always a potentially aesthetic medium. In sum, Bakhtin heightens our ability to experience verbal and written expression in a rich and complex way, thus serving as an antidote to a simplified, exclusive concern with purely formal aspects of writing instruction.

Perhaps the best way to begin discussing Bakhtin's importance is with the rhetorical triangle. In describing verbal and written communication as consisting of speaker-listener-subject (through language) Aristotle provided the world with an enduring paradigm. Bakhtin alters this paradigm slightly. He maintains the "speaker" and the "listener," but in place of the "subject" he puts a concept known (at least in translation) as the "hero." According to Bakhtin, a speaker does not communicate to a listener about a "subject"; instead, "speaker" and "listener" engage in an act of communication which includes the "hero" as a genuine rhetorical force. The difference here is significant. In our conventional analyses of discourse, we talk of the way writers "treat" subjects, the way they research, describe, develop, analyze, and attack them. Subjects are actually conceived as objects. They are passive, inert, powerless to shape the discourse. In Bakhtin's terms, the hero is as potent a determinant in the rhetorical paradigm as speaker or listener. The hero interacts with the speaker to shape the language and determine the form. At times, the hero becomes the dominant influence in verbal and written utterance.

Novelists and poets have known this for a long time. When William Thackeray was asked why his character Henry Esmond married his own mother, he replied that it was not he who had married them: "They married themselves." It is perhaps easy to see how a created character becomes a hero. But so do ideas, objects, locations. In Bakhtin's terms, the city of New York becomes the hero in Woody Allen's film, *Manhattan*; freedom becomes the hero in a speech by Martin Luther King, Jr. In *this* essay, Bakhtin's work dominated my thinking, forcing me into certain kinds of developmental structures and syntactic constructions, and affecting my diction and style. His ideological language has infiltrated my own so that not only do I appropriate terms such as "the word," "dialogical," and "heteroglossia," but find the overall style and treatment of this subject becoming bakhtinian. The hero often is a strong determiner within discourse. Speaker-hero-listener—the three elements introduce equivalent pressures on speaking and writing.

Bakhtin's paradigm, of course, is based on a dialogue between a speaker and a listener. This is important to remember because dialogue lies at the heart of Bakhtin's rhetoric. For Bakhtin, dialogue is no static model of speaker making utterance to listener concerning hero. The three elements of the dialogue speak, listen, and influence each other equivalently. It is easy enough to see that the speaker becomes the listener when the listener speaks, and that each influences the words, tones, attitudes, beliefs of the other. But the hero also "speaks"; it too contains its own accumulation of values and terms. It too carries with it a set of associations, an ideological and stylistic profile. In essence, it has as much an identity as the speaker and listener. Speaker and listener, in the act of engaging with the hero (which is, like them, both a speaker and listener), become charged by the hero's identity. They change as a result of the association, for they are just as affected by the hero as they are by their close association with each other. And so, too, is the hero. Like planets in a solar system, each element affects the orbits of the other whirling participants by means of its own gravitational pull. The rhetorical triangle, with its three distinct points, is transformed by Bakhtin's theory into a rhetorical circle with speaker, hero, and listener whirling around the circumference. That circumference consists of all three elements fused together in language. Bakhtin's paradigm is a model of complex interaction. Subject and Object lose their distinctive ontological status. Each is altered by the semantic shaping given to it through the "dialogic" interaction, to use Bakhtin's term.

This term, "dialogic," is a key one for Bakhtin. It describes the interactive nature of language itself which inevitably proceeds according to a dialogic model. Language development is dialogical because it occurs as a result of speaker-hero-listener interaction. Words come to us from other speakers; our job is to lay claim to this verbal property. Bakhtin states the situation as follows:

> The word in language is half someone else's. It becomes "one's own" only when the speaker populates it with his own intention, his own accent, when he appropriates the word, adapting it to his own semantic and expressive intention. Prior to this moment of appropriation, the word does not exist in a neutral and impersonal language (it is not, after all, out of a dictionary that the speaker gets his words!), but rather it exists in other people's contexts, serving other people's intentions: it is from there that one must take the word, and make it one's own. (*Dialogic* 293–94)

All speakers must grasp words and learn to possess them because these same words already belong to another. Accordingly, all language contains the semantic intention of both self and other; it expresses both the speaker's (or writer's) meaning as well as the meanings of its other speakers, heroes, listeners, usages. All individuals struggle to replace alien meanings with their own semantic and expressive intentions. Only by doing so do they begin to develop their own stylistic profiles. That struggle never ceases; throughout the linguistic history of an individual, a society, a nation this continuous dialogic interaction occurs as speakers struggle to infuse language with their own intentions. This dialogism is characteristic of both spoken and written forms of the word. As Bakhtin states:

> Any utterance—the finished, written utterance not excepted—makes response to something and is calculated to be responded to in turn. It is but one link in a continuous chain of speech performances. Each monument [written utterance] carries on the work of its predecessors, polemicizing with them, expecting active, responsive understanding, and anticipating such understanding in return. (*Marxism* 72)

It is in this sense that language is dialogical. In his attempt to describe this quality, Bakhtin reifies language, making it into not a living being but a vital medium which expresses the continuous energy of its speakers:

> When a member of a speaking collective comes upon a word, it is not as a neutral word of language, not as a word free from the aspirations and evaluations of others, uninhabited by others' voices. No, he receives the word from anoth-

er's voice and filled with that other voice. The word enters his context from another context, permeated with the interpretations of others. His own thought finds the word already inhabited. Therefore the orientation of a word among words, the varying perception of another's word and the various means for reacting to it, are perhaps the most fundamental problems for the metalinguistics study of any kind of discourse. . . . (*Problems* 202)

Language is essentially a rich stew of implications, saturated with other accents, tones, idioms, meanings, voices, influences, intentions. Words carry with them their own histories, their own previous and potential significations. It is this interactive quality that Bakhtin describes as "the dialogical." Language—whether spoken or written—is a perpetual hybrid which expresses the various contexts within which it exists. These contexts include not only the syntactic structuring of the utterance and the localized setting of the speaker or writer but also the social, historical, ideological environments in which that utterance exists and participates (*Dialogical* 271). Dialogism is an inherent quality of language; it also seems to me to represent a basic model for epistemology, for how we come to know. As Bakhtin's contemporary, Lev Vygotsky, expressed it in *Thought and Language:* "A word is a microcosm of human consciousness" (153).[2]

Bakhtin's view of language as dialogic compels us to redefine the traditional concept of style in our composition classes. Style has generally been represented as a quality separable from language itself. As defined by most rhetoricians, it has been considered the dress of thought, the rouge applied at a late stage of composing. Louis Milic, for example, argues that "If we want to teach something in our composition classes, it may be that we must return to some form of rhetoric, which is honestly and unashamedly concerned with form and not with content" (126). Following this view, teachers have often given separate evaluations for "style" and "content" as if one could be skimmed from the other like cream from milk.[3] Bakhtin argues that style *is* language, that to create a style is to create a language for oneself. If we can agree with Vygotsky that language and thought develop symbiotically from about the age of two onward, if we can agree with Janet Emig that writing is a mode of learning, then perhaps we can also agree with Bakhtin that stylistic concerns in the composition classroom are not merely the fluff of writing instruction but a fundamental concern with our students' ability to claim thought and meaning for themselves.

Furthermore, to attend to style in language is, according to Bakhtin, to perceive the interpretive richness of discourse. When we think of the kinds of accents and intonations that can enter into language from other speakers, heroes, listeners, and languages we begin to establish a perspective from which we can understand more sophisticated language use such as sarcasm, parody, and irony. We begin to see how style develops through the imitation of—and association with—other styles. We begin to see how ideological and normative influences seep their way into another's words. Such insights are of substantial use to rhetoricians who must concern themselves with analysis of all kinds of narrative and expositional writing produced both by students and by published authors.

In describing language in these terms, Bakhtin elevates it into an eschatology. Meaning, experience, consciousness can only be understood in terms of the word. Bakhtin is eloquent on this issue of the primacy of language as the means by which we conceive the world:

> There is no such thing as experience outside of embodiment in signs. . . . It is not experience that organizes expression, but the other way around—*expression organizes experience.* Expression is what first gives experience its form and specificity of direction. (*Marxism* 85)

Without the word, there is no word. Language is not just a bridge between "I" and "Thou," it *is* "I" and "Thou." Language is thus fundamental not only to learning, but to mind; it both creates and is created by the human intelligence. When we speak and write, we create ourselves and the world. No intellectual construct—no expression or idea—can exist without language, and language is itself continuously interactive in its nature. Worlds whirl within worlds in Bakhtin's circular—or is it spherical—rhetorical paradigm.

Bakhtin's perspective on style and language allows us to see that meaning is always both explicit and implicit, a result of the word's semantic and extra-semantic configurations. Traditional rhetorical theorists have, to some extent, acknowledged the importance of implicit meaning, but generally have tiptoed carefully around the subject. In his landmark study, *The Rhetoric of Fiction,* Wayne Booth worries over the problems of interpretation created by irony and ambiguity. His reading of Jane Austen's *Emma* lops off various edges of uncertainty, a result made inevitable by his later lamentation that because of the unreliable narrator, "it becomes more and more difficult to rely, in our criticism, on the old standards of proof; evidence from the book can never be decisive" (369). (Interestingly, Booth has become increasingly persuaded by the Bakhtinian point of view, as indicated in his preface to *Problems of Dostoevsky's Poetics.*) Chaim Perelman considers implication only in terms of argumentation; the general thrust of his work is toward the empirical and verifiable. He has little of value to say about the importance of suggestion and connotation in persuading readers except that "the elimination of all interpretation is part of an exceptional and artificial situation" (126). James Kinneavy states that ambiguity plays a role in the various aims of discourse, but he offers scant information about the capacity of language to express meanings indirectly. Even when discussing literary discourse, he focuses on the concern for clarity and coherence: "In conclusion, then, organization in literature must give primacy to structure by making it conspicuous, these conspicuous structures must have an intense horizontal and vertical unity, and they must be harmonious and fit" (357). Kinneavy does say that ambiguity is "frequently a necessary virtue in exploratory discourse" (189) and that persuasive discourse employs words that " 'refer' to emotional associations, attitudes, affective and conative elements" (287). He is almost entirely concerned, however, with explicit, denotative meaning. All these theorists have developed their work from the traditional Aristotelian paradigm as it has evolved through the centuries, which is most inadequate when it is used to describe multi-modal language, tonal variations, parody, irony, ambivalence, ambiguity. Bakhtin's paradigm, the rhetorical circle, is particularly useful at helping us to understand these blurred usages which, it seems to me, represent much of the language use we most value.

I shall return to this argument momentarily, but first it is important to illustrate the ways that Bakhtin allows us to analyze more clearly certain kinds of dialogical language use where the burring of the elements is most clearly evidenced. Bakhtin calls such blurrings "double-voiced" and they occur often, particularly in narratives where a narrator's (speaker's) language comes into a zone of dialogical contact with a character's (hero's). In double-voiced usages, it is usually possible to identify two different semantic orientations—almost as if two voices were speaking the same words at once. Double-voiced utterances represent one of the clearest instances of the dialogic. Here, for example, is what appears to be a short and unremarkable narrative description:

> Edward sat down heavily. Where could he go? What should he do? He had no idea which session to attend next.

A conventional analysis of this passage would suggest that a third person narrator is describing the physical and mental actions of Edward. But Bakhtin draws our attention to the second and third interrogative sentences. Who is the speaker of those lines? They represent questions within the mind of Edward, yet they are not offered as interior monologue. On the other hand, they do not seem to be spoken entirely by the narrator. In fact, they are double-voiced utterances which simultaneously belong to both speaker and hero. The voice of the third person narrator (the speaker) has become shot through with the accents and intentions of the character (the hero). Such double-voiced utterances are common to narration, since that form of discourse customarily posits at least two distinct consciousnesses. In less obvious ways, double-voiced utterances also occur in other forms of exposition and analysis.[4]

The historical writer, David McCullough, provides another useful example of the dialogical merging of speaker with hero, one of many that could be drawn from his work. McCullough's prose does more than record factual events from the past; it resonates in such a way that observation merges with speculation, "author" with "subject." McCullough as writer engages dialogically with his hero, be it the Johnstown Flood, the Brooklyn Bridge, the Panama Canal, or young Teddy Roosevelt. That dialogic interaction creates the potential for double-voiced discourse which contributes substantially to the meaning and overall aesthetic effect. Here is such a passage from *Mornings on Horseback*; in it, McCullough describes one of the most traumatic incidents in the boyhood of Teddy Roosevelt: the death of his father. In an expositional paragraph, McCullough states the family's explanation of the elder Theodore's untimely passing:

> His father's fatal illness, it had been concluded among the family, stemmed from a hike he had taken in Maine the previous summer. Theodore had

strained himself somehow mountain climbing, during the stay at Mount Desert with Bamie. Beyond that there seemed no possible explanation why someone of such vigor—such a "splendid mechanism"—could have been brought down. With his Maine guide, a large, bearded, kindly man named William Sewall, a man as large as Theodore had been, the boy now hiked twenty, thirty miles a day, all such feats being recorded in his diary, just as during another summer in the mountains of Switzerland when he was ten. (190)

The paragraph begins with a possessive pronoun linking the point of view to the young Teddy, third-person subject of the preceding paragraph. Such usage is, of course, transitional, but it also closely associates what follows with the young Roosevelt. The noun phrase, "it had been concluded among the family," expands that point of view to include the entire family and it does so emphatically by virtue of its placement between subject and verb. Within the context of the entire chapter, such a phrase sends a clear signal that the narrative is veering toward an identification, a dialogic interaction, with the surviving Roosevelts. Infiltrated by the ideas and attitudes of the family, the narrative voice becomes dialogized, as is apparent in the subsequent sentences. The language assumes a double orientation as if issuing from both narrator and family. One can feel the groping of the family toward some explanation with the use of the adverb "somehow" in the second sentence. Even more apparent is the futility of supplying any explanation implied in the third sentence, which seemingly expresses the narrator's point of view but stylistically and emotionally expresses the family's position that "there seem d no possible explanation" for Theodore's death. McCullough's use of direct quotation here, " 'splendid mechanism,' " introduces the family's idiom directly, but the familial viewpoint is also strongly implied by the use of indirectly quoted words such as "vigor" and "brought down," terms particularly associated in this context with the nineteenth century (and, at least in the case of "vigor," with Teddy Roosevelt). The ironic tone being introduced here is an expression of narratorial skepticism, directed in this case toward the family's struggle to cling to a purely physical explanation as the cause for the Theodore's death. McCullough's position is that the elder Roosevelt's political struggles, particularly with Roscoe Conkling who led the successful fight against Roosevelt's nomination for the Collectorship of the Port of New York, contributed directly to his fatal bout with intestinal cancer. McCullough's undercutting of the family's explanation is, in this instance, accomplished rhetorically through a parodic re-statement of the official Roosevelt explanation. The final sentence of the paragraph moves back to a more particular identification with the young son and returns the paragraph to the point of view established in the first sentence. It has, however, become semantically charged by its context. Appearing here without a transition, it seems almost a non sequitur. But McCullough is once again conveying his meaning implicitly. By noting the similarity between William Sewall and the elder Roosevelt, McCullough suggests an implicit identification. Sewall, at least for a time, functions as a kind of surrogate father to the young Roosevelt, the two of them engaged in an activity that is itself a replication of earlier, happier days. Taken in its entirety, this passage reveals how closely McCullough identifies with his subject. This identification assumes a stylistic profile, in this case a strong suggestion of the ironic created by the fusion of speaker with hero. One of the rhetorical lessons that David McCullough teaches is that it is not only direct quotation which anchors historical narrative to history, but a dialogic fusion of speaker with hero. Perhaps a more important lesson for us as readers and teachers of writing is the degree to which McCullough develops his argument implicitly through tonal shifts and the use of double-voiced language.

Both of the above examples depict double-voiced, dialogic interaction between two characters or psychological entities (narrator and Edward; narrator and the Roosevelt family). But, as stated earlier, dialogic interaction can occur even when the hero is not a character or living being. The following example, from my own prose, illustrates one of these more abstract dialogical interactions:

> Theory and practice are equally necessary in the study of mathematics. They depend upon each other, much the way gluten and yeast are needed to make bread. Problem solving within a numerical universe takes long hours, muscle, and sweat; it requires both "know-how" and "know-that," so that when the loaf falls—as all loaves occasionally do—we can use our experience to prevent future failures.

In these sentences, "theory and practice" are being compared to "gluten and yeast"; studying mathematics is thus analogous to making bread. Comparison alone is not dialogical, but in the process of making this one the language becomes, at least to some extent, dialogized. This is apparent in the third sentence which states that problem solving demands "long hours, muscle, and sweat." The language of manual labor here has been transposed into a numerical context. The words create associations of the factory, rather than of an academic subject. In the remainder of this sentence, the language is balanced between these two ideologically opposed contexts, so that simple and complex verbal and syntactical constructions are created consecutively within the same sentence. Moreover, the pun apparent in "*needed* to make bread" is another example of rudimentary dialogism. Puns by their very nature imply two meanings at once. They are a focal point for clashing points of view, irreconcilable meanings. Their humor, such as it is, results from that dialogical interaction.

Even in such brief examples, I hope it is clear that Bakhtin's paradigm leads us toward aesthetic concerns in language. Bakhtin is most concerned with sophisticated language use, with forms that convey multiple orientations and interpretations. As experienced readers, writers, and teachers of fictional and nonfictional prose, so are we. Our post-romantic view of the aesthetic is inextricably bound up with this concept of the polysemantic because of our preoccupations with continuing interpretation and the primary role of the reader in making meaning. Bakhtin's theories of language provide a firm vantage point from which one can explore such linguistic territory—not just the symbolic and the ambiguous, but the more common forms of dialogically charged language. The passages analyzed above, for example, are not ambiguous, but they can be characterized as having a capacity for meaning that doubles upon itself, as if the words were layered semantically. The conclusion I would like to draw is that much of the writing (fictional *and* nonfictional) that we most value can be characterized as being dialogical in these ways. Dialogism in language leads insistently to the aesthetic.

Robert Pirsig reinforces this Bakhtinian argument in *Zen and the Art of Motorcycle Maintenance*. For Pirsig, as for Bakhtin, Quality (the aesthetic) is possible only when traditional categorical distinctions are broken down, when classical and romantic conceptions of reality are fused. Pirsig argues that

> Quality is not just the *result* of a collision between subject and object. . . . It is not subordinate to them in any way. It has *created* them. They are subordinate to *it*! (234)

Quality unites traditional oppositions in a moment of pre-rational perception before traditional categorization asserts itself. Throughout *Zen*, Pirsig struggles to describe and define Quality using the dualistic terms of western civilization while simultaneously denying the dualism explicitly in his argument and implicitly within the plot structure of the motorcycle journey. Quality, for Pirsig, is identification (290); it is unselfconsciousness (288); it is a relationship between the human and the experiential (363). "Quality is not a *thing*," he says. "It is an *event*" (233). Like the dialogic that Bakhtin describes, Quality is elusive and peripheral. States Pirsig:

> You point to something as having Quality and the Quality tends to go away. Quality is what you see out of the corner of your eye. . . . (335)

It is "reality itself, ever changing, ultimately unknowable in any kind of fixed, rigid way" (373). According to Pirsig, rhetoric has too passionately attached itself to empirical formulations and rigid taxonomies. It has created inflexible oppositions that have falsified our relations with the world and ourselves. In arguing for Quality, Pirsig's *Zen* establishes the philosophical and rhetorical assumptions for Bakhtin's theory of language and aesthetics. Bakhtin's work represents a renewed effort to continue the kind of rhetorical tradition that Pirsig extols among the ancient sophists. Bakhtin's passionate concern is to analyze the interrelationships between words, linguistic forms, styles. For Bakhtin, as for Pirsig, the word is a mirror image of consciousness that is forever in flux; thus it continually refracts the brilliant light of analysis that is concentrated upon it. In order to prevent ourselves from being blinded, we must develop our peripheral vision so that we can see not only Truth but Quality.

Clearly, then, Mikhail Bakhtin's ideas about language and aesthetics are reiterated by Robert Pirsig. Both insist on complicating our view of language and urge us to resist the natural human drive to understand through rigid definition and concrete specification. Not everything that matters can be pointed to on a page. Indeed, much of what really matters in writing is immanent. We attach metaphors to such concepts in order to understand them—metaphors such as voice, style, tone, image. As writing teachers, we tend not to pay attention to such elements probably because we are afraid of their elusiveness. It is much safer to point to poor usage, an awkward construction, a botched paragraph. Reading Bakhtin develops our ability to read for these qualities in language and reaffirms their importance. Without allowing for these transcendent possibilities, we are bound to conceive of the world in terms that deny the very quality we most value.

There is much more to Bakhtin than just this thumbnail sketch of a few of his ideas on language. Instead of continuing to paraphrase and condense what should be read in full, however, I would like to conclude by illustrating the usefulness of his perspective by analyzing a text, specifically John McPhee's most recent work of nonfiction, *La Place de la Concorde Suisse,* a book which presents the particular and idiosyncratic genius of the Swiss Army. McPhee is celebrated as one of the finest journalistic writers in America, praise which his work deserves. What is generally unacknowledged is the degree to which aesthetic elements in his work ensure him a more enduring place in literary history as one of the finest practitioners of aesthetic nonfictional prose in the twentieth century. Bakhtin's critical insights encourage use to see these elements in McPhee. For the purposes of this essay, I will limit my analysis to the opening paragraph of the section which describes Luc Massy, a patrol leader in the Swiss Army, as he engages in his fulltime civilian occupation as winemaker in the Epesses vineyard he owns along with his father. It is a substantial paragraph, but it needs to be quoted in full:

> The cave was a ganglion of hoses and tubes: Massy fixing leaks with surgical cotton, Massy on a ladder with a light bulb and a cord, Massy inside the cuves. He was wearing high rubber boots, bluejeans, and a rubber apron over a cotton football shirt bearing the number "26" and the name "BROWNS." He was racking a new white—in its taste a hint of something foul. Time had come to separate the wine from its lees. The ladder was leaning against the tiled wall of a cuve—a tall and narrow chamber full of wine. On the outside of the cuve, a column of wine in a clear-plastic tube reported the depth inside. In this cave were twenty-one cuves, also a big oak cask—in all, a hundred and thirty-five thousand litres of wine. Massy was working alone. He was working like a soldier. With a hose that could have put out a fire, he sent most of the contents of a cuve into an aeration tub, where it spilled like a fountain into a foaming pool and by another hose was sucked away. The wine was not at all attractive. It looked like floodwater, like weak tea with skim milk in it, like something a chemical company had decided to hide. Sometimes he was interrupted by people who came to the cave to buy the product from the oenologist himself. Between rackings, he might have a few moments to sit and read *La Tribune du Matin,* but scarcely enough time to turn a page. He was racking at the rate of thirty-two thousand litres a day. Now and again, he picked up something that

looked like a flamethrower and shot needles of cold water with steamlike force over the walls and floor of the cave. "If you are clean—if everything that touches the wine is clean—it is easy to make wine," he said. From time to time, he would pick up a small hose and let a slow downbending stream of wine fall past his tongue until he found the moment where the quality stopped. When a cuve was drawn down and its wine transferred, he opened a small oak door at the bottom and mucked out the offensive lees. They came forth like a warm coffee ice cream that had begun to sour. Putting on a yellow rain slicker, an impermeable yellow hat, Massy then crawled inside the cuve. If odor could kill, he would have fallen dead. He hosed out the interior. This had been a most unusual year, he said from inside—his voice distorted, tympanic, echoing, fermenting. He said he would be making about a hundred and seventy thousand litres—a volume approaching twice his annual average. There had been a fine spring, a better summer, with ample but not excessive rain. "Also," he added, "for four years the vines have not given much." (37–38)

Bakhtin encourages us to be sensitive to the ideological implications of language, to read for tone and suggestion, concerns which are particularly appropriate to this McPhee passage. Most particularly, Bakhtin is concerned with interpretive doubling, with usages that exhibit twofold orientations, like parody and irony. The term "dialogical," as I have explicated it in this essay, is an umbrella term which describes this merging of voices, speaker with hero and listener, one writer with another. Language, for Bakhtin, is a conversation where a great many people talk at once. M⁻Phee's writing exemplifies a great many of these concerns, for McPhee may best be characterized as a writer of understatement and consolidation, that is, one who compresses his meanings, folding them within language.

Up until this paragraph, McPhee has written of Massy as soldier in the Swiss Army, that is, he has been defined within a military context as a patrol leader on a practice reconnaissance in the Swiss country surrounding the Simplon Tunnel. Only at the very end of the preceding section does McPhee reveal that Massy is one of the premier wine-makers and wine-testers in Switzerland and that three days earlier he was in Epesses making wine. Suddenly he is in a cave, which is later explained to be the basement of his home (and winery). The word, "cave," however accurately and literally it describes Massy's work area, also creates a bridge between the mountainous setting of the previous section and this one; it suggests a double context of natural and constructed, outside and inside. McPhee is a master at creating these kinds of double associations which produce a semantic tension in his language. As Massy works inside the cave, McPhee uses descriptive terms such as "floodwater" and "slow downbending stream" to reinforce this doubling. He introduces a new thematic element with his use of "ganglion," an anatomical term, which finds an echo in the phrase "Massy fixing leaks with surgical cotton." Winemaker has become surgeon, with cave as body. Throughout this paragraph which describes Massy's activities, one finds the stylistic influence of the contexts of mountain and operating room, soldier and surgeon. Both professions are physically demanding; both emphasize decisiveness, thoroughness, precision, attention to detail. Massy's concern for cleanliness, his "working like a soldier," his use of "something that "looked like a flamethrower" clearly suggest the military. His continuous hosing and scrubbing, and the description of the wine which "by another hose was sucked away" suggest, to a lesser extent, surgical procedures. Surgeon, soldier, winemaker—Massy is stylistically created as all of these within this one passage.

One effect this has is to undercut Massy at the same time that his expertise is being extolled. Massy's activities, after all, cannot be favorably compared to that of surgeon or soldier. The stylistic analogies create an ideological tension that expresses itself through irony. The gently ironic point of view is established in other ways as well. The opening sentence creates a parodic militaristic parallel in its syntax and rhythm. The three absolute clauses beginning with "Massy," each piling up on top of the other, suggest Tennyson's "Charge of the Light Brigade" with its famous three-line refrain, "Cannon to right of them,/Cannon to left of them,/Cannon behind them . . ." Even without a direct echoing of the line, the highly stylized absolutes evoke epic phrasing. Neither as winemaker nor as soldier can Massy be construed as epic hero; the parallel is an ironic one. And irony, as was pointed out earlier, is one form of the dialogical.

Literate and literary as he is, McPhee frequently creates phrasing that echoes other popular and literary expressions. Such phrasings can be felt elsewhere as well. The sentence "Time had come to separate the wine from its lees" attracts attention to itself because of its lack of an opening article; it echoes the famous line from Lewis Carroll, " 'The time has come,' the Walrus said, 'To talk of many things' "—a poem which describes a different kind of harvest. The allusion is all the more indirect (and perhaps even unconscious) by virtue of the omitted article. McPhee's usage of "They came forth" to describe the draining of the lees suggests a biblical context, perhaps the going forth of Noah and all the living creatures from the ark, after another kind of flood and redemption, or the story of Jonah swallowed up, like Massy, inside the belly of a beast. His employment of the term "oenologist" (which is, after all, a studier rather than a maker of wine) creates an ironic scientific and technical aura around Massy as he works in his Cleveland Browns shirt. The word contributes to the ironic cast of the passage all the more for its academic connotation. It also establishes, as does the use of technical terms and detailed place names elsewhere, the authority of McPhee. Bakhtin forces us to pay attention to such rhetorical and dialogical possibilities in word and phrase, and they provide an ever-widening set of associations and evaluative responses to the reader.[5]

The last section of this paragraph also deserves mention; here McPhee employs language that is most clearly dialogical. He begins by indirectly quoting Massy, and then describes his voice inside the cuve as "distorted, tympanic, echoing, fermenting." That last participle shifts the ground of the comparison: Massy's voice has become the grape inside the vat. McPhee continues to use indirect quotation in the next sentence. But the following declarative shifts toward the double-voiced, for it is not quite clear whether Massy, McPhee, or the two together state that "There had been a fine spring, a better summer, with ample but not excessive rain." The sentence conveys the meaning of Massy but the diction and syntax of McPhee. Immediately McPhee anchors it to Massy by his use of "he added" in the following sentence. Yet the effect of the dialogical persists, creating a blend of voices which adds a resonance to the end of the paragraph.[6]

What I hope such an analysis suggests is the interpretive richness of language. It may well be that other readers—and John McPhee himself—would disagree with my reading, wanting to limit or expand it further. Yet I would hope that all readers would concur that such an interpretation is only unusual in the degree to which it attends to the kinds of language issues that Bakhtin so brilliantly articulates. Such analysis is, of course, possible with all discourse. Bakhtin's insights encourage us to produce richer discourse as writers and more fully participate in the rich discourse produced by others. Once we realize the extent to which all language is saturated with other styles, idioms, and modes of speaking and writing, we become better readers and, by extension, better teachers of reading and writing. Bakhtin's perspectives on language suggest an exciting new development for contemporary rhetorical theory.

NOTES

1. Scholars disagree on this point, which may never be resolved. In his introduction to *The Dialogic Imagination*, Michael Holquist explains that "There is a great controversy over the authorship of three books that have been ascribed to Bakhtin: *Freudianism* (1927) and *Marxism and the Philosophy of Language* (1929; 2nd ed. 1930), both published under the name of V. N. Voloshinov, and *The Formal Method in Literary Scholarship* (1928), published under the name of P. N. Medvedev. . . . The view of the present editor is that ninety percent of the text of the three books in question is indeed the work of Bakhtin himself" (xxvi). This is a reasonable conclusion. The ideas presented in these works are sufficiently complex and sophisticated that it is difficult to imagine two individuals writing so similarly at the same time within the same community. More likely, Voloshinov may have readily agreed to publish the works under Bakhtin's name so that the latter's ideas could be brought into academic currency. Some intellectual collaboration among the individuals in Bakhtin's circle was inevitable in any case. In the final estimate, it makes little difference whether there was one author named Bakhtin, or several named Bakhtin-Voloshinov-Medvedev; what is important is that the works exist and provide an illuminating perspective on language. Concerning this question, see in particular Katerina Clark's and Michael Holquist's fine biography, *Mikhail Bakhtin*, especially ch. 6.

2. The parallels between Vygotsky and Bakhtin are striking. Born within a year of each other in czarist Russia, both men followed similar studies and both ran afoul of Stalinist ideology. Both men studied language as it manifested itself within the social setting, although Vygotsky's concern is developmental while Bakhtin's is more literary-critical. Both celebrate language as the means through which human beings understand the world and themselves. Vygotsky's famous statement in *Thought and Language* that "A word devoid of thought is a dead thing, and a thought unembodied in words remains a shadow" (153) could just as easily be ascribed to Bakhtin. According to Katerina Clark and Michael Holquist, Bakhtin had read Vygotsky's early work, but I think it is safe to say that

there is little direct influence there (382). Although Bakhtin cites a wide range of historical and contemporary theorists, critics, and linguists throughout his work, he never mentions Vygotsky. For another perspective on the relationship of Bakhtin's work to Vygotsky's see, Caryl Emerson, esp. 251–57.

3. For the unfortunate consequences of Milic's line of thinking see the insightful analysis by C. H. Knoblauch and Lil Brannon (41–47).

4. In *The Dialogic Imagination,* Bakhtin states that "Form and content in discourse are one, once we understand that verbal discourse is a social phenomenon—social throughout its entire range and in each and every of its factors, from the sound image to the furthest reaches of abstract meaning" (259). As is so often the case in Bakhtin's work, verbal discourse is quickly extended to represent all discourse, verbal and written. (See, for example *Marxism and the Philosophy of Language,* where Bakhtin states that "A book, i.e., a *verbal performance in print,* is also an element of verbal communication" [95]). Bakhtin's statement concerning "form and content" opens his masterful, lengthy analysis of stylized forms of writing, "Discourse in the Novel." Later in this essay, he struggles toward another definition of style: "Style can be defined as the fundamental and creative [triple] relationship of discourse to its object, to the speaker himself and to another's discourse; style strives organically to assimilate material into language and language into material" (*Dialogical Imagination,* [378]). For Bakhtin, style emerges out of the interaction that is a precondition for all language development.

5. Bakhtin develops his ideas about this form of discourse most directly in *Marxism and the Philosophy of Language,* esp. chs. 3 and 4. See also *Problems,* ch. 5. In an excellent summarizing article in *PTL,* Brian McHale concludes that of all the contemporary theorists who have analyzed this form of utterance, Bakhtin is the most insightful.

6. One other line deserves specific mention—McPhee's statement that "He was racking a new white—in its taste a hint of something foul." There is a resonance to this line that I find difficult to explain. It suggests the horror genre with its emphatic placement of "foul," or perhaps *Hamlet* ("Something is rotten in the state of Denmark"). Whatever it is, I cannot identify it, though the line shimmers with interpretive possibility.

WORKS CITED

Bakhtin, Mikhail. *The Dialogic Imagination.* Trans. Caryl Emerson and Michael Holquist. Austin: U of Texas P, 1981.

———. *Problems of Dostoevsky's Poetics.* Ed. and trans. Caryl Emerson. Theory and History of Literature 8. Minneapolis: U of Minnesota P, 1984.

Booth, Wayne. *The Rhetoric of Fiction.* Chicago: U of Chicago P, 1961.

Clark, Katerina, and Michael Holquist. *Mikhail Bakhtin.* Cambridge: Belknap P of Harvard UP, 1984.

Emerson, Caryl. "The Outer Word and Inner Speech: Bakhtin, Vygotsky, and the Internalization of Language." *Critical Inquiry* 10 (1983): 245–64.

Kinneavy, James. *A Theory of Discourse.* Englewood Cliffs, NJ: Prentice, 1971.

Knoblauch, C. H., and Lil Brannon. *Rhetorical Traditions and the Teaching of Writing.* Upper Montclair, NJ: Boynton/Cook, 1984.

McCullough, David. *Mornings on Horseback.* New York: Simon, 1981.

McHale, Brian. "Free Indirect Discourse: A Survey of Recent Accounts." *PTL* 3 (1978):249–87.

McPhee, John. *La Place de la Concorde Suisse*. New York: Farrar, 1984.

Milic, Louis. "Theories of Style and Their Implications for the Teaching of Composition." *CCC* 16 (1965):66–69, 126.

Perelman, Chaim, and L. Olbrechts-Tyteca. *The New Rhetoric*. Notre Dame: U of Notre Dame P, 1969.

Pirsig, Robert. *Zen and the Art of Motorcycle Maintenance*. 1974. New York: Bantam, 1975.

Voloshinov, V. N. *Marxism and the Philosophy of Language*. Trans. Ladislav Matejka and I. R. Titunik. New York: Seminar P, 1973.

Vygotsky, Lev. *Thought and Language*. Cambridge: MIT P, 1962.

Gary A. Olson, ed.

"Jacques Derrida on Rhetoric and Composition: A Conversation"

Jacques Derrida's work has forever altered how we perceive the relationships among writers, readers, and texts and has transformed our very notions of "rhetoric" and "writing." Not only have composition theorists drawn on his work, but recently some have attempted to apply it to the classroom. The publication of Gregory Ulmer's *Applied Grammatology*, G. Douglas Atkins and Michael Johnson's *Writing and Reading Differently*, Jasper Neel's *Plato, Derrida, and Writing*, and Sharon Crowley's *A Teacher's Introduction to Deconstruction* indicates just how influential his ideas have become in our field.

While Derrida has, of course, had much to say about writing and rhetoric, this interview is his first extended discussion of rhetoric and composition *per se.* He describes his own growth as a writer, proposes a model of composition instruction, discusses problems compositionists should avoid, and comments on a range of other related topics, including liberatory learning, social constructionism, logocentrism, and feminism.

The theme that perhaps will most surprise at least some readers is that Derrida vigorously asserts the importance of the "canon," the "tradition," and rigorous academic discipline. He concludes that many critics have seriously misrepresented his ideas. Pointing to his own rigorous academic training, Derrida maintains that even as he seeks to deconstruct pedagogies and ways of thinking, he is "at some level true" to the "classical" training he received in the French educational system. He stresses that deconstruction "doesn't mean simply destroying the norms or pushing these norms to utter chaos." In fact, if what passes as deconstruction produces "neglect of the classical authors, the canonical texts, and so on, we should fight it."

This theme recurred throughout the session, indicating how strongly he feels that deconstruction has been misrepresented and maligned. He is convinced that "if deconstruction is only a pretense to ignore minimal requirements or knowledge of the tradition, it could be a bad thing." Apparently, it is often supporters of deconstruction themselves who feed this misunderstanding: "Sometimes the most ferocious critics who react vehemently and passionately and sometimes with hatred understand more than supporters do." Those who "play at decon-struction, try to behave deconstructively" before reading "the great texts in our tradition" give deconstruction a bad name. Certainly, we need to open the canon, to broaden it, to question it, but we can't do so before acquiring at least a "min-imal knowledge of the basic foundations of the canon." Only then can we devel-op "a deconstructive practice." As if to warn supporters as well as to answer crit-ics, Derrida insists, "If you're not trained in the tradition, then deconstruction means nothing. It's simply nothing."

Derrida also has firm convictions about how composition should be taught. Although there is no formal composition instruction in the French system, he believes there should be. He speaks of "much anxiety" in France over the level of students' writing competency. While he hesitates to call this situation a "liter-acy crisis," he says that many of his generation feel that the young no longer "respect the same norms," the same values—that they "don't read and write the way they should." Derrida perceives this problem as a "restructuring of the norms." He suggests that it is not that students are less intelligent but that "their intelligence is applied differently." However, he contends that instruction in composition would be beneficial, that there should be "parallel teaching of com-position everywhere: in the teaching of French literature, of history, and so on."

It's no mistake that this sounds like a writing-across-the-disciplines model of writing instruction; Derrida fully endorses such a model. While he is not sure how such a model would work, he is certain that writing instruction centralized in a single academic department will lead to the "hegemony of some kind of norm in writing." Aside from "minimal requirements in grammar, clarity of exposition, and so on," writing competence is inextricably linked to the dis-course conventions of specific disciplines. He questions whether it is possible to teach writing without being "competent in the content of a discipline." After all, he argues, "you can't teach writing simply as a formal technique." Of course, he is quick to point out that he does not advocate establishing "boundaries"; yet, he is concerned that writing instruction detached from specific discourse commu-nities will be artificial and, therefore, ineffective—a mere matter of mechanical, formal "technique."

On the other hand, he does not propose that compositionists be "scattered" helter-skelter throughout the university. While he does think it important that writing instruction take place within particular disciplines and therefore that writing specialists be associated with and competent in those disciplines, he feels just as strongly that compositionists must have "something in common"; that is, they must have shared training and expertise in the teaching of composition—in effect, a common discipline of their own. Thus, fully aware of the complexity of the subject and the contradictory nature of his response, Derrida says, "I would not rely on a model in which composition instructors are confined simply with-in one discipline; nor would I rely on a model in which they are simply dis-persed, scattered among a variety of disciplines."

Nor does he recommend that compositionists form their own academic departments apart from English departments. While he acknowledges that "it's important that a large number of composition teachers belong to the English department," he reiterates that it would be counterproductive to "confine" compositionists to any single department.

Clearly, Derrida has a keen grasp of the complexity of the very issues we ourselves are struggling with, and his reluctance to seek security in a "unilateral solution" may well be an example we should follow in shaping the future of writing instruction and our own professional relationships within the structure of the university.

Moreover, we would do well, Derrida advises, to "deconstruct" not only written texts but the institution of composition and the very notion of "composition" itself. He cautions against imposing rigid schemes of writing on students and suggests that we continually question and destabilize the authority of models of composition and that we seek to "invent each time new forms according to the situation." Echoing the recent concerns of many composition theorists, Derrida reminds us that writing is always contingent upon context—the "situation, the audience, your own purpose"—not on preestablished, formulaic models. So we should "analyze these models" and determine "where their authority comes from" and "what interests they serve."

Compositionists should be especially wary of what Derrida calls "rhetoricism": "thinking that everything depends on rhetoric." Certainly, rhetoric is central to almost every facet of life, but we must not attribute to rhetoric more power than it has—an "inherent danger" in the teaching of rhetoric and composition. This is not to say that "rhetoric is simply subordinate," but that "rhetoric is not the last word." Derrida believes that "a self-conscious and trained teacher, attentive to the complexity, should at the same time underline the importance of rhetoric and the limits of rhetoric." We need to help students understand the full complexity of language use—its power *and* its limitations.

It is evident from the conversation recorded here that Derrida takes writing instruction quite seriously and shares with compositionists many of the same concerns, both theoretical and pedagogical. He supports our attempts to improve composition pedagogy and applauds our efforts to deconstruct ourselves—our self-reflexive examination of the notion of "composition," the field, and our institutional relationships. Such continual analysis and self-examination will lead to productive change and growth. Not only is his support somewhat comforting, but his insights, I believe, contribute productively to the ongoing dialogue in rhetoric and composition about who we are and who we should be.

Q. Do you think of yourself as a writer?

A. It's difficult to answer this question without some preliminary precautions. I don't think of myself as a writer if by "writer" you mean merely a literary writer, an author of poems and fiction in the traditional sense. From that point of view, I'm not a writer. But neither am I a philosopher who writes or a theoretician who writes without being attentive to writing—to the form, techniques, and so on. So, I think of myself neither as a writer (in the sense of working within literary genres) nor as a scientist or philosopher who wouldn't be interested in questions of writing. I'm interested in the way I write, in the form, the language, the idiom, the composition. When I write a text—and I write different kinds of texts—I'm as attentive to, let's say, the content as to the formal style and also to the performative shape, the genre, all the aspects that belong to a given genre. All those problems which are traditionally called "formal" are what interest me most. To that extent, I think of myself as a sort of writer. But I'm unhappy with the boundaries between, let's say, literary writing and philosophical writing. I'm not a writer, but writing to me is the essential performance or act. I am unable to dissociate thinking, teaching, and writing. That's why I had to try to transform and to extend the concept of writing, which is not simply "writing down" something. So, "yes and no" would be the answer to the first question.

Q. Who were key "writing teachers" for you? By that I mean not necessarily people who held official faculty positions, but people who advised you well about your writing or whose writing inspired your own composition processes.

A. There are a number of possible answers to this. Paradoxically, I learned a lot from my teachers both in high school and in what we call the *khâgne*—a grade between high school and the *Ecole Normale Supérieure*—the university. We had to prepare a composition we call the *concours d'entrée*. This instruction was very hard and heavy, very demanding according to classical norms. I was trained in those very classical norms. And probably people who read me and think I'm playing with or transgressing norms—which I do, of course—usually don't know what I know: that all of this has not only been made possible by but is constantly in contact with very classical, rigorous, demanding discipline in writing, in "demonstrating," in rhetoric. Even if I feel, or some of my readers think, that I am free or provocative toward those norms, the fact that I've been trained in and that I am at some level true to this classical teaching is essential. I think that perhaps my American readers—when they read me in English, for example—don't or can't pay attention to the fact that this classical superego is very strong in terms of rhetoric, whether it's a question of rhetoric in the sense of the art of persuasion or in the sense of logical demonstration. When I take liberties, it's always by measuring the distance from the standards I know or that I've been rigorously trained in. So, my classical training in France has been a great influence—all those competitions that I suffered from. The French system was and still is terrible from that point of view, you have to go through a number of selective competitions which make you suffer to make you better. I'm politically against this system and I fight it; nevertheless, I had to go through it. Yet, however negative it may be from some point of view, it's good discipline and I learned a lot from it. The way I write is probably marked by this experience. So, first, there are those teachers at school. But then, you learn from everything you read; every writer or philosopher you admire is a kind of writing teacher. So I learned from many, many writers.

Q. Anyone in particular?

A. No, because it depends on the type of text I write. I write different types of texts. I won't say I imitate—that's certainly not true—but I try to match in my own idiom the style or the way of writing of the writers I write on. When I write on Mallarmé, I don't write the same as when I write on Blanchot or Ponge. It's not a mimetic behavior, but I try to produce my own signature in relation to the signature of the other, so I don't learn a model way of writing. It's not learning; it's listening to the other and trying to produce your own style in proportion to the other. It's not a lesson you learn; it's something else.

Q. Would you describe this as being "influenced" by these authors?

A. It's not an "influence." Even though I write differently when I write on Mallarmé or Blanchot or Ponge, this difference doesn't mean that I'm under their influence. But I adjust. I don't write like Blanchot, but my tone changes; everything is differently staged, but I wouldn't speak of "influence."

Q. So it's a matter of "responding."

A. Yes, responding; that's it. Responding is responding to the other. Blanchot remains other, and I don't write the way he writes so my writing is other, too. But this otherness is responding or co-responding, so to speak.

Q. Most European universities do not offer courses in writing. Is composition taught in French universities? If not, do you think that formal courses in writing should be taught there?

A. No, there is no such instruction in France. We don't teach composition, as such. Of course, through the teaching of French and literature, there has been, or there should be, the concurrent teaching of composition. The teacher of French literature, for example, requires students to write correctly, elegantly, and so forth. There are grammatical and stylistic norms. But this is a very mobile situation. Now we are seeing problems which look or sound like yours. I wouldn't call it "illiteracy," but there has been a massive change during the last two decades. The level of what is required seems to have dropped, and this is something that everyone in my generation complains about. But it's not that simple, and I don't share these complaints. It is true that our norms are not respected, and we cannot recognize in children and young people now the same respect we had for spelling, and so on. In France the pedagogy which was built through the ideology of the Third Republic was very rigorous, and the social authority of the teacher was enormous. This meant that there was an ethics of spelling, of *orthographe,* and every transgression, every misspelling, was a crime. This was the case in my generation and before me. Now, of course, this is no longer the case, and respect for these values has disappeared, for the students and for the young teachers, too. But this doesn't mean that these people have given up any respect for anything; it's that the norms have changed. They're not less intelligent but their intelligence is applied differently, and it's very difficult for people from my generation to understand this shifting, this restructuring of the norms. So there is no teaching of composition, as such. There should be parallel teaching of composition everywhere: in the teaching of French literature, of history, and so on. Now, everyone believes that French young people, however intelligent they may be, don't read and write the way they should. This is the cause of much current anxiety in France.

Q. What university department do you think should teach writing? Would it be the French department? Would it be a separate department?

A. I wouldn't think that one single department should be in charge, because if you concentrate the teaching of composition in a single department—for instance, the literature department—then you'll have the hegemony of some kind of norm in writing. The people in mathematics and history and law don't have to write the same way. Of course, the minimal requirements in grammar, clarity of exposition, and so on can be addressed everywhere. But then you have to adjust the transformations of the way you write according to each discipline, the discourse of the discipline. There is writing competence for a lawyer, for a historian, and there are also changes in those competencies. So if you concentrate composition teaching in one single place, you won't be able, first, to differentiate between the different requirements, and then to take into account the necessary transformations in style. And, of course, I'm in favor of transformations in rhetoric and in the mode of argument. Such changes have to be specific to each discipline. And, if possible, crossing the boundaries would be good, too. I have no model for this, but I would not rely on a model in which composition instructors are confined simply within one discipline; nor would I rely on a model in which they are simply dispersed, scattered among a variety of disciplines. There should be a specificity and also a crossing of the boundaries. So, it's a very difficult question.

Q. In fact, there's a model here that we call "writing across the disciplines" in which all or many of the academic departments are involved in the teaching of writing.

A. I don't know what your feeling is, but is it possible to teach writing without being competent in the content of a discipline? You can't teach writing simply as a formal technique. Each technique is determined by the specific content of the field. So the one who teaches writing in law school should, I think, be informed about the laws and not simply a rhetorician.

Q. You say that the ideal situation would be to teach within the discourse of each particular discipline and not isolate rhetoric in a particular department. However, the political situation in American universities is such that rhetoric and composition specialists typically hold faculty positions in English departments, along with specialists in traditional literary areas and critical theory. Composition programs (and their faculty) are beginning to emerge as powerful components of many English departments because of the increasing political, economic, and curricular importance of writing instruction. Understandably, the co-existence in many institutions of traditional literature professors and these newer composition professors has created a certain amount of tension and professional rivalry. Given this political situation, do you believe that writing/rhetoric programs should be housed in English—that is, *literature*—departments? Or should they, as in a few American institutions, exist as independent departments devoted exclusively to the study of and instruction in language, writing, and rhetoric?

A. Both, I would say. I'm not attempting to avoid your question, but I would say that any unilateral solution would be bad. First, there's the question of English in this country. And this is a political question: why should composition and the teaching of rhetoric be linked not to English as English literature but to English as the English language, the American language? There are linguistic minorities in this country, so, to some extent, you have to teach English, including composition. Of course, English is and will remain the predominant language in this country, but if it's not the only spoken and written language in this country, if there are also the languages of minorities and also people who know other foreign languages—French or Spanish or Chinese or Japanese—then you have to respect this diversity. How to do so I don't know, but if English remains the only vehicle for the teaching of rhetoric and composition, that would be limiting, especially in this country. That's one level of this question. Another level is exactly the one you mentioned: whether it's a good thing that writing teachers be in English departments because the English departments are the most powerful and the largest, even though differences among colleagues may occur. Many of my best students in this country are in English departments; their fields are more differentiated, and there are more struggles. So, I think it's important that a large number of composition teachers belong to the English department. But it would be a bad thing that they be confined in them because there are other perspectives and, of course, other disciplines which are not literary disciplines. So, it's important, too, that to some extent, in some ways, teachers of rhetoric and composition not remain confined in the English department. My answer is apparently contradictory, but that's politics. You have to be contradictory in a sense; you have to do both.

Q. You wouldn't, then, put them in their own department by themselves—a department of rhetoric and composition?

A. No, but there must be some specificity, something in the training of teachers in rhetoric, something in common. They should have something in common, as well as a specialization in a field or discipline. So my answer is what we call in French *une réponse de Normand*, which is "yes and no; on the one hand and on the other hand." Any unilateral solution would be bad.

Q. A few other questions about the teaching of writing. One connection between deconstruction and composition may be a recognition of the incredibly complex nature of communication processes and a recognition of the "fleeting uncertainty" of knowledge. Do you see any specific implications for composition studies in the recognition that we are trapped in a logocentric world? If so, what are they?

A. Of course there is a connection between deconstruction and composition. Of course composition should recognize the complexity of communication processes and the uncertainty of knowledge. But before reaching the level of these concerns—the university level, where we should really face these questions—I think deconstruction should go through a reflection on the institution of composition. As you know, deconstruction is not simply a critical questioning about, let's say, language or what is called "communication processing."

It's not only a way of reading texts in the trivial sense; it's also a way of dealing with institutions. Not only with content and concepts, but with the authority of institutions, with the models of institutions, with the hard structures of institutions. And we know that "the complex nature of communication processes, and so on" depends on many institutions, and, to begin with, on schools. So, the connection between deconstruction and composition should be problematized—first, I would say, in political and institutional terms. The word *composition*, as you know, is an old word, implying that you can distinguish between the meaning, the contents of the meaning, and the way you put these together. As you know, *deconstruction* means, among other things, the questioning of what synthesis is, what thesis is, what a position is, what composition is, not only in terms of rhetoric, but what *position* is, what *positing* means. Deconstruction questions the *thesis*, the theme, the positionality of everything, including, among other things, *com*position. Writing is not simply a "composition." So once you realize that writing is not simply a way of positing or posing things together, a number of consequences follow.

Without remaining at this level, which is radical—but we have to mention this radicality—I would say that in the university, or in high school, or in any academic field, deconstruction should provoke not only a questioning of the authority of some models in composition, but also a new way of writing, of composing—composing oral speeches and composing written papers. Now, this new way is not simply a new model; deconstruction doesn't provide a new model. But once you have analyzed and questioned and destabilized the authority of the old models, you have to invent each time new forms according to the situation, the pragmatic conditions of the situation, the audience, your own purpose, your own motivation to invent new forms. And these depend on what I was just calling the "pragmatic" in the sense of speech act theory. In each situation you have to write and speak differently. Teachers should not impose a rigid scheme in any situation. A moment ago, I was speaking of my training in France; the rigidity of those forms, those norms for rhetoric and composition, was terrible. It had some good aspects too, but it was terrible. You had to write what we called a *dissertation* according to a certain pattern: in the introduction you should ask a question after having played naive; that is, you should act as if you do not know what the question is, then you *invent* the question, you justify the question, and at the end of the introduction you ask the question. Then in three parts you. . . . Well, there's no need to describe the formula, but it was terribly rigid. So I think through deconstruction you should study and analyze these models and where they come from, where their authority comes from, what the finality of these models is, what interests they serve—personal, political, ideological, and so on. So we have to study the models and the history of the models and then try not to subvert them for the sake of destroying them but to change the models and invent new ways of writing—not as a formal challenge, but for ethical, political reasons.

Q. As a matter of fact, there have been at least three new books published in the

1980s in America that attempt to apply your work in the classroom: Gregory Ulmer's *Applied Grammatology,* G. Douglas Atkins' and Michael Johnson's *Writing and Reading Differently,* and Sharon Crowley's *A Teacher's Introduction to Deconstruction.* Are you familiar with any of these texts and, if so, what is your response to them? Generally, are you satisfied with how your work has been applied pedagogically?

A. I must confess that the only one you mentioned that I know is Greg Ulmer's *Applied Grammatology.* I greatly admire Gregory Ulmer's book—not only this book but everything he writes. It's very important for me and very rigorous. I think what he did in *Applied Grammatology* is, first, very original, which means that it's not simply an "application." It moves very far from, let's say, the premises, what he would call "the premises"; it's not simply an applied grammatology. It goes much further. This means to me that he opens a new field; he's not only applying something relating to the field, but he has discovered a field of new possibilities. I agree with him that in *Of Grammatology* pedagogical problematics were not applied but *implied.* This doesn't mean I would apply these implications the way he does. I don't know; I haven't done such work. But I'm sure he's right in trying to propose a new pedagogy that takes into account new technologies, the new space opened by those questions, and that is not frightened by the modernity of telecommunications, video, etc. I'm not sure I would agree or disagree with his approach; I don't have anything very specific to say about the methodology he would practice. But I'm sure that an awareness of the problematics is absolutely necessary, and it's what is expected from all of us. [Note: A week after this interview, Derrida wrote in a personal correspondence, "I'm currently reading another book, as new and as important, by Greg Ulmer: *Teletheory: Grammatology in the Age of Video* (Routledge, 1989). I find it illuminating for the questions we were discussing in New York."]

Q. So you're encouraged by such attempts.

A. Of course, absolutely.

Q. For close to two decades, Roland Barthes has been refining a classroom practice of deconstruction aimed at throwing literary texts into disorder and deconstructing academic, professional discourse. He lets classroom discourse "float," "fragment," and "digress." Do you believe these techniques would be appropriate not only in the literature classroom but in the *writing* classroom? If so, in what way?

A. I wouldn't approve of simply throwing literary texts into disorder. First, deconstructing academic, professional discourse doesn't mean simply destroying the norms or pushing these norms to utter chaos. I'm not in favor simply of disorder. In fact, there are many ways of practicing order and disorder. I'm sure that there are very conservative ways of throwing texts into disorder, or very conservative ways of disorganizing the classroom. On the contrary, there are very disturbing ways of teaching quietly and, apparently, according to the most traditional forms. I'm not presenting myself as a model for pedagogy, far from it, but people who have a certain image of deconstruction and associate it with me would be very surprised by the way I teach, the way I read papers, the way I give advice to students; it's apparently a very traditional way. The scenario is very classical. In my case, in order to convey what I want to say or to provoke what I want to provoke, I need a very quiet and classical staging of the teaching. But this is not a model; my situation is very specific. When I started teaching, I arrived in the classroom (as everyone does) with a few notes, spoke according to these notes, asked questions, and so on. Now, I just lecture. I arrive with a written paper. I don't change a word for two hours. Everybody is quiet (which is usually the case in France). In some ways it's a liberal way of teaching, in that everyone can cooperate and interrupt me—though, in fact, no one does except when I stop and say, "Well, now we'll start the discussion." Nevertheless, I think that through these very academic, very quiet and conservative ways of teaching, something nonconservative and disturbing arises. But it depends on the situation. At CUNY, for instance, I don't teach the same way. I've only a few notes, and I improvise. So, I don't think there is a model for teaching and an alternative between, let's say, a conservative and a progressive teaching.

What we have to do, perhaps, once the minimal requirements are fulfilled in terms of language, grammar, comprehension, and so on, is to let each teacher have maximum freedom for his or her idiom in teaching, according, again, to the situation. And the situation depends on the audience and the teacher, and the situation is different in New York and Florida, even in some sections in New York and other sections. You have to adjust your teaching according to the situation. I call my students in France back to the most traditional ways of reading before trying to deconstruct texts; you have to understand according to the most traditional norms what an author meant to say, and so on. So I don't start with disorder; I start with the tradition. If you're not trained in the tradition, then deconstruction means nothing. It's simply nothing.

Q. What about those teachers who are afraid of what deconstruction might bring to the classroom, afraid, perhaps, of confusing students, afraid that it may just undermine some of the goals they thought they had? Is there anything we can tell them?

A. First, I would say, when they say this in good faith, I understand them and I approve. I think that if what is called "deconstruction" produces neglect of the classical authors, the canonical texts, and so on, we should fight it. I wouldn't be in favor of such a deconstruction. I'm in favor of the canon, but I won't stop there. I think that students should *read* what are considered the great texts in our tradition—even if that's not enough, even if we have to change the canon, even if we have to open the field and to bring into the canonical tradition other texts from other cultures. If deconstruction is only a pretense to ignore minimal requirements or knowledge of the tradition, it could be a bad thing. So when those colleagues complain about the fact that some students, without knowing the tradition, play at deconstruction, try to behave deconstructively, I agree that that's a mistake, a bad thing, and we shouldn't encourage it. However, sometimes some colleagues refer to these situations simply in order to *oppose* deconstruction: "Well, the effect of deconstruction is this, so we must exclude deconstruction." That's what I would call bad faith in the service of conservative politics. So, I would say that we should require, according to the situation—which may be very different from one country to the other, one city to the other—a minimal (the definition of *minimal* is problematic, I know) culture and minimal knowledge of the basic foundations of the canon. On this ground, of course, students could develop, let's say, a deconstructive practice—but only to the extent that they "know" what they are "deconstructing": an enormous network of other questions.

Q. Vincent Leitch says that deconstructive pedagogy moves "beyond" traditional liberalism in that it could serve conservative or liberal agendas. Such "heterogeneity," says Leitch, is the "hallmark of deconstructive productions." Peter Shaw, on the other hand, says that deconstruction is the child of French radical, leftist politics; it is by nature already political and "leftist." Which perspective is more in line with your own?

A. I understand why Vincent Leitch says what he says. In fact, according to the privilege you give to one or another aspect, deconstruction may look conservative. I'm in favor of tradition. I'm respectful of and a lover of the tradition. There's no deconstruction without the memory of the tradition. I couldn't imagine what the university could be without reference to the tradition, but a tradition that is as rich as possible and that is open to other traditions, and so on. That's conservative; tradition is conservative to that extent. But at the same time deconstruction is not conservative. Out of respect for the tradition, deconstruction asks questions; it puts into respect for the tradition and even the concept of "question" (which I did in *Of Spirit: Heidegger and the Question* [Chicago UP, 1989])—and this, clearly, is a nonconservative stand. So this oscillation is not pertinent here. Deconstruction is, at the same time, conservative and nonconservative. This political translation is not pertinent here either. If you use these political criteria, these old criteria, to describe the effects of deconstruction in the academy, you say, "Well, sometimes, of course, some professors are comforted by deconstruction because it helps them to reinforce the tradition and to exclude other politically subversive questions." That may happen, of course; or it may happen the other way around. That's why there is not one deconstruction, and deconstruction is not a single theory or a single method. I often repeat this: deconstruction is not a method or a theory; it's something that happens—it happens. And it happens not only in the academy; it happens everywhere in the world. It happens in society, in history, in the army, in the economy, and so on. What is called deconstruction in the academy is only a small part of a more general and, I would say, older process. There are a number of deconstructions occurring everywhere.

Now, if we refer to deconstruction as an organized discourse which appeared under that name some twenty-five years ago, of course, this phenomenon, as such, appeared in France. Nevertheless, it was not originally French; it appeared in France as already the heritage of a number of old things—German things, for instance. It was a new hybrid or graft, the French graft, of something older which implies Marxism, Heideggereanism, psychoanalysis, structuralism, and so on. So if it's a child, it's a bastard, I would say. As a child of French leftist politics, it was already a bastard, a hybrid. Now, I should say, since deconstruction is always associated with me, that I consider myself a leftist, I won't say it's visceral, but I never thought of myself as anything other than a leftist. But this doesn't mean that deconstruction, as such, is leftist. Depending on the situation, it can be a weapon to resist, let's say, liberal capitalism; in other situations, a way of resisting leftist totalitarianism. So it's not intrinsically one or the other. This doesn't mean that I have a relativistic view of deconstruction. I would say it's not a theory that can be abstracted from a given field of forces—political, economical, etc. You see, even in France it's not always considered radical and leftist. It's considered such by some and the other way around by others. If it were really only the child of French radicalism, how could you account for its success in the United States, which is more widespread than in France? For me, deconstruction is rather an American child. The fact that apparently it came from France and landed in the States but received in the States a welcome and extension which is out of proportion with what it has been in Europe, and the fact that now it is beginning to come back to Europe through the United States means that the real birthplace, if we follow this metaphor—which I would not want to follow very far—the richer, most fecund birthplace is the United States, and probably for very serious reasons. I apologize for quoting myself, but in *Mémoires for Paul de Man*, the three lectures I gave at Irvine a few years ago about deconstruction in America, I ventured to say at some point that "deconstruction *is* America." It's for essential reasons that deconstruction has had such a development in this country. And we have to understand why—for what historical, political, and theological reasons in the tradition of the United States—deconstruction is such a phenomenon. So if it's a child, it's as well a child of the United States.

Q. Many compositionists draw on the work of Paulo Freire and his notions of "critical literacy" and "liberatory learning." Are you familiar with Freire's work? If so, do you believe that deconstruction and liberatory learning share similar goals?

A. This is the first time I've seen his name.

Q. He's a Marxist educator in Brazil, and he's got quite a following in America and internationally. He is interested in subverting the traditional kinds of teaching which help to reinforce and reproduce the ideology of the ruling class and that keep people illiterate in the name of literacy. Freire wants to subvert such hierarchies.

A. Well, I'm not familiar with his work, but, referring to your description, I would say that in some situations—and we have to take such situations into account—deconstruction would help liberatory learning. I think that you couldn't compare, for instance, the situation in industrial, rich societies and the situation in oppressed, Third World countries. But in the situation of a repressive teaching institution, in the situation in which learning and culture are used in order to confirm the given hegemony, I think that deconstruction could help, could have some emancipatory effect. However, I can imagine some perverse use of deconstruction in the hands of the authorities, who might, for instance, maintain the given order by using apparently deconstructive arguments. So you have to suspect the strategy of self-appointed deconstructionists. To act in a liberatory or emancipatory way, it's not enough to *claim* to be a deconstructionist or to apply deconstruction. In each situation you have to watch, and I can imagine (of course, I try not to do so) someone using deconstruction with reactionary and repressive effects or goals. That's why you can't stop watching and analyzing. You can't simply rely on names, titles, or claims.

Q. Hélène Cixous and other French feminists advocate that women create a "women's language"—a language that inscribes femininity, a "new insurgent" language that liberates, ruptures, and transforms "phallogocentric" discourse. Such a language aims "to break up, to destroy," to "wreck partitions, classes, rhetorics, regulations and codes." Do you see these strategies as identical to those of deconstruction? Can deconstruction serve to help bring about the goals and aspirations of feminism? Or do you believe that such attempts are merely replacing one hierarchy with another?

A. Sometimes it does; it depends on the way women and sometimes men practice this writing, teaching, speaking, and so on. Sometimes feminism replaces phallogocentrism with another kind of hegemony. I wouldn't say that all women do that, but it's a structural temptation. It's perhaps inevitable at some point that they try to reverse the given hierarchy, but if they do only that—reverse the hierarchy—they would reinscribe the same scheme. Sometimes feminism, as such, does that, and I know that some women are not happy about that. You are quoting Hélène Cixous, a very old friend of mine whom I admire deeply, and she is, I would say, one of the greatest writers in France today. She, at some point, of course, spoke of "feminine writing," but I don't think she would still do that, if by "feminine writing" you refer to a specific essentially feminine way of writing. At some points in history, women have had to claim that there is some irreducible feminine way of writing—themes, style, position in the field of literature—not in order to essentialize this, but as a phase in the ongoing war or process or struggle. But if some of them—and I don't think this is the case with Hélène Cixous—would try to say it's the eternal essential feminine which is manifested in this feminine writing, then they would repeat the scheme they claim they are fighting.

Q. Several composition theorists are especially interested in social constructionism because if you posit that all "facts" and knowledge, even *reality* itself, are community created and maintained, then rhetoric becomes the central, paradigmatic epistemic activity. That is, if all of our knowledge and facts and reality are created by social groups, by discourse communities, then rhetoric is the key to it all. What are your thoughts about social constructionism?

A. I must confess, I'm not familiar with the term "social constructionism."

Q. It's a movement drawing in part from the work of Thomas Kuhn and others that posits that all knowledge, all facts, even the ways we think are not "essential" but rather depend on the social group. So, for example, if the community of, let's say, philosophers believes such and such, then that becomes the current "knowledge" until the community of philosophers decides to change this knowledge.

A. I wouldn't be inclined to think that the beliefs, the values, the norms in the community depend on, let's say, thinkers or philosophers, as such. This doesn't mean that philosophy or thinking is simply a symptom, but it's not a *cause* of the shared values. The social structure doesn't obey this kind of causality. I would say that philosophy is neither just an epiphenomenon, nor the cause of or the place where everything is decided on or constructed. Although I'm unfamiliar with social constructionism, I'd like to make a point about rhetoric becoming the central paradigmatic, epistemic activity. On the one hand, I would think that we should not neglect the importance of rhetoric, as if it were simply a formal superstructure or technique exterior to the essential activity. Rhetoric is something decisive in society. On the other hand, I would be very suspicious of what I would call "rhetoricism"—a way of giving rhetoric all the power, thinking that everything depends on rhetoric as simply a technique of speech. Certainly, there are no politics, there is no society without rhetoric, without the force of rhetoric. Not only in economics but also in literary strategy, rhetoric is essential. Even among diplomats, rhetoric is very important; in the nuclear age much depends on some kind of rhetoric. (I tried to show this in an article called "No Apocalypse, Not Now" in *Diacritics*.) Now, this doesn't mean that everything depends on verbal statements or formal technique of speech acts. There are speech acts everywhere, but the possibility of speech acts, or performative speech acts, depends on conditions and conventions which are not simply verbal. What I call "writing" or "text" is not simply verbal. That's why I'm very interested in rhetoric but very suspicious of rhetoricism.

Q. How might composition teachers and theorists avoid falling into this rhetoricism? How can they be cautious; what steps can they take?

A. There is an inherent danger of rhetoricism in the teaching of rhetoric. You can't avoid that. It's intrinsic. When you teach rhetoric you are inclined to imply that so much depends on rhetoric. But I think that a self-conscious and trained teacher, attentive to the complexity, should at the same time underline the importance of rhetoric and the limits of rhetoric—the limits of verbality, formality, figures of speech. Rhetoric doesn't consist only in the technique of tropes, for instance. First, rhetoric is not confined to what is traditionally called figures and tropes. Secondly, rhetoric, as such, depends on conditions that are not rhetorical. In rhetoric and speaking, the same sentence may have enormous effects or have no effects at all, depending on conditions that are not verbal or rhetorical. I think a self-conscious, trained teacher of rhetoric should teach precisely what are called "pragmatics"; that is, the effects of rhetoric don't depend only on the way you utter words, the way you use tropes, the way you compose. They depend on certain situations: political situations, economical situations—the libidinal situation, also.

Q. Ever since Plato's opposition to rhetoric as a discipline, philosophy and rhetoric seem to have existed in a state of continual tension. Why does there seem to be tension between these disciplines? Aren't these disciplines—rhetoric and philosophy—necessarily bound together? Aren't they necessarily intricately and complexly tied?

A. Well, from that point of view I would be on the side of philosophy. The tension comes first from the fact that rhetoric as a separate discipline, as a technique or as an autonomous field, may become a sort of empty instrument whose usefulness or effectiveness would be independent of logic, or even reference or truth—an instrument in the hands of the sophists in the sense that Plato wanted to define them. So contrary to what some people think I think—for instance, Habermas—I would be on the side of philosophy, logic, truth, reference, etc. When I question philosophy and the philosophical project as such, it's not in the name of sophistics, of rhetorics as just a playful technique. I'm interested in the rhetoric hidden in philosophy itself because within, let's say, the typical Platonic discourse there is a rhetoric—a rhetoric against rhetoric, against sophists. I've been interested in the way concepts or arguments depend intrinsically on metaphors, tropes, and are in themselves to some extent metaphors or tropes. I'm not saying that all concepts are essentially metaphors and therefore everything is rhetoric. No, I try to deconstruct the opposition between concept and metaphor and to rebuild, to restructure this field. I'm not at ease with metaphor either. I'm not saying, "Well, we should just substitute metaphor for concept or simply be content with metaphors." What I say, for example, in *White Mythology* is that the concept of metaphor, first, is a metaphor; it's loaded with philosophy—a very old philosophy—and so we shouldn't keep the concept of metaphor the way it is commonly received. So I would distrust, suspect, the couple concept and metaphor. And I would, for the same reasons, be suspicious of the opposition between philosophy and rhetoric. To the extent that I am caught up within this couple, I'm a philosopher, but I try not to remain within this opposition. I try to understand what has happened since Plato and in a recurrent way until now in this opposition between philosophy and rhetoric.

Q. Let me ask you more about the sophists. Recently, several historians of rhetoric have sought to revive the legacy of certain "good" sophists—Gorgias, Protagoras, and Prodicus, for example—finding them lost exemplars of an anti-Platonism attuned to the ways that the contexts for rhetorical acts can shift. In your deconstruction of the *Phaedrus* in "Plato's Pharmacy," you seem to offer support for a sophistic stance toward rhetoric and philosophy. Yet, at times you seem to retreat from a full-fledged endorsement of the sophists. Would you elaborate on your attitude toward the sophists for these historians? Do you think that we know enough about them to conceptualize their legacy?

A. Your question implies the answer, and, in a way, I've already suggested an answer. I've resisted the way Plato attacked or imprisoned the sophists, captured the sophists, in the figure of the sophists. To that extent, it's as if I were simply counterattacking Plato from the position of the sophists. But as you've said, it's not that simple: if the sophists are what Plato thinks they are, I'm not in favor of the sophists; however, I think it's much more complicated. We don't have enough knowledge; the question of what the sophists really were is an enormous question. I wouldn't venture to simplify this. Considering how little we know of what the sophists were, I think today we must be interested in the challenge philosophy was to the sophists, as well as the challenge the sophists were, and still are in their modern form, to philosophy. This has had, again, a recurrent form in many epochs, including Nietzsche's and ours. So today, first, we should remember what happened between Plato, Socrates and the sophists—remember all the subsequent figures of this opposition. But also we must try not to reduce modern conflicts to this opposition. There are people who say, "Well, today we have to restore philosophy against the modern sophists." And usually deconstructionists are considered the modern sophists. Such people are reducing the complexity and the singularity of the situation. We're not in the same situation. We have, of course, to refer to these Greek situations because they are part of our heritage, but some essential things have changed, and we have to take these changes into account. There are no more sophists today and I would say no more philosophers in the given sense. So I'm not in favor of sophistics. But neither am I against the sophists, against Protagoras and the others. I would try to give an accurate analysis if possible of what is inherited, but also of what is new in our culture. And I think the battle between Plato and the sophists is not pertinent enough.

Q. Rhetoric is defined in many disciplines as Aristotle's "discovery of the available means of persuasion." Yet, in many English departments, the notion of "rhetoric" that has become increasingly familiar is the view promulgated by Nietzsche, Paul de Man, J. Hillis Miller, Barbara Johnson, and others. They seem to equate rhetoric with the cognitively disruptive interplay of tropes—the status of text as an allegory of its ultimate unreadability. Some rhetoricians tend to regard this notion as an undue truncation of what appears to be a Western rhetorical tradition. Would you agree with this judgment? By giving such importance to their own particular sense of "rhetoric," can these deconstructionists be accused of "rhetoricism"? Or does this set of questions unfairly characterize them?

A. This is a very delicate question since names are dropped. It's very difficult. As you know, I'm very close to the people you mention here, but at the same time I'm not doing exactly what they're doing with regard to rhetoric. All of them are attentive, and I think rightly so, to rhetoric. First, I wouldn't agree with this opposition. Paul de Man, for example, is interested in rhetoric also as a means of persuasion. And his theories precisely of grammar, rhetoric, tropes, and persuasion are very complex ones.

Q. So you don't think that this work necessarily subverts the ancient rhetorical tradition?

A. I would not simply reduce these people, these works, to a single, homogeneous set; however new these works are, they aren't simply inventing a new rhetoric or breaking with the tradition. Their relation to the tradition is more complex: it disrupts and it inherits at the same time. For instance, when Paul de Man speaks of "unreadability," he's not simply a rhetoricist (although in comparison what I'm doing is less rhetoricist than his work). There are so many differences here between de Man and myself that this is difficult to answer, but let me try an answer that would do justice to the complexity without really being able to engage in the full complexity of this subject. I would say, for instance, that de Man and Hillis Miller, differently, are very much, and I would say rightly so, interested in rhetoric in literature and in the problem of rhetoric. Sometimes it's as if rhetoric could have the last word for both of them, especially for Paul de Man. Then, perhaps, someone could speak of rhetoricism. Sometimes I'm tempted to say, "There is a danger of rhetoricism here—that is, of claiming to exhaust the text, the reading of the text, through the means of rhetorical questions." But at some point, what de Man and Miller do goes further than rhetoric. For instance, when de Man speaks of the aporia between performative and constative, when he speaks of unreadability and so on, he exceeds the classical field of rhetoric, although through a new problematic of rhetoric. Another example is when Hillis Miller asks questions, when he not only reads Victorian novels in a new way, in a deconstructive way, being attentive to all the rhetorical figures, but when he asks ethical questions, when he speaks of the ethics of reading, and so on; the ethics of reading cannot be reduced to rhetoric.

This doesn't mean that rhetoric is simply subordinate, not simply, but rhetoric is not the last word. Rhetoric is subordinate to something which is not simply rhetorical. When sometimes I've used the word *rhetoricism,* it was not simply in reference to rhetoric. I remember having used this word as an accusation. I was not referring to what we call "rhetoric" or to the attention given to rhetoric. On the contrary, I am in favor of the most rigorous and most generous attention given to rhetoric. What I'm suspicious of under the name "rhetoricism" is the authority of language. *Rhetoric* comes from, as you know, a Greek word meaning *speaking.* So, the charge of logocentrism or phonocentrism is, by itself, a charge against rhetoricism—not the narrow field of what we call rhetoric, but simply the authority of speech, the authority of speaking. If you give absolute privilege to rhetoric you fall into what I call logocentrism or phonocentrism; that's what I meant when I spoke of rhetoricism. I was not charging anyone with being too attentive to rhetoric. I think we should be attentive to rhetoric and to language as much as possible, but the hegemony of speaking over anything else—writing, acting, and so on—is a kind of rhetoricism. So for me, rhetoricism in that context is synonymous with logocentrism or phonocentrism.

Q. Some of your remarks on Chinese characters in *Of Grammatology* suggest that logocentrism may be less prevalent in non-Western cultures. If so, can we turn to these other cultures as a model of a post-logocentric culture, or are we doomed to remain within logocentrism and struggle against it?

A. Well, for these very, very difficult questions there are many possible answers.

Let me attempt an immediate answer, not a learned or scholarly answer. I wouldn't say that logocentrism, as such, is less prevalent in non-Western cultures. I would speak of "phonocentrism"; I would say that the phonocentrism of a culture linked to a technique of writing, which submits, for instance, writing to speech, is less prevalent in cultures in which non-phonetic writing prevails—the Chinese language, for instance. But I would dissociate here phonocentrism from logocentrism, because even in a culture which is non-phonocentric with respect to its technique of writing, the logocentric scheme may prevail with all its essential features, even all the oppositions, the hierarchies which are linked to logocentrism in Western cultures. So I would say that phonocentrism has prevailed in Western cultures. Logocentrism, however, is a universal structure.

That's the unlearned answer, using the word *logos* in the wide sense. Now, if you refer to *logos* in its Greek, determined sense, then, of course, logocentrism is only a Western phenomenon. Then we'll have to understand what logos is. Last week I gave a lecture on Heidegger and precisely on the tradition of logos, what he wrote about logos. I tried to show how Heidegger was logocentric, not because logos was considered the center, but because, for Heidegger, logos is a gatherer; it's something which assembles, unifies, gathers everything. Logocentrism wouldn't mean in that case that logos is at the center of everything, but that logos is the centering structure; it is the structure or the experience of re-gathering—that is, re-assembling around the circle, re-forming the circle, not being at the center of the circle but gathering instead of dissociating the authority of the one as opposed to the multiple, to the other. So from that point of view, if you interpret the tradition of logos—which, of course, you can't do improvising in front of these little tape recorders—then I would say logocentrism is essentially Western. Logocentrism literally, as such, is nothing else but Greek. Everywhere that the Greek culture is the dominant heritage there is logocentrism.

I wouldn't draw as a conclusion, as a consequence of this, that we should simply leave it behind. Perhaps modern China is Greek and as logocentric as any other culture. I wouldn't say that we have to "leave" logocentricism It's something that we can't simply turn our back on and say, "enough." There's another way of, let's say, living with this memory and transforming it and thinking it, and to think of it is not simply living within it. You can travel all your life and go very far from Europe without stopping being logocentric, and you can live in Athens or in New York or in Rome and already have left logocentrism to some degree. I think that the deconstruction of logocentrism is not a matter of decision, it's not a matter of deliberate politics; it happens—it just happens.

Q. Have the non-Western cultures been an influence on your thought?

A. Unfortunately not. The *existence* of such cultures, the *fact* that they limit or delimit or make a pressure on our own, of course, has an influence. I can't simply sleep and ignore this. But if by "influence" you mean: do I really know from the inside a non-Western culture, then no, unfortunately; of course, I should but I don't. I would like to, but that's a limitation on my part. What is interesting to me—and unfortunately I'm not able to follow this work—is that there have been a number of publications on the relationship between deconstruction and some non-Western cultures—Buddhism and Zen, etc. So I read to some extent these books, but I can't really say they've influenced me.

Q. Final question: your work has been cited extensively by countless scholars from numerous disciplines. Such frequent citation necessarily increases the opportunity for misunderstanding or misrepresenting your views. Are you aware of any specific misunderstanding that you would like to take issue with at this time? Any analyses or critiques of your work that have been misinformed?

A. First, there are no simple misunderstandings. Each time you read a text—and this is my situation and the situation of every reader—there is some misunderstanding, but I know of no way to avoid this. Misunderstanding is always significant; it's not simply a mistake, or just an absurdity. It's something that is motivated by some interest and some understanding. Sometimes the most ferocious critics who react vehemently and passionately and sometimes with hatred understand more than supporters do, and it's *because* they understand more that they react this way. Sometimes they understand unconsciously, or they know what is at stake. Sometimes I think that this enemy, because he's so ferocious, so nervous, is more aware of what is at stake than a friendly ally is. So, sometimes misunderstanding is understanding, and the other way around.

After these preliminary cautions, I would say, very briefly, that the misunderstandings that I deplore most would be, in the broad sense, political and institutional. I think that the people who try to represent what I'm doing or what so called "deconstruction" is doing, as, on the one hand, trying to destroy culture or, on the other hand, to reduce it to a kind of negativity, to a kind of death, are misrepresenting deconstruction. Deconstruction is essentially affirmative. It's in favor of reaffirmation of memory, but this reaffirmation of memory asks the most adventurous and the most risky questions about our tradition, about our institutions, about our way of teaching, and so on. When people try to confine deconstruction in negative models as something nonpolitical, noninstitutional or as something confined to books, to speculative speeches, to what is in the library, when they interpret text as something which is written down and not in the generalized concept that I've tried to elaborate, I think it's a very serious misrepresentation. But it's the symptom of a resistance; it's not simply a mistake. It's precisely a resistance to what is happening through deconstruction. So I try to understand what this resistance is, where it comes from; and sometimes this resistance is at work within myself, within the people who are supposed to be in favor of deconstruction. These prejudices about the notion of text, the notion of writing, are as old as what I call "deconstruction," which is about twenty-five years old. From the beginning, I tried again and again to say, "Well, a text is not simply an alphabetic note or a book." And from this statement a number of consequences should follow. But from the beginning and from the most authorized

Rhetoric and Science

Science (from Latin *scire*, "to know") is ostensibly concerned with investigating and elucidating the nature of observable phenomena, and rhetoric plays an important role in the process of communicating just what these phenomena are. Modern interest in the rhetoric of science was given much of its impetus by Thomas Kuhn's reevaluation of the history of science, *The Structure of Scientific Revolutions*, first published in 1962. Kuhn presents the history of science as a series of competing explanations of the phenomenological universe. Scientific revolutions are only the more dramatic historical instances of one explanation replacing another. A "paradigm shift" occurs when, for instance, the heliocentric explanation of the universe replaces the geocentric explanation; such revolutionary shifts are initiated by the discovery of phenomena for which the old paradigm does not account. To do "normal science," then, is to confirm hypotheses within the current paradigm, and to achieve the expected; thus the discovery of a previously unobserved planet rotating around the sun constitutes scientific progress but not scientific change. It maintains the heliocentric paradigm.

Kuhn's work is important for understanding the rhetoric of science because it ultimately calls into question the ways in which language is used to construct knowledge and to compose official explanations of the truth. The very metaphor of the paradigm, appropriated from the study of natural languages, illustrates Kuhn's interest in science as a creation and consequence of discourse. However, Kuhn's critics note that he never makes quite clear exactly what a paradigm is. (Margaret Masterman has observed that Kuhn uses the term "paradigm" in twenty-two different senses in *The Structure of Scientific Revolutions*.) Nonetheless, the phrase *paradigm shift* has moved from regard as an unfamiliar and intrusive concept when Kuhn first employed it to a widely used explanatory term, both for historians of science and for scholars in fields as diverse as sociology and composition studies who have reconstructed their own histories as series of paradigm shifts. The fact that *paradigm shift* was once a strange idea and has now become central to "normal" scholarship in a number of fields, and in popular culture as well, suggests that—keeping Kuhn's model in mind—we have now passed through a "revolution" in the rhetoric of science and other disciplines. Our explanatory language has been altered.

Although one implication of Kuhn's insights is that it is impossible *not* to be working within some sort of paradigm, one might observe that the field of rhetoric has never had a paradigm of its own. Rhetoric makes use of the operative paradigms, discursive practices, and organizing principles at work (or "at play," to borrow a term from postmodern theorists such as Derrida and Lyotard) in the various academic disciplines, as well as in other realms of human endeavor. In this sense, rhetoric is "unsophisticated" (yet still, at times, "sophistic") because it lacks a disciplinary identity. It feasts upon the features of verbal and nonverbal discourse, using and exploiting the paradigms that are already in place to describe them as such or to use them for, as Aristotle proposes, "the available means of persuasion." Although we may say that science and its paradigms are constructed through rhetoric, because the content of science is at any given moment relatively stable and well-defined, whereas the content of rhetoric is ambiguous, the two fields remain distinct from one another.

In *Against Method*, Kuhn's contemporary Paul K. Feyerabend underscores the relationship between science and rhetoric: Subtitled "Outline of an Anarchistic Theory of Knowledge," *Against Method* provides a critique of rationalistic approaches to science and calls attention to the ideological dimension of "factual" assertion. Proclaiming himself a "flippant Dadaist and *not* a serious anarchist," Feyerabend defends a radical (yet playful) argument against empirically based methods that—although he claims they are involved in a quest for ultimate scientific truths—are essentially politically charged language games. Feyerabend realizes that his own proposal "against method" represents a scientific philosophy that is not without its own method. Seeming to anticipate the charge that the position of *Against Method* is as much a truth-claim as those it refutes, the index to the first edition (1975) of the book includes the entry, "rhetoric, 1-309," suggesting that all of the book's 309 pages comprise the intellectual play associated with rhetoric rather than the absolutism associated with science.

A recent attempt to address the subject of science and rhetoric has come with the work of Alan G. Gross: His *The Rhetoric of Science* is the fullest contemporary treatment of scientific discourse from a rhetorical point of view. Writing as a rhetorician, Gross recently argued in *Rhetorica* that, in order to "get science across," rhetoric is necessary. According to Gross, "there is no line that can successfully be drawn between rhetoric and scientific knowledge." Advocating a "radical rhetoric of science," Gross admits that there may be "a limit to rhetorical analysis" of scientific texts, but he nevertheless takes issue with scientists whom he believes distinguish between rhetoric and science on the basis of *a priori* considerations about the nature of both enterprises. His critics charge him with a privileging of rhetoric over science and a relativizing of "brute scientific facts" as manipulation of linguistic entities. (For the response of two scientists to Gross's position, see J. E. McGuire and Trevor Melia's essay in the same issue of *Rhetorica*.)

The following selection of readings contains excerpts from Gross's *The Rhetoric of Science*, Feyerabend's *Against Method*, Herbert Schnädelbach's essay "Against Feyerabend," and portions of an early essay by linguist Kenneth L. Pike, "Language as Particle, Wave, and Field," which suggests how the lexicon of science might be appropriated to a theory of rhetorical invention.

FURTHER READING

Briggs, John C. *Francis Bacon and the Rhetoric of Nature.* Cambridge, Harvard UP, 1989.

Gross, Alan G. "Rhetoric of Science without Constraints." *Rhetorica* 9.4 (1991): 283–299.

Gutting, Gary, ed. *Paradigms and Revolutions.* Notre Dame: U of Notre Dame P, 1980.

Kuhn, Thomas. *The Structure of Scientific Revolutions.* Chicago: U of Chicago P, 1970.

McGuire, J. E. and Trevor Melia. "The Rhetoric of the Radical Rhetoric of Science." *Rhetorica* 9.4 (1991): 301–316.

Popper, Karl R. "Normal Science and Its Dangers." *Criticism and Growth of Scientific Knowledge.* Eds. Imre Lakatos and Alan Musgrave. Cambridge: Cambridge UP, 1970,. 50–58.

Alan G. Gross

"Rhetorical Analysis"

We readily concede that the law courts and the political forum are special cases of our everyday world, a world in which social reality is uncontroversially the product of persuasion. Many of us can also entertain a possibility Aristotle could never countenance: the possibility that the claims of science are solely the products of persuasion. We live in an intellectual climate in which the reality of quarks or gravitational lenses is arguably a matter of persuasion; such a climate is a natural environment for the revival of a rhetoric that has as its field of analysis the claims to knowledge that science makes.

Rhetorically, the creation of knowledge is a task beginning with self-persuasion and ending with the persuasion of others. This attitude toward knowledge stems from the first Sophistic, an early philosophical relativism made notorious by Socrates. In spirit, the *Rhetoric,* my master theoretical text, is also Sophistic, its goal "to find out in each case the existing means of persuasion." It is a spirit, however, that Aristotle holds firmly in check by limiting the scope of rhetoric to those forums in which knowledge is unquestionably a matter of persuasion: the political and the judicial. If scientific texts are to be analyzed rhetorically, this Aristotelian limitation must be removed; the spirit of the first Sophistic must roam free.

Whether, after rhetorical analysis is completed, there will be left in scientific texts any constraints not the result of prior persuasion, any "natural" constraints, remains for the moment an open question. In the meantime, as rhetorical analysis proceeds unabated, science may be progressively revealed not as the privileged route to certain knowledge but as another intellectual enterprise, an activity that takes its place beside, but not above, philosophy, literary criticism, history, and rhetoric itself.

The rhetorical view of science does not deny "the brute facts of nature"; it merely affirms that these "facts," whatever they are, are not science itself, knowledge itself. Scientific knowledge consists of the current answers to three questions, answers that are the product of professional conversation: What range of "brute facts" is worth investigating? How is this range to be investigated? What do the results of these investigations mean? Whatever they are, the "brute facts" themselves mean nothing; only statements have meaning, and of the truth of statements we must be persuaded. These processes, by which problems are cho-sen and results interpreted, are essentially rhetorical: only through persuasion are importance and meaning established. As rhetoricians, we study the world as meant by science.

Thirty years ago the humanistic disciplines were more easily definable: histo-rians of science shaped primary sources into chronological patterns of events; philosophers of science analyzed scientific theories as systems of propositions; sociologists of science scrutinized statements aimed at group influence (Markus 1987, p. 43). In the last two decades, however, the humanities have been subject to what Clifford Geertz has called "a blurring of genres." As a result, "the lines grouping scholars together into intellectual communities . . . are these days run-ning at some highly eccentric angles" (1983, pp. 23–24).

David Kohn, Sandra Herbert, and Gillian Beer on Darwin: are they writing intellectual history or literary criticism? Ian Hacking on gravitational lensing: is he doing philosophy or sociology? Arthur Fine on Einstein: is he producing phi-losophy or intellectual history? Are Steve Woolgar and Karin Knorr-Cetina studying the scientific paper from the point of view of sociology or rhetorical criticism? Is Evelyn Keller's work on Bacon epistemology, psychology, or liter-ary criticism? When Michael Lynch analyses laboratory shop talk, is he doing ethnomethodology or rhetoric of science?

These intellectual enterprises share a single methodological presupposition; all, to paraphrase Barthes, "star" their texts; all assume with Geertz that "the road to discovering . . . lies less through postulating forces and measuring them than through noting expressions and inspecting them" (1983, p. 34). To address Einstein's philosophy, Fine becomes a historian. Latour and Woolgar discover the intellectual structure of science not through philosophical analysis but through the ethnomethodology of the laboratory. Keller approaches Bacon's epistemology not by reconstructing his arguments but by analyzing his metaphors; Beer treats the *Origin* less like an argument than like a novel by George Eliot or Thomas Hardy.

Rhetorical analysis describes what all of these scholars of science are doing; it defines the intellectual enterprise of workers as different in outlook and training as Gillian Beer and Steve Woolgar. For such scholars, the speculative knowledge of the sciences is a form of practical knowledge, a vehicle of practical reasoning, whose mark "is that the thing wanted is *at a distance* from the immediate action, and the immediate action is calculated as the way of getting or doing or secur-ing the thing wanted" (Anscombe 1957, p. 79). The *Origin of Species* is specula-tive knowledge, certainly; from a rhetorical point of view, however, it is also practical knowledge, the vehicle by means of which Darwin attempted to per-suade his fellow biologists to reconstitute their field, to alter their actions or their dispositions to act.

To call these intellectual activities rhetoric of science, then, is only to register a claim already staked and mined; to view these apparently distinct enterprises as rhetoric is merely to make available to all a coherent tradition, a set of well-used intellectual tools.

Rhetoric of science differs from literature and science, a branch of study that also "stars" its texts. The texts privileged by literature and science are traditionally literary; the science of an era is studied for its ability to illuminate the literary productions of that era: Katherine Hayles's *The Cosmic Web* trains the concepts of scientific field theory on a set of contemporary novels influenced by this theory. In contrast, rhetoric of science proposes by means of rhetorical analysis to increase our understanding of science, both in itself and as a component of an intellectual and social climate. From this perspective, when Gillian Beer studies the impact of Darwin on Victorian intellectual life, she is doing not literature and science but rhetoric of science.

To say that a rhetoric of science views its texts as rhetorical objects, designed to persuade, is not to deny that there is an aesthetic dimension to science. From a rhetorical point of view, however, this dimension can never be an end in itself; it is always a means of persuasion, a way of convincing scientists that some particular science is correct. In science, beauty is not enough: Descartes's physics is beautiful still, but it is not still physics.

• • •

LOGOS

The common topics are a staple of classical rhetorical invention; comparison, cause, definition—these and their fellows are the traditional places where rhetoricians can find arguments on any given topic. These same common topics are also an important source for arguments in science—in Newton, for example. In his *Opticks*, Newton defines a light ray twice. Early in this work he provides a definition in terms of the observable: light behaves *as if* it were made up of tiny particles. Later Newton defines light in terms of a hypothesis concerning the constitution of matter: light *may actually consist* of tiny particles. The difference in these definitions reflects a change in persuasive purpose. By means of the first definition, Newton hopes to persuade the skeptical scientist of the truth of his analysis of light; to agree, this scientist need not subscribe to Newton's speculative atomism. By means of the second, Newton hopes that this same scientist will seriously entertain atomism as a scientific hypothesis.

In Newton's optical works, the common topics are used heuristically as well as persuasively. Newton undermines Descartes's analysis of color by means of the topic of comparison: he contrasts Descartes's theory with his own incontrovertible experimental results. Concerned about the material constitution of light, he addresses the topic of cause: the sensation of light, he speculates, is evoked when its tiny particles impinge on the retina. In his presumption of the rectilinear propagation of light, he relies on the topic of authority; everybody since Aristotle has taken this as true.

In each case, we might say that Newton defines scientifically, compares scientifically. But in none of these instances is it possible to define a scientific sense for the common topics that is qualitatively distinct from their rhetorical sense: these sources for arguments in science and rhetoric do not differ in kind.

In addition to the common topics suitable to all argument, there are special topics that provide sources of argument for each of the three genres of speeches: forensic, deliberative, and epideictic. Forensic texts establish past fact; they are so named because their paradigm is the legal brief; their special topics are justice and injustice. Epideictic texts celebrate or calumniate events or persons of importance; their paradigms are the funeral oration and the philippic; their special topics are virtue and vice. Deliberative texts establish future policy; their paradigm is the political speech; their special topics are the advantageous and the disadvantageous, the worthy and the unworthy.

Scientific texts participate in each of these genres. A scientific report is forensic because it reconstructs past science in a way most likely to support its claims; it is deliberative because it intends to direct future research; it is epideictic because it is a celebration of appropriate methods. Analogously, scientific textbooks strive to incorporate all useful past science, to determine directions for future research, and to commend accepted methods. But science also has special topics of its own, unique sources for its arguments. Precise observation and prediction are the special topics of the experimental sciences; mathematicization is the special topic of the theoretical sciences. But there is considerable reciprocity. In the experimental sciences, mathematization is also a topic, and it provides arguments of the highest status; and in the theoretical sciences, at least by implication, arguments from mathematics are anchored in the special topics of prediction and observation.

But are observation, prediction, and mathematization *topics?* Science is an activity largely devoted to the fit between theories and their brute facts; the better the fit, the better the science. Surely, observation, prediction, and mathematization are not topics, but means to that end. In prediction, the confrontation between theory and brute fact is at its most dramatic. Einstein's theory of general relativity forecast the never-before observed bending of light in a gravitational field; Crick's theory of the genetic code predicted that an otherwise plausible variant—the codon UUU—would never occur. Both predictions insisted on the participation of nature; nature, not human beings, would clinch the argument. Einstein's theory was confirmed by the bending of stellar light as measured during a total eclipse; Crick's was disconfirmed by the discovery of a UUU codon. In both cases, it seems, we have left rhetoric behind. We seem to be in direct contact with the brute facts as the criterion for theoretical truth: stellar photographs in the first case, instrument readings in the second.

But this line of argument fails: in neither case did the brute facts point unequivocally in a particular theoretical direction. In fact, in no scientific case do uninterpreted brute facts—stellar positions, test-tube residues—confirm or disconfirm theories. The brute facts of science are stellar positions or test-tube residues *under a certain description;* and it is these descriptions that constitute meaning in the sciences. That there are brute facts unequivocally supportive of a particular theory, that at some point decisive contact is made between a theory and the naked reality whose working it accurately depicts, is a rhetorical, not a scientific, conviction. Observation, prediction, measurement, and their mathematization: these are sources for the arguments in science in the same way—exactly the same way—that the virtuous is the source of arguments for the epideictic orator.

The Structure of Argument. For Aristotle, scientific deduction differs in kind from its rhetorical counterpart. True, both are conducted according to the "laws" of thought. But rhetorical deduction is inferior for two reasons: it starts with uncertain premises, and it is enthymematic: it must rely on an audience to supply missing premises and conclusions. Since conclusions cannot be more certain than their premises, and since any argument is deficient in rigor that relies on audience participation for its completion, rhetorical deductions can yield, at best, only plausible conclusions. Rhetorical induction, reasoning from examples, is equally marked by Aristotle as inferior to its scientific counterpart because of its acknowledged inability to guarantee the certainty of its generalizations: examples illustrate rather than prove.

Aristotle notwithstanding, rhetorical and scientific reasoning differ not in kind but only in degree. No inductions can be justified with rigor: all commit the fallacy of affirming the consequent; as a result, all experimental generalizations illustrate reasoning by example. Deductive certainty is equally a chimera; it would require the uniform application of laws of thought, true in all possible worlds; the availability of certain premises; and the complete enumeration of deductive chains. But of no rule of logic—not even the "law" of contradiction—can we say that it applies in all possible worlds. Moreover, even were such universal rules available, they would operate not on certain premises but on stipulations and inductive generalizations. In addition, all deductive systems are enthymematic: the incompleteness of rhetorical deduction is different only in degree, not in kind, from the incompleteness of scientific deduction. No deductive logic is a closed system, all of whose premises can be stipulated; every deductive chain consists of a finite number of steps between each of which an infinite number may be intercalated (Davis and Hersh 1986, pp. 57–73). Because the logics of science and rhetoric differ only in degree, both are appropriate objects for rhetorical analysis.

ETHOS AND PATHOS

Scientists are not persuaded by *logos* alone; science is no exception to the rule that the persuasive effect of authority, of *ethos*, weighs heavily. The antiauthoritarian stance, the Galilean myth canonizing deviance, ought not to blind us to the pervasiveness of *ethos*, the burden of authority, as a source of scientific conviction. Indeed, the progress of science may be viewed as a dialectical contest between the authority sedimented in the training of scientists, an authority reinforced by social sanctions, and the innovative initiatives without which no scientist will be rewarded.

Innovation is the *raison d'être* of the scientific paper; yet in no other place is the structure of scientific authority more clearly revealed. By invoking the authority of past results, the initial sections of scientific papers argue for the importance and relevance of the current investigation; by citing the authority of past procedure, these sections establish the scientist's credibility as an investigator. All scientific papers, moreover, are embedded in a network of authority relationships: publication in a respected journal; behind that publication, a series of grants given to scientists connected with a well-respected research institution; within the text, a trail of citations highlighting the paper as the latest result of a vital and ongoing research program. Without this authoritative scaffolding, the innovative core of these papers—their sections on results, and their discussions—would be devoid of significance.

At times, the effects of scientific authority can be stultifying: collective intellectual inertia blocked the reception of heliocentric astronomy for more than a century; Newton's posthumous authority retarded the reemergence of the wave theory of light. At other times, perhaps more frequently, authority and innovation interact beneficially; consider heliocentric astronomy between Copernicus and Kepler, the theory of light between Descartes and Newton, the concept of evolution in Darwin's early thought: in each of these cases we can see the positive results of the dialectical contest between authority and innovation. These examples alert us to the fact that there is no necessary conflict between originality and deference. One of the persuasive messages of authority in science is the need to exceed authority; indeed, the most precious inheritance of science is the means by which its authority may be fruitfully exceeded: "Was du ererbt von deinen Vätern hast/Erwirb es, um es zu besitzen" ("You must earn what you inherit from your fathers; you must make it your own"; Goethe, quoted in Freud 1949, p. 123).

At the root of authority within science is the relationship of master to disciple. To become a scientist is to work under men and women who are already scientists; to become a scientific authority is to submit for an extended period to existing authorities. These authorities embody in their work and thought whatever of past thought and practice is deemed worthwhile; at the same time, they are exemplars of current thought and practice. In their lectures, they say what should be said; in their laboratories, they do what should be done; in their papers, they write what should be written.

As long as science is taught as a craft, through extended apprenticeship, its routes to knowledge will be influenced by the relationships between masters and disciples. The modern history of heliocentricity is one of progress from epicycles to ellipses. But this theoretical development was realized only through a chain of masters and disciples, surrogate fathers and adopted sons: Copernicus and Rheticus, Maestlin and Kepler. By this means, research traditions are founded, and the methodological and epistemological norms that determine the legitimacy of arguments are passed on as tacit knowledge.

An examination of the forms of authority within science reminds us that epistemological and methodological issues cannot be separated from the social context in which they arise: the early members of the Royal Society decided what science was, how it would be accomplished, how validated, how rewarded. But we need also to be reminded of another set of authority relationships: those between science and society at large. It was the paradoxical promise of early science that it would benefit society best when wholly insulated from larger social concerns. This ideological tenet becomes difficult to justify, however, in an age of nuclear power and gene recombination. Justification is especially difficult when science converts its exceptional prestige into a political tool to protect its special interests, perhaps at the expense of the general interest. The recombinant DNA controversy is a case in point.

Emotional appeals are clearly present in the social interactions of which science is the product. In fact, an examination of these interactions reveals the prominent use of such appeals: the emotions are plainly involved, for instance, in peer review procedures and in priority disputes. Anger and indignation are harnessed in the interest of a particular claim; they are part of the machinery of persuasion. When science is under attack, in cases of proposed research in controversial areas, emotional appeals become central. The instance of proposed research in gene recombination is a good example of the fundamental involvement of science in issues of public policy, and of the deep commitment of scientists to a particular social ideology.

In addition, the general freedom of scientific prose from emotional appeal must be understood not as neutrality but as a deliberate abstinence: the assertion of a value. The objectivity of scientific prose is a carefully crafted rhetorical invention, a nonrational appeal to the authority of reason; scientific reports are the product of verbal choices designed to capitalize on the attractiveness of an enterprise that embodies a convenient myth, a myth in which, apparently, reason has subjugated the passions. But the disciplined denial of emotion in science is only a tribute to our passionate investment in its methods and goals.

In any case, the denial of emotional appeal is imperfectly reflected in the scientific texts themselves. The emotions, so prominent in peer review documents and in priority disputes, are no less insistently present in scientific papers, though far less prominent. In their first paper Watson and Crick say of their DNA model that it "has novel features which are of considerable biological interest" (1953b, p. 737). In his paper on the convertibility of mass and energy, Einstein says: "It is not impossible that with bodies whose energy-content is variable to a high degree (e.g., with radium salts) the theory may be successfully put to the test" (1952, pp. 67–71). In these sentences, key words and phrases—"novel," "interest," "successfully," "put to the test"—retain their ordinary connotations. Moreover, in Watson and Crick, "considerable" is clearly an understatement: the topic is the discovery of the structure of the molecule that controls the genetic fate of all living organisms.

Our science is a uniquely European product barely three centuries old, a product whose rise depended on a refocusing of our general interests and values. Its wellspring was the widening conviction that the eventualities of the natural order depended primarily not on supernatural or human intervention but on the operation of fixed laws whose preferred avenue of discovery and verification was quantified sensory experience. The ontological results of this epistemological preference defined the essence of nature and founded a central Western task: to control nature through an understanding of its laws. To this task, the specific values of science—such as the Mertonian norms of universalism and organized skepticism—are instrumentally subordinate. Equally subordinate are the values on which theory choice depends: simplicity, elegance, power. In such a view, *ethos, pathos,* and *logos* are naturally present in scientific texts: as a fully human enterprise, science can constrain, but hardly eliminate, the full range of persuasive choices on the part of its participants.

• • •

Paul Feyerabend

From Against Method

Thus science is much closer to myth than a scientific philosophy is prepared to admit. It is one of the many forms of thought that have been developed by man, and not necessarily the best. It is conspicuous, noisy, and impudent, but it is inherently superior only for those who have already decided in favour of a certain ideology, or who have accepted it without ever having examined its advantages and its limits. And as the accepting and rejecting of ideologies should be left to the individual it follows that the separation of state and church must be complemented by the separation of state and science, that most recent, most aggressive, and most dogmatic religious institution. Such a separation may be our only chance to achieve a humanity we are capable of, but have never fully realized.

The idea that science can, and should, be run according to fixed and universal rules, is both unrealistic and pernicious. It is *unrealistic,* for it takes too simple a view of the talents of man and of the circumstances which encourage, or cause, their development. And it is *pernicious,* for the attempt to enforce the rules is bound to increase our professional qualifications at the expense of our humanity. In addition, the idea is *detrimental to science,* for it neglects the complex physical and historical conditions which influence scientific change. It makes our science less adaptable and more dogmatic: every methodological rule is associated with cosmological assumptions, so that using the rule we take it for granted that the assumptions are correct. Naive falsificationism takes it for granted that the laws of nature are manifest and not hidden beneath disturbances of considerable magnitude. Empiricism takes it for granted that sense experience is a better mirror of the world than pure thought. Praise of argument takes it for granted that the artifices of Reason give better results than the unchecked play of our emotions. Such assumptions may be perfectly plausible *and even true.* Still, one should occasionally put them to a test. Putting them to a test means that we stop using the methodology associated with them, start doing science in a different way and see what happens. Case studies such as those reported in the preceding chapters show that such tests occur all the time, and that they speak *against* the universal validity of any rule. All methodologies have their limitations and the only 'rule' that survives is 'anything goes'.

Modern science, on the other hand, is not at all as difficult and as perfect as scientific propaganda wants us to believe. A subject such as medicine, or physics, or biology appears difficult only because it is taught badly, because the standard instructions are full of redundant material, and because they start too late in life. During the war, when the American Army needed physicians within a very short time, it was suddenly possible to reduce medical instruction to half a year (the corresponding instruction manuals have disappeared long ago, however. Science may be simplified during the war. In peacetime the prestige of science demands greater complication.) And how often does it not happen that the proud and conceited judgement of an expert is put in its proper place by a layman! Numerous inventors built 'impossible' machines. Lawyers show again and again that an expert does not know what he is talking about. Scientists, especially physicians, frequently come to different results so that it is up to the relatives of the sick person (or the inhabitants of a certain area) to decide *by vote* about the procedure to be adopted. How often is science improved, and turned into new directions by non-scientific influences! It is up to us, it is up to the citizens of a free society to either accept the chauvinism of science without contradiction or to overcome it by the counterforce of public action. Public action was used against science by the Communists in China in the fifties, and it was again used, under very different circumstances, by some opponents of evolution in California in the seventies. Let us follow their example and let us free society from the strangling hold of an ideologically petrified science just as our ancestors freed *us* from the strangling hold of the One True Religion!

The way towards this aim is clear. A science that insists on possessing the only correct method and the only acceptable results is ideology and must be separated from the state, and especially from the process of education. One may teach it, but only to those who have decided to make this particular superstition their own. On the other hand, a science that has dropped such totalitarian pretensions is no longer independent and self-contained, and it can be taught in many different combinations (myth and modern cosmology might be one such combination). Of course, every business has the right to demand that its practitioners be prepared in a special way, and it may even demand acceptance of a certain ideology (I for one am against the thinning out of subjects so that they become more and more similar to each other; whoever does not like present-day Catholicism should leave it and become a Protestant, or an Atheist, instead of ruining it by such inane changes as mass in the vernacular). That is true of physics, just as it is true of religion, or of prostitution. But such special ideologies, such special skills have no room in the process of *general education* that prepares a citizen for his role in society. A mature citizen is not a man who has been *instructed* in a special ideology, such as Puritanism, or critical rationalism, and who now carries this ideology with him like a mental tumour, a mature citizen is a person who has learned how to make up his mind and who has then *decided* in favour of what he thinks suits him best. He is a person who has a certain mental toughness (he does not fall for the first ideological street singer he happens to meet) and who is therefore able *consciously to choose* the business that seems to be most attractive to him rather than being swallowed by it. To prepare himself for his choice he will study

Herbert Schnädelbach

"Against Feyerabend"

---

*"Despise but reason or science or both—the highest of all mankind's gifts—
and you have surrendered to the devil and to perdition are doomed". (Free
adaptation of Hegel's free adaptation of Goethe)*

". . . the propaganda which is termed 'argumentation' "—A debate with a
Dadaist is not without its dangers, for if you take him or her seriously, you are
the very least in danger of making a laughing stock out of yourself. "The
Dadaist's favorite pastime is confounding rationalists by inventing compelling
reasons for irrational theories". One might be inclined to dismiss Feyerabend as
a philosophical clown—"it is jokes, entertainment, and illusion that are liberating, and not 'truth' "—were it not for the fact that he is not amusing enough to
fit the role. If you criticize him in such a way as to annoy him, then you know
what to expect: namely to be classified as a "someone who reads only on
Sundays", an "illiterate", or a "propagandist".

• • •

". . . that reason is not a standard for our thoughts and action, but itself a particular form of thinking and acting, on the same level as other forms of thought
and action."

For over a decade now Feyerabend has been trying to shock people whom he
seems to be painfully fixated on, yet of whom it is not quite clear whether they
actually exist or not: the rationalists, the ratiomanics, and the ratiofascists.
Admittedly, it has to be left to the observer whether s/he actually feels injured
or not. As a rule, the response will probably be "how refreshing!" and s/he will
be happy that once again it is the others who are the target. Feyerabend is not
against reason; far from it; it is only a matter of pruning reason down to the
appropriate size. And it is circumstances which determine what is appropriate:
"There may, of course, come a time when it will be necessary to give reason a
temporary advantage and when it will be wise to defend its rules to the exclusion of everything else. I do not think that we are living in such a time today".

Against this it would be simplest to exclaim "Objection: I think we are!" and the discussion would already be over. . . . But we had wanted the focus to be on argumentation. Let us thus investigate more closely that with which Feyerabend believes he can maintain a tactical relationship, namely "reason", "rationality". For him, rationalism is "the idea that there are general rules and standards for conducting out affairs." Rationality is, for the rationalist, "agreement with certain general rules and standards", and the rationalist desires "that people always act rationally (in this sense, H.S.)". It may well be that someone has defined "reason" to be something like this—and that person should thus also be compelled to regard programmed computers, trained bats, indeed even washing machines, as rational. Is it reasonable to define rationality in such a manner? Did Karl Popper, the "propagandist" and an "established" philosopher, define it thus? Feyerabend continually confuses the rational and the obsessive-compulsive, and yet he nevertheless believes he must "instruct" the rationalists. Instead of immediately setting out to combat all the compulsions in the world—I would gladly join ranks in such an undertaking—it would be better if we were first to ask ourselves what it is that distinguishes a rational person from his/her obsessive-compulsive counterpart. To my mind, the rational person not only obeys simple universal rules and standards, but also has them at his/her *disposal*: s/he *controls* them and not vice versa. The *use* of these rules and standards must also be reasonable, and it is obvious that this implies not merely following rules, for this would just involve a meta-compulsion. Philosophers have always been aware of this. One needs think only of the manner in which Aristotle describes *logistikon* or *phrónesis*. After all, why does Kant introduce *judgment* into the argument. He states that "deficiency in judgment is just what is ordinarily called stupidity, and for such a failing there is no remedy". What Feyerabend attacks as the "reason" of the rationalists is simply stupidity and "even the Gods battle against it in vain". Even the critical rationalists cannot simply be accused of stupidity if they in principle think that their principle of criticism can be criticized; if things look different in practice and they really have founded a "barren, dogmatic church" then it was at least not the fault of the principle involved.

• • •

Kenneth L. Pike

"Language as Particle, Wave, and Field"

What is the nature of language? What are its parts? How is the structure of language related to structural problems in other areas of investigation?

Language, in my view, can be viewed profitably from three distinct standpoints. One of these is traditional, and views language as made up of PARTICLES—'things', pieces, or parts, with sharp borders. The second view is not at all thought of in lay circles perhaps, and is largely neglected on the technical front. This second view treats language as made up, not of parts which are separated one from the other and added like bricks on a row, but rather as being made up of WAVES following one another. This second view is one which I have recently been developing, and leads to some very stimulating insights as to the nature of language structure. A third view consists in viewing structure as a total FIELD. Technicians have studied semantic fields as part of language, but the handling of the concept systematically in terms of the more ordinary structuring of sentences has not even been attempted. Some components which could enter such a possible view, however, have been developed for other purposes, and I have found the concept fruitful in certain practical situations of applied linguistics.

These three views of language can be summarized in different terms. Language, seen as made up of particles, may be viewed as if it were STATIC—permanent bricks juxtaposed in a permanent structure, or as separate 'frames' in a moving-picture film. The view of language made up of waves sees language as DYNAMIC—waves of behavioral movement merging one into another in intricate, overlapping, complex systems. The view of language as made up of field sees language as FUNCTIONAL, as a system with parts and classes of parts so interrelated that no parts occur apart from their function in the total whole, which in turn occurs only as the product of these parts in functional relation to a meaningful social environment.

It is extraordinary that in the twentieth century we should still be viewing language almost entirely from a static, particle-like view rather than in a dynamic fashion. Only recently have approaches of a dynamic type begun to appear. In my own work the insistence on a wavelike hierarchical blending and fusion of units is designed in part to fill this gap. In the so-called 'prosodic' approach in London, developed by Firth and his colleagues, there are also dynamic elements.

In spite of the importance of the wave and field concepts of language we shall first, however, discuss the structure of language as made up of particles, since it is easiest for us to grasp psychologically, closest to the lay view of language, and most fully developed in technical exposition. (Later, we will affirm that each of the three views must be retained, supplementing one another, if we wish to preserve an empirically and theoretically adequate view of language.) This particle view reflects a commonsense attitude: Language is made up of words, with sharp boundaries between them. A language, for some people, would appear to be ideally comprised of a dictionary. Once one has the dictionary of a language one seems to have under control the heart of the language, if one thinks in this way. This view appears to be very common in some areas of our culture.

A more sophisticated particle view aims at an analysis of great simplicity. It attempts to reduce high-level language structures to combinations of a few small units in more and more restricted groupings. The unit chosen is the sound—the PHONEME—or a component of a phoneme. If one has a list of the sounds and the possible restrictions on the combination of these sounds, one is assumed to know the structure of the language. This view—though I have oversimplified it—has had high prestige in the United States in the past few years.

Harris has attempted, for example, to study the combinatorial structure of language without reference to meaning and has attempted to go as far as possible in finding the lexical units—the MORPHEMES—by purely distributional techniques. That is, by studying the fashion in which one sound may follow another, he has tried to arrive at successive groupings of sounds in structurally significant combinations on higher and higher levels of organization until the words and sentences are analyzed without reference to the meaning or identification of the morphemes or words or sentences as such. For example, after a sequence of sounds such as represented by the English letters *I th-o-u-g-h-t th-*, there are only a few specific letters which could follow, such as *a* of the word *that*. (The scholars referred to, however, would be very careful to handle such a problem in reference to the pronounced sounds, not in reference to spelling by letters.) Here, then, is a 'thing-centered' view of language, but with the particular parts made up of small sound units rather than of word units. It tends towards a philosophical reductionism, with sounds or sound components as the ultimate and only primitive units and with all other units as merely combinations of these in a distributional relationship.

This view has been very fruitful in stimulating linguistic discussion and development. Some of us feel, however, that characteristics inherent in language structure will prevent its complete fulfillment. (The pendulum has in the last year or two begun to swing for these authors, however, away from complete rejection of meaning to a basic reliance upon it in specified areas of study. Harris, for example, now treats of some grammatical problems in which a basic constant necessary to identify the relations between, for example, *John hit Bill* and *Bill was hit by John* is a retention of certain lexical meanings. He appears to avoid destroying his earlier work—that based on an attempted rejection of meaning-relevance in grammar—by a semantic device. He calls the one type 'combinatorial' or 'descriptive' grammar, and the kind based on meaning relations 'transform' grammar. In my view, a synthesis of these extremes into a single hierarchical approach would seem to reflect the data more effectively.) Most linguists have not in practice attempted as formally 'rigorous' an analysis of language into meaningless discrete parts as this latter view seems to imply (with 'rigor' used in a mathematical sense as 'nonintuitive'—rather than as 'coherent, consistent presentation of the data'). Nevertheless, the development of the analysis both of the phoneme and of the morpheme is very intricate, very extensive, and represents one of the greatest achievements of twentieth-century linguistic science.

A phoneme may include within its various pronunciations a large number of different varieties of pronunciation. The *t* at the beginning of the word *time,* for example, is much different from the single consonant sound in the middle of an American pronunciation of *Betty* (which in turn is very different from the pronunciation of the *t* in *bought*). (The first has a puff of breath following it, the second is made by a quick flip of the tongue, and the last may be heard sometimes as cut off rather sharply at the end of an utterance.) Some scholars, however, prefer to work more extensively with a unit smaller than the phoneme as the basic unit, namely one or more of the components which make up the phoneme, as atoms can make up a molecule. The sound *d,* for example, has a component of voicing—produced by the vibrating vocal chords—as well as a component of mouth closure by tongue tip, plus a component of nasal passage closure by the soft palate, and so on.

The second unit, the morpheme, would include such lexical items as *boy, dog, house,* and, in addition, meaningful lexical units such as the suffix *-s* of *cups* or the prefix *un-* of *unpleasant.* Morphemes, like phonemes, have been studied heavily in reference to their varieties. The plural suffix *-s* of *cups,* for example, occurs in a special form *-es,* in *houses,* and in further forms in *feet, children,* and *data.* The development of techniques to discover, describe, and systematize the phonemic and morphemic variants has required a great deal of research by some of the most competent linguistic scholars of our generation and is by no means finished.

While still keeping within the view of language as made up of parts, pieces, or units, a third small unit, it appears to me, must be postulated. This is a unit of grammar, comparable to the units of phonology and lexicon just discussed. Some of my recent research has been the introduction of a TAGMEME unit into linguistic theory, on a par with the phoneme and the morpheme. (The term itself is given to us by Bloomfield, although his particular attempt to define, describe, or isolate such a unit has not been fruitful and has not entered into current linguistic theory or practice.) The new concept (of the same name) has already proved helpful in analyzing languages in field situations. The layman would recognize some such units or unit classes if he were told, for example, that there may be in an English sentence several kinds of subject, each of which is a separate tagmeme. Thus a subject-as-actor unit in the sentence *John came home* would be one tagmeme, whereas subject-as-person-affected would be a distinct tagmeme in the sentence *John was hit by Bill.*

In my current researches I am applying to such units the same kind of linguistic development which has been so successfully applied to the phoneme and morpheme. Variants of tagmemes occur just as one finds variants of phonemes and morphemes. A subject variant, for example, might be a simple one such as *John* in the sentence just quoted, or a complex subject in a sentence such as *My big Johnny came home yesterday.* Both the simple subject and complex subject here are variants of the English subject-as-actor tagmeme. The tagmeme concept, it should be noted, resists the reductionism of language structure to meaningless sounds. It points in the direction both of preserving a meaningful lexical unit and of introducing a meaningful grammar unit as primitive terms in linguistic theory.

The structure of a complex word in the Candoshi language of northern Peru may serve to illustrate the way morpheme, phoneme, and tagmeme pieces function together. (The data utilized are chosen from those published by Doris Cox in the *International Journal of American Linguistics* and by Lorrie Anderson and me in *Lingua Posnaniensis*.) In the word *kopáako* 'She washes' the consonants and vowels are quite audible and easily analyzed with an 'ordinary' (from the English viewpoint) stress on the first part of the second syllable. A few 'special' sounds, however, occur in the language. The phrase 'She cooks', for example, differs from the one quoted only by the fact that the first vowel is whispered rather than spoken aloud. We may write that vowel with a capital letter thus: *kOpáako*. Only once elsewhere in the history of the world, in the information which has reached me, has careful documentation been published of this phenomenon; this other instance concerns the Comanche of Oklahoma, as found in the researches of Canonge. (Such differences are highly important to Bible translators, such as Cox and Anderson, in pairs of words such as these, in passages like Revelation 1:5 " [Christ] washed us from our sins in His own blood". In a head-shrinking or cannibal culture these must not be confused!)

The consonants and vowels make up the parts which, going together, produce words. Compare the word *táyanchshatana* which means 'I have stayed there then'. It is made up of the parts *tá* (the stem, 'to be'); *ya* 'recently'; *nch* 'completely'; *sha* 'next'; *t* 'individually'; *a* 'I'; *na* 'emphatically';—that is, 'Emphatically-I-individually-next-completely-and-recently-was-there'.

In turn these morphemes, made up of phonemes, are members of classes of morphemes which are replaceable in particular slots in a potential structure. The combination of such a functional slot, along with the class of morphemes which can fill that slot, makes up one of the tagmemes interior to the verb. Note the chart of independent indicative suffixes (Fig. 1), which suggests how (with certain unimportant exceptions) words—among them the word quoted—can be made on this particular 'mapping' pattern. The ± on the chart means that a particular class is optional in the verb. The ∓ followed by ± within the parentheses indicates that some one or more of these classes must be represented. A + indicates obligatory occurrence of some member of the class in every word of that type. In the particular form quoted, furthermore, certain special sub-varieties of these morphemes occur. In our illustration above, for example, the first person instead of being represented by the vowel -*i* is represented by -*a* (which is found always replacing -*i* after the *t*), while the normal variety -*ya* 'emphatic', is replaced following *i* by a variety spelled -*na*, which is especially restricted to its occurrence there.

With some special restrictions, any morpheme can be chosen from its respective column to go toward making up a word.

Other quite different mapping must be made for independent desiderative suffixes, independent imperative suffixes, independent optative suffixes, dependent conditional suffixes, and nonpersonal dependent suffixes.

The tagmemes in the chart are represented (1) by the column (which indicates

±	±	±	+(∓	±	±	±)	±	+	±
-ka locative	-ya recent	-ran past	-k indicative	-ma durative	-ch incomplete	-sha 2nd order	-t individualizer	-i 1st person singular	-ya emphatic
-mpa intensive	-ta punctiliar		-r current	-shin movement	-nch complete	-masi 1st order		-ish 2nd person singular	-pa potential
				-tar habitual				-o 3rd person singular	-shi negative
				-ts possible				-ini 1st person plural	-a interrogative
								-is 2nd person plural	
								-ana 3rd person plural	
								-ich impersonal	

Fig. 1. Chart of independent indicative suffixes.

the functional positions of the suffixes), correlated (2) with the particular class of morphemes listed in that column. For the learning of the language, such a chart provides the morphemes and tagmemes upon which practical substitution drills can be based for the assimilation of the language structure.

The minimal particles—phoneme, morpheme, tagmeme—are not the only 'particles', however, which some of us treat as basic. Each of the three is rather, in a hierarchical view of language, merely the smallest unit of several units in an increasing complexity of organization leading to larger and larger units. The phonological minimal unit of sound (the phoneme) is part of a larger phonological unit which may be called the SYLLABLE.

In much of the technical linguistics in America during the past two decades, however, due to a phonological reductionism and nonhierarchical treatment, the syllable has either been denied theoretical status or ignored in theoretical treatments. It is only within the last few years that this unit, so well known to the layman, has begun to be handled in our country by more structural theoreticians. The reason for this has been a kind of reductionism which has wished to eliminate all higher level units of complexity as primitive terms (although occasionally they replace these units, in description, with units of the same name which were defined merely as aggregations of sequences of lower level units; that is to say, that the term SYLLABLE while appearing in such writings would be treated not as a new KIND of unit, but merely as the resultant of specific distributions of sounds which gave the characteristic effect we call syllables). A scholar by the name of Stetson for many years objected to this, but only recently has his work had the impact necessary to force a few structuralists to begin to work the syllable into their theories as both a physiological and distributional element.

Above and beyond the syllable in size and complexity within the phonological hierarchy lie other units. These include the stress group (or rhythm unit), the pause group, and other units with phonological characteristics such as the rhetorical period.

In a hierarchical approach we assume that the morpheme is at the base of a lexical hierarchy, distinct from the phonological hierarchy in structure. Groups of morphemes make up specific words on a higher level of that hierarchy. Thus *boy* plus *-s* makes up the word *boys*.

For the layman, some of the most easily seen units on the next levels of the lexical hierarchy are idioms. *To step on the gas* is a high-level unit of the lexical hierarchy. It differs from a different kind of high unit, *putting one's foot on top of the gasoline*. Still higher in this same hierarchy are items like sonnets, limericks, and other integrated specific verbal pieces.

The grammatical hierarchy, on the other hand, may be illustrated as proceeding from a particular kind of subject (but with the particular subject unspecified—whether it be *John, Bill, Joe*) to a higher unit such as a subject–predicate complex which makes up a clause. Clauses in turn make up complex sentences, and so on. The problem of distinguishing between the lexical and grammatical hierarchies is a very technical one which is crucial to this point of view—but which at the moment seems to be more in doubt from the point of view of the technician than from that of the layman. I shall not set forth here the intricate arguments which I have been developing to attempt to make the essentiality of this distinction clear to my colleagues.

Thus far it has been difficult to show how modern linguistics and current literary criticism have much in common, although some scholars such as Hill and Jakobson have attempted to exploit this area. It seems to me clear, however, that once linguistics turns its attention more fully to higher hierarchical levels, it will begin to look at many of the problems which have taken part of the attention of literary scholars. In some of their formal aspects, linguistics study and literary study of such high-level units might mutually complement one another in a way more fruitful than can be seen at present.

In my own hierarchical emphasis, for example, I am attempting to develop techniques by which the separate lexical, phonological, and grammatical hierarchies can maintain their identity in the analysis, and yet at the same time, the intricate overlappings between each of the three, at various levels of the three, can be pointed out. It seems to me that one would achieve only a 'flat' picture of communication—especially of literary communication—if one were to attempt to treat literary structure exclusively with low-level units such as phoneme, morpheme, and tagmeme. Even when these three are supplemented by studies of pause, intonation, and stress—as is currently being done—the result comes far from reaching the subtlety of actual literary communication. It would seem to me that the subtlety with which the poet operates can begin to be analyzed or approximated by the linguist only when he is able to study the crisscrossing of effects of one hierarchy upon another at various levels. The level of sound-sequence structure must be seen to affect the choice of words, as in alliteration. The level of word choice affects the structure of syllable-type sequences, for meter. The level of grammatical functional units provides key turning points for forced interpretation of homophonous words or for simultaneous dual meanings of passages. The simultaneous double function of one physical unit in two separate hierarchies, or on two levels of one hierarchy, allows for some of the extraordinary richness of interplay of subtle innuendo which must be accounted for if one is to analyze literary composition. These and other items not adequately explored by the linguist must be developed further in a hierarchical multiphase conceptual framework before the linguist can hope to have full converse with his literary colleagues.

Nevertheless, once these views are developed more fully, it is clear that a particle view of language will allow for an understanding of an enormous amount of complexity built from a few elegantly simple items such as morpheme, phoneme, and tagmeme in intricate crisscrossing hierarchical arrangements.

Once one has sensed the thrill of understanding language organization as such an interweaving of sound and sound complexes, lexical units and lexical complexes, grammatical units and grammatical complexes, it comes as a shock to find that despite this insight it is possible to deny the relevance of almost every statement made thus far by beginning from a different point of view. Language, one can affirm, is not made up of particles at all! Language contains no phonemes, no morphemes, no tagmemes! One must not go around looking for bits and pieces, whether small or large, whether on a low hierarchical level like phonemes and morphemes, or on a higher hierarchical level like syllables, pieces of sentences.

In this second view there are no sounds as such, no syllables as such, no words as such, no isolatable sentences as such. Rather what one meets is a constant flux of total physiological or acoustic movement in a total physiological or acoustic field. Here, language is seen as a sequence of waves of activity; the train of waves is one continuous behavioral event. That which was labelled earlier as a sequence of 'separate' sounds would in this view be nothing but a series of waves of movement or of sound with the peak of a particular wave identifying the place in a sequence where a particular 'segment' was supposed to have occurred.

One's natural view of a language sequence, after one has been taught to read by letters of an alphabet, is that there are little 'gaps' between each pair of sounds in a sequence. Sounds would appear to hang together by some kind of mysterious, invisible cement. But in the view which we must now consider, the wave view, no such thing occurs. Investigation by acoustic instruments shows that the sound sequence may be a continuous unbroken chain. In a sentence such as *Bob did go there?* no single gap appears in the acoustic record. One sound flows into another with no point at which the voice completely ceases. Where, then, are the 'separate' sounds? They have disappeared.

This conclusion is strengthened by articulatory studies through motion-picture X rays in which one sees that the articulations of the mouth form continuous sweeping movements. There are no points of rest in a rapid sentence to allow for gaps between sounds.

What then shall we do to salvage in some fashion the idea of 'sounds'? And units of sound? The answer, in part, is that we must treat sounds not as separate bits or pieces but as waves in a wave train. At the peak of each movement—at the peak of a 'wave of articulation'—we recognize the fact that a sound has been uttered even though the borders between the sounds are not sharp-cut. That is, we replace the concept of a bead-like separation with that of a wave fusion, but retain the general idea of sounds as sounds in a fused sequence. This leads tentatively to a 'wave segmentation', with no sharp division of sounds at their borders, but with the general principle of units in sequence undisturbed.

Even this comfort, however, is soon torn from us. Joos tells us that if one pronounces syllables such as *pop* versus *tot* and records them on tape, and if one then, with a pair of scissors, cuts off the consonants from the tape at the point where segmentation would seem to occur by either a particle view or a wave view of the type just mentioned, and if one then plays back on the recorder the vowel sound only, the two syllables are still distinguishable as *pop* and *tot*! This extraordinary and unexpected result forces us to investigations which show clearly that not only is there fusion at the points where sounds bump into one another in the sequence, but that sounds which are 'due to appear' late in the sequence may actually be in part anticipated early in a sequence. The anticipation affects the early sounds. And sounds which appear early in the sequence, from the point of view of normal, ordinary segmentation, actually decay so slowly in articulation and resultant effect that their influence is felt late in the sequence.

Practical phoneticians recognize, furthermore, that these anticipatory or decay characteristics of a sound are oftentimes extremely important for the recognition of the sound. If, for example, one wishes to listen to certain kinds of *r* sounds or pharyngeal consonants, it is frequently much easier for the beginner to 'recognize' the presence of the consonants by listening to the neighboring vowels which are modified by these consonants than it is to try to listen directly to the consonants themselves. More recent acoustic experiments on the nature of perception would seem to indicate that this is true not only for the phonetics beginner, but that to some extent it reflects the normal experience of the native speaker.

Where does this lead us? Certainly to the view that sounds cannot be considered as segmentable in the sense that one can cut up with a pair of scissors a sequence on tape and have left in segment form all the relevant components of one sound after another. It leads to the view that the totality of any one sound is not necessarily found in any one segmentable section of the sequence. Rather, part of the sound's relevant characteristics may be at the wave peak in the sequence, but various other parts may be extended forwards and backwards over several segments. Since this is true in experiment and practice, where then does a 'sound' lie? AND HOW CAN ONE SPEAK OF A 'PARTICLE' ANY MORE? The particle view is seen to be inadequate at this point.

Does the wave view, however, do any better? Yes. To begin with we spoke of a wave view as if it dealt with a train of waves as in Fig. 2.

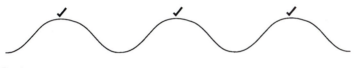

Fig. 2

This diagram would imply that one sound 'follows' another; that at each peak (identified by a little check above it) a sound is heard, but that the borders fuse into each other in the troughs of the waves. Our later comments implied that this diagram must be revised, however, in order to allow for the overlapping characteristics which we discussed. Note the diagram of Fig. 3.

Fig. 3

In this diagram each wave begins and ends at the same two spots respectively. The difference in the waves is in the place where they come to a peak, and in the relative concentration of their characteristics at any one spot in the total sequence. The linguistic interpretation of such a sequence includes the fact that there are a number of sounds, phonemes, each sound identified by its respective peak, but with its borders completely indeterminable. Borders within the continuum cannot be found by any practical experiment, on the one hand, and from the theoretical point of view it is hopeless to expect to develop future experiments to do so inasmuch as their characteristics are smeared throughout. Here, then, seems to be the death of a simple particle view. It would appear that a wave view must replace it. (Later, however, we shall affirm that BOTH the particle AND the wave view must be retained simultaneously.)

What has been said for sounds applies also to syllables, on a higher level of the phonological hierarchy. Syllables may occasionally be sharply separated—just as on occasion sounds may be sharply separated—but on other occasions they may fuse in such ways that the borders between them are not clear. Thus in *bad dog* a boundary may be clear in slow speech, but in *biting,* the *t* phoneme comes at the syllable juncture and makes indeterminate the point at which the first syllable begins or ends. This is similar to the fact that phonemes fuse into one another at their border points. Syllables may also be partially anticipatory of each other, within higher units of the phonological hierarchy, so that their phonetic characteristics must in part be picked out as waves just as phoneme characteristics must. Syllables, too, disappear as 'particles'—as sharp-cut segments—and can only be identified by peaks in a complex wave train. Similarly, on a still higher level of the phonological hierarchy, stress groups fuse into one another within pause groups, and so on.

The general relation of a low-level unit to its including high-level unit may be made more clear by an analogy: The small phoneme waves may be related to the higher syllable waves and to the still higher stress group waves much as a ripple may occur on a wavelet which is part of a wave which is part of an ocean swell. All may be seen at once, all interrelated, and yet none exists without the other. A further figure of speech—though it must be used with caution—suggests that a stress-group wave is like a low harmonic, a syllable wave a higher harmonic, and a phoneme a still higher harmonic. These articulatory movements all fuse into a total articulatory complex which in turn produces a single complex sound wave which reflects components of these differing articulatory wave sources.

It is not only in the phonological sphere that particles seem to disappear and waves to appear, once attention is focused in this direction. It is true also with units of the lexical hierarchy. Thus, for example, if one says *as you like,* slowly, the words *as* and *you* may be quite distinct. If, however, the pronunciation is speeded up, the *-s* and *y-* usually fuse into a single palatal sibilant which is technically only one segment in length. Now a difficult question of linguistic theory arises: Should that one sibilant be considered part of the first word but not of the second? Or part of the second word but not of the first? Or should it be somehow divided into components so that the sibilant component belongs to the first word but the palatal component belongs to the second? Current particle linguistic theory has no answer to this question except the arbitrary one which leaves alternate solutions equally valid (although a particular linguist may find one of the solutions preferable or more economic for certain purposes). Our wave view of language, however, would insist that all three of these answers are artificial and that the empirical facts require that one flatly refuse to segment at such points. One must rather insist that the two words *as* and *you* have an indeterminate border which is fused in a wave-like fashion. In spite of this fusion the PRESENCE of the two words is fully clear, in that the vocalic peak of each of the words serves as the peak of the syllables by which the two words are respectively pronounced. The wave view insists, furthermore, that this indeterminancy is an essential part of a language—the wave-like fusion of forms in sequence—and that, rather than force an artificial segmentation upon language, one should adopt a wave theory of language which does not require this artificial treatment.

Going still further, one can look for illustrations on the lexical level which are somewhat parallel to the phonological ones wherein there was anticipation and decay of sounds which affected more than adjacent sounds. For example, in such a pronunciation of *Why did not you go?* as *Wainchago* the total pronunciation of *did* may disappear; *not* also may disappear as such (including the segment *n* written here), except for a residue of nasalization throughout the first syllable or two. The abstraction of these words from the total sequence cannot then be easily handled by a particle theory, whereas wave theory has not yet remotely come to the place where it can systematically handle such things smoothly. Nevertheless, the wave theory toward which I am pointing indicates clearly that some such approach must be developed if we are to handle language as it actually functions.

In grammar, also, such fusions exist in grammatical situations where one word functions doubly in two constructions. Note, for example, the following sentence (from Fries) in which the second *have* serves simultaneously in reference to the infinitive relation and in reference to the verb *pay*: *They have to have the students pay.*

The language of a wave view may include words such as PROCESS, DYNAMICS, CHANGE, FUSION, and the like. The language of particles includes phrases such as IS FOUND IN SUCH AND SUCH DISTRIBUTION, OCCURS UNDER THESE CONDITIONS, IS ENCOUNTERED IN VARIOUS ALTERNATE FORMS, etc. Currently the latter set of terms is in favor in the United States because of the heavy emphasis upon a particle view. The earlier set of terms was found in earlier American literature of a generation ago, but has been largely abandoned in current presentations. In a wave view of language, these former terms must be re-utilized, with more careful definition. A wave view implies process, development, change, and fusion.

It would seem probable, also, that no variety of a static, particle view of language can provide the most useful conceptual framework for the description of dynamic historical change. Within a wave view of language, change over a period of time or over a geographical area could presumably be described more easily through intermediate, transitional, fusion stages than is provided by a particle view. To allow for this approach, however, one must assume that fusion can take place not only between particular segments in a sequence, but between systems in time, and that these systems in some sense act as waves with identifiable components.

It is here that the wave view is seen to be a dynamic one. The dynamics of change in time are the dynamics of waves of movement of one system to another system with indeterminate areas between. In a historical change one system does not cease and another one begin with a gap between them. Rather there are transition states. And yet all is not transition in a single 'flat' sense. Rather there are periods and peaks when certain items or certain phases of systems are prominent. The dynamics of a wave view of language and of historical change would allow this to be treated in a sense that cannot easily be handled by the particle, static view of human behavior which by extension treats a system 'synchronically' (i.e., in terms of a fiction, extremely convenient for certain purposes, that a system can be studied at a point of time as if change were irrelevant to it at that time).

Reference to system, however, forces us to turn to the discussion of a field view of language. As with the wave view of speech, so within this view separate particles as such disappear and melt into one another. There is one major difference, however. Instead of looking at language as a sequence of waves in a single flat wave train, language is viewed somehow in 'depth'. A word is seen not as part of a sequence alone, but as part of a whole class of words which are not being uttered at that particular time but are parts of the total potential behavioral field. A word is viewed against this larger background; it is viewed in reference to its contrastive relationships with words which are not being uttered at that particular moment. A word is seen as part of a total language system. It exists only as part of that system. Its meanings develop only in contrast to other words in the system. Its function is explicable only against the backdrop of the total language behavioral events of that system.

In this view, therefore, CLASSES of words or language events come more into prominence, and patterns of language behavior occur and are analyzable and describable only as part of and in reference to the over-all total behavioral potential of the community. This total behavioral potential, this reservoir of possible activities within a behavioral system, comes into focus, and any one particular sequence of events drops in significance as over against the whole dynamic potential or structure of the system.

This field view is a necessary antidote to an over-segmentation which treats as the only object of study the particular bits and pieces in a particular sequential relation or event. The necessity for this correction derives from the nature of language behavior itself. Language is a vehicle for communication. Yet communication cannot be done with abstract sequences by themselves. Communication requires understanding, and understanding requires a MEMORY reservoir, or pool of common experience, or field, against which particular speech events at a particular moment stand out as figure on ground, and provide the structure which provides the potential for patterned events. Without the total ground, the figure has no meaning, and no perceptual impact.

The concept of field is also useful in terms of fused forms, but on a much more restricted plane. Instead of viewing words as bits which are pasted together in a line (in a particle view), or instead of viewing them merely as fused at their borders, or overlapping (in a wave view), in a field view one is more ready to deal as wholes with elements which resist analysis by the earlier two approaches. Here one is able to deal with a total complex and state that in the complex two or more elements are PRESENT, but that it is impossible to abstract or identify phonologically these two elements without doing violence to the data. It emphasizes the 'wholistic' nature of phenomena. It emphasizes that in communication it is not the bits and pieces which communicate, but the total speech event which carries communication impact only against a behavioral background of structured experience, structured memory, and structured potential.

Specifically, from this field view, we get clues to the reason why, when fusions go far enough, it is no longer useful on a practical level—and in the field view it is seen to be no longer useful on a theoretical level—to try to separate and indicate exactly the formative parts as they currently are present in the fused whole. In a rapid pronunciation of *Did you enjoy it?*, in which the first syllable rhymes with *gin* for *ginjoyit*, a field view would imply that the total overlapping of *did* with *you* and with the first part of *enjoy* is such that it is no longer useful to try to segment the separate elements. If one rejects a field view at this point, one is faced with the alternative of an elaborate particle or wave analysis of a type. Notice, for example, the following conjugation which might result in rapid speech of a certain type:

Die enjoy it?	'Did I enjoy it?'
Dee enjoy it?	'Did he enjoy it?'
D'they enjoy it?	'Did they enjoy it?'
D'we enjoy it?	'Did we enjoy it?'
Jew enjoy it?	'Did you enjoy it?'

So far no one has seriously attempted the analysis of any extensive body of English of this general type. It seems to me that before it can be done neatly a field theory must be more fully developed.

Turning now to look at the problem as a whole, in the light of these three views of language—particle, wave, and field—what attitudes should we now adopt? Should we consider, for example, that the particle view is invalid since a wave view is useful for describing physical continua? And must the wave view then be discarded because a field view provides better for functional relationships? By no means. As I see language structure, we need the three views, all preserved in our total descriptive statement, to approximate more closely the manner in which language operates as a behavioral structure in an active community.

The phoneme concept, specifically, must not be discarded, but supplemented. It reflects more truly than any other approach some of the structuring of data which is called to one's attention as one watches people struggle to learn languages other than their native one, as they attempt to understand the articulatory characteristics of their own speech sounds, and as they begin first to read and write. No wave view, nor field view, as adequately accounts for such psycholinguistic phenomena.

Moreover, in an attempt to avoid the particle implications of the phoneme we must not rely upon a retreat to the syllable, or to other pieces of the sentence, as basic units. This stratagem merely leads to a delay in facing the basic issue. Syllables, words, stress groups, or other units are also types of particles—a part of a segmenting approach—and are ultimately subject to the same attacks which can be leveled against the phoneme. To retreat from phoneme to syllable is to remain within the same phonological hierarchy, of the same basic particle view. If the syllable can be preserved, so can the phoneme. If the phoneme disappears, so inevitably will the syllable and—from another particle hierarchy—the particular morpheme, and word, and sentence!

The solution to our problem does not lie in this direction. Rather, a view of the multiple structuring of data, in three particle hierarchies of phonology, lexicon, and grammar, must be retained. But this hierarchical-particle approach must be supplemented by wave and field outlooks for providing dynamic and functional components within the analysis.

It is worth pointing out another major conclusion—by no means accepted by many linguists—that seems evident to this writer, at least. This is the conviction that LANGUAGE IS A VARIETY OF BEHAVIOR (not merely a code, or set of symbolic forms, or a mathematical logical pattern). This I firmly hold. It comes as no surprise, therefore, that problems of figure and ground which are relevant to perception and to other behavioral forms are relevant to language. The problem of relevant segmentation of non-language behavior, furthermore, requires a concept of purpose which is analogous to meaning in language study, and is essential for the detecting of those parts of events which are significant to the participants in those events. The conflict between studying ordinary behavior from the point of view of significant events, with indeterminate borders between events, as over against studying them as physical continua in which no gaps or borders as such can be found, is also common to language and other behavioral forms. In language, however, the particle view of behavior has been very heavily developed. If we can add to it wave and field views of behavior and develop them as extensively, we should then be ready to apply some of these concepts to other forms of behavior in a way that will help us to focus on some structural characteristics of events whose relevance has previously evaded us.

Language study is the first discipline to exploit in mathematical detail certain structural relationships which may also be found in other forms of behavior. It is, from this point of view, a historical accident that behavior structure, studied in quasimathematical terms and in terms of particle and wave, is developing in linguistics before developing in the same sense in other behavioral sciences. As a matter of fact, my interest in the extension of such language structural concepts to non-language areas was an accident. In 1949 when I was developing the theoretical material which I have referred to in this article, I was trying to get an over-all definition for any and all language units. Part of the definition required a component of distribution of the unit in a larger matrix of some type. When, however, I tried to define language itself within this same framework, the distribution requirement forced me to state that language was distributed in culture. Once culture entered the formulas at this point, it was only a matter of time until culture itself, in order to help meet this requirement adequately, had to be viewed within a framework sufficiently comparable to allow it to enter into unified statements with language. The transition therefore was gradual and forced upon me empirically rather than being set up *a priori*.

Now, following this experience, I am convinced that all forms of human behavior can be studied in terms of a hierarchy of particles, a sequence of waves of events, and a background field within which there are manifested concentrations of energy which we call events.

Rhetoric and Linguistics

Rhetoric and linguistics meet at the crossroads of structure, meaning, and context. Linguistics seeks to explicate the basic features of ordinary human language by describing its phonetic, syntactic, and semantic structures. *Rhetorical linguistics*, then, would be the study of how the structure and meaning of language vary according to changing circumstances. Scholars in sociolinguistics and psycholinguistics pursue this study, and may be said to differ from rhetorical theorists to the extent that rhetoric is more often concerned with *planned* discourse, the sort deliberately composed in advance of its presentation in particular circumstances; and linguistics is more often concerned with *unplanned* discourse, presented more-or-less spontaneously.

Ironically, modern excitement about linguistic contributions to rhetoric began in the heyday of an insistently arhetorical linguistics, when Noam Chomsky posited the innateness of syntactic structures in human cognition. With the appearance of *Syntactic Structures* in 1957, Chomsky initiated the argument that certain innate "deep structures" in the mind are the universals of human language and allow us to distinguish "grammatical" from "ungrammatical" speech. Deep structure comprises a basic grammar from which we can generate an infinity of possible grammatical statements by combining or transforming simple statements into more complex statements. The theory that all humans are able to generate complex "surface structures" by performing generative transformations upon a common deep structure led to revolutionary attempts to teach effective grammar and style in the composition classroom. Setting aside the formal teaching of grammar, researchers such as John Mellon and Frank O'Hare contributed to the development, during the 1960s and 1970s, of transformational sentence combining as a process that offered students practice in the transformation and elaboration of syntactic structures and yielded writing judged to be more fluent and mature. In sum, Chomsky's arhetorical concern with positing linguistic universals gained currency as a basis for enriching the style and the associated rhetorical power of student writing.

Case grammar is another movement away from Chomsky and toward understanding of the *functional* roles of grammatical structures. Charles Fillmore attempts to improve upon transformational grammar by taking participant–action relationships into an account of meaning. Consider these sentences:

John broke the window.
A *rock* broke the window.
The *window* broke.

In each instance, the italicized word may be called the grammatical *subject* if we ignore its function, as transformational grammar allows. For Fillmore, however, *John* is *agentive,* instigating the action; *rock* is *instrumental,* an inanimate force causing the action; and *window* is *objective,* a thing affected by the action. Fillmore takes our conception of grammar a step closer to J. R. Firth's claim that *meaning* is *use,* the product of a transaction among participants.

Case grammar cannot, however, address the question of *purpose,* although it might be argued (see Winterowd below) that Fillmore's terminology can help us understand the values implied by case relationships. It remains for speech act theory, psycholinguistics, and sociolinguistics to consider matters such as *intention* and *interpretation;* it is these areas of linguistics that expand the relationship of grammar and meaning to include social and psychological contexts.

Speech act theorists J. L. Austin and John Searle recognize that sentences are designed to serve specific functions—to inform, to warn, to order, to question—and they show that language is more than a signaling system by presenting a theory for exploring the transaction between speaker and hearer. While noting the importance of their work, we must look elsewhere for an analysis of language that considers all the variables. Between the 1962 appearance of Austin's book and the 1970 appearance of Searle's, a theory more broadly based than theirs began influencing linguistic notions of communication competence. At Berkeley in the early 1960s, Del Hymes, John Gumperz, and Susan Ervin-Tripp began to develop a language-focused school with the theoretical underpinnings of the new ethnography perspective current at the University of Pennsylvania, and additionally related to the symbolic anthropology of Victor Turner, Clifford Geertz, and Gregory Bateson at the University of Chicago. Moved by hostility toward transformational grammar, these proponents of the ethnography of speaking began to argue that communicative competence must be understood as a function of both grammatical competence and *use* competence. In 1974, Hymes represents sociolinguistics as the relationship of language structures to social structures, and says that a linguistic ethnographer should consider any language act an interrelationship among psychological, logological, and social components. One of the most recent applications of this theoretical position, excerpted here, is Marcia Farr's ethnographic study of *mexicano* verbal performances. Farr presents such performances as a contrast to "essayist" literacy, which is the register of academic writing characterized by "a decontextualization of written language from actual situations and an idealization of readers and writers as rational minds and of text as perfectly rational."

Psycholinguistic research has contributed much to our understanding of the processes of writing and reading. Frank Smith in particular has shown that the meaning of a written text, for the writer and the reader, consists in the *reduction of uncertainty* (see below) and that the meaning-making process depends at least as much on what is *not* on the page as on what is. A writer's presuppositions, purposes, experiences, abilities, and environment affect the production, interpretation, and evaluation of written words; the interaction of this context with the writer's desire to get "clearer" on what he or she is writing results in a series of changing intentions and goals that materialize in the words on the page. In other words, writing cannot be the stable and steady realization of a fixed thesis because of the dynamic psychological and social complexities we bring to the act.

FURTHER READING

Austin, J. L. *How To Do Things With Words.* Eds. J. O. Urmson and Marina Sbisa. 2nd ed. Cambridge: Harvard UP, 1962.

Bateson, Gregory. *Steps to an Ecology of Mind: Collected Essays in Anthropology, Psychiatry, Evolution, and Epistemology.* San Francisco: Chandler, 1972.

Chomsky, Noam. *Syntactic Structures.* The Hague: Mouton, 1957.

Fillmore, Charles J. "The Case for Case." *Universals in Linguistic Theory.* Eds. Emmon Bach and Robert T. Harms. New York: Holt, 1968.

Geertz, Clifford. *The Interpretation of Cultures.* New York: Basic, 1973.

Hymes, Del. *Foundations in Sociolinguistics.* Philadelphia: U of Pennsylvania P, 1974.

O'Hare, Frank. *Sentence Combining: Improving Student Writing Without Formal Grammar Instruction.* Urbana, IL: National Council of Teachers of English, 1973.

McQuade, Donald, ed. *Linguistics, Stylistics, and the Teaching of Writing.* Akron, OH: L & S, 1979.

Searle, John L. *Speech Acts: An Essay in the Philosophy of Language.* London: Cambridge UP, 1969.

Turner, Victor. *Dramas, Fields, and Metaphors: Symbolic Action in Human Society.* Ithaca: Cornell UP, 1974.

W. Ross Winterowd

"The Rhetoric of Beneficence, Authority, Ethical Commitment, and the Negative"

In the following discussion, I would like to explore rhetorical force in sentences. Arguments in the rhetorical sense can, of course, never be mere sentences (or at least I cannot imagine a sentence which is also a rhetorical argument), even though they can be such in the logical sense. However, as I will suggest toward the end of this paper, what we find out concerning the rhetorical force of sentences can be extended to true rhetorical arguments and to literature. In fact, starting with analysis of the sentence has the virtue of concision and neatness, advantages to be prized in an area so large and essentially messy as rhetoric.

The first point I want to make concerning *intention* has been stated again and again. Simply, we cannot fully interpret a sentence until we can supply an intention for it. If I say to you, "I'll be here tomorrow," you cannot really take the sentence as anything but a mere utterance (which it undeniably is) until you can determine what I'm getting at. The ambiguity of the sentence (which, undoubtedly, a context would eliminate) concerns precisely what I am calling intention. Namely, you must know whether I am *promising* or *stating.* I can clarify this point—if it needs clarification—through an anecdote. Suppose that Dorothy comes into my office and I say to her, "You're looking lovely today." And suppose that she answers, "What do you mean by that?" The fact that she must ask my meaning indicates that meaning has not been *consummated,* indicates, in fact, she is suspicious of my intention, though it would never occur to me or to you that she wanted a definition of the sentence in the conventional sense. Her question has indicated her uncertainty about my intention.

It turns out that there is a class of verbs which can be used to specify intention whenever and wherever it is in doubt. These are the *performatives,* verbs with which the saying is the doing. When an ordained minister in the proper setting (etc.) says, "I hereby *pronounce* you man and wife," he is not only saying something; he is doing it. To state the point another way: the saying is the doing.

Among the performative verbs are the following: advise, answer, appoint, ask, authorize, beg, bequeath, beseech, caution, cede, claim, close, command, condemn, counsel, dare, declare, demand, empower, enquire, entreat, excommunicate, grant, implore, inform, instruct, offer, order, pledge, pronounce, propose, request, require, say, sentence, vow, warn, write.

If you put any of these verbs into declarative, positive, first person sentences in the present tense, you have performative sentences. Thus:

NONPERFORMATIVE
Advise me to stop smoking.
I don't answer your question.
They appoint you chairman.
I asked you the time.

PERFORMATIVE
I (hereby) *advise* you to stop smoking.
I (hereby) *answer* your question.
I (hereby) *appoint* you chairman.
I (hereby) *ask* you the time.

Notice that we gain some clarification of the nature of performatives by the fact that they easily take the modification of the adverb *hereby*.

That much is interesting, and has been extremely useful to ordinary language philosophers such as Austin and Searle. But it turns out that performatives are extremely interesting to rhetoricians also. A minor interest has already been stated. When a declarative sentence is nonperformative, its intention can be made explicit by stating the sentence in question as the object of a performative verb.

Let me give just a couple of brief examples to clarify this point. The sentence *You should stop smoking* might well be ambiguous as to intention, even in context, but the following sentence is unambiguous: *I (hereby) advise you that you should stop smoking*. Such also is the case with the following two sentences: *I'll never take another drink. I (hereby) vow that I'll never take another drink*.

Performative verbs *state* intentions, and thus I like to call them "verbs of intention." Each of the verbs, like all verbs, can, of course, be nominalized, and thus they give us names for intentions:

I'll pick the strawberries. I (hereby) *state* that I'll pick the strawberries. (The sentence is a statement.)
You might like sherry. I (hereby) *suggest* that you might like sherry. (The sentence is a suggestion.)

It seems self-evident (to me, at least) that intention is a part of meaning in sentences, and ordinary language philosophy lends me support, for the total speech act consists, roughly, of *utterance acts* (the mere uttering of morphemes, words, etc.), *propositional acts* (predicating and referring), *illocutionary acts* (stating, questioning, promising, threatening, etc.), and *perlocutionary acts* (achieving effects, such as frightening, convincing, informing). And I am arguing that performatives are verbs of intention.

But, indeed, the discussion so far has been pretty much old hat, covering a hoary noggin. The rhetorician will become interested in the concept of performatives just at the point where the grammarian will be roused from his lethargy by the possibility of structural analysis. And it is to the structure of the performative proposition that I would now like to turn.

I draw my first premises (which, I think, will finally be pretty much self-evident) from the concepts advanced by Charles Fillmore in his now classic essay "The Case for Case." Fillmore argues that, from one point of view, a sentence is a two-part structure, consisting of modality and proposition. The modality consists of such functions-on-the-sentence-as-a-whole as tense, modal auxiliaries, and so on. Thus, in *I smoke cigars*, the modality is simply present tense, and in *Norma can make pancakes*, the modality is present tense plus the modal *can*. The modality, however, need not concern us; it is the proposition that we must explore. The proposition in a sentence is made up of a predicate plus the grammatical "roles" or "cases" that function with the predicate and in relation to one another. Thus, for instance, we can analyze the proposition of *Jeff changes the oil* as

PREDICATE	AGENT	NEUTRAL
change:	Jeff	the oil

The proposition of *George gives Mary a whack with a bat* is something like this:

PREDICATE	AGENT	GOAL	NEUTRAL	INSTRUMENTAL
give:	George	Mary	a whack	with a bat

The names that I have chosen to give the roles in the example sentences are not significant. Fortunately, in our analysis of the propositions of performative sentences we need not concern ourselves with identifying and naming the various roles that can enter into nonperformative sentences, for performatives are relatively simple in their propositional structure.

PREDICATE	AGENT	OBLIQUE	NEUTRAL
advise:	I	you	to be cautious
(I advise you to be cautious.)			
close:	I		this session
(I close this session.)			
pledge:	I	(to you)	that I'll be there
(I pledge [to you] that I'll be there.)			

Arbitrarily, we will choose the terms *agent, oblique,* and *neutral.* As we have seen, the Agent will always be expressed by a first person pronoun (I or we), and as we have already seen, there will frequently be an Oblique role, normally expressed by *you.* Finally, there is a third role, the one which we have chosen to call Neutral. This is easily demonstrated, and is more easily explained through demonstration than otherwise: Clearly, however, this analysis, in its simplicity, leaves out virtually all of the information that is of interest to rhetoricians in their analysis of propositions. What it omits, in fact, is what I call the principle of *bene-faction*. Take the following sentence as an example: *I hereby bequeath you my watch*. It is a fact of the meaning of the sentence that the referent of the Oblique case will be the beneficiary of the consequence of my statement, and that person must believe that I intend him or her to be the beneficiary or the meaning of the sentence is not consummated. Compare this with *I hereby ask you to give me a dollar*. Clearly, the intent is that the speaker (Agent) will benefit. On the basis of this evidence alone, we can posit that the proposition of the performative sentence contains either Agent or Agent-Beneficiary (as the subject); either Oblique or Oblique-Beneficiary (in some sentences, as the indirect object usually); and Neutral. It is also the case that with some verbs, the benefit that Oblique receives will be *negative,* as in *I hereby condemn you to death*. (Later we will give full discussion to the principle of the negative. For the moment, I only want to argue that we can begin to understand the nature of the performative proposition by positing a feature—Beneficiary.) A survey of the performatives that we are dealing with will illustrate how the principle of beneficence works in the proposition. The following chart (fig. I) will be incomplete, in that it will deal with only one use of each performative when, in fact, more than one use or "sense" might be possible.

Undoubtedly, the chart raises a great many questions, and it is admittedly sketchy. It is merely intended to suggest how benefaction is a grammatical-rhetorical principle just a bit further, stopping short, I hope, of running it into the ground. If I say, "I inform you that you've won the lottery," clearly the Oblique role is beneficiary, but if I say, "I inform you that you are guilty," the Oblique role is hardly beneficiary in any ordinary sense of that word. Thus, I posit the feature +/- Beneficiary.

Figure I. Role Structure

Sentence (Pred. italicized)	Agent	Agent Benef	Oblique	Oblique	Neutral
I *advise* you to save your money.	+			+	×
I *answer* your question.	+			+	×
I *appoint* you chairman.	+			+	×
I *ask* you the time.		+	+		×
I *authorize* you to act for me.	+			+	×
I *beg* your indulgence.		+	+		×
I *bequeath* you my watch.	+			+	×
I *beseech* you to stop.		+	+		×
I *caution* you to be careful.	+			+	×
I *cede* my claim to you.	+			+	×
I *claim* my rights from you.		+	+		×
I *close* this session.	+				×
I *command* you to stop.	+		+		×
I *condemn* you to death.	+		−		×

	1	2	3	4	5
I *counsel* you to study.	+			+	×
I *dare* you to jump.	+		+		×
I *declare* a moratorium.	+				×
I *demand* satisfaction from you.		+		−	×
I *empower* you to vote.	+			+	×
I *enquire* after the answer (from you).		+	+		×
I *entreat* you to stop.		+	+		×
I *excommunicate* you.	+			−	
I *grant* (you) your claim.	+			+	×
I *implore* your forgiveness.		+	+		×
I *inform* you of my intention.	+			+	×
I *instruct* you to turn right.	+		+		×
I *offer* you a cigar.	+			+	×
I *order* you to study.	+		+		×
I *pledge* my support to you.	+			+	×
I *pronounce* you man and wife.	+			+	×
I *propose* marriage to you.		+		+	×
I *request* your presence.		+	+		×
I *require* your reply.		+		+	×
I *say* X to you.	+		+		×
I *sentence* you to jail.	+			−	×
I *vow* revenge on you.	+			−	×
I *warn* you of X.	+			+	×
I *write* my opinion.	+				×

In any case, I think that "playing around" with the semantics of benefaction will tell anyone a good deal about the rhetorical force of performative sentences. As I will point out later, we need other principles to account for the force of such sentences as *I command you to stop,* for we feel, I think, that accounting for the force of this and others in terms of benefaction is highly tenuous and makes us uneasy. For the moment, I am content if I have demonstrated that benefaction is a rhetorical principle in performatives. (Regardless of whether or not anyone agrees with my individual analyses.)

• • •

Marcia Farr

"Essayist Literacy and Other Verbal Performances"

• • •

In the following section, persuasive oral performances by Mexican immigrants in Chicago are presented as yet another contrast to essayist literacy. Instances of the *mexicano* performances were gathered as part of an ongoing ethnographic study of oral language and literacy in the Mexican-origin community. The examples to be examined here come from recordings made at public meetings in the community, which consisted of predominately two groups: *mexicanos* (immigrants who were primarily enculturated, or raised, in Mexico) and Mexican-Americans (those primarily enculturated, and, in this case, educated, in Chicago). The recordings reveal at least two discourse styles: a *mexicano* style of public oratory and a Mexican-American style that demonstrates some characteristics of essayist literacy. These particular Mexican-Americans may have acquired such characteristics from formal educational experiences in Chicago. Only the performances by the *mexicanos* are explored here.

MEXICANO *VERBAL PERFORMANCES*

The *mexicano* discourse style evidenced in these performances emphasizes a personal, human stance (in contrast to the "detached and objective" stance of essayist literacy) and features such qualities as *sabor* (flavor), *sinceridad* (sincerity), and *emoción* (emotion) in discourse as often more appealing and persuasive than "objectively" presented information. Examples of this discourse style can be found throughout a corpus of audiotapes made in public settings in the heart of the Mexican-origin community in Chicago. Settings in which the audiotapes were made include monthly meetings of a Chicago City Council alderman with his precinct representatives, block club meetings, annual conventions of local community organizations, and local school council meetings. These settings were chosen because they provided ample opportunity for persuasive discourse to occur.

The observational and audiotaped data from the public settings were supplemented with data from informal interviews; specifically, perceptions of effective and persuasive speaking were elicited from members of one social network of Mexican immigrant families. The instances of public persuasion performed by various residents of the neighborhood and the perceptions of effective speaking provided by network members together yield a coherent portrayal of a *mexicano* discourse style that contrasts sharply with the characteristics of essayist literacy.

In the interviews, network members characterized their enjoyment of language with a number of expressions that, to them, encapsulated what they valued in "good speakers." Four of these values are presented here: *gracia* (grace, wit), *sabor* (flavor, taste), *sinceridad* (sincerity), and *emoción* (emotion).

Gracia (grace, wit) is used to refer to wittiness in talk; people who *tiene gracia* (have grace, are witty) are seen as clever and funny. Not everyone illustrates this quality, but those who do are obvious from the moment they speak. As one middle-aged male said,

> . . . *cuando ellos empiezan a hablar, desde el momento que los oyes hablar, tienen gracia. Entonces, la gente que tiene gracia, se va juntando gente a oírlos. Y hay gente más desabrida, diría yo. No tiene, no le quedan sus chistes. Aunque cuente uno una charrita . . . ya no te vas a reír igual.*
> [. . . when they start to speak, from the moment that you hear them speak, they are witty. So then, the people who are witty begin to have a listening crowd gather about them. And then there are people who are more boring, I would say. They don't have, their jokes just don't make it. Even though they may tell a joke . . . you're not going to laugh in the same manner.]

Sabor (flavor, taste) is another crucial ingredient in good speaking, and *hablar sabroso* (literally, "to speak deliciously") describes a way of conversing that is intensely pleasurable. As an activity, this kind of conversing is often preferred by older network members, and by many younger ones as well, to watching television. In fact, several adults in the network have complained on different occasions about households in which television viewing takes the place of such pleasurable conversing. The best description of this kind of talk was provided by a young woman:

> . . . *cuando yo llego muy sabroso con una persona, se me va rápido el tiempo así, y sus pláticas le pone uno atención, y se hayan entre dos personas, yo a eso lo llamo sabroso . . . sabroso es entretenida . . . por la vista, la expresión, sí . . . pero no más en especial que dé la mímica . . . Lo sabroso es lo que, la plática que tenga, te gusta, te interesa. Te entretiene su plática, eso es para nosotros sabroso.*
> [. . . when it gets real delicious with a person, the time goes by quickly that way, and you pay attention to the talk, and the two people click, that is what I call delicious . . . "delicious" is entertaining . . . because of the look, the expressions,

yes . . . but especially because of the mimicking. . . . What is delicious is the talk that you have, that you like, that interests you. If someone's talk entertains you, that for us is delicious.]

Sinceridad (sincerity) refers to the genuineness and honesty evidenced by a speaker. One person said that a good speaker "tells a story with earnest desire." Another reported what her own father had told her to do in order to evaluate other speakers for their *sinceridad:*

"M'ija, cuando alguien de verdad le estima a uno, mírele a la cara y en sus ojos verá su expresión, si le gustó usted, sí o no. Cuando usted vaya a una así, siempre una cosa . . . usted vea." Y yo decía, "¿Pero cómo? ¿Cómo le voy yo a ver en la cara?" Pero con el tiempo, los años, usted ve que sí. Sí es verdad.
["My daughter, when someone truly respects you, look the person in the face and in the person's eyes you will see the expression, if the person likes you or not. When you go to someone like that, always remember . . . you look." And I said, "But how? How am I going to tell by the face?" But with time, the passing of years, you see that it's true. Yes, it's true.]

Thus one is able, with experience, to "read" others' faces for *sinceridad,* to determine whether or not their words can be trusted.

Emoción (emotion) is as important in impressive speaking as *sinceridad, sabor,* or *gracia,* and in practice all of these qualities are often intimately related, together being what one man referred to as *encantable* (enchanting). For example, a person who speaks "from the heart," or sincerely, speaks with emotion, and those who converse "deliciously" put emotion into their performances, as well as deriving pleasure emotionally from the talk itself. As a young woman indicated,

O sea que lo cuentan en un modo que lo hace más interesante que otras personas. Otras personas nomas te lo cuentan. Tal vez lo cuentan nada más con palabras, así, y otras, como que lo hacen más emocionante, más mejor.
[In other words, they tell it in a way that makes it more interesting than other people. Other people just tell it to you. Perhaps they tell it only with words, like that, and others, it's as if they make it more emotional, much better.]

Another young woman added to this description of speaking with emotion:

Será la expresión que hacen, la expresión de su cara como lo dicen. Que a veces uno les mira, y como expresan las cosas, uno cree que en verdad. . . . Es lo que llama a uno mucho atención, la expresión que hacen en su cara . . . cuando plátican, mueven las manos así, y las caras, y hacen las cosas como si en verdad estuvieran pasando.
[It must be the expression that they make, the expression on the face as they tell it. Sometimes you look at them, and how they express things, and you believe that it is true. . . . It's what catches your attention, the expression that they make on the face . . . when they talk, they move their hands all about, and their faces, and they do it as if it were really happening.]

These four characteristics of "good speaking" are clearly in evidence in the two public verbal performances discussed below. Both of the speakers, at one point or another, however, were interrupted in their attempts to display the discourse style described by network members above. The interrupters, who were managing the public meetings, were Mexican-Americans with higher levels of education received in the United States than the *mexicano* speakers and with discourse styles more characteristic of essayist literacy than of *mexicano* traditions.

The first performance to be discussed occurred at a ward-level political meeting that was run by the alderman elected by the ward to the Chicago City Council. In addition to the alderman, the meeting included members of his staff and block-level representatives from around the ward. Such meetings occur on a monthly basis in the alderman's office in the neighborhood. Most of the people who attend these meetings are of Mexican origin, either *mexicanos* or Mexican-Americans.

At this particular meeting, there were 35 people: 26 Latinos (almost all of whom were either *mexicanos* or Mexican-Americans), 6 African-Americans, and 3 Whites. The meeting ran for about 90 minutes and consisted primarily of discussion about which, if any, Democratic mayoral candidate should be supported in the upcoming primary election. Most of the meeting took place in English; toward the end, however, a few people presented their views in Spanish. What they had to say was in most cases summarized in English by the Mexican-American political leader who was managing the meeting.

Choosing which mayoral candidate to support in the upcoming election was especially difficult, because it involved racial politics. At the time of the meeting, there were three candidates for the Democratic primary: Richard Daley (son of Chicago's famous Mayor Daley), Eugene Sawyer (the incumbent mayor who was elected—quite controversially—in the aftermath of the sudden death of Harold Washington, the charismatic, and first Black, mayor of Chicago), and Juan Soliz, an alderman from another Latino ward who briefly threw his hat into the ring. Timothy Evans, who had narrowly lost to Sawyer right after Washington died, also was still a viable candidate for mayor; he was, in fact, the true candidate of choice for this group because he was the widely recognized "heir-apparent" to Harold Washington, and this alderman and his supporters had been part of Washington's Black/Latino/liberal-White coalition. Evans, however, had pulled out of the Democratic primary in order to run in the general election as an independent. Because Daley is White and both Sawyer and Evans are Black, the dilemma at this meeting was how to avoid splitting the "minority" vote without either supporting Daley or reducing Evans's chances to win in the general election.

Various people at the meeting reported to the group what they had heard on their blocks, at their churches, or in other places in the community about preferences for the various candidates. From a tape of the meeting, one episode was selected for analysis; this episode consisted of a series of turns by four different people called on by the leader to report what they were hearing. This episode began and ended with a shift in topic. Within this episode, a smaller stretch of discourse contained a rather extensive verbal performance, although an interrupted one.

This stretch of discourse was selected because it contained an example of *mexicano*-style oratory and the responses of others to this style. Elsewhere on the tape, there are abundant examples of essayist literacy-style discourse by a White and by the Mexican-American leader who was raised and educated, through college, in Chicago. There are also examples of what is usually thought of as "Black" rhetoric by, interestingly, not only the African-Americans present, but also occasionally by the Mexican-American leader. For example, the leader said, in referring to a Latino alderman who had just endorsed Daley, "One monkey don't stop no show" in a distinctly "Black" cadence. This remark, intended to cheer up those who were discouraged by a Latino alderman's decision to support Daley, the White candidate, elicited much laughter and clapping; it shows a sensitive use of discourse styles to build a multiethnic political coalition.

In the transcribed discourse below, three people take turns at speaking; they are represented by pseudonyms: M (Sr. Martinez), F (Mr. Fuentes), and R (Sra. Rodriguez). The transcription begins when Sr. Martinez is trying to get the floor; access to the floor and turn-taking are being controlled by Mr. Fuentes, the leader. The talk is overlapping at first, with Mr. Fuentes winning out by loudly introducing Sr. Martinez as someone active at a local church who can report what is going on within that large congregation.

M = Uh, want to say {overlapping with following by F}
F = Mr. M. is also active at one of the churches here so, he can, he can let us know what's going on in a large congregation . . . overlapping with following by M}
M = I'm gonna use, uh, uh, speak in Spanish OK? Uh, concern about what the lady, what she said. *Es muy importante que nos eduquemos, que sepamos analizar la situación. Si nos mencionan de Juan Soliz es muy importante darle a conocer a las personas la historia de Juan Soliz. Yo fui, fui uno de los primeros que andaba con Juan, con Juan Soliz. Cuando yo no lo conocía, ṿé. No más porque era Juan Soliz. Pero este, es importante que e, ya de su historia Juan Soliz entre nosotros. Es importante que sepamos quien es la persona y darle a conocer a los que nos preguntan, nos interrogan, quien es la persona. Darles a conocer que la última elección . . . era . . . ganó por unos cuantos votos. ¿Porque la gente de él no lo quería? Hay que, hay que preguntar esa, hacer esa pregunta.*

[It is very important that we get educated, that we learn to analyze the situation. If they mention Juan Soliz to us it is very important that we tell the people about Juan Soliz's history. I was, was one of the first who went with (i.e., supported) Juan, with Juan Soliz. When I did not know him yet, you see. Just because he was Juan Soliz. But it is important that uh, Juan let his history be known among us. It is important that we know who the person is and introduce him to those that ask us about him, those who question us who the person is. To let them know that the last election . . . was . . . won with about a couple more votes. Why did his people not like him? One has to, one has to ask that, to ask that question.]

Why he was, you know, har'ly makin' it the las' time. He was incumbent, he har'ly made it, you know. So this very important to educate ourselves, so we know what to, you know, to answer. To neutralize the ignorance of that people, of those people, you know, whoever they might be. But it's important to know who we are support—not because he's a Black person, a Hispanic per-, person, a White person. But what that person is doing for us, what we gonna get for peo-, for our community, for our children, for our families.
R = [begins without pause] *OK. Yo hablé con ellos, perdón, yo hablé con ellos y les dije los, lo que dije, no?*

> [O.K. I spoke with them, excuse me, I spoke to them and told them the, what I said, no?]

M = Yeah?
R = *Lo que nosotros sabemos. Pero a ellos no les importa, ellos lo que ven en él es un Latino, eso es lo que ellos ven en él, eso es lo que ellos a mí me indicaron. Y eso es lo que yo vengo a explicar aquí.*

> [What we know. But they do not care, what they see in him is a Latino, that is what they see in him, that is what they indicated to me. And that is what I have come to explain here.]

M = *Si ellos no han oído a él, no pueden más el dos por ciento, el dos por ciento de la gente. ¿Que va a hacer con el dos por ciento? Y la última vez apenas lo hizo por ahora menos. {laughter} No olviden*

> [If they have not heard of him, he can't do better than two percent, two percent of the people. What is he going to do with the two percent? And the last time he barely made it, for now it will be less. {laughter} Do not forget]

that we have to educate ourselves, who that person is, why they have, you know, the history of what they been doing. We all make history ever' day of our lives.
F = {without pause, immediately recognizes next speaker} OK, Manuel?
M = I'm sorry, thank you, *gracias.*
F = Thank you.

Mr. Martinez is fluent in both languages, having lived in various Mexican states as well as Texas during his childhood. Although the predominant language used for discussion at this meeting was English, Sr. Martinez's verbal performance began, as he announced beforehand, in Spanish, perhaps because he felt that this genre would be more appropriately carried out in Spanish or that he could perform it better in Spanish. He switches to English twice, however, both times after beginning a turn in Spanish, possibly because of some felt pressure to return to the predominant language of the meeting. The switches also could have been carried out as an attempt to be more persuasive with his audience, which included both Spanish and English speakers, or to signal his own membership in both worlds.

Regardless of his choice of language, however, his verbal style throughout his performance remained the same. He certainly made particular "points" that contributed to the ongoing discussion at the meeting, but he embedded them in a verbal performance that illustrated a very different style from that of the leader. He began by admonishing his audience to educate themselves, to learn to analyze situations, and to spread the word about what they conclude. He then went off on what some non-*mexicanos* at that meeting perceived to be "tangents," or side issues: He made an inexplicit reference to the "history" (or past) of the Latino candidate who briefly threw his hat into the ring, saying that he himself even had supported him before he knew anything about him. He explained that this candidate was barely elected alderman by his own people during the last election, and asked, rhetorically, why his own people did not like him. He ended, in English, by stressing the importance of knowing well the person one decides to support and making that decision not on the basis of race, but by judging what that person can do for the community.

Sr. Martinez builds to a climax in this presentation, using sudden changes in pitch and stress, as well as repeated intonation patterns in parallel phrases to do so. He says, " . . . not because he's a Black person, a Hispanic person, a White person" and also, " . . . what that person is doing for us, what we gonna get for peo-, for our community, for our children, for our families." Both of these examples illustrate several kinds of parallelism, a feature of oral poetry that has been noted in a number of widely different cultures (Bricker, 1974; Jakobson, 1968). Parallelism is shown in the repeated intonation pattern in the following two examples: [raised portions were spoken at a higher pitch]

1. a ^{Black} person, a His^{pan}ic person, a ^{White} person
2. for our com^{mun}ity, for our ^{chil}dren, for our ^{fam}ilies

In addition to parallelism in the intonation pattern, these phrases also illustrate syntactic and semantic parallelism. In the first example, each repetition consists of three words: an indefinite article (*a*), an adjective (*Black, Hispanic, White*), and a noun (*person*); the three adjectives are semantically related. In the second example, each repetition consists of a preposition (*for*), a possessive adjective (*our*), and a noun (*community, children, families*); here the nouns are semantically related. Thus parallelism is marked simultaneously by intonation, syntax, and semantic associations.

After a dramatic pause, Sr. Martinez was interrupted by a woman (Sra.

Rodriguez) who disagreed with him, saying that she has explained all these things to the people she has talked to, but that what they still saw in the short-lived Latino candidate was that he was Latino. After a rejoinder by Sr. Martinez in which he again began to increase in intensity, the leader, Mr. Fuentes, interrupted, seemingly eager to move on in the discussion. Again there was overlapping talk, and again the leader maintained control of the discourse. The struggle for the floor at the beginning, middle, and end of Sr. Martinez's performance, although handled politely, was clearly signaled by the use of such phrases as "excuse me," "I'm sorry," and "thank you." That the speaker probably knew he had been allowed to speak reluctantly was indicated by his apology at the end: "I'm sorry, thank you, *gracias*." After the meeting, the Mexican-American leader commented privately, "sometimes that guy just goes on and on." Throughout the meeting, the leader appeared to prefer discourse that moved quickly to its point, stated that point explicitly, and avoided tangential references, accounts of personal experiences, and hortatory discourse with poetic qualities.

This incident illustrated a clear difference—in fact, a conflict—in discourse styles. The one used by the leader and expected by him and some others at this meeting generally fits the description of essayist literacy discussed above. The other discourse style, that used by Sr. Martinez in his brief holding of the floor, is more "oratorical" in its style, emphasizing oral devices such as intonation, repetition, and parallelism, and it is more intense in its tone, exhorting listeners to follow a certain course of action. Finally, it is more figurative than the "plain-style" essayist literacy discourse of much of the rest of the meeting.

This verbal style, as it was performed here, accentuates the personal, and it features the valued qualities described by our informants: sincerity, "flavor," wittiness, and emotion. Sr. Martinez argues that it is the *person* who is important ("who that person is"), not whether he is Black, White, or Hispanic. He shows sincerity by including personal testimony: "I was … one of the first who went with … Juan Soliz. When I did not know him, you see." He adds "flavor" and wit to his argument by claiming that during the last election this particular incumbent received only two percent of the vote of "his own people," and insists that this time it would be even less! Pointing out that this man was barely elected by his own people is somewhat embarrassing in this public setting; it makes fun of the candidate and draws laughter from the audience. Finally, he relies on shared values to persuade by urging his audience to take actions ("tell the people about Juan Soliz's history") for the larger good: "for our community, for our children, for our families." In using the pronouns *we* and *us* (rather than *you*), and by using both Spanish and English, he identifies himself closely with the audience, positioning himself and his audience within the same communities.

Sr. Martinez's discourse style may derive from a centuries-old and highly valued Mexican tradition of oratory (Vaughn, 1988) that is well-suited to many contexts. Apparently, however, it was not well-suited to this meeting, at least not from the perspective of the political leader of the meeting. There is no inherent reason it should not be appropriate, because the meeting was a political one, conducted in public, and because it was entirely orally based (even the oral discussion did not involve any written text other than a list of agenda items held by the leader). The difference, I think, was at least partly a cultural one. Some would argue that the perceived inappropriateness of this style was due to time constraints, but attitudes toward time are themselves embedded in cultural traditions. In many parts of Mexico, such oratory and orality itself are highly valued; it is assumed that written texts, especially in classrooms, must be explicated and recited orally for learning to take place (Rockwell, 1991). Moreover, as our informants have made clear, verbal performances that are full of flavor, sincerity, and emotion are highly valued among *mexicanos*. At this meeting in Chicago, led by a Mexican-American raised and educated there, however, this style of oratory was assumed by some of the participants to be inappropriate; some people were impatient with it, wanting the speaker to get to his point, to relay his information explicitly and concisely, without oratorical embellishments. Other participants, of course, indicated their enjoyment of the oratory by responding with laughter at relevant points in the performance.

•   •   •

Frank Smith

"Information and Uncertainty"

We should not expect to be able to identify and measure information by look-ing for something with unique and manifest characteristics in the world around us. Information can be found in a multitude of guises—in marks on paper, in facial expressions and other bodily gestures, in the configuration of clouds, trees (and sometimes tea leaves), and in the sounds of speech. Obviously sources of information have little in common, and neither do the channels through which information passes.

Consider the mutations of information when we listen to a broadcast record-ing of someone talking. What we hear begins as an intention in the speaker's mind, represented in some complex and deeply mysterious way in the flux of chemical and bioelectrical activities in the structures of the brain. This intention is then translated into bursts of neural energy, dispatched from the brain at differ-ent times, rates, and directions to the musculature of the jaw, mouth, lips, tongue, vocal cords, and chest, orchestrating the expulsion of breath in such a manner that distinctive pressure waves of contrasting intensity and frequency radiate through the surrounding atmosphere. These fleeting disturbances in the molecules of the air cause the tiny diaphragm of a microphone to resonate in sympathy, triggering a flow of electrical energy along a wire quite unlike the corresponding patterns of neural energy in the nervous systems of the speaker or listener. Amplified and modulated, the electrical impulses from the microphone impress subtle combina-tions of magnetic forces onto a plastic tape or etch wavy lines into a plastic disk. Through further mechanical and electronic incarnations, the information may then be diffused by radio transmission (perhaps diverting through the transistors of an earth-orbiting satellite) before being reconstituted by a receiver and loud-speaker into airborne pressure waves that lap against the listener's ear. And still the transformations are not done. The oscillation of the eardrum is conveyed to another resonating membrane of the inner ear across a tiny bridge of three artic-ulating bones—the hammer, the anvil, and the stirrup. And then, perhaps most bizarrely, a pressure wave pulses back and forth through liquid in the coiling canals of the inner ear, a labyrinth carved into the skull itself, where microscopic hair cells wave like reeds with the movement of the fluid in which they are con-tained. The roots of these fronds are the tiny beginnings of the mighty auditory nerve, and they generate the final relays of neural impulses that travel its hundreds of thousands of separate nerve fibers, through half a dozen booster and transformer stations in various recesses of the brain, to be transformed at last into subjective experiences of meaningfulness and sound. And this meaningfulness of acoustic events can be congruent with a subjective meaningfulness and visual experience from perhaps the same words written down and reaching the brain by a completely different route through the eyes. How can all or even part of this complexity be identified and evaluated as "information"?

ON MAKING DECISIONS

The answer is by looking at what it enables the "receiver"—the listener or the reader—to do. Information enables a person to make decisions, to choose among alternative possibilities or competing courses of action. Information can be discriminated and assessed, not from its source or from the various forms that it can take during transmission, but from what it enables the recipient to do. Reading involves decisions, whether by a child striving to identify a single letter of the alphabet or by a scholar struggling to decipher an obscure medieval text. And anything that helps a reader to make a decision is information.

Put into other words again, *information reduces uncertainty*. The change of focus from the facilitation of decisions to the reduction of uncertainty may not seem to be much of a conceptual gain, but in fact it permits information to be measured, or at least estimated comparatively. Information cannot be quantified directly—it is not possible to assess the dimensions of a piece of information, or to weigh it. In the same way the size or weight of a decision cannot be calculated directly. But it is possible to put a number to uncertainty, and thus indirectly to the amount of information that eliminates or reduces that uncertainty. The trick is accomplished by defining uncertainty in terms of the number of alternatives confronting the decision-maker. If you are confronted by a lot of alternatives you have a great deal of uncertainty; there are many different decisions you could make. If you have fewer alternatives, it may be just as hard for you to make up your mind but theoretically your uncertainty is less; there are fewer alternative decisions you might make. The argument has nothing to do with the importance of the decision to you, only with the number of alternatives. Theoretically, your uncertainty is the same whether you must decide for or against major surgery or for having your morning eggs scrambled or fried. The number of alternatives is the same in each case, and so therefore is your uncertainty.

And now information can be defined more fully: *Information reduces uncertainty by the elimination of alternatives*. Information, very reasonably, is anything that moves you closer to a decision. It is beside the point whether the decision concerns the identification of particular objects or events or the selection among various choices of action. Uncertainty and information are defined in terms of the *number* of alternative decisions that could be made no matter *what* the alternatives are. However, it is easier to reach an understanding of these concepts if particular situations are taken as examples.

Suppose that the information is available in a single letter of the alphabet. Or to put the matter into plain English, suppose a child is given the task of identifying a letter written on the chalkboard. There are 26 letters of the alphabet, and the reader's uncertainty requires a decision or choice among these 26 alternatives. If the situation involves bidding in a bridge game, then the uncertainty may perhaps concern a player's strongest suit, and the number of alternatives will be four. For the simple toss of a coin, the number of alternatives is two; for the roll of a die, it is six. Sometimes the exact number of alternatives is not immediately apparent—for example, if a word rather than a letter is being read. But it may still be possible to determine when this indefinite amount of uncertainty has been reduced—for example, if the reader learns that the word begins with a particular letter or is of a particular length. Either of these pieces of information will reduce the number of alternative possibilities of what the word might be.

We can now return to the definition of information as the reduction of uncertainty. Just as the measure of uncertainty is concerned with the number of alternatives among which the decision-maker has to choose, so information is concerned with the number of alternatives that are eliminated. If the decision-maker is able to eliminate all alternatives except one, and thus can make a complete decision, then the amount of information is equal to the amount of uncertainty that existed. A bridge player who receives the information that the partner's strongest suit is red has had uncertainty reduced by one-half; if the information is that the strongest suit is hearts, uncertainty is reduced completely. Similarly, a child who knows the letters well enough to decide that the letter on the board is a vowel has acquired information reducing uncertainty from 26 alternatives to five. If the letter is correctly identified, then the information gained from the letter must have been equal to the original uncertainty.

Some aspects of reading involve the acquisition of information in order to make decisions, to reduce uncertainty. For the visual identification of letters and words and possibly some aspects of "reading for meaning," uncertainty can be calculated, and therefore also the amount of information required to make a decision. The exact number of alternatives can be specified for letters, an approximate figure can be put to the number of words, but the number of alternatives for a meaning, if it can be estimated at all, must obviously be closely related both to the text being read and to the particular individual who is doing the reading.

Rhetoric and Education

❦

Rhetoric and education have always been intimately related, in part because of the role rhetoric has played in education throughout history, particularly at the secondary and postsecondary levels, and in part because the art of rhetoric is, by nature, heuristic—that is, rhetoric leads a speaker or writer to examine what he or she knows and needs to know.

Although young students in pre-Socratic Greece would certainly have had the opportunity to study rhetoric, either in academies such as Aristotle's or through private study with a sophistic teacher, the institution of rhetoric as a school subject is a feature of Roman culture. From the second century BCE onward, the standard curriculum for a Roman student would have been the subjects known as the *trivium*—grammar, logic, and rhetoric—and then the subjects called the *quadrivium*—mathematics, music, astronomy, and natural philosophy, or science. So firmly established was this classical curriculum, with rhetoric at its center, that it became the pattern for all secondary and postsecondary schooling in the West for nearly two millennia after its institution.

The Romans' decision to install rhetoric at the center of their curriculum was intimately related to their culture's definition of eloquence. To the Romans, especially Cicero, an orator could not be truly eloquent unless he was liberally educated in a vast number of subjects. In the dialogue *De Oratore*, Cicero has the wise Crassus describe the breadth of knowledge that an orator must acquire:

> The poets must . . . be studied; an acquaintance must be formed with history; the writers and teachers in all the liberal arts and sciences must be read, and turned over, and for the sake of exercise be praised, interpreted, corrected, censured, and refuted; . . . The civil law must be thoroughly studied; laws in general must be understood; all antiquity must be known; the usages of the senate, the nature of our government, the rights of our allies, our treaties and conventions, and whatever concerns the interests of the state must be learned.

Later in the dialogue, Crassus once again emphasizes the relation between liberal learning and training in eloquence: "[B]y an orator, everything that relates to human life, since that is the field on which his abilities are displayed, and is the subject for his eloquence, should be examined, heard, read, discussed, handled, and considered, since eloquence is one of the most eminent virtues."

The Romans did their best to incorporate this array of subject matters into the actual pedagogy of their education in rhetoric. A prominent feature of secondary education was the *progymnasmata,* a series of gradually more challenging exercises in written composition. Through preparing to write these compositions, students were led to learn about Roman poetry and history, natural philosophy, and laws and government: These were the subject matters, the substance, students wrote *about* as they learned how to speak and write effectively.

To a certain extent, the philosophy underlying the rhetoric–education connection in ancient Rome recurs in contemporary schooling. Instructors who teach the art of rhetoric, the *practice* of effective speaking and writing, may not always agree on what exactly their students should read and write about, but they generally agree that surveying the world with a rhetorician's eye—that is, with the intention of writing or speaking about a subject—is one of the most effective ways of learning about it.

The selections in this section illustrate the rhetoric–education connection from antiquity to the present. James J. Murphy in the introduction to his translation of Quintilian's *Institutio Oratoria* describes the Roman concept of schooling that placed rhetoric at its center. Donald Lemen Clark shows how one of the major figures in British literature, John Milton, would have encountered this classical education in his training at St. Paul's School. Melinda Fine illustrates how students in a multicultural middle school learn about extremely difficult problems in world history by having the opportunity to engage in lively, open discussions. Finally, Barry Brummett characterizes rhetorical theory as being essentially different from other bodies of theory in the social sciences in its emphasis on the ultimate morality involved in *finding* perspectives on challenging issues that face a rhetor.

FURTHER READING

Antczak, Frederick J. *Thought and Character: The Rhetoric of Democratic Education.* Ames, IA: Iowa State UP, 1985.

Bizzell, Patricia. *Academic Discourse and Critical Consciousness.* Pittsburgh: U of Pittsburgh P, 1992.

Clark, Donald Lemen. *Rhetoric in Greco-Roman Education.* New York: Columbia UP, 1957.

Fox, Thomas. *The Social Uses of Writing: Politics and Pedagogy.* Norwood, NJ: Ablex Publishing Corporation, 1990.

Kimball, Bruce. *Orators and Philosophers.* New York: Teachers College, 1986.

Secor, Marie and Davida Charney, eds. *Constructing Rhetorical Education.* Carbondale: Southern Illinois UP, 1992.

James J. Murphy

"The Concept of 'School'"

In one sense this is the story of a successful approach to teaching speaking and writing, and in another sense it is the story of the one ancient book which best typifies that approach.

Democratic education in ancient Greece, as one famous historian has pointed out, was necessarily of a collective character because it aimed to provide learning opportunities to all free men. This led to the creation and development of a remarkable social tool—the "school." It is often difficult for the modern student to understand that the concept of "school" had to be invented. But it was a deliberate cultural choice at a certain stage in Western civilization, one which has so dominated our subsequent thinking that for most people today it would be difficult to imagine any kind of civilization without schools. Yet there have always been alternatives. It has always been possible for the very rich or the very reclusive to hire one tutor for one son or one daughter, and for the ignorant or the religious zealot to reject any learning at all. Nevertheless, over the centuries the predominant choice of societies as diverse as the Roman Empire and Christian monasticism has been to gather the young in groups to receive purposeful instruction in the methods and values dear to those societies.

For the Greeks, and for the Romans who inherited Greek thought, such instruction always began with the matter which made all other learning possible—that is, it began with language and the uses of language. The interplay of speaking and writing was an integral part of this instruction from the beginning.

These are historical truisms of our culture, but they are worth repeating here because they illustrate the central importance of our author's concerns. Quintilian not only describes for us the educational processes which he had inherited and which were to be replicated substantially down into our own century, but he explains to us why these processes are superior to their alternatives and what they can accomplish for society by educating citizens who are both humane and effective. His frequent discussions of alternative ideas provide us with a depth of understanding which could not be reached by a bare statement of a single viewpoint.

It must be noted that the Romans were a systematic people. Their remarkable feats of hydraulic engineering created aqueducts for the water supply of cities;

they built paved roads which in some parts of the world are still usable today; they introduced central heating for buildings; they pioneered the mass production of chariots and naval vessels with interchangeable parts to support a carefully designed military force which dominated Europe, Asia Minor, and North Africa for half a thousand years. The governmental structure of the republic was delicately balanced to prevent any one man from seizing absolute power, with paired executives (the Consuls), a parliamentary body (the Senate), and representatives of the people (the Tribunes) with the power of veto; this pattern of government worked so well, in fact, that when the republic finally succumbed to personal dictatorships it was possible even then for the emperors to keep the old mechanisms intact while they wielded the real power. The worldwide system of public administration under the empire was a marvel of meticulous record keeping. In short, the Romans were social engineers as well as mechanical and military experts.

It should not be surprising then to discover that the Roman approach to schools was equally systematic. We know that the subject of rhetoric was so highly schematized by the lifetime of Cicero (born 106 B.C.) that even as an adolescent (aged fifteen to seventeen) Cicero was able to rehearse what he had learned and produce a major treatise on rhetoric—his *De inventione.* This systematization of rhetoric, a product of Hellenistic efforts during the second century before Christ, may well have been a by-product of the increasing standardization of the schools in which rhetoric was the core subject. As George A. Kennedy remarks, "practically all of the additions to rhetorical theory made in Hellenistic times stem from a desire to create an academic discipline, a list which could be memorized, or something which applied to classroom exercises." Naturally there was a good deal of variety among specific schools, and the official Censors closed down at least one rhetorical school in 92 B.C. for promoting "a new kind of study," but there is such a clear overall pattern of subject matter and teaching methodology over many centuries of Roman schooling that it seems fair to think of Roman education as a "system" with identifiable characteristics.

By the time of Emperor Vespasian (A.D. 70–79), the schools had become an instrument of public policy. Vespasian initiated the practice of granting teachers immunity from certain municipal taxes, a practice which was confirmed and expanded by many later emperors, on the grounds that their service was a benefit to the state. It was also Vespasian who established official professorships to be paid from the state treasury; Quintilian was the first to receive the chair for Latin rhetoric, with its annual stipend of 100,000 sesterces (a large sum, possibly equivalent to a modern quarter-million dollars). Quite apart from this kind of official privilege or endowment, there was a larger social force which ensured a close relation between the schools and the world power of Rome. The military administration which enforced Roman rule was founded on permanent garrisons; these garrisons required civilian support by merchants, suppliers, and clerks. In due course garrisons became towns and cities. The parents of children in York, Beirut, Marseilles, Cologne, or Carthage could demand the same educational advantages accruing to residents of Rome itself, and there is ample evidence of municipal support for such schools down at least into the sixth Christian century. Where the soldiers went, the schools went as well.

The schools outlasted the empire. While there were some zealous Christians like Tertullian and Cyprian who wanted to renounce learning in favor of a simple faith, the fifth-century church decided instead to pursue the values of the educational system already in place. The example of Aurelius Augustinus (340–430) shows how firmly imbedded was the concept of school. After attending school in his hometown of Tagaste in North Africa, Augustinus taught in Carthage but moved to a better teaching job in Rome; once in Rome, he moved again to a position in Milan. It was in Milan that he went to hear a popular Christian speaker, Ambrose, and through him became interested in Christianity. Ultimately Saint Augustine became bishop of Hippo in North Africa, a prolific writer and speaker on behalf of Christianity, and one of the four Latin Fathers of the church. His teaching background led him to write one of the most influential documents of the fifth century, *On Instruction in Christianity (De doctrina Christiana),* arguing for the use of rhetoric to promote the faith. His career would not have been possible without the schools.

If the schools outlasted the empire, it was also true that the teaching methods outlasted the Roman schools themselves. The history of medieval education is only now being written, but there is increasing evidence that the basic pedagogy which the Romans had inherited from the Greeks was passed on into the Middle Ages substantially unchanged. The methods persisted long after their sources were forgotten—perhaps because the methods worked well—and were already familiar to the humanists who created in the fifteenth and sixteenth centuries what has come to be called the Renaissance. One of the reasons for the great popularity of Quintilian in the early Renaissance, in fact, was that his work provided an explicit rationale for an educational program in literary culture which was already under way. The English poets William Shakespeare and John Milton, for instance, each had an education remarkably similar to that outlined in Quintilian's *Institutio oratoria*—but remarkably similar as well to that of John of Salisbury in the twelfth century, of Gasparino Barzizza in the fourteenth, and of Winston Churchill in the nineteenth. The continuity of method did not depend on any single book, but rather on the pragmatic conclusion that what was successful was worth continuing.

The modern reading of Quintilian, then, is not a mere antiquarian exercise. His book epitomizes the best of a humane approach to literacy. To understand his role in promoting that approach, it will be useful to examine his career, his work, and his influence before turning to the text itself.

Donald Lemen Clark

"The Progymnasmata"

There have been many references to Aphthonius in our discussions of theme writing as practiced in the schools of Milton's day. Aphthonius has been someone we have been looking forward to and preparing for. Erasmus recommended him, Brinsley thought him difficult but essential, Hoole recommended him, school statutes required him. Why? The one thing that made Aphthonius' *Progymnasmata* so valuable to schoolmaster and to schoolboy is that Aphthonius shows how themes are written. He gives patterns. He presents a graded series of elementary exercises in theme writing that proceeds from the easy to the more difficult, and builds each exercise on what the boy has learned from previous exercises, repeating somewhat from the previous exercise and adding something that is new. He never takes anything for granted save a teacher in a room full of boys, assembled for the purpose of learning to write themes.

The elementary exercises in theme writing which Aphthonius teaches should be good. They are based on many centuries of grammar school experience. Quintilian explained them in the first century A.D. briefly but with approval. Suetonius describes some of them as taught by the earliest Roman teachers in the first century B.C. Three textbooks survive to show us what ancient schoolmasters had evolved. These are the *Progymnasmata* of Theon, Hermogenes, and Aphthonius, all Greek teachers of grammar and rhetoric. Hermogenes, a native of Tarsus, lived in the second century. His textbook, translated into Latin by Priscian the grammarian in the fifth century, was very popular in postclassical times and in the Middle Ages. The most recent of the ancient textbooks to present the elementary exercises is that of Aphthonius, who taught rhetoric in Antioch in the fourth century. His strongest bid for popularity was that he added a brief model theme to each pattern of his formulary. It was this textbook, translated into Latin, annotated elaborately, and amplified with many additional model themes, which held the lead in the English grammar schools from the middle of the sixteenth century.

The *Aphthonius* which Milton probably used was, as I have just indicated, a composite product. The underlying strata are composed of a Latin translation of the original Greek *Aphthonius* edited and combined by Reinhard Lorich from previously published translations by Rudolph Agricola and Joannes Maria Cataneo. In Lorich's edition of 1542 this is overlaid by Lorich's elaborate scholia and augmented by the addition of many more model themes, some written by Lorich and some collected by him from other Renaissance writers. A revised and somewhat enlarged edition appeared in 1546.

Lorich also quotes, sometimes rather fully, from other writers on the elementary exercises, more especially from Quintilian and Priscian. I have found no references to this "Priscian" which do not refer to Priscian's Latin version of Hermogenes' *Progymnasmata*. Where Aphthonius echoes Hermogenes closely, as he often does, Lorich does not introduce material from Hermogenes, but does so very freely whenever Hermogenes gives a fuller explanation, or a different example, than Aphthonius. Lorich's failure to identify "Priscian" as Hermogenes, so confusing to modern scholars, resulted naturally enough from the traditional title which displays the translator more emphatically than the author. Thus in the Aldine collection of minor rhetoricians (*De Rhetori*, 1523) we find: *Priscianus de Rhetoricae praeexercitamentis ex Hermogene*, and in *Antiqui Rhetores Latini* (1599) it is entitled *Prisciani Grammatici Caesariensis de Praeexercitamentis Rhetoricae ex Hermogene Liber*. It was Lorich's edition of Aphthonius in Latin with additions from Priscian's Latin Hermogenes that became standard for one hundred and fifty years from its publication in 1546.

The nature of the exercises in Aphthonius, Lorich makes explicit in his scholia to the first exercise. There are fourteen exercises, which introduced the boys to all three classes of rhetoric: Demonstrative rhetoric is represented by Fable, Narrative, Chreia, Proverb, Thesis; Judicial rhetoric, by Confirmation, Refutation, Common Place; Demonstrative rhetoric, by Encomium, Vituperation, Impersonation, and Comparison. I shall endeavor to explain these exercises, point out how they were taught, and illustrate briefly in the order of their appearance in Aphthonius, where each exercise is treated in a separate chapter, the numbers of which I follow.

1. Fable

This first assignment was a very simple one for little boys, who were required to do little more than retell the stories from Aesop in an extended or condensed paraphrase, or to turn it from indirect to direct discourse. The boys were to acquire good morals from the fables, a stock of illustrative stories to use in mature oratory, and an increasingly flexible command of Latin style. Milton's *Apologus de Rustico & Hero* is such a fable, but treated as a more advanced exercise because done in verse.

2. Narrative

The next assignment involved the retelling of stories from the poets and historians the boys were reading. It aimed, as Quintilian had said, not at eloquence but at knowledge. Aphthonius points out that the narrative themes should make clear: I) Who performed the action; 2) What was done; 3) The time when; 4) The place where; 5) How it was done; 6) The cause why. The stories, he adds, should possess the virtues of clarity, brevity, probability, and propriety of word use. They were in effect imitative exercises in paraphrase such as I have already explained.

3. Chreia

The chreia, like the proverb which follows it as Exercise 4, is an exercise in the amplification or dilation of a theme. In fact the chreia is the Theme par excellence. Both exercises of chreia and proverb taught the pupil both *inventio* and *dispositio*. But let Aphthonius, following Hermogenes very closely, define. "A chreia is a brief account of what a person said or did, for the purpose of edification." The following is his example of a verbal chreia: "Socrates said the root of learning is bitter, but the fruit is pleasant." The following is a chreia of action: "Diogenes, seeing a rude boy, struck his tutor, saying, 'Why did you teach him thus?' " In either sort of chreia the schoolboy was to develop the theme according to the formula laid down as follows: Begin with praise of the sayer or doer; Then a paraphrase or exposition of the theme; Tell why it was said or done; Introduce a contrast; Then a comparison; And an example; Support with confirmatory testimony; Conclude with a brief epilog. [*Laudativo, paraphrastico, causa, contrario, parabola, exemplo, testimonio veterum, brevi epilogo.*]

4. Proverb

Both the Latin Hermogenes and Latin Aphthonius call this exercise *sententia*, a summary saying or statement of general application, persuading, dissuading, or edifying, in Greek *gnome*. It is much the same as the chreia, save that the name of the author of the words is not named. According to Aphthonius it follows the same formula for sequence and is otherwise treated in the same way. Lorich, in his additions to the basic teachings of Aphthonius, quotes an example of a theme developed from a proverb from Priscian's Hermogenes, which I shall now translate for the interesting light it throws on the kind of theme writing Milton's schoolmasters were trying to teach.

EXAMPLE OF A PROVERB DRAWN FROM PRISCIAN

THEME: "A counsellor should not sleep all night."

Laudativo. Briefly praise the author of the proverb.

Paraphrastico. Then explain the meaning of the proverb simply, thus: "It is not fitting for a responsible leader of great power to be oppressed by sleep from sunset to dawn or to lie torpid with sloth."

Causa. "A leader should always be alert and ready to give counsel to his followers, while sleep takes away counsel and causes forgetfulness."

Contrario. "As a private citizen differs from a king, so sleep differs from wakefulness. Thus there is no harm if a private citizen sleeps all night, but it is intolerable if a king is not wakeful, pondering the welfare of his subjects."

Comparatio. "Just as the helmsman of a ship must keep watch for the common safety, even though the others sleep, so an emperor must be fraught with solicitude for his own people."

Exemplo. "Hector, watchful at night and taking thought for the republic, sent Dolon to reconnoiter the Greek ships. The wakeful Scipio stormed the camp of the sleeping Syphax. *(Livy, Book 10, of the Punic War.)*

Testimonio veterum. "This Sallust confirms, saying, 'Many mortals dedicated to their bellies and to sleep, bring their ignorant and uncultivated lives to an end like vagrants.' "

Conclusio. This should be hortatory. "We should take counsel with the greatest care and wakefulness concerning all undertakings which we command."

I shall now quote McCrea's translation of *An Early Prolusion by John Milton* as an example of how a schoolboy followed the formula in Aphthonius. I think the reader will recognize that it was composed not only according to the formula but also with some attention to the foregoing example as a model to be imitated. To draw attention to its pattern I shall break it up into paragraphs and insert the designations as Lorich did for Priscian's version of Hermogenes.

IN THE MORNING RISE UP EARLY

Laudativo. "'Tis a proverb worn with age, 'It is most healthy to rise at break of day.' Nor indeed is the saying less true than old, for if I shall try to recount in order the several advantages of this, I shall seem to undertake a task of heavy labor."

Paraphrastico. "Rise, then, rise, thou lazy fellow, let not the soft couch hold thee forever."

Causa (Pleasant). "You know not how many pleasures the dawn brings. Would you delight your eyes? Look at the sun rising in ruddy vigor, the pure and healthful sky, the flourishing green of the fields, the variety of all the flowers. Would you delight your ears? Listen to the clear concert of the birds and the light humming of the bees. Would you please your nostrils? You cannot have enough of the sweetness of the scents that breath from the flowers."

Causa (Profitable). "But if this please you not, I beg you to consider a little the argument of your health; for to rise from bed at early morn is in no slight degree conducive to a strong constitution; it is in fact best for study, for then 'you have wit in readiness.' "

Comparatio. "Besides, it is the part of a good king not to pamper his body with too much sleep, and live a life all holidays and free from toil, but to plan for the commonwealth night and day."

Testimonio veterum. "As Theocritus wisely urges 'It is not well to sleep deep.' And in Homer the Dream thus speaks to Agamemnon
'Sleepest thou, son of wise-minded, horse-taming Atreus?
'Tis not well for a man of counsel to sleep all night through.' "

Exemplo. "Why do the poets fable Tithonus and Cephalus to have loved Dawn? Surely because they were sparing of sleep; and, leaving their beds, were wont to roam the fields, decked and clad with many-colored flowers."

Contrario. "But to extirpate somnolence utterly, to leave no trace of it, I shall attempt to lay bare the numberless inconveniences that flow to all from it. It blunts and dulls keen talent, and greatly injures memory. Can anything be baser than to snore far into the day, and, to consecrate, as it were, the chief part of your life to death?"

Conclusio. "But you who bear rule, you especially should be wide awake, and utterly rout gripping sleep as it creeps upon you. For many, coming upon enemies, whelmed by heavy sleep, and as it were, buried therein, have smitten them with slaughter, and wrought such havoc as it is pitiful to see or hear of. A thousand examples of this kind occur to me which I could tell with an inexhaustible pen. But if I imitate such Asiatic exuberance, I fear lest I shall murder my wretched listeners with boredom."

Milton clearly found the formula for his theme in Aphthonius as well as a model for imitation. The material about the good king who keeps awake to counsel for the good of the commonwealth is right out of the model. Moreover he need not have gone directly to Homer for his pat quotation, "'Tis not well for a man of counsel to sleep all night through." He would have found it readily in Lorich's scholia to Aphthonius' own example of a proverb, all in Greek, or he may have found it where Lorich seems to have found it, for that worthy scholiast translates from the Greek, "Haud dignum duce, noctem dormire per omnem, ut reddit Erasm. in Proverb." The proverb which Dr. Gil set his boys for their theme, "It is most healthy to rise at break of day," can doubtless be found in a number of collections, but Dr. Gil, or Milton if he chose his own theme to write on, could have found it in Lily's *A Short Introduction of Grammar.* Lily uses it to illustrate *The First Concorde* of the verb: "Somtime the Infinitive mode of a verb . . . may be the nominative case to the verb: as Diluculo surgere, saluberrimum est, To arise betime in the morning, is the most holsome thing in the worlde."

5. Refutation

Aphthonius calls this exercise *Destructio,* but it falls in better with modern usage to follow Priscian's Hermogenes where it appears as *Refutatio.* (Hermogenes includes with it as one exercise *Confirmatio,* of which Aphthonius makes a separate exercise.) It is a very old exercise, one described by Suetonius: "Frequently they attacked the credibility of fables. This type of thesis the Greeks called destructive and constructive." This was the first exercise which gave the boys an opportunity to argue for or against anything. Lorich quotes Quintilian as pointing out that the boys need not argue the credibility of myths alone, but the credibility of legends from early history as well. The subject matter was thus well adjusted to the capacity and experience of the boys who were reading the poets and the historians and were hence familiar with the stories.

Aphthonius gives as the formula for treatment: "First blame the teller of the story; then give an expository summary of the story; and finally attack it under the following heads. It is obscure, incredible, impossible, does not follow logically, unfitting, unprofitable." As his example Aphthonius attacks the credibility of the story of Daphne and Apollo, pointing out that if she were the daughter of the river god Ladon and the Earth, she would have drowned if she were brought up by her father and would have been invisible if brought up by her mother underground. Lorich assembles other model themes including an attack on the stories of Arion and the dolphins and the story of Elphenor turned to a swine by Circe.

6. Confirmation

Confirmatio has the same topics and the same formula as *Refutatio,* only the arguments are turned inside out. Thus Aphthonius directs: "First praise the teller of the story; give an expository summary; and confirm the story by showing that it is manifest, probable, possible, follows logically, fitting, profitable." He then produces a model theme supporting the credibility of the story of Daphne and Apollo. He points out that if Daphne was the daughter of the river god she would take after his nature and would be in no danger of drowning if she lived under water. And what if she would be invisible to men if brought up underground by her mother? It is no more than decent that a young girl should live a sheltered life. Lorich in turn supplies themes supporting the credibility of the stories of Arion and of Elphenor.

This exercise helped to open the boys' minds to the amazing truth that something can be said for as well as against the credibility of an implausible story, just as the exercise in refutation helped them to recognize the equally amazing truth that they need not believe credulously everything they read in a book. These exercises also introduced them, on an elementary level, to "the art of discovering all possible means to persuasion in any subject."

7. Common Place

"A commonplace," says Aphthonius, "is an oration enlarging on [*augmentans*] the good or evil which resides in anyone. It is called commonplace because it deals with matter common to all men who partake of the good or evil discussed." Lorich correctly quotes in his scholia the statement of Quintilian that in a commonplace one declaims, not against a person, but against the vices, such as adultery, gambling, theft, and quotes from Priscian's Hermogenes that the commonplace is an amplification [*exaggeratio*] of what is acknowledged to be true. The commonplace, then, assumes the "facts" and gives the boys practice in coloring, dilating, and amplifying the good or bad, throwing a favorable or unfavorable light on the "facts" assumed.

Aphthonius points out that the commonplace gives the student practice in perorating, in rousing the feelings of the auditors, as one needs to do in the epilog of an actual speech. The formula for the *dispositio* of the commonplace and the places of invention to be used are as follows:

> Begin with the contrary, analysing it, not to inform, for the facts are assumed, but to incite and exasperate the auditors. Then introduce a comparison to heighten as much as possible the point you are making. After that introduce a proverb, upbraiding and calumniating the doer of the deed. Then a digression, introducing a defamatory conjecture as to the past life of the person accused; then a repudiation of pity. Conclude the exercise with the final considerations of legality, justice, expediency, possibility, decency, and the consequences of the action.

The model theme which Aphthonius supplies is one against tyranny, a theme always popular with Milton, as with the teachers of declamation in antiquity. Lorich's additional themes are against drunkenness, sacrilege, disobedience, and avarice.

8. Encomium

Quintilian, and Hermogenes after him, included themes in praise and dispraise in one exercise, but Aphthonius separates them to give the boys additional practice in this most important aspect of oratory; for here we have a grammar school adaptation of that part of rhetoric which Aristotle called epideictic and Cicero, demonstrative. The exercise called commonplace was a preparation for it. Commonplace enlarged on praise of virtue and dispraise of vice. Encomium praised a person or thing for being virtuous; vituperation attacked a person or thing for being vicious.

Aphthonius defines encomium or praise as "an oration enumerating the good qualities belonging to any thing." Things which can be praised he lists as persons, moral qualities, seasons of the year, places, dumb animals, and plants. The most characteristic encomium is of course that of a person. Aphthonius gives for an encomiastic theme the following elaborate formula:

> Begin with an exordium. Then subjoin what stock the person is, divided as follows: of what people, of what country, of what ancestors, of what parents. Then explain his education under the heads of instruction, art, laws. Then introduce the chief of all topics of praise, his deeds, which you will show to be the results of 1. his excellences of mind as fortitude or prudence, 2. his excellences of body as beauty, speed, vigor, 3. his excellences of fortune as his high position, his power, wealth, friends. Then bring in a comparison in which your praise may be heightened to the uttermost. Finally conclude with an epilog urging your hearers to emulate.

The extent to which encomium was encouraged to go in exaggeration is suggested by Milton's own comments, in his *Second Defense,* on his elogium of the Queen of Sweden, whose approval of his *First Defense* had delighted him:

> And if I had happened to have written what I have, when a young man [*adolescenti*], and the same liberty were allowed to orators as to poets, I should in truth not have hesitated to prefer my fortune to that of some among the gods; forasmuch as they, being gods, contended only for beauty, or in music, before a human arbiter; and I, being a man, with a goddess for my arbitress, have come off victorious in the noblest far of all contests.

As a model theme in encomium Aphthonius offers one in praise of Thucydides. Lorich adds model themes in praise of wisdom, Demosthenes, Philip of Macedon, eloquence, the University of Marburg, and city life.

9. Vituperation

Although he makes a separate exercise of dispraise, Aphthonius follows

Hermogenes in pointing out that it is based on the same places of invention as praise and that the same things can be dispraised as praised. His own model theme is a vituperation of Philip of Macedon. Lorich adds model themes vituperating Paris, Hannibal, and, important for the student of Milton's school days, Phalaris.

Milton mentions, in a passage which I have already quoted, in his discussion of the benefits to be derived from the practice of theme writing in school, declamatory vituperation of this Phalaris, the Agrigentine tyrant who roasted his victims in a brazen bull. Phalaris is the subject of two declamations by Lucian, which Milton may have read in school, but it is much more probable that he learned to declame against Phalaris while he was writing themes based on the formularies and models of Aphthonius.

Another tyrant whom Milton mentions in the same passage as an object of vituperation is Mezentius, who was expelled by his subjects on account of his cruelty. Milton may well have met him in the *Æneid* or in Livy, but his interest in Mezentius as a tyrant to dispraise would have been heightened by a reference to him in Aphthonius, under the second sort of *chreia,* amongst the additional examples "ex Stephano Nigro."

That Milton had been exercised in declamation on the theme of the tyrant Mezentius receives further support from other references to him. In *The Doctrine and Discipline of Divorce* (1643), describing the misery of mismated man and wife, he says: "Instead of being one flesh, they will be rather two carkasses chain'd unnaturally together; or as it may happ'n, a living soule bound to a dead corps, a punishment too like that inflicted by the tyrant *Mezentius.*" Milton again refers to the tyrant Mezentius in the *First Defense.*

In his mature writings praising and blaming were not unusual themes with Milton, as has been frequently noticed. That he carried vituperation to extremes even more than he did encomium undoubtedly received strong support from the grammar school exercises taught according to the formularies of Aphthonius. In *L'Allegro* and *Il Penseroso* he handles the topics of encomium and vituperation more playfully. In the former he assigns a defamatory ancestry to Melancholy; in the latter, an encomiastic one. Both poems owe a great deal to a rhetorical training which taught Milton to argue on both sides of a theme.

10. Comparison

Comparison as a rhetorical exercise taught little new. The boys had already been taught to introduce a brief comparison as one of the places of argument in earlier and simpler themes. But Comparison was valuable in summing up earlier exercises and preparing for more advanced ones. As Aphthonius defines it, "Comparison is an oration in which one likens one thing with another, showing one of the things to be either equal or superior to the other." It uses, as he points out, the same places of argument as the commonplace, the encomium and the vituperation. Aphthonius gives as his model theme a comparison of Achilles and Hector. Lorich adds only one model theme of his own, a comparison of Demosthenes and Cicero. He cites, however, a number of Plutarch's parallel lives as examples. Clearly the schoolboys were to compare historical, legendary, or fictitious characters whom they had met in their reading of school authors.

11. Impersonation

This rather difficult exercise might be called today the composition of dramatic monologs. In antiquity it was most frequently called *prosopopoeia*. Aphthonius defines it as "The imitation and expression of the character of a person assigned." Lorich quotes Quintilian and Priscian's Hermogenes as in substantial agreement with Aphthonius. The exercise required the boys to compose lines for a person, real or imaginary, to speak under given circumstances. Aphthonius gives three subdivisions to this exercise: *Ethopoeia*, when the writer composes lines for a known person to speak, as what Hercules might say to Eurysthenes; *Eidolopoeia*, when lines are composed as for the dead to speak; *Prosopopoeia*, when both persons and lines are feigned, as in a dramatic poem or play.

Aphthonius gives as his model theme the lines Niobe might speak over the bodies of her slain children. In his scholia Lorich quite properly leans heavily on the poets. His own model themes include a speech for Hercules to Eurysthenes, for Dives reduced to want, for Hecuba after the fall of Troy, for Andromache after Hector's death, for Medea after she has slain her children, this last in the translation of Erasmus from the Greek of Libanius, the fourth century sophist. Lorich concludes by pointing out examples in Plutarch: What Cornelia said when she heard that Pompey was defeated by Caesar; What Cleopatra said when she learned that Antony was dead. Difficult as the exercise is, it could be a benefit to schoolboys in bringing alive to their imaginations dramatic scenes from classical literature. Moreover, the exercise emphasizes decorum or propriety to the person speaking, the person spoken to, and to the emotional coloring of the attendant circumstances. The value of such an exercise to a future poet was quite clear to Quintilian, who wrote, "Prosopopoeiae appear to me the most difficult of all [exercises] ... But the exercise is extremely beneficial, both because it requires double effort, and because it improves the powers of those who would be poets or historians."

That Milton was familiar with the exercise and with the lessons to be learned from it is clear from his references to the indecorum of Bishop Hall's letter addressed to the Church, "a Letter to a prosopopoea a certain rhetoriz'd woman whom he calls mother," and from his explanation of the theory of dramatic decorum in *The First Defense*. Here he points out that Salmasius misrepresented the sentiments of Aeschylus by quoting him out of context:

> We must not regard the poet's words as his own, but consider who it is that speaks in the play, and what that person says; for different persons are introduced, sometimes good, sometimes bad, some times wise men, sometimes fools, and they speak not always the poet's own opinion, but what is most fitting to each character [*sed quid cuique personae maximè conveniat*].

The oratorical nature of this exercise as taught in the grammar schools also accounts, I believe, in some measure for the superiority of the speeches Milton composed for characters to deliver in *Comus, Paradise Lost, Paradise Regained* and *Sampson*, to his efforts at dramatic dialog.

12. Description

"Description is an oration expository or narrative which aims to place the subject as it were before the eye." In his scholia Lorich quotes definitions from Priscian's Hermogenes and from Quintilian, both of whom use the image of "bringing before one's eyes what is to be shown." The Greek term is *ecphrasis,* which is probably more commonly used today than "description" to name the rather formal set piece the exercise aimed at, exemplified for modern readers by Pater's Mona Lisa and Ruskin's St. Marks.

As Aphthonius points out an ecphrasis can describe persons, things, dumb animals, and plants. It may be simple, as a description of a battle or a time of day; or complex, as Thucydides' description of a battle which took place at night. The treatment should involve the use of many descriptive figures, both schemes and tropes, in presenting a vivid imitation of the subject.

For his model theme Aphthonius describes in detail the acropolis of Alexandria, comparing it and contrasting it with the acropolis of Athens, and going into great detail over the halls, porticos, temples, and the library. Lorich picks out for mention such famous exphrases from the poets as the storm in the first book of the *Æneid,* the house of fame in Ovid's *Metamorphoses* (which Milton imitated in *In quintum Novembris*), and Cleopatra's barge from Plutarch's *Life of Antony* (which Shakespeare imitated). Then Lorich offers as model themes a description of the habitation of St. Antony from Jerome's life of Hilary, and a long description of his own grammar school at Hadamar [*Descriptio gymnastica domûs Reinhardi Lorichii Hadamarii*]. Would Milton had left us an ecphrasis on St. Paul's School!

Quintilian had warned against the theatricality resulting from overdoing ecphrasis, Horace had warned against the purple patch, and Lucian had urged restraint and done a burlesque ecphrasis which Milton refers to appreciatively, but Aphthonius gives no warning. In their ecphrases the boys, it seems, might go as far as they liked.

13. Thesis

The thesis was the first exercise that gave the boys an opportunity to speak and write on a theme that had two sides. The previous themes held them to the full dilation of what was accepted as true. Priscian's Hermogenes, as quoted in Lorich's scholia, makes this distinction explicit: "This is the difference between a thesis and a commonplace. The commonplace is an amplification [*exaggeratio*] of a subject matter admitted; the thesis is a debate on a matter still in doubt."

"A thesis, or consultation," says Aphthonius, "is an investigation or examination of a question in an oration. It may be political or speculative. Political as 'Should one take a wife? Go on a journey? Build walls?' Speculative as 'Are the heavens spherical? Are there many worlds?' " He further points out an important difference between a thesis, which discusses a general question [*quaestio infinita*], and a hypothesis, which discusses a particular question [*quaestio finita* or *causa*]. "Should one fortify a city?" is a thesis: "Should the Lacedaemonians fortify Sparta against the Persian invasion?" is a hypothesis. Cicero, in his *Orator* points out the difference between them in the following passage, part of which Lorich quotes in his scholia to Aphthonius:

> Wherever he can the orator will divert the controversy from particular persons and circumstances to universal abstract questions, for he can debate a genus on wider grounds than a species. Whatever is proved of the whole is of necessity proved of the part. A question thus transferred from specific persons and circumstances to a discussion of a universal genus is called a thesis. Aristotle used to have young men argue a thesis as an exercise.

Milton shows his awareness of the differences between thesis and hypothesis and the persuasive value of thesis when he says: *"A thesi ad hypothesin,* or from the general to the particular, an evincing argument in Logick."

Since the thesis is the first exercise of the *Progymnasmata* which deals with debatable questions, Aphthonius points out that the *dispositio* of a thesis should be the same as that of an oration. The thesis begins with an exordium, to which one may add a *narratio,* proceeds to confirmatory argument and rebuttal, and concludes with an epilog. "The arguments," he says, "are drawn from the final headings of justice, legality, expediency, and possibility."

Aphthonius offers a model theme supporting the thesis that a man should take a wife. Lorich adds a model theme urging a man not to take a wife. So we can be very sure that Milton had been introduced in boyhood to the theme of his divorce tracts and had, perhaps, debated the thesis, for or against, as an exercise at St. Paul's School. Lorich's other model themes illustrating the thesis argue that old age is not troublesome to bear and that wealth is not the greatest good.

The thesis has had a long life as a school exercise. In Milton's day, at least, it was much practiced at Cambridge as well as in the grammar schools. All seven of the *Prolusiones* which Milton wrote as a student at Cambridge and published in the edition of 1674 along with his Latin epistles are theses. Each was written to support one side of what Aphthonius called a political or speculative question. The themes of the seven theses are as follows: 1) That day is more excellent than night; 2) Pythagoras' theory of the harmony of the spheres is true at least poetically; 3) That scholastic philosophy is neither pleasant nor profitable; 4) (The only one entitled *Thesis*) In the destruction of any thing a resolution to primary matter does not occur; 5) Partial forms do not occur in an animal in addition to the whole; 6) (Entitled *Oratio*) That sometimes sportive exercises are not prejudicial to philosophical studies; 7) (Entitled *Oratio*) That knowledge renders man happier than ignorance. Of these the fourth and fifth are characteristic examples of the scholastic disputation, so important in the Cambridge of Milton's day, which the third prolusion is at pains to attack. The first and seventh are the most characteristic examples of the thesis as it was taught by Aphthonius.

The thesis is also susceptible of poetic treatment. Thus the first seventeen of Shakespeare's sonnets are theses on the theme, Should a man marry? Milton's *L'Allegro* and *Il Penseroso* are companion theses arguing whether the active or contemplative life is more desirable or, as Tillyard suggests, whether the pleasures of night are superior to those of day.

14. Legislation

The exercise in finding arguments for and against a law gave the boys their first taste of deliberative oratory on the mature level of public legislation. To be sure they were not encouraged to propose new laws or in other ways overturn the existing establishment of the government, but to debate the pros and cons of ancient laws or even of fictitious laws. Thus Aphthonius gives as his model theme an attack on the ancient law which permitted the injured husband to kill the adulterers if he took them together in the act of adultery. To attack the cruelty and savagery of the law without seeming to palliate adultery involved careful footwork for the schoolboys who debated the theme from the fourth century to the eighteenth.

The arguments against a law, according to Aphthonius, are drawn from the final headings of justice, legality, expediency, and possibility, a procedure Milton is careful to follow in *Areopagitica,* where he points out that the licensing act is *impossible,* of enforcement, *unjust* and *dishonorable,* and finally that the act is *inexpedient* in hampering the discovery and dissemination of truth.

Lorich offers three additional model themes. The first is a speech in support of the law proposed by C. Oppius, tribune of the people, against women's extravagance in dress. The second is a speech in favor of a law which would require children to support their parents under penalty of imprisonment. Lorich's third model theme, quoted from Petrus Mosellanus, supports a law, ascribed to the Swiss, which stipulates that guests should not be urged to drink. It is clear that Lorich's models, at least, would encourage the boys in modesty of dress, filial devotion, and sobriety.

In his precepts for the *dispositio* of a speech on legislation, exemplified by his models, Aphthonius encourages a mechanical arrangement, involving the statement of one objection at a time followed by an immediate confutation, then another objection followed by its confutation. This mechanical arrangement Milton follows in his *Animadversions upon the Remonstrants Defense,* and to a smaller degree in other tracts. To some degree, at least, Milton as well as his contemporaries was influenced by the instruction in theme writing he received under the guidance of the *Progymnasmata* of Aphthonius.

Melinda Fine

"You Can't Just Say That the Only Ones Who Can Speak Are Those Who Agree with Your Position: Political Discourse in the Classroom"

In this article, Melinda Fine describes the classroom dynamics surrounding the discussion of controversial issues in a middle school classroom. Through observation and interviews, she creates a detailed portrait of the interactions among teachers and students, revealing that while discussions of emotionally charged social and political issues are often heated and difficult, they can still be constructive. Fine maintains that students are more resilient and able to handle disagreement than is often believed. She concludes by arguing that education in a democracy requires that teachers and students learn to deal constructively with political and social differences.

Cambridge, Massachusetts, lies just across the Charles River from Boston. Known best for its stately, well-kept colonial homes and the ivy-clad brick buildings of Harvard University, this three-hundred-and-fifty year old city is generally perceived as a White, middle-class, intellectual enclave. While this perception is at least partially true, this densely packed city of almost 100,000 is in fact far more heterogeneous than its popular image suggests. One-fifth of all Cambridge residents are foreign-born, and one-half of these arrived during the past decade. A majority of the city's African Americans, as well as immigrants from Cape Verde, Brazil, Southeast Asia, Central America, and Haiti, tend to reside in neighborhoods that look quite different from the tree-lined streets and white-trimmed mansions surrounding Harvard University.

The Medgar Evers School is located in one of the poorer neighborhoods of Cambridge.[1] Here, mostly Black, Latino, Haitian, and Asian families live in multi-family homes that are usually close together, and often in need of paint or new siding. Many of Medgar Evers' students come from the large housing project just across the street; 44 percent of the student population qualifies for free or reduced-price lunches. Because of the city's desegregation program, however, the school's roughly six hundred K-8 students are more racially balanced than the neighborhood in which the school is located: in 1992–1993, the school was 43 percent White, 34 percent African-American, 16 percent Asian, and 7 percent Latino.

Medgar Evers is a long, three-story, beige concrete building of irregular geometric design. Surrounded by few trees, the school appears cold and austere when viewed from the street. Once inside, however, one gets an entirely different impression. Classrooms, offices, the school library, and the auditorium spin off from an airy central space that is open from the third floor to the basement. Sunlight streams in through skylights on the school's slanted roof, infusing all three floors of the building with light. Terracotta-tiled floors, clean hallways, notices for bake sales and other school events, as well as abundant displays of student artwork make the school feel cheery and welcoming. An enormous map of the world hangs on a wall across from the school's central office. This map is covered with push pins, each connected to a string that leads to a flag representing the country pinpointed. "We have children and families in our school representing *at least* sixty-four countries of the world," a card next to the map states. "We want to encourage children to become familiar with the world map, to identify all of the countries of origin, and to help celebrate our diversity!"

I have visited a classroom in this school nearly every day for the past four months, acting as a participant/observer while carrying out research for my doctoral dissertation in education. I have come to study how the teacher and students in one classroom grapple with an interdisciplinary social studies unit called "Facing History and Ourselves."[2]

This program seeks to provide a model for teaching history in a way that helps students reflect critically upon a variety of contemporary social, moral, and political issues. It focuses on a specific historical period—the Nazi rise to power and the Holocaust—and guides students back and forth between an in-depth historical case study and reflection on the causes and consequences of presentday prejudice, intolerance, violence, and racism.[3]

Facing History's decision to use the Holocaust as a case study and a springboard for exploring contemporary issues is complex and merits some discussion. When middle school teachers in Brookline, Massachusetts, created Facing History and Ourselves in 1976, relatively few Holocaust curricula existed. Perceiving the Holocaust to be a watershed event of the twentieth century, these teachers felt that their students should, indeed, learn about such a critical historical moment. At the same time, however, they felt that the Holocaust's "meaning" to students must lie not only in understanding its unique historical dimensions, but also in grappling with its more generalizable lessons about human behavior. Historically examining the escalation of steps through which individuals living under Nazi rule were made to follow Hitler—from the use of propaganda to influence one's thinking, to the threats against one's economic and personal security, to the use of terror to compel obedience—course designers sought to help students identify how opportunities for resistance were gradually eroded with the demise of German democracy and the rise of a totalitarian state. Using historical understanding as a catalyst for more personal, critical reflection, they intended to foster students' awareness of the social conditions that can undermine democracy and promote their sense of moral and political responsibility as future citizens.

It might well be asked whether these goals could not also be achieved by undertaking a different, perhaps more relevant case study—of the Middle Passage (the transatlantic slave trade), for example, or the genocide of Native Americans. No doubt they could be. Program designers, teachers, and promoters do not argue that the Holocaust is the only genocide—or even the most important genocide—to teach about. In fact, Facing History has developed other curricular materials that deal more directly with these "closer-to-home" events, and the Facing History Resource Text includes a chapter on the Armenian Genocide.[4]

Program advocates do contend, however, that discussions about contemporary racism and violence may in fact be facilitated by focusing on a period of history more tangential to the cultural backgrounds of the course's ethnically diverse students. As Larry Myatt, a longtime teacher of the course and the director of an inner-city high school in Boston, says, Facing History offers "a way to talk about these issues in a *removed* way so that we don't hit people over the head with a two-by-four and say 'racism!' 'scapegoating!' "[5]

In keeping with the program's educational priorities, the semester-long curriculum is structured to move back and forth between a focus on "history" and a focus on "ourselves." Initial chapters of the program's resource book encourage thinking about universal questions of individual identity and social behavior. From here the course moves on to its more specific case study of prejudice and discrimination: an examination of the history of anti-semitism, beginning as far back as ancient Rome, Students undertake a rigorous, multifaceted study of German history from 1914 to 1945, examining, for example, the impact of Nazi racial policies in education and the workplace, the nature of propaganda, and the various roles played by victims, victimizers, and bystanders during the Third Reich. These lessons provide critical historical content and serve as structured exercises for thinking about the choices that individuals, groups, and nations faced with regard to action and resistance. These exercises, in turn, prepare students for later discussions about how they themselves can assume responsibility for protecting civil liberties and becoming active citizens.[6]

Facing History's complex intellectual content is undergirded by a pedagogical imperative: to foster perspective-taking, critical thinking, and moral decision-making among students. It is specifically geared toward adolescents who are developmentally engaged in a fierce (and somewhat contradictory) struggle to become distinct individuals *and* to fit in with their peers. These students, curriculum developers argue, have the most to gain from a course that "raises the problem of differing perspectives, competing truths, the need to understand motives and to consider the intentions and abilities of themselves and others."[7] Rather than shying away from the conflicts that are inevitably generated when a diverse group of adolescents work to clarify their own beliefs and values, teachers encourage students to view complexity and conflict as potentially conducive to personal growth and social exchange.

I chose to observe the implementation of Facing History and Ourselves in the Medgar Evers school for specific reasons—reasons undoubtedly operative in my interpretation of the course and, consequently, important to acknowledge here. First and foremost, I am a supporter of the program's goals. Educational efforts to foster moral and social responsibility are difficult undertakings, not only because of the conflictual nature of the material inevitably confronted with the students, but also because of the embattled position many such education programs—including Facing History—find themselves in today. I consider them socially necessary, nonetheless.

I also find compelling Facing History's claim that using historical subject matter somewhat tangential to the lives of racially diverse students may quite effectively reach and motivate students in multicultural urban settings. For this reason I have observed Facing History courses in several urban schools over the past few years, while completing my own doctoral work and serving as a research consultant to the Facing History organization.[8] My professional collaboration with Facing History has deepened my understanding of the program, but also demanded that I be vigilant in pushing myself to view its classroom practice in a critical light.

Consequently, while at the Medgar Evers school, I observed class daily for an eleven-week period. I hoped to learn how students and their teacher interpreted issues raised by the course, recognizing that their interpretations would no doubt shift during the semester and assuming, too, that they would at times produce conflict among classroom participants. I intended to describe how these conflicts were negotiated within the classroom.

To carry out my objectives, I felt that I needed to know as much as possible about the students, their teacher, and the school culture that surrounded the classroom study. I needed to have all classroom participants speak freely with me, and thus I needed to be known and trusted by them. These requirements dictated a qualitative, descriptive, phenomenological, and self-consciously personal approach to my subject, involving, among other things, participant/observation, in-class and post-class writing, lengthy individual interviews with students and their teacher, and ongoing review of students' written work.

My relations with the teacher and students were open and friendly. Over the course of the semester, I was invited to a bar mitzvah, sock hop, viola recital, and soccer match, and after the school year ended, I received a letter from one student asking me out to lunch. Since my intent was to get to know classroom participants and to let them get to know me, I never tried to hold myself aloof or maintain the stance of a completely distant, "objective" observer. Though I didn't, for the most part, participate actively in class discussion, I nonetheless tried to act in a style compatible with the school's "open" atmosphere. My constant, in-class writing was obvious to all present (in fact, students often teased me about how quickly I wrote), and I did comment on topics when asked by either the teacher or students. I also frequently asked, and was told, about students' basketball games, dances, baby-sitting, and dates. In turn, students asked and were told about me: that I was a teacher, an activist, and at that time a graduate student, and that I was writing a book about them.

I identify what I did and where I stand in relation to Facing History not to suggest that researcher "bias" qualifies the validity of my observations—as if some wholly neutral position were a preferable point of departure or even possible to attain. I believe all researchers stand in some relation to their subject; the reader simply deserves to know where I stand before watching these classroom events along with me.

• • •

It is an unseasonably hot day in May. The twenty-three students in Marysa Gonzalez's seventh/eighth-grade class sit fanning themselves with their spiral notebooks as late-morning sun pours into the classroom through a large, partially closed window on the far side of the room. Of the twelve girls and eleven boys in this room, six are African-American, four are Asian, and thirteen are White, one of whom is a Latina. Nursing her latest sports injury, Jess limps to her seat clad in navy blue shorts and a University of Michigan tee-shirt. Abby sports a summer-bright turquoise shirt, matching socks, and white stretch pants. The top piece of her shoulder length, sandy-blond hair is pulled back in a clip, and her bangs remain loose and hanging. Sandra's clothing and hairstyle are almost identical. Alan and Josh each sport marginally punk hairdos. Alan wears an earring in his left ear. Chi-Ho's pressed, beige cotton shirt remains buttoned at both the neck and cuffs, and he removes his thick, black-rimmed glasses every now and then to wipe the sweat from his brow. Jamal and Amiri both wear oversized tee-shirts and baggy cotton pants.

The teacher, Marysa Gonzalez, searches intently through piles of paper on her desk. A handsome Latina in her late forties, her style is informal and unpretentious: she wears light khaki slacks, a loose-fitting red cotton shirt, and no make-up. Her long black hair, pulled back in a loose braid, is streaked with grey.

It is the eleventh and second-to-last week of the Facing History course. Using students' understanding of the Holocaust as a lens through which to approach more immediate concerns, Marysa focuses the remaining class discussions around contemporary political problems in order to highlight students' own social and political responsibilities. This way of bringing closure to the course is in keeping with the final chapter of the Facing History Resource Text:

> This curriculum must provide opportunities for students to explore the practical applications of freedom, which they have learned demand a constant struggle with difficult, controversial, and complex issues. . . . This history has taught that there is no one else to confront terrorism, ease the yoke and pain of racism, attack apathy, create and enforce just laws, and wage peace but us. . . . We believe that participating in decision-making about difficult and controversial issues gives practice in listening to different opinions, deciphering fact from opinion, confronting emotion and reason, negotiating, and problem-solving.[9]

Marysa circulates around the uncomfortably hot classroom handing out the syllabus for the week. Listing all reading and homework assignments for the next five days, the syllabus begins with a quote from radical community organizer Saul Alinsky, which is directly relevant to this week's discussion: "Change means movement, movement means friction, friction means heat, and heat means controversy. The only place where there is no friction is in outer space or a seminar on political action."

Intended as a comment upon political conflicts in the world at large, Alinsky's remark is equally telling about classroom dynamics. Over the next several days, students will view provocative documentary films about individuals and/or organizations holding controversial and differing political beliefs. These films (and related readings) are intended to impress upon students the importance of clarifying one's own political beliefs and raise complex questions about how a democratic and pluralistic society should best handle the conflicts generated by political diversity. In discussing these films, political differences within the classroom itself will be illuminated and debated, and dilemmas raised by the course's intellectual content will be mirrored in the lived curriculum of classroom dynamics.

From my perspective, these classroom dynamics reveal tensions about conflicting values and ideologies among teachers, students, and the Facing History curriculum itself, demonstrating the enormous complexity of the endeavor to catalyze critical, moral thinking among adolescent students. On the one hand, the Facing History program advocates bringing forth multiple points of view, developing students' understanding of multiple perspectives, and promoting tolerance among diverse peoples of often differing backgrounds. In the classes I have observed, teacher practice is to a considerable extent in keeping with these curricular values; teachers often actively engage with students of diverse political perspectives and encourage them to remain fair-minded and open to at least hearing alternative points of view. On the other hand, the program unequivocally rejects moral relativism, condemning social attitudes and beliefs that in any way repress or discriminate against individuals or social groups. Tensions inevitably arise when teachers and students differ in their feelings about which beliefs actually further or hinder these stated curricular objectives. Whose standards should determine what is morally "right" or "wrong"? Do these determinations align with an individual's own political beliefs? How should beliefs that some regard as "wrong" be handled in the classroom? What are the repercussions of silencing these viewpoints or, alternatively, allowing them to be voiced freely? As the recent controversy over New York City's "Children of the Rainbow" curriculum demonstrates, these questions are increasingly the subject of national educational debate.

Marysa and her students also clearly struggle with questions such as these. A close look at how they are dealt with here—within the safety of a trusted school community—may help to illuminate how they are negotiated within a broader social context. What follows, then, is a portrait of classroom life. It is intended not as an evaluative critique of the Facing History program's success or failure in meeting its stated goals, but rather as an analytic exploration of the dynamics encountered in attempting to do so. As a matter of both research inquiry and writing style, social science portraiture investigates, describes, and analyzes characters, settings, and events in context and in relation to one another, and is informed by an awareness of the researcher's own relationship with his or her subject.[10] Equally important, portraiture offers a style of writing designed to engage the reader in the particular experience described and, in so doing, give him or her a sense of a larger whole. I offer the following in the spirit of what the writer Eudora Welty has noted in another context: "One place comprehended can make us understand other places better."[11]

•   •   •

Friday, May 11
"Remember yesterday? What did we see?" Marysa asks about a film in which the subject of political difference is raised. Sandra answers, "A story about a man who taught his students that the Holocaust never happened, and that Jews wanted to rule the world." Abby adds, "He also said that all the banks and the finances were controlled by Jewish people." "Yeah," agrees Alan, "he thought there was an international Jewish conspiracy."[12]

Students take turns passionately describing "Lessons in Hate," an early 1980s documentary about Jim Keegstra, a popular and charismatic mayor and teacher in a small town in Alberta, Canada, who taught anti-semitic beliefs to students for more than a decade. The film extensively documents Keegstra arguing that the Holocaust was a "hoax" that in no way singled out Jewish people. He also argues that the French revolution was a product of the "international Jewish conspiracy"; that John Wilkes Booth, the man who shot Abraham Lincoln, was a Jew; and that Jews caused the American Civil War. Young, vulnerable, and with little access to alternative beliefs or perspectives, Keegstra's students uncritically absorbed his teachings, or, in a few cases, adopted them ambivalently in order to receive a passing grade. More problematic still, Keegstra's statements were tacitly accepted by the school's principal and faculty, and by most of the town's council and citizens. When the mother of one student finally challenged Keegstra's teachings, she was vehemently opposed by members of her community. The school board eventually fired Keegstra, but not until after a long and difficult battle had been waged that painfully divided members of the small town.[13]

The Keegstra film raises questions about how a community can tolerate conflictual beliefs among its members while still maintaining cohesion. Showcasing the struggles experienced by both Keegstra and those who oppose him, it demonstrates how difficult it can be to stand up for one's beliefs, regardless of their content. After what they have read, seen, and been taught throughout the semester, Marysa's students are outraged that anyone could minimize the horror of the Holocaust, much less deny its very existence. Distancing themselves from their Canadian peers, some make disparaging remarks about Keegstra's seemingly docile and gullible students:

Abby: It seems like these people just *feed* on people who are torn apart. They just suck them up by providing them with an excuse to hate! They probably want to find a way to place the blame on someone else just to explain their own situation.

Marysa: Exactly! What's the vocabulary word which describes that? (Several students shout out, "scapegoating!") Well, what can you do to help people when they're in this condition? What can you do to turn their beliefs around?
Josh: Kill them!
Marysa: What?! Kill them?!
Josh: Yes. If they say those things, and if they start a war or something, you have to fight back.
Alan: But if you go out and fight these people, and you kill six hundred or seven hundred of them, it won't stop *anything!* More will just come and fight back!
Marysa: What I'm really trying to push is that this is not just a problem that happened in history, a long time ago—the Dark Ages, when I was born. These issues are here, in the present. And you're a part of it. You have to be aware of it so you are not brainwashed or indoctrinated in the future.

For the next several minutes, students discuss the apparent differences between their own multicultural community and Keegstra's ethnically homogeneous school and town. Marysa asks students to identify similarities between Nazi doctrine and what Keegstra taught, and Abby brings up the international Jewish conspiracy theme. Drawing this argument closer to home, Marysa suggests parallels between the historical claim that Jews have controlled the financial industry and the present-day fear that Japanese increasingly dominate the U.S. economy. Chi-Ho raises his hand and quietly drops a bombshell: "I think that a Jewish international conspiracy *does* exist, but not quite as much [as] they say. So many people are talking about it, it must be some way true." "What?!" several students exclaim at once. Josh stares in disbelief at the boy who sits next to him, suddenly a stranger. Susie and Jess yell out in disbelief. Marysa responds in a strained but consciously even-tempered voice, "Chi-Ho, why do you think this?" Chi-Ho answers in a somewhat muffled voice, "I don't know, but I do." Marysa continues, "Don't you think that if there was a conspiracy it could have stopped the Holocaust?" "No, I don't," Chi-Ho replies, "because it's more recent. It's developed since the fifties only, I think." Marysa responds emphatically, "Chi-Ho, we need to talk!"

Animated one-on-one conversations spring up between students who sit next to each other in all corners of the room; the whole class seems to be buzzing. Abby raises her hand and (deliberately or not) turns up the heat several notches. She says, "I'm against what some people are doing with Israel, with the way it was established and with killing the Palestinians and everything. But that's different from an international Jewish conspiracy." "*What* are you talking about?" Josh exclaims furiously. "We weren't even talking about that!" Sandra adds critically, "What are you against now, Abby?" Abby answers, "I'm against the way the country was set up." Marysa asks incredulously and slightly sarcastically, "The UN vote?" Abby replies, "Not that, but what happened to the Palestinian people *through* that. Elie Wiesel and people like that were involved, and millions of Palestinian people were massacred and forced to leave their homes, just like in the Holocaust."

All hell breaks loose. It seems like everyone begins yelling at Abby, and Chi-Ho's earlier remark is left by the wayside. Abby steadfastly holds her ground. Though her words remain strong and her claims unqualified, she slumps further and further into her seat with each new attack by her classmates. She strikes me as being both scared and defiant. Confused about historical facts, Josh defends the state of Israel.

Josh: They were *attacked* in an eight-day war!
Abby: Well, it's still not right to be killing people to set up a country!
Josh: That's exactly what *we* did to set up *our* country!
Abby: So? I'm against that, too! I don't believe in that either!
Sandra (becoming increasingly exasperated): Well, what *are* you for? What *do* you believe in?
(Alison and Susie nod emphatically in agreement.)
Abby (matter-of-factly): I believe in control by the people.
Marysa: But how do you determine which people should have control, Abby? In the film we saw, the Canadian teacher thinks he should have control, 'cause he thinks he's right. How are you going to decide who gets to speak and who doesn't?

Students debate the conundrum of free speech for the remaining few minutes of class. Though Marysa has (perhaps self-consciously) shifted discussion away from a contentious and personalized debate, the classroom atmosphere remains charged.

I am scheduled to interview Abby later on this same day. As students get ready for lunch, I watch Abby self-consciously gather her books, seeming proud yet uncomfortable about being isolated. Calling out to her, I suggest that we can discuss the points she has raised during our interview, if she is interested; she smiles appreciatively.

Sandra, Alison, and Angela note my overture and come up to speak with me on their way out of the room. "Look, I don't know much about the Jewish religion, or any religion, really," Sandra says, "but isn't it true that in the Bible it says that the land was originally Jewish land, and that's why they wanted it? Or, why didn't the Jewish people just go to a different country?"

I try to answer as best as I can, explaining that Jews, Christians, and Moslems have all lived on the land, and that all have laid claim to it at different periods of history. "But doesn't the Bible say that the Jews were there *first*?," Angela retorts, "and then the Moslems came when the Jews went to Egypt?" Trying to grant each group its legitimacy, I speak to the importance of finding contemporary political solutions to the problem. Seeing myself more as a participant/observer than an arbiter of divergent viewpoints, I refuse to choose sides despite the girls' best efforts to make me do so. The three girls head off for lunch less angry, but still visibly confused.

Josh leaves class upset by the comments made by both Abby and Chi-Ho. He speaks to Marysa for almost an hour after class, refusing to sit next to Chi-Ho and demanding that his seat be changed. In keeping with the curriculum's intent to foster students' ability to listen to alternative perspectives, Marysa tells me later:

I tried to explain to Josh that Chi-Ho was the same person Josh thought he was before he made that statement. I told him that the way to respond to problems is not to refuse to speak to someone, but to talk together to try to figure it out and to help people to change their beliefs.

But "talking together" is not always easy. True to Alinsky's comment, "frictions" caused by Abby and Chi-Ho seem to circulate around the class as a whole (several students shout at Abby and Chi-Ho); between students and their teacher (Marysa expresses unequivocal disapproval of both students' comments); and, perhaps most poignantly, within students' individual relationships (friendships between Josh and Chi-Ho as well as Abby and Sandra are strained).

Marysa leaves class as upset as many of her students and uncertain about how to proceed. In fact, her confusion seems to have been manifest in her classroom dealings. Confronted with views she finds repugnant and even dangerous, she does, nevertheless, encourage students to remain open-minded, independent in their thinking, and respectful of difference. She even engages Abby and Chi-Ho in a critical debate, urging them to clarify their thinking and to defend their controversial points of view. At the same time, however, Marysa implicitly undermines the views of both of these students. By publicly acknowledging her disagreement with Abby and Chi-Ho, she uses her implicit authority as the "teacher" (the one empowered to design seating plans, assign homework and grades, and so forth) to undermine, rather than muzzle, these students' perspectives. Given the power differential between teacher and student, the critical debate between them is unevenly weighted.

For example, Marysa challenges Chi-Ho's remarks before the full classroom community, but then seeks to remove them from the public arena. "Chi-Ho, we need to talk," she says after only a brief exchange, simultaneously displacing disagreement to the private realm and suggesting that, once there, she will set the record straight. Moments later Marysa chooses not to intervene when several students jump on Abby, and her own questions of Abby sound slightly facetious. Finally, she eventually steers discussion away from the Middle East and toward freedom of speech in the midst of an unresolved debate.

Admittedly uncomfortable with the arguments raised and feeling unequipped to handle them, Marysa avails herself of her proximity to the Facing History and Ourselves national office and calls in staff member Steve Cohen to address the controversial issues raised by Abby and Chi-Ho. While I believe Marysa is making good use of an available resource, I also wonder whether she is bringing Steve in to quell controversy and, in essence, to set the record straight. A balding, wiry man in chinos and tennis shoes, Steve visits class a few days later.

Monday, May 14
"Why did Hitler choose to focus on the Jews?" Steve asks to open this morning's complex agenda. Alan replies, "He said that they were in charge of the money." Jess adds, "He said they were the people who put Germany in the economic state they were in." "Well, why did people believe it?" Steve continues. Abby says,

"It's like that quote, 'If you tell a lie big enough and long enough, people will start to believe it.' " Steve asks, "Do you think that's true, from your own experience?" "Well, I've always been someone who doesn't like to just go along with what other people are saying," Abby replies, "but *yeah*, if you hear something long enough, it affects you … you kind of forget what your own principles are."

Steve bounces around the room, weaving around students' desks and speaking quickly in an animated voice that is often squeaky with excitement. Focusing directly on each student with whom he speaks, and referring to each by name, he engages the class in a discussion about how basic emotions and stereotypes take over when you "forget your own principles" and are "no longer able to think." "I want you to think about how stereotypes and propaganda work," Steve explains, "because, as you know, Hitler didn't invent anything new. Before Hitler, there was plenty of hatred of Jews." He continues with the following example:

In the 1890s, a book appeared, and it was called . . . *Protocols of the Elders of Zion*. (Steve writes the title of the book on the board, and students copy it into their journals.) It appeared in Russian in 1890. And it explained that there was an international group of Jews who used to get together and meet in a Jewish cemetery in Prague, at night, and they would plan *everything* that was going to happen in the world. (Josh taps Chi-Ho on the shoulder, as if to suggest that he should listen closely.) This book was republished in England in 1919. It was republished in the United States in the 1920s—in a newspaper owned by Henry Ford, one of the two or three most important men in the country! In England it was published in the most important newspaper—the *Times* of London. And the most interesting thing about this book is—it's a fraud! It's complete nonsense! It's made up! (Josh again prods Chi-Ho and whispers something to him; Chi-Ho smiles awkwardly.)

How do you know it's a fraud? Well, in the 1890s, this book was written by members of the Russian police force. (Steve writes "1890—Russian police force" hurriedly on the board.) And how do you know that? Well, because this book was actually copied (Steve's voice cracks in excitement) from a book that was written in 1864 in France that didn't blame *Jews,* but that said the ruler of France, Napoleon III, was trying to take over the world (he writes "Napoleon, 1864" on the board). And everywhere where Napoleon appears in this book (Steve points to the original text), the word *Jews* appears in this one (he points to the words "Elders of Zion"). Think about this for a second! A French book in 1864 was copied by the Russians in 1890. The British copied the Russians. And the Americans copied the British. And it's a complete fraud! It's hocus pocus! It's untrue! It's a *lie.* And millions and millions of people believed it. (Pause). How come?
Susie: Because nobody told them any differently.
Alan: Because they believed it was written by someone who knew!
Josh: A lot of people want to blame somebody else for all of their problems.
Chi-Ho: Because then you're not responsible for what happens to people.

"Exactly!" Steve exclaims. "There are a lot of things that happen that are really beyond our control. An idea like this says—even if it's someone you hate, *somebody* is in control. Somebody is in charge of what's going on. And even if things are *lousy*, it's nice to be able to say, it wouldn't be lousy if it weren't for these bums. Let me show you how this happened in real life! This should take about five hours, but I'll do it in three minutes. You ready?" Students nod that they are.

For the next several minutes, Steve gives a remarkably clear and concise account of the infamous turn-of-the-century case in which Alfred Dreyfus, one of the few Jewish officers in the French Army, was falsely accused of giving military secrets to the Germans, convicted in two trials, and sentenced to prison on Devil's Island. "Many people said, 'How could Dreyfus have done it alone?' And others said, 'Aha, he didn't! He was part of this!' " (Steve points again to "Elders of Zion" on the board).

Abby asks, "Is that thing called the international Jewish conspiracy?" Steve explains: "In France, they called it the 'Syndicat.' And they referred to it as the 'international Jewish conspiracy.' There's a tremendous *power* in this kind of idea. Why were people so willing to believe it of Jews? Would they have believed it if this was . . . about Catholics? Would that have been popular in Europe?" "No," answers Sandra, "there are a lot of Catholics, so it wouldn't be as easy as singling out one Jew." Abby interjects, "What things you believe in will also depend upon the family you grow up in." Steve agrees, and draws the thorny issue of an international Jewish conspiracy to a close by reinforcing the curriculum's valuation of critical thinking. He says, "One of the things you're going to have to decide is whether you're going to believe what people say, or whether you're going to try to figure it out on your own."

Chi-Ho has remained conspicuously silent throughout this entire discussion. Often quiet in class, his behavior today is not unusual. Today's lecture, however, is given in response to his earlier remark, and it would seem to call for his participation. While only Josh makes a point of publicly acknowledging the connection between the previous class and today's by tugging at Chi-Ho's shirtsleeve and whispering to him repeatedly, other students shoot furtive glances in Chi-Ho's direction. Chi-Ho seems to studiously ignore all meaningful looks. Though he appears to be listening throughout class and assiduously copies Steve's blackboard notes into his journal, he does not acknowledge that today's lecture was, however subtly, directed at him.

This is by no means the case with Abby when the second item on today's agenda is discussed. Referring to a set of maps of the pre- and post-World War I period, Steve shows how the world has changed since the fall of the Ottoman Empire. He points to the Middle East region and says: "There are White people, Black people, and Brown people living here. It's a whole Rainbow Coalition! After World War I, one of the major questions was—should people like this be able to rule *themselves*? And the winners of the war—France, Britain, and the United States—say 'No!' They give them independence with training wheels, and the winners of the war are gonna be the training wheels! These people end up living in countries which are *invented* after World War I. It's all a product of politics! Well, what kinds of problems might the 'training wheels' encounter?"

"They had to make sure the new boundaries wouldn't get people mad because they don't want to start another war," Alan answers thoughtfully. Nora adds, "They needed to keep people together with their own people so they'll be content." Drawing his finger across a large section of the map, Steve describes how Transjordan was ruled by the victorious British until 1948."And who lived here?" he asks simply, pointing to Palestine."Palestinians," Abby replies. Steve continues, asking, "Who were they, and what was their religion?" "They were Arabs," Abby responds. "They were Moslems, Jews, and Christians," corrects Steve."To be a 'Palestinian' meant literally to live in Palestine. And they all lived under British rule."

For the next several minutes, Steve helps the class review what happened to Jews in the years leading up to and immediately following World War II. Josh remembers that Jews tried to get out of Europe, but often had no place to go. Angela believes many headed for Palestine because they had "religious ties there." Nora comments that it was often impossible to return to their homes because "they were taken by people, like their neighbors." Zeke adds that their possessions were taken, too.

"Lots of Jews live in detention camps for two or three years after the war," Steve explains. "The Jews in Palestine want the European Jews to come there, but the Arabs and Christians don't want them to. The British have control of Palestine and they don't know what to do with it. Since the British can't figure it out, they give the problem to the United Nations, which functions as an international government with representatives from different countries. This is the U.N.'s big moment! Well, in 1947 the U.N. votes to divide Palestine again, into a state for Jews and a state for non-Jews."

"Is this when the eight day war took place?" Josh interjects, reviving his previous comment, "No," Steve answers, "that took place later." Nora comments, "The U.N. is made up of representatives from all different countries, right? So, what did the Palestinian representative do?" Supportive and genuinely impressed, Steve exclaims, "That's a great question! There wasn't one, since Palestine was under British rule." "Well," Nora continues, "did the majority of the non-Jews in Palestine agree with the decision?" Steve responds, "Absolutely not! The majority of people were not happy. So in 1948 a war occurs—it's a small war compared to World War I and World War II—and in that war, the *Jewish* side of Palestine manages to survive, but the *non-Jewish* region gets taken—not by Israel, but by 'Transjordan.' . . . The Jewish part becomes Israel, but the non-Jewish part becomes Jordan and Egypt."

Abby is getting frustrated with Steve's version of history. She breaks in in a loud and exasperated voice, "But there was lots of violence between the Jews and non-Jews! A lot of people were killed! People were kicked off their homes. It was just like in the Holocaust!" Steve acknowledges the complexity of the situation, but is direct in his rebuttal. Calmly and with authority, he asserts, "That's not quite true; part of it's true, but it's *very* complex. There were broadcasts telling people to leave their land, and many people *wanted* to leave because they wanted to get away from the war. When the Israeli government came in, they didn't know what to do with the Arab land. The people that fled their homes *do* end up living in camps, but that was the choice of the Jordanians, not the Israelis."

Abby objects, saying, "But they shouldn't have had to leave in the first place!" "They *chose* to leave," Steve responds, "There's *no* question that this displaced people and that people lost their homes who didn't want to. But there's also *no* question that extermination was *not* the policy. . . . The other thing is that many Jews in these Arab countries also lost *their* homes. One of the things that happens in times of war is that international human rights are *completely* neglected. This should make us think very closely about the policies of international government—they're *not* extermination policies, but they're also not policies that make it very easy for people to live their lives in the way they would like to." Abby isn't satisfied. "But if the Palestinians hadn't been kicked off . . ." she begins. Steve breaks in, "Do you mean the Palestinian non-Jews?" Accommodating Steve's language, Abby continues, "OK, if the Palestinian non-Jews hadn't been kicked off, why should they be so angry about not having their land?" "Oh, well! They've spent the past forty years living in camps and wanting to be on their parents' land!" Steve responds.

Most students have remained silent yet attentive during this exchange. Sandra sits close by Abby and does not come to her aid, despite Abby's frequent, beseeching looks in her direction. Josh only half-hides a smirk, seemingly pleased that Steve is taking Abby on. He now contributes to the discussion, "But there was another war!" and Steve replies, "There have been *lots* of wars. The tension Abby speaks to developed more after the land was taken in 1967. Many people believe that land should be exchanged for peace. There's a large Peace Now movement in Israel today saying that those territories should be given back to the Palestinian Arabs."

"But they *won* the war!" Josh repeats emphatically. "I learned that in Temple!" Steve responds by briefly highlighting different points of view within contemporary Israeli (Jewish) society. He is careful to distinguish between current policies and those on which the state was founded. Though he admits the existence of conflicting perspectives within contemporary Israeli society, he leaves less room for alternative interpretation when it comes to the founding of the state ("The tension Abby speaks to developed more after the land was taken in 1967," he says, and he suggests that Palestinians were not "kicked off" their land but "*chose*" to leave it). Though Steve is by no means alone in articulating this perspective (and in distinguishing it from current Israeli policies), it nonetheless reflects only one particular viewpoint in a complex and contentious historical debate.[14]

Some of Steve's other interventions are also grounded in a particular political stance. While acknowledging that the founding of the State of Israel was accompanied by some human rights violations, he denies that those violations were systematic or a matter of official policy. Moments later, he "corrects" Abby's language by recommending that she refer to Arabs as "Palestinian non-Jews"—a categorization that is itself not politically neutral, and arguably comparable to referring to Blacks as non-Whites or women as non-men. Like Marysa in the earlier classroom incident, Steve acts in somewhat contradictory ways, eliciting students' diverse viewpoints on the one hand while undermining the legitimacy of those with which he disagrees on the other.

Class nearly over, students begin to close their notebooks and put them inside their desks. Marysa and Steve turn to each other and begin speaking privately in the front of the room; they express pleasure and relief at having gotten through a potentially difficult session without drawing too much fire.

That neither Steve nor Marysa entirely transcended their own political beliefs in interpreting and responding to political differences within the classroom is not surprising; I would argue that no one can do so. These beliefs are a part of our internal make-up, as operative within these teachers as they are within my own interpretations of their practice. I did not leave my own political beliefs at the door when I entered the classroom; they were within me as I observed each class. These perspectives no doubt influenced how I interpreted classroom tensions between eliciting and muting student voice. As a Jewish woman strongly committed to a peaceful resolution of the Israeli-Palestinian conflict, I felt strongly opposed to Chi-Ho's remarks and to Abby's more extreme comments, even though I disagreed with how the teachers at times responded to both of these students.

Interviews conducted individually with Chi-Ho, Abby, Josh, and Sandra shortly after these classes took place support my interpretation of these classroom events as political in nature.[15] By "political" I mean to suggest not only the content of the classroom debate (in which a diversity of political views were expressed), but also the process by which it was negotiated (whereby controversial voices were silenced by those with greater authority and power). In these instances, power was exercised between students and their teachers; between Marysa and Steve; and among the students themselves. So, too, the relations among these players were hierarchical: some were given (or assumed) more authority to speak than others. And, depending on one's point of view, opposing positions were granted legitimacy or invalidated. In the process, some students felt silenced and subordinated, while others felt empowered and privileged.

In the course of our interviews, Chi-Ho and Abby express discomfort at feeling "unheard" and "misunderstood" in class, while Sandra and Josh enjoy the fact that these students were silenced. Expressing frustration with being "misunderstood," Chi-Ho remarks, "[Josh] wouldn't listen! . . . [It felt] terrible . . . I was disappointed. I *really* think that Marysa didn't really listen to me very carefully, and, if she *did*, she would understand what I meant."

Abby's response to the classes under study is multifaceted. She initially admits to being confused by Steve's alternative reading of historical events and expresses concern for (what she imagines to be) *his* discomfort. Portraying *herself* as the agent of her silencing (rather than Steve), Abby notes:

> I *really* was confused by what he said, because, from what *I* had read (because my parents have a lot of books about that), it *really* was the total *opposite* of what he was saying. And, I mean, I *didn't* want to make a scene, so I didn't really, you know, say as much as I could have? I *didn't* want to totally contradict him, 'cause it would have made him feel uncomfortable. So I just kind of left it.

Moments later, however, Abby suggests that this self-censorship was not entirely voluntarily. Though she hesitantly adopts Steve's terminology, she nevertheless defends her own perspective and argues that he was unable to hear it:

> I thought about it a lot *during* and *afterwards* and, I *really* think that this point of view was *really, really* closed-minded! I mean, he thought about what I had to say, but he basically said it was totally wrong! ... I was *trying to tell him* that from what *I've learned,* the situation between (pause) Palestinian non-Jews and the *Jews* was *very* oppressive, and one-sided, and it was really an awful situation! And he kind of *glorified* it in a way, and made it sound like it wasn't as violent as it really was!

While Abby eventually admits to having modified some of her own thinking in response to Steve, she seems frustrated that he has not done the same:

> I didn't really mean *millions* because there weren't that many Palestinian non-Jews in the country. ... *He* was right, because I thought about it and it wasn't really *extermination.* But they *really* wanted them to move off that land! And it was *their* homeland in the first place! And I *meant* that by taking them out of their home, as the Nazis did with the Jews, they put them in something that was like a *camp* where they weren't allowed to have any *human* rights that most people take for granted. I agree with him that the methods weren't exactly extermination but I *don't* agree with him when he says it wasn't as bad as in the *first* steps [of the Holocaust].

In contrast, neither Josh nor Sandra expresses discomfort with classroom dynamics, but they instead express pleasure in Steve's having silenced those with whom they disagree. Sandra notes with satisfaction, "When Steve came in and told Abby, 'You're wrong!' well, it was kind of funny, because she got like, *really* mad." Josh similarly notes, "Steve, he's great! He came in and he said this is total nonsense." Whispering "Don't tell her, but Abby talks a lot!" Josh takes pleasure in describing a contentious class in which his own beliefs reflect majority opinion while Abby's are seen as marginal. "I like when people make sure people know what's going on," he says later of Steve's also having put Chi-Ho in his place.

These excerpts suggest a confluence between my interpretation of classroom dynamics and students' experience of the course. Though students differed among themselves in their feelings about classroom dynamics, they shared my belief that both Marysa and Steve conveyed their own sense of "right" and "wrong" to the class and made sure, as Josh says, that "people know what's going on."

• • •

Students' contradictory yearnings for both closure and openness may be irresolvably in tension. Teachers' efforts to foster tolerance for alternative perspectives may be similarly at odds with their efforts to promote moral thinking. The ambiguities, conflicts, and tensions that arose during these three classroom sessions demonstrate the enormous challenge of debating contemporary social and political issues in the classroom.

There are those who oppose interjecting contemporary issues into the classroom for precisely these reasons. Conservative activists like Phyllis Schlafly, for example, have in the past attacked the Facing History and Ourselves program precisely because it encourages adolescents to reflect critically on current social issues. Condemning the program in national public hearings in 1984, she charged that it (and other so-called "therapy education" initiatives) could "depress the child" by "forc[ing] [him] to confront adult problems which are too complex and unsuitable for his tender years."[16] By causing the child to be "emotionally and morally confused," they could, she felt, lead to the "high rates of teenage suicide, loneliness, premarital sex, and pregnancies" that plague contemporary society.[17]

The Department of Education's National Diffusion Network—an agency that reviews curricula and funds their dissemination—reflected Schlafly's concerns in 1986–1988 when it denied funds to the Facing History program. The Department's action sparked a Congressional hearing and heated debate among public-policy makers, educators, and other concerned citizens.[18]

But one need not look as far back as the mid-eighties to find opposition to classroom discourse on contemporary social and political debates. Only recently, the New York City Board of Education ousted Chancellor Joseph A. Fernandez, largely because of his support for initiatives that included AIDS education, condom distribution, and a curriculum that advocated tolerance for diverse social groups, including homosexuals. According to Carol Ann Gresser, the New York School Board's newly elected chair, parents were upset by Fernandez's promotion of a "social agenda" in the schools. "You can't bring into the classroom issues that haven't even been decided by the society," she said.[19]

I would argue exactly the opposite: one cannot possibly avoid bringing into the classroom issues over which society is still divided because students themselves are well aware of these issues and hungry to discuss them with their peers. The liveliness of the classroom sessions presented here testify to students' investment in just such debates. While these students were at times discomforted by what transpired in class, they were also vitally invested, excited, and engaged in the struggle. Though Sandra begged for closure, she tolerated not getting it; though Josh demanded separation from Chi-Ho, he remained sitting next to his friend; though Marysa opposed Abby, she engaged with her in open debate; though Abby felt intimidated, she hung in and held her ground. In short, while tempers were high, feelings impassioned, and intellects fiercely engaged, the group never closed down or fell apart. Highly conscious of their differences and the fault lines that divide them on specific issues, the class remained a community throughout. Their ability to do so reflects the skill with which Marysa created an environment of relative trust and safety within the classroom, and Facing History's engendering of personal, critical reflection no doubt contributed to that effort. But the strengths and capacities that students bring with them into this or any other classroom—their hunger to sort out where they stand and their ripeness for engaging in just such debates—must also be taken into account.

Thus, though opponents may argue that the inevitable consequence of such classroom interactions is either political indoctrination or the promotion of moral relativism, I would contend that neither is a necessary outcome nor an accurate characterization. What does seem inevitable is ambiguity and conflict—on this point, at least, advocates and opponents both agree. But here, too, programs encouraging engagement with social, moral, and/or political issues may offer a possible passageway through trouble—not by denying conflict through positing an unproblematized, homogeneous ideal, but by helping students to take well-thought-out stands and to listen closely to each other. Hopefully, by doing so they will learn to tolerate more fully the conflicts they will inevitably encounter in the world beyond the classroom. At their best, what programs like Facing History and Ourselves may offer students is not a blueprint for creating a single ideal community, but practice in making webs between multiple ones. And that is essential to education in a democracy.

NOTES

1. At the request of school administrators, the names of the school and its students and teachers have been changed.

2. Information about this curriculum can be obtained from Facing History and Ourselves, 16 Hurd Road, Brookline, MA 02146 (617-232-1595). The organization develops and disseminates curricular materials and runs an extensive training program to prepare teachers to teach the curriculum.

3. Throughout this article, the term "Holocaust" is used to refer to the Nazi genocide of Jews.

4. See Alan Stoskopf and Margot Stern Strom, *Choosing to Participate: A Critical Examination of Citizenship in American History* (Brookline, MA: Facing History and Ourselves, 1990); Margot Strom and William Parsons, *Facing History and Ourselves: Holocaust and Human Behavior* (Watertown, MA: Intentional Educations, 1982).

5. See Melinda Fine, "Collaborative Innovations: Documentation of the Facing History and Ourselves Program at an Essential School," *Teachers College Record*, 94, No. 4 (1993), 776.

6. Strom and Parsons, *Facing History.*

7. Strom and Parsons, *Facing History*, p. 14.

8. See Melinda Fine, "Facing History and Ourselves: Portrait of a Classroom," Special Issue: "Whose Culture?" *Educational Leadership* (1991/1992), 44–49; Fine, "Collaborative Innovations," pp. 771–789; Melinda Fine, "The Politics and Practice of Moral Education: A Case Study of Facing History and Ourselves," Diss., Harvard Graduate School of Education, 1991; and Melinda Fine, *Dilemmas of Difference: A Case Study of Moral Education Policy, Politics, and Practice* (Jossey-Bass: San Francisco, forthcoming).

9. Strom and Parsons, *Facing History*, pp. 383, 387.

10. See, for example, Sara Lawrence Lightfoot, *The Good High School: Portraits of Character and Culture* (New York: Basic Books, 1983). For an excellent discussion of the similarities and differences between portraiture and other forms of social science inquiry, see Marue

Walizer, "Watch With Both Eyes: Narratives and Social Science: Sources of Insight into Teachers' Thinking," Diss., Harvard University Graduate School of Education, 1987, pp. 12–47 and 101–129.

11. Eudora Welty, *The Eye of the Storm: Selected Essays and Reviews* (New York: Vintage Books, 1979), p. 129.

12. All quotations of in-class-comments are from written notes taken while class was in session.

13. "Lessons in Hate," distributed by Intersection Associates, Cambridge, Massachusetts, and available through the Facing History and Ourselves Resource Library.

14. See, for example, Zachary Lockman, "Original Sin," in *Intifada: The Palestinian Uprising Against Israeli Occupation,* eds. Zachary Lockman and Joel Beinin (Boston: South End Press, 1989), pp. 185–204.

15. All interviews with students were tape recorded. Students' verbal emphases are indicated in the text in italics.

16. Phyllis Schlafly, *Child Abuse in the Classroom* (Illinois: Pere Marquette Press, 1984), pp. 435–437.

17. Schlafly, *Child Abuse*, p. 12.

18. For a fuller discussion of this controversy, see Fine, *Dilemmas of Difference.*

19. "A Full-Time Volunteer," *New York Times,* May 13, 1993, p. B3.

Barry Brummett

"Rhetorical Theory as Heuristic and Moral: A Pedagogical Justification"

This essay develops a perspective on rhetorical theory and the criticism which supports it. By rhetorical theory I do *not* mean those works that are sometimes called rhetorical theory but are actually better described as rhetorical philosophy: articles that explore the epistemological, ontological, axiological, or ethical dimensions of communication.[1] Nor does this essay have anything to say about those many valuable critical studies of discourse that have as their goal historical, aesthetic, literary, or similar judgments about particular works.[2] Rather, by rhetorical theory I mean essays that systematically assert propositions about how rhetoric actually works in the world, essays that identify some rhetorical tactic, strategy, device, etc., and attempt to account for its effectiveness in *general*. This essay focuses on the sort of work typified by Osborn's discussions of metaphor, Burke's theories of symbolic action such as scapegoating, or Bormann's claims concerning fantasy in public discourse.[3] Scholars typically expect this sort of rhetorical theory to produce knowledge similar to that produced by social science theory, but rhetorical theory is in fact very different. The peculiarities of rhetorical theory are such that traditional ways of accounting for it are insufficient; I shall propose instead that it be regarded as primarily pedagogical. This essay does not propose new ways of doing theory and criticism, but a new perspective on what theory and criticism are good for. In trying to understand what a rhetorical theory is, and what sort of knowledge it produces, one might first consider what rhetorical theory is not.

WHAT RHETORICAL THEORY IS NOT

Rhetoricians often seem to regard their theories as close parallels to more conservative, hypothetical-deductive, social science theories. Gronbeck sounds like a social scientist when he claims that Burkean scholars try to generate "a systematic set of covering propositions."[4] Black argues that rhetorical theory, apart from the more insignificant theories derived from logical necessity, is grounded in "regularities" of psyche or discourse.[5] McGee explicitly claims that "if it is to achieve the status of 'theory,' any prose must reliably describe, explain, and predict."[6] Zarefsky agrees that rhetorical theory should be both testable and predictive.[7] Swanson demands that a rhetorical study pass "objective tests of its accuracy."[8]

Many rhetoricians view rhetorical criticism as the means to test the regularities asserted by rhetorical theory; criticism is to rhetorical theory what experiment and other methods are to social science theory.[9] Swanson argues that rhetorical criticism contributes to rhetorical theory and to its predictive power.[10] Campbell's "enduring" criticism contributes more to theory than to an understanding of the particular object of criticism.[11] Although Clevenger sees criticism as primarily descriptive, he explicitly argues that it can and should *test* a rhetorical theory.[12] Farrell's theoretical "models" are informed and tested by criticism.[13] In short, rhetorical scholars often see their work as paralleling some of the social science theory and research done by their colleagues in interpersonal or organizational communication; let us examine this social science model more closely to see what it is that rhetorical theory and its supporting criticism are supposed to be doing.

To be a social science theory, a set of systematic propositions must assert that some regularities exist in the world. Those regularities are sometimes expressed as laws,[14] sometimes as rules which guide action,[15] sometimes as forms or patterns.[16] Because a theory asserts something systematically about the world, it is above all testable, one can look at the world to see if it behaves as theory says it does.[17] Hempel has called testability "the minimum scientific requirement."[18] As researchers employing a theory examine the world, they pile up data which tend to confirm or disconfirm the theory.[19] Although philosophers disagree over what it takes to confirm or disconfirm theory,[20] they do agree that theories are usually tested, refined, and rejected by the *cumulation,* in Merton's terms, of data from several studies.[21] Single studies rarely establish or destroy a theory's usefulness.[22] A single study may provoke research towards a theory, but for the scientific community at large, the single study by itself hardly ever warrants a theory. The accuracy of a theory, the amount of agreement between what it says about the world and the way the world objectively is, thus becomes the chief criterion for judging theory.[23]

A second characteristic of social science theory is quite obvious: it is almost always distinct from the *methods* which are used in studies designed to prove or disprove theory. That is not at all to say that there is no relationship between theory and method, but the two are distinct. A given social science theory can usually be tested by several different methods. A given theory of voting behavior, for instance, might be tested by laboratory experiments or by survey research. The distinction is reflected even in the structure of social science journal articles, which usually begin with theory and set method off under a separate heading. The learning of a method, of how to test a theory, is a complicated and difficult course of study; thus methodology is a branch of social science in its own right, and one can take courses in methods that are quite distinct from the theories which methods will eventually test.

Rhetorical theory and its supporting criticism as actually written, on the other hand, have characteristics which disqualify social science theory and research as models for understanding rhetorical studies. First, theory-centered criticism does not in fact seem to be *testing* theory. Indeed, a closer examination reveals that rhetorical theory is *never* tested in the sense that social science theories are.

Unlike social science theory, a rhetorical theory is established without the need of *much* accumulating evidence. Black correctly notes that only one rhetorical criticism is necessary to establish a rhetorical theory.[24] Leff says that criticisms need not accumulate as do scientific experiments in order to confirm a theory.[25] One need only compare the number of critical essays clustering around any rhetorical theory to the studies tied to theories concerning communication apprehension, or reticence, to see the relative lack of accumulation in rhetorical theory. Some rhetorical theories were accepted as useful on the basis of one or a few critical studies for example, theories concerning apologia,[26] archetypal metaphor,[27] or fantasy themes.[28]

Any social science theory must not only be testable, but a study using the theory must specify how the theory is being tested and what the consequences are of the theory's failure. Criticisms rarely or never say how they are testing a theory. Rather, criticism seems to illustrate theory. The usefulness of the theory is *assumed*. The spate of essays on fantasy theme analysis has demonstrated a number of subject areas to which that theory might be applied, but one senses that the later essays did not *need* to appear in order to justify Bormann's theory, that it could walk by itself from birth.[29] The testing of a rhetorical theory rarely involves a comparison with another theory to see which best accounts for data, as is often done in comparing "trait" vs. "state" accounts of communication apprehension, for instance.[30] Nor does the failure of a theory to make sense in a critical application ever deny that theory. A critic who finds that he or she cannot apply fantasy theme analysis to a piece of discourse will simply turn to Burke, Aristotle, or some other theory, and the "failure" of the rejected theory never sees the light of published day. As Black put it, "There is not a single case in the literature of our field in which a rhetorical theory has been abandoned as a result of having failed an application in criticism."[31] Such a statement could not be made about social science theory. Rhetorical theories are like fishing lures: they are discarded only if they *never* seem useful. That a lure fails to hook *this* bass *today* is not really a test of it. Rhetorical theories are like vampires: you need see one in action only once to believe in what it can do, and it is nearly impossible to kill.

A second major difference between rhetorical studies and the social science model is that in rhetorical studies, the distinction between theory and method is much weaker. Usually a method is the exercise of an insight engendered by the theory itself. Method uses ordinary skills of research such as reading, library techniques, etc., as guided by the extraordinary sensibilities given to one by the theory. That such is the case can be seen clearly when theories are imported into rhetoric. Kenneth Burke, trained in other disciplines, has proposed a number of theories (or one grand theory) of symbolic action. One can find in his writings clear distinctions between theory which posits propositions about frames of acceptance, the pentad, scapegoating, ultimate terms, and the like, and his methods whereby he would have one test his theories by seeking out associational clusters, puns, images of killing, etc.[32] Burke's disciple in sociology, Hugh Duncan, also draws a clear distinction between theoretical and methodological propositions in adapting Burke to social science.[33]

But when rhetorical scholars take up Burke's theories, the major points of his theories are usually treated as categories of critical analysis. His methods are submerged within theory. If Burke says, for instance, that scapegoats must bear the guilt of victimizers, must be representative, and must be powerful, a rhetorical criticism *based* on that theory will use *those* concepts rather than distinct methodological tactics as the categories of analysis around which the study is formed.[34] I am not claiming that theory-based criticism has no method, but rather that the method is merged with and subordinated to the theory. Unlike the mysteries of quantitative method, the methods of theory-related rhetorical criticism[35] involve no more esoteric an action than reading a newspaper or journal, or watching television. To show that a given discourse is engaged in mortification, one simply reads it looking for what Burke's theory says to look for. This is not to say that anybody can do rhetorical criticism with no training, for a method is the exercise of a trained sensibility. The sensibility is given to the critic not by taking a course in statistics but by studying the theory itself. Complexity is kept to a minimum in favor of clear and direct application of a theory to discourse. To take an example, Bormann's notion of "fantasy themes" treats theory and method as practically one. Bormann presents theory about what sometimes happens in rhetorical transactions; mastering that theory, the critic develops a sensitivity to certain kinds of utterances which one can then look for in public discourse. This sensitivity, augmented by an ordinary ability to read speeches looking for what one has been sensitized to look for, is also the method of fantasy theme analysis. Or in a final example, classical rhetorical theory tells one to look for logos, pathos, and ethos as the persuasive forces of a discourse. To do so, one must know what those terms mean, but the meaning is given by the theory. Armed with that theoretical sensibility, the rhetorical critic employs the everyday tactic of reading a speech and looking for utterances that seem to fit the theoretical categories.

A glance at any theory-related criticism shows that while the rhetorical theories to which they refer do make assertions about what the world is like, rarely are specific predictions made, no consideration is given to what sort of outcome is likely to confirm or disconfirm the theory, few competing theories are mentioned, and there is little sense that the criticism at hand fits cumulatively with other work to support or deny a theory. Theory and method are also merged as I have described that merger.[36]

For example, Rushing and Frentz's recent article on "The Deer Hunter" proposes a theory "based on the works of Carl Jung."[37] The article includes a single criticism of one film, yet the authors offer their theory as a way to explain other rhetorical discourses.[38] The theory is stated in broad terms that suggest no clear ways to test hypotheses derived from it, and certainly no alternative theoretical possibilities. For instance, "We contend that individuation ... would be most probable for the postwar warrior who entered the battle with a strong persona, because his shadow would be less likely to overcome it."[39] A social science theory would test such an "hypothesis" by examining several such warriors, by rigorously operationalizing key terms such as *strong persona* or *overcome,* and by specifying what sort of outcome would confirm or disconfirm the theory and why. Yet one feels that the theory could usefully be assumed in future analysis and that a systematic test of the psychological ritual model is irrelevant to its usefulness. Other studies with theoretical import yield similar results upon examination.[40]

One might therefore conclude that rhetorical theory is simply unworthy of the name theory, not ready to take its place among more rigorous disciplines. Bowers' view of criticism as "pre-scientific" seems to regard rhetorical criticism and theory as a sort of immature social science. Rhetorical criticism, in his view, contributes to verifiable statements about the world which may be formulated as laws. Real testing of that theory, however, is conducted through scientific experiment, according to Bowers, because criticism can only produce statements of probability, not the precise pronouncements needed for testability, predictability, etc.[41] Bower's view of rhetorical criticism and theory is thus much like Merton's "orientations,"[42] or Max Black's "metaphor"[43] in social science. Although Bowers' views may be professionally unappealing to rhetoricians, they may be unavoidable as long as current assumptions hold about models appropriate to rhetorical theory and criticism.

WHAT IS RHETORICAL THEORY ABOUT?

We saw in the first section of this essay that if "theory" means a set of systematic, testable propositions about regularities in the world, then rhetorical studies cannot be regarded as theoretical because of the peculiar ways in which its "theories" are proposed and judged. In this section we will see that what rhetorical theory is *about* is also extremely problematic. Can rhetorical theory account for the way rhetoric is actually experienced?

Let us turn to an essay which has not received the attention it deserves, Samuel Becker's article in *The Prospect of Rhetoric.*[44] Becker undertook to explain how people actually experience and respond to the phenomenon of rhetoric in a culture dominated by mass media. Becker describes rhetorical transactions from the point of view of the audience, of those masses who experience the transactions, rather than from the point of view of the sources of messages. Becker argues that people typically move through an environment full of "bits" of messages, bits which are speeches, snatches of informal conversation, mass media broadcasts, nonverbal events, and the like. These bits form a "mosaic," and what people actually experience in terms of rhetoric are *message sets* that they, the audience, construct for themselves from that mosaic.[45]

Believing that "in most important communication situations, the message is scattered and unorganized,"[46] Becker holds that rhetoric-as-experienced is the result of employing a form or pattern to assemble those message bits so that they make sense to individuals. He gives the example of his own experiencing of the "message" of Martin Luther King's death, which he assembled from bits and pieces of discourse heard over the course of a day as well as from nondiscursive elements of his environment. Furthermore, the message that Becker assembled was, because of his unique position in time and space, different from messages that might have been assembled by other people. The message within that experience was not something decreed for the masses by a few rhetors, it was something made for each person by him or herself. One might then examine a given eulogy for its aesthetic or ideological import, but one would be very mistaken to treat it as *the* message or even *a* message that ordinary people ended up with. It was a "bit" that people may or may not have extracted, wholly or in part, from the "mosaic" in making messages for themselves. Now, if Becker describes accurately the way rhetoric occurs in a technological age,[47] can rhetorical theory account for it?

We saw in the first section of this paper that a rhetorical theory cannot be about how people make messages out of the mosaic *in general*. Such assertions of generality are not tested, perhaps not even testable. Instead, rhetorical theories are *illustrated*. If a critic applied a rhetorical theory about mythic heroes to the King assassination, for example, for the reasons given in part one such a theory could not be tested exhaustively in that one study and would not be tested subsequently by the accumulation of studies.

If rhetorical theory (and its attendant criticism) accounts at all for Becker's mosaic, perhaps it tells us about the ways in which the rhetorical transaction, the message sets, were actually manifested in one particular instance. Perhaps emphasis should be placed on the critical studies that are linked to the theory being presented; thus a given critical study might hold that the message *was made* in such and such a way in this particular instance.

Two objections arise to that possible role of rhetorical theory and criticism. First, message sets are actually assembled in many ways, in potentially as many different ways as there are people to assemble them. Since rhetorical criticisms usually present *one* perspective on a rhetorical transaction, they cannot really claim to be about how the rhetoric actually was manifested from the points of view of perhaps millions of active participants. A second objection is that if the critic claims that the message was manifested in such and such a way, the critic should prove that this was so. That would entail actually going to the public and asking them, ascertaining how John and Jane Doe assembled message sets last Friday. Not only is this never done in rhetorical studies, it would take the rhetorical scholar out of his or her proper area and into survey research. At best, rhetorical critics examine some of the available bits themselves; if citizens' reactions are ever taken into account, it is the sort of reaction that makes its way into the popular press and thus becomes part of the rhetorical mosaic itself. In short, it does not seem possible that rhetorical theory and its attendant criticism can be about the ways in which message sets and rhetorical transactions were actually assembled by the masses of participant observers moving through the mosaic.

A more promising line would be to argue that a rhetorical criticism is the way in which the critic himself or herself, perhaps acting as a representative participant, actually did assemble message sets in a rhetorical transaction. A rhetorical theory might thus be the logic or pattern behind that experience. To assert that the rhetoric of a certain experience illustrated Burkean scapegoating is to say that the form or pattern of scapegoating guided the critic's direct experience of a rhetorical transaction, or his or her reconstruction of the transaction from recorded texts, press clippings, photographs, and the like. This account raises the problem of significance, however. Why should anybody care how critic Jane Smith experiences a transaction if what the study is about is nothing more than her own experiences? A final attempt to account for rhetorical theory might hold that a rhetorical criticism illustrates how anybody in a given time and space *might* have experienced a rhetorical transaction. The rhetorical theory employed is again the logic guiding the choice of bits from the mosaic to be assembled into message sets. We are closer to the position that this paper finally defends, but two more problems arise. First is the problem of significance again; why should a theorist study possible ways of experiencing a single rhetorical transaction that is already finished?[48] And a second objection takes us back to conclusions we drew in the first section, which is that we are now very far from being able to use social science theory as a model for rhetorical theory. This last statement of what rhetorical theory and its criticisms can be about seems to have little to do with testable and systematic propositions about how things really are. A reformulation of rhetorical theory and criticism is now in order. This reformulation must account for how theory and criticism are actually written, and find a use for it in saying something about the mass media dominated culture in which much rhetoric now occurs.

RHETORICAL THEORY AS HEURISTIC AND MORAL

We might start by considering the *audience* for rhetorical theory and criticism. Most of us who publish write for the community of scholars as our primary audience. I am not indicting those who do so, for scholarly writing allows the author to make subtle and complex claims, and there are well-entrenched social and practical forces that will keep scholars as our *first* audience. But while this essay does not call for a change in how rhetorical theory and criticism is *done*, I do call for a change in what can be *done with* it. To think of scholars as our chronologically *first* audience does not entail regarding them as our logically *primary* audience. Let us begin to think of the community of rhetorical scholars as gatekeepers, as interpreters who pass on what they read to theory and criticism's primary audience. That audience I propose to regard as ordinary people, and since rhetoricians confront ordinary people most often and most directly in their classrooms, let us think of rhetorical theory and criticism's audience as properly and primarily our *students*. Rhetorical scholars and teachers would then become more involved than I suspect we now are as translators of the sometimes weighty articles in learned journals, as popularizers of scholarship. This conception of rhetorical theory and criticism's audience would cause one to start thinking of theory not as contributing to the store of scholarly knowledge possessed by the academic community, but as enriching the stock of general knowledge possessed by ordinary people.[49]

Now let me present the heart of this alternative perspective on theory and criticism, which I shall then develop at length: a rhetorical theory is a form, pattern, or recipe, a statement in the abstract, of how a person might experience a rhetorical transaction. I mean "experience" in Becker's sense: a rhetorical theory is the logic that might guide one's choice of bits from the mosaic in assembling message sets. A rhetorical criticism in support of theory is an illustration of how such a theory might in fact have guided rhetorical experience in one particular instance. That kind of learning is practical, and it adds to one's repertoire of action in the world. If we regard ordinary people (students) as the primary audience for rhetorical theory and its criticisms, then rhetorical theory and criticism's ultimate goal and justification is pedagogical: *to teach people how to experience their rhetorical environments more richly.* The more dance steps one knows in the abstract, the better able one will be to dance no matter what the circumstances. The more rhetorical theories one is familiar with, the more one can consciously and richly see, understand, and appreciate rhetoric no matter what the circumstances. Let me try to elaborate upon this perspective by describing rhetorical theory and its criticism as both heuristic and moral.

People experience an expansion of consciousness when learning new ways of making sense of the world. Architects go about seeing things in buildings that the rest of us do not, civil engineers experience traffic intersections and neighborhood layouts more richly than do others, etc. This ability to see and to experience *more* comes about by enlarging one's conceptual repertoire, by expanding the number of forms or patterns through which one can apprehend the world. To master a form or pattern of apprehending the world is to master a heuristic device that helps us learn about the world.

Rhetorical theory should also be viewed as such a heuristic device. Cleaned of the sometimes ponderous jargon through which it is presented in academic journals, a rhetorical theory can be part of a student's conceptual repertoire for apprehending rhetorical experience. To learn a theory concerning the rhetoric of Presidential "rose garden strategies," for instance,[50] and to see an illustration of how such a theory might have been used to understand a particular instance of intentional political silence, is to adopt a new way of assembling message sets from the rhetorical mosaic. Learning more rhetorical theories enables one to experience rhetoric more richly, for it both expands one's ability to assemble message sets consciously and to understand rhetorical transactions on several levels at once. Just as a drama critic's appreciation of a play from a number of different perspectives at once is richer, so could a trained observer experience a given rhetorical transaction from a number of different points of view, each grounded in a rhetorical theory. Rhetorical theory and criticism are heuristic because they are a set of "how to" instructions, they are guides to symbolic action in the real world.

People *do* assemble message sets, and if people are not trained to be focally aware of how they do so, then they will do so uncritically, perhaps even unconsciously. To learn a rhetorical theory is to learn a way of experiencing rhetoric more consciously and intentionally. I may have experienced Presidential rhetoric guided by the forms and structures of heroic myth all my life; but if I learn rhetorical theories that bring such forms and structures to my attention, then I can *choose* whether or not to continue experiencing Presidential rhetoric from that point of view. The more rhetorical theories in my repertoire, the more choices I have for ordering my rhetorical world.

Such choices are moral choices, for how one chooses to structure one's world shapes what one sees in it and how one acts in response to it. Any such choices would be moral ones, born of a heightened awareness of *how to* understand rhetoric.[51]

Rhetorical theory and criticism are also moral from the point of view of the teacher. If, as this essay argues, theory and criticism are ultimately justified by being taught to our students, then we as teachers must make the moral choice of which theories to pass on to students. For instance, the teacher of classical rhetoric should consider a number of essays that have suggested that Aristotelian theories have an inherently conservative bias.[52] It is not my intention to suggest that one sort of theory or ideology be passed on to students, but rather to call to the teacher's attention that (1) it is probably impossible to teach students *every* rhetorical theory in a way that will be useful to them, allowing them to incorporate the theory into their conceptual repertoires, but that (2) the choice of *which* theories to give students is also a moral choice on the teacher's part if we are indeed equipping the student for seeing and responding to rhetoric in his or her own life. Specifically, then, how does this perspective better account for the absence of testing in theory and criticism, for the blurred distinction between theory and method, and for the difficulties of accounting for rhetoric as Becker describes it?

The requirements that a theory be testable in asserting general propositions about regularities in the world, that tests of the theory accumulate before the theory is accepted or rejected, are both appropriate if the theory is designed to say something about what *already is* and perhaps, on the basis of that description, to predict what *will be* if current assumptions hold. A theory can be tested if it is about something which exists apart from the theory, so that the thing (the world) can be examined to see if the theory passed or failed the test. But this essay proposes that rhetorical theory be regarded as neither descriptive of what objectively is, not predictive of what will probably be. Instead, rhetorical theory is *creative* insofar as it gives people the conceptual means by which to experience in the future. A theory may have its source in what is already happening, as did Burke's scapegoating theory for instance. But when it emerges in *rhetorical* studies, Burke's theory does not *systematically* show where scapegoating occurs, for whom, or under what conditions. The theory only shows that it *might* happen, and the same thing is true for every other rhetorical theory. A rhetorical theory is not tested as are social science theories because it is not about something that already exists; it is about a potentiality of experience, and its supporting criticisms illustrate that potentiality. That is why criticisms illustrate rather than test, and why they need not accumulate; to see once how a rhetorical theory might be used is enough to enable one to *use* it. Rhetorical theories are discarded (if they are ever discarded) only when they never seem to be useful in helping anyone experience any rhetorical tradition. Rhetorical theory is not like a kinesiological statement of how leg muscles contract and extend in dancing; instead, it is like a dance instructor's statement that people sometimes dance thus and so, and here's how to do it should it seem useful and possible for *you* to use this step.

Theories and methods of rhetorical criticisms are often blurred because a theory *is* a method of experiencing rhetoric in the real world. Rhetorical theory addresses, or should address, action in real life rather than the store of scholarly knowledge; and so the method for carrying it out or applying it is nothing more than the everyday real life actions of looking and hearing *with sensibilities sharpened by the theory*. As noted above, a theory is a set of instructions or guidelines of "how to experience," and "how to" is a methodological word. Methods are usually ways of testing theories, but because rhetorical theories are themselves methods of experiencing and are not subject to the usual tests of social science theories, rhetorical theory and its methods are often merged with one another. Therefore, if we see rhetorical theory as equipping people to experience rhetorical transactions more richly and consciously, and its supporting rhetorical criticism as illustrating how such experience might be done, then some of the problems and embarrassments of rhetorical studies disappear. Such theory is not pre-scientific at all in Bowers' sense, for it equips students for practical experience in the world rather than adding to the store of scholarly knowledge about the world.

This pedagogical perspective on rhetorical theory and criticism also avoids many of the possible problems raised earlier in accounting for rhetoric in Becker's sense. Rhetorical theory and criticism would no longer be held accountable for describing or predicting the world; instead, it would prepare people for acting in, even for *making* the world. There is no longer any question of theory having to account for the several ways in which people assemble message sets. Instead, rhetorical theory sensitizes and trains people to assemble message sets in future experience. Rhetorical theory grows or advances as it adds to people's conceptual repertoire of ways of experiencing, illustrated in criticism that shows how such a form or pattern might have guided experience in one set of circumstances.

The most good that rhetorical scholars can do in the world probably lies in the ways in which we affect the students who come before us. Rhetoric is, of course, a dimension of experience that underlies all sorts of experience; one can hardly move through an hour without finding an opportunity to appreciate the rhetorical dimension of life. Rhetorical studies can thus serve as the kind of integrative, underlying perspective on which liberal arts education is based. A more conscious direction of the efforts of rhetorical theorists and critics to our best audience, students, may go a long way towards restoring rhetoric to the foundations of liberal arts education.

NOTES

1. Such as those essays reviewed by Michael Leff, "In Search of Ariadne's Thread: A Review of the Recent Literature on Rhetorical Theory," *Central States Speech Journal*, 29 (1978), 73–91. Leff divides his review into "meta-rhetorical" essays, which are the philosophical sort of essays which I am avoiding, and "historical textual studies," which are not quite my subject either. I am interested in essays which primarily assert or develop a systematic statement about how rhetoric works in general; such statements are often illustrated by historical/textual studies, but their primary concern is the articulation of a theory rather than the study of a particular era or discourse.

2. Ernest G. Bormann, in *Theory and Research in the Communicative Arts* (New York: Holt, Rinehart, and Winston, 1965), seemed to have these works in mind when he placed rhetorical studies under the rubric of "scholarship" rather than art or science, p. 38. "Rhetorical theory" does not appear in his index; many of the sorts of works that I have in mind have been published since his book was written.

3. Michael Osborn, "Archetypal Metaphor in Rhetoric: The Light-Dark Family," *Quarterly Journal of Speech*, 53 (1967), 115–126; Kenneth Burke, *The Philosophy of Literary Form* (1941; rpt. Berkeley: University of California Press, 1973), 191–200; Ernest G. Bormann, "Fantasy and Rhetorical Vision: The Rhetorical Criticism of Social Reality," *Quarterly Journal of Speech*, 58 (1972), 396–407. Some recent examples of the sort of essay with which this paper deals are Kathleen Hall Jamieson and Karlyn Kohrs Campbell, "Rhetorical Hybrids: Fusions of Generic Elements," *Quarterly Journal of Speech*, 68 (1982), 146–157; Noreen Wales Kruse, "The Apologia in Team Sport," *Quarterly Journal of Speech*, 67 (1981), 270–283; Lance Bennett, "Assessing Presidential Character: Degradation Rituals in Presidential Campaigns," *Quarterly Journal of Speech*, 67 (1981), 310–321; and Barry Brummett, "Gastronomic Reference, Synecdoche, and Political Image," *Quarterly Journal of Speech*, 67 (1981), 138–145.

4. Bruce E. Gronbeck, "Dramaturgical Theory and Criticism: The State of the Art (or Science?)," *Western Journal of Speech Communication*, 44 (1980), 328.

5. Edwin Black, "A Note on Theory and Practice in Rhetorical Criticism," *Western Journal of Speech Communication*, 44 (1980), 333–4.

6. Michael Calvin McGee, " 'Social Movement': Phenomenon or Meaning?" *Central States Speech Journal*, 31 (1980), 233.

7. David Zarefsky, "A Skeptical View of Movement Studies," *Central States Speech Journal*, 31 (1980), 245.

8. David L. Swanson, "A Reflective View of the Epistemology of Critical Inquiry," *Communication Monographs*, 44 (1977), 210.

9. As noted earlier, I am not denying at all that criticism may serve purposes having nothing to do with theory: aesthetic judgment, historical study, etc. My concern is with criticism that is used to "test" or support a theory.

10. David L. Swanson, "The Requirements of Critical Justification," *Communication Monographs*, 44 (1977), 317.

11. Karlyn Kohrs Campbell, "Criticism: Ephemeral and Enduring," *Speech Teacher,* 23 (1974), 9–14.

12. Theodore Clevenger, Jr., "The Interaction of Descriptive and Experimental Research in the Development of Rhetorical Theory," in *Contemporary Rhetoric,* ed. Douglas Ehninger (Glenview, IL: Scott, Foresman: 1972), 174–8.

13. Thomas B. Farrell, "Critical Models in the Analysis of Discourse," *Western Journal of Speech Communication,* 44 (1980), 300–314.

14. Abraham Kaplan, *The Conduct of Inquiry* (San Francisco: Chandler, 1946), 22; Robert Dubin, *Theory Building* (New York: The Free Press, 1969), 19; A. R. Louch, *Explanation and Human Action* (Berkeley: University of California, 1966), 11.

15. Donald P. Cushman and Robert T. Craig, "Communication Systems: Interpersonal Implications," in G. Miller, ed., *Explorations in Interpersonal Communication* (Beverly Hills: Sage Publications, 1976).

16. Hugh Dalziel Duncan, *Symbols in Society* (New York: Oxford University Press, 1968).

17. Jack P. Gibb, "Identification of Statements in Theory Construction," *Sociology and Social Research,* 52 (1967), 72–87; Louch, 12; Robert K. Merton, *Social Theory and Social Structure* (New York: Free Press, 1957), 8.

18. Carl G. Hempel, "The Logic of Functional Analysis," in May Brodbeck, ed., *Readings in the Philosophy of the Social Sciences* (New York: Macmillan, 1963), 185.

19. Peter R. Monge, "Theory Construction in the Study of Communication: The System Paradigm," *Journal of Communication,* 23 (1973), 5–16.

20. See the exchange between followers of Popper and Kuhn in Imre Lakatos and Alan Musgrave, eds., *Criticism and the Growth of Knowledge* (Cambridge: Cambridge University Press, 1970).

21. Merton, 7.

22. Kaplan, 34.

23. May Brodbeck, "General Introduction," in *Readings in the Philosophy of the Social Sciences,* 4.

24. Edwin Black, *Rhetorical Criticism* (New York: Macmillan, 1965), 137.

25. Michael C. Leff, "Interpretation and the Art of the Rhetorical Critic," *Western Journal of Speech Communication* 44 (1980), 346.

26. B. L. Ware and Will A. Linkugel, "They Spoke in Defense of Themselves: On the General Criticism of Apologia," *Quarterly Journal of Speech,* 59 (1973), 273–283.

27. Osborn.

28. Bormann, "Fantasy and Rhetorical Vision."

29. See Farrell's review of some of that literature, 311–12.

30. James C. McCroskey, "Oral Communication Apprehension: A Summary of Recent Theory and Research," *Human Communication Research,* 4 (1977), 78–96.

31. Black, "A Note on Theory and Practice," 333.

32. William H. Rueckert, in *Kenneth Burke and the Drama of Human Relations* (Minneapolis: University of Minnesota Press, 1963), clearly classifies Burke's theoretical pronouncements apart from his methods esp. 83–110.

33. Hugh Duncan, op cit., discusses theory on 63–150, and method from 151–232.

34. As is done in Barry Brummett, "Symbolic Form, Burkean Scapegoating, and Rhetorical Exigency in Alioto's Response to the Zebra Murders," *Western Journal of Speech Communication,* 44 (1980), 64–73.

35. I must stress again that I am referring to critical studies that are directed toward theory; historical rhetorical criticism, for instance, does use more specialized methods of historical research.

36. This review of examples of theory-based criticism should not at all be taken as derogatory of those studies. I simply wish to show that they cannot be doing what theorists have often claimed they are doing; I shall propose a different justification for these studies later.

37. Janice Hocker Rushing and Thomas S. Frentz, " 'The Deer Hunter': Rhetoric of the Warrior," *Quarterly Journal of Speech*, 66 (1980), 393.

38. Rushing and Frentz, 405–6.

39. Rushing and Frentz, 396.

40. See also, among others, Kurt W. Ritter, "American Political Rhetoric and the Jeremiad Tradition: Presidential Nomination Acceptance Addresses, 1960–1976," *Central States Speech Journal*, 31 (1980), 13–171; David Zarefsky, "Lyndon Johnson Redefines 'Equal Opportunity:' The Beginnings of Affirmative Action," *Central States Speech Journal*, 31 (1980), 85–94; Robert L. Ivie, "Progressive Form and Mexican Culpability in Polk's Justification for War," *Central States Speech Journal*, 30 (1979), 311–320.

41. John Waite Bowers, "The Pre-Scientific Function of Rhetorical Criticism," in Ehninger, 163–173. An attempt to treat rhetorical studies pre-scientifically is M. Lee Williams, "The Effect of Deliberate Vagueness on Receiver Recall and Agreement," *Central States Speech Journal*, 31 (1980), 30–41.

42. Merton, 5.

43. Max Black, *Models and Metaphors* (Ithaca, NY: Cornell University Press, 1962), 10.

44. Samuel L. Becker, "Rhetorical Studies for the Contemporary World," in Lloyd F. Bitzer and Edwin Black, eds., *The Prospect of Rhetoric* (Englewood Cliffs, NJ: Prentice-Hall, 1971).

45. Becker, 33.

46. Becker, 24.

47. The accuracy of Becker's insight is also indicated by those rhetorical scholars who have called upon their colleagues to investigate rhetoric from the point of view of the "active audience." See Robert L. Scott, "On *Not* Defining 'Rhetoric,' " *Philosophy and Rhetoric*, 6 (1973), 81–96; James Chesebro and Caroline D. Hamsher, "Contemporary Rhetorical Theory and Criticism: Dimensions of the New Rhetoric," *Speech Monographs*, 42 (1975), 311–33.

48. The single rhetorical transaction is certainly of interest to the historian/critic; my concern here is with the theorist as I have defined him or her.

49. "Ordinary people" is not meant to be condescending; I simply mean people who are not trained as rhetoricians, as they go about their everyday lives. The most brilliant musician, chemist, or physician would thus be an ordinary person in this sense.

50. Keith V. Erickson and Wallace V. Schmidt, "Presidential Political Silence: Rhetoric and the Rose Garden Strategy," *Southern Speech Communication Journal*, 47 (1982), 389–401.

51. See Robert P. Newman, "Under the Veneer: Nixon's Vietnam Speech of November 3, 1969," *Quarterly Journal of Speech*, 56 (1970), 168–178; Hermann G. Stelzner, "The Quest Story and Nixon's November 3, 1969 Address," *Quarterly Journal of Speech*, 57 (1971), 163–172; Karlyn Kohrs Campbell, *Critiques of Contemporary Rhetoric* (Belmont, CA: Wadsworth, 1972), 50–8; Forbes Hill, "Conventional Wisdom—Traditional Form—The President's Message of November 3, 1969," *Quarterly Journal of Speech*, 58 (1972), 373–386. Each of these articles represents its author's moral choices about how to assemble message sets from the rhetorical swirl that surrounded Richard Nixon.

52. For instance, Parke G. Burgess, "The Rhetoric of Moral Conflict: Two Critical Dimensions," *Quarterly Journal of Speech*, 56 (1970), 120–130; Franklyn S. Haiman, "The Rhetoric of the Streets: Some Legal and Ethical Considerations," *Quarterly Journal of Speech*, 53 (1967), 99–114.

Rhetoric and Literacy

❧

Literacy is a term that, like *rhetoric*, has been defined in a number of ways. Apart from any particular definition, literacy refers to ways in which people use language to communicate and to understand their world, and in this respect the kinship of literacy and rhetoric is apparent. William Covino has recently called rhetoric "the performance of literacy," stressing that any prevailing definition of literacy determines what sorts of rhetorical performances are deemed appropriate and allowable. In other words, literacy implies rhetoric.

Sylvia Scribner has described three metaphors that can categorize and contain the wide variety of definitions that fall under "literacy." They are *adaptation*, *power*, and *state of grace*. The adaptation metaphor serves to "capture concepts of literacy that emphasize its survival or pragmatic value." Current discussions of "functional literacy" fall into this category. Coined originally by the U.S. Army, the term is now widely used to indicate the minimal skills necessary to survive in today's technological society. Its currency rests on the presupposition that if one is to function in an institution (such as the military) or a society, one needs the ability to decode and respond to instructions and information. Significantly, radical literacy theorist Paulo Freire explains adaptation as a dehumanizing activity in *Education for Critical Consciousness:*

> To the extent that man loses his ability to make choices and is subjected to the choices of others, to the extent that his decisions are no longer his own because they result from external prescriptions, he is no longer integrated. Rather, he has adapted. He has "adjusted." Unpliant men, with a revolutionary spirit, are often termed "maladjusted."

Countering the adaptation metaphor, Freire emphasizes literacy as revolutionary power, power attendant to a critical perspective on culture. Critical literacy—especially as it has been developed by American theorists such as Ira Shor, Ann Berthoff, and Henry Giroux—requires the view that language is an open and ambiguous system, that meaning is always contingent rather than fixed, and that literacy is not restricted to the mastery of any particular code (e.g., standard written English), but should be reconsidered as the global awareness of and sensitivity to the diversity of ways in which we make meaning.

The "state of grace" metaphor presupposes that the literate person has access to special knowledge from which others are shut away. This metaphor informs Augustine's influential medieval treatise *On Christian Doctrine*, in which both the literate reader of the Bible and the effective Christian rhetor are described as enjoying a state of grace that makes them receptive to hidden spiritual meaning when reading, and to the divine gift of uttering a "good speech." The state of grace metaphor also informs *The Autobiography of Malcolm X*, at the several points when X notes that his inclination and ability to read lifted him from the life of a huckster to demigogic prominence.

Concern over the nature of literacy reaches back to the classical age in the West, when Plato's Socrates worries in *Phaedrus* that writing "will produce forgetfulness in the souls of those who have learned it. They will not need to exercise their memories, being able to rely on what is written." The belief that full literacy requires a strong and active memory continues through the Middle Ages, and we might note a restatement of that belief in the current emphasis on the size and versatility of RAM (random access memory) in computer technology. To the extent that the computer is understood as an extension of a writer's intellect, the power of its memory is an extension of a writer's literacy.

Many who write about the effects of the development of writing technology on society propose that the ability to think logically and critically corresponds to the replacement of orality with writing, and that a culture that can write is one we can call literate. This view is central to the Great Divide Theory, which emphasizes the historical and cultural transition from orality to literacy, and has provoked considerable discussion and debate. One of the articles presented in this section, Eric Havelock's "The Coming of Literate Communication to Western Culture," argues that the development of writing in classical Greece led to a different way of thinking. He has also acknowledged that, although writing provides us the kind of language that makes abstract conceptual thought possible, what we understand as literate behavior can remove us from physical and emotional feelings and experiences.

Thomas J. Farrell's "A Defense for Requiring Standard English" is concerned with the orality/literacy split as it operates in U.S. locales that are in many respects "oral" cultures, particularly African-American communities in which black English is spoken. Farrell argues for language use that is functional in the larger society, that helps its users toward economic improvement. Harriet Malinowitz's "The Rhetoric of Empowerment in Writing Programs" offers a different model for teaching students who are marginalized from the mainstream society. Malinowitz argues that "when writing, including the tools of mastering the code, is integrated into a curriculum in which the outsider's vision is nourished, students become owners, rather than renters, of language." Echoing Freire's concern with literacy as adaptation, she discusses a number of literacy programs that are both liberatory and empowering. William A. Covino's "Magic, Literacy, and the *National Enquirer*" studies a particular case of literacy (reading the *National Enquirer*) and—with reference to Freire's distinction between "magic consciousness" and "critical consciousness"—proposes that the *Enquirer* offers its readers a discourse of "false magic."

FURTHER READING

Covino, William A. *Magic, Rhetoric, and Literacy: An Eccentric History of the Composing Imagination.* New York: SUNY P, 1994.

Freire, Paulo. *Education for Critical Consciousness.* Trans. Myra Bergman Ramos. New York: Continuum, 1973.

Goody, Jack, and Ian Watt. "The Consequences of Literacy." *Perspectives on Literacy.* Eds. Eugene R. Kintgen, Barry M. Kroll, Mike Rose. Carbondale: Southern Illinois UP, 1988: 3–27.

Ong, Walter J. *Orality and Literacy: The Technologizing of the Word.* London: Methuen, 1982.

Pattison, Robert. *On Literacy: The Politics of the Word from Homer to the Age of Rock.* Oxford: Oxford UP, 1982.

Scribner, Sylvia. "Literacy in Three Metaphors." *Perspectives on Literacy.* Eds. Eugene R. Kintgen, Barry M. Kroll, Mike Rose. Carbondale: Southern Illinois UP, 1988: 71–80.

Thomas J. Farrell

"A Defense for Requiring Standard English"

Many English teachers considered themselves in support of civil rights when they voted, 79–20, at the 1974 CCCC convention, for the resolution on the "Students' Right to Their Own Language." I questioned whether the means proposed by the defenders of that resolution—teacher sensitivity to students' feelings and extensive teacher knowledge of dialects—would actually contribute to the positive realization of the noble aim of civil rights. I spent several years questioning my professional colleagues at St. Louis Community College at Forest Park and elsewhere in the country about the adequacy of the means suggested by the advocates of the students' so-called right, to help students develop their abilities to read and write well. During those years of questioning, I continued to study the growing body of research on primary orality and literacy, especially the work of Walter J. Ong and Eric A. Havelock. I eventually came to the conclusion that people from a residual form of primary oral culture needed to learn the surface forms of the standard grammar of a literate language to a certain extent in order to develop their own literate thought. I reported and explained this conclusion in an article in the December 1983 *College Composition and Communication* and defended this position against four commentators in the December 1984 *CCC.* I proposed in the December 1984 *College English* that the study of primary orality and literacy raises serious questions about the appropriateness of the means suggested by the advocates of the students' so-called right to their dialects, for helping students from an oral tradition to develop their potential for literate thought. James Sledd responded to my comment in the same issue of *CE.* My three pieces and his response were the subject of lively discussion at the 1984 MLA Convention. That discussion in turn was the subject of the lead story in the January 9, 1985 issue of *The Chronicle of Higher Education* (Coughlin 1, 10). The purpose of this essay, then, is to respond to the various arguments presented by Sledd and others against my opposition to the resolution about the students' right.

First, some definitions. By the term "standard English" in the title of this paper, I mean primarily the standard surface forms of English grammar, which were developed in print culture and which are used in carefully edited publications, and secondarily the lexicon. I emphatically do not mean phonology. I use the following terms as synonyms for standard English: educated English, the literate language, the language of literacy and literate modes of thought, and the grapholect. The term "literate" encompasses both non-vowelized and vowelized systems of phonetic alphabetic writing, but it does not include syllabic or pictographic systems of writing. As a matter of fact, in this paper I refer only to the vowelized system employed in English. In addition, I follow Ong's lead in speaking of literate culture as encompassing a matrix of personality and behavioral structures. Those who are familiar with Sigmund Freud's *Civilization and Its Discontents* will understand the kind of inter-dependent interaction to which Ong is referring. However, in this essay my primary concern is cognitive development, although I do mention matters related to personality structures towards the end.

Now, the argument. I wish to note at the outset that I am not going to discuss how to eliminate real racism. Real racism does exist in the USA. Anti-white racism exists, just as anti-black racism exists, and other forms of real racism exist in various people in the USA. Real racism is a deep-seated personal malady. I am not going to discuss possible measures that might be taken to help real racists overcome their racism. However, I am going to discuss the charge of racism that has been levelled against those who advocate, as I do, that all students, regardless of race, be required to learn the standard surface forms of English grammar used in most books, including the standard forms of the verb "to be." For I maintain that this is the only truly non-racist position.

I am going to defend the position that this requirement is not racist, and I am going to argue that the failure to require students to learn standard English is *in effect* racist. I know that some people believe that black ghetto students should not be required to learn standard English, and I am *not* suggesting that those who advocate that are themselves necessarily motivated by anti-black racism, even though I am arguing that their position is in effect racist. Since I am on the subject of motives, I wish to say something about my own motives. If I were a real anti-black racist, I would not be presenting the argument I am presenting and withstanding the impassioned outcries of people like Sledd. For the very logic of my argument would lead a real anti-black racist to discourage black ghetto students from becoming literate, as real anti-black racists actually did in the nineteenth century by effectively forbidding most blacks to learn to read and write. That is obviously not the logic I am following. But it is in effect the logic followed by Sledd and others even though they may not be aware that that is the logical implication of their position. Because they are probably not aware of that, they most likely are not motivated by real anti-black racism. Nevertheless, their position is dangerous. Therefore, it is imperative to respond to the arguments put forth in support of their position concerning the so-called right of students to their dialects.

Now, I claim that it is an expression of anti-white racism to *identify* standard English with whites and to argue from this putative linkage, as Sledd and others argue, that it would be racist to require non-white students to learn standard English. Standard English as such is race-neutral or race-independent in the sense that whether or not one can learn it does not depend on one's race. Educated blacks in various parts of the world have learned standard English, and so have other non-whites who have learned to read and write English well. Since non-whites in various parts of the world have learned standard English, this demonstrates that standard English is not intrinsically connected with being white. Moreover, it clearly shows the anti-white racism of those who identify standard English with whites and argue from this putative linkage that non-whites should not be required to learn standard English. Therefore, the only non-racist position is to require all normal students regardless of race to learn standard English.

Sledd and others wish to convince us that Ong's work, and my work are ethnocentric. There is substantial evidence to suggest that reputable editors do not agree with their verdict on this matter, however. Dexter Fisher included Ong's "Oral Culture and the Literate Mind" in the collection of essays entitled *Minority Language and Literature,* which was published by MLA in 1977, and Houston A. Baker, Jr., included an introduction by Ong in the collection of critical essays about Chicano, Native American, and Asian-American literature entitled *Three American Literatures,* which was published by MLA in 1982. Norman Simms chose to reprint Ong's "Literacy and Orality in Our Times" in an issue of *Pacific Quarterly Moana* devoted to oral tradition, which issue featured essays about works from Serbia, the South Pacific, Maori, Malay, Cameroun, and the third world in general. Those three editors undoubtedly considered that Ong's various contributions are not ethnocentric, or else they would not have included them. Moreover, the editors of *New Literary History* did not consider Ong's "African Talking Drums and Oral Noetics" to be ethnocentric; the editors of *America* did not consider Ong's "Mass in Ewondo" (a language used in Cameroun) to be ethnocentric; and the editors of *Mosaic* did not consider Ong's magnificently sensitive and deeply insightful essay on "Truth in Conrad's Darkness" to be ethnocentric. Considerations of space preclude quoting at length from these six essays. Readers who wish to consult these six works can judge the matter for themselves. But the fact that the editors of six different publications accepted them suggests that ethnocentrism is not likely to be found in them. From a ninety-page review of research on open admissions, completed as part of my dissertation, I became convinced that I knew a more suitable way to describe the situation of black ghetto students. Subsequently, I have produced a number of articles describing the situation of these students in terms of orality and literacy. Thomas Kochman published a study of orality and literacy as factors in black and white communication at about the same time as my earliest articles (1974). A number of editors have now accepted my essays on orality and literacy in a wide range of journals suggesting that ethnocentrism is not likely to be found in them.

Perhaps Sledd and others fear what might happen if real anti-black racists were to discover Ong's work or mine. Real racists probably would ignore Ong's many comments designed to undercut *their* mentality and twist his work to their end. Moreover, real racists would probably be able to do the same with my work.

Those are real possibilities. But neither Ong's work nor mine is addressed to real racists. Moreover, apprehension over the possible twisted misuses real racists might make of something cannot deter Ong and me from addressing our fellow teachers, who as teachers have the power to use orality-literacy studies to achieve great good. Furthermore, Sledd's position is dangerous precisely because it could keep teachers from achieving that great good—and thereby play into the hands of the real anti-black racists in the USA. But teachers who take the non-racist position of requiring all students regardless of race to learn standard English can contribute to the civil rights movement by helping all Americans realize the potential with which they are endowed: to learn to read and write reasonably well and to experience thereby the intellectual liberation that can result from such empowerment.

To sidestep the argument about the potential danger of the so-called students' right position, Sledd and his followers caricature the work of Havelock by referring to it as the great leap theory. But their caricature merely reveals their lack of familiarity with Havelock's work. For nobody who has carefully studied *The Greek Concept of Justice: From Its Shadow in Homer to Its Substance in Plato* could so characterize Havelock's work. In this monumental study Havelock traces the gradual development of abstract thinking as it emerged over a period of several centuries. Today, the gradual development of abstract thinking in children in an essentially literate culture occurs over a period of several years, as studies by Piaget, Vygotsky, and others show. Children in an essentially literate culture proceed from the seminal forms of abstract thinking that Jensen finds in most white children, through the stage of developed concrete operational thinking to the stage of developed abstract thinking that Piaget describes (Farrell "IQ"). In either the historical or the contemporary case, the so-called great leap takes place gradually. But what about the intellectual development of children from a residual form of primary oral culture? Jensen does not find the seminal form of abstract thinking among black children out of oral tradition that he finds among white children from an essentially literate culture, as I explain in my *CCC* pieces. Because of the early non-development of certain intellectual potentials, it will be a greater leap for black ghetto students out of an oral tradition to develop their potential for the stage of abstract thinking that Piaget describes, than it will be for most of their white counterparts who have grown up in the print culture of the USA. Moreover, if they do not learn the literate language to some extent, they are not likely to develop to the stage of developed abstract thinking as Piaget describes it, and their low scores on standardized tests will continue to show their nonlearning.

Sledd and others have decried my privileging of the literate language over the dialects developed in a residual form of primary oral culture as cultural imperialism, oppression, and racism. Now, if the real anti-black racists of the past who forbade blacks to learn to read and write were to return to life, they would no doubt howl with delight at Sledd's arguments. For from the point of view of real racists, the claim that dialects are separate but equal must be as much of a hoot as the claim that those separate schools were equal. For that claim about dialects is a devious way to discourage many black ghetto schoolchildren from learning educated English. The charge of cultural imperialism is misleading, because it can distract us from the fact that if the schools fail to require the students to learn standard English, the students are probably not going to become reasonably well educated, and their failure to become reasonably well educated will continue to be reflected in their low scores on standardized tests. The development of the literate language and the development of the cognitive abilities measured by standardized tests are correlated, as Siegmar Muehl and Lois B. Muehl found. Here is their own modest summary of their report in *Language and Speech* (28):

> Eighty black students enrolled in a pre-freshman year college program were divided into four standard English ability groups based on standardized scores. Group dialects were obtained by asking the students in each of the groups to translate orally a standard English reading selection. Quantitative and qualitative analyses of these dialect translations showed differences among the groups in dialect facility that were positively and significantly related to group rankings in standard English ability. Initial differences among the groups in reading ability and geographical background did not appear to account for the differences in dialect facility. Comparing the results of the quantitative analyses in the present study with findings in language development studies suggested a developmental hypothesis to account for the group differences in both dialect and standard English communication skill for these black students.

Their research supports Geraldine Van Doren's (70) recent observation: "The trouble later on is not that some children cannot learn to read and write well because they have low I.Q.'s, but rather that these children have low I.Q.'s because they have not been taught to read and write well enough. Literacy, the acquisition of knowledge, and the ability to think are interdependent." In short, the charge of cultural imperialism conveniently overlooks the liberating power that learning to read and write reasonably well can have on people regardless of race.

Of course, the spurious claim of cultural imperialism and/or racism levelled against standardized tests also needs to be answered. Just as standard English is not intrinsically connected with the white race, so too the learning tested by standardized tests is not intrinsically connected with any particular racial group. On the contrary, that which is learnable is open to all who apply themselves to learning it—regardless of race. To identify that which is learnable with whites and to argue from this putative linkage that non-white students should not be tested for their learning of learnable material, is to express anti-white racism. Because that which is being tested is learnable, it is race-neutral or race-independent in the sense that whether or not one can learn it does not depend on one's race. Since learning can be liberating for all learners regardless of race, sentimentality should not keep educators from encouraging all students to learn as much as they can with their native potential. While it appears that all human beings are not endowed with equal potential intelligence for abstract thinking, it is nevertheless a truism that the potential intelligence of people from a residual form of primary oral culture for abstract thinking cannot be known until their potential is actuated. It can be actuated, I claim, by their actually learning the surface forms of the grammar of standard English to a certain extent as well as the lexicon of educated English. The study by the Muehls supports this claim.

To avoid possible misunderstanding, let me emphasize that the term "potential intelligence" here refers specifically to the potential for abstract thinking, as I repeatedly specified in my CCC pieces. Of course, the term "intelligence" can be used more generically. For example, Ong ("Writing" 10) clearly is referring to the larger, generic sense of the term "intelligence" when he questions the validity of so-called intelligence tests: "most if not all of which show little indication if any of understanding the mental processes of oral cultures or of residually oral subcultures . . ." I unequivocally accept this point of Ong's. Nevertheless, I still maintain that so-called intelligence tests are reliable and valid measures of abstract thinking. Since abstract thinking is one kind of intelligence (the literate kind), those standardized tests are not totally misnamed "intelligence tests." But they are not perfect tests. For even as measures of abstract thinking, their reliability and validity needs to be expressed in terms of degrees; their measures do not yield certitude, but probability. In addition, they are probably dreadfully imperfect as measures of the kind of intelligence developed by primary orality—the kind of intelligence of which Athena in ancient Greece was the goddess. However imperfect standardized tests may be in this respect, the kind of intelligence fostered by primary orality may ultimately prove to elude measurement. However that may be, an observation made by Ong ("Literacy" 15) bears repeating: "Orality sometimes provides nonanalytic short-cuts into the depths of human issues."

Two minor arguments often put forth by Sledd and other defenders of the CCCC resolution on the so-called right of students to their dialects can be readily challenged. One spurious argument says that teachers need to be sensitive to the feelings of the students when they correct them. Of course, no one is going to argue that teachers should be insensitive. But it is important to note two things. First, teachers cannot avoid correcting students if they are actually going to teach them, and, second, teachers cannot predict how their corrections will register on students. Frankly, some students are simply not open to being corrected. Those students need to be told to listen to their teachers. I for one believe that a campaign to tell students to listen to their teachers would do far more to facilitate student learning than would a campaign to tell the teachers to be more sensitive to the unpredictable feelings of their students. Another spurious argument says that teachers should learn a lot about the dialects of the students before they attempt to teach them standard English. This is simply an unreasonable demand. For teachers of English as a second language beyond the rudimentary level are not required to learn the various languages of their students before they attempt to teach them. The same is true beyond the rudimentary level of teachers of Spanish as a second language, teachers of Japanese as a second language, teachers of Arabic as a second language and so on. Extensive knowledge of the students' languages and/or dialects is not necessary in order to teach them in another language or dialect. It is simply self-serving for sociolinguists to demand that teachers acquire extensive knowledge of sociolinguistics before they attempt to teach students standard English.

The major argument put forth by Sledd and other sentimental defenders of the so-called right of students to their dialects states that black ghetto students *may* be taught standard English if they *choose* to learn it. School *policy* is the matter of concern here. Several points need to be made in order to adequately challenge this spurious argument. Perhaps an analogy will help clarify the situation. School policy in the USA dictates that students will be required to learn the decimal system of computing, not, say, the binary system. School policy does not say that students *may* be taught the decimal system of computing if they *choose* to learn it. The policy is to require all the students to learn it. Of course, some learn to compute better than others with the decimal system. Student choice may in some sense very well account for some differences in actual learning. After all, the students are the principal agents of their own learning. If they do not apply themselves to learning, then they will not learn. In this respect, the students always either choose to apply themselves to learning or choose not to. But the policy of the schools with respect to what the students will be required to learn is a different issue from the issue of whether or not students will apply themselves to learning what is required of them. In other words, school policy and student practice are separate issues. While there may be great diversity in student practice, school policy should be uniform in the sense of requiring the same standard of all, regardless of race. In the USA the policy is to require all students to learn to compute in the decimal system. By analogy the policy should be to require all students to learn standard English. For no other policy position is defensible as a policy position. If, for example, the schools were to adopt the policy of *explicitly* allowing the children to choose whether or not they wish to attempt to learn standard English, as Sledd advocates, then the schools would not be acting responsibly, for they would be allowing some students to make a choice between resting satisfied with the dialects they have acquired outside of school, on the one hand, and attempting to learn the relatively unfamiliar features of the grammar of standard English and the new words in the lexicon of educated English on the other. One course of action would require no effort, while the other would probably require considerable effort. Students are simply not well enough informed to make such a choice. The schools would be acting irresponsibly if they were to allow students to make such a choice. For the schools would then be officially sanctioning a double standard, and in the final analysis that is an untenable position as a policy position.

Moreover, if one were to argue against *requiring all* American students to learn standard English, as Sledd seems to argue, then one would be implying that perhaps not all those children have the intelligence to learn standard English (Farrell "A Comment"). Specifically, to argue against requiring black ghetto students to learn standard English is to imply that perhaps they lack the intelligence to learn it. Of course, if they actually did lack the potential to learn it, it would be unreasonable to require them to attempt to learn it, for it would be impossible for them to do so. But the example of educated blacks shows that it was possible for *them* to learn standard English, and so it is reasonable to assume that it would be possible for all normal black students to learn standard English. Thus, to argue for requiring all normal students to learn standard English is to imply that they actually have the potential intelligence to do so.

Those like Sledd who argue that the students have a so-called right to the dialects they happened to learn outside of school are the unwitting perpetuators of the caste system, I claim. The dialects collectively known today as black English—with their non-standard forms of the verb "to be"—developed in the residual form of primary oral culture of black Americans at a time when they were forbidden by law or custom to learn to read and write. Those who forbade blacks to learn to read and write were real anti-black racists. That form of racism continued long after the Emancipation Proclamation, and it forestalled for many black Americans the intellectual liberation that can result from learning to read and write well. Of course, other factors due to real racism compounded and prolonged the unfortunate circumstances of the caste system in the USA. In recent years this situation has been protracted further by the ostensibly well-intentioned but nevertheless sentimental talk about the students' so-called right to their dialects. While there may be some truth in the claim that dialects do not hamper students from learning to read and write, that claim is beside the point, and so as an irrelevant point it does not bear on the issues under consideration here concerning so-called rights versus requirements. The important point to note is that students probably need to learn the surface forms of standard English to a certain extent as well as the lexicon of standard English in order to learn to read and write *well*. These "learnings" may be concomitant with one another. If dialects do not interfere with such learning, fine. The more important point to recognize is that instruction in the surface forms of standard English may very well result in optimal learning. This is far more likely to happen with the aid of explicit instruction than with the willy-nilly concomitant learning just referred to. But if a sentimental concern for the dialects of black ghetto students keeps the schools from requiring them to learn standard English, then they most likely are not going to learn in the optimal way how to read and write. They may very well not learn to read and write well, and consequently they may not experience the intellectual liberation that can result from learning to read and write well. Moreover, even if they are socially promoted through primary and secondary school and perhaps even admitted to an open admissions college, they will not have acquired the knowledge and modes of thought required by more and more jobs in our highly technological society. In short, the honoring of the so-called right of students to their dialects will leave them ill-prepared for anything but the most menial labor at a time when positions requiring only menial labor are shrinking in number. Of course, those black students who do learn the grapholect and learn to read and write reasonably well will most likely fare well later in life in terms of jobs. But those poor blacks who are victimized by sentimental educators concerned with their so-called right to their dialects will prob-

ably continue to suffer economically, unless they happen to be talented as athletes or entertainers. In other words, the sentimentality of certain educators will
unwittingly perpetuate the effects of the caste system by failing to require those
who are now at the lowest socioeconomic echelons to acquire in school the basic
intellectual skills that could enable them to find more rewarding jobs later in life.

If all jobs are rank-ordered, somebody is going to be at the bottom. In this
respect, the lowest socioeconomic echelons in one sense will always be there. But
if we consider the unemployment of black Americans and the relatively low economic status of many blacks over the last twenty-five years—at the very time of
the civil rights movement—then we need to note that the American economy
experienced a phenomenal growth in jobs over the last fifteen years. In *Freedom
with Justice* (49) Michael Novak reports these figures:

> In 1970 there were 78.7 million civilians employed in the United States. The labor
> force was not much larger; only 4.9 million persons who sought work were
> unemployed. A moderate majority of married women (57 percent) sought no
> work outside the home. . . . The US economy performed better during the peri-
> od 1970-1984 than anybody expected. It created an unprecedented 24 million
> jobs, raising the number of employed civilians from 78.7 million to 104.1 million
> by March 1984. In short, the number of new civilian jobs grew by 25.4 million, a
> herculean increase of 32 percent. No other nation came even close to that.

Unfortunately, Novak does not mention the percentage of married women who
sought work outside the home by March, 1984. But it is obvious that many of the
new jobs mentioned by Novak were held by women, most of whom, I would
argue, were essentially literate and acculturated in the print culture of the USA
out of which our contemporary secondary oral culture has grown. Conversely, I
would argue that most blacks and other normal people who are perennially in the
lower socioeconomic echelons are people from a residual form of primary oral
culture. Since the sustained economic development of the West emerged when
the West moved into what Ong styles print culture, I infer that a certain degree of
acculturation to print literacy is probably a necessary but not sufficient condition
for sustained economic development (Farrell, "Democratic Capitalism"). I am
arguing that this is necessary for individuals within the USA, unless they are athletes or entertainers or otherwise talented in a special way, and I am also arguing
that this is necessary for countries throughout the world, unless they are oil-rich
or otherwise endowed with an abundant high-value natural resource. (Even then
sustained economic development over decades and centuries probably would
require the assimilation of what Ong calls print culture.) I obviously do not subscribe to the Marxist reduction of the world to a struggle of good guys vs. bad
guys, where the good guys are the people who are still living in a residual form
of primary oral culture and the bad guys are the people living in a print culture.
On the contrary, I consider what Novak styles democratic capitalism to be the
only viable socioeconomic system available to the world today, but I recognize
that many parts of the world have yet to move into the print culture that fosters

the development of democratic capitalism. However, since print culture and democratic capitalism have been worked out in the West, other people should be able to assimilate the best aspects of these developments without repeating the mistakes made in working them out.

Because I consider the Marxist scenario laughable, I fully expect self-proclaimed radical English teachers to object to my valorization of print literacy over primary orality. In response to their predictable objections, I would challenge them to reflect honestly on what they themselves really desire. If they truly desire to perpetuate primary orality, then they should not seek to teach people to read and write well. In other words, they should not be English teachers. But if they desire to teach people how to read and write well, then they should not object to my valorization of print literacy over primary orality—for I am just making explicit what is implicit in their desire to teach people to read and write well. Of course, they could still object to my valorization of democratic capitalism. This, I believe, is the real difference between me and the radical English teachers. It is beyond the scope of this essay to try to resolve such large differences. But I would encourage those who are interested in the subject to read Novak's *Spirit of Democratic Capitalism.* Moreover, those who are concerned about the noble aim of civil rights need to consider carefully Thomas Sowell's penetrating analysis in *Civil Rights: Rhetoric or Reality?* as well as his other fine works.

In sum, I am arguing that teachers as such probably have more power than anybody else in the USA to effect the noble aim of the civil rights movement. For teachers can play a positive gatekeeping role, as Charles Timothy Summerlin has recently reminded us, by empowering students to read and write reasonably well. Of course, teachers will need the strong cooperation of the adult community as well as the students themselves. If that cooperation were forthcoming, the phenomenal expansion of the American economy from 78.7 million jobs in 1970 to 104.1 million jobs in 1984 suggests that great strides could be made in a comparatively short time to fulfil the noble aim of the civil rights movement.

WORKS CITED

Coughlin, Ellen K. "Literacy: 'Excitement' of New Field Attracts Scholars of Literature." *The Chronicle of Higher Education* 9 January 1985: 1, 10.
Farrell, Thomas J. "From Orality to Literacy: Teaching Writing to the Disadvantaged." *Oral English* 1 (Fall 1982): 1–5.
———. "Kelber's Breakthrough." *Semeia* 39 (1987): 27–45.
———. "Early Christian Creeds and Controversies in the Light of the Orality-Literacy Hypothesis." *Oral Tradition* 2 (1987): forthcoming.
———. *Opening the Door: An Analysis of Some Effects of Different Approaches to Educating Academically High-Risk Students at Forest Park Community College 1971–72.* Ph.D. dissertation, Saint Louis University, 1973. Ann Arbor, MI: University Microfilms, 1974, Order No. 74–24,070.

———. "Open Admissions, Orality, and Literacy." *Journal of Youth and Adolescence* 3 (1974): 247–60.

———. "Literacy, the Basics, and All That Jazz." *College English* 38 (1976–77): 443–59. Reprinted in *Sourcebook for Basic Writing Teachers*. Theresa Enos, ed. Random House, 1987. Forthcoming.

———. "Developing Literacy: Walter J. Ong and Basic Writing." *Journal of Basic Writing* 2 (Fall/Winter 1978): 30–51.

———. "Differentiating Writing from Talking." *College Composition and Communication* 29 (1978): 346–50.

———. "Scribes and True Authors." *ADE Bulletin* 61 (May 1979): 9–16.

———. "The Lessons of Open Admissions." *The Journal of General Education* 33 (1981): 207–18.

———. "Havelock on Literacy." *Cross Currents* 33 (1983): 214–16.

———. "A Comment on Edward Anderson's 'Language and Success' " *College English* 45 (1983): 616–18.

———. "Democratic Capitalism and Psycho-Cultural Evolution." *Catholicism in Crisis* 2.1 (December 1983): 41–43.

———. "IQ and Standard English." *College Composition and Communication* 34 (1983): 470–84.

———. "Reply by Thomas J. Farrell." *College Composition and Communication* 35 (1984): 469–78.

———. "Two Comments on James Sledd's 'In Defense of the Student's Right.' " *College English* 46 (1984): 821–22.

———. "On Biology and Composition." *The University Bookman* 24.2 (Winter 1984): 42–44.

Freud, Sigmund. *Civilization and Its Discontents*. Trans. by Joan Riviere. London: Hogarth Press, 1930.

Havelock, Eric A. *The Greek Concept of Justice: From Its Shadow in Homer to Its Substance in Plato*. Cambridge, MA and London, ENG: Harvard UP, 1978.

Kochman, Thomas. "Orality and Literacy as Factors of 'Black' and 'White' Communicative Behavior." *Linguistics* 136 (15 September 1974): 91–115. The contents of this issue are identical to the contents of *International Journal of the Sociology of Language* No. 3.

Muehl, Siegmar, and Lois B. Muehl. "Comparison of Differences in Dialect Speech among Black College Students Grouped by Standard English Test Performance." *Language and Speech* 19.1 (January 1976): 28–40.

Novak, Michael. *The Spirit of Democratic Capitalism*. New York: Simon and Schuster/American Enterprise Institute, 1982.

———. *Freedom with Justice: Catholic Social Thought and Liberal Institutions*. San Francisco: Harper and Row, 1984.

Ong, Walter J. "Mass in Ewondo." *America* 131.8 (28 September 1984): 148–51.

———. "African Talking Drums and Oral Noetics." *New Literary History* 8 (1976–77): 411–29.

———. "Truth in Conrad's Darkness." *Mosaic* 11.1 (Fall 1977): 151–63.

———. "Oral Culture and the Literate Mind." *Minority Language and Literature: Retrospective and Perspective*. Ed. by Dexter Fisher. New York: Modern Language Association of America, 1977. 134–49.

———. "Introduction: On Saying We and Us to Literature." *Three American Literatures: Essays in Chicano, Native American, and Asian-American Literature for Teachers of American Literature*. Ed. by Houston A. Baker, Jr. New York: Modern Language Association of America, 1982. 3–8.

————. "Literacy and Orality in Our Times." *Pacific Quarterly Moana* 7.2 (1982): 8–20.

————. "Writing and the Evolution of Consciousness." *Mosaic* 18.1 (Winter 1985): 1–10.

Sledd, James. "James Sledd Responds." *College English* 46 (1984): 822–29.

Sowell, Thomas. *Civil Rights: Rhetoric or Reality?* New York: Morrow, 1984.

Summerlin, Charles Timothy. "Toward Defining 'Basic' Once Again." *ADE Bulletin* 81 (Fall 1985): 32–35.

Van Doren, Geraldine. "English Language and Literature." *The Paideia Program: An Educational Syllabus.* Ed. by Mortimer J. Adler. New York: MacMillan, 1984. 59–70.

Harriet Malinowitz

"The Rhetoric of Empowerment in Writing Programs"

For people who are relatively powerless in society—such as workers, people of color, and women—there can be a contradiction in the idea that writing is a tool of empowerment. In traditional writing courses, students have been taught rhetorical patterns that define, describe, analyze, classify, tell what happened, show causal relation, and argue to convince an audience; yet teachers usually haven't acknowledged that these rhetorical techniques are taught within a social context that systematically repudiates their authentic use. For example:

> Workers can be fired for describing, defining, or analyzing their experiences in the workplace because the result is likely to be the argument of unionization.
>
> People of color are defined and described primarily by white people in the media and the academic disciplines, and are classified by them in business, industry, health care, education, and government, from the Moynihan Report to our welfare and legal systems.
>
> Women in most states still can't legally classify a rape as such if it occurs in marriage, and narrating an experience of sexual harassment on the job will more likely lead to public humiliation for the narrator than justice for the perpetrator.

Recent trends in writing pedagogy veer away from the use of rhetorical modes and formulaic paragraph arrangements. The new process theorists of the past fifteen to twenty years focus on the internal dynamics of composing, emphasizing its essentially recursive quality and techniques such as prewriting, freewriting, drafting, revising, and problem solving. Old buzzwords like *thesis statement* and *topic sentence* have been supplanted by a content-oriented vocabulary, including *thinking, meaning, ideas,* and *transactions*. To make instruction more student-centered and to make students feel more empowered in their capacity for personal expression, teachers sometimes try to restructure authority arrangements in the classroom. The process people define writing as something other than just the acquisition of writing *skills*; they try to take a more holistic view of the writer in the world and of the meaning at the root of the writing act.

Writing process theory has brought us a long way from the alienating dogma of the five-paragraph theme and has been indisputably pivotal in the evolution of composition studies. At the same time, its focus needs to be broadened if its intentions are to be fully realized. It is artificial to search for meaning and to reconfigure power when the goals and the arrangements of the classroom are not related to the power relationships that exist outside the classroom, including the social roles of teachers and administrators and the bureaucracies of schools and literacy programs. For the process people, as well as for the traditionalists they have been deposing, there is a schismatic sense of concern with what Paulo Freire calls the world and the word. The world is brought into writing classrooms as an adjunct in the development of students' writing processes, instead of writing's being seen as part of a larger process, a process of engagement in a dialectic with history and culture. The process approach, like its product-centered antecedents, draws no necessary connection between students as people who write and think in a classroom and people who live in a sociopolitical universe. The process people do link form to content; but the process that students are expected to negotiate is often personal and individualistic, and the context, instead of being the ideologically and materially complicated real world, is frequently, as the introduction to one textbook in the vanguard of this school asserts, "the writing workshop" (Brannon, Knight, and Neverow-Turk 1). James Berlin calls the field of apolitical writing process theory "cognitive rhetoric," one that "rest[s] secure . . . in its scientific examination of the composing process," yet one that he believes is "eminently suited to appropriation by the proponents of a particular ideological stance, a stance consistent with the modern college's commitment to preparing students for the world of corporate capitalism." According to this school of thought, says Berlin, "the structures of the mind correspond in perfect harmony with the structures of the material world, the minds of the audience, and the units of language" (480–82).

Like most academics and professionals, process theorists and teachers tend to be middle-class, and they are most often white. Like members of most dominant groups in society, they have the privilege of presuming their experiences to be normative or universal and to view education as culturally neutral; diversity in race, class, and gender is often boiled down to the image of the classroom as a benevolent melting pot of experiences and perspectives. These ideas, which I believe arise more from self-perpetuating naivete and apoliticism than from a conscious desire to strangle students' writing powers, nevertheless engender an intellectual vigilantism, in which the insiders—that is, the students who demographically most resemble their teachers—swim, while the outsiders sink. The problem is that writing instructors see themselves as purveyors of technique, in which meaning has an important role; yet the real context of the writer may be invisible to them. As Adrienne Rich says, "For young adults trying to write seriously for the first time in their lives, the question 'Whom can I trust?' must be an underlying boundary to be crossed before real writing can occur" ("Teaching

Language" 64). Process classes often pretend that class peers are the intended audience of student writing, but it is still understood that anything not accessible to a white, middle-class teacher may be seen as the product of a process gone awry. What the field of writing pedagogy needs, especially that part concerned with nontraditional students, is a shift from student problems, attitudes, and fears as the sources of scrutiny to a serious questioning of teacher ideology.[1]

A good example is something that happened a few years ago, when I was a new adjunct instructor in a developmental writing program. A group of us who taught different sections of the same course met to create a recommended list of novels or full-length works of nonfiction that could be used as a content addition to the course. Each of us was responsible for writing synopses of a few books of our choosing. When we met a few weeks later to pare down the list, all books written by nonwhite authors were eliminated for one reason or another. Maya Angelou's *I Know Why the Caged Bird Sings* was rejected as being "strongly anti-white." Zora Neale Hurston's *Their Eyes Were Watching God* was considered a poor choice because her use of "dialect" might overrun everything we were trying to teach our students about correct usage. Winnie Mandela's *Part of My Soul Went with Him*—a book about her life and that of her husband, jailed African National Congress leader Nelson Mandela—was deemed too "inaccessible," as were *Down Second Avenue: Growing Up in a South African Ghetto* by Ezekiel Mphehlele and *The Woman Warrior* by Maxine Hong Kingston. Such books as Eudora Welty's *One Writer's Beginnings* and Carson McCullers's *Heart Is a Lonely Hunter* remained on the list.

I'd heard rumors that the department had been accused of racism. It was clear from the discussion of the book list that both a wish to redress the department's image and the personal anxieties of individual instructors were in play. The six of us in the meeting were all white, but most students in the program were people of color. One of the instructors in the meeting said that Maya Angelou's problems with white people made her "uncomfortable" and that she could not teach the book "because of its consistent attitude throughout the story." Others agreed, adding that they were afraid their students might understand more of these books than they did. Finally, the department's reputation was alluded to, and it was agreed that the best way to steer clear of any further misunderstandings was to use only white (thus, safe and teacherproof) texts in the classroom. This was a program that claimed a commitment to "writing as process" and "writing as a social act"; but the instructors' own processes and social perceptions unfortunately remained unanalyzed, including their process of trying to socialize the largely nonwhite worker-student body into white, middle-class reality.

In his introduction to *Freire for the Classroom,* an anthology of essays on liberatory teaching, Ira Shor proposes that teachers join students in creating a critical pedagogy that is *"participatory, critical, values-oriented, multicultural, student-centered, experiential, research-minded, and interdisciplinary"* (22). Most of these items are priority areas for process theorists. The difference between theories of politically liberating pedagogy and writing process goes back to the gap between the word and the world. Shor's "desocializing model for teacher education" is one in which teachers ground themselves in ethnography and cross-cultural communication, in an understanding of inequities in society, in the history of egalitarian movements that have been socially transforming, and in models of community change (24–25). Process pedagogy at its best makes writing possible, enabling students to achieve some academic and social legitimacy; at its worst it so neglects student writers' realities that it becomes simply another setup for failure. In any case, process theory ignores the paradox it presents for nontraditional students by, on the one hand, urging them to find their voices and the tools to name their perceptions and experiences while, on the other hand, ignoring the dangers that can arise when these tools are used in the real world and proposing no ways to overcome the voicelessness and passivity that the larger society delegates to them. Generating a pedagogy that is not political, writing process theory can implicitly impart to such students the rules of false expression—fostering, in the words of several Marxist educators, the "reproduction of subordinate consciousness." Even attempts to decenter authority in the classroom are ineffectual as long as they fail to acknowledge the dissonance, confusion, and outright resistance that result for students who are simultaneously interacting with the larger institutions that contain the classroom and that directly refute such arrangements. The reorganization of authority in the classroom can't be just a way of encouraging students to write; to make any real sense, the reorganization must also be a model for using language to reshape authoritative structures in the world.

To engage in this collaboration sincerely, teachers must be willing to give up some of their own power. To give up power does not mean to make oneself neutral, inconspicuous, ignorant, unavailable, irresponsible, or value-free. Rather, it means to investigate the social foundations and the limits of one's own process of making meaning, recognizing that this construction is political, as well as technical. As Henry Giroux says,

> illiteracy as a social problem cuts across class lines and does not limit itself to the failure of minorities to master functional competencies in reading and writing. . . . As a part of the larger and more pervasive issue of cultural hegemony, illiteracy refers to the functional inability or refusal of middle- and upper-class persons to read the world and their lives in a critical and historically relational way. . . . Fundamental to [the struggle toward literacy] is the need to redefine the nature of teachers' work and the role of teachers as transformative intellectuals. (12, 24–25)

In this context, to give up power means to question the assumptions that have delimited one's worldview or, put simply, to engage in consciousness-raising. The women's movement has probably offered the best model for this process, starting in the late 1960s, when women gathered together and discussed the truths about their lives. As similar personal problems surfaced again and again and surprising commonalities among women's experiences were more fully understood, these narratives were alchemized from confessions into sociopolitical parables and gave birth to the feminist maxim that the personal is political. Later, in the 1970s, awakened by Third World women who challenged the white, middle-class foundations of contemporary feminist theory and activism, some white women within the movement went back to consciousness-raising. This time they attempted to confront honestly their own racism, to discover how it functioned in their personal lives and in the alternative institutions they were creating, and to learn much of what they did not know about the lives of women of color. The realization that they were reproducing in another form the subordination that feminism sought to eradicate was enormously disturbing to many white women, yet, for those who were interested in building a viable and global movement, the challenge became a galvanizing force toward growth.

In 1979 four feminists, two black and two white, published a set of consciousness-raising guidelines for women's groups that were working on the issue of racism (Cross et al.). They began by asserting that theoretical and analytical discussion alone was not sufficient to bring about meaningful change in social, human relationships. Their suggested topics for discussion ranged from early memories and childhood experiences to contemporary feminist issues. Some of the questions were the following: "What did you learn at home about Black people and people of color?" "What kind of contact did you have with people of different races? Were they adults, children, playmates?" "In what ways was race used by you or your friends as a subject of so-called teenage rebellion?" "If you were growing up during the 50s and 60s, what kind of information did you get about Black people through the media?" (Cross et al. 54–56). The questions guided discussions that have taken place in women's groups around the country through the 1980s and that have given us important insights into how we have come to see ourselves and others as people in the world. Just as the early days of feminism opened up the idea that we are not just people but women, so does racism consciousness-raising open up the idea for white people that we are not just generic people. For teachers, as well as activists—and it is a Freirian precept that to teach really is to be an activist—dispensing with the facile notion of global humanness and confronting the politics of difference must be the first part of any liberatory process. The second part might be called divestiture; having recognized difference, one must be willing to help break the monopolistic hold of one's (or one's group's) experience on mass consciousness.

Liberating education is not just an idea; it is a practice with a history. Here are a few instances of educational practice in which the *process* that teachers and learners collaborated in was the transformation of their own lives.

The Highlander Folk School began in the early 1930s in Tennessee. Highlander, a name derived from a popular term for Appalachian, was founded and led by Myles Horton, who wanted to create a school for mountain people in a time when most of the local population was on relief. Modeled on the folk school tradition that had begun in nineteenth-century Denmark, Horton's pedagogy was unabashedly partisan and aimed to provoke imaginative leaps from actual to possible social conditions. Horton promoted the idea of adult education as worker education, and he tapped an incipient revolutionary consciousness by using the conditions of the students' lives as the source material of learning. Most worker-education programs then, as now, emphasized basic skill-focused literacy and the acquisition of pragmatic job-related knowledge, but Highlander taught literacy in the context of music, dance, poetry, and the theater arts—all steeped in the principles of collective organizing. Highlander worked with unions and farmers' organizations, often educating on the picket line. The school openly violated Tennessee's jim crow laws and worked to open the labor movement to all working people. Among the creative fruits of the Highlander community was an early incarnation of the song "We Shall Overcome."

By the end of World War II, as unions expanded their membership, literacy skills were cultivated at Highlander through the making of posters and leaflets and the writing of news releases and shop papers; students also learned about parliamentary procedures, public speaking, and community relations. In the 1950s and 1960s the school's focus shifted to the civil rights movement and in the 1970s to community organizing around regional issues.

As Highlander evolved, many of its middle-class educators discovered that traditional academic methods had no value where people struggled daily to meet the most basic material needs. At the same time they discovered that within the struggle for food and jobs lay the foundations of the educational process. Mutual learning centering on the most critical problems and conflict situations in students' lives, what Freire has called "dialogic learning," was the key to Highlander's success. As Horton once wrote in a letter:

> The tie-in with the conflict situations and participation in community life keeps our school from being a detached colony or utopian venture. But our efforts to live out our ideals makes possible the development of a bit of proletarian culture as an essential part of our program of workers' education. (Adams 517)

The Citizenship Schools, started in the racially segregated Sea Islands of South Carolina in 1954, represented another program spearheaded by Highlander, though the schools later ended up under the auspices of the Southern Christian Leadership Conference (Graves 3). The Citizenship Schools were initiated by Esau Jenkins, a bus driver who wanted to create a literacy program that would enable black people to register to vote. Highlander provided critical start-up support, and by 1963 the Southern Christian Leadership Conference reported that more than four hundred schools had been started across the South, with an estimated 100,000 students who had learned to read and write through the program (Adams 513).

Asked to explain the success of this program when other literacy projects had failed, Horton said:

> It isn't a kind of mass education gimmick that you can plunk down anywhere and it works. That's why they couldn't get people to come to those state-financed literacy programs. It wasn't that people wanted to read and write because it was a good thing. They wanted to read for a purpose. That's why so

many programs don't work; they are based on the thought that everybody if given a chance would learn to read and write. It's obviously not true . . . you must start where people are. That means their perception of where they are, not yours. . . . In the case of the Citizenship School, the basis was their everyday experiences and their ambition, their goal, which was voter registration. The content comes from what the people want to learn. (Graves 4)

Another successful, internationally celebrated literacy program that read the world and, consequently, helped people read the word was the national literacy crusade in Nicaragua. Begun in 1980, less than a year after the dictator Somoza was ousted by the popular Sandinista revolution, and staffed largely by young students, the crusade brought the Nicaraguan illiteracy rate down from fifty percent to twelve percent in five months of intensive work and spawned numerous adult education programs that still continue. Since then, local adult literacy programs have steadily continued to build on the crusade's groundwork. The crusade was mounted as a tangible tool of empowerment, most tellingly in that it was accompanied by a revolution in health care and the government's arming of the people with weapons to defend themselves. As Myles Horton said, "The purpose of education is to serve whatever system it's part of" (Graves 5). The system the Nicaraguan literacy crusade was avowedly serving was a revolutionary one, a system that had not been given to the people but, rather, had been claimed by them. Roberto Saenz, one of the crusade's planners and later vice-minister of adult education in Nicaragua, said:

It is a political project with pedagogical implications, not a pedagogical project with political implications. There are no neutral projects, not in Nicaragua, not in the United States, not anywhere. Every social project carries with it an ideology—in order to maintain a system, to reproduce a system, or to sustain a process of profound change. (qtd. in Hirshon 7)

In September 1980 the National Literacy Crusade of Nicaragua received UNESCO's first prize for "distinguished and effective contribution on behalf of literacy" (Hirshon 215); the country ranked third in literacy in Latin America, only after Cuba (which had undergone a similar national literacy effort) and Argentina. By contrast, as Jonathan Kozol has amply documented, the United States, a country with incomparably greater economic resources, ranks forty-ninth among the 158 member nations of the United Nations in its literacy level, with more than 60 million people—more than one-third the adult population—being illiterate. Estimates indicate a fifty percent illiteracy rate by 1990 (4). Kozol says: "Illiteracy in any land as well-informed and wealthy as the USA in 1985 is not an error. It is not an accident" (89). Pointing out that at one time "laws throughout the nation made it a crime to teach black people how to read and write" (93), Kozol demonstrates that our history has institutionalized literacy as a ruling-class privilege and that only a radical shift in national priorities and consciousness, not superficial panaceas, will alter the devastating trend, as happened in Cuba and Nicaragua.

Two educational programs in which I played a part have presented important alternatives in learning. One was a women's studies program at a large state university in the late 1970s, when I was a graduate student in creative writing. A chance encounter with a women's literature seminar drew me to my first penetrating look at the social context that encompassed me as a woman, the literature I had always loved, and, inevitably, the literature I wrote. I continued to take and to audit feminist literature, history, and theory courses. Not only was the content of the courses central to my own living but the form was different. Students were involved in policy and planning, in hiring faculty, in proposing courses, and in shaping course content. The instructors had had nothing in their graduate training or professional experience that specifically prepared them to teach this discipline; many of the ground-breaking classics of the field were being published while we sat in our classrooms, collaboratively digging our own way. As the boundaries of what we felt we needed to know expanded, so did our networks; our courses began to overlap with and at times consolidate with those in other "special studies" programs, like African-American studies and labor studies. These were the programs that the university considered the most expendable, indulgent frills, the first to be reduced or axed in budget cuts; and yet, because of the unusual level of involvement and passion they ignited, they were the only programs students actively fought to keep.

Around this time, May 1979, Adrienne Rich gave a commencement address at Smith College in which she posed some of the fundamental questions about the purposes and sources of education that women's studies sought to answer:

> Suppose we were to ask ourselves simply: What does a woman need to know to become a self-conscious, self-defining human being? Doesn't she need a knowledge of her own history, of her much-politicized female body, of the creative genius of women of the past—the skills and crafts and techniques and visions possessed by women in other times and cultures, and how they have been rendered anonymous, censored, interrupted, devalued? . . . [D]oesn't she need an analysis of her condition, a knowledge of the women thinkers of the past who have reflected on it, a knowledge, too, of women's world-wide individual rebellions and organized movements against economic and social injustice, and how these have been fragmented and silenced? . . . Without such education, women have lived and continue to live in ignorance of our collective context, vulnerable to the projections of men's fantasies about us as they appear in art, in literature, in the sciences, in the media, in the so-called humanistic studies. I suggest that not anatomy, but enforced ignorance, has been a crucial key to our powerlessness. ("What Does a Woman" 1–2)

Years later, Rich's questions come back to me manifested in new forms through my work in a college program housed in a labor union. The Institute of Applied Social Science is a Hofstra University branch campus at District 65 (now a United Auto Workers affiliate), a historically progressive union that Martin Luther King, Jr., once called "the conscience of the labor movement." The institute is a small (about 140 students), fourteen-year-old enterprise founded to empower workers to shape the conditions of their lives. Many of the students had been out of school for twenty years or more, got high school equivalency diplomas in mid-life, and began college, often to their surprise, when their children were fully grown; the median student age is thirty-nine. As Barbara Joseph, director of the program, explained:

> People come to the institute because ordinary people who work finally have a chance to be validated. It isn't that they need approval from faculty and leadership—it's that they have to have their reality recognized by themselves collectively as co-students and by a curriculum that addresses their experience, the conditions of their lives, their hopes, their visions, and their ability to create the conditions that they want and need for themselves, their families, and their communities. Empowerment is a very important issue in our school. Empowerment comes from dealing with people at their basic level of need, and that need for education is demonstrated over and over again.

The students' writing and reading skills are at varying levels of proficiency, but a significant number of the students begin the program in need of developmental work. The basic writing courses at the institute have been taught in a variety of ways; I have taught the same course differently at different times. But the important feature that distinguishes them from basic writing courses I have known elsewhere is the fact that they are nested in a context that draws on, rather than draws away from, the students' real experiences: their lifelong disjointed experiences as outsiders in academe, where writing performance has always loomed as the most notoriously vulnerable front line, and their experiences as social outsiders, denied credit for their roles as actors in history. Most students start the program with an adult education seminar that introduces them to andragogy, an essentially Freirian concept in which adults are seen as active learners through their own initiative, rather than as the obedient receptors of didactic teaching. Through discussions and written journals, the students' past experiences with infantilizing, paternalistic schooling constitute the primary text of the course, which then becomes a backdrop for their theoretical reading. Students critically rethink the nature of their education, gaining confidence as they proofread the past with new eyes and see their "failures" as acts of resistance and survival, a healthy response to an intellectually abusive society. Most students say that the course becomes a spur to self-realization and self-direction, affecting not only their relations to school but also their relations to work, family, and community life. Because of this effect, they bring to the basic writing class and to their other classes the beginnings of that sense of self infused with conviction that is the primordial feature of all real writing: a voice. As they continue in their other courses—studying the history and the culture of working people, the relations of groups in society, the theory and the practice of social transformation—that voice further crystallizes into what Adrienne Rich calls the "outsider's eye," which can be "her real source of power and vision" ("What Does a Woman" 6).

Mina Shaughnessy writes that "a person who does not control the dominant code of literacy in a society that generates more writing than any society in history is likely to be pitched against more obstacles than are apparent to those who have already mastered that code" (13). When writing, including the tools of mastering the code, is integrated into a curriculum in which the outsider's vision is nourished, students become owners, rather than renters, of language. To own language, one must own some piece of reality that feels worth describing. This is the beginning of exploring a writing process.[2]

NOTES

1. For a working definition of the nontraditional student, I use a modified version of a description developed by Bruce Carmel, Maureen McDonogh-Kolb, and Adam Haridopolous. Nontraditional students often possess at least some of the following traits: they are working-class, people of color, and older than conventional college age; they speak English as a second language or a nonformal dialect of English; and they are the first or among the first in their families to attend college.

2. Several parts of this paper draw on some collaborative thinking with Deborah Mutnick, Sheila Smith-Hobson, and Barbara Henning. The entire paper benefited from the editorial advice of Sara Cytron. Many thanks go to them all.

WORKS CITED

Adams, Frank. "Highlander Folk School: Getting Information, Going Back and Teaching It." *Harvard Educational Review* 42 (Nov. 1972): 497–520.

Berlin, James."Rhetoric and Ideology in the Writing Class." *College English* 50 (1988): 477–94.

Brannon, Lil, Melinda Knight, and Vara Neverow-Turk. *Writers Writing.* Upper Montclair: Boynton, 1982.

Cross, Tia, Freada Klein, Barbara Smith, and Beverly Smith. "Face to Face, Day to Day— Racism CR." *But Some of Us Are Brave.* Eds. Barbara Smith, Gloria Hull, and Patricia Bell Scott. Old Westbury: Feminist, 1981. 52–56.

Freire, Paulo, and Donaldo Macedo. *Literacy: Reading the Word and the World.* South Hadley: Bergin, 1987.

Giroux, Henry. "Literacy and the Pedagogy of Political Empowerment." Freire and Macedo 1–27.

Graves, Bingham. "What Is Liberating Education? A Conversation with Myles Horton." *Radical Teacher* May 1979: 3–5.

Hirshon, Sheryl. *And Also Teach Them to Read.* Westport: Hill, 1983.

Joseph, Barbara. Interview. *Building Bridges: Community Labor Report.* Prod. Mimi Rosenberg. WBAI, New York. 12 Nov. 1987.

King, Martin Luther, Jr. Speech at District 65's thirtieth anniversary meeting, Madison Square Garden, 23 Oct. 1963. *Dr. Martin Luther King, Jr., Speaks to District 65 DWA.* District 65 Wholesale-Retail Office and Processing Union, n.d.

Kozol, Jonathan. *Illiterate America.* New York: Anchor, 1985.

Rich, Adrienne. "Teaching Language in Open Admissions." *On Lies, Secrets, and Silence: Selected Prose 1966–1978.* By A. Rich. New York: Norton, 1979. 51–68.

———. "What Does a Woman Need to Know?" *Blood, Bread, and Poetry: Selected Prose 1979–1985.* By A. Rich. New York: Norton, 1986. 1–10.

Shaughnessy, Mina. *Errors and Expectations.* New York: Oxford UP, 1977.

Shor, Ira. *Freire for the Classroom: A Sourcebook for Liberatory Teaching.* Portsmouth: Boynton, 1987.

Eric A. Havelock

"The Coming of Literate Communication to Western Culture"

THE INVENTION OF THE ALPHABET CREATED A CULTURAL TENSION "BETWEEN THE ARTS AND WAYS OF ORAL COMMUNICATION AND THOSE OF THE WRITTEN, AS THE EYE SLOWLY INVADE[D] THE PROVINCE OF THE EAR."

During the centuries between 1100 and 600 B.C., when the civilization we know as classical Hellenism was born, the Greeks came to live as a dispersed people speaking various dialects of a common tongue, not only on the European peninsula we still call Greece, but in all the islands of the Aegean Sea, on the coasts of Anatolia, Thrace, and the Black Sea, and on the coasts of Sicily, South Italy, and North Africa. Essentially the Greeks were at this time a maritime people, clinging to the edges of the mainland rather than occupying and subduing it. Yet in thinking of the Greeks, it is always tempting to plant one's feet firmly on the Acropolis of Athens and survey the rest of the population from that vantage point. It is more correct in this instance, however, to regard the circumference as more significant than the center. And the circumference was the birthplace of the earliest Greek composition we have, known as the poems of Homer.

THE CLASSICAL AGE BECOMES A MATTER OF RECORD AT THE MOMENT WHEN THE HOMERIC POEMS WERE TRANSCRIBED.

Possibly, as I have said elsewhere, the transcription was not a matter of a moment, but was a process spread over decades, not finalized in Athens until perhaps as late as the sixth century B.C. (There are scholars, including myself, who would accept such a conclusion, but it is controversial, and not crucial.) At some time—the year 1000 B.C. is often taken as a convenient starting point marking the inception of the manufacture of geometric pottery—the Greeks of the dispersion, as I have called it, began to develop the initial stages of what became the hallmarks of

Greek classical culture: an architecture, a visual art, a poetry, and a political structure, the Greek *polis*. It seems indisputable that these were in position at a time when the people who placed them there could still neither read nor write.

Therefore an understanding of literacy must begin with non-literacy.[1] Literacy when it came did not create a culture; it transmuted one which it inherited, and the process must have taken time. Non-literacy in Greece represented a cultural condition of immemorial antiquity during which evolutionary pressures molded the capacities of the human brain to the point where it could use language and form communities. Biologically we are all oralists, who have become literate only through cultural conditioning. Past and present intermingle in us, and it is possible that if literacy presents us with certain problems, these may not be soluble without reference to the habits of non-literacy.

Human culture is a creation of human communication; this I take to be a truism. My central concern is with language, both spoken and written. Borrowing a theoretic paradigm from social anthropology, the transmission of social culture can be described thus: as our genes hold in storage coded sets of information to guide the developing organism, from conception to death, a storage transferred from generation to generation, so at the level of social culture, societies in order to exist and enjoy their own forms of organic continuity have to place accumulated information in storage for re-use. The main method for doing this is linguistic. It is easy to see this in the case of documented information covering our law and literature, our science and technology, with which we educate ourselves and from which we absorb our values and attitudes, as we receive it and re-use it and make additions to it.

How does one get the same kind of results in a non-literate culture? In such a culture, storage and transmission between the generations can be carried on only in individual memories. Linguistic information can be incorporated in a transmissible memory, as against some one person's memory, only as it obeys two laws of composition: it must be rhythmic and it must be mythical, in the original Greek sense which the word "mythical" implies, meaning two things. Overall, it must be cast in the form of mythos as a tale; piecemeal, it must be cast in the form of mythos as a saying; the bits and pieces of cultural information must be governed by the syntax of the tale, one which describes an action performed by an agent rather than a law or principle or formula. The oral memory is unfriendly to such statements as "the angles of a triangle are equal to two right angles." But if you say "the triangle strode over the field of battle on its two straight legs defending its two right angles against the enemy," you are remodeling the equation retroactively to accord with the linguistic requirements of oral transmission. If you transfer the tense to the present or imperative and say "a triangle (always) protects its two right angles," or "it (is) better that it do so," or "it must do so," you have produced the equivalent of a saying, an oral maxim, apothegm, or aphorism—supposing strictly oral cultures were ever interested in triangles, which does not seem to be the case.

The felt need of the group for a sense of cultural identity and historical continuity cannot be satisfied by the mere transmission by word of mouth of a body of maxims and sayings or even by separate short stories, i.e., myths. It needs a great story within which these can be amalgamated in some way into that construct we call "national epic," essentially an oral form of composition. Such epics seem to have been recited and sung wherever oral cultures reached a given level of sophistication. They report and illustrate and recommend, indirectly through narrative, the mores and manners, law, religion, and government of the people concerned, who entrust the formation and recitation of such epics to professional singers and are continuously instructed by them as they listen to the recited poems and are encouraged to quote and repeat them. The mass of information is suspended like sediment in the great sweep of the tale.

Such is the theoretic or anthropological framework within which to place the two Homeric epic poems.[2] Seen in this light, they can be viewed as owing less to individual authorship—strictly a literate conception—than to a collegiate activity on the part of generations of composers, not excluding the possibility of individual genius among them. It is not appropriate to base critical judgments of such poetry on strictly literate standards of criticism, which means "literary" standards, provided, that is, that we possess the poetry in something like its original oral form, which for most national epics, for example the Icelandic Eddas or the Niebelungenlied, is not strictly the case. While both Homeric poems upon transcription entered the world of dawning literacy and became works of "literature" for us, they represent a condition of the strictly oral word as composed and sung in a non-literate society.

THE TWO HOMERIC POEMS LEFT THEIR ORAL SOURCE BEHIND AND BECAME WORKS OF LITERATURE THROUGH THE INSTRUMENT WE CALL THE ALPHABET.

Textbooks and histories which deal in any way with these matters commonly use the word alphabet generically to cover a variety of early writing systems, the Greek one being only the latest in a series of such "alphabets." This failure of distinction is unfortunate, for it helps to obscure the fact that the adaptation when carried out amounted to a transformation of function and technological capability which was truly radical. The invention was revolutionary, even if like all inventions it arose through a fresh combination of previously experienced observations. The history of literacy would be served by restricting the term alphabet to the Greek system, as I propose to do.

The phonetic technology of the invention calls for brief exposition, since it was a technology with far reaching effects upon the history of Western culture. Not later than circa 700 B.C.,[3] plus or minus a few years, the invention was available to those who could use it. Its borrowing of written characters previously used by the Phoenicians illustrates the law that new invention is continuous with previous experience. The effort to symbolize the sounds of spoken speech, following upon the earlier and primitive uses of picture writing, had been going on in the Near East for centuries. The problem of these systems was that the sounds symbolized were the possible syllables of words, not the components of the syllables. The possible total of syllables in any tongue is too large, and their exhaustive definition too difficult, to be manageable except in some approximate and incomplete fashion. Systems of shorthand had to be devised to cut down the number and reduce the variety to be symbolized. The Phoenicians carried the shorthand principle to its ultimate by arranging a table of syllables in sets, according to their initial consonants, and then indexing the consonants, and then assigning a single character to each. The signs, the phonetic values, the names, and the memorized list the Greeks borrowed from the Phoenicians with some approximations to fit their own tongue. But they still did not have an instrument fit to translate that tongue fluently from sound to sight, from speech to sign, because the index supplied consonants but no vowels; in effect it applied a single label to a whole group of syllables.

It is usually said that the Greek contribution was to "invent" the five vowels *a, e, i, o, u,* and to assign "unwanted" signs of the Phoenician list to their signification. It is more to the point to say that by identifying all five vowels (some had been already identified in previous systems) in separation from the consonants, they isolated the consonants as separate components of language. Now, a consonantal sound by itself has a theoretic but not an actual existence in any tongue. It normally requires the addition of some vocalization to be pronounced. So what the Greeks really achieved in their act of "adaptation," as their borrowing of Phoenician is called, was an act of abstraction. They decided to use their ABC to symbolize sounds that existed analytically as mental objects but not empirically as spoken sounds. Once this happened, a language could be atomized exhaustively into less than thirty components, any two, three, or four of which could be combined to produce adequate symbolization for any required actual sound, i.e., syllable, with relative accuracy, as it was pronounced.

Recognition (the original Greek work for "reading") became automatic and swift. Ambiguity was banished, and fluency released. A universal instrument for recording the phonemes of any spoken tongue exhaustively and simply was now available, with the proviso that some residual approximation remained. The instrument devised proved to be precise enough for practical purposes.[4]

THIS INVENTION, GIVEN THE RIGHT SOCIAL CONDITIONS FOR TEACHING IT (A LARGE ORDER), COULD BE LEARNED BY A MAJORITY OF A GIVEN POPULATION, THUS CREATING THE POSSIBILITY OF A POPULAR LITERACY.

Yet at the time of the invention, and for some time after, the theoretic possibilities of literacy, either political or psychological, lay far in the future. The Greeks could not become literate overnight. Two things stood in the way. There was, obviously, as yet no ready supply of documented material which would make it worth one's while to learn to read it; and there was no technology for teaching it to preadolescent children, at an age when its use can be readily mastered: the institutional arrangements necessary for this purpose did not exist. A still more important factor which stood in the way was represented by the existing system of "musical" education[5] in the Greek sense. Any indoctrination in letters, i.e., reading or writing, was treated as strictly ancillary to oral competence. To preserve and transmit the traditions of Greek society remained the province of the poets for over two centuries after the documentation of poetry became possible. The poets[6] were essentially still oral poets, down to the time when a reading public came into existence, ready to comprehend new forms of written composition. The poets were called on to continue the didactic functions performed by Homer, most strikingly exemplified in the Athenian drama, in which traditional myths, i.e., orally remembered stories, are continually worked up in varying versions to entertain but also to instruct.

During this time the alphabet was becoming an instrument of some government and some law and some economic activity—but to a limited extent. It is only in the latter half of the fifth century that the evidences for its application begin to multiply. Thus in reconstructing an image of antique Greek history, one must imagine the beginning and slow increase of a cultural tension between the arts and ways of oral communication and those of the written, as the eye slowly invades the province of the ear, the reader the province of the listener. The character of classic Greek literature, during this period, is explicable by the fact that it is reproducing this unique tension in a form which could never recur except in a society starting from scratch, in which all knowledge of the alphabet had perished.

THE INITIAL USE OF THE GREEK ALPHABET THEREFORE INVOLVES A PARADOX.

Though its technology was such as to provide a capacity for designing and recording new forms of discourse, i.e., non-oral forms, for a long time it was used primarily for recording and perpetuating what had first been composed orally. This is strikingly evidenced even in the earliest inscriptions. If they attempt to say anything coherent, they do so in meter—sometimes of the roughest kind. The proper interpretation of this phenomenon is turned upside down by those whose notions of poetry and poetic function are derived from their own literate societies. The early appearance of inscribed verse is taken to indicate a sophistication on the part of ordinary people who must have already become highly literate in order to be able to use poetry for minor occasions. The reverse and correct judgment would estimate the practice of such verse making as a popular art widely and instinctively practiced in a society innocent of letters, and so unable to preserve a statement of some individual importance for even a generation unless it was first versified. The alphabet made possible not the creation but the transcription of the first European literature in the full sense of that word, and yet initially and for some time the original genius remained oral.

But the effects were to go deeper than that, affecting the structure of language and of thought. It must be borne steadily in mind that in tracing what happened our concern is not with that ephemeral speech pronounced in conversation, but the speech preserved for re-use by a given culture, placed in storage to be repeated and added to, a repository of useful experience and necessary knowledge. It is the character of this kind of communication that controls the character of the culture. The range of experience and knowledge expressed in casual unrecorded speech never exceeds what is possible in preserved speech, and usually falls well below it.

Vocabulary and syntax had been controlled by the pressure to memorize. This limited anything that was said to what could be said rhythmically, and in narrativized form, meaning actions performed by agents, or events which happened to them. Even the wording of what is more easily recognizable as preserved wisdom—the maxims, aphorisms, parables, and proverbs—had to conform to these laws. Once the same speech is placed in documented form, the pressure to memorize is relieved, though not at first abolished. The document can lie around available for re-reading and re-consultation without prior necessity of oral recall. Therefore the pressures for poetry as a preservative, and for a restriction to narrative syntax, are relieved also. The twin possibilities exist of a preserved prose, and a prose which no longer tells a story. It can allow itself to express other types of discourse.

Of what precisely will these types consist? Let us begin with the subject of a sentence. Orally preserved speech requires this to be an agent doing something: the most readily available such is a human being, a hero let us say, but there are many varieties of non-human subjects which can be represented as functioning as agents. For example, the opening lines of the *Iliad* speak of a man's anger, to us a psychological phenomenon, which however behaves as a destroyer, that places afflictions upon people, and hurls their souls to Hades. This is the kind of standard idiom for describing in orally preserved speech what goes on in the world. We can reword by saying this is Homer's *description* of the *psychology* of the hero and its negative *effect* upon the *situation* of the Greek army, but in so doing, we are substituting our vocabulary of subjects and objects (which I have italicized) in place of his. This kind of vocabulary, conceptual and abstract, only became possible as an end product of the literate revolution. We speak as we think—speech indeed is the only perceptible evidence that thought exists. It is easy to fall into the supposition that though Homer spoke thus and so, he did so "poetically" as a "convention"; that if he had wanted to, he too could have described his story in terms of connections between abstractions like *description* and *situation* and *cause* and *effect*; in other words, that he could "think" as we do. But is this true? Could an oral culture "think" in this sense?

The premise that the technology of communication controls the content of what is communicated has been popularized in connection with modern radio, cinema, and television. I am applying it in a more radical fashion to a shift in the character of the human consciousness which occurred in ancient Greece, and which we inherit. Briefly I am arguing that the history of the human mind, as of the human language, falls into roughly two epochs, the pre-alphabetic and the post-alphabetic. The possibilities of the latter took time to realize themselves in

Greece, and emerged in the writings of Plato and Aristotle. Even then they were not fully realized. The effects of the resolution accelerated after the European Renaissance and are still going on in our own day.

A linguistic statement requires verbs as well as subjects and objects. Orally preserved speech required these to be performative as when an agent, like Achilles' anger, does something—or else, situational, as when something happens or is present, or is born or dies. The oral syntax is unfriendly to that kind of statement which tries to place two subjects, or a subject and object, in a steady, unchanging relationship to each other, one fixed by their respective natures or essences, as we would say. Once this happens, the subject, or its "name," escapes from the narrative syntax. It tends to be connected by the verb *to be* used solely as a copula, as in the example cited earlier. The angles of a triangle *are* equal to two right angles. The removal of the memorization pressure, meaning the pressure to think of every phenomenon as an act or event, made it possible to document statements of this sort. An analytic syntax is slowly invented, and perfected in prose by Plato and Aristotle. As this happens, the symbols or names as the Greeks would say for subjects and predicates related to each other cease to symbolize agents and become symbolic of concepts, mental constructs which have been wrested and wrestled, so to speak, from the flux of the narrative.

One way of putting this is to say that alphabetic literacy substituted the abstract for the concrete, but we must be careful here to distinguish the abstractions represented in a mere word like Homeric anger and that which is expressed when anger becomes a phenomenon defined in analytic terms. The psychological and semantic revolution was one which involved changes in the syntax, by which terms are connected, not the terms by themselves as found in a dictionary.

IN ADDITION TO THE TWO ADVANCES REGISTERED IN THE ALPHABET—INCREASED FLUENCY OF RECOGNITION AND THE REMOVAL OF THE PRESSURE TO MEMORIZE—IS A THIRD FACTOR, THE SUBSTITUTION OF THE EYE FOR THE EAR IN THE RECEPTION OF COMMUNICATION.

The teaching and practice of literacy has thus involved some considerable manipulation in the use of the senses, and has done some violence to the way in which we have been programmed during our evolution as a species. Literacy is a late comer, a parvenu, in human history. For millenia we have been biologically conditioned to use and understand language only as it is spoken and heard, and in the interest of preserving some of that language for recall we have schooled ourselves as a species to develop a poetic language. Does one discard this inheritance overnight without some psychological damage to the organism—whether an individual or a society—which uses it? If it is desirable that a large majority of a modern population be literate, can this be accomplished without a prior linkage to the poetic and musical inheritance—in short, should children be rushed into reading before they have learned to speak fluently, to recite, to memorize, and to sing suitable verse available in their own tongue? Furthermore, can a society which values the abstract above the poetic ever understand societies which do not? I am thinking here in particular of what we call the Third World, on which we have occasionally made war, as in Vietnam, or occupied, as the European powers have done, or restructured with our technology, as in Iran, always it would appear to small purpose in the long run.

However, asking such questions is only a modern diversion. My tale is of that uniquely interesting people, the ancient Greeks. In their growing literature, aside from the slow emergence of abstract discourse, can be seen also a growing movement towards a more extended organization of what is said, and to a wider sweep of comprehension of what the content can be. In particular I am speaking of the birth of history and historical writing, which again emerged in the late fifth century in Athens. It is here, I think, that the evidence shows most clearly what the help of the eye was doing to recorded speech. It enables a composer to range over what he has said, and review it and rearrange it according to principles which I will call architectural rather than acoustic. The Homeric composer relied on an echo principle to produce his forms of unity and there is evidence in Greek drama of the persistence of the same technique. The complete writer may still use echo—he never forgets he is symbolizing a spoken tongue—but he also is guided by a vision which appreciates shape, and the arrangement of shapes.

This brings me to my last item among the effects of the alphabet, and not the least. Language increasingly available in visual documented form ceases to be an unseen impulse carried through the air—the winged word—and becomes an artifact, a thing in itself, an object of its own study. The evidence again is that this is exactly what occurred in Athens in the fifth century, as the sophists began to name the parts of speech and investigate their "grammar," which means the rules governing the written characters, the *grammata.*

As this happens to language, something happens to its users. In orality, the speaker and his speech remained one; what was spoken was his creation, in a sense it was himself, and it was difficult to think of this self apart from the words it spoke. As language assumed a new identity, so did the personality that spoke and used it. The composer began to separate himself from the written composition and believe in himself as an "authority," an "author." The separation attracted the attention of the philosophers, those first experimenters with a truly conceptual discourse. They began to propose the need for a vocabulary which would describe a man not just doing something, or saying something, but being himself and using language in order to think about himself. The twin concepts of the individual ego, the "soul," and the "intellect" which is part of the ego or soul, or which the ego employs to form concepts, were on their way to achievement when Plato was born. But would they have emerged into the discourse of Europe without the help of the alphabet?

REFERENCES

1. Coldstream, John Nicholas. *Geometric Greece.* New York: St. Martin's, 1977, chapter 11, "The Recovery of Literacy."
2. Havelock, Eric. *Preface to Plato.* Cambridge, Mass.: Belknap/Harvard University Press, 1963.
3. Havelock, Eric. *The Greek Concept of Justice: From Its Shadow in Homer to Its Substance in Plato.* Cambridge, Mass.: Harvard University Press, 1978.
4. Havelock, Eric. *Origins of Western Literacy.* Toronto: Ontario Institute for Studies in Education, Monograph Series 14, 1976.

NOTES

1. This is in marked difference from illiteracy, which describes a personal failure to become literate, an option which must be present in order for literacy to be possible.

2. In my *Preface to Plato* (2), and still more in my *Greek Concept of Justice* (3), I have offered analyses of extensive portions of both *Iliad* and *Odyssey* to demonstrate that these information materials do indeed inhere in the text.

3. The latest discussion (1) places the invention of the alphabet in the first half of the eighth century B.C. The dating problem would be only of marginal importance in the general context of the Greek literate revolution were it not for my conviction that the assignment of a date for the Greek alphabet to the first half of the eighth century owes as much to a preconceived bias in favor of literacy as it does to scholarship, a bias arising from a conviction conscious or otherwise that no culture worth the name can have been non-literate, certainly not the Greek. I am tempted to repeat what I first wrote in 1963, speaking of "scholars of the written word," that when they "turn their attention to the problem of written documentation they betray a consistent tendency to press the positive evidence for it as far as they can and as far back as they can" (2).

4. For a more extended explanation of alphabetic technology, see my *Origins of Western Literacy* (4).

5. *Mousike* refers to the joint arts of poetry, instrumentation, and dance as devised and produced in a partnership which is, I believe, typical of all oral culture in varying degree, and of a kind unique to them. This partnership is fundamentally a response to the need to memorize verbal statements already cast into rhythm by reinforcing this rhythm through the accompanying addition of the rhythms of melody and of bodily motion. As you recited you sang; as you sang you played an instrument; as you played you danced, these motions being performed collectively. Their unusually sophisticated partnership supplied mutual reinforcement. The tenacity with which Athens clung to this method of educating its youth is revealed by indirect reference to it as still a going concern as late as the last half of the fifth century. The schoolmaster was the *kitharistes,* the lyre player. His pupils, besides being taught deportment and discipline, along with the gymnastic practiced in the wrestling school, were trained in the memorization and recitation of the poets and in performance on musical instruments.

6. In viewing the orality of Greek civilization, we must not restrict our perspective to Homer and the Homeric age. What we call Greek literature, produced for 250 years after the alphabetic invention, remains overwhelmingly poetic, composed under audience control, published orally and preserved orally.

William A. Covino

"Magic, Literacy, and the National Enquirer*"*

You can get rid of negative thoughts—and get on with your life—by follow-
ing an expert's simple four-step program. . . . Admit that you don't know
what's causing your problem. . . . Accept responsibility for your problem, but
don't blame yourself for it. . . . Gain a fresh perspective. . . . Think positive.
—National Enquirer

This quotation from the *National Enquirer* is one example among many of that publication's coercive incantations, language that seeks to control and transform readers by declaring that they can overcome difficulties through patterned behavior. Discussing the *Enquirer* as a specimen text of such pronouncements allows us to distinguish between "good" and "bad" magic and advances a lexi-con for evaluating coercive rhetorics and the literacies they enfranchise. More generally, I propose that magic and magic consciousness are foundations of rhetoric and literacy, and, as they are exploited in language, magic formulas and magic consciousness define mass culture.

MAGIC AS RHETORIC

It is possible to distinguish between magic in the strict, or real, sense and magic in the weak, or metaphorical, sense; we might restate this distinction as one between magic as such and magical rhetoric. Magic as such includes medical magic (e.g., the curative spells of the "medicine man"), black magic (witchcraft, sorcery), ceremonial magic (rainmaking), religious magic (exorcism), occultism (fortune-telling), and the paranormal (ESP, flying saucers). Daniel O'Keefe, who has written the most comprehensive recent social theory of magic, distinguishes magic in the strict sense from magical rhetoric by pointing out that, in real magic, "speeches are not extemporaneous or composed, but entirely traditional; and audience response is preordained." Further, real magic "does not try to 'per-suade' [as does rhetoric], but to compel." O'Keefe does admit, however, with reference to Plato and Aristotle, that the function of rhetoric (as persuasion) may be "wrenching the consensus and foreclosing it" and that "there is some resemblance to magic in this operation—in the attempt to suspend communal dialogue, in the first person singular speaking as the first person plural ['we believe'], in the partialism of the viewpoint." But "magic itself" is rigidly scripted, while rhetoric is "much freer and more plastic." Strictly speaking, rhetoric "reminds us of magic" (O'Keefe 82–83).

I suggest that we may borrow terms from magic to illuminate rhetoric and, in particular, to understand the workings of coercive discourse. Although my subject is the rhetoric of coercion, addressed in the terms of magic, you should understand that when I use the word *magic* I mean *rhetoric*. I argue here for the synonymy of magic and rhetoric; after sketching that argument, I leave off any mention of rhetoric, with the hope that magic will sound like rhetoric to you as well.

Consider, for instance, that illusion is the common goal of both magic and rhetoric. Jacqueline de Romilly emphasizes this point in *Magic and Rhetoric in Ancient Greece,* holding the Sophists responsible for illusions of truth achieved through the incantatory spell of language and reminding us that Plato's Socrates often charged his opponents with bad magic, while also weaving his own spells (see esp. 26–27, 36). The Sophists made a world of multiple forms appear and disappear, while Plato's Socrates kept rehearsing one trick—making dialogue disappear into essence but continually admitting that it can't be done because the essence of language is illusion.[1]

While Aristotelian and Ciceronian rhetorics contributed to the establishment of rhetoric as *techne* without magic, as a pursuit associated with political and institutional control and stability, the link between magic and rhetoric persisted. Through the Middle Ages and into the Renaissance, many prominent humanists were also occultists, and while the emphasis on technical rhetoric continued, "a revival of the Greek sophistic notion of rhetoric as magic" also occurred (Ward 109). From John O. Ward's recent study of magic and rhetoric, we learn that teachers such as Isidore of Seville wrote textbooks on both rhetoric and magic, and a typical government adviser in the Middle Ages was a "practicioner of magic and rhetoric, a supplier of skills to ruler and crown—administrative, ideological, rhetorical, historical, liturgical, and architectural skills" (101; note the analogy between this characterization of government advisers and the astrologer Joan Quigley's role in the Reagan administration).

The need for magic, which Susanne Langer posits as part of the "inventory of human needs" (38), seems to coincide with the need for technical rhetoric; as Ward points out, "high points in the history of rhetoric are also high points in devotion to the occult" (87). In particular, the proliferation of new facts, the "steady increase of certain knowledge" (Ward 115) that accounts for the beginning of each traditional epoch of progress in Western history, provokes doubt about what is "really" true and drives those who manage a newly more complex world to magic and to magic rhetoric. Thus the overtly magical sophistry of early antiquity, the renewed reliance on both magic and technical rhetoric in the late Middle Ages and the Renaissance (Ward 107-109), the appropriation of magic to empirical methodology in the Enlightenment (O'Keefe 557), and the growth of both New Age occultism and data-management systems in our own "information age" may all reflect the appeal of both magic and rhetoric, or of magic as rhetoric, at times when the influx of new knowledge and of new living patterns makes us search for a spell to control the demons of change. Recent best-sellers include both Shirley MacLaine's *Out on a Limb,* which offers a reactionary mysticism that looks backward for selfhood and constructs identity by invoking past lives, and E. D. Hirsch's *Cultural Literacy: What Every American Needs to Know,* a reactionary pedagogy that looks backward for a common language of established facts and constructs identity through a dictionary of cultural literacy, a list of terms we must memorize and speak to transmigrate into the mainstream, a virtual lexicon of incantations.

Insofar as programs such as Hirsch's provide schemata for public discourse, they constitute a technical rhetoric. The congeniality of magic and technical rhetoric results from the real power of rhetoric to design and alter reality: the mastery of institutional discourse makes one an insider who can, in turn, invoke and impose facts and formulas. As Kenneth Burke writes, this power exists because "the magical decree is implicit in all language; for the mere act of naming an object or situation decrees that it is to be singled out as such-and-such rather than as something-other." Magic is a "coercive command," the "establishment or management by decree," and insofar as it is intrinsic to language, it is unavoidable. Further, all magic is a strategy calculated to address a situation "in the name of" a certain power (*Philosophy* 3–5). For Burke, strategy, situation, and power are the elements of magic and (I would add) the elements of rhetoric, when embodied in discourse: "Stop in the name of the law." Herbert Marcuse emphasizes the force of these elements as they operate on mass culture:

> At the nodal points of the universe of public discourse, self-validating, analytical propositions appear which function like magic-ritual formulas. Hammered and rehammered into the recipient's mind, they produce the effect of enclosing it within the circle of the conditions prescribed by the formula. (88)

For Marcuse, "the closing of the universe of discourse" is effected by "magical, authoritarian and ritual elements [that] permeate speech and language. . . . It is the word that orders and organizes, that induces people to do, to buy, and to accept" (84–86). Abbreviated thought and thoughtless behavior are the consequences of the tendency in media and government institutions to prefer the abridgment of information: "In its immediacy and directness, [media language] impedes conceptual thinking; thus, it impedes thinking" (95). A popular and obvious current magic-ritual formula is "just say no," which at once makes the victims of the drug problem responsible for eliminating it and prescribes an incantation that will make it disappear, all in the name of (again) the law. (As I propose more fully later, victims who don't use magic words effectively are typically left to blame themselves.)

TRUE MAGIC AND FALSE MAGIC

Burke sketches the conditions for a true magic, a correct magic, and a false or incorrect magic. True magic is the result not of formulaic incantation that attempts to suspend or control "the laws of motion" but of action that creates action, words that create words. It is consequential, producing "something out of nothing," and it is generative (*Grammar* 66). Writers are assistants to the magic of words causing words, to the play of language

> where the act of the writing brings up problems and discoveries intrinsic to the act, leading to developments that derive not from the scene, or agent, or agency, or extrinsic purposes, but purely from the foregoing aspects of the act itself. . . . Our act itself alters the conditions of action, as "one thing leads to another" in an order that would not have occurred had we not acted. (67)

The power that generates true magic is novelty.

Like true magic, correct magic also entails revelation and change, but instead of the "pure" magic of words causing words, correct magic is social, a decree that is least coercive and most inclusive, approachable through the "collective revelation of testing and discussion," that is, dialectically and dialogically. Thus, correct magic entails what Burke calls "scope" (*Grammar* 59); it accounts more fully for facts by subjecting them to the broadest inquiry. (The ideal practice of correct magic is "possible only to an infinite, omniscient mind" [*Philosophy* 4, 7].)

With Burke as a guide, I propose that while all magic is always coercive because it constitutes reality by decree, true-correct magic is practiced as *constitutive inquiry* or the *coercive expansion of the possibilities for action,* while false-incorrect magic—distinct from both the pure novelty of true magic and the shared creativity of correct magic—is practiced as *enforced doctrine* or the *coercive reduction of the possibilities for action*: "Stop in the name of the law."[2] Other distinctions between true-correct and false-incorrect magic (listed below) extend the definitions I have presented for each and point us toward further explanation and illustration with reference to that widely read American medium for false-incorrect magic, the *National Enquirer.*

TRUE-CORRECT MAGIC
generative
enlarges the grounds for action by the creation of choices
originates on the margins of mass culture, as critique
practiced as dialogue
results in integration

FALSE-INCORRECT MAGIC
reductive
exploits the laws of motion by the restriction of choices
originates in the center of mass culture, as technique
practiced as inculcation
results in adaptation

I abbreviate true-correct magic as true magic and false-incorrect magic as false magic—collapsing correctness into truth and incorrectness into falsehood—partly for stylistic economy and partly to stress the moral distinction between one magic and another.

MAGIC AND THE NATIONAL ENQUIRER

Magic power appeals, on the one hand, to aspiring insiders who want to be part of the intellectual or political or economic establishment that issues decrees. On the other hand, the more marginalized and oppressed one is, the more susceptible to magic and to technical rhetoric (Ward 69). Roland Barthes and Jacques Ellul complain that the burden of "facts" accounts for this susceptibility; a world that seems to contain too much knowledge and too many associations makes us more inclined to accept magical solutions (O'Keefe 476). Paulo Freire contrasts "critical consciousness" with this "magic consciousness," associating the latter with the oppressed classes. Magic consciousness "apprehends facts and attributes them to a superior power, [leading people to] fold their arms, resigned to the impossibility of resisting the power of facts" (*Education* 44). Such resignation finds its common expression in "that's the way it is," which is an acceptance not of truth examined but of circumstance enforced.

Widely circulated and widely read by the American working class, the *National Enquirer* may represent a habit of false inquiry rooted in magic consciousness. Advertising the "largest circulation of any paper in America," the *Enquirer* (established in 1926) sells over 4 million copies of each issue, reaching a total adult audience of nearly 19 million. Its closest newspaper rival is *USA Today*, which advertises a national readership of 5.3 million (on every front page) and whose audience is probably in a different class than that of the *Enquirer* audience.

While *USA Today* devotes a good deal of space to news about financial markets and yuppie trends, thus appealing to the upwardly mobile, the typical *Enquirer* reader is a working-class woman who has not attended college. According to a profile of the 1987 *Enquirer* audience, 77% of all readers have not attended college, and annual household income for nearly 64% is under $30,000. Female readers outnumber male readers 2 to 1. They are older (36.7 is the median age for women, 33.6 for men), they are less well-educated (80% of the women have no college, compared with 73% of the men), and they earn less (65% of the female respondents have annual household incomes of less than $30,000, compared with 60% of the male respondents).[3]

While proposing that such numbers indicate a majority of working-class women readers, I must also admit the difficulty of defining *working class*. The color of one's collar on the job and the possession of a job outside the home are questionable determinants; beliefs and feelings about one's status and group identity may be the significant factors (Jackman and Jackman 38). Identifying class with the power and authority enjoyed by its members, we might, at least, distinguish the working class from the middle class by adopting O'Keefe's definition that middle-class people are "those who do not run things, but are treated well in return for their loyalty" (O'Keefe 467); consequently, working-class people are those treated less well, those Paul Fussell calls "people things are done to" (44). According to the 1980 census, this definition certainly applies to working-class women, who "suffer disproportionately from economic marginality, unsatisfying jobs, poor working conditions, inadequate social and municipal services, deteriorating neighborhoods, and alienation from the American mainstream" (Hunter and Harman 388). In general, *Enquirer* readers lack the resources and experience that make upward mobility possible, and thus they are relegated to the status that Fussell describes. *Enquirer* readers need magic, and the *Enquirer* provides it, with all the characteristics of false magic that I proposed above.

False Magic Is Reductive.   Most *Enquirer* stories are tethered—often explicitly—to governing maxims: the same ones, repeated in similar stories from issue to issue, are "hammered and rehammered into the recipient's mind," so that they become "proverbial" examples of Marcuse's magic-ritual formulas (88). A handful of "proverbs" recurs in each issue:[4]

Self-Improvement Is Simple. "Simply Eating Certain Foods Will Make You Smarter" (2 Aug. 1988; 23); "Living a Long, Happy Life Is Easier Than You Think" (12 Apr. 1988; 9); "52 Simple Tips That Will Put Thousands in Your Pocket" ("Bone your own chicken breasts. . . . Don't let the water run while you're brushing your teeth. . . . Don't buy premium paper towels" [10 Jan. 1989; 6–7]). Articles such as these are virtual extensions of the proverbial wisdom that defined *Poor Richard's Almanack,* which set aside complexity and difficulty and advertised discipline.

Success Techniques Apply to Everyone. The *Enquirer* sets aside individuality along with complexity and difficulty. Generalized schematic advice—advertising better living through sameness—aligns success with following universal rules. There are five rules for handling mistakes on the job (22 Dec. 1987; 12), seven rules for saving time in the kitchen, seven rules for getting a promotion (27 Sept. 1988; 15, 20), ten ingredients in the "recipe for a happy marriage," and three steps to falling asleep (23 Aug. 1988; 13, 48). In a world where individual differences are homogenized into generalized behaviors, individual psychology is understood only as an instance of universal categories. For example, "The Way You Celebrate Your Birthday Reveals Your Personality" (23 Aug. 1988; 12), but you have just nine personalities to choose from; similarly, the way you take compliments, give gifts, and smile, along with your favorite ice-cream flavor, allow you to type yourself.

Failure Is an Attitude Problem. Success results from the imposition of mind—equipped with the prescribed rules and principles—over matter. And the proper mind-set is a positive attitude, a Reaganesque image of "morning in America," in which sniveling about pains and problems is taboo (a regular *Enquirer* feature is "$10 for Happy Thoughts"). The sky diver whose chutes don't open saves himself by refusing to imagine his imminent death and instead picturing his family:

"We're so happy!" I thought. "Our future looks so bright!" I saw a mental picture of my mischievous little son Ben, a fantastic little 4-year-old who's everything a father could want. I saw his 18-month-old brother Matt, with that dribbly chin that melts my heart whenever I see it. Nope, no way would death meet up with me at this point in my life. (30 Aug. 1988; 3)

Determined not to die, he meditates himself into "a ball of fat, a rubber ball. I won't get hurt. I'll just melt into the earth or bounce off it," and bounce he does, surviving a two-mile fall. This is an extreme instance of the "you can be anything you wanna be" attitude that the *Enquirer* insists on continually, through the very frequency of its success prescriptions.

Medical Technology Can Fix Anything. The power of attitude and technique to make life better is rivaled by the power of technology, mainly medical technology. New machines, drugs, and surgical procedures can make blood clots disappear, eliminate hemorrhoids, remove fat, grow hair, smooth wrinkles, cure arthritis. While numerous *Enquirer* articles reveal such breakthroughs, *Enquirer* advertising, with its decided emphasis on fixing one's body, represents the most strident and substantial appeal to those who want to make pain, age, and mortality disappear. Typically, nearly half the ads in each issue are selling skin treatments, body beautifiers, reducing programs, indigestion and pain relievers, or ambulatory aids.

Nobody's Safe. Although technique, attitude, and technology ensure personal and professional success, anyone can become a victim or a freak. *Enquirer* articles describe Australians who are violently allergic to plastic and chemical additives, little girls who are dying from exposure to light, a boy who won't grow, a boy who can't stop eating, women who have been unable to stop having babies, a house possessed by demons. Celebrities, the culture heroes of the *Enquirer,* are just as vulnerable: Liz Taylor fights back pain, alcoholism, and suicide; television star Alan Thicke is pursued by a terrifying, lovesick fan; Ringo Starr fights drug addiction. From issue to issue, the diseases, deaths, and divorces of the rich and famous illustrate a world of misfortune and tragedy from which no one is protected.

Implicitly, we are all already victims of technical and technological advances; they reduce the latitude of human behavior and individuality. The threat that technology will overcome humanity is occasionally explicit, in articles about machines taking over human labor:

"Robots will take over the Earth!" declares a university robotics expert [Hans Moravec, director of the Mobile Robot Laboratory at Carnegie Mellon University]. . . . "They won't need us. They will be knowledgeable enough to handle their own maintenance, reproduction and self-improvement. It seems that the takeover by robots is almost inevitable." (3 Jan. 1989; 4)

While mimicking science fiction, this piece is also the logical extension of the *Enquirer* view that facts and formulas exert more control in the world than people do.

Survival Is in the Hands of Providence. A grizzly bear and a "man-eating crocodile" number among the murderous animals who miraculously end their attacks, to sighs of "thank God" from their victims. Renegade machines—airplanes, tanks, cars—level property but leave inhabitants unhurt, each survivor repeating the sentiments of Stephen Bright, whose car was sliced in half by a runaway airplane: "I'll thank God every day for the miracle that saved my life" (18 Oct. 1988; 3). Escapes from a monstrous death get providential credit from issue to issue, reinforcing both the traditional belief that life-saving reversals of fortune are ordained by heavenly forces and the idea that individuals are powerless; Stephen Bright joins the other *Enquirer* survivors who remind readers "how easily life can be lost."

The *Enquirer* joins God as an agent of good luck, advertising its power as an amulet for the suffering. Reading the *Enquirer* is itself featured as the way to survival and happiness. Once or twice a month, the paper prints testimony from grateful readers; Petta Bourdreault writes, "Thank God for the *National Enquirer*—it saved me from a lifetime of agony!" and explains that her seven years of "living in hell" with the pain of shingles ended with an *Enquirer* story about a new cream that "cleared up her pain completely" (2 Aug. 1988; 17).

Altogether, the *Enquirer* names the world as, on the one hand, a threatening realm of inexplicable forces and, on the other, a realm where formulas and technology and a subscription to the *Enquirer* can overcome human pain and poverty. Its maxims define a "circle of . . . conditions" (Marcuse 88) that reduces the possibilities for human action, by prescribing devotion to the magic of technique, attitude, and technology while also saying that they are no insurance against disaster. Participating in the contradictory worlds of the *Enquirer* has its domesticating effect: one must meet each day with happy thoughts, discipline, and fear.

False Magic Exploits the Laws of Motion by the Restriction of Choices. Any behavior that occurs as an unwitting reduction of complexities may be classed as motion rather than action. Burke makes the distinction by saying that

> insofar as a vote is cast without adequate knowledge of its consequences, one might even question whether it should be classed as an activity at all; one might rather call it passive, or perhaps sheer motion (what the behaviorists would call Response to a Stimulus). (*Grammar* xx).

And insofar as false magicians create "simple" solutions to complex problems, they appeal to motion rather than action; a closer look at one typical *Enquirer* formula for overcoming personal problems, "*Enquirer's* No. 1 Plan to Conquer Shyness," reveals the magicians' work:

> Top experts have worked with us in developing this special plan—which will enable you to greatly reduce this crippling problem within a matter of weeks. . . . Accept the fact that you are shy. . . . Realize that you have nothing to be afraid of. . . . Observe how confident people behave. Watch people who

do well in social situations. You'll see that during conversations, they: Smile frequently. Stand and act naturally instead of folding their arms defensively across their chest. Speak loudly enough to be clearly heard. Lean forward to demonstrate interest in the person they're talking to. Make frequent eye contact. Occasionally touch the other person on the arm or shoulder. Nod often to show interest. . . .

Don't try to be the life of the party. . . . Set realistic goals for situations that make you shy. . . . Make your conversation totally positive—don't criticize. . . . Meet other people through your hobbies. . . . Practice in simple "safe" situations. . . . Review your social successes—and congratulate yourself.

Dr. Danilo Ponce, professor of psychiatry at the University of Hawaii School of Medicine and one of the experts who helped devise the plan, told the *Enquirer:* "Shyness is far from being incurable. By following the advice of this plan you can greatly reduce your problem within a matter of weeks." . . . And Dr. Gordon Deckert, professor of psychiatry at the University of Oklahoma Health Sciences Center in Oklahoma City, added, "By consistently following the advice in this plan, you'll be able to overcome your shyness—no matter what degree—and become happier, more popular and more successful." (22 Nov. 1988; 2)

The emphasis here on watching and imitating, and the focus on symptoms rather than causes, is the typical *Enquirer* attempt to prescribe motion rather than action, patterned behavior rather than critical understanding or reflection.

False Magic Originates in the Centers of Mass Culture, as Technique. Significantly, the "experts" who advertise magic formulas are almost always university professors (mainly in social sciences and medicine), that class which inhabits an academic otherworld unknown to the typical *Enquirer* reader who has not been to college. The magicians of culture—those who either invent magic formulas for success (the professors) or are themselves transformed by the magic of determination, discipline, and luck (the celebrities)—are called, respectively, experts and insiders. These secular oracles speak to a working class on the margins of the happiness, popularity, and success that Dr. Deckert promises.

False Magic Is Practiced as Inculcation. The chant of maxims and prescriptions that recurs in each *Enquirer* identifies knowledge with the invariable, suggests that learning about the world means remembering facts and procedures, and proposes that any fact is worth knowing. The bimonthly feature that lists miscellaneous statistics, "What Happened since You Last Read the *Enquirer*," joins the other numerical facts that make headlines in each issue, all restating the importance of simplistic empiricism:

Video rentals soar 1900% in five years . . . 8 in 10 grocery shoppers bring along coupons . . . 1 in 4 students is a college grad . . . last week Americans spent almost $2 million on maps and atlases . . . last week Americans bought 24,000 guitars, mandolins, banjos and ukeleles . . . there are over 41,000 pizzerias in the U.S. . . . gasoline costs $4.24 a gallon on the Ivory Coast . . . 6 to 12 iron tablets can kill a child . . . 2,760 American teens become pregnant daily. . . . Between 10 billion and 12 billion pennies are minted every year. . . . (3 Jan. 1989; 11, 12, 13, 40, 42, 46, 60)

This is the *Enquirer* narrative of American life: if it can't be quantified and memorized, it didn't happen; if it can be quantified, it's worth knowing. It's not that some things count more than others; whatever can be counted counts.

False Magic Results in Adaptation. Freire distinguishes integration from adaptation, associating adaptation with magic consciousness:

> *Integration* with one's context, as distinguished from *adaptation*, is a distinctively human activity. Integration results from the capacity to adapt oneself to reality *plus* the critical capacity to make choices and to transform that reality. To the extent that man loses his ability to make choices and is subjected to the choices of others, to the extent that his decisions are no longer his own because they result from external prescriptions, he is no longer integrated. Rather, he has adapted. He has "adjusted." Unpliant men, with a revolutionary spirit, are often termed "maladjusted." (*Education* 4)

Enquirer magic appeals to the desire for normalcy. Shyness, weakness, anxiety, anger, disaffection, and infidelity are debilitating maladjustments. They make happiness, popularity, and success less likely; they make a person more like the *Enquirer* freaks of nature, who represent what it means to be abnormal. Nobody's safe, but adaptation, with its attendant docility, is a hedge against adversity.

MAGIC AND LITERACY

Other, less established and less glossy "prole weeklies" (Fussell's term) such as the *National Examiner* and the *Weekly World News* appeal to incredulity by featuring blatantly weird phenomena like two-headed babies and repeated Elvis sightings. The *Enquirer,* with its emphasis on normalcy rather than the paranormal and its avoidance of the extremely lurid and grotesque, asks to be taken seriously. (A colleague of mine recently cut the *Enquirer* from a popular culture course because "it isn't sleazy enough"—its pseudojournalism is too subtle, too factual, too difficult to dismiss.) Regular *Enquirer* readers may be aware of its negative reputation, but the paper's straight-faced appeal to conservative mainstream values, the apparent veracity of its prescriptions and statistics, and its disdain for complexity and confusion ensure it a good measure of credibility. A middle-aged married couple who have read the *Enquirer* regularly and thoroughly for several years told me recently that (while they seldom admit it) the *Enquirer* helps them feel well-informed. Such anecdotal evidence aside, the

Enquirer appeals to—and accounts for the leisure reading of—a substantial number of working-class people and may be used as an index to working-class literacy. Taking the *Enquirer* seriously and reading it uncritically demonstrates a literacy limited by the information, beliefs, and attitudes that the paper enfranchises. It is a literacy limited by the dictates of false magic, a literate susceptibility to the coercive reduction of the possibilities for action. I say this not to continue castigating the *Enquirer* per se but to propose that uncritical literacy—the ability to read and write unreflectively that is often called functional literacy—invites and sustains false magic. To the extent that mass media generally advertise a reductive, technocratic ideology of adaptation, they are the agents of false magic. More important, to the extent that education and educators generally advertise a reductive, technocratic ideology of adaptation, *they* are the agents of false magic.

Recall that the *Enquirer* magicians are usually professors whose work contributes to both the formulaic management of abnormality and the ideology of career success. Their characterization as *Enquirer* experts alerts us to the ambiguous position of the academy and academics; the more proximate the academy's mission and the work of academics are to the center of mass culture, the more likely they are to entail false magic. The professors attacked by the *Enquirer* are those who get government grants for projects that offer no practical benefits for mainstream Americans; a typical attack, "Should You Foot the Bill to Dig Up Ancient Mexico?" responds with outrage to a $73,000 National Science Foundation grant for studying "Prehistoric Political Economy in Mesoamerica's Northern Periphery" (24 Jan. 1989; 30).

True magic, because it is a dialogic critique that seeks novelty, originates at a remove from the mass culture it would interrogate. Efforts to identify literacy with true magic have not become popular in American education, which is, paradoxically, as it should be; such popularity would entail the transmutation of dialogic critique into slogans, the disappearance of one magic into another. And so, true magic remains the work of radicals: Freire's literacy program—with Ira Shor as its American publicist—is a striking revolution against false magic, founded in generative language, reflection and action, and continual dialogue and critique (see Freire's *Education for Critical Consciousness* and Shor's *Freire for the Classroom*). Freire's opposition of a mechanistic, servile literacy to a dialogic, critical literacy parallels the opposition of false magic to true magic, so that we may think of his insistence on a liberatory literacy as his magic remedy for magic consciousness. Literacy is itself the offer of a new magic:

> We wanted to offer the people the means by which they could supersede their magic or naive perception of reality by one that was predominantly critical, so that they could assume positions appropriate to the dynamic climate of the transition. (*Education* 44)

Grounded in an "active, *dialogical,* critical and criticism-stimulating *method,*" literacy brings with it "an attitude of creation and re-creation, a self-transformation producing a stance of intervention in one's context" (*Education* 45, 48). Noting Freire's emphasis on the transformative magic of dialogue, I stress that a Freirean educator's task is precisely the coercive expansion of the possibilities for action, that constitutive inquiry I have posited as the true magic method.[5]

Grounded in false magic, literacy becomes, effectively, the perpetuation of the *National Enquirer*; grounded in true magic, literacy enlarges both exploration and community. The very identification of literacy with magic asks that we define our roles as teacher-magicians and makes it more difficult for us to measure progress in our students in terms of adaptation and career success; to do so may contribute to the world of *Enquire*ry rather than inquiry.

NOTES

1. For recent discussions of the play of essence and illusion in the *Phaedrus,* see Covino 10–21 and Neel 1–29.
2. My distinction here between true and correct and false or incorrect magic is an elaboration of hints by Burke, especially in *Grammar* 59, 66, and in *Philosophy* 3–4.
3. To get a profile of *Enquirer* readers, I first wrote to the senior editor, Iain Calder, explaining,

> I am currently conducting a scholarly study of the reading habits of working-class Americans and have concluded that the *National Enquirer* is the publication they read most often. I am asking your help to verify this conclusion. Might you supply me with (1) the circulation figures for the *Enquirer* and (2) any information regarding the types of readers who tend to buy and read the *Enquirer* (socioeconomic level, sex, race, etc.)?

Calder responded with a courteous refusal, saying, "We receive hundreds of requests like yours for assistance, and we simply do not have the time or the staff to help everyone who asks" (6 Oct. 1988).

However, when I phoned the *Enquirer* advertising department and said that I wanted to buy ad space but needed demographic information first, they immediately sent me a state-by-state breakdown of paid circulation and a profile of the 1987 *Enquirer* audience, with breakdowns according to age, education, and household income.

I offer this tale as a contribution to scholarly research methods and leave its further implications to you.

4. For the analysis that follows, I examined *Enquirer* issues from 29 September 1987 through 31 January 1989.
5. Jonathan Kozol, with his insistence that literacy is more than the incorporation of "adult nonreaders into the accepted mainstream of noncritical America" (182), has also identified "fundamental humane literacy" with characteristics that would disallow false magic; they are:

1. informed irreverence
2. tolerating indecision
3. political sophistication
4. respect for history

5. counteraction of violence
6. wise anger
7. taste ("the willingness to state that some things count a lot, others much less, and some things not at all")
8. global literacy (as against "geographical myopia")
9. ability to decode doublespeak (174–182)

Brian V. Street reminds us that

> what governments and companies want from literacy is primarily techno-logical competence and improvement. The relationship between this and "intellectual competence" is problematic. . . . Literacy programmes will still be justified on the grounds of "productivity." (185)

By defining the literate individual as broadly informed, critical, participatory, and skeptical, Kozol realizes that he "portends some danger for the social system as a whole" (133), as he counteracts the public emphasis on literacy as unreflective and obedient behavior.

WORKS CITED

Burke, Kenneth. *A Grammar of Motive*. Berkeley: U of California P, 1969.
———. *The Philosophy of Literary Form*. Los Angeles: U of California P, 1974.
Covino, William A. *The Art of Wondering: A Revisionist Return to the History of Rhetoric*. Portsmouth: Boynton, 1988.
Kozol, Jonathan. *Illiterate America*. Garden City: Anchor, 1985.
Neel, Jasper. *Plato, Derrida, and Writing*. Carbondale: Southern Illinois UP, 1988.
Street, Brian V. *Literacy in Theory and Practice*. Cambridge: Cambridge UP, 1984.

Rhetoric and Composition

The terms *rhetoric* and *composition* are yoked together so firmly in some people's minds that they tend to see the two concepts as somehow naturally complementary, like *love* and *marriage* or *salt* and *pepper*. The facts, however, show that rhetoric and composition have had a rather uneven relationship. It is only within the past 30 years that rhetoric's revival as a legitimate field of study in American universities has rescued composition teaching from a relatively arhetorical mishmash and has reestablished traditional rhetorical theory as the source of concepts upon which composition curricula and pedagogy should be based.

Two perspectives on the teaching of composition in the United States, a historic one and a demographic one, help to clarify its relation to rhetoric. There have been courses in rhetoric at colleges and universities as long as postsecondary education has existed, but in American institutions these courses have taken two significant turns: The composition curriculum gradually evolved to emphasize almost solely written composition, and it changed from a progressively more difficult series of courses in the theory of effective speaking and writing that students took in all four undergraduate years to a single course in "expository" writing of "correct" prose that students took in their first year.

In American colleges and universities in the seventeenth, eighteenth, and early nineteenth centuries, students took courses in rhetorical theory, as well as in principles of public speaking and effective writing. In the middle and late nineteenth century, however, with increasing numbers of people enrolling and a mission emerging for colleges and universities to prepare graduates to work in business and industry, as well as the professions of law, religion, and medicine, courses came to emphasize a rather utilitarian training in written composition, in contrast to what was seen as more genteel, old-fashioned preparation in rhetoric and oratory. The singular emphasis on written composition was largely complete by the end of the nineteenth century.

The shift from a four-year unified curriculum in rhetoric, oratory, and written composition to a single course for first-year students came about in the last third of the nineteenth century. In 1874, suspecting that students were coming to college without adequate preparation in written composition (a refrain heard again and again since that time), Harvard began to require an entrance examination in essay writing, a move that eventually led the college to concentrate composition instruction in a single, required first-year course that would remediate students whose secondary school training was deficient. Most colleges and universities around the country followed Harvard's lead, and freshman comp was born.

From a demographic perspective, it is worth noting that the United States is one of the few countries with well-developed educational systems in which all college and university students are required to take composition courses after they have been admitted to an institution. The difference between the United States and many other countries hinges on the American ideal of access to higher education for all students who want it, an ideal that emerged in the second half of the nineteenth century and has grown stronger since that time. In countries where access to higher education is restricted to the brightest or most fortunate students, educators assume—perhaps erroneously—that students enter a university already prepared to write effective, correct academic essays. In the United States, on the other hand, educators have long assumed that composition instruction must be offered to all incoming students in order to prepare them for the new demands that their college or university studies will place on them as readers and writers.

These historical and demographic influences for many years hindered educators from perceiving traditional rhetorical theory as a legitimate basis for composition curricula and pedagogy. From the last third of the nineteenth century to the beginning of the 1960s, American colleges and universities grew in number and size, particularly in the three postwar surges following the Civil War and the two World Wars. As the number of students enrolling in college grew, many universities came to rely solely on novice faculty, part-time instructors, and graduate teaching assistants to teach composition. These instructors usually lacked any formal preparation to teach college composition and many felt little commitment to it. Their primary interest was in the study and teaching of literature, and they generally saw teaching composition courses as a service, often an unwelcome one, to the college or university. Moreover, for most of this century, literary study was dominated by the principles of new criticism, which saw texts as verbal artifacts intended to be studied as self-contained "icons," not as products of a writer's composing process or entities that come to life only when they are received by real, situated readers. Traditional rhetorical theory, with its emphasis on the interaction of readers and writers that gives rise to invention, arrangement, and style, was far removed from literary studies—and thus from most composition instruction—for most of this century, until a revival of rhetoric as a legitimate field of study took hold in the 1960s.

From our perspective some 30 years later, it is possible to contrast a reductive view of rhetoric that was promulgated in much composition instruction before the revival with a more productive view of rhetoric, one that is more faithful to traditional rhetorical theory, that has come to be inscribed in the best composition curricula and pedagogy since that time. The older, reductive view has even been given a name in the composition literature: Richard Young, in a famous essay titled "Paradigms and Problems: Needed Research in Rhetorical Invention" calls it the "current-traditional rhetoric." According to Young, current-traditional rhetoric ignores invention, assuming that gifted writers some-how tap into vital veins of engaging subject matter or gain their ideas solely from extensive reading regimens. Current-traditional rhetoric, in addition, mandates inflexible structural guidelines for two genres deemed of primary importance to composition instruction: the informal essay and the research paper. It dwells heavily on the traditional "modes of discourse"—description, narration, exposition, and argument—as basic organizational paradigms. It focuses too much attention on abstract, decontextualized rules of usage, such as syntax and spelling, and abstruse qualities of style, such as economy and unity. Student writers in composition curricula dominated by the worst excesses of current-traditional rhetoric are seen as an isolated, unthinking "objective" reporters, unaffected by either their own or their audiences' ideologies, simply following the rules of organization, format, and style that they have been taught to follow.

Composition scholarship in the past three decades has repudiated this reductive view of rhetoric, offering perspectives on the ways composition courses can embody principles of invention, arrangement, and style that are congruent with traditional rhetorical theory. Rather than ignoring invention, many composition instructors have seen it as their primary duty not to teach precepts of correct organization and format, but instead to teach students how to generate and support clear, cogent, and defensible ideas. For these instructors, as Janet Emig maintains in the essay reprinted in this chapter, writing is a mode of learning, not just of reporting what one has learned. As John Gage's essay "Why Write?" illustrates, instead of assuming that gifted writers can simply come up with something engaging to write about, composition scholars now see their most important task as teaching students to inscribe a philosophy of "good reasons" in their writing. As James Berlin's "Rhetoric and Ideology in the Writing Class" argues, rather than seeing writers as "objective" reporters of reality, composition instructors are now urged to help their students understand themselves as ideologically situated writers in real rhetorical situations. In sum, rhetorical theory in the past three decades has revived the teaching of composition as a challenging, exploratory intellectual exercise, not one dominated simply by rote and drill.

FURTHER READING

Harkin, Patricia, and John Schilb, eds. *Contending with Words: Composition and Rhetoric in a Postmodern Age.* New York: Modern Language Association, 1991.

Lindemann, Erika, and Gary Tate, eds. *An Introduction to Composition Studies.* New York: Oxford UP, 1991.

McQuade, Donald A., ed. *The Territory of Language: Linguistics, Stylistics, and the Teaching of Composition.* Carbondale, IL: Southern Illinois UP, 1986.

Young, Richard. "Paradigms and Problems: Needed Research in Rhetorical Invention." In Gary Tate and Edward P. J. Corbett, eds. *Teaching Composition: Ten Bibliographical Essays.* New York: Oxford UP, 1987.

John T. Gage

"Why Write?"

There is no question that students *should* write. Without exception, it seems, reports and studies dealing with educational quality in recent years have advocated more writing, at every phase of learning.[1] This renewed interest in writing results from the belief that writing is not simply a "skill" to be mastered and then applied neutrally to knowledge, but the ongoing reflection of students' developing understanding of ideas. The slogan "writing to learn" seems to have replaced "learning to write" for many teachers, because they believe that there is a direct relationship between students' development as thinkers and the discovery of meaning in the struggle to compose discourse. It seems inconceivable that any suggestion to have students write *less* would be taken seriously, so powerful is the current belief that composing lies at the center of learning. In the face of nearly universal agreement that students should write, it might seem unnecessary to discuss the reasons. After all, if we agree that students should write, the relevant question changes from *why* writing should be emphasized to *how* to do it. With all this agreement, however, I think the need to address the question *why* is even greater, because if we assume the answer we are in danger of forgetting that different justifications for writing depend on different assumptions about what education is for, and these will yield different pedagogies.

The question of why students should write needs attention, then, lest we adopt methods that do not fulfill genuine educational objectives. In response to the recent call for "writing to learn," we might inquire "Writing to learn what?" It happens, I think, that the answer to this question, in relation to some ways of teaching writing, is not consistent with certain values of a liberal education. Other ways, however, support those values. Behind every methodology is an ideology. The neglect of ideological discussion in favor of exclusive attention to method, then, is risky indeed.

The ideological, or philosophical, assumptions behind composition will concern me in this essay. It is necessary that I write somewhat abstractly, although I do not wish to ignore some practical implications that follow from such a concern. I trust that the essays in the rest of this volume will adequately survey available techniques of teaching composition. In discussing the justifications that might support such techniques, however, I would like to begin with a reminder that these justifications are not of recent origin. They are not responses to any recent "literary crisis," but echo the earliest attempts to reason about human knowledge and its relation to the written word. I want to begin, therefore, with a sketch of some ancient responses to the question "Why write?" These responses raise issues that are never resolved once and for all but require rethinking by every generation. The ideas discussed by Greek philosophers about the value of writing continue to be relevant to current pedagogy, and a brief look at them can help to clarify major issues facing those who would defend the teaching of writing today.

SOME OLD WINE: ELOQUENCE VERSUS WISDOM

In Plato's *Phaedrus,* the philosopher Socrates attacked writing as a false art, which, if taught to youth, would lead them away from the honest pursuit of the truth. Socrates practiced an oral art of discussion which he called "dialectic" and which consisted of questions and answers between people who sought to discover transcendent truths. In order for dialectic to proceed *toward* new discoveries, it required that people be able to question each other, a process that is not possible, Socrates maintained, when the written word separates a speaker from the living presence of an audience. More importantly, however, Socrates questioned the motives of the would-be writer: a writer was someone who wished to persuade an audience of a predetermined conclusion, entering into the process of communication only in order to prevail. Socrates saw writing as manipulative and therefore dishonest. In such a one-way communication, a writer's own mind could not be changed, since the object of persuasion was to win one's argument, not to discover truth in dialectic fashion. Socrates maintained that he engaged in the oral art of dialectic, not to persuade, but to arrive at self-knowledge. He thought of this as the genuine end of education, and he thought of writing as an obstacle to this process.

Socrates' critique of writing takes place in the context of his attack on a group of philosophers called the sophists, who were the first teachers of composition. They were professional speech-writers who used their knowledge of "rhetoric" to compose speeches on any subject, with no regard—as Socrates complained—for the truth. They also wrote and sold handbooks containing techniques of speech writing. Socrates' most critical discussion of these handbooks, and of the sophists' advice to writers, is found in Plato's *Gorgias,* where he charged that the sophists are skilled liars, people who make a living by making "the worse case appear the better." Their handbooks of persuasive devices were morally indefensible, for Socrates, since the better the sophists were at manipulating language—the more skilled technically—the worse they were as spokesmen for the truth. Knowing and practicing the art of writing persuasively, for Socrates, were dangerous to the soul, because they did not depend on knowing the truth. This art depended instead on knowing how to write well on any idea indiscriminantly, whether true or not. Socrates condemned the art of rhetoric, then, as a false version of dialectic, because even though it seemed to use the same techniques of argumentation, it disregarded the thing that mattered most: a desire to "know oneself." It substituted "belief," gained through persuasion, for genuine self-knowledge. It was because of the tremendous power of the rhetoricians' techniques for gaining belief that Socrates feared writing would have a bad effect on those who practiced it. Socrates advised his student Phaedrus to avoid the rhetoricians, lest he be seduced by their skills into giving up his search for wisdom.

Aristotle, as a student of Plato, was familiar with such ethical objections to the art of rhetoric: that it substituted eloquence for wisdom. Aristotle, however, sought to provide a different kind of defense of this art, one which did not defend writing as a means of gaining power, as the sophists had done, nor which condemned writing as an obstacle to the truth, as Socrates had. Aristotle instead attempted to relate the art of persuasion to the discovery of knowledge. In the first place, Aristotle did not believe that the way to protect students from the harmful effects of the skilled rhetoricians was to avoid teaching the skills. He believed that the answer to the problem of people being led to believe lies by means of the rhetoricians' tricks was to teach them what the tricks are. Aristotle thought that if people understood where the persuasive power of language came from, what "the available means of persuasion" are, they would be less likely to be easily persuaded by them. His antidote to the power of sophistical rhetoric was to advocate teaching people how it works, unlike Socrates' solution, which was to keep this knowledge from corrupting his students. Aristotle believed that if people understood how skilled writers attempt to manipulate them, they would be less manipulable, and the effect would be a greater ability to detect false arguments. He thought, in other words, that the best defense against powerful writers was to educate the audience in the art of persuasive writing, so that "the worse case" could not appear the better. He wrote a treatise on rhetoric, then, which taught people how persuasion works. His was not a handbook on how to persuade, but a critical anatomy of persuasive techniques.[2] In that treatise, Aristotle emphasized the importance of honest persuasion, but acknowledged that dishonest persuasion also uses the same techniques. He said it was not the art that made the sophist, but the motive. The ability to write well could be used as a means of promoting the truth as well as promoting falsehood, as Socrates had said, but Aristotle added that only if people understood good writing could they be alert to the difference between honest uses of rhetoric and dishonest ones.

Aristotle believed that the process of honest persuasion was a means by which people could discover what they should believe. Socrates had distinguished truth from mere belief. Aristotle was not so quick to make this distinction. For Aristotle, there are many questions which people must decide for which knowledge of the truth is simply not available. The process of attempting to persuade other people of answers to such questions should involve a search for the best reasons one could discover. Thus, when Aristotle discussed the art of rhetoric, he did so in an entirely different way from the way in which the sophists had done in their handbooks. The sophists taught writing as a "bag of tricks," a set of persuasive techniques that one could use to prevail on any side of a question. They advocated the use of many techniques for making ideas sound better than they really were, techniques for hiding weaknesses in one's own argument, and for giving one's writing eloquent stylistic flourishes for the sake of diminishing the audience's capacity for judgment. Aristotle, on the other hand, taught rhetoric as an intellectual, rather than as a technical skill. For him, it was an art of searching for the best available reasons for believing something, and of arranging those reasons in logical order and in a clear style. The sophists believed that any reason was good if it worked. Aristotle taught that a writer's skill actually amounted to an ability to reason well. It required that the writer be willing to argue only for positions for which good reasons could be found. Thus, Aristotle believed that the honest practice of rhetoric, as a search for good reasons, could result in one's changing one's own mind.

Two premises underlie Aristotle's defense of writing, at least for the purposes of this discussion. The first is that there is such a thing as "contingent, probable truth,"[3] a category of knowledge that Socrates had rejected as false and self-deceptive. Socrates sought a pure method of dialectic which would provide only pure truths, truths untainted by human motives and conditions. Rhetoric, for Socrates, was the opposite of dialectic. For Aristotle, rhetoric and dialectic were parallel arts. Both were means of discovering knowledge in the realm of ideas where absolute truth is beyond reach.

Thus, as a second underlying premise, Aristotle did not think that there could be anything like a "systematic" set of "rules" that could lead to knowledge. Argumentation, or rhetorical inquiry, led to knowledge by means of circumstantial reasoning which was not logically pure, even though it tried to be reasonable. Aristotle admitted, in other words, that people believe for reasons that are not always strictly logical, and thus writing could not be reduced to any set of systematic and logical procedures. Aristotle thought of rhetoric as unsystematic, but no less valid for that reason.

In this controversy in antiquity, essentially three ideologies of composition are represented, three very different answers to the question "Why write?" The first is that of the sophists, for whom writing was a source of power. Writing well enabled one to manipulate the beliefs of others, and it was one of the skills one needed, therefore, to get ahead in the world of politics and commerce. The second is that of Socrates, who thought of writing as an obstacle to knowledge of the truth. In reaction to the sophists, he saw the *mere* skill of writing well as a means of self-deception. The third is that of Aristotle, who, in reaction to both the sophists and to Socrates, viewed writing itself as a means of discovering knowledge. The practice of persuasion, when it involved the search for the best available means of reaching a conclusion, led the writer through a process that enabled the discovery of adequate, sharable grounds for belief. Technical skill was necessary, of course, but for Aristotle writing was essentially a thinking skill.

These three ideologies relied, furthermore, on three essentially different theories of what knowledge is. The sophists justified their approach to teaching writing skills because they did not believe that there was such a thing as knowledge. They thought that all ideas were equally unknowable and sought to substitute the ability to win one's case for the unattainable goal of wisdom. Socrates, on the other hand, believed in the human capacity to know transcendent truths, and he valued reason as the only means by which such absolute knowledge could be attained. It was knowable, then, but not necessarily sharable in human discourse. Aristotle, as I have already suggested, admitted another kind of knowledge and a way of knowing it. Aristotle thought that contingent, changing truths, unlike certainties, could be known through reason, but not without taking human motives, passions, egos into account. Thus, knowledge about such matters was the same as agreement, and it was attained by the rational use of persuasion. In similar ways, theories about what knowledge is and how one gets it continue to provide tacit support for ways of teaching writing.

You will be happy to know that I do not intend to trace these three ideologies "throughout history," as my students like to say. These issues never go away, and different times have produced different ways of viewing them. I intend to leap forward to the present day, instead, and to say how I think these ideologies look to us. The forms in which we encounter these controversies have changed, but the basic issues nevertheless persist. The relation between writing and knowledge, the ethical question of writing as a technical skill, the question of whether writing and thinking rely on "rules"—these issues continue to be debated, and positions on them continue to give rise to teaching methods.

SOME NEW BOTTLES: COMPETENCY VERSUS INDEPENDENT THOUGHT

The difference between writing as a technical skill and writing as an intellectual process continues to divide writing pedagogies. While there are few modern-day sophists claiming that ideas do not matter, numerous approaches to teaching writing are carried out *as if* ideas do not matter. Such approaches simply ignore content in the interest of form. If the teacher's mission is to drill students in the basic rules of correctness, then chances are that the ideas contained in the students' sentences will not be subject to the teacher's assessment. No one is telling these students that their ideas are unimportant; but the students are not being asked to write ideas at all—they are being asked to write sentences. Such approaches are usually defended on the ground that writing is a *competency*, that is, an ability to construct written artifacts that have certain definable, formal attributes, such as subject–verb agreement or, at a higher level of sophistication, topic sentences for every paragraph. In effect, this technical approach to composition assumes that writing can be mastered by learning *what* the attributes are and by practicing them in exercises, apart from real writing situations. When competency in writing is attained, students are assumed to be able to perform in situations where writing is called for. But this competency is thought to be developed in the English classroom, where approaches to composition may stress drill and error-avoidance, define forms of sentences and compositions, or prescribe the use of different strategies of organization or diction. Whenever the prescribed form is independent of the specific intellectual content of the student's composition—when assignments prescribe that a theme be five paragraphs long, for instance, or that each paragraph contain three supporting details, whether they are required by the writer's purpose or not—it is apparent that ideas serve only as a convenient means to the end of learning such patterns, rather than the very substance of the writing. To facilitate the practice of such skills, students are usually provided with topics to write about, as if students can be expected to write as well about other people's ideas as about their own. Composition textbooks are full of such topics: "Write a narrative essay about the first time you . . ."; "Write a 500-word essay that compares and contrasts. . . . " Such topics at times attempt to imitate real writing situations, but the need to master a given form usually makes easily controlled, and therefore inherently uninteresting, topics preferable to the adventurous and sloppy kind that emerge from the students' own thinking.

The method I have just described—the prescribed form to be filled in with arbitrarily selected content—has come under attack by those who would exchange its "product" emphasis for teaching students the "process" of writing instead. The recent popularity of teaching the "writing process" has not, however, guaranteed that the quality of the student's thinking will be relevant to the processes the student is guided through. The "process-approach" to teaching writing emphasizes the stages of composing by offering students procedures that will help them in choosing topics, gathering information, organizing their thoughts, composing, and revising. While the approach is a clear alternative to the drudgery of filling in empty rhetorical forms, following prescribed procedures for each "stage" of the writing process does not necessarily invite students to do their best thinking. Any of these procedures, such as the use of different "heuristic" strategies for inventing things to say about a topic, can be reduced to a repetitive exercise and taught as a skill to be mastered in a thoughtless way, as if competency in the prescribed heuristic procedure were more important than the quality of the ideas it may (or may not) help the student to discover. The new demand for "process over product" answers only part of the objection to technical mastery as the aim of writing instruction.

The exclusive teaching of technique will always be accompanied by the claim that writing is, of course, *more* than drill, and error-avoidance, and practicing organizational and heuristic strategies, and all of the other separate tasks of the classroom. No one denies that writing also requires independent thinking. But such approaches, at least in their extreme forms, give only lip-service to the aim of independent thinking and do not address it directly through teaching. This is the case, presumably, because some of a writer's activities are assumed to be teachable while others are assumed to be unteachable. Sentence structure, grammar, mechanics, organizational forms, heuristic procedures—these are teachable. Having ideas, being sensitive to issues, caring about whether one is right, taking responsibility for finding good reasons—these are not teachable.

So, even while it may be admitted that the latter activities, or attitudes, are essential for writers, these are not among the "skills" that technical methods teach. Students are assumed to be able to gain them on their own, at some point after the skills are mastered.

Based on a standard like that of Socrates, we might say that a strictly technical approach to composition, or a "competency in writing" model, assumes that "good writing" is defined by the same characteristics whether it is applied to a good or bad idea. Sentences can be manipulated according to different grammatical or syntactical principles, heuristic or editing procedures can be followed, and essays can be written that adhere to the required form or length—all without the quality of the ideas contained in that writing coming under any scrutiny at all, by the student writer or by the teacher. If the terms of a writing assignment are strictly formal, as in the traditional "five-paragraph theme" or the equally traditional term paper which must have citations from x number of sources, then it is clear that such an assignment can be fulfilled with good or bad ideas indiscriminately. And, if students have been taught to view success on such assignments as fulfillment of the technical requirements, however these may be defined, then it will no doubt occur to them that the best way to ensure success is to keep the ideas as simple and meaningless as possible. If successful writing is defined as technical skills only, then students may be learning an unspoken lesson that is unintended by the pedagogy, namely, that ideas do not matter. Socrates would say, I think, that they are learning that the truth does not matter, or that the way to succeed in writing is to *seem* to be saying something without really troubling to ask whether it is true.

If writing pedagogies stress the technical at the expense of the intellectual (even while claiming that the intellectual is important), then we may indeed question their effects in terms similar to Socrates' complaints about the handbooks of the sophists. Are we, by our ways of teaching writing, encouraging students to think that it is more important to be correct than to be right? Indeed, since "being right" is likely to be seen as the province of instruction in content areas alone, where the textbook presents the information and the teacher tests whether students have learned it, technical methods of teaching writing may be reinforcing the already prevalent notion that good ideas are judged more on the basis of authority than on the basis of the adequate presentation of reasons in writing. Such methods may well encourage an uncritical acceptance of ideas independent of the quality of the writing in which they are argued. From Socrates' point of view, what appears to be good writing as defined by the handbooks of composition may in fact be the worst sort, if the assessment of writing is entirely independent of whether one ought to believe what it says. The better the writing is in a technical sense, the worse it may be in an ethical sense, if "good writing" brings with it no responsibility to examine ideas for their truth. A stupid idea is no less stupid for having been written correctly, or eloquently. In his *Philosophy of Composition*, E. D. Hirsch, Jr., has written, similarly, that "An A-plus success in achieving a trivial or harmful intention is a trivial or harmful success, and ought to be so judged."[4] For Socrates, the more eloquently such an idea might be written, the worse it is for the author and for the audience, since eloquence has the power to compel belief.

SOME SUPERSTITIONS ABOUT WRITING IN SCHOOL

We do not need Socrates to guide us in speculating about the potential effects of strictly technical writing pedagogies, however. We can ask, simply: What habits of mind, or attitudes, do they encourage? It seems to me that strictly technical approaches to composition risk some specific effects that need our consideration. I would like to consider for a moment the possibility that some of the superstitions that students frequently have about writing in school may be the result of how they have been taught to write. These are superstitions which students often have to be painfully untaught when they reach college—that is, of course, unless the college classes they encounter continue to reinforce them.

"My only writing problem is grammar." This is a comment I frequently hear from students in writing classes. I have decided that students believe it because they have been taught grammar and little else. They have probably been subjected to prescriptions and proscriptions deriving from principles they do not understand and in jargon they do not comprehend. They believe that grammar is a mystery, known only to English teachers, and that their own failure to learn every nuance of grammar is going to get them into trouble as writers—because it always has in the past. When these students write, they think about having to follow the rules, and in consequence their attention is diverted from what they are trying to say. Writing becomes, as I mentioned above, error-avoidance. For such students, grammar is a gigantic, invisible mine field through which they must navigate or be destroyed—when they least expect it—by red ink. They have often suffered this sort of injury; their teachers paid attention to the correctness of their writing and never noticed whether they had an interesting idea or not. Shell-shocked, they stopped trying to have interesting ideas, because these only made errors more likely. Such students express the hope that someone will finally provide them with the easy explanation of those complicated rules that will demystify writing for them. But, of course, they will be forever disappointed in this hope and will eventually give up, deciding that they cannot be writers, simply because they have never been able to learn "how to write," by which they usually mean spell or punctuate or distinguish "who" and "whom."

A corollary of this superstition is another: "Some people are writers and some are not." If students believe this, it is also because they have not mastered some technical competency that has been the focus of their writing instruction, some competency that has been taught as the *sine qua non* of all good writing. But, more importantly, they have seen other students succeed as writers and have finally decided that such students differ from them in an undefinable but essential way. Writers, they assume, are different. Writers know how to do something that other people cannot learn. This belief is mixed up with another general superstition, perpetuated by the culture, that writers are special people, an idea that has its origin in the romantic adulation of writers as a class. "Writers are born, not made." "Writers are sensitive people, gifted with imagination." Writers, of course, are simply people who engage in the activity of writing, and everyone is a writer sometimes and no one is a writer all the time. This should not need saying, but it does. The romantic belief is a strong one, and it helps to kill the motivation of students who have struggled with mastery of technique.

I encounter the mirror image of this superstition in students who think writing classes are beneath their dignity. "I already know how to write," they argue, as if writing competency were a matter of doing one thing—writing as analogous to tying one's shoes—over and over. The technical definition of competency suggests that a skill is something that one either acquires or one does not and that it is acquired once and for all. It is as if there were a "writing" switch inside each student's mind, with an *on* and *off* position. The metaphor is odious. No one knows how to write in that sense. Writing is not a competency in that sense. It is an activity, always undergone in new situations which change the nature of the task, with greater and lesser degrees of challenge and uncertainty. There are learnable techniques and attitudes that can help one to approach a writing problem, but there are no techniques that will make it go away. The student who believes, "I already know how to write," is self-deceived. He or she has no doubt had teachers who rewarded technical competency as if the constantly challenging and imperfectable problem of thinking had nothing to do with it. No student who had always been pushed in writing assignments to think better, simply because better thinking is *always* possible, could come away with such an easy and deceptive confidence.

Both the confident and the unconfident writers I have just described might share the further superstition that "there is a right and a wrong way to write." In other words, many students have learned to view the technical principles of good writing as good because these principles have been taught as absolutes, on the basis of the authority of the teacher or the textbook. "Why follow this rule? Because it is a rule, that's why." Writing becomes, if not a quasi-religion, then a quasi-science, in which the essentials are taken on faith. It is something that students are told to do in certain ways, theirs not to reason why. And, not surprisingly, students find this comforting. None of the responsibility of thinking about writing is really theirs; all they need do is follow the "rules."

Finally, students sometimes reveal the unexpressed attitude that writing is not important to them because they can do without it. And what they do when they do without it has been more important to them in their education than what they accomplish when they compose. "I get good grades in other courses," students sometimes tell me, or "My other teachers don't care whether I write well." I recently read a student evaluation of a literature class in which the student attempted to argue that the teacher had been unfair because he had included writing skills as a basis for grading. Writing for such students is separated in their minds from learning. They think of it as something that can be done *in addition to* learning, but not as directly related to what they know or how well they think.

This attitude does not develop solely as a result of what they have accomplished, as students, without writing. It can also result from their success as writers, in a technical sense. Students who develop mastery of formal principles, but who are nevertheless left unchallenged intellectually by writing tasks, can readily come to view writing as unrelated to the rest of their education. Furthermore, they can be reinforced in this attitude when they know that they have written on mindless subjects (by their own account) but have been rewarded for their technical skill— as well as when they have written thoughtfully but have been wholly excused for technical lapses in their writing. In either case, they will view writing itself as an intellectually inferior "subject" for the same reasons many teachers do, because it is not somehow the real stuff of learning. Writing teachers are often assumed by their colleagues in other fields to be no more than grammar cops, people who police "good writing" but who have no real function in the intellectual development of students. Composition programs, likewise, can be viewed by colleagues and administrators as providing "service courses"—those necessary but unfortunate auxiliaries to real education.[5]

UTILITY VERSUS RESPONSIBILITY

If technical approaches to writing are justified by the goal of competency, what justifies the idea of competency as an end of education? The answer most frequently heard is a utilitarian argument, which amounts to an ultimate superstition about writing and education in general. Students are said to need to write in order to carry on the business of their lives, whether to get better grades while in school or to get better jobs later on. The payoff, they often believe, will be a tangible one. Good writers, they believe, are wanted by business. Students who do not learn to write will find themselves behind in their advancement toward economic prosperity. For similar reasons, good writers are said to be needed to benefit the society. While these aims are not easily disregarded, we might recall Socrates' complaint against the teaching of the sophists, to the effect that their art was dangerous because it gave one power while it led one away from the pursuit of wisdom. The sophists were vocational education specialists *par excellence.* They promised to provide one with a marketable skill, a capacity to stay on top of situations and to advance one's own cause successfully. But, as Socrates observed, the skill did not distinguish between good causes and bad ones, it did not make one more able to perceive goodness or justice, and it provided one only with standardized tricks that work in standard situations. It did not teach independent thought or the ability to reason.

The difference between teaching writing as a strictly technical skill and teaching writing as the exercise of independent thought and the ability to reason can be found in the answer to a simple question: Is it possible to succeed fully in this writing task (whether from a textbook's or the teacher's directives) without having a good idea of one's own? If the answer is yes, then what is learned by performing the writing task can be said to exercise the student's competency at the expense of failing to exercise the student's judgment. Such tasks may teach a limited procedure, or process, but they may also misrepresent what the procedure is good for. If writing is good for the writer in any other than a utilitarian sense— if it serves to clarify or improve the writer's understanding—then it must provide the occasion for genuine inquiry and the exercise of responsible judgment. These are what writing teaches students, if it requires them to have ideas of their own and to accept the responsibilities that come with having them. All of the technical aspects of writing can be taught in this context, because those aspects— such as correctness, efficient sentence structure, or a coherent organization—are among the responsibilities that writers accept when they are engaged in the communication of ideas that matter to them. But when taught as isolated skills, apart from the writer's commitment to an idea, these matters can reduce a student's sense of commitment to thought rather than increase it.

This "test" is not so simple as it sounds, however, since by asking the question we are faced with the inherent difficulty of saying what a "good idea" is. What makes an idea "good"? Certainly we cannot expect to agree on the answer, especially if we were to set out to say whether this or that idea measures up. A few generalizations might help us remain aware of the need to keep asking the question, however, as we assess the kinds of writing we ask students to perform.

In the first place, a good idea need only mean one that a student comes up with through independent thought and decides is significant enough to require communicating. While it is unlikely that such ideas can be invented by teachers and assigned to students, this does not mean that teachers will encourage students to look for them by allowing them to write about anything at all. Such ideas do not occur to people spontaneously, apart from their confrontation with issues of some kind. In other words, thinking is situational, in the sense that we respond with ideas of our own when we find ourselves in situations that demand ideas from us. Robert Frost once remarked that students cannot be taught to think by rapping them on the knuckles and shouting "Think!" They can, however, be put into situations that require thinking from them. Such situations are created for us by our presence in an audience—it is when confronted by the ideas of others that we look for our own. The desire to inquire after an idea presupposes the need to find one: thinking, like writing, is at its best when it is a search for an answer to a problem of some kind.

In the context of learning to write, a good idea need not be profound, nor does it need to represent the writer's final judgment on the subject. These qualities alone are needed: A good idea is one that a student comes up with in response to being confronted by a genuine conflict of thought. ("Genuine," like "good," is continually subject to our best judgment.) Such an idea, then, must emerge from exposure to the thinking of others, nor for the purpose of accepting it as true, but for the purpose of measuring it against one's own convictions. A good idea for writing, by these standards, cannot be one that a student feels solves no problem or one that solves a problem that is of no significance. It is an idea that the writer's audience does not already understand or accept—and it is this condition that makes it necessary for the writer to use all of the writing skills at his or her command to earn the reader's assent. Earning a reader's assent is not the same as persuading a reader to believe anything. When we have an idea that we feel ought to be of genuine interest to someone else, our first responsibility is to be sure that we have sufficiently good reasons for believing it ourselves.

Although I have criticized the utilitarian-competency justification for teaching writing by appealing to principles derived from Socrates, it should now be clear that I am speaking of "good" ideas for writing from the point of view of Aristotle. Writing about such ideas becomes a search for good reasons, motivated by the writer's response to an issue that demands attention. It is motivated neither by the sophist's desire to win the argument at the expense of truth, nor by the philosopher's desire to know truth in an ultimate sense. It is rather an encounter with ideas that demand attention but do not necessarily lend themselves to permanent answers or to ultimate conviction. These are the kinds of ideas that face us every day, as we confront issues of ethics and politics, of interpretation and evaluation, and they demand our best thinking because they urge themselves on us insistently as we listen to others take positions. If they are urgent enough, we attempt to find grounds for agreement; and if this really matters, then we attempt such persuasions by honest means. It is by this process that we teach ourselves to reason better, because in any genuine exchange of ideas our reasons will encounter resistance, calling for equivocation, qualification, and improvement. This is the responsible exercise of rhetoric as Aristotle conceived it: inquiry and honest argumentation practiced for the purpose of achieving cooperation among members of an audience who must continually struggle to come up with adequate, though not final, answers.

It is no wonder that these Aristotelian premises for defining ideas in student writing are less in evidence in classrooms and textbooks than the sophistical forms and strategies that seem most popular. The Aristotelian concept of a good idea for writing puts responsibility for thinking on each person who undertakes to write and on each person who undertakes to assess what is written. Teachers, in other words, are made responsible for exercising reasoning and judgment when they invite their students to do so. This responsibility hardly recommends itself to teachers who must show evidence in quantifiable terms—to students, parents, and administrators—that they are teaching students "skills." The problem of learning to write responsibly and well is only magnified in an educational setting where the measured result must be objective, and where human judgments are distrusted as an adequate basis for assessment.

Teaching students to write in order to solve genuine problems of thought is inevitably constrained by the way students learn to confront such problems in other educational contexts. Just as students are led to believe that there are technical approaches to writing situations, they are encouraged to think of learning as memorizing easy, reliable formulas for solving problems. Confronted by problems of thought, in whatever arena of knowledge, students are confident that there is a simple, dependable "key" that will unlock the answer. This key is not one that they have to forge for themselves, they think, but one that can be found somewhere, perhaps written as a rule or as a missing piece of information. And it is one which, when found, will guarantee a single unambiguous answer. Thus, students learn, I believe, to take no responsibility for finding their own answers by means of critical and rational thought, since they are confident that there will be a formula which, when applied, will make such thought unnecessary. Those who struggle to learn are those who have not yet learned some necessary technique or bit of information, they think, that will make the solution easy. Those who do not struggle may relax into the easy confidence that the techniques and bits of information they do possess will see them through. This habit of mind, encouraged perhaps by adopting the model of scientific education for all other fields,[6] is one reason that some students give up on learning—whether they are poor students or good ones—either because the mysterious element eludes them or because they have found success so easy they do not wish to risk going beyond it.

What has been missed in the education of such people is the difficult but significant habit of "critical judgment." In an essay that argues for critical judgment as the principle aim of education, Wayne C. Booth offers this definition: "To be genuinely critical—to judge on the basis of thought—is to have no easily predictable relationship with belief or doubt, with yes or no, with joining or splitting. The critical mind does not know in advance which side it will come out on."[7] What is hard for many to accept about this definition is that it really means that the critical habit of thought requires two very difficult attitudes: it requires the willingness to take responsibility for thinking for oneself, and it requires the ability to live with the perpetual condition of uncertainty.

These two attitudes are ones that writing can teach, perhaps better than any other academic process. But it cannot do so, as I have indicated, if technical mastery is viewed as an end in itself. How does writing instruction as something more than technique lead to the justification of writing as a way of learning? Aristotle thought that the honest practice of persuasion was a means by which people could come to know contingent and probable truths that could not be known in any other way. What does this mean in today's terms?

BETTER WRITING AND BETTER THINKING

Writing pedagogies do not have to place technique above content. It is possible for writing pedagogies to place students' responsibility for thinking and for judging their own ideas at the very center of the enterprise. The question of how writing might fulfill these ends depends on understanding that "thinking" and "judging," as such, can be taught only by indirect means. These are available to be assessed only through some kind of performance, such as writing. And good thought, good judgment, the kind we wish to teach students to practice, is in fact undefined, except in hopeful generalities like Booth's. Such definitions are themselves acts of human judgment, and our judgments of how well our students make judgments are obviously limited by our own capacities to reason—without finally being able to ground that reasoning on the solid foundation of quantifiable knowledge.

This is where Aristotle's defense of writing becomes a defense of education in humanistic terms: Since we cannot know many truths with absolute certainty, and since we nevertheless need to act on the basis of thought, we must learn somehow to seek and accept the best available grounds for assent, however limited "best" may be. Rhetorical assent, the kind we daily forge out of genuine situations of disagreement, is not the same as truth. But it does the same job, in the absence of the possibility of truth in all situations. The practice of looking for good reasons, which for Aristotle is what a writer does, is justified, then, because good reasons provide the only basis for rational behavior. Without knowing exactly what it is, we wish to give our students the ability to exercise judgment, because without this ability their technical skills cannot serve them as rational participants in a world that is ever ambiguous but always calls for acts of judgment in new situations.

Judgment is not something that students should be assumed to lack when they enter any given stage of their education, or to possess fully when they leave that stage. It is a human activity that everyone exercises all of the time. But everyone exercises it better or worse at different times, and no one exercises it well all the time. This is why the growth of students' ability to exercise good judgment is harder to measure than the growth of their store of knowledge. It may even be impossible to measure. Students may not feel that they are thinking better when in fact they are, since, after all, as they become better thinkers the kinds of problems that they think about will naturally become more complex and they will continue to feel a familiar uneasiness about their ability to solve them. This uneasiness should not be something that students are conditioned to worry about. It is something that they need to recognize as the fate of thinking people, and to learn to live with, and to enjoy.

Students improve as thinkers in small, undetectable increments of change, brought about by the level of challenges they face. It is only when they are put into situations where better thinking is called for that they will be challenged to produce it. Such situations, of one kind or another, at whatever degree of difficulty, should be the aim of each course that students take. But lacking such consistency, students should at least know that they can create such situations for themselves, by looking for questions or problems within the material they encounter. This is a practice that is encouraged by writing, if writing is understood to be a means of clarifying problems and of inquiring into potential solutions.

Learning to become a better writer happens in the same way that learning to become a better thinker does. Students are not expected to take writing classes because they do not yet know how to write, nor should they be expected to have become perfect writers when those classes are over. Students always enter a writing class knowing something about how to write that that class will not teach. Some write well and others write poorly, but none would be in class if they were starting from zero or if they had nothing to learn. No writing class can complete the job of teaching students to write at their best. All writers, even if they seem to write effortlessly, are always learning to write better each time they take on and complete a new writing challenge—and each new writing task should be a challenge to them in some sense. The rate at which they will become better writers will be just as imperceptible as the rate at which they can be expected to become better thinkers; it will happen slowly, in small increments of change, in intuitive stages of progress that they may not even notice.

Just as they may not realize it when they are thinking better, students may not know that their writing is improving when in fact it is. The reason for this is the same one I mentioned before: As they improve as writers, they will naturally take on slightly more challenging writing tasks and find themselves in somewhat more difficult writing situations, and they will naturally attempt more sophisticated effects. As they do these, they may continue to feel inadequate to each new writing task, simply because it will involve using what they already know how to do to go beyond it. Again, this feeling of inadequacy is nothing to worry about. It is the way students should feel if they are learning. It is only when they give up in despair, because they have been promised too much, or when they feel too satisfied with their writing, that we should worry, because at that point they will have stopped trying to write better.

One difference, of course, between writing and thinking is that writing is tangible—it results in a finite product—while thinking is intangible and just goes on and on (or, sometimes, around and around). But this difference is also a reason why learning to become a better writer results in better thinking. Writing is thinking-made-tangible, thinking that can be examined because it is "on the page" and not all "in the head," invisibly floating around. Writing is thinking that can be stopped and tinkered with. It is a way of making thought hold still long enough to examine its structures, its possibilities, its flaws. The road to a clearer understanding of one's own thoughts is travelled on paper. It is through the attempt to find words for ourselves, and to find patterns for ourselves in which to express related ideas, that we often come to discover exactly what we think.

But notice that I said "attempt to find for ourselves." The idea that students must create the patterns of discourse that they use, when movitated to say something in the best way possible, is contrary to what I have been calling "technical" approaches to composition throughout this chapter. The forms cannot be *given* to students, whose task is then to fill them up with ideas, since in such cases the ideas will not have a purpose in themselves other than to satisfy the demands of the form. It is ideas which come first, in writing, and forms which satisfy the demands that face a writer who has them.

Thus, there is yet another important benefit to thinking that comes from the process of learning to write better, even if this benefit, too, is an intangible one. Writing is a process of finding and structuring ideas. Having ideas is what creates the responsibility for searching for a way to express them. Writing is an occasion for making ideas matter, and without ideas to compel it, it is empty exercise. Writing is the search, not only for the right words in the right order, but also for the right *reasons*. It is in this way that the serious attempt to compose one's thoughts in writing is what can lead one to the very important discovery not only of *what* to think, but *why*.

This is the most significant sense in which writing is a way of learning. Any student, in any class, can listen, read, collect information, pass multiple-choice tests, and even think deliberately about the problems or implications of the information learned about a given subject. But writing about that information has an effect that none of these activities alone can produce: It causes one to *need* to clarify that information, those problems, and those implications for oneself, to put them into relationships, and to explore reasons for saying what one has decided to say about them. Writing does this because it is sustained discourse, as opposed to the temporary and fragmented nature of thinking. Writing does this, furthermore, because it externalizes, for an implied if not a real audience, what is otherwise private and inaccessible. Thus, the possibility of being *read* creates responsibilities that thinking alone can neglect. Writing, because it is undertaken as a decision to be clear, forces clarity. But if it is also undertaken as a decision to be *believed,* it forces more than clarity. Any act of writing that does not stop with the mere assertion of random bits of information will force a writer to look for good reasons, and in the process of looking for good reasons the writer's judgment is being exercised along with the writer's composing skills.

William Irmscher has discussed all of the advantages I have ascribed to writing in a way that demonstrates that these are not separate advantages, but take place simultaneously. "Writing," he says,

> is a way of counteracting our distractedness. It requires concentration, focus, and discipline, usually in a silent and solitary setting. Because writing is so much more deliberative than talking, it helps us determine what we know and what we don't know. In our minds, we can fool ourselves. Not on paper. . . .
>
> Writing is often thinking about our own thoughts; that is, it permits us to distance ourselves from our thoughts, to separate the thought from the thinker—a kind of analyzing and assessing, a resolving of differences, and a final structuring. Perhaps most important of all, writing permits us not just to say what we have to say, but to *see* what we have to say. Thus we have a new concern for the *how* as well as the *what*, the manner as well as the substance.[8]

This justification for writing as a way of exercising and improving critical judgment implies a very different kind of pedagogy from the promulgation of technical knowledge and practice. This pedagogy will not be one in which the technical aspects of writing are ignored, however. Technical advice about composition can be taught as an end in itself, or it can be taught as a consequence of the responsibilities that follow from having ideas and wanting to express them.

THE WRITING CLASSROOM WHERE IDEAS MATTER

It is the responsibility of teachers, and of those who administer curriculum, to attempt to make the writing class a place where ideas matter more than technique, so that technique can be taught as a means to a significant end rather than as an end in itself. The difficulty we all face is how to encourage students to want to be right, first, and correct only as a consequence of wanting to be believed. While many different pedagogies will satisfy this condition, certain features must be shared by them, it seems, if the writing class is to create problematic situations that call for the student's best thinking—situations that the students must write their way out of. What are these features?

First of all, a writing class must be a place where students encounter ideas and where they are free to respond to them honestly and critically. This means that reading the thoughts of others is necessary, not only to provide students with "models" of decorous writing, but to stimulate them to assert their own agreements and disagreements so that they can explore their own reasons along with the available arguments of others. The reading students do in a writing class must be critical reading, in the sense that students are not required to accept and memorize information on the basis of the writer's authority but encouraged to question the writer's conclusions on the basis of the quality of the writer's reasons. Critical reading is a process of measuring one's agreement with a conclusion against the quality of the case made in its defense. Writing students who are encouraged to undertake this process will not need to learn complicated or arbitrary "heuristic strategies" in order to come up with ideas for writing. Their ideas will result from their having adopted "stances" in relation to problematic ideas.[9]

Second, students must know that they do not write exclusively for the teacher. Instead, they write for an audience of other inquiring minds, who share their concern for finding answers. This definition of audience places the teacher-critic in the role of eavesdropper on a communication that is intended for others. The teacher helps the student achieve that communication, but it is the members of the class, with whom the student has engaged in critical dialogue about issues, that comprise the student writer's audience. (Or, if not the class, then some other real audience outside the class.) This implies that students also ought to be reading each other's writing and offering their responses. Too often, students write without any sense of a real audience who reads in order to hear what they have to say. Students know that teachers read in order to mark their mistakes. Teachers, as members of the student's audience and yet as authorities on writing, should not think of themselves as "correcting" student compositions so much as explaining aspects of the student's writing which inhibit or enhance its communication. This means that they ought to comment on technical matters as well as respond to ideas. They should respond as people who share an interest in the student's ideas and who are capable of judging those ideas based on the clarity of the writing and the adequacy of the support offered.

Third, thoughtful revision should be taught as a writer's responsibility, given the reasons for writing we have discussed. Revision is ordinarily perceived by students as a perfunctory exercise in cosmetic editing: correcting only the surface faults that the teacher has marked. When students revise in this way, they are responding to revision as a kind of punishment for their errors, rather than as a further opportunity to rethink what they have to say and their reasons for saying it. Revision cannot be a penalty for crimes against grammar; it must be an occasion for reassessing every aspect of the writing after having had the opportunity to see how others respond to it. Students must be encouraged to revise in order to satisfy themselves that they have presented their best thinking and that they have presented this thinking in such a way that the reader's potential understanding and objections are taken into account. Revision, in other words, is essential not because it is forced on students by writing teachers but because it serves the end that writing students should be aiming for: the earned assent of readers who are capable of deciding on the basis of the quality of the writer's reasons.

These are but three considerations that follow from the attempt to make writing serve the ends of a liberal education. Obstacles to bringing these pedagogical considerations to bear on teaching are plentiful, but teachers and administrators must ask themselves occasionally whether the reasons that make change difficult are becoming excuses for not trying. One reason, and potential excuse, that I see as especially important is that teachers who feel inadequate to judge the quality of students' ideas fall back on grading for mechanics and grammar because they can have confidence in their ability to recognize faults in these areas. Recognizing faults in thinking is not only much harder, it is much more unreliable. It puts the teacher at risk, because of course, when it comes to judging ideas we are all equally dependent on our own ability to reason. No handbook of grammar, no computer editing program, no sentence-combining exercise, can tell us how to recognize a good idea. This is not a rule-governed activity, and consequently it is imperfect. To chance being wrong threatens the teacher's authority in the classroom, and consequently, for the writing teacher, it is always easier to get through the day if all ideas are allowed to stay safely equal.

Teachers *can* judge thought because they do it every day, when they read critically writing that is addressed to them as thinking persons. They must be as free to exercise their critical judgments in their writing classes as they are elsewhere. For students to develop their own critical capacities, they need to be in active, honest dialogue about their ideas with a writing teacher. If this puts the teacher at risk, it is only because thinking always puts a person at risk: It always creates the possibility of being wrong, and if it did not, we would never learn to think better. The risk of honestly facing real human issues, as Aristotle taught, requires abandoning systematic means of testing knowledge and engaging in the messy and unpredictable business of argumentation, not knowing where you might come out, but knowing that by entering the dialogue you are demonstrating an ability to live with uncertainty.

CONCLUSION

Why write, then? My answer is because writing, more than any other task, brings one face to face with important human responsibilities. These include the responsibility to clarify and structure one's ideas. More importantly, they include the responsibility to continue to inquire and argue, *toward* the truth as we are able to discover it through the shared means of discourse, even while knowing that the whole truth will always be beyond our means. These responsibilities are as necessary for students as they learn to respond as thinking members of the audience for others' writing, as much as they are for them as they learn to compose their thoughts. Thus, while writing as a competency is justified by claims to offer students power, writing as the responsible exercise of judgment is justified by a plea for tolerance.

NOTES

1. A summary of such reports is contained in *Education Week* 4 (September 5, 1984): L-51. The entire issue of this journal is devoted to literacy, with thorough discussion, from many viewpoints, of the relationships between writing and learning. For a review of eight recent reports on education that illustrates the technical/intellectual distinction I discuss in this chapter, see Walter Karp, "Why Johnny Can't Think: The Politics of Bad Schooling," *Harper's Magazine* 270 (June 1985): 69–73. For discussions of teaching writing as a thinking skill in the lower grades, see *Perspectives on Writing in Grades 1–8*, ed. Shirley Haley-James (Urbana, Ill.: National Council of Teachers of English, 1981).

2. Aristotle wrote, for instance, that the function of rhetoric "is not so much to persuade, as to find out in each case the existing means of persuasion." See The *"Art" of Rhetoric*, trans. John Henry Freese (Cambridge, Mass.: Harvard University Press, 1926), p. 13.

3. For my extended discussion of this concept and its relation to methods of teaching composition, see "An Adequate Epistemology for Composition: Classical and Modern Perspectives," in *Essays on Classical Rhetoric and Modern Discourse*, eds. Robert Connors, Andrea Lunsford, and Lisa Ede (Carbondale, Ill.: Southern Illinois University Press, 1984), pp. 152–69.

4. E. D. Hirsch, Jr., *The Philosophy of Composition* (Chicago: University of Chicago Press, 1977), pp. 182–83.

5. For further discussion, see my "Freshman English: In Whose Service?" *College English* 44 (September 1982): 15–20.

6. See Wayne C. Booth, *Modern Dogma and the Rhetoric of Assent* (Chicago: University of Chicago Press, 1974), esp. pp. 3–40.

7. Wayne C. Booth, "The Uncritical American: or, Nobody's from Missouri Any More," in Wayne C. Booth, *Now Don't Try to Reason with Me: Essays and Ironies for a Credulous Age* (Chicago: University of Chicago Press, 1970), p. 66.

8. William Irmscher, *Teaching Expository Writing* (New York: Holt, Rinehart and Winston, 1979), p. 20.

9. See Wayne C. Booth, "The Rhetorical Stance," in Booth, *Now Don't Try to Reason with Me*, pp. 25–33.

James Berlin

"Rhetoric and Ideology in the Writing Class"

The question of ideology has never been far from discussions of writing instruction in the modern American college. It is true that some rhetorics have denied their imbrication in ideology, doing so in the name of a disinterested scientism—as seen, for example, in various manifestations of current-traditional rhetoric. Most, however, have acknowledged the role of rhetoric in addressing competing discursive claims of value in the social, political, and cultural. This was particularly evident during the sixties and seventies, for example, as the writing classroom became one of the public arenas for considering such strongly contested issues as Vietnam, civil rights, and economic equality. More recently the discussion of the relation between ideology and rhetoric has taken a new turn. Ideology is here foregrounded and problematized in a way that situates rhetoric within ideology, rather than ideology within rhetoric. In other words, instead of rhetoric acting as the transcendental recorder or arbiter of competing ideological claims, rhetoric is regarded as always already ideological. This position means that any examination of a rhetoric must first consider the ways its very discursive structure can be read so as to favor one version of economic, social, and political arrangements over other versions. A rhetoric then considers competing claims in these three realms from an ideological perspective made possible both by its constitution and by its application—the dialectical interaction between the rhetoric as text and the interpretive practices brought to it. A rhetoric can never be innocent, can never be a disinterested arbiter of the ideological claims of others because it is always already serving certain ideological claims. This perspective on ideology and rhetoric will be discussed in greater detail later. Here I merely wish to note that it has been forwarded most recently by such figures as Patricia Bizzell, David Bartholomae, Greg Myers, Victor Vitanza, and John Schilb and John Clifford. I have also called upon it in my monograph on writing instruction in twentieth-century American colleges. I would like to bring the discussion I began there up to date, focusing on ideology in the three rhetorics that have emerged as most conspicuous in classroom practices today: the rhetorics of cognitive psychology, of expressionism, and of a category I will call social-epistemic.

Each of these rhetorics occupies a distinct position in its relation to ideology. From the perspective offered here, the rhetoric of cognitive psychology refuses the ideological question altogether, claiming for itself the transcendent neutrality of science. This rhetoric is nonetheless easily preempted by a particular ideological position now in ascendancy because it encourages discursive practices that are compatible with dominant economic, social, and political formations. Expressionistic rhetoric, on the other hand, has always openly admitted its ideological predilections, opposing itself in no uncertain terms to the scientism of current-traditional rhetoric and the ideology it encourages. This rhetoric is, however, open to appropriation by the very forces it opposes in contradiction to its best intentions. Social-epistemic rhetoric is an alternative that is self-consciously aware of its ideological stand, making the very question of ideology the center of classroom activities, and in so doing providing itself a defense against preemption and a strategy for self-criticism and self-correction. This third rhetoric is the one I am forwarding here, and it provides the ground of my critique of its alternatives. In other words, I am arguing from ideology, contending that no other kind of argument is possible—a position that must first be explained.

Ideology is a term of great instability. This is true whether it is taken up by the Left or Right—as demonstrated, for example, by Raymond Williams in *Keywords* and *Marxism and Literature* and by Jorge Larrain in *The Concept of Ideology*. It is thus necessary to indicate at the outset the formulation that will be followed in a given discussion. Here I will rely on Göran Therborn's usage in *The Ideology of Power and the Power of Ideology*. Therborn, a Marxist sociologist at the University of Lund, Sweden, calls on the discussion of ideology found in Louis Althusser and on the discussion of power in Michel Foucault. I have chosen Therborn's adaptation of Althusser rather than Althusser himself because Therborn so effectively counters the ideology-science distinction of his source, a stance in which ideology is always false consciousness while a particular version of Marxism is defined as its scientific alternative in possession of objective truth. For Therborn, no position can lay claim to absolute, timeless truth, because finally all formulations are historically specific, arising out of the material conditions of a particular time and place. Choices in the economic, social, political, and cultural are thus always based on discursive practices that are interpretations, not mere transcriptions of some external, verifiable certainty. The choice for Therborn then is never between scientific truth and ideology, but between competing ideologies, competing discursive interpretations. Finally, Therborn calls upon Foucault's "micropolitics of power" (7) without placing subjects within a seamless web of inescapable, wholly determinative power relations. For Therborn, power can be identified and resisted in a meaningful way.

Therborn offers an especially valuable discussion for rhetoricians because of his emphasis on the discursive and dialogic nature of ideology. In other words, Therborn insists that ideology is transmitted through language practices that are always the center of conflict and contest:

> The operation of ideology in human life basically involves the constitution and patterning of how human beings live their lives as conscious, reflecting initiators of acts in a structured, meaningful world. Ideology operates as discourse, addressing or, as Althusser puts it, interpellating human beings as subjects. (15)

Conceived from the perspective of rhetoric, ideology provides the language to define the subject (the self), other subjects, the material world, and the relation of all of these to each other. Ideology is thus inscribed in language practices, entering all features of our experience.

Ideology for Therborn addresses three questions: "What exists? What is good? What is possible?" The first deals with epistemology, as Therborn explains: "what exists, and its corollary, what does not exist: that is, who we are, what the world is, what nature, society, men and women are like. In this way we acquire a sense of identity, becoming conscious of what is real and true; the visibility of the world is thereby structured by the distribution of spotlights, shadows, and darkness." Ideology thus interpellates the subject in a manner that determines what is real and what is illusory, and, most important, what is experienced and what remains outside the field of phenomenological experience, regardless of its actual material existence. Ideology also provides the subject with standards for making ethical and aesthetic decisions: "*what is good*, right, just, beautiful, attractive, enjoyable, and its opposites. In this way our desires become structured and normalized." Ideology provides the structure of desire, indicating what we will long for and pursue. Finally, ideology defines the limits of expectation: "*what is possible* and impossible; our sense of the mutability of our being-in-the-world and the consequences of change are hereby patterned, and our hopes, ambitions, and fears given shape" (18). This last is especially important since recognition of the existence of a condition (poverty, for example) and the desire for its change will go for nothing if ideology indicates that a change is simply not possible (the poor we have always with us). In other words, this last mode of interpellation is especially implicated in power relationships in a group or society, in deciding who has power and in determining what power can be expected to achieve.

Ideology always carries with it strong social endorsement, so that what we take to exist, to have value, and to be possible seems necessary, normal and inevitable—in the nature of things. Ideology also, as we have seen, always includes conceptions of how power should—again, in the nature of things—be distributed in a society. Power here means political force but covers as well social forces in everyday contacts. Power is an intrinsic part of ideology, defined and reinforced by it, determining, once again, who can act and what can be accomplished. These power relationships, furthermore, are inscribed in the discursive practices of daily experience—in the ways we use language and are used (interpellated) by it in ordinary parlance. Finally, it should be noted that ideology is always pluralistic, a given historical moment displaying a variety of competing ideologies and a given individual reflecting one or another permutation of these conflicts, although the overall effect of these permutations tends to support the hegemony of the dominant class.

COGNITIVE RHETORIC

Cognitive rhetoric might be considered the heir apparent of current-traditional rhetoric, the rhetoric that appeared in conjunction with the new American university system during the final quarter of the last century. As Richard Ohmann has recently reminded us, this university was a response to the vagaries of competitive capitalism, the recurrent cycles of boom and bust that characterized the nineteenth-century economy. The university was an important part of the strategy to control this economic instability. Its role was to provide a center for experts engaging in "scientific" research designed to establish a body of knowledge that would rationalize all features of production, making it more efficient, more manageable, and, of course, more profitable. These experts were also charged with preparing the managers who were to take this new body of practical knowledge into the marketplace. The old nineteenth-century college had prepared an elite to assume its rightful place of leadership in church and state. The economic ideal outside the college was entirely separate, finding its fulfillment in the self-made, upwardly mobile entrepreneur who strikes it rich. The academic and the economic remained divided and discrete. In the new university, the two were joined as the path to success became a university degree in one of the new scientific specialities proven to be profitable in the world of industry and commerce. The new middle class of certified meritocrats had arrived. As I have indicated in my monograph on the nineteenth century, current-traditional rhetoric with its positivistic epistemology, its pretensions to scientific precision, and its managerial orientation was thoroughly compatible with the mission of this university.

Cognitive rhetoric has made similar claims to being scientific, although the method called upon is usually grounded in cognitive psychology. Janet Emig's *The Composing Process of Twelfth Graders* (1971), for example, attempted an empirical examination of the way students compose, calling on the developmental psychology of Jean Piaget in guiding her observations. In studying the cognitive skills observed in the composing behavior of twelve high school students, Emig was convinced that she could arrive at an understanding of the entire rhetorical context—the role of reality, audience, purpose, and even language in the composing act. Richard Larson was equally ambitious as throughout the seventies he called upon the developmental scheme of Jerome Bruner (as well as other psychologists) in proposing a problem-solving approach to writing, once again focusing on cognitive structures in arriving at an understanding of how college students compose. James Moffett and James Britton used a similar approach in dealing with the writing of students in grade school. For cognitive rhetoric, the structures of the mind correspond in perfect harmony with the structures of the material world, the minds of the audience, and the units of language (see my *Rhetoric and Reality* for a fuller discussion of this history). This school has been the strongest proponent of addressing the "process" rather than the "product" of writing in the classroom—although other theories have also supported this position even as they put forward a different process. Today the cognitivists continue to be a strong force in composition studies. The leading experimental research in this area is found in the work of Linda Flower and John Hayes, and I would like to focus the discussion of the relation of ideology and cognitive rhetoric on their contribution.

There is no question that Flower considers her work to fall within the domain

of science, admitting her debt to cognitive psychology (Hayes' area of specialization), which she describes as "a young field—a reaction, in part, against
assumptions of behaviorism" (*Problem-Solving* vii). Her statements about the
composing process of writing, furthermore, are based on empirical findings, on
"data-based" study, specifically the analysis of protocols recording the writing
choices of both experienced and inexperienced writers. This empirical study has
revealed to Flower and Hayes—as reported in "A Cognitive Process Theory of
Writing"—that there are three elements involved in composing: the task environment, including such external constraints as the rhetorical problem and the
text so far produced; the writer's long-term memory, that is, the knowledge of
the subject considered and the knowledge of how to write; and the writing
processes that go on in the writer's mind. This last is, of course, of central importance to them, based as it is on the invariable structures of the mind that operate
in a rational, although not totally predictable, way.

The mental processes of writing fall into three stages: the planning stage, further divided into generating, organizing, and goal setting; the translating stage,
the point at which thoughts are put into words; and the reviewing stage, made up
of evaluating and revising. This process is hierarchical, meaning that "components
of the process [are] imbedded within other components" ("A Cognitive Process"
375), and it is recursive, the stages repeating themselves, although in no predetermined order. In other words, the elements of the process can be identified and their
functions described, but the order of their operation will vary from task to task and
from individual to individual, even though the practices of good writers will be
very similar to each other (for a rich critique, see Bizzell). The "keystone" of the
cognitive process theory, Flower and Hayes explain, is the discovery that writing
is a goal-directed process: "In the act of composing, writers create a hierarchical
network of goals and these in turn guide the writing process." Because of this goal
directedness, the protocols of good writers examined consistently "reveal a coherent underlying structure" ("A Cognitive Process" 377).

It is clear from this brief description that Flower and Hayes focus on the individual mind, finding in the protocol reports evidence of cognitive structures in
operation. Writing becomes, as Flower's textbook indicates, just another instance
of "problem-solving processes people use every day," most importantly the
processes of experts, such as "master chess players, inventors, successful scientists, business managers, and artists" (*Problem-Solving* 2–3). Flower's textbook
says little about artists, however, focusing instead on "real-world" writing. She
has accordingly called upon the help of a colleague from the School of Industrial
Management (vi), and she includes a concern for consulting reports and proposals as well as ordinary academic research reports—"the real world of college and
work" (4). This focus on the professional activity of experts is always conceived
in personal and managerial terms: "In brief, the goal of this book is to help you
gain more control of your own composing process: to become more efficient as a
writer and more effective with your readers" (2). And the emphasis is on self-
made goals, "on your own goals as a writer, on what you want to do and say" (3).

As I said at the outset, the rhetoric of cognitive psychology refuses the ideological question, resting secure instead in its scientific examination of the composing process. It is possible, however, to see this rhetoric as being eminently suited to appropriation by the proponents of a particular ideological stance, a stance consistent with the modern college's commitment to preparing students for the world of corporate capitalism. And as we have seen above, the professional orientation of *Problem-Solving Strategies for Writing*—its preoccupation with "analytical writing" (4) in the "real world" of experts—renders it especially open to this appropriation.

For cognitive rhetoric, the real is the rational. As we observed above, for Flower and Hayes the most important features of composing are those which can be analyzed into discrete units and expressed in linear, hierarchical terms, however unpredictably recursive these terms may be. The mind is regarded as a set of structures that performs in a rational manner, adjusting and reordering functions in the service of the goals of the individual. The goals themselves are considered unexceptionally apparent in the very nature of things, immediately identifiable as worthy of pursuit. Nowhere, for example, do Flower and Hayes question the worth of the goals pursued by the manager, scientist, or writer. The business of cognitive psychology is to enable us to learn to think in a way that will realize goals, not deliberate about their value: "I have assumed that, whatever your goals, you are interested in discovering better ways to achieve them" (*Problem-Solving* 1). The world is correspondingly structured to foreground goals inherently worth pursuing—whether these are private or professional, in writing or in work. And the mind is happily structured to perceive these goals and, thanks to the proper cognitive development of the observer—usually an expert—to attain them. Obstacles to achieving these goals are labelled "problems," disruptions in the natural order, impediments that must be removed. The strategies to resolve these problems are called "heuristics," discovery procedures that "are the heart of problem solving" (36). Significantly, these heuristics are not themselves rational, are not linear and predictable—"they do not come with a guarantee" (37). They appear normally as unconscious, intuitive processes that problem solvers use without realizing it, but even when formulated for conscious application they are never foolproof. Heuristics are only as good or bad as the person using them, so that problem solving is finally the act of an individual performing in isolation, solitary and alone (see Brodkey). As Flower explains: "Good writers not only have a large repertory of powerful strategies, but they have sufficient self-awareness of their own process to draw on these alternative techniques as they need them. In other words, they guide their own creative process" (37). The community addressed enters the process only after problems are analyzed and solved, at which time the concern is "adapting your writing to the needs of the reader" (1). Furthermore, although the heuristics used in problem solving are not themselves rational, the discoveries made through them always conform to the mensurable nature of reality, displaying "an underlying hierarchical organization" (10) that reflects the rationality of the world. Finally, language is regarded as a system of rational signs that is compatible with the mind and the external world, enabling the "translating" or "transforming" of the non-verbal intellectual operations into the verbal. There is thus a beneficent correspondence between the structures of the mind, the structures of the world, the structures of the minds of the audience, and the structures of language.

This entire scheme can be seen as analogous to the instrumental method of the modern corporation, the place where members of the meritocratic middle class, the twenty percent or so of the work force of certified college graduates, make a handsome living managing a capitalist economy (see Braverman, ch. 18). Their work life is designed to turn goal-seeking and problem-solving behavior into profits. As we have seen in Flower, the rationalization of the writing process is specifically designated an extension of the rationalization of economic activity. The pursuit of self-evident and unquestioned goals in the composing process parallels the pursuit of self-evident and unquestioned profit-making goals in the corporate marketplace: "whatever your goals are, you are interested in achieving better ways to achieve them" (*Problem-Solving* 12). The purpose of writing is to create a commodified text (see Clines) that belongs to the individual and has exchange value—"problem solving turns composing into a goal-directed journey—writing my way to where I want to be" (4)—just as the end of corporate activity is to create a privately-owned profit. Furthermore, while all problem solvers use heuristic procedures—whether in solving hierarchically conceived writing problems or hierarchically conceived management problems—some are better at using them than are others. These individuals inevitably distinguish themselves, rise up the corporate ladder, and leave the less competent and less competitive behind. The class system is thus validated since it is clear that the rationality of the universe is more readily detected by a certain group of individuals. Cognitive psychologists specializing in childhood development can even isolate the environmental features of the children who will become excellent problem solvers, those destined to earn the highest grades in school, the highest college entrance scores, and, finally, the highest salaries. Middle class parents are thus led to begin the cultivation of their children's cognitive skills as soon as possible—even in utero—and of course there are no shortage of expert-designed commodities that can be purchased to aid in the activity. That the cognitive skills leading to success may be the product of the experiences of a particular social class rather than the perfecting of inherent mental structures, skills encouraged because they serve the interests of a ruling economic elite, is never considered in the "scientific" investigation of the mind.

Cognitive rhetoric can be seen from this perspective as compatible with the ideology of the meritocratic university described in Bowles and Gintis' *Schooling in Capitalist America*. Power in this system is relegated to university-certified experts, those individuals who have the cognitive skills and the training for problem solving. Since social, political, and cultural problems are, like the economic, the result of failures in rational goal-seeking behavior, these same experts are the best prepared to address these matters as well. Furthermore, the agreement of experts in addressing commonly-shared problems in the economic and political arenas is additional confirmation of their claim to power: all trained observers, after all, come to the same conclusions. Once again, the possibility that this consensus about what is good and possible is a product of class interest and class experience is never seriously entertained. Cognitive rhetoric, then, in its refusal of the ideological question leaves itself open to association with the reification of technocratic science characteristic of late capitalism, as discussed, for example, by Georg Lukács, Herbert Marcuse, and Jürgen Habermas (see Larrain, ch. 6). Certain structures of the material world, the mind, and language, and their correspondence with certain goals, problem-solving heuristics, and solutions in the economic, social, and political are regarded as inherent features of the universe, existing apart from human social intervention. The existent, the good, and the possible are inscribed in the very nature of things as indisputable scientific facts, rather than being seen as humanly devised social constructions always remaining open to discussion.

EXPRESSIONISTIC RHETORIC

Expressionistic rhetoric developed during the first two decades of the twentieth century and was especially prominent after World War I. Its earliest predecessor was the elitist rhetoric of liberal culture, a scheme arguing for writing as a gift of genius, an art accessible only to a few, and then requiring years of literary study. In expressionistic rhetoric, this gift is democratized, writing becoming an art of which all are capable. This rhetoric has usually been closely allied with theories of psychology that argued for the inherent goodness of the individual, a goodness distorted by excessive contact with others in groups and institutions. In this it is the descendant of Rousseau on the one hand and of the romantic recoil from the urban horrors created by nineteenth-century capitalism on the other. Left to our own devices, this position maintains, each of us would grow and mature in harmony. Unfortunately, hardly anyone is allowed this uninhibited development, and so the fallen state of society is both the cause and the effect of its own distortion, as well as the corrupter of its individual members. In the twenties, a bowdlerized version of Freud was called upon in support of this conception of human nature. More recently—during the sixties and after—the theories of such figures as Carl Rogers, Abraham Maslow, Eric Fromm, and even Carl Jung have been invoked in its support. (For a fuller discussion of the history and character of expressionistic rhetoric offered here, see my "Contemporary Composition," and *Rhetoric and Reality* 43–46, 73–81, 159–65).

For this rhetoric, the existent is located within the individual subject. While the reality of the material, the social, and the linguistic are never denied, they are considered significant only insofar as they serve the needs of the individual. All fulfill their true function only when being exploited in the interests of locating the individual's authentic nature. Writing can be seen as a paradigmatic instance of this activity. It is an art, a creative act in which the process—the discovery of the true self—is as important as the product—the self discovered and expressed. The individual's use of the not-self in discovering the self takes place in a specific way. The material world provides sensory images that can be used in order to explore the self, the sensations leading to the apprehending-source of all experience. More important, these sense impressions can be coupled with language to provide metaphors to express the experience of the self, an experience which transcends ordinary non-metaphoric language but can be suggested through original figures and tropes. This original language in turn can be studied by others to understand the self and can even awaken in readers the experience of their selves. Authentic self-expression can thus lead to authentic self-experience for both the writer and the reader. The most important measure of authenticity, of genuine self-discovery and self-revelation, furthermore, is the presence of originality in expression; and this is the case whether the writer is creating poetry or writing a business report. Discovering the true self in writing will simultaneously enable the individual to discover the truth of the situation which evoked the writing, a situation that, needless to say, must always be compatible with the development of the self, and this leads to the ideological dimension of the scheme.

Most proponents of expressionistic rhetoric during the sixties and seventies were unsparingly critical of the dominant social, political, and cultural practices of the time. The most extreme of these critics demanded that the writing classroom work explicitly toward liberating students from the shackles of a corrupt society. This is seen most vividly in the effort known as "composition as happening." From this perspective, the alienating and fragmenting experience of the authoritarian institutional setting can be resisted by providing students with concrete experiences that alter political consciousness through challenging official versions of reality. Writing in response to such activities as making collages and sculptures, listening to the same piece of music in different settings, and engaging in random and irrational acts in the classroom was to enable students to experience "structure in unstructure; a random series of ordered events; order in chaos; the logical illogicality of dreams" (Lutz 35). The aim was to encourage students to resist the "interpretations of experience embodied in the language of others [so as] to order their own experience" (Paull and Kligerman 150). This more extreme form of political activism in the classroom was harshly criticized by the moderate wing of the expressionist camp, and it is this group that eventually became dominant. The names of Ken Macrorie, Walker Gibson, William Coles, Jr., Donald Murray, and Peter Elbow were the most visible in this counter effort. Significantly, these figures continued the ideological critique of the dominant culture while avoiding the overt politicizing of the classroom. In discussing the ideological position they encouraged, a position that continues to characterize them today, I will focus on the work of Murray and Elbow, both of whom explicitly address the political in their work.

From this perspective, power within society ought always to be vested in the individual. In Elbow, for example, power is an abiding concern—apparent in the title to his recent textbook (*Writing With Power*), as well as in the opening pledge of his first to help students become "less helpless, both personally and politically" by enabling them to get "control over words" (*Writing Without Teachers* vii).

This power is consistently defined in personal terms: "power comes from the words somehow fitting the *writer* (not necessarily the reader) . . . power comes from the words somehow *fitting what they are about*" (*Writing With Power* 280). Power is a product of a configuration involving the individual and her encounter with the world, and for both Murray and Elbow this is a function of realizing one's unique voice. Murray's discussion of the place of politics in the classroom is appropriately titled "Finding Your Own Voice: Teaching Composition in an Age of Dissent," and Elbow emphasizes, "If I want power, I've got to use *my* voice" (*Embracing Contraries* 202). This focus on the individual does not mean that no community is to be encouraged, as expressionists repeatedly acknowledge that communal arrangements must be made, that, in Elbow's words, "the less acceptable hunger for participation and merging is met" (98). The community's right to exist, however, stands only insofar as it serves all of its members as individuals. It is, after all, only the individual, acting alone and apart from others, who can determine the existent, the good, and the possible. For Murray, the student "must hear the contradictory counsel of his readers, so that he learns when to ignore his teachers and his peers, listening to himself after evaluating what has been said about his writing and considering what he can do to make it work" ("Finding Your Own Voice" 144–45). For Elbow, the audience can be used to help improve our writing, but "the goal should be to move toward the condition where we don't necessarily need it in order to speak or write well." Since audiences can also inhibit us, Elbow continues, "we need to learn to write what is true and what needs saying even if the whole world is scandalized. We need to learn eventually to find in *ourselves* the support which—perhaps for a long time—we must seek openly from others" (*Writing With Power* 190).

Thus, political change can only be considered by individuals and in individual terms. Elbow, for example, praises Freire's focus on the individual in seeking the contradictions of experience in the classroom but refuses to take into account the social dimension of this pedagogy, finally using Freire's thought as an occasion for arriving at a personal realization of a "psychological contradiction, not an economic one or political one," at the core of our culture (*Embracing Contraries* 98). The underlying conviction of expressionists is that when individuals are spared the distorting effects of a repressive social order, their privately determined truths will correspond to the privately determined truths of all others: my best and deepest vision supports the same universal and external laws as everyone else's best and deepest vision. Thus, in *Writing Without Teachers* Elbow admits that his knowledge about writing was gathered primarily from personal experience, and that he has no reservations about "making universal generalizations upon a sample of one" (16). Murray is even more explicit in his first edition of *A Writer Teaches Writing*: "the writer is on a search for himself. If he finds himself he will find an audience, because all of us have the same common core. And when he digs deeply into himself and is able to define himself, he will find others who will read with a shock of recognition what he has written" (4).

This rhetoric thus includes a denunciation of economic, political, and social pressures to conform—to engage in various forms of corporate-sponsored thought, feeling, and behavior. In indirectly but unmistakably decrying the dehumanizing effects of industrial capitalism, expressionistic rhetoric insists on defamiliarizing experience, on getting beyond the corruptions of the individual authorized by the language of commodified culture in order to re-experience the self and through it the external world, finding in this activity possibilities for a new order. For expressionistic rhetoric, the correct response to the imposition of current economic, political, and social arrangements is thus resistance, but a resistance that is always construed in individual terms. Collective retaliation poses as much of a threat to individual integrity as do the collective forces being resisted, and so is itself suspect. The only hope in a society working to destroy the uniqueness of the individual is for each of us to assert our individuality against the tyranny of the authoritarian corporation, state, and society. Strategies for doing so must of course be left to the individual, each lighting one small candle in order to create a brighter world.

Expressionistic rhetoric continues to thrive in high schools and at a number of colleges and universities. At first glance, this is surprising, unexpected of a rhetoric that is openly opposed to establishment practices. This subversiveness, however, is more apparent than real. In the first place, expressionistic rhetoric is inherently and debilitatingly divisive of political protest, suggesting that effective resistance can only be offered by individuals, each acting alone. Given the isolation and incoherence of such protest, gestures genuinely threatening to the establishment are difficult to accomplish. Beyond this, expressionistic rhetoric is easily co-opted by the very capitalist forces it opposes. After all, this rhetoric can be used to reinforce the entrepreneurial virtues capitalism most values: individualism, private initiative, the confidence for risk taking, the right to be contentious with authority (especially the state). It is indeed not too much to say that the ruling elites in business, industry, and government are those most likely to nod in assent to the ideology inscribed in expressionistic rhetoric. The members of this class see their lives as embodying the creative realization of the self, exploiting the material, social, and political conditions of the world in order to assert a private vision, a vision which, despite its uniqueness, finally represents humankind's best nature. (That this vision in fact represents the interests of a particular class, not all classes, is of course not acknowledged.) Those who have not attained the positions which enable them to exert this freedom have been prevented from doing so, this ideology argues, not by economic and class constraints, but by their own unwillingness to pursue a private vision, and this interpretation is often embraced by those excluded from the ruling elite as well as by the ruling elite itself. In other words, even those most constrained by their positions in the class structure may support the ideology found in expressionistic rhetoric in some form. This is most commonly done by divorcing the self from the alienation of work, separating work experience from other experience so that self discovery and fulfillment take place away from the job. For some this may lead to the pursuit of self expression in intellectual or aesthetic pursuits. For most this quest results in a variety of forms of consumer behavior, identifying individual self expression with the consumption of some commodity. This separation of work from authentic human activity is likewise reinforced in expressionistic rhetoric, as a glance at any of the textbooks it has inspired will reveal.

SOCIAL-EPISTEMIC RHETORIC

The last rhetoric to be considered I will call social-epistemic rhetoric, in so doing distinguishing it from the psychological-epistemic rhetoric that I am convinced is a form of expressionism. (The latter is found in Kenneth Dowst and in Cyril Knoblauch and Lil Brannon, although Knoblauch's recent *College English* essay displays him moving into the social camp. I have discussed the notion of epistemic rhetoric and these two varieties of it in *Rhetoric and Reality* 145–55, 165–77, and 184–85.) There have been a number of spokespersons for social-epistemic rhetoric over the last twenty years: Kenneth Burke, Richard Ohmann, the team of Richard Young, Alton Becker and Kenneth Pike, Kenneth Bruffee, W. Ross Winterowd, Ann Berthoff, Janice Lauer, and, more recently, Karen Burke Lefever, Lester Faigley, David Bartholomae, Greg Myers, Patricia Bizzell, and others. In grouping these figures together I do not intend to deny their obvious disagreements with each other. For example, Myers, a Leftist, has offered a lengthy critique of Bruffee, who—along with Winterowd and Young, Becker and Pike—is certainly of the Center politically. There are indeed as many conflicts among the members of this group as there are harmonies. They are brought together here, however, because they share a notion of rhetoric as a political act involving a dialectical interaction engaging the material, the social, and the individual writer, with language as the agency of mediation. Their positions, furthermore, include an historicist orientation, the realization that a rhetoric is an historically specific social formation that must perforce change over time; and this feature in turn makes possible reflexiveness and revision as the inherently ideological nature of rhetoric is continually acknowledged. The most complete realization of this rhetoric for the classroom is to be found in Ira Shor's *Critical Teaching and Everyday Life*. Before considering it, I would like to discuss the distinguishing features of a fully articulated social-epistemic rhetoric.

For social-epistemic rhetoric, the real is located in a relationship that involves the dialectical interaction of the observer, the discourse community (social group) in which the observer is functioning, and the material conditions of existence. Knowledge is never found in any one of these but can only be posited as a product of the dialectic in which all three come together. (More of this in a moment.) Most important, this dialectic is grounded in language: the observer, the discourse community, and the material conditions of existence are all verbal constructs. This does not mean that the three do not exist apart from language: they do. This does mean that we cannot talk and write about them—indeed, we cannot know them—apart from language. Furthermore, since language is a social phenomenon that is a product of a particular historical moment, our notions of the observing self, the communities in which the self functions, and the very structures of the material world are social constructions—all specific to a particular time and culture. These social constructions are thus inscribed in the very language we are given to inhabit in responding to our experience. Language, as Raymond Williams explains in an application of Bakhtin (*Marxism and Literature* 21–44), is one of the material and social conditions involved in producing a culture. This means that in studying rhetoric—the ways discourse is generated—we are studying the ways in which knowledge comes into existence. Knowledge, after all, is an historically bound social fabrication rather than an eternal and invariable phenomenon located in some uncomplicated repository— in the material object or in the subject or in the social realm. This brings us back to the matter of the dialectic.

Understanding this dialectical notion of knowledge is the most difficult feature of social-epistemic rhetoric. Psychological-epistemic rhetoric grants that rhetoric arrives at knowledge, but this meaning-generating activity is always located in a transcendent self, a subject who directs the discovery and arrives through it finally only at a better understanding of the self and its operation— this self comprehension being the end of all knowledge. For social-epistemic rhetoric, the subject is itself a social construct that emerges through the linguistically-circumscribed interaction of the individual, the community, and the material world. There is no universal, eternal, and authentic self that beneath all appearances is at one with all other selves. The self is always a creation of a particular historical and cultural moment. This is not to say that individuals do not ever act as individuals. It is to assert, however, that they never act with complete freedom. As Marx indicated, we make our own histories, but we do not make them just as we wish. Our consciousness is in large part a product of our material conditions. But our material conditions are also in part the products of our consciousness. Both consciousness and the material conditions influence each other, and they are both imbricated in social relations defined and worked out through language. In other words, the ways in which the subject understands and is affected by material conditions is circumscribed by socially-devised definitions, by the community in which the subject lives. The community in turn is influenced by the subject and the material conditions of the moment. Thus, the perceiving subject, the discourse communities of which the subject is a part, and the material world itself are all the constructions of an historical discourse, of the ideological formulations inscribed in the language-mediated practical activity of a particular time and place. We are lodged within a hermeneutic circle, although not one that is impervious to change.

This scheme does not lead to an anarchistic relativism. It does, however, indicate that arguments based on the permanent rational structures of the universe or on the evidence of the deepest and most profound personal intuition should not be accepted without question. The material, the social, and the subjective are at once the producers and the products of ideology, and ideology must continually be challenged so as to reveal its economic and political consequences for individuals. In other words, what are the effects of our knowledge? Who benefits from a given version of truth? How are the material benefits of society distributed? What is the relation of this distribution to social relations? Do these relations encourage conflict? To whom does our knowledge designate power? In short, social-epistemic rhetoric views knowledge as an arena of ideological conflict: there are no arguments from transcendent truth since all arguments arise in ideology. It thus inevitably supports economic, social, political, and cultural democracy. Because there are no "natural laws" or "universal truths" that indicate what exists, what is good, what is possible, and how power is to be distributed, no class or group or individual has privileged access to decisions on these matters. They must be continually decided by all and for all in a way appropriate to our own historical moment. Finally, because of this historicist orientation, social-epistemic rhetoric contains within it the means for self-criticism and self-revision. Human responses to the material conditions of existence, the social relations they encourage, and the interpellations of subjects within them are always already ideological, are always already interpretations that must be constantly revised in the interests of the greater participation of all, for the greater good of all. And this of course implies an awareness of the ways in which rhetorics can privilege some at the expense of others, according the chosen few an unequal share of power, perquisites, and material benefits.

Social-epistemic rhetoric thus offers an explicit critique of economic, political, and social arrangements, the counterpart of the implicit critique found in expressionistic rhetoric. However, here the source and the solution of these arrangements are described quite differently. As Ira Shor explains, students must be taught to identify the ways in which control over their own lives has been denied them, and denied in such a way that they have blamed themselves for their powerlessness. Shor thus situates the individual within social processes, examining in detail the interferences to critical thought that would enable "students to be their own agents for social change, their own creators of democratic culture" (48). Among the most important forces preventing work toward a social order supporting the student's "full humanity" are forms of false consciousness—reification, pre-scientific thought, acceleration, mystification—and the absence of democratic practices in all areas of experience. Although Shor discusses these forms of false consciousness in their relation to working class students, their application to all students is not hard to see, and I have selected for emphasis those features which clearly so apply.

In falling victim to reification, students begin to see the economic and social system that renders them powerless as an innate and unchangeable feature of the natural order. They become convinced that change is impossible, and they support the very practices that victimize them—complying in their alienation from their work, their peers, and their very selves. The most common form of reification has to do with the preoccupation with consumerism, playing the game of material acquisition and using it as a substitute for more self-fulfilling behavior. In pre-scientific thinking, the student is led to believe in a fixed human nature, always and everywhere the same. Behavior that is socially and self destructive is then seen as inevitable, in the nature of things, or can be resisted only at the individual level, apart from communal activity. Another form of pre-scientific thinking is the belief in luck, in pure chance, as the source of social arrangements, such as the inequitable distribution of wealth. The loyalty to brand names, the faith in a "common sense" that supports the existing order, and the worship of heroes, such as actors and athletes, are other forms of this kind of thought, all of which prevent "the search for rational explanations to authentic problems" (66). Acceleration refers to the pace of everyday experience—the sensory bombardment of urban life and of popular forms of entertainment—which prevents critical reflection. Mystifications are responses to the problems of a capitalist society which obscure their real sources and solutions, responses based on racism, sexism, nationalism, and other forms of bigotry. Finally, students are constantly told they live in the most free, most democratic society in the world, yet they are at the same time systematically denied opportunities for "self-discipline, self-organization, collective work styles, or group deliberation" (70), instead being subjected at every turn to arbitrary authority in conducting everyday affairs.

Shor's recommendations for the classroom grow out of an awareness of these forces and are intended to counter them. The object of this pedagogy is to enable students to *"extraordinarily reexperience the ordinary"* (93), as they critically examine their quotidian experience in order to externalize false consciousness. (Shor's use of the term "critical" is meant to recall Freire as well as the practice of the Hegelian Marxists of the Frankfurt School.) The point is to "address self-in-society and social-relations-in-self" (95). The self then is regarded as the product of a dialectical relationship between the individual and the social, each given significance by the other. Self-autonomy and self-fulfillment are thus possible not through becoming detached from the social, but through resisting those social influences that alienate and disempower, doing so, moreover, in and through social activity. The liberatory classroom begins this resistance process with a dialogue that inspires "a democratic model of social relations, used to problematize the undemocratic quality of social life" (95). This dialogue—a model inspired by Paulo Freire—makes teacher and learner equals engaged in a joint practice that is "[l]oving, humble, hopeful, trusting, critical" (95). This is contrasted with the unequal power relations in the authoritarian classroom, a place where the teacher holds all power and knowledge and the student is the receptacle into which information is poured, a classroom that is "[l]oveless, arrogant, hopeless, mistrustful, acritical" (95). Teacher and student work together to shape the content of the liberatory classroom, and this includes creating the materials of study in the class—such as textbooks and media. Most important, the students are to undergo a conversion from "manipulated objects into active, critical subjects" (97), thereby empowering them to become agents of social change rather than victims. Shor sums up these elements: "social practice is studied in the name of freedom for critical consciousness; democracy and awareness develop through the form of dialogue; dialogue externalizes false consciousness, changing students from re-active objects into society-making subjects; the object-subject switch is a social psychology for empowerment; power through study creates the conditions for reconstructing social practice" (98).

This approach in the classroom requires interdisciplinary methods, and Shor gives an example from the study of the fast-food hamburger: "Concretely my class' study of hamburgers not only involved English and philosophy in our use of writing, reading, and conceptual analysis, but it also included economics in the study of the commodity relations which bring hamburgers to market, history and sociology in an assessment of what the everyday diet was like prior to the rise of the hamburger, and health science in terms of the nutritional value of the ruling burger" (114). This interdisciplinary approach to the study of the reproduction of social life can also lead to "the unveiling of hidden social history" (115), the discovery of past attempts to resist self-destructive experience. This in turn can lead to an examination of the roots of sexism and racism in our culture. Finally, Shor calls upon comedy to reunite pleasure and work, thought and feeling, and upon a resourceful use of the space of the classroom to encourage dialogue that provides students with information withheld elsewhere on campus—"informational, conceptual, personal, academic, financial" (120)—ranging from the location of free or inexpensive services to the location of political rallies.

This survey of the theory and practice of Ira Shor's classroom is necessarily brief and reductive. Still, it suggests the complexity of the behavior recommended in the classroom, behavior that is always open-ended, receptive to the unexpected, and subversive of the planned. Most important, success in this classroom can never be guaranteed. This is a place based on dialectical collaboration—the interaction of student, teacher, and shared experience within a social, interdisciplinary framework—and the outcome is always unpredictable. Yet, as Shor makes clear, the point of this classroom is that the liberated consciousness of students is the only educational objective worth considering, the only objective worth the risk of failure. To succeed at anything else is no success at all.

It should now be apparent that a way of teaching is never innocent. Every pedagogy is imbricated in ideology, in a set of tacit assumptions about what is real, what is good, what is possible, and how power ought to be distributed. The method of cognitive psychology is the most likely to ignore this contention, claiming that the rhetoric it recommends is based on an objective understanding of the unchanging structures of mind, matter, and language. Still, despite its commitment to the empirical and scientific, as we have seen, this rhetoric can easily be made to serve specific kinds of economic, social, and political behavior that works to the advantage of the members of one social class while disempowering others—doing so, moreover, in the name of objective truth. Expressionistic rhetoric is intended to serve as a critique of the ideology of corporate capitalism, proposing in its place an ideology based on a radical individualism. In the name of empowering the individual, however, its naivety about economic, social, and political arrangements can lead to the marginalizing of the individuals who would resist a dehumanizing society, rendering them ineffective through their isolation. This rhetoric also is easily co-opted by the agencies of corporate capitalism, appropriated and distorted in the service of the mystifications of bourgeois individualism. Social-epistemic rhetoric attempts to place the question of ideology at the center of the teaching of writing. It offers both a detailed analysis of dehumanizing social experience and a self-critical and overt-

———. *Writing with Power: Techniques for Mastering the Writing Process.* New York: Oxford UP, 1981.

Emig, Janet. *The Composing Process of Twelfth Graders.* Research Report No. 13. Urbana: NCTE, 1971.

Flower, Linda. *Problem-Solving Strategies for Writing.* 2nd ed. San Diego: Harcourt, 1985.

Flower, Linda, and John R. Hayes. "A Cognitive Process Theory of Writing." *College Composition and Communication* 32 (1981): 365–87.

Knoblauch, C. H. "Rhetorical Constructions: Dialogue and Commitment." *College English* 50 (1988): 125–40.

———, and Lil Brannon. *Rhetorical Traditions and the Teaching of Writing.* Upper Montclair: Boynton/Cook, 1984.

Larrain, Jorge. *The Concept of Ideology.* Athens: U of Georgia P, 1979.

Larson, Richard. "Discovery Through Questioning: A Plan for Teaching Rhetorical Invention." *College English* 30 (1968): 126–34.

———. "Invention Once More: A Role for Rhetorical Analysis." *College English* 32 (1971): 665–72.

———. "Problem-Solving, Composing, and Liberal Education." *College Composition and Communication* 23 (1972): 208–10.

Lutz, William D. "Making Freshman English a Happening." *College Composition and Communication* 22 (1971): 35–38.

Murray, Donald. *A Writer Teaches Writing.* Boston: Houghton, 1968.

———. "Finding Your Own Voice in an Age of Dissent." *College Composition and Communication* 20 (1969): 118–23.

Myers, Greg. "Reality, Consensus, and Reform in the Rhetoric of Composition Teaching." *College English* 48 (1986): 154–74.

Ohmann, Richard. "Literacy, Technology, and Monopoly Capital." *College English* 47 (1985): 675–89.

Paull, Michael, and Jack Kligerman. "Invention, Composition, and the Urban College." *College English* 33 (1972): 651–59.

Shor, Ira. *Critical Teaching and Everyday Life.* 1980. Chicago: U of Chicago, 1987.

Therborn, Göran. *The Ideology of Power and the Power of Ideology.* London: Verso, 1980.

Vitanza, Victor. " 'Notes' Towards Historiographies of Rhetorics; or, Rhetorics of the Histories of Rhetorics: Traditional, Revisionary, and Sub/Versive." *PRETEXT* 8 (1987): 63–125.

Williams, Raymond. *Keywords: A Vocabulary of Culture and Society.* Revised Edition. New York: Oxford UP, 1977.

———. *Marxism and Literature.* Oxford UP, 1977.

Janet Emig

"Writing as a Mode of Learning"

Writing represents a unique mode of learning—not merely valuable, not merely special, but unique. That will be my contention in this paper. The thesis is straightforward. Writing serves learning uniquely because writing as process-and-product possesses a cluster of attributes that correspond uniquely to certain powerful learning strategies.

Although the notion is clearly debatable, it is scarcely a private belief. Some of the most distinguished contemporary psychologists have at least implied such a role for writing as heuristic. Lev Vygotsky, A. R. Luria, and Jerome Bruner, for example, have all pointed out that higher cognitive functions, such as analysis and synthesis, seem to develop most fully only with the support system of verbal language—particularly, it seems, of written language.[1] Some of their arguments and evidence will be incorporated here.

Here I have a prior purpose: to describe as tellingly as possible *how* writing uniquely corresponds to certain powerful learning strategies. Making such a case for the uniqueness of writing should logically and theoretically involve establishing many contrasts, distinctions between (1) writing and all other verbal languaging processes—listening, reading, and especially talking; (2) writing and all other forms of composing, such as composing a painting, a symphony, a dance, a film, a building; and (3) composing in words and composing in the two other major graphic symbol systems of mathematical equations and scientific formulae. For the purposes of this paper, the task is simpler, since most students are not permitted by most curricula to discover the values of composing say, in dance, or even in film; and most students are not sophisticated enough to create, to originate formulations, using the highly abstruse symbol system of equations and formulae. Verbal language represents the most *available* medium for composing; in fact, the significance of sheer availability in its selection as a mode for learning can probably not be overstressed. But the uniqueness of writing among the verbal languaging processes does need to be established and supported if only because so many curricula and courses in English still consist almost exclusively of reading and listening.

WRITING AS A UNIQUE LANGUAGING PROCESS

Traditionally, the four languaging processes of listening, talking, reading, and writing are paired in either of two ways. The more informative seems to be the division many linguists make between first-order and second-order processes, with talking and listening characterized as first-order processes; reading and writing, as second-order. First-order processes are acquired without formal or systematic instruction; the second-order processes of reading and writing tend to be learned initially only with the aid of formal and systematic instruction.

The less useful distinction is that between listening and reading as receptive functions and talking and writing as productive functions. Critics of these terms like Louise Rosenblatt rightfully point out that the connotation of passivity too often accompanies the notion of receptivity when reading, like listening, is a vital, construing act.

An additional distinction, so simple it may have been previously overlooked, resides in two criteria: the matters of origination and of graphic recording. Writing is originating and creating a unique verbal construct that is graphically recorded. Reading is creating or re-creating *but not* originating a verbal construct that is graphically recorded. Listening is creating or recreating but not originating a verbal construct that is *not* graphically recorded. Talking is creating *and* originating a verbal construct that is *not* graphically recorded (except for the circuitous routing of a transcribed tape). Note that a distinction is being made between creating and originating, separable processes.

For talking, the nearest languaging process, additional distinctions should probably be made. (What follows is not a denigration of talk as a valuable mode of learning.) A silent classroom or one filled only with the teacher's voice is anathema to learning. For evidence of the cognitive value of talk, one can look to some of the persuasive monographs coming from the London Schools Council project on writing: *From Information to Understanding* by Nancy Martin or *From Talking to Writing* by Peter Medway.[2] We also know that for some of us, talking is a valuable, even necessary, form of prewriting. In his curriculum, James Moffett makes the value of such talk quite explicit.

But to say that talking is a valuable form of pre-writing is not to say that writing is talk recorded, an inaccuracy appearing in far too many composition texts. Rather, a number of contemporary trans-disciplinary sources suggest that talking and writing may emanate from different organic sources and represent quite different, possibly distinct, language functions. In *Thought and Language,* Vygotsky notes that "written speech is a separate linguistic function, differing from oral speech in both structure and mode of functioning."[3] The sociolinguist Dell Hymes, in a valuable issue of *Daedalus,* "Language as a Human Problem," makes a comparable point: "That speech and writing are not simply interchangeable, and have developed historically in ways at least partly autonomous, is obvious."[4] At the first session of the Buffalo Conference on Researching

Composition (4–5 October 1975), the first point of unanimity among the participant-speakers with interests in developmental psychology, media, dreams and aphasia was that talking and writing were markedly different functions.[5] Some of us who work rather steadily with writing research agree. We also believe that there are hazards, conceptually and pedagogically, in creating too complete an analogy between talking and writing, in blurring the very real differences between the two.

WHAT ARE THESE DIFFERENCES?

1. Writing is learned behavior; talking is natural, even irrepressible, behavior.
2. Writing then is an artificial process; talking is not.
3. Writing is a technological device—not the wheel, but early enough to qualify as primary technology; talking is organic, natural, earlier.
4. Most writing is slower than most talking.
5. Writing is stark, barren, even naked as a medium; talking is rich, luxuriant, inherently redundant.
6. Talk leans on the environment; writing must provide its own context.
7. With writing, the audience is usually absent; with talking, the listener is usually present.
8. Writing usually results in a visible graphic product; talking usually does not.
9. Perhaps because there is a product involved, writing tends to be a more responsible and committed act than talking.
10. It can even be said that throughout history, an aura, an ambience, a mystique has usually encircled the written word; the spoken word has for the most part proved ephemeral and treated mundanely (ignore, please, our recent national history).
11. Because writing is often our representation of the world made visible, embodying both process and product, writing is more readily a form and source of learning than talking.

UNIQUE CORRESPONDENCES BETWEEN LEARNING AND WRITING

What then are some *unique* correspondences between learning and writing? To begin with some definitions: Learning can be defined in many ways, according to one's predilections and training, with all statements about learning of course hypothetical. Definitions range from the chemo-physiological ("Learning is changed patterns of protein synthesis in relevant portions of the cortex")[6] to transactive views drawn from both philosophy and psychology (John Dewey, Jean Piaget) that learning is the reorganization or confirmation of a cognitive scheme in light of an experience.[7] What the speculations seem to share is consensus about certain features and strategies that characterize successful learning. These include the importance of the classic attributes of reinforcement and feedback. In most hypotheses, successful learning is also connective and selective. Additionally, it makes use of propositions, hypotheses, and other elegant summarizers. Finally, it is active, engaged, personal—more specifically, self-rhythmed—in nature.

Jerome Bruner, like Piaget, through a comparable set of categories, posits three major ways in which we represent and deal with actuality: (1) enactive—we learn "by doing"; (2) iconic—we learn "by depiction in an image"; and (3) representational or symbolic—we learn "by restatement in words."[8] To overstate the matter, in enactive learning, the hand predominates; in iconic the eye; and in symbolic, the brain.

What is striking about writing as a process is that, by its very nature, all three ways of dealing with actuality are simultaneously or almost simultaneously deployed. That is, the symbolic transformation of experience through the specific symbol system of verbal language is shaped into an icon (the graphic product) by the enactive hand. If the most efficacious learning occurs when learning is reinforced, then writing through its inherent reinforcing cycle involving hand, eye, and brain marks a uniquely powerful multi-representational mode for learning.

Writing is also integrative in perhaps the most basic possible sense: the organic, the functional. Writing involves the fullest possible functioning of the brain, which entails the active participation in the process of both the left and the right hemispheres. Writing is markedly bispheral, although in some popular accounts, writing is inaccurately presented as a chiefly left-hemisphere activity, perhaps because the linear written product is somehow regarded as analogue for the process that created it; and the left hemisphere seems to process material linearly.

The right hemisphere, however, seems to make at least three, perhaps four, major contributions to the writing process—probably, to the creative process generically. First, several researchers, such as Geschwind and Snyder of Harvard and Zaidal of Cal Tech, through markedly different experiments, have very tentatively suggested that the right hemisphere is the sphere, even the *seat*, of emotions.[9] Second—or perhaps as an illustration of the first—Howard Gardner, in his important study of the brain-damaged, notes that our sense of emotional appropriateness in discourse may reside in the right sphere:

> Emotional appropriateness, in sum—being related not only to *what* is said, but to how it is said and to what is *not* said, as well—is crucially dependent on right hemisphere intactness.[10]

Third, the right hemisphere seems to be the source of intuition, of sudden gestalts, of flashes of images, of abstractions occurring as visual or spatial wholes, as the initiating metaphors in the creative process. A familiar example: William Faulkner noted in his *Paris Review* interview that *The Sound and the Fury* began as the image of a little girl's muddy drawers as she sat in a tree watching her grandmother's funeral.[11]

Also, a unique form of feedback, as well as reinforcement, exists with writing, because information from the *process* is immediately and visibly available as that portion of the *product* already written. The importance for learning of a product in a familiar and available medium for immediate, literal (that is, visual) re-scanning and review cannot perhaps be overstated. In his remarkable study of purportedly blind sculptors, Géza Révész found that without sight, persons cannot move beyond a literal transcription of elements into any manner of symbolic transformation—by definition, the central requirement for reformulation and reinterpretation, i.e., revision, that most aptly named process.[12]

As noted in the second paragraph, Vygotsky and Luria, like Bruner, have written importantly about the connections between learning and writing. In his essay "The Psychobiology of Psychology," Bruner lists as one of six axioms regarding learning: "We are connective."[13] Another correspondence then between learning and writing: In *Thought and Language*, Vygotsky notes that writing makes a unique demand in that the writer must engage in "deliberate semantics"—in Vygotsky's elegant phrase, "deliberate structuring of the web of meaning."[14] Such structuring is required because, for Vygotsky, writing centrally represents an expansion of inner speech, that mode whereby we talk to ourselves, which is "maximally compact" and "almost entirely predicative"; written speech is a mode which is "maximally detailed" and which requires explicitly supplied subjects and topics. The medium then of written verbal language requires the establishment of systematic connections and relationships. Clear writing by definition is that writing which signals without ambiguity the nature of conceptual relationships, whether they be coordinate, subordinate, superordinate, causal, or something other.

Successful learning is also engaged, committed, personal learning. Indeed, impersonal learning may be an anomalous concept, like the very notion of objectivism itself. As Michael Polanyi states simply at the beginning of *Personal Knowledge*: "the ideal of strict objectivism is absurd." (How many courses and curricula in English, science, and all else does that one sentence reduce to rubble?) Indeed, the theme of *Personal Knowledge* is that

> into every act of knowing there enters a passionate contribution of the person knowing what is being known. . . . this coefficient is no mere imperfection but a vital component of his knowledge.[15]

In *Zen and the Art of Motorcycle Maintenance*, Robert Pirsig states a comparable theme:

> The Quality which creates the world emerges as *a relationship* between man and his experience. He is a *participant* in the creation of all things.[16]

Finally, the psychologist George Kelly has as the central notion in his subtle and compelling theory of personal constructs man as a scientist steadily and actively engaged in making and re-making his hypotheses about the nature of the universe.[17]

We are acquiring as well some empirical confirmation about the importance of engagement in, as well as self-selection of, a subject for the student learning to write and writing to learn. The recent Sanders and Littlefield study, reported in *Research in the Teaching of English,* is persuasive evidence on this point, as well as being a model for a certain type of research.[18]

As Luria implies in the quotation below, writing is self-rhythmed. One writes best as one learns best, at one's own pace. Or to connect the two processes, writing can sponsor learning because it can match its pace. Support for the importance of self-pacing to learning can be found in Benjamin Bloom's important study "Time and Learning."[19] Evidence for the significance of self-pacing to writing can be found in the reason Jean-Paul Sartre gave last summer for not using the tape-recorder when he announced that blindness in his second eye had forced him to give up writing:

> I think there is an enormous difference between speaking and writing. One rereads what one rewrites. But one can read slowly or quickly: in other words, you do not know how long you will have to take deliberating over a sentence . . . If I listen to a tape recorder, the listening speed is determined by the speed at which the tape turns and not by my own needs. Therefore I will always be either lagging behind or running ahead of the machine.[20]

Writing is connective as a process in a more subtle and perhaps more significant way, as Luria points out in what may be the most powerful paragraph of rationale ever supplied for writing as heuristic:

> Written speech is bound up with the inhibition of immediate synpractical connections. It assumes a much slower, repeated mediating process of analysis and synthesis, which makes it possible not only to develop the required thought, but even to revert to its earlier stages, thus transforming the sequential chain of connections in a simultaneous, self-reviewing structure. Written speech thus represents a new and powerful instrument of thought.[21]

But first to explicate: Writing inhibits "immediate synpractical connections." Luria defines *synpraxis* as "concrete-active" situations in which language does not exist independently but as a "fragment" of an ongoing action "outside of which it is incomprehensible."[22] In *Language and Learning,* James Britton defines it succinctly as "speech-cum-action."[23] Writing, unlike talking, restrains dependence upon the actual situation. Writing as a mode is inherently more self-reliant than speaking. Moreover, as Bruner states in explicating Vygotsky, "Writing virtually forces a remoteness of reference on the language user."[24]

Luria notes what has already been noted above: that writing, typically, is a "much slower" process than talking. But then he points out the relation of this slower pace to learning: This slower pace allows for—indeed, encourages—the shuttling among past, present, and future. Writing, in other words, connects the three major tenses of our experience to make meaning. And the two major modes by which these three aspects are united are the processes of analysis and synthesis: analysis, the breaking of entities into their constituent parts; and synthesis, combining or fusing these, often into fresh arrangements or amalgams.

Finally, writing is epigenetic, with the complex evolutionary development of thought steadily and graphically visible and available throughout as a record of the journey, from jottings and notes to full discursive formulations.

For a summary of the correspondences stressed here between certain learning strategies and certain attributes of writing see Figure 1.

Figure 1   Unique Cluster of Correspondences Between Certain Learning Strategies and Certain Attributes of Writing

Selected Characteristics of Successful Learning Strategies	*Selected Attributes of Writing Process and Product*
(1) Profits from multi-representational and integrative reinforcement	(1) Represents process uniquely multi-representational and integrative
(2) Seeks self-provided feedback:	(2) Represents powerful instance of self-provided feedback:
(a) immediate	(a) provides product uniquely available for *immediate* feedback (review and re-evaluation)
(b) long-term	(b) provides record of evolution of thought since writing is epigenetic as process-and-product
(3) Is connective:	(3) Provides connections:
(a) makes generative conceptual groupings, synthetic and analytic	(a) establishes explicit and systematic conceptual groupings through lexical, syntactic, and rhetorical devices
(b) proceeds from propositions, hypotheses, and other elegant summarizers	(b) represents most available means (verbal language) for economic recording of abstract formulations
(4) Is active, engaged, personal— notably, self-rhythmed	(4) Is active, engaged, personal— notably, self-rhythmed

This essay represents a first effort to make a certain kind of case for writing—specifically, to show its unique value for learning. It is at once over-elaborate and under-specific. Too much of the formulation is in the off-putting jargon of the learning theorist, when my own predilection would have been to emulate George Kelly and to avoid terms like *reinforcement* and *feedback* since their use implies that I live inside a certain paradigm about learning I don't truly inhabit. Yet I hope that the essay will start a crucial line of inquiry; for unless the losses to learners of not writing are compellingly described and substantiated by experimental and speculative research, writing itself as a central academic process may not long endure.

NOTES

1. Lev S. Vygotsky, *Thought and Language,* trans. Eugenia Hanfmann and Gertrude Vakar (Cambridge: The M.I.T. Press, 1962); A. R. Luria and F. Ia. Yudovich, *Speech and the Development of Mental Processes in the Child,* ed. Joan Simon (Baltimore: Penguin, 1971); Jerome S. Bruner, *The Relevance of Education* (New York: W. W. Norton and Co., 1971).

2. Nancy Martin, *From Information to Understanding* (London: Schools Council Project Writing Across the Curriculum, 11–13, 1973); Peter Medway, *From Talking to Writing* (London: Schools Council Project Writing Across the Curriculum, 11–13. 1973).

3. Vygotsky, p. 98.

4. Dell Hymes, "On the Origins and Foundations of Inequality Among Speakers," *Daedalus,* 102 (Summer, 1973), 69.

5. Participant-speakers were Loren Barritt, University of Michigan; Gerald O'Grady, SUNY/Buffalo; Hollis Frampton, SUNY/Buffalo; and Janet Emig, Rutgers.

6. George Steiner, *After Babel: Aspects of Language and Translation* (New York: Oxford University Press, 1975), p. 287.

7. John Dewey, *Experience and Education* (New York: Macmillan, 1938); Jean Piaget, *Biology and Knowledge: An Essay on the Relations Between Organic Regulations and Cognitive Processes* (Chicago: University of Chicago Press, 1971).

8. Bruner, pp. 7–8.

9. Boyce Rensberger, "Language Ability Found in Right Side of Brain," *New York Times,* 1 August 1975, p. 14.

10. Howard Gardner, *The Shattered Mind: The Person After Brain Damage* (New York: Alfred A. Knopf, 1975), p. 372.

11. William Faulkner, *Writers at Work: The Paris Review Interviews,* ed. Malcolm Cowley (New York: The Viking Press, 1959), p. 130.

12. Géza Révész, *Psychology and Art of the Blind,* trans. H. A. Wolff (London: Longmans-Green, 1950).

13. Bruner, p. 126.

14. Vygotsky, p. 100.

15. Michael Polanyi, *Personal Knowledge: Toward a Post-Critical Philosophy* (Chicago: University of Chicago Press, 1958), p. viii.

16. Robert Pirsig, *Zen and the Art of Motorcycle Maintenance* (New York: William Morrow and Co., Inc., 1974), p. 212.

17. George Kelly, *A Theory of Personality: The Psychology of Personal Constructs* (New York: W. W. Norton and Co., 1963).

18. Sara E. Sanders and John H. Littlefield, "Perhaps Test Essays Can Reflect Significant Improvement in Freshman Composition: Report on a Successful Attempt," *RTE,* 9 (Fall, 1975), 145–153.

19. Benjamin Bloom, "Time and Learning," *American Psychologist,* 29 (September 1974), 682–688.

20. Jean-Paul Sartre, "Sartre at Seventy: An Interview," with Michel Contat, *New York Review of Books,* 7 August 1975.

21. Luria, p. 118.

22. Luria, p. 50.

23. James Britton, *Language and Learning* (Baltimore: Penguin, 1971), pp. 10–11.

24. Bruner, p. 47.

Rhetoric and Technology

To assert that technical writing is rhetorical, though not a wholly original idea, would certainly raise a few eyebrows. Typically, we imagine technical writing—the presentation of complex, specialized data—to be neutral and objective, set apart from the strategically stylized prose associated with rhetoric. To go one step further and suggest that technology *itself* is rhetorical—an agent of strategic discourse—is stranger still. Readings in this section, by scholars in computer programming, classics, composition studies, literature, and art history, all address the rhetorical character of modern mechanisms. They point out that we live in an electronic age that has narrowed the gap between humans and machines. Software and hardware vendors regularly hawk the newest "friendly" software and the latest "smart" microprocessors. The machines themselves seem to bear up all this advertising, particularly when they soundly beat the world's best chess players, when they point out our spelling and grammatical errors, or when they write poems and create original drawings.

The Greek roots of the word *technology, techne* and *logos,* suggest its connection with language use. *Techne* refers to art, as the result of productive reason, and *logos* is generally translated as word or explanation. Technology, then, is "words about productive art," itself a form of rhetoric. One of the most striking linguistic shifts that occurred during the industrial revolution was the metamorphosis of the meaning of technology from an explicitly discursive *process* to a *product* that stands on its utility and efficiency (we call palm-top computers "high-tech"). In this change from process to product, the "rhetoric" in *technology* has disappeared.

The modern invisibility of the *logos* in *technology* corresponds with the inaccessibility of technical and scientific writing to wide understanding. If scientists and technicians increasingly rely on an esoteric logos, the language of equations and diagrams, who—beyond the community of experts—will understand the discourse explaining their art? If science and technology are to be professions that epitomize communal knowledge in their attempts to discover, distribute, and apply new explanations of how the universe operates, then, as S. Michael Halloran notes, they need the rhetorical skill and scope to effectively publicize that knowledge.

Students in both the pure and applied sciences, including technological sciences such as material and agricultural engineering, often express the belief that they "speak" the language of mathematics, whereas people in English and philosophy departments are assumed to have their own language. This creates a division between the sciences and the humanities, not solely along lines of interest, but at the level of communication. This division can be traced back to Socrates's assertion in Plato's *Cratylus* that words are the tools of the dialectician—they are a technology that only professionals can work. Socrates's worry about discourse specialization continues today in the proliferation of discourse-community-specific and discourse-function-specific professions. Just as most literary critics would not entertain the relevance of linear algebra to an analysis of Borges's *Labyrinths*, civil engineers would not use Quintilian's *Institutio Oratoria* to prepare a proposal on snowplow routing for a state highway system, though it contains a good deal of relevant advice. When the relationship between scientists, technicians, and humanists becomes deferential rather than cooperative, the possibility for disciplinary integration is severely impaired. The problem is brought into focus when we begin to learn that many companies worldwide market themselves as exclusive technical discourse specialists. Lexicon Naming, Inc., a company that creates, copyrights, and sells new product names, recently collected several million dollars when Intel Corporation, the company that designs and builds the central processing chip in most IBM and IBM-compatible machines, rejected all in-house suggestions for the name of their latest chip, and bought the word Pentium from Lexicon. Taking Socrates's cue, we have developed a culture in which naming is itself an exclusive technology.

The specific questions and issues that the following authors address range widely within the relationship between rhetoric and technology, but issues concerning language and its power are to be found in them all. In an excerpt from *Gödel, Escher, Bach: An Eternal Golden Braid*, Douglas Hofstadter introduces the importance of the linguistic interaction between computer programmers and their machines. Using Walter Ong's and Eric Havelock's tripartite history of consciousness (from primary orality to literacy to secondary orality), Kathleen Welch argues for the revitalization of the humanities by "electrifying rhetoric"; she suggests that an understanding of how media, especially electric media, can facilitate ideas, allows one to master an extremely persuasive mode of discourse. Jay Bolter briefly but energetically contends in an excerpt from *Writing Space* that the linear, hierarchical reality we are experiencing now is being replaced, by popular demand, with a nonlinear, weblike society where all knowledge and all experience is equally shared and valued. Finally, in a piece of short fiction by George Landow, some of the problems faced by a struggling author in a future where language is monitored by machines are presented in uncomfortable detail.

One important writer who is not represented here is Jacques Ellul, whose book *The Technological Society* is the most thorough critique of "technique" available. By technique Ellul means the highly rational methodology of solving a specific problem to achieve a specific end. It is humanity's obsession with finding the most efficient solution possible, Ellul argues, that keeps people from being spontaneous and critical. As new techniques are developed to solve existing

Kathleen E. Welch

"Electrifying Classical Rhetoric: Ancient Media, Modern Technology, and Contemporary Composition"

Electronic discourse, or secondary orality, compels us to reappropriate the writing and speaking careers of Gorgias, Isocrates, and Plato, among others, as new sources for reflection and action in rhetoric and in the humanities in general.[1] One of the writers to recognize this cultural necessity is Walter J. Ong, who writes in *The Presence of the Word* that classical culture in all its aspects must be reconsidered in light of the emergence of secondary orality:

> Our entire understanding of classical culture now has to be revised—and with it our understanding of later cultures up to our own time—in terms of our new awareness of the role of the media in structuring the human psyche and civilization itself. (18)

We can now begin to particularize this agenda by reconceptualizing Gorgias, Isocrates, and Plato, whose writings and "traditions" must be re-created in light of the new technology we all live in, live with, and live through, whether we are aware of that newness or not.

All three writers helped enable writing—or literacy—to form. They wrote and spoke in a world of language fluctuation and so helped to create literacy. Their formations—including abstraction, written dialogue, and prose crafted on a page rather than ordered in the memory—remain very much with us. As Tony M. Lentz argues in *Orality and Literacy in Hellenic Greece*, speaking and writing competed with each other, and their strife led to stunningly original work. The experience of these three writer/rhetorician/innovators resembles in some striking ways the struggle and denial of the new technology consciousness that we have been experiencing for about the last century as secondary orality becomes recognized by some and denied by many.

Since the word *literacy* in particular needs to be problematized, and since many readers find the phrase *secondary orality* opaque, I will sketch an overview of the three-part construction. The primary orality/literacy/secondary orality hypothesis relies on Ong's and Eric A. Havelock's three-part division of the history of consciousness. Primary orality, responsible for the construction of consciousness before the Greek alphabet was invented (between 720 B.C. and 700 B.C.), enabled people to store cultural knowledge and educate young people through spoken performance. This stage is evident to us in the written-down version of the Homeric poems. The second stage, literacy, emerges with the use of a workable Greek alphabet that, as it gradually became interiorized, enabled people to think differently, more abstractly. Literacy became an even more powerful constructor of ways of thinking when movable print type made the writing and reading of the written word even more pervasive. The third stage is secondary orality. Largely electronic, this stage began with the invention of the telegraph in the 1840s and gathered more power as motion pictures, video, computers, and other forms became dominant communication modes. Havelock states that secondary orality represents a "cultural recall" of primary orality because the emphasis on speaking and hearing acquires new significance with electronic forms of communication. Crucially, the three communication-consciousness forms are not mutually exclusive; rather, they are cumulative. Secondary orality could not exist without literacy, and the residue of primary orality remains very much with us, contributing to the empowerment of secondary orality.

One of the changes provoked by our emerging awareness of secondary orality lies in the necessity of reinterpreting classical rhetoricians with a recognition of how secondary orality conditions our own critical sensibilities.[2] At least two immediate complaints arise in recasting writers such as Gorgias, Isocrates, and Plato. The first complaint is a disagreement that secondary orality forms consciousness. The second is an unhappiness that many writers and readers experience when they see Gorgias, Isocrates, and Plato placed on the same plane, as I am doing here for the rhetorical moment. More writers and readers will be unhappier still to see Plato put on the same level as Gorgias and Isocrates. This placement appears to contradict all the known "facts" about Plato, as well as the common sense of many interpreters, who take it as a given that Plato is superior in knowledge, in text, and therefore as a person. For some, it is a heretical act. Nonetheless, while it is easy to grant that Plato exerted more influence over the centuries than did Isocrates or Gorgias, it is helpful in making the sophists' writing and teaching understandable to us to put Plato on the same plane as Gorgias and Isocrates for the interpretive moment or longer. Plato has not been made superior to all his peers because his work was inherently superior; he has been made superior because his work was appropriated in various strands of thought for particular reasons.

Plato railed against the old-fashioned treatment of language as it appeared in the out-of-step Homeric poems—texts which dominated fourth-century Greek thought and educational practice to a degree we tend to forget. Havelock demonstrates in *Preface to Plato* and elsewhere that Plato's agenda consisted partly in transferring the power of the spoken and written-down Homeric poems to a language that was more abstract and less antiquated. The words that appear in a Homeric dictionary differ from those that appear in a dictionary that includes Attic prose.[3] More words, and more abstract words, occur in the fourth century. This difference in vocabulary reflects the linguistic reality that Plato faced (with some sadness): the Greek world had changed as a result of writing. It had changed not only on the outside (communication, or exterior discourse) but on the inside as well (expression to self, or interior discourse). Consciousness itself began to take on the constraints and possibilities presented by the written word. Plato wanted to change what we now call "the canon." Like Isocrates, Plato exploited writing fully. Both of them realized that they needed to be writers and that encoding with the new technology presented a force that could not be ignored or relegated to the status of an addition or a decoration.

REHISTORICIZING CLASSICAL WRITERS

Lodged as we are one-hundred years into secondary orality, or since the advent of effective motion picture technology, we are in a position to reinterpret these three ancient writers (as well as others) in ways that take into consideration radical changes in communication (including interior discourse, or the part of thinking that is in one's primary language or languages). When one first studies the intermingling in the orality/literacy/secondary orality hypothesis, a natural resistance can occur because it may seem rather far-fetched, or too neat. This concern is an important one. Sweeping claims can frequently lead to the settling of unsettleable problems and the closure of inquiry and dialectic. The analogy in this context acts as a tentative beginning for the analysis of burgeoning literacy and burgeoning secondary orality. The pressures and possibilities of fourth-century B.C. literacy and for modern electronic discourse systems remain radically different in many ways. People's perceptions have changed radically. Nonetheless, a peculiar characteristic remains in common: the dominance of oral discourse has become more important since film and video have become dominant symbol systems than at any time since the ancient period. Modern revolutions in ways of thinking have taken place, and they resemble in substantial ways the revolutions in thinking of the fourth century B.C. These revolutions occur with great pain and difficulty and have made a lot of people angry, including Plato to a limited extent in the ancient era, and literacy hounds such as Allan Bloom to a great extent in the present era. The belief persists now that visual texts are inherently inferior to written texts, a belief that has gone through many permutations since the invention of the camera and that has resulted in discussions about the nature of "realism." The unexamined belief in the inferiority of visual texts continues to permeate the academy in the United States.

Many people now will routinely acknowledge the idea that film and video are "artistic" media. However, their own responses to these media often indicate that these newer symbol systems are not in fact taken as seriously as symbol systems such as print or painting or music. The most compelling evidence for this marginalization of newer discourse technologies lies in their nonintegration in general education requirements. They are regarded as peripheral concerns, unrelated to the study of print texts. When courses do appear in the electronic media, they tend to be segregated or marginalized. Their placement in the curriculum announces their secondary status. The written text of the canon reigns supreme; a remarkable sameness of response exists in the entrenched unawareness of the issues involved. When educational resources become scarce, as they do from time to time and from region to region, the study of electronic media is one of the first kinds of training to be dropped. Its marginality is taken for granted. The conditioning that most people have toward electronic texts leads to statements (either explicit or, more frequently, implicit) that print texts are by nature superior. The situation can be characterized as a class system in texts: Great-Book texts are the aristocrats; some best-seller titles (for example, the books of James Michener) and European art films (the films, for instance, of Ingmar Bergman), contribute to the large middle class of texts; and television and "popular" films comprise the proletarian class. The underclass exists in student writing.

An additional and larger obstruction has occurred in promoting visual literacy. Film and video texts have frequently been taught as if they were print texts. For example, plot issues that might dominate the novel are transferred to the visual realm. "Hollywood Aristotelianism," as it has been called, derives from print culture. The grammar of film and the grammar of video have not been integrated into enough film pedagogy. Consequently, film and video courses frequently (especially in English departments) appear to be pale versions of courses in great print texts and so remain all the more susceptible to marginalization or deletion.

CHANGING CONCEPTUALIZATIONS OF AUDIENCE

Several alternatives exist for synthesizing literacy and secondary orality in the modern era and for recognizing their silences as well. Recognizing changes in the nature of audiences can lead to a better understanding of discourse technologies and their effects on writerly and readerly consciousness. In the realm of primary orality—when Homeric poets, for example, spoke poems to a community, or when an Acoma tribal leader spoke the Origin Myth of Acoma to one of the Pueblo tribes—the audience consisted of many people. The poet or leader was in charge of the group and spoke for the group as well as to it. In other words, performance was central to primary orality and to its residual existence in modern cultures. Literacy—both in manuscript cultures and in print cultures—required removal from the group, as Ong has pointed out. Writing generally required a certain amount of isolation, or at least a turning inward that is very much the inverse of the turning outward that performance requires. In the shifts that have occurred with the accretion of primary orality, literacy, and secondary orality, the constitution of audiences has changed. Oratory has always dealt partly with large audiences. Electronic discourse mostly speaks to large audiences. But as Plato's Socrates is made to say in *Phaedrus,* rhetoric "has to do with all audiences, great as well as small"; the private discourse of the household is as much the province of rhetoric as the discourse of the legislative assembly. It appears that Plato understood the constraints of literacy—including its requirement of more isolation from groups—than he is generally given credit for.

Secondary orality has brought about a redefining of a central characteristic of primary orality and a central characteristic of literacy. In the former case, performance has reemerged in a powerful way as people communicate on film or videotape with actual or perceived simultaneity of performance and reception. In the latter case, the isolation brought about by writing and reading has reemerged as people decode the texts of electronic discourse either alone or with a small group. Disembodied communication (literacy) has been re-embodied through visual mechanisms such as video monitors and film screens. This technology has made the fifth canon of delivery (medium) take on the urgency of simultaneous communication. The lag time of print seems to disappear. I write "seems to" because electronic discourse in most of its manifestations appears to be "live" but in fact is stored on film or tape and only appears to be live. The immediacy of this appearance, the attractiveness of the liveness, holds part of the performative power of the symbol systems of secondary orality. In other words, the lag time that modern writers and readers associate with print and regard as "normal" exists in many of the forms of secondary orality as well. Something is lost, but something else is gained.

Deciding on a medium in which to encode, or determining how to use the fifth canon of delivery, or medium, has become a major issue for many encoders in art, business, entertainment, and, to a lesser extent, academics. In addition, the widespread use of telephones provides one obvious example of simultaneous, disembodied communication; it is in fact so familiar that it appears to be nearly a natural part of life. In a less obvious way, the facsimile machine has provided live, simultaneous, disembodied discourse in a way that includes the first demand of literacy: documents exist as part of and as a result of the instantaneous communication. The nature of performance has undergone radical change. Depending on the decision an encoder makes about the fifth canon (that is, which medium or symbol system to use), a different emphasis on a way of knowing will occur. But electronic discourse will contribute to the way of knowing even if one writes. Regardless of which medium is chosen, primary orality, literacy, and secondary orality will exist in each one; they will inform one another, infuse one another, and create one another. They are not mere additions or accumulations; they are changes in consciousness, that is, in the ways we conceptualize.

We do not have a choice about removing video from our lives and our individual or group consciousness. Even if an individual decides to remove all video monitors from his or her environments, that person will remain significantly formed by the small screen. Written discourse and electronic discourse do not compete as much as they change and reinforce each other, even if the encoder appears to be working only in one symbol system.

The implications for pedagogy of these performance issues remain staggering. The institution of the teaching of writing remains in a very tentative phase now, partly because the merging of primary orality, literacy, and secondary orality hovers in a tenuous—and very exciting—place.

MAKING DISCOURSE ACTIVE AND PROMOTING EMPOWERMENT

Choosing a medium in which to communicate (and therefore its attendant power) preoccupies Hans M. Enzensberger in "Constituents of a Theory of the Media." His theory of electronic discourse necessarily includes reference to written discourse. Enzensberger writes,

> The new media are orientated towards action, not contemplation; towards the present, not tradition . . . The media produce no objects that can be hoarded and auctioned. They do away completely with "intellectual property" and liquidate the "heritage," that is to say, the class-specific handing-on of nonmaterial capital." (106)

The activity that inheres in electronic forms of discourse provides one of its great strengths because it can help to create dialectic, or a productive, interactive clash of legitimate views, in its decoders. The activity that comprises dialectic is one of the promises the electronic forms of discourse offer. Ong makes this point in "McLuhan as Teacher: The Future Is a Thing of the Past":

> All a teacher can ever do is get other people to think. Without a teacher, learners may be impoverished, unable to find much to learn. The teacher sets things up, whether by enlivening familiar matter or by providing new things for the learners to think about. But, even with the most brilliant teacher, if the learners are to do any learning, they are the ones who have to do it. The pipeline information-transfer model does not really work for the teacher-learner relationship, for it presents learners as passive recipients. Learners are doers, not recipients. (129)

Activity in the mind must be present for learning to take place. Both these writers recognize the fundamental issue of the power of activity in creating or transferring knowledge, or the enabling of the learner to extend his or her already-present abilities.

Michael C. Flanigan explores the primacy of activity in "Composition Models: Dynamic and Static Imitations." He discusses the way professional writing can be used to promote thinking in student writers to enable them to become more effective writers. He also describes the more familiar role of professional models in writing classes: the static model that students are assigned to read, mysteriously absorb, and then mysteriously imitate.

All these critics realize that in making decoding active (whether as readers or as spectators of visual media) change must occur. In other words, the decoder will undergo an activity that leads to reconceptualization. We can call the change "new encoding." The popular concepts of critical writing and critical thinking appear to be related to the concept of active, new encoding on the part of the decoder.

When students are made aware of the varying constraints imposed by each symbol system (for example, the grammar of film as opposed to the grammar of dominant-culture written English), they are able to engage the symbol system in active ways. Raising an awareness of medium empowers students in at least two ways: (1) it makes them (and us, their teachers) conscious of the technology that will to a large extent determine the result of their decoding (that is, the "meaning"); and (2) knowledge of what a medium consists of and where it came from shows students more of the possibilities of all media and connects students' usually isolated relationships to the media.

Conventionally, expertise in encoding with a video camera remains isolated from the experience of encoding with a pen or a word processor or any other media. When encoders increase their consciousness of medium, it can help them to transcend the frequently antagonistic relationship between language theory and language practice. Knowing that one is choosing a medium for expression empowers a writer who will consider the constraints that each medium imposes as well as the possibilities it offers. Within one medium—for instance, writing—students who study this reasserted canon can think about the kind of text production they want to engage in. Handwriting, typewriting, and word processing offer three possible technologies for writing texts. Each one has particular powers as well as limitations. The recent rehistoricizing of classical rhetoric allows us to see the connections between the fifth canon (in Greek, *hypocrisis*; in Latin, *pronuntiatio,* or *actio*: delivery or medium) as it gathered power in the fourth century B.C. and the fifth canon as it exists differently but also similarly in the twentieth century.

We can extrapolate from Enzensberger's preoccupation with writing, film, video, and so on, that making students active encoders is a dangerous activity. If students achieve adequate consciousness of the ways they have been conditioned to respond, and if they empower themselves through writing and the dialectic of inquiry, then the status quo might be in danger. If we empower too many students, they might want to change substantially the general culture we all partake of and help to create.

The potentially dangerous activity of writing is bypassed by constructing many—perhaps most—writing classes as passive reading classes (as opposed to active reading classes), a point that process compositionists such as Peter Elbow and James Moffett have been making forcefully and persuasively for a generation. Writing textbooks appear in most writing classes partly because they are comforting to teachers and partly because they allow passive reading (as opposed to critical reading) to dominate the class. They reassure the apprentice writing teacher by providing a map of uncharted territory, and they reassure many experienced writing teachers who are overwhelmed by the results of student writing (so unordered, so unlike a book with its neat typeface and margins). Reading a "perfectly" produced textbook can be a tidy, organized, lovely, and passive experience. Looking at writing before it reaches this lovely state requires developing alternative sensibilities. It requires looking at tentativeness, messy lines, and blips of invention that appear to go nowhere. In other words, compelling students and teacher to "write" the course text as the class emerges throughout the semester creates a mess and a mass of disorganized documents that appear to contradict the "rules" of literacy, including order and neatness. Keeping track of drafts and distributing student writing intimidates many writing teachers, both apprentice and experienced.

An even more substantial fear exists in the presence of the activity that comprises dialectic: print culture/print thinking leads us to believe that whatever resides in typeset possesses authority. Moreover, the romantic tradition of English studies makes belletristic writing of the kind reproduced in most textbooks appear to be inherently superior. Both issues—the beauty of the professionally-printed page and the attitude of reverence toward sanctified writers— lead to deemphasizing student activity in the form of writing. It reinforces the class structure of texts discussed above: the underclass of student texts cannot remain the center of attention very long.

Perhaps the largest class of all in the textual class system is the student-writing group of texts. It comprises the underclass, that huge pool of texts produced in huge quantities every year by students working their ways through educational systems. Many people working in the academy prefer not to have contact with this kind of text production or even to be aware of it. This hierarchy dominates the way most readers are trained to interpret written texts as well as texts from other symbol systems. The reintegration of student writing as a center of concern in higher education that the renaissance of rhetoric and composition studies brought has meant that student writing is regarded in some quarters as worthy of attention. Nonetheless, student writing remains the underclass, and many instructors are distressed when they have to come into contact with it for an extended period.

Enzensberger's formulation of "contemplation" versus "action" summarizes one of the major conflicts in both fourth-century B.C. language and twentieth-century A.D. language. In each era, a new form of activity challenged the contemplativeness of the status quo and the many comforts it invariably offers. Plato's complaints against writing resemble the complaints of many people in higher education against training students in the electronic media.

People in the late twentieth and early twenty-first centuries need to be aware of technology and consciousness so that they can participate in the encoding (and so find one way of achieving dialectic) and so that they can understand the modes of persuasion and manipulation that immerse everyone. Becoming aware of one's place in print culture empowers student writers and writing instructors. Taking print culture for granted enables the still-powerful formalist devaluation of culture and context to remain unexamined.

Classical rhetoric as it has been reappropriated by the writers in the

Dialectical School can strengthen student writing ability by revealing the inter-connections of print culture and electronic culture. Making language pedagogy active rather than passive can be done in a number of ways. One of them is through a study of technologies.

THE NEW RHETORIC IS THE OLD RHETORIC

Electronic discourse and the changes in consciousness resulting from it have made classical rhetoric a compelling issue once again. The triviality and bore-dom associated with much of classical rhetoric (traits it continues to possess for many, and understandably so, given its presentation), can be regarded as pres-sures resulting from the domination of print literacy. The cultural situation of print domination probably required that two of the primary functions of rhetoric—memory and delivery—move underground to the realm of the trivial, to the realm of tropes-for-tropes' sake.

A primary characteristic of rhetoric in all historical eras lies in its adaptabili-ty. Rhetoric adapts so well that it is alien to virtually nothing. However, this strength easily becomes a problem: its adaptability makes it the chameleon of disciplines. If rhetoric can adapt to any kind of language and symbol system, then what is it? Where is its substance? Since it is partly a faculty, it can be applied to anything.

The adaptability of rhetoric—its power and its danger—leads inevitably to the construction and communication of value systems. Rhetoric as a faculty and a systematic form of study has been throughout its history, beginning with its systematization in the fifth century B.C. and leading to the present moment, appropriated by people for negative purposes. This complaint formed the center of Plato and Aristotle's long-lasting attack against the sophists. These patriarchs of Western philosophy (who came to appropriate—one could say "colonize"— the field of ethics), Plato and Aristotle, disagreed on many issues, but they in a sense collaborated in their rigorous denunciation of the sophists. The totalizing effect of their stance silenced the sophists virtually until the nineteenth century, as various recent commentators have demonstrated. In the political realm, dic-tators have always adapted rhetoric to their ends. But then so too have benefi-cent rulers. So what can be done with a faculty or an ability that can go out of control so readily?

Rhetoric's adaptability, more than the characteristics of any other field, points to the need for examinations of value systems. It points, in fact, to the need for the analysis of many kinds of value systems. Couched in different terms, it requires us to study ideology, or the interconnecting systems of values and beliefs that inform attitudes and behaviors. Most significantly, rhetoric can teach people to become aware of these systems that are usually tacit and assumed to be factual, or based on "reality," partly because they feel so "normal," so "nat-ural." This enterprise leads to the emphasis on rhetorical consciousness.

RHETORIC, CONSCIOUSNESS, AND THE "CONSCIOUSNESS INDUSTRY"

Print texts possess power that readers tend to take for granted. Print literacy has conditioned us to view published texts as more authoritative than manuscript texts or nonprint texts produced on videotape, film, or other media. Some electronic texts have come to enjoy the same authoritativeness. (This is one reason why live television has become rare: its authoritativeness is jeopardized by mistakes or by unprogrammed material that enters the visual field.) The authoritativeness of printed texts leads to a greater emphasis on the text and, in turn, its life as a finished object. The completed nature of print texts appears to be natural or even inevitable.

If we move the focus from the text and its apparent objectivity and refocus on which institutions control the distribution of the printed or electronic text, then we confront Enzensberger's point: a consciousness industry possesses enormous control over the population. Enzensberger writes in "The Industrialization of the Mind,"

> While radio, cinema, television, recording, advertising, and public relations, new techniques of manipulation and propaganda, are being keenly discussed, each on its own terms, the mind industry, taken as a whole, is disregarded. Newsprint and publishing, its oldest and in many respects still its most interesting branch, hardly comes up for serious comment any longer, presumably because it lacks the appeal of technological novelty. (6)

These institutions help comprise the fifth canon of rhetoric, delivery (or medium). So great is the distribution power of the mind industry that the fifth canon, it can be maintained, is now the most powerful canon of the five. The fifth canon has become the consciousness industry, and the fifth canon remains the function of rhetoric most frequently (one could say most avidly) ignored by writing instructors and their institutions.

Rhetoric, particularly when the fifth canon is fully considered, helps to create the consciousness industry. Rhetoric as both a faculty and a field of study provides not only the means of analysis for all these symbol systems but the means of producing new kinds of material as well. No other system for the production and reception of texts in all symbol systems possesses the completeness of rhetoric and its definitive connection to systems of education and to cultures.

Rhetoric, including the composition of texts in all media, has the capacity to make people conscious of the unprecedented power of print and electronic texts as systems of communication and of indoctrination. Along with the raising of fifth-canon consciousness, rhetoric provides one means for people to enact their own encoding; it enables writing, filming, taping, and so on. Part of the potential dialectic that inheres in all media occurs when decoders become encoders in a particular medium. For example, when a reader turns to writing, the nature of writing texts changes for him or her. The same situation holds true for filming, taping, and so on.

Because of the power of encoding of all kinds, rhetoric as it applies to the various symbol systems needs to be studied by novices as well as by more experienced encoders. In addition to being studied by critics (a rather small, privileged group) rhetoric in literacy and in secondary orality must become part of the agenda of general education. Studying the technology of literacy and secondary orality has become a necessity for even a minimally educated population. Ink and paper, the word processor and printer, the film camera, the video camera, the frames of big and small screens—all must be studied for an understanding of cultural dynamics. Remaining unconscious of the media of literacy and secondary orality means that cultures will have functionally illiterate populations.

Functional illiteracy in this context means that the power of print and visual texts will remain centered in privileged groups; it also means that the status quo will appear to sustain itself. Appropriate training in print and visual literacy—when students encode as well as decode—would make students less passive. It would promote the interactive thinking that is dialectic. However, the institutionalization of visual literacy is not action enough. Educational institutions themselves must give up their marginality. The passivity of most educational practice (the student as empty vessel waiting to be filled with the knowledge of teacher and print text) is supplemented by an implied moral superiority that frequently accompanies the disciplines ordered under the rubric, "the humanities." An unapparent transaction takes place: the humanities are given tacit moral superiority in exchange for being relatively useless.[4]

POWER IN THE ORDINARINESS OF LANGUAGE

The visual illiteracy of modern cultures, along with the sustained unconsciousness of delivery, or medium, means that the ability to understand systems of communication (including various forms of manipulation and control) remains at an elementary level. Only when the ordinariness of language is recognized—in exterior discourse as well as in the interior discourse that partly constitutes thinking—can extraordinary uses (artistic or literary discourse) be understood. The everyday uses of language exist in constant flux, like Heraclitus's river. Less noticeably, the uses of ordinary language exist in flux as well. While a true rhetoric may exist for some people, that trueness is largely unlocatable. Fluid discourse—rhetoric and the mutual discovery and challenge of dialectic—remains the source of power in classical rhetoric. In this fluidity and dialectic, one may discover (as Plato believed possible at various points in his career as a writer) ultimate realities.

The fact that a primary reception of classical rhetoric has been made utterly definite (that is, static) in positivistic presentations illustrates the moribund state not only of Cartesian dualism but of discourse education that remains marginalized, ghettoized, and useless. Walter Benjamin, in "The Work of Art in the Age of Mechanical Reproduction," explores the idea that electronic media enable oral discourse to gain a kind of power that it did not have in pre-electronic eras: permanence. Films, videos, and computer disks can maintain texts as readily as writing can. In primary orality, the dynamism of the word is powerful but transitory. In secondary orality, the dynamic of the spoken word is not only powerful, it is lasting. We have returned to a much more powerful state of interdependence of oral and written discourse. With the technology of secondary orality, the spoken word and the written word are empowering each other in ways that previously were not possible. Oral discourse is now largely electric. This situation makes classical rhetoric—which accounts for encoders, decoders, and cultures, as well as texts—a newly powerful area. After residing in the nether world of tropes and figures for many centuries, classical rhetoric is newly resuscitated by the interdynamics of literacy and secondary orality. Benjamin writes,

> Around 1900 technical reproduction had reached a standard that not only permitted it to reproduce all transmitted works of art and thus to cause the most profound change in their impact upon the public; it also had captured a place of its own among the artistic processes. For the study of this standard nothing is more revealing than the nature of the repercussions that these two different manifestations—the reproduction of works of art and the art of the film—have had on art in its traditional form. (220)

The fifth canon of delivery as it has come to exist in various electronic forms in the twentieth century influences all forms of art, as Benjamin was one of the first to recognize. Art's reproducibility can empower people who may not have had access to the power of encoding. The means of producing discourse in several symbol systems is available to a large population. In order for people to become persuaded of the empowerment that is possible for them through encoding, they must see the relationship between their own ordinary language—including interior discourse—and that of artistic discourse. This issue provides a powerful means of persuasion for writing instructors. Connecting a student's interior discourse—something that is lived and felt—to a class essay or to a play by Shakespeare acts as an effective means of empowering students. This connection treats conceptualizations or "how" questions, not "content" or "what" questions. In addition, this connection enables students to comprehend the interconnections of all language use and its existence as a communal activity rather than as the merely private, hermetic possession that many people assume it to be.

Plato and Isocrates appear in their writing to have understood the primary relationship between inner speech (and its relationship to the soul) and outer speech. Plato's rhetoric and dialectic, difficult though they are to define, connect to both kinds of speech in a person engaged in a search, or a process, that is not readily identifiable. Rhetoric and dialectic are communal as well as singular activities; their push and pull require conversation (in any medium) with another person, but, like rhetoric, they require interior change as well. Virginia N. Steinhoff has written about these relational activities:

> The Platonic stance toward rhetorical arts and instruction is synthetic and art-ful, shaped from unexpected material into new forms that are, at best, sugges-tions of things not seen. The Socratic role requires, in addition, a kind of play-fulness and suspension of goal-directed behavior that is unlikely to sit well with responsible institutions of higher learning or teachers anxious about pro-ductivity in the classroom, specifically about written products—papers, essays, themes, theses, scholarly articles, and so on. (39)

These outward manifestations, or artifacts of the movement between interior and exterior discourse, have been privileged over the syntheses Steinhoff alludes to. But the signature of Platonic rhetoric as well as of Isocratean rhetoric remains the subjectivity of thinking rather than the objectivity of texts.

Plato obviously and Isocrates less obviously impelled their readers to use their own subjective selves to make contact with versions of reality and therefore to improve perceptive reality. While Isocrates remained more committed to ordi-nary communication, he nevertheless resembles Plato in his commitment to inte-rior discourse. The impressionism that accompanies rhetoric and encoding in all symbol systems constitutes part of its definition. Positivists of the Heritage School and other groups do not take well to impressionism and subjectivity. It appears to interrupt the definiteness that tends to be reassuring. Writing that is relegated to the status of a mere "skill" partakes of this definiteness. As we have seen, however, writing as a skillbound activity, as the mastering of the produc-tion of definite objects that reflect more or less definite interior realities, quickly becomes boring for encoders and for decoders alike.

Secondary orality and its brief century of life have changed the nature of rhetoric, including that of classical rhetoric. In addition, the ways people per-ceive have changed radically. The changes brought about in audience as well as in interior discourse resemble (even as they in other ways do not resemble) the changes in epistemology that Plato, Isocrates, Gorgias, and other writers and performers experienced with the spreading of literacy as a dominant form of consciousness in the fourth century B.C. There is no point in worshipping these early writers, as has been done perennially. The hierarchy created by the wor-shipper and the almost divine means that a huge gap of utter inequality exists. This space may be appropriate in religious practice but hinders discourse prac-tice and pedagogy.

The study of secondary orality as a continuing dynamic will not progress if analogizing to the possibilities and constraints of fourth-century B.C. discourse leads to more of the tired, old fetishizing of classical rhetoric texts and the inevitable and tired, old response of rejecting those texts for being fetishized. Instead, the study of secondary orality can bring about a democracy of texts, in which student texts are produced and studied with the rigor and care that Great-Book texts (of whatever discipline) are studied. In addition, continuing to privi-lege one medium over the other media that the fifth canon offers us means that the power of delivery will never be realized. Instead, the status quo will remain.

It has remained the sincere task of many language educators to remain unconscious of the fifth canon, of medium, and therefore to act as if only one or two significant systems of delivery exist. This ingrained rhetorical unconsciousness is accompanied by a tacit assumption that good speaking and good writing are somehow innate. In other words, they act as if (that is, their performances as educators state) that good speaking and writing do not at all connect to technology but instead are basically natural traits, the result of good breeding. Those students unfortunate enough (according to these promoters of the rhetorical unconscious) not to have received this language goodness at home (usually the children of the underprivileged) must be trained in it. These spokespeople for the status quo tend to see good writing and speaking as inborn qualities rather than as acquired capabilities. If one is unfortunate enough to be ill-bred, then schools should train the student to acquire the discourse habits of good breeding. In this way, the status quo can go on and on, with its native born and with its recruits reinforcing the power structure that feels familiar.

Literacy hounds such as Allan Bloom and William Bennett have committed themselves to this elitism, and they have taken up the task of rushing toward their valorized past as reinforcement of the way things are rather than reconstituting the past according to modern demands. Embracing the "whatness" of a definite history, with definite categories that feel natural and normal and require no questioning, these new literacy masters are among the first to recoil from the study of visual texts or the study of the revolutions in symbol systems that have been one of the major sources of intellectual advancement and liberation in the twentieth century.

Unknown to these guardians of the elitist version of the humanities, the way people think has changed. The revolutions they insistently deny include the revolutions of delivery, or medium. The canons of classical rhetoric have been reconstituted and revivified by secondary orality. If we continue to lapse into rhetorical unconsciousness, the status quo—the uselessness of not only rhetoric but of "the humanities"—will continue. The commonplace that the discipline of classics committed suicide in the United States remains a lesson that the literacy masters need to consider. It is a lesson that the promoters of the enfeebled, wholesome, enriched version of "the humanities" need to consider. Any work in the historicizing of classical rhetoric needs to take account of this phenomenon. Will other forms of discourse study follow the path of the classics in the United States? Or will false issues of breeding, correctness, and unacknowledged elitism lead to the continued appropriation of print and electronic media by business people and by social scientists who record "taste" (desire), while academics hoard the diminishing artifacts of the humanities among themselves?

The unusual adaptability of classical rhetoric and its preoccupation with producing discourse and not merely analyzing it after someone has produced it make it one of the most powerful discourse systems we have. The fact that it has been appropriated by elitists from many centuries and traditions who invest particular ancient texts and writers with religious properties is no reason to dispense with it. In fact, its adaptability and usefulness make it an extraordinarily powerful way of studying texts—written, visual, painted, or any other kind—

and their contexts. Classical rhetoric, like the humanities in general, is simply too important to be left to the positivists and to the elitists. Instead, we need to continue the reappropriation begun by dialectical critics such as Enzensburger and Benjamin and to re-encode and reinterpret classical rhetoric with the emerging critical sensibilities that have so enlivened and politicized discourse studies in the last generation.

A new agenda lies before us, and part of that newness is as old as Isocrates, who figured out what was going on with the burgeoning power of writing (the exploding power of delivery, the medium of writing). The agenda confronting us now, one-hundred years into secondary orality, is to figure out how literacy has been transformed and what that elaborate change holds for us. Electric rhetoric is upon us. If we want to demarginalize discourse education (and perhaps the moribund state of the humanities as well), if we want the humanities to give up its profound and self-inflicted uselessness in the general culture, then we can look to electric rhetoric as one way to make the humanities something more substantial than the gentrifying of generations of upwardly mobile or already-arrived students who pass through the assembly lines of "English" and other disciplines and roll off the line better prepared to buy and use up not only the usual consumer durables such as cars and furniture but who are better prepared to use up "the arts" in exactly the same way. We live in a state (in both senses) in which "the arts" and "the humanities" have been enfeebled to the point of becoming just some more consumer durables. It does not have to stay that way.

NOTES

1. I address many of the issues that appear here in *The Contemporary Reception of Classical Rhetoric: Appropriations of Ancient Discourse.*

2. Vitanza has argued, along with not enough others, that we cannot retrieve any historical era "as it was." We cannot, for instance, read anything without being influenced by thinkers such as Freud and Marx. Returning to some pristine classical rhetoric, in denial of many centuries of interpretation and events, is not possible.

3. See Cunliffe, for example.

4. Anthony Grafton and Lisa Jardine have traced some of the historical ramifications of this phenomenon in *From Humanism to the Humanities.*

WORKS CITED

Acoma Tribe. "Origin Myth of Acoma." *American Indian Literature: An Anthology.* Ed. Alan R. Velie. Norman: U of Oklahoma P, 1979. 12–28.
Cunliffe, Richard John. *A Lexicon of the Homeric Dialect.* Norman: U of Oklahoma P, 1980.
Benjamin, Walter. "The Work of Art in the Age of Mechanical Reproduction." *Illuminations.* Trans. Harry Zohn. New York: Schocken, 1969.

Enzensberger, Hans M. "Constituents of a Theory of the Media." *The Consciousness Industry: On Literature, Politics, and the Media.* Ed. Michael Roloff. New York: Seabury, 1974. 95–128.

———. "The Industrialization of the Mind." *The Consciousness Industry: On Literature, Politics, and the Media.* Ed. Michael Roloff. New York: Seabury, 1974. 3–15.

Flanigan, Michael C. "Composition Models: Dynamic and Static Imitations." *Theory into Practice.* 19 (1980): 211–19.

Havelock, Eric A. *Preface to Plato.* Cambridge: Harvard UP, 1963.

———. *The Muse Learns to Write: Reflections on Orality and Literacy from Antiquity to the Present.* New Haven: Yale UP: 1986.

Welch, Kathleen E. *The Contemporary Reception of Classical Rhetoric: Appropriations of Ancient Discourse.* Hillsdale, NJ: Erlbaum, 1990.

Douglas Hofstadter

"Are Computers Super-Flexible or Super-Rigid?"

One of the major goals of the drive to higher levels has always been to make as natural as possible the task of communicating to the computer what you want it to do. Certainly, the high-level constructs in compiler languages are closer to the concepts which humans naturally think in, than are lower-level constructs such as those in machine language. But in this drive towards ease of communication, one aspect of "naturalness" has been quite neglected. That is the fact that inter-human communication is far less rigidly constrained than human–machine communication. For instance, we often produce meaningless sentence fragments as we search for the best way to express something, we cough in the middle of sentences, we interrupt each other, we use ambiguous descriptions and "improper" syntax, we coin phrases and distort meanings—but our message still gets through, mostly. With programming languages, it has generally been the rule that there is a very strict syntax which has to be obeyed one hundred per cent of the time; there are no ambiguous words or constructions. Interestingly, the printed equivalent of coughing (i.e., a nonessential or irrelevant comment) is allowed, but only provided it is signaled in advance by a key word (e.g., COMMENT), and then terminated by another key word (e.g., a semicolon). This small gesture towards flexibility has its own little pitfall, ironically: if a semicolon (or whatever key word is used for terminating a comment) is used inside a comment, the translating program will interpret that semicolon as signaling the end of the comment, and havoc will ensue.

If a procedure named INSIGHT has been defined and then called seventeen times in the program, and the eighteenth time it is misspelled as INSIHGT, woe to the programmer. The compiler will balk and print a rigidly unsympathetic error message, saying that it has never heard of INSIHGT. Often, when such an error is detected by a compiler, the compiler tries to continue, but because of its lack of insihgt, it has not understood what the programmer meant. In fact, it may very well suppose that something entirely different was meant, and proceed under that erroneous assumption. Then a long series of error messages will pepper the rest of the program, because the compiler—not the programmer—got confused. Imagine the chaos that would result if a simultaneous English–Russian interpreter, upon hearing one phrase of French in the English, began trying to interpret all the remaining English as French. Compilers often get lost in such pathetic ways. *C'est la vie.*

Perhaps this sounds condemnatory of computers, but it is not meant to be. In some sense, things had to be that way. When you stop to think what most people use computers for, you realize that it is to carry out very definite and precise tasks, which are too complex for people to do. If the computer is to be reliable, then it is necessary that it should understand, without the slightest chance of ambiguity, what it is supposed to do. It is also necessary that it should do neither more nor less than it is explicitly instructed to do. If there is, in the cushion underneath the programmer, a program whose purpose is to "guess" what the programmer wants or means, then it is quite conceivable that the programmer could try to communicate his task and be totally misunderstood. So it is important that the high-level program, while comfortable for the human, still should be unambiguous and precise.

SECOND-GUESSING THE PROGRAMMER

Now it is possible to devise a programming language—and a program which translates it into the lower levels—which allows some sorts of imprecision. One way of putting it would be to say that a translator for such a programming language tries to make sense of things which are done "outside of the rules of the language". But if a language allows certain "transgressions", then transgressions of that type are no longer true transgressions, because they have been included inside the rules! If a programmer is aware that he may make certain types of misspelling, then he may use this feature of the language deliberately, knowing that he is actually operating within the rigid rules of the language, despite appearances. In other words, if the user is aware of all the flexibilities programmed into the translator for his convenience, then he knows the bounds which he cannot overstep, and therefore, to him, the translator still appears rigid and inflexible, although it may allow him much more freedom than early versions of the language, which did not incorporate "automatic compensation for human error".

With "rubbery" languages of that type, there would seem to be two alternatives: (1) the user is aware of the built-in flexibilities of the language and its translator; (2) the user is unaware of them. In the first case, the language is still usable for communicating programs precisely, because the programmer can predict how the computer will interpret the programs he writes in the language. In the second case, the "cushion" has hidden features which may do things that are unpredictable (from the vantage point of a user who doesn't know the inner workings of the translator). This may result in gross misinterpretations of programs, so such a language is unsuitable for purposes where computers are used mainly for their speed and reliability.

Now there is actually a third alternative: (3) the user is aware of the built-in flexibilities of the language and its translator, but there are so many of them and they interact with each other in such a complex way that he cannot tell how his programs will be interpreted. This may well apply to the person who wrote the translating program; he certainly knows its insides as well as anyone could—but he still may not be able to anticipate how it will react to a given type of unusual construction.

One of the major areas of research in Artificial Intelligence today is called *automatic programming,* which is concerned with the development of yet higher-level languages—languages whose translators are sophisticated, in that they can do at least some of the following impressive things: generalize from examples, correct some misprints or grammatical errors, try to make sense of ambiguous descriptions, try to second-guess the user by having a primitive user model, ask questions when things are unclear, use English itself, etc. The hope is that one can walk the tightrope between reliability and flexibility.

AI ADVANCES ARE LANGUAGE ADVANCES

It is striking how tight the connection is between progress in computer science (particularly Artificial Intelligence) and the development of new languages. A clear trend has emerged in the last decade: the trend to consolidate new types of discoveries in new languages. One key for the understanding and creation of intelligence lies in the constant development and refinement of the languages in terms of which processes for symbol manipulation are describable. Today, there are probably three or four dozen experimental languages which have been developed exclusively for Artificial Intelligence research. It is important to realize that any program which can be written in one of these languages is in principle programmable in lower-level languages, but it would require a supreme effort for a human; and the resulting program would be so long that it would exceed the grasp of humans. It is not that each higher level extends the potential of the computer; the full potential of the computer already exists in its machine language instruction set. It is that the new concepts in a high-level language suggest directions and perspectives by their very nature.

The "space" of all possible programs is so huge that no one can have a sense of what is possible. Each higher-level language is naturally suited for exploring certain regions of "program space"; thus the programmer, by using that language, is channeled into those areas of program space. He is not *forced* by the language into writing programs of any particular type, but the language makes it *easy* for him to do certain kinds of things. Proximity to a concept, and a gentle shove, are often all that is needed for a major discovery—and that is the reason for the drive towards languages of ever higher levels.

Programming in different languages is like composing pieces in different keys, particularly if you work at the keyboard. If you have learned or written pieces in many keys, each key will have its own special emotional aura. Also, certain kinds of figurations "lie in the hand" in one key but are awkward in another. So you are channeled by your choice of key. In some ways, even enharmonic keys, such as C-sharp and D-flat, are quite distinct in feeling. This shows how a notational system can play a significant role in shaping the final product.

Jay Bolter

"The Electronic Hiding Place"

There is another, more positive way to view the loss of a stable core for our culture. Although we do lose the satisfaction of belonging to a coherent cultural tradition, we gain the freedom to establish our own traditions in miniature. The computer offers people the opportunity to build liaisons with other readers and writers and to work in relative isolation from other such groups. A group does not need to convince a major publishing house of its importance or saleability; it can use electronic mail and diskettes to disseminate its materials. A group does not need to feel answerable to a cultural norm, but can pursue its own definition of literacy. This feature of electronic writing will be as useful to traditionalists as to the avant-garde. Scholars in esoteric subjects will be able to communicate and publish their results by fax machine or electronic mail. Unlike television, which promotes uniformity (even through the apparent diversity of cable and satellite stations), the microcomputer and the phone network really do permit special literacies to survive.

The computer is an ideal writing space for our networked society, because it permits every form of reading and writing from the most passive to the most active. A large group of users (perhaps the largest) will use the resources of the machine to shop, read the weather report, and play fantastic video games under the rubric of virtual reality. There will be a large market for the electronic equivalents of how-to books and interactive romances, science fiction, and the other genres. Small groups will read and write "serious" interactive fiction and nonfiction. Tiny networks of scholars will conduct esoteric studies in ancient and modern literature and languages. Hundreds or thousands of different interest groups from fundamentalist religion to space exploration will publish and read each other's messages and hypertexts—on commercial, academic, or governmental communication networks. Government and business will produce electronic documents by the billions. All these groups will be in contact at various levels for various purposes. In other words, the chaos of publication and communication in the late age of print will continue. The ideal of stability and cultural cohesion will largely disappear. Few will feel the need to assert such cohesion, since even the smallest group of writers and readers can function happily in its niche in the electronic network. The computer can in fact provide a quiet place for readers and writers to pursue such interests, relatively secure from the noise of what remains of shared cultural elements. The computer as a writing space can also be a place to hide from the sensory overload of the daily world of work and leisure and the other electronic media. In this space, all the various definitions of cultural literacy can survive, but no single definition can triumph at the expense of all others.

George Landow

"Ms. Austen's Submission"

———————————

She knew that some like to make their Submissions in the privacy of their own living quarters. Other fragile souls, who had to work themselves up to such an important act, made theirs on the spur of the moment by making use of a foneport they encountered while away from home. Austen, however, had decided to do it the traditional way, the right way, as she thought of it, or perhaps, she had admitted to herself, it was just that she found such older forms comforting. At any rate, she had risen early, bathed, put on her best outfit, treated herself to an elegant breakfast at Rive Gauche, the restaurant frequented by would-be's, and then made her way to the Agency of Culture, outside of whose main portal she now stood.

Taking several deep, careful breaths to remain calm, she entered the forbidding building and sought the elevator that would take her to the eighty-ninth floor of the west tower. She found herself alone in the elevator for the last half of her ascent, and superstitiously taking anything she encountered as an omen, she wondered if that meant that she was to be one of the lucky ones who would rise fast and alone, one of those few who would make it. As the elevator eased to a halt and its bronze-colored doors slid back, she automatically stepped out of the elevator; but before proceeding down the long corridor, she carefully checked the number of the floor, though, like any other Apprentice Author, she had recognized it immediately. Smiling wryly at the way her nervous hesitation masked itself as a traveler's caution, Austen began an inner harangue that she sometimes carried on for hours at a time. "Come on, you know this is the right floor, and you recognized it immediately. Jane, you can recite the names of the worthies whose portraits line the halls, since they haven't changed in a hundred years. They certainly haven't since your disastrous last visit. There's Shakespeare, Homer, Dante, the first three on the left, and Woolf, Dickinson, Johnnes, and all the rest on the right."

Arriving at the end of the corridor, Austen paused, took a deep breath, and opened the door marked "Submissions." Now that she was here, she began to worry that perhaps she had been too hasty. Perhaps her story was not quite ready. Maybe she had better go home and let it sit for a few days or maybe a week. Her mouth was dry, so dry she licked her lips several times without much effect. "Relax," she told herself. "There's no sense in waiting any longer. You know it's the best thing you've ever done; you can feel it in your bones, and you knew this was the one as soon as it began to take shape last week. Besides," she added, "it's only your second Submission. If something crazy happens and it is not accepted, you still have one more."

Deciding that this was no time to hesitate, the young woman stepped firmly up to the central console, pressed her palm against the recognition pad, plugged in her Authorpad, and said in a voice that was slightly deeper and more hoarse than usual, "I, Jane Austen, Apprentice Author, would like to make a Submission."

"Thank you, Ms. Austen," a rich alto voice answered. "This is your second Submission. Are you fully aware that if this one is not accepted, you have only a single opportunity remaining?"

"I am."

"Please press the white button to make your Submission."

She had promised herself that, win or lose, she would make her Submission like a true Author. She would not close her eyes, take a deep breath, or mumble any prayers. She would just press the white button that had been pressed by so many thousands of fingers before her and would be pressed by so many thousands after.

Austen tried to summon courage by recalling how full of confidence and how eager to complete her Submission draft she had been yesterday. In fact, when the clerk at the writing bureau, a man in his sixties who always wore an old-fashioned ill-fitting suit, had looked in her direction, she had left her chair in the waiting room and headed directly toward the door even before he called her name. "Fourteen, Ms. Austen," he said in his sad, thin voice, when she looked back at him before opening the door to the workrooms. Silently counting the rooms on her right—"one, two, three, four"—she made her way to number fourteen, which she recognized immediately as one of the newly reconditioned units. Pressing her hand against the recognition pad that would charge her time in the workroom to her personal account at CenterBank, Austen waited until the door opened and then, full of barely repressed excitement, entered the little chamber that would be her working place for the next four hours, unslung the case containing her Authorpad, and proceeded to open its battered light blue case. Glancing at the portable writer that had been hers since the Agency of Culture had assigned it to her six years ago when she declared for authorship as a career, Austen plugged it into the narrow shelf before her and seated herself in the authorship chair, which immediately shaped itself to her back and sides.

"Welcome, Ms. Austen," she heard slightly behind her and to her left—that's where the sound always seemed to emanate from in this unit, she recalled. "Today we can offer you a fine selection of environment suitable for inspiration or editorial activities. First, we have Off Puerto Rico, 25 June, a calm seascape whose quiet waves many have found most suitable, and which Andros van Hulen, the recent winner of the Prix de Rome, used while composing the crucial third chapter of his brilliant prose epic. Second, you might like to work within Far Himalayas, 1 August, a bare, chilling setting far from human and other distractions. The third environment that is new since your last session is entitled Jungle Vista, Amazon Basin, 3 February, which, in contrast to the other new offerings, seethes with energy and strange life forms and is well worth the supplementary fee. Several of our young authors," the huckstering machine continued, "have already worked with it and claim that the reluctant work produced within this surround is simply wonderful."

"Thank you, Surround, but today I think I need something better known, more familiar. Please let me have Browning's study, personalized version no. 32-345B." Immediately, the narrow confines of her cramped workunit appeared to shift until she found herself seated at a large oak work table covered with manuscript and leather-covered rectangular solids in a walnut-paneled room the likes of which had not existed for several hundred years. She had no idea who this Robert Browning had been or even what kind of work he had created—whether it was, say, adventure tales or erotic epics—but she had felt at home in his work room since she first came upon it while idly browsing through infrequently used scenarios. Austen felt the temperature of the air around her drop slightly as Surround changed it to match the qualified realism that marked her own personalized version of this ancient writer's workplace.

Turning on her Authorpad model 73.2 automatically called up the last word-file she had entered before going to sleep a very few hours before. Austen had caught fire late yesterday afternoon, and unwilling to spare attention or energy for anything else, she had composed until her latest tale—her best, she knew—arrived at the conclusion for which she had been searching. Anxious lest the passages that seemed so perfect before she had returned home and thrown herself down on her rumpled sheets and slept at last would now appear awkward and imprecise, she nervously rubbed her left hand over her mouth and cheek. She had waited long for this one, so long that she was terrified lest she had deluded herself into thinking, as all beginners must, that she had a winner. No, she was certain. This time her Submission would move the Agency to promote her from Apprentice Author Class 1C to Author.

Like all those many thousands of student and apprentice authors, she had wasted far too much creative energy, she knew, dreaming of making it. She wanted the enormously greater convenience of having her own workunit at home, of course, and like everyone else, she naturally wanted the stipend that came with promotion as well. And the status of being a real Author and not one of the hangers-on, the would-be's, so many of whom eventually dropped out of the struggle and ended their days as clerks or worse, well, that was wonderful, to be sure. But it was publication, gaining access to the literary network, that made it all worthwhile.

Sure, it wasn't much, not like achieving the status of Mass Author or even Serious Author, but it was a first step, the one that allowed and encouraged her to take others. Some legendary Apprentice Authors had made it real big. Why, not more than two or three years ago, she remembered, a young man had shot out of obscurity, scored big with a Mass Novel about the last war that had made international network where it had been picked up and used for videos throughout the world. There was even one of those weird pop fairy-tale versions in New Delhi, and the French had taken it, dividing the main character into six states of consciousness or moods, and creating a phantasmagoria that made the art channels.

Today she felt hopeful, energetic, sure that she would make it to the network. Moods are funny, she thought, for not more than a week ago she had felt crushed beneath the base of this massive pyramid that stretched from students, authors-in-training, and would-be authors to fully accredited practitioners and from them upward to the minor and major Mass Authors, and above them, in turn, to the Serious ones, whose works would be allowed to exist for one hundred years after their death. And, then, way off in the distance, at the peak of this pyramid, there were the Canonical Authors, those whose works had lasted and would be allowed to last, those whose works could be read and were even taught in schools to those who didn't want to be writers.

She knew how difficult creating something new had proved. And she certainly had learned the hard way that there were no easy shortcuts to success. In particular, she remembered with embarrassment how she had tried to crash through the gates of success with a little piece on a young author struggling to succeed, and she still squirmed when she remembered how Evaluator, the Agency of Culture's gateway computer, had responded to her first Submission with an extreme boredom and superior knowledge born of long experience, "Ah, yes, Ms. Austen, a story on a young author, another one. Let's see, that's the eighth today—one from North America, one from Europe, two from Asia, and the rest from Africa, where that seems a popular discovery of this month. Your ending, like your concentration on classroom action and late night discussions among would-be authors, makes this a clear example of Kunstlerroman type 4A.31. Record this number and check the library, which at the last network census has 4,245 examples, three of which are canonical, 103 Serious Fiction, and the remainder ephemera.

"Your submission has been erased, and the portions of your Authorpad memory containing it have been cleared, thus allowing you to get on with more promising work. Thank you for your submission. Good day, Apprentice Author Austen."

That, she thought, must be her most painful memory, but another concerning her attempt at truly original creativity rivaled it. A year before the first incident, which took place this past November, she had decided that she had been relying too much on the Authorpad's tie-ins to the Agency's plot, character, and image generators. No, she promised, she would be her own woman, and though she had found it difficult working without the assistance of that friendly voice that made suggestions and allowed her to link instantly to source texts and abundant examples, she had forced herself to slog on, hour after hour, confident that she would return the craft of authorship to its past glories, the glories of the BackTime when computers had not offered their friendly assistance and authors, so it was rumored, actually created heavy things called books (though how one was supposed to store or even read them she wasn't quite certain). She remembered her chagrin when the Practice Evaluator at school, which was programmed to emulate the Agency's official one, pointed out how sadly derivative her contribution had turned out to be. When she emphasized how she had composed it entirely "on her own"—that was the phrase she used—the knowing voice commanded, "Look, Austen," and then before she realized what the evaluator was doing, the scene vanished from her Surround, replaced by sets of flow charts, concept maps, and menus, some of which bore labels like "Parallels to Plots of Submitted Work" or "Forty-One Types of Novels about Young Authors." She found herself particularly embarrassed to discover that even the title of which she was so proud, "A Portrait of the Artist as a Young Man," had already been used by an obscure twentieth-century author who resided in the distant reaches of the canon.

Worst, she had had to listen, this time forced to pay close attention, to another lecture on the foolish egotism of would-be authors. She had taken all the requisite courses in literary theory, naturally, and now Evaluator was accusing her of theoretical naiveté and ideological illiteracy. Her main problem, she had to admit, was that she had such a firm sense of herself, such a firm conviction that she existed apart, different, that she found the Culture Agency's emphasis on inevitable creation uncongenial, and well, yes, threatening as well. It all went back, the machine was reminding her, to language, the condition of all intelligence, whether human, artificial, or combination of the two. "All of us, Apprentice Austen, use it to communicate our thoughts and to shape our reality, but although you speak ComEnglish, you do not create it, even though no one may ever have combined those words that you use at this instant in precisely that way before. In fact, as your teachers have reminded you so many times, the thoughtful Author confronts the fact that language speaks her as much as she speaks language. And since literature is but another level of language and linguistically organized codes, you cannot assume that you are in sole control of the stories you produce. Your job as an author, Ms. Austen, involves recombinations and possible discoveries, not origins, not originations. An author is a weaver of tapestries and not a sheep producing wool fibre."

Austen learned her lesson, she felt sure, and this story would be the one to realize all that potential her teachers had seen so many years earlier.

Austen pressed the white button, transmitting her story from the Authorpad to Evaluator in the legally required act of Submission. She thereupon stepped back and waited. Slightly more than seven seconds later, Evaluator's melodious womanly voice, now warmer and more enthusiastic than before, announced, "Congratulations, Author Austen, your story has been accepted. It will appear this Thursday on the regional network and we predict solid interest. Please check the official reviews and abstract that will be circulated on this date in order to provide author's confirmation of the abstract. Additional congratulations are in order, Ms. Austen: Requests have just been received for translation rights from Greater Germany, Nepal, and Japan."

Austen lifted her finger to press the white button that would transmit her story from the Authorpad to Evaluator in the legally required act of Submission. She placed her finger near the white button, paused a second, and then another. Slowly unplugging her Authorpad, she left the cell, and holding herself rigid by sheer force of will, walked briskly back toward the elevator.

Austen pressed the white button, transmitting her story from the Authorpad to Evaluator in the legally required act of Submission. She was still seated, eyes shut and holding her breath, when less than ten seconds later, Evaluator announced, "Congratulations, Author Austen, your story has been accepted for a collaborative fiction! Your text will mingle with those of eleven other authors, only two of them brand new like yourself. That is quite an honor, I must say. Would you like to learn the identities of your collaborators?"

Austen pressed the white button, transmitting her story from the Authorpad to Evaluator in the legally required act of Submission. She had not time to remove her index finger from the button, when the firm motherly voice of Evaluator gently announced, "I am sorry, Ms. Austen. Your Submission is not accepted. Please try not to be upset. At another time, your work might have been admitted to the Net, but this past week has seen an unusual number of texts submitted. If you find yourself in need of a tranquilizing agent now or something to help you sleep later, I am authorized to prescribe one at your local pharmacia."

Several years after writing the above speculative fiction, I encountered Gordon Wu's review of Paula Milne's *Earwig*. According to Wu's description, in Milne's play a "feminist novelist in need of money" works on "soap operas plotted by a committee of tired hacks working for a television network. Their success is judged by a computer, EARWIG, which projects audience ratings for their scripts." When I first wrote my description of a future author's experience of trying to publish her work, I thought Ms. Austen's new world of publishing as a dystopia, though one, of course, that takes the form of extrapolating strands found in contemporary England and America. However, after reading Richard Ohmann's account of the relations that obtain among authors, publishers, advertisers, reviewers, and leading periodicals in contemporary America, I wonder if machines could do worse. Then, of course, I recalled Ulmer's observation that machine intelligence necessarily reproduces someone's ideology. . . .

Rhetoric and Oratory

❧

In its earliest Western varieties, oratory took the form of sophistic disputation in the courts of ancient Greece. Later, the Socratic dialogues, most notably *Phaedrus,* suggested the privileging of speech over writing, thereby entailing a philosophy of oratory; and Aristotle's *Rhetoric* described judicial, deliberative, and epideictic speech as the three kinds of oratory. Cicero's *De Oratore* expressed the mature thought of Rome's most influential public speaker, followed only a century and a half later by "the good man speaking well" of Quintilian's *Institutio Oratoria.* We might say that the history of Western rhetorical theory is in many ways a footnote (or endnote?) to the canonical early Graeco-Roman philosophers and teachers for whom oratorical expression was the chief means—if not the *goal*—of life.

In its narrowest sense, oratory comprises the art of *speaking* (or praying, as expressed in the proverb *Ora et labora*: "pray and work"). Oratory's association with persuasion brings it into the realms of power: the law court, the pulpit, and the political arena. Nowhere is the (narrowly defined) art of oratory more readily observable than in the speeches and debates of those aspiring to, or striving to maintain, public office. Decades of half-truths, equivocation, and unfulfilled promises have resulted in the modern public's heightened sensitivity to and skepticism about the power of words used by political orators. Political oratory has become identified as "mere rhetoric" that seeks votes and defends party lines more than it respects truth.

However, with each passing election we find the word *rhetoric* used more and more frequently not only in its colloquial sense of insincere persuasion, but in scholarly and journalistic analyses that appreciate the diverse positive functions of speech and communication. For instance, our current understanding of oratory is not limited to human speechmaking. We recognize the oratorical function of phenomena such as exit polls, photography, video images, and clothing; each of these constitutes a public appeal with persuasive power. After the 1988 campaign for the United States presidency, some political commentators proposed that a decisive moment determining Michael Dukakis's loss to George Bush came when the two candidates appeared together to shake hands after one of the debates: Bush was significantly taller than Dukakis, and the image of Dukakis looking up to Bush suggested, in the minds of some, the superiority of the Republican party platform. Kathleen Jamieson has analyzed the oratorical content of televised political commercials in *Packaging the Presidency,* noting that often the most persuasive appeals are made without words at all. Jamieson describes how these appeals often backfire, as did the 1988 campaign ad footage of Michael Dukakis tooling around in circles in an M1 tank, smiling and waving to the folks back home.

Oratory—be it verbal or nonverbal—is necessarily dramatic, or dramatistic. Ernest Bormann's work has, since the publication of his seminal 1972 essay, "Fantasy and Rhetorical Vision: The Rhetorical Criticism of Social Reality," focused on the social construction of rhetorical situations. Influenced by Robert Bales's *Personality and Interpersonal Behavior,* Bormann examines how groups of individuals participate in elaborate, dramatic fantasy-events made up of small-er units of the "fantasy-theme," which he defines as a "recollection of something that happened to the group in the *past* or a dream of what the group might do in the future." As the participants act out these fantasies, they make increasing use of a collective, group imagination, a shared sense of myth, hero, villain, story, and subplot. Bormann analyzes examples from recent political history such as the media's portrayal of the release of American hostages from Iran at the time of Ronald Reagan's presidential inauguration. Similar applications might be made of Bormann's theory to George Bush's oratory at the onset of the 1991 Persian Gulf war.

Using a different approach, Walter Fisher has emphasized the important role played by a community's shared sense of story in his important work on narra-tive paradigms. Fisher contends that oratorical success is closely bound to the orator's ability to tell stories effectively. Formal argumentation, inference, deduction, and syllogism are not as important as the speaker's ability to con-struct a narrative that makes use of biographical, autobiographical, and histori-cal elements: "[R]easoning need not be bound to argumentative prose or be expressed in clear-cut inferential or implicative structures. . . . [R]easoning can be discovered in all sorts of symbolic actions—nondiscursive as well as discursive." Appropriating Kenneth Burke's definition of "man" as the "symbol-using (sym-bol-making, symbol-misusing) animal," Fisher proposes that *Homo narrans* is a fitting metaphor that represents "the essential nature of human beings," as it is evinced in texts as different as Plato's *Gorgias* and Ronald Reagan's oratory.

The following readings address the nature of oratory in its most obvious arena—politics. "Speech and Power: The Tools of Presidential Leadership," from Roderick P. Hart's 1987 book *The Sound of Leadership: Presidential Communication in the Modern Age,* argues that American presidents are "less flesh and blood per-sons than they are widgets in a political machine," and that their oratory—how-ever influential—is a function of the power perceived to rest in the office of the presidency. In an excerpt from *Eloquence in an Electronic Age: The Transformation of Political Speechmaking,* Kathleen Jamieson contrasts conventional notions of "manly" and "womanly" discourse, and concludes with an analysis of Geraldine Ferraro's oratorical style in her 1984 presidential debate with George Bush. The concluding chapter of Jamieson's *Packaging the Presidency: A History and Criticism of Presidential Campaign Advertising* summarizes the pervasive influence of short television commercials, and how these function as oratory in an age of mass media. Finally, Ronald K. Burke's essay on the historical background and rhetorical features of Martin Luther King, Jr.'s "Letter from Birmingham Jail" reveals how one of the twentieth century's greatest orators transformed an act of racial injustice into a moving *apologia* in defense of civil rights.

FURTHER READING

Benson, Thomas W. (ed.). *American Rhetoric: Context and Criticism*. Carbondale and Edwardsville, IL: Southern Illinois UP, 1989.

Bormann, Ernest. *The Force of Fantasy: Restoring the American Dream*. Carbondale, IL: Southern Illinois UP, 1985.

Campbell, Karlyn Kohrs, and Kathleen Hall Jamieson. *Deeds Done in Words: Presidential Rhetoric and the Genres of Governance*. Chicago and London: U of Chicago P, 1990.

Fisher, Walter. *Human Communication as Narration: Toward a Philosophy of Reason, Value, and Action*. Columbia: U of South Carolina P, 1987.

Pearce, Kimber Charles, and Dean Fadely. "Justice, Sacrifice, and the Universal Audience: George Bush's Address to the Nation Announcing Allied Military Action in the Persian Gulf." *Rhetoric Society Quarterly* 22 (1992): 39–50.

Tulis, Jeffrey. *The Rhetorical Presidency*. Princeton: Princeton UP, 1987.

Roderick P. Hart

Speech and Power: The Tools of Presidential Leadership

Chapter Three

SPEECH AS COMMODITY

To say that politics is dehumanizing is to sound hackneyed, but this seems truer now than it has ever been before. In a very real sense, presidents are less flesh and blood persons than they are widgets in a political machine—cut, shaped, planed, and polished until the machine hums smoothly. Presidents are described in the press as making moves and countermoves, as if they were but blinking lights in a video arcade game. Citizens cynically associate the president with "government" in general and presume that he is enmeshed in a cavernous political system devoid of human feeling. Foreign governments view the president less as an individual with unique fears and hopes and more as simply the current emanation of a Western democracy. Given the political constraints placed on the president of the United States, each of these viewpoints has credence.

But there is an even more fundamental way in which presidents become dehumanized—they sell their speech. A presidential speech is now a prize bought and paid for with political capital. The right to host the president when he speaks is a right purchased either with monetary contributions or with votes (at the polls or in Congress). How long a president will talk ("a major announcement," "just a few brief remarks," etc.) is also a point of negotiation, as is the time of day for his speech, its location, who will introduce him, what access the local press will have, and so forth. The White House is thus the nation's most active, most expensive, and (undeniably) most powerful lecture bureau. This all makes a certain amount of sense for, as an officeholder, a president has little to offer but himself and his words. He can make some political appointments, favor this federal contractor over that one, call up the marines rather than the National Guard. But the more frequent decision he makes is rhetorical—to involve himself or not involve himself in a congressional squabble, to favor a visiting dignitary with a formal banquet or a working dinner, to travel North versus South in the off-year elections. The political costs of each of these potential contracts are calculated when the president makes his decision. The political contractors themselves do all that they can to sweeten the deal, hoping against hope that they have political funding sufficient to "get Reagan" for their fundraiser (as opposed to Bush, or Baker, or Kemp, or worse).

When most Americans think of their president, they imagine him delivering a televised talk from his desk in the White House or facing media personalities during a press conference. But as table 3.6 demonstrates, over 40% of the president's speeches in Washington are delivered to special interest groups or to invited guests (a good many of whom also represent special interests). Americans may choose to think of the nation's Capitol as a counterpart to the Roman agora, and they may choose to think of Richard Nixon's chat with the student protestors at the Lincoln Memorial as normal presidential activity. But a great deal of the chief executive's public speaking is really private public speaking, speech acts designed to woo or placate or impress or apologize to a politically influential group.

Table 3.6 Audiences for Presidents' Washington, D.C., Speeches

Audience	N	%
Government employees	106	1.7
Local/press	2797	44.9
National	688	11.0
Invited guests	1147	18.4
Special interest group	1496	24.0

To some extent, a president thus becomes known by his audiences. In one month, for example, Ronald Reagan addressed the Associated General Contractors, the National Association of State Departments of Agriculture, the Conservative Political Action Conference, the Sister Cities International Program, the White House Correspondents Association, the Young Republican Leadership Conference, and a National Conference of the AFL-CIO. Depending upon their relative political clout, these groups received either a general speech or one carefully adapted to their organizational goals and procedures. Collectively, the above groups point toward the constraints imposed upon an American president by business, labor, bureaucracy, party politics, the media, and political activists. The following peroration was offered by Mr. Reagan to the AFL-CIO, but it is clearly composed of interchangeable words. From an audience's perspective, the power of a presidential speech is binary power—he speaks to them or he doesn't. Very few groups demand more than boilerplate:

> I'm here today because I salute what you've done for America. In your work you build. In your personal lives, you sustain the core of family and neighbor-

hood. In your faith, you sustain our religious principles. And with your strong patriotism, you're the bulwark which supports an America second to none in the world. I believe the American people are with us in our cause. I'm confident in our ability to work together, to meet and surmount our problems, and to accomplish the goals that we all seek.

Now, I know that we can't make things right overnight. But we will make them right. Our destiny is not our fate. It is our choice. And I'm asking you as I ask all Americans, in these months of decision, please join me as we take this new path. You and your forebears built this Nation. Now, please help us rebuild it, and together we'll make America great again.

Thank you very much.

It is not hard to see why a presidential speech is such a high-priced commodity in the political world. Reporters may scoff at most of the speeches they hear by a chief executive, but that is because they hear them all. Most listeners are meeting their president for the first time. Even though they may not sit close to the speaker's podium, they sense that they are very much "there" and that some important bit of news might be shared with them and them alone. Moreover, the presidency is a major repository for the nation's history and sacred truths, and that also makes speeches by the head of state—even in a massively public setting—highly attractive.

Perhaps the most "expensive" presidential speech of all is the special appearance, the "miscellaneous speech"—fluid in structure, spontaneous in appearance and comparatively rare (6.2% of all presidential speeches). It should not be surprising, then, that such speeches (there were roughly 600 of them between 1945 and 1985) are often delivered to members of "invited" audiences. As we saw in Chapter One, speeches of this type were heavily used by Presidents Kennedy, Johnson, and Nixon, each of whom had special talents as public flatterers. These speeches are particularly valuable political tokens for distribution *because they seem so apolitical.* Consider, for example, the remarks Richard Nixon made on March 16, 1974, at the Grand Ole Opry in Nashville, Tennessee. His performance that evening was unusually well received because (1) he had not been making public appearances up to that point; (2) he wandered from topic to topic during the speech, signaling that he was relaxed, among friends; (3) he mixed somber and lighthearted moods and formal and informal language; and (4) even played the piano and put on a yo-yo exhibition for his enraptured audience. One snippet from his speech indicates why listeners regard these speeches as more than worth the price of admission:

Mr. Acuff [handing the president a Yo-Yo]: Now let it come over this way. Hold your hand like this. [Laughter] We are not in any hurry. He don't need to get back up there quick anyway. [Laughter] We need him down here for a while.

Now, turn your hand over and let it ride. Now jerk it back.
The president: I will stay here and try to learn how to use the Yo-Yo. You go up and be President, Roy.

Mr. Acuff: That is just what it takes to be a great President, is to come among people and be among we working people, we common people, and then be one of us. That is what it takes to be a real President . . .

Mr. President, do you belong to the union, the musician's union? You will get some talk on this if you don't. Come on up here. I want you to take the piano.
The president: I am an honorary member of the musicians union in New York City.
Mr. Acuff: That is great. There will be no argument.
The president: No, but I don't pay dues.
Mr. Acuff: He says he is an honorary member of the union in New York City.
The president: Roy, because of the remarks that I made, it occurred to me that what would be most appropriate at this time on this opening evening—and you still can play in the key of G?
Mr. Acuff: Yes.
The president: Okay, fine. You will know this song when I start playing it—I think they will know it when I start playing it. [Laughter] But anyway, you remember on that prisoners-of-war affair, that dinner, that one of the highlights was when Irving Berlin who had been very ill, came down and brought the original score of the great song that he wrote that everybody sings since then—
Mr. Acuff: Yes, I remember.
The president: I thought possibly we would try that one.
Mr. Acuff: Oh, do, that would be great. "God Bless America." [The President played "God Bless America" on the piano.]

Presidential speeches like these are gifts, but such gifts are earned by their recipients. During his administration, Jimmy Carter made three different trips to the State of Iowa (in *non*electoral years) to pay back in speech a debt he had incurred in votes. On his first visit back, he reminded Iowans that they had helped launch his campaign for the presidency ("When I was lonely you took me in. When I needed support, you gave it to me") and that his gratitude had not abated after the election. Such speaking trips were, quite clearly, good politics, for they showed that Mr. Carter paid his debts with the coin of his realm—his time, his voice. Mr. Carter's speeches in Iowa were hardly exalted (a radio call-in show, a town meeting in Burlington, a speech from the deck of the *Delta Queen*), but he knew the rhetorical rules attendant to such gift giving: (1) *indicate that the speech is being given freely, with no ulterior motives* ("I feel like I'm coming home"); (2) *show that the gift has been purchased with this, and only this, audience in mind* ("Iowa is number one in corn production, number one in hog production"); (3) *allay suspicion of opportunism by linking the giving of the gift to the larger relationship shared* ("You introduced me to your friends. I got to know you. You got to know me"); and (4) *designate the gift/speech as but a token of the relationship, a mere bauble when contrasted to the larger truths shared by speaker and audience* ("If you'll stand with me . . . I'll try to . . . work with you to make sure that we keep our Nation as it has always been—the greatest country on Earth").

Although it is not frequently recognized as such, the giving of a gift can itself be an exercise in the use of power. When giving another a gift, we sometimes engender in them a sense of obligation to us, enhance our social image by appearing munificent, and, in general, constrain how the other person will relate to us in the future. This is not the pretty side of gift giving, but it is a real side—especially in political circles. Thus, when analyzing the motives of a political benefactor, it is important to know how much the gift really cost him or her. During the first six months of his administration, for example, Richard Nixon spoke to such groups as the Department of Housing and Urban Development, the National Association of Broadcasters, the American Cancer Society, the League of Women Voters, the Organization of American States, and many other groups. During his *last* six months in office, however, Mr. Nixon's largess was considerably more circumscribed: the Young Republican Leadership Conference, the Veterans of Foreign War, the U.S. Chamber of Commerce, the Daughters of the American Revolution, and, naturally, the National Citizens Committee for Fairness to the President. What the president giveth, he too can taketh away.

In connection with this latter point, to deny another a gift can also be an exercise in power relations. One political curiosity demonstrates this: between October 30, 1964, and April 17, 1975, no president spoke in the tenth largest state in the nation—Massachusetts. No other state could boast (or be ashamed) of such a record. During this period Utah had three speeches, as did South Carolina and Vermont, and even the citizens of Wyoming had a chance to meet their president. In fact, *no* state was deprived like Massachusetts. Lyndon Johnson declared in his first speech there that he was part of an "Austin to Boston" pact, that Massachusetts would henceforth be known "as the home of the Kennedys and the Johnsons," and that he had "more men from Massachusetts in the White House than from all the other States put together." Despite his professions of ardor, however, Lyndon Johnson never came back "home."

As we see in figure 3.9 (which plots the New England speaking of the two presidents), Mr. Johnson did manage to return to Windsor Locks, Connecticut; Lewiston, Maine; Manchester, New Hampshire; Kingston, Rhode Island; and Burlington, Vermont. We see that Richard Nixon also visited every New England state except its most populous one. Not until Gerald Ford returned in April of 1975 did Bay Staters hear a president speak in person. This is not to say, of course, that the good citizens of Massachusetts felt particularly deprived during this decade of presidential reticence. Neither Presidents Johnson nor Nixon were especially loved there—after all, one of its native sons tried to remove LBJ from office in 1968, and it was the only state to vote for Richard Nixon's rival in 1972. From the standpoint of political economics, the citizens of Massachusetts clearly deserved their fate.

It would be gross speculation, of course, to suggest that there was something truly conspiratorial about all of this, but given what we now know about the personalities of the presidents involved (Johnson felt inferior around Harvard men; Nixon detested student activists; both had a "Kennedy complex"), their behavior seems understandable. After all, the media in Massachusetts are notoriously vigilant as well as notoriously liberal, and its citizens are not known for suffer-

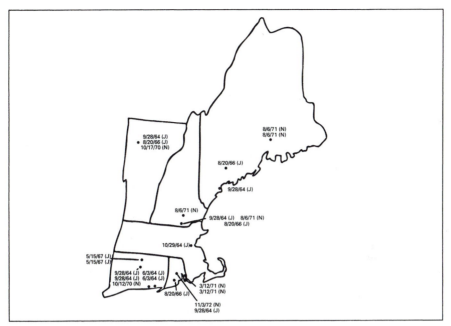

Figure 3.9. Speechmaking in New England by Presidents Johnson and Nixon.

ing in silence when a president they do not like comes to address them. Were Presidents Johnson and Nixon intentionally snubbing the people of Massachusetts? Were these presidents flaunting the authority of their office by traveling everywhere but there? Clearly, no definitive answers are possible here, but the questions raised about speech and power are fascinating indeed. To speak to another is, in some small way, to honor that person. To refuse to speak, to have forgotten to speak, or to be too busy to speak, makes a statement of a very different kind.

CONCLUSION

To speak is to be a power monger. To tell others that we love them is to constrain their behavior, to insure that they do not leave us. To ask for directions is to avoid being incapacitated—late for an appointment, unable to reach town before dark. To give advice is to insinuate ourselves into the lives of others; to give good advice is to make them dependent upon us for future advice. To teach is to control the mind of another, at least in part; to preach is to direct people's lives, at least for awhile. Most of us do not like to think of speech in these ways. Most of us like to think of speech as mutuality, as two souls sharing space and time, as a gift freely given. But a closer inspection of the speech act always finds power—

power unacknowledged, power disguised, power even denied. Unless we wish no control of our lives, however, we insist on having our say. In contrast, some authorities describe the schizophrenic as suffering from marginality, an implicit decision to forgo social impact by using random, unintelligible speech patterns. The corollary is that the impulse to be influential through speech is quite normal and, in a human society, ultimately desirable. After all, speech is not the only route to power. Adolph Hitler knew this route, but he knew other routes too.

All speech is not created equal. The speech of presidents is more powerful than most. This power derives in part from the office of the presidency, but it also derives from the attitudes presidents have toward the speech act itself. Most presidents, certainly most modern presidents, use speech aggressively. The position they hold and the information at their command give them the tremendous advantages of saying a thing first and saying it best. Modern presidents engage in repartee with the press, knowing all the while that such polite jousts are really struggles for attitudes and hence votes and hence money and hence might. Modern presidents can be as stern as a deacon in the pulpit or as frivolous as youngsters rolling Easter eggs, but whether silly or serious they are always serious. Modern presidents play politics, a game about the distribution of power. Speech is how they play.

Kathleen Hall Jamieson

"Eloquence in an Electronic Age"

THE MANLY SPEAKER

For millennia, effectiveness and manliness were synonyms. To call a woman manly was to praise her. In 1843 Margaret Fuller noted that a friend meant the phrase "a manly woman" as a high compliment. By deifying "manly" speech and devaluing "effeminate" or "womanly" speech, theorists implied that nature had privileged the speech of men.

The distinction between the manly and the effeminate was rooted in the conviction that because their minds govern their discourse, men and their speech are inherently superior. Its origin in the emotions meant that the speech of women was defective. The widespread notion that the man is the head of the family, the woman the heart, translated to the notion that men had the right and obligation to control female speech.

Because it was presumably driven by emotion, womanly speech was thought to be personal, excessive, disorganized, and unduly ornamental. Because it was presumably driven by reason, the manly style was thought to be factual, analytic, organized, and impersonal. Where womanly speech sowed disorder, manly speech planted order. Womanly speech corrupted an audience by inviting it to judge the case on spurious grounds; manly speech invited judicious judgment.

The view that public virtues are the by-products of the manly was underscored by the Queen who proclaimed that were she "turned out of the realm" in her petticoat, she would be able to live anywhere in Christendom. Elizabeth I told the troops braced for the assault by the Spanish Armada that "I have but the body of a weak and feeble woman; but I have the heart of a King, and of a king of England, too." Since the heart not the head was presumed to control female speech, Elizabeth's kingly heart certified that her claims were trustworthy, not effeminate. Only a sovereign uttering manly speech could claim credibly that should Britain be invaded, "I myself will take up arms—I myself will be your general, judge and rewarder of every one of your virtues in the field."

Although some men deliver "effeminate" speech and some women master "manly" speech, theorists held that speakers generally stayed true to their gender. Those women willing to forego reproduction for the conception and delivery of ideas were presumed to aspire to be men. If a wife "still wants to appear educated and eloquent," noted Juvenal, "let her dress as a man, sacrifice to men's gods, and bathe in the men's baths." This aspiration was not taken to be the sincerest form of flattery because, said women's rights opponents, "when she unsexes herself, and puts on the habiliments and claims to exercise the masculine functions of man in society, she has lost the position which she should occupy. When woman violates the law which God has given her, she has no law, and is the creature of hateful anarchy."

Under rare circumstances, a woman's "manly" speech won praise. But even then, it was male control that accounted for its success. The credit for their accomplishments was given to the men who had taught them, which was the case with Laela and Hortensia, the daughters of famous Roman orators. Like Elizabeth, whose "heart" was that of a king, the eloquence of these famous daughters was attributed to the bloodline that enabled them to transcend their gender.

If a woman spoke as a stand-in for an absent male and did so to "preserve her female nature," her chances for a favorable reception increased. So, for example, in 42 B.C., Hortensia delivered a widely acclaimed speech in which she argued: "You have already deprived us [women] of our fathers, our sons, our husbands, and our brothers on the pretext that they wronged you, but if, in addition, you take away our property, you will reduce us to a condition unsuitable to our birth, our way of life, and our female nature."

The state was civilized by manly speech, corrupted by effeminate speech. Not only could speaking cost a woman her ability to bear children, it would cost the body politic its capacity to bear arms. Apparently believing that female speech would drain the nation of its testosterone, opponents of women's rights claimed that "the transfer of power from the military to the unmilitary sex involves national emasculation." To save the country from the dustbins of history, women would have to return to their dustpans and aprons.

The distinction between manly and effeminate speech is long-lived. The Romans distinguished between a manly style, which was revered, and the effeminate style, which was reviled. However, what constituted manly and effeminate speech has varied from decade to decade and century to century. Some in Cicero's time thought his loose structure, high level of repetition, and general "tumidity" "effeminate," for example.

By the late nineteenth century the scientific style was enshrined as manly. "The eloquence of Mr. Adams resembled his general character, and formed, indeed, a part of it," noted Daniel Webster. "It was bold, manly, and energetic." Nineteenth-century textbooks lauded the "plain, manly, oratorical style."

THE RATIONAL, INSTRUMENTAL, IMPERSONAL STYLE AND ITS OPPOSITE

The "logical" manly style appealed to "reason." The eloquence used to address judges "is grave, composed, luminous, compact," nineteenth-century Boyleston chair holder Edward Channing told his students. "It is under such restraints as a man's good taste will impose, when he is in the presence of his acknowledged superiors, who are to decide upon the strength of his reasoning, and who have made such questions as he is investigating the serious study of their lives. The style of this eloquence is masculine, earnest and impressive."

Manly discourse works in the service of "ambition, business, and power," noted eighteenth-century theorist Hugh Blair. Accordingly, it is impersonal, unemotional, and competitive. Where manly discourse persuades, effeminate discourse pleases. Manly discourse inhabits the public forum where it engages in debate about public affairs. The proper place for effeminate discourse is either the parlor or the corrupt government.

The interchangeability among the terms rational, manly, and scientific discourse dictates the exclusion of women from the domain of each. According to "nineteenth-century stereotypes or rhetorical idealizations, a woman scientist was a contradiction in terms—such a person was unlikely to exist, and if she did (and more and more of them were coming into existence), she had to be 'unnatural' in some way."

Where women were seen as "delicate, emotional, noncompetitive, and nurturing," science was viewed as "tough, rigorous, rational, impersonal, masculine, competitive, and unemotional." The emphasis of the scientific method on objectivity contrasts with the supposed feminine focus on subjectivity. The scientist who aspired to distance himself from the subject, control the environment, and manipulate variables expressed his findings in impersonal dispassionate prose. Within this frame of reference scientists were heirs of Descartes living in his world of extension and motion; women by contrast, were projected into the world of Pascal who held that the heart has reasons that reason could not know. Judged by the scientific standard, the behaviors and style supposedly native to women were considered defective; those native to scientific man were desirable.

WOMANLY DISCOURSE IS SHRILL; MANLY DISCOURSE IS ROBUST

For centuries, their opponents argued that women's fundamental irrationality and congenital emotionalism should disqualify them from public speaking and public office. The high pitch of the woman's voice was seen as symptomatic not of physiological differences in the vocal mechanism but of excessive emotionalism. "[H]igh-pitched vocalizations tend to be strongly associated with emotional or irrational outbursts," observes contemporary theorist Max Atkinson, "a deeply rooted cultural assumption that no doubt derives from, and is sustained by, the screams of each new generation of infants."

Noting that shrillness characterized the voices of eunuchs, women, and invalids, Quintilian recommended that men increase the robustness of their voices by abstaining from sexual intercourse. Later theorists were equally concerned that men not sound womanish. "Some have a womanish squeaking Tone," wrote John Mason in *An Essay on Elocution and Pronunciation* (1748) "which, Persons whose Voices are shrill and weak, and overtrained, are very apt to fall into." Unlike Quintilian, Mason did not recommend sexual abstinence as a solution.

Eager to mute the inference that their voices signalled irrational or emotional natures, female politicians, Margaret Thatcher among them, have sought voice retraining. Under the supervision of a tutor from the National Theatre, Mrs. Thatcher lowered the natural pitch at which she spoke in public.

Women's emotional natures supposedly accounted for their inability to either produce or understand rational discourse, and for their disposition to speak too much and too often, to employ a shrill tone, and finally to overdress discourse in ornamental language.

THE MANLY STYLE IS PERSPICACIOUS; THE EFFEMINATE, ORNAMENTAL

The belief that language is the dress of thought is a commonplace among rhetorical theorists. The cultural assumption that ornamental dress was appropriate only for Roman women disposed the Romans to identify the stylistic devices that ornament the dress of language as feminine. In drawings of Dame Rhetoric, the figures of speech beautify her garments.

As theorists grappled with the relationship between thought and language, the notion took hold that the figures of diction were soft, ornamental, dispensable, and feminine while figures of thought were vital and virile. "The figure of diction (*figura dictionis*) is a figure by which speech is formed from words resonating pleasingly and smoothly among themselves," noted Omer Talon, in 1567. "The figure of thought (*figura sententiae*) is a figure by which speech is fashioned from some kind of sententious statement affecting movement of the will." Figures of thought provide a "virile dignity, superior to a soft and delicate beauty (*venustate*)." Where figures of diction adorn and color an oration, figures of thought supply its vigor.

Striking parallels ally effeminate discourse and the traditional role of women. Both are expected to please and soothe but not engage in the rigors of vigorous public debate. Both are soft and ornamental. Both flourish when their freedom is circumscribed. To prevent them from veering into excesses of one sort or another, both require control by men. In both, ambition and a desire for power are vices.

The scientific revolution argued that rhetoric's ornamental dress obscured the essentials of discourse. So, we hear Thomas Sprat dismissing "specious tropes and figures" because they cloud our knowledge with "mists and uncertainties." The Royal Society, for which Sprat spoke, sought to disrobe rhetoric. The ideal of that Society was "a naked, natural way of speaking" that was "as near Mathematical plainness" as possible. Ultimately, the debate over whether expression should be naked or clothed was rendered pointless when inorganic metaphors replaced organic ones. A naked engine is hardly the object of a voyeur's attentions or affections. Nor are the naked extension and motion that survived Descartes' skepticism.

In the aftermath of the scientific revolution, the notion that language was the dress of thought gave way to the belief that language expressed thought. Then that view too was displaced by the conviction that language and thought are indistinguishable.

From the late 1800s to the present, the woman's movement debunked pejorative uses of "womanly." These attacks drove the labels effeminate and manly from the vocabularies of theorists.

By embedding a condemnation of effeminate speech in the language in which eloquence was defined, theorists ensured that if a woman rose to speak she would embrace "manly" norms of discourse, thereby in some important sense counterfeiting her identity. Before the notion of a manly style lost currency, female speakers had absorbed its norms.

By embracing such "manly" norms, women created an ironic situation for their descendants. The age of television, not even envisioned as the Grimke sisters took to the circuit, would invite the style once spurned as "womanly." In the television age, men would have to learn and women recapture the "womanly" style. Unfolding that irony is my remaining task.

We judge discourse today by standards set by the "manly" style. Insofar as it was combatively argumentative and saw overcoming its audience as a desired end, the rhetoric of fire and sword was manly. In the scientific age, manly discourse took on additional meanings: it was impersonal, rational, direct, and data-based.

Whether men and women are naturally disposed to different communicative styles is difficult to ascertain. The task of separating stereotypes about male and female communication from actual behavior is complicated by our tendency to internalize the behaviors and attitudes approved by society. Incorporating societal expectations into our concept of self can transform stereotypes into behaviors. Countering this tendency is the ability of stereotypes to warn against and hence minimize disapproved behavior. Also difficult to know is whether dissimilar communicative behaviors are the by-product of nature, nurture, or the biased perception of the observer. Additional complications arise because much research on the role of gender in communication is suggestive rather than conclusive. Nonetheless, one might conclude that women are neither irrational nor more talkative than men. Whatever their cause, and despite the fact that the assertiveness of female speakers is on the rise, gender-associated differences remain.

THE FEMALE STYLE AND TELEVISION

The intimate medium of television requires that those who speak comfortably through it project a sense of private self, unself-consciously self-disclose, and engage the audience in completing messages that exist as mere dots and lines on television's screen. The traditional male style is, in McLuhan's terms, too hot for the cool medium of television. Where men see language as an instrument to accomplish goals, women regard it as a means of expressing internal states. In conversation, men focus on facts and information, women on feelings. In group settings, men focus on accomplishing the task, women on maintaining the harmony and well-being of the group.

Once condemned as a liability, the ability to comfortably express feelings is an asset on television. Women are more inclined than men to verbally indicate emotion. This does not mean, however, that women respond to events more emotionally. Instead, it seems that women are more disposed to display their reactions in emotional terms. Females are advantaged in conveying emotion by their more expressive faces and body movements and their general skill in deciphering the nonverbal cues of others. Consistent with their harmonizing tendencies, women look more at the person they are conversing with than men do. Overall, females are more empathic than males; they tend to both give and receive more emotional support than men.

The inability to disclose some sense of private self on an intimate mass medium has proven a barrier for most men in politics today. Here too the "manly" style is a noose. While "the speech of men is characterized by action and the projection of themselves as actors upon their environment; women are concerned with internal states and behaviors which would integrate other persons with themselves into the social situation." The self-disclosure of men and women is consistent with their instrumental and expressive differences. Women reveal themselves in service of expressive or affiliative needs where men tend to disclose about goals related to instrumental needs.

As I noted earlier, television favors a conciliatory style over a combative one. Here too the style once demeaned as effeminate is desirable.

Because girls identify positively with their mothers and then recreate the mothering role in their own lives, some psychologists believe that their capacities for nurturance and empathy are more developed than boys'. Accordingly, it is natural for a woman to define herself through her social relationships. By contrast, male exposure to the military and to competitive sports may engender such traditional male values as aggressiveness.

Whatever the cause, where women tend to cooperate, men tend to compete. Whether in public or private communication, men are more comfortable than women in a combative "debate" style. Lecturing, arguing, pivoting on claims from reason or logic, and demanding or providing evidence are more typically male than female behaviors. Consistent with these findings, women use less hostile verbs than men. Men are more likely than women to engage in verbal dueling.

Not only are the messages of women less verbally aggressive but they tend to be more pro-social, particularly in their stress on relationships rather than on autonomous action. In their political ads, women usually stress their strengths rather than counteract their weaknesses.

THE PERSONAL FEMALE STYLE AND TELEVISION

The impersonal nature of male speech is evident in a male disposition toward using numbers to describe. By contrast, for women "[t]he implied relationship between the self and what one reads and writes" and presumably says "is personal and intense." Consequently, women's novels and critical essays are often autobiographical. "Because of the continual crossing of self and other, women's writing may blur the public and private." Denied access to the public sphere, women developed facility in such private forms of communication as conversation and storytelling. Accordingly, the poems of the twelfth-century female troubadours employ "the more straightforward speech of conversation." Since educated men spurned the oral form of the ballad for the prestige of learned written poetry, women became the custodians of the ballad tradition. "[B]allads are old-wives' tales which were able to develop and change in authentically feminine ways mainly because men left them alone."

In the French salons of the Renaissance and seventeenth and eighteenth centuries, women perfected the art of conversation. Literary breakfasts and evening conversational parties performed the same function in Britain.

Because the mass media are fixated on differences between the private and public self of public figures, a comfort with expressing rather than camouflaging self, or at the minimum an ability to feign disclosure, is useful for a politician. That utility benefits females. And because the broadcast media invite an intimate style, their conversational and narrational skills also advantage women.

WOMANLY NARRATIVE IS WELL-SUITED FOR TELEVISION

The cliché old-wives' tales remind us that traditionally women are a family's storytellers. So, for example, Goethe credits his father with engendering in him "the seriousness in life's pursuits" but praises his mother for transmitting "the enjoyment of life, and love of spinning fantasies." When this skill is seen as a liability, its mistresses are condemned as gossips. Sixteenth-century critic Steven Guazzo noted that although gossip was a vice common to many, "it is most familiar with certain women." Such gossips retell the misfortunes of their neighbors in "speeches." "Have you not hearde the hard hap of my unfortunate neighbor," they ask. "[A]nd thereupon making the storie, they rehearse howe the husbande by means of his servant, took her tardie in her hastie business. Then they tell (the details of) the wall, and the way whereby her lover got downe: next, how cruelly her husband beate her, and her maid, and thinke not that they leave anything behind untolde, but rather will put too somewhat of their own devise." The indictment of the female gossip survived the centuries. "The second kind of female orator," writes Addison in the *Spectator*, "are those who deal in invectives, and who are commonly known by the name of the censorious. . . . With what a fluency of invention and copiousness of expression will they enlarge upon every little slip in the behavior of another! With how many different circumstances, and with what variety of phrases, will they tell over the same story!" Television's bias prizes the narrative skills that once were pilloried.

It is a skill women retain. In both primitive and advanced cultures, women are the repositories of parable-like dramatic vignettes, concise stories that transmit the common wisdom from woman to woman and generation to generation.

The talent for capturing ideas and lessons in brief dramatic narratives is one cultivated by mothers telling bedtime stories to their children. It is a talent of use as well to those who transmit the goings-on of the community. Because society has encouraged women to cultivate these dispositions to narrative, they are better able than men to respond to television's narrative demands.

Television invites a personal, self-disclosing style that draws public discourse out of a private self and comfortably reduces the complex world to dramatic narratives. Because it encompasses these characteristics, the once spurned womanly style is now the style of preference. The same characteristics comprise a mode of discourse well suited to television and much needed in times of social stress or in the aftermath of divisive events. By revivifying social values and ennobling the shared past, epideictic or ceremonial discourse helps sustain the state. In a later chapter I argue that the early 1980s required leaders to have a talent for the epideictic.

POLITICIANS AND THE MANLY AND WOMANLY STYLE

Capitalizing on the newly recognized strengths of their once disdained style is not as simple for women as it at first seems. Before they can bring centuries of acculturation to television, women must overcome their socially reinforced fear of public speech; they must then abandon the "manly" style they adopted in order to deliver socially acceptable public discourse.

Such beliefs as "Little girls should be seen and not heard" couple with other means of devaluing women's speech to dispose women to avoid the public forum. Females report more difficulty than males in expressing themselves in public and in gaining either a hearing or respect for their ideas. Consistent with social sanctions against aggressive speech by women, they are also less likely than men to speak on controversial topics.

Although no one seriously credits the view that women pay in shrivelled uteruses for speaking in public, women's role as child bearer continues to affect perception of her public role. Because they have raised their families before entering public service, women seeking high public office for the first time are generally older than their male counterparts. Being the married mother of young children is a political liability for a female politician because it reminds the public of a role that voters have been socialized to believe "makes women less suitable and available for public office." The presumption that women bear responsibility for child rearing and maintenance of the family means that a mother of young children cannot as readily appeal to those family values that her presence on the public stages appears to violate.

Those who invade the linguistic domain of men must overcome their own sense of the inadequacies of a woman's speech. Unsurprisingly, then, political women are more "assertive, more venturesome, more imaginative and unconventional, and more liberal in their attitudes" than women in the population at large. The pressures of deviating from expected social roles exact a price. Female politicians tend toward "a serious and dutiful manner and . . . a fretful uncertainty about themselves and their situation."

In constructing campaign strategies, consultants are mindful of the existence of stereotypes. When Evelyn Gandy faced William Winter in the Mississippi Democratic gubernatorial primary in 1979, Winter's consultant Bob Squier redefined the governorship as a manly, military job. In spot ads Winter was shown confidently striding among armored tanks. The governor is the commander-in-chief of the National Guard argued Winter's ads. "The Guard is the first line of national defense," proclaimed the candidate. Since the federalized National Guard had played an important role in confrontations with Southern governors in the 1960s there was a certain remote plausibility to the claim. Meanwhile, by showing her looking feminine and sounding maternal, Gandy's ads played into Squier's hands. The woman portrayed in her ads did not seem able to fulfill the requirements of the role Squier had defined as central to the governorship. Winter won.

To disassociate the role of California state attorney general from that of tough, rugged, male policeman, consultant Michael Kaye dissolved from pictures of his candidate, Yvonne Braithewaite Burke, in a police uniform to a picture of her in a suit. Nonetheless, voters elected her male opponent.

Republican consultant Ed Blakely, whose firm has helped elect three female congressional candidates, advises women seeking public office to "stick to the facts and the issues. They should be tough without losing their femininity, smart but not in a threatening way." Whenever possible, he shows them holding their own against male bureaucrats.

The belief that women speak from emotion grounded the assumption that females respond to political cues "irrationally," focusing on good looks, style, character, or personality rather than on candidates' stands on public policy. In fact, women are as issue-oriented as men. Even in campaigns in which issue distinctions are clear, men and women alike consider personal evaluations of candidates as important or more important than their stands on issues.

The difference in our expectations of men and women was highlighted in the 1984 vice-presidential debate between George Bush and Geraldine Ferraro. There, Ferraro was asked a question that presupposed that, unlike a man, a woman might be unable to initiate an act of war. "How can you convince the American people and the potential enemy that you would know what to do to protect this nation's security, and do you think that in any way that the Soviets might be tempted to try to take advantage of you simply because you are a woman?" Three days later on "Meet the Press" Marvin Kalb asked Ferraro a question that had not been asked of Bush or the male presidential contenders: "Are you strong enough to push the button?"

Sex stereotypes about female leaders both advantage and disadvantage them. When a male attacks his male opponent, he is behaving in a culturally accepted way. But should a woman do likewise, she risks the perception that she is unfeminine, shrill, and nagging. "[T]he United Nations is an institution which specializes in talking," noted former UN Ambassador Jeane Kirkpatrick. "It's a place where people make speeches and listen to speeches. But if I make a speech, particularly a substantial speech, it has been frequently described in the media as 'lecturing my colleagues,' as though it were somehow peculiarly inappropriate, like an ill-tempered schoolmarm might scold her children. When I have replied to criticisms of the United States (which is an important part of my job), I have frequently been described as 'confrontational.' . . . Terms like 'tough' and 'confrontational' express a certain very general surprise and disapproval at the presence of a woman in arenas in which it is necessary to be—what for males would be considered—normally assertive."

In the vice-presidential debate, Bush too felt social constraints. We disapprove of men who bully, attack, or patronize women. The interplay of stereotypes and behavior was evident when Bush said, "Let me help you with the difference, Mrs. Ferraro, between Iran and the embassy in Lebanon." The patronizing edge in the offer would have been less noted had it been made to a male opponent. Although warned by his coaches of the hazards of patronizing, Bush had stumbled. Ferraro responded, "I almost resent, Vice President Bush, your patronizing attitude that you have to teach me about foreign policy." The response was widely replayed in news synopses of the debate.

Sex stereotypes were at play as well in Bush's identification of Ferraro as Mrs. Ferraro rather than Congresswoman Ferraro; subtly, the fact of her marriage invited hostility from those disposed to hear the founders' discussion of "domestic tranquility" as a claim that a woman's place is in the home.

Like members of other disenfranchised groups, women tended to adopt the socially approved style. Until recently, women who attained political power did so by adopting the manly approach. Here Ferraro was a victim. Because her communicative style was forged in the clashes of law school and the courtroom, she reverted to a combative, impersonal, data-deluged form at key points in the debate. At the same time, reliance on the notes she took to rebut Bush led her to focus eye contact on the note cards rather than on the audience, a move that undercut her credibility.

Ferraro's style manifests the double bind in which television traps a female politician. The style traditionally considered credible is no longer suitable to television. But only a person whose credibility is firm can risk adopting a style traditionally considered weak. So a male candidate whose credibility is in part a function of presumptions made about those of his sex is more likely to succeed in the "womanly" style than is an equally competent but stereotypically disadvantaged female candidate. Ronald Reagan can employ a female style, Geraldine Ferraro cannot. Only after Ronald Reagan and other credible male leaders have legitimized television's preferred style will females running for high office be able to reembrace the "womanly" style without risk. Meanwhile, females holding state and local offices can pave the way for the change in perception of the style appropriate to the nation's highest elective offices.

The natural compatibility between the "womanly" style and television is not the only factor propelling candidates toward that style. Two bodies of evidence invite the "womanly" style as the natural marriage of political substance and expression. Both favor female candidates over males.

The gender gap revealed that female voters differ from their husbands, brothers, and fathers on humanitarian issues and matters of war and peace. Moreover, female candidates are more credible than males on those "human" issues that tie intuitively to a maternal role. These include nutrition for infants, food stamps, aid to the elderly, Social Security, and initiatives that would prevent sons from dying in war.

Style and substance coalesced. Not only were women more inclined to personal speech but they were more inclined to favor issues that lent themselves to such speech. Not only were women inclined to oppose military intervention but they also were ill disposed to hostile verbs, aggressive verbal behavior, and clear refutative postures. Not only did women favor a nurturant, incorporative style but they also supported programs that nurtured.

At the same time, women's sense of political efficacy increased and with it their disposition to participate in politics. In 1960, the authors of *The American Voter* concluded that "Men are more likely than women to feel they can cope with the complexities of politics and to believe that their participation carries some weight in the political process." By 1976 women and men of the same age had developed similar senses of political efficacy.

Female candidates for local and statewide office responded to this convergence by returning to a more personal womanly style. Bella Abzug gave way to Barbara Jordan; Barbara Jordan to Geraldine Ferraro. What most clearly distinguishes the political ads for male and female candidates is the females' emphasis on their compassion and warmth. By contrast, men stress their toughness.

Since society approved their use of the "manly" style in public but the "womanly" style in private, many women entered the televised age proficient in both. Increasingly, female candidates felt comfortable blending the strengths of each style. Barbara Mikulski, elected to the Senate from Maryland in 1986, "fights" for humanitarian causes and comfortably combines data-giving and dramatizing.

The broadcast age has rendered the combative, data-driven, impersonal "male" style obsolete. Two ironies result: only to the extent that they employ a once spurned "womanly" style can male politicians prosper on radio and television; meanwhile, in their surge toward political equality, women abandoned and must now reclaim the "womanly" style. Later, I will argue that by employing a self-disclosive, narrative, personal, "womanly" style, Ronald Reagan, an ideological conservative, pioneered a revolution not only in televised communication but, implicitly, in women's participation in politics on their own terms. But his was not the quintessential art. Sacrificed in Reagan's preoccupation with pictures was the additional power his discourse might have drawn from a well-argued case capsulized in a memorable phrase.

Packaging the Presidency

Political advertising is now the major means by which candidates for the presidency communicate their messages to voters. As a conduit of this advertising, television attracts both more candidate dollars and more audience attention than radio or print. Unsurprisingly, the spot ad is the most used and the most viewed of the available forms of advertising. By 1980 the half hour broadcast speech—the norm in 1952—had been replaced by the 60 second spot.

Ads enable candidates to build name recognition, frame the questions they view as central to the election, and expose their temperaments, talents, and agendas for the future in a favorable light. In part because more voters attend to spot ads than to network news and in part because reporters are fixated with who's winning and losing instead of what the candidates are proposing, some scholars believe that ads provide the electorate with more information than network news. Still, ads more often successfully reinforce existing dispositions than create new ones.

Ads also argue the relevance of issues to our lives. In the 1950s the public at large did not find political matters salient to it. From the late 1950s to the early 1970s the perception of the relevance of political matters to one's day-to-day life increased at all educational levels. Citizens saw a greater connection between what occurred in the political world and what occurred in their lives.

TV ads' ability to personalize and the tendency of TV news to reduce issues to personal impact have, in my judgment, facilitated that change. Ads argued, for example, that a vote against nonproliferation could increase the Strontium 90 in children's ice cream. As the salience of political issues increased so too did the consistency of the beliefs of individual voters. Dissonant views are less likely to be simultaneously held now than before. This tendency is also reinforced by political advertising, for politicians have increasingly argued the interconnection of issues of importance to them. In 1980 Reagan predicated a strong defense on a strong economy. In 1968 Nixon tied crime, lawlessness, and the war in Vietnam into a single bundle and laid it on Humphrey's doorstep.

Ads also define the nature of the presidency by stipulating the attributes a president should have. In the process they legitimize certain occupations. Ike polished the assumption that being a general was a suitable qualification. Carter argued that being an outsider plus an engineer, a farmer, a businessman but not a lawyer qualified him. Reagan contended that being the governor of a large state as well as a union leader were stronger qualifications than being an incumbent president. Eisenhower, Nixon, Johnson, Ford, and Carter argued that being the incumbent qualified one for the presidency.

This book was premised on the assumption that advertising provides an optic through which presidential campaigns can be productively viewed. In the ten campaigns I have focused on we have seen, for example, various styles of leadership reflected in the candidates' treatment of their advertisers and advertising. Where Nixon maintained tight control over advertising decisions in 1960, Kennedy delegated all responsibility for advertising to others. At the same time, ad campaigns that lurched uncertainly from one message form to another, from one set of strategists to another, as did Ford's, Mondale's, and Dukakis's, suggested perhaps that the candidate and his advisers were unable to provide a clear sense of the direction in which they wanted to take the country, an observation consistent with the failure of these campaigns to forecast their candidates' visions of the future.

Occasionally, a candidate's response to the requirements of advertising raises troublesome questions about his suitability for the office or, perhaps, about the intensity of his desire to hold it. Adlai Stevenson's perpetual quest for the perfect word or perfectly phrased argument and his apparent need to continue to perfect texts even as he was walking to the stage invite doubts about his ability to act decisively.

When the acceptance speech and the election eve telecasts are taken as the brackets bounding advertising, a focus on paid messages can reveal a campaign's fundamental coherence or incoherence. In a coherent campaign, the acceptance speech at the convention synopsizes and polishes the message the candidate has communicated in the primaries as a means of forecasting both the themes of the general election campaign and of this person's presidency. The message is then systematically developed in the advertising of the general election and placed in its final form on election eve where the candidate tries on the presidency by indicating for the country his vision of the next four years under his leadership. When from the first campaign advertising of January through the last on election eve in November, candidates offer consistent, coherent messages about themselves and the future as they envision it, they minimize the likelihood that their record or plans will be distorted effectively by opponents, and create a clear set of expectations to govern their conduct in office, expectations that may haunt them when they seek reelection.

Viewing campaign advertising as an extended message rather than a series of discrete message units also enables us to see how a candidate's response to attacks in the primaries can either strengthen or strangle the candidate's chances in the general election. When attacks are raised in the primaries and effectively neutralized, as were questions about Kennedy's age and religion in 1960, the issues can be effectively dispatched in the general election. Kennedy's widely aired speech to the Houston ministers builds on a structure of belief first cemented in Kennedy's speeches and ads in the West Virginia primary. Accordingly, those including NCPAC, Glenn, and Hart, whose ads in 1984 exploited Mondale's vulnerability to the charge that he was the captive of special interests, may have done Mondale a favor since the charges forced him to demonstrate that he had called and would continue to call for sacrifices from every segment of the electorate including those whose endorsements fueled his candidacy. At the same time, these charges against Mondale forced his natural constituencies to accept a fact they might otherwise have rejected—that if they demanded Mondale's public and total embrace of their agendas, that embrace would enfeeble his candidacy and the credibility of their endorsements.

Preventing candidates from using advertising to create a sense of themselves discrepant from who they are and what they have done is the vigilant presence of opponents and the potentially vigilant presence of the press. Throughout this book we have seen instances in which candidate's words and actions in settings they did not control undermined the crafted images of their ads. So, for example, the image of the sweating, gaunt, pale Nixon of the first debate in 1960 clashed with the polished presence in his ads. When ads lie, the vigilance of press and opponents can, but do not necessarily, protect the public.

In many ways televised political advertising is the direct descendant of the advertised messages carried in song and on banners, torches, bandannas, and broadsides. Ads continue to ally the candidate with the people, only now that takes the form of showing the candidate pressing the flesh or answering questions from groups of citizens. Candidates continue to digest their messages into slogans, yet these now appear at the end of broadcast ads rather than on banners and torches. Candidates continue to overstate their accomplishments and understate their failures. So, for example, as governor, despite his claims to the contrary, Ronald Reagan did not increase welfare benefits 43%, although he did increase them just as, contrary to his advertising, Andy Jackson had served in one, not two wars.

What differentiates the claims of Jackson's time from those aired today is the role the press has now assumed as monitor of presidential advertising. While the partisan papers controlled by his opponent revealed Jackson's actual war record and noted that his was not the hand that guided the plow, those papers were not a credible source of information for Jackson's likely supporters. By contrast, in the 1980 presidential and 1990 statewide races, articles and news stories—bearing the imprint of neither party—publicly scrutinized the adequacy of candidates' claims. The difficulty in relying on news to correct distortions in advertising is, of course, that comparatively few people consume news while many are exposed to ads.

One of the argumentative ploys born in the political and product advertising of the nineteenth century was refined by politicians in the age of television and then shunted aside by Watergate. By visually associating the favored candidate with pictures of well-fed cattle, happy families, large bundles of grain, and bulging factories, banners and broadsides argued to literate and illiterate alike that this candidate stood for prosperity. The opponent, on the other hand, was visually tied to drawings of starving cattle, poverty-ravished families, empty grain bins, and fireless factories. Some of the associations seemed to have no direct bearing on what sort of president the candidate would make.

Political argument by visual association flowered for the same reason it appeared in product advertising. Initially, advertising for products simply identified the existence, cost, function, and way to obtain the product. As success bred success, products performing the same function proliferated. Distinguishing attributes—some real, some fictional—were sought to persuade customers that one product rather than its twin should be purchased. Van Buren and Harrison were parity products, differentiated by the associations sculpted by their respective campaigns. Since the advertising of the early nineteenth century relied on drawings rather than photographs the range of possible associations was limited only by the artist's imagination.

The wizardry of videotape and film editing did not change the nature of argument from visual association—it simply increased its subtlety. In the process, the evidentiary burden that candidates should assume dropped. So, for example, Goldwater's ads juxtaposed a picture of Billie Sol Estes with scenes of street riots and then intercut a picture of Bobby Baker. Goldwater then appeared on screen to indict the Democrats for their disregard of law, order, and morality. Estes' relation to Baker, the relation of either to the street riots, or the relation among the three and Lyndon Johnson are not explicitly argued.

In 1968 this type of argument reached a new level of complexity in the Republican ad that intercut scenes from the Vietnam War and from the riots outside the Democratic convention with pictures of Hubert Humphrey, including one in which he appears to be smiling. The juxtaposition of highly evocative images invites the audience to impute causality.

The form of argument embodied in this ad is as powerful as it is irrational. It solicits a visceral and not an intellectual response. As a vehicle of attack, this type of ad was vanquished by Watergate because Watergate forced politicians and public to consider what is and is not fair attack in a political campaign. Lurking in the McGovern and Bush campaigns are the forms of attack that replace it: the personal witness, neutral reporter, and pseudo-documentary furlough ad. These mimic some of the features of news. The personal testimony ads consist of actual individuals reporting their opinions of the opposing candidate's performance. They resembled person-in-the-street interviews and are almost a survey; the opinions expressed are not scripted—indeed, their ungrammatical nature underscores their spontaneity. They do not appear to be unfair because, first, we are taught that everyone is entitled to express his or her opinion and, second, these people are voicing opinions that the electorate presumably is disposed to share. In 1976 Ford pioneered this form against Carter.

In the neutral reporter spot, an announcer whose delivery is deliberately low key details facts about the opponent. The ad itself rarely draws any conclusion from the data. That task is left to the audience. Ford did this in a 1976 ad comparing Carter's statements in the campaign with his actual record as governor of Georgia. An ad by Carter did the same to Reagan in 1980.

Pseudo-documentary ads dramatize supposedly real conditions. Here the "revolving door" ad is a prime illustration. As strange as it may seem since the independent PACS have been roundly criticized for their advertising against Democratic senators, the PAC presidential ads also fall, in the main, in 1980, into the neutral reporter category. A typical one simply quotes a promise by Carter and demonstrates that he had not kept it. The most cogent are those by the National Conservative Political Action Committee that edit from the Carter-Ford debates specific promises by Carter, show him making them, freeze the frame, and print across the screen the evidence establishing that the promise has been broken. The Horton ad of 1988 also is a straightforward presentation of presumed fact.

By replacing attack ads that use visual not verbal means to prompt sweeping inferences with attack ads that verbally and visually invite judgments based on verifiable facts, Watergate temporarily transformed a form of presidential attack advertising from an exercise in the prompting of false inferences to an exercise in traditional argument. In 1988, invitations to false inference were back with a vengeance.

Just as political attack advertising survives, but in a circumscribed form, so too the political speech survives, albeit in shortened form, in televised advertising. Contrary to popular belief, the speech remains the staple of paid political broadcasting. There is not a presidential general election campaign in the televised age in which each candidate did not deliver at least two nationally broadcast speeches. In most campaigns far more are given and the candidates deliver short speeches in spot ads as well. Speeches and segments of speeches also recur in telecast campaign biographies. The rise of C-Span means that over 50% of viewing households can watch campaign speeches daily.

The reason we mistakenly think the broadcast speech is an object of antiquity is that half hour speeches tend to draw smaller, more highly partisan audiences than spots. Additionally, when a candidate such as Nixon or Ford delivers addresses by radio, he is speaking on a medium to which many of us do not routinely attend. Moreover, we tend not to think of five minute or 60 second statements by the candidate as speeches. Finally, a televised speech by a presidential candidate was more novel in the 1950s than it is now and so we are more likely to have noted and to long remember its occurrence then than now. Still, if judged by number of minutes on the air in which the candidate is speaking directly to the audience, Reagan's total exceeds Eisenhower's from either 1952 or 1956. If judged by the total number of televised appearances each made speaking directly to the audience, Reagan leads by a substantial margin.

The widespread perception that being able to present broadcast messages persuasively to a mass public would emerge as a criterion governing selection of presidential candidates is not convincingly confirmed from 1952 to 1980. Of the candidates to receive their party's nomination since 1952, Kennedy, Bush, and Dukakis were adequate speakers, Goldwater and Nixon often excellent, and only Reagan a master. In short, the ability to deliver televised messages artfully, while certainly an asset for those who possess it, has not become so central a qualification for the presidency that it has exiled candidates who lack it.

Another misconception about political advertising holds that spots and paid programming are somehow alien to the political speech, a thing apart, a bad dream, an aberration. An analysis of both the stock campaign speeches and the acceptance addresses of the presidential candidates suggests instead that the advertising is rarely anything but a digest of the speeches being delivered throughout the country. Occasionally, but not often, the candidate will say something important in a stump speech that does not appear in the paid broadcasting. But these things are usually strategic blunders such as Carter's assertion that Reagan will rend the country North from South.

As I have noted in each chapter, the convention acceptance speeches are a highly reliable predictor of the content of the candidate's ads in the general election. For those who read the campaign's position papers, examine its brochures, and listen to its stump speeches, the ads function as reinforcement. Those who ignore the other campaign-produced materials receive a digest of them in the ads. This is true both of the advertising against the opponent and the advertising supporting the candidate.

The cost of reaching voters through broadcast advertising poses other problems. Since spot advertising is both costly and often the most cost efficient means of reaching a mass of voters, the contemporary reliance on spots means that those who cannot afford to purchase them, with rare exceptions, are denied the ability to have their ideas either heard or taken seriously in presidential primaries.

For these and related reasons, as I noted in the Introduction, public concern over the nature and influence of political advertising has been rising. Responding to this escalating public concern, legislators drafted or considered drafting bills that can be grouped into three broad categories. The first would have either the public or the radio and TV stations assume the burden of financing some or all of candidate advertising; the second would give candidates attacked by PACs free response time or—regardless of the origin of attack—would give the attacked candidate free response time; the third, still in the talking stage as this book goes to press, would promote changes in the form by offering free time to those agreeing to certain formats (e.g., mandate talking head ads) or lengths (e.g., specify a minimum length or make available free time in no less than five minute and half hour blocks).

Underlying the debate over these and like proposals is widening consensus that the electoral process would benefit if the candidates' cost of reaching a mass audience could be reduced; if all bona-fide candidates could be provided with sufficient access to communicate their basic ideas; if politicians made greater use of longer forms of communication and the electorate as a whole attended more readily to such forms; if candidates assumed or could be enticed to assume the obligation of being viewed by the public in forms such as debates that they do not control; if the advantage PACs can bring to a presidential candidate could be countered or muted.

Still, if political advertising did not exist we would have to invent it. Political advertising legitimizes our political institutions by affirming that change is possible within the political system, that the president can effect change, that votes can make a difference. As a result, advertising like campaigns in general channels discontent into the avenues provided by the government and acts as a safety valve for pressures that might otherwise turn against the system to demand its substantial modification or overthrow.

Political advertising does this, in part, by underscoring the power of the ballot. Your vote makes a difference, it says, at the same time as its carefully targeted messages imply that the votes that would go to the opponent are best left uncast.

Political ads affirm that the country is great, has a future, is respected. The contest they reflect is over who should be elected, not over whether there should be an election. The very existence of the contest suggests that there is a choice, that the voters' selection of one candidate over the other will make a difference.

Ronald K. Burke

Eight Alabama Clergy vs.
Martin Luther King, Jr.

Protest by blacks in the United States extends as far back as the latter half of the seventeenth century when the slave population in America began to expand. The impulse to resist oppression continued into the twentieth century with the formation of the National Association for the Advancement of Colored People (NAACP) in 1909.

In 1948, the Congress of Racial Equality (CORE) sponsored a "Journey of Reconciliation" in which racially mixed groups defied Jim Crow laws and rode together on buses through several border states. A year later, after continuous hostility from Southern Democrats, the Democratic party adopted a strong civil rights plank. About this time, President Harry S Truman desegregated the United States Army.

In 1954, the Supreme Court ruled in *Brown vs. the Board of Education* that separate but equal schools were unconstitutional. Then, in 1955 Rosa Parks refused to yield her seat on a bus to a white man in Montgomery, Alabama. Mrs. Parks was taken to the police station and fingerprinted. Immediately, a young black minister named Martin Luther King, Jr., organized the Montgomery Improvement Association that successfully boycotted the city's transit system. This bus boycott is considered to be the major turning point for the most sweeping social movement in United States history. From this time to the early 1960s, blacks and whites conducted "sit-ins" at restaurants throughout the South, rode on segregated buses as "Freedom Riders," integrated swimming pools and churches, marched for freedom, and worked to integrate the public schools. With this intensified protest permeating all levels of society in the South, King went to Birmingham—a fortress of racism—to confront segregationists.

On Good Friday, April 12, 1963, the Reverend Martin Luther King, Jr., openly defied an Alabama Supreme Court order forbidding demonstrations by leading a march of fifty or more followers "and some one thousand onlookers" through the streets of Birmingham, Alabama to protest the city's racial policies. Not the least bit intimidated by this symbolic act, a phalanx of police officers and fire fighters led by an outspoken segregationist, Commissioner of Public Safety Eugene "Bull"

Connor, "moved swiftly, dispersing and arresting King and about fifty demonstrators."[1] To spur a dramatic breakthrough in the civil rights movement, King selected Birmingham as the location for the protest marches. As historian Lerone Bennett, Jr., noted: "On Wednesday April 3, 1963 Martin Luther King, Jr. stepped from an airliner and announced that he would lead racial demonstrators in the streets of Birmingham until 'Pharaoh lets God's people go.'"[2]

During King's stay in the Birmingham jail cell, there appeared in the newspaper a plea signed by eight leading white churchmen urging protestors to call off their demonstrations. Those eight priests, rabbis, and ministers criticized the marches for being "unwise and untimely."[3] Having the clergy enter the situation proved to be an unexpected boon to the campaign. King, who had a remarkable flair for the dramatic and an imagination peculiar to charismatic leaders, replied with a civil rights classic, "Letter from Birmingham Jail." Melinda Snow remarked that it was "an eloquent expression of the philosophy of the American civil rights movement of the fifties and sixties."[4] Richard Fulkerson reported that it "has already become an American classic," and Haig Bosmajian believed: "We can now place among the lists of great public letters Martin Luther King's 'Letter from the Birmingham Jail,' dated April 16, 1963."[5]

Although a public letter is not a speech, it can serve a rhetorical end. Bosmajian declared that "The public letter, in the tradition of Emile Zola's 1898 letter to the President of the French Republic denouncing the Dreyfus decision and Thomas Mann's 1937 public letter to the Dean of the Philosophical Faculty of the University of Bonn, has long been a means of persuasion used by reformers and politicians, writers, and prisoners." Since King was a person in jail, he was not at liberty to deliver a traditional apologetic speech. Furthermore, Snow believed the letter was sermonic, observing that King, like St. Paul, "shrewdly used his prison cell as an ironic pulpit and the letter as a means to reach his audience."[6] In King's case, the letter was his available means of persuasion.

ACCUSATION BY THE ALABAMA CLERGY

In their letter to King, the eight Alabama clergymen attacked King's policy as well as his character. They wanted to subvert King's policy of confrontation and they aimed to undermine King's character by what Walter Fisher labeled a "subversive rhetoric."[7]

At the beginning of the letter, the clergymen presented three facts appropriate to the rhetorical situation. The first fact reminded the reader that in January of 1963 the clergy had presented "An Appeal for Law and Order and Common Sense." The second fact stated that there has been a "call for honest and open negotiation of racial issues and some citizens have taken to work to various problems." The third fact was that the city has been "confronted by a series of demonstrations by some of our Negro citizens."[8] Upon close examination the so-called facts were accusatory. For example, when reference was given to the fact that they had appealed for law and order, they implied that King's policy would lead to chaos; moreover, they indirectly charged that the activists were not using their common sense. By calling for "honest and open negotiation," they directed the audience's attention to the notion that as men of God they wished to sit down with the dissenters and solve the problem, but King did not. The insinuation was: "We are willing to negotiate, why aren't you?" In noting that the demonstrators were "some of our Negro citizens," the innuendo was that those who were not white were not peaceful. Through the application of the stasis of fact to the statement of accusation, the clergy cleverly positioned themselves as highly principled men of God searching for a way to quell potential social unrest, but the Reverend King was not.

As to the stasis of quality regarding King's policy, the accusers implied that the protestors were irresponsible. They noted that the disruptions "have not contributed to the resolution of our local problem." Quality was again argued when they implied that the wisdom of the leader should be questioned because the demonstrations were "unwise and untimely." In essence, the clerics said that the activists avoided any attempt to take constructive actions to create more desirable conditions in Birmingham.

Not only did the clergy undermine King's policy, but they attacked King's character by alluding to him as an interloper. For instance, in the third paragraph of their letter, they said the demonstrations were "directed and led in part by outsiders." In the next paragraph they charged that outsiders were not needed to settle their local disputes:

> We agree rather with certain local leadership which has called for honest and open negotiation on racial issues in our area. And we believe this kind of facing the issues can best be accomplished by citizens of our own metropolitan area, white and Negro, meeting with their knowledge and experience of the local situation. All of us need to face that responsibility and find proper channels for its accomplishment.

By using such phrases as "local leadership," "our area," "Our own metropolitan area," and "local situation," the clerics tried to limit the negotiations to Birmingham residents. They implied that outsiders were not wanted. They let their audience infer that King and his people made it their business to foment the kind of demonstrations that had already occurred in the city, and that perhaps they really sought to gain control of the city. The clerics' strategy corresponded precisely to what Fisher labeled a "subversive rhetoric": "Subversive rhetoric is an anti-ethos rhetoric; that is, it invariably is an attempt to undermine the credibility of some person, idea, or institution. One of its chief modes accords with what is sometimes called the 'devil theory' of persuasion. The strategy is to make a man, idea, or institution consubstantial with Satanic attributes and intentions."[9] In brief, the clergy intimated that members of the protesting group were "consubstantial with Satanic attributes and intentions." The analysis of the letter showed that the clerics attacked King's policy and character by arguing definition and quality. There matters stood until King responded to the letter.

MARTIN LUTHER KING, JR.'S, APOLOGIA

As stated earlier, the clergy's public statement created an unexpected boon to the civil rights campaign. The clerics' accusation gave King the opportunity to deliver a detailed explanation of the movement's *raison d'etre* in his now famous "Letter from Birmingham Jail." In investigating King's *apologia*, B. L. Ware and Wil Linkugel isolated the factors and postures in verbal defense, and these are helpful in the present study.[10]

In King's letter, three factors were present: denial, bolstering, and transcendence. Denial is defined as: "the simple disavowal by the speaker of any participation in, relationship to, or positive sentiment toward whatever it is that repels the audience."[11] In the letter, King repudiated the accusation that he was an outsider by offering reasons for being in Birmingham. "I think I should indicate," he asserted, "why I am here in Birmingham, since you have been influenced by the view which argues against 'outsiders coming.'"[12] King offered four reasons why he was not an intruder. The first reason was that "I along with several members of my staff, am here because I was invited here." Second, he reminded them that "I have basic organizational ties here." The Southern Christian Leadership Conference, based in Atlanta, Georgia, of which King was president, had affiliations in the South, and the Alabama Christian Movement for human rights was one of them. His third and fourth reasons criticized the notion of the "outsider." Hence, his third reason was that he traveled to places where injustice existed, as the prophets of the eighth century B.C., did and as Paul did to spread the gospel of Jesus Christ. Lastly, King replied that there was an interrelatedness of communities and states.

King effectively denied the charge that he was an outsider on legal and moral grounds. By definition, he had a legal right to be there because an organization to which he belonged invited him to Birmingham. Morally, he had every right to be there. Inasmuch as he believed that all men and women are brothers and sisters under the skin, he felt compelled to be where persecution occurred. The ministers could not easily ignore King's persuasive argument. Was it not their duty as ordained clerics to be present where there were violations of human rights? Was it not difficult for these men of the cloth to indict one who practices the word of Christ? King also used bolstering which is defined as "any rhetorical strategy which reinforces the existence of a fact, sentiment, object, or relationship."[13] Bolstering is a form of identification because it reaffirms audience perceptions. For instance, King first used it to express discontent with states below the Mason-Dixon line: "Too long has our beloved Southland been bogged down in a tragic effort to live in monologue rather than dialogue." The phrase "too long" reminded the audience of decades of strained race relations. "Our beloved Southland," moreover, invoked what Kenneth Burke referred to as consubstantiality, that is, "men have common sensations, concepts, images, ideas, attitudes that make them consubstantial."[14] The word "Southland" was meant, therefore, to bring to mind sensations, concepts, and images of the South. King effectively identified with his audience's roots and love of the region. Additionally, the term "bogged down" conveyed the notion of regression and not progress. By invoking the neutral word "Southland," King hoped to establish the idea that blacks and whites should work together enthusiastically to overcome the deteriorating relations. This argument also helped to reinforce the image that King was not an outsider—he was from the South, too.

Moreover, King said the lack of communication between blacks and whites had been a "tragic effort to live in monologue rather than dialogue." He used the word "tragic" in the sense that racial strife could have been avoided, but in place of coexisting, blacks and whites retreated from interacting with one another. By bolstering, King tried to unify the parties by appealing to love of homeland, of "Southland." He appealed to common sense by implying that rather than being divided by monologue they could be united in dialogue.

The final rhetorical strategy King used was transcendence. According to Ware and Linkugel, transcendence strategies "psychologically move the audience away from the particulars of the charge at hand in a direction toward some more abstract general view of his character."[15] King's use of transcendence is illuminating. He wrote that segregationists may have a legitimate concern since activists were breaking the law. But he recognized that there are two kinds of law: just and unjust. He agreed with St. Augustine that "an unjust law is no law at all." He countercharged that the city of Birmingham reflected injustices in its laws in three ways: (1) it required some to obey while others were not required to obey the same law; (2) it was unjust "if it is inflicted on a minority that as a result of being denied the right to vote, had no part in enacting or devising the law"; and, (3) it was unjust when laws were employed "to maintain segregation and to deny citizens the First Amendment privilege of peaceful assembly and protest." After describing the distinction between a just and an unjust law, King defended his policy and character by transcending to a more elevated plane by saying:

> Of course, there is nothing new about this kind of civil disobedience. It was evidenced sublimely in the refusal of Shadrach, Meshach, and Abednego to obey the law of Nebuchadnezzar, on the ground that a higher moral law was at stake. It was practiced superbly by the early Christians who were willing to face hungry lions rather than submit to certain unjust laws of the Roman Empire.

These Biblical examples were well chosen. The clergymen could not deny the applicability of the Biblical times to the present. Moreover, these examples would have persuasive efficacy with the audience because they could easily infer how King responded to the "higher moral law" that liberates and not to the earthly immoral law that subjugates.

The posture King assumed in his *apologia* was explanation. He hoped that "if the audience understands his motives, actions, beliefs, or whatever, they will be unable to condemn him."[16]

King defended the protests by explaining them: "In any nonviolent campaign there are four basic steps: collection of the facts to determine whether injustices exist, negotiation, self-purification, and direct action." He gave a detailed elucidation of each one of the four basic steps. As to "whether injustices exist," King noted that Birmingham had an "ugly record of police brutality," "unjust treatment of Negroes in the courts," and "bombings of Negro homes and churches." When he tried to negotiate, King said the city fathers "consistently refused to engage in good-faith negotiation." For self-purification King said they had workshops on nonviolence and asked themselves a series of questions about entering into violent encounters. Needless to say, the final step of direct action was implemented.

King then replied to the charge that the protests were ill-timed. He explained that "freedom is never voluntarily given by the oppressor, it must be demanded by the oppressed." This notion of timing was significant insofar as *kairos* (see Glossary) was concerned. Having been told that the demonstrations were ill-timed, King replied that he never participated in any direct action that was well-timed. He turned the point back on his accusers: "For years now I have heard the word 'Wait!' It rings in the ear of every Negro with piercing familiarity. This 'Wait' has almost always meant 'Never.' As one of our distinguished jurors once said, 'Justice too long delayed is justice denied.'"

In the next section of the letter King continued to exercise his rhetorical posture of explanation. In perhaps the most moving statement on the deprivation of black people's God-given rights to emerge from the civil rights movement, King showed how a society spawned segregation, lynchings, drownings, police brutality, and intimidated children. He decried widespread poverty amidst an affluent society:

> Perhaps it is easy for those who never felt the stinging darts of segregation to say "Wait." But when you have seen vicious mobs lynch your mothers and fathers at will and drown your sisters and brothers at whim; when you have seen hate-filled policemen curse, kick and even kill your black brothers and sisters with impunity; when you see the vast majority of your 20 million Negro brothers smothering in an air-tight cage of poverty in the midst of an affluent society. . . . then you will understand why we find it difficult to wait.

One passage in particular was notably powerful: "When you suddenly find your tongue twisted as you seek to explain to your six-year-old daughter why she can't go to the public amusement park that has just been advertised on television, and see tears welling up when she is told that Funtown is closed to colored children, and see ominous clouds of inferiority beginning to form in her little mental sky. . . ." King easily assumed an explanatory posture because he had confronted hatred and bigotry most of his life.

CONCLUSION

In this encounter, the eight Alabama clergymen expressed dissatisfaction with the black community's determination to redress their grievances by making an appeal for law and order and calling for negotiations. Further, in an attempt to discredit King, the clergy charged that "outsiders" were leading the demonstrations. The clergy's letter criticized King's course of action and questioned his moral character.

King responded to these criticisms with three of the four factors of verbal self-defense, denial, bolstering, and transcendence. He denied the allegations that he was an outsider by demonstrating that he had ties to the area and that he was invited there. He built on that kind of defense by using language that supported his consubstantiality with his audience by referring to the "Southland" of which he was clearly a member. And in one of the most moving parts of his letter, he appealed to a higher moral law that bound his accusers with him: as clerics, they were all obliged to do God's work.

King was wise to select explanation for his posture of self-defense. The efficacy of explanation was that it allowed him to detail the reasoning behind the civil rights movement and thereby to imply the justification for his policy in Birmingham. Thus, he was able to defend his policy by elucidating his character that informed the policy, and the righteous policy he championed was a positive indication of his moral habits. Although the eight Alabama clergymen's letter is not as famous as King's letter, it must be credited with motivating the Reverend King to compose in the crucible of confrontation an efficacious personal *apologia* that ranks as one of the most eloquent civil rights proclamations of the twentieth century.

NOTES

1. Lerone Bennett, Jr., *Before the Mayflower: A History of the Negro in America 1619–1964* (Baltimore, Penguin Books, 1966), p. 334.

2. Ibid., p. 330.

3. "Public Statement by Eight Alabama Clergymen" is in Charles Muscatine and Marlene Griffith, eds., *The Borzoi College Reader*, 3rd ed. (New York: A. A. Knopf, 1976), pp. 233–34; also reprinted in Melinda Snow, "Martin Luther King's 'Letter from Birmingham Jail' as Pauline Epistle," *Quarterly Journal of Speech* 71 (1985):321.

4. Snow, " 'Letter from Birmingham Jail' as Pauline Epistle," p. 318.

5. See Richard P. Fulkerson, "The Public Letter As A Rhetorical Form: Structure, Logic, And Style in King's 'Letter From Birmingham Jail,' " *Quarterly Journal of Speech* 65 (1979): 121, and Haig A. Bosmajian, "Rhetoric of Martin Luther King's Letter From Birmingham Jail," *Midwest Quarterly* 8 (1967): 127.

6. Snow, " 'Letter from Birmingham Jail' as Pauline Epistle," p. 319.

7. Walter R. Fisher, "A Motive View of Communication," *Quarterly Journal of Speech* 56 (1970): 131–39.

8. Muscatine and Griffith, "Public Statement by Eight Alabama Clergymen," pp. 233–34.

9. Fisher, "A Motive View of Communication," p. 138.

10. B. L. Ware and Wil A. Linkugel, "They Spoke in Defense of Themselves: On the Generic Criticism of Apologia," *Quarterly Journal of Speech* 59 (1973):273–83.

11. Ibid., p. 274.

12. I quote from the "Letter" published in *The Christian Century* 80 (1963):767–73.

13. Ware and Linkugel, "They Spoke in Defense of Themselves," p. 277.

14. Kenneth Burke, *A Rhetoric of Motives* (New York: The World Publishing Co., 1950), p. 545.

15. Ware and Linkugel, "They Spoke in Defense of Themselves," p. 280.

16. Ibid., p. 283.

INFORMATION SOURCES ON THE SPEECH SET

Eight Alabama Clergymen's Accusation

The "Public Statement by Eight Alabama Clergymen" first appeared in the *Birmingham Post Herald* on Saturday April 13, 1963. Also the letter is included in Charles Muscatine and Marlene Griffith, eds., *The Borzoi College Reader*, 3rd ed. (New York: A.A. Knopf, 1976), pp. 233–34 and Melinda Snow, "Martin Luther King's 'Letter from Birmingham Jail' As Pauline Epistle," *Quarterly Journal of Speech* 71 (1985):321.

Martin Luther King, Jr.'s, Apology

King wrote the "Letter" on the margins of the newspaper in which the clergymen's statement appeared while he was in jail. He continued the letter on scraps of writing paper supplied by a friendly black trusty and then concluded on a pad of paper his attorneys gave him. The American Friends Service Committee had 50,000 copies of the letter printed for distribution. Later, after refining, it became a significant chapter in *Why We Can't Wait* (1964). This analysis is based on the copy in *The Christian Century* 80 (1963):767–73. The letter is included in several college anthologies: Charles Muscatine and Marlene Griffith, eds., *The Borzoi College Reader*, 3rd ed. (New York: A.A. Knopf, 1976); Arthur M. Eastman et al., eds., *The Norton Reader*, 4th ed. (New York: W.W. Norton, 1977); Caroline Shrodes, Harry Finestone, and Michael Shugrue, eds., *The Conscious Reader*, 2nd ed. (New York: Macmillan, 1978); Richard E. Young, Alton L. Becker, and Kenneth L. Pike, *Rhetoric: Discovery and Change* (New York: Harcourt, Brace & World, 1970); Halsey P. Taylor and Victor N. Okada, eds., *The Craft of the Essay* (New York: Harcourt Brace Jovanovich, 1977); and Forrest D. Burt and Cleve Want, eds., *Invention and Design: A Rhetorical Reader* (New York: Random House, 1978). It also appears in Edward P. J. Corbett, *Classical Rhetoric for the Modern Student*, 2nd ed. (New York: Oxford, 1971); Staughton Lynd, ed., *Nonviolence in America: A Documentary History* (Indianapolis: Bobbs-Merrill, 1966); George Ducas and Charles Van Doren, eds., *Great Documents in Black American History* (New York: Praeger, 1970); and Herbert J. Storing, ed., *What Country Have I? Political Writings by Black Americans* (New York: St. Martin's, 1970).

Index to Introductions and Glossary

Pennsylvania State University. Reproduced by permission of The Pennsylvania State University Press.

Paul Oskar Kristeller. "The Renaissance." From *Renaissance Thought and its Sources.* Copyright © 1979 by the Board of Trustees of Oberlin College. Reprinted by permission.

George Landow. "Ms. Austen's Submission." From *Hypertext: The Convergence of Contemporary Critical Theory and Technology.* Copyright © 1992 Johns Hopkins University Press. Reprinted by permission of The Johns Hopkins University Press.

Lao-tzu. Excerpts from *Tao Te Ching* by Gia-fu Feng/Jane English. Copyright © 1972 by Gia-fu Feng and Jane English. Reprinted by permission of Alfred A. Knopf, Inc.

Harriet Malinowitz. "The Rhetoric of Empowerment in Writing Programs." Reprinted by permission of the Modern Language Association from *The Right to Literacy,* edited by Andrea A. Lunsford, Helene Moglen, and James Slevin. Copyright © 1990 the Modern Language Association.

James J. Murphy. "The Concept of 'School'." From Murphy, James J., *Quintillian on the Teaching of Speaking and Writing,* pp. ix–xiii. Copyright © 1987 by the Board of Trustees, Southern Illinois University. Reprinted by permission of the publisher.

Cary Nelson. "Always Already Cultural Studies: Two Conferences and a Manifesto." Originally appeared in *The Journal of the Midwest Modern Language Association,* 24(1991). Pages 24–38. Reprinted by permission of the Midwest Modern Language Association and the author.

Andrea Nye. Reprinted from *Words of Power: A Feminist Reading of History* (1990) by permission of the publisher, Routledge, New York, and of the author.

Robert T. Oliver. "Culture and Rhetoric." From *Communication and Culture in Ancient India and China.* Copyright © 1971. Reprinted by permission of Syracuse University Press.

Gary A. Olson, ed. "Jacques Derrida on Rhetoric and Composition: A Conversation." Originally appeared in *Journal of Advanced Composition* 10.1 (1990). Pages 1–21. Reprinted by permission.

Chaim Perelman. "Logic, Dialectic, Philosophy, and Rhetoric." From *The Realm of Rhetoric* by Chaim Perelman. © 1992 by the University of Notre Dame Press. Reprinted by permission of the publisher.

Kenneth L. Pike. "Language as Particle, Wave, and Field." Originally appeared in *The*

Texas Quarterly, 2.2, 1959. Pages 37–54. Reprinted by permission of the author.

Donald Preziosi. "Overview: Linguistic and Architectonic Signs." From *Architecture, Language, and Meaning,* by Donald Preziosi. Copyright © 1979 Mouton de Gruyter. Reprinted by permission.

Herbert Schnädelbach. "Against Feyerabend." From *Beyond Reason,* edited by Gonzalo Munevar. Copyright © 1991 Kluwer Academic Publishers. Reprinted by permission of Kluwer Academic Publishers.

Charles I. Schuster. "Mikhail Bahktin as Rhetorical Theorist." Originally appeared in *College English,* October 1985. Copyright 1985 by the National Council of Teachers of English. Reprinted with permission.

Eve Kosofsky Sedgwick. "Axiom 5." From *Epistemology of the Closet.* Copyright © 1990 The Regents of The University of California. Reprinted by permission of The University of California Press, and of the author.

Frank Smith. "Information and Uncertainty." From *Understanding Reading,* 4th edition. Copyright © Frank Smith 1988. Reprinted by permission of the author and of the publisher, Lawrence Erlbaum Associates.

Richard E. Vatz. "The Myth of the Rhetorical Situation." Originally appeared in *Philosophy and Rhetoric,* 6.3 (1973). Pages 154–161. Copyright 1973 by The Pennsylvania State University. Reproduced by permission of The Pennsylvania State University Press.

Brian Vickers. "Epilogue: The Future of Rhetoric." © Brian Vickers 1988. Reprinted from *In Defence of Rhetoric* by Brian Vickers (1988) by permission of Oxford University Press.

Kathleen E. Welch. "Electrifying Classical Rhetoric: Ancient Media, Modern Technology, and Contemporary Composition." Originally appeared in *Journal of Advanced Composition.* 10.1 (1990). Pages 22–38. Reprinted by permission.

Audrey Wick. "The Feminist Sophistic Enterprise: From Euripides to the Vietnam War." Originally appeared in *Rhetoric Society Quarterly,* 22.1 (1992). Pages 27–38. Reprintd by permission.

W. Ross Winterowd. "The Rhetoric of Beneficence, Authority, Ethical Commitment, and the Negative." Originally appeared in *Philosophy and Rhetoric,* 9.2 (1976). Pages 65–83. Copyright 1976 by The Pennsylvania State University. Reproduced by permission of The Pennsylvania State University Press.